D0742829

ABD-RU-SHIN

IN THE LIGHT OF TRUTH · THE GRAIL MESSAGE

This book "In the Light of Truth", The Grail Message, by Abd-ru-shin, contains the translation according to the sense of the original German text. In the translation the expressions and sentences used by Abd-ru-shin to mediate the Living Word to the human spirit can only be rendered approximately. The reader should therefore realise that this translation cannot replace the original. However, if he makes the effort – as is desired by the Author – to absorb the contents intuitively, he will recognise the significance of this work for mankind, despite the deficiencies arising out of a translation.

ABD-RU-SHIN

IN THE LIGHT
OF TRUTH

THE GRAIL MESSAGE

GRAIL FOUNDATION PRESS
GAMBIER, OHIO

Abd-ru-shin
"In the Light of Truth"
The Grail Message. Edition in one volume.

Tenth edition 1996. Only authorized edition.

Copyright 1990 by Stiftung Gralsbotschaft, Stuttgart, Germany, under special license to
Grail Foundation Press, Gambier, Ohio.

All rights are reserved in whole or in part concerning translation
and dissemination through public lectures, films, radio, television,
any kind of sound carrier, copying, photographic reproduction or any other
form of duplication or storage by computer.

Library Systems and Services Cataloging in Publication Data

Abd-ru-shin, 1875–1941.
[Im Lichte der Wahrheit. English]
In the Light of Truth :
The Grail Message / Abd-ru-shin.
p. cm.
Translation of: Im Lichte der Wahrheit.
Includes index.
ISBN 1-57461-006-6 (3 vols. in 1)
1. Grail movement (Bernhardt). I. Title.
BP605.B43232 1995 299'.93 – –dc20
Printed in Germany

FREE YOURSELF FROM ALL DARKNESS!

HE WHO

MAKES NO EFFORT TO

GRASP THE WORD OF THE LORD

ARIGHT BURDENS HIMSELF

WITH GUILT!

VOLUME 1

FOR YOUR GUIDANCE!

THE BANDAGE falls, and belief becomes conviction. Liberation and redemption lie only in conviction!

I am addressing earnest seekers only. They must be able and willing to examine this matter objectively! Religious fanatics and irresponsible enthusiasts may hold aloof, for they are detrimental to the Truth. As for the malevolent and prejudiced, they shall find their sentence in the very words.

The Message will strike only those who still carry within them a spark of truth, and the yearning to be true human beings. To all such it will become the shining light and staff. It will lead them unswervingly out of all the chaos of the present-day confusion.

The following Word does not bring a new religion, but is intended as the torch to help all serious listeners or readers find the right path, which leads them to the longed-for height.

Only he who bestirs himself can advance spiritually. The fool who uses extraneous aids for this, in the form of the ready-made opinions of others, only walks his path as if on crutches, while ignoring his own healthy limbs.

But the moment he boldly uses all the abilities which lie dormant within him awaiting his call, to help in his ascent, he is employing the talent entrusted to him in accordance with his Creator's Will, and will easily overcome all obstacles that seek to divert him.

Therefore awake! Genuine faith lies only in conviction, and conviction comes solely through an inflexible weighing and examining! See that you are truly alive in the wonderful Creation of your God!

Abd-ru-shin

WHAT SEEK YE?

WHAT *seek ye?* What is all this tumultuous agitation? It permeates the world like a ferment, and a flood of books overwhelms all peoples. Scholars pore over ancient writings, investigating and pondering until spiritually exhausted. Prophets arise to warn, to predict . . . suddenly from all sides people strive feverishly to spread new light!

Thus it rages now over the troubled soul of mankind, not refreshing and invigorating, but scorching, consuming, absorbing the last vestiges of strength still left to the afflicted one in this gloominess of the present time.

Here and there also a whispering is heard, rumours of a growing expectation of something impending. Every nerve is restless, tense with subconscious longing. There is seething and surging, and over everything lies a kind of ominously brooding stupor. Fraught with disaster. What *must* it bring? Confusion, despondency and ruin, unless a mighty hand tears asunder the dark layer that now envelops the terrestrial globe spiritually. With the slimy tenacity of a dirty morass, absorbing and smothering every ascending free light-thought before it has become strong; with the gruesome silence of a swamp, suppressing, disintegrating, and destroying every good volition even in the bud, before any action can arise from it.

But the seekers' cry for light, imbued with strength to cleave through the mire, is turned aside and dies away beneath an impenetrable canopy, assiduously set up by the very people who think they help. *They offer stones for bread!*

Look at the innumerable books:

They do not animate, they only weary the human spirit! And this is the proof of the barrenness of all they offer; for whatever wearies the spirit is never right.

Spiritual bread immediately refreshes, Truth revitalises and Light animates!

Simple people must surely despair when they see what walls are being built around the beyond by so-called psychic science. Who among the simple is to grasp the learned sentences and strange expressions? Is the beyond, then, intended exclusively for psychic scientists?

They speak of God! But is it necessary to set up a university in order first of all to acquire the abilities to recognise the conception of the Godhead? To what lengths will this mania, which is mostly rooted only in ambition, drive them?

Readers and listeners stagger along like drunkards from one place to another – unsteady, not free in themselves, one-sided, because they have been diverted from the simple path.

Listen, you despondent ones! Lift up your eyes, you who are seriously seeking: *The way to the Highest lies open to every human being! Proficiency in learning is not the gate to it!*

Did Christ Jesus, that great example on the true path to the Light, choose His disciples among the learned Pharisees? Among the Scribes? He took them from the simple, natural people, because they had no need to struggle against this great delusion that the way to the Light is hard to master, and must be difficult.

This thought is man's greatest enemy, it is a lie!

Thus turn away from all scientific knowledge, where it is a question of what is most sacred in man, which must be *fully grasped!* Leave it alone; for science, being a product of the human brain, is piecework and must remain piecework.

Consider, how should scientific knowledge, acquired by laborious study, lead to the Godhead? *What, after all, is knowledge?* Knowledge is what the brain can conceive. Yet how very limited is the perceptive capacity of the brain, which remains firmly bound to space and time. Even eternity and the meaning of infinity cannot be grasped by a human brain. Just that which is inseparably linked with the Godhead.

But the brain stands silent before the incomprehensible power streaming through all that exists, from which it derives its own activity. The power which everyone intuitively perceives as a matter of course every day, every hour, every moment, whose existence science too has always recognised; whereas with the brain, that is with the knowledge and intellect, one seeks in vain to grasp and comprehend it.

So inadequate is the activity of a brain, the basis and instrument of science, and this limitation naturally also affects what it produces, hence all science itself. Thus science does indeed *subsequently* help to elucidate, classify and arrange all that it receives ready-made from the creative power which precedes it; but when it seeks to assume leadership or offer criticism, it must inevitably fail so long as it binds itself so firmly to the intellect, that is, to the perceptive capacity of the brain, as it has done hitherto.

For this reason erudition, along with those who adjust themselves to it, always remains clinging to details; whereas each man carries within himself, as a gift, the great inconceivable whole, and is fully capable of attaining to the noblest and highest without laborious study!

Therefore away with this needless torture of spiritual enslavement! Not for nothing does the great Master exhort us: "Become like children!"

He who bears within himself the firm volition for what is good, and strives to give purity to his thoughts, *has already found the way to the Highest!* All else will then be added unto him. This requires neither books, nor spiritual strain; neither asceticism, nor solitude. He will become sound in body and soul, freed from all pressure of morbid pondering; for all exaggeration is harmful. You are meant to be human beings, not hothouse plants which through one-sided cultivation succumb to the first puff of wind!

Awake! Look around you! Listen to your inner voice! That alone can open the way!

Heed not the dissensions of the churches. The great Bringer of Truth, Christ Jesus, the personification of Divine Love, did not concern Himself with creeds. After all, what are the creeds today? A shackling of the free spirit of man, enslavement of the Divine spark dwelling within you; dogmas that seek to compress the work of the Creator, and also His great Love, into forms moulded by the human mind. This indicates a dishonouring of Divinity, a systematic disparaging.

Every serious seeker is repulsed by such things, because they prevent him from ever experiencing the great reality within himself. As a result his longing for the Truth becomes increasingly hopeless, and finally he despairs of himself and of the world!

Therefore awake! Shatter the walls of dogma within you, tear off the bandage, so that the pure Light of the Highest may reach you undimmed. Then your spirit will soar aloft in exultation, jubilantly sensing all the great Love of the Father, which knows no limitations of earthly intellect. You will at last know that you are a part of this Love; you will grasp It easily and completely, unite with It, and thus gain new strength daily and hourly as a gift, enabling you to ascend out of the chaos as a matter of course!

THE CALL FOR THE HELPER

Just let us look more closely at all those people who today with special eagerness are seeking a spiritual helper, those who, inwardly uplifted, are awaiting him. In their opinion they themselves are already thoroughly prepared spiritually to recognise him and to hear his word!

On calm observation we notice a great many factions. Christ's Mission, for instance, affected so many people in a strange way. They formed a false picture of it. As usual, this was due to their wrong self-assessment, their presumption.

Instead of the former veneration and the preservation of a natural gulf and sharp demarcation towards their God, there has arisen on the one hand a plaintive begging which always wants only to receive, but on no account to contribute anything itself. They certainly accepted the "pray", but refused to acknowledge that this was also coupled with "and work" – "work on yourself".

Again, on the other hand, people imagine they are so self-reliant, so independent, that they can do everything themselves, and with a little effort even become Divine.

There are also many people who only demand and expect God to run after them. Inasmuch as He had already once sent His Son, He proved thereby how greatly concerned He is that mankind should draw near to Him, indeed that He probably even needs them!

Wherever one turns there is nothing but presumption to be found in all things, no humility. True self-assessment is lacking. –

In order *really* to be a *human being,* and begin his ascent as *such*, it is first of all necessary for man to descend from his artificial height.

Today, spiritually puffed up, he is sitting in a tree at the foot of the mountain, instead of standing with both feet firmly and securely on the ground. Thus unless he first comes down or falls from the tree he will obviously never be able to climb the mountain.

Meanwhile, however, all those who went their way calmly and sensibly on the ground beneath his tree, and upon whom he looked down so haughtily, have probably arrived at the summit.

But events will come to his aid; for in the very near future the tree *will* fall. When he is so roughly shaken down from his precarious perch, perhaps man will then once more come to his senses. But for him it will then be high time, he has not a single hour left to waste.

Many now think that life can continue in the old way, as it has done for thousands of years. Stretched out comfortably in their armchairs, they are awaiting a strong helper.

But *how* do they depict this helper! It is really pathetic!

In the first place they expect or, just to be quite correct, *demand* that *he* should prepare the way upward to the Light for each individual! *He* must exert himself to build bridges to the path of the Truth for the adherents of *every* religious faith! *He* must make it so easy and intelligible that everyone can understand it without effort. His words must be so chosen that their rightness will immediately convince one and all.

As soon as man must exert himself and think for himself, then the helper is not a proper helper. For if he is called to lead and to show the right way through his word, he must then naturally also exert himself for men. It is *his* duty to convince men, to awaken them! After all, Christ also gave His life.

Those who think in this way today – and there are many who do so – need not begin to trouble themselves, for they are like the foolish virgins, they face the "too late"!

The helper will surely *not* awaken them, but will let them sleep quietly on until the gate is closed and they can find no entrance into the Light, because they cannot free themselves in time from the sphere of matter, for which the word of the helper showed them the way.

For man is not as valuable as he imagined. God does not need him, but he does need his God!

Since in their so-called progress mankind today no longer know what they really *want,* they will at last have to experience what they *must!*

As they both seek and criticise in a supercilious way, this type of people will pass by, just as even at that time so many also passed by *Him* for Whose coming everything had already been prepared through the revelations.

How can one possibly envisage a spiritual helper *thus!*

He will not *budge an inch* to make concessions to mankind, and wherever he is expected to give he will *demand!*

That man who is capable of serious reflection, however, will immediately recognise that *just this strict and uncompromising demand* for attentive thinking contains what is best, and what mankind, already so deeply entangled in spiritual indolence, need for their salvation! It is just by demanding spiritual alertness right from the beginning, together with an *earnest* volition and self-exertion for the understanding of his words, that a helper easily separates the grain from the chaff already at the outset. An automatic working lies in this, as it is in the Divine Laws. Here, too, men receive exactly according to their actual volition. –

But there is yet another class of people who fancy themselves particularly alert!

Naturally these have formed an entirely different picture of a helper, as can be read from reports. It is no less grotesque, however, for they expect him to be … a spiritual acrobat!

In any case, thousands already suppose that clairvoyance, clairaudience, clairsentience, etc., indicate great progress, which is really *not* so. These arts, whether acquired, cultivated, or even a natural gift, can never rise above the constraint of this earth, thus they only operate within low limits, can never claim to any height, and are therefore almost worthless.

Is *that* the way to help the ascent of mankind – showing them, or teaching them to see and hear, ethereal things which are on the same level as they are?

This has nothing to do with the actual ascent of the spirit, and is to equally little purpose for earthly happenings! They are minor spiritual tricks, nothing more, interesting to the individual, *but utterly useless* to mankind as a whole!

That all such people wish for the same kind of helper, but one even more proficient than themselves, is indeed readily understandable. –

Yet there are a great many who carry matters much further in this respect, even to the point of absurdity. And who are nevertheless perfectly serious about it.

For example, one of the fundamental conditions they impose to prove he is genuine is that a helper … must be immune from catching a cold! He who does so is already disqualified; for in their opinion this does not correspond

15

to an ideal helper. At all events, a strong helper must as a first essential be completely above these trifles with his spirit.

This may sound fanciful and ridiculous; but it is only based on facts, and suggests a faint repetition of the former cry: "If Thou be the Son of God, save Thyself and come down from the cross!" – They are already calling out the same today, even before such a helper is in sight at all!

Poor, ignorant men! He who trains his body so *one-sidedly* that it is rendered temporarily insensible under the power of the spirit is by no means great or eminent. Those who admire him are like children of former times, watching with open mouth and shining eyes the antics of travelling clowns, and filled with a burning desire to emulate them.

And a great many so-called spirit-seekers or God-seekers of today are no further advanced in the *spiritual* field than the children of bygone days were in this quite *earthly* field!

Just let us consider a little further: The vagrants of olden times, of whom I have just spoken, developed themselves increasingly and became acrobats in circus and music-hall. Their skill grew prodigious, and even now thousands of sophisticated people watch these feats every day in perpetual wonder, often inwardly shuddering.

Yet do they *themselves gain* anything from it? What do they take away with them after such hours? Although many an acrobat even risks his life during his performances. Nothing whatever! For even at the peak of perfection all these things will *always* remain strictly limited to music-hall and the circus. They will always serve only to amuse, but never lead to any advantage for mankind.

Yet people now look for *such* acrobatic feats in the *spiritual* field as the standard by which to measure the great helper!

Let such people keep their spiritual clowns! They will soon enough experience where this leads! They have really no idea *what* they are actually pursuing thereby. They imagine that only he is great whose spirit so controls his body that it no longer suffers illness!

All such development is one-sided, and one-sidedness brings only what is unhealthy and diseased! These things do not *strengthen the spirit,* but only *weaken the body!* The balance necessary for healthy harmony between body and spirit is disturbed, and as a result such a spirit finally severs itself much sooner from the maltreated body, which can no longer provide the strong healthy resonance needed for earthly experience. But then the spirit lacks this experience, and enters the beyond while still *immature*. It will have to live its earth-life *once again*.

These are spiritual tricks, nothing more, performed at the expense of the earthly body, which should in reality *help* the spirit. The body *belongs* to an epoch in the spirit's development. But if it is weakened and suppressed it cannot be of much use to the spirit either; for its radiations are too feeble to provide the full power that the spirit needs in the World of Matter.

If a man wishes to suppress an illness he must spiritually bring about the pressure of an ecstasy on the body, just as in a minor degree fear of the dentist may suppress toothache.

The body may be able to stand such intense stimulation once, perhaps even several times, unharmed, but not continually without suffering serious damage.

And if *that* is the practice or advice of a helper, he is not worthy to be a helper; for he is thereby transgressing the Natural Laws in Creation. Man on earth should cherish his body as property entrusted to him, and strive to achieve healthy harmony between spirit and body. To disturb this through one-sided suppression is neither progress nor ascent, but a decisive obstacle to the fulfilment of his task on earth, as *in the World of Matter* in general. The full power of the spirit as regards its effectiveness *in the World of Matter* is thereby lost, since this definitely calls for the strength of a physical body which is not enslaved but which harmonises with the spirit!

He who is accounted master on such grounds is less than a pupil who knows nothing whatever of the tasks of the human spirit, nor of what is required for its development! He is even detrimental to the spirit.

They will come soon enough to the painful recognition of their folly.

Every false helper, however, will have to undergo *bitter* experiences! His ascent in the beyond can only begin *when the very last* of all those whom he has held up or even led astray by spiritual trifling has come to recognition. As long as his books and writings continue to influence men on earth, he will be held fast in the next world, even if in the meantime he has come to a better understanding there.

He who recommends occult training gives men stones instead of bread, thereby proving that he has not even the faintest idea of what *actually* takes place in the beyond, still less of the complete mechanism of the Universe! –

17

MEN! WHEN the hour comes in which, according to the Divine Will, the purification and winnowing must take place on earth, then watch for the predicted and partly supernatural signs *in the sky!*

Do not then allow yourselves to be confused by *those* men and also churches who have already long ago surrendered to Antichrist. It is sad that until now not even the churches have known *where* to look for this Antichrist, although he has already been active among all men for so long. If they had only been a little on the alert they must have recognised it! Who can possibly act in a more anti-Christian manner than those who at that time fought against *Christ Himself* and finally also murdered Him! Who could have revealed themselves in a worse and also more obvious way as antagonistic to Christ!

They were the leaders and representatives of earthly religion; and the *true* teaching of God, as revealed in and through the Son of God, did not agree with what they had built up. Indeed, the true Message of God could not be reconciled with it, because the structure set up by priestly dignitaries was aimed at earthly influence, earthly power and expansion.

They proved quite clearly thereby that they were servants of the human intellect, which is directed solely towards earthly knowledge and earthly power, and is hostile and obstructive to everything that lies beyond earthly comprehension! Now since God remains completely outside the range of earthly intellectual knowledge, as also does the spiritual, the intellect is clearly the only real obstacle thereto! Thus by its nature it is opposed to all that is Divine and all that is spiritual! And with it logically therefore all men who acknowledge their intellect as of paramount importance, and seek to build only upon *that!*

The religious leaders of those days were afraid of losing influence among the people through the enlightenment of the Son of God. As everyone today knows, *this* was the main reason for the slanders they sought to spread against

Christ, and ultimately also for the execution of the Son of God. They nailed Him to the cross as a blasphemer of the very God by Whom He was sent to bring enlightenment, and Whose servants they professed to be!

They tried to make people believe they were serving God; but how little did they really know *this* God and His Will, for Whose honour and earthly defence this Son of God, the Divine Messenger, was however ... murdered by them!

This was clearly the disastrous result of their enslavement to the earthly intellect, which fought solely to maintain its influence thereby. They allowed themselves to become the executioner as tools of the Antichrist, whom they had secretly enthroned in their hearts. For this satisfied their human weaknesses – their presumption, arrogance and vanity.

Whoever expects clearer proof cannot be helped; for there is nothing more antagonistic to Christ, the Son of God, and His Words! And indeed Antichrist signifies the fighter *against* Christ, against man's redemption in God's Message. The earthly intellect drove them to it! This very intellect, as a poisonous product of *Lucifer,* is an instrument for him which has become the greatest danger to mankind!

Thus the disproportionate over-development of the human intellect in the past has grown into the hereditary sin for man! Behind this, however, stands Lucifer himself as Antichrist in person! *He* it is who through men was able to raise his head! He, the only real enemy of God! He acquired the name of Antichrist through his hostile struggle against the Mission of the Son of God. None other would have had the strength and the power to become the Antichrist.

And in his warfare against the Will of God, Lucifer makes use not merely of *one* man on earth but of nearly all mankind, thus leading them to destruction under the effect of the Divine Wrath! Whoever cannot grasp *this* most obvious fact, that only *Lucifer himself* could be *the Antichrist* who dares to oppose God, will never be able to understand anything of all that takes place outside the World of Gross Matter, that is, outside what is purely earthly.

And as it was then, *so is it still today!* Indeed far worse. Today, too, many religious representatives will wish to fight bitterly to maintain the earthly intellectual ordinances hitherto upheld in the temples and churches.

It is precisely this human intellect, blunting all nobler intuition, that is one of the most insidious growths of Lucifer which he was able to spread among mankind. All slaves of the intellect, however, are in truth *Lucifer's servants*, who are accomplices in the terrible collapse which must thus befall mankind!

Since no one suspected that Antichrist lurked beneath the intellect, he could extend his sinister influence all the more easily! Lucifer triumphed; for he thereby cut off mankind from any comprehending of all that lies outside the World of Gross Matter. From *real life!* From that place where contact is first made with the spiritual, which leads to the proximity of God!

With this he set his foot upon this earth as lord of the earth and of the greater part of mankind!

No wonder, then, that he could penetrate to the altars, and that representatives of earthly religions, also of the Christian churches, were bound to become his victims. For they too expect the Antichrist just before the predicted Judgment. Up till now the great Revelation in the Bible, like many other things, has never yet been understood in this respect.

The Revelation says that this Antichrist *will raise his head* before the Judgment, but not that he will first appear then! If it is said therein that he raises his head, this clearly indicates that he must be here already, but not that he is yet to come. It means that *he will have reached the zenith of his dominion* just before the Judgment!

Listen to this cry of warning, you who are not yet spiritually deaf and blind! Take the trouble for once to think quite seriously about it *yourselves*. If you remain indolent in this respect you give yourselves up as lost!

If you lift the protecting cover from the lair of a poisonous snake that suddenly realises it is exposed, it will naturally try to rear up and bite this ruthless hand.

It is no different here. Finding himself exposed, the Antichrist will quickly protest through his servants; on being unmasked he will make a great outcry, and try in every possible way to maintain himself on the throne which mankind so willingly offered him. But all this he can only do through those who inwardly revere him.

Therefore now keep a sharp watch on your surroundings when the conflict begins! By their very outcry you will all the more surely recognise them, everyone who belongs to him! For once *again*, as before, fear of a pure truth will make them side with its opponents!

The Antichrist will again try desperately to retain his influence on earth. Observe his dubious methods in defence and attack; for he will once more make use only of slander and insinuations, since his followers are incapable of doing anything else. To stand before the Truth and refute it is impossible.

Thus Lucifer's servants will also fight the Messenger of God, just as they once fought the Son of God!

Be on the alert where such an attempt is made; for thereby such people only wish to protect Lucifer in order to uphold his reign on earth. A centre of Darkness lurks there, even if the people habitually appear in bright earthly garments, even if they are servants of a church.

Do not forget what happened when the Son of God was on earth, but reflect that still today the *same* Antichrist, with a far greater human following, is striving to retain dominion over the earth, to escape destruction and to go on obscuring the true Will of God.

Therefore watch carefully for all the promised signs! Each individual must make his *final* decision. Salvation or destruction! For this time it is God's Will that everything which again dares to oppose Him shall be lost!

Every act of negligence will rise up against you in the Judgment! – The Divine Insignia will not appear above some church, nor will any priestly dignitary on earth bear the sign that he is the Messenger of God! But only He Who is inseparably linked with the Signs, Who therefore also carries them living and radiating with Him, as once the Son of God did when He dwelt on this earth. They are the Cross of Truth, living and radiating within Him, and the Dove above Him! They will become visible to all those who are blessed to see spiritual things, so that they may give testimony of it to all people on earth; for there will be among all peoples those who will this time be permitted to "see", as the last Grace of God! – – –

These Sublime Signs of the Holy Truth can never be simulated. Not even Lucifer, who must retreat before them, can achieve this, much less a human being. Therefore he who still seeks to set himself against these Signs of God henceforth sets himself against God as an enemy of God. He shows thereby that he neither is nor ever was a servant of God, no matter what he has hitherto pretended to be on earth.

Be on your guard, lest you also be found among such!

MORALITY

It is as though a dark thunder cloud were hanging over humanity. The atmosphere is sultry. Man's intuitive faculty labours sluggishly under a heavy pressure. Only the nerves affecting the senses and animal instincts of the bodies are in a highly-strung condition. Artificially stimulated through the error of a wrong education, of a false attitude, and self-delusion.

In this respect the man of today is not normal, but is burdened with a morbid sexual instinct, aggravated tenfold, for which in a hundred forms and ways he seeks to establish a cult that is bound to become the ruin of all humanity.

Infectious and contagious as a plague, all this gradually influences also those who still seek desperately to cling to an ideal that floats half-hidden in their subconscious mind. They indeed stretch forth their arms longingly towards it, but ever again, after a glance at their surroundings, drop them with a sigh of hopelessness and despair.

Utterly helpless, they observe with horror how swiftly the clear vision regarding morality and bad habits is obscured, how the capacity to judge is lost, and how these concepts change to such an extent that so much which only a short time before would still have aroused disgust and contempt is very soon regarded as quite natural, not even causing surprise.

But the cup will soon be filled to the brim. A terrible awakening must come!

Already now these sensually overwrought masses will sometimes quite involuntarily and unconsciously recoil in sudden misgiving. A momentary feeling of uncertainty grips many a heart; but it brings no awakening, nor any clear perception of their unworthy conduct. They thereupon only redouble their efforts to shake off such "weakness" or "last remnants" of old-fashioned ideas, if not to suppress them altogether.

Progress at any price, that is what it must be. However, one can progress in two directions. Upwards or downwards. As one chooses. And as things now stand it is downwards, with horrifying speed. When the hour strikes for those hurtling downwards to encounter a strong resistance, the impact must shatter them.

In this sultry atmosphere the thunder-cloud grows ever more dense and ominous. At any moment now the first flash of lightning may be expected, rending and lighting up the darkness, and brilliantly illuminating the most obscure corner so relentlessly and sharply as to bring liberation to those striving for light and clarity, but destruction to those who have no longing for the Light.

The longer this cloud has time to grow in darkness and density, the more dazzling and terrifying will also be the lightning it generates. Gone will be the soft enervating atmosphere whose sluggish embrace hides a lurking sensuality; for the first flash of lightning will quite naturally also be followed by a current of fresh, bracing air, bringing new life. In the cold clarity of the light, all the products of morbid imagination will suddenly stand stripped of their dazzling falsehoods before the eyes of horrified humanity.

The awakening will strike the souls like the shock of a mighty thunderclap, so that the living spring water of undimmed Truth can pour forth and rush over the loosened soil. The day of freedom dawns. Deliverance from the spell of an immorality that has existed for thousands of years, and that is now reaching its climax.

Look around you! Observe what people read, how they dance, how they dress! By tearing down all barriers between the two sexes, the present time is more than ever anxious systematically to obscure the purity of the intuitive perception, thus to distort it and give it misleading masks, and ultimately, if at all possible, to smother it.

When misgivings arise they are quietened by high-sounding talk, which however proves on investigation to emanate only from the inwardly vibrating sexual instinct, in order to provide ever fresh nourishment for the carnal lusts in countless ways, skilful and clumsy, open and covert.

They speak of the emergence of a free independent humanity, of a development of inner stability, of physical culture, the beauty of the nude, ennobled sports, and of education to bring to life the saying: "To the pure all things are pure!" In short: Upliftment of the human race by laying aside all "prudery", thus producing the noble and free human being who is to carry the future! Woe to him who dares to remonstrate! With a great outcry, accusations are immediately hurled at such an audacious person, similar to the assertions that only impure thoughts can make him "find anything wrong in it"!

It is a mad whirlpool of foul water, spreading a stupefying, poisoning atmosphere which, like the effect of morphine, induces mental delusions into which thousands upon thousands continually allow themselves to slide until they become so weakened that they go under.

A brother seeks to enlighten his sister, and children their parents. Like a storm-driven tide it sweeps over all mankind, and wild breakers surge round the few who, gripped with repugnance, have retained their balance and still stand like solitary rocks in the sea. To these cling many whose strength threatens to fail them in the violent storm. It is good to see these small groups standing like refreshing oases in the desert, inviting the traveller to find rest and recuperation after grimly battling his way through the sandstorm that threatened to overwhelm him.

What is being preached today under the fine guise of progress is nothing but a veiled encouragement of utter shamelessness, the poisoning of every higher intuitive perception in man. It is the greatest pestilence that ever befell humanity. And strange: it seems as if so many had only been waiting for a plausible excuse to debase themselves. To countless people it is very welcome!

But he who knows the spiritual laws operating in the Universe will turn away in disgust from today's pursuits. Let us take just one of the "most harmless" pleasures: "Mixed bathing".

"To the pure all things are pure!" These words have such a pleasant sound that many things are permissible under their protection. But just let us consider the most simple ethereal happenings in such a bathing-place. Let us assume that of thirty persons of both sexes, twenty-nine are really pure in every respect. This is an assumption which is completely impossible from the very start; for the opposite would be more correct, and even then still rare. But let us assume it.

Stimulated by what he sees, impure thoughts arise in the mind of the one, the thirtieth bather, although his outward behaviour may be absolutely irreproachable. These thoughts are immediately embodied ethereally in living thought-forms, which move towards and attach themselves to the object of his glances. This is a defilement, whether or not it leads to any remarks or improprieties!

24

The person thus contaminated will carry about this dirt, which is capable of attracting similar straying thought-forms. Thereby they become denser, ever denser around this person, and may finally confuse and poison the victim, as a parasitic creeper often destroys the healthiest tree.

Such are the ethereal happenings in so-called "harmless" mixed bathing, at party games, dances or the like.

It should be borne in mind, however, that in any case it is just all those particularly desirous of having their thoughts and senses excited by such exhibitions who will visit these bathing-places and pleasure haunts! It is not difficult to explain what filth is thus generated, without anyone being outwardly aware of it in the gross material sense.

It is also obvious that this steadily increasing and condensing mass of sensual thought-forms must gradually influence countless people who of themselves do not seek such things. At first vague thoughts of a similar nature arise in them; in time these grow stronger and more alive, being ceaselessly nourished by the various expressions of so-called "progress" around them. And so one after another they glide along into the viscous dark stream, in which the power to apprehend true purity and morality is ever more obscured, until finally everything is dragged into the depth of uttermost darkness.

First of all, these opportunities and incitements for such rapidly growing abnormalities must be done away with! They are nothing but breeding centres into which the pestilential vermin of immoral human beings can cast their thoughts, which then spring up luxuriantly and spread destruction over all humanity; creating ever new breeding grounds which finally form only one huge field of noxious growths, exuding a poisonous stench that also suffocates the good.

Wrench yourselves out of this delirium, which like a narcotic only appears to invigorate, but in reality has a weakening and destroying effect!

It is natural, though sad, that it is just the female sex which is again the first to exceed all bounds, and which has sunk without any scruple to utter shamelessness in their attire.

However, this only proves that the explanation about ethereal happenings is correct. It is just woman, gifted by nature with a stronger intuitive ability, who first and more deeply absorbs this poison of the tainted ethereal world of thought-forms, albeit quite unconsciously. She is more at the mercy of these dangers, for which reason she is also the first to be carried away, and oversteps every limit incredibly quickly and conspicuously.

Not for nothing is it said: "When a woman becomes bad she is worse than a man!" This holds good in everything, be it in cruelty, in hatred or in love! The behaviour of woman will always be a product of the Ethereal World around her! There are exceptions, of course. Nor is woman on this account free from responsibility; for she is able to observe the influences assailing her, and can guide her own volition and actions according to her will if ... she so desires! That the majority of women unfortunately fail to do this is a fault of the female sex, which is entirely due to the absolute ignorance in these matters.

It is a great misfortune for the present time, however, that the future of the people actually lies in the hands of woman. She carries it because her psychic condition influences her descendants more incisively than that of the man. What a decline, then, must the future bring! Inevitably! It cannot be halted by arms, money, nor discoveries. Nor by kindness or diplomacy either. More incisive means are required here.

Yet this enormous guilt does not fall upon woman alone. She will always be only the true reflection of that world of thought-forms which hovers over her people. This must not be forgotten. *Respect and honour* woman *as such,* and she will form herself accordingly; she will become *what you see in her,* and in this way you uplift your whole people!

However, before this can happen, a great process of transformation must take place among women. As they are now a cure can only be effected through a radical operation, by a forceful and relentless intervention, removing any growth with sharp knives and casting it into the fire! Otherwise it would also destroy all the healthy parts.

Towards this essential operation on all mankind the present time is irresistibly rushing, faster, ever faster, and will finally bring it about of itself! This will be painful and terrible, but the end will be restoration to health. Not until then will it be the time to speak of morality. Today it would die away like the word spoken in the wind.

But when the hour is past, in which corrupt Babylon had to perish, because it collapsed from inner decay, then observe the female sex! What they do and what they leave undone will always show you *how you stand,* because through their finer intuitive ability they live what the thought-forms desire.

This fact also gives us the assurance that when the thinking and intuitive perceiving are pure, womanhood will be the first to soar upwards to that ideal which we regard as a truly noble human being. Then morality, in the full glory of its purity, will have entered!

AWAKE!

AWAKE, ye men, out of your leaden slumber! Recognise the ignoble burden you bear, that weighs upon millions with enormous pressure. Throw it off! Is it worth bearing? Not for a single second!

Of what does it consist? Empty husks which the breath of Truth will scatter in the wind. You have wasted time and energy for nothing. Therefore burst the fetters that hold you down, and free yourselves at last!

The man who remains inwardly bound will always be a slave, even if he were a king.

You bind yourselves with all that you aspire to learn. Reflect: In acquiring knowledge you force yourselves into alien forms thought out by others; you willingly adopt an alien conviction, making your own only what others have experienced within, *for themselves.*

Consider: What applies to one does not apply to all! What helps one person may harm the other. Each individual must make his own way to perfection. The abilities he carries within him are his equipment for this. He must adjust himself to them and build upon them! Otherwise he will remain a stranger to his real self, will always stand *beside* what he has learned, which can never come to life in him. Thus he is barred from any gain. He will vegetate, all progress being impossible.

Listen, you who seriously aspire to Light and to Truth:

Each individual must inwardly experience the way to the Light, he must discover it *himself* if he wishes to be sure of the way. Only what a man experiences inwardly, what he perceives intuitively in all its variations, has he fully grasped!

Both sorrow and joy are constantly rapping at the door to encourage and arouse man to awaken spiritually. He is then very often freed for a few seconds from the trivialities of everyday life, and in happiness or grief vaguely senses his affinity with the spirit pulsating through all that lives.

And *everything* is life, nothing is dead! Happy is he who seizes and holds

28

on to such moments of affinity, using them to soar upwards. In so doing he must not keep to rigid forms, but everyone must develop himself, from within.

Ignore the scoffers, who are still strangers to spiritual life. They stand before the great Work of Creation, which offers us so much, like drunkards, like sick people. Like blind men who grope their way through life on earth without seeing all the splendour around them!

They are confused, they sleep; for how can anyone still affirm, for instance, that only what he can see exists? That where his eyes perceive nothing there is no life? That with his physical death he himself also ceases to exist, all because in his blindness he could not, up till now, convince himself to the contrary through his eyes? Does he not already know from many things how very limited is the capacity of the eye? Does he not yet know that it is related to the capacity of his brain, which is bound to time and space? That because of this he *cannot* recognise with his eyes anything rising *above* time and space? Has this logical, intellectual reasoning not yet become clear to any of these scoffers? Spiritual life, let us also call it the beyond, is after all merely something that stands completely above the earthly division of time and space, and therefore requires a similar nature in order to be recognised.

Yet our eyes do not even see all that can be classified within time and space. Think of a drop of water, which appears immaculately pure to every eye; and which on examination under the microscope is shown to contain millions of living organisms mercilessly fighting and destroying each other. Are there not sometimes bacteria in both water and air that have the power to destroy human bodies, and that are imperceptible to the human eye? But they become visible by means of powerful instruments.

Who then will still dare to maintain that there is nothing new and as yet unknown to be seen when the power of these instruments is further increased? Increase their power a thousandfold, a millionfold, and there will be no end to what may be seen, but ever new worlds which previously you could neither see nor feel, yet which nevertheless existed, will unfold before you.

Logical thinking also leads to the same conclusions about everything the sciences have hitherto been able to collect. There is a prospect of continuous progress and development, but never of an end.

What, then, is the beyond? The *word* confuses many. The beyond is simply all that cannot be perceived by earthly means. And earthly means are the eyes, the brain and all other parts of the body, also the instruments that help them to do their work still more accurately and precisely, and to extend its scope.

Therefore one could say: the beyond embraces all that is beyond the perceptive capacity of our physical eyes. *But there is no division between this world and the beyond!* Nor any gulf! All is united, as is the whole of Creation. *One* power streams through this world and the beyond, everything lives and works from this one life stream, and is thus quite inseparably linked. Thus the following becomes clear:

If one part of it sickens the effect must be felt in the other part, as with a physical body. Through the attraction of homogeneous species, diseased matter from this other part will then flow across to the sick part, thus further aggravating the illness. But should such a disorder become incurable, it will absolutely be necessary forcibly to sever the ailing member, if the whole is not to suffer permanently.

For this reason change your attitude. There is no such thing as this world and the beyond, but only one united existence! The idea of a division has been invented solely by man, because he is unable to see everything, and imagines himself to be the centre and focal point of the surroundings visible to him. Yet his sphere of action is greater. With the erroneous idea of a division, however, he forcibly limits himself, hinders his progress, and allows his imagination to run riot and conjure up grotesque pictures.

Is it surprising then, if as a consequence many only smile incredulously, while others adopt an unwholesome form of worship that becomes servile or degenerates into fanaticism? Who can then still be astonished if some people develop a nervous fear, even terror and consternation?

Away with all this! Why these torments? Break down this barrier which human error sought to erect, but which never existed! Your past wrong attitude also gives you a false foundation, on which you vainly endeavour continually to build up the true belief, that is, inner conviction. You consequently encounter points, obstacles, which must make you waver and doubt, or compel you to tear down the whole structure, perhaps abandoning everything out of despair or resentment.

The loss is then yours alone, because this is not progress for you, but standstill or retrogression. The road which in any case you must follow one day will only be lengthened thereby.

5. AWAKE!

When you have at last perceived Creation as a complete whole, as it is, and do not separate this world from the beyond, then you have found the direct path, the true goal draws nearer and the ascent gives you joy and satisfaction. You are then much better able to feel and understand the reciprocal actions pulsating warmly through this uniform whole, since all activity is driven and sustained by the one power. Then the Light of Truth will dawn upon you!

You will soon realise that many who scoff only do so out of indifference and indolence, just because it would require a certain effort to throw over existing ideas and learning and erect something new. Others would find it interferes with their customary mode of living and thus becomes uncomfortable for them.

Leave all such alone, do not argue, but offer your knowledge helpfully to those who are not satisfied with fleeting pleasures, to those who seek for something *more* in their earthly lives than merely to fill their stomachs like animals. Do not then bury your talent, impart to them the recognition you are granted; for in giving, your knowledge will in turn be enriched and strengthened.

An Eternal Law operates in the Universe: That only in giving can one receive where lasting values are concerned! Like a sacred legacy of its Creator, this Law deeply permeates the whole of Creation. To give unselfishly, to help where help is needed, and to understand both the suffering and the weaknesses of your fellow-men, means to receive, because it is the simple and true way to the Highest!

And to will this seriously brings you immediate help and strength! By one single, honest and ardent wish to do good, the wall which your thoughts have hitherto erected as a barrier is cleaved as with a flaming sword from the other side that is now still invisible to you; for you are indeed one with the beyond which you so fear, deny or long for, you are closely and inextricably linked with it.

Try it, for your thoughts are the messengers you send forth, which return heavily laden with similar thought-forms, good or evil as the case may be. This actually happens! Remember that your thoughts are realities that shape themselves spiritually, often becoming forms outliving the earth-life of your body, then much will become clear to you.

Thus it is quite rightly said: "For their works will pursue them!" Thought-creations are works which will one day await you! Which form

31

light or dark rings around you, which you must traverse in order to enter the spiritual world. Neither protection nor intervention can help in this, because the decision lies with you. Therefore you yourself must take the first step in everything. This is not difficult; it lies solely in the volition, which expresses itself through thoughts. Thus you carry heaven or hell within you.

You are free to decide, but you are then irrevocably subject to the consequences of your thoughts, of your volition! You yourselves create these consequences, and that is why I exhort you:

Keep the hearth of your thoughts pure, by so doing you will bring peace and be happy!

Do not forget that every thought you produce and send out attracts all similar thoughts on its way, or attaches itself to others, thus continually increasing in strength and finally also reaching a goal, a human brain which is perhaps off its guard just for a moment, thereby offering such floating thought-forms the opportunity to penetrate and operate.

Just consider what responsibility will fall upon you if at some time or other the thought becomes a deed through some person whom it was able to influence! This responsibility already arises through the fact that every single thought keeps a constant link with you just as if by an unbreakable thread, so as to return with the strength gained on its way, either to burden you or to bring you joy, according to the kind you produced.

Thus you stand in the world of thoughts, and according to your way of thinking at the time make room for similar thought-forms. Do not therefore waste the power of thinking, but gather it for defence and for *keen* thinking, which goes forth like spears and affects everything. Thus create out of your thoughts the *Holy Spear* which fights for the good, heals wounds and furthers the whole of Creation!

Adjust your thinking, therefore, towards activity and progress! To do this you must shake many a pillar supporting traditional ideas.

Often it is some concept wrongly understood that hinders man from finding the right way. He must return to the starting-point. One flash of light will destroy the whole structure so painfully erected over decades, and following a shorter or longer period of stunned inertia, he will make a fresh start! He *must* do so, for there is no standing still in the Universe. Let us take, for instance, the concept of time:

Time passes! Times change! We hear this said everywhere, and automatically a picture arises in the spirit: *We see changing times marching past us!*

This picture becomes so engrained that for many it also forms a solid foundation on which they continue to build, adjusting their whole research and speculation to it. Before long, however, they encounter obstacles which contradict each other. However hard they try, not everything will fit in. They lose their way, leaving gaps that can no longer be filled in spite of all their pondering.

Many then believe that in such places *faith* must act as a substitute for the failure of logical reasoning. But this is wrong! Man should not believe in things he cannot grasp! He must try to understand them; for otherwise he opens wide the door to errors, and with errors the Truth is always debased.

To believe without understanding is just indolence, mental laziness! It does not lead the spirit upwards, but presses it down. Look upward, therefore, we are to test and investigate. Not for nothing does the urge to do so lie within us.

Time! Does it really pass? Why does one encounter obstacles when thinking more deeply about this axiom? Simply because the fundamental idea is *wrong; for time stands still!* We, however, hurry towards it! We rush into time, which is eternal, and seek the Truth in it.

Time stands still. It remains the same, today, yesterday and a thousand years hence! Only the forms change. We plunge into time, to cull from her records for the purpose of enriching our knowledge from what has been collected there! For time has lost nothing, it has recorded all things. It has not changed, because it is eternal.

You too, O man, are always just the same, whether you appear young or old! You remain what you are! Have you not already sensed this yourself? Do you not clearly notice a difference between the form and your "ego"? Between the body that is subject to change and yourself, the spirit, which is eternal?

You seek the Truth! What is Truth? What you still feel to be truth today you will recognise even tomorrow as error, in which, however, you will later again discover grains of truth! For the manifestations also change their forms. Thus your seeking continues, yet amid these changes you mature!

Truth, however, remains always the same, it does not change, for it is eternal! And being eternal it can never be clearly and truly grasped by the earthly senses, which are familiar only with the change of forms!

Therefore become spiritual! Free from all earthly thoughts, and then you will *possess* the Truth, will stand in the Truth, and will bathe in it, constantly surrounded by its pure Light, for it will envelop you completely. As soon as you become spiritual, you will swim in it.

Then you need no longer study so painstakingly what science has to offer, nor need you fear errors, but you will already have the answer to every question in the Truth itself. Moreover, you will no longer have any questions, because without thinking you will know all things, will embrace all things, because your spirit will *live* in the pure Light, in the Truth!

Therefore become spiritually free! Burst all the fetters that hold you down! If obstacles present themselves welcome them joyfully; for they show you the way to freedom and strength! Look upon them as gifts from which you will benefit, and you will overcome them with ease.

Either such obstacles are put in your way to teach and develop you, in which case you add to the means of your ascent, or they are the reaction to some debt you have incurred, which you can redeem in this way and thus free yourselves. In either case they help you to advance. Therefore set out to meet them with a bold heart, it is for your own good!

It is foolish to talk of reverses of fortune or of trials. Every conflict and every sorrow means *progress*. Men are thus offered the chance to dispel the shadows of former misdeeds; for not a single farthing can be remitted to the individual, because here also the cycle of the Eternal Laws in the Universe is inflexible. The Creative Father-Will reveals Himself in them, and thereby forgives us and dispels all Darkness.

So clearly and wisely is everything arranged that the minutest swerving from this would have to plunge the world into ruins.

But what of the man who has very much to redeem from former times, must he not then despair, will he not tremble at the thought of the misdeeds he has to atone for?

As soon as he *honestly wills* he can hopefully and gladly begin with it, free from all worry! For a *balance* can be brought about by the counter-current of the power of good volition, which like other thought-forms takes life in the spiritual, forging a strong weapon capable of removing every dark burden, every weight, and leading the "ego" towards the Light!

Power of volition! A mighty force, unsuspected by so many! Attracting similar powers like a never-failing magnet, it grows like an avalanche.

Uniting with similar spiritual forces, it works backwards, again reaching the starting-point, thus the origin, or rather, the producer, uplifting him high to the Light, or pressing him deeper into the mud and filth! Exactly in accordance with what the author himself originally willed.

He who is acquainted with this steady, never-failing reciprocal effect inherent in all Creation, which manifests and unfolds itself with absolute certainty, knows how to make use of it; he must love it and fear it! Gradually the invisible world around him becomes alive to him; for he feels its influence so distinctly that it silences all doubt.

If he only pays a little attention to it he must intuitively sense the strong waves of ceaseless activity that affect him from out of the great Universe. Finally he feels himself the focal point of strong currents, like a lens that absorbs the rays of the sun, concentrating them on one point and producing a combustive power which can burst forth to singe and destroy, but also to heal, animate and bring blessing; and likewise can start a blazing fire!

And you, too, are such lenses, capable through your volition of gathering these invisible power-currents that reach you, and sending them forth as a united force for good or evil, to bring blessing or indeed destruction to mankind. Through this you can and should light a blazing fire in the souls of men, a fire of enthusiasm for the good, for the noble and for perfection!

This only requires a strength of volition, which in a certain sense makes man lord of Creation and master of his own fate. It is man's own volition which brings him destruction or redemption, reward or retribution, with inexorable certainty!

Do not fear then, that this knowledge will alienate you from the Creator, or weaken your present faith. On the contrary! The knowledge of these Eternal Laws, which you can put to use, makes the entire work of Creation appear even more sublime to you. Its magnitude forces him who searches more deeply to his knees in veneration!

Man will then never wish for evil things. He will joyfully grasp at the best support that exists for him: Love! Love for the whole wonderful Creation, and love for his neighbour, that he too may be led to the glory of this enjoyment, of this consciousness of power.

SILENCE

WHEN a thought suddenly strikes you, keep it back, do not utter it at once, but nourish it; for it will condense through being retained in silence, and gain strength like steam under counter-pressure.

Pressure and condensation produce the quality of a magnetic activity, in accordance with the Law that all that is stronger attracts what is weak. Similar thought-forms are thus attracted from all sides and retained, constantly reinforcing the power of your own, your original thought, yet working in such a way that through the joining of other forms the originally produced form is refined, changes, and takes on different shapes until it comes to maturity. Indeed you sense all this inwardly, but you always think it is entirely your own volition. *But you never give purely your own volition in any matter, there are always other influences as well!*

What does this process tell you?

That only in the union of many elements can anything perfect be created! Created? Is that right? No, but formed! For there is really nothing new to be created; in everything it is merely a matter of producing new forms, since all the elements already exist in the vast Creation. But these elements are to be pressed into service for the way to perfection, which is brought about through union.

Union! Do not pass over this lightly, but try to become absorbed in the concept that maturity and perfection are achieved through union. The principle rests in all Creation as a treasure that needs to be unearthed! It is closely related to the Law that only in giving can there also be receiving! And what is required to grasp these principles aright? Thus to experience them? Love! And therefore love indeed stands as the highest power, as unlimited might, in the mysteries of the great Life!

As with a single thought, union moulds, refines and forms, so is it with man himself and with the whole of Creation, which in a never-ending fusion of existing, individual forms undergoes transformations through the power of volition, and thus becomes the way to perfection.

A single individual cannot offer you perfection, but the whole of humanity, with all its varied characteristics, may do so! Each individual has something which is definitely part of the whole. And this is also why one so far advanced as no longer to know any earthly desires loves all mankind, not one individual, because only the whole of mankind can make the strings of his mature soul, laid bare through purification, sound the chord of heavenly harmony. He bears the harmony within himself, because all strings vibrate!

Let us return to the thought that attracted the other forms, and thereby became strong and ever stronger. It finally emerges beyond you in firmly united power-waves, breaks through your own personal aura, and exerts an influence upon your wider environment.

Mankind call this personal magnetism. The uninitiated say: "You radiate something!" According to your nature, either unpleasant or pleasant. Attractive or repulsive. It is felt!

But you do not radiate anything! The process which engenders the feeling in these others has its origin in the fact that like a magnet you draw to yourself all that is spiritually similar. And it is this drawing that is felt by those around you. Yet in this, too, lies the reciprocal effect. Through the connection the other person then clearly senses your strength, and thereby "sympathy" awakens.

Always bear in mind: Expressed according to our concepts, all that is spiritual is magnetic, and you also know that the stronger always overcomes what is weak through attraction, through absorption. In this way "from him that hath not (the weak one), even that which he hath shall be taken away". He becomes dependent.

There is no injustice in this, but it takes place according to the Divine Laws. Man only needs to pull himself together and will aright, and he will be protected from it.

You will now probably ask: What happens when all want to be strong? When there is nothing left to be taken from anybody? Then, dear friend, *there will be a voluntary interchange,* based on the Law that only in giving can there also be receiving. There will be no standstill on that account, but all that is inferior is eliminated.

Thus it happens that through indolence many become spiritually dependent, and sometimes, in the end, they hardly possess the ability to develop thoughts of their own.

It must be emphasised that only the homogeneous will be attracted. Hence the proverb: "Birds of a feather flock together." Thus drinkers will always find each other, smokers will have "fellow feelings", likewise gossips, gamblers, and so on; yet noble characters will also come together for a high aim.

But it goes further: Whatever is drawn to another spiritually will eventually also manifest *physically,* since everything spiritual penetrates into the gross material, whereby we must bear in mind the Law of Returns, because a thought always remains connected with its origin and radiates back to it through this link.

I am always speaking here only of *real* thoughts, which carry within them the vital power of the psychic intuition. Not of the power wasted by the brain-substance entrusted to you as a tool, which forms but fleeting thoughts that only manifest in a wild medley as shadowy phantoms, and fortunately very soon fade away. Such thoughts merely waste your time and energy, and thereby you fritter away a gift entrusted to you.

If, for instance, you seriously ponder over something, this thought becomes strongly magnetic within you through the power of silence, attracting all that is similar and thus becoming fructified. It matures and rises above the commonplace, thereby even penetrating into other spheres, from which it receives an influx of higher thoughts ... inspiration! Hence, in contrast to mediumship, the basic thought in inspiration must proceed from yourself, must form a bridge to the beyond, to the spiritual world, in order to draw consciously from a spring there. Inspiration has therefore nothing whatever to do with mediumship.

In this way the thought is brought to full maturity within you. You approach its realisation, and *bring* into effect, *condensed through your power,* what already in countless elements was floating in the Universe before as thought-forms.

Through unification and condensation of what has long existed spiritually you thus produce *a new form*! So in the entire Creation it is always only the forms that change, because all else is eternal and indestructible.

Beware of confused thoughts, of all shallowness in thinking. Carelessness will exact a bitter revenge; for it will speedily debase you to the level of a playground for alien influences, through which you very easily become sullen, moody and unjust to your surroundings.

If you have a genuine thought and cling to it, then the gathered power must eventually also press towards realisation; for the evolution of everything takes place entirely in the spiritual, *since every power is purely spiritual!* What then becomes visible to you are always only the final effects of a preceding spiritual-magnetic process, which takes place continually and uniformly according to a firmly established order.

Observation of your thoughts and feelings will soon prove to you that all real life can in truth *only be spiritual life*, in which alone the origin and also the development lie. You must come to the conviction that everything you see with your physical eyes is in reality only the manifestations of the eternally driving spirit.

Every action, even the slightest movement of a human being, is indeed always first spiritually willed. The physical bodies merely act as spiritually animated instruments, which themselves only took shape through the power of the spirit. The same applies to trees, stones and the whole earth. Everything is animated, permeated and driven by the Creative Spirit.

However, since all matter, thus all that can be physically seen, is simply the outcome of spiritual life, it is not hard for you to comprehend that *conditions on earth* are also formed according to the nature of the spiritual life which *immediately* surrounds us. What logically follows from this is clear: Through the wise ordering of Creation man has been given the power to shape conditions for himself with the Power of the Creator. Happy is he who uses it only for good! But woe unto him who succumbs to the temptation to use it for evil!

The spirit in men is only encompassed and darkened by earthly desire, which clings to it like dross, burdens it and drags it down. However, his thoughts are acts of will endowed with spiritual power. *The decision to think in a good or evil way lies with man, and he can thus guide the Divine Power to good or evil purpose!* Therein lies the responsibility that man bears, for reward or retribution will infallibly be his, as all the consequences of his thoughts return to the starting-point through the established reciprocal action, which never fails, and which is quite inflexible in this matter, thus inexorable. Thereby also incorruptible, stern and just! Do people not also say the same of God?

If today many opponents of religion reject the existence of a Godhead, this cannot in any way alter the facts I have cited. People need only omit the little word "God", and engross themselves deeply in science, and they will find *exactly the same*, only expressed in different words. Is it not absurd, therefore, still to argue about it?

There is no getting round the Laws of Nature, no man can defy them. God is the Power that activates the Natural Laws; the Power that nobody has yet grasped or seen, but whose *effects* every one, daily, hourly, indeed in every fraction of a second, must see, intuitively sense and observe, if only he *wants* to do so – in himself, in every animal, every tree, every flower, in every fibre of a leaf swelling and bursting its sheath to come to the light.

Is it not blindness to oppose this so obstinately while everyone, including these stubborn repudiators themselves, confirms and acknowledges the existence of this Power? What is it that prevents them from calling this acknowledged Power God? Is it childlike obstinacy? Or is it a certain shame at being obliged to confess that they have been obstinately trying all the time to deny something, the existence of which has always been clear to them?

Probably nothing of all this. The cause may well lie in the caricatures of the great Godhead held up to mankind from so many sides, which on serious investigation they could not accept. Any attempt to press the all-embracing and all-pervading Power of the Godhead into a picture must certainly debase and dishonour It!

On serious reflection no picture can be brought into harmony with It! Just because every man bears within him the awareness of God, he rejects with misgiving the narrowing down of the great inconceivable Power that created and guides him.

It is *dogma* that is to blame for a great number of those who, in their antagonism, seek to overstep the mark altogether, very often against the certainty living within them.

The hour is not far distant, however, when spiritual awakening will come! When the words of the Redeemer will be rightly interpreted and His great Work of Redemption rightly grasped; for Christ brought redemption from the Darkness by pointing out the way to the Truth, by showing as a man the path to the Luminous Height! And with His blood shed on the cross He set the seal to His conviction!

Truth has never yet been different from what it was even then, and is today, and still will be tens of thousands of years hence; for it is eternal!

Therefore learn to know the Laws contained in the great Book of the entire

Creation. To submit to them means: To love God! For then you will bring no discord into the harmony, but will help to bring the resounding chord to its full magnificence.

Whether you say: I voluntarily submit to the existing Laws of Nature because it is for my own good, or: I submit to God's Will, Which manifests in the Laws of Nature, or to the unfathomable Power Which activates the Laws of Nature ... would the effect be any different? The Power is there and you recognise it, you simply *must* acknowledge it, because as soon as you reflect a little there is nothing else you can do ... and thereby you acknowledge your God, the Creator!

And this Power also operates within you when you are thinking! Therefore do not misuse it to evil purpose, but think good thoughts! Never forget: When you are producing thoughts you are using Divine Power, with which you can achieve the purest and highest!

Try never to forget here that all the consequences of your thoughts always fall back upon you in proportion to the power, importance and extent of the *effect* of the thoughts for good or evil.

Since thought is spiritual, however, the consequences will return *spiritually.* They will thus affect you no matter whether here on earth, or later in the spiritual after your departure. Being spiritual they are by no means bound to the material either. Thus it follows *that the disintegration of the body does not prevent the consequences from taking effect!* The requital in the reaction will surely come, sooner or later, here or hereafter, with all certainty.

The spiritual link with all your works remains firm; for indeed earthly, material works also have a spiritual origin through the creative thought, and will remain in existence even when everything earthly has passed away. It is therefore rightly said: "Your works await you, in so far as the effect has not yet reached you through the reaction".

If you are still here on earth when a reaction is due, or if you are again here, the consequences coming from the spiritual will exert their force *according to their nature* either for good or for evil, through your circumstances and your environment, or directly on yourself, on your body.

Here it must once more be specially emphasised: *The true real life takes place in the spiritual!* And that knows neither time nor space, and therefore no separation either. It stands above earthly conceptions. For this reason the consequences will strike you, wherever you may be, at the time when, according to the Eternal Law, the effect returns to its starting-point. Nothing is lost in the process; it is bound to come.

This now also answers the question so often asked: Why is it that obviously good people must sometimes suffer such bitter adversity in their earth-lives as to make it appear unjust? *These are reciprocal effects, which must strike them!*

Now you know the answer to this question; for your existing physical body plays no part in it. Your body is not you personally, it is not your entire "ego", but an instrument which you have chosen or which you were obliged to take according to the existing Laws of the spiritual life, which you may also call Cosmic Laws if that makes them easier to understand. The particular earth-life is but a short span of your real existence.

A crushing thought if there were no escape, no protecting power to counteract it. On awakening to the spiritual many a person would then have to despair, and wish rather to go on sleeping in the same old way. For he has no idea *what* awaits him, what will still strike him in the shape of reaction from former times! Or as people say: "What he has to make good."

But take comfort! In the wise provision of the great Creation, as you awaken a path is also shown to you through that *power of good volition* to which I have already called special attention, and which mitigates or entirely pushes aside the dangers of the karma that is taking effect.

This, too, the Father's Spirit has given into your hands. The power of good volition forms a circle around you capable of disintegrating the evil pressing upon you, or at least of greatly modifying it, exactly as the atmosphere also protects the earth.

But the power of good volition, this strong protection, is fostered and nourished by the power of silence.

Therefore I once more urgently exhort you, seekers:

"Keep the hearth of your thoughts pure and then, above all, exercise the great power of silence if you wish to ascend."

The Father has already endowed you with the strength for everything! You have only to use it!

ASCENT

You who are striving for recognition, do not entangle yourselves in a web, but become seeing!

Through an Eternal Law you are burdened with an irrevocable obligation to make atonement, which you can never cast upon others. What you burden yourselves with through your thoughts, words or deeds can be redeemed by no one but yourselves! Consider, were it otherwise Divine Justice would be but an empty sound, in which case everything else would also crumble into ruins.

Therefore free yourselves! Do not delay a single hour in setting a limit to this enforced atonement! The honest volition for what is good, for something better, reinforced by a truly heartfelt prayer, *will bring redemption!*

Without the honest, steadfast volition for good there can never be atonement. Evil will then perpetually find ever fresh nourishment to keep it alive, and thus require ever new atonement, unceasingly, so that through constant renewal it only appears to you as a *single* vice or affliction! Whereas it is a whole chain without end, continually binding anew even before the old could be severed.

Then there will never be redemption because of the demand for constant atonement. It is like a chain that keeps you fettered to the ground; and there is very great danger of being dragged still further down. Therefore, you who are still in this world or already in what you regard as the beyond, pull yourselves together at last and concentrate your volition on what is good! With steadfast good volition the end of all atonements *must* come, since he who wills what is good and acts accordingly will incur no fresh debts demanding further atonement. This will then bring deliverance, redemption, which alone permit ascent to the Light. *Listen to the warning! There is no other way for you! For no one!*

But thereby everyone also receives the certainty that it can never be too late. For the individual deed, that you will have to redeem and settle, certainly; yet in the moment when you earnestly begin to strive for the good you mark the end of your atonement. Rest assured that this end *must* come one day, and your ascent will therewith begin! You can then joyfully start working off all your karmaic burden. Whatever you then still encounter is for your own good and brings you nearer to the hour of redemption, of liberation.

Do you now understand the value of my counsel to start exerting yourselves with all your strength for what is good, and to keep your thoughts pure? Not giving up, but pursuing this course with all your longing, all your energy? It will uplift you! It will change you and your environment!

Bear in mind that every life on earth is a short time of schooling, and that you yourselves do not cease to exist when you lay aside your physical body. You will continually live or continually die! Continually enjoy bliss or continually suffer!

Whoever imagines that with earthly burial everything is also ended and balanced for him, may turn and go his own way; for he is only trying to delude himself thereby. Horrified, he will come face to face with the Truth and ... will *have* to begin his path of suffering! His true self, deprived of the protection of his body, whose density surrounded him like a wall, will then be attracted, enveloped and held fast by what is homogeneous.

It will be more difficult for him, and for a long time impossible, to arouse the earnest volition for what is better, which could liberate and help him to ascend, because he is entirely subject to the influence of the homogeneous surroundings, which does not carry the kind of light-thought that might awaken and support him. He must suffer doubly under everything he has created for himself.

For this reason ascent is much harder than when he was in the flesh, where good and evil dwell side by side, which only the protection of the physical body makes possible because ... this earth-life is a school in which every "ego" is given the opportunity of further development according to its free will.

Therefore rouse yourselves at last! The fruit of every thought will return to you, here or there, and you have to taste of it! No one can escape this fact!

Of what use is it to try and bury your head timidly in the sand like an ostrich, to evade this reality? Face the facts boldly! You thereby make it easy for yourselves; for here progress is quicker.

Make a start! But realise that all old debts must be settled. Do not expect blessings to rain down upon you immediately, as many fools do. Perhaps some of you still have a long chain to expiate. But he who despairs on that account only harms himself, because it cannot be spared and remitted him. Through hesitation he only makes everything more difficult for himself, perhaps for a long time impossible.

This should spur him on not to delay another hour; for he only begins to live when he takes the first step! Happy is he who plucks up the courage to do so, for link by link he will be released. He can rush ahead with giant strides, jubilantly and gratefully overcoming also the last obstacles; for he becomes free!

The stones that his previous wrong-doing had heaped up before him like a wall, *inevitably* barring his advance, will indeed not be cleared away, but on the contrary will be carefully laid out before him so that he may recognise and surmount them, because he must bring about the balance for all his errors. However, filled with astonishment and admiration, he will soon see the love that surrounds him as soon as he only evidences his goodwill.

With tender forbearance the way will be made as easy for him as a child's first steps, aided by its mother. Should there be things in his former life that were a silent source of apprehension to him, and which he would rather let sleep forever ... quite unexpectedly he will be placed directly before them! He must decide, must act. In a striking way he is urged to do so through the enchainments. If he then ventures to take the first step, trusting in the victory of the good volition, the fateful knot is severed, he passes through and is freed from it.

But hardly is this debt settled than already the next one in some form or other presents itself to him, requesting as it were also to be settled.

Thus one by one the fetters that restricted and were bound to weigh him down are burst. He feels so light! And the feeling of lightness which some of you have surely experienced at one time or another is no illusion, but the effect of reality. The spirit thus freed from pressure becomes light and, in accordance with the Law of Spiritual Gravity, leaps upwards, to that region to which in accordance with its lightness it now belongs.

And so it must rise steadily upwards towards the longed-for Light. An evil volition presses the spirit down and makes it heavy, whereas a good volition uplifts it.

For this, too, Jesus has already shown you the simple way leading unerringly to the goal; for deep truth lies in the simple words: *"Love thy neighbour as thyself!"*

With these words He gave the key to freedom and ascent! Because it is an irrefutable fact: What you do for your neighbour you do in reality only for yourselves! Solely for yourselves, since according to the Eternal Laws everything returns to you without fail, good or evil, either already here or there. It will surely come! Thus you are shown the simplest of ways in which this step to the good volition is to be understood.

You should give to your neighbour with your *being,* your nature! Not necessarily with money and goods. For then those without means would be excluded from the possibility of giving. And in this being, in this "giving yourself" in the relation with your neighbour, in the consideration and respect you voluntarily offer him, lies the "love" of which Jesus speaks; lies also the help you give to your neighbour, because it enables him to change himself or ascend further, and because he gains strength from it.

The returning radiations of this, however, will quickly uplift you in their reciprocal action. You will receive continually new strength through them. With a soaring flight you will then be able to strive towards the Light ...

Poor fools are they who can still ask: "What do I gain by giving up so many old habits and changing myself?"

Is it a question of a business deal? And were they only to gain as human beings, to become ennobled as such, that alone would be reward enough. But there is infinitely more to it! I repeat: The moment a man begins to exert his good volition he also marks the end of his obligation to make atonement, which he must fulfil and can never escape. In this respect no one else can take his place.

Thus with this resolution the end of the enforced atonement is in sight. Of such great value is this that all the treasures of this world cannot outweigh it. He thus struggles free from the chains that fetter him, which he is constantly forging for himself. Therefore rouse yourselves from your enervating sleep. Let the awakening come at last!

Away with the intoxication that brings the paralysing delusion that redemption through the Saviour has become a letter of safe conduct, enabling you to spend your whole life in careless selfishness, provided that in the end you embrace the faith, turn back, and depart this earth believing in the

Saviour and His Work! Fools to expect such miserable, defective piecework from the Godhead! That indeed would mean cultivating evil! Remember this, and free yourselves!

Cult should be the endeavour which has taken on form, to make in some way acceptable to the earthly senses something that is beyond earthly comprehension.

It *should* be the endeavour which has taken on form, but unfortunately this is not yet so; for otherwise many things would have to have quite different forms if they had *emerged* from the endeavour itself. The *right* way for this requires the breaking forth of the outward forms from the inmost being. But all we see today is an *intellectual* upbuilding, into which the intuitive perceptions are only *afterwards* to be pressed. Thus the opposite way is taken, which naturally might just as well be called the reverse or wrong way, that can never really be inwardly alive.

As a result many a thing appears clumsy or obtrusive, which in another form would come much nearer to the *real* volition, and only then could have a convincing effect.

Much that is well-intentioned must repel rather than convince, because the right form for it has not yet been found, which the intellect can never give for something that is beyond earthly comprehension!

So is it also in the churches. The intellectual upbuilding here, which is directed towards earthly influence, is only too evident, and much that is good fails to impress because it has an unnatural effect.

On the other hand only that which does not conform to the Laws of Creation can have an unnatural effect. Just such things, however, are very much in evidence in the present-day cults, where simply everything that is opposed to the natural Laws of Creation is shrouded in a mysterious darkness.

However, just by unconsciously never speaking of a mysterious light in such matters, but always only of a mysterious darkness, men strike the right note; for the Light knows no veiling, therefore also no mysticism either, which should have no place in the Creation that arose out of the perfect Will of God, and works automatically in accordance with an unchangeable rhythm. Nothing is more clear in its weaving than just Creation, which is the Work of God!

Therein lies the secret of success and continuity, or of collapse. Where something is built on these living Laws of Creation, there they help, bring success and also continuity. But where these Laws are not observed, either through ignorance or self-will, sooner or later collapse must inevitably follow; for nothing that does not stand on a firm and solid foundation can endure permanently.

That is why so much of man's work is transient when it need not be so. This includes many kinds of cults, which have to undergo continual changes to prevent them from complete collapse.

In the simplest and clearest manner, the Son of God gave to earthmen in His *Word* the *right* path on which to lead their lives on earth in accordance with this weaving of Creation; so that through the Laws of God that operate in the weaving of Creation they might be helped, sustained and uplifted to Luminous Heights, and so also attain to peace and joy on earth.

Unfortunately, however, the churches have not followed the way to the redemption and upliftment of mankind, quite clearly explained and given to them by the Son of God Himself. Instead they have added to His teaching many of their own ideas as well, thereby naturally creating confusion, which was bound to cause dissensions because it was not in accordance with the Laws of Creation, and therefore, strange as it may sound, is also opposed to the clear teaching of the Son of God, although they call themselves Christians after Him.

So is it, for example, with the mariolatry of the papal Christians. Did Jesus, Who taught men *everything,* how they should think and act, yes even speak and pray, in order to do what is right and what lies in the Will of God, ever say even one single word of the kind? *No, He did not!* And this is a proof that He did not wish it either, that it was not to be!

There are even statements by Him which prove the opposite of what mariolatry implies.

And surely Christians would wish through honest living to follow only Christ, otherwise they would not *be* Christians.

If still more has now been added by men, and the papal churches act otherwise than as Christ taught, it is proof that this church has the effrontery to set itself *above* the Son of God; for it tries to improve on His Words by instituting practices which the Son of God did *not* want, because otherwise He would undoubtedly also have taught them, judging by all He gave to men.

Certainly, there *is* a Queen of Heaven, Who according to earthly conceptions could also be called the Primordial Mother, and Who yet possesses the purest virginity. She however has dwelt from all eternity in the *Highest Heights*, and has never been incarnated in an earthly body!

And it is She, Her *radiated picture*, but not in reality Herself, that can occasionally be "seen" or "intuitively perceived" by persons who have been profoundly moved. Through Her, help often comes at such an accelerated speed that people call it a miracle.

However, it is never possible, even for the most matured human spirit, to have an actual vision of this Primordial Queen *Herself*, because in accordance with the inflexible Laws of Creation each species can only always see the same species. Thus the physical eye can only see earthly things, the ethereal eye only ethereal things, the spiritual eye only spiritual things, and so on.

And since the human *spirit* can only see the spiritual, from which it has emerged, it is unable actually to behold the Primordial Queen, Who is of a much higher species. But should anyone ever be so blessed, it would *only* be possible to see *Her spiritually radiated picture.* This, however, appears so lifelike, and can be so strong even in its radiation, that it works miracles wherever it finds the soil prepared for it, through unshakable faith or the deep emotions arising out of suffering or joy.

This lies in the working of Creation, which issues from and is sustained by the perfect Will of God. In this working also lies all help for men from the beginning and unto all eternity, providing they themselves do not turn away from it in their pretentious learnedness.

God manifests in Creation; for it is His perfect Work.

And it is just on account of this perfection that the earthly birth of the Son of God had also to be preceded by a physical procreation. Whoever asserts the contrary throws doubt on the perfection of the *Works* of God, and thus also on the perfection of God Himself, out of Whose Will Creation issued.

An *immaculate* conception is a conception in purest love, as opposed to a conception in sinful lust! But no earthly birth without procreation.

If an earthly conception, that is, a physical procreation as such could not be immaculate, then every motherhood would have to be regarded as unclean!

Through Creation God also speaks, and clearly shows His Will.

To recognise this Will is the duty of man. And the Son of God in His Holy Word showed the right way to do so, because men had made no effort towards it, and had thus entangled themselves more and more in the self-acting Laws of Creation.

This inflexible weaving of Creation was bound to destroy men in time through their ignorance and misapplication; whereas it will raise mankind on high if they live aright according to the Will of God.

Reward and punishment for man lie in the weaving of Creation, which is perpetually and unswervingly guided by the Will of God Itself. In it also lies rejection or redemption! It is relentless and just, always impartial, never arbitrary.

In it lies the indescribable Greatness of God, His Love and Justice. That is, in *His Work,* which He made over to man and to many other beings, as a dwelling-place and a home.

The time has now come for men to acquire the *knowledge* of it, so that with complete conviction they will come to the recognition of *God's activity,* which is expressed in His *Work!*

Then every earthman will stand quite unshakable here on earth, filled with the most joyful eagerness to work, most gratefully looking up to God, because recognition links him for all time through the *knowledge!*

In order to convey to mankind such knowledge, which gives them a clear and intelligible conviction of the working of God in His Justice and Love, I have written the work "In the Light of Truth", which leaves no gap, contains the answer to *every* question, and clearly shows to mankind how wonderful are the ways in Creation that are upheld by many servants of His Will.

But God alone is Holy!

RIGIDITY

EVERYTHING in Creation is movement. Brought into being strictly according to Law by the pressure of the Light, movement produces heat through which forms are able to unite. Thus without Light there could be no movement, and therefore man can also imagine that in the proximity of the Light the movement must even be far more rapid and strong than at a vast distance from It.

In fact the greater the distance from the Light, the slower and more sluggish becomes the movement. In time it may even lead to the rigidity of all the forms which had already taken shape when at first the movement was still more animated.

The expression "Light" in this connection does not, of course, refer to the light of some planet, but to the *Primordial Light,* which is Life itself, therefore God!

Following this picture of a great survey of what takes place in Creation, I wish for once today to direct attention to the earth, which is now revolving at a far greater distance from the Primordial Light than it did many millions of years ago, because it has been increasingly exposed to the weight of the Darkness through men, who in their ridiculous and stubborn conceit, due to a one-sided over-development of the intellect, drew away from God. The intellect is and will always continue to be directed only *downwards* towards coarse matter, because *that is the purpose* for which it was provided; on the assumption, however, that it should be able to receive absolutely undimmed all radiations and impressions emanating from above, out of the Luminous Heights.

All the work of the intellect for outward activity in coarsest matter, that is, in material substance, falls to the frontal brain. On the other hand, the back brain has the task of taking in from above impressions which are lighter and more luminous than coarse matter, and passing them on for further use.

This harmonious co-operation of the two brains, given to men for their benefit, was disturbed by man's one-sided surrender to purely earthly, that is, to gross material activities. In the course of time it was completely stifled and tied off, as it were, because owing to its excessive activity the frontal brain was bound gradually to over-develop in proportion to the neglected back brain, which consequently became still less capable of receiving and also weakened. Thus over thousands of years the *hereditary evil* came into being through physical reproduction; for even newly-born children brought with them a frontal brain proportionately far more developed than the back brain. This held the danger of the awakening of the *hereditary sin*, through which man is compelled from the outset to direct his thoughts solely towards earthly things, and thus away from God.

All this will be easily comprehensible to every man of sincere good-will; moreover, I have given many and detailed explanations of it in my Message.

All the evil on earth came into being because man, owing to his spiritual origin, could exert a pressure with his volition upon everything else existing on earth; whereas just because of this spiritual origin he could and also should have had an *uplifting* influence; for that was and is his real task in Subsequent Creation, in which all that is spiritual naturally takes the lead. It can lead up-wards, which would be the natural thing, but it can also lead downwards if the volition of the spiritual is mainly striving only after earthly things, as is the case with earthmen.

In the knowledge of Creation which I have given in my Message, and in the related explanation of all the Laws automatically working in Creation, which may also be called the Laws of Nature, the whole weaving of Creation is dis-played without a gap; it allows every process to be clearly recognised, and therewith the purpose of man's whole life. With unassailable logic it also un-folds his "whence" and his "whither", thus giving an answer to every question, provided man seriously seeks for it.

Even the most malevolent opponents must halt here, because their cunning is insufficient to be able to invade and destroy the perfect completeness of what has been said, and thus also rob man of this help. – –

I have said that the movement in Creation must become progressively slower the further away anything is from the Primordial Light, the starting-point of the pressure which subsequently brings about movement.

So is it with the earth at the present time. Through the guilt of earthmen its orbits have become increasingly distant. As a result the movements are becoming slower, ever more sluggish, and thereby much has already approached the stage where rigidity sets in.

Rigidity also has very many stages; in its beginnings it is not so easy to recognise. Even while it is progressing, recognition remains impossible unless a flash of light for once stimulates the keenest observation.

This recognition is difficult simply because everything living within the sphere of the steadily slackening movements is also drawn uniformly into the increasing denseness that leads to rigidity. This applies not only to the body of a human being, but to everything, including his thinking. It affects even the most minute things. Imperceptibly every concept also changes and becomes distorted, even those concerning the actual meaning of the language.

Since he himself is drawn along in the same sluggish vibration, man cannot notice this in his neighbour, unless from out of his inner being he seeks once more to fight his way upwards spiritually with the strongest volition and with tenacity, so as again to come a little nearer to the Light. His spirit will then gradually become more mobile, thus lighter and more luminous, and will influence his earthly recognition.

Terrified and aghast with horror, however, he will then see, or at least intuitively perceive, how far the distortions of all concepts have already progressed in rigidity on this earth. The far-seeing view of how things really are is lacking, because everything has been pressed into narrow and obscure limits which can no longer be penetrated, and must in time completely stifle everything they embrace.

I have already often pointed out distorted concepts; but now, through the steady withdrawal from the Light, these are slowly proceeding on the downward path to rigidity.

It is unnecessary to give individual examples, for either no attention whatever would be paid to such explanations, or they would be described as tiresome quibbling, because man is much too rigid or too indolent to want to give them serious reflection.

I have also already spoken sufficiently of the power of the word, of the mystery that even the *human word* can, for a time, work constructively or destructively on the weaving of Creation within the sphere of the earth. This is because through the sound, tone and composition of a word, creative forces are set in motion which do not work according to the intention of the speaker, but according to the sense of the *word* in its meaning.

The meaning, however, was originally given through the forces which the word sets in motion, and which are therefore exactly adjusted to the *true* meaning, or vice versa, but not to the volition of the speaker. Meaning and word arose out of the corresponding movement of forces, therefore they are inseparably *one!*

Again, man's *thinking* sets in motion *other* currents of force which correspond to the essence of his thinking. Man should therefore endeavour to choose the right words to express his thinking, thus in so doing to perceive intuitively in a more accurate and clear manner.

Suppose a man is asked about something of which he has heard, and part of which he may even have seen. When questioned he would maintain without hesitation that he *knows* it!

In the opinion of many superficial people this answer would be correct, and yet in truth it is *wrong* and objectionable; for "to know" means to be able to give *exact information* about everything, every detail from beginning to end, without any omission and from one's own experience. Only *then* can a man say that he *knows* it.

Great responsibility attaches to the expression, and to the concept of "knowledge" associated with it!

I have also already pointed out the great difference between "knowledge" and what has been "learned". Learnedness is by no means real *knowledge*, which can only be absolutely personal; whereas what has been learned remains the acceptance of something outside the personal.

To hear something, and perhaps even to see part of it, is far from being the *knowledge* itself! A man should not assert: I *know* it, but the most he could say is: I have heard of it or seen something of it. If he wishes to act *correctly*, however, truth would oblige him to say: I do not know it!

This would be far more correct in every way than to report about something which he himself has nothing to do with, and which cannot therefore be a real *knowledge* either; whereas through incomplete reports he would only cast suspicion on or incriminate other people, perhaps even plunge them unnecessarily into misfortune, without knowing the actual ins and outs. Therefore carefully weigh with your intuitive perception *every* word you intend to use.

He who thinks more deeply, who will not be satisfied with already rigid concepts as a personal excuse for loquacious pomposity and malevolence, will easily understand these explanations, and in quiet examination will learn to look further in everything he says.

A multitude of such restricted concepts, with their fatal consequences, have already become habitual among earthmen. They are greedily snatched up and promoted by slaves of the intellect, who are the most willing adherents of the Luciferian influences of deepest Darkness.

Learn to observe attentively and to use properly the currents in this Creation, which bear the Will of God, and thus God's Justice in pure form. Then you will again find the true humanity which has been wrested from you.

How much suffering would thereby be avoided, and how many ill-disposed persons among mankind would also be deprived of the opportunity to commit their deeds.

This evil is also responsible for the description of the earthlife of the Son of God Jesus not corresponding at all points with the facts, as a result of which a totally false picture has gradually arisen in the minds of men up till now. The words given by Him were also distorted, as has happened with *every* teaching that was made into a religion and which was intended to bring upliftment and perfection of spirit to mankind.

And therein also lies the great confusion among all men, who increasingly fail really to understand one another, thus allowing discord, distrust, slander, envy and hatred to grow and flourish.

All these are unmistakable signs of advancing rigidity on earth!

Arouse your spirit, and begin to think and speak in a *far-seeing* and comprehensive way! This naturally also demands that you not only work with the intellect, which belongs to coarsest matter, but also make it possible once more for your spirit to guide your intellect, which should serve the spirit as ordained by your Creator, Who from the very beginning has permitted you to come undistorted into existence here on earth.

So much is already in the first stage of rigidity. Soon your entire thinking may already be gripped by it and must flow through rigid, iron channels, bringing you nothing but uneasiness, suffering upon suffering, and finally forcibly degrading you from a human being to the state of an empty machine serving only the Darkness, far away from all Light. –

56

CHILDLIKENESS

THE WORD "childlike" is an expression which is in most cases wrongly applied by human beings in their careless and thoughtless manner of speaking.

Hampered by indolence of the spirit, this expression is not perceived intuitively enough to be properly grasped. But he who has not grasped it in its entirety will never be able to use it aright either.

And yet it is just childlikeness that offers mankind a strong bridge for ascent to Luminous Heights, for giving every human spirit the possibility to mature, and for reaching perfection in order to live eternally in this Creation, which is the House of God the Father that He places at the disposal of men, provided ... they remain guests therein who are *agreeable* to Him. Guests who do not cause damage in the rooms so graciously made over to them solely for their use, with a table at all times richly spread.

But how far removed is man now from the childlikeness he so needs!

Yet without it he can achieve nothing for his spirit. The spirit *must* possess childlikeness; for it is and remains a child of Creation, even when it has gained full maturity.

A child of Creation! In this lies the deep meaning; for the spirit must develop into a child of God. Whether it will ever achieve this depends entirely on the degree of recognition it is willing to acquire on its wanderings through all the Spheres of Matter.

But with this willingness the *deed* must also manifest. In the Spiritual Planes will is at the same time also deed. There will and deed are always *one*. However, this is only so in the *Spiritual* Planes, not in the Worlds of Matter. The more dense and heavy a plane of the World of Matter is, the further removed is the deed from the will.

The fact that density causes obstruction is demonstrated even by sound, which as it travels has to struggle through material substance, which ob-

57

structs it according to the nature of the density. This can be clearly observed even over shorter distances.

When a man chops wood or drives nails into the timbers of a building, the impact of his tool can be clearly seen, yet the sound of it only arrives a few seconds later. This is so noticeable that everybody must have experienced it at one time or another.

The process is similar, but still more ponderous, between the will and the deed of man on earth. The will flares up in the spirit, and is immediately deed in the spirit. But to make the will visible in the Gross Material World, the spirit also needs the physical body. Only on impulse does a physical body already act within a few seconds of the flaring up of the will. Thereby the more tedious work of the frontal brain is eliminated, which otherwise has to mediate the way of the will right up to the impression on the activity of the body.

The normal way takes rather longer. Sometimes the result is only a feeble action, or none at all; because on its extended way the volition is weakened, or altogether suppressed, by the pondering intellect.

In this connection, although not strictly relevant here, I would like to make a reference to the effects of Creation's Law of the Attraction of Homogeneous Species, which are overlooked and yet so clearly visible also in human activity:

Human-earthly laws have been worked out by the earthly intellect, and are also carried into effect by it. *For this reason* schemes pondered with the intellect, thus premeditated actions, are as such more severely punished and judged as more evil than actions committed on the impulse of the moment, thus unpremeditated. In most cases these latter are treated more leniently.

In reality, there is a connection which is imperceptible to men, in the homogeneity of intellectual activity under the compulsion of the Law of Creation, for all those who unconditionally submit to the intellect. To them this is quite understandable.

Without knowing about it, the greater part of the atonement for an impulsive action is therewith assigned to the *Spiritual Plane*. Legislators and judges have no idea of this, because they proceed from quite different, purely intellectual principles. With deeper reflection, however, and knowledge of the active Laws of Creation, all this appears in an entirely different light.

Nevertheless, in other earthly sentences and judgments, the Living Laws of God in Creation work quite independently on their own, uninfluenced by earthly-human laws and conceptions. It will surely not occur to any serious-minded person to think that real guilt, not merely what men first designate as guilt, could also be expiated at the same time before the Laws of God through a paid penalty dictated by the earthly intellect!

Already for thousands of years these have been, as it were, two separate worlds, separated by men's actions and thoughts, although they should only be *one* world in which *God's* Laws alone operate.

Through such earthly punishment, atonement can only ensue if the laws and the punishments are completely in accord with God's Laws in Creation.

Now there are two kinds of unpremeditated actions. Firstly, those already described, which should really be called *impulse;* and then the kind that flashes up in the frontal brain, thus not in the spirit, and belongs to the intellectual category. The latter are unpremeditated, but should not receive the same mitigation as impulse-actions.

However, to find out exactly the just difference between the two will only become possible to *those* human beings who know all the Laws of God in Creation and are familiar with their effects. This must be reserved for a time to come, when there will also be no more arbitrary actions among men, because they will have a spiritual maturity that lets them swing only in the Laws of God in all their deeds and thoughts.

This digression is merely to induce reflection, it did not belong to the real purpose of the lecture.

Take note, then, that in the Spiritual Planes will and deed are *one,* but in the Material Planes they are separated through the nature of the substance. That is why Jesus once said to men: *"The spirit is willing, but the flesh is weak!"* The flesh, which refers here to the gross material substance of the body, does not convert into deed everything that has already been will and deed in the spirit.

But also on earth the spirit in its gross material garment could compel its volition always to become a gross material deed, if it were not too lazy to do so. It cannot hold the body responsible for this indolence; for the body was given to each spirit only as an instrument, which it must learn to control in order to use it properly. –

Thus the spirit is a child of Creation. And it must be *childlike* therein if it wishes to fulfil the purpose for which it stands in Creation. The arrogance of the intellect caused the spirit to withdraw from childlikeness, because the intellect could not "understand" what it really is. As a result, however, the spirit lost its foothold in Creation, which in order to remain healthy itself must now expel it as a stranger, an intruder and a dangerous creature.

And so it will come to pass that through their wrong thoughts and actions men will dig their own graves. –

How strange it is that every man who wishes to experience the Christmas Festival in the true sense must first try to recall his childhood!

This can surely be regarded as a clear enough sign *of the fact* that as an adult he is quite incapable of experiencing the Christmas Festival with his *intuitive perception.* It is definite proof that he has lost something he possessed as a child! Why does this not make men reflect!

Again it is spiritual indolence that prevents them from serious reflection on such matters. "That is for children," they think, "and grown-ups have simply no time for it! They have to think about *more serious matters.*"

More serious matters! By these more serious matters they mean only the pursuit of earthly ends, thus the work of the intellect! The intellect quickly represses memories, so as not to lose its supremacy if the intuitive perception is for once yielded to!

The *greatest* things could be recognised in all these apparently so trivial facts, if only the intellect would allow time for it. But it has the upper hand, and fights for it with all craftiness and cunning. That is to say, it is not the intellect that fights, but actually that which uses it as a tool and hides behind it: the Darkness!

The Darkness does not want the Light to be found in memories. And *how* the spirit longs to find the Light, to draw new strength from It, can be recognised by the fact that with the memories of childhood Christmas Festivals there also awakens an undefined, almost painful longing, able to move many people for a brief moment to tenderness.

If such tenderness were used at once and with all one's strength, it could become the best soil for the *awakening!* But unfortunately this only sends adults into a reverie, whereby the rising power is wasted and lost. And in the reverie the opportunity also slips by without the possibility of bringing benefit, or of having been used.

Even though many a person sheds a few tears, he feels ashamed and tries to hide them, pulling himself together with a physical jerk that so often betrays unconscious defiance.

How much could people learn from all this. It is no coincidence that a tender sadness also weaves itself into the memories of childhood days. It is the subconscious sensing that something has been lost, leaving an emptiness, the inability still to perceive intuitively like a child.

But you have surely often noticed the wonderful and refreshing influence of the mere quiet presence of any person from whose eyes a *childlike* radiance sometimes glows.

The adult must not forget that childlike is not childish. But you do not know whence the childlike has such an effect, what it really is! And why Jesus said: "Become as little children!"

To fathom what childlike is, you must first be clear that the childlike is by no means bound up with the child itself. No doubt you yourselves know children who lack the true beautiful childlikeness! Thus there are children without childlikeness! A malicious child will never have a childlike effect, nor an unruly one who is really ill-bred!

This clearly shows that childlikeness and the child are two things independent in themselves.

That which is called childlike on earth is a branch of the effect from out of *Purity!* Purity in its higher, not merely earthly-human sense. The human being who lives in the ray of Divine Purity, who makes room for the ray of Purity within himself, has thereby also acquired childlikeness, whether it be still in childhood or already as an adult.

Childlikeness is the result of inner purity, or the sign that such a human being has submitted to Purity and serves It. All these are merely different modes of expression, but in reality they always amount to the same thing.

Thus only a child who is pure within itself, and an adult who cultivates purity within himself, can have a childlike effect. That is why he has a *refreshing* and vitalising effect, and also inspires confidence!

And wherever there is true purity, genuine love can also enter, for God's Love works in the ray of Purity. The ray of Purity is the path It treads. It could not possibly walk on any other.

The ray of Divine Love can never find its way to him who has not absorbed the ray of Purity!

Man, however, has deprived himself of childlikeness by turning away from

61

the Light through his one-sided intellectual thinking, to which he has sacrificed everything that might have uplifted him. Thus he has firmly chained himself with a thousand fetters to this earth, that is, to the World of Gross Matter, which will hold him in its grip until he liberates himself from it. This, however, cannot come to him through earthly death, but only through *spiritual* awakening.

CHASTITY

CHASTITY is a concept that has been so unbelievably narrowed down by earthmen that absolutely nothing of its real meaning is left. It has even been dragged on to a wrong course; and as the natural and inevitable consequence this distortion has brought needless oppression, and even very often untold suffering, upon many people.

Ask where you will what chastity is, and everywhere in reply you will find explained in one way or another the concept of physical virginity; in any case, this is the highest that the perception of earthmen can reach.

This proves completely the inferior way of thinking of those who subordinate themselves to the intellect, which has itself set the limits to everything earthly, because it cannot reach any further with its faculties that are born of the earthly.

How easy it would then be for man to be regarded as chaste and so create a reputation, while sunning himself in vain self-glorification. But this does not bring him one step upwards on the road to the Luminous Gardens, which as Paradise are the blissful and final goal of a human spirit.

It is of no avail to earthman if he keeps his physical body chaste and defiles his spirit, which can then never cross the thresholds that lead upwards from one step to the next.

Chastity is different from men's idea of it, far more comprehensive and greater. It does not demand that man should go against nature; for this would be an offence against the Laws vibrating in God's Creation, and could only have harmful results.

Chastity is the *earthly* concept of Purity, which is *Divine*. For every human spirit it is the endeavour to manifest gross-materially what is sensed as a reflection of something that really exists in the Divine Sphere. Purity is Divine, chastity its representation by the human spirit; thus a spiritual image, which can and should become evident in earthly conduct.

This should suffice as a fundamental Law for every *matured* human spirit

63

in order to realise chastity. But on earth, urged on by many a selfish desire, man is inclined to imagine he possesses something which he actually does not, solely for the purpose of having his wishes fulfilled.

Selfishness takes the lead, and dulls the truly *pure* volition! Man will never admit this to himself, but simply allows himself to drift along. And when he can no longer persuade himself otherwise, he describes this often very obvious attempt to satisfy his questionable selfish desires as a decree of fate to which one must submit.

Therefore to guide and support him he needs still other hints which will let him experience and recognise what in truth chastity *is* as it lies in the Will of God, Who does not want any separation from nature on earth.

In the Divine Sphere Purity is closely united with Love! Hence if he is to derive blessing from them, man must not try to separate the two on earth either.

But on earth love is also no more than an evil caricature of what it *really* is. Thus unless it first undergoes a change it cannot unite with the true concept of purity.

To all those who strive to attain chastity, I herewith give a hint which provides the support that man needs on earth in order to live *in such a way* as rests in the Law of Creation, and as is therefore also pleasing to God:

"He who in his actions always remembers not to harm his fellow-man who reposes trust in him, not to do anything that may later oppress him, will always act *in such a way* as to remain spiritually unburdened, and may therefore be called truly chaste!"

These simple words, rightly understood, can fully protect and guide man through the entire Creation, and lead him upwards into the Luminous Gardens, his true home. These words are the key to all rightful activity on earth; for genuine chastity lies in them.

The Son of God Jesus expressed precisely the same in the words:

"Love thy neighbour as thyself!"

But you must beware of falling back into the old human faults, and of once more construing and partly distorting the meaning of the words so as to make them serve your own purpose, soothe you in your wrong-doing, and lull your fellow-men into carelessness or even help to mislead them.

Absorb such words as they are truly meant to be absorbed, not as appears convenient to you and suits your stubborn volition. Then for you they will be like the keenest sword in your hand, with which you can slay all Darkness if you but will. Let them become alive within you in the right way so that, filled with gratitude, you may grasp life on earth as jubilant victors!

THE FIRST STEP

LET MY Word become *alive* within you; for *this* alone can bring you *that* benefit which you need, enabling your spirit to ascend to the Luminous Heights of the Eternal Gardens of God.

It is of no avail to *know* of the Word! And if you could recite my entire Message sentence by sentence from memory, in order to teach yourselves and your fellow-men ... it is of no avail unless you *act* accordingly, *think* in the sense of my Word, and adjust your whole earth-life to it as a matter of course, as something which has become an integral part of your being, which cannot be separated from you. Only then will you be able to draw from my Message the eternal values it holds for you.

"By their *works* ye shall know them!" This saying of Christ is *primarily* intended for all the readers of my Message! By their works means by their *activity,* that is, by their thinking and deeds in their daily life on earth! Your deeds also include your speech, not only your actions; for speaking *is* action, the effect of which you have hitherto under-estimated. Even your *thoughts* are included here.

Men are in the habit of saying that thoughts are "free". By this they wish to imply that they cannot be held accountable on earth for their thoughts, because these are on a level which is inaccessible to human hands.

Therefore they often *play* with thoughts in the most careless way or, better expressed, they play *in* thoughts. Unfortunately often a very dangerous game, in the light-hearted illusion that they can emerge from it unharmed.

But here they err; for thoughts too belong to the *World of Gross Matter,* and must in all circumstances also be redeemed in it before a spirit becomes capable of swinging itself freely upwards, once it has severed the connection with its earthly body.

Therefore seek at all times to swing even with your thoughts in the sense of my Message, in such a way that you desire only what is *noble,* and do not lower yourselves because you imagine that nobody can see or hear it.

Thoughts, words and the visible deed all belong to the Realm of Gross Matter in this Creation!

Thoughts operate in the World of *Fine* Gross Matter, words in the World of *Medium* Gross Matter, and visible actions take form in the World of *coarsest,* that is, *densest* Gross Matter. These three kinds of your activity are *gross material!*

But the forms of all three are closely connected with each other, their effects are interwoven. What that implies for you, how incisive and decisive its effect often is in the course of your existence, you cannot estimate all at once.

It means nothing else than that also a thought, automatically working on according to its nature, can strengthen a homogeneous type in the World of *Medium* Matter, thereby producing more powerful forms; likewise then, deducing from this, it again continues to work on within this intensification, and arises in a visible active form in the *coarsest* World of Matter, without you yourselves seeming to be directly concerned with it.

It comes as a shock to know this, when one realises how superficial and careless these earthmen are in their thinking.

Thus without knowing it you *participate* in many a deed perpetrated by one or other of your fellow-men, simply because he has received the intensification in the way I have just explained to you. It became capable of driving him to the crudest perpetration of something that had hitherto slumbered within him, with which previously he had always merely toyed in his thoughts.

Thus many a person on earth very often looks with disapproval upon some action of one of his fellow-men, angrily repudiating and condemning it, and yet he is *partially responsible* for it before the Eternal Laws of God! In this someone who is a complete stranger to him may be involved, and it may concern a deed which he himself would never have committed in the Realm of Coarsest Matter.

Think yourselves deeply into such happenings for once, and you will then all the more understand why I call to you in my Message: *"Keep the hearth of your thoughts pure, by so doing you will bring peace and be happy!"*

But when you have become sufficiently strong in this respect through your own purification, far fewer crimes than hitherto, in which many have been unknowingly implicated, will be committed on earth.

The time and place of such deeds as you may become implicated in are of no importance here. Even if they occurred at the opposite end of the earth to where you live, in places where you have never set foot, of whose existence you have no knowledge whatever. Through your toying with thoughts intensifications will strike *wherever* they discover homogeneous types, independent of distances, nation and country.

Thus in the course of time thoughts of hate and envy may thrust themselves upon individuals, groups or whole nations, wherever they find homogeneity, impelling them to actions expressed in forms entirely different from those that first arose through your toying with thoughts.

The final result may then manifest according to the inner state of the *perpetrator* at the time of the deed. Thus you may have contributed to the perpetration of such horrible deeds as you yourselves have never really contemplated, and yet you are connected with them, and a part of the reaction must burden your spirit, must hang on it like a weight when it severs itself from the body.

But on the other hand you can also contribute even more powerfully to the peace and happiness of humanity, and through pure, joyful thinking can have a share in works that develop through total strangers.

From this the blessing also naturally flows back to you, and you do not realise why.

If you could but once *see* how the immutable Justice of God's All-Holy Will is always fulfilled in the self-acting Laws of this Creation for every single thought you harbour, you would strive with all your might to attain purity in your thinking!

Only then will you have become *such* human beings as the Creator in His Work will mercifully guide to the knowledge that bestows eternal life upon them, allowing them to become helpers in Creation worthy to receive the high blessings destined for the human spirit; so that these may be joyfully and gratefully transformed and passed on to *those* creatures who are only able to absorb them through such a transformation by man, and who today, through the decline of the human spirit, remain wantonly cut off from them, after it had already been possible for them to come into existence in times of a better and more purely swinging humanity.

With this, however, you will have made only *one* sentence from my Message glow with vitality for yourselves on earth!

For you it is the *most difficult one*, which will then make all the rest much easier, whose fulfilment must already let miracle upon miracle arise before you in earthly *visible* and tangible form. –

When you have conquered yourselves *in this,* you will be confronted on your path with yet another danger resulting from the distortion of human thinking: You will recognise in it a power which you will wish to press all too readily into quite definite forms, so that it may serve this or that special purpose made up of selfish desires!

Already today I wish to *warn* you against this; for the danger can engulf you, you would perish in it, even after you have set out on the right path.

Beware of a *desperate struggle* to enforce this purity of thoughts; for in so doing you would already press them into definite channels, and your effort would become an illusion, would always be only *artificially* enforced, and could never have the great effect that it should have. Your efforts would bring harm rather than benefit, because they lack the genuineness of the free intuition. Again it would be a product of your *intellectual volition,* but never the work of your spirit! Against this I warn you.

Remember my Word of the Message which tells you that all true greatness can lie only in *simplicity,* since true greatness *is* simple! You may be better able to understand *that* simplicity which I mean here, if for the time being you use instead the human-earthly concept of *being unassuming.* This perhaps comes nearer to your comprehension, and you will hit upon the true meaning.

You cannot give the purity that I mean to your thoughts through your thought-volition; but the pure volition, *unassuming* and boundless, must well up within you from your intuitive perception, not compressed into a word which can only give rise to a limited concept. That must not be; but an all-embracing urge for the good, able to envelop your thoughts as they arise and to permeate them even before they take form, is the right thing which you need.

It is not difficult, indeed much easier than the other attempts, once you become unassuming, whereby intellectual conceit about your own abilities and your own power cannot arise. Empty yourselves of thoughts, and set free within you the urge for what is noble and good. Then you will have *that* foundation for thinking which comes from the volition of your *spirit;* and whatever arises *from that* you can then safely leave to the work of your intellect to carry out in the Realm of Densest Gross Matter. Nothing wrong can ever develop.

Cast off all the torment caused by thoughts, and trust instead in your *spirit,* which will surely find the right way if you yourselves do not wall it up. Become *free in spirit,* which means nothing else than *let the spirit within you have its way!* Then it simply *cannot* do other than journey towards the height; for its very nature draws it upwards with all certainty. Hitherto you have restrained it so that it could no longer unfold, thereby you had restricted its flight or bound its wings.

The foundation for the upbuilding of a new humanity, which you cannot and must not evade, rests in the one sentence: *Keep the hearth of your thoughts pure!*

And it is *with this* that man must begin! That is his *first* task which will make him *what* he *must* become. An *example* to all who strive for Light and Truth, who wish to serve the Creator gratefully through the nature of their whole being. He who fulfils *this* needs no further directions. He *is* as he should be, and will thus receive the full measure of help that awaits him in Creation and leads him upwards without interruption.

THE WORLD

THE WORLD! When man uses this word he often utters it thoughtlessly, without forming a picture of *what* this world he speaks of is really *like*.

Many, however, who try to picture something definite visualise countless celestial bodies of the most varied nature and size arranged in solar systems, pursuing their courses in the Universe. They know that ever new and more celestial bodies can be seen as stronger and more far-reaching instruments are produced. The average man is then satisfied with the word "infinity", and thereby the error of a *wrong* conception sets in with him.

The World is not infinite. It is the material Creation, that is, the *Work* of the Creator. This Work, like every work, stands *beside* the Creator, and as such is finite.

So-called advanced thinkers often pride themselves on having the recognition that God rests in all Creation, in every flower, every stone; that the driving forces of nature are God, thus everything that is beyond investigation, what is sensed but cannot really be grasped. An ever-active Primordial Energy, the Source of Power, Itself eternally evolving anew, the Unsubstantiate Primordial Light. They consider themselves mightily advanced in the consciousness of finding God everywhere, of encountering Him everywhere, as an all-pervading driving Power, ever working towards the one goal of further development to perfection.

But only in a certain sense is this true. What we encounter in all Creation is only His Will and thus His Spirit, His Power. He Himself stands far above Creation.

From its very inception the Material Creation was bound to the unalterable Laws of evolution and dissolution; for what we call the Laws of Nature are the Creative Will of God, which in its activity is continually forming and dissolving worlds. This Creative Will is *uniform* in all Creation, to which the Ethereal World and the Gross Material World belong as *one*.

The absolute and immutable uniformity of the Primordial Laws, thus of

71

the Primordial Will, ordains that in the most minute process of the gross material earth the course is always exactly the same as it must be in every happening, thus also in the most stupendous events of the entire Creation, and in the creative process itself.

The strict form of the Primordial Will is plain and simple. Once it is recognised we easily discover it in everything. The complexity and incomprehensibility of many happenings lies solely in the manifold interlacing of the detours and by-paths formed by the varied volitions of men.

Thus the Work of God, the World, is as Creation subject to the Divine Laws, which are constant in all things and perfect; it also issued from them, and is therefore finite.

The artist, for example, also is in his work, merges with it, and yet personally stands beside it. The work is limited and transient, but not the talent of the artist on that account. The artist, that is, the creator of the work, can destroy his work, in which lies his volition, without himself being affected by it. Nevertheless he will still remain the artist.

We recognise and discern the artist in his work, and he becomes familiar to us without our needing to see him personally. We have his works, his volition lies in them and influences us, he confronts us in them, and yet may himself be living his own life far away from us.

The creative artist and his work faintly reflect the relation of the Creation to the Creator.

It is only the *cycle* of Creation, in its continuous coming into being, disintegration and re-formation, that is eternal and without end, thus infinite.

All the revelations and prophecies, too, are fulfilled within this happening. Finally the "Last Judgment" for the earth will also be fulfilled in it!

The Last, that is, the *Final* Judgment, comes one day for *each* material celestial globe, but it does not take place simultaneously in the whole of Creation.

It is a process necessary in that particular part of Creation which reaches the point in its cycle where its disintegration must set in, so that it can form itself anew on its further course.

This eternal cycle does not refer to the orbit of the earth and other stars around their suns, but to the great and mightier cycle which must in turn be followed by all the solar systems, while they in themselves also carry out their own movements separately.

Again, by reason of the consistency of the Natural Laws, the point at which disintegration of each celestial globe must begin is precisely determined. A very definite place at which the process of disintegration *must* develop, irrespective of the condition of the celestial globe concerned and of its inhabitants.

The cycle drives every celestial globe irresistibly towards this point, the hour of disintegration will be fulfilled without delay; as with everything in Creation this actually denotes only a transformation, the opportunity for a further development. Then the hour of the "either – or" has come for every human being. Either he is raised high towards the Light if he strives for the spiritual, or he remains chained to the World of Matter, to which he clings if out of conviction he declares that only material things are of value.

In that case, through the lawful consequence of his own volition, he is unable to rise from the World of Matter, and on the last stretch of the way he is drawn with it into disintegration. This then is spiritual death! Equivalent to effacement from the Book of Life.

This process, in itself quite natural, is also designated as eternal damnation, because he who is thus drawn along into disintegration "must cease to be personal". It is the most dreadful thing that can befall man. He is considered as a "rejected stone", which cannot be used for a spiritual building and must therefore be ground to dust.

This separation of spirit from matter, likewise taking place by reason of quite natural processes and Laws is the so-called "Last Judgment", which is connected with great upheavals and transformations.

Surely everyone will readily understand that this disintegration will not take place in *one* earth day; for in world events a thousand years are as one day.

But we are well into the early stages of this epoch. The earth now approaches the point at which it diverges from its hitherto existing course, which must also make itself strongly felt in gross matter. Then the separation among all men, which has already been prepared for some time, but which until now has only manifested itself in "opinions and convictions", will set in more sharply.

Every hour of an earth-life is therefore more precious than ever. He who earnestly seeks, and is willing to learn, should exert all his strength to tear himself from base thoughts, which must chain him to earthly things. Otherwise he is in danger of remaining attached to the World of Matter, and being drawn with it towards complete disintegration.

Those who strive for the Light, however, will gradually become detached from the World of Matter, and will finally be uplifted to the home of all that is spiritual.

Then the division between Light and Darkness will be finally accomplished, and the Judgment fulfilled.

It is not "the World", that is to say all Creation, which will perish thereby, but the celestial globes will only be drawn into the disintegrating process when their course reaches the point where dissolution, and with it also the preceding separation, is due to set in.

This is accomplished through the natural effect of the Divine Laws, which have lain in Creation from its very beginnings, which brought forth Creation itself, and which also now and in the future unswervingly bear the Will of the Creator. In the eternal cycle there is a perpetual creating, sowing, ripening, harvesting and dissolving, so that, newly invigorated through the change in the combination, other forms may again evolve, speeding towards a new cycle.

In considering this cycle of Creation, one may picture a gigantic funnel or a gigantic cave, from which in an incessant stream there perpetually gushes forth primordial seed, striving in rotating movements towards fresh union and development. Exactly as science already knows and has correctly noted.

Through friction and amalgamation dense nebulae are formed, and from these again celestial globes, which through immutable Laws group themselves with absolute consistency into solar systems; and rotating individually, they must unitedly follow the great cycle which is the eternal one.

Exactly as it is in the process that is visible to the physical eye in connection with plant, animal and human bodies, where there ensue from the seed the development, forming, maturity and harvest or decay, thus entailing a change, a disintegration, leading to further development, so is it also in great world events. The gross materially visible celestial globes, surrounded as they are by a far greater ethereal environment that is therefore invisible to the physical eye, are subject to the same process in their eternal cycle, because the same Laws are active in them.

Not even the most fanatical sceptic is able to deny the existence of primordial seed, and yet it cannot be seen by any physical eye because it is of a different substance which lies in the "beyond". Let us again simply call it ethereal.

Nor is it difficult to understand that in the natural order of things the world that *first* forms itself from primordial seed is equally ethereal, and not discernible with the physical eyes. Only *later* the *coarsest* precipitation further resulting from it gradually forms, dependent on the Ethereal World, the Gross Material World with its gross material bodies; and it is *only that* which can be observed from its minutest beginnings with the physical eyes and with all additional gross material aids.

It is no different with the covering of the real man in his spiritual nature, of whom I shall yet speak later. During his wanderings through the various worlds his garment, cloak, shell, body or instrument, no matter what one cares to call the covering, must always be of the same substance as the particular environment which he enters, so that he can make use of it as a protection and necessary aid if he wishes to be able to work *directly* and effectively therein.

Since the Gross Material World is dependent upon the Ethereal World, it follows that whatever happens in the Gross Material World also reacts on the Ethereal World.

This immense ethereal environment has likewise been created from the primordial seed. It takes part in the eternal cycle, and is finally also driven towards and sucked into the rear end of the aforesaid gigantic funnel, where disintegration takes place, in order to be thrust out again at the other end as primordial seed for a new cycle.

As with the action of the heart and the blood circulation, the funnel is like the heart of material creation. Thus the process of disintegration involves the whole of Creation, including the ethereal part, because *everything* that is material is again dissolved into primordial seed in order to form itself anew. There is nothing arbitrary in this, but everything develops out of the natural consistency of the Primordial Laws, which permit of no other course.

Hence at a certain point of the great cycle the moment arrives for all that is created, whether gross material or ethereal, when the process of disintegration is prepared independently from out of what is created, and finally breaks through.

Now this Ethereal World is the transitional dwelling-place of the earthly departed, the so-called beyond. It is closely connected with the Gross Material World, which is part of it and one with it. At the moment of death man, with his ethereal body, which he bears along with the gross material body, enters the homogeneous ethereal environment of the Gross Material World, while he leaves the gross material body behind on the latter.

Now this Ethereal World, the beyond, belonging as it does to Creation, is subject to the same Laws of continuous development and disintegration. With the setting-in of decay, a separation of the spiritual from the material again takes place in a perfectly natural way. According to man's spiritual state in the Gross Material World as well as in the Ethereal World, the spiritual man, the real "ego", must either move upwards or remain chained to the World of Matter.

The serious longing for Truth and Light will, by virtue of the change it works in him, make each person spiritually purer and thus more luminous, so that this condition must naturally detach him more and more from dense matter, and drive him upwards in proportion to his purity and lightness.

However, he who believes only in matter keeps himself bound to matter by his conviction, remaining chained to it, and thus cannot be driven upwards. Through a decision personally desired by each individual, a separation therefore takes place between those striving towards the Light and those connected with the Darkness, in accordance with the existing natural Laws of Spiritual Gravitation.

Thus it becomes clear that one day there will be a *definite end* also to the possibility of development through the purification-process in the so-called beyond for those who have departed this earth. A final decision! Men in both worlds will either be so far ennobled that they can be uplifted to the Regions of Light, or they will remain bound in their base nature through their own volition and thereby be finally hurled down into "eternal damnation". This means that together with matter, from which they cannot detach themselves, they will be drawn towards disintegration, will themselves suffer painful disintegration, and therewith cease to be personal.

They will be scattered like chaff in the wind, crumbled to dust and thereby erased from the Golden Book of Life!

Hence this so-called "Last Judgment", that is, the Final Judgment, is likewise a happening which through the operation of the Laws upholding Creation takes place in an absolutely natural manner, and in such a way that it could not be otherwise. Here, too, man always receives only the fruits of what he himself has willed, that is to say, what he himself brings about through his conviction.

It does not diminish the greatness of the Creator, but can only give cause to regard Him as even more sublime, to know that all that happens in Creation is strictly consistent and takes place automatically, that the direction of men's fate is always determined by themselves alone through their wishes and volition, and that the Creator does not look on and intervene to reward or punish.

The greatness lies in the *perfection* of His Work, and this compels us to look upwards in reverential awe, since the greatest Love and the most incorruptible Justice must lie without distinction in the mightiest as well as in the most minute happening.

Great also is man, placed as such in Creation as master of his own destiny! Through his will he is able to lift himself out of the Work, and at the same time contribute to its higher evolution; or he can drag it down and become entangled in it so that he can no longer free himself and will continue with it towards dissolution, whether in the Gross Material World or in the Ethereal World.

Therefore strive to free yourselves from all ties arising from base feelings; for it is high time! The hour approaches when the period allotted for this will have expired! Awake in yourselves the longing for the pure, the true and the noble! –

Far above the eternal cycle of Creation there floats like a crown in the centre an "Azure Island", the abode of the blessed, of the purified spirits, who may already dwell in the Regions of Light! This Island is separate from the World. Therefore it has no part in the cycle; but in spite of its height above the rotating Creation, it constitutes the support and the centre for the outgoing spiritual forces. It is the island that bears on its height the much-praised city with its streets of gold. Here nothing is subject any longer to change. No "Last Judgment" is to be feared any more. Those who can dwell there are "at home".

But as the last, as the highest on this Azure Island, inaccessible to those not specially called, stands the ... Grail Castle, so often spoken of in poetry! Encompassed by legends, the object of longing to so many, it stands there in the Light of Greatest Glory and harbours the Sacred Vessel of the Pure Love of the Almighty, the Grail!

The purest of spirits are appointed as guardians. They are bearers of Divine Love in its purest form, which is very different from what men on earth imagine it to be, although they experience it daily and hourly.

Through revelations, tidings of the Castle were brought down stage by stage the immense distance from the Azure Island through the Ethereal World, until finally, through a few deeply inspired poets, they also became known among people of the gross material earth. Passed on downwards step by step, the Truth also unintentionally suffered various misrepresentations, so that the final version could only be an increasingly dimmed reflection, which gave rise to many errors.

If now from some part of the great Creation in dire distress, suffering and ardent appeals rise to the Creator, then a Servant of the Vessel is sent forth as a bearer of this Love to intervene helpingly in the spiritual need. What floats merely as a myth and a legend in the Work of Creation then enters Creation as a living reality!

Such missions, however, do not often occur. Each time they are accompanied by incisive changes and great upheavals. Those who are thus sent bring Light and Truth to the erring, Peace to the despairing; with their message they stretch forth their hands to all who seek, offering them new courage and new strength, and guiding them through all Darkness up to the Light.

They come only for those who long for help from the Light, but not for the scoffers and the self-righteous.

THE STAR OF BETHLEHEM

THERE shall now be Light here on earth, as once it should have been when the Star of Promise shone radiantly above a stable in Bethlehem.

But at that time only a few accepted the Light, and those who listened to them very soon distorted and misrepresented it, as men on earth are apt to do. What they forgot they tried to replace with ideas of their own, thereby creating only a confusion that nowadays is meant to pass as inviolable Truth.

Out of alarm that everything will collapse if even the smallest pillar proves to be unsound, every ray of Light that can bring recognition is resisted, defiled and, if there is no other way, at least ridiculed with a malice and cunning which plainly indicates to clear thinking that it springs from fear! But clear thinking is only rarely to be found on earth.

In spite of this the light of true recognition *must* at last come over all mankind!

The time has arrived when everything unhealthy invented by the human brain will be swept out of Creation, so that it no longer suppresses the enlightenment that the Truth wears a *different* aspect from the unsteady images which boastful conceit and commercialism, morbid imagination and hypocrisy, in a craving for earthly power and earthly admiration, have created out of the sultry swamp of base narrow-mindedness.

Accursed now be those who through leading millions of people astray have so enslaved them that today they no longer dare to open their eyes to the Light, but blindly revile anything coming to their knowledge that sounds different from what they have hitherto heard, instead of at last listening attentively and examining inwardly to see whether the new does not come nearer to their understanding than what they have learned in the past.

Their ears are stopped, and anxiously they see to it that no breath of fresh air penetrates to them. Actually just out of laziness and fear that this fresh air, through the ensuing recovery, implies *spiritual activity*, demanding and enforcing self-exertion. In contrast to the present apparently comfortable spiritual slumber, which is followed by the heavy permanent sleep, and thereby only gives a free hand to the cunning of the distorted, debased intellect!

But it is of no avail to stop your ears against the new Word, to shut your eyes lest the Light dazzle and startle you! You will now be *forcibly* roused from this deplorable stupor! You will have to stand shivering before the cold Light that mercilessly strips you of all false wrappings. Shivering because your spirit-spark can no longer be kindled *within you,* and thus generate the warmth from within that will unite with the Light.

Indeed it is all too *easy* for you to *believe* the *unbelievable;* for then you need not trouble to think and examine for yourselves. Just because it cannot stand up to any test that is in accordance with the Divine Laws of Nature, you simply *have* to believe, without questioning the why or wherefore; you have to believe *blindly,* and this you imagine to be *great!* You who so conveniently imagine you are particularly devout, simply raise yourselves above all doubts in this matter, and ... feel happy, secure, noble, pious and sure of a place in Heaven!

However, you have not thereby raised yourselves above all doubt, but only bypassed it in a cowardly way! You were too spiritually indolent to bestir yourselves, and preferred blind faith to a knowledge of the natural happening in the Law of God's Will. Fictions devised by the human brain aided you in this. For the more absurd and incomprehensible the things you are supposed to believe, the easier it also becomes literally to believe in them *blindly,* because in such matters it is quite impossible to do otherwise. Knowledge and conviction *must* be eliminated then.

Only the impossible demands blind, unreserved faith; for whatever is possible immediately stimulates independent thinking. Wherever there is Truth, which is always characterised by naturalness and consistency, thinking and deep intuitive sensing automatically set in. This only ceases where it no longer finds anything natural, thus where Truth does not exist. And it is *only* through deep intuitive sensing that anything can become conviction, which alone brings values to the human spirit.

So now, along with everything else, the cycle which begins with the Holy Night in Bethlehem is also closing! And the closing of this cycle must cast out all inaccuracies in the transmissions, and in their stead bring the Truth to victory. The Darkness created by humanity is dispelled by the penetrating Light!

All legends which in the course of time have been woven around the life of Jesus must fall away so that it may at last emerge in purity, in accordance with Divine Laws, as indeed it could not have been otherwise in this Creation. Hitherto you have credulously and wantonly denied the Perfection of the Creator, your God, with your self-established cults.

You deliberately and consciously represent Him in these cults as imperfect in His Will! I have already spoken about this and, turn and twist as you will, not a *single* subterfuge can acquit you of having been too indolent to think about it yourselves. You do not honour God by blindly believing in things that are not in accordance with the Primordial Laws of Creation! On the contrary, if you believe in the Perfection of the Creator, then you must know that nothing can happen here in Creation that does not also precisely conform to the logical sequence in the firmly established Laws of God. Only therein can you truly honour Him.

He who thinks otherwise thus doubts the *Perfection* of the Creator, his God! For where alterations or further improvements are possible, there is not and never has been perfection! Development is something different. This is provided for and intended in this Creation. However, it must follow unconditionally *as a logical sequence* of the effect of already existing Laws. But all this cannot produce such things as many believers take for granted, especially in the life of Christ!

Wake up from your dreams at last and become inwardly *true!* Let it be said once more that according to the Laws in Creation it is impossible for bodies of earthmen ever to be born without previous physical procreation, and equally impossible for a physical body to be raised into the Ethereal Realm after its earthly death, still less into the Animistic or even the Spiritual Realm! And since Jesus had to be born here on earth, this event was also subject to the gross material Divine Law of a previous procreation.

If it had happened with Christ as transmissions report, God would have to act against His own Laws. But this He cannot do since He is *perfect from the very beginning,* and thus also His Will, Which lies in the Laws of Creation. Whoever still dares to think otherwise doubts this Perfection and thus ultimately also doubts God! For God without Perfection would not be God. There can be no subterfuge! No human spirit can quibble about this simple certainty, even if the foundations of many a former opinion must now be shaken thereby. Here there is only either – or. All or nothing. There can be no compromise, because nothing incomplete or unfinished can exist in the Godhead! Nor in anything concerned with God!

Jesus was procreated *physically*, otherwise an earthly birth would not have been possible.

At that time only a few recognised the Star as the fulfilment of the prophecies. Among them were Mary herself, and also Joseph who, deeply stirred, hid his face.

Three kings found their way to the stable and presented earthly gifts; but then they went away, leaving without protection the Child Whose earthly path they should have smoothed with their wealth and power, so that no harm might befall Him in the fulfilment of His Mission. Although they received enlightenment enabling them to find the Child, they did not fully recognise their sublime call.

Disquietude drove Mary away from Nazareth, and Joseph, seeing her silent suffering and longing, granted her wish solely to make her happy. He handed over the management of his carpenter's shop to his oldest employee, and with Mary and the Child journeyed to a distant country. In the course of their everyday life of work and cares, the memory of the Radiant Star slowly faded from their minds, especially as in His early years Jesus displayed nothing extraordinary, but like all children was quite natural.

It was only on his deathbed, after returning to his native town, that Joseph, who had always been the best of fatherly friends to Jesus, saw in his passing, during his last moments on earth, the Cross and the Dove above Jesus, Who stood alone at his bedside. Deeply stirring were his last words: "So Thou art He after all!"

Jesus Himself knew nothing of this until something urged Him to go to John, of whom He had heard that he was proclaiming wise teachings and baptising at the River Jordan.

With this gross material act of baptism, the beginning of the Mission was firmly anchored in the World of Gross Matter. The bandage fell. From this moment Jesus Himself was conscious that He was to carry the Word of the Father among mankind on earth.

His whole life as it really was will unfold itself before you, divested of all the fantasies invented by human brains! With the closing of the cycle of this

14. THE STAR OF BETHLEHEM

event, it will be revealed to all during the Judgment through the victory of the Truth, which for a long time to come may no longer be obscured!

Mary fought an inward battle with her doubts, which were strengthened through motherly anxiety for her son, right up to the grievous walk to Golgotha. Purely human and not supernatural. Only there did recognition of His Mission, and with it belief, finally come to her.

But now, at the return of the Star, all errors shall henceforth be redeemed through the Grace of God; and likewise all the faults of those who, without obstinacy or evil intent, rendered Christ's way more difficult at that time; and who now at the closing of the cycle come to recognition, and try to make good their neglect or failures.

Through their desire to make good, redemption arises for them with the Radiant Star; liberated, they can give jubilant thanks to Him Who in His Wisdom and Goodness created the Laws by which all creatures must judge and also redeem themselves.

83

THE CONFLICT

Up TILL now there could be no question as yet of a sharp confrontation between two world views. Conflict is therefore an ill-chosen term for what is actually happening between the intellectuals and serious seekers for the Truth.

All that has so far taken place has consisted of one-sided attacks by the intellectuals, which to any dispassionate observer must appear obviously unfounded and often absurd. Scorn, hostility, and even persecution of a most serious kind await all those who seek to develop themselves higher in a purely spiritual sense, even when they maintain silent reserve. There are always some who try by ridicule or force to pull back and drag down such aspiring ones to the dull insensibility or hypocrisy of the masses.

Thus many were bound to become actual martyrs, because not only the masses but therewith also the earthly power has been on the side of the intellectuals. What these have to offer is already clearly indicated in the word "intellect". That is: A narrowing of the range of the perceptive capacity to purely earthly matters, and thus to the minutest part of real existence.

It is easily understandable that this can produce nothing perfect, nothing good whatever for a humanity whose existence moves mainly through spheres which the intellectuals have closed to themselves. Especially so when one considers that just one brief earth-life should become a significant turning-point for the whole existence, entailing as it does decisive interventions in those other spheres which are completely inconceivable to the intellectuals.

The responsibility of the intellectuals, who rightly considered have already fallen deeply, is thus enormously increased, and as heavy pressure it will help to push them more and more swiftly towards the goal of their choice, so that they will at last have to partake of the fruits of what they have persistently and presumptuously advocated.

By intellectuals are to be understood those who have unconditionally submitted themselves to their own intellect. These people, strange to say, have for thousands of years believed that they had an absolute right to impose their limited convictions by law and by force also upon those who wished to live according to another conviction. This utterly illogical presumption again lies only in the intellectuals' narrow perceptive capacity, which is incapable of lifting itself higher. This very limitation brings them a so-called peak of comprehension, whereby such presumptions are bound to arise in the imagination, because they believe they really are standing on the utmost height. This is actually true so far as they are concerned, since they have arrived at the boundary which they cannot cross.

But their attacks on seekers for the Truth, so often inexplicably malevolent, clearly show on closer observation the whip of the Darkness brandished behind them. Seldom does one find in these hostile acts a trace of honest volition, which might somewhat excuse their often shocking manner of proceeding. In most cases there is only blind fury devoid of any real logic. Just examine such attacks dispassionately. How seldom is there among them an article whose contents indicate an attempt to enter really *objectively* into the speeches or essays of a seeker for the Truth.

The unfounded and paltry nature of the attacks is always quite strikingly apparent from the very fact that these are *never kept purely objective!* They are always a veiled or open defilement of the *person* of the Truth-seeker. *This is only done by someone who is incapable of replying objectively.* After all, a seeker for the Truth or a bringer of the Truth does not give himself *personally*, but he brings what he *says*.

The word must be examined, not the *person!* It is a habit of the intellectuals to seek always to regard the person first, and then to consider whether they can listen to his words. Owing to the narrow limitation of their perceptive capacity, these people *need* such an outward hold, because they must cling to externals to prevent them from becoming confused. Indeed just this is the hollow structure which they erect, which is inadequate for men and a great hindrance to their advancement.

If they had a firm inner hold they would simply let fact speak against fact, excluding the personal element altogether. But this they are unable to do. Indeed, they intentionally avoid it because they feel or partly know that in a well-ordered tournament they would be quickly unseated. The ironic reference to "lay preacher" or "lay interpretation", so often used, shows such a degree of ridiculous presumption that every serious person immediately senses: "This is a shield used to conceal shallowness at all costs. To cover their emptiness with a cheap signboard!"

Clumsy strategy which cannot last for long. Its purpose is from the beginning to place seekers for the Truth who may become troublesome on an "inferior" if not even a ridiculous level in the eyes of their fellow-men, or at least to classify them as "dabblers" so that they will not be taken seriously.

In so doing they seek to prevent anyone from seriously paying attention to the words. The motive for this proceeding, however, is not anxiety lest their fellow-men be delayed in their inner ascent through erroneous teachings, rather it is a vague apprehension of losing influence and thereby being compelled to penetrate more deeply than before, and having to change much that till now was supposed to be unassailable, and which suited them.

It is just this frequent reference to "laymen", this strange looking down upon those who through their strengthened and less influenced intuitive perception stand much nearer to the Truth, and who have not built walls for themselves through rigid intellectual forms, that exposes a weakness whose dangers cannot escape the notice of any thinker. *He who believes in such opinions is at the outset excluded from being an unprejudiced teacher and guide,* for he stands much further away from God and His Activity than any other man.

Knowledge about the development of religions, with all the errors and faults, does not bring men nearer to their God, and just as little does the intellectual interpretation of the Bible or of other valuable writings of the different religions.

The intellect is and remains bound to time and space, that is to say earthbound; whereas the Godhead, and thus also the recognition of God and His Will, are above time and space and above all that is transitory, and therefore can never be grasped by the narrowly-confined intellect.

For this simple reason the intellect is not called upon to bring enlightenment in eternal values. Indeed it would be a contradiction. Therefore he who in *these* matters boasts of university qualifications, and would look down upon those who are not so influenced, thereby declares his own incompetence and limitation. Thinking people will at once sense intuitively the one-sidedness, and use caution against him who cautions them in such a manner!

Only those who are called can be true teachers. Called ones are those who carry the ability within them. These abilities, however, do not ask for university training, but for the vibrations of a refined intuitive faculty, able to soar above time and space, thus beyond the limit of comprehension by the earthly intellect.

Moreover, any inwardly free man will always assess a matter or a teaching according to *what* it brings, not according to *who* brings it. The latter is the strongest possible evidence of his unfitness to be an investigator. Gold is gold, whether a prince or a beggar holds it in his hand.

But just in the most valuable things of the spiritual man, one seeks obstinately to disregard and to alter this irrefutable fact. Naturally without any more success than in the case of gold. For those who are really seeking seriously do not permit themselves to be influenced by such distractions from examining the matter itself. But those who do allow themselves to be so influenced are not yet mature to receive the Truth. It is not for them.

But the hour is not far distant when a conflict, which has been lacking as yet, must now break out. The one-sidedness will end, and a sharp confrontation will follow which will destroy all false presumption.

MODERN PSYCHIC SCIENCE

MODERN psychic science! What gathers beneath this flag! What comes together there, and what also opposes each other beneath it! A playground for earnest seeking, little knowledge, great plans, vanity and stupidity; in many cases also for empty boasting, and still more for the most unscrupulous commercialism. Out of this confusion there frequently blossom envy and boundless hatred, which finally results in the basest kind of malicious vindictiveness.

In such a state of affairs it is naturally not surprising if many people shun all these strange activities, fearing to poison themselves by coming into contact with them. They are not far wrong either; for countless adherents of psychic science are anything but engaging in their behaviour, still less attractive; on the contrary, everything about them warns others to exercise the greatest caution.

It is strange that the whole field of so-called psychic science, which is often confused by the malicious or ignorant with *ghost* science, is today still considered a sort of *free territory* where everyone may go on in his own way and get up to his tricks unhindered, even unrestrained and unpunished.

Such is it *considered* to be. But already experiences have very often taught that it is *not* so!

Countless pioneers in this field who were rash enough to venture a few steps forward in their investigations, equipped with only an imagined knowledge, have become helpless victims of their carelessness. The only sad thing about this is that all these victims fell without bringing even the slightest benefit to humanity thereby!

Now each of these cases should really have proved that the way followed is not the right one, because it brings only harm and even destruction, but no blessing. Yet with singular persistence these false ways are still retained, and fresh victims continually sacrificed; a great clamour is raised over every small detail that is discovered and newly recognised, although self-evident in the mighty Creation, and innumerable treatises are written which must repel many serious seekers, because the uncertain groping therein is clearly perceptible.

All investigations until now can really rather be called dangerous pastimes, based on good intentions.

The field of psychic science, which is considered free territory, can never be entered upon with impunity as long as one does not *first* know how to take into account the *spiritual* Laws to their full extent. Every conscious or unconscious opposition to these Laws, that is "non-observance" of them, which is equivalent to a transgression, must through its inevitable reciprocal action strike the bold, frivolous or careless person who does not or cannot pay close attention to them.

Trying to explore the non-earthly with earthly means and possibilities is no different from placing and leaving an undeveloped child, as yet unfamiliar with earthly dangers, alone in a virgin forest, where only a man adequately equipped for it and at the height of his strength, exercising the greatest precaution, can have any prospect of surviving unharmed.

For modern psychic scientists with their present methods it is no different, even if their intentions are absolutely serious, and if they are really taking great risks for the sole purpose of gaining knowledge to help men advance across a boundary, before which they have long stood knocking and waiting.

Today these investigators still stand before it like children, helpless and groping, unaware of the dangers that may stream towards them at any moment, or pour forth through them on to others if their bungling efforts breach the natural defences, or open a door that for many had better remain closed.

As long as those desiring to forge ahead are not absolutely certain that they will be able completely and instantly to master all dangers which may arise, not only for themselves but also for others, all this can only be termed rashness, not courage.

Those "investigators" who engage in experiments act most irresponsibly of all. Attention has already been repeatedly called to the crime of hypnotism.*

Investigators experimenting in yet other ways in most cases make the regrettable mistake, knowing nothing themselves – for otherwise they would

---

* Lecture: "The Crime of Hypnotism"

surely not do it – of putting other very sensitive or mediumistic persons into either a magnetic or even a hypnotic sleep, in order to bring them nearer to the physically invisible influences of the "other world", in the hope of there-by hearing and observing various things that would not be possible if the person experimented upon was in a fully day-conscious condition.

In at least ninety-five out of a hundred cases they thus expose such persons to great dangers, which they are not yet qualified to meet; for *every kind* of artificial help towards deeper penetration is a binding of the soul, forcing it into a sensitiveness that goes further than its natural development would permit.

The result is that such a victim of experiments suddenly stands psychically in a region where he is robbed of his natural protection by the artificial help, or for which he does not have his natural protection, which can only be formed through *personal,* sound inner development.

One must picture such a pitiable person as if he stood naked, tied to a stake and pushed far out into a dangerous country as a bait, to attract and even let himself be affected by the as yet unknown life and activity there, so that he can report upon it; or so that various manifestations will also become visible to others, through his co-operation, by the giving off of certain earthly sub-stances from his body.

A person thus experimented with is able at times, through the connection his projected soul must maintain with his earthly body, to report as through a telephone all that happens, and transmit it to the observer.

However, should the outpost thus artificially pushed forward be in some way attacked, he cannot defend himself through lack of his natural protec-tion. He is helplessly abandoned, because with the aid of others he has been only artificially pushed into a domain where, according to the state of his own development, he either does not yet or does not at all belong. And the so-called investigator, whose thirst for knowledge pushed him into it, can do just as little to help him, since he himself is strange and inexperienced in the place whence the danger comes, and therefore unable to do anything to pro-vide protection.

Thus it happens that the investigators unwittingly become criminals, who cannot be apprehended by earthly justice. However, this does not prevent the *spiritual* Laws from exercising their reciprocal action with full force, and chaining the investigator to his victim.

Many a person used for experiments has suffered ethereal attacks which in due course, often also quickly or immediately, have a gross-material-physical effect as well, so that physical illness or death follows, but without eliminating the harm done to the soul.

The observers who call themselves investigators, however, who push their victims into unknown regions, in most cases stand during such hazardous experiments under good earthly cover through the protection of their body and day-consciousness.

It is seldom that they share simultaneously in the dangers confronting the persons experimented with, thus that such dangers are immediately communicated to them. But then at their physical death, the transition into the Ethereal World, because they are chained to their victims they *must* inevitably go wherever these may have been drawn, so that together with them they may slowly begin to ascend once more.

The artificial projection of a soul into another domain must not always be taken to mean that the soul leaves the body and floats away to another region. In *most* cases it remains quietly in the body. But the magnetic or hypnotic sleep makes the soul unnaturally sensitive, so that it responds to much finer currents and influences than would be possible in its natural state.

It is self-evident that in this unnatural condition the full strength is not available, which the soul would otherwise possess if it had attained this point through its own inner development, and would therefore stand firmly and securely on this new and more refined soil, bringing an equal strength to bear on all influences.

Because of this lack of sound full vigour, the artificiality produces an inequality which is bound to entail disturbances. As a result all intuitive perceptions become absolutely blurred, giving rise to distortions of reality.

The cause of the false reports and countless errors is again always given only by the investigators themselves, through their harmful assistance. That is also why in the many "investigated" matters from the occult field already available so much does not accord with strict logic. They contain countless errors, which until now could not yet be recognised as such.

Absolutely nothing that could be of the slightest use or blessing to mankind is gained by these obviously wrong methods.

Actually only that which helps men *upwards,* or at least points a way thereto, can be of any use to them. But from the outset there can be absolutely no question of this as far as these experiments are concerned!

Sometimes, however, an investigator through artificial assistance may ultimately be able to crowd some sensitive or mediumistic human being out of his earthly gross material body into the Ethereal World nearest to him, but *not* a hair's breadth *above* the region to which in any case he belongs by virtue of his inner development. On the contrary, through artificial assistance he cannot even bring him that far, but always only to the environment nearest to all that is earthly.

However, this environment nearest to the earthly can only contain all that of the beyond which is still closely earthbound, which remains chained to the earth by its inferiority, its vice and passion.

Naturally, now and then something more advanced will also make a short stay in this environment. But it is not always to be expected. Something exalted cannot be there, purely by virtue of the Natural Laws. Sooner would the world be turned upside down, or ... a foundation for anchoring the Light exist in a human being!

It is hardly to be assumed, however, that this should be sought either in a person experimented upon or in such a groping investigator. Thus the danger and uselessness of all experiments remains.

Moreover it is certain that unless there is a human being of advanced development, whose presence purifies all coarseness, something really higher can *not* approach a medium, much less speak through him. Materialisations from *higher* circles are altogether out of the question, to say nothing of such popular pastimes as knocking, movements of objects, and so on. The gulf for this is far too wide to be easily bridged.

Even with a medium, all these things can only be carried out by such souls in the beyond as are still very closely connected with matter. Were it otherwise possible, that is to say, if an exalted being could so easily make contact with humanity, then there would have been no need whatever for Christ to become man, but He could have accomplished His Mission also without this sacrifice.* Men of today, however, are certainly no more highly developed psychically than in Jesus' earth-life, so it cannot be assumed that it is easier to establish a link with the Light now than it was in those days.

* Lecture: "The Redeemer"

Now psychic scientists declare, of course, that their primary aim is to establish that there is life in the beyond, and especially that life continues after physical death; and that in view of the scepticism prevailing today very strong and forceful arguments are needed, hence *earthly tangible* proofs, to breach the defences of the adversaries.

But this reasoning does not justify the repeated endangering of human souls in such a wanton way!

Besides, there is really no compelling need to set about convincing malevolent opponents at all costs! Surely it is well known that even if an angel came directly from Heaven to proclaim the Truth to them they would not be prepared to believe. As soon as he had gone they would simply affirm that it was a mass hallucination and no angel at all, or trump up some other excuse. And if any thing or any body were brought, which or who remains in an earthly state, thus neither vanishing nor becoming invisible, there would again be other excuses, just because it would then be too earthly for those who do not wish to believe in a beyond.

They would not hesitate to declare such a proof a swindle, and the person a visionary, a fanatic, or likewise a swindler. Whether it be too earthly or too unearthly, or both together, they will always have some fault to find and doubt to express. And if they know of no other way to help themselves, then they will take to abuse, proceed to even more vigorous attacks, and will not shrink from violence.

Therefore, to convince *these,* sacrifices are not called for! Still less, however, for many of the so-called adherents. With a strange kind of arrogance, due to their generally rather vague and fantastic belief in life in the beyond, these think they can make certain demands on it whereby they in turn must "see" or "experience" something. They expect signs from their guides in the beyond as a reward for their good behaviour.

The expectations they harbour, which they consider to be their natural due, are often as utterly ridiculous as the much-knowing, leniently forgiving smile with which they mask their real ignorance. It is poison to wish even to give performances to these masses; for since they imagine they know so much, the experiments are little more to them than well-earned hours of entertainment, in which those in the beyond are expected to act as music-hall artistes.

But just let us leave the big experiments now and consider the small ones, such as table-turning. These are by no means as harmless as people imagine, but because of the extreme ease with which these practices can spread they are a *very grave danger!*

Everyone should be warned against this! Enlightened persons must turn away in horror when they see how lightly these things are treated. How many adherents seek to display their "knowledge" in various circles by suggesting experiments in table-turning, or by introducing into families, with smiles or mysterious whispers, the almost playful practice with letters and a glass, or some other aid, which when the hand is lightly laid on it glides or is drawn along to various letters, thus forming words.

With uncanny rapidity all this has developed into party games carried out amid laughter, derision and at times a kind of pleasant thrill.

Every day older and younger ladies, in families or also alone, are seated at a little table before a piece of cardboard on which letters have been drawn, which if possible must even be of a very special design, so that the hocus-pocus stimulating the imagination is not lacking. Actually this is quite un-necessary; for the object would also be accomplished without it, if the person concerned has only some tendency towards these things. And those who have are innumerable!

Modern psychic scientists and leaders of occult societies are glad of this, because real words and sentences are formed of which the person practising has neither consciously nor unconsciously been thinking. He must thereby become convinced and increase the number of adherents of the "occult".

Publications of occult societies point to this, speakers support it, and app-liances are made and sold, which facilitate all this nonsense, and thus almost the entire occult world acts as *an efficient underling of the Darkness,* in the honest conviction of being a priest of the Light!

These occurrences alone prove the utter ignorance that lies in occult endeav-ours of this kind! They show that of all these people nobody is *really a "see-ing" one!* If now and then some good medium has developed from these be-ginnings, or rather, to be more correct, if in the early stages a good medium has been temporarily attracted to them, this must not be regarded as proof to the contrary.

The few people destined for this from the outset have in their own natural development a totally different protection, carefully watching over every step, which others do *not* enjoy. However, this protection is only effective in natural self-development, *without any artificial aids!* Because only in all that is natural does protection lie as a matter of course.

As soon as there is the slightest assistance, whether through practices by the person concerned or from another source in the form of magnetic sleep or hypnotism, it becomes unnatural, and is thus no longer completely in harmony with the Natural Laws which can alone grant protection. When to this there is added ignorance such as exists everywhere today, then it becomes disastrous. *Volition* alone will never replace ability when it comes to action. But no one should go further than his own ability will carry him.

It is naturally possible that among the hundreds of thousands who engage in this dangerous pastime there may be here and there one who really escapes unpunished and enjoys good protection. There are also many who will only be harmed in such a way as is not yet apparent on earth; and not until they pass on must they suddenly realise in what follies they have actually indulged. But there are also many who already bear physical evidence of harm, although they will never recognise the real cause during their life on earth.

For this reason the ethereal and spiritual happenings during these pastimes must for once be explained. It is just as simple as everything in Creation, and not at all so complicated, and yet again more difficult than many imagine.

In the present state of the earth the *Darkness* has, through the volition of mankind, gained the upper hand over everything material. Thus in all material things it stands to all intents and purposes on its own familiar ground, and can therefore manifest to the fullest extent in the material. Hence it is in its element there, fighting on soil with which it is well acquainted. Thereby, for the time being, in all that is material, that is gross material, it is superior to the Light.

The consequence is that in all things material the power of the Darkness becomes greater than that of the Light. Now with such pastimes as table-turning, etc., the Light, thus what is exalted, is completely out of the question. At the most we can speak of something bad, thus dark, and something better, thus more luminous.

Now when a person makes use of a table, or a glass, or indeed of any gross material object, he thus enters upon the battle-ground which is familiar to the Darkness. A soil which all Darkness calls its own. From the start he thereby yields to the Darkness a power against which he cannot summon up adequate protection.

Let us for a moment consider a spiritist pastime, or simply a party game with the table, and then follow the spiritual, or rather the ethereal happenings.

When one or more persons approach a table for the purpose of contacting through it those living in the beyond, either so that these should make knocking sounds or, as is more usual, move the table, so that words can be formed from these signs, then through the connection with material substance the first to be attracted is also the Darkness, which will take over the manifestations.

Those in the beyond often use high-sounding language with great skill, and seek to answer the thoughts of men, which they can read quite easily, in the manner these desire; but if serious questions arise they invariably lead them astray and, if it is done often, try gradually to bring them under their ever-increasing influence, and so slowly but surely to drag them down. Yet they very cunningly leave the dupes in the belief that they are ascending.

But if perhaps at the very start, or at some other opportunity, a relative or friend who has passed over can communicate through the table, which very often happens, the deception is then much more easily accomplished. The people will recognise that it must really be a specific friend who manifests, and then will believe that it is always he when any utterances are transmitted through the table and the name of the friend is given as the author.

But this is not the case! Not only does the ever watchful Darkness make cunning use of the name to make deceptions appear as authentic as possible, and gain the confidence of the questioners; but it even goes so far that a dark one will interfere in the middle of a sentence begun by the real friend, and purposely give it a false ending. Thereupon emerges the scarcely known fact that in a smoothly and flowingly given sentence *two* have taken part. First the real, and perhaps quite luminous, therefore purer friend, and then a dark entity of evil volition, without the questioner noticing anything of it.

The results of this are easy to imagine. The trusting person is deceived and his faith shaken. The opponent uses the incident to support his ridicule and doubts, and occasionally to make violent attacks on the whole subject. But in fact both are wrong, which can only be traced back to the ignorance still prevailing on the whole matter.

What occurs, however, takes place in all naturalness: If a more luminous and real friend is at the table to comply with the wish of the questioner and to make himself known, and a dark spirit crowds to the table, then the more luminous one must retreat from it, since the darker one can develop greater strength through the material substance of the table acting as an intermediary, because at the present time all that is material is the actual domain of the Darkness.

The mistake is made by the person who chooses material objects, and thus from the outset provides unequal ground. What is dense, heavy, and therefore dark, certainly stands by virtue of its density nearer to gross matter than what is luminous, pure and lighter, and through the closer connection it can develop greater strength.

On the other hand what is more luminous and still able to manifest through a material object, likewise still possesses a certain degree of density corresponding with the object, otherwise a link with physical matter for the purpose of some communication would no longer be possible at all. This in itself presupposes a closer approach to matter, which in turn involves the possibility of defilement as soon as the connection with the Darkness is made through matter.

To avoid this danger the more luminous one has no option but quickly to withdraw from the material, thus from the table or some other appliance, as soon as a dark one reaches out for it, in order to cut off the intermediary link, which would form a bridge over the natural separating and thereby protecting gulf.

It is then unavoidable in the beyond that in such cases the person experimenting through the table must be left at the mercy of base influences. Indeed, his own action proves that he wished for nothing else; *for ignorance of the Laws cannot protect him here either.*

With these occurrences much that has hitherto been inexplicable will become clear to many, numerous puzzling contradictions will be solved, and it is to be hoped that in future many people will really leave such dangerous playthings alone!

Also the dangers attaching to all other experiments, which are much bigger and more powerful, can now be described in the same detailed manner. But for the time being it should suffice to mention these most common and widespread instances.

Only one other danger must yet be mentioned. Through this kind of questioning and seeking for replies and advice, people make themselves very dependent and lose their self-reliance. This is the reverse of life's purpose on earth.

In every respect it is the wrong course! It only brings harm, no benefit. It is a grovelling on the ground where there is danger of constantly encountering disgusting vermin, wasting one's strength, and finally collapsing exhausted by the wayside … all for nothing!

With this "desire to investigate", however, much damage is also done to those in the beyond!

Many dark ones are thus offered an opportunity, indeed they are thereby even directly tempted to commit evil and to burden themselves with fresh guilt, which they could not so easily do otherwise. And others are retarded in their upward striving through the constant link formed by such wishes and thoughts.

In clearly observing the nature of these investigations it often appears so childishly obstinate, so imbued with a most ruthless egotism, and withal so clumsy, that one must shake one's head and ask oneself how anyone could possibly want to open out to the general public a region of which he himself does not really know the first thing.

It is also wrong for all these investigations to take place before the general public. To do so opens the way for visionaries and charlatans, making it difficult for mankind to gain confidence.

This has never happened in any other field. And every investigation whose complete success is now acknowledged was subject to numerous failures during the previous period of research. But the public were not allowed to take part in them to the same extent! They are fatigued by them, and in due course lose all interest. The result is that when the Truth is at last discovered the impetus for a revolutionary and sweeping enthusiasm was bound to be lost beforehand. Mankind can no longer rouse themselves to an exultant joy, so convincing that it carries everything along with it.

When it is realised what wrong courses have been pursued, the repercussions become sharp weapons in the hands of many enemies, who in the course of time are able to instil such distrust in the minds of hundreds of thousands of people that, when the Truth emerges, these unfortunates will no longer desire to examine it seriously for sheer fear of a new delusion! They close their ears, which they would otherwise have opened, and so miss the last span of time that could still grant them the opportunity to ascend to the Light.

Thereby the Darkness will then have won a further victory! It can offer its gratitude to the investigators who to that end extended their hands to it, and who are pleased and proud to proclaim themselves leaders of modern psychic sciences!

WRONG COURSES

With few exceptions, mankind labour under a boundless delusion which is fatal for them!

God has no need to run after them and beg them to believe in His existence. Nor are His servants sent out forever to admonish people on no account to turn away from Him. This would indeed be absurd. To think and expect such things is a dishonouring and debasing of the sublime Godhead.

This erroneous conception causes great harm. It is fostered by the behaviour of many truly earnest pastors who, out of a real love for God and men, try again and again to convert people who turn only to material things, to convince them and win them over to the church. All this only tends immeasurably to increase man's conceit in regard to his importance, of which there is more than enough already, and in the end really to place many under the delusion that they must be begged to strive for what is good.

This is also the cause of the strange attitude of the majority of all "believers", whose example is more often a deterrent than an inspiration. Thousands upon thousands feel a certain inner satisfaction, an exaltation, in the consciousness that they believe in God, that they utter their prayers with such earnestness as they are capable of bringing up, and that they do not intentionally harm their neighbours.

In this inner "exaltation" they feel a certain reward for goodness, thanks from God for their obedience, and they sense a being linked with God, of Whom they also think at times with a certain sacred thrill that produces or leaves behind a state of bliss, in which they revel.

But these legions of believers take the wrong course. Living happily in a self-created delusion, they are unaware that it numbers them with those Pharisees who, with the genuine but mistaken feeling of gratitude, bring their small sacrifices: "Lord, I thank Thee that I am not as other men are". This is not expressed in words, nor really in thought, but the inner "uplifting feeling" is nothing more than this unconscious prayer of thanks, which Christ too has already shown to be false.

In these cases the inner "exaltation" is nothing more than the setting free of self-satisfaction engendered by prayer or forced good thoughts. Those who call themselves humble are mostly very far from really being humble! It often requires self-restraint to speak with such believers. In such a frame of mind they will never at any time attain to the bliss which they are confident they already possess! Let them take heed lest they be altogether lost through their spiritual arrogance, which they consider to be humility.

It will be easier for many who now are still absolute unbelievers to enter the Kingdom of God than for all the legions with their conceited humility, who do not really stand before God in simple supplication, but indirectly demanding that He reward them for their prayers and pious words. Their petitions are demands, their inner being hypocritical. They will be swept away like empty chaff before His Countenance. They will have their reward, certainly, but it will be different from what they imagine. They have already satiated themselves long enough on earth in the consciousness of their own value.

The feeling of well-being will rapidly disappear on passing into the Ethereal World, where the inner intuitive perception, which is scarcely sensed here, will come to the fore, while the feeling hitherto mainly produced only by thoughts will be blown to nothing.

This inner, silent, so-called humble expectation of something better is really nothing but a demand, even though it be expressed differently, in however beautiful words.

Every demand, however, is a presumption. God alone has to demand! Nor did Christ come pleading to mankind with His Message, but warning and demanding. He certainly gave explanations about the Truth, but He did not enticingly hold out rewards before the eyes of His hearers to spur them on to become better. Calmly and sternly He commanded serious seekers: "Go thou and do likewise!"

God stands before humanity *demanding,* not enticing and pleading, not lamenting and grieving. He will calmly abandon to the Darkness all the wicked, even all the wavering ones, so that those who are striving upwards shall no longer be exposed to their attacks; enabling the others thoroughly to experience everything they consider to be right, and thus come to the recognition of their error!

LIKE deepest night ethereal darkness lies spread over this earth! For a very long time already. So dense and firm is the suffocating embrace in which it holds the earth that every ascending light-perception is like a flame which, without oxygen, loses its power and quickly fading dies out.

This ethereal condition, now manifesting at its worst, is dreadful. Anyone permitted for only five seconds to glimpse what is happening would from sheer horror be deprived of all hope of salvation! –

And all this has been brought about through the guilt of men themselves. Through the guilt of their propensity for what is base. Here mankind have been their own worst enemy. Now even those few who are once more earnestly striving upwards are *also* in danger of being swept into the depths, towards which others are now developing at a sinister speed.

It is like a close embrace, which is followed inevitably by fatal absorption. Absorption into the sultry, tenacious swamp, in which everything sinks without a sound. There is no longer a struggling, but only a still, silent, gruesome choking.

And man does not recognise it. Spiritual indolence blinds him to this fateful happening.

But all the time the swamp is sending forth its poisonous emanations, which slowly weary those who are still strong and alert, so that they, too, will fall asleep and sink away powerless.

That is the state of affairs on earth today. It is not a picture that I am unfolding therewith, but *life!* Since all ethereal matter bears forms, created and animated through men's intuitive perceptions, such a happening actually takes place continually. And this is the environment that awaits men when they must leave this earth, and cannot be led upwards to the more luminous and beautiful regions.

But the Darkness grows ever *more* dense.

Therefore the time draws near when for a while this earth must be left to the rule of Darkness, without direct help from the Light, because humanity enforced this through their volition. The consequences of the volition of the majority *were bound* to bring this ending. – It is the time which John was once permitted to behold, when God will veil His Countenance. –

Everywhere there is night. Yet during the deepest affliction when everything, including what is better, is also in danger of sinking away, at the same time dawn will now break! But the dawn will first bring the travail of a great purification, which is inevitable before the salvation of all serious seekers can begin; for *no* helping hand can be offered to all those who pursue base ends! They shall fall headlong into those terrible depths where alone they can still hope for an awakening through such torments that they must come to loathe themselves.

Those who with sneers and apparent impunity have hitherto been able to hinder the upward striving ones will become silent and more pensive, until finally, begging and whimpering, they will supplicate for the Truth.

Then it will not be so easy for such; they will be irresistibly led through the millstones of the inexorable Laws of Divine Justice, until in the *experiencing* they come to the recognition of their errors. –

In the course of my travels I could see that a firebrand was hurled among the indolent human spirits with my Word, which declares that no man can lay claim to Divinity; whereas just at this time much effort is bent upon discovering God *within* oneself, so that ultimately man himself might also become God!

Hence disquiet has often awakened with my Word, mankind rebelliously seeking to defend themselves against it, because they only wish to hear soothing and reassuring words that seem *pleasant* to them!

Those who so rebel are simply cowards, who would like nothing better than to evade the personal issue, only to remain in obscurity, where they can indulge in sweet and peaceful dreams to *their* heart's content.

Not everyone can bear to be exposed to the Light of Truth, which clearly and mercilessly shows up the defects and spots on one's garment.

With smiles, scoffing or with enmity such people would like to prevent the coming of the day when the feet of clay supporting that flimsily constructed idol, their "ego", will be clearly revealed. Such fools are only masquerading with themselves, which will be relentlessly followed by the grey Ash Wednesday. With their wrong views they really want only to idolise themselves, and thereby they feel well and comfortable on earth. From the outset they regard *anyone* who disturbs them from this indolent placidity as an enemy!

However, *this time* no resistance will be of any avail to them!

The self-idolatry evident in the assertion that there is Divinity in man is a base attempt to grasp at the sublimity and purity of your God, *thereby defiling* for you the most Holy, to which you look up in the most blissful trust! –

There is within you an altar which should serve for the worship of your God. This altar is your intuitive faculty. If this is pure it is directly connected with the Spiritual Realm and thus with Paradise! Then there are moments when you too can fully perceive the nearness of your God, as often happens in times of deepest sorrow and greatest joy!

You then perceive His nearness in the same way as is constantly experienced by the eternal Primordial Spirits in Paradise, with whom you are closely connected at such moments. The strong vibration caused by the emotion of great joy or deep sorrow for a few seconds pushes everything earthly and low far into the background, thereby setting free the purity of the intuitive perception, which thus immediately forms the bridge to the homogeneous purity that animates Paradise!

This is the most supreme happiness for the human spirit. The eternal ones in Paradise live in it continually. It brings the glorious certainty of being protected. They are then fully conscious of the nearness of their great God, in Whose Power they stand, yet at the same time they also realise as a matter of course that they have reached their greatest height, and will never be able to behold God.

This, however, does not depress them, but in the recognition of His unapproachable Majesty they give jubilant thanks for the inexpressible mercy He has always shown in regard to the arrogant creature.

And this happiness can already be enjoyed by man on earth. It is quite right to say that in deeply solemn moments earthman senses the nearness of his God. But it is sacrilege if man asserts that he himself possesses a spark of the Godhead within, because of this wonderful bridge which grants him the awareness of Divine nearness.

Hand in hand with this assertion also goes the debasing of Divine Love. How can God's Love be measured by the standard of human love? Moreover, how can It be valued even *below* this human love? Look at those people who picture Divine Love as the highest ideal, just silently enduring and also forgiving everything! They want to recognise Divinity *by the fact* that It tolerates any misbehaviour from lower *creatures,* such as only the greatest weakling or the most cowardly human being would do, for which they are despised. Just reflect what a monstrous insult this implies!

Men would like to sin unpunished, and then finally even please their God by allowing Him to forgive their wrong-doing without having to atone for it themselves! Such presumption shows either the utmost narrow-mindedness, unpardonable laziness, or the realisation of how hopelessly weak they are in bringing forth the good volition to strive upwards: The one, however, is as reprehensible as the other.

Picture to yourselves Divine Love! Crystal clear, radiant, pure and great! Can you then imagine that It is as sentimentally weak and ignobly yielding as mankind would so like it to be? They want to build up a false greatness where they *wish* for weakness, they give a false picture only to deceive and reassure themselves about their own shortcomings, which make them willing servants of the Darkness.

Where then is to be found the freshness and power that unquestionably belong to the crystal purity of Divine Love? Divine Love is inseparable from the utmost severity of Divine Justice. Indeed It even is Divine Justice. Justice is Love, and Love again lies only in *Justice.* In this alone lies also Divine Forgiveness.

The churches are right in saying that God forgives *everything!* And *really* forgives! Contrary to man, who goes on condemning a person even after he has atoned for some trivial offence, and thus burdens himself with a double guilt by such thoughts, because he does not act according to the Will of God. Here human love is lacking in justice.

The activity of the Divine Creative Will purifies every human spirit of its guilt as soon as it strives upwards, whether through its own experiences or through its voluntary efforts at improvement.

If it returns to the Spiritual Realm from these mills in the World of Matter, it will then stand pure in the Kingdom of its Creator; it matters not *what* its guilt may have been! Just as pure as one who has never yet sinned. But *first* his path will take him through the activity of the Divine Laws, and in *this* fact lies the guarantee of Divine Forgiveness, of His Mercy!

Do we not often hear today the fearful questioning: How could God allow such years of tribulation? Where does love, where does justice come in? The question is asked by *mankind,* by *nations,* often by families and the individual human being! Should this not rather prove to him that, *after all,* God's Love is probably *different* from what many would like to imagine it? Just try *in this way* to visualise to the *end* the all-forgiving Love of God, as man insists on portraying It! Demanding no self-atonement, tolerating everything, and ultimately even offering generous forgiveness. It must produce a lamentable result! Does man consider himself so precious that his God should suffer under this? Thus more precious even than God Himself? To what lengths does men's presumption go. –

On thinking it over calmly you must stumble over a thousand obstacles, and can *only* come to a conclusion when you belittle God and make Him imperfect.

But He was, and is, and remains perfect, regardless of men's attitude to this.

His Forgiveness lies in *Justice.* Nothing else. And in this unconditional Justice also lies the great Love which has hitherto been so misunderstood!

Rid yourselves of the habit of measuring according to earthly standards! God's Justice and God's Love are concerned with the human *spirit.* Material substance has nothing whatever to do with this. It is only *formed* by the human spirit itself, and has no life without spirit.

Why do you so often torment yourselves with mere earthly trifles which you perceive to be sin, but which are not really so.

It is only what the *spirit wills* in any action that is decisive for the Divine Laws in Creation. This spiritual will, however, is not thought-activity, but the deepest intuitive perception, the actual volition within man, which alone can set in motion the Laws of the beyond, and indeed does so automatically.

Divine Love cannot be degraded by men; for in It rest in Creation also the inexorable Laws of His Will, Which is borne by Love. And these Laws take effect according to how man adjusts himself in Creation. They may link him with the proximity of his God, or they form a dividing wall that can never be destroyed unless man at last adapts himself to them, which means obeys them, in which alone he can find his salvation, his happiness.

It is *one* perfect whole, the great Work shows no flaws, no gaps. Any fool or simpleton who would have it otherwise will meet with his doom. –

Divine Love weaves therein only what *benefits* every human spirit, but not what pleases and seems agreeable to it on earth. Divine Love goes *far* beyond this, because it governs the whole of existence. –

At present many a person very often thinks: If tribulation and destruction are to be expected in order to bring about a great purification, then God must be so just as to send out in advance preachers calling for repentance. Man must certainly be forewarned. Where is John who proclaims what is to come?

These are wretched ones who think themselves so wise, but are so empty-minded! Such cries merely conceal an utterly hollow presumption. They would only scourge him and throw him into prison!

Do open your eyes and ears! But man goes *dancing* frivolously away over all the suffering and misery of his fellow-men! He does not *want* to see and hear! –

Already two thousand years ago a preacher also first appeared, calling for repentance, and following on his heels the Word Incarnate. Yet mankind have made strenuous efforts to efface and obscure the pure lustre of the Word, so that the magnetic power of Its radiance should gradually become extinct. –

And all those who wish to disentangle the Word from the clinging vines must soon perceive how desperately the messengers of Darkness try to prevent every joyful awakening!

But today there will be no recurrence of what happened in Christ's time! At that time the Word came! Mankind had their free will, and the majority then decided to reject and repudiate this Word! From that time onwards they were subject to the Laws, which were automatically linked to the free decision then carried out in this way. Thereafter men found all the fruits of their own volition on their self-chosen path.

Soon the ring will close. Things are piling up ever more, rising like a rampart which will soon collapse and crash down upon mankind, who go on living unsuspectingly in spiritual apathy. Finally, at the time of fulfilment, they will naturally no longer have the free choice!

They must now just reap what they sowed at that time, and also later on their wrong ways.

All who once rejected the Word at the time of Christ are today reincarnated on this earth to settle accounts. Now they no longer have the right to be forewarned, and to make a second decision. In the two thousand years they have had time enough to change their minds! Also he who absorbs a wrong interpretation of God and His Creation, and does not exert himself to grasp It more purely, has *not* absorbed It *at all.* Indeed, it is far worse, for a wrong belief keeps one back from grasping the Truth.

But woe unto him who, in order to attract followers, *falsifies* or *perverts* the Truth because men find it more agreeable in an easier form. He not only burdens himself with the guilt of falsification and deception, but in addition he also bears the whole responsibility for those whom he was able to attract to himself by making it more convenient or acceptable. When his hour of retribution comes he will *not* be helped. He will fall into the abyss from which there can be no return, and rightly so! – This John was also permitted to see and warn against in his Revelation.

And when the great purification begins man will now have no time to rebel, or even to stem this happening. The Divine Laws which man so much likes to picture wrongly will then take inexorable effect.

Just in the most terrible tribulation of the times that the earth has ever experienced, humanity will at last learn that God's Love is far removed from the softness and weakness which man so audaciously ascribed to It.

More than half of all the men living at the present time do not belong on this earth at all!

Already for thousands of years this mankind have sunk so low, and live *so* strongly in the Darkness, that through their unclean volition they have built many bridges to dark spheres which are far *below* this earth-plane. There live those who have sunk deeply, whose ethereal weight would never have permitted the possibility of their rising to this earth-plane.

This formed a *protection* both for all those living on earth and for these dark ones themselves. They are separated by the natural Law of Ethereal Gravity. Down below they can give full vent to their passions, and all baseness, without doing any harm. On the contrary. There their unrestrained indulgence only strikes those of a like nature, whose base way of living similarly also affects them. Thus they suffer mutually, which leads to maturing but not to further guilt. For through the suffering, loathing for themselves may in time awaken, and with it also the desire to escape from this region. Gradually the desire leads to an agonising despair, which may finally result in the most fervent prayers, and therewith in an earnest volition to do better.

This is how it should be. But through men's wrong volition things developed differently!

Through their *dark* volition men built a bridge to the region of Darkness. Thus they held out a hand to those living there, making it possible for them to rise to the earth through the power of attraction of similar species. Here they naturally also found the opportunity for a fresh incarnation, which was not yet intended for them in the normal course of world events.

For on the earth-plane, where through the medium of gross matter they can live *together* with those who are more luminous and better, they only do harm and thereby burden themselves with *fresh* guilt. This they cannot do in their lower regions; for the depravity is only beneficial to their homogeneous kind, because ultimately they only recognise themselves as they really are, and come to abhor their baseness, which helps towards improvement.

Man has now *disrupted* this normal course in all development through the base use of his free will, with which he formed ethereal bridges to the region of Darkness, so that those who had sunk there could be thrown onto the earth-plane like a rabble, who now joyfully populate the greater part of it.

Since luminous souls must retreat before the Darkness wherever the latter has gained a firm foothold, it was easy for the darker souls, who had no right to be on the earth-plane, also to incarnate sometimes where otherwise only a luminous soul would have entered. In such a case the dark soul has found an anchorage through some person near the prospective mother, enabling it to assert itself and push aside the light soul, even when mother or father belong to the more luminous ones.

This also clears up the puzzle of how many a black sheep could come to good parents. However, if a prospective mother takes more heed of herself and of her immediate surroundings, of those with whom she associates, this can *not* happen.

Thus one can recognise it only as *Love* when at last the final effect of the Laws sweeps away from the earth-plane in full justice those who do *not* belong here, so that they fall into that realm of Darkness to which by their nature they definitely belong. Thus they can no longer hinder the ascent of the more luminous ones, nor burden themselves with fresh guilt, but perhaps still, after all, mature through disgust at their own experiences. –

The time will certainly come when the hearts of *all* men will be seized with an iron grip, when spiritual arrogance will be uprooted in every human creature with terrible relentlessness. Then every doubt which today prevents the human spirit from recognising that Divinity is not *in* him, but high *above* him, will also disappear. That It can only stand as the purest *image* on the altar of his inner life, to which he looks up in humble prayer. –

It is no error but sin when a human spirit confesses his desire also to be Divine. Such presumption must cause his fall; for it is equivalent to an attempt to tear the sceptre from the Hand of his God, and degrade Him to the same level as man occupies, and on which until now he has never even fulfilled his task, because he wanted to be *more*, and aspires to heights which he can never possibly reach, nor even recognise. Thus he heedlessly overlooked all reality, not only making himself quite useless in Creation, but far worse, making himself directly *harmful!*

In the end, brought about through his own wrong attitude, it will be proved to him with uncanny clarity that in his present so degenerated state he does not even represent the shadow of Divinity. The whole hoard of earthly knowledge that he has laboriously accumulated over these thousands of years will then prove before the horrified gaze of his eyes to be as *nothing;* helpless, he will experience with himself how the fruits of his one-sided earthly aspirations become useless and sometimes even a curse to him. *Then he may reflect upon his own divinity, if he can! – –*

A mighty voice will sound forth and compel him: "Down on your knees, creature, before your God and Lord! Do not sacrilegiously try to lift yourself up to the level of God!" – –

The self-centredness of the indolent human spirit cannot continue.

Only then can this humanity really think of an ascent. That will also be the time when everything that does not stand on a sound foundation will collapse. The sham forms of life, the false prophets and the organisations surrounding them, will disintegrate from within! Therewith the wrong courses that have hitherto prevailed will also be exposed.

Then many a self-complacent person will probably also be terrified to realise that he is standing on the brink of an abyss and, through being wrongly guided, is swiftly gliding downwards when he proudly imagined himself already to be ascending and nearing the Light! That he opened protective gates without having the full strength of defence behind them. That he attracted dangers which in the natural course of events he would have passed over. Happy is he who then finds the right way back!

ONCE UPON A TIME ...!

Four words only, yet they are like a magic formula; for they bear within them the quality of instantly arousing some special intuitive perception in every human being. Seldom is this intuitive perception of the same kind. Similar to the effect music has. Exactly as with music, these four words also find their way straight to the spirit of man, his real "ego". Naturally only to those who do not keep the spirit completely locked within them, and have thus already lost their real humanity here on earth.

On hearing these words, however, every *human being* will involuntarily and instantly think back to some former experience. This rises vividly before him, and with the picture also a corresponding intuitive perception.

With one it will be a yearning tenderness, a melancholy happiness, or also a silent longing impossible of fulfilment. With others, however, pride, anger, horror or hatred. Man will always think of some experience which made an exceptional impression upon him, but which he also thought long since extinguished within him.

Yet nothing has been extinguished in him, nothing lost of what he once really *experienced* within himself. All of it he can still call his own, as really acquired by himself, and thus imperishable. But only that which has been experienced! Nothing else can arise with these words.

Man should for once closely heed this with care and with an alert mind, then he will soon recognise what is really alive within him, and what can be designated as dead, as a soulless shell of useless memories.

Only what has so deeply affected him during his earth-life as to stamp an indelible and ineffaceable imprint on his *soul* serves to benefit man, by whom we must not imagine the physical body. Only such imprints have an influence on the forming of the human soul and thereby, going further, also on the advancement of the spirit for its continual development.

In reality, therefore, only *that* which leaves such a deep impression is experienced and thus made one's own. All else flits ineffectively by, or at best serves to help in the development of events that are capable of calling forth such great impressions.

Happy is he who can call his own many such powerful experiences, no matter whether called forth by joy or sorrow; for the impressions they leave will one day be the most precious that a human soul takes with it on its way into the beyond. –

Purely intellectual work, such as is customary today, *when properly applied* serves only to facilitate *physical* life on earth. Closely considered, that is the actual ultimate aim of *all* intellectual activity! In the final analysis there is never any other result. With *all* erudition, irrespective of which branch of education, and also with all activities whether in public affairs or in the family, with every individual or with nations, as also finally with humanity as a whole.

But unfortunately *everything* has subjected itself quite unconditionally to the intellect alone, and therefore lies in heavy chains of earthly limitation of the perceptive capacity, which was naturally bound to bring in its wake disastrous consequences in every activity and happening, and will continue to do so.

To this there is only *one* exception on this whole earth. This exception, however, is not perhaps offered to us by the church, as many will think and indeed as it should be, but by *art!* Here now the intellect unquestionably takes *second* place. But where the intellect gains the upper hand, art is at once reduced to *craftsmanship;* it is immediately and quite incontestably degraded from its lofty position. This is a logical consequence which in its simple naturalness cannot possibly be otherwise. Not one exception to it can be pointed out.

Of course, the same conclusion must also be drawn in all else! Does this not make man think? Surely it must be as though scales fell from his eyes. This quite plainly indicates to the thinking and discriminating person that with everything else dominated by the intellect he can indeed obtain but one substitute, the inferior! From this fact man should recognise the place assigned by nature to the intellect, if anything that is right and of value is to arise!

So far only art is still born out of the activity of the living spirit, out of the intuitive perception. Art alone has had a natural and therefore a normal and healthy origin and development. The spirit, however, does not *express* itself in the intellect, but in the *intuitive perceptions,* and only *manifests* in what is

112

generally called *"deep inner feeling" ("Gemuet")*. That is just what the intellectual man of today, who is so inordinately proud of himself, likes to mock and ridicule. Thus he derides what is most valuable in man, yes, the very thing that really makes man a human being!

Spirit has nothing to do with the intellect. If at length man wishes for improvement in all things he must take heed of Christ's words: *"By their works ye shall know them!"* The time is at hand when this will come to pass.

Only the works of the *spirit* from their very origin bear *life* within them, and with it permanence and stability. Everything else must collapse from within when its time of blossoming is past. As soon as the fruits of it are due to appear, the barrenness will be exposed!

Just look at history! Only the work of the spirit, that is to say art, has outlived the peoples who have already collapsed through the activity of their intellect, which in itself is lifeless and cold. Their great, much-praised knowledge could not offer them any salvation from collapse. Egyptians, Greeks and Romans went this way; later also the Spaniards and the French, now the Germans – *yet the works of genuine art have outlived them all!* Nor can they ever perish. But no one has perceived with what strict regularity these events have recurred. No person thought of getting to the real root of this great evil.

Instead of searching for this root, and for once calling a halt to the ever-recurring decline, men have blindly submitted to it, and with laments and complaints have resigned themselves to the idea that "nothing can be changed".

Now finally it will strike all mankind! Much misery already lies behind us, still greater is to come. And deep affliction moves through the dense ranks of those who have even now to some extent been affected by it.

Think of all the peoples who have already had to fall on reaching full bloom, the zenith of the intellect. The fruits which developed from the blossom-time were *everywhere the same!* Immorality, shamelessness and debauchery in various forms, inevitably followed by decline and ruin.

The complete similarity is very obvious to everyone! And also every thinking person must discover a very definite nature and consistency of the strictest Laws in this happening.

One after the other these peoples had finally to recognise that their greatness, their power and their glory were only apparent, upheld solely by force and compulsion, and not secured by an inner soundness.

If you would only open your eyes, instead of despairing! Look about you, learn from the past, and compare it with the messages that have reached you already thousands of years ago from the Divine, and you *must* discover the root of the devouring evil, which alone forms the obstacle to the ascent of all mankind.

Only when the evil has been thoroughly eradicated will the path to general ascent be open, not before. And this will then be lasting, because it will be animated by the living spirit, which has hitherto been impossible. –

Before going into this subject more deeply, I want to explain what spirit, as the only really living part in man, is. Spirit is not wit, and not intellect! Nor is spirit acquired knowledge. It is erroneous, therefore, to call a person "rich in spirit" because he has studied, read and observed much and knows how to converse well about it, or because his brilliance expresses itself through original ideas and intellectual wit.

Spirit is something entirely different. It is an independent *consistency,* coming from the world of its homogeneous species, which is different from the part to which the earth and thus the physical body belong. The spiritual world lies higher, it forms the upper and lightest part of Creation. Owing to its consistency, this spiritual part in man bears within it the task of returning to the Spiritual Realm, as soon as all the material coverings have been severed from it. The urge to do so is set free at a very definite degree of maturity, and then leads the spirit upwards to its homogeneous species, through whose power of attraction it is raised.*

Spirit has nothing to do with the earthly intellect, only with the quality which is described as "deep inner feeling" ("Gemuet"). To be rich in spirit, therefore, is the same as "having deep inner feelings" ("gemuetvoll"), but not the same as being highly intellectual.

Just to discover this difference more easily, man should now make use of the expression: "Once upon a time!" That alone will help very many seekers to find clarification. If they observe themselves carefully they can recognise what has so far proved beneficial to their *souls* in their earth-life, or what has merely served to ease the conditions of their life and work in the earthly environment. In other words, what is of value to them not only on earth but also in the beyond, and what serves only earthly purposes but remains valueless for the beyond. The one can be taken over by man, but the other he leaves

---

* Lecture: "I am the Resurrection and the Life...!"

114

behind on his departure as belonging only here, because it can be of no further use to him. What he leaves behind, however, is but the tool for earthly events, an aid for the *time on earth*, nothing more.

If a tool is not used solely as such, but is valued much more highly, it obviously cannot come up to the higher demands made upon it; it is in the wrong place and will thereby naturally also produce many kinds of deficiencies, which in time will have quite disastrous consequences.

The first and foremost of these tools is the *earthly intellect* which, as a product of the human brain, must bear within itself the limitation to which anything physical-gross-material by its own consistency is always subject. And the product cannot possibly be different from its origin. It always remains bound to the nature of the origin. Likewise the works that develop through the product.

For the intellect this naturally results in the most limited, purely earthly comprehensive capacity, closely bound to time and space. Since it originates in the World of Gross Matter, itself inert and with no life of its *own*, the intellect is also without living power. This condition, of course, is likewise perpetuated in all the activities of the intellect, for which it thereby remains impossible to impart life to its works.

In this inflexible natural happening lies the key to the unhappy events during man's life on this small earth.

We must at last learn to differentiate between the spirit and the intellect, the vital core of man and his tool! When this tool is placed *above* the living core, as it has hitherto been, the result will be something unsound, which even at its inception must bear within it the germ of death; and thereby the vital, the highest and most valuable part, is constricted, bound and cut off from its necessary activity, until in the inevitable collapse of the lifeless structure it rises free but incomplete from the ruins.

Instead of "once upon a time" let us now picture to ourselves the question: "What was it like in former times?" How different is the effect. The great difference is immediately perceived. The first question speaks to the intuitive perception, which is linked with the spirit. But the second question is directed to the intellect, and entirely different pictures emerge. From the outset they are limited, cold, without warmth of life, because the intellect has nothing else to give.

From the very beginning, however, mankind's greatest guilt has lain in

115

placing this intellect, which can only produce what is incomplete and without life, on a high pedestal, and virtually dancing around it in worship. It was given a place that should have been reserved *for the spirit alone.*

This action is entirely opposed to the ordinances of the Creator and thus to nature, because these are anchored in what takes place in nature. Therefore nothing can lead to a true goal either, but everything must fail at the point where the harvest is due to set in. It cannot be otherwise, but is a natural happening that is to be expected.

Only in *purely technical science,* in all industry, is it different. This has reached great heights through the intellect, and will even advance much further in the future! This fact, however, serves to prove the truth of my explanations. Technical science in *all* its aspects is and will always remain purely earthly, lifeless. Now since the intellect likewise belongs to all that is earthly, it is able to develop brilliantly in the technical sciences, and can accomplish really great things. Here it stands in its right place, in its real task!

But wherever anything "living", thus purely *human,* has to be considered as well, the intellect by its nature is not adequate, and *must* therefore fail if it is not then guided by the spirit! For spirit alone is life. Success of a specific kind can always be achieved only by the activity of the homogeneous kind. The earthly intellect will therefore never be able to do spiritual work! For this reason placing the intellect above life has become the grave offence of this mankind.

Contrary to the creative, thus wholly natural ordinance, man has therewith directly *reversed* his task, and has, so to speak, turned it upside down by yielding the supreme place that belongs to the living spirit to the intellect, which comes in the second and purely earthly place. Through this it is again quite natural for man now to be obliged painfully to seek from below upwards, whereby the superimposed intellect, with its limited capacity to comprehend, obstructs any broader view, instead of his being able to look down from above through the spirit.

If he wishes to awaken he is compelled first to "transpose the lights". To put the intellect, which is now above, in the place given to it by nature, and restore the spirit to the supreme position. This necessary transposition is no longer so easy for the man of today. –

The change of order that men introduced in bygone times, so incisively directed against the Will of the Creator, thus against the Laws of Nature, was the actual *"fall of man"*, the consequences of which cannot be more terrible; for in due course it developed into "inherited sin", because the elevation of the intellect to the position of sole ruler again brought in its wake the natural consequence that, in the course of time, such one-sided cultivation and activity also strengthened the brain one-sidedly, so that only the part which has to do the work of the intellect grew bigger, and the other part was bound to become stunted. Thereby the part that has become stunted through neglect can only operate today as an unreliable dream-brain, even then being still under the powerful influence of the so-called day-brain, which activates the intellect.

Thus the part of the brain which should form the bridge to the spirit, or rather the bridge from the spirit to everything earthly, is thereby paralysed; a connection is broken, or at least very much loosened, whereby man has cut off for himself all spiritual activity, and with it also the possibility of "animating", spiritualising and inspiring his intellect.

Both parts of the brain should have been developed absolutely *equally,* for joint harmonious activity, like everything in the body. The spirit leading and the intellect carrying out here on earth. It is obvious that because of this all the activity of the body too, and even the body itself, can never be what it should be. For naturally what has taken place affects everything! Because the most essential factor for all earthly things is thereby missing!

It is easy to understand that the cutting off was simultaneously linked with the withdrawal and estrangement from the Divine. Indeed, there was no longer any way to It.

Finally this in turn had the disadvantage that already for thousands of years, owing to the ever-increasing hereditary factor, every child's body that is born brings with it to the earth the frontal intellectual brain so large that, from the outset and because of this condition, each child is again readily submitted to the intellect the moment this brain develops its full activity. The gulf beween the two parts of the brain has now grown so wide, and their functions so proportionately unequal, that with the majority of all mankind an improvement can no longer be achieved without catastrophe.

The intellectual man of today is no longer a *normal* human being, but lacks any development of the principal part of his brain that belongs to the complete human being, because he has allowed it to become stunted for thousands of years. Without exception, every intellectual has only a *crippled* normal brain! Therefore *brain-cripples* have been ruling the earth for thousands of years; they regard the normal human being as an enemy and seek to subjugate him. In their crippled condition they imagine that they accomplish a great deal, and they do not know that the normal human being is in a position to achieve *ten times as much*, producing works of a *permanent* nature which are more perfect than the present efforts! The way is open to every really serious seeker to acquire this ability!

An intellectual, however, will no longer so easily become able to grasp something that belongs to the activity of this stunted part of his brain! He is simply *incapable* of it, even if he should desire it; and solely because of his voluntary restriction he ridicules everything that he is unable to attain, and which owing to his really *retarded*, not normal brain will never at any time be understood by him either.

Just therein lies the most terrible part of the curse of this unnatural aberration. The harmonious co-operation of both parts of the human brain that absolutely belongs to a normal human being, is definitely impossible for the present-day intellectuals, who are called materialists. –

To be a materialist is really no recommendation, but evidence of a stunted brain.

Thus the *unnatural* brain has hitherto ruled on this earth; and finally its activity must obviously also bring about the inevitable collapse in all things, since everything, no matter what it wishes to produce, naturally contains discord and ill-health even from the very start, owing to the stunting.

Nothing of this can now be changed any more, but one must calmly let the naturally developing collapse come about. *Then, however, will be the day of resurrection for the spirit, and also for a new life!* The slave of the intellect, who has held the reins for thousands of years, will thus be disposed of for ever! Never again will he be able to arise, because the evidence and his own experience will finally compel him voluntarily to submit at last, ill and spiritually impoverished, to *that* which he was unable to grasp. Never again will he be given the opportunity to oppose the spirit, either by scoffing or by the semblance of right through imposing force, such as was also used towards the Son of God, Who had to fight against it.

Then there would still have been time to avert such misery. But now it is too late; for in the meantime the loosened connection between the two parts of the brain can no longer be bridged.

Many intellectuals will again try to ridicule the explanations in this lecture, but except for empty platitudes, they will be unable to present even *one really objective counter-argument*. Yet any serious seeker and thinker will have to take such blind zeal simply as fresh proof of what I have set forth herein. However hard they try, it is *impossible* for these people. Let us therefore regard them from now on as sick persons, who will soon be in need of help, and ... let us calmly await the time.

No struggle and no act of violence are needed to enforce the necessary progress; for the end will come of itself. Here too, through the immutable Laws of all reciprocal actions, the natural course of events will take effect quite inexorably, and also punctually. - -

Then, according to various prophecies, a "new generation" shall arise. However, this will not only be made up of the newly-born, such as are now already observed in California and also in Australia to be endowed with a "new sense", but mainly of *people already living*, who in the near future will become "seeing" through the many impending events. They will then possess the same "sense" as those now newly-born; for this is nothing more than the ability to stand in the world with an open and unrestrained spirit, no longer allowing itself to be suppressed by the limitation of the intellect. *Inherited sin will thereby be eliminated!*

But all this has nothing to do with what has been hitherto described as "occult faculties". *It is then simply the normal man as he should be!* To "become seeing" has nothing to do with "clairvoyance", but signifies *"insight"*, recognition.

Men will then be in the position to observe everything impartially, which means nothing else than to assess. They will see the intellectual man as he really is, with the limitation so dangerous to himself and his environment, in which there simultaneously arise the arrogant lust for power, and the disputing that is actually part of it.

They will also see how, with strict consistency, all humanity has suffered under this yoke in one form or another for thousands of years; and how this cancerous sore, as the hereditary enemy, has always been directed against the development of the free human *spirit*, which is the main object in human existence! Nothing will escape them, also not the bitter certainty that affliction, *all* suffering, and every downfall, were bound to come about through this evil, and that there could never be any betterment because from the start all insight was ruled out owing to the limitation of the perceptive capacity.

But with *this* awakening all influence, all power of these intellectuals has ceased. For *all* time; for then begins a new and better epoch for mankind, in which the old can no longer survive.

Therewith the necessary victory of the spirit over the failing intellect, already longed for by hundreds of thousands today, will come. Many of the masses who have hitherto been led astray will then still recognise that until now they had completely misinterpreted the term "intellect". The majority simply accepted it as an idol, without examination, just because the others also did so; and because all its adherents always knew how through force and the laws to pose as infallible, absolute rulers. That is why many do not even take the trouble to expose the real hollowness of these people, and the deficiencies it has concealed.

There are certainly also some who already for decades have been fighting against this enemy with tenacious energy and conviction, in secret and to some extent also openly, occasionally also being exposed to most bitter suffering. *But they fight without knowing the real enemy!* And this has naturally made success more difficult. Indeed, it has made it impossible from the outset. The warriors' sword was not well sharpened, because they were always striking at non-essential things that dented it. With these non-essentials, however, they have always struck to one side, missing the mark, wasting their own strength, and only causing disunion among themselves.

In reality there is only *one* enemy of mankind all along the line: *The hitherto unrestricted rule of the intellect! That* was the great *fall of man,* his most grievous guilt, which brought all evil in its wake. *That* became the *hereditary sin,* and *that also is the Antichrist* of whom it is proclaimed that he will raise his head. More plainly expressed: The mastery of the intellect is his tool, through which men have fallen prey to him. To him, the enemy of God, the Antichrist himself ... Lucifer!*

We are in the midst of this time! He dwells today in *every* human being, ready to ruin him; for his activity immediately brings estrangement from God as quite a natural consequence. As soon as he is allowed to rule he cuts off the spirit.

* Lecture: "The Antichrist"

Therefore, let man be keenly on his guard. –

He must not on that account belittle his intellect, but must make it what it is, *his tool;* not, however, his authoritative will. Not his master!

The man of the coming generation will be able to regard past times only with disgust, horror and shame. Rather as we feel on entering an old torture chamber. There, too, we perceive the evil fruits of the cold, calculating domination of the intellect. For it is surely quite undeniable that a person *possessing only a little inner feeling,* and thus spiritual activity, could never have devised such atrocities! Still, on the whole it is no different today, only somewhat more camouflaged; and the miseries of the masses are just as rotten fruits as was the individual torture in olden times.

On looking back into the past, man will only be able to shake his head in sheer amazement. He will ask himself how it was possible to suffer these errors calmly for thousands of years. The answer, of course, is simple: by force! Wherever one looks it can be recognised quite clearly. Leaving aside the times of remote antiquity, we need only enter the aforementioned torture chambers which can still be seen everywhere today, and the use of which does not lie so very far back.

We shudder as we look at these old implements. What cold brutality, what bestiality do they reveal! Hardly anyone today will doubt that the most grievous crime lay in those past proceedings. Upon the criminals an even greater crime was thus perpetrated. But also many an innocent person, dragged away from family and freedom, was roughly cast into these dungeons. What lamentations, what shrieks of suffering died away here from those who, completely defenceless, were at the mercy of their tormentors. People were compelled to suffer things the contemplation of which simply fills one with horror and loathing.

Involuntarily every one asks himself whether it was really humanly possible – all that happened to these defenceless ones, and moreover under the guise of justice. Of a justice that after all once had only been obtained by force. And now again, through physical pain, confessions of guilt were forced from those under suspicion, so that they could then be murdered at leisure. Even though these confessions of guilt were only extracted under compulsion, in order to escape these insane physical tortures, yet they nevertheless satisfied the judges, because they needed them to comply with the "letter" of the law. Did these so narrow-minded ones really imagine that in this way they could also whitewash themselves before the Divine Will, and escape the inexorable working of the basic Law of Reciprocal Action?

Either all those who dared to pass judgment on others were the scum of the most hardened criminals, or it clearly showed the unhealthy limitation of the earthly intellect. There can be nothing between.

According to the Divine Laws of Creation every person in authority, every judge, no matter what office he holds here on earth, should never stand in his *actions* under some protection of his office, but like any other person he must alone and purely *personally, unprotected,* bear full responsibility *himself* for all he does in his office. Not only in the spiritual but also in the earthly sense. Then everyone would regard things much more seriously and carefully. And so-called "errors", whose consequences are forever irreparable, will certainly not so easily occur again. To say nothing of the physical and psychic suffering of the victims and their relatives.

But let us further consider another aspect of this subject, the trials of so-called "witches"!

Anyone who has ever had access to the court records of such trials would wish, in an outburst of burning shame, never to be numbered among this mankind. In those days if anyone even had knowledge of healing herbs, either through practical experience or tradition, and if he used this knowledge to aid sufferers asking him for help, he was relentlessly tortured for it. Final release from these tortures only came with death at the stake, if his body had not already succumbed to these cruelties.

Even physical beauty, especially chastity that did not yield willingly, could in those days give rise to such tortures.

And then the horrors of the Inquisition! Comparatively speaking, only a few years separate us from "that time"!

Just as today we recognise this injustice, so also did the populace feel at that time. For the "intellect" had not yet limited them to such an extent, and here and there the intuitive perception, the spirit, broke through in them.

Do we not recognise today the absolute narrow-mindedness in all this? The irresponsible stupidity?

Although these things are spoken of with an air of superiority and a shrugging of the shoulders, yet fundamentally nothing has changed. The stupid presumption towards everything not understood is still exactly the same! Except that instead of these tortures men now publicly scoff at everything which, owing to their narrow-mindedness, they do not understand.

Many a person would do better to search his heart for once and think seriously about this without sparing himself. Upholders of the intellect, which means those who are not quite normal, and often even the law courts, will from the outset regard as a swindler every person who possesses the ability to know something that is concealed from others; he may be able also to see the Ethereal World with his ethereal eyes as a natural occurrence, which will very soon no longer be doubted, much less brutally opposed.

And woe unto him who does not himself know what to make of it, but naively speaks of what he has seen and heard. He must fear the consequences as did the first Christians under Nero, with his helpers always ready for murder.

Should he even possess still other abilities which can *never* be grasped by the out-and-out intellectuals, then he will most certainly be mercilessly hunted, slandered and ostracised unless he complies with everyone's wishes; if at all possible he will be rendered "harmless", as it is so charmingly expressed. Nobody has any qualms of conscience about it. Even today such a man is regarded as the free prey of anyone, and sometimes of inwardly very unclean persons. The more narrow-minded, the greater the delusion of cleverness and the propensity to conceit.

Man has learned nothing from these happenings of the olden days, with their tortures, burnings at the stake, and records of ridiculous trials! For even today anyone is still free to defile and insult with impunity all that is unusual and not understood. In this respect it is no different now from what it was then.

The proceedings of the Inquisition, which were instigated by the Church, were even worse than those of the courts of law. Here the shrieks of the tortured were drowned by pious prayers. It was a mockery of the Divine Will in Creation! The ecclesiastical representatives of those days thus proved that they had no idea of Christ's true teaching, nor of the Godhead and Its Creative Will, Whose Laws lie irrevocably anchored and work on in Creation, the same even from the very beginning to the end of time.

God endowed the human spirit by its very nature with the free will to decide. Only through *this* can it mature *as it should,* refine itself and develop fully. Only therein lies the possibility for it to do so. However, should this free will be cut off, then this is a hindrance, if not a violent throwing back.

But in those days the Christian churches, as well as many religions, fought this Divine ordinance, opposing it with the greatest cruelty. By means of torture and finally death, they sought to compel people to pursue courses and make confessions which were against their conviction, thus *against their will*. Thereby they violated the Divine commandment. And not only that, but they hindered men's spiritual progress, even throwing them back centuries.

If only a spark of real intuitive perception, thus of the spirit, had shown itself, this should and could never have happened! Therefore such barbarities were only the cold-blooded work of the intellect.

As history proves, many a Pope even permitted the use of poison and dagger to realise his purely earthly wishes and aims. *That* could only happen under the domination of the intellect, which in its triumphal march subjugated *everything* and stopped at nothing. –

And supreme over all the Will of our Creator inexorably manifested and manifests in the irrevocable march of events. On passing into the beyond every human being is divested of earthly power and its protection. Name, position, everything is left behind. Only a poor human soul passes over, there to receive and experience what it sowed. Not a *single* exception is possible! On its path it is led through all the wheels of the relentless reciprocal action of Divine Justice. There is no church, no state, but only individual human souls who must personally account for every error they have made!

He who acts against God's Will, and thus commits a sin in Creation, is subject to the consequences of this transgression. It matters not who he may be and on what pretext he acted. Be it an individual under the cloak of the church or of the law ... a crime committed against body or soul is and remains a crime! Nothing can alter it, not even the *semblance* of justice, which is by no means always justice; for of course the laws, too, were made only by intellectuals, and therefore must be subject to earthly limitations.

Just consider the law in so many states, especially in Central and South America. The man who today presides over the government, enjoying all the honours connected with it, may even tomorrow be thrown into prison or executed as a criminal, if his opponent succeeds in seizing the reins of this government through an act of violence. Should he not be successful, then it is *he* who, instead of being recognised as the ruler, will be looked upon as a criminal and persecuted. And all the public officials are as willing to serve the one as the other. Even a world traveller, to remain in good standing everywhere, must change his conscience as often as he would his clothes when passing from one country to another. What in one country is considered a crime is very often permitted in another and, what is more, may even be welcomed.

This is naturally only possible in the achievements of the earthly intellect, but never where the intellect must occupy its natural place as a tool of the living spirit; for he who listens to the spirit will never neglect the Laws of God. And where these are used as the foundation there can be no flaws, no gaps, but only a uniformity that brings in its wake happiness and peace. In their basic features the expressions of the spirit can always and only be exactly the same everywhere. They will never contradict each other.

Also the arts of justice, healing and statesmanship are bound to remain merely deficient crafts where only intellect can form the foundation, and the spiritual is lacking in them. It cannot possibly be otherwise. Here naturally always starting from the true conception of "spirit". –

Knowledge is a product, but spirit is life, the value and power of which can only be measured according to its connection with the origin of the spiritual. The closer this connection the more valuable and powerful will be the part which emanated from the origin. But the looser this connection becomes, the more distant, alien, isolated and weak must also be the emanated part, thus the human being concerned.

All these are such simple self-evident facts that it is impossible to comprehend how the erring intellectuals can pass them by over and over again as if they were blind. For what the root provides, sustains the trunk, the blossom and the fruit! But here also this hopeless self-limitation in understanding reveals itself. They have toiled to erect a wall before themselves which they can now no longer see over, much less see through.

However, with their conceited, superior and mocking smile, with their arrogance and looking down upon others less deeply enslaved, they must sometimes appear to all spiritually alive people like poor, sick fools who, in spite of all pity, must be left to their delusion, because their limited understanding even allows facts that prove the contrary to slip by without making any impressions. Every effort to bring about an improvement must simply prove as fruitless as trying to heal a sick person by hanging a new and resplendent cloak around his shoulders.

Even today materialism is past its climax, and now, failing everywhere, it must soon collapse. Not without also tearing down much that is good. Its devotees are already at the end of their ability, and will soon become confused about their work and then about themselves, without perceiving the abyss that has opened up before them. They will soon be like a flock without shepherds, one not trusting the other, each pursuing his own way, and yet still proudly looking down upon others. Not thinking matters out carefully, but merely following old habits.

With all signs of the outward semblance of their hollowness, they will end by blindly falling into the abyss. They still regard as spirit what are only the products of their own brains. But how can lifeless matter produce living spirit? They are proud of their meticulous thinking in many things, but quite unscrupulously and most irresponsibly leave gaps in the most important.

Every new step, every attempt at improvement, will ever again have to carry within it all the barrenness of the intellectual work, and thus the germ of inevitable doom.

All that I am saying here is neither prophecy nor loose prediction, but the unalterable consequence of the all-animating Creative Will, Whose Laws I explain in my lectures. He who follows with me in spirit along the paths that are clearly indicated therein must also survey and recognise the necessary end. And all the signs for it are already here.

People complain and cry out, they see with disgust how the excrescences of materialism today take on scarcely believable forms. They beg and pray for deliverance from the affliction, for improvement and recovery from the overwhelming downfall. The few who have managed to save some stirring of their inner life from the tidal wave of the incredible happenings, who have not suffocated spiritually in the general downfall that deceptively bears the name of "progress" proudly on its brow, feel like outcasts and backward people, and are also regarded and ridiculed as such by the soulless followers of modern life.

A laurel wreath to all those who had the courage to refrain from joining the masses! Who have proudly stayed behind on the steeply sloping path!

He who today still considers himself unfortunate because of this must be a *sleepwalker! Open your eyes!* Do you not see that everything that oppresses you is already the beginning of the sudden end of materialism, which at the moment only appears still to rule? The whole structure is already collapsing, without any assistance from those who have suffered and must still suffer under it. Intellectual mankind must now reap what for thousands of years they have produced, nourished, reared and acclaimed.

In human reckoning it is a long time, but for God's self-acting mills in Creation a brief span. Wherever you look there is failure everywhere. It surges back and heaps itself up menacingly like a heavy rampart that will soon topple over and crash down upon its admirers, burying them beneath the ruins. It is the inexorable Law of Reciprocal Action which during this manifestation must have a terrible effect, because in spite of the many kinds of experiences gained there has never in thousands of years been any change towards higher things, but on the contrary the same wrong road has been trampled wider and wider.

Despondent ones, the time is at hand! Hold up your heads, which you have so often had to hang in shame when injustice and stupidity were able to cause you such deep suffering. Now look calmly at the opponent today who thus sought to suppress you!

Already the fine raiment worn up till now is very badly tattered. The figure in its true form is at last visible through all the rents. The exhausted product of the human brain, the intellect, which allowed itself to be enthroned as spirit, less confident but no less conceited, looks forth confounded!

Just confidently take the bandage from your eyes and look about you more keenly. Alone the perusal of newspapers which are otherwise quite good reveals all sorts of things to the clearsighted. There are desperate efforts still to cling to all the old illusions. With arrogance, and often very coarse jokes, people seek to cover up the lack of comprehension that becomes more and more evident. A person will frequently use absurd language to judge something, of which in reality he has quite obviously no shred of understanding.

Today even people with quite good abilities helplessly take refuge in questionable courses rather than confess that so many things are beyond the grasp of their own intellect, on which alone they have hitherto sought to rely. They do not sense the absurdity of their behaviour, do not see the weaknesses which they only help to increase thereby. Confused and dazzled, they will soon stand face to face with the Truth, and mournfully look back over their bankrupt life, at last recognising with shame that stupidity lay just where they thought themselves wise.

What have things already come to today? *The man of muscle is the hero!*

Has an earnest scientist, who after decades of arduous research has discovered a serum giving protection and also help against fatal diseases year after year to hundreds of thousands, young and old, ever been able to celebrate such triumphs as a boxer, who with purely physical, crude brutality overpowers his fellow-man? Yet does this in any way benefit even one human *soul?* It is only earthly, all earthly, which means *low* in the whole Work of Creation! Entirely corresponding to the golden calf of intellectual activity. As the triumph of this so earthbound clay effigy of a monarch over narrow-minded mankind! – –

And no one sees this mad rush downwards into the gruesome abyss!

He who intuitively perceives this will still keep silent for the present, in the shameful awareness of being ridiculed in any case should he speak. It is already a wild frenzy in which, however, there is a dawning recognition of powerlessness. And with the growing awareness of *that* recognition people become even more rebellious, out of sheer obstinacy, out of vanity, and last but not least from fear and horror of the impending events. They simply *refuse* already to think of the end of this colossal error! Convulsively they cling to the proud structure built up over past millennia, which closely resembles the Tower of Babel, and which will end in the same way!

This hitherto uncurbed materialism carries within it a foreboding of death, which becomes more evident every month! –

Yet in many human souls, in all places, on the entire earth, something is astir! The radiance of the Truth is still only covered by a thin layer of old, false conceptions, which the first gust of a purification will sweep away, thus setting free the core, whose light will unite with that of so many others to unfold its cone of rays, rising like a fire of gratitude to the Realm of Pure Joy, to the Feet of the Creator.

That will be the time of the much-longed-for Millennium, which lies before us in brilliant promise as the great Star of Hope!

And with this the grievous *sin* of all mankind *against the spirit*, which has kept the spirit bound on earth through the intellect, is at last redeemed! Only *that* then is the right way back to what is natural, to the way of the Will of the Creator, Who desires men's works to be great, and suffused with living intuitive perceptions! The victory of the spirit, however, will at the same time also be the victory of purest Love!

ERRORS

THERE is many a man who lifts up his eyes seekingly for Light and Truth. His longing is great, but very often he lacks earnest volition! More than half of the seekers are not genuine. They bring their own preconceived opinion. Should they have to change it in the slightest degree, then they would much rather reject all that is new to them, even if it contains the Truth.

Thus thousands must go under because, entangled as they are in erroneous convictions, they have restricted the freedom of movement which they need to swing themselves upward to salvation.

There are always some who imagine they have already grasped all that is right. They have no intention of subjecting *themselves* to a strict examination based on what they have heard and read.

I am naturally *not* addressing such as these!

Nor do I speak to churches and political parties, to fraternities, sects and societies, but only in all simplicity to *man* himself. Far be it from me to pull down what exists; for I am building up and completing the answers to questions as yet unsolved, questions that must arise in everyone as soon as he thinks just a little.

Only one basic condition is essential for every listener: Earnest seeking for the Truth. He should inwardly examine *the words* and let them come to life, but not heed the speaker. Otherwise he derives no benefit. All who do *not* strive to do this are simply wasting their time from the start.

It is incredible how naively the great majority of people cling tenaciously to their ignorance on such questions as whence they come, what they are, and whither they go!

Birth and death, the inseparable poles of all life on earth, should not be a secret to man.

There is a great deal of contradiction in the views of what constitutes the inner core of man. This is the result of the morbid self-aggrandisement of the earth-dwellers, who presumptuously boast that their inner core is *Divine!*

Look at humanity! Can you discover anything Divine in them? Such a foolish statement should be branded as blasphemy, because it denotes a debasement of Divinity.

Man does not carry a grain of Divinity within him!

This idea is just morbid presumption, the cause of which is simply the consciousness of being unable to understand. Where is the man who can honestly say that for him such a belief has also become conviction? Whoever examines himself seriously must deny it. He will feel distinctly that it is only a longing and a desire to harbour something Divine within him, but not a certainty! It is quite right to say that man carries within him a spark of God. But this *spark* of God is *spirit!* It is not a part of Divinity.

The term spark is a perfectly correct designation. A spark develops and flies out without taking along or bearing within it anything of the quality of the producer. It is the same here. *A spark* of God is not itself Divine.

Where such mistakes can already be found in regard to the *origin* of a being, there failure *must* ensue in the whole development! If I have built on a wrong foundation, then one day the whole structure must totter and fall.

For it is the origin that provides the *mainstay* for everyone's whole existence and development! Anyone who seeks to reach far beyond his origin, as usually happens, reaches for something he cannot grasp, and thereby loses all support in the quite natural course of events.

If, for instance, I reach for the branch of a tree which through its material consistency is similar to my earthly body, I can gain a hold on this branch and thus swing myself up on it.

But if I reach beyond this branch, then through the different consistency of the air I can find no support, and ... cannot therefore pull myself up either! Surely this is clear enough.

It is exactly the same with the *inner* consistency of man, called the soul, and its core, the spirit.

If this spirit wishes to have the essential support that it needs from its origin, then it must not of course seek to reach into the Divine. That would be unnatural; for the Divine lies much too far above it, and is of an entirely different consistency!

And yet in his conceit man seeks contact with that sphere to which he can never attain, and thus interrupts the natural order of things. His wrong desire

130

is like a *dam* forming an obstruction between himself and his necessary supply of power from the origin. He cuts himself off from it.

Therefore away with such errors! Not until then can the human spirit develop its full power, which it still heedlessly disregards today, and become what it can and should be, *lord in Creation!* But mark well, only in Creation, not standing *above* it.

Only *Divinity* stands above all Creation! –

God Himself, the Origin of all being and life, is Divine, as the very word implies! Man was created by *His Spirit!*

Spirit is the *Will* of God. Now out of this *Will* the *first* Creation came into being. Do let us keep to this simple fact; it provides the possibility for a better understanding.

By way of comparison, just picture your own will. It is an act, but not part of man himself; otherwise man would in time dissolve in his many acts of will. There would be nothing whatever left of him.

It is no different with God! His Will created Paradise! But His Will is the Spirit, designated as the "Holy Spirit". Paradise, again, was only the *work* of the Spirit, not part of the Spirit Itself. There is a gradation *downwards* in this. The Creative Holy Spirit, that is, the Living Will of God, was not absorbed in His Creation. He did not even give one part of Himself to it; but He Himself remained wholly *outside* Creation. The Bible already states this quite clearly and plainly with the words: "And the *Spirit* of God moved *upon* the face of the waters", not God Himself! After all, that is different. Thus man does not carry within him anything of the Holy Spirit Itself either, but only of the *spirit* which is a work of the Holy Spirit, an act.

Instead of concerning himself with this fact, man already exerts all his energy to form a gap here! You have only to think of the prevalent conception of the *First* Creation, of Paradise! It absolutely had to be on this earth. The small human intellect thereby compressed the event requiring millions of years within its own sphere, limited by space and time, imagining himself to be the centre and axis of all that happens in the world. As a result he immediately lost the way to the actual starting-point of life.

In place of this clear path of which he could no longer command a view, a substitute had to be found in his religious conceptions, if he was not to designate himself as the creator of all being and life, and thus *as God*. The term "faith" has given him this substitute until now! And all mankind has suffered ever since from the word "faith"! What is more, this misunderstood word, which was meant to restore all that was lost, became a cliff against which everything was wrecked!

Only the *indolent one* is content with faith. It is also faith which can become the butt of *scoffers*. And the word "faith", *wrongly* interpreted, is the barrier which today obstructs the road to mankind's progress.

Faith is not meant to be the cloak generously covering all slothful thinking, which like a sleeping-sickness gradually steals over and paralyses the spirit of man! Faith should really become *conviction*. Conviction however demands life, the keenest examination!

Where even *one* gap, *one* unsolved riddle remains, conviction becomes impossible. Therefore no one can have genuine faith so long as he has a question unanswered.

Even the words "blind faith" show that there is something unsound!

Faith must be *alive*, as Christ already once demanded, otherwise it serves no purpose. But to be alive means to bestir oneself, to weigh and also to examine! Not dumbly accepting the thoughts of others. After all, blind faith plainly means lack of understanding. What a person does not understand, however, cannot bring him spiritual benefit either, for through lack of understanding it cannot come to life within him.

But whatever he does not fully experience within never becomes his own either! And only what is his own helps him to ascend.

After all, no one can walk and go forward along a road containing great yawning clefts. Where man's knowledge cannot take him any further he must come to a spiritual standstill. This fact is irrefutable and no doubt also easily understood. Hence he who wishes to advance spiritually should awaken!

He can never proceed on his path to the Light of Truth in his sleep! Nor with a bandage or a veil over his eyes.

The Creator wants to have His humanity seeing in Creation. To be seeing, however, means to be knowing! And knowledge does not go with blind faith. Only indolence and slothful thinking lie in such a belief, not greatness!

The privilege of being endowed with the ability to think also brings man the duty to *investigate!*

In order to avoid all this, man out of laziness has simply so belittled the great Creator as to ascribe to Him arbitrary actions in proof of His Omnipotence.

He who will but think a little must again find a great error therein. An arbitrary act implies the possibility of diverting the existing Laws of Nature. However, where such a thing is possible, perfection is lacking. For where there is perfection there can be no alteration. Thus a large part of humanity erroneously represents the Omnipotence of God in such a way that those who think more deeply would have to regard it as a proof of imperfection. And therein lies the root of much evil.

Give God the honour of perfection! Then you will find the key to the unsolved riddles of all life. –

It shall be my endeavour to bring serious thinkers to this point. A sigh of relief shall go through the circles of all seekers for the Truth. Finally they will joyfully recognise that there is no mystery, no gap in the entire course of world events. And then ... they will see clearly before them the road to ascent. They only need to follow it. –

In all Creation there is no justification whatever for mysticism! There is no room for it, because everything should lie clearly and without gaps before the human spirit, right back to its origin. Only what is *above* that will have to remain a most sacred mystery to every human spirit. Therefore it will never be able to grasp what is Divine. Not with the best will and the greatest knowledge. But in this inability to grasp what is Divine lies the *most natural* thing for man that one can think of; for as everyone knows, it is not possible for anything to go beyond the composition of its origin. Nor for the spirit of man either! A boundary is always set by the difference in composition. And the Divine is of an entirely different consistency from the spiritual, in which man originates.*

The animal, for instance, can never become a human being, however highly developed its soul may be. From its animistic substance there cannot possibly blossom forth the spiritual which brings forth the human spirit. In the composition of all animistic substance the spiritual basic species is missing. Man, who has issued from the spiritual part of Creation, can in turn never become Divine either, because the spiritual has not the nature of Divine substance. The human spirit may well be able to develop to the highest degree of perfection, but must nevertheless always remain *spiritual*. It can never go above itself into the Divine. Here again the different consistency naturally

* A still more extensive breakdown in regard to this will be given in later lectures.

forms the ever impassable limitation upwards. The World of Matter does not come into it at all here since it has no life of its own, but serves as a covering, motivated and formed by the spiritual and the animistic.

The mighty field of the spirit extends through all Creation. Therefore man can, should and must fully grasp and recognise Creation! And through his knowledge he will rule therein. But rightly understood, to rule, however severely, simply means to serve! –

At no point in the entire Creation, up to the highest spiritual, is there any deviation from the natural happening! This fact alone surely makes all things much more familiar to everyone. The unhealthy and secret fear, the reluctance to face so many things as yet unknown, thus fall away of their own accord. With *naturalness* a fresh breeze blows through the sultry atmosphere formed by the morbid imaginings of those who like to cause a great stir. Their sickly fantastic creations, which terrify the weak and are mocked by the strong, have an absurd and childishly foolish effect on the sight that is becoming clear, and that finally, joyful and happy, takes in the glorious naturalness of every happening, which always moves only in simple straight lines that can be clearly recognised.

It runs through everything uniformly, in the strictest regularity and order. And this makes it easier for every seeker to obtain the broad, free view right to the point of his actual origin!

For this he needs neither painstaking research nor imagination. The main thing is for him to stand aloof from all those who in their muddled secretiveness try to make a scanty part-knowledge appear greater.

It all lies *so* simply before men that owing to the very simplicity they often do not come to recognition, because from the outset they assume that the great work of Creation must be much more difficult and intricate.

Here in spite of the best volition thousands stumble, they raise their eyes seekingly to the heavens, not realising that without effort they have only to look *before* and around them. They will then see that through their existence on earth they are already standing on the right road, and need only go calmly ahead! Without haste and without effort, but with *open* eyes and a free, unprejudiced mind! Man must at last learn that true greatness lies only in the most simple and natural happening. That greatness implies this simplicity.

So is it in Creation, so also in himself, who belongs to Creation as a part of it!

Only *simple* thinking and intuitive perceiving can give him clarity! Such simplicity as children still possess! Calm reflection will show him that, in the ability to comprehend, simplicity is identical with clarity and also with naturalness! The one simply cannot be thought of without the others. They form a triad that expresses *one* concept! Whoever makes it the foundation-stone of his search will soon break through the nebulous confusion. Everything that has been added artificially will then collapse into nothingness.

Man will realise that the natural order of events may nowhere be eliminated, and that at no place is it interrupted! And therein the greatness of *God* also reveals itself! The unchangeable vitality of the self-acting Creative Will! For the Laws of Nature are the inexorable Laws of God, continually visible to all men, appealing to them, testifying to the Greatness of the Creator, of an unshakable regularity, admitting of no exception! Of no exception! For a grain of oats can again bring forth only oats, likewise a grain of wheat only wheat, and so forth.

So is it also in that first Creation, which as the Creator's own Work stands nearest to His Perfection. There the fundamental Laws are anchored in such a way that, driven by the vitality of the Will, they were bound in the most natural order of events to result in the coming into being of the further Creation, right down finally to these celestial globes. Only becoming coarser the further Creation draws away in the process of development from the Perfection of the origin. –

Let us first of all just consider Creation.

Imagine that all life therein, no matter in what part it is found, is of two kinds only. The one kind is self-conscious and the other unconscious of itself. It is of the utmost value to observe these two different categories! This is connected with the "origin of man". The differences also give the stimulus to further development, to the apparent struggle. The unconscious is the basis of all the conscious, but its composition is of exactly the same nature. To become conscious is progress and development for the unconscious, which through association with the conscious is continually being stimulated also to attain to this consciousness.

In the process of developing downwards, the first Creation itself brought successively three great basic divisions: As uppermost and highest is the *spiritual*, the Primordial Creation, followed by the denser and thus also gradually heavier Sphere of Animistic Substance. Lastly as the lowest, and because of its greatest density the heaviest, still follows the great Realm of Matter which, severing itself from Primordial Creation, has gradually sunk down! Through this there finally remained as the uppermost only the Primordial Spiritual Substance, because in its pure nature it embodies what is lightest and most luminous. It is the oft-mentioned Paradise, the crown of all Creation.

With the sinking down of that which becomes denser we already touch upon the Law of Gravitation, which is not only anchored in matter, but has an effect in all Creation, from the so-called Paradise down to us.

The Law of Gravitation is of such decisive importance that everyone should hammer it into his mind; for it is the main lever in the whole evolution and process of development of the human spirit.

I have already said that this gravitation applies not only to earthly consistencies, but also works uniformly in those parts of Creation which earth-men can no longer see, and which they therefore simply call the beyond.

For a better understanding I must still divide the *World of Matter* into two sections. Into *ethereal matter* and *gross matter*. Ethereal matter is that matter which cannot become visible to the physical eye, owing to its different nature. And yet it still is matter.

The so-called "beyond" must not be confused with the longed-for Paradise, which is purely spiritual. The spiritual must not be taken as something "to do with thoughts", but the spiritual is a *consistency*, just as the animistic and the material are each a consistency. Therefore now this ethereal matter is simply called the "beyond", because it lies beyond earthly vision. Gross matter, however, is this side, all that is earthly, which on account of its similar species becomes visible to our gross material eyes.

Man should get rid of the habit of regarding things that are invisible to him as also incomprehensible and unnatural. *Everything* is natural, even the so-called beyond, and Paradise, which is still an immense distance from it.

Now just as here our physical body is sensitive to its surroundings of a *homogeneous* nature, which it can therefore see, hear and feel, so is it exactly the same in those parts of Creation whose consistency is not like ours. The ethereal man in the so-called beyond feels, hears and sees only his homogeneous *ethereal* environment; the higher spiritual man again can only feel his *spiritual* environment.

Thus it happens that many an earth-dweller now and then already sees and hears also the Ethereal World with his ethereal body, which he bears within, before the separation from the gross material earthly body takes place through physical death. There is absolutely nothing unnatural in this.

Side by side and co-operating with the Law of Gravitation is also the no less valuable Law of Homogeneous Species.

I have already touched upon this in saying that one species can only recognise the same species. The proverbs: "Birds of a feather flock together", and "like father, like son" seem to have been sensed from the Primordial Law. Together with the Law of Gravitation it swings throughout Creation.

In addition to those already mentioned there is a third Primordial Law in Creation: The Law of Reciprocal Action. The effect of this Law is that man must reap what he has once sown, unconditionally. He cannot reap wheat where he sowed rye, nor clover where he sowed thistles. In the Ethereal World it is exactly the same. In the end he will not be able to reap kindness where he felt hatred, nor joy where he nourished envy!

These three fundamental Laws form the corner-stones of the Divine Will! They alone automatically work out reward or punishment for a human spirit, with inexorable justice! So incorruptibly, in the most wonderful delicate gradations, that the thought of a slightest injustice in the gigantic world happening becomes impossible.

The effect of these simple Laws brings every human spirit exactly to the place where, according to his inner attitude, he does belong. Any error here is impossible, because the manifestation of these Laws can only be set in motion by the *inmost* condition of a human being, which will, however, set it in motion without fail in every case! Thus to bring this about the spiritual power of the *intuitive perceptions* which is *in* man is needed as the lever! Nothing else has any effect. For this reason only the real *volition*, man's *intuitive perception*, is decisive for what develops for him in the world that is invisible to him, and which he must enter after his earthly death.

There neither pretence nor self-deception will help him. He must then unconditionally reap what he has sown through his *volition!* What is more, exactly according to the strength or weakness of his volition, it sets in motion to a greater or lesser degree the homogeneous currents of the other worlds, no matter whether they are hatred, envy or love. An absolutely natural process, of the greatest simplicity, and yet with the inexorable effect of adamantine justice!

He who tries to go seriously and deeply into these happenings in the beyond will recognise what incorruptible justice lies in this automatic working, and will see in this alone the inconceivable Greatness of God. He does not need to interfere, after having given His Will as Laws, thus perfect, into Creation.

He who in the course of his ascent again enters the Spiritual Realm is purified; for he had first to pass through the self-acting mills of the Divine Will. No other road leads to the proximity of God. And *how* these mills work on the human spirit depends on its former inner life, its own *volition*. They can carry it blissfully into the Luminous Height; or on the other hand they can also pull it agonisingly down into the night of horror, indeed even drag it to complete destruction. –

It should be realised that at the time of its earthly birth the human spirit which has matured to the point of incarnation already wears an ethereal cloak or body, which it has needed on its journey through the Ethereal World. During its earthly existence this also remains with it as a connecting link to the physical body. Now the Law of Gravitation always exerts its main effect upon the densest and coarsest part. Thus during life on earth upon the physical body. But when this dies and falls away, the ethereal body again becomes free, and in this moment, being unprotected and now the coarsest part, is subject to this Law of Gravitation.

When it is said that the spirit forms its body, that is true as regards the ethereal body. The inner quality of man, his desires and his actual volition lay the foundation for it.

In the volition lies the power to form ethereal matter. Through the urge for what is base or for mere earthly pleasures the ethereal body becomes dense, and therewith heavy and dark, because the fulfilment of such desires lies in the World of Gross Matter. Thereby man binds himself to what is coarse and earthly. His desires draw along the ethereal body, that is to say, it is formed so densely that its consistency resembles as nearly as possible that of the earthly body. This alone holds the prospect of being able to participate in earthly pleasures or passions, as soon as the physical body has fallen away. Whoever strives after such things must sink through the Law of Gravitation.

But it is different with those people whose minds are mainly directed towards higher and nobler things. Here the volition automatically makes the ethereal body lighter and thus also more luminous, so that it can draw near to

138

what to these human beings is the goal of their earnest aspirations! That is, to the purity of the Luminous Height.

Expressed in other words: Through the prevailing goal of the human spirit, the ethereal body in earthman is at the same time so equipped that after the death of the physical body it can strive towards this goal, whatever kind it may be. Here the spirit really forms the body; for its volition, being spiritual, also bears within it the power to make use of ethereal substance. The spirit can never evade this natural process. It happens with every volition, no matter whether it is pleasant or unpleasant for the spirit. And these forms remain clinging to it as long as the spirit nourishes them through its volition and intuition. They advance or retard the spirit according to their nature, which is subject to the Law of Gravitation.

Yet the moment the spirit changes its volition and intuition new forms will thereby immediately arise, whereas the old ones, no longer receiving nourishment because of this change, must fade and dissolve. In this way man also changes his fate.

Now as soon as the earthly anchorage falls away through the death of the physical body, the ethereal body which is thereby released either sinks down or floats up like a cork in the Ethereal World, which is called the "beyond". Through the Law of Gravitation it will be held fast exactly in that place which corresponds with its own weight; for then it cannot move further, either up or down. Here it will naturally also find all homogeneous species or all like-minded people; for like nature implies like weight, and like weight of course like nature. According to how man was himself, so will he have to suffer or be able to rejoice among those of like nature, until he changes anew inwardly, and with him his ethereal body, which under the effect of the altered weight must either lead him further upwards or downwards.

Therefore man can neither complain nor need he give thanks; for if he is raised towards the Light it is his own consistency that inevitably causes him to be raised; if he falls into the Darkness, it is again his condition that forces him to do so.

But every human being has reason to glorify and praise the Creator for the perfection that lies in the working of these three Laws. The human spirit is thereby unreservedly made the absolute master of its own fate! For its true volition, thus the genuine inner condition, must cause it either to rise or to sink.

If you try to get a true picture of the effect of these Laws, singly and working together, you will find that they contain reward and punishment, mercy or also damnation, minutely weighed for each one according to his inner state. It is the most simple process, and shows the lifeline provided by every serious volition of a human being, which can never break and never fail. It is the greatness of such simplicity that forcibly drives him who recognises to his knees before the infinite Sublimity of the Creator!

In every happening and in all my explanations we always again and again meet clearly and distinctly the effect of these simple Laws, whose wonderful interaction I must yet describe especially.

Once man knows this interaction he thus also has the step-ladder to the Luminous Realm of the Spirit, to Paradise. But he then also sees the road that leads down to the Darkness!

He need not even tread these steps himself, but the automatic mechanism raises him on high or drags him down, entirely according to how he adjusts the mechanism for himself through his *inner* life.

Which way he wishes to let himself be borne along is always left to *his* decision.

Man must not allow himself to be confused by scoffers.

Rightly viewed, doubt and derision are nothing but the expression of wishes. Quite unconsciously every doubter expresses what he wishes for himself, thus exposing his inner self to the searching glance. For denial and defence also harbour deeply hidden wishes which can be easily recognised. It is sad, or even revolting, to see what negligence or poverty of mind is thus sometimes revealed, because just through this a man often drags himself inwardly down below the level of any ignorant animal. One should have compassion for such people without, however, being indulgent; for indulgence would indeed mean cultivating indolence in serious investigation. He who seeks earnestly must become sparing with indulgence; otherwise he will ultimately harm himself without helping the other thereby.

But with growing recognition man will jubilantly stand before the wonder of such a Creation, and consciously let himself be borne aloft to the Luminous Heights which he may call his home!

THE HUMAN WORD

As a great grace for your maturing in the coarse World of Matter, the ability to form words has been bestowed upon you human beings by the Creator! You have never recognised the true value of this sublime gift, because you did not trouble yourselves about it, and treated it carelessly. Now you must suffer bitterly under all the consequences of your wrongdoing.

You stand in this affliction, and do not yet know the *causes* which bring such suffering in their wake.

No one may trifle with gifts of the Almighty without harming himself; such is the Law which rests and works in Creation, and which can never be diverted.

And when you consider that this being able to speak, thus your ability to form words, which anchor your volition in the World of Gross Matter through speaking, is an especially high gift of your Creator, then you will also know that it involves obligations for you, and that an immense responsibility arises therefrom; for it is with the language, and through it, that you are to work in Creation!

The words you form, the sentences, shape your outward fate on this earth. They are like seed in a garden which you build around you; for each human word is part of the most vital thing that *you* can weave for yourselves in this Creation.

Today I give you this, with an admonition, to think it over: there is a releasing quality in every word, because all words are firmly anchored in the Primordial Laws of Creation!

Every word shaped by man has come into being under the pressure of higher Laws and, according to its application, must manifest formingly in a very definite way!

The *application* lies in man's hands according to his free volition; however he is unable to control the effect, which is strictly and justly governed in conformity with the Holy Law by a power hitherto unknown to him.

Therefore in the final reckoning woe will now fall upon every human being who has abused the mysterious working of the word!

But where is *the* man who has *not* yet sinned in this respect! For thousands of years the whole earthly race has been deeply entangled in this guilt. What harm has already been spread throughout this earth by the wrong application of this gift of being permitted to speak!

Through ruinous, thoughtless and idle talk all men have sown poison. The seed has duly sprung up, the plant has blossomed forth, and now bears the fruit which you must harvest, whether you like it or not; for it is all the consequences of *your* actions that are now thrown into your lap!

That this poison *must* bring forth the most repulsive fruits will not surprise anyone who knows the Laws in Creation, which do not conform to the ideas of men, but serenely pursue their great course, irresistibly, without deviation, from the primordial beginning, and also unchanged unto all eternity.

Look around you, men, clearly and without bias: You *must* easily recognise the self-acting Divine Laws of the Most Holy Will, because you do have before you the fruits of your sowing! Wherever you look you will find that today high-sounding talk predominates and leads in everything. This seed *had* to come swiftly to such flower, to reveal now in the ripening its true kernel, whereby it will then collapse as useless.

It *had* to ripen under the increased pressure from the Light, and must shoot up as if in a hothouse; so that, losing every support through its hollowness, it will fall and bury all who with light-hearted confidence or selfish hope imagined themselves safe under its protection.

The time of harvest has already begun! Therewith all the consequences of wrong speaking now fall back upon the individual, as upon the entire masses who encouraged such talk.

It is quite *natural,* and shows the strict consistency of the effects of the Divine Laws, that now on the eve of the harvest the greatest talkers must in the end also gain the strongest influence and greatest power, as culmination and fruit of this continual wrong use of the word, whose mysterious working foolish humanity could no longer know, because they have long since closed themselves to the knowledge of it.

They did not listen to the warning voice of Jesus, the Son of God, Who already at that time said:

"Let your communication be yea or nay; for whatsoever is more than these cometh of evil!"

There is more in these words than you imagined; for they hold upbuilding or decline for mankind!

Through your propensity for much and useless talk you have chosen *decline,* which has already come to you. Finally, before the general collapse in the Judgment, it also still shows you quite clearly, as a help towards the saving recognition, all the fruits which you have forcibly brought into being through the wrong application of the word.

The reciprocal power now raises the masters at your own sins to the top, in such a way that you are in danger of being crushed by them, so that through recognition you will at last free yourselves from or be destroyed by them.

That *is* at the same time justice and help, as only the Will of God in His Perfection can offer you!

Just look around you! You *must* recognise it, if only you will. And for those who still hesitate to do so, the veil which they themselves hold before their eyes will yet be forcibly torn away from the fruits of their volition through still greater suffering than in the past, so that this earth may be cleansed from the pressure of your great guilt!

The entire mankind has actively participated in this, not merely individuals. They are the blossoms of all the wrongdoing over past centuries, which now had to ripen in these last fruits for the Judgment, so as to perish in this ripeness.

The frivolous, senseless and thoughtless chatter which, however, is always wrong and out of harmony with the Primordial Laws of Creation, had to culminate in the *universal* disease which is evident today, and must now in fever spasms, as in a storm, also shake off the fruits ... they drop into the lap of mankind.

Hence no people should be pitied who must now groan and suffer under this; for these are the fruits of their *own* volition, which must be consumed even if they taste rotten and bitter and bring destruction to many, because from poisonous seed only poison can be harvested. I have already said: where you sow thistles, no wheat can grow!

Thus out of agitation, mockery and harming your fellow-men there can never come any upbuilding whatever; for each kind of expression and attitude can only bring forth something *similar,* can only attract what is homo-geneous! You must *never* forget this Law of Creation! It works *automatic-ally,* and all human volition can never act against it! Never, do you hear that? Impress it upon yourselves, so that you may always heed it in your thinking, speaking and acting; for everything germinates from this and grows into your fate! Therefore never hope for anything else as fruit than always and only the same kind as the seed!

This after all is not so difficult, and yet it is just in this that you continually fail! Slander can again only produce slander, hate only hate, and murder only murder. But dignity, peace, light and joy can in turn only arise from a *dignified* way of thinking, never otherwise.

Liberation and redemption do not lie in the clamour of individuals and of the masses. A people that permits itself to be led by talkers must inevitably and rightfully fall into bad repute, into sorrow and death, into distress and misery; it is forcibly pushed into the mire.

And if hitherto the fruit and the harvest have so often not appeared in *one* earth-life, but only in later ones, this is now different; for the fulfilment of the Holy Will of God enforces *immediate* release of every happening on earth, and therewith also the unravelling of all the fates of men and of the peoples! Final reckoning!

Therefore guard your word! Pay careful attention to your speech; for the human word is also a deed which, however, can only produce forms in the Plane of Fine Gross Matter, that sink into and have an effect on everything earthly.

Yet do not imagine that promises are fulfilled according to their wording and thus grow into deeds, unless at the same time the speaker bears the *purest* intentions in his soul; but the words form *that* which from out of the *inner-most being of the speaker* simultaneously vibrates with them. So the same word can produce two kinds of results, and woe unto him with whom it did not truthfully vibrate in complete purity!

I lift the veil covering your ignorance which has prevailed up to now, so that you may henceforth consciously experience the evil consequences, and benefit from them for the future.

As a further help I therefore give you:

Heed your word! Let your speech be simple and true! In accordance with the Holy Will of God, it contains an ability to form in an upbuilding or also in a destroying way, depending on the nature of the words and of the speaker.

Do not squander these sublime gifts which God so mercifully granted you, but seek to recognise them aright in their full value. Up till now the power of speech has been a curse to you through such people, who as Lucifer's satellites have misused it under the evil influence of the distorted and one-sidedly developed intellect!

Therefore beware of people who talk much; for with these goes disintegration. *You,* however, are to become *upbuilding ones* in this Creation, not talkers!

Heed your word! Do not talk merely for the sake of talking. And speak only when, where and how it is necessary! In the human word there shall be a reflection of the splendour of the Word of God, which is Life and will eternally remain Life.

You know that all Creation swings in the Word of the Lord! Does this not make you think? Creation vibrates in Him, as also do you yourselves, who are indeed part of Creation; for it arose out of Him and is maintained through this Word.

It has been clearly proclaimed to mankind:

"In the beginning was the Word! And the Word was with God! And the Word was *God!*"

Herein lies all knowledge for you, if you would only draw it. But you skim over it and do not heed it. Plainly it tells you:

The Word came *out of* God! It was and is a part out of Him.

A faint reflection of the power of the *Living* Word of God, which contains all and embraces all that is outside of God, a faint reflection of this also lies in the *human word!*

It is true that the human word is only able to send out its effect into the Planes of Fine Gross Matter, but that is enough retroactively to shape the destinies of men and also of peoples *here on earth!*

Remember that! He who talks much stands only on the ground of the distorted, one-sidedly developed intellect! The two always go hand in hand. By that you can recognise it! And these are words emanating from the low earthly planes, that can never build up. Yet in accordance with the Divine Law the word *is* to build up. Wherever it does not obey this command it can only bring about the opposite.

Therefore always heed your word! And *stand* to your word! You have still to be taught the right way to do this in the building up of the Kingdom of God here on earth.

You must first learn to recognise the power of the words which you have hitherto so thoughtlessly and frivolously debased.

Just think for once of the most Holy Word that has been given to you, of the Word: GOD!

You very often speak of God, *too* often for *that* awe still to resound in It which would indicate the right *intuitive perception* when you utter this Word: the awe which will allow you only to *whisper* the Sublime Word in reverential devotion, so as to shield It carefully from any kind of desecration.

But what have you men made of the most Sacred of all concepts in the Word! Instead of humbly and joyfully preparing your spirit for this most Sublime Expression, so that it may gratefully open itself to an unspeakable Radiation-Power of the Unsubstantiate Light-Sublimity of real Being, Who first permits you as well as all creatures to breathe, you have dared to drag It down to the low planes of your most trivial thinking, using It carelessly as an every-day word, which thereby had now to form itself in your ears into only an empty sound, and thus can find no entrance to your *spirit*.

It is then obvious that the effect of this most Sublime of all words will be different from the effect on those who whisper It with the proper awe and recognition.

Therefore pay attention to *all* words; for they hold joy or sorrow for you, they build up or disintegrate, they bring clarity but can also confuse, according to the manner *in which* they are spoken and applied.

I will later also give you recognition *for this*, so that you can *give thanks* with *every* word which the Creator still permits you to speak now! Then you shall also have earthly happiness, and peace will reign here on this hitherto troubled earth.

THE WOMAN OF SUBSEQUENT CREATION

THESE words touch upon the sorest spot in Subsequent Creation. *That* spot which needs the greatest change, the most lasting purification.

Although man of Subsequent Creation has made himself the slave of his own intellect, woman has transgressed to a far greater extent.

Equipped with the greatest delicacy of intuitive perceptions, she should easily swing herself up to the purity of Luminous Heights, and form the bridge to Paradise for all humanity. *Woman!* Streams of Light should flow through her. Her entire physical, gross material nature is adapted to this. Woman only needs to will honestly, and all the offspring from her womb *must* be strongly protected and encompassed by the power of the Light even before birth! It could not possibly be otherwise, because every woman through the wealth of her intuitive perception can almost entirely alone influence the spiritual nature of the fruit! Therefore she remains *primarily* responsible for all her descendants!

In addition she has been richly endowed with unlimited possibilities to influence the entire people, indeed even the whole of Subsequent Creation. Her starting-point of the greatest power is, for her, home and hearth! There alone lies her strength, her unlimited might, but not in public life! In home and family her abilities make her queen. From the quiet, intimate home her incisive virtue extends through the whole people, present and future, and pervades everything.

There is nothing upon which her influence cannot absolutely be brought to bear, if she stands *in that place* where her inherent *womanly* abilities fully unfold to blossom. But only if woman is truly *womanly* does she fulfil the mission which is assigned to her by the Creator. Then she is completely what she can and should be. And it is only genuine womanliness that silently educates the man who, supported by this quiet activity containing undreamed-of power, feels like storming the heavens. Out of an inner naturalness he will then gladly and joyfully seek to protect true womanhood as soon as it only shows itself to be *genuine*.

But womankind of today trample underfoot their real power and their high mission, they blindly overlook them, wantonly destroy all the sacred gifts they carry within them, and instead of being an upbuilding influence they bring about disintegration, thus being the most poisonous element in Subsequent Creation. They push man as well as children down with them into the abyss.

Look at the woman of today! Just let a ray of Light fall upon her with all the relentlessness and dispassion which are always accompanying conditions of Purity.

You will hardly recognise the high qualities of genuine womanhood, those in which there can be unfolded that pure might which is given only to the finer sensitiveness of womanhood, to be used solely as a *blessing*.

A man can never develop this pervading nature. The silent weaving of that invisible power which the Creator allows to move through the Universe, *first* and completely seizes *the woman* with her more delicate intuitive perception. Man receives it only partially, and then converts it into deeds.

And just as the Living Power of the Creator remains invisible to all men, while yet upholding, nourishing, moving and driving the whole Universe, *so* the weaving of all genuine womanhood is intended to be; it is *that for* which she has been created, and *that* is her high, pure and wonderful goal!

It is ridiculous to use the expression "weak woman", for woman is psychically stronger than man. Not in herself, but through being more closely connected with the Creative Power, which grants her the more delicate intuitive faculty.

And this is just what the woman tries to hide today; she exerts herself to coarsen or suppress it altogether. In boundless vanity and stupidity she surrenders the most beautiful and valuable gift bestowed on her. Through this she makes herself an outcast from the Light, to whom the way back will remain closed.

What has thereby become of these images of queenly womanhood! One must turn away from them with horror. Where does one still find in the woman of today the genuine feeling of shame, which is the expression of the most delicate intuitive perception of *noble* womanhood. It is so grossly distorted that is must be exposed to ridicule.

The woman of today is certainly ashamed to wear a long dress if fashion decrees a short one, but she is not ashamed to expose almost three-quarters of her body, offering it to the glances of all on festive occasions. And of course not only to their glances but also, when dancing, unavoidably to their hands! Without hesitation she would also uncover still more if fashion required it, probably even everything judging by present experiences!

This is no exaggeration. For hitherto we have had enough of this disgraceful conduct. It was not a wrong but, alas, only too true a saying that "woman begins to *dress* herself when she retires for the night"!

Besides, delicate intuitive perceptions also demand a sense of beauty! Unquestionably. But if today the delicacy of womanly intuitive perceptions is still to be assessed on that basis, then affairs are in a deplorable state. Indeed, the type of dress often and plainly enough tells the opposite, and these thinly-stockinged legs of a woman, or even of a mother, are very difficult to reconcile with womanly dignity. Bobbed hair and modern sports for women are no less harmful to genuine womanhood! Coquetry is the inevitable accompaniment of vain fashion follies, which result in grave dangers for body and soul, to say nothing of the simple domestic happiness. Often enough many a woman prefers the coarse and really insulting flattery of some idler to the faithful labour of her husband.

Thus much, very much more could be cited as visible evidence that a woman of today is lost to her *real* task in this Subsequent Creation! And likewise all the high values entrusted to her, of which she must now give an account. Accursed be these empty human beings! They are not the victims of circumstances, but they have forced these circumstances into being.

All this talk about progress does not alter the fact that these zealots of progress, together with their faithful followers, only sink deeper, ever deeper. Already they have all buried their real values. The majority of womankind no longer deserve to bear the name of honour, woman! And they can never represent nor become men, thus in the end they remain nothing but drones in Subsequent Creation, which must be exterminated according to the inflexible Laws of Nature.

Of all the creatures in Subsequent Creation, woman stands least in the place where she should stand! In her way she has become the saddest figure among all creatures! She simply *had* to become corrupt in soul, since she wantonly sacrifices her most noble intuitive perception, her purest power, to outward, absurd vanity, thereby ridiculing and scorning the decree of her Creator. With such superficiality there can be no salvation; for these women would reject words, or be no longer able to understand and grasp them at all.

Thus out of the horrors the new, true woman must first arise, who has to become the mediator, and therewith also provide the foundation for the new God-willed life and human activity in Subsequent Creation, the woman who will have become free from poison and corruption!

SUBMISSION

"THY WILL be done!" People who believe in God utter these words submissively! But a certain sadness always vibrates in their voices or lies in their thoughts, in their intuitive perceptions. These words are used almost exclusively where *sorrow* that was *inescapable* has entered. Where man realises that he could do nothing more about it.

Then, if he is a believer, he will say in passive submission: *"Thy Will be done!"*

It is not humility, however, that prompts him to speak thus, but the words are meant to calm him in face of something he has been powerless to deal with.

That is the origin of the submission which man expresses in such a case. If, however, he were offered the slightest opportunity to alter things in any way, he would not care about the Will of God, but his submissive attitude would again quickly be changed to the form: *"My will be done!"*

Such is man! – – –

"Do with me as Thou wilt, O Lord!" and similar hymns are often to be heard at funerals. But every mourner bears within him the unshakable wish: "If I could alter it I would do so at once!"

Human submission is *never* genuine. Deeply implanted in a human soul lies the opposite. Rebellion against the fate that befalls it; and it is this very protest that causes the soul's suffering, which "oppresses" and bows it down.

What is unhealthy in this is due to the wrong application of the meaning of these words: "Thy Will be done!" They do not belong where man and churches use them.

The Will of God lies in the Laws of this Creation! Whenever man says: "Thy Will be done!" it is tantamount to affirming: "I will honour and obey Thy Laws in Creation!" To honour means to *observe* them, but to observe them demands to live accordingly! Only thus can man honour the Will of God!

151

But if he wants to observe It, if he wants to live accordingly, he must also first of all *know* It!

That is just the point, however, against which mankind on earth has transgressed in the worst way! Until now man has never concerned himself with the Laws of God in Creation! Thus not with the Holy Will of God! And yet he utters over and over again: "Thy Will be done!"

You see how unthinkingly earthman approaches God! How senselessly he seeks to apply the sublime words of Christ. Plaintively, often writhing in anguish, feeling himself defeated, but never with a joyful pledge!

"Thy Will be done" actually means: "I will act according to It" or "I desire Thy Will!" One can just as well also say: "I will obey Thy Will!"

But he who obeys also *acts*. One who obeys is not inactive; that is implied in the very word. He who obeys also *does something*.

Yet as the man of *today* says: "Thy Will be done!" he wishes *to do nothing himself*, but puts into his intuitive perception the meaning: "I remain still, *You do it!*"

He considers himself great in this, believing that he has conquered himself and "become merged" with the Will of God. Man even imagines himself superior to all others thereby, and believes he has made a tremendous advance.

All such people, however, are useless weaklings, idlers, enthusiasts, visionaries and fanatics, but no useful links in Creation! They are numbered among those who must be rejected in the Judgment; for they do not want to be *labourers* in the vineyard of the Lord! The humility of which they boast is nothing but indolence. They are idle servants!

The Lord demands *life*, which lies in *movement!* —

Submission! This word should not exist at all for believers in God! Simply replace it with "joyful volition"! God does not want dull submission from men, but joyful activity.

Just look closely at those who are described as "resigned to God's Will". They are hypocrites who bear a great lie within them!

Of what use is it to cast a glance of submissive resignation upwards, if at the same time man looks around with cunning, lust, arrogance, conceit or malice! This only makes him *doubly* guilty.

Submissive people bear the lie within, for submission is absolutely incompatible with "spirit"! Therefore also with a human spirit! All that is "spirit" is utterly unable to bring the quality of true submissiveness to life within itself! Wherever it is attempted it must remain artificial, thus self-delusion or even conscious hypocrisy! But it can never be genuinely felt because the human spirit, being spiritual, is incapable of it. The pressure under which the human spirit stands does not allow the quality of submissiveness to become conscious. The pressure is too strong for this. And therefore man cannot practise it either.

Submissiveness is a quality that lies solely in the animistic! Only in the animal does it find genuine expression. The *animal* is submissive to its master! But the spirit does not know this designation! Therefore it *always* remains unnatural for the human being.

Submission was drilled into slaves with difficulty and harshness, because they were put on a par with animals in sale and purchase, as personal property. Yet the submission could never become really genuine in these slaves. It was either dullness, fidelity or love that lay hidden under the submission and gave it expression, but never true submission. Slavery is unnatural among men.

The submission of the animistic finds its enhancement in the spiritual in conscious and willed loyalty! What denotes submission in the animistic, therefore, is loyalty in the spiritual!

Submission does not befit man; because he is of the spirit! Just pay closer attention to the language itself, which indeed expresses in its words what is right, and bears the true meaning in it. It gives you the right picture.

For instance, the victor also says to the vanquished: "Submit!" In this word lies the meaning: "Surrender yourself to me unconditionally so that I may deal with you as I see fit, even over life or death!"

But in this the victor acts wrongly; for even in victory man has to conform strictly to the Laws of God. Otherwise with every neglect of them he makes himself guilty before the Lord. The reciprocal action will then strike him without fail! This applies to the individual as well as to entire peoples!

And now the time has come when everything, everything that has hitherto taken place in the world, must be redeemed! What has been wrong, what is happening on earth *today, not one word will remain unatoned for!*

The atonement is not reserved for a distant future, but is already taking place in the *present time!*

Thus the *speedy* release of *all* the reciprocal actions is not opposed to the Law of Creation, but lies quite correctly in the Law itself.

The action of the mechanism is at present accelerated by the increased radiation of the Light, which enforces final effects by first driving everything to fruition and over-ripeness, so that the false will decay therein and in withering away judge itself, while the good will become free from the hitherto existing pressure of the wrong and can gain strength!

In the near future this radiation will be so intensified that in very many cases the reciprocal action will come *at once, instantaneously!*

This is the power which will soon alarm earthmen, and which they will then have to fear in the future! But only *those* who have done *wrong* need fear it, and rightly so. Whether they have thought themselves in the right, or have tried to make others believe they were, it will not save them from the blow of the reciprocal effect that operates in the Laws of God!

Even though men have devised different laws on earth, under whose protection many act wrongly and unjustly in the delusion that they are thereby also in the right, it does not absolve them of one particle of their guilt.

The Laws of God, thus the Will of God, do not concern themselves with the opinions of these earthmen, which they have laid down in their mundane laws, even though the whole world has now considered them to be right. Whatever is not in harmony with the Divine Laws, there also the blow of the sword will now strike! Judging in the process of redemption!

All those who in the light of God's Laws have suffered *innocently* at the hands of men may now rejoice; for henceforth they shall receive justice, while their adversaries or judges are delivered up to the Justice of God.

Rejoice; for this Divine Justice is near! It is already working in every country on earth! Look at the confusion! This is the effect of the *approaching* Will of God! It is the setting-in of the purification!

For this reason everything that is wrong among men is already *now* meeting with its doom, be it in economics, the state, politics, the churches, sects, peoples, families and also in the individual! Everything, everything is now dragged before the Light, *so that it may reveal and simultaneously judge itself therein!* Also what has hitherto been able to remain hidden *must* reveal itself as it *really* is, must become active, and thus finally, despairing of itself and others, disintegrate and turn to dust.

Thus even now there is a boiling up under the pressure of the Light in all countries, everywhere. Every kind of tribulation is increasing to the point of despair, until finally nothing remains but hopelessness, with the realisation that the would-be saviours had *only empty words* besides selfish desires, but could offer no help! Spiritual warriors are sweeping over all humanity, and striking sharply where a head refuses to bow.

Only then will there be the right soil that pleads once more for *God's* help! After murder and fire, starvation, pestilence and death, after man has recognised his own incapacity.

The great upbuilding begins.

Then the despairing ones shall become free, free from the pressure of the Darkness! But they shall also become free *within themselves!* To become free within, however, can only be achieved by each individual *alone.* Yet for this he must know what freedom means, what it *is.*

Only the man who lives in the Laws of God is free! Thus and not otherwise does he stand unoppressed and unconstrained in this Creation. Everything then serves him instead of obstructing his path. It "serves" him because he uses it in the right way.

God's Laws in Creation are in truth simply all that every man needs for a healthy, happy life in Creation. They are, as it were, nourishment for his well-being! Only he who knows the Will of God and lives accordingly is really free! All the others must bind themselves in many threads of the Laws of this Creation, because they entangle themselves.

Creation originated only in the Will of God, in His Laws. Working together, the threads of these Laws sink deeper and deeper, everywhere enforcing movement towards development, and inevitably branching out more and more in the course of development, while in the continuous movement new creations are perpetually formed around the threads. Thus these Laws provide at the same time the support, the possibility of continued existence and the further expansion of Creation.

Nothing exists without this Will of God, Which alone gives movement. Everything in Creation conforms to It.

Only the human spirit has *not* adjusted itself to these threads! It has tangled them and thereby entangled itself, because it wanted to follow new roads according to *its* will, and disregarded those already prepared and in existence.

The increasing power of the Light is now changing this. The threads of all the Divine Laws in Creation are being charged with increased energy, so that they become powerfully taut. This enormous tension causes them to spring back into their original position. What is tangled and knotted is thereby disentangled, so suddenly and irresistibly that everything that cannot still adapt itself to the right position in Creation is simply torn down in this process!

Whatever it may be, whether plant or animal, whether mountains, streams, countries, states or man himself, all will collapse that cannot prove itself at the last moment to be genuine and willed by God!

INDOLENCE OF THE SPIRIT

THE COSMIC Clock can be heard on earth as it now booms out the hour of twelve through the Universe! Frightened, Creation holds its breath, and every creature bows down in fear; for the Voice of *God* rings down and demands! Demands that you render account, you who have been permitted to live in this Creation!

You have mismanaged the bounty which God in His Love made over to you. All those servants who have thought only of *themselves* and never of their Master will now be expelled! And all those who sought to make themselves the master. –

You men shy away from my words, for you do not consider severity Divine! But that is only *your* fault, because until now you have imagined everything Divine, everything that comes down from God, to be tenderly loving and all-forgiving, since that is what the churches have taught you!

But these false teachings were only intellectual schemes aimed at the mass-capture of human souls on earth. In order to catch something, a bait is needed that is attractive to everything at which it is aimed. The right choice of bait is the main thing for each catch.

Now as this was intended for *human souls,* a plan based on *their* weaknesses was skilfully devised. The lure had to correspond to the main weakness! And this main weakness of the souls was love of ease, the indolence of their spirit!

The church knew very well that it was bound to achieve great success as soon as it showed much leniency towards *this* weakness, and did not require it to be overcome!

Recognising this aright, it built for earthmen a broad and easy road that was ostensibly to lead to the Light, and displayed it enticingly to these earthmen who would prefer to give one-tenth of the fruits of their labour, go on their knees and murmur prayers by the hundred, rather than exert *themselves spiritually for even one moment!*

Therefore the church took the spiritual effort away from men, also pardoning all their sins if they were obedient outwardly and in the earthly sense, and carried out what *the church* required of them in mundane ways!

Whether in the way of church attendance, confessions, in the number of prayers, in tributes or in donations and bequests, no matter what, the *church* was satisfied. They left the believers under a delusion that everything they did for the *church* would also secure them a place in Heaven.

As if the church could allot these places!

However, the achievements and the allegiance of all believers links them only *with their church*, not with their God! Neither the church nor its servants can take away from or even forgive a human soul one particle of its guilt! Just as little are they permitted to canonise a soul, and thereby interfere in God's perfect eternal Primordial Laws of Creation, which are immutable!

How can *men* presume to vote and also to decide on matters that rest in the Omnipotence, the Justice and the Omniscience of God! How dare earthmen try to make their fellow-men believe such things! And it is no less sacrilegious for earthmen credulously to accept such claims, which so plainly carry within them only a dishonouring of the Sublimity of God!

Anything so incredible can only be possible with thoughtless people of herd mentality, who by such action brand themselves with the mark of the greatest spiritual indolence; for the most simple reflection must enable anyone instantly and easily to realise that such persumptions cannot even be explained by human conceit or arrogance, but contain grave blasphemies!

The reciprocal effect must be terrible!

The time of God's forbearance is now indeed over. Holy Wrath strikes the ranks of those offenders who thereby seek to dupe humanity on earth in order to increase and preserve their authority, whereas within themselves they clearly sense that here it is a question of matters far beyond the level to which they can ever be entitled to rise!

How dare they dispose of the Kingdom of God in Eternity? Overnight the Ray of Divine Wrath will awaken them from their unbelievable spiritual slumber and ... *judge* them! – – –

What does a man give to his God by obedience to the church! He does not have with it a single, *natural* intuitive urge, which alone can help him to ascend.

I say to you that men can in truth only serve God with just *that* which did *not* come to life through the churches: With their *own* thinking and *independent* investigation! Everyone must journey *alone* through the mills, through the mechanism of the Divine Laws in Creation. And therefore it is necessary for *every man himself* to become acquainted at the right time with the nature and function of the mills.

But this is just what many a church has persistently withheld, so that the believers could not develop the necessary *personal* reflection and intuitive perception. Thereby they robbed man of that staff which alone can guide him safely and direct him towards the Light, and tried instead to force upon every man an interpretation, the acceptance of which was bound to bring benefit only to the *church*. Benefit, influence and power!

Human souls can serve their Creator only by the *activity of their own spirit!* Thereby, however, in the first place they are also simultaneously serving themselves. Only *that* human spirit which stands bright and alert in this Creation, aware of its Laws and adapting itself to them in thought and deed, is pleasing to God, because it is then fulfilling the purpose of existence, which every human spirit has in this Creation!

But this never lies in the observances that the churches demand of their believers! For these lack naturalness and free conviction, knowledge, as the *main requisite* of true service to God! There is a lack of vigour and joy in helping all creatures to advance, in letting their souls exult in the happiness of knowing that they can contribute to the beauty of this Creation as a part of it, and *thereby* thank and honour the Creator!

Instead of joyful, free worshippers of God, the church has cultivated church-slaves for itself! It has thrust *itself* before men's free upward gaze! Thereby obscuring true Light. It has only bound and gagged the human spirits, instead of awakening and liberating them. Wantonly it has kept the spirits in slumber, oppressed them, restrained their desire for knowledge, and forbidden the knowledge itself through regulations that are contrary and opposed to the Will of God! All this in order to uphold its *own* power.

Even as in olden times the churches have not shrunk from various forms of torture, torment and murder, so today they do not hesitate to slander their fellow-men, speak ill of them, undermine their reputation, agitate against them, and put every available obstacle in their way if they are not willing to join the host of church-slaves! They work with the most sordid means only for *their* influence, *their* earthly power.

But through the reciprocal action this now will also be the very first to waver and collapse; for it is the opposite of what *God* wills! It shows how far removed they are from humbly serving *God!* –

Enticed by the sanctioned indolence of the spirit, endless multitudes have allowed themselves to be drawn into the fold of the church, which lulls them to sleep! They believed the wicked delusion of a cheap atonement for their sins, and as the spiritually indolent masses grew so did the earthly influence, with the final goal of earthly power! The people did not see that the false view and teaching obscured and defiled the Sacred Justice of Almighty God; they saw only the thus simulated broad and easy road to the Light, which in reality does not exist at all! Through its arbitrary, illusory forgiveness it leads to Darkness and destruction!

The self-glorification of all the churches, which is hostile to God, separates their believers from God instead of leading them to Him. The doctrines were false! But the people should easily have found this out *themselves,* for they clearly contradict the simplest sense of justice! And therefore the church believers are *just as guilty* as the churches themselves!

The churches proclaim in the words of Christ from the Gospel of John:

"Howbeit when he, the Spirit of truth, is come, he will guide you into all truth. And when he is come, he will reprove the world of sin, and of righteousness! And will bring the Judgment. I, however, go to the Father and you will henceforth not see me. I came forth from the Father and am come into the world. Again, I leave the world and go to the Father!"

These words are read in the churches without understanding; for it is quite clearly stated by the Son of God that *another* than He will come to proclaim the Truth and to bring the Judgment. The Spirit of Truth Who is the Living Cross! And yet in this matter, too, the church teaches wrongly and against these clear words.

Even though Paul also once wrote to the Corinthians: "For *we* know in part. But when that which is perfect is come, then that which is in part shall be done away!"

Here the Apostle shows that the coming of Him Who will proclaim the Perfect Truth is yet to be expected, and that the prophecy of the Son of God concerning it should not be taken to refer to the well-known outpouring of the Power of the Holy Spirit, which at that time had already taken place when Paul wrote these words.

He testifies thereby that the Apostles did *not* regard this outpouring of Power as the fulfilment of the mission of the Comforter, the Spirit of Truth, as strange to say many churches and believers now try to interpret it at Whitsuntide, because these things would not otherwise fit into the structure of their faith, but would form a gap which must cause serious shocks to this false edifice.

Yet it avails them nothing; for the time has come for the recognition of all these things, and everything that is false collapses!

Until now there could not yet be a true Pentecost for mankind; the recognition through spiritual awakening could not come to them, since they acquiesced in so many false interpretations, in which the churches especially have a great share!

Nothing of their great guilt will be remitted to them! –

Now you men stand amazed before the new Word, and many of you are no longer even capable of perceiving that It comes from the Luminous Heights, because It is so different from what you had imagined! For in you, too, there certainly still lives some of the tenacious indolence in which the churches and the schools have enveloped you, so that you would remain faithful followers, and have no longing for the awakening of your own spirit!

Until now men on earth have been indifferent to what *God* demands! Once more, however, I say to you: "The broad and easy road which the churches have hitherto tried to simulate for their own advantage is *wrong!* With its promise of an arbitrary, illusory forgiveness, it does not lead to the Light!"

MEN, WHAT has been your attitude towards your God up till now! Hypocritically you have sought to deceive Him, even as you have always wished to deceive yourselves with the false piety which was only lip-service, but never shared by your spirit. *You* have established rules and observances, in your temples, your churches, without asking whether this way was pleasing to *God*. If only they pleased *you*, then that settled the service to God for you!

Do you not see how arrogant all this was. *You* wanted to decide the way everything should be arranged. In doing so you have never cared about *God's* Will. What *you* termed great was to be equally acceptable to God. You wanted to force *your* opinions in all things upon God as justified, irrespective of what you were dealing with.

What *you* considered right was to be rewarded by God as righteous; what *you* chose to call wrong God was to punish.

You have never seriously wanted to find out what *God* regards as right, and what before *His* Eye is wrong. You have paid no attention to the Divine Laws, nor to the inexorable Holy Will of God, Which has existed from all Eternity and has never yet changed, nor ever will change!

It will now shatter you, and with you all the false works of man, which have created laws to serve *your earthly desires*. But you human beings yourselves stand before God as scheming, neglectful servants who in their selfishness, self-conceit and ridiculous claim to know everything have never respected *His* Will.

You have been and still are servants who thought themselves masters, and who out of arrogance and spiritual indolence have tried to resist and drag down all that they could not understand, if it did not agree with the attainment of the base earthly ends which they wished to be regarded as of the highest order.

You miserable ones, who could so transgress! Everything was only to serve *you, even the Laws!* Only what served you, regardless of its form, only what helped you towards the fulfilment of your earthly desires – only *that* did you acknowledge as right, only such thin_ᵍ did you still want to know about.

But should it now be required of you that you yourselves should eagerly and loyally serve your Lord, to Whom you owe your existence, then you are quite astonished, since in your opinion it is only He Himself Who should serve you with His Power, with His Glory and His Great Love!

How could it possibly be *otherwise,* in view of the high opinion you have of yourselves! For you thought it was service enough to God if you acknowledge Him, and ask in thought for His help to fulfil all the wishes you carry within you. To put it plainly, that He should *serve you* with the Omnipotence that is His own, and make your life pleasant! Nothing else enters your mind.

At its best your service to God has been *begging!*

Just think it over very carefully for once; it has never yet been otherwise.

When you examine yourselves in this respect, are you not seized with both shame and anger about yourselves?

The majority of mankind think that the only object of this earth-life is the purpose of acquiring material gain! Also at best the purpose of a family and children! He who does not *think* so still *acts* accordingly! But on such a basis what is the use of propagation, as you call it, which in reality does not mean propagation at all, but simply provides opportunities for other human spirits to incarnate so that these may continue to improve themselves and cast off old faults. By your behaviour you add to the burden of your guilt; for you thereby prevent all those spirits from ascending, whom you bring up as your children for the same empty purposes!

What is the good of building up an earthly kingdom if it is not intended for the honour of God, if it does not work according to the Wishes of God, about Which you are still completely ignorant, and have hitherto not wanted to learn anything either, since *your* wishes are more important to you than anything else. You only want to satisfy *yourselves*, and then even expect God to bless your poor efforts! You do not care to serve and to fulfil your duty towards your God.

The strange activities of mankind on earth, who in their folly even dare to drag the Name of God into everything that is false, thereby defiling what is most sacred, will now be shattered!

You will be thrust from the throne of your intellectual artifice so that at least some of you may still become able, in pure humility, to receive true Wisdom from Divine Heights, Which alone can make you human beings; for you would never mature for this of your own accord.

What does not suit you, you slander, and you are quick to pick up stones to do away with anything that is irksome enough to disturb you from the continued belief in yourselves.

You would rather hail Luciferian satellites who, in flattering your vanities and encouraging your self-conceit, then all the more surely cut you off from the Light and keep you in spiritual indolence, which must lead to the sleep of death for your true being!

But I say to you that you are now awakened from the intoxication, the oppressive delirium, that is already holding you in its iron grip. You must awaken *against* your will, be it only to recognise with the most terrible despair, even at the last moment, all you have freely abandoned with such wanton indifference – before you are thrust into the bottomless pit that seems so desirable to you!

This earth and the whole world is now being purified! No longer shall any of the filth remain; so that the creatures will be able peacefully and joyfully to serve their Lord, the Almighty God, Who in His Love once granted them the conscious enjoyment of all the blessings of Creation.

He who again tries to bring disturbance into it by disregarding or even opposing the Laws of God in Creation will be mercilessly eliminated; for with such conduct he brings to you only envy, hate, suffering, disease and death!

All this tribulation can only still be avoided if you really seek to recognise and honour the *Word of the Most High!* To do so, however, It must first be understood in *Its true nature!* But hitherto you have always construed It only as It pleased *you!* And not as It was given by God for your help, your salvation, out of the greatest need!

However, you have not shrunk from making even the Holy Word the slave of your arrogance, so that through the distortion of Its true meaning It might serve only *you*; instead of *you* serving the Word for your own salvation in *that* sense in which It was given to you!

What have you made of the Word of God in your explanations, and even in the Scriptures! That you can quarrel about It, that you as human beings can come together and deliberate this way and that way over It, even this in itself is evidence of an unsound foundation and of a lack of clarity in what you have dared to set up as the pure, sublime Word of God! The Word of the Lord is inviolable, simple, clear and indestructibly hewn into Creation.

Where It is not obscured and distorted there can be no analysing, no deliberation! It is clear to *every* creature.

But for you, with your ridiculous conceit, the greatness of this simplicity was still too small! In the gloom of your mental workshop you have laboriously toiled away at the Word until you could distort and mould It *in such a way* that It pleased *you*, so that It conformed to your petty earthly desires, your weaknesses, and also to your great opinion of yourselves and your importance.

In this way you created something that had to serve you, that flattered your vanity.

For also that humility which you display when you speak of your great sins, for which a *God* brought the sacrifice of atonement, is nothing but the basest vanity. *A God for you!* How valuable you must imagine yourselves! And you need do nothing further about it than graciously condescend, after much persuasion, merely to ask for remission!

This train of thought must surely make even the most conceited feel somewhat uneasy in his hypocritical humility.

But this is only one thing among many. You have thus distorted *everything* that is intended to clarify your relation as a self-conscious creature towards the great Creator!

Nothing of it has remained pure and sublime under the conceit of this humanity on earth. Therefore the right attitude towards God has automatically changed and become false.

Presumptuously expecting a good reward or disdainfully begging, only *thus* have you stood before your Lord – if indeed you have ever taken the trouble and time really to think of Him, forced to do so by many a misfortune that had to strike you in the reciprocal effect of your actions!

But now you must at last awaken and must accept the Truth as It *really is*, not as *you* think It is! With this what is false collapses, and the gaps due to your hypocritical claim of knowing everything better become apparent. Nothing can hide in the Darkness any longer; for through the Will of God there will henceforth be Light, so that the Darkness will fall and perish!

Now there will be Light also on earth and in the whole great World of Matter! It blazes forth radiantly in every part, disintegrating and burning all evil as well as all evil volition. Everything false must show itself wherever it seeks to hide, must collapse of itself before the Ray of God's Light, which now illuminates the entire Creation! All that is not and does not wish to live in accordance with the Sublime Laws of God will sink down to the region of destruction, where it can never arise again! –

ALL THAT IS DEAD IN CREATION SHALL BE AWAKENED, SO THAT IT MAY PASS JUDGMENT UPON ITSELF!

THE DAY of Judgment! Every prophecy that is connected with this proclaims the resurrection of all the dead for the Final Judgment! But this mankind have again introduced an error into the concept of the expression; for it is not meant to denote: Resurrection of *all the* dead, but resurrection of *all that is* dead! That is: The animating of all that is without movement in Creation, so that it may become *alive* for the Divine Judgment, either to be strengthened in its activity or annihilated!

Today nothing remains motionless; for the Living Power that now flows with greater intensity through all Creation urges, presses and forces everything into motion. Thereby it grows stronger, including that which has hitherto been inactive or dormant. It is awakened, strengthened, and thus *must* become active; in this awakening activity it is, so to speak, dragged before the Light, even if it wished to hide. It can also be said that it comes to the Light of itself and must reveal itself; it can no longer remain dormant, wherever it may be. As the popular saying is: "It comes to light!"

Everything becomes life and activity in this entire Creation through the new penetration of the Light! The Light thereby exerts a powerful attraction ... whether that which rests or perhaps even hides in this Creation wishes it or not; and finally it will also come into contact with this Light, it cannot escape It, even if it had the wings of the morning no place in the entire Creation can grant it protection from the Light. There is nothing which will not be lit up.

But in the movement of being attracted, anything that cannot endure the radiation, thus anything that is not already voluntarily striving towards this Light, must be shattered and burnt up by the Light. What is attuned to the Light, however, will blossom and grow strong in the purity of its volition!

So is it also with all the *qualities* of the souls of these earthmen. What has hitherto appeared to be dead, what has slumbered in them, often unknown to men themselves, will awaken and become strong under the Power, will develop into thought and deed, so that according to its nature it will in manifesting judge itself by the Light! Reflect, whatever is slumbering *in you* will come to life! Therein lies the resurrection of all that is dead! The Living Judgment! The Day of Judgment!

Then you must deal with all that is within you, must purify yourselves, or you will perish with the evil if it is able to become too powerful in you. It will then *hold* you fast, break over your head with foaming and bubbling, to sweep you down with it into the abyss of disintegration; for it can no longer exist in the radiance of Divine Power! – –

To you I have now given the Word showing the way that, in the awakening of this Creation, leads you unerringly to the Luminous Heights, the way that will not let you fall, whatever happens and tries to flare up within you! If you have turned your gaze to the Light in loyal conviction, if you have rightly grasped my Word and absorbed it in your souls, then you will calmly ascend out of the chaos, cleansed and purified, free from everything that might once have hindered you from entering Paradise.

Watch and pray, therefore, that you do not let your clear outlook be dimmed by vanity and conceit, the most dangerous snares for these earthmen! Beware! As you have now prepared the soil within you, so will it happen to you during the purification of Creation! –

EVEN as the Darkness moved over Golgotha when Jesus, the Living Light, departed from this earth, so is it now moving over mankind, returning to them the great suffering they inflicted upon the Love of God in the cruel way of the cunning intellect, which is utterly incapable of any intuitive vibrations, and which as Lucifer's most powerful tool you have held sacred! –

Now try if you can, you human beings, to protect yourselves with your intellect against God's All-Holy Wrath! Defend yourselves against the Omnipotence of Him Who graciously made over for your use *that* part of Creation which you have devastated and defiled like a stable of the most neglected animals, so that only suffering and misery can still dwell therein, because all peace and joy flee before your wrong actions and dark volition, and all purity conceals itself in horror.

Try to hide from God's inflexible Justice! It strikes you *everywhere* in the inexorable execution of Divine Will, without remitting anything of the enormous guilt with which you have laden yourselves in your self-will and obstinacy.

You are judged even before you are able to stammer a single word of excuse, and all petitioning, all supplicating, all blaspheming or cursing avails you nothing; for now you have unpardonably wasted the last respite for searching your soul and turning back, merely on fostering your vices! –

I do not tell you this as a warning; because it is too late for that. Far be it from me to continue to admonish you as I have done for years. You are only to think of it in the coming *experiences!* For this reason I state once more what this time has in store for you. Perhaps the knowledge of it will help to *alleviate* many an affliction for you, although it can no longer prevent anything.

You know it is the clearing of the debt with which you have voluntarily burdened yourselves, since nobody has forced you to do this. If through my words you can come to recognition in the suffering, and if thereby a yearning

169

for Light and for Purity arises within you and forms a humble petition, you may still be granted salvation as you are sinking; for God's Love is ever watchful.

Then you will also be permitted to see the new life, which the Lord will grant only to *those* who willingly swing in the sacred Laws of His Creation, to those who will keep His Mansion in which you are but guests free from all activities that are hostile to the Light, and who will not again wantonly devastate the beautiful gardens, in whose splendour and purity they shall evermore rejoice in order to grow strong therein.

Oh, you deluded ones, why would you not awaken! You could have been spared so much hardship. But as it is, your existence must be shrouded in grey veils of deep sorrow, from which only through the piercing flashes of the Holy Wrath of God can liberation and redemption once more be granted to you!

And this Wrath will break over you with unsuspected might in the Holy Judgment! –

But the Judgment is *different* from your conception of it. You know of a Book of Life which will be opened by the Judge of God at the appointed hour for *each* one!

The Book of Life shows *the names* of all creatures who have come to life, and nothing else.

But the inscribed pages belonging to the great Book of Life, which show the for and against of every single thought and every single deed of the individual, are *the souls themselves,* upon whom has been imprinted all that they have experienced or done in the course of their existence.

The Judge can clearly read *therein* all the for and against. But again you also picture the reading wrongly. This too is much simpler than you try to imagine.

The Judge does not order each soul to step separately before Him, before His Judgment Seat, but in the Name of God He sends His sword-thrusts *into the Universe!* The sword-thrusts are *radiations,* which go forth and strike *everything* in Creation!

Realise the great simplicity and amazing naturalness! The Judge does not send the rays consciously or intentionally to this one or that one; no, He simply sends them *out* at God's Holy Command; for it is the Power of *God*, nothing else but His All-Holy Will could operate in this way!

Thus the radiation-thrusts or radiations penetrate all Creation, but in such force as they have *never been before.*

Nothing can hide from the effect! And thus, in the Law of the Working of Creation, the Ray of Divine Power also strikes *every soul* at the appointed hour.

When the Divine Ray, which is completely invisible to the human soul, falls upon it, everything that still clings to it must revive and also become manifest, active, *thereby* enabling the last link in the cycle to be closed, either pressing the soul down or raising it up.

Whatever of wrong or evil such a soul in the course of its existence has already been able to throw off, through redemptive experiences according to the Laws of Creation, is obliterated, and in such a way as if it had never been; thus it no longer clings to the soul, it is then no longer imprinted upon it. The soul is freed from it and pure, and therefore can suffer no harm from it.

Only that which has *not* yet come to the closing of its cycle, and therefore still clings to and is connected with the soul, is forthwith driven to the closing of the cycle in the pressure of the Light, in that as it comes to life it *reveals* itself as it attempts to become active, and in so doing also receives the blow it deserves.

The actual blows depend entirely on the strength of the individual volition which, being released in the *reciprocal action,* is directed *against* the soul as the point of origin! Everything, be it good or evil, is now strengthened by the irresistible pressure of the Light and thrust back to the starting-point, to the soul.

And everything which otherwise, in the cumbersome movement of the condensed, hardened environment of all the human souls on earth, might still have required many thousands of years to close the cycle, is now, through the power of the blows from the Light, compressed into a few months in the impetus that is unexpected by mankind.

Such is the manifestation of the World Judgment in its simple naturalness! This time it *is* the *"Last Judgment",* so often proclaimed to you! But its manifestations are entirely different from what you thought. What was formerly proclaimed to you was given *in pictures,* because you would not otherwise have understood it at all.

By means of the Grail Message, however, your knowledge of the working in Creation goes further, and therefore more and more can be revealed to you; for today you are already able to understand it through my Message.

The sword-thrusts of the Judgment-Day strike as strong Light-radiations into Creation, and flow through all the channels that have already been formed through the automatic working of the Divine Laws in Creation, which are based on all the intuitive perceptions, thoughts, volitions and also actions of men as starting-points.

The judging rays are therefore guided with infallible certainty through these existing channels to all souls, and there take effect according to the state of the souls concerned, but in *such* an accelerated way that their whole existence is brought to the *final closing of the cycle* of all past activities within a few months; and in exact accordance with their actual condition these souls will be uplifted or cast down, animated and strengthened or destroyed!

Such is the Judgment! *Today* you are able through the Message to understand the process thus described.

Formerly you could not have grasped it, and therefore everything had to be revealed in simple pictures which correspond more or less to the operation of the process. –

And these blows of the Last Judgment are already on their way to you, to each one in Creation, no matter whether he is with or without his physical body.

The first blows have already reached you, and everything that still clings to your souls is revived.

But also the *final* blows bringing destruction or upliftment have been sent out with an all-overwhelming severity to complete the purification upon this earth! Already they are rushing towards mankind, and nothing can check them anywhere. At the exact hour appointed by God, mankind will be inexorably but justly struck by them! –

THE MILLENNIUM

LIKE a legend it floats in the minds of many people who know of the prophecy, but it is vague, without form, because no one knows how to come to the right conception of it!

The Millennium! Wiseacres have tried again and again to put forward an explanation of how this great period of peace and joy that is implied in it is going to be realised. But it has never yet been possible to come any nearer the truth! They have all gone wrong because they have assigned far too great a role to earthmen, as always happens with everything men think. Moreover, they approved of and built upon existing concepts, and thus every one of these theories had to be regarded as wrong from the start, no matter what its nature.

And then man forgot the principal thing! He did not take into account the condition that was also foretold, that *before* the thousand-year Reign of Peace *everything* has to become *new* in the Judgment! That is the essential foundation for the New Kingdom. It cannot be built up on the existing soil! *Everything* that is old has first to become new!

This does not mean, however, that the old is to be revitalised in its existing form, but the expression "new" implies a change, a transformation of the old!

In his pondering man failed to take this into consideration, and therefore never made any progress towards a right conception.

What must first change most drastically in the Judgment is man himself; for he alone has brought the confusion into Subsequent Creation. From him, from his wrong volition, the evil went forth into the world.

The original beauty, purity and health that always result from a swinging in the Primordial Laws of Creation were gradually distorted and perverted through the wrong volition of this humanity. Instead of a healthy maturing towards perfection, nothing but caricatures could still form in the unceasing process of development!

Just picture to yourselves a potter sitting at his wheel, before him the clay, pliable enough to be moulded to any shape. The wheel, however, is not turned by the potter himself but by a driving-belt, which in turn is kept in motion by the power of an engine.

By a pressure of his fingers the clay is now shaped in continual rotation, carried out by the wheel on which the clay was placed. Now *as* the finger presses *so* the shape develops, either beautiful, plain or ugly.

The spirit of man also works in the same way in this world, in Subsequent Creation. Through his volition he exercises leadership, thus as spirit he exerts pressure upon certain animistic substance, which shapes both ethereal and gross matter. For a spirit, animistic substance is the finger that exercises the pressure according to the spirit's volition. The clay is ethereal and gross matter; but the movement, which is independent of the human spirit, comprises the automatic movements of the Primordial Laws of Creation, which like currents ceaselessly drive towards the development of everything man forms in his volition.

Thus the volition of the human spirit is answerable for much that develops in Subsequent Creation; for *man* as spirit exercises the pressure that determines the nature of the form. He cannot exercise his will without simultaneously forming! No matter what it is! Thus he can likewise never evade this responsibility for all the forms created by him. His volition, his thinking and his actions – everything takes on form in the mechanism of this world. That man has neither known it, nor wanted to know it, is his concern, is his fault. His ignorance does not alter the effect.

Thus through his wrong volition, his obstinacy and self-conceit, he has not only held back any true blossoming, but has ruined Subsequent Creation and brought about only harm instead of blessing!

Admonitions through prophets, then through the Son of God Himself, were not enough to change man and induce him to take the right course! He did not *want* to, and increasingly nourished his conceited idea of being a world-ruler, in which already lay hidden the germ for his inevitable downfall. This germ grew with his conceit, and prepared the catastrophes that must now be unleashed according to the Eternal Law in Creation, which man failed to recognise because his conceited idea of being the master prevented him from doing so.

The sole cause of the coming horrors lies in the distortion of the Divine Primordial Laws through the false volition of these human spirits in Subsequent Creation! For this wrong volition threw into confusion all the power-currents that take effect automatically. The diversion of their course, however, cannot go unpunished since, knotted and entangled as they are, they will then *forcibly* detach themselves at a certain time. The detaching and disentangling shows itself in the manifestations that we call catastrophes. It makes no difference whether this occurs in public affairs, in families, with individuals or entire peoples, or with the forces of nature.

Thereby all that is false will collapse, judging itself through the power that is in these currents, which have been wrongly directed by humanity's conceit, contrary to what God willed; for these currents can *only* bring about blessing when they follow *those* courses which are intended for them by Primordial Law, thus ordained for them by the Creator. Never otherwise.

That is also why the end could be foreseen already thousands of years ago, because owing to the wrongly-willed attitude of men it could not possibly come about any differently, since the final result of anything that happens always remains strictly bound to the Primordial Laws.

Now since the human spirits have proved their utter inability to recognise their task in this Creation, since they proved their unwillingness to fulfil it by repudiating and misinterpreting all the warnings given by called ones and prophets, even those by the Son of God Himself, sealing their enmity by the crucifixion, God now *forcibly* intervenes.

Hence the Millennium!

Only by *force* can Subsequent Creation still be helped, as well as mankind, who have proved that they would never voluntarily be persuaded to take the right path which they must follow in Creation in order to live in it according to God's Will, and also to work and bring blessing as *the* beings that they really are by virtue of their spiritual nature.

For this reason mankind now, in the Judgment, are being *deprived of their rights,* they are for a time *disinherited* of the right they have possessed up till now, the right that the *human will* rules over this Subsequent Creation, guiding and forming it! Disinherited for a thousand years, so that at last there may be peace, and a striving towards the Light in accordance with the Primordial Laws in Creation, to which man has hitherto been hostile.

Disinheriting humanity of all the rights hitherto held in Subsequent Creation therefore makes possible and safeguards the establishment of the long-wished-for Kingdom of Peace! *Thus* does man stand before his God! *For that* must he now render account. *That* is the meaning of and the necessity for the thousand-year Kingdom of God here on earth. A sad truth, which cannot be more shaming for this mankind! But ... it is the only way to help them.

Thus the Millennium will become *a school for mankind,* in which they must learn *how* they have to stand in this Subsequent Creation, how to think and to act in order to fulfil their appointed task correctly, and thereby to achieve happiness themselves!

To this end the will of mankind as ruler in Subsequent Creation is now suspended for a thousand years, after whatever he has wrongly sown and wrongly guided has been destroyed in the Judgment!

During the thousand years the Will of God alone will reign supreme, to Which every human spirit must submit as soon as he has been able to pass through the Judgment!

But should there be another failure as in the past, then mankind must count on complete annihilation!

Such is the Millennium and its purpose! In their self-conceit and the delusion of their own importance, mankind have imagined it to be quite different. But they will have to learn and experience it as it actually is!

Therein also lies only a *Grace* of God, to help those who are really of a pure volition!

A NECESSARY WORD

BE ON your guard, spirit of man, for your hour has come! The time which you so ardently desired, which is granted to you for your development – you have spent it only in wickedness!

Beware, in your presumptuous intellectual conceit that has thrown you into the arms of Darkness, which today holds you triumphantly in its clutches!

Look upwards! You are standing in the Divine Judgment!

Awake and tremble, you who in your narrow-mindedness and limited outlook swarm around the golden calf of earthly transience, like moths attracted by a deceptive brightness. It was because of you that Moses, in his wrath of disappointment, once shattered those tablets of the Laws of your God that were to help you to ascend to the Light.

This breaking of the tablets was the living symbol that the entire humanity did not deserve to have knowledge of this Will of God, of the Will Which they rejected in their wanton behaviour and earthly arrogance, in order to dance round a self-made idol and thereby follow their own desires!

Now, however, the end is at hand in the final reaction, in the consequences, in the retribution! For now *you* will be shattered by the Will once so frivolously rejected!

Neither lamentations nor pleading will help any more; for you were given thousands of years to come to your senses! But you never had time for that! You did not want to, and even today, with incorrigible arrogance, you think yourselves much too wise. That *just in this* the greatest stupidity reveals itself, you do not want to see. Thereby you have finally become troublesome vermin in this world, no longer knowing anything other than wilfully to revile all Light, because with your persistence in grubbing about only in the Darkness you have lost every possibility of seeking with a free upward gaze, of recognising or of being able to bear Light.

Thus you are now branded by yourselves!

Therefore as soon as the Light once more shines forth you will stagger back dazzled, and beyond help sink into the abyss that has even now opened up behind you, waiting to engulf those who have thus been rejected!

There you shall be bound in an inescapable grip, so that all those who strive to aspire to the Light may find the way thereto in blissful recognition, free from your presumption and your hankering to accept tinsel instead of pure gold! Sink into that death-dealing horror, which you have prepared for yourselves with the most stubborn efforts! In future you shall no longer be able to obscure the Divine Truth!

How zealously they try, these little human beings, to push their ridiculous pseudo-knowledge well into the foreground, and how do they thereby confuse so many souls who could be saved if they did not fall into the hands of spiritual highwaymen, who like brigands still prowl about the first stretch of the right path, *apparently* following the same road. But what is it that they really offer? With great pompousness and hackneyed phrases they proudly take their stand on traditions, the true meaning of which they have never understood.

Very apt is the popular saying about this: they are threshing empty straw! Empty because they have not also picked up the real kernels, for which they lack understanding. One comes up against such narrow-mindedness everywhere; with dull obstinacy they ride upon the phrases of others, because they themselves have nothing to contribute.

There are thousands of these, and again thousands who imagine that they *alone* possess the true faith! Wherever they meet with anything beyond their comprehension they humbly, and with inner satisfaction, warn against arrogance! *These belong among the worst!* They are the very ones who are even now rejected, because their religious obduracy makes it impossible ever to help them. Once they realise their error no dread, no lamenting and no petitioning will be of any avail. They did not want it otherwise, they missed their opportunity. There shall be no mourning over them. Each moment is far too precious still to be wasted on those who think they know everything better; for they will never in any case come to an awakening from their obstinacy, but will blindly perish in it! With nauseating words and assurances of their faith in God, their purely imaginary recognition of Christ!

In no better case are the masses of those who attend their Divine Services with the regularity and duty they apply to other work; because it is necessary and advantageous, expedient. Partly also out of habit or because it is the "custom". Perhaps also out of simple prudence because, after all, "one never knows to what good it might ultimately lead". *Like a breath in the wind they will vanish!* –

More to be pitied are those investigators who with their really earnest inquiring mind fail still to rise from the brushwood in which they tirelessly rummage, expecting to discover *in it* a way to the beginning of Creation. Nevertheless it is all useless, and there is no excuse for it! Besides there are only a few, a very few. Most of those who call themselves investigators become lost in meaningless trifling.

The great remainder of mankind, however, *have no time* for "introspection". Apparently they are very harassed human beings, burdened with quite enough work in order to achieve fulfilment of their earthly desires, their daily needs, but ultimately also of things going far beyond that. They do not notice that with the fulfilment their wishes also increase, whereby a final aim never comes in sight, and thus the striving one can *never* find the peace or the time for *inner* awakening! Without any high goal for eternity, he allows himself to be hurried through his earth-life, enslaved to his earthly desires.

Exhausted by such activities, he must finally also care for his body through rest, change and diversion. So of course he has no time left for anything beyond the earthly, for the spiritual! But should his intuitive perception occasionally and very softly make itself felt with the thought of what comes "after death", then at best he becomes somewhat pensive for a few moments, but never allows himself to be stirred and awakened by it; instead, he then brusquely and quickly represses all such things, complaining that he cannot occupy himself with them even if he really wanted to! He simply has not *any* time for it!

Many a one would even like to see *others* creating the opportunity for it. Quite often there are also accusations against fate and murmurings against God! Naturally every word is wasted on such as these, because they are *never willing* to acknowledge that it depended solely upon themselves to shape their lives differently!

For them there are only *earthly* needs, which always increase with every success. They have never *seriously* wished for anything else. They have always raised all kinds of obstacles against it. They have frivolously relegated it to the fifth or sixth place, only to be thought of in dire need or at the approach of death. Until now it has remained a matter of secondary importance for all ... who have time!

And if one day there presented itself, *plainly recognisable, the opportunity* to concern oneself seriously with it, then immediately new and special wishes, which are really nothing more than excuses, would arise, such as: "But *first* I still want to do this and that, then I am quite prepared to study it." Exactly as Christ once said!

Nowhere is there to be found that seriousness which is absolutely imperative for this most essential of all matters! It seemed to them too remote. For this reason they are now *all* rejected, all of them! Not one of them will be admitted into the Kingdom of God!

Rotten fruit for ascent, who only spread further decay around them. Now reflect for yourselves, who *then* can still remain! A sad picture! But unfortunately only too true. –

And when now the Judgment causes mankind to yield they will very quickly kneel in the dust! But just envisage already *today how* they will kneel: In all wretchedness, but at the same time once more arrogantly; for again they will only be lamenting and *begging that help may be given to them!*

The heavy burden which they have imposed on themselves, and which finally threatens to crush them, *should be taken from them! That* then is what they petition for! Do you hear it? Their petitions are for alleviation of their torment, but without at the same time one thought for their own inner improvement! Not *one* honest wish for voluntary alteration of their hitherto wrong thinking, of their purely earthly pursuits! Not *one* wish to recognise and bravely acknowledge their present errors and faults.

And then, when the Son of Man comes among them in the great affliction, no doubt all their hands will be stretched out to Him, with whining and beseeching, yet again only in the hope that He will *help them in the way they wish*, thus ending their suffering and leading them to new life!

But He will push away the majority of these petitioners like poisonous vermin! For after receiving help, all such imploring ones would immediately relapse into their old faults, poisoning their environment at the same time. He will accept *only* those who plead to Him for strength finally to pull themselves together for permanent improvement, who humbly strive to throw off all former stubbornness, and joyfully greet the Word of Truth from the Light as redemption! –

But an understanding of the Grail Message, as well as of the previous Message of the Son of God, will only become possible when a human spirit casts aside *everything* that it has built up with its imagined understanding, *and starts from the very beginning!* In this they must first become like children! A leading across from the present errors is impossible. From the ground up there must be a complete *newness,* which grows and becomes strong out of simplicity and humility.

If mankind were helped in the way they ask in the hour of danger and need, then everything would once more be quickly forgotten as soon as their terror was removed. With their lack of understanding they would again unscrupulously begin to criticise instead of to reflect.

Such a waste of time is quite impossible in the future, since the existence of this part of the world has to hasten towards its end. Henceforth for every human spirit it is: Either – Or! Salvation from self-created entanglements or destruction therein!

The choice is free. But the consequences of the decision are definite and irrevocable!

As though released from a great pressure, those saved will then breathe freely and exult after the repulsive, unclean Darkness, with the creatures that gladly cling to it, has at last had to go down where it belongs, through the sword-thrusts of the Light!

Then the earth, purified of all pestilential thoughts, will arise like a virgin, and peace will blossom for all mankind!

THE GREAT COMET

FOR YEARS now "knowing ones" have been speaking of the coming of this especially significant Star. The number of those who await it is continually increasing, and the indications become more and more definite, so much so that in fact it is to be expected soon. But *what* it really signifies, what it brings, whence it comes, has not yet been rightly explained.

It is thought that it brings upheavals of an incisive nature. But this Star portends more.

It *can* be called the Star of Bethlehem, because it is of exactly the same nature as that was. Its power sucks the waters up high, brings weather catastrophes and still more. When encircled by its rays the earth quakes.

Since the event in Bethlehem there has been nothing like it. Like the Star of Bethlehem, this Star has also detached itself from the Eternal Realm of Primordial Spirit at such a time as to take effect on this earth exactly when the years of spiritual enlightenment are to come to all mankind.

The Star takes its course in a *straight* line from the Eternal Realm to this part of the Universe. Its core is filled with high spiritual power; it envelops itself in material substance, and will thereby also become visible to men on earth. Unerringly and unswervingly the Comet pursues its course, and will appear on the scene at the right hour, as already ordained thousands of years ago.

The first direct effects have already begun in recent years. For anyone who wishes neither to see nor to hear this, and who does not perceive how ridiculous it is still to maintain that all the *extraordinary* things which have already happened are of everyday occurrence, there is naturally no help. He either wishes to act like an ostrich out of fear, or he is burdened with an extremely limited understanding. Both types must be allowed to go serenely on their way; one can only smile at their easily refutable assertions.

But the knowing ones could also be told where the first *powerful* rays are striking. However, since the rays are gradually also encompassing the whole earth, there is no use in being more explicit. It will take years to come to this point, and years before the Comet again releases the earth from its influence.

And *then* the earth is *purified* and *refreshed* in *every respect* for the blessing and joy of its inhabitants. It will be more beautiful than it has ever been. Therefore every believer shall look forward to the future with tranquil confidence, and not be alarmed at anything that may happen in the coming years. If he can look up with confidence to God no harm will come to him. – –

THE WORLD TEACHER

He is called World Teacher not because He is to teach the World, and will perhaps found a religion that unites the World, or more specifically the earth, or better still humanity on earth, or that holds sway over the earth; but He is called World Teacher because He *explains* the "World" and brings the teaching about the World. That which man really must know! He teaches how to *recognise* the "World" in its automatic activity, so that earthman may adjust himself accordingly, and thereby be able consciously to ascend in the recognition of the actual Laws of the World!

Thus it is really a question of cosmology, of instruction about the World, about Creation.

Behind this *true* World Teacher, visible to *pure clairvoyants*, stands radiantly the great *Cross of Redemption*, as once it did with Christ! It can also be said: *"He bears the Cross"*! But that has nothing to do with suffering and martyrdom.

This will be one of the signs which, "living and radiating", no sorcerer or magician however accomplished is able to simulate, and by which the absolute genuineness of His Mission can be recognised!

This "beyond-earthly" happening is not disconnected, not merely arbitrary, therefore not unnatural. The connection will immediately be understood as soon as the true significance of the actual "Cross of Redemption" is known. The Cross of Redemption does not have the same meaning as Christ's Cross of Suffering, through which indeed mankind could not be redeemed, as I explain in detail in the lecture "The Crucifixion of the Son of God and the Lord's Supper", and repeat many times. It is something quite different, again of apparent simplicity, yet of immense greatness!

The Cross was already known before Christ's time on earth. It is the sign of Divine Truth! Not merely the sign, but the living form for It. And since Christ was the Bringer of Divine Truth, of the genuine One, and came from the Truth, was in direct connection with It, bearing a part of It within Himself, It also clung to Him inwardly and outwardly in a living form! It is *visible* in the living, thus shining and independently *radiating* Cross! It may be said that It is the Cross itself. Where this Radiant Cross is, there also is Truth, since this Cross cannot be separated from Truth; rather they are both one, *because this Cross displays the visible form of Truth*.

The Cross of Rays or the radiating Cross *is* therefore the Truth in its original form. And since man can ascend only through the Truth, and in no other way, the human spirit finds true *redemption* only in the recognition or knowledge of Divine Truth!

Again, since redemption lies only in the Truth, it follows that the Cross, that is, the Truth, is the redeeming Cross, or the *Cross of Redemption!*

It is the Cross of the Redeemer! *The Redeemer, however, is the Truth* for mankind! Only knowledge of the Truth and, connected therewith, making use of the way that lies or is shown in the Truth, can lead the human spirit out of its present derangement and error upwards to the Light, can liberate and redeem it from its present state. And as the Son of God Who was sent, and the Son of Man now coming, are the *sole* Bringers of the *undimmed* Truth, bearing It within Themselves, They must both naturally also bear inseparably the Cross within Themselves, that is, They must be Bearers of the Cross of Rays, Bearers of Truth, Bearers of Redemption, which for humanity lies in the Truth. They bring redemption in the Truth to those who receive It, who thus walk on the path shown. – What is all the clever talk of men beside this? It will fade away in the hour of need.

For that reason the Son of God told men that they should take up the Cross and follow Him, which means *to accept the Truth and to live accordingly!* To adapt themselves to the Laws of Creation, to learn to understand them fully and make only the best use of their automatic effects.

But what has the restricted mind of man once more made of this simple and natural fact! A doctrine of suffering desired neither by God nor the Son of God! And thereby they have taken a *wrong* path, that is not in accord with the path indicated, but leads far away from the Will of God, Which desires only to lead to joy instead of suffering.

It is naturally a terrible symbol for mankind that at that time the Son of God was nailed by them just to the earthly representation of the form of Truth, and tortured to death, thus going to His earthly destruction on the symbol of the Truth which He brought! The Cross of Suffering of the churches, however, is *not* the Cross of Redemption!

It is said of the Son of God: "He who stands in the Power and the Truth". The Power is the Will of God, the Holy Spirit. Its visible form is the Dove. The visible form of Truth is the independently radiating Cross. Both were seen – living – with the Son of God, because He stood in them. Thus with Him it was a natural and self-evident manifestation.

The same will also be seen with the Son of Man! The Dove above Him, the Cross of Redemption behind Him; for He again is inseparably linked with them as the Bringer of Truth, "Who stands in the Power and the Truth"! *They are the infallible signs of His genuine Mission to fulfil the prophecies.* The signs that can never be imitated, which are indestructible, warning, and despite the fearfulness of the severity also promising! Before these alone must the Darkness yield!

Look upwards! As soon as the inexorable harbingers of His coming have appeared, clearing the way for Him of the obstacles that human conceit heaps upon it, *the bandage will fall from the eyes of many* to whom is granted the grace to recognise Him *thus!* Then, forced by the power of the Light, they will *have* to bear witness openly.

Not one of the false prophets and of the leaders, today still so numerous, is able to stand his ground against *this;* for in these two sublime signs, which no one but the Son of God and the Son of Man can bear, God Himself speaks for His Servant, and all human wisdom must become silent because of them. –

Watch for that hour, it will be nearer than *all* men think.

THE STRANGER

ONCE more Darkness had settled over the earth. Triumphantly it over-shadowed men, and barred their way to the Primordial Spiritual Realm. The Light of God had withdrawn from them. The body that had served It as an earthly vessel hung bleeding and mutilated on the Cross, as a victim of the protest of those to whom It wished to bring happiness and holy peace.

At the summit of the entire Creation, in the radiant vicinity of God, stands the Grail Castle as the Temple of Light. Deep grief prevailed there over the erring human spirits far below who, blindly imagining that they knew every-thing better, closed themselves in hostility to the Truth, and allowed them-selves to be driven so far by the hate-filled Darkness as to commit this crime against the Son of God. The curse thus created by mankind fell heavily on the whole world, pressing them into an even greater limitation of under-standing. –

Gravely perplexed, a youth beheld this monstrous happening from the Castle of the Grail . . . the future Son of Man. He was then already being pre-pared for His Mission, a process which took thousands of years; for He was to descend well-equipped into those lower regions where, through the vol-ition of mankind, Darkness reigned.

A woman's hand was gently laid on the shoulder of the dreaming one. The Queen of Womanhood stood beside Him, and spoke in a sad and loving voice:

"Let this event impress itself upon you, dear son. *Such* is the battlefield through which you will have to pass in the hour of fulfilment; for at the re-quest of the murdered Saviour God the Father grants that before the Judg-ment you shall once more proclaim His Word to the faithless, in order to save those who are still willing to listen to It!"

The youth bowed His head in silence and sent up a fervent prayer for strength, for such great Divine Love re-echoed mightily within Him!

The tidings of the last, of another possibility of Grace spread rapidly through all the spheres, and many souls besought God to grant that they might be permitted to help in the great work of the redemption of all those who still wish to find the way to God. The Love of God the Father granted this to many a soul, who was thereby helped in its ascent. In grateful joy the host of these so blessed ones jubilantly gave a solemn pledge of loyalty to fulfil the opportunity of serving that was granted them.

Thus *those* Called ones were trained, who were later to hold themselves at the disposal of the Envoy of God when His hour of fulfilment on earth came. They were carefully developed for these tasks and incarnated on earth at the right time, so that they might be ready whenever the Call reached them, *and their first fulfilment of duty remained to listen for this Call!*

Meanwhile the legacy of the murdered Son of God, His Living Word, was exploited on earth solely for selfish purposes. Mankind had no conception of the true Principles of Christ. On the contrary, they gradually grew into such a wrong and purely earthly doctrine of love that finally they rejected anything else as not coming from God, and they still today reject and revile whatever does not conform to this nauseating sentimentality desired by them, and what does not practise a similar and very unwholesome servile worship of mankind.

Everything that does not have as its foundation the acknowledgment of the supremacy of man is simply labelled as false, and not belonging to the Word of God. This behaviour, however, actually only conceals the uneasy apprehension that the long-felt hollowness of the false edifice might become apparent.

This is what had been made of the sacred legacy of the Son of God! On such degrading assumptions His clear words were interpreted and passed on in all too human a way. Adherents were solicited through courting human frailties, until some earthly power could be developed, which has always remained the ultimate goal. Then, however, by their brutal cruelties they very soon showed how far the bearers of the misconstrued Christ-Principle were from the real understanding of it, and how little they lived it.

Continually and ever more clearly there was proof that the very ones who wished to be the bearers of the Christ-Principle were shamelessly and unpardonably the worst enemies and greatest offenders against the true Christ-Principle! After Christ's life on earth the whole of history, from the beginning of the churches, sets forth these facts so clearly, in letters so indelibly engraved and branded, that they can never be denied or glossed over. The stigma of conscious hypocrisy was undisguisably established throughout the long history of individual and mass murders under unpardonable invocations of God, and even today this is being extended in many places, but in different forms adapted to the present time.

Thus, thanks to the willingness of all the human spirits, the Darkness became ever denser as the time approached when the Son of Man had to be incarnated upon earth.

Joyful activity in the elements heralded the earthly birth. Angels lovingly accompanied Him down to this earth. Primordial Beings formed a solid rampart around Him and around His earthly childhood. His earthly youth was allowed to be bright and sunny. In the evenings He saw the Comet, radiant above Him, like a greeting from God the Father; He regarded it as nothing unusual, as one of the other stars, until the bandage which He had to wear during His bitter training on earth was put before His eyes.

Then life around Him seemed strange; only a great unquenchable longing filled His soul, increasing to a restlessness, to a continual nervous seeking. Nothing the earth offered could satisfy it.

With the ethereal bandage over His eyes, He now stood on hostile ground facing the Darkness, on a battlefield where everything dark could have a firmer foothold than He Himself. Therefore it was only natural that wherever He sought to undertake something He could find no response and no success, but only the Darkness hissed up in enmity every time.

As long as the time of fulfilment for Him had not arrived, the Darkness could always remain stronger, and could inflict material damage upon Him wherever He engaged in some earthly affairs; for everything earthly quite naturally *had* to oppose the Envoy of God with nothing but hostility, because all human volition today is directed *against* the true Will of God in spite of the alleged search for Truth, behind which there always lurks only self-conceit in various forms. The Darkness easily found willing creatures everywhere to hinder the Envoy from the Light, and to injure Him grievously and painfully.

Thus His time of learning on earth became the path of suffering.

Just as spiritual substance, with great power, appears to have a magnetically attracting and holding effect upon animistic, ethereal and gross material substances, so in a similar and much more powerful way whatever has its origin above the spiritual in Subsequent Creation must exert an influence on *everything* that lies below it. This is perfectly natural, it could not be otherwise. However, it only resembles the power of attraction in its manifestation. The power of attraction in the ordinary sense is effective only among homogeneous species.

But *here* it is a question of the existing *power of the stronger* in a purely objective and most noble sense! It is not to be thought of in an earthly human way; for in the World of Gross Matter this Law, like everything else, has been coarsened in its effect through the actions of men. The natural effect of this dominant power reveals itself outwardly like a magnet attracting, uniting, holding together and controlling.

Now because of this Law, men too felt themselves magnetically drawn to this veiled, more powerful Stranger from On High, although often resisting Him with enmity. The thick veils He wore around Him could not entirely prevent the emanation of this power that was alien on earth; while on the other hand this power could not yet radiate freely either to exert *that* irresistible might which it has after the falling away of the covering veils in the hour of fulfilment.

This brought conflict among the intuitive perceptions of men. The very being of the Stranger was enough to awaken in those who met Him hopes of the most varied kinds which alas, because of their attitude, were always brought down to merely earthly wishes, which they nourished and fostered within themselves.

The Stranger, however, could never heed such wishes, since His hour had not yet come. Thereby many were often greatly disappointed through their own imaginings and, strange to say, even felt themselves deceived. They never reflected that in reality it was *only their own* selfish expectations which were not fulfilled and, indignant about this through their disappointment, they laid the responsibility for it on the Stranger. Yet He did not call them; but they forced themselves upon and clung to Him because of this Law which was unknown to them, and they often became a heavy burden to Him, with which He journeyed through *those* years on earth that were ordained for Him as His time of learning.

Men on earth perceived something mysterious and unknown about Him, which they could not explain, they sensed a hidden might which they did not understand, and in the end through their ignorance they naturally suspected only intentional suggestion, hypnotism and magic, according to the nature of their lack of understanding; whereas there was no question of any of these. Their original attachment, the consciousness of being strangely attracted, then very often turned into hatred, which expressed itself in moral stone-throwing and attempts to defile Him from Whom they had expected much – too soon.

No one took the trouble to make a just self-examination, which would have revealed that the Stranger, living apart with different views and ideals, was the one made use of by those who crowded towards Him, but not that He had taken advantage of anyone, as the obtruders, in their bitterness over the non-fulfilment of their desires for a life of ease, encouraged themselves and others to believe. Blindly they repaid the friendliness shown them with senseless hate and enmity, similar to the deed of Judas.

But the Stranger on earth had to bear everything patiently; for it was only a quite natural consequence of His existence, so long as mankind were still living in error. By this alone He, to Whom all wrong-doing and wrong thinking were entirely alien, was able to recognise what earthmen in their nature could become capable of. At the same time, however, such experiences also gave Him the necessary hardening, which slowly laid itself like an armour around His otherwise ever-present helpfulness, and thus created a gulf between that and mankind ... through the wounds inflicted upon His soul, which brought about a separation, and which can only be healed through the complete change in mankind. These wounds inflicted on Him have formed from that hour the gulf which can be bridged only by *that* man *who wholly* follows the road of the Laws of God. This alone can serve as a bridge. Everyone else must be dashed to pieces in the abyss; for there is no other way over it. And to remain standing before it means destruction.

At the exact hour, even before the end of this arduous time of learning, the meeting came to pass with *that* Companion Who as a Part of Him was to journey with Him through earthly life, to participate in the great task according to Divine Ordinance. Herself a Stranger on earth, She joyfully entered the Will of God through Her own recognition, and gratefully merged with It.

Only then came the time for the Called ones, who had once solemnly pledged to God their loyalty for service! The granting of their petition had been carefully carried out. At the appropriate time they were incarnated on earth. Through faithful guidance they were equipped in the earthly sense with everything they needed for the fulfilment of their respective tasks. It was brought, given to them, so noticeably that they simply could not consider it other than as a gift, as a loan for the hour of fulfilment of their former promise.

At the precise moment they came into contact with the Envoy, through His Word, and then also personally ... but many of them, although they sensed the Call and intuitively perceived something unusual in their souls, had meanwhile in the course of their earth-life permitted themselves to be so ensnared by purely earthly matters, and to some extent even by the Darkness, that they could not summon up the strength to conquer themselves for the true service, to fulfil which they were permitted to come to earth for this great time.

A few did show a faint willingness to fulfil, yet their earthly faults held them back from it. Unfortunately there were also others who certainly set out on the path of their mission, but who from the very beginning sought *first* of all to gain earthly advantage for themselves thereby. Even among those of earnest volition there were several who expected Him Whom *they* had to serve to smooth their way to the fulfilment, instead of the reverse.

Only a few isolated ones really showed themselves capable of growing into their task. To these was then given in the hour of fulfilment ten times greater strength, so that the gaps were no longer perceptible, and in loyalty they became capable of accomplishing even more than the great throng could ever have achieved. –

It was with grief that the Stranger on earth saw the havoc among the group of the Called ones. *That was one of the most bitter experiences for Him!* Much as He had learned, much as He suffered at the hands of men ... before this last fact He stood uncomprehending; for He found no excuse whatever for this failure. In His conception a Called one who, in the granting of his petition, was specially guided and incarnated, could do no other than faithfully carry out his task in the most joyous fulfilment! For what other purpose was he on earth! Why had he been faithfully guarded up to the hour when the Envoy needed him! Everything had been given to him solely for the sake of his necessary service.

So it was that the Stranger, on meeting the first Called ones, put His full trust in them. He regarded them only as friends, who simply could not think,

192

intuitively perceive and act in any other way than in the most steadfast loyalty. Was it not the highest, the most precious privilege that could fall to the lot of a human being. The possibility never entered His mind that even Called ones could have become impure during their time of waiting. It was inconceivable to Him that any human being, in view of such grace, could wantonly neglect and trifle away the real purpose of his earth-life. With the faults clinging to them they only appeared to Him as being in need of great help ... And so the dreadfulness of a recognition struck Him all the more severely when He had to experience that even in such exceptional cases the human spirit is not reliable, and that it shows itself unworthy of the highest blessing even with the most faithful spiritual guidance!

Deeply shaken, He suddenly saw before Him mankind in all their unspeakable inferiority and depravity. They filled Him with disgust.

Misery fell more oppressively upon the earth. The instability of the false structure of all that mankind had hitherto produced became ever more apparent. Proof of their incapacity came more plainly to light. With the increasing confusion everything slowly began to sway, with one exception: Man's conceit in his own imagined abilities.

This was just what sprang up more luxuriantly than ever, which was quite natural, because conceit always needs the soil of narrow-mindedness. The increase of narrow-mindedness must also bring with it an abundant growth of conceit.

The craving for importance increased to a feverish frenzy. The less man had to offer the more his soul, which forebodingly sensed only too well that it was sinking, cried out anxiously within him for liberation, the more he then, in his false desire to keep his balance, obtrusively pursued *outward earthly trifles* and human honours. Even if in quiet moments men at last began to doubt themselves, this only made them the more eager to have at least a *reputation* for knowledge. At *all* costs!

Thus things went rapidly downhill. In the fear-producing recognition of the approaching collapse, each in his own way finally thought to dull himself, letting the outrageous state of affairs continue to take its course. He closed his eyes to the menacing responsibility.

"Wise" men, however, proclaimed the time of the coming of a strong helper out of the distress. But most of them wanted to see this helper in themselves or, if they were modest, at least to find him within their circle.

The "faithful" prayed to God for help out of the confusion. But it became evident that these petty earthmen, even while praying in expectation of a fulfilment, sought inwardly to impose conditions upon God by wishing for *such* a helper as would correspond with *their views*. So far-reaching are the results of earthly narrow-mindedness. Mankind can believe that an Envoy of God needs to adorn Himself with earthly honours! They expect Him to adapt Himself to their narrow-minded earthly opinions in order to be acknowledged by them, and *thereby* to win their faith and confidence. What incredible conceit, what arrogance, lie in this fact alone! In the hour of fulfilment the conceit will be completely shattered, along with all those who inwardly indulged in such a delusion! –

Then the Lord called to His Servant, Who was walking the earth as a Stranger, that He should speak and give tidings to all those who were thirsting for it!

And behold, the knowledge of the "wise ones" was false, the prayers of the faithful were not genuine; for they did not open themselves to the Voice that came forth from the Truth, and which therefore could only be recognised where the spark of Truth within man had not been buried by earthly wrongdoing, the domination of the intellect, and all those things that tend to crowd the human spirit from the right path and cause its downfall.

It could only awaken an echo where the petition came from a truly humble and honest soul.

The Call went forth! Wherever it struck it brought disquiet and dissension. But in those places where it was earnestly awaited it brought peace and happiness.

The Darkness began to stir restlessly, and massed ever more densely, heavily and gloomily around the earth. Here and there it was already hissing up malignantly, and spitting in hate into the ranks of those who wished to obey the Call. Ever more closely it surrounded *those* Called ones who, through their failure, were forced to sink away into the Darkness, to which they had thereby voluntarily held out their hand. Their former solemn vow bound them fast to the Envoy spiritually, and drew them to Him at the hour of the approaching fulfilment, while their faults formed obstacles and repelled them from Him, because a connection with the Light was thus impossible.

Now from this there could in turn only arise a bridge for hate, for the whole hate of the Darkness against all that is Light. And so they intensified the path of suffering of the Envoy from the Light until it became a Golgotha, and the majority of mankind only too gladly joined in making it more difficult; especially those who imagined that they already knew and were following the path of the Light themselves, as once the Pharisees and Scribes did.

All this created a situation in which mankind could prove once more that they would again behave in exactly the same way today as long ago they acted against the Son of God. Only this time in a more modern form, a symbolic crucifixion through an attempt at *moral murder*, which according to the Laws of God *is no less punishable than physical murder*.

It was fulfilment after the last opportunity of mercy had been frivolously neglected. Traitors, false witnesses and slanderers came from the ranks of those who had been called. Base minions of the Darkness ventured to approach in ever increasing numbers, since they felt themselves secure, because in fulfilment the Stranger on earth kept silent when confronted with this filth, as He had been commanded to do, and as once the Son of God also was silent before the howling mob that wanted to have Him nailed to the cross as a criminal.

But when the faithless deserters in their blind hate already thought themselves close to victory, and the Darkness once more assumed that the Work of the Light had been destroyed, because it hoped that the Bearer of this Work had been rendered quite impotent on earth, then this time God revealed *His Will with Omnipotence!* And then ... even the mockers sank trembling to their knees, but ... for them it was too late!

SALVATION! REDEMPTION!

SALVATION! Redemption! How often already have human beings pictured these words wrongly to themselves, when they wanted to see in them unconditional help from the Light, to the exclusion of the All-Holy Justice! This implies a total error, that is already evident today in everything devised by the human mind. They want to make God into their helpful slave, who is only to be considered in connection with the welfare of insignificant earthmen.

Just ask yourselves for once about this, throw light on your thoughts without extenuation, delve into them clearly and objectively, then you will have to confess that your whole thinking has never been attuned other than to the idea that, upon your petitions, God should always serve and help you to fulfil your wishes.

Of course you do not speak of it in terms that would be more according to the nature of your being, but as always give another name to your false volition, putting on little cloaks of deceptive humility, and only speaking of "granting" instead of serving; yet this does not alter the fact that your whole conduct, even when praying, is dominated by evil and cannot be pleasing to God!

At last be honest with yourselves for once, and tremble at the recognition of how you have hitherto always stood before your God, stubborn, arrogant and discontented, hypocritical because of your superficiality, thinking of Him only in misery and distress so that He may help you out of the consequences of your actions; but you have never asked beforehand whether your decisions really were according to *His* Will.

What are you men before the Omnipotence and Sublimity of the Lord, Whom you would have rule over you just *as* it pleases you! With what presumption you would like to enforce here on earth *those* laws that come from your narrow way of thinking, and that are not in harmony with the Divine Laws that He placed in Creation. You so often exercise your wrong volition, with a cunning and evil-mindedness that is inexcusable before God, harming your neighbours thereby to gain advantages for yourselves, either in money or goods, or to acquire a reputation with those for whom you do it.

All this will now fall heavily upon you with the weight of a mountain; for nothing of all your wrong-doing could be cancelled in the Law of Reciprocal Action as having been redeemed, unless you freed yourselves through the change in your volition for what is good.

The barriers that still hold back the collapse of the piled-up mass of reprisals are torn away! Everything rolls down irresistibly on earthly humanity, who would like to continue in spiritual indolence and arrogance in order to enforce their will, which has long since strayed far from the Will of God.

This, however, is the end for the dominion of all Darkness on earth! It will collapse, and drag down all those human beings who have sided with it.

But in the midst of the thundering roar of the collapse, the Word rings out! Victoriously It resounds through the lands, so that those who honestly *strive* for It may still save themselves.

The condition implied is that each one must himself strive to recognise the Word of the Lord as salvation! If he doubts and allows this last opportunity to pass without making use of it with all his strength, he will never again be in this position, and the moment for him to find redemption is forever lost.

Salvation, redemption, will only come to him in the Word, Which he must absorb, so that by living in accordance with It he may release himself from the bonds that hold him down through misunderstanding and distorting the true concepts.

You have been most seriously poisoned and endangered by the false representation of the Love of God, which you sought to divest of all vigour, all power and clarity, enveloping it instead in an unhealthy weakness and harmful indulgence, which was bound to plunge you all together into spiritual indolence and thus into ruin.

Beware of the fatal distortion of the concept of the Holy Love of God! You therewith fall into a slumber which at first is pleasant, but which becomes the sleep of death.

True love does not lie in indulgence, and in a kindness that is expected to forgive everything. This is wrong, and acts like a drug that only lulls the spirits into lassitude and weakness, finally bringing on complete paralysis and enforcing eternal death, since an awakening at the right time is then impossible.

Only the severe coolness of Divine Purity can penetrate the lassitude, and pave the way for the true Love that leads to your spirits. Purity *is* severe, It knows neither extenuation nor excuse. Therefore It will probably appear ruthless to many a person who only too willingly tries to deceive himself. But actually It only hurts where something is not in order.

Weakness brings harm to yourselves as well as to those whom you imagine you are pleasing by it. In time you will be judged by a *Higher One* with the kind of justice that has become strange to you for a long time through yourselves, for you have withdrawn from it.

It is the *Divine Justice,* unchangeable from eternity to eternity, and independent of the opinions of men, free of their partiality, of their hate and their malice, their power. It is *Al*mighty, for it is of God!

Unless you devote *all* your strength to severing yourselves from the old, you will not learn to comprehend this Justice either. But you will then likewise not be able to become new within! And only the *new* man, who stands in the Word of Life and strives towards the Light, will receive the help that he needs to pass through the Judgment of God.

Man must help himself through the Word, which shows him the ways he must follow! Only *thus* can he find redemption, otherwise it will not fall to his lot! He must grow strong in the battle that he wages for himself, or he must perish in it!

Awake, and present a fighting front to all Darkness, then you will also be given strength to help you. Weaklings, however, will lose even what strength they still possess, because they do not know how to use it properly. The little they have will thereby be taken away from them because, according to the Law of Attraction of Homogeneous Species, it flows to those who use this strength with zeal and in the *right manner.* Thus an ancient promise is fulfilled.

THE LANGUAGE OF THE LORD

IT IS the sacred duty of the human spirit to investigate why it is living on earth, or in general in this Creation, in which it is suspended as if by a thousand threads. No man considers himself so insignificant as to imagine that his existence is without purpose, unless *he* makes it purposeless. In any case he deems himself too important. And yet there are only a few men on earth capable of laboriously detaching themselves from their spiritual indolence, *so* far as seriously to concern themselves with the investigation of their task on earth.

Again it is solely indolence of the spirit that makes them willing to accept the firmly-established doctrines of others. And it is indolence that lies in the reassurance that comes from thinking that it is great to adhere to the faith of their parents, without submitting its underlying principles to keen, careful and independent examination.

In all these matters men are now eagerly supported by calculating and selfish organisations, which believe that the best way to extend and safeguard their influence, and thus to increase their power, is by adding to the number of their adherents.

They are far from true recognition of God; for otherwise they would not bind the human spirit with the fetters of a firmly-established doctrine, but would have to educate it for the personal responsibility ordained by God, which fundamentally stipulates *full freedom of spiritual decision!* Only a spirit free in this respect can come to the true recognition of God that matures within him to the complete conviction which is essential for anyone who wishes to be uplifted to Luminous Heights; for only free, sincere conviction can help him to achieve this. –

But what have you done, you men! How have you suppressed this highest Grace of God and wantonly prevented it from developing, and from helping all earthmen to open up *that* path which safely leads them to peace, to joy, and to the highest bliss!

Consider this: that also in making a choice, in agreement or in obedience, which as a result of spiritual indolence may be done only from habit or general custom, a *personal decision is involved,* laying upon the individual who makes it personal responsibilities according to the Laws of Creation!

Those who influence a human spirit to do this naturally bear a personal responsibility, which is inevitable and irrevocable. No thought or action, however trivial, can be erased from Creation without similar consequences. In the web of Creation the threads both for the individual and for the masses are accurately spun, awaiting redemptions, which in turn must eventually be received by the originators or producers, either as suffering or as joy, according to how they once issued from them; only now they have grown and are thus strengthened.

You are caught in the web of your own volitions, of your actions, and are not released from it until the threads can fall away from you in the redemption.

Among all creatures in Creation the human spirit is the only one to have *free will,* which until today he could not explain and did not understand, because within the narrow bounds of his intellectual pondering he found no essential facts to prove it.

His free will lies solely in the *decision,* of which he may make many every hour. In the independent weaving of the Laws of Creation, however, he is unswervingly subject to the consequences of every one of his personal decisions! Therein lies his responsibility, which is inseparably connected with the gift of free will to make decisions, which is peculiar to and an absolute part of the human spirit.

Otherwise what would become of Divine Justice, which is firmly anchored in Creation as support, balance and maintenance of all the working therein?

In Its effects, however, It does not always take account of the short span of only one earth-life for a human spirit; but here there are entirely different conditions, as readers of my Message know.

You have often brought harm upon yourselves, and sometimes force it upon your children, through many superficial decisions. Even though you yourselves have proved too indolent still to summon up the strength to decide for yourselves in your deepest intuitive perception whether, regardless of all you have learnt, each word to which you decided to adhere can hold Truth, at least you should not seek to force the consequences of your indolence also upon your children, whom you thus plunge into misfortune.

Thus what in one case is caused by spiritual indolence, in others is brought about by the calculating intellect.

Through both these enemies of spiritual freedom in decision mankind is now bound, except for a few who still try to summon up the courage to burst this bond within them in order to become real human beings themselves, as follows from obedience to the Divine Laws.

The Divine Laws are true friends in everything, they are helpful blessings from the Will of God, Who thus opens the paths to salvation for everyone who strives towards it.

There is not a single other road to this than the one clearly shown by the Laws of God in Creation! The whole of Creation is the Language of God, which you should earnestly strive to read, and which is by no means as difficult as you may think.

You belong to this Creation as a part of it, and therefore you must swing with it, work in it, and mature in learning from it; and thus through gaining in understanding you must rise ever higher, from one step to the next, drawing along through the radiation in order to ennoble everything that comes in contact with you on your way.

There will then spontaneously develop around you one beautiful miracle after another, which through reciprocal action will raise you ever higher.

Learn to recognise your path in Creation, and you will also know the purpose of your existence. Then you will be filled with grateful rejoicing, and the greatest happiness a human spirit is able to bear, which lies solely in the recognition of God!

The supreme bliss of the true recognition of God, however, can never grow out of an acquired blind faith, much less come to flower; but convinced knowledge, knowing conviction, alone gives to the spirit what is necessary for this.

You earthmen are in this Creation to *find* supreme happiness! In the Living Language which God speaks to you! And to understand this Language, to learn it, and to sense inwardly the Will of God in it, *that* is your *goal* during your journey through Creation. In Creation itself, to which you belong, lies the explanation of the *purpose* of your existence, and at the same time also the recognition of your *goal!* In no other way can you find either.

This demands of you that you *live* Creation. But you are only able to live or *experience* it when you really *know* it.

With my Message I now open the Book of Creation for you! The Message clearly shows you the Language of God in Creation, which you must learn to understand so that you can make it completely your own.

Just imagine a child on earth who cannot understand his father or mother because he has never learned the language they speak to him. Indeed, what is to become of such a child?

He does not even know what is expected of him, and will thus fall into one difficulty after the other, draw upon himself one sorrow after another, and probably end up utterly useless for any purpose or enjoyment on earth.

If he is to amount to anything, must not every child *personally* learn the language of his parents for himself? Nobody can do it for him!

Otherwise he would never adjust himself, nor would he ever be able to mature and work on earth, but he would remain a hindrance, a burden to others, and would finally have to be segregated to prevent him from causing harm.

Could you expect anything else then?

You have of course inescapably to fulfil such a duty of the child towards your God, Whose Language *you* must learn to understand as soon as you desire His help. God, however, speaks to you in His Creation. If you want to advance in it, you must first recognise this His Language. Should you neglect it, you will be cut off from those who know the Language and adjust themselves to it, because you would otherwise cause harm and obstruction, without necessarily wishing to do so!

You must therefore do it! Do not forget this, and see that it is done now, otherwise you will be helplessly abandoned to whatever threatens you.

My Message will be a faithful helper to you!

NOW STRIDE UPWARDS

VIGOROUSLY!

VOLUME 2

RESPONSIBILITY

THIS question is always one of the first, because the vast majority of people would be only too glad to throw off all responsibility, and cast it on anything rather than themselves. That this is in fact self-humiliation causes them no concern here. In this respect they are really remarkably humble and modest, but only so that they can go on living all the more merrily and unscrupulously.

It would indeed be so wonderful to be permitted to gratify all one's wishes and calmly to let all one's desires run riot, even at other people's expense, without having to atone for it. If necessary, the earthly laws can be evaded and conflicts avoided. Under their cover the more adept can even rake in quite a successful haul, and do many a thing that would not stand up to any moral examination. In addition they often even enjoy the reputation of being especially capable people.

Thus with a little shrewdness one could really live very comfortably according to one's own ideas, if ... there were not something somewhere that awakened an uneasy feeling, if from time to time there did not appear a rising disquiet that after all many a thing might be somewhat different from how one's own wishes shape it.

And indeed it is so! The reality is serious and inexorable. The wishes of men can bring about no deviation whatsoever in this respect. Adamantine stands the Law: "What a man sows he will reap many times over!"

These few words hold and convey much more than many a person thinks. They correspond minutely and exactly to the actual process of the reciprocal action resting in Creation. No more appropriate expression could be found for it. Just as the harvest yields a multiple of the seed, so man always receives back greatly multiplied what in his own intuitive perceptions he awakens and sends out, according to the nature of his volition.

Thus man bears spiritually the responsibility for everything he does. This responsibility begins already with the making of the resolution, not just with the accomplished deed, which is simply a consequence of the resolution. And the resolution is the awakening of an earnest volition!

There is no division between this world and the so-called beyond, but all is only one single immense existence. The whole mighty Creation, visible and invisible to man, gears together like an amazingly ingenious, never-failing mechanism; it does not function separately. *Uniform* Laws support the whole, penetrating everything like nerve-strands, holding it together and affecting each other in constant action and reaction!

When schools and churches speak of Heaven and hell, of God and the devil, this is right. It is wrong, however, to explain it as good and evil powers. That must at once plunge every serious seeker into error and doubt; for where there are *two* powers there must also logically be two rulers, hence in this case two gods, a good one and an evil one.

And this is not the case!

There is only *one* Creator, one God, and hence only *one* Power which streams through all that exists, animating and furthering it!

This pure, creative Power of God flows continually through the whole Creation, lies in it and is inseparable from it. It is to be found everywhere: in the air, in every drop of water, in the growing rock, the struggling plant, the animal, and naturally also in man. There is nothing where it would not be.

And just as it flows through everything, so it also streams unceasingly through man. Now the latter is so constituted that he resembles a lens. Just as a lens collects the sun's rays streaming through it, and passes them on in concentrated form, so that the heat-giving rays, united on one spot, singe and set on fire, so man by virtue of his specific nature collects through his intuitive perception the Power of Creation streaming through him, and passes it on in concentrated form through his thoughts.

According to the nature of this intuitive perceiving and the thoughts connected with it, he thus *guides* the self-acting creative Power of God to good or evil effect!

And that is the responsibility which man must bear! Therein also lies his free will!

You who often seek so strenuously to find the right way, why do you make it so hard for yourselves? In all simplicity picture to yourselves how the pure Power of the Creator flows through you, and how you guide it with your thoughts in a good or in an evil direction. There you have it all, without trouble and without racking your brain!

Consider that it lies with your simple intuitive perceiving and thinking whether this mighty Power will evoke good or evil. What a furthering or destructive power is thus given to you!

You need not exert yourselves till you perspire, you need not convulsively cling to some so-called occult practice in order to reach, through every conceivable and inconceivable physical and spiritual contortion, some stage that is completely worthless for your true spiritual upward-swinging!

Cease this time-wasting trifling, which has so often become painful torment, signifying nothing else than the former self-scourgings and mortifications practised in the monasteries. It is only another form of the same thing, which can bring you as little gain.

The so-called occult masters and pupils are modern Pharisees! In the truest sense of the word. They are the true reflection of the Pharisees at the time of Jesus of Nazareth.

Realise in pure joy that through your simple, good-willing intuitive perceiving and thinking you are able without effort to guide the one and mighty Power of Creation. The Power will then take effect exactly according to the nature of your intuitive perceiving and your thoughts. *It works by itself,* you need only guide it.

This takes place in all simplicity and unassumingness! No erudition is required for this, not even reading and writing. It is given to *each* of you in the same degree! In this no difference exists.

Just as a child playing with a switch can turn on an electric current that produces tremendous effects, so is it given to you, through your simple thoughts, to guide Divine Power.

You may rejoice over this, may be proud of it, when you use it for the good! But tremble if you fritter it uselessly away, or even employ it for impure purposes! For you cannot escape the Laws of Reciprocal Action that rest in Creation. And if you had the wings of the morning, the Hand of the Lord Whose Power you thus misuse would strike you through this automatic reciprocal action, wherever you wished to hide.

Evil is brought about with the same pure Divine Power as good!

And it is the kind of use made of this uniform Power of God, left to the free choice of each one, that bears within it the responsibility which no one can escape. Therefore I call out to every seeker:

"Keep the hearth of your thoughts pure, by so doing you will bring peace and be happy!"

Rejoice, you ignorant and weak ones; for to you is given the same power as to the strong! Therefore do not make it too hard for yourselves! Do not forget that the pure, self-creating Power of God also streams through you, and that you too, as human beings, are enabled to give a definite direction to this Power through the nature of your inner intuitive perceptions, that is of your volition, for good as well as for evil, destructively or constructively, bringing joy or sorrow!

Since there is only this one Power of God, the mystery of why in every serious final struggle the Darkness must retreat before the Light, evil before good, is also cleared up. If you guide the Power of God to the good, it remains undimmed in its original purity and thereby develops a much greater force, whereas with the dimming into the impure a weakening takes place at the same time. Thus it is the *purity* of the Power which in any final struggle will always work effectively and be decisive.

Everyone feels to the very finger-tips what is good and what is evil, without a word said. To brood over it would only cause confusion. Dull brooding is a waste of power, it is like a swamp, a clammy mire which paralysingly clutches and suffocates all within its reach. But a brisk cheerfulness tears apart the spell of brooding. You need not be sad and depressed!

At any moment you can set out on your way to the Height and make good the past, whatever it may be! Do nothing more than think of the process of the pure Power of God always streaming through you, then you yourselves will shrink from guiding this purity into the unclean channels of evil thoughts, because without any effort you can equally attain to what is highest and noblest. You only need to *guide* it, the Power then works on by itself in the direction you desire.

Thus you have happiness or unhappiness in your own hand. Therefore raise your head proudly, and face everything freely and courageously. Evil cannot approach unless you call it! As you *wish* it, so will it happen to you!

FATE

MEN SPEAK of deserved and undeserved fate, of reward and punishment, retribution and karma.

All these are only part-designations of a Law resting in Creation: *The Law of Reciprocal Action!*

A Law which lies in the entire Creation from its earliest beginning, which has been inseparably interwoven with the great, never-ceasing evolution as an essential part of creating itself, and of development. Like a gigantic system of the finest nerve-strands, it supports and animates the mighty Universe, and promotes continual movement, an eternal giving and taking!

Plainly and simply, and yet so aptly, Jesus Christ has already expressed it: *"What a man sows that shall he reap!"*

These few words render the picture of the activity and life in the entire Creation so excellently that it can hardly be expressed differently. The meaning of the words is inflexibly interwoven with life. Immovable, inviolable, incorruptible in its continual operation.

You can see it if you *want* to see! Begin by observing the surroundings now visible to you. What you call Laws of Nature are, of course, the Divine Laws, are the Creator's Will. You will quickly recognise how unswerving they are in constant activity; for if you sow wheat you will not reap rye, and if you scatter rye it cannot bring you rice!

This is so obvious to every man that he simply never reflects on the actual process. Therefore he does not become at all conscious of the strict and great Law resting in it. And yet here he faces the answer to a riddle, which need be no riddle to him.

Now the same Law which you are able to observe here takes effect with equal certainty and force also in the most delicate things, which you are only able to discern through magnifying glasses, and, going still further, in the ethereal part of the whole Creation, which is by far the larger part. It lies immutably in *every* happening, also in the most delicate development

209

of your thoughts, which also still have a certain element of material substance.

How could you imagine that it should be different just where you would like to have it so? Your doubts are in reality nothing more than the expression of your inner wishes!

In all existence, visible and invisible to you, it is no different, but each kind produces its own kind, no matter what the substance. Just as continual are the growing and developing, the bearing of fruit and reproducing of the same kind. This process runs *uniformly* through everything, it makes no distinctions, leaves no gap, it does not stop at some other part of Creation, but carries the effects through like an unbreakable thread, without interruption or cessation.

Even though the greater part of mankind, in their limitation and conceit, have isolated themselves from the Universe, the Divine or Natural Laws have not ceased on that account to regard them as belonging to it, and to go on working without change, calmly and evenly.

But the Law of Reciprocal Action also stipulates that whatever a man sows, thus where he causes an effect or consequence, he *must* also reap!

Only at the beginning of every matter is man free to resolve, free to decide where the Omnipotent Power flowing through him is to be guided, in what direction. He *must* then bear the consequences arising from the Power that was set in motion in the direction willed by him. In spite of this, many persist in asserting that even so man has no free will if he is subject to fate!

This foolishness is only meant to serve as a narcotic, or to be a grudging submission to something inevitable, a discontented resignation, but mainly a self-excuse; for each of these consequences falling back on him had a beginning, and at *this beginning* the cause of the subsequent effect lay in a previous *free decision* by man.

This free decision has at some time or other preceded *every* reciprocal action, thus every fate! With a first volition man has each time produced or created something in which he himself has to live afterwards, sooner or later. *When* this will happen, however, varies greatly. It can still be in the same earth-life in which his first volition made the beginning for it, but it can equally well happen in the Ethereal World, when the gross material body has been laid aside, or later still in yet another gross material earth-life.

The variations are not important here, they do not free man from the consequences. He carries the connecting threads with him continually, until he is redeemed from them, that is to say, "detached" through the final effect that ensues through the Law of Reciprocal Action.

The one who forms is bound to his own work, even if he has intended it for others!

If therefore a man today decides to do another an ill turn, either in thought, word or deed, he has thereby "put something into the world", quite irrespective of whether this is generally visible or not, thus whether gross material or ethereal; it has within it power and therefore life, which continues to develop and work on in the desired direction.

How it will affect the person for whom it is intended depends entirely on the psychic condition of the one concerned, to whom it may thereby bring either much or little harm, perhaps also different from what was intended, or even none whatever; for again the psychic state of the one concerned is solely decisive for himself. Hence no one is exposed to such things unprotected.

It is different with him who through his decision and his volition has given rise to this movement, that is to say, who was its producer. His product remains unconditionally bound to him, and after a short or long journeying in the Universe returns to him reinforced, laden like a bee, through the attraction of similar species.

Here the Law of Reciprocal Action takes effect in that every single product in its movement through the Universe attracts, or is itself attracted by, various similar species, through whose union a source of power then comes into being, which sends back as from a power station reinforced power of the same kind to all those who through their products are connected as if by cords with the assembly-point of similar species.

Through this reinforcement an ever greater density also occurs until there finally arises from it a gross material precipitation, in which the one-time producer must now live and experience to the full what he once willed, in order at last to be freed from it.

That is the origin and development of the so dreaded and misunderstood fate! It is just, down to the minutest and finest shading, because through the attraction of *only similar species* it can never bring in the returning radiation anything other than what was actually willed personally in the beginning.

Whether for a particular individual or in general makes no difference here; for it is naturally also the self-same process when man does not specifically direct his volition to one or several persons, but lives generally in some kind of volition.

The kind of volition which he decides upon determines the fruits he must eventually reap. Thus countless ethereal threads cling to man, or he to them, all of which let whatever he once willed flow back to him. These currents result in a mixture that constantly has a strong influence on the forming of his character.

Thus in the mighty machinery of the Universe there are many things which contribute to how man "fares", but there is nothing to which man has not himself first given cause.

He furnishes the threads out of which in the untiring loom of life the cloak he has to wear is made.

Christ plainly and distinctly expressed the same when He said: "What a man sows, that *shall* he reap". He did not say, "can" he reap, but he "*shall*". That is the same as saying: he *must* reap what he sows.

How often does one hear otherwise very sensible people say: "It is incomprehensible to me that God should allow such a thing!"

But it is incomprehensible that men can speak thus! How small they imagine God to be with this remark. They prove thereby that they think of Him as an "*arbitrarily* acting God".

But God does not at all directly intervene in all these small and great cares of men, such as wars, misery and other earthly matters! From the very beginning He has woven into Creation His perfect Laws, which automatically carry out their incorruptible work so that all is accurately fulfilled, forever taking effect uniformly, thus preventing any preference as well as any prejudice, an injustice being impossible.

Hence God has no need to trouble Himself especially about this, His Work is without flaws.

But one of the principal mistakes so many people make is that they only judge according to gross matter, regarding themselves as the centre therein, and taking into consideration *one* earth-life, whereas in reality they already have *several* earth-lives behind them. These, as well as the intervening times in the Ethereal World, are equal to one *uniform* existence, through which the threads are tightly stretched without breaking, so that in the effects of a particular earthly existence only a small part of these threads therefore becomes visible.

Hence it is a great mistake to believe that at birth an absolutely new life begins, that a child is thus "innocent", and that all happenings can be accounted for in only the short life on earth. If this were true, then the existing Justice would naturally require the combined causes, effects and reactions to occur during the span of one earth-life.

Turn away from this error. You will then soon discover in everything that happens the logic and justice which are now so often missed!

Many are alarmed at this and afraid of what they still have to expect from the past through the reaction in accordance with these Laws.

But such are unnecessary worries for those who are in earnest about the good volition; *for in the self-acting Laws also lies at the same time the certain guarantee of mercy and forgiveness!*

Quite apart from the fact that, with the firm beginning of the good volition, a limit is immediately set for the point where the chain of evil reactions must come to an end, yet another process of immense importance comes into force:

Through the continuing good volition in every thought and deed, a constant reinforcement also flows retroactively from the homogeneous source of power, so that the good becomes more and more firmly established in man himself, emerges from him, and first of all forms accordingly the ethereal surrounding that envelops him like a protective covering in much the same way as the atmospheric layer round the earth affords it protection.

Now when evil reactions from the past return to this man to be redeemed, they slide off the purity of his surrounding or covering, and are thus deflected from him.

But should they nevertheless penetrate this covering, the evil radiations are either immediately disintegrated or at least appreciably weakened so that the harmful effect cannot manifest at all, or only to a very minor extent.

In addition, through the resulting transformation, the actual inner man to whom the returning radiations are adjusted has also become much more refined and lighter through the continuous striving for the good volition, so that he no longer has any homogeneous affinity with the greater density of evil or base currents. Similar to wireless telegraphy, when the receiver is not tuned in to the energy of the transmitter.

The natural consequence of this is that the denser currents, because they are of a different species, cannot take hold of anything, and thus pass harmlessly through without evil effect, redeemed by some unconscious symbolic action, the various kinds of which I will speak about at some later time.

Therefore set to work without delay! The Creator has placed everything in Creation into your hands. Make use of the time! Every moment holds disaster or gain for you!

THE CREATION OF MAN

"GOD CREATED man after His own image and breathed into him His breath!" These are two happenings: the creating and the animating!

Both processes, as with everything, were strictly subject to the existing Divine Laws. Nothing can go beyond their scope. No Divine Act of Will will oppose these immovable Laws, which bear the Divine Will Itself. Also every revelation and promise takes place in regard to these Laws, and must be fulfilled in them, not otherwise!

So also the coming into existence of man on earth, which was a step forward of the mighty Creation, the transition of the gross material to an entirely new, higher state.

In order to speak of the incarnation of man it is necessary to know of the Ethereal World; for man in flesh and blood is placed as a furthering connecting-link between the ethereal part and the gross material part of Creation, while his root remains in the spiritual.

"God created man after His own image!"

This making or creating was a long chain of development, which took place strictly within the Laws which God Himself has woven into Creation. Put into effect by the Highest, these Laws work inflexibly and steadfastly at the fulfilment of His Will; automatically, as a part of Him, towards perfection.

So also with the creation of man as the crown of the whole work, in whom all the species that lay in Creation were to unite. Hence in the Gross Material World, physically visible matter, there was gradually formed in the further evolution the vessel in which a spark from the Spiritual that was immortal could be incarnated.

Through the continuously striving forming there grew up in time the most highly developed animal which, by thinking, already made use of various aids for its sustenance and defence. Even today we can observe certain species of animals which make use of certain aids to secure and store their necessities of life, and which often show astounding cunning in defence.

The aforesaid most highly developed animals, which were swept away by upheavals that took place on earth, are today described as "primeval men". But to call them the *ancestors of men* is a great error! With equal right the cow could be described as "part-mother" of mankind, because in the first months of their lives most children need the cow's milk to build up their bodies, and thus with her help remain alive and grow.

The noble and thinking animal "primeval man" has also not much more to do with the real man than that; for the gross material body of man is nothing more than the indispensable instrument that he needs to enable him to work in all directions in the gross material earthly, and to make himself understood.

To assert that man is descended from the ape is a great exaggeration! This is going much too far. Raising part of the process to represent the absolute full fact. The main point is lacking!

It would be right if man's body really were "the man". As it is, however, the gross material body is only his cloak, which he lays aside as soon as he returns to the Ethereal World.

How then did the first man come into existence?

The highest stage in the Gross Material World having been reached with the most perfect animal, a change for the purpose of further development had to come if there was not to be a standstill, which with its dangers could become retrogression. And this change was foreseen, and came:

Having issued as a spirit spark, sinking down through the Ethereal World and at the same time uplifting everything, there stood at its boundary, at the moment when the gross-material-earthly vessel rising upwards in its development had reached the highest point, the ethereal-spiritual human being also ready and prepared to unite with gross matter, in order to further and uplift it.

Thus while the vessel in the World of Gross Matter had grown to maturity, the soul in the Ethereal World had developed so far that it possessed sufficient strength to retain its independence upon entering the gross material vessel.

The union of these two parts now signified a closer union of the Gross Material World with the Ethereal World, right up to the Spiritual.

Only this event was the birth of man!

Procreation itself is still a purely animal act with men even today. Higher or baser intuitive perceptions attending it have nothing to do with the act itself, but they bring spiritual consequences whose effects become of great importance in the *attraction* of absolutely similar species.

Also of a purely animal nature is the development of the body up to the middle of pregnancy. Purely animal is really not the right expression, but for the time being I will call it purely gross material, and only enter into it more fully in later lectures.

In the middle of pregnancy, at a certain maturity of the growing body, the spirit intended for the birth is incarnated, which until then stays very much in the vicinity of the mother-to-be. The entrance of the spirit causes the first twitches of the small developing gross material body, thus the first movements of the child.

At this point there also arises the peculiarly blissful feeling of the pregnant woman, in whom quite different intuitive perceptions set in from this moment: the awareness of the presence of the second spirit within her, the sensing of it. And her own intuitive perceptions will also be in accordance with the nature of the new, second spirit within her.

Such is the process with every incarnation. But now let us return to the first coming into existence of man.

Thus the great epoch in the development of Creation had come: On the one side in the Gross Material World stood the most highly developed animal, which was to provide the gross material body as a vessel for the coming man; on the other side in the Ethereal World stood the developed human soul who was waiting to unite with the gross material vessel, and thereby give a further impetus for spiritualisation to everything gross material.

Now when an act of procreation took place between the noblest pair of these highly developed animals, there was incarnated at the hour of incarnation not an animal soul, as hitherto, but instead the waiting human soul bearing within it the immortal spirit spark. The ethereal human souls with predominantly developed positive abilities incarnated in male animal bodies, corresponding to the homogeneity; those with predominantly negative, more delicate abilities in female bodies, which were closer to their nature.

This process does not support the assertion that man, whose real origin lies in the spiritual, descends from the animal "primeval man", which could only provide the gross material intermediate vessel. Even today it would not occur to the most extreme materialists to consider themselves directly related to an animal, and yet there is now, as there was then, a close physical relationship, hence a gross material homogeneity, whereas the really "living" man, that is, the actual spiritual "ego" of man, has no homogeneity with or derivation from the animal whatever.

Now after his birth the first earthman really stood alone, without parents, because in spite of their high development he could not recognise the animals as parents, and was unable to have any communion with them.

Nor did he need it; for he was a completely intuitively-perceptive human being, and as such also lived in the Ethereal World, which gave him values that made up for everything else.

The severance of the woman from the first human being was an ethereal-spiritual one. It did not take place in a gross-material-earthly way, as in fact the descriptions in the Bible and ancient religious writings mainly refer just to spiritual and ethereal events. Man as such stood alone, and during his growth primarily used the rougher, sterner intuitive perceptions for his subsistence, as a result of which the more delicate ones were increasingly pushed aside and isolated until, as the more delicate part of the spiritual man, they were completely severed.

Now this second part, in order not to remain inactive in the gross material, where in the first place it was absolutely necessary for upliftment, was incarnated in a second vessel, which in accordance with its fineness was of the female sex, while the rougher intuitive perceptions were left to the gross materially stronger man. Exactly corresponding to the Laws of the Ethereal World, in which everything immediately takes on form, the delicate and weak manifesting in female forms, the stern and strong in male forms.

Through her more valuable spiritual qualities, woman should and could in reality be more perfect than man, if she had only exerted herself to clarify ever more harmoniously the intuitive perceptions bestowed upon her, whereby she would have become a power that was bound to have a revolutionising and greatly furthering effect in the entire Gross Material Creation.

But unfortunately it was just she who above all failed, because she surrendered herself as a plaything to the strong powers of intuitive perception assigned to her, which in addition she even dimmed and defiled through feeling and imagination.

What deep significance lies in the Biblical narrative of the tasting from the

218

tree of knowledge! How the woman, incited by the serpent, offered the apple to the man. A better illustration of the event in the material sphere simply could not have been given.

The offering of the apple, emanating from the woman, was the woman's becoming conscious of the effect of her charms upon man, and their *intentional exploitation*. But the taking and eating by the man was his response to it with the awakening urge to draw the attention of woman only to himself by beginning to make himself desirable through accumulating treasures and appropriating various things of value.

With this began the cultivation of the intellect, with its accompanying manifestations of greed, falsehood and oppression, to which men finally subjected themselves completely, thus of their own free will making themselves slaves of their instrument.

But with the intellect as ruler it inevitably followed that, in accordance with its very nature, they also chained themselves firmly to time and space, thereby losing the ability to grasp or experience anything above time and space, such as everything spiritual and ethereal.

This was the complete *severance* from the real Paradise and from the Ethereal World, which they brought upon themselves; for it was now inevitable that with the horizon of their ability to comprehend firmly bound to earthly matters through the intellect, and thus narrowly limited, they could no longer "understand" all that is ethereal, which does not know the earthly concept either of time or of space.

Thus the experiences and visions of the intuitively-perceptive men, as well as the misunderstood traditions, became "fairy tales" to the intellectual men. The ever-increasing number of materialists, that is, those who are only able to acknowledge coarse matter bound to earthly time and space, finally ridiculed the idealists to whom, through their much deeper and more expansive inner life, the way to the Ethereal World was not yet quite barred; they called them dreamers, if not fools or even impostors.

All this was a long-lasting period of development, comprising millions of years.

But now at last we are very near the hour when the next great epoch in Creation sets in, which is unconditional upward-swinging, and brings what the first epoch with the coming into existence of man should already have brought: the birth of the spiritualised complete man! Of the man who has a furthering and ennobling effect on the whole of Gross Material Creation, which is the real purpose of man on earth.

Then there will be no more room for the oppressive materialist, chained solely to earthly conceptions of time and space. He will be a stranger in every country, homeless. He will wither away and perish like chaff that separates from the wheat. Take care that in this separation you are not found too light!

MAN IN CREATION

MAN IS not really meant to live according to the conceptions which have hitherto prevailed, but should be more of an *intuitively-perceptive human being*. In that way he would form an essential connecting-link for the further development of the whole Creation.

Because he unites in himself the ethereal of the beyond and the gross material of this world, it is possible for him to survey both and to experience both simultaneously. In addition he also has at his disposal an instrument that puts him at the head of the entire Gross Material Creation: the intellect. With this instrument he is able to guide, thus to lead.

Intellect is the highest of what is earthly, and is meant to be the *steering element* through life on earth, whereas the *driving power* is the intuitive perception, which originates in the Spiritual World. The basis of the intellect therefore is the physical body, but the basis of the intuitive perception is the spirit.

As a product of the brain, which belongs to the gross material body, the intellect, like all that is earthly, is bound to the earthly conception of time and space. The intellect will never be able to work outside time and space, although it is actually more ethereal than the body, but nevertheless still too dense and heavy to rise above earthly conceptions of time and space. Hence it is completely earthbound.

But the intuitive perception (not the feeling) is timeless and spaceless, and therefore comes from the Spiritual.

Thus equipped, man could be closely connected with the finest ethereal, indeed even be in touch with the spiritual itself, and yet live and work in the midst of all that is earthly, gross material. Only man is endowed in this way.

He alone, as the only bridge between the Luminous Heights and the gross material earthly, should and could provide the healthy, fresh connection! *Only through him in his special nature could the pure Life from the Source of Light pulsate downwards into the deepest gross material, and from there up-*

wards again in the most glorious, harmonious reciprocal action! He stands as a link between the two worlds, so that through him these are welded into *one* world.

However, he did *not* fulfil this task. He *separated* these two worlds instead of keeping them firmly united. *And that was the Fall of Man!* –

Through the special nature just explained man was really destined to become a kind of lord of the Gross Material World, because the Gross Material World depends on his mediation, inasmuch as, according to his nature, it was forced to suffer with him or could be uplifted through him, depending on whether the currents from the Source of Light and Life could flow *in purity* through mankind or not.

But man *cut off* the flow of this alternating current necessary for the Ethereal World and for the Gross Material World. Now just as a good blood circulation keeps the body fresh and healthy, so is it with the alternating current in Creation. Cutting it off must bring confusion and illness, finally ending in catastrophes.

This serious failure on the part of man could come about because he did not use the intellect, which originates only in gross matter, solely as an instrument, but completely subjected himself to it, making *it* ruler over all. He thus made himself the slave of his instrument and became merely intellectual man, who is in the habit of proudly calling himself a materialist!

By subjecting himself entirely to the intellect, man chained himself to all that is gross material. Just as the intellect cannot grasp anything beyond the earthly conception of time and space, obviously the man who has completely subjected himself to it cannot do so either. His horizon, that is his ability to comprehend, became narrow together with the limited ability of the intellect.

The connection with the Ethereal was thus severed, a wall was erected which became dense and ever denser. Since the Source of Life, the Primordial Light, God, is far above time and space and still stands far above the Ethereal, naturally every contact must be cut off through the binding of the intellect. For this reason it is quite impossible for the materialist to recognise God.

The eating from the tree of knowledge was nothing more than the cultivation of the intellect. The resulting separation from the Ethereal was also the closing of Paradise as a natural consequence. Mankind locked themselves out by inclining wholly towards the gross material through the intellect, thus de-

222

grading themselves, and voluntarily or of their own choice placing themselves in bondage.

But where did this lead? The purely materialistic, thus earthbound and inferior thoughts of the intellect, with all their accompanying manifestations of acquisitiveness, greed, falsehood, robbery, oppression, sensuality and so on, *were bound* to bring about the inexorable reciprocal action of what is homogeneous, which formed everything accordingly, drove men onwards, and will finally burst over everything with ... annihilation!

A World Judgment, which in accordance with the existing Laws of Creation cannot be avoided. As with a gathering thunderstorm, which must finally burst and bring destruction. But at the same time also purification!

Man did not, as was essential, serve as a connecting-link between the ethereal and the gross material parts of Creation, did not let the ever refreshing, animating and furthering necessary alternating current flow through, but separated Creation into two worlds by evading his obligation, and chaining himself wholly to gross matter. Consequently both parts of the World were gradually bound to become diseased.

The part which was completely deprived of the Light-stream, or received it too weakly through the few human beings who still provided a connection, naturally much more severely. This is the gross material part, which is therefore driving towards a terrible crisis and will be utterly convulsed by mighty fever spasms, until all that is diseased therein has been consumed, and it can at last be restored to health under a new, strong influx from the Fountain-Head.

But who will be consumed in this process?

The answer to this lies in the natural happening itself: Through the creative power dwelling in it, every *intuitively perceived* thought immediately takes on an ethereal form corresponding to the content of the thought, always remaining connected as by a cord with its producer, but being drawn off and away from him through the power of attraction of homogeneous species in all that is ethereal, and driven through the Universe with the currents constantly pulsating through it, which like everything in Creation move in ellipses.

Thus the time approaches when the thoughts that have come to life and reality in the Ethereal, together with the similar species attracted on their way, *will fall back* upon their origin and *starting-point,* because in spite of their wandering they remain linked with him, in order now to discharge, to release themselves there.

223

Hence in the final combined effect that is now to be expected, annihilation will *first of all* strike those who through their thinking and intuitive perceiving have been producers and constant supporters. That the destructive rebounding force will describe still wider circles, and in passing will affect even near homogeneous species of these human beings, is inevitable.

But then men will fulfil *that* which they should fulfil in Creation. They will be the connecting-link, will through their quality draw from the Spiritual, that is, will let themselves be guided by the purified intuitive perception, and translate this into the Gross Material, thus into the earthly, to this end using their intellect and accumulated experiences only as an instrument, in order to carry through these pure intuitive perceptions in gross material life, taking into account everything earthly, whereby the entire Gross Material Creation will be continually furthered, purified and uplifted.

This will make it possible in the reciprocal action for something more healthy to flow back from the Gross Material to the Ethereal; and a new, uniform and harmonious world will arise.

In the proper fulfilment of their activity men will be the longed-for complete and noble human beings; for through the right adjustment to the great Work of Creation they too will receive quite different powers than hitherto, which will let them intuitively experience contentment and bliss unceasingly.

HEREDITARY SIN

HEREDITARY sin was a consequence of the original Fall of Man.

The sin or wrong-doing lay in the over-cultivation of the intellect, associated with which was the voluntary chaining of man to space and time. There were additional effects resulting from purely intellectual activity, such as love of gain, imposing upon others, oppression, etc., which again brought many other, in fact all, evils in their train.

This process naturally had an ever-increasing influence on the forming of the physical body of those people who developed themselves in a purely intellectual way. Through being continually exerted, the frontal brain which produces the intellect became disproportionately enlarged. It was therefore quite natural that this change in structure expressed itself in the procreation of the physical body, and that at birth children entered the world with an increasingly developed and stronger frontal brain.

This contained, and still today contains, a predisposition or tendency towards an intellectual power dominating all else, which harbours the danger that the bearer of such a brain, on awakening it fully, not only chains himself to space and time, but also to everything that is earthly and gross material. He then becomes incapable of grasping anything that is ethereal or primordial, and in addition entangles himself in all sorts of evil, which is inevitable where the intellect dominates.

It is the coming into the world with this voluntarily over-cultivated frontal brain, containing the danger of a mere intellectual domination with its inevitable evil manifestations, which *is the hereditary sin!*

It is the physical inheritance of this part, called on account of its excessive artificial cultivation the "great" brain (cerebrum), which exposes man from birth to the danger of too easily entangling himself in evil. At any rate the narrow-mindedness which results from enchainment to coarse matter makes it more difficult to recognise God.

This, however, does not free him from responsibility, which he retains, for

225

he inherits only the danger, not the sin itself. He is in no wise compelled to allow his intellect to rule unconditionally and thus submit himself to it. On the contrary, he can wield the great power of his intellect like a sharp sword to clear his path in the daily bustle of life, as directed by his intuitive perception, which is also called the Inner Voice.

But if through education and training a child's intellect is brought to the point where it completely dominates, then the child is absolved of part of the guilt, or better, of part of the reactions brought about by the Law of Reciprocal Action, because that part will then fall upon the educator or teacher who caused it. From this moment onward he is tied to the child till the latter is freed from this mistake and its consequences, even if this takes hundreds or thousands of years.

What a child so educated does after it has had the opportunity to consider and retrace its steps, would then react upon it alone. Such opportunities arise through the spoken or written word, through emotional shocks in life or similar happenings, which forcibly bring about a moment of deep intuitive feeling. Such opportunities are bound to come.

It would be useless to say more on this subject or to multiply examples, which would only be a repetition and lead to the same conclusion. He who reflects upon the matter will soon find a veil lifted from before his eyes. He will then have solved many questions within himself.

GOD

Why do human beings so timidly evade this word, which should be more intimate to them than anything else?

Is it veneration? No! You are confused because neither school nor church ever gave you any clear explanation that could satisfy your inner longing for the Truth. The actual Trinity still remained fundamentally a puzzle to you which you tried to solve as best you could.

Can a prayer in these circumstances ever become so heartfelt, so confiding, as it should be? It is impossible!

Yet you should and must approach nearer to your God! How foolish it is to say that it might be wrong to concern oneself more completely with God! The indolent and comfort-loving even maintain it is sacrilege!

But I say to you that all Creation testifies that it is a necessary condition that you should draw near to God! Therefore he who evades this is not showing humility but, on the contrary, boundless presumption! It is equivalent to demanding that God should approach man, instead of man trying to approach God in order to recognise Him.

Wherever you look, wherever you listen, there is hypocrisy and indolence, all under the cloak of a false humility!

You, however, who no longer wish to sleep, who are fervently seeking and striving for the Truth, take note of this and seek to grasp it properly...

There is but *one* God, but *one* Power! What then is the Trinity? God the Father, God the Son, and the Holy Spirit?

When mankind shut themselves out of Paradise by no longer heeding the guidance of the intuitive perception, which is spiritual and therefore near to God, but freely chose to cultivate the intellect, subjecting themselves to it and thus becoming slaves of the tool given them to use, they naturally fell further and further away from God.

The cleavage occurred when humanity gave preference to worldly matters, which are unconditionally bound to space and time. This is alien to the nature of God, and therefore makes it impossible to comprehend Him.

The gulf became wider with each generation, and men chained themselves more and more exclusively to the earth. They became the earthbound intellectuals who call themselves materialists. They even do so with pride because they have not the faintest idea of how they are chained. Through being firmly bound to space and time it was natural that their horizon simultaneously became narrowed.

How could the way to God be found in such conditions?

It was impossible, unless help came from God! And He was merciful! God in His Purity could no longer reveal Himself to the debased intellectual human beings, because they were no longer capable of sensing, seeing or hearing His Messengers. Those few still able to do so were ridiculed because the materialists, with their limited horizon bound to space and time, rejected as impossible all thought of any expanse beyond that. Such a thing was quite inconceivable to them.

Therefore the prophets whose penetrative power was too weak no longer sufficed, because even the fundamental thoughts of all religious movements had finally become purely materialistic.

Thus it was necessary that a Mediator between the Godhead and erring humanity should come, One endowed with greater power than all the others had possessed, so that He would be able to penetrate. Shall one say for the sake of the few who, in the midst of utter materialism, still longed for God? This would be right, but the adversaries would prefer to call it presumption on the part of the believers, instead of realising the Love of God as well as the strict Justice in it, offering redemption equally through reward and punishment.

For this reason God in His Love, through an Act of His Will, severed a *Part* of Himself and incarnated It in flesh and blood, in a physical body of male sex – Jesus of Nazareth, Who thus became the Incarnate Word, the Incarnate Love of God, the Son of God.

This was a process of radiation which will receive further explanation later.

Through this act the severed, but nevertheless closely-linked part became *personal.* Even after laying aside the physical body and re-uniting closely with God the Father, He still remained personal.

God the Father and God the Son are two, yet in reality only one!

And the "Holy Spirit"? Christ Himself said that sins against God the Father and against God the Son could be forgiven, but never those committed against the "Holy Spirit"!

Does the "Holy Spirit" then stand higher or is It more than God the Father and God the Son? This question has occupied and worried many a soul and confused many a child.

The "Holy Spirit" is the Will of God the Father, the Spirit of Truth Which, severed from Him, works separately in all Creation, and yet like the Love, in the form of the Son, remains closely connected with the Father and one with Him.

The inexorable Laws of Creation which spread through the whole Universe like a network of nerves and bring about the unconditional reciprocal action forming man's fate or karma ... are of the "Holy Spirit" or, more explicitly, are the activity of the "Holy Spirit"!*

That is why the Saviour said that no one may sin against the "Holy Spirit" unpunished, because through Its inexorable and immovable reciprocal action the retribution falls back on the originator, on the starting point, whether it be good or evil.

As the Son of God, Jesus, is of the Father, so also is the "Holy Spirit". Both are Parts of Him, belonging completely to Him, and inseparable from Him. They are like the arms of a body which can act independently, but still belong to the body if this is to be complete. Yet they can only carry out independent actions as a part of the whole.

Such is God the Father, in His Omnipotence and Wisdom! At His right hand, as Part of Himself, is God the Son, Love; and on His left is God the "Holy Spirit", Justice. They have both emanated from God the Father and belong to Him as a unity. This is the Trinity of the *One* God!

Before Creation came into existence God was One! During the process of creating He severed a Part of His Will to work independently in Creation, and thus became two-fold. When later it became necessary to provide a mediator for erring mankind, because the Purity of God did not permit a direct connection to self-enchained humanity, out of His Love He severed a Part of Himself to act as a temporary bridge, in order to make Himself once more understood. Thus, with the birth of Christ, He became a *Trinity!*

* Lecture: "The development of Creation".

6. GOD

The difference between God the Father and God the Son was already clear to many, but the conception of the "Holy Spirit" was still confused. "The Holy Spirit" is Executive Justice, Whose eternal, irrevocable and incorruptible laws pulsate throughout the Universe. Up till now these laws have only been guessed at and variously described as . . . Fate . . . Karma . . . Divine Will!

THE INNER VOICE

THE SO-CALLED "inner voice", the spiritual part of man, to which he can listen, is the intuitive perception. It is not without reason that people say: "The first impression is always right!"

As all such expressions and proverbs harbour profound truths, so also here. By the word "impression" is meant "intuitive perception". For example, what a man intuitively senses at a first meeting with a stranger can either be a kind of warning to be careful, which may even go as far as absolute repugnance, or something pleasant mounting to a feeling of complete affinity. In some cases it may also be indifference!

If now, in the course of conversation or further intercourse, this impression is brushed aside or entirely effaced through the judgment of the intellect, so that the thought arises that the original intuition was wrong, it almost invariably turns out at the end of such an acquaintance that the very first intuition was the right one. And this often occurs to the bitter suffering of those who allowed their intellect to mislead them through the deceptive nature of the other person!

The intuitive perception, which is not bound to space and time but connected with its homogeneous kind, with the spiritual, immediately recognised the true nature of the other person and did not allow itself to be deceived by the cleverness of the intellect.

It is absolutely impossible for the intuitive perception to err!

Whenever man is led astray there are two reasons for his errors - either the intellect or the feeling!

How often one hears it said: "In this or that matter I allowed myself to be guided by my feelings and got into trouble! One should only rely on one's intellect!"

Such persons have mistaken their feelings for their inner voice. They praise their intellect and have no idea that it is just the intellect which plays such an important part in their feelings.

Therefore be on your guard! Feeling is not intuitive perception! Feeling emanates from the physical body. This generates instincts which, guided by the intellect, produce feeling. It differs greatly from the intuitive perception. The combined working of feeling and intellect, however, gives birth to imagination.

Thus on the spiritual side we have only the intuitive perception which is far above space and time*, while on the earthly side we have in the first instance the physical body, which is bound to space and time. From this body emanate instincts which, in co-operation with the intellect, arouse *feelings*.

The intellect, being a product of the brain bound to space and time and the finest and highest element in matter, is able with the co-operation of feeling to produce *imagination*.

Imagination, therefore, is the result of the working together of feeling and intellect. It is ethereal, but *without* spiritual power. For this reason imagination has only a *retroactive effect*. It can only influence the feelings of its creator, but never of itself send out a wave of power to others.

Thus imagination only works *backwards* upon the feeling of its originator. It can only inflame *his* enthusiasm, but never influence his surroundings. This clearly stamps it as belonging to an inferior order. It is different with the intuitive perception. This bears within itself a spiritual power, creative and animating, and sending forth radiations which fire and convince others.

Thus we can observe on the one side the intuitive perception, and on the other side the body, instincts, intellect, feeling and imagination.

The intuitive perception is spiritual and stands above earthly conceptions of space and time. Feeling belongs to fine gross matter, depending on instincts and intellect, and is therefore of a lower order.

Although feeling consists of fine gross matter, it can *never coalesce* with and thus cannot dim spiritual intuition. The intuition will always remain pure and clear because it is spiritual. And it will always be clearly sensed or "heard" by men if ... it really is the intuitive perception which speaks!

But the majority of people have closed themselves to this intuition by pushing their feelings in front of it like a dense veil or wall. Then they mistake the feeling for the inner voice, as a result of which they experience many disappointments. This prompts them to rely even more on their intellect,

---

* Lecture: "Intuitive perception".

never suspecting that it was just through the co-operation of the intellect that they could be deceived.

As a result of this error they are quick to reject everything spiritual, with which their experiences had absolutely nothing to do, and turn more and more to that which is inferior.

The fundamental evil here, as in many other matters, lies in the voluntary subjection of these people to their intellect, which is bound to space and time.

The man who completely subjects himself to his intellect also subjects himself completely to the *limitations* of the intellect which, as a product of the gross material brain, is fast bound to space and time. In this way man chains himself exclusively to gross matter.

All that a man does he does himself and of his own free will. Thus he is not being fettered, but he fetters himself. He permits himself to be dominated by the intellect (this could never happen unless he desired it himself), which by its very nature binds him to space and time and prevents him from recognising or understanding anything which lies beyond.

Through the limitation of the perceptive capacity a veil firmly bound to space and time therefore covers the intuition, which goes beyond space and time. This acts like a boundary, and man can either no longer hear anything whatever – his "pure inner voice" having been stifled – or he can only "hear" his feeling, which is closely connected with the intellect, instead of his intuition.

It would create a false idea to say that feeling suppresses the pure intuitive perception, for nothing is more powerful than the intuition! It is man's highest power and can never be suppressed or prejudiced by anything. It is more correct to say that man makes himself incapable of recognising his intuition.

If man fails it is always through his own fault, never because of the strength or weakness of his specific gifts; for just the fundamental gift, the actual power, the strongest part of man, which is the bearer of all life and immortal, is given to all *alike*. In this respect no man has an advantage over another. All differences are due only to the way in which it is *used*.

Neither can this fundamental gift, the immortal spark, ever be dimmed or tarnished. It remains pure, even amid the greatest filth. You need only tear the veil which you have wrapped around you through the voluntary limitation to which you have subjected your perceptive ability! Then, without any transition whatever, it will flare up again as pure and clear as it was at the beginning, unfolding itself fresh and strong to unite with the spiritual.

Rejoice that this treasure lies inviolable within you! It is of no importance whether you are esteemed by your neighbours or not. Every bit of dirt that has gathered like a dam around this spirit-spark can be cast aside through honest goodwill. If you have achieved this and again liberated the treasure, you are worth just as much as he who never buried it.

But woe unto him who through indolence completely closes himself to willing what is good. In the hour of Judgment this treasure will be taken from him, and he will then cease to be.

Therefore awake, you who keep yourselves closed, you who have drawn the cover of your intellect, with its limited ability to understand, over your intuitive perception! Take heed and listen to the warnings that assail you! Whether it be in the form of a terrible grief, a great emotional upheaval, severe suffering, or a supreme pure joy, all of which are capable of bursting through the dark layer of base feelings, do not let any such thing go by without profiting from it! They are aids which show you the way!

It is better if you do not first wait for them, but set out with the earnest volition for all that is good and for spiritual ascent. In so doing the separating layer will soon become thinner and lighter again, till finally it disintegrates altogether, and the still pure and untarnished spark bursts forth into a blazing flame.

But this first step must and can *only* be taken *by the individual himself*, otherwise he cannot be helped!

Therefore you must discriminate sharply between desire and volition. Nothing is achieved by mere "desiring", it brings no advance. There must be a volition which impels and carries it into action. A serious volition is the beginning of a deed.

Even if many a man must travel on various bypaths, because in the past he had entirely enslaved himself to the intellect, he should have no fear on that account. He also will gain! For him it means to clarify his intellect and slowly to detach himself from and remove all hindrances through every single experience he has to undergo on all the bypaths.

Therefore, advance bravely! With an earnest volition every path will finally lead to the goal!

THE RELIGION OF LOVE

THE RELIGION of Love has been misunderstood, because the concept of *love* has in many ways been distorted and misrepresented, for the greater part of true love is severity!

What is *now* called love is anything but love! If all so-called love were relentlessly sifted to the bottom, nothing would remain but selfishness, vanity, weakness, desire for ease, conceit or instinct.

Genuine love will take no account of what gratifies the other, of what is agreeable to him and gives him joy, but will only direct itself towards what will *benefit* him, regardless of whether it affords him pleasure or not. That is genuine love and service!

If, therefore, it is written: "Love your enemies", it means: "Do that which will benefit them! Punish them if they cannot otherwise be made to understand!" That is serving them! But justice must prevail, for love cannot be separated from justice – they are one!

Misplaced indulgence would mean fostering the faults of the enemies and thus letting them slide further on the downward path. Would that be love? On the contrary, by acting thus one would burden oneself with guilt!

Through the unexpressed wishes of man alone the Religion of Love has deteriorated to a religion of laxity, as also the personality of the Bringer of Truth, Christ Jesus, has been dragged down to one of weakness and yielding, characteristics which He never possessed. It was just because of His all-embracing Love that He was so harsh and severe among the men of intellect.

That He was often overcome with sadness is natural when one considers His high mission and the human material He had to deal with. This sadness had nothing whatever to do with weakness.

After eliminating all distortions and dogmatic restrictions, the Religion of Love will be a doctrine of the strictest consistency, in which no weakness or illogical indulgence is to be found.

THE REDEEMER

THE SAVIOUR on the Cross! These crucifixes are erected by the thousands as a token that Christ suffered and died for the sake of humanity. On all sides they call out to the faithful: "Remember it!"

In the lonely meadow, in the bustling city streets, in the private sanctuary, in churches, on graves and at wedding celebrations – everywhere they serve to comfort, strengthen and admonish. Remember it! Because of your sins the Son of God, Who came to earth to bring you salvation, suffered and died on the Cross!

The faithful Christian tremulously approaches them, in deep veneration and full of gratitude. With a glad feeling he leaves the place, conscious that he also has been released from his sins by the sacrificial death.

But you who are earnest seekers go and stand before the sacred, solemn token and strive to understand your Redeemer! Cast aside the soft cloak of ease that keeps you so pleasantly warm and creates a comfortable feeling of well-being and safety, allowing you to doze on till your last hour on earth! Then you will be vigorously aroused from your half-slumber and, freed from your earthly fetters, you will suddenly find yourself facing the naked truth. The dream to which you clung so persistently, and in which you surrendered yourself to inertia, will then quickly come to an end.

Therefore awake! Your time on earth is precious! Because of our sins the Saviour came – that is unassailably and literally true! It is also true that He died because of the guilt of humanity.

But this does not mean that your sins have been taken from you! The Saviour's work of redemption was to take up the battle with Darkness in order to bring Light to mankind, *to open the way to the forgiveness of all sins.*

But each one must tread this path alone in accordance with the irrevocable laws of the Creator. Christ did not come to overthrow the laws but to fulfil them. Do not fail to recognise Him Who should be your best friend! Do not attach a wrong meaning to such true words!

When it is quite rightly said that for the sake of man's sins all this happened, it means that the coming of Jesus became necessary only because mankind could no longer find their way alone out of their self-created darkness, nor release themselves from its clutches.

Christ had to show mankind the way. Had they not entangled themselves so deeply in sin, that is, had they not taken the *wrong* road, then the coming of Jesus would not have been necessary. He would have been spared His life of struggle and pain.

Therefore it is quite right to say that He was obliged to come for the sake of men's sins, if the latter in their pursuit of the wrong road were not to sink into the abyss, into darkness.

This does not mean, however, that the personal guilt of every individual is therewith remitted *at a moment's notice,* as soon as he really believes in and lives according to the words of Jesus. But if he does live according to the words of Jesus his sins *will* be forgiven him. Of course only gradually, as soon as redemption sets in through the reciprocal action ensuing from the counter-activity of his good volition. Not otherwise! It is different with those who do not live according to the words of Jesus; for them forgiveness is absolutely impossible.

This does not imply, however, that only members of the Christian religion can attain to the forgiveness of sins.

Jesus proclaimed the *Truth!* His words must therefore also embrace all the truths in other religions. He did not want to found a church, but to show mankind the right path, which can equally well lead through the truths of other religions. For this reason His words often accorded with the religions already existing.

Jesus did not take these truths out of them but, as He brought the Truth, It must necessarily contain all that was true in the other religions.

He who does not know the words of Jesus personally, but who seriously strives for the Truth and for ennoblement, often lives completely in harmony with the sense of these words, and will surely attain to pure faith and the forgiveness of his sins. Beware, therefore, of a one-sided outlook! It would be debasing the work of the Redeemer.

He who strives earnestly after truth and purity will also not be lacking in love. Though sometimes beset with serious doubts and struggles, he will be led upwards spiritually step by step and, *regardless of what religion he may belong to,* he will either here or later in the Ethereal World meet the Christ-

Spirit, which in *the final end* will lead him on towards recognition of God the Father. Thus the Word will be fulfilled: "No man cometh unto the Father but by me!"

"The final end", however, does not begin with your last hours on earth, but at a certain stage in the development of spiritual man, for whom the passing from the Gross Material World to the Ethereal World is but a transition.

And now to turn to the great work of Redemption itself. Mankind was erring in spiritual darkness. They had created this themselves by subjecting themselves more and more to the intellect, which they had so assiduously cultivated. In so doing they limited their perceptive ability more and more until, like their brain, they became unconditionally bound to space and time, and could no longer grasp the way to what is infinite and eternal.

Thus they became completely earthbound, limited to space and time. All connection with the Light, with Purity, with the spiritual, was cut off thereby. The volition of man was only capable of directing itself to earthly things, with the exception of a few who, as prophets, did not have the power to penetrate and make a free path to the Light.

This situation opened all the gates to evil. Darkness welled up and flooded the earth, bringing disaster. This could only have *one* end – spiritual death! The most terrible fate to befall mankind!

The guilt for all this misery lay upon mankind. They brought it upon themselves by voluntarily choosing this course. They had wanted it to be so and cultivated it. In their utter blindness they were even proud of their achievement without recognising the terrible consequences arising from their limited understanding, which they so painstakingly forced upon themselves. To open a path to the Light from a humanity in such a state was impossible. The self-imposed limitation was already too great.

If there was still to be any possibility of salvation help must come from the Light. Otherwise the downfall of man into darkness was inevitable.

Darkness itself, through its impurity, has a greater density, which brings about a heaviness. Because of this heaviness Darkness cannot of itself rise above a certain weight-level, unless from the other side some attracting power comes to its aid. Light, however, possesses a lightness corresponding to its purity, which makes it impossible for the Light to descend to the level of Darkness.

Thus there is an unbridgeable gulf between both parts, in the middle of which stands man and his earth.

According to the nature of his volition and wishes, man now possesses the choice of approaching the Light or of approaching the Darkness, of opening the gates and smoothing the way so that either Light or Darkness can flood the earth. In this process men themselves are the mediators through whose power of volition either Light or Darkness can gain a firm foothold there, from which it can operate more or less powerfully.

The more Light or Darkness thereby gains in power on earth, the more each can pour over mankind what it has to give – either good or evil, well-being or disaster, happiness or unhappiness, the peace of Paradise or the torment of hell.

The pure volition of man had become too weak to be able to offer an anchorage for the Light in the heavy stifling Darkness, which had already gained the upper hand on earth. This anchorage was needed for the Light to hold on to and unite with in such a way that its undimmed purity and consequent unimpaired power could cleave the Darkness and thus deliver mankind. They would then be able to draw strength by tapping this source and find their way upward to the Luminous Heights.

It was impossible for the Light Itself to descend so far into the mire unless a firm anchorage was offered to It. Consequently a mediator had to come. Only a messenger from the Luminous Heights could, *by incarnating*, break through the dark wall which men's volition had built and, in the midst of all the evil, create for the Divine Light *that* gross material foothold which would stand firm amid the heavy darkness. From this anchorage the pure rays of the Light would then be able to cleave through and disperse the dark layers so that humanity would not sink completely and suffocate in the Darkness.

Thus Jesus *came* for the sake of mankind and their sins!

This newly-created connection with the Light could not – because of the purity and strength of the Messenger from the Light – be cut off by the Darkness. Thus a new road to the spiritual heights was opened up for mankind.

From Jesus, who had become the earthly foothold of the Light, rays penetrated the Darkness through the Living Word which brought the Truth. He could transmit this Truth unblemished as He Himself was the Word and the Truth.

People were aroused from their spiritual lethargy through the miracles that happened simultaneously. In following these up they came upon the Word. Hearing the Truth that Jesus brought and reflecting upon It, there gradually awakened in hundreds of thousands the wish to follow this Truth and know more about It. By so doing they slowly strove upwards towards the Light.

Through this wish the Darkness surrounding them had to loosen its grip, and ray after ray of Light victoriously penetrated as people thought about these words and found them to be true. It became brighter and brighter around them and the Darkness, being no longer able to retain a firm hold on such persons, finally fell back and thus lost more and more ground. In this way the Word of Truth worked in the Darkness like a germinating mustard seed, as yeast does in bread.

And *this* was the work of redemption of the Son of God, Jesus, the Bringer of Light and Truth!

The Darkness, which imagined it was already master of all humanity, rebelled against this in a wild struggle to make the work of redemption impossible. It could get no hold on Jesus Himself, for it fell back before His pure intuition. Thus it naturally made use of the willing tools at its disposal for the battle.

These were the people who quite rightly called themselves "intellectuals", who yielded to the intellect and who, like the intellect, were fast bound to space and time. Consequently they could no longer grasp the higher spiritual concepts, which lie far beyond space and time, and it thus became impossible for them to follow the teaching of the Truth.

All these had the conviction that they stood on too "realistic" a ground, just as so many do today. Realistic ground, however, really means a very limited ground. The majority of these people represented power, being in positions of authority in government and church.

Thus the Darkness, in furious self-defence, whipped up these people to commit the brutal assaults against Jesus through the earthly power that lay in their hands.

By this the Darkness hoped to destroy the work of redemption. That it was at all possible for it to exert this power on earth was due solely to the guilt of humanity which, through their self-chosen wrong attitude, limited their perceptive ability and thus gave the Darkness the upper hand.

And because of this sin of humanity Jesus had to suffer! The Darkness continued to fan the flame to the uttermost! Jesus would have to suffer death on the Cross if He stood firm in His assertion that He was the Bringer of Truth and Light. It was the final decision! To flee or withdraw from it all could save Him from death on the Cross. But that would have meant victory to the Darkness at the last moment, because all the work of Jesus would then gradually have run to sand, and the Darkness would have victoriously engulfed everything. Jesus would not have fulfilled His Mission and the work of redemption started by Him would have remained unfinished.

The inner struggle in Gethsemane was sharp but short! Jesus did not shun physical death, but calmly faced it for the sake of the Truth He brought. With His blood on the Cross He put the seal upon all He had said and lived.

With this deed He vanquished the Darkness completely, which had then played its last trump. Jesus won the victory – out of love for mankind, whose way to freedom and Light thus remained open, because His death fortified their faith in the Truth of His words.

If He had withdrawn and fled and so given up His work, doubts would inevitably have assailed them.

Thus Jesus died for the sake of humanity's sins! If mankind had not sinned, nor turned away from God by limiting themselves through the intellect, then Jesus could have spared Himself His coming as well as His path of suffering and His crucifixion. Therefore it is quite right to say: "On account of our sins Jesus came, suffered and died on the Cross!"

But this does not mean that you do not have to redeem your own sins yourselves!

It is only that now it is easy for you, because by bringing the Truth Jesus has *shown you the way in His Words.*

Neither can the crucifixion of Jesus simply wash away your sins! Before such a thing could happen all the laws of the Universe would first have to be overthrown. But that will not happen! Jesus Himself often enough referred to "all that is written", that is, to the Old Covenant. The new Gospel of Love does not intend to overthrow or annul the old Gospel of Justice, *but to supplement* and unite with it.

Therefore do not forget the Justice of the mighty Creator of all things, which cannot be moved by even so much as a hair's breadth, and which stands inviolable from the very beginning of the world until its end! It could never permit any person to take another's guilt upon his shoulders in order to redeem it.

So for the sake of the guilt of others, or because of the guilt of others, Jesus could come, suffer and die – could step forth as the Warrior for the Truth, but He Himself remained pure and untouched by this guilt. That is why He was unable to take it upon Himself personally.

This does not lessen the work of redemption; instead it is a sacrifice that could not be greater. Jesus came down for you out of the Luminous Heights into the mire. He fought for you, suffered and died for you, in order to bring you Light and to show you the right way upward, so that you will not become lost in the Darkness and sink!

That is *how* your Redeemer stands before you! *That* was His tremendous work of Love!

The Justice of God continued to exist, severe and strict, in the Laws of the Universe. For what a man sows that shall he reap, as Jesus Himself said in His Message! Divine Justice does not permit one farthing to be remitted.

Think of this when you stand before this sacred, solemn token! Give fervent thanks that with His Word the Redeemer re-opened the way to the forgiveness of your sins, and leave the spot with the earnest intention to go the way shown to you so that forgiveness may really be yours!

To go that way does not mean just to learn the Word and believe It, but *to live* the Word! To believe It, to regard It as right, and yet not to act according to It in everything, would not benefit you at all. On the contrary, you would be worse off than those who know nothing of the Word.

Therefore awake! Your time on earth is precious!

THE MYSTERY OF BIRTH

WHEN men declare that great injustice lies in the unequal circumstances into which children are born, they do not know what they are saying.

One person persistently affirms: "How, if justice exists, can it happen that a child is born burdened with a hereditary disease? The innocent child must be helping to bear the sins of its parents!"

Another declares: "One child is born in rich circumstances, the other in misery and bitter poverty. How then can one believe in justice!"

Or again: "Granted that the parents deserve punishment, but it is not fair that this should happen through the illness and death of a child. That means that the innocent child must suffer!"

These and similar assertions circulate among men by the thousand. Even serious seekers sometimes rack their brains over it.

The simple statement that "the inscrutable ways of God are all for the best" does not dispose of the urge to find the answer to the "why". He who is supposed to be satisfied with such a statement must either *dumbly* acquiesce or immediately suppress every questioning thought as wrong.

That is not what is intended! Through questioning one finds the right way. Apathy or forced suppression are reminiscent only of slavery. God, however, does not want slaves! He does not want apathetic subjection, but a free, cognizant looking upwards!

His wonderful and wise dispositions do not require to be enveloped in mystic darkness. They can only gain in their sublime, inviolable greatness and perfection when they lie exposed before us. Immutable and incorruptible, with even deliberation and certainty, they unceasingly carry on their eternal activity.

They take no heed either of man's grumbling or of his acknowledgement, nor do they consider his ignorance, but they return to each individual with minutest accuracy the ripened fruits of the seeds he has sown.

"The mills of God grind slowly, but they grind exceeding fine" is a common saying that so aptly describes this weaving of the inexorable reciprocal action in the whole Creation, the immutable laws of which bear and carry out Divine Justice. It trickles, flows, streams and pours over all mankind whether they wish it or not, whether they yield to it or rebel against it. They must accept it as just punishment and forgiveness, or as a reward when they are uplifted!

If a grumbler or doubter could but once catch a glimpse of the transcendental surging and weaving carried and pervaded by the inexorable Spirit, which penetrates and embraces the whole Creation, in which Creation rests, and which in itself is part of this Creation, a living never-ceasing loom of God, he would immediately be shamed into silence and realise with horror the presumption contained in his words!

The serene grandeur and infallibility that he would see there would force him apologetically into the dust.

How small he imagined his God to be! And what sublime magnitude he finds in His works! He will then realise that his highest earthly conceptions are nothing but an attempt to belittle God and depreciate the perfection of His great work, through his futile efforts to compress it into the narrow confines brought about by the over-cultivation of the intellect, which can never rise above time and space.

Man must never forget that he stands in the *work* of God, that he himself is part of this work, and thus unconditionally subject to its laws!

The work, however, not only embraces things visible to the physical eye but also the Ethereal World, in which the greatest part of man's actual existence and activity takes place. His occasional lives on earth are only small sections of it, *nevertheless always great turning points.*

Birth on earth only forms the beginning of a special section in a man's entire existence, but not the beginning of man himself.

When man as such starts out on his course in Creation he stands free, without any threads of fate attached to him. These emanate from him later through his volition and proceed into the Ethereal World. On their way they are continually strengthened through the power of attraction of similar species, they cross and interweave with others, and react upon their originator, with whom they had remained connected, thus bringing about fate or karma.

When certain threads return at the same time their effects intermingle, with the result that the originally sharp and distinct colours of the threads take on other shades and produce new combined pictures*.

Each thread serves as a channel for the reactions until the originator no longer provides an anchorage for similar species in his inner being, i. e., when he himself no longer maintains this channel in good condition. Then these threads can no longer retain a foothold, cannot attach themselves to him, and must wither and fall away, regardless of whether they are good or evil.

Thus every thread of fate is ethereally formed through an act of will in making a decision to take some action. This leaves its author and yet remains anchored to him, thus forming a secure path to homogeneous species, bringing them reinforcement and receiving from them in return added strength which flows back to the starting point.

In this happening lies the help which has been promised to those who strive towards the good, or it contains the condition that "evil must continue to give birth to evil"**.

The reactions of these existing threads, to which he adds new threads daily, constitute the fate every man has created for himself and to which he must submit. All arbitrariness, and therefore all injustice, are thus precluded. The karma which a man bears with him and which seems one-sided predestination is, in reality, the inevitable *result* of his past, in so far as it has not yet been redeemed through reciprocal action.

The actual beginning of man's existence is *always* good and so also is the end for many; with the exception of those who have become lost of their own accord, when through their decisions they first stretched out their hands to evil, which then completely dragged them down into perdition. The vicissitudes in man's existence only occur in the between time, in the period of inner growth and maturing.

Thus man always shapes his future life himself! He provides the threads and thereby decides the colour and design of the garment which is woven for him in the loom of God through the Law of Reciprocal Action.

The causes working to determine the conditions into which a soul is born often lie far back, just as they determine the period under the influence of which the child will enter the physical world, so that during its earthly pilgrimage these conditions may continually influence it and achieve what this

* See Lecture: "Fate".
** See Lecture: "Man and his free will".

particular soul needs for its redemption, moulding, casting off karma, and further development.

But this does not happen in a one-sided manner for the child only, but the threads spin on automatically so that the reciprocal action is also felt in the earthly surroundings.

The parents give the child just what it needs for its further development, just as vice-versa the child gives to its parents, be it good or evil. For further development and advancement it is of course necessary in this connection to become free from an evil by personally experiencing it, whereby it will be recognised for what it is and cast off. It is the reciprocal action which always brings about the opportunity for this. Without the operation of this law man could never become really free from anything that has happened to him.

Thus the Laws of Reciprocal Action hold as a great gift of mercy the road to freedom or ascent! Therefore there can be no question of any punishment. Punishment is a wrong expression, for in these laws lies the greatest love – the hand of the Creator stretched out towards forgiveness and liberation!

The coming of man to earth comprises procreation, incarnation and birth. Incarnation is the actual entrance of the human being into earthly existence*.

A thousandfold are the threads that co-operate to determine an incarnation. But in these happenings, as always in Creation, the most scrupulous and absolute justice prevails and contributes to the advancement of *all* concerned.

Therefore the birth of a child is far more important and valuable than is generally accepted. For its entrance into the physical world holds a new and special act of grace of the Creator, not only for the child but at the same time for its parents, even for its brothers and sisters if it has any, and for others who come in contact with it, in that they thereby all get a further opportunity to progress in some way.

Through the necessary nursing during an illness, through heavy worries or misery, an opportunity may be offered to the parents to advance spiritually, be it the simple means to achieve some aim, the actual discharge of an old debt, or perhaps even a pre-redemptive measure against some threatening karma.

With a person who has already begun to will what is good it very often happens that, through his voluntary decision to devote himself to nursing his

---

* Lecture: "The creation of man".

own or some other child, a serious illness which was to have afflicted *him* as karma, according to the Law of Reciprocal Action, will mercifully be *pre-redeemed* in consequence of his good volition.

A real redemption can only ensue in the intuitive perception, in the full experience. A genuinely devoted nursing often brings an even deeper experience than that of one's own illness. There is deeper anxiety and pain during the illness of a child or of one who is really considered a loved one. And the joy at his recovery is equally great.

The deep intensity of this experience stamps its imprint so firmly on the intuitive perception, on the spiritual man, that it helps to change him, and in this process the threads of fate that would otherwise still have struck him are cut off.

Through their severance or falling away the threads rebound like stretched elastic in the opposite direction, to the homogeneous ethereal centres, the power of attraction henceforth pulling them from one side only. Thereby all further influence on the reformed human being is out of the question, because the connecting link is missing.

Thus, if a person will freely and willingly take upon himself some duty towards another out of pure love, there are thousands of ways of achieving redemption in this manner!

In His parables Jesus has given the best examples. In the Sermon on the Mount and in all His other sayings He has clearly pointed out the good results of such practices. In so doing He always spoke of "thy neighbour", thus pointing out the best, the simplest and truest way towards redemption of karma and towards ascent.

"Love thy neighbour as thyself" He charged, thus giving the key to the gate leading to all ascent! It need not always involve a case of illness. The necessary care and education of children quite naturally offer so many opportunities that they embrace in themselves *all* that comes into consideration to free a man from his karma. For this reason children are a blessing, no matter how they are born and developed.

What applies to parents applies equally to brothers and sisters and to all who have a lot to do with children. They also have opportunities to profit by this newcomer, be it only through striving to cast aside bad habits or similar things, by practising patience and giving careful help of different kinds.

The child itself, however, is no less helped. Birth gives each individual the possibility to advance a mighty step upwards. If this does not happen it is the fault of the individual himself, because he did not want it.

Hence every birth should be regarded as a benevolent and impartially distributed gift of God. Those who, being childless, adopt a strange child will be no less blessed, indeed the blessing will be all the greater on account of the adoption, provided that it is done for the child's sake and not for personal satisfaction.

In an ordinary incarnation the power of attraction of what is spiritually homogeneous plays a leading role together with reciprocal action. Qualities regarded as inherited are not really inherited, but are merely due to this power of attraction. Nothing spiritual is inherited from mother or father, for the child is as distinct a being as is each of the parents. It is only that the child has similar qualities through which it felt attracted to them.

But it is not only this power of attraction of the homogeneous that is decisive in an incarnation; other existing threads of fate, to which the soul to be incarnated is bound, also play a part. Perhaps they are in some way connected with a member of the family into which it is led. All this contributes, attracts and finally causes the soul to incarnate.

The case is different where a soul volunteers to undertake a mission, either to help some particular persons or to engage with others in some benevolent work for all mankind. Out of its own free will that soul then accepts in advance all that will happen to it on earth, so that here also there is no question of injustice. If all has been done in self-sacrificing love without thought of any reward, the reward must come as a result of reciprocal action.

Into families with hereditary diseases souls will be incarnated which, through the reciprocal action, need these diseases for redemption, for purification, or for advancement.

The guiding and supporting threads do not allow a wrong and thus unjust incarnation to take place. They exclude the possibility of any error. It would be like trying to swim against a current which follows its orderly course with iron and inexorable power, eliminating all resistance from the start, so that even an attempt to swim against it is altogether out of the question. However, if its characteristics are precisely respected, it will bring nothing but blessing.

All circumstances are carefully taken into consideration, also with voluntary incarnations in which diseases are voluntarily accepted in order to attain a certain purpose. If perhaps the father or mother burdened themselves by some sin with a disease, maybe only by neglecting the strict laws Nature lays down for the health of the body entrusted to their care, then the grief at seeing the same illness appear in the child would in itself be atonement and, if the grief is genuinely felt, would lead to purification.

There would be little point in giving specific examples, since every single birth would give a new picture differing from the others because of the many intermingled threads of fate. Even every homogeneous type must offer thousands of variations on account of the fine gradations of the manifold reciprocal actions.

Let us give just one simple example! A mother loves her son so dearly that she resorts to all manner of means to prevent him from marrying and leaving her. She continually chains him to herself. Such love is wrong, purely selfish, even if the mother, in her opinion, does everything to make her son's life on earth as pleasant as possible. With her selfish love she has wrongly interfered in the life of her son.

Genuine love never thinks of itself, but always of the advantage of the beloved one, and acts accordingly, even if it involves self-sacrifice!

The mother's hour to be called away arrives, and the son stands alone. Now, however, it is too late for him to arouse that joyful enthusiasm for the fulfilment of his wishes, which only youth has at its command. But, in spite of all, he has made some gain, for he redeems something through this imposed renunciation. It may be a similar characteristic in a former life, thereby avoiding the inner loneliness of marriage, which he would otherwise have had to experience, or it might be something else. He can only benefit through such things.

The mother, however, has taken over her selfish love with her. Therefore the power of attraction of what is spiritually homogeneous draws her irresistibly to people of similar qualities, for in their vicinity she is able, through the intuitive life of such people, to experience a small part of her own passion when they practise their selfish love towards others. Therefore she remains earthbound.

Should a procreation take place with persons in whose vicinity she continually finds herself, she will incarnate there through the link of her spiritual enchainment.

But then the tables will be turned! As a child she will now have to suffer from the same characteristic in her father or mother as she once caused her child to suffer. In spite of her longing to leave the parental home, and the opportunities to do so, she cannot free herself. Not until she recognises through personal experience the injustice of such qualities will she atone for her guilt and be freed from it!

Through his union with the physical body, that is, through his incarnation, a bandage is placed before the eyes of every human being, which prevents him from surveying his past existence. Like everything that happens in Creation, this also is for the benefit of the person concerned. Here again is a proof of the wisdom and love of the Creator!

If everyone could precisely recall his previous existence he would merely stand aside and remain a calm onlooker in his new life on earth, in the consciousness that by so doing he was making progress or redeeming something. However, instead of helping him to advance, this would expose him to the great danger of sliding downwards.

Life on earth must be really *experienced* if it is to have any purpose! Only what has been inwardly lived through in all its heights and depths, what has been thoroughly perceived in one's intuition, only that may one truly call one's own! If a man could always clearly know from the very outset the exact course that would benefit him, there would be no occasion for him to weigh and decide. Hence he could acquire neither the strength nor the independence that are absolutely necessary for him.

As it is, he takes every situation of his earth-life with greater realism. Every genuine experience leaves a firm imprint upon his intuition, upon the immortal part which, newly fashioned by these impressions, man takes over with him as his own, as a part of himself. But *only* that which he has really experienced, for all else is extinguished at physical death! That which has been *experienced* remains, however, as the clear extract of his earthly existence, as his gain.

Not all that has been learned has been experienced; but only that which has been learned through experience becomes one's own. All the rest of the learned lumber, for which many a man sacrifices his whole life, remains behind as husks. Therefore each moment of life can never be taken too seriously, so that our thoughts, words and deeds shall not deteriorate into meaningless habits, but pulsate with vital warmth!

Through the bandage placed before its eyes at the time of its incarnation the newly-born child seems to be completely ignorant, and is therefore often erroneously regarded as being innocent. But it often brings a mighty karma with it which offers opportunities to redeem past errors by living through them and fully experiencing them. In cases of predestination karma is only the necessary consequence of all that has happened. Where it is a question of a mission karma, in so far as it does not belong to the mission itself, is voluntarily undertaken for the purpose of gaining earthly understanding and maturity in order to fulfil the mission.

Therefore man should no longer grumble about injustice at birth, but gratefully look up to the Creator, Who only grants new mercies with every single birth!

IS OCCULT TRAINING ADVISABLE?

THIS question must be answered with a definite "no"! Occult training, which generally includes exercises for the attainment of clairvoyance, clairaudience, etc., is a hindrance to a free development and to real spiritual ascent. As soon as the training is fairly sucessful it results in what in former times was described as a magician.

It is a process of one-sided groping forward from below upwards, whereby the so-called terrestrial limits can never be crossed. All the phenomena likely to be achieved in such conditions will be of a lower and most inferior order, which cannot actually uplift a man inwardly, but may well lead him astray.

Through these efforts man is only able to penetrate into his immediate ethereal environment, where the entities are often more ignorant than man on earth himself. All that he accomplishes here is that he exposes himself to unknown dangers, from which he otherwise remains protected by not opening himself.

One who has become clairvoyant or clairaudient through such training will often see or hear things on this low plane which appear to be sublime and pure, and yet which are far from it. In addition there is his own imagination which, even more stimulated by his training, also creates a surrounding that the student actually sees and hears, with resultant confusion.

A man thus artificially trained stands insecurely on his feet. He cannot discriminate, nor with the best will can he draw a sharp line between truth and deception or between the thousandfold ways in which the formative power works in ethereal life. Finally there are the base and, for him, decidedly injurious influences to which he voluntarily and with arduous efforts opens himself, and which he cannot oppose with a higher power. Thus he soon becomes a rudderless wreck on an unknown sea, which is liable to be a menace to everything that comes into contact with it.

It is exactly the same as with a person who cannot swim. He is quite capable of sailing in perfect safety over the unfamiliar element in a boat. This can be compared to earthly life. But if during the voyage he removes one of the protecting planks from the bottom, then he tears a hole in his boat through which the water will enter, depriving him of his protection and drawing him down. Through his inability to swim he will thus become a victim of the unfamiliar element.

Such is the procedure in occult training! Man only removes a plank from his protecting boat, *but does not learn to swim!*

There are swimmers, however, who call themselves experts. In this category are those swimmers already possessed of a certain talent, which with a little training they make more effective, and also continually try to develop further. In such cases, then, a more or less natural talent will unite with artificial training. However, even the best swimmer is confined within rather narrow limits. Should he venture too far his strength will give out, and he will finally be just as lost as a non-swimmer unless, indeed, help comes to them both.

In the Ethereal World such help can only come from the Luminous Heights, from the pure spiritual realm. And this help again can only approach if the one in danger has reached a certain degree of purity in his psychic development, with which it can unite to give a firm hold. Such purity cannot be obtained through experimental occult training, but only through developing true inner integrity by constantly looking upwards to the purity of the Light.

If a man has followed *this* path it will in time bring him a certain measure of purity which will naturally be reflected in his thoughts, words and deeds. Then by degrees he will obtain a link with purer heights from which, through reciprocal actions, he will also receive increased strength.

Throughout all the intermediary steps he then has a connection which will hold him and to which he can cling. It will not be long before all that the swimmer has vainly tried to achieve will be given to him without any effort. But it is given with the care and precaution which are inherent in the inexorable Laws of Reciprocal Action, so that he gets only as much of it as his own strength can counterbalance, whereby all danger is excluded from the outset.

At last the separating partition, which may be compared to the planks of a boat, becomes thinner and thinner, and finally falls away altogether. That then is the moment when, in the same way as a fish is at home in water, he himself will feel quite at home in the Ethereal World right up to the Luminous Heights. That alone is the right way!

What has been artificially forced by training is wrong. It is only the fish that is free from danger in water, because that is "its element", for which it has been properly equipped in a way which a trained swimmer can *never attain*.

When a man intends to take up this training, it is preceded by a voluntary decision, to the consequences of which he is then subjected. Therefore he cannot anticipate that help *is certain* to be given him! He had the freedom to decide beforehand!

But a man who induces others to take up such training, as a result of which they are exposed to all sorts of dangers, must take a great part of the consequences of the guilt of each individual upon his own shoulders. He will become ethereally chained to them all. After laying aside his physical body he must irrevocably descend to those who have departed before him, to those who have succumbed to the dangers, right down to him who sank lowest of all.

He is unable to ascend himself until he has helped every single one to rise again, until their wrong path has been obliterated and everything neglected through such training has been retrieved. Such is the balance brought about by reciprocal action and, at the same time, the merciful means by which he can put right the injustice and himself ascend.

If such a man has not only influenced others through his words, but also through his writings, he will be hit even more severely, because his writings go on doing harm even after his earthly death. He must then wait in the Ethereal World till the last person he has led astray, and whom he is obliged to help on to the right path, has crossed over. Centuries may well elapse in this process!

However, this does not mean that the field of the Ethereal World should remain untouched and unexplored during life on earth!

At the appropriate hour it will be given to those who are inwardly matured to feel at home where others would still be in danger. They will be permitted to see the Truth and pass it on. But at the same time they will also be able clearly to survey the dangers which threaten those who, by means of occult training, wish to penetrate one-sidedly into the lower spheres of unknown regions. They will never advocate occult training.

SPIRITISM

SPIRITISM! Mediumship! A hot battle rages over them, for and against. It is not my task to say anything about its opponents and their eager denials. That would be a waste of time, for every logical thinker needs only to read of the way the so-called tests and investigations are carried out to perceive the complete ignorance and definite incapacity of these "experimenters".

Why? If I want to investigate the earth, I must adapt myself to its nature. If, on the contrary, I wish to explore the sea, I have no choice but to adapt myself to the nature of water and to use such aids as conform to that.

To tackle water with spade and shovel or with drilling machines would not carry me far in my investigations. Or should I perhaps deny the existence of water because my spade passes right through it, contrary to what happens when I place it in the more familiar solid earth? Or because I cannot walk upon water as I do upon solid earth?

Opponents will declare: "But that is different, for I can both *see* and feel that water exists, and nobody can deny it!"

How long ago was it that man energetically denied the existence of myriads of colourful organisms in a drop of water, which every child now knows about? And why was their existence denied? Only because man could not see them! It was not until an instrument adapted to their nature had been invented that man could recognise, see and observe this new world.

The same applies to the Ethereal World, the so-called beyond. First learn to perceive, and *then* you may permit yourself to judge! It rests with *you*, not with the "other world"! Apart from your physical body you also have the substance of the other world within you, while those in the beyond no longer possess your gross material substance.

You demand and expect that those in the beyond, who no longer have gross matter at their disposal, should approach you (give signs, etc.). You wait for them to prove their existence to *you*, who have at your disposal the substance of the beyond as well as your physical substance, while you yourself sit waiting with the attitude of a judge!

You should span the bridge, which *you can do!* Work at last with the same substance, which is also at your command, and learn to perceive in the process! Or keep silent if you cannot manage this, and continue to nourish gross matter, which weighs upon ethereal substance more and more!

The day will come when the ethereal part must sever itself from the gross material part and remain prostrate, because it never practised soaring upwards, for like the physical body the ethereal body is also subject to the physical laws.

Only movement brings strength! You do not need mediums in order to perceive ethereal substance! Just observe the life of the ethereal part within you! Let your will give it what it needs to grow strong! Or do you want to dispute the existence of your will because you can neither see nor touch it?

How often do you feel the after-effects of your willing within yourselves! You sense them, but you can neither see nor touch them, whether it be exaltation, joy or sorrow, anger or envy. As soon as the will gets to work it must also possess the power to create a pressure, for without pressure there can be no activity, no sensing. And where there is pressure something solid of the same substance must be active, otherwise no pressure could be exerted.

Thus there must be solid forms of a substance that you can neither see nor touch with your physical body. And such is the substance of the beyond, which you can only perceive by means of the similar substance also dwelling within you.

The battle for and against life after physical death is extraordinary, and really verges upon the ludicrous. He who is able to reflect and observe calmly, without prejudice and self-desires, will soon find that *everything*, positively everything, speaks for the probability of an existing world of other substance which the average person of today is unable to see. There are so many happenings which repeatedly remind us of this fact and which simply cannot be heedlessly pushed aside as non-existing.

On the other hand, the only thing which favours an absolute cessation of life after physical death is contained in the desire of many persons who would thereby like to evade every spiritual responsibility because neither cleverness nor cunning carry any weight therein, but only genuine intuitive perception.

But to turn to the *adherents* of spiritism, spiritualism, etc., or whatever name they choose to give it! In the end they all suffer from the same thing – great errors!

The adherents are often more dangerous and harmful to the truth than the adversaries!

There are only a few among the millions who will allow themselves to be told the truth. Most of them are entangled in a huge web of small errors, which hinders them from finding the path to the plain truth. Where does the blame lie? In the beyond, perhaps? No! Or in the mediums? No, not there either! *Only in the individual himself!* He is not severe and stern enough with himself. He does not want to throw over his preconceived opinions, and shrinks from destroying the self-constructed picture of the beyond which has long *filled* him with a *sacred awe and a certain feeling of well-being,* though in fact this only exists in his imagination.

And woe to him who would dare to touch upon this! Every adherent has a stone ready to throw at him! He clings firmly to his opinions and is quite prepared to call those in the beyond lying or teasing spirits, or to charge the mediums with deficiency, rather than calmly to examine himself and reflect whether *his conception* may be wrong.

Where, then, should I begin to root out the many weeds? It would be work without end! Therefore let what I say here be only for those who are really seriously seeking, for only such shall find!

Here is an example! A man visits a medium, whether one of note or not is of no importance! There are others with him, and a "sitting" begins. The medium "fails" and nothing happens! What are the consequences? Some say the medium is no good. Others declare that all spiritism amounts to nothing. Investigators boastfully assert: "The frequently tested mediumistic qualities of the medium were all a swindle, for as soon as *we* come the medium does not dare to do anything and the 'spirits' are silent!"

Believers and those who are convinced, however, go away depressed. The reputation of the medium suffers and, if there are repeated "failures", it is ruined.

If the medium has a sort of manager and money is charged, the manager will nervously urge the medium to make greater efforts when people pay money for it, etc. In short there will be doubt, derision and discontent and, in a new attempt, the medium will make convulsive efforts to get himself into a trance and, in a sort of nervous self-delusion, perhaps unconsciously say something he imagines he has heard, or simply resort to direct deception which, in fact, is not very difficult for a speaking medium.

The sentence passed is: All a swindle, and a denial of spiritism altogether because some mediums, due to the circumstances mentioned above, may have resorted to deception to avoid the increasing animosity!

Here are a few questions:

1. Is there any class of society where no swindlers are to be found? Does one in other cases immediately condemn the ability of honest workers on account of a few swindlers?

2. Why just in these matters and actually nowhere else?

Everyone can easily answer these questions for himself!

But who is principally to blame for such unworthy conditions? Not the medium, but most certainly the people themselves! Through their extremely one-sided views, and particularly through their utter ignorance, they force the medium to choose between suffering from unjust animosity or practising deception.

Mankind does not easily leave a middle course open to a medium!

I am here speaking only of a medium who can be taken seriously, not of the numerous would-be mediums who try to push their insignificant abilities into the foreground. It is also far from my desire in any way to take the part of the great number of followers of mediums because the spiritists who throng round mediums have real value only in very rare cases, with the exception of serious investigators who approach this unexplored region in order *to learn* and not ignorantly to pronounce judgment.

To the greater number of the so-called believers these visits or "seances" bring no progress, but rather standstill or retrogression. They become so dependent that they cannot decide anything themselves, but always want to get the advice of "those in the beyond", often about the most ridiculous things, and mostly for earthly trivialities.

A serious investigator or an honest seeker will always be indignant at the incredible narrow-mindedness of those who for years have been constant visitors to mediums, with whom they feel quite "at home".

With an exceedingly shrewd and superior air they talk the greatest nonsense and then sit with hypocritical devotion enjoying the agreeable tickling of the nerves, which they imagine to be due to intercourse with invisible powers.

Many mediums sun themselves in the flattering talk of such visitors who, in reality, are only expressing a selfish wish to "experience" as much as possible themselves. The "experiencing" in their case, however, is only the same as hearing or seeing, in other words, being entertained. Nothing ever comes to "real experience" within them!

What should a *serious* person take into consideration in such matters?

1. That a medium can contribute nothing whatever to ensure "success" apart from inwardly opening himself, that is, surrendering himself, and then waiting. A medium is a tool who is used, an instrument which of itself cannot give forth any sound until it is played upon. Therefore there can be no question of what is termed as a *failure!* He who talks in this way only shows his narrow-mindedness, and he should keep his hands off! Nor should he express any opinion because he cannot judge in the matter, just as he who finds learning arduous should avoid the university! A medium is therefore simply a bridge or a means to an end.

2. It is the *visitors* who play a great role in this, not by their outward standing or even by their social standing, but *by their inner life!*

The inner life, as the greatest scoffers also realise, is a world of itself. Naturally their intuitions, with their generative and nourishing thoughts, cannot be just "nothing", but there must logically be ethereal bodies or things which through pressure or influence awaken intuitive feelings, which could not otherwise arise.

Neither could pictures be seen in spirit where there is nothing. Just such a conception would indicate the greatest gap in the laws of the exact sciences.

Thus something *must* be there, and something *is* there, for the generative thought immediately creates in the Ethereal World (in the beyond) corresponding forms, the density and vitality of which depend on the intuitive power of the generative thought concerned. Therefore what is called the "inner life" of a man produces a corresponding and similarly formed environment around him.

And it is this surrounding which must affect a medium, who is more open and sensitive to the Ethereal World, either in a pleasant or disagreeable, if not painful, way. Thus it may happen that genuine messages from the Ethereal World are not transmitted so correctly if the medium is hindered, oppressed or confused by the presence of people who have an ethereally or spiritually impure inner life.

But it goes still further. This impurity constitutes a barrier to purer ethereal matter, so that no message can be transmitted save one of an equally impure ethereal nature.

With visitors who have a *pure* inner life, contact with a correspondingly pure ethereal environment is naturally possible. But everything different to that forms an unbridgeable gap! That is why such differences exist in the so-called seances, often bringing about complete failure or causing confusion. This all rests on inexorable, purely physical laws which operate in exactly the same way in the beyond as they do in this world.

The unfavourable reports of "investigators" are now seen in a different light. And he who is able to observe the ethereal happenings must smile at many an investigator who, in his report, pronounces judgment on *himself*, exposing his own inner life and only criticising the state of *his own* soul.

Here is a second example! A man visits a medium. It happens that a departed relative speaks to him through the medium. He asks his advice perhaps on quite an important earthly matter. The departed one gives him a few directions which the visitor looks upon as gospel truth, as a revelation from the beyond, which he obeys minutely, with the result that he is taken in and often suffers heavy damage.

What is the result? The visitor will first of all doubt the medium. In his disappointment and perhaps annoyance at his loss he may work against the medium. In some cases he will even feel obliged to proceed publicly against him in order to save others from similar loss and deception.

In connection with this I should now explain life in the beyond, how by doing this such a person opens himself to similar ethereal currents through the attraction of what is spiritually homogeneous, and how, as a tool of such counter-currents, he may then develop into a fanatic in the proud consciousness of standing up for the truth, thereby rendering a great service to mankind! In reality, however, he makes himself a slave to impurity and burdens himself with a karma which it will take a lifetime and more to redeem. New threads will continue to emerge from this, weaving a net in which he will entangle himself, until finally he can no longer find his way about and, in his antagonism, becomes increasingly furious.

Or, if the disappointed visitor does not regard the medium as a swindler, he will at least have grave doubts about the entire beyond, or may take the usual easy road as thousands do, and say: "What concern of mine is the other world? Let others rack their brains about it! I have better things to do!" The "better things", however, are serving the physical body by acquiring wealth and thus withdrawing still further from ethereal things.

Where, then, does the actual guilt lie? *Again only with man himself!* He had formed a *false* picture when he accepted what was said as gospel truth. That was *his* fault alone, nobody else was to blame! He took it for granted that a departed spirit, by virtue of its ethereal nature, became at the same time partly omniscient, or at least possessed greater knowledge.

Many hundreds of thousands make this mistake. The only additional knowledge that a departed being possesses following his transformation is that he has not really ceased to exist after so-called death.

But that is all – so long as he makes no use of the opportunity to advance in the Ethereal World, which also depends on his own free decision, as well as on his honest and diligent efforts!

Therefore, when he is questioned about worldly matters, he will give his opinion with the good intention of fulfilling the wish of the questioner, convinced that he is giving the best advice. But he himself is not conscious of the fact that he is in no position to judge material matters and conditions as clearly as a man still living there in flesh and blood, because he lacks the gross material substance which is absolutely necessary to form a proper judgment.

His view of the matter, therefore, must be quite a different one. Still he gives what he can and, with the best intention, the best he knows. Thus neither he nor the medium can be blamed. Nor is he a "lying spirit". In fact we should only distinguish between "knowing" and "unknowing" spirits, for as soon as a spirit sinks, i. e., becomes more impure and dense, his horizon simultaneously and automatically narrows.

He gives and expresses only what he feels; *he lives only with his intuition,* not with his calculating intellect, which he no longer possesses, since this was bound to his earthly brain and thereby limited to space and time. As soon as that fell away at death, there was no more thinking and reflecting for him, but solely intuitive perception, *an immediate and continuous experiencing!*

The fault lies with those who still ask about earthly matters bound to space and time from those who are no longer so limited and who therefore cannot understand.

Those in the beyond are in a position to discern what is the right or wrong course in any matter, but then man must weigh and consider with his earthly aids, i. e., with his intellect and experience, how best to follow the right course. He must bring it into accord with earthly possibilities! That is *his* work!

Even when a spirit who has fallen deeply gets the opportunity of influencing and speaking, nobody can say that he lies or tries to mislead, for he only reflects what he lives and tries to convince others of it as well. He cannot give anything else!

Thus there are innumerable errors in the conceptions of spiritists.

"Spiritism" has come into great disrepute, not of itself, but through the majority of its adherents, who after only a few and often very meagre experiences, enthusiastically imagine that the veil has been drawn aside for them. Then they eagerly try to make others happy with a picture of ethereal life which they thought out themselves, which was created by an unbridled imagination, and which, above all, completely satisfies their own wishes. But these pictures are seldom in complete accord with the Truth!

EARTHBOUND

THIS word is often used, but who really understands what it means? "Earth-bound" sounds as if it were some terrible punishment. Most people have a rather uncanny feeling about those who are still earthbound and fear them. Still, the significance of the word is not so bad after all!

Certainly there is much that is dark to make this or that soul earthbound, but more often than not quite simple matters inevitably lead to this condition.

Let us, for instance, take the case of: "The sins of the fathers revenge themselves unto the third and fourth generation!"

A child puts some question or other to the family concerning the beyond, or about God, something it has heard in school or church. The father curtly dismisses it with the remark: "Stop such stupid nonsense! When I am dead it is all over!"

The child is startled and begins to doubt. The disdainful remarks of father or mother are repeated. The child also hears the same from others, and finally accepts their opinion.

The hour now arrives when the father must pass on. He realises to his dismay that with this he has not ceased to exist. The ardent wish will now awaken within him to impart this knowledge to his child. This wish binds him to the child.

But the child neither hears him nor feels his nearness; for it now lives in the conviction that its father has ceased to exist. This stands like a firm, impenetrable wall between it and the father's efforts. The father is obliged to witness how through him his child now takes the wrong path, which leads further and further away from the truth. To his anguish is added the fear lest the child may not be able to avoid the danger of sinking still further, a danger to which it is now more than ever exposed. At the same time all this forms the father's so-called punishment for misleading his child.

Very seldom will he be able to bring this knowledge in any way to the notice of the child. He must witness how his wrong idea is conveyed from the child to his grandchildren and so on, all as a result of his own failing. He cannot be released until one of his descendants recognises and follows the right way and also influences the others, whereby he will gradually be freed and can begin to think about his own ascent.

Here is another case! A habitual smoker takes over with him the strong craving to smoke, for this craving is a propensity which verges on the intuition, on that which is spiritual, although only at its outermost edge. It becomes a burning desire and holds him where he can obtain gratification – on earth! He finds this by pursuing smokers and enjoying *their inner sensations with them.*

If no heavy karma binds such persons to any other place, they feel quite pleasant and very seldom become conscious of the fact that this is really a punishment. Only he who can survey the whole complexity of existence can recognise the punishment in the inevitable reciprocal action, which prevents the person in question from rising higher as long as the perpetual desire for gratification by "experiencing" binds him to people still living on earth in the flesh, through whose sensations alone he can find satisfaction.

This is also the case with sexual gratification, with drinking, yes, even with a pronounced love of eating. Here, too, many are bound by the latter propensity to rummage in kitchens and cellars, and to be present when the food is being enjoyed by others so as at least to sense a small part of their enjoyment.

Taken seriously, of course, this is "punishment". But the craving of these "earthbound" souls, which overshadows all else, prevents them from perceiving it. Therefore, the yearning for something nobler and higher cannot grow so strong as to become the principal experience, which would then free them from the baser desire and uplift them.

They never realise the opportunity they are missing until this desire for gratification, which at best can only be a part gratification, enjoyed through others, on this account slowly wanes and dies out. Then other sensations accompanied by lesser craving, which he still carries with him, come forward and rise to first place, as a result of which they immediately become experience and with that attain to the power of reality.

The nature of the sensation which has come to life brings him to the place where there are similar types, either higher or lower, until this, too, like the first one, is overcome and gradually disappears, only to be followed by the next one to be dealt with.

This purification of all the dross he took over with him will be achieved in due course. But will he not come to a standstill somewhere at the last sensation? Or will the power of the intuition be diminished? No! For when at last base sensations are gradually outlived or discarded, and ascent begins, then the constant yearning for what is higher and purer awakens and steadily drives him upwards.

This is the *normal* course! But there are a thousand variations. The danger of a fall or of remaining stationary is much greater than when in the flesh on earth. If you have already attained a certain height and yield but for a moment to a base intuition it will immediately become an experience and thereby reality. You become denser and heavier and you will sink down into analogous regions. Thus your horizon narrows and you will gradually have to work yourself upwards again, if it does not happen that you sink lower and lower.

"Watch and pray!" is therefore no empty phrase. At the present moment the ethereal part in you is still protected by your body as if held with a firm anchor. But when severance comes with so-called death and dissolution of the body, you are then without this protection and, being ethereal, will be irresistibly attracted by similar species, whether high or low. You cannot escape it! Only one great driving power can help you upwards, your strong volition towards that which is good and sublime. This will develop into a yearning and an intuitive perception, becoming also an experience and a reality, in accordance with the law of the Ethereal World, which knows only intuitive perception.

Therefore, prepare yourself now to start with this volition so that when you are called away, which can happen at any hour, it is not overruled by a more powerful earthly desire! Be on your guard, man, and keep watch!

DOES SEXUAL CONTINENCE FURTHER
SPIRITUAL DEVELOPMENT?

THERE will be far less unhappiness if people will only free themselves from the error of the merits of sexual continence. Compulsory continence is an interference which may have dire consequences.

Wherever one looks the Laws in all Creation show the way plainly enough. Suppression is unnatural. All that is unnatural is a rebellion against the Natural and thus the Divine Laws, which in this as in all else can never yield any good results.

No exception is made on this particular point! Man must simply never permit himself to be mastered by the sexual impulse, nor must he become a slave to his instincts, otherwise they will develop into a passion whereby what is natural and healthy will become a morbid vice.

Man should stand *above* this, which means that he should not force continence upon himself but, with a pure inner morality, practise self-control so that neither he nor others will come to any harm.

If some people think that through continence they can rise higher spiritually, it may well happen that they achieve just the opposite. According to individual disposition, there will be a more or less continual conflict with the natural instincts. This struggle consumes a great part of the person's spiritual powers, keeping them in constraint so that they cannot be active in other directions. Hence the free unfolding of these spiritual powers is hindered. Such persons will at times suffer from a depressing melancholy which will hinder them from an inner joyful soaring upwards.

The physical body is a gift which God entrusted to man and it is his duty to take care of it. Just as he cannot abstain with impunity from satisfying the body's needs of food, drink, rest and sleep, and of relieving bladder and bowels; and just as lack of fresh air and sufficient exercise will soon make him feel uncomfortable; so precisely the same applies to the healthy desire of a mature body for sexual intercourse, with which he cannot toy without doing some harm or other to himself.

Fulfilling the natural desire of the body can only further and never hinder the inner man, i. e., the development of the spiritual, otherwise the Creator would not have placed this desire within him.

But here as in everything else excesses are harmful. Great care must be taken that this desire is not the result of an imagination artificially stimulated by reading or some other cause, or the consequence of an enfeebled body or overwrought nerves. It should really be only the demand of a healthy body, which by no means often occurs with men.

It will only occur when there has previously set in between both sexes a perfect spiritual harmony which, in its consummation, sometimes strives towards physical union as well.

All other reasons are dishonouring to both parties, are impure and immoral, *even in marriage.* Where there is no spiritual harmony, the continuance of a marriage becomes absolutely immoral.

If the social order has not yet found the right way in this matter, this defect can in no way change the Laws of Nature, which will never adapt themselves to human dispositions or to wrongly fostered ideas. There will, however, be no other choice left to man but finally to adapt the State and social institutions to the Laws of Nature, i. e., to the Divine Laws, if he ultimately wants to have inner peace and become healthy.

Sexual continence has nothing to do with chastity, either! At best it could be included in the concept of "decency", resulting from discipline, education or self-control.

By true chastity is meant *purity of thought,* but in *all* things right down to everyday business. Chastity is a purely spiritual and not a physical quality. Even in the act of satisfying the sexual instinct, chastity can be fully preserved where purity of thought reigns on both sides.

Physical union not only serves to procreate, but from it ensues the equally valuable and necessary process of an intimate fusion and a mutual exchange of vibrations, thus producing greater power.

THOUGHT-FORMS

Take a seat in any cafe or restaurant and observe the people sitting at the tables around you! Listen to their conversation and note what they have to say to one another! Go into families, watch your most intimate friends in their hours of leisure when work no longer presses!

You will be shocked at the hollowness of their conversations when they cannot talk about their various occupations. If you observe them closely you will sense with disgust the emptiness of their thoughts and the oppressively narrow sphere of their interests, as well as their terrible superficiality.

The few exceptions you encounter, those whose words in their *leisure hours* of everyday life are penetrated by a longing for a greater development of their souls, will appear to you as solitary strangers in the midst of a fair.

It is just in his so-called leisure hours that you can best recognise the real inner man, when his daily work is done and he has lost the outer hold on life provided by his special field of knowledge. What *then* remains is the actual man. Watch him and listen dispassionately to his words! You will soon cease your observations because they will become intolerable.

You will be filled with deep sadness when you realise that many people are not very much different to animals, not quite so dull and equipped with a higher intellect, but on the whole the same. They go through life on earth as if with blinkers, never seeing more than one aspect, i.e., what is purely material. They attend to eating and drinking and aim to increase to a greater or lesser extent their hoard of earthly treasures, seeking for physical enjoyment and regarding all reflection on things they cannot see as a waste of time, which they consider would be better employed in "rest and recreation".

They cannot and will not understand that life on earth, with all its pleasures and joys, only gets its real meaning when one has become more or less familiar with the Ethereal World, and knows about the reciprocal actions connecting us with it, for then one no longer has the feeling of being at the mercy of chance. They repudiate this idea under the misapprehension that, if an ethereal world really exists, it would only bring them discomfort or even dismay as soon as they concern themselves with it.

To them it is a strange idea that life on earth only gets real value through striving upwards, and that then a delightful, vital warmth also pulsates through all earthly joys and pleasures. These latter are not pushed aside; on the contrary, those who yearn for and earnestly seek what is pure and high will, as a beautiful result of reciprocal action, attain an ardent love of life, often ending in jubilant enthusiasm for all that exists and is proffered.

Fools are they who pass this by! Cowards, to whom the glorious joy of those who advance courageously will ever be denied!

Rejoice that all around you *lives,* far away to regions that seem immeasurable! Nothing is dead, nothing is void as it would appear! Everything is working and weaving in reciprocal action, in the centre of which you stand as men continually forming and directing the threads, being both starting point and final goal.

Mighty rulers are you! Each one of you is establishing his own kingdom in such a way that it will either uplift you or bury you beneath its ruins. Awake! Use the power given to you in the full knowledge of this mighty happening, lest in your stupidity and obstinacy, or even in your indolence, you bring forth only harmful deformities which choke all that is healthy and good and finally cause you as their author to totter and fall!

Even man's nearest ethereal surrounding can contribute much to uplift or debase him. This is the strange world of thought-forms, the vital activity of which comprises only a small section of the giant mechanism of the whole Creation. Their threads, however, penetrate both into the Gross Material World, and further up into the Ethereal World, as well as descending into the realm of Darkness. Like a gigantic network of veins or nerve-strands, all is intertwined and interwoven, untearable and inseparable! Mark this well!

There are favoured ones who here and there can see a part of this, but much they can only divine. In this way some things have come to the knowledge of mankind, who have sought to build further upon this knowledge in order to obtain a complete picture. But in so doing gaps and mistakes were bound to occur. Many investigators of the ethereal realm jumped to conclusions which inevitably caused the proper sequence to be lost. Others again filled the gaps with fantastic imagery, bringing disfigurements and distortions which consequently shattered faith in the whole matter. The result was a justifiable derision which, based on the lack of logic of the so-called spiritual investigators, was certain to be victorious.

If these matters are to be spoken of at all it is necessary that first of all a cord should be drawn through all that happens in the working of Creation, which the onlooker can grasp in order to help him climb upwards. Many of the processes which perplex him have their origin in his immediate vicinity. One glance into the world of thought-forms should suffice to make him understand several things that seemed inexplicable before.

In dealing with many a case the Judiciary would also find the real originators to be quite different persons to those accused, and would first of all call such persons to account. The key to this lies in the connection between the individual and the world of thought-forms, which stands closest to humanity.

It is certainly a blessing for many that they are blindfolded and cannot see further than their physical eyes will permit, for the nature of the existing thought-forms would give them a fright.

Paralysing horror would grip many who today naively or frivolously lead unscrupulous lives. For *every thought that is generated,* like everything in the Ethereal World, immediately takes a form which embodies and expresses the essential meaning of the thought.

The Living Creative Power which flows through man collects ethereal substance through the volition of a completed thought and moulds it into a form which gives expression to the will of this thought. Thus this form is something real, something living, which now, in accordance with the Law of Attraction of Homogeneous Species, attracts what is homogeneous in this world of thought-forms or is attracted by them, depending on the strength it possesses.

Just as a thought when it arises is simultaneously *perceived intuitively,* with greater or lesser intensity, so its ethereal form will bear an equivalent *life.* This world of thoughts is densely populated. Through the mutual power of attraction complete centres have been formed which, by means of their accumulated energy, exercise a great influence upon human beings.

In the first place those persons will always be influenced who tend towards a similar nature, that is, who bear something similar within themselves. Such persons will thereby be strengthened in their corresponding will, and encouraged to continue producing new and similar forms which, working in the same manner, enter the world of thought-forms.

But also other people who do not possess these special tendencies can be bothered by these influences and gradually be attracted to them, if these centres are continually reinforced and so obtain unsuspected power. Only those are protected who possess other tendencies in greater strength, making a connection with what is dissimilar impossible.

Unfortunately, however, it is hate, envy, jealousy, lustfulness, avarice and all other evils which, through their greater numbers of adherents, form the strongest power centres in the world of thought-forms. Far less great are those of purity and love! This is the reason why evil is spreading with such uncanny rapidity. In addition these power centres of thought-forms in turn obtain a connection with analogous spheres of darkness. From there they are specially roused to ever greater activity so that as a consequence they are able to create downright devastation among mankind.

Therefore, blessed be the hour when thoughts of pure love will once more take a greater place among mankind, so that similarly strong centres will develop themselves in the world of thought-forms, which can be reinforced from the more luminous spheres and thus not only strengthen those striving towards what is good, but also slowly work on darker minds with a gradually purifying effect!

Yet another activity is to be observed in the Ethereal World. According to the wishes of their originator, thought-forms are sent out to certain persons to whom they may then cling.

If these thought-forms are of a pure and noble nature, they will beautify the person for whom they are meant, strengthen the shield of purity around him and, if they meet with inner intuitive perceptions of a similar nature, they can uplift him further and strengthen him for his ascent.

Impure thoughts, however, cannot fail to soil the person for whom they are meant in just the same way as a physical body is soiled if mud and dirt is thrown at it. If a man so attacked is not inwardly anchored firmly to the centres of light-streams, it may very well happen that in time his intuitive perception may become confused under this barrage of impure thoughts. This is possible because these impure thought-forms clinging to him are able to attract others of a like nature, which strengthen them so that by degrees they poison the thoughts of the person so encompassed.

The greater part of the responsibility naturally falls back upon the man who generated the impure thoughts and whose wish or desire sent them out to the person concerned, for the thought-forms also remain attached to their author and react upon him accordingly.

It is therefore necessary repeatedly to call out to all true seekers: "Give heed to the purity of your thoughts!" Put all your energy into this effort! You have no idea what you are thus doing; something stupendous lies in it! You can work with this like mighty warriors and pioneers for the Light, and thus liberate your fellow-men from the poisonous creepers that infest the world of thought-forms!

If now the bandage could be removed from the eyes of a man so that he could look into his immediate ethereal environment, he would at first be alarmed and terrified at the wild confusion he would see there. But this would only last until he realised the power within him, with which, as with a sharp sword, he can without effort clear a free passage merely by exerting his volition.

He would see thought-forms in a hundred thousand varieties in all possible and, to the physical eye, often impossible shapes. Each one, however, is sharply defined, showing and expressing what was the actual volition, unadorned and without artificial disguise, when the thought was generated.

Still, in spite of the thousands of varieties, one learns in time to recognise at a glance the nature of each thought-form, that is to say, one knows to which category they belong in spite of their different shapes. Just as one can distinguish a man from an animal by his face, or indeed recognise the different human races by certain facial characteristics, so in precisely the same way thought-forms have also quite marked expressions that clearly indicate whether the form belongs to hatred, envy, lust, or some other basic type.

Each of these fundamental types has its own particular stamp which has been impressed on each thought-form as the foundation of the characteristics embodied in it, no matter what outer shape each form has taken through the generating thought. Thus, in spite of the most grotesque distortion of a form, which may reach the most terrible deformity, one can immediately recognise to what fundamental type it belongs. Once this is recognised that which appears to be wild confusion no longer remains so.

One sees the inexorable order and strictness of the fundamental laws governing all Creation which, if one knows them and has adapted oneself to their course, afford unbounded protection and great blessing.

He, however, who opposes these laws will naturally be attacked and, if not utterly cast down and crushed, will at least undergo a severe grinding between the great millstones which, through pain and bitter experiences, will remodel him until he fits into the working of these laws and is no longer an obstacle. Only then can he be carried along upwards!

These thought-forms not only return their effects to humanity, but go further. For to the same Ethereal World belong the greater number of the elementals. He who has reconciled himself to the fact that all is alive and also has a form, whether physically visible or not, will not find it difficult to go a step further and realise that the elemental powers also have forms.

To these belong the gnomes, elves, sylphs, water-sprites, etc., the earth, air, fire and water elementals, which have been seen by many, but formerly more often than now. These are being influenced by the thought-forms so that also there much good or evil arises. And so it goes on! One thing gears into another like cogwheels in the finest and most highly-perfected mechanism.

In the midst of all this "machinery" stands man! He is equipped with the means to decide the nature of the weaving that shall proceed from the loom of Creation and to set the mechanism in motion in different directions.

Be conscious of this immeasurable responsibility, for it all takes place only within the circle of your earthly limits. By the wise ordinance of the Creator nothing goes beyond this, but falls back upon you yourselves. Through your wishes, your thinking and your volition you are able to poison this world and the beyond, or you may purify and uplift them towards the Light. Therefore direct your destiny so that it may lead upwards through the purity of your thoughts!

WATCH AND PRAY!

HOW OFTEN are these words of the Son of God quoted as well-meant advice and warning! But neither the giver of the advice nor the recipient take the trouble to reflect upon the real meaning of these words!

Every man knows what is meant by "praying", or rather he *thinks* he knows, although in truth he does *not* know. He also imagines that he knows what "to watch" means, but he is far from doing so!

"Watch and pray" is a figurative rendering of the admonition to keep the ability to perceive intuitively on the alert, i. e., to keep the spirit active! Spirit in its *true* sense, and not the activity of the brain, for the way the living human spirit expresses itself is only and solely through the *intuitive perception! In no other way* does the spirit of man, i. e., the original kernel which evolved into his true "ego" in the course of its wanderings through Subsequent Creation, become active.

"Watch and pray" is therefore nothing less than the demand to refine and strengthen man's ability to perceive intuitively, which is equivalent to vitalising the life of the spirit. The only eternal value man possesses is his spirit, which alone can return to the Paradise from which it issued. It *must* return there, either matured and self-conscious, or again in an unconscious state; either welcome to the Light as a living ego which has become useful in Creation, or as a dismembered and dead ego if it has proved itself useless.

The admonition to "Watch and pray" is therefore one of the most serious which the Son of God bequeathed to mankind. At the same time it is a grave warning to stand as useful beings in Creation, lest damnation inevitably follows through the automatic working of the Divine Laws.

Look at woman! She has, as the most precious gift of womanhood, a delicacy of intuitive perception which no other creature can attain. *For this reason* one should be able to speak only of *noble* womanhood in this Creation, because womanhood possesses within itself the strongest gifts towards the realisation of all that is good.

This, however, places the greatest of responsibilities upon woman. For *this* reason Lucifer, with all the host that belong to him, aimed primarily at woman in order thus to subjugate the whole Creation to his power.

Unfortunately Lucifer found only too superficial a basis in the woman of Subsequent Creation! With open eyes she flew into his meshes and, in her own way, poisoned the entire Subsequent Creation by changing pure concepts into distorted images, which inevitably brought confusion to all human spirits.

The pure flower of noble womanhood, the crown of this Subsequent Creation, debased itself under the influence of the tempter and soon became the poison plant which, with its glittering colours and seductive fragrance, attracts all to the spot where it flourishes, to the *swamp*, into the sultry softness of which the victims thus allured sink.

Woe unto woman! Because she did not make proper use of the highest of all values bestowed upon her, she will inevitably be the first upon whom the Sword of Divine Justice will fall, unless she decides to use the special mobility of her spiritual intuition, so peculiarly her own, to take the lead in the necessary ascent of mankind out of the ruins of such a faulty structure of perverted conceptions, which only arose through Lucifer's promptings!

Instead of setting the example of honestly striving for the white blossom of noble purity and adorning herself with it, she chose to indulge in coquetry and vanity, the playground of which is a wrongly cultivated social life.

Woman fully sensed that she was losing thereby the genuine ornament of womanhood, and grasped at the substitute offered to her by the Darkness. She sought to offer her physical charms for sale and became a shameless slave of fashion, as a result of which she sank still further into the abyss, dragging men along with her by stimulating their instincts, which inevitably hindered the unfolding of their spirits.

All those who thus failed and became rotten fruit in this Creation had planted within themselves the seed which now, in the necessary Judgment, must cause their destruction through the reciprocal action, because it made them incapable of withstanding the roaring and purifying storms!

Let no one soil his hands by helping the worshippers of the idol of vanity and coquetry if they stretch out their arms to be saved in their hour of need! Let them sink, push them away, they have no valuable qualities which could be used in the new building up that has been promised!

They do not see how absurd and hollow are their actions! They laugh at and ridicule the few who try to preserve for themselves the decency and purity of true womanhood, at those who did *not* permit the delicate feeling of shame, the most beautiful ornament of girl and woman, to be extinguished, but their mocking shall soon change to cries of dismay and thus be stifled!

It is as if the woman of Subsequent Creation is standing on the sharp edge of a knife, because of the great gifts bestowed upon her. She must now give an account of what she has done with them up to the present! There can be no excuse for her! It is impossible to turn and retrace her steps, for the time is up! They should all have thought of it before, and should have known that *their* opinion cannot oppose the adamantine Will of God, in which there is nothing but *Purity,* clear as crystal!

The woman of the future, however, who has been able to preserve herself and her values during the dissolute period of a modern Sodom and Gomorrah, together with those who will be newly born, will at last bring womanhood to that blossom where all who approach her do so in holy awe and *purest* veneration. She will be *the* woman who lives according to God's Will, that is, who *so* stands in Creation that she is like the radiant crown, which indeed she can and shall be, permeating everything with the vibrations she absorbs from the Luminous Heights and passing them on undimmed by virtue of her ability, which lies in the delicacy of the feminine intuitive perception.

The Son of God's words "Watch and pray" will be embodied in *every* woman of the future, as they should already be in every woman of today, *for in the vibrations of the feminine ability to perceive intuitively lies that perpetual watchfulness and most beautiful praying which are pleasing to God, providing she strives towards purity and the Light!*

Such a vibration brings the experience of heartfelt gratitude and joy, and *that* is prayer as it should be! At the same time the vibrations contain a constant warning to be on guard at all times, that is, *to watch!* For everything nasty that tries to approach, and every evil volition, is sensed by such delicately sensitive vibrations and is noticed before it can become a thought. Thus it is made easy for the woman *always* to protect herself in time, unless she herself *wants it otherwise!*

In spite of the fineness of these vibrations they hold a power which can remodel *everything* in Creation. There is nothing which could resist this power, for in it is Light and therefore Life!

This was well known to Lucifer! Therefore he mainly directed his attacks and temptations towards womanhood! He knew that *everything* would succumb to him if he succeeded in winning over woman. And unfortunately he succeeded only too well, as everybody who wishes to can clearly see today.

For this reason the Call from the Light is again addressed in the first place to woman! She *ought to be able* to recognise to what depths she has fallen! She ought to, if ... her vanity permitted it! But *this* snare of Lucifer holds all womanhood so fast bound that she can no longer recognise the Light, and even *no longer wishes to!* She no longer wishes to because modern woman cannot forgo her life of frivolous trifling, although she is vaguely aware of what she has lost through it. *Indeed she knows it only too well!* And to dull this warning intuitive perception, which is the equivalent of "knowing", she throws herself headlong and as if struck with blindness into the newest folly – *emulating man in his profession and in his whole being!*

Instead of returning to genuine womanhood, the most precious of possessions in all Creation, and thus to the task allotted to her by the Light!

It is *she* who robs man of all that is sublime and thereby prevents the flowering of noble manhood!

No nation and no people can flourish and prosper where the man is unable to look up to the woman in her womanliness!

Only genuine, purest womanhood can awaken and lead a man to great deeds! Nothing else! And *that* is the vocation of woman in Creation according to God's Will! Through this she uplifts her nation and all humanity, yes even the whole of Subsequent Creation, for in her gentle working alone lies that sublime power which is irresistible and compelling and, if of the purest volition, blessed by Divine Power. There is nothing to equal it, for she carries beauty in its purest form into everything she does and everything that proceeds from her!

That is why her weaving should permeate the whole Creation, refreshing, uplifting, furthering and animating, like a breath from the longed-for Paradise!

This was the pearl among the gifts of your Creator that Lucifer grasped at *first of all,* with all his cunning and malice, knowing that that was the best method with which to tear away your hold and your striving towards the Light! For in woman lies the precious secret that is able to set free the purity and sublimity of every thought, the inspiration to the greatest activity and noblest deeds – provided that she is the woman the Creator intended her to be when He lavished these gifts upon her.

You let yourselves be duped too easily! You succumbed to the temptations without a fight! As a willing slave of Lucifer woman now directs her beautiful Divine gifts to serve a contrary purpose, and thereby brings the entire Subsequent Creation under the domination of the Darkness.

Of everything that God wanted to come into existence for the joy and happiness of all creatures in this Creation, only repulsive caricatures are present! Of course everything did come into existence, but changed and distorted through the influence of Lucifer. Wrong!

The woman of Subsequent Creation made herself the mediator in this matter. A gruesome bog spread over the clear soil of purity, and radiant enthusiasm was replaced by sensual orgies! *Now* you are willing to fight, but against every demand of the Light, so that you can remain in that state of vain self-satisfaction which intoxicates you!

There are not many who today are capable of meeting a clear gaze steadfastly. The majority turn out to be leprous, whose beauty – true womanhood – has already been eaten away and can never be restored again. If after some years many who can still be saved recall all that they regard today as being beautiful and good, they will be disgusted with themselves. It will seem like awakening and recovery from the most terrible fever-dreams!

Just as woman was able to drag the whole Subsequent Creation down deeply, so also has she the power once more to uplift and further it, for man will follow her lead in this.

The time will come soon after the purification when one can joyously call out: "Look at woman as she should be, the *genuine* woman in all her greatness, her noblest purity and power!" Then you will experience through her the words of Christ, "Watch and pray", in all naturalness and in the most beautiful form!

MARRIAGE

MARRIAGES are made in heaven! These words are often uttered by married couples with resentment and bitterness. But they are also used hypocritically by those who are furthest removed from heaven! The natural consequence is that one has taken to shrugging one's shoulders, to smiling, mocking and even sneering at these words!

This is understandable when a person considers all the marriages with which he has become acquainted in his own and wider circles during the course of years. Those who mock are right! Only it would be better not to ridicule the saying but the marriages themselves! In the majority of cases *these* deserve not only ridicule and scorn, but even contempt!

Marriages as they are today, and as they have already been for centuries, have so discredited the truth of this saying as to prevent anyone from believing in it. Unfortunately, with but very few exceptions, they are distinctly immoral! They cannot be brought to an end quickly enough in order to save thousands from the disgrace into which they blindly run because of present-day habits! They imagine that it cannot be different because it is customary. Added to this, everything at the present time is shamelessly directed towards dimming and suffocating every purer intuitive perception. No one thinks of making the personality what it should, could and must be by also showing the necessary respect for the physical body.

The body, like the soul, must be regarded as something precious and therefore untouchable, something that should not be exhibited in order to entice! Thus in this particular respect also the body on earth is inseparable from the soul. Like the soul it must be equally respected and preserved as something inviolable, if it is to have any value at all! Otherwise it will become rubbish with which one soils oneself, deserving nothing better than to be thrown into a corner and picked up cheaply by the first passing hawker.

If today an army of such hawkers and second-hand dealers came swarming over the earth they would discover untold quantities of this rubbish. At every step they would find new heaps waiting to be added to their collection. And truly such hawkers and second-hand dealers are already wandering about in great numbers. They are envoys and tools of darkness, who greedily seize their cheap booty to drag it triumphantly down further and further into their dark realm, till they are all swallowed up in blackness and can never find their way back to the Light.

It is no wonder that everyone laughs when somebody seriously affirms that marriages are made in heaven!

Civil marriage is nothing but a sober business contract. Those who thus bind themselves do not do so in order seriously to tackle a joint task, which would raise the inner and outer value of the persons concerned, and also enable them to strive together for high aims, thereby becoming a blessing for themselves, for mankind and also for the whole Creation; but they regard it as a simple bargain ensuring each other's material security, so that mutual physical surrender may follow without any further cogitation.

The position of the woman in this matter is a degrading one. In eighty out of a hundred cases she hires or sells herself simply to serve her husband, who does not seek in her a companion of equal worth but, apart from showing her off, merely uses her as a cheap and willing housekeeper to make his home comfortable, with whom he can also indulge his sensual appetite undisturbed and under the cover of a false respectability.

Young girls often leave their parents to marry for the most trivial reasons. Sometimes they are tired of being at home and long for a sphere of action in which they have the say. Others think it would be fascinating to play the role of a young wife or hope to get more excitement out of life. They may also believe they can better their material position.

There are also cases where a young girl marries out of spite to annoy some other person. Marriage can also be entered into merely out of physical desires, which have been awakened and artificially nourished by reading bad literature, through wrong conversation and by playing around.

It is seldom the true love of the soul that urges them to take this most important step of their earth-lives. Aided and abetted by many parents, girls are supposedly "too clever" to allow themselves solely to be guided by their purer intuitions, and thus they rush all the more easily into unhappiness. Such persons will already pay in part for their superficiality in their married life. But only in part! The bitter experience of reciprocal action in consequence of such false marriages comes much later, for the main fault lies in irresponsibly neglecting the opportunity to advance.

Many an earth-life is thereby completely lost to the real *purpose* of personal existence. This may even bring serious retrogression which must be laboriously retrieved!

How different when a marriage has been contracted on the right foundation and develops harmoniously! Joyfully and voluntarily serving each other, the couple grows upward together towards spiritual ennoblement. Shoulder to shoulder they smilingly face all mundane trials. Such a marriage through its sheer happiness becomes a gain for their whole existence! And in this happiness lies a swinging upwards, not only for the individuals concerned, but for all humanity.

Therefore, woe unto those parents who drive their children into false marriages by persuasion, cunning, compulsion or subtle reasoning! The burden of responsibility, which extends further than that concerning the child only, will sooner or later fall back with such persistence upon them that they will wish never to have entertained such "brilliant ideas"!

The marriage ceremony in church is considered by many as only part of a purely mundane celebration. The churches themselves or their representatives use the words: "What God hath joined together, let not man put asunder!"

In religious cults the fundamental thought is that those contracting the marriage are through this act being united by God. "Advanced persons" give it the meaning that the couple is thus united *before* God. The latter interpretation is more justifiable than the former.

Such an explanation, however, is not intended by these words, which are meant to convey something entirely different! For they are based on the fact that marriages are really made in heaven.

When all false conceptions and interpretations are removed from these words, then every cause for laughter, ridicule or sneering will cease immediately. Their meaning will lie before us in all its seriousness and unalterable truth. The natural result will then be the realisation that marriages are meant and desired to be something entirely different from what they are today, that is, that marriage may only be entered upon under entirely different conditions, with entirely different views and convictions, and with absolutely pure motives.

"Marriages are made in heaven" indicates in the first place that already at birth every human being brings along certain qualities, the harmonious development of which can only be achieved through those with matching qualities. These matching qualities are not identical, however, but complementary to the others, and in completing each other they obtain their full value.

In this state of full value all the strings sound in a harmonious chord. If the one partner is complemented to full value by the other partner, then the latter will also receive full value through the former, and in their union, that is, in their living and working together, the harmonious chord will resound. *Such* is the marriage which has been made in heaven!

However, this does not mean that for each person there is only *one* other very special person on earth with whom he can enter upon a harmonious marriage, but there are generally *several* who possess the qualities to complete the other person.

It is therefore unnecessary to wander about the earth for decades to find this really suitable and complementary partner. It is only a question of exercising the necessary seriousness, keeping eyes, ears and heart open and, above all, giving up all those conditions which have so far been demanded for a marriage. Just what is regarded as important today shall *not* be!

Working together and having the same high aims are as necessary for a *sound* marriage as exercise and fresh air are indispensable for a healthy body. Whoever counts on having comfort and the greatest possible freedom from cares, and tries to build up a mutual life on this, will in the end only harvest something unhealthy, with all its accompanying consequences. Therefore seek at last to contract marriages that are made in heaven! Then happiness will be yours!

"Made in heaven" signifies that the two people were already destined for each other before or upon entering this earth-life. This "being destined" for each other, however, depends only on the qualities that each brought along, with which the two complement each other. Such persons are thereby meant for each other!

You could just as well express "destined for each other" by "suited for each other", thus really complementing each other. In this lies the predestination.

"What God hath joined together, let not man put asunder!"

282

Much harm has already been caused by a misunderstanding of these words of Christ. Up till now many imagined that "what God hath joined" referred to the marriage. But this, however, had so far nothing to do with the meaning of the words. That which God has joined is a union where the conditions required for complete harmony are fulfilled, and it is thus made in heaven. Whether or not the permission of the State and the Church has been given for this union makes no essential difference.

It is, of course, also necessary to observe civil laws. If, then, with such a bond, a wedding takes place according to a prevailing religious cult and with appropriate devoutness, it is quite natural that, through the inner attitude of those concerned, the union will receive a much higher consecration, which will bring a real and strong spiritual blessing to the couple. Such a marriage is then really united *by* God and *before* God, and is made in heaven!

And now follows the warning: "Let not man put asunder!" To what insignificance has the high meaning of *these* words also been reduced!

Yet the truth is clearly evident! Wherever one finds a union that is made in heaven, that is where two people so complement each other that a full and harmonious chord results, there no third person shall attempt to bring about a separation. Whether it be to create discord, to make a union impossible, or to cause a separation, whatever the case, such an attempt would be a sin! It would be an injustice which in its reciprocal action must cling heavily to its originator, since two persons would be simultaneously affected by it, together with the blessing which through their happiness would have spread throughout the Gross Material and Ethereal Worlds.

The simple truth that lies in these words is evident to all. The warning is intended to protect only such unions as have been made in heaven under the aforesaid conditions, which is confirmed by the fact that they brought along with them the necessary psychic qualities to complement each other.

No third person should intervene between two such souls, not even the parents! It will never occur to the two partners to wish for a separation. The divine harmony which is based on their mutual psychic qualities does not permit such a thought to arise. The happiness and permanence of their marriage is consequently assured from the start.

If a divorce is proposed by one of the marriage partners it is the best proof that the necessary harmony is *not* the basis of the marriage, and therefore that it cannot have been made in heaven. In such cases the marriage should be definitely ended in order to reinstate the moral self-respect of the couple living in such an unsound state.

Such wrong marriages now form the great majority. The cause of this evil lies primarily in the moral retrogression of mankind, as well as in the prevailing worship of the intellect.

Parting those whom God joined together applies not only to the marriage, but also to the period which precedes it, the time of approach of the two souls who, through their complementing qualities, can only develop harmony and are thus destined for each other. If they enter into such a union and a third party tries to intervene by slandering or by similar well-known means, then this intention is already absolute adultery.

The meaning of the words: "What God hath joined together, let not man put asunder!" is so simple and clear that it is hard to understand how they could be so erroneously interpreted. This was only possible by wrongly separating the Spiritual World from the Material World. This resulted in a narrow intellectual conception becoming prominent, which has never yet produced anything of real value.

These words issued from the Spiritual World and it is only in the spiritual sense that they can be truly interpreted.

THE CLAIM OF CHILDREN ON THEIR PARENTS

MANY children live under an unfortunate delusion in regard to their parents, which will do them great harm. They believe they can charge their parents with being the cause of their existence on earth. One often hears the remark: "Of course my parents must take care of me, for they brought me into the world. It is not my fault that I am here!"

Nothing more foolish could be said! Every person is here on earth either at his own request or because of his own fault. The parents merely provide the possibility for an incarnation, and nothing else. And every incarnated soul must be grateful for the opportunity offered!

The *soul* of the child is only the *guest* of its parents. This fact alone gives sufficient explanation to enable one to know that in reality a child can claim no rights in regard to its parents! It has no spiritual claim on its parents! Earthly rights, however, have arisen solely out of a purely mundane social order, brought about by the State so that it need not take any obligations upon itself.

Spiritually the child is a complete personality in itself. Apart from its physical body, which it needs as a tool for its activity on this gross material plane, it has received nothing from its parents – only a dwelling which the already independent soul can make use of.

Still, through procreation the parents assume the obligation to care for the dwelling place they have thus created, and to maintain it until the soul which has taken possession of it is itself capable of undertaking its maintenance. The natural development of the body will indicate when the moment for this has come. Whatever is done beyond this is a gift from the parents.

Therefore children should finally cease to rely upon their parents, and would do better to think of standing upon their own feet as soon as possible.

In that respect it is really immaterial whether the child works in the home of its parents or elsewhere. But it must be an activity other than mere pleasures and the fulfilment of so-called social duties. It must definitely be a really useful duty, such as would have to be performed by some person specially engaged if the child no longer did it. Only in this way can one speak of a useful life on earth, which brings about the maturing of the spirit.

If a child, male or female, fulfils such a task in the parental home, then the parents should give it the *same* wage as they would have to pay a stranger engaged for the purpose. In other words, the child must be regarded and treated as a really independent human being while fulfilling its duty!

If the parents and children are linked by special bonds of love, confidence and friendship, it is so much the nicer for both, for then it is a voluntary tie born of inner conviction, and therefore all the more precious. Then it is genuine, and the bond will endure into the beyond for their mutual advancement and joy.

But when children have reached a certain age, it is unsound and objectionable that they should continue subject to family customs and servitude.

Naturally there should also be none of the so-called claims of kinship on which particularly aunts, uncles, cousins, and whoever else tries to come within the category of a relative, so often depend. It is exactly these claims of kinship which are an objectionable abuse, and which must always disgust a person who is free and independent.

Unfortunately tradition has caused this sort of thing to become such a habit that a person usually does not bother to think differently, but quietly submits to it, even though with aversion! But he who ventures to take the small step of thinking it over freely will, from the bottom of his soul, find it all so ridiculous and repulsive that he will indignantly turn away from such presumption.

Such an unnatural state of affairs must be cleared up! As soon as a new and healthy race of men awakens inwardly, then this type of abuse will definitely be tolerated no longer because it is contrary to every sound sense.

Anything really great could never arise out of such artificial distortions of natural life, because on account of this human beings remain far too bound. A terrible bondage arises out of these apparently minor matters!

It is *here* that the individual must begin to free himself by breaking away from these unworthy customs! True liberty lies only in the proper *recognition* of duties, to which their voluntary *fulfilment* is linked. *Rights* are only obtained by the fulfilment of duties. This also applies to children who can only claim rights if they loyally perform their duties.

There is, however, a long list of the strictest duties incumbent upon all parents, which have nothing to do with the rights of the children.

Every adult must be aware of what procreation really involves. The frivolity, thoughtlessness and wrong views hitherto existing in this respect wreak a terrible vengeance.

You must know and understand that there are in the immediate beyond a great number of souls standing ready and awaiting the opportunity to reincarnate on earth. They are mostly human souls bound by threads of karma, which they are seeking to redeem in a new earth-life.

As soon as the possibility is presented, they attach themselves to where an act of procreation has taken place in order to await and follow up the growth of the new human body as a prospective dwelling. During this waiting period ethereal threads are spun from the young body to the soul – which keeps itself persistently in the immediate vicinity of the prospective mother – and from the soul to the young body. At a particular stage of maturity these threads serve as the bridge which permits the alien soul from the beyond to enter the young body and immediately take full possession.

Thereby a strange guest moves in whose karma can cause its educators many worries. A strange guest! What an uncomfortable thought! Everyone should always bear this in mind and never forget that he *also* can have a say in the choice between the waiting souls, if he does not carelessly waste his time.

The incarnation is certainly subject to the Law of Attraction of Homogeneous Species. However, it is not absolutely necessary that one of the procreators should serve as the homogeneous pole; sometimes it may be a person who is often near the prospective mother.

Many an evil can be averted as soon as mankind really understand the whole process and consciously concern themselves with it. As it is they frivolously trifle their time away, attending games and dances, giving parties, and paying little attention to the important event which is being prepared during this period, and which later on will forcefully intervene in their whole lives.

Through prayer which is always based on fervent wishes, they should consciously take a guiding hand in these matters, thus lessening the evil and strengthening the good, so that the strange guest who then comes to them as a child would remain *welcome* to them in *every* way. Much nonsense is talked in the usual manner about pre-natal education – a misunderstanding or half understanding of certain outwardly observable effects.

As often happens the conclusions drawn by men from such observations are wrong. There is no possibility of pre-natal education, but instead there is a definite possibility of *influencing the attraction*, if it is done at the right time and with the appropriate seriousness! This is a difference, the consequences of which reach further than any pre-natal education could ever accomplish.

If this has become clear and people still carelessly and thoughtlessly enter into a union, they deserve nothing better than that a human spirit should penetrate into their circle with the risk of bringing only disquietude, if not evil.

For spiritually free human beings procreation should be nothing but the proof of their willingness to take a strange human spirit into the family as a permanent guest, offering it the opportunity on earth to atone and to mature! Only when both sides have the fervent wish *to achieve this purpose* should the opportunity for procreation be sought!

If you now take into account only these facts as regards parents and children much will automatically change. Their treatment of one another, their education and everything will rest upon a different and more serious foundation than has up till now been customary in many families. There will be more consideration and respect shown towards one another. The consciousness of independence and the striving for responsibility will make itself felt, resulting in a natural social advance for the nation.

The children, however, will soon learn to desist from claiming rights which never existed.

PRAYER

IF PRAYER is to be spoken of at all, then the following words are naturally only meant for those who concern themselves with prayer.

He who does not feel the inner urge to pray may well refrain from doing so, for his words or his thoughts would inevitably dissolve into nothingness. If prayer is not felt deeply within, through and through, it has no value, and therefore will have no effect.

The best foundation for a prayer which may be expected to have effect lies in those moments of spontaneous thankfulness arising out of great happiness or of deepest pain resulting from heartfelt grief. In such moments a person is filled with one particular intuitive perception which dominates all else. This enables the main wish of the prayer, be it gratitude or a request, to receive undimmed power.

People often have a wrong picture of how a prayer comes into existence, what happens to it, and how it further develops. Not every prayer penetrates to the Highest Ruler of the Universe. On the contrary, it is a very rare exception when a prayer is actually able to ascend to the steps of His Throne. Here also the basic Law of the Power of Attraction of Homogeneous Species plays the principal role.

A prayer which is seriously and deeply felt will be attracted to and itself attract those of similar nature, and come into contact with a power-centre of a kind identical to the main theme of the prayer. These power-centres can also be called sections of the spheres or something similar – basically it all amounts to the same!

The main wish of the prayer will become effective through reciprocal action. It will either bring calmness, strength, recovery, plans suddenly arising in the mind, the solution to difficult problems, or other things. Something good will always come of it, be it only increased composure and balance of mind, which will in turn lead to a solution and some way out of the difficulty.

It is also possible that the prayers sent out, having received increased power through the reciprocal action of homogeneous power-centres, will find an ethereal path to people who, being stimulated through this, will in some way bring help and thus fulfilment of the prayer.

All these happenings will be easily understood by observing ethereal life. Here again justice lies in the fact that it is always the inner quality of the one who prays which is decisive. The fervour with which he prays determines the power, i.e. the vitality and effectiveness of the prayer.

In the great ethereal happenings in the cosmos each variety of intuitive perception finds the homogeneous species to which it belongs, because not only could it not be attracted by others, but it would even be repelled. Only when meeting its similar kind does a connection take place with a consequent increase in strength.

A prayer embodying various intuitive perceptions, which still contain a certain measure of strength through the deep absorption of the one praying, will, in spite of its unconnected parts, thereby attract different things, and will also return different kinds of reciprocal effects.

Whether this results in any kind of fulfilment will depend entirely on the nature of the separate parts, which can either foster or hinder each other. However, in every case when praying it is better to send out only *one* thought as an intuitive perception in order to prevent confusion.

Nor did Christ intend the Lord's Prayer to be prayed all at once, but in it He summarised *that* for which a person with an earnest volition may in the first instance ask with the certainty of being heard.

These petitions contain the foundation for *everything* which man needs for his physical well-being and spiritual ascent. They even give much more! They also indicate the *lines* which man should strive to follow during his life on earth. The composition of the petitions is a masterpiece in itself.

The Lord's Prayer alone provides *everything* for the seeker if he penetrates into it deeply and grasps it aright. He would need nothing more than the Lord's Prayer! It shows him the whole gospel in concentrated form. It is the key to the Luminous Heights for him who knows how to experience it rightly. It can be both a *staff* and a *torch* for the advance and ascent of everyone! What it contains is absolutely immeasurable!*

* Lecture: "The Lord's Prayer".

The real purpose of the Lord's Prayer is evident in the wealth of its contents. In the Lord's Prayer *Jesus* gave humanity *the key to the Kingdom of God! It is the very essence of His Message!* But He did not intend that it should be rattled straight off!

Man needs only to take note when he is praying to realise how often his attention wanders and how much the depth of his intuitive perception is weakened by repeating the separate petitions one after the other, even when he knows them fluently. It is impossible for him to pass from one petition to the other with the fervour necessary to a genuine prayer!

In His own way Jesus made everything easy for mankind. The right expression would be "easy enough for a child to understand"! Jesus particularly observed: "Become as little children!" That is, think as simply and look for difficulties as little as they do! He would never have expected anything so impossible from mankind as to pray the Lord's Prayer, with the deep concentration it requires, straight through.

This should also convince humanity that Jesus wanted something different, something greater. He gave humanity the key to the Kingdom of God, and not merely a prayer!

It always weakens a prayer to make it manifold. Neither does a child come to its father with seven requests at a time, but only with that which is nearest to its heart, whether a grief or a wish.

This is the way in which man in his distress should also approach his God with a petition about that which oppresses him. In most cases it will be just *one* particular matter, not many at once! Man should not pray for something that does not really bother him. Since such a prayer cannot come to life deep within his intuition, it becomes an empty form and quite naturally weakens some other and perhaps really necessary request.

Therefore man should only pray for what is really necessary! All empty phrases should be avoided, as they are bound to fall to pieces and in time must foster hypocrisy!

Prayer requires profound earnestness. Pray in quietness and purity, so that the power of the intuitive perception will be increased through quietness and receive through purity that luminous lightness which will enable the prayer to be carried upward to the heights of all that is light and pure! Then the supplicant will receive that fulfilment which will be most beneficial for him and really advance him in his whole being!

The *power* of a prayer is *not* able to impel or force it upward; *only purity* with its corresponding lightness can do so. As soon as the urge to ask becomes alive within him, every person can achieve purity in prayer, although perhaps not in all prayers. It is not necessary for his whole life already to be based on purity, but while praying he will now and then be able at least to uplift himself for a few seconds in the purity of his intuitive perception.

Not only do the peace of seclusion and the deeper concentration made possible thereby help to strengthen the power of a prayer, but also every strong emotional feeling, such as fear, anxiety or joy.

This does not mean that the fulfilment of a prayer will necessarily always correspond to and harmonise with man's *earthly* ideas and wishes. The fulfilment, in his best interests, reaches out far beyond these, leading towards what is best *for the whole,* not just for the earthly moment. If the prayer does not appear to be fulfilled this will be recognised later as the only right and best fulfilment, and the person will then be happy that things did not go according to his wish of the moment.

Now for the question of intercession! People often wonder how the reciprocal effect of a prayer of intercession, i. e. a petition for someone else, can find its way to a person who has not himself prayed, since the reaction must flow back to the petitioner along the way he has paved for it.

Here also there is no deviation from the firmly established laws. During a prayer the interceder thinks so intensively of the one for whom he is praying that his wishes are thereby first *anchored* or tied firmly to the person, and then start in their upward course from there. They can thus return to the other person, since the strong wishes of the petitioner have already become alive and circle around him. The one indispensable condition, however, is that the soil within the person being prayed for is receptive and, being of a like nature, offers an anchorage and puts no obstacle in the way.

If the soil is not receptive, thus unworthy, the fact that the intercessory prayer glances off reveals once more the wonderful justice of the Divine Laws, which cannot permit that help from outside through another person should fall on stony ground. This repulsing or glancing off of an intercession seeking anchorage in the person being prayed for, whose inner state has proved him unworthy, makes it impossible for help to come to him.

Here again we find something so perfect in this automatic and natural activity that man stands amazed before the unwavering and just distribution of the fruits of what men themselves willed!

Intercessions by people who have no definite inner urge from their intuitive perception have neither value nor success. They are as chaff before the wind!

There is still another way in which genuine intercession can take effect. That is when it acts as a signpost! The prayer immediately rises upwards and points to the one needing help. If now, in view of the way shown to him, a spiritual messenger is sent to give aid, the possibility of help reaching the person in need is subject to the same laws of worthiness or unworthiness, thus whether he is open to it or will repulse it.

If the person needing help has an inward leaning towards darkness, the messenger sent to help him in answer to the prayer cannot get in touch with or influence him, and must return without having accomplished anything. Thus the intercession could not be fulfilled because the living laws did not permit it.

But if the soil is suitable then a genuine intercession is of immeasurable value! Either it brings help without the person in need knowing it, or it unites with the wish or prayer of the person in need, thus giving him greatly increased strength.

THERE are but few people who try to realise *what* they actually want when they say the Lord's Prayer. Still fewer are those who really know the *meaning* of the sentences which they "rattle off". To rattle off is about the only right expression for what in this instance men call praying.

He who unsparingly examines himself in this respect *must* admit this, otherwise he only proves that his whole life is spent on a similar basis, i. e., a superficial one, and that he is not capable of deep thinking, nor ever was! There are more than enough of such people on this earth who take themselves seriously but who, with the best will in the world, cannot be taken seriously by others.

Ever since the earliest days the beginning of this prayer in particular has been wrongly perceived intuitively, although in different ways. When saying the introductory words, or shortly thereafter, a certain sense of safety, of psychic calm, is felt by those who try to utter this prayer earnestly and thus with a good volition. This feeling predominates for several seconds after saying the prayer.

This explains two things! In the first place the one who is praying can only maintain his earnestness during the first words which arouse this feeling; and secondly, that the feeling thus aroused proves how far removed he is from grasping what he is saying with these words.

This shows plainly either his inability to carry on any deep thinking or his superficiality. Otherwise the succeeding words, as soon as they really come to life within him, should immediately arouse a *different* feeling, corresponding to the different meaning of the words.

Thus he only retains what the first words awake in him. But had he grasped the right sense and true meaning of those words, they should have aroused a quite different feeling to that of being comfortably sheltered.

Again those people who are more arrogant see in the word "Father" the confirmation that they are directly descended from God, and that therefore with the right development they will themselves ultimately become divine, since already now they definitely possess something of the divine within them! Many such errors concerning this sentence exist among men!

Most people, however, consider it as simply the form of *address* in the prayer, the invocation! This requires the least effort in thinking! And accordingly the prayer is uttered thoughtlessly, despite the fact that the invocation to God should carry the greatest fervour of which man's soul can ever become capable.

But this first sentence is not meant either to convey or to be an invocation! By His choice of words the Son of God at the same time explained or indicated *the way in which a human soul* should set about praying; *how* it may and indeed must approach its God if the prayer is to be heard. He tells exactly what quality the soul must possess at that moment, and in what condition the pure intuitive perception must be if the soul wants to lay its petition before the steps of God's Throne.

Thus the prayer is divided into three parts. In the first part the soul approaches and surrenders itself completely to God. Figuratively speaking the soul unfolds itself before Him and thus gives testimony to its pure volition ere it brings forth its request.

Here the Son of God wants to make clear which intuitive perception alone may form the basis for approaching God! Therefore the words: "*Our Father Who art in Heaven!*", with which the prayer starts, come as a great sacred vow.

Bear in mind that a prayer is not synonymous with a request! Otherwise there would be no prayer of thanksgiving, which contains no request! To pray does not mean to beg! In this respect the Lord's Prayer has so far always been misconstrued because of man's evil habit of never approaching God without at the same time expecting or even demanding something from Him. For every expectation contains a demand! Actually man *always* expects something when praying! This he cannot deny! It may be, generally speaking, merely a vague feeling within himself of one day securing a place in heaven!

Man does not know what it is to give jubilant thanks while happily enjoying the conscious life granted to him; while co-operating in the great Creation in the way God wants, and justly expects of him, for the benefit of his environment! He does not even suspect that just in this and *only* in this lies his real welfare, as well as his advance and ascent!

It is on such a basis, according to God's Will, that the Lord's Prayer really stands! The Son of God, Who only desired man's welfare, which entirely depends on the proper observance and fulfilment of the Will of God, could not have worded it in any other way!

Thus the prayer He gave is anything but a begging petition. It is a great, all-embracing vow in which man lays himself at the feet of his God! Jesus gave it to His disciples who, at that time, were willing to live in the pure worship of God, to serve God through their life in Creation, and by this service to honour His Holy Will.

Man should think over carefully whether he may dare to make use of and utter this prayer at all, and should examine himself earnestly as to whether, in using it, he is not trying to deceive his God!

The introductory sentences admonish each one plainly enough to examine himself as to whether he really is what he professes to be in this prayer; and whether he thereby dares to approach God's Throne without guile!

But if you experience the first three sentences of the prayer within you, then they will lead you to the steps of God's Throne. *They are the way thereto* if they become a living experience in the soul! No other way but this way leads there! If these sentences are not experienced, however, none of your petitions can reach there.

When you dare to say: "Our Father, Who art in Heaven!" it shall be a devout but at the same time joyful outcry!

This outcry voices your sincere affirmation: "To Thee, O God, I give all a father's rights over me and wish to submit humbly to them like a child! With this I also acknowledge Thy Omniscience, O God, in everything that Thou hast ordained! I beg Thee to treat me as a father has to treat his children! I am here, Lord, to listen to Thee and to obey Thee like a child!"

The second sentence: *"Hallowed be Thy Name!"*

This contains the assurance of the worshipping soul as to how seriously it takes everything it dares to say to God, that the full intuitive perception controls its every word and thought, and that it does not misuse God's Name through superficiality, because it regards the Name of God as being too holy to do so!

Bear in mind, you who pray, what you are vowing with this! If you want to be absolutely honest with yourselves you must confess that so far it is precisely in this that you have lied in the face of God; for you were never *so* earnest in your praying as the Son of God made *conditional* in these words!

The third sentence: *"Thy Kingdom come!"* is again no petition, but another vow, a vow in which a human soul declares it is prepared to make life here on earth *such* as it is in the Kingdom of God!

Hence the expression: *"Thy* Kingdom come!" That means we will also develop so far on earth that Thy perfect Kingdom may be established down here! We shall so prepare the soil that everything lives only according to Thy Holy Will, thus completely fulfilling Thy Laws in Creation. Then it will become *as it is* in Thy Kingdom, the Spiritual Realm, where the matured spirits who are freed from all guilt and burdens live only to serve God's Will. Since Thy Will is perfect, good can only come from unconditional obedience to It. Thus, it is man's assurance that he wishes to develop *in such a way* that the earth will also through the human soul become a kingdom where God's Will is fulfilled!

This assurance is strengthened to an even greater extent through the next sentence: *"Thy Will be done on earth as It is in Heaven!"*

This is not only the declaration of willingness to conform entirely to the Divine Will, but it also promises that man will concern himself about this Will and strive ardently to recognise It. Of course this striving must precede the effort to conform to God's Will, for as long as man does not really know this Will he is not able to adjust himself to It in his intuitive perception, his thoughts, words and deeds!

What appalling, punishable carelessness everyone shows by continually repeating these assurances to his God, when in reality he never troubles to find out what is His Will, firmly anchored as It is in Creation! Man utters a lie with every word when he dares to say this prayer! He stands before his God as a hypocrite! He keeps on adding new sins to the old ones, and when he breaks down ethereally, as he must under this burden in the beyond, he even feels he ought to be pitied.

It is only when a soul has really fulfilled the preliminary condition imposed by these sentences that it can go on to say:

"Give us this day our daily bread!"

This means to say: "When I have fulfilled what I promised, let Thy Blessing rest upon my earthly work so that, in attending to my physical needs, I may always retain the time to live according to Thy Will!"

"And forgive us our trespasses as we forgive them that trespass against us!"

In this sentence lies the knowledge of the incorruptible and just reciprocal action of the spiritual laws ordained by the Will of God. At the same time it expresses the assurance of complete confidence therein. For the plea for forgiveness or redemption from guilt is *conditional* upon the petitioner having *previously* forgiven all the wrongs inflicted upon him by his fellow-men.

He who is capable of *that*, i. e., who has already forgiven his fellow-men everything, is *so* inwardly purified that he will never *intentionally* do wrong! He is then free of all guilt before God, for with God only that is considered wrong which is done with *evil desire and intention.* It is only that which makes it wrong! This is very different to all the human laws and opinions current in the world today.

The basis of this sentence again contains a promise to its God by each soul striving towards the Light. It proclaims the true volition which the soul hopes to receive strength to fulfil through deep concentration and self-clarification in the prayer. With the right attitude this power will be given to the soul according to the Law of Reciprocal Action.

"And lead us not into temptation!"

Man has a wrong conception when he tries to interpret these words as if God would tempt him. God tempts no one! In this case, owing to a doubtful transmission, the unfortunate choice of the word "temptation" was made. The right meaning would include such concepts as erring, going astray and thus going wrong, and seeking the Light on the wrong path.

It means: "Let us not take the wrong road, nor seek in the wrong direction! Let us not lose, waste nor fritter away time in such seeking! But if necessary restrain us *forcibly* from doing so, even if we need to be stricken with sorrow and pain!"

Man should have grasped this meaning from the words of the next sentence, which according to its contents evidently belong to it:

"But deliver us from evil!"

This "but" shows clearly enough that the sentences are connected. The meaning is similar to: "Let us recognise evil at whatever cost, even at the cost of suffering! Let every error we commit help us to do so through Thy reciprocal actions!" For in the recognition of evil lies the redemption for those who show goodwill!

With this, man's converse with God, the second part of the prayer ends. The third part completes it:

"For Thine is the Kingdom, the Power and the Glory, for ever and ever, Amen!"

When the soul has laid all it pledged in the prayer at the feet of its God, these last words come as a jubilant avowal of feeling protected by His Omnipotence.

Thus the prayer given by the Son of God has two parts – the introduction or approach to God and the converse with God. Through Luther there was finally added the jubilant confession of the realisation of the help available for everything in the second part of the prayer, and of the strength received to fulfil what the soul vowed to God. And this fulfilment *must* then carry the soul upward into the Kingdom of God, to the region of Eternal Joy and Light!

And so the Lord's Prayer, if it is truly experienced, becomes the support and the staff for ascent into the Spiritual Realm!

Man should not forget that when praying he need only obtain the strength to enable him *to bring into being himself* what he is praying for! That is how he should pray! That is how the prayer which the Son of God gave to His disciples is meant!

IT CAN safely be stated that man has never yet understood, much less practised, the worship of God, which should be absolutely natural to him.

Just consider for a moment how the worship of God has been carried on so far! Man only knows how to plead, or still better said, how to beg! Only now and then does it happen that prayers of thanksgiving ascend which really come from the heart. However, that is a great exception and occurs only when a person *unexpectedly* receives a very special gift or when he is *suddenly* rescued from a great danger. Unexpectedness and suddenness are necessary before he will arouse himself to utter a prayer of thanks.

The most tremendous things may fall undeserved into his lap, but so long as this happens in a quiet and normal way, it would never occur to him, or only very seldom, to think of offering thanks.

If he and all his loved ones are always blessed with good health, and if he has no material cares, he will hardly bring himself to utter an earnest prayer of thanksgiving.

In order to arouse a stronger emotion within himself man unfortunately needs a very *special* incentive. When all is well with him he will never bestir himself of his own free will. He may perhaps talk about it now and then or go to church in order to murmur a prayer of thanks, but it will never occur to him to put his whole soul into it, not even for a single minute!

Only if real misfortune befalls him will he *then* very quickly remember that there is One Who is able to *help* him. Fear finally drives him to stammer a prayer for once! However, even then it is always merely begging, and never worshipping!

Such is the man who still thinks he is *good* and calls himself a believer! But there are few enough of them on earth and even they are laudable exceptions!

Just ponder over this deplorable state of affairs! After careful consideration how does it strike you as human beings? Then how much more despicable must such a person appear in the eyes of his God! Yet unfortunately this is reality! Turn and twist as you will, these facts remain when you trouble to investigate closely and without trying to make excuses. It must leave you somewhat depressed, for neither begging nor thanksgiving belong to worship!

Worship means *reverence!* But this is really not to be found anywhere on earth! Just look at the festivals or celebrations which are intended to honour God and in which, as an exception, begging and pleading are for once left out! There are oratorios! Pick out the singers who worship God with their singing! Observe them as they prepare themselves in the concert hall or church! They all want to achieve something that will please the *people.* In this respect God is a matter of indifference to them! Just He in Whose honour it is supposed to be given! Look at the conductor! He invites applause – he wants to show the people what he can do!

Then go further! Look at the proud buildings, the churches and cathedrals, which are supposed to have been raised in honour of God! The artist, the architect and the builder only strive for earthly acknowledgement. Every city *shows off* these buildings – for its own renown! They must even serve to attract strangers, not indeed for the purpose of worshipping God, but so that their money shall flow into the town through increased business! Wherever you look it is nothing but a craving for earthly externals! And all this under the pretext of worshipping God!

Here and there one may still find a person whose soul will unfold in the forest or on the mountain heights, and who may even give a fleeting thought to the greatness of the Creator of all the beauty around him, but a Creator pushed into the far distant background. His soul unfolds, but not to take jubilant flight upwards – it really expands in a luxurious feeling of enjoyment!

This may not be mistaken for soaring upwards! It really has no other value than the pleasure a glutton derives from a richly-laden table! Such an expansion of the soul is erroneously taken for worship; but it remains a shallow ecstasy, a *personal* feeling of well-being, which is mistakenly sensed as gratitude to the Creator. But it is merely an earthly happening! There are also many nature enthusiasts who take their ecstasy to be genuine worship of God. They also imagine that they are far superior to those who have no possibilility of enjoying the scenic beauties of the earth. It is a crude, pharasaical view, having its origin only in a personal feeling of well-being – sham gold, utterly worthless!

301

When the time comes for such people to seek in their souls for the treasures which can be used for their ascent, they will find their inner shrine completely empty, for what they imagined to be a treasure was only ecstasy at the sight of beauty, nothing else! Genuine veneration for their Creator was lacking!

The real worship of God does not show itself in ecstasy, in murmuring prayers, in begging, kneeling, and wringing one's hands, nor in blissful shuddering – but in joyful *activity!* In the jubilant acceptance of life on earth! In the thorough enjoyment of every moment! This means to make full use of it, which in turn means – to experience! Not, however, in gambling and dancing or wasting time, which are harmful to body and soul, and which the intellect seeks and needs as a balance and stimulant to its activity, but in looking upwards to the Light and *Its* Will, which alone furthers, uplifts, and ennobles *all* that exists in Creation!

The fundamental condition for this, however, is the exact knowledge of the Divine Laws in Creation. These show man how he must live if he wishes to be healthy in body and soul; they point with precision to the path leading upwards to the Spiritual Realm. But they also enable him to recognise clearly the horrors he will have to face if he opposes these laws!

As the inexorable and adamantine Laws in Creation operate vitally and automatically, with a power against which human spirits are entirely helpless, it stands to reason that the most urgent need of every human being must be the *thorough recognition* of these laws, to the effects of which he remains absolutely defenceless in every respect.

And yet men are so narrow-minded that they heedlessly try to overlook this clear and simple necessity, although there is nothing of greater importance to them! It is well-known that mankind never hits on the *simplest* thoughts! In this, strangely enough, every animal is wiser than man. It adapts itself to Creation and is furthered therein as long as man does not seek to hinder it.

Man, however, wants to be master over something to which, with its independent activity, he is and will always remain subject. No sooner has he learned to turn to his profit minute fractions of certain radiations, or learned to apply in some small way the effects of air, water, and fire, than he thinks in his conceit that he is already *master over* these forces! But he does not consider that before he can make his relatively minor applications he *first has to learn* and observe how to make complete use of the already existing conditions or

302

forces, according to *their specific nature.* He must try to adapt himself if he wishes for success! *He* is the one who must do so!

This is not ruling or conquering, but submitting and adapting himself to the existing laws.

Through this man should at last realise that only by adapting himself can he learn and receive any benefit! With this in mind he should gratefully go forward! But no! Instead he gives himself airs and acts even more arrogantly than ever! And in those particular instances where for once he bows to and serves the Divine Will in Creation, thereby immediately receiving visible benefits, he childishly tries to pose as conqueror, a subduer of nature!

This senseless attitude is the climax of stupidity, as a result of which he blindly overlooks that which is really great. For if he had the right attitude he would actually be a conqueror – over himself and his vanity! Because he would see on sober examination that in all his notable achievements he had previously bowed to and studied what already existed! This alone will bring him success!

Every inventor and everyone achieving something really great have adapted their thinking and volition to the existing Laws of Nature. Whatever resists or even wishes to oppose these laws will be smothered, crushed and shattered. It could never really come to life!

As it is with minor experiences, so also with man's whole existence, and with man himself!

Man, who not only has to live the short span on earth but also wander through the whole Creation, must of necessity possess the knowledge of the laws to which the *whole Creation,* and not merely the nearest visible environment of man, remains subject. If he does not possess this knowledge he will be hampered, delayed, hurt, thrown back or even crushed, because in his ignorance he could not go along *with* the power-currents of the laws, but fitted himself into them so wrongly that they had to press him down instead of lifting him up.

A human spirit who stubbornly and blindly tries to reject facts, the effects of which he *must* daily recognise everywhere, does not appear great or admirable but rather ridiculous if he makes fundamental use of them for his activity and for every kind of technical work, yet not for himself and his soul. In his earthly life and activity the spirit *always* has the opportunity to observe the absolute steadiness and uniformity of all the basic effects of the laws, providing he does not thoughtlessly or even hostilely close himself to them and remain asleep.

In this respect there is no exception in all Creation, not even for a human soul! It *must* submit to the Laws of Creation if their activity is to further its progress! In the most superficial way men have up till now completely overlooked this simple self-evident fact.

So simple did it appear that by virtue of its very simplicity it was bound to become the most difficult thing for him to recognise, so difficult indeed that in time it proved impossible for him to do so. So today man faces ruin, the psychic breakdown, which must demolish everything he has built up!

Only one thing can save him – a thorough knowledge of the Divine Laws in Creation! This alone will help him onward and upward again, and with him all that he attempts to build up in the future!

Do not argue that, being human spirits, you cannot so easily recognise the Laws in Creation, and that it is difficult to distinguish between the truth and false conclusions! That is not so! Whoever says this is either trying once more to use it to conceal his indolence and to hide the indifference of his soul, or is making excuses for the sake of his own peace of mind.

But it is of no use! For all those who are indifferent or indolent will now be rejected! Only he who musters all his strength so as to devote it *unremittingly* to achieve what is most indispensable for his soul has any prospect of being saved! All half measures count for nothing! Every hesitation, every postponement, is the same as a complete neglect of duty! Mankind have no more time left because they have already waited until the limit of their allotted period!

This time, naturally, it will not be made so easy for man, nor will he find it so easy, since through the most careless negligence in these matters he robbed himself of the slightest capacity even to believe in the profound seriousness of a necessary *final* decision! And it is exactly *this* point which is his greatest weakness, which will inevitably cause the downfall of many!

For thousands of years much has been done to enlighten you about God's Will or the working of the Laws in Creation, at least in so far as you need it in order to ascend and find your way back to the Luminous Heights whence you came! This was not achieved through the so-called earthly sciences, nor through the churches, but only through the servants of God, the prophets of olden times, and later through the Message brought by the Son of God!

Although it was given to you quite simply, so far you have only *talked* about it, but never seriously troubled to understand it aright, still less to live accordingly! In your indolent opinion this was asking too much of you, although it is your only salvation! You wish to be saved without exerting yourselves in any way! If you reflect upon this you must surely come to this sad conclusion!

You turned every Divine Message into a religion! For your own convenience! *And that was wrong!* You placed religion upon a special pedestal, removed from everyday life! That was the greatest mistake you could have made; for in so doing you also removed God's Will from your daily life or, what amounts to the same thing, you separated *yourselves* from God's Will, instead of uniting with It and making It the centre of your daily life and activity, thus becoming *one* with It!

You must absorb every message from God quite *naturally* and interweave it in a practical manner into your work, your thoughts and your whole life! You must not set it apart by itself, as you have now done, only paying it a visit in your leisure hours in order to indulge for a short time in contrition, gratitude or relaxation! As a result it never became something natural, a part of you, such as hunger or sleep!

Understand this aright at last! You shall *live* in this Will of God so that you may find your way on all the paths which bring you benefit! God's Messages are precious hints which you *need!* Without knowing and obeying them you are lost! Therefore you must not place them as something sacred in a glass shrine, to gaze upon them in awe and trembling only on Sundays, or to retreat there in fear and distress in order to receive strength! You wretched ones, you shall not only venerate the Message, but *make use* of It! You shall grasp It with hearty goodwill, not only when you are in Sunday attire, but with the fist hardened by daily toil, which never shames or debases, but only *honours* everyone! The precious gem shines with greater purity and brilliance in a rugged hand discoloured by sweat and dirt, than in the well-cared-for fingers of a lazy idler who spends his time on earth only in contemplation!

Every Divine Message was granted to you so that *it should become an integral part of you!* You must try and grasp what this means!

You should not look upon it as something separate, something that remains outside yourselves, which you accustom yourselves to approach with timid reserve! *Absorb* the Word of God so that each one of you may know *how* he must live and proceed in order to attain to the Kingdom of God!

Therefore at last awake and learn to know the Laws in Creation! No worldly cleverness will help you in this matter, nor the small amount of technical knowledge derived through observation! Something so meagre will not suffice for the path your soul must take! You *must* lift your eyes far *beyond* this earth and recognise where your path leads after this earthly life, so that at the same time you may become aware of why and for what purpose you are here on earth!

And whatever your conditions are in *this* life, whether rich or poor, healthy or ill, at peace or in conflict, in joy or sorrow, so you will learn to recognise the reason and purpose of it all! This will make you glad and happy, grateful for the experiences which have come your way. You will learn to value every single second as precious and, above all, learn to use them for your ascent to joyful existence and purest happiness.

And because you so badly entangled and confused yourselves, the Divine Message was brought to you by the Son of God as a means of salvation, after the warnings of the prophets had remained unheeded. The Divine Message showed the way, the only way, to save you from the swamp which already threatened to smother you! The Son of God sought to lead you to this way by parables! Those who wanted to believe and who were seekers listened with their *ears,* but it penetrated no further. They never tried to live in accordance with them!

Religion and daily life have always remained also for you two separate things! You always stood beside it, never in it! The effects of the Laws of Creation explained in the parables remained absolutely incomprehensible to you because you never looked for them in those parables!

And now, through the Grail Message, the explanation of the laws comes to you in a form more understandable in the present time! In reality they are precisely the same as those Christ already brought in the form suitable *at that time.* He showed men how they should think, speak and act so that they could mature spiritually and advance upwards in Creation! Humanity needed no more than that! There is not a single gap in the Message given at that time.

He who at last adapts himself to It in his thoughts, words, and deeds *thus practises the purest worship of God, for this lies only in deeds!*

He who willingly submits himself to these laws will always do the right thing! *In so doing* he proves his veneration for the wisdom of God and joyfully submits to His Will expressed in His Laws. Its effects will then further and protect him, and he will be freed from all sorrow and uplifted into the realm of the Luminous Spirit. There, in a jubilant experiencing, the Omniscience of God will become visible in all its perfection to everyone! There the worship of God is life itself! There every breath, every intuitive perception, every action speaks of joyous gratitude and thus becomes a lasting delight – a delight born of happiness, disseminating happiness, and therefore reaping happiness!

The worship of God in your life and in your experiences consists solely of keeping the Divine Laws! This alone ensures happiness! So shall it be in the coming Kingdom, in the Millennium, which will be called the Kingdom of God on earth!

MAN AND HIS FREE WILL

IN ORDER to give a complete picture of this, much that is extraneous but which more or less influences the main question must be taken into consideration.

Free will! This is something which even many eminent persons ponder over, because the laws of justice decree that where responsibility exists there must also unquestionably be a possibility to make a free decision.

Wherever one turns, from all sides one hears the question: Where does free will come in if in fact man is subject to Providence, guidance, destiny, the influence of the stars, and karma? Man gets pushed, polished and moulded whether he wishes it or not!

Serious seekers eagerly seize upon all that is said about free will, rightly discerning that it is just on this subject that an explanation is very necessary. As long as this is lacking man cannot adjust himself properly so as to maintain the position in this great Creation which is rightfully his. If he is not properly attuned to Creation he must remain a stranger in it. He will roam about and have to submit to being pushed, polished and moulded because he is not conscious of the purpose of life.

His great deficiency is that he does not know where his free will comes in and how it functions. This fact alone shows that he has completely lost the way to his free will and no longer knows how to find it.

The entrance to the path leading to this knowledge is blocked by drifting sands and is no longer visible. All traces are effaced. Man runs around irresolutely in circles, tiring himself out, till a fresh wind comes at last to make the path clear again. It is obvious that in this process the drifting sands will first be violently whirled up and, before they are carried away, will blind the eyes of many who continue hungrily to seek the entrance to the path.

For this reason everyone must exercise the greatest care to keep his vision free until the last grain of drifting sand is blown away. Otherwise it might well happen that, although he sees the way, his somewhat obscured vision may cause him to take a false step, stumble and fall, and thus sink away when the path is right in front of him.

The lack of understanding which men stubbornly show regarding the actual existence of free will has its roots mainly in the fact that they do not know what the free will really is.

Although the explanation is already given in the words themselves, here as elsewhere man overlooks such simple things because of their utter simplicity. Instead he searches in the wrong place, thereby preventing himself from getting a clear picture of free will.

The great majority of men today regard the will as something forcefully brought into being by the earthly brain when the intellect, which is bound to time and space, indicates and decrees a certain definite direction for thoughts and feelings.

However, that is not free will, but the will *bound* by the earthly intellect!

The confusion of these two concepts by many people brings about great errors, and erects the wall which makes recognition and understanding impossible. Then man is surprised when he comes upon gaps and contradictions and cannot find any logic in it!

The free will which alone has such an incisive effect upon actual life that it reaches far into the world beyond, and which imprints its stamp upon the soul and is able to mould it, is of quite a different nature. It is too great to be limited to things of this earth. Hence it has no connection whatever with the earthly physical body, nor with the brain. Free will is inherent in the spirit alone, in the soul of man!

If man would not always give unlimited sway to the intellect, then the free will of his actual spiritual "ego", which has a wider vision, could through its finer intuition prescribe the direction the intellectual brain should take. Then the "bound" will, so absolutely necessary for all earthly purposes, which are limited to time and space, would very often choose another course than is now the case.

That fate would also then hold different possibilities is easily comprehensible because, owing to the different course taken, karma would also weave different threads and bring about a different reciprocal action.

This explanation is naturally not sufficient to give a right understanding of what free will is. To give a complete picture it is necessary to know how free will has already manifested, also how the many intricate entanglements of an existing karma came about, the effects of which can so conceal the free will that it is hardly possible, or completely impossible, to recognise its existence.

Again, such an explanation can only be given if the entire course of development of the spiritual man is taken into consideration, beginning with the moment in which the spirit-germ of man for the first time descended into the ethereal covering on the very outskirts of the World of Matter.

Then we see that man is in no way what he prides himself on being. He can by no means claim the absolute right to eternal bliss and eternal individual existence! The expression: "We are all God's children" is wrong in the sense that man has given to it. *Not* every man is a child of God, only he who has developed into one!

Man is sent down into Creation as a spirit-germ. This germ contains everything it needs to enable it to develop into a child of God, conscious of its personality. The condition is, however, that he unfolds and cultivates the corresponding abilities and does not allow them to perish.

Great and mighty is the process and yet quite natural in its every stage. Nothing goes outside logical development, for there is logic in all Divine activity, because this is perfect, and what is perfect cannot be wanting in logic.

Each of these spirit-germs carries the same abilities within itself, as they are all of the *same* spirit. Each of these abilities contains a promise which will be unconditionally fulfilled as soon as the ability has been developed. But only then! That is what *each* germ has in prospect when it is sown. And yet...!

A Sower went forth to sow! The region where the finest ethereal substance of Creation borders upon the Realm of Animistic Substantiality* is the field in which the human spirit-germs are sown. Small sparks go out from this Animistic Sphere across the border and sink away into the virgin soil of the finest ethereal part of Creation, similar to the electric discharges during a thunderstorm. It is as if the Creative Hand of the Holy Spirit were sowing seeds in the World of Matter.

While the seed develops and slowly ripens towards the harvest many of them are lost. They do not germinate, that is, they have not developed their higher qualities, but have let them decay or wither, and they must therefore lose themselves in the World of Matter. But those which have germinated and

* See Appendix.

310

work up above the surface are strictly sifted at the harvest, and the dead ears are separated from the full ears. Then, after the harvest, once more the chaff is carefully separated from the wheat.

That is the general outline of the development, but to come to a better understanding of human free will it is necessary to go more thoroughly into the actual development *of man*.

When spirit-sparks fly over into the soil of the ethereal outskirts of the World of Matter, a gaseous covering of the same substance as this most delicate of all the regions of the World of Matter immediately envelops them. Thereby the spirit-germ of man has entered Creation which, like all that is material, is subject to change and disintegration. It is still free from karma and awaits the things which are to come.

The vibrations of the powerful experiences which continually take place in the midst of Creation, in the process of development and decay, penetrate to the furthest outskirts of that ethereal region*.

Even if they are but the most delicate of vibrations that pass like a breath through the World of Ethereal Substance, yet they are sufficient to awaken the sensitive volition in the spirit-germ and arouse its attention. It desires to "taste" of this or that vibration, to follow it or, to express it differently, to let itself be drawn by it, which is the same as allowing itself to be attracted by it.

Therein lies the first decision of the spirit-germ which, with its manifold tendencies, is now attracted here or there according to the choice it makes. Thus the first delicate threads are woven for the fabric that later is to become its tapestry of life.

The rapidly developing germ can now use every moment to indulge in vibrations of other kinds, which are constantly crossing its path in many variations. As soon as it determines to do so, thus wishing it, it will change its course and follow the newly-chosen kind or, rather, allow itself to be drawn by it.

Its wish is like a rudder through which it can change its course in the currents as soon as the one it is following no longer pleases it. In this way it is able to "taste" here and there.

Through this tasting it matures more and more. It gradually develops the capacity to distinguish and finally the ability to judge until, in the end,

---

* For the moment only the wider aspect of all this is given, but in later lectures it will be explained in greater detail.

becoming ever more conscious and assured, it follows a certain definite direction. The choice of vibrations it is willing to follow has a deep effect upon it.

In accordance with their own characteristics it quite naturally follows that the vibrations in which of its free volition the spirit-germ "swims", so to speak, exercise an influence upon it through the reciprocal action.

The spirit-germ itself, however, possesses *only pure and noble* qualities. These are the talents which it should put to the highest use in Creation. If it indulges in noble vibrations, these through the reciprocal action will arouse its latent qualities, stir them up, and strengthen and cultivate them, so that they may, in time, bear good fruit and bring great blessing to Creation. A man developing spiritually in this manner will become a good householder.

If, however, the spirit-germ decides principally in favour of ignoble vibrations these can, in due course, influence it so strongly that their nature remains clinging to it, and also envelop its own pure qualities, suffocating them and preventing them from awakening and developing. These must finally be considered as "buried", whereby the person concerned becomes a bad householder of the talents entrusted to him.

Thus a spirit-germ itself cannot be impure as it comes from the region of purity and carries only purity within it. But after it has sunk into the World of Matter it can sully its cloak, which is also of material substance, by voluntarily "tasting" impure vibrations, as through temptations. In doing so it can even outwardly make *its own* the inward impurity which has superimposed itself upon the noble characteristics, whereby it also receives impure qualities in contrast to the inherited qualities of the spirit which it brought along.

All guilt and karma are *only material,* existing only within material Creation and nowhere else! Nor can they become part of the spirit as such, but can only cling to it! Therefore it is possible to be *washed clean* of all guilt!

The recognition of this does not upset anything but only confirms what religion and church say allegorically. Above all we recognise more and more the great Truth which Christ brought to mankind.

It is quite natural that a spirit-germ, having burdened itself with impurity in the World of Matter, cannot return with this burden to the Spiritual Realm, but must remain in the Material World until it has cast off this burden and redeemed itself from it. In this process it must naturally remain in that region to which the weight of its burden forces it, depending on the greater or lesser degree of impurity.

If it does not succeed in ridding itself of and casting off its burden before the Day of Judgment, it will not be able to rise in spite of the purity always retained by the spirit-germ. This could not unfold itself according to its actual qualities, because it had been overlaid with impurity. The impurity holds it down by its weight and draws it along into the dissolution of all that is material.

The more conscious a spirit-germ becomes in the course of its development, the more does its outer covering take on the nature of its inner qualities, striving either towards what is noble or ignoble, and thus becoming beautiful or ugly.

Every deviation it makes forms a knot in the threads dragging behind it which, through the following of many wrong paths and going to and fro, become looped and form an intricate network in which the spirit is entangled, either perishing through being held fast, or having forcibly to extricate itself.

The vibrations in which it indulged while nibbling or enjoying during its wandering remain attached to it and drag after it like threads, continually sending their particular radiations to it.

If it keeps to the same direction for a long time, then both the threads further back and the new threads can operate with undiminished vigour. Whenever it changes its course, however, the influence of the further vibrations will slowly be weakened by being crossed, for they must first pass through a knot. This hinders them because, in making the knot, they joined and fused with new vibrations of quite a different nature.

Thus it goes on and on. As the spirit-germ grows the threads become denser and stronger and form karma, the ultimate effect of which may become so powerful that it may attach to the spirit this or that "propensity", which is finally able to influence its free decisions and give it a direction that can already be estimated in advance. Then the free will has been darkened and can no longer operate as it should.

Thus from the beginning free will has existed, but later many a free will becomes burdened to such an extent that it is strongly influenced in the way already described and so can no longer act as a free will.

The spirit-germ which is developing in this way more and more must come ever nearer to the earth, for from there the vibrations emanate more strongly.

Steering more and more consciously, the spirit-germ follows these or, more precisely, lets itself be "attracted" by them, so that it may enjoy ever-increasingly those kinds which its inclination chooses. It wants to pass from "nibbling" to the real "tasting", and finally to "enjoying".

The reason why the vibrations from the earth are so strong is that something new and powerful has been added – physical, material, generative power*!

The latter has the mission and the capacity to set the whole spiritual intuitive perception *"aglow"*. It is only through this that the spirit gets the proper connection with material Creation and consequently it can only then work in it with full vigour. It then embraces all that is requisite to gain complete authority in the Material World, to stand firmly in it in every respect, to be able to work in it decisively and forcefully, and to be armed and protected against everything.

Hence the mighty waves of power issuing from man's experiences in his life on earth! It is true they only go as far as material substance in Creation, but they penetrate to the furthest and most delicate regions therein.

If there was on earth a human being of spiritually high and noble character, who was therefore able to bring to his fellow-men a high spiritual love, he would remain a stranger to them and could not come inwardly near them as long as his generative power was missing. Through this a bridge to understanding and to the psychic sensing of the intuitive feelings of others would be lacking, leaving a gap.

However, at the moment in which this spiritual love enters into a pure union with the generative power and is thereby set aglow, the emanation from this receives an entirely different vitality for all material substance. It becomes more real in the earthly sense and is thereby able to work more completely and understandably upon humanity and upon the whole World of Matter. Only then can this emanation be absorbed and finally perceived intuitively, bringing into Creation the blessing which the spirit of man should bring.

There is something mighty about this union. *This* is the actual purpose, at least the *main purpose,* of this natural instinct, so immense and yet so mysterious to many, namely that it permits the spiritual to unfold in the World of

* Lecture: "The significance of man's generative power for his spiritual ascent".

Matter to its fullest working power. Without it the spiritual would remain too alien to material substance to be able to work in it properly. The purpose of procreation only comes in the *second* place. The main thing resulting from this union is the "swinging upwards" of the human being. This gives the human spirit its full powers, its warmth and vitality. With this happening it is, so to speak, completed. *It is at this moment, therefore, that its full responsibility sets in!*

At this important turning point the wise Justice of God gives man not only the opportunity but at the same time the natural urge easily to shake off all the karma with which he has burdened his free will up till then. This enables man once more completely to free his will, so as to become a child of God, standing consciously and powerfully in Creation, working according to God's Will, and ascending in his pure and sublime intuitive perceptions to those heights to which he will later be attracted as soon as he has laid aside his physical body.

If man does not do this it is his own fault, for when his generative power sets in he is first of all stirred by a mighty upward impulse to all that is ideal, beautiful and pure. This can always be clearly observed with unspoiled youth of both sexes. Hence the enthusiasms in the years of youth, not to be mistaken for the years of childhood, which are unfortunately often laughed at by adults!

This also accounts for the inexplicable, rather melancholy but none the less serious intuitive perceptions in these years. The hours in which it seems as if the young man or maiden were burdened with all the sorrows of the world, when presentiments of a deep seriousness come over them, are not altogether without reason.

Also their frequent feeling of not being understood has in reality much truth in it. It arises from their occasional recognition of how wrong is the world around them, a world which cannot and will not understand the sacred wish of their soul to soar on high. A world which is not satisfied until these strongly warning intuitive perceptions in the maturing soul are dragged down to a level people can better understand, thus something "more real" and matter-of-fact, which they consider better suited to man and, with their one-sided intellectual mind, the only normal state of affairs!

In spite of this there are many out-and-out materialists who during this period of their lives have perceived these same serious warnings, and who now and then enjoy speaking of the golden days of their first love with a slight tinge of sentiment, even melancholy, thus unconsciously expressing a certain sadness at having lost something they cannot define more closely.

And indeed they are all correct in this respect! The most precious thing has been taken away from them, or they themselves carelessly threw it away when, in the dull routine of every-day work, or under the ridicule of their so-called "men and women friends", or again by reading bad books or through bad examples, they faint-heartedly buried the treasure. And still its radiance shines forth from time to time during their further life and, for a moment, makes their disappointed heart beat faster, oppressed and bewildered by an inexplicable feeling of sadness and longing.

Even if these intuitive feelings are always quickly pushed away and laughed at in bitter self-contempt, they still bear witness to the existence of this treasure. Fortunately there are but few who can assert that they never had such feelings! Such men would indeed only excite pity, for they have never really lived!

But even such depraved ones, or let us rather call them pitiable ones, intuitively sense a longing when they have an opportunity to meet a person who makes use of this energy with the right attitude, through which he has become pure and already attained an inner maturity on earth.

The first effect of such a longing in these people is in most cases the involuntary recognition of their own baseness and negligence which then turns into hatred and may culminate in blind rage. It often happens that a man whose soul has attained to an exceptionally high degree of maturity attracts the hatred of the masses without himself having given them any outwardly visible cause. Such masses know nothing better than to cry: "Crucify him! Crucify him!" This is the reason for the long series of martyrs in the history of mankind.

The real cause is their violent grief at seeing something precious in others which they themselves have lost, a grief which they only feel as hatred. When people who have more inner warmth, and who have only been kept down or dragged in the mud by the bad example of others, meet a person of high inner maturity, the longing for something they have not attained themselves will often call forth an unbounded love and veneration. Wherever such a man goes there will always be a for and against, but indifference towards him is impossible.

The mysterious radiating charm of an unsullied maiden or youth is nothing but the *pure* upsurge of the awakening generative power which, united with spiritual power, strives for what is highest and noblest, and is intuitively perceived by their environment through the strong vibrations emanating from it.

With careful forethought the Creator provided that this awakening should come at an age when man can be fully aware of his volition and actions. This is the time when, in conjunction with the full power now resting in him, he can and should easily shake off all that lies in the past. It will even fall away of itself, if man only keeps his volition for the good, which he is being unceasingly urged to do during this time. Then, as the intuitive perceptions quite rightly intimate, he could rise without any effort to that level to which he as a human being belongs!

Behold the dreaming of unsullied youth! It is but the perception of this upsurge, the wish to be free from all baseness, the ardent longing for the ideal! Their uneasy restlessness, however, is the signal not to waste time, but energetically to cast off their karma and start on their spiritual ascent.

That is why the earth is the great turning-point for mankind!

How glorious it is to stand in this all-embracing power, to work in it and with it! At least as long as the direction man chooses remains a good one! But there is nothing more pitiable than one-sidedly to dissipate these powers in blind sensual orgies, thereby enfeebling one's spirit and depriving it of a great part of the impetus it so urgently needs to advance upwards!

And yet in most cases man fails to profit by this priceless period of transition and allows himself to be led by those in his environment who think they "know" on to wrong paths, which hinder him from rising and, alas, only too often lead him downwards! Consequently he is unable to throw off the dark vibrations clinging to him; on the contrary these only attract reinforcement, and he will more and more entangle his free will till he can no longer recognise it.

This is what happens with the *first* incarnation on earth. In later incarnations which become necessary man brings a much heavier karma with him. But in spite of this the possibility of shaking it off recurs in every life, and no karma could be stronger than a human spirit which has acquired its full vigour as soon as it receives, through the generative power, the complete connection with the World of Matter to which karma belongs.

But if man fails to make use of these periods to cast off his karma and

317

thereby regain his free will, and should he have further entangled himself or perhaps even sunk deeply, in spite of this a powerful ally is offered to help him fight his karma and ascend. It is the greatest conqueror existing, able to overcome everything!

The wisdom of the Creator has ordained that the times mentioned above are not the only ones in the World of Matter in which mankind may find the possibility of quick help, in which he is able to discover himself and his true worth, and in which he even receives an exceptionally strong impetus to draw his attention to it.

This magic power which every person during his whole life on earth has at his disposal in constant readiness to help, which also originates from the same union of generative power with the spiritual power, and which can liberate from all karma, is *the love*. Not the demanding love of the material world, but the high pure love which only knows and wishes the welfare of the beloved one, and which never thinks of itself. This love also belongs to material Creation, and it demands no renunciation, no asceticism, but only wishes what is best for the other. It fears for him, suffers with him, but also shares in his joy.

The basis of this love is similar to the intuitive longing for the ideal which unsullied youth has when its generative power sets in. But it also spurs on the responsible, i. e. the mature human being to the full power of all his abilities, even to heroism, so that the creative and competitive powers are exerted to their utmost extent. In this no limit is set as to age! As soon as a human being opens his heart to pure love, whether it be man's love for a woman or vice versa, or the love for friends, parents or children, it is all the same! If only it is pure it will bring as its first gift the opportunity to cast off all karma, which will then only be redeemed "symbolically"*, so that the free and conscious will, which can *only* strive upwards, may blossom forth. As a natural consequence ascent will then begin, that is, redemption from the unworthy fetters that hold him down.

The first intuitive feeling which stirs the heart at the awakening of pure love is thinking oneself unworthy of the beloved one. This can be described in other words as the dawn of modesty and humility, thus the acquisition of two great virtues. With this comes the desire to protect the other so that no possible harm could come to him from any direction, and so that his way

---

* Lecture: "Symbolism in the fate of man".

should lead over flowery, sunny paths. This desire "to wait hand and foot upon a person" is no empty saying, but quite rightly marks the rising intuitive perception.

Inherent in this is the surrendering of one's personality, a strong desire to serve, which alone could suffice to cast off all karma in a short time, provided the volition remains uppermost and does not give way to mere sensual instincts. Finally, with pure love comes the ardent desire to do something really great and noble for the beloved one, not to offend or hurt him by look, thought or word, much less by an unworthy action. The most delicate consideration is engendered.

The important thing is to hold fast to these pure intuitive perceptions and to place them above all else! Then no one will desire or do anything wrong. He will simply be unable to do so! On the contrary, through this he will enjoy the best protection, the greatest power, and the most benign helper and adviser.

That is why Christ refers again and again to the supreme power of love! Love alone can overcome and accomplish all things, always provided, however, that it is not the earthly demanding love, which harbours jealousy and kindred evils.

With this the Creator in His Wisdom has thrown a lifebuoy into Creation, with which *every* individual comes more than once into contact during his life on earth, so that he may grasp it and swing himself upwards.

This help is there for all! No distinctions are made, either in age or sex, between rich or poor, high or low! Therefore love is the greatest of God's gifts! He who grasps this can be certain of salvation from every tribulation, and however deep he may have fallen. He frees himself and thus quickly and easily regains an undimmed free will, which leads him upwards.

And even if he had fallen to such a depth as to make him despair, love is able to sweep him upward with the impetuosity of a whirlwind to the Light, to God, Who Himself is Love! As soon as pure love stirs within a man, no matter what has caused it, he obtains the most direct connection with God, the Primordial Source of all Love, and thus the strongest help. But should a man possess all things and have *no* love, he would be but "sounding brass or a tinkling cymbal" – without warmth, without life ... nothing!

However, if he does find true love for some fellow being, a love striving only to bring light and joy to the beloved one, and not to drag him down through senseless desires, but a love that protects and uplifts him, then he *serves* the other without being aware that he is doing so. Through this he becomes more of an unselfish giver, and this serving sets him free.

Many will here say to themselves: "That is exactly what I do or, at least, what I am already striving to do! Using all the means in my power I try to make life on earth easy for my wife or family, offering them pleasures while I exert myself to obtain sufficient resources to enable them to lead a comfortable and agreeable life, free from all care!"

Thousands will give themselves airs, feeling uplifted and imagining they are undeniably good and noble. But they err! *That* is *not* the living, vital love! Such living love is not so one-sidedly material, but simultaneously urges much more strongly towards that which is high, noble and ideal. Certainly no one may venture to forget earthly necessities with impunity, i. e., without detriment to himself! He should not disregard them, but at the same time they must not become the principal aim of his thoughts and actions. Hovering above all this, great and strong, is the desire, so mysterious to many, to be able actually to *attain to what* they are considered to be in the eyes of those who love them.

With this desire they are on the right path, which will only lead upwards!

Genuine pure love needs no further explanation! Every man feels exactly what it is! Man often tries to deceive himself about it on seeing his mistakes and realising how far away he really is from loving truly and purely. But he must then pull himself together, he may not hesitate or stop and finally give up, for without genuine love there can no longer be any free will for him.

How many opportunities thus offered to men to pull themselves together and swing upwards are left unused! The complaint and seeking of the majority are therefore not genuine. They simply do not want to be bothered if it means that they themselves must contribute something, be it but a slight re-arrangement of their habits and views. To a great extent it is falsehood and self-deception! God should come to them and lift them upwards to Him without the necessity for them to forgo their precious comfort and self-worship! Then they would possibly condescend to go along, but not, however, without expecting special thanks from God for so doing!

Let these drones go their own way to destruction! They are not worth any trouble! Over and over again they will let the opportunities presented to them pass by while lamenting and praying. If ever such a person does grasp an opportunity, he would surely rob it of its most noble adornment of purity and unselfishness in order to drag this precious treasure into the mire of passion.

Those who seek and those who know should finally make up their minds to avoid such people! They should not think they are doing the Almighty a favour in spreading His Word and His Holy Will in such a cheap manner, offering it by trying to teach others, so that it almost appears as if the Creator were forced, with the help of His faithful ones, to go begging in order to extend the circle of adherents. It is defilement to offer His Word to such as would grasp it with unclean hands. The saying should not be forgotten which forbids "casting pearls before swine"!

And that is what it amounts to in such cases! An unnecessary waste of time, which may no longer be wasted to such a degree without ultimately causing harmful reactions! Help should be given only to those who seek!

The increasing disquietude felt by many people, and the searching and seeking for the whereabouts of the free will, are perfectly justified, and a sign that it is high time to set about it! This feeling is strengthened by an unconscious premonition that there may come a time when it is too late. That is what keeps the searchers constantly active at the present time. But for the greater part it is in vain! *The majority of people of the present day can no longer make use of their free will because they have entangled themselves too gravely!*

They have sold and bartered it ... for nothing!

They cannot hold God responsible for this, however, as is so often and continually being tried through all kinds of interpretations by which they erase from their minds all thought of the personal responsibility awaiting them, but they must accuse themselves! Even if this self-accusation was of the greatest bitterness and accompanied by the deepest pain, it could not be severe enough to counterbalance, even in a small measure, the value of the lost gift which has been senselessly suppressed or squandered!

Yet, in spite of this, man can still find the way to regain what he lost as soon as he seriously exerts himself, always provided, of course, that the wish to do so comes from deep within, that it is really *alive* in him and never weakens. He must carry the greatest longing for it! And should he need to spend his whole life on it, he could only benefit, for it is an urgent necessity for mankind to regain their free will! Instead of "regain" we could also say "dig it out" or "wash it free". It would be all the same!

As long as man only *thinks* and *ponders* on the subject, however, he will attain nothing. The greatest efforts and perseverance must then fail him, because through thinking and pondering he can never reach beyond the limits of time and space, which means that he cannot get to where the solution lies. And since at present thinking and pondering are considered as the high road to all research, there is no prospect that any progress, apart from mere earthly matters, may be expected. Unless, indeed, men would fundamentally change in this respect!

Make use of your time on earth! Remember the great turning-point which always brings full responsibility with it!

For this reason a child is spiritually still under age, because the union between the spiritual and the material has not been established through the generative power. Not until the moment when this power sets in will its intuitive perceptions be sufficiently strong incisively to penetrate the entire World of Matter, reforming and transforming it. With this he automatically takes full and complete responsibility. Previous to this the reciprocal action is not so strong either, because the intuitive faculty is much weaker.

Therefore in the first incarnation* on earth karma cannot be so powerful. At the utmost it could influence the circumstances into which a child is born, so that these can help the spirit in its earth-life to redeem its karma by recognising the qualities it possesses. The question of the attraction of homogeneous species would play an important role in this. But all these influences would be rather weak. The actual powerful and incisive karma only sets in when the generative power unites with the spiritual power in man, whereby he not only becomes of full value in the World of Matter, but can far surpass the material in every respect if he adapts himself accordingly.

Until then darkness and evil are unable to approach man directly. The child is protected against this by the gap which exists between itself and the material world. It stands as if isolated, because the bridge is missing.

Many readers will now more readily understand why children enjoy much greater protection from evil; this is even proverbial! However, on the same path which the bridge forms for the entering generative power, and over which a man in his full power can stride forth to do battle, naturally also everything else can approach him, unless he is on his guard. But in no case can

* The entrance of man into life on earth.

322

this happen until he possesses the necessary means of defence! Not for one moment does an inequality exist which could serve as an excuse!

This enormously increases the responsibility of the parents. Woe unto those parents who through misplaced ridicule or a wrong education, if not even by bad example, which also includes all sorts of ambitious desires, rob their children of the opportunity to rid themselves of their karma and to ascend! The temptations of life on earth lure men hither and thither as it is. And since adolescent youth are not enlightened as to the scope of their power, they either do not use it at all or too little, or they squander it in an irresponsible manner, if not even put it to an improper or evil use.

Thus, because of ignorance, their karma inevitably grows ever greater! Through some propensity or other its radiations influence decisions on this or that matter in advance, thereby limiting actual free will to the extent that it is no longer free. That is why the *majority* of people today can no longer make use of their free will. They have bound, chained and enslaved themselves through their own guilt.

How childish and unworthy do men make themselves when they try to reject the thought of an absolute responsibility, preferring to blame the Creator for injustice in this matter! How ridiculous it sounds to pretend that they never really possessed free will, but were guided, pushed, polished and moulded without being able to do anything against it!

If they could but realise for a moment what a pitiable role they actually play with such behaviour! Above all, if they could but once critically observe themselves in view of the position of power bestowed upon them, so as to recognise how senselessly they squander this power in petty and transitory things, how they raise trifles to a contemptible position of importance, and how they feel themselves great in things in which they must appear very small in comparison with their real vocation as human beings in Creation!

The man of today may be likened to one to whom a kingdom is given, but who prefers to idle away his time with the most simple of children's toys!

It is only natural, and not to be expected otherwise, that the mighty powers which have been given to man must crush him if he cannot guide them!

It is high time to awake! Man should make full use of the time and the grace accorded to him with each earth-life! He has still no idea how urgent this already is! In the moment when he once more frees his encumbered will, everything that now so often seems to be against him will then help him. Even the radiations of the stars, feared by so many, are only there to help him, no matter what their nature!

And everyone can do it regardless of how heavily karma weighs upon him, even when the radiations of the stars appear to be predominantly unfavourable! The effect of all this is only unfavourable when the will is not free. This, however, is only apparently so, for in reality it is only for his benefit when he is at a loss to help himself. It forces him to defend himself, to awaken and to be on the alert.

Fear of the radiations of the stars is quite out of place, however, because the reactions they call forth are always and only linked up with the threads of karma attached to the person concerned. The radiations of the stars are merely channels into which is drawn all the karma hanging about a person at that time, in so far as the karma is homogeneous to the existing radiations. If the radiations of the stars are unfavourable then only the unfavourable karma clinging to a person will be drawn into these channels, exactly as it corresponds to the nature of the radiation, and nothing else! It is the same with favourable radiations. Jointly guided in this way, karma can have a much more perceptible effect on mankind. However, where there is no bad karma outstanding, even unfavourable radiations of the stars cannot have bad effects. The one cannot be separated from the other.

Here again the great Love of the Creator can be recognised. The stars control or direct the effects of karma. Therefore bad karma cannot manifest without interruptions because the stars send out their radiations alternately, and this leaves man time to breathe in the intervals, for evil karma cannot take effect at the times of favourable radiations. As it must then cease and wait until unfavourable radiations again set in, it cannot so easily oppress a man completely. If, apart from the evil karma, a man has no good karma which could manifest when the radiations of the stars are favourable, then at least the favourable radiations would give him some respite from his suffering during the time they are active.

Thus also here one wheel in the course of events gears into the other. In strict consistency the one draws the other along, simultaneously controlling it, so that there can be no irregularities. And so it continues, as in a gigantic machine! On every side the teeth of the wheels gear sharply and exactly into each other, moving everything onward, driving it forward in its development.

And in the midst of all this stands man, with the immeasurable power entrusted to him to direct this mighty mechanism through his volition. *But always and only for himself!* It can lead him upward or downward. The direction he gives it alone decides the outcome.

But the machinery of Creation does not consist of rigid substance, but is entirely composed of living forms and beings who, in co-operating, create a much greater impression. The whole wonderful weaving, however, has the sole purpose of helping man, so long as he does not obstruct it by childishly squandering and misusing the power given to him. It is time man adapted himself in a different way in order to become what he should be! To obey really means nothing else than to understand. To serve is the same as to help. And to help means to rule. Within a short period every man can make his will free, as it should be. In doing so everything will change for him, because he himself has first changed inwardly.

But for thousands, for hundreds of thousands, indeed for millions, it will become too late because they do not wish it otherwise. It is quite natural that the wrongly-applied power, which would otherwise have served the mechanism so as to accomplish a work full of blessing, must now destroy it.

And when everything breaks down all those who hesitated will suddenly bethink themselves of prayer, but they will be unable to find the right way to pray, which alone can bring them help. If they recognise their failure they will, in desperation, speedily start to curse, declaring accusingly that there can be no God if He permits such things to happen. They will neither believe in an inexorable justice, nor that they had the power given to them in time to change everything, and that they were told of this often enough.

With childish obstinacy they demand for themselves a loving God as they want Him to be, a God Who forgives everything! Only in that do they want to recognise His greatness! But how then should this God of their imaginings deal with those who have always sought Him seriously, but who, on account of their seeking, were downtrodden, scorned and persecuted by those who now expect forgiveness?

Fools who in their continually self-chosen blindness and deafness rush on to their destruction, who diligently create their own doom! Let them be abandoned to darkness, towards which they stubbornly strive in their self-sufficiency! Only through their own experiences can they still come to their senses! Therefore the Darkness will be their best school. But there will come a day and an hour when this way will also be too late, because there will not be time enough left, after they have finally come to a recognition through their experiences, to tear themselves from darkness and ascend. For this reason it is high time seriously to concern yourself with the Truth!

PERHAPS we had better say human beings who wish to be ideal! But here we must first of all very carefully exclude all those who already consider themselves or would like to be considered such, but who cannot be classed with those who wish to be ideal!

They form the large class of gushing, sentimental enthusiasts of both sexes, to whom must also be added persons gifted with imagination, who could never learn to control and employ their gift usefully. We must also exclude those who are always dissatisfied with existing conditions, and who attribute their dissatisfaction to the fact that they tend to be more ideal than all their contemporaries and therefore do not fit in with their time.

Then there is the great army of the so-called "misunderstood" of both sexes, of which the greater number are girls and women. People of this type imagine that they are misunderstood. In plain English they live continually under the illusion that they possess valuable treasures which the other person with whom they happen to be associated at the time is unable to recognise. In reality, however, there is no treasure at all hidden in these souls, merely an inexhaustible source of endless wishes that can never be satisfied.

One can safely and simply call all these so-called misunderstood people "useless" people, because they prove how useless they are to live properly in the present time, being addicted only to what is unreal, and even to some extent to looseness. They always incline to what is unsuitable for a healthy life on earth. Unfortunately the path of these eternally misunderstood girls and women very frequently leads to a life commonly described as "carefree" and immoral, because they only too gladly, too readily and too often let themselves be "consoled", which is well known to a certain type of man, who unscrupulously exploits it.

The fact is that these misunderstood people are and will always remain unreliable in every respect. They think themselves ideal, but they are completely worthless, so that a serious person who harbours no bad intentions had better avoid them. It would be vain to try to help them. Almost invariably it will be "comforters" with *evil* intentions who approach them. Here the reciprocal action quickly falls back upon them, for on the breast or in the arms of a so-called comforter the misunderstood girl or woman will again feel "misunderstood" after a few days or weeks, and will once more long to be understood, for in fact she does not really know what she wants!

To all these useless groups of people must finally be added the group of the harmless dreamers! Apparently as harmless as children! But such a dreamer is only harmless in his effect upon himself and his own personality, but is not so harmless in regard to his own environment and all the people he meets. On *many* people mere conversation with such a person immediately acts like a slow, corroding poison, destructive and consuming, because by developing his ideas he is able to tear his listeners out of their normal and therefore healthy life, and lead them into the realm of what is unsuitable and unreal for their time on earth.

However, be it noted that I do not say such a dreamer is impure or even bad! On the contrary he may have the *best* intentions, but it will always be something that is unreal for the earth, unfeasible in practice! Therefore his influence is not furthering, but hindering and destructive to life on earth.

But even among the remaining men "striving for the ideal" we must observe keenly so as to make a further distinction between two kinds – those who are only "longing for the ideal" and those who are really striving towards the ideal.

The former are mostly weaklings who are always longing for something which can never be attained, at least not on earth, and who, therefore, can never be really happy nor even glad. They are not far removed from the group of the "misunderstood". In time they fall a prey to a morbid sentimentality which leads to nothing good.

Having thus keenly sifted them, we must now indeed, figuratively speaking, look for the remaining few with a lantern in broad daylight, so scarce are they! Even these few cannot be called "ideal people", but as I have already said they are people who "strive towards the ideal". This striving towards the ideal to be considered a personal quality which becomes active on earth!

These then are the people who can be regarded as having full value, who have a great, often a stupendous, goal in view, but who never allow themselves to live in the clouds. They keep both feet firmly planted on earth, so as not to lose themselves in what is unreal for life here. With sound outlook and skilled hand they strive step by step towards their high and distant goal without harming anybody undeservedly.

Whatever benefit is brought about by such people will seldom be confined to a few individuals. There is no question of their taking unfair advantage of anyone, as that would not justify their title of "striving towards the ideal". And every human being should and could strive towards the ideal, no matter what is his occupation here on earth! In doing so he can ennoble every kind of work and give it a wider goal, only he must never forget to keep everything within the compass of *life on earth!* If he goes beyond that it becomes unreal and therewith unsound for this earth. The result is that the *progress* which remains the basic condition and mark of all that strives towards the ideal can never be achieved.

It is man's duty on earth to set himself the highest attainable goal, and to strive for this goal with all the powers at his disposal. But as a *human being!* This excludes from the beginning that, like an animal, he should merely trouble himself about food and drink as, unfortunately, many men do; or let himself be goaded by the intellect into striving only for worldly greatness or fame without keeping in view as the main purpose the general welfare and advancement of mankind. All such people have less value on earth than the animals, because an animal is always *completely* and unaffectedly what it should be, even if it only serves to keep other creatures on the alert so that no hampering indolence sets in, which might lead to decline and disintegration, for *movement* is a vital condition of life in Creation.

Be on the alert! The person who really strives towards the ideal can be recognised by his efforts to *uplift* existing things on earth, not in the intellectual sense of increasing power and position, but towards *ennobling* them.

All his ideas will possess the possibility of being realised on earth, and will bring gain to the individual as well as to mankind in general. But those who only wish to be ideal wallow in notions that cannot possibly be put into practice in a sound earth-life. On the contrary these ideas merely divert them and draw them into a dream world, with the harmful result that man neglects to make use of the present time for the maturing of his spirit, which every man should cultivate and develop through the experiences of the moment!

Serious consideration will prove that also those people who hold idealistic communistic thoughts are dangerous to mankind, because the realisation of their ideas would only bring about unhealthy conditions, although they themselves only want what is good. They are like builders who carefully construct *in their building yard* a house which is to be put up elsewhere. It looks trim and beautiful . . . in the yard! But when erected on the actual site it stands unsteady and askew so that nobody can live in it, for the ground there is uneven and it is impossible to level it in spite of the greatest efforts and exertions. The builders had forgotten to take this into account. They neglected properly to evaluate the exact conditions prevailing at the site of erection. He who really strives for the ideal would not do this!

When put into practice idealistic communistic ideas cannot sprout from such soil, cannot be anchored in nor connected with it, because as the ground is composed of human beings they are not suited to it. It is too uneven, and will always remain so, because a uniform maturity of all men on earth cannot be achieved.

There will always be a great variation in the maturity of human beings in a specific period, because spiritually individuals are and remain completely *independent* personalities who can only develop in varied ways, since the free will *to decide for themselves* shall never be taken from these spirit-persons!

Now try to recognise the people who truly strive for the ideal here on earth, and help them with their activity, because their building up will only bring benefit!

CAST ALL YOUR GUILT UPON HIM!

THIS expression, so often used, is one of the principal sedatives of all those who call themselves believing Christians. But it is a poison which intoxicates. Like many poisons which are only used to deaden physical pain arising from disease, thus creating apparent comfort, so a similar condition is brought about spiritually with the words: "Cast all your guilt upon Him; for He has redeemed us and through His wounds we are healed!"

Since this is accepted by the faithful as one of the basic tenets of the doctrines of the Christian churches, its effect upon them is so much the more destructive. Their whole inner attitude is built up on it.

Through this, however, they fall a prey to the deadly embrace of blind faith, in which they are only able to view everything else as in a dense mist, until finally the whole picture is blurred and a grey veil descends over the Truth. Thus they are only able to find a hold on the artificial structure of distorted theories, all of which must collapse on the day of recognition!

"Cast all your guilt upon Him ...!"

Foolish delusion! Like a fire the shining Truth will sweep in between the hosts of false teachers and indolent believers, and consume all that is untrue! Yet even today the masses bask comfortably in the belief that everything the Saviour suffered and did was done for them! With their indolent thinking they describe as presumptuous and sacrilegious all those who imagine that they themselves must also contribute something in order to be able to enter Heaven. In this respect many show an astonishing humility and modesty, qualities which in other directions are completely lacking in them!

In their opinion it would be blasphemy to harbour the thought, however faint and timid, that the Saviour's descent to earth, and the suffering and death He therewith took upon Himself, were not sufficient to wipe away the sins of all those human beings who no longer doubt that He lived on earth at that time.

"Cast all your guilt upon Him ...!" they think with fervent devotion, without knowing what they are really doing! They sleep, but the time will come when they will have a terrible awakening! Their faith, apparently so humble, is nothing but self-complacency and boundless arrogance in imagining that a Son of God would come down to serve them, and prepare a path on which they can stupidly saunter along straight into Heaven!

Every one should really be able to recognise the hollowness of this without further ado! It can only arise out of an indescribable love of ease and frivolity; unless, indeed, shrewdness suggested it as a bait to gain earthly advantages!

Mankind have lost themselves in a maze of a thousand paths, and deceive themselves in their foolish faith! What a debasement of God this implies! What is man that he has the effrontery to expect God to send His Inborn Son, a part of His Own Unsubstantiate Essence, so that men can cast their load of sin upon Him, only in order to avoid the trouble of washing their own dirty linen and clearing away the dark burden they had heaped upon themselves!

Woe to those who will one day have to account for such thoughts! It is the most insolent defilement of the Sublime Godhead! The Mission of Christ was not of such a low order, but sublime and demanding in pointing to the Father!

I have already referred to the Son of God's great work of redemption*. The seeds sown by His great Work of Love have come up in this world and in the beyond, bringing forth all kinds of fruit. In the meantime many who were elected by men have frequently claimed to be called by God. They seized these pure teachings with unholy hands, dragging them down to their own level, and thereby dimming their clarity!

Mankind, who trusted them without first seriously examining the very Word which they taught, fell with them! The sublime kernel of Divine Truth was ringed about with earthly narrow-mindedness. The form remained, but all luminosity was destroyed through the mania for earthly power and advantage. Only dim twilight exists where the brightest radiance of spiritual life could reign. Pleading humanity was robbed of the precious jewel which Christ Jesus brought *to all who long for it.* Distorted by a veil of selfish desires, seekers are shown a false path which not only makes them lose precious time, but very often even drives them into the arms of darkness.

False doctrines grew up rapidly. They choked simplicity and truth, covering them with an iridescent garment, the brilliant colours of which, like pois-

---

* Lecture: "The Redeemer".

onous plants, hold dangers benumbing all who approach, whereby the alertness of the believers with regard to themselves is paralysed and finally dies. With this every possibility for an ascent to the true Light dies also.

Once more the mighty Call of Truth will reverberate through every land! Then for each one will come the final reckoning through the fate he himself has woven! Men will finally receive what they have so persistently advocated in the past. They will have to live through the errors which they sought to advance in their desires or presumptuous thoughts, or which they tried to follow! For many this will result in a wild outcry, with chattering of teeth from fear, anger or despair!

Those who are badly stricken by evil and those who are rejected will suddenly feel it as unjust and cruel when they are thrust into *that* reality which, during their earth-life, was the only one they wanted to recognise as being true, and which they also continually offered to their fellow-men. Then they expect the God they faced with such boundless presumption to help! They will beseech and call upon Him, expecting that He in His Divinity will easily forgive even the worst sins of the "ignorant" little human beings! In their imagination He will suddenly be far too "great" to be able to resent such things! He Whom they have so debased in the past!

But He will *not* listen to them, *nor* will He help them any more, because previously they did not want to listen to His Word which He sent them! And herein lies that Justice which can never be separated from His great Love!

Like thunder a Voice will reverberate towards them: "You did not wish to! Therefore you will now be destroyed and erased from the Book of Life!"

THE CRIME OF HYPNOTISM

STRANGE, but at one time men raged against the assertion that such a thing as hypnotism really exists, and foremost among them were many members of the medical profession! They did not shrink from describing hypnotism as humbug and fraud, just as a short time before they had also done with magnetic healing, which today has become a great blessing to so many. Practitioners in this field were bitterly attacked and called charlatans and deceivers.

Today it is again the medical profession which has largely appropriated hypnotism. What at one time they denied in the strongest terms they now advocate!

This may be judged in two ways! He who quite objectively observed the bitter conflict at that time naturally cannot refrain from smiling today when he again sees how those who formerly showed excessive hostility now try to apply with even greater zeal the hypnotism they disdained. On the other hand, however, it must be acknowledged that this almost grotesque change of front nevertheless deserves respect! It requires a certain amount of courage to expose oneself to the risk of being ridiculed, which just in this case is quite probable!

We must recognise in this the earnestness which really desires to benefit humanity, and for this reason does not even shrink from facing such a risk!

It is only to be regretted that people have not learned from this for the future by becoming more careful in passing judgments and – let us be honest – in showing hostility when it concerns things which belong to the same field as hypnotism! In spite of every experience many other subjects in this field are unfortunately today treated in exactly the same way, perhaps even worse!

In the end the same display will inevitably be repeated – that suddenly, without any transition, something is being eagerly advocated which until then they stubbornly sought to deny! What is more, they will unscrupulously attempt with every means at their disposal to obtain possession of and exploit many things, the research into and discovery of which was first carefully left to others, mostly so-called "laymen", who had to face their continual hostility!

Whether this can still be termed creditable and courageous is open to question! On the contrary, it is much more likely that this eternal repetition will throw a different light upon actions considered meritorious! Such is the issue considered from the *external* aspect!

But it becomes much more serious when one really knows the *effects of the application* of hypnotism. It is good that the *existence* of hypnotism has at last been recognised and confirmed, and that the verbose attacks of the scientists, which according to present experience only reveal the ignorance of those making them, have ceased. But that its *application* should consequently have been so widely extended under the aegis of the suddenly enlightened former opponents proves that these wiseacres are much further removed from real knowledge than the much-abused laymen who made the first researches.

It is appalling to know what harm is done to thousands who today confidently place themselves in the hands of the supposedly qualified in order to submit to hypnosis, either voluntarily or through persuasion or, worst of all, who are forced into it without their knowledge. Even if all this is done with the best intention to achieve something good, it does not alter the fact that this practice causes immeasurable harm *in every case!* Those who employ hypnotism are *not* qualified to do so! Only he can be called qualified who is fully familiar with the sphere to which all that he uses belongs. In the case of hypnotism this would be the Ethereal Sphere. And he who really knows this sphere, and not only imagines in his presumption that he does, *will never make use of hypnotism* as long as he desires what is best for his fellow-men. Unless, of course, he quite consciously intends to harm them gravely!

Therefore where hypnotism is used a sin is committed, whatever the circumstances; no matter whether by a layman or not. In this there is no single exception!

When in all simplicity one tries to regard the matter from the logical point of view alone, one must then come to the conclusion that it is in fact boundless frivolity to work with something the range of which one can only overlook to a very limited degree, and the final effect of which is not yet known!

It is no consolation to know that such frivolity concerning the weal and woe of one's fellow-men not only harms the person experimented upon, but also doubles the burden of responsibility which falls upon the experimenter. It would be better if people did not consent so confidently to something they do not themselves thoroughly understand! If it is done without their knowledge and wish, then it amounts to a downright crime, even if it is performed by a so-called qualified person!

Since it cannot be assumed that all who use hypnotism intend to harm their fellow-men, there remains nothing else but to state the fact that they are entirely ignorant of the nature of hypnotism, and face the results of their activity with a complete lack of understanding. There is not the slightest doubt about this; it is either the one or the other! Therefore all that remains is the lack of understanding!

When a person employs hypnotism *he binds the spirit* of the one hypnotised! This binding is in itself a spiritual transgression or crime. To use hypnotism for the purpose of healing a bodily disease or as a means towards psychic recovery does not excuse it. Nor can it be defended by the argument that the resulting psychic change for the better has also improved the volition of the patient, so that he has benefitted by hypnotic treatment.

To live and act in this belief is self-deception; for only what a human spirit undertakes with a perfectly *free* and uninfluenced volition can bring it that benefit which it needs for its real ascent. All else is extraneous and only capable of bringing about a temporary and apparent benefit to them.

Every binding of the spirit, no matter for what purpose it was done, forms an absolute check on the possibility of the necessary progress. Apart from the fact that such a binding brings far more dangers than advantages, a spirit bound in this way is not only subject to the influence of the hypnotiser but also remains to a certain extent defencelessly exposed to other ethereal influences, despite the possible prohibition of the hypnotiser, because in its bound state it lacks the sorely-needed protection which only freedom of movement can offer.

Just because men notice nothing of these perpetual conflicts, the attacks, and their own successful or unsuccessful efforts at defence, this does not exclude the activity in the Ethereal World or their co-operation with it.

Thus every man who is effectively hypnotised is more or less permanently hindered in the true development of his innermost ego. Whether the outward circumstances thereby become still more unfavourable, or show an apparent temporary benefit, is only of secondary consideration, and is therefore no criterion for any judgment. *The spirit must remain free in any case,* because in the final analysis only the spirit is concerned!

Supposing there is a noticeable outward improvement, upon which hypnotists so much like to build, the person concerned has in reality received no benefit from it at all. His bound spirit is unable to work as creatively in the Ethereal World as a spirit which is completely free. The ethereal forms created by his bound or forced volition are without power, because they were formed at secondhand and very soon wither away in the Ethereal World. Therefore even his improved volition cannot bring him the same benefit through the reciprocal action that can certainly be expected of the creative activity of a free spirit!

It is naturally the same with a bound spirit which wills and carries out something evil at the direction of the hypnotiser! Because of their lack of power, the ethereal forms will soon fade away or be absorbed by other similar types, despite the evil gross material deeds, so that an ethereal reciprocal action cannot set in. Consequently an earthly responsibility can fall upon those under compulsion, but not a spiritual responsibility! *The process is exactly the same with those who are insane!*

In this one sees again the complete Justice of the Creator, operating in the Ethereal World through the living laws which are unexcelled in their perfection. Thus the person compelled to perform evil deeds through an alien will cannot be accounted guilty, neither will he receive blessings for carrying out good actions through an alien will, because his independent "ego" played no part in them!

Instead something else happens! Through the hypnotism which forcibly binds the spirit the hypnotiser is simultaneously bound to his victim as if with the strongest chains. He cannot be released until he has helped the person whom he forcibly retarded in his free development to advance as far as he would have done if his spirit had not been bound. After his earthly death the hypnotiser must go where the spirit he formerly bound goes, be it even down to the deepest depths!

One can easily see from this what is in store for those who regularly practise hypnotism. When after their earthly death they awake and regain their senses in the beyond they will perceive with horror how many ties connect them with those who have already passed on as well as with those still on earth! Nothing of this can be remitted! Such a man must redeem one link after the other, even if he loses thousands of years in the process!

However, it is probable that he will be unable to reach the end of this task before he is drawn into the disintegration which will destroy the personality of his own "ego" – *for he has gravely sinned against the spirit!*

ASTROLOGY

ASTROLOGY is called the royal art, and not without reason. Not that it is the most exalted of arts, nor reserved only for earthly monarchs; but whoever proved really capable of practising it could take royal rank in the spiritual sense, since he would be able to guide the course of events in many respects!

However, there is not a single human being on earth to whom these abilities have been entrusted. Hence all work in this field must remain only pitiable efforts, unreliable if seriously meant by the practitioner, and malicious if conceit and morbid imagination play a part in it instead of deep earnestness!

On the whole the calculation of star aspects alone can be of little value, for there must also be included with the stellar radiations the ground radiations of the earth prevalent at the time, as well as all the activity of the living substance of the Ethereal World, such as the world of thought-forms, karma, vibrations of the Darkness and of the Light in the World of Matter, and much else. Now what human being can boast that he is able clearly and sharply to survey all this from the deepest depths to the highest heights of the World of Matter?

The radiations of the stars only form the paths and channels through which all the living ethereal substance can penetrate in a more concentrated form to the human soul in order to become effective there. Figuratively speaking, one can say that the stars give the signal for the times when the returning reciprocal actions and other influences can, through the guidance of their radiations, flow to the human being in a more complete and concentrated form. Unfavourable or hostile stellar radiations become united with evil vibrations floating in the Ethereal World in connection with a certain person; on the other hand favourable radiations will only unite with beneficial ethereal vibrations, all according to homogeneity.

Therefore such calculations are not in themselves entirely worthless. But there is a definite condition that with unfavourable stellar radiations a person also receives unfavourable reciprocal actions, and with favourable radiations he will experience favourable reciprocal actions. Otherwise there can be no manifestation! In turn, however, the stellar radiations are not a mere illusion in themselves, ineffective when not linked with other powers, but they do have certain automatic effects which act to a certain extent as a *check*.

If in the Ethereal World there are nothing but bad reactions due to and working upon a person, their activity will, according to the type of radiation, be stopped, pushed back or at least strongly restrained on the days and during the hours when the stellar radiations are favourable. Naturally also *vice versa* – when good reactions are at work, unfavourable radiations will intercept that which is favourable so long as such radiations are active.

Even when the *channels* of the stellar radiations *become empty,* due to the lack of *homogeneous* reactions, they still serve as a temporary *check* to other reactions that may be operating, so that they are never altogether without influence. Thus unless the corresponding reactions are lying ready for the person in question, good radiations do not always bring benefit or evil radiations harm.

Astrologers cannot exclaim here: "There, you see, we are right after all!" They are only right conditionally and in a very *limited* sense. This does not justify their frequent presumptuous assertions and commercial self-praise. The empty channels of the stellar radiations can indeed bring interceptions, but nothing else, neither good nor evil.

Again, it must be admitted that the temporary interception of evil reactions is to some extent beneficial! For the one who is sorely harassed by evil it creates a breathing spell, which will enable him to gain strength for further endurance.

In addition these intercepting radiations should induce the human spirit to exert greater power, which will awaken and strengthen it. The effort to overcome these interceptions will set the spirit more and more aglow.

In spite of everything the calculations of the astrologers could be welcomed if the perpetual boasting and advertising of so many of them were disregarded. However, still other important factors come into it, making the calculations very unreliable, so that they actually do more harm than good to the public.

For instance, not only the few stars which are today at the disposal of astrologers for their calculations come into consideration. There are countless other stars, not even known to astrologers, which play a great role in decreasing, strengthening, crossing or displacing the effects, so that the final picture of the calculations can often be exactly the opposite to what the best astrologer of today is capable of stating.

Finally there is still another decisive point – the greatest and most difficult of all – and that is the *soul* of each individual! Only he who, in addition to all the other requirements, can assess each one of these souls, with all its abilities, characteristics and karmaic entanglements, as well as the aims for which it is striving; in short, judge to a nicety its real maturity or immaturity in the spiritual sense; only he could venture to make calculations!

If, owing to the condition of his soul, a human being is surrounded by many dark influences, nothing luminous or good can reach him, however favourable the stellar radiations may be. If on the other hand the condition of a person's soul permits only purity and light to surround him, then the most unfavourable stellar radiations will not be able to oppress him to the extent of seriously harming him, for in the end the circumstances must always become beneficial.

The Omnipotence and Wisdom of God are not as one-sided as the disciples of astrology imagine them to be in their calculations. God does not make the fate of human beings, that is, their weal and woe, dependent only upon stellar radiations.

Of course they do have a powerful influence, not only for the individual, but in all world happenings. Still they are only tools, the activity of which is not only bound up with many other influences, but the possible manifestations of which also remain dependent upon them. Even if some astrologers imagine that they work intuitively, by impulse or inspiration, this cannot deepen their insight sufficiently to warrant greater confidence in the correctness of their calculations.

These remain one-sided piecework, inadequate, and with many gaps – in short, imperfect! They create disquiet among men, and disquiet is the soul's most dangerous enemy, for it breaks down the soul's natural defences and often lets in evil which would otherwise have found no entrance.

Many people feel uneasy when they tell themselves that they are at the moment under the influence of evil radiations; often, however, they become over-confident and unwise when convinced that they are subject to good radiations. In view of the inadequacy of all these calculations they are only burdening themselves with unnecessary worries instead of always exhibiting a free, joyous spirit, which sets up a more powerful defence than the most malevolent radiations could break down.

If they are so bent upon it, astrologers should quietly continue their work and try to perfect themselves in it; but only in private and for themselves, *which is what those who are really in earnest do!* For the time being they should spare other people such imperfections, since these would only have a destructive influence, resulting in an undermining of self-confidence and harmful fettering of free spirits! This should be avoided at all costs!

SYMBOLISM IN THE FATE OF MAN

IF MEN were not so entirely absorbed in the necessities and many trivialities of every-day life, but would also pay some attention to and observe more closely both the great and small happenings around them, they would soon come to a new understanding. They would be astonished at themselves, and hardly believe it possible that up till now they could so thoughtlessly have overlooked something so obvious!

And there is every reason why they should sorrowfully shake their heads at themselves! If they were only a little observant a whole world of strictly-ordered, living happenings would suddenly reveal itself to them, enabling them clearly to recognise the stern guidance of a higher Hand – the world of symbolism!

While its roots reach deep down into the ethereal part of Creation, only the very outskirts of this world of symbolism appear as visible effects on the material earth. It is just like a sea which appears perfectly calm, and which has a continuous but imperceptible movement only to be observed by its last effects, i. e., by the ripples lapping upon the beach.

Man does not realise how clearly he can observe the dreaded and incisive activity of karma, if he only devotes a little effort and attention to it. It is possible for him to become more familiar with it, however, so that the fear which is often awakened in thinking people will gradually fade and karma lose its terror.

If they learn to perceive and to trace the deeper vibrations of ethereal life through the visible happenings on earth, as a result of which they gradually become convinced of the existence of absolutely consistent reciprocal actions, this may develop into a way upwards for many people.

Once a person has arrived at this stage, he will slowly adjust himself step by step, until he finally recognises the strictly logical and complete driving power of the conscious Divine Will in all Creation; thus in the Gross Material as well as in the Ethereal World. From that moment onward he will reckon with it and submit to it of his own free will. This means that he will "swim" in the power, the effects of which can only be of advantage to him. It serves him because he knows how to make use of it by adapting himself to it in the right way.

Thus the reciprocal action can only bring him happiness. Smilingly he sees every biblical word being literally fulfilled whereas previously, because of its childlike simplicity, this often tended to become a stumbling block for him. A fulfilment often threatened to become difficult because in the opinion he held up till then it required a servile attitude. But as his eyes are opened the demand for obedience, regarded as so unpleasant, will gradually become the highest distinction that can befall a creature. It will truly become a Divine gift carrying within itself the possibility for an immense spiritual unfolding of power, which will permit a personal and conscious co-operation in the magnificent Creation.

The expressions: "He that humbleth himself shall be exalted"; "Man must humble himself before his God in order to enter His Kingdom"; he should "obey", "serve", and similar biblical counsels; all these somewhat repulse the modern man at the outset because of their simple, childlike, and yet striking form of expression. They offend his pride, rooted as it is in the consciousness of intellectual knowledge. He no longer wants to be led so blindly, but desires to understand and consciously co-operate in all things in order to obtain *through personal conviction* the inner upswinging necessary to accomplish everything great. *And this is not wrong!*

In his further development man *should* stand more consciously in Creation than he has done previously. And when he has joyfully recognised that the simple biblical expressions, the nature of which seems so foreign to the present times, counsel precisely what he voluntarily and with complete conviction decides upon through his knowledge of the mighty Laws of Nature, it will be as though a bandage falls from his eyes. He will be deeply shaken by the fact that hitherto he only rejected the old teachings because he interpreted them wrongly, and never seriously tried to penetrate them aright so as to bring them into harmony with the perceptive capacity of today.

Whether it is said: "Submit in humility to the Will of God" or "having recognised the mighty Laws of Nature aright, use them according to their kind and activity", *it is one and the same thing!*

Man can only make use of the powers that bear the Will of God when he studies them exactly, thus recognising them and adapting himself to them. To reckon with or adapt oneself to them really means nothing less than to adjust oneself to them, thus to submit oneself to them! It means not to go *against* these powers, but to go *with them!* Only when man adapts his will to the special nature of these powers, thus going in the same direction, can he make use of the might of these powers.

This is not mastery of the powers, but humbly submitting oneself to the Divine Will. Even if man ascribes much to his own sagacity or to scientific achievement, this does not alter the fact that it is nothing but a so-called "discovery" of the effects of the existing Laws of Nature, that is, of the Divine Will, which man has thereby "recognised", "adjusting" himself to this Will by the evaluation or use of these laws. This unquestionably *is* humble submission to the Will of God; it is "obeying"!

But now to symbolism! Every happening in Creation, thus in the World of Matter, must come to a proper ending of its cycle; or it can also be said, it must close its cycle! Therefore, according to the Laws of Creation, everything unconditionally returns to its starting point, where alone it can find its end and thus be severed, dissolved or extinguished as a working unit. This applies to the entire Creation as well as to each single happening, and it is the cause of the unconditional reciprocal action which in turn brings symbolism in its wake.

Since all actions must end where they originated, it follows that each action must end in the same species of substance whence it arose! Thus an ethereal beginning must have an ethereal ending, and a gross material beginning a gross material ending! Men cannot see the ethereal, but the gross material ending of every happening is visible to all. For many people, however, the actual key to it, the beginning, is missing, because in most cases it lies in a previous gross material existence.

Although the greater part of all happenings of reciprocal action takes effect only in the Ethereal World, the operating karma can never be completely redeemed unless in some way the end manifests in the Gross Material World and becomes visible there. Only when a visible happening corresponds to the nature of the reciprocal action can an open cycle be closed and thus bring about complete redemption; no matter whether, through the nature of the beginning, the redemption brings good or evil, happiness or unhappiness, blessing or forgiveness! This final visible effect *must* return to the place of its origin, and to *that* person who, through some action or other, initiated it! In no single case can this be avoided!

If in the meantime the person concerned has changed inwardly to such an extent that something better than the original action came to life in him, then the reaction of that original type cannot gain a firm foothold. It no longer finds homogeneous ground in the upward-striving soul, which has become more luminous and thus lighter in accordance with the Law of Spiritual Gravity*.

The natural result is that when it approaches the more luminous environment of the person concerned a darker reaction becomes permeated and thereby considerably weakened. But despite this the Law of Revolution and of Reciprocal Action must be entirely fulfilled in its automatic operating power! It is impossible to annul any of the Laws of Nature!

Consequently even such a weakened returning reciprocal action must, in accordance with the immovable laws, become visibly effective in the World of Gross Matter in order really to be redeemed and extinguished. The end must flow back into the beginning. The dark karma, however, is unable to bring harm to the person concerned because of his more luminous surroundings; and so it happens that the weakened reciprocal action can only work on his immediate *surroundings* in such a way as to provide the person concerned with the opportunity to do something voluntarily, the nature of which corresponds only to the *tendency* of the returning reciprocal action.

In comparison with the original unbroken strength of the returning dark reaction intended for him there is the difference, however, that it causes neither suffering nor harm, but may even bring joy.

This comprises a *purely symbolical* redemption of many a *heavy* karma, but still completely accords with the Laws of Creation, which operate automatically in that way through the change in the condition of the soul. Therefore most people often remain unaware of it. The karma, however, has been redeemed and Immutable Justice has been satisfied to its most delicate vibrations. But these happenings, which accord so naturally with the Creative Laws, hold such mighty acts of Grace as only the Omniscience of the Creator could bring forth in His Perfect Work.

* Lecture: "Fate".

There are many such purely symbolic atonements where otherwise reciprocal action would strike heavily!

Let us take an example! A once hard, domineering character has burdened himself with heavy karma through indulging these attributes in the oppression of his fellow men. Active according to its specific nature, this karma proceeds on its course, and must then fall back upon him with the same characteristics, but many times reinforced! This vibration of ruthless despotism, often immensely reinforced through the Law of Attraction of ethereal homogeneous species, will in approaching him so interpenetrate his whole ethereal environment that it will have an incisive effect on his gross material environment, which is closely connected with it; thereby creating conditions forcing the originator to suffer to a far greater extent from a similar tyranny than did the people he once tormented.

Meanwhile if such a person has arrived at a better understanding and has, through his genuine efforts to ascend, gained a more luminous and lighter environment, then of course the nature of the final effect will also be changed! The returning waves of denser darkness will be more or less permeated by the degree of luminosity of the new surrounding of the person concerned and will thus be rendered more or less harmless. If the former tyrant has made great progress, that is, if the guilty person has made an exceptional improvement, it may happen that the final reaction will be as good as annulled, and that he will only do something in passing which outwardly resembles atonement.

Let us suppose it be the case of a woman! Then it would suffice for her to take the brush out of her maidservant's hand to show her in all kindness how to scrub the floor. Even if there are only a few such movements, they satisfy the symbolism of service! This little action results in a redemption that had to happen *visibly* and which, despite its insignificance, can end a heavy karma.

In the same way the re-arrangement of even one room can become a symbol ending and redeeming a guilt, the atonement or reaction of which would really have required a greater, more revolutionary change, with painfully incisive effects. Such things occur in one way or another through the weakened influence of a reaction; or incidental actions are often skilfully used by the spiritual guidance to bring about a redemption.

In all this it is naturally presumed that an exceptionally great upsurge, with a corresponding change in the condition of the soul, has already set in. These are circumstances that an astrologer is actually unable to take into account, as a result of which he often occasions unnecessary worries with his calculations, sometimes even evoking such fear that the power of this alone is able to call forth or form something unpleasant. Thus the calculation may be apparently fulfilled, when without such fear it would have proved to be wrong. In such cases, however, the person concerned has through his fear opened a door in the circle of light surrounding him.

Whenever a man voluntarily stretches out his hand beyond his protecting cover no help can come to him from any direction. His own will breaks *every* protection from within, as unless he exercises his own volition nothing can reach him through the Light from outside.

Hence the smallest kindness to a fellow man, a genuinely felt sorrow with a neighbour, even a single friendly word, can lead to the symbolic redemption of a karma, as soon as the underlying motive is an earnest striving for what is good!

Naturally this earnest striving for the good must come first; for otherwise there can be no question of symbolic redemption, and every reaction due would have to work out to the fullest extent!

As soon as a person's serious volition to ascend sets in, however, he will quickly notice how his surroundings become gradually more and more animated, as if everything possible were being put in his way which, however, always turns out well. This is immediately obvious to him and finally, and just as striking, there will come a more peaceful period or a time when all that happens will plainly help him to rise in the material sense. Then the time for atonement is over!

With joyful thanks he may gratefully indulge the thought that much guilt has fallen from him, for which he would otherwise have had to do heavy penance! He must then be on his guard that his volition and desires only weave good threads of fate so that only good may return to him!

FAITH

WHAT is exhibited by the majority of the so-called faithful is not faith! Real faith can only arise when a man has made the contents of the Divine Messages completely his own, and thereby turned them into a spontaneous, living conviction.

Divine Messages are received through the Word of God and also through His Creation. Everything bears witness to Him and to His Will. As soon as a man is able consciously to *experience* the entire process of genesis and existence, all his intuitions, his thoughts and his deeds will unite in joyful affirmation of God.

Then, however, he will become silent, and will not speak about it much. He will have become a person who through this silent devotion to God, which can also be called trust in God, stands firmly and securely in the entire Creation. He will not lose himself in fantasies or fits of ecstasy, nor live an exclusively spiritual life here on earth, but attend to his earthly duties fearlessly and with common sense, thereby skilfully using his keen intellect as a sharp weapon, necessary for his defence when attacked, without of course being unjust in doing so.

In no case should he silently tolerate being treated with injustice, because he would thereby encourage and strengthen evil!

Now there are many who only *imagine* themselves to have faith! In spite of inwardly acknowledging the existence of God and His Divine activity, they fear the smile of the doubters. It is disagreeable and painful to them. In the course of conversation they silently let it pass with an inscrutable expression on their faces, and in their embarrassment they constantly make concessions to the doubters through their attitude. This is not faith, but merely an inward *yielding!* In reality they are denying their God, to Whom they pray in silence and from Whom they consequently expect every blessing.

This false consideration for the doubter cannot be excused by saying that to the "faithful" the subject is "too sacred and too serious" to allow it to be exposed to possible ridicule. Nor can one call it modesty, for it is nothing but mean cowardice! Speak up at last and show whose spiritual children you are! With the pride that becomes every child of God fearlessly face *every* man! Only then will the doubters be finally forced to bridle their sneers, which only betray their uncertainty. At the present time, however, their mockery is only fostered and encouraged by the frightful behaviour of many of the "faithful".

These people deceive themselves, because they have ascribed an entirely different meaning to the word "faith" from what it demands. Faith must be a *living* thing, that is to say, it must become even more than conviction, it must become a deed! It becomes a deed as soon as it permeates everything – all intuitions, all thoughts, all actions. Coming from within the man, it must unobtrusively become visible and noticeable as a matter of course in all that appertains to him! It must not only be hung out as a mask or a shield, but all that becomes manifest outwardly should merely be a result of the natural radiation of the inner spiritual core!

In plain words, true faith must be a power which, radiating from the spirit of man, permeates his flesh and blood and so becomes something quite natural – nothing artificial or forced, nothing studied, but normal life!

Observe many of the faithful! They declare their absolute belief in life after death and apparently order their thoughts accordingly. If, however, at some opportune moment they receive proof of life in the beyond, somewhat outside the ordinary course of events, they are terrified or deeply shaken! Thereby they show that fundamentally they were not so convinced after all of this life in the beyond, for otherwise such an occasional proof would seem quite natural. Consequently they should neither be frightened nor specially shaken by it!

In addition there are countless happenings which clearly reveal how little faith the so-called faithful have. Theirs is no living faith!

EARTHLY POSSESSIONS

A QUESTION which very often arises is whether a man should part with his earthly possessions or disregard them altogether when he is striving for *spiritual* gain.

It would be foolish to lay down such a principle! When it is said that a man should not cling to earthly possessions as soon as he strives towards the Kingdom of Heaven, this does not mean that he should give or throw them away and live in poverty. Man may and should gladly enjoy what God provides for him through His Creation!

"That he should not cling" to earthly possessions only means that man should not allow himself to go so far as to make their accumulation the main object of his life on earth, and thus "cling" mainly to this one idea!

Such an attitude is naturally bound to distract him from higher aims, for which he would have no time left. Indeed, with his whole being he would only cling to this one aim of acquiring earthly possessions! Whether it be for the sake of the possessions themselves, for the sake of the pleasure they give him, or for whatever other reason, the result would always be fundamentally the same. Such a man clings and thereby binds himself to what is purely material, thus losing the ability to look upwards and ascend.

The erroneous conception that material possessions are incompatible with striving spiritually upwards is responsible for the absurd view held by the majority of people that all spiritual endeavours, if they are to be taken seriously, may never have anything in common with earthly possessions. The harm mankind have done themselves through this view has strangely enough never occurred to them!

As a result they debase the spiritual or highest gifts that may fall to their share. Because of this peculiar attitude all spiritual endeavours in the past had to depend on offerings and charity, just as *beggars* did. Thus the same attitude as was shown towards beggars crept in unnoticed towards spiritual endeavours, which could therefore never command the respect that in the first place they are really entitled to!

For the same reason, however, these endeavours were always doomed to perish from the very beginning, because they could never stand firmly on their own feet, but always remained dependent upon the good will of men. What is most sacred to him, the *spiritual part,* must be protected and preserved against his fellow men, and it is just on this account that anyone striving seriously should not despise earthly possessions, which must now mainly serve him as a shield in the Gross Material World to ward off like with like!

It would create an unhealthy position if, in the age of the materialist, those striving spiritually upwards should despise the strongest weapon of their unscrupulous opponents! This would show a levity which might revenge itself heavily upon them.

Therefore, all you true believers, do not despise worldly possessions, which could also have only been created through the Will of God, Whom you seek to honour! But do not let the comfort which such earthly possessions can afford lull you to sleep, but make sound use of them!

The same applies to the special gift of such powers as serve to heal various illnesses, or to similar beneficial abilities. In a most naive or, better said, impudent manner people assume that such abilities, because they were given as a special gift from spiritual spheres to be used on earth, should be placed at their disposal free of cost. It even goes so far that some people expect to be met with special expressions of joy when in their great distress they "condescend" to avail themselves of such help! Such people must be excluded from all help, even if it were the only way to save them!

Those so gifted, however, should themselves first learn to set a greater value on this gift of God, so that they do not continually cast pearls before swine! To achieve real results they need *far more* physical and ethereal power, as well as more time, than a barrister needs to give to his best plea in defence, a doctor to visit many patients, or an artist to create a picture. It would never occur to anybody to expect the barrister, the doctor or the artist to do their work for nothing, although their intellectual ability, as every other talent, is also but "a gift of God" and nothing else! Now, at last, cast aside these beggar's rags and don the garment that befits you!

DEATH

THERE is one thing in which all men believe without exception. It is death! Everyone is convinced that it will come. It is one of the few facts about which there is no dispute or ignorance.

Although everybody from childhood onward reckons with the fact that they must eventually die, yet the majority always try to ward off the thought. Many people indeed are even irritated if the subject is broached in their presence. Others again carefully avoid cemeteries and funerals, and if by chance they meet a funeral procession in the street, they seek to efface every impression as soon as possible.

They are always oppressed at such moments by a secret fear that death may one day suddenly surprise them. An indefinable horror prevents them from seriously grappling with this irrefutable fact.

There is hardly another event that is so inevitable and yet so constantly pushed aside in their thoughts as death; and hardly so important an event in life on earth, except for birth! It is a striking fact that man wishes to concern himself so little just with the beginning and the end of his earthly existence, whereas to all other events, even quite trivial matters, he tries to ascribe a deep significance.

He examines and ponders over all the intermediate happenings much more than upon that which would enlighten him on everything – the beginning and the end of his life on earth! Death and birth are so closely linked because one is the result of the other.

In the first place how little serious thought is given to the act of procreation! Only in very rare cases is there anything to be found worthy of the dignity of a human being! Just in this matter man cheerfully places himself on a level with the animal, yet without being able to preserve its innocence. This, indeed, puts him *below* the animal, which acts according to the level it occupies in Creation.

Man, however, can not or will not keep to the level that befits him, but descends to a lower one, and then wonders why the whole of humanity gradually deteriorates in various respects.

To start with all the customs at weddings are so designed as to make marriage appear merely an earthly affair. It even goes so far in many cases that more serious-minded people would like to turn away in disgust from the suggestive details which hint at nothing more than earthly intercourse. Wedding festivities have in many cases degenerated into absolute match-making orgies, which parents conscious of their great responsibility should strictly forbid their children to attend!

However, youths and young women who do not themselves feel disgust at the customs and insinuations during such festivities, and who although responsible for their own actions still do not stay away, may already be counted as belonging to the same base level, and can thus be left out of all consideration. It appears as if even in this matter people were trying through a drunken revelry to deceive themselves over something they do not want to think about.

If, then, life on earth is built up on such a frivolous foundation, as has indeed already become customary, one can understand that man also tries to deceive himself about death by striving desperately not to think of it. This pushing aside of all serious thoughts is closely connected with his own base attitude during the act of procreation. The indefinable fear which accompanies man like a shadow during his whole life on earth largely originates in the fact that he is fully aware of all that is wrong in his frivolous and unworthy actions.

And if he cannot get peace any other way, as a last resort he artificially and frantically clings to the delusion that either death is the end of all things, whereby he consciously acknowledges his inferiority and cowardice at possibly being called to account, or the hope that he is not much worse than others.

But all these illusions do not alter the fact in the slightest degree that earthly death is approaching – coming nearer day by day, hour by hour!

How pitiful it so often appears when the majority of those who so rigidly tried to deny any responsibility in a life after death begin, in their last hours, fearfully to ask the great questions, thus proving they have suddenly become confused about their own convictions! But their questioning is of little avail then, for again it is only cowardice which, shortly before the great step out of this earth-life, suddenly conjures up the possibility of a continuation of life and of being called to account therein.

However anxiety, fear and cowardice can no more diminish or redeem the unconditional reaction arising from every deed than can stubbornness. Real comprehension, i. e., a true understanding, cannot be attained in this way. Prompted by fear, their intellectual cunning, which often enough proved trustworthy during their earth-life, plays a mean trick on dying people during their last hours by inducing them, out of ordinary prudence, suddenly to become outwardly pious; this at the moment when the severing of the ethereal man, who continues living, from the physical body has so far advanced that during this process of separating the intuitive life has become equal in strength to the intellect, which up till then had forcibly subjugated it.

But they gain nothing from this! They will reap what they sowed through their thoughts and deeds during their life on earth! Nothing has been improved or changed in the slightest degree! They will be irresistibly drawn into the network of the strictly operating Laws of Reciprocal Action, so as to experience in the Ethereal World all the errors they perpetrated in thought and deed as a result of wrong convictions!

Such people have every reason to dread the hour when they must leave their physical bodies, which for a time offered protection against many ethereal happenings. This protection was given to them as a shield and a cover so that behind it they could have changed for the better in undisturbed peace, and even completely redeemed many a thing which would otherwise have hit them severely.

It is doubly sad, yes even ten-fold so, for those who spend this time of mercy which every earth-life represents in frivolous deception, as if it were a drunken revel. Many there are who have every reason for alarm and apprehension!

The case is quite different with those who have not wasted their existence on earth but who, although at a late hour yet still in time and not impelled by fear and anxiety, have set out on the road to spiritual ascent. They will take their serious seeking over with them as a staff and support in the Ethereal World. Without fear and anxiety they can venture to take the step from the Gross Material World into the Ethereal World which is inevitable for everyone, because all that is transient, such as the physical body, must sooner or later perish again! They may welcome the hour of this release, for it means definite progress for them, no matter what they have to experience in the ethereal life! Their good experiences will then bring them happiness and the evil ones will be made surprisingly easy, for their good volition will help them in this far more powerfully than they ever dreamed.

The process of dying in itself is nothing but birth into the Ethereal World, similar to the process of birth into the Gross Material World. After the separation the ethereal body remains attached to the physical body for a time as if with a navel cord. The higher the soul now born into the Ethereal World has already developed itself towards this Ethereal World during its life on earth, the looser this cord will become.

The more a man's volition has chained him to this earth, i. e., to gross matter, indicating thereby a refusal to acknowledge any continuation of life in the Ethereal World, the more firmly will this volition bind him with this cord to his physical body and consequently also bind the ethereal body, which he needs as a garment for his spirit in the Ethereal World.

The denser his ethereal body is the heavier it becomes according to the prevailing laws, and the darker it must appear. Such great resemblance and close relation to matter makes it very hard for the ethereal body to detach itself from the physical body, so that it happens in such cases that it must still undergo and feel the last physical pains as well as the whole process of decay. Neither does it remain insensible with cremation.

After the final severance of this connecting cord, the ethereal body sinks to that level in the Ethereal World where its surroundings are of corresponding density and weight. There, in this environment of equal weight, it will find only those of similar tendencies. It is understandable that conditions there are worse than when on earth in the physical body, because in the Ethereal World all intuitive feelings express themselves in *full* force and without restraint.

It is different with those people who during their life on earth have begun to strive for all that is noble. Because they bear within themselves a living conviction about the step into the Ethereal World, the severance is much easier. The ethereal body of such a person and its connecting cord are not dense. Their texture is alien to that of the physical body, and this permits the severance to be very quickly effected. Thus during the entire so-called death struggle or the last muscular twitchings of the physical body, the ethereal body is already standing *beside* the latter, if indeed one can speak of a death struggle at the normal death of such a person. The loose and slender condition of the connecting cord prevents the ethereal being standing beside the body from feeling any pain because, being so frail and light in substance, this cord cannot transmit pain from the physical body to the ethereal body.

Owing to its finer nature such a strand severs the connection more quickly, setting the ethereal body completely free in a shorter space of time to soar to the region consisting of this finer and lighter substance. There it can only find kindred souls and gain peace and happiness through the increasingly high quality of the intuitive life. Such a light and less dense ethereal body naturally appears brighter and more luminous, until finally it becomes so transparent that the inner spiritual core begins to break through radiantly before it enters the spiritual sphere as a completely luminous radiant spirit.

Those, however, who are present at a death bed should take warning not to break out into loud lamentations! When the grief at parting is too strongly expressed, the person in the process of detaching himself, or who is perhaps already standing beside his body in ethereal form, may hear or feel it and be emotionally disturbed by it. If then pity awakens in him, together with the wish to say a few words of consolation, this again binds him more strongly to his physical body through the desire to make himself *understood* by the grief-stricken mourners.

He can only make himself understood on earth by the use of his brain. This effort, however, makes for a closer connection with the physical body, and indeed this is a necessary condition. The result is that not only does an ethereal body still in the process of detaching itself re-unite itself more closely to the physical body but, if it is already standing detached beside the physical body, it will be drawn back into it once more. The final result is that he will once again feel all the pains from which he had already been delivered.

When the process of detachment is renewed it is much more difficult, and may even last for some days. This brings about the so-called prolonged death struggle, which becomes really painful and difficult for the soul wanting to depart. The blame lies with those who, through their selfish grief, have called it back from its natural course of development.

Through this interruption of the normal course, be it only the weak attempt at concentrating on making itself understood, a new and forced connection has taken place. To dissolve this unnatural connection again is not so easy for one who is completely inexperienced in this matter. And, because it desired this reconnection itself, no help can be afforded.

Such a connection can easily be effected as long as the physical body is not yet completely cold and the connecting strand, which often does not tear till after many weeks, is still in existence. It is unnecessary suffering for the dying man, a rudeness and want of consideration on the part of the bystanders.

Therefore absolute quiet should reign in the chamber of death, a dignity and seriousness corresponding to the importance of the hour! People who cannot control themselves should be forcibly removed, even if they be the nearest relatives.

DEPARTED THIS LIFE!

PERPLEXED and lonely, a soul stands in the chamber of death! Perplexed because the human being lying on the death-bed refused while on earth to believe in the continuity of life after the death of the physical body! He had therefore never seriously considered the matter and ridiculed all who spoke of it.

Confused, he looks around! He sees himself lying on his death-bed, sees people he knows standing about it weeping, hears the words they speak, and senses their grief as they lament his passing. He would like to laugh and call out that he is still alive! He does so, but is surprised to observe that they do not hear him. He calls again and again, louder and ever louder. The people do not hear it, but go on lamenting. Fear begins to arise within him, for he himself hears his own voice quite clearly, and is also distinctly aware of his own body.

Again he calls out in anguish, but nobody pays any attention to him! Weeping, they gaze upon the lifeless body, which he recognises as his own yet suddenly regards as something strange that is no longer part of him, for he now stands beside it in a body free from all the pain he had suffered up till then!

Now he lovingly calls the name of his wife who is kneeling beside the death-bed, but her weeping does not cease and there is no word or movement to show that she has heard him. In desperation he walks up to her and shakes her shoulder vigorously. She does not notice it. He does not know that he is only touching and shaking the ethereal body of his wife, not the physical one, and that the woman, who like him never gave a thought to the existence of anything beyond the physical body, therefore cannot feel his touch upon her ethereal body.

An unspeakable feeling of dread makes him shudder! A feeling of being utterly forsaken makes him so weak that he sinks to the floor and loses consciousness!

The sound of a voice he used to know gradually awakens him again. He sees the body he used on earth surrounded by flowers. He would like to fly away, but he finds it impossible to sever himself from this cold, lifeless body. He distinctly feels he is still connected to it. Again he hears the voice which awoke him from his slumber. It is his friend speaking to another person. They have each brought a wreath and are talking together while laying them down. No one else is in the room.

His friend! He wishes to attract his attention, also that of the other man; they were often welcome guests together in his home. He must tell them that strange as it may seem he is still alive, that he can still hear what they are saying! He calls out! But his friend calmly turns to his companion and goes on talking. But *what* he says gives him a shock! Is *that* his friend? Is that the way he talks about him now?

Petrified, he listens to the words of these people with whom he had so often drunk and laughed, and who only flattered him while sitting at his table enjoying the hospitality of his home!

They left and others came. *How clearly* he could now see through people! So many whom he had highly valued now filled him with disgust and anger, and several whom he had always disregarded he would like to shake hands with gratefully. But they neither heard nor sensed him, although he shrieked and raved at them to prove he was still alive!

In a great procession the body was carried to the grave. He sat astride the coffin! Embittered and desperate, he could now but laugh and laugh! But his laughter quickly gave way to deepest despondency, and a great feeling of desolation assailed him. He became tired and fell asleep.

When he awoke darkness surrounded him. How long he had been asleep he could not tell, but he felt that he could no longer be connected to his physical body, for he was free! But free in a strangely oppressive darkness!

He called out, but no sound came. He could not hear his own voice. He sank back groaning, and in so doing struck his head hard against a sharp stone. When after a long time he awoke once more there was still the same darkness, the same sinister silence. He wanted to jump up, but his limbs were heavy and refused to do their work. With all the strength born of fearful desperation he struggled to his feet, staggering and groping his way to and fro. He often fell down and injured himself, and bumped against corners and edges to right and left, but he was allowed no respite – for a strong urge drove him to grope onwards unceasingly and to seek. To seek! But what? His thinking was confused, tired and without hope. He was seeking something that he could not comprehend. He was seeking!

It drove him onward, ever onward, until he again sank down, only to rise once more and resume his wanderings. Years passed in this way, decades, till finally tears welled up in his eyes and sobs shook his breast and ... a thought arose in him, a petition, the outcry of a tired soul yearning for an end to this condition of dark hopelessness!

This outcry of utter despair and hopeless suffering, however, gave birth to the first thought of longing to escape from this condition. He tried to understand what had brought him to this terrible plight, and what had so cruelly forced him to wander in darkness. Around him he could feel nothing but stark rocks! Was this the earth, or perhaps after all the other world in which he had never been able to believe?

The other world! Then he must be physically dead and yet alive, if he could call this condition being alive! He found thinking the greatest difficulty. And so he groped onwards in his seeking. Again years passed. Oh, for a way out of this darkness! The wish grew into a powerful urge, which gave way to longing. Longing, however, is the purer intuition born out of the coarse urge, and out of this longing very timidly a prayer arose.

Finally this prayer of longing burst forth from him like a spring, and a feeling of soothing, comforting peace, humility and submission, entered his soul. When he arose to continue his wanderings he experienced a warm glow coursing through his body, for now twilight surrounded him and he could suddenly see!

Far away in the distance he recognised a light, like a torch that greeted him. Jubilantly he stretched forth his arms towards it, and filled with deep happiness he again sank down, his heart overflowing with gratitude, and gave thanks to Him Who had granted him this light! With renewed strength he then strode towards the light. It came no nearer to him, but after his experiences he still hoped to reach it even if it should take centuries. What had now happened to him might happen once again, and thus finally lead him out of this stony desert into a warmer and lighter region, if he humbly prayed for it!

"My God, help me in this!" broke forth from his hope-filled breast. And, what joy, he could again hear his own voice! Even though at first quite weak, still he could hear it! His happiness at this gave him new strength, and full of hope he again went forward.

Such is the story of the initial experiences of a soul in the Ethereal World! This soul could not be called bad, on earth he had even been considered very good. He had been the head of a large industrial establishment, always busy and meticulously concerned to comply with the mundane laws.

Let me add an explanation to this case! The man who in his life on earth refuses to acknowledge that there is also life after death, and that sooner or later he will be forced to render account for all that he has done and all that he has left undone, is blind and deaf when he one day has to pass over into the Ethereal World. Only during the days and weeks while he still remains connected with his discarded physical body will he be able partially to observe what goes on around him.

However, once he is free from his disintegrating physical body this possibility is lost to him! He no longer sees or hears anything. That, however, is not punishment, but quite natural, because he did not *want* to see or hear anything of the Ethereal World. His own will, which can quickly form ethereal matter corresponding to it, prevents his ethereal body from seeing as well as hearing until gradually a change takes place in his soul. Whether this takes years or decades, perhaps even centuries, is the concern of each individual. He can exercise his free will untrammelled. Help will only come to him when he himself longs for it. Not before! It will never be forced upon him!

The light which this soul greeted with such great joy when it started to see again was always there, but previously the soul was unable to see it. This light is also clearer and stronger than it appears at first sight to the hitherto blind soul. *How* the soul sees it, whether strong or weak, depends entirely on the condition of the soul itself. The light does not come closer of its own accord, but it is there! The soul can enjoy it at any time, if it humbly and earnestly wishes to do so.

However, what I am explaining here applies only to this *particular kind* of human soul. It does not necessarily apply to others. In the region of darkness and its planes there is no light. There it is impossible for him who advances inwardly to be able suddenly to see the light, for he must first be led out of the surroundings which hold him.

The condition of the soul depicted here may surely be called miserable, because it is filled with a great fear and is void of all hope, but it did not wish it otherwise. It now receives only what it forced upon itself. It had refused to believe in a conscious life after physical death. But the soul cannot abolish this continuation of life for itself, because it has no jurisdiction over it. It only builds for itself a barren ethereal plane, paralysing the senses of the ethereal body, so that it can neither see nor hear ethereally until ... *the soul itself* finally changes its attitude.

These are the souls which can be found by the million on earth today. Apart from the fact that they refuse all knowledge about God and eternity, they can still be called *decent*. The fate of the evil-minded is naturally much worse, but we shall not speak about them here, only about the so-called *respectable* people.

When it is said that God will stretch forth His Hand to *help*, this is done *in the Word* which He sends out to mankind, showing them how they can redeem themselves from the guilt in which they have become entangled. From the very beginning He has shown His Mercy in all the great possibilities placed freely at the disposal of human spirits in Creation. This is so overwhelming that the man of today cannot even conceive it because he never concerned himself with it seriously enough! Wherever he did, however, it was only as a pastime or for the purpose of vain self-aggrandisement!

MIRACLES

THE EXPLANATION for this lies in the word itself. A miracle is a happening that sets men wondering; it is something they do not believe to be possible! But they only *think* it is so, for that it is possible is proved by the fact that it does happen.

But miracles such as many of the believers in God imagine them to be do *not* exist! They consider a miracle as something that happens outside the Laws of Nature, even something contrary to those laws, and it is just on this account that they see the hand of God in it. They think a miracle is something possible only to their God, Who thereby shows His especial Grace and uses His Omnipotence to accomplish it.

Such poor creatures erroneously imagine that omnipotence implies the capability to act arbitrarily, and they regard miracles as such arbitrary acts! But they do not reflect how they thereby belittle God, for such miracles would be anything but Divine!

In the first place Divine Activity shows an absolute perfection, without fault or gap. And perfection demands the strictest logic and absolute consistency in every respect. Consequently a miracle can only work itself out with flawless consistency in the course of events. Although it happens in the usual way the only difference with a miracle is that the process of development, which according to earthly conceptions should take a longer time, occurs with such immense rapidity, either through the special power granted to some individual or through some other channel, that it appears miraculous by reason of its extraordinary speed; in short, it may be called a miracle!

Occasionally it may be something reaching beyond the present state of development that finds its fulfilment through concentrated power. But it will never in any circumstances occur outside or even contrary to the existing Laws of Nature! In such a case, which is an impossibility anyway, it would lose all its Divine essence and become an arbitrary act. Thus it is exactly the opposite to what so many of the faithful believers imagine it to be.

364

32. MIRACLES

Nothing that is deficient in strict consistency can emanate from God. Every miracle is an absolutely natural happening, only occurring with exceptional speed and concentrated power. It is completely out of the question that anything unnatural can ever happen in this connection.

When diseases are healed which up till now were regarded as incurable, this does not mean that the Natural Laws have been changed, but merely exposes the great deficiencies in human knowledge. All the more should it be recognised as a mercy of the Creator when here and there He endows individual human beings with special powers which they can use for the benefit of suffering humanity. But it will always be those who have kept themselves far away from every conceit of science, because earthbound knowledge quite naturally suffocates the ability to receive higher gifts.

Worldly scholarship exerts itself to achieve something, but can never receive in a pure, childlike way. The powers coming from a sphere beyond time and space may, however, only be received in simplicity, but can never be acquired by exertion. This circumstance alone shows which is the more valuable, the stronger and, therefore, the more correct.

BAPTISM

If a child is baptised by a clergyman who regards it as merely a duty of his office, it is absolutely meaningless, doing neither good nor harm. On the other hand, when an adult person is baptised, the strength and purity of his inner preparedness to receive will contribute to the possibility as to whether he really will receive something spiritual or not.

In the case of a child, only the belief of the one who administers the baptism can serve as a means of achieving the purpose. According to the strength and purity of this belief, the child receives a certain spiritual strengthening through this act, as well as a protection against evil radiations.

Baptism is an act which not every human being ordained by earthly church dignitaries can perform effectually. For this purpose a human being is needed who is connected with the Light. Only such a person is able to transmit light! This ability, however, is not attainable through earthly studies, nor through church consecration or ordination. It has nothing whatever to do with mundane customs, but is purely a gift of the Almighty Himself.

One so endowed thereby becomes a Called One! There are not many such, for this gift demands the condition that there be suitable soil within the person himself. If this condition does not exist the connection from the Light cannot be established. The Light cannot penetrate into soil which has not been loosened or into soil hostile to it, because like everything else this process is also strictly subject to the all-pervading Primordial Laws.

Such a Called One, however, can really transmit spirit and power through the act of baptism, which thereby receives *that* value which it expresses symbolically! In spite of this it is always preferable only to baptise those persons who are fully conscious of the effect of this act and who have the ardent desire for it. Therefore, if it is to become of real value, baptism requires a certain age of maturity and the voluntary wish of the person to be baptised, as well as a Called One to do the baptising.

John the Baptist, who today is still regarded as a truly Called man by all the Christian churches, found his greatest adversaries just among the Scribes and Pharisees, who at that time imagined themselves to be the most highly called to judge over this matter.

The people of Israel *were* themselves Called at that time. There is no doubt about that! In their midst the Son of God was to accomplish His Mission on earth. Accordingly the priests of that nation should also at that time have been the most highly Called Ones to baptise! But in spite of this John the Baptist had to come so that, as the only Called One, he could baptise the Son of God in His earthly vessel at the beginning of His actual Mission on earth.

This happening also shows that earthly appointments to office have nothing to do with Divine callings. And again only Called Ones can effectively fulfil commissions in the name of God, thus be commissioned by Him, as it should be in the case of baptism. The Called One, John the Baptist, who was not acknowledged by the existing high priest of the Called people, described his adversaries as a "generation of vipers"! He denied them the right to come to him!

Nor did these same high priests of the then Called people even recognise the Son of God Himself! They persecuted Him ceaselessly and worked for His earthly destruction, because He was superior to them and therefore a source of trouble.

If Christ were again to come among men at the present time in a new form, He would undoubtedly meet with the same denial and animosity as He then experienced. A similar fate would befall one sent by Him. All the more so because mankind today imagine themselves to be more "advanced"!

Not only in this one case of John the Baptist, but in many similar cases, it is clearly shown that consecrations by the earthly churches, and ordinations which as such are actually a part of "church organisation" only, can never bring a greater ability to carry out spiritual acts if the officiating person has not already been called for it.

Considered in the correct way, therefore, baptism administered by church dignitaries is nothing more than a preliminary act of admission into the organisation of a religious union. It is not admission to God, but admission into the respective *church community on earth*. The confirmation which follows later, including confirmation by a bishop, can only be regarded as a repeated acknowledgement and a further admission to the customs of these communities. The minister acts as the "accredited servant of the church", thus in a purely earthly sense, because the church and God are not one and the same thing!

THE HOLY GRAIL

Manifold are the interpretations of the legends which exist about the Holy Grail. The most serious scholars and investigators have occupied themselves with this mystery. Much of their work has high moral value, but it all shows one great fault – that they have only built from the earth upwards, while the essential thing, the ray of light from above, which alone could bring animation and enlightenment, is missing.

All who strive from below upwards must come to a halt at the boundary line of the material sphere, even if they are granted to conceive the greatest possible heights! In most cases, however, even under the most favourable conditions, barely half this road can be covered. And how great is the distance from there to the real understanding of the Holy Grail!

This feeling that it is so unattainable finally grows upon the investigators, with the result that they try to regard the Grail purely as the symbolic expression of an idea, so as to give it the high place they rightly feel is its proper due. But in so doing they actually go backwards, not forwards; downwards instead of upwards. They deviate from the right way, which is already indicated to some extent in the legends.

These legends faintly reflect the truth, but only very faintly, because the lofty inspirations and visionary pictures of the poets were pressed into far too material a concept through the intervention of the intellect during the transmission. In their reproductions they portrayed what they received spiritually in pictures conforming to their own worldly surroundings, with the object of making the meaning of the legends more readily understandable to men. In this, however, they failed because they themselves could not arrive at the essence of the truth.

Thus from the very outset the subsequent research and investigation was founded upon an uncertain basis, and any success was bound to be very limited! Therefore it is not surprising that finally only the thought of something purely symbolic remained, and redemption through the Grail was transferred to every man's inmost self.

The existing interpretations are not without great ethical value, but they cannot claim to be an explanation of the legends, much less to approach the truth about the Holy Grail.

Nor is the Holy Grail meant to be the cup which the Son of God used during His last meal with His Disciples at the end of His Ministry on earth, and in which His blood was afterwards caught when He was on the cross! This vessel is a sacred memento of the Son of God's sublime work of redemption, but it is not the Holy Grail of which the poets of the legends were mercifully granted to sing praises. These legends have been misinterpreted by mankind!

They were meant to be promises from the Highest Heights, the fulfilment of which mankind is to await! Had they been interpreted as such, surely another way would have long since been found to take the investigations a little further. As it was, however, all their interpretations had finally to come to a dead stop because a full and complete solution could never be reached; owing to the false conceptions of the past, all the investigations started on a wrong basis from the very beginning!--

No human spirit, even if it has finally attained its greatest perfection and immortality, will ever be able to face the Holy Grail Itself! It is for this reason that, unless a Messenger is sent *from there,* no detailed tidings about It can ever reach the World of Matter! Thus the Holy Grail will remain a mystery to the human spirit for all eternity!

Man should keep to what he can grasp spiritually and, above all, he should try to fulfil what lies in his power and develop it to its most noble state of perfection! Unfortunately, however, he is always too anxious to reach out far beyond these limits without developing his essential abilities! Thereby he is guilty of a negligence which prevents him even from reaching what he otherwise could, whereas in any case he could never attain the goal of his desires. He thus deprives himself of the most beautiful and sublime part of his true being with the result that he completely fails to fulfil the purpose of his existence!---

Parsifal is a great promise! The defects and errors which the poets have added to the legends through their too earthly way of thinking distort the true essence of this figure. Parsifal is identical with the Son of Man, Whose coming the Son of God Himself proclaimed.

As a Divine Messenger with His spiritual sight blindfolded, He will have to go through the most bitter hardships on earth, outwardly a man among men.

370

After a certain time, when His spiritual sight is restored, He will inevitably recognise His origin and therewith Himself, as well as clearly realising His mission. This mission will also bring redemption to those who are seriously seeking, and goes hand in hand with a stern judgment.

For this purpose not just anybody can be chosen, much less can the possible experiences of many people, or even of all the people, be seen in it. On the contrary, it will only be a very definite and special Messenger!

The immutable lawfulness of Divine Will decrees that everything, after it has completed its cycle of development and reached its highest state of perfection, may return to the starting point of its original substance, but never beyond it. Thus also the human spirit! The human spirit originates as a spirit-germ in the Sphere of Spiritual Substantiality, to which it may return as a conscious spirit embodied in a substantiate form if, after its course through the World of Matter, it has achieved its highest state of perfection and attained a living purity.

No spirit belonging to this sphere, however sublime, pure and radiant, can cross the boundary line into the Divine Sphere! The boundary line here, and the impossibility of crossing it, as in the spheres or planes of material Creation, is in the nature of things simply a question of the difference between the species.

The highest and most sublime is God Himself in His Divine Unsubstantiality. Next, and somewhat lower, comes Divine Substantiality. Both are eternal. Adjacent to this, going deeper and deeper, follows the work of Creation which, descending in planes or spheres, becomes denser and denser down to the World of Gross Matter, which is finally visible to mankind.

The ethereal part within the World of Matter is what men call the beyond, thus what lies beyond their earthly or physical capacity to see. Both, however, belong to the Work of Creation and are not eternal with regard to their form, but subject to change for the purpose of renewal and regeneration.

At the summit of the eternal Sphere of Spiritual Substantiality stands the Castle of the Grail, spiritually visible and tangible, because it is still of the same species of spiritual substantiality. This Castle of the Grail contains a Sanctuary which lies on the outermost border adjacent to the Divine Sphere, and is thus of still finer consistency than the rest of spiritual substantiality. In this Sanctuary, as a pledge of the eternal Goodness of God the Father, as a symbol of His Purest Divine Love, and the point from which Divine Power issues, stands *the Holy Grail!*

This is a chalice in which it bubbles and surges unceasingly like red blood without overflowing. Enveloped as it is in the most Luminous Light, it is granted only to the purest of all spirits in the Realm of Spiritual Substantiality to look into this Light! *These* are the Guardians of the Holy Grail! If it is said in the legends that the purest of men are destined to become Guardians of the Grail, this is a point about which the blessed poet has drawn all too earthly a picture, because he was unable to express himself differently!

No human spirit can enter this holy Sanctuary! Even in its most perfect state of spiritual substantiality, after having returned from its wanderings through the World of Matter, it is still not so fine that it could cross this threshold, i. e., the boundary line! Even in its highest state of perfection it is still too dense to do so!

A still further etherisation would be equivalent to its complete disintegration or combustion, because the origin of its nature does not lend itself to assuming even greater radiance and luminosity, thus becoming still more etherised. It cannot bear it!

The Guardians of the Grail are Eternal Primordial Spiritual Beings, who never were human beings. They are the highest of all in the Realm of Spiritual Substantiality. However, they are in need of Divine Unsubstantiate Power, are dependent upon It, as all else is dependent on Divine Unsubstantiality, the Source of all Power, God the Father!

From time to time on the Day of the Holy Dove, the Dove appears above the Chalice as a renewed token of the unalterable Divine Love of the Father. It is the hour of communion which brings about the renewal of power. The Guardians of the Grail receive it in humble devotion and can then transmit this magic power.

On this depends the existence of the whole Creation!

It is the moment in which the Love of the Creator radiantly flows forth in the Temple of the Holy Grail, bringing new life and a new urge to create, pulsating downwards and diffusing itself through all the Universe. A trembling and a holy awe, with forebodings of joy and great happiness, vibrate through all the spheres. Only the spirit of earthman still stands aside, without intuitively sensing what is happening particularly to him at that moment; or in what a dull-witted manner he accepts such an immeasurable gift, because the limitations he imposed upon himself through his intellect no longer permit him to grasp such greatness!

It is the moment when a new supply of vital energy is sent out into the entire Creation!

It is the necessary, ever-recurring ratification of the Covenant between the Creator and His Work! Should this supply ever be cut off, should it ever fail to come, inevitably all that exists would slowly dry up, grow old and disintegrate. The end of all days would then come, and only God Himself would remain, as it was in the very beginning, because He alone is Life!

This process is related in the legend. How everything must grow old and decay if the Day of the Holy Dove, the "uncovering" of the Grail, does not recur is even hinted at in the description of the growing old of the Knights of the Grail, during the time in which Amfortas no longer uncovers the Grail till the hour in which Parsifal appears as King of the Grail.

Man should cease to regard the Holy Grail as only something intangible, for It really exists! The human spirit, however, owing to its nature, can never behold It. But the blessing radiating forth from It, which can be and is being passed on by the Guardians of the Grail, can be absorbed and enjoyed by those human spirits who open themselves to it.

In this sense some of the interpretations cannot be called wrong, as long as they do not try to draw the Holy Grail Itself into their explanations. They are correct, and yet again they are also not correct!

The appearance of the Dove on the special Day of the Holy Dove indicates the sending of the Holy Spirit on each occasion, for this Dove stands in very close connection with the Holy Spirit.

But this is something which the human spirit is only able to grasp figuratively, because by the very nature of things, even if he has attained the highest perfection, he can really only think, know and perceive intuitively up to the point from which he himself came, i.e., to the species *homogeneous* to the purest nature of his origin. This is the eternal Realm of Spiritual Substantiality.

Even in his thoughts he will never be able to cross this boundary! Nor can he ever grasp anything beyond it. This is so self-evident, so logical and simple, that every human being can follow this train of thought!

Whatever goes beyond this boundary will and must, for this reason, remain a perpetual mystery to mankind!

Every man, therefore, who imagines that he bears God within himself or that he is himself Divine, or can become so, lives under a foolish delusion. He bears *spirituality* within himself, but *not* Divinity! And therein lies an unbridgeable difference. He is a creature, not part of the Creator, as so many try to make themselves believe. Man is and remains a *work* and can never become a master!

Thus it is also wrong to say that the human spirit issues from God the Father Himself and returns to Him. The origin of man lies in the Realm of *Spiritual Substantiality*, not in Divinity Unsubstantiate. Therefore, even if he has attained perfection, he can only return to the Sphere of Spiritual Substantiality. It is right to say that the human spirit originates from the *Kingdom of God* and therefore can, when it becomes perfect, return to the *Kingdom* of God, but not to God Himself.

Later there will follow detailed lectures about the individual divisions of Creation, which are totally different in their fundamental nature.

At the summit of each of these planes of Creation stands a Castle of the Grail as the necessary transition and power transmitting stage.

Fashioned according to the nature of the sphere of Creation concerned, this is always a reflection of the real highest Castle of the Grail situated at the summit of the whole of Creation which, through the radiations of Parsifal, constitutes the starting point of the entire Creation.

Amfortas was priest and king in the *lowest* of these reflections of the Grail Castle, standing at the summit of the sphere of the human spirits who have developed from spirit-germs. It is the one closest to man on earth.

THE MYSTERY OF LUCIFER

A GREY veil shrouds all that appertains to the figure of Lucifer, and it is as though everybody shrinks from lifting a corner of it.

In truth this shrinking back is nothing but man's inability to penetrate into the realm of Darkness. Again this inability simply lies in the order of things, for here as elsewhere a limit is set upon the human spirit owing to its nature, which prevents it from penetrating so far. Just as it is unable to reach the Highest Heights, so also is it unable to penetrate to the deepest depths, nor will it ever be able to do so!

Thus the imagination created substitutes for what was missing; it created a diversity of beings! People speak of the devil in the most adventurous forms, of the fallen and expelled archangel, of the embodiment of the evil principle, and all the rest of it. Nothing is understood of Lucifer's true nature, although the human spirit is often struck by him, and consequently thrown into a state of great inner conflict, which can be likened to a battle!

Those who speak of a fallen archangel, as also those who speak of the embodiment of the evil principle, come closest to the truth. But here also a false attitude prevails, giving a false picture of everything. An embodiment of the evil principle makes one think of the summit, of the final goal, of all evil having been invested with life and body, thus the crowning, the complete culmination!

On the contrary, however, Lucifer is the *origin,* the *starting point* and the driving power of the wrong principle! One should really not call the principle he brings forth the *evil* principle, but the *wrong* principle! The field of action of this wrong principle is the World of Matter.

It is only here that the effects of the Light and the effects of Darkness, the two opposing principles, meet with one another, and constantly influence the human soul while it is developing on its journey through the World of Matter. Whichever of the two the human soul favours, in accordance with its own wishes, proves decisive for its ascent toward the Light or for its descent toward Darkness.

The gulf which lies between Light and Darkness is immense. It is filled by that part of Creation called the World of Matter, which is subject to the transient nature of the forms, that is, to the disintegration of the forms existing at the time and to a subsequent reconstruction.

Since according to the Laws which the Will of God the Father has placed in Creation a cycle can only be considered completed and fulfilled when it ends up by returning to its origin, so also the cycle of a human spirit can only be considered fulfilled when it returns to the Spiritual Realm, because that is where its spirit-germ originated.

If a human spirit permits itself to deviate towards Darkness, it runs the risk of being drawn beyond the outermost circle of its normal course towards a depth from which it can then no longer find its way back in order to ascend. Nor can it step even deeper over the extreme boundary of densest and deepest ethereal darkness and thus completely out of the World of Matter, as it could do in the upward direction into the Realm of Spiritual Substantiality, because the latter is its point of origin. And so it is constantly drawn along in the mighty cycle of material Creation until it is finally drawn into disintegration, because its ethereally dark and therefore dense and heavy garment, which is also called the ethereal body, holds it down.

This disintegration then dissolves the spiritual personality it has acquired on its course through Creation, so that it suffers spiritual death and is dispersed to primordial spiritual seed.

Lucifer himself stands *outside* material Creation and will therefore *not* be drawn into the disintegration which is the fate of the victims of his principle, because Lucifer is eternal. His origin lies in a part of the Sphere of Divine Substantiality. The dissension started after the creation of all matter had begun. Sent out to support Spiritual Substantiality and further its development in the World of Matter, he failed to carry out his mission in accordance with the Creative Will of God the Father but, through a volition which came to him while working in matter, he chose ways other than those ordained by this Creative Will.

Misusing the power delegated to him, he introduced among other things the principle of temptation in place of the principle of supporting help, which is identical with serving love; serving love in the Divine sense, which has nothing in common with slavish servility, but only has the spiritual ascent and thereby the eternal happiness of his fellow man at heart and acts accordingly!

The principle of temptation, however, is identical with the setting of snares which cause creatures who are not sufficiently strong within themselves quickly to stumble, fall and become lost, whereas others, it is true, grow stronger and more alert so as to blossom forth powerfully towards spiritual heights. But all that is weak is irrevocably abandoned to destruction from the start. This principle knows of no goodness, no compassion; it is wanting in the love of God the Father, and therewith also in the mightiest power to ascend and in the strongest support available.

The temptation in Paradise described in the Bible shows the effect produced by the application of the Lucifer principle. It depicts how, through temptation, it tries to test the strength or steadfastness of the human couple, only to thrust them pitilessly on the road to destruction at the least sign of wavering.

Steadfastness would have been identical with a joyful adjustment to the Will of God which lies in the simple Laws of Nature or Laws of Creation. And this Will, the Divine Command, was well known to the human couple. Not to hesitate would have been the same as obeying these laws. Only through such obedience can man make proper and unlimited use of them and thus become truly "a lord in Creation", because he is "in harmony with them"! If he does not put himself into opposition, all the powers will serve him and work automatically in his favour.

This then holds the fulfilment of the Creator's commandments which have but one aim – to preserve and maintain undimmed and unhampered all the possibilities of development that lie in His wonderful work. The simple observance of this means in turn consciously to co-operate in the further sound development of Creation or of the World of Matter.

He who fails in this is an obstacle which must either be hewn into the right shape or left to be crushed in the wheels of the world's mechanism, that is, in the Laws of Creation. He who will not bend must break, as there can be no stagnation!

Lucifer refuses to wait with kindness for man gradually to mature and become strong. He refuses to be the loving gardener that he should be, caring for, supporting and tending the plants entrusted to him. With him "the wolf" literally "came to mind the sheep"! His goal is the destruction of all that is weak, and he works relentlessly towards that end.

At the same time he despises the victims who succumb to his temptations and snares, and it is his wish that they should be destroyed in their weakness!

He is also contemptuous of the baseness and meanness which these fallen victims show in the working out of his principle, for it is only men who turn it into the loathsome villainy which is so evident. Through this they only incense Lucifer the more to regard them as creatures who deserve nothing but destruction, not love and care!

To achieve this destruction not a little is contributed by the principle of "letting oneself go", which follows as a natural consequence of the principle of temptation. This "letting oneself go" takes place in the lower regions of Darkness but, through so-called psycho-analysis, some practitioners have already accepted it on the assumption that here on earth also "letting oneself go" liberates and matures.

But what dreadful misery must the practice of this principle cause here on earth! What mischief must it bring since, in contrast with the regions of Darkness where only homogeneous species are together, on earth both darker and lighter souls dwell side by side! In this respect you need only to think of sexual life and similar things. If such a principle was put into practice and let loose on mankind, it must ultimately create nothing but a Sodom and Gomorrah from which there would be no escape, and only the most abject terror could bring it to an end!

Quite apart from this, however, one already sees numerous victims of similar therapies wandering about today without any hold on life, whose little bit of self-reliance and, on the whole, all their individual thinking have been completely picked to pieces and destroyed when they had confidently expected help. They are like people whose clothing has been systematically torn from their bodies so that they are then forced to put on the new garments handed to them. However, in most cases these denuded ones unfortunately can no longer see why they should put on any new clothing at all!

Through the systematic intrusion into their most intimate affairs and rights they have gradually lost the feeling of shame which is an integral part of personal self-consciousness, a part of the personality, and without which there can be nothing individual.

On such uprooted soil no new solid building can then be erected. With few exceptions these people remain dependent and sometimes actually become helpless, because the small hold they formerly possessed has been taken from them.

Both the principles of "letting oneself go" and of temptation are so closely connected that temptation must without doubt precede "letting oneself go". The latter is thus a direct following and spreading of the Lucifer principle.

The true physician of the soul does not need to tear down. He recognises the slumbering good qualities, awakens them and then builds upon them. The true principle brings about a transformation of wrong desires through a spiritual understanding!

The application of his loveless principle, however, quite naturally separated Lucifer more and more from the Loving Will of the Almighty Creator, causing him to be cut off and cast out from the Light. Consequently he fell ever deeper. Lucifer is one who has severed himself from the Light, which is equivalent to having been cast out.

This expulsion was also bound to occur according to the existing Primordial Laws, the irrevocable Holy Will of God the Father! It could not possibly happen otherwise!

Since only the Will of God the Father, of the Creator of all things, is omnipotent, and is also firmly anchored in material Creation and its development, Lucifer can quite well send his principle into the material sphere, but the resulting effects will always and only operate within the Primordial Laws ordained by God the Father and must form themselves accordingly!

Thus, in pursuit of his erroneous principle, Lucifer can incite men to set out on a road dangerous to them, but he is unable in any way to force men into something unless they themselves decide upon it voluntarily!

In fact Lucifer can only lure! But man as such stands more firmly in material Creation than he does, therefore with much greater security and power than any influence Lucifer could ever wield over him. Thus every man is so well protected that it is a tenfold shame upon him if he permits himself to be enticed by this power, which is a relatively weaker power than his! He should remember that Lucifer himself stands *outside* the material sphere, while he himself is firmly rooted in familiar soil!

In order to apply his principle Lucifer is forced to make use of his auxiliary troops, composed of human spirits who have succumbed to his temptations!

The spirit of every man striving upwards is not only fully able to deal with them, but is far superior in strength. One single, serious volition suffices to make an army of them vanish without trace, providing their enticements meet with no response or approval to which they can cling.

Lucifer would indeed be quite powerless if mankind would make the effort to recognise and follow the Primordial Laws given by the Creator. Unfortunately, however, men increasingly support the wrong principle through their present behaviour, and the greater part of them will therefore have to perish!

It is impossible for any human spirit to fight a battle against Lucifer himself for the simple reason that, owing to the difference in the nature of their species, it cannot penetrate to him. The human spirit can only come in contact with those who have fallen through the wrong principle because they are basically of the same species.

The origin of Lucifer requires that only he who is of the same or of a higher origin can personally approach and face him, and so none other can penetrate to him. It must be a Divine Envoy, armed with the sacred seriousness of His Mission and with perfect trust in the Source of All Power, in God the Father Himself!

This task has been delegated to the prophesied Son of Man!

The combat will be a personal one, face to face, not only a general symbolical one, as many investigators want to interpret from the prophecies. It is the fulfilment of the promise given in Parsifal. Lucifer has wrongly used the "Holy Spear", the Power, and through his principle inflicted a painful wound with it upon humanity and thus upon the Sphere of Spiritual Substantiality. The Spear will be wrested from him in this combat. Then, in the "proper hands", that is, by applying the true Grail principle of pure, severe love, it will heal the wound previously inflicted by it while in the wrong hand, that is, through its wrong use.

Through the Lucifer principle, that is, through the wrong application of Divine Power, which is the same as the "Holy Spear" being wielded in the wrong hand, a wound *that cannot heal* has been inflicted upon the Sphere of Spiritual Substantiality. In the legend this thought is portrayed in striking manner, for the happening does resemble an open wound that will not heal.

It should be realised that the human spirits, as unconscious spirit-germs or sparks, leap or flow over the boundary of the lowest region of Spiritual Substantiality into material Creation! The expectation is that these outflowing particles, having been awakened and developed to personal consciousness during their wanderings in the World of Matter, will return thereafter to the Sphere of Spiritual Substantiality in order to complete their cycles. This is similar to the circulation of the blood in the physical body.

The Lucifer principle, however, diverts a large portion of this circulating spiritual stream. Thus the necessary cycle cannot be closed, the result being a weakening as from the continual *draining* of an open wound!

When now the "Holy Spear", i.e., the Divine Power, is wielded in the *proper* hand, acting according to the Will of the Creator and showing the right way to spiritual substance which constitutes an animating factor in Matter, thereby leading it upwards to its point of origin, to the luminous Kingdom of God the Father, the spiritual substance will no longer become lost, but will flow back to its origin as the blood does to the heart. As a result the exuding wound, which up till then weakened the Sphere of Spiritual Substantiality, will be *closed!* Thus the healing can only take place through the same Spear as inflicted the wound!

To achieve this, however, the Spear must first be wrested from Lucifer and come into the proper hand, and this takes place in the *personal* combat between Parsifal and Lucifer!

The further battles which extend into the Ethereal and Gross Material Worlds are but the after-effects of this one great combat, which must bring about the promised binding of Lucifer and herald the beginning of the Millennium! They mean the extermination of the consequences of the Lucifer principle!

This principle is opposed to the reign of Divine Love, the blessings of which fall to man's share on his journey through the World of Matter. If men would simply strive after this Divine Love they would immediately become completely invulnerable to every temptation of Lucifer, and he would be robbed of all the terror the human spirit has woven around him.

The monstrous and hideous forms which man erroneously tries to give to Lucifer are but the confused phantasies of the human brain! In truth, for the simple reason that there is a difference in species, no human eye was ever able to behold him, not even the eye which already during life on earth is often able to recognise the Ethereal World of the beyond!

Contrary to all ideas Lucifer may be called proud and stately, of a supernatural beauty and sombre majesty, with large, clear blue eyes which, however, in their ice-cold expression bear witness to a lack of love! He is not only a conception, as he is generally represented when all other interpretations fail, but he is personal!

Mankind should learn to understand that for them too, on account of their particular species, a limit is set which they can never cross, naturally not even in their thoughts, and that messages can only come to them from beyond this limit as an act of Grace. This cannot happen through mediums, who are unable to change their species even under supernatural conditions, and just as little through science. Indeed it is just science which by means of chemistry has the opportunity to discover that the difference of species can create insurmountable barriers! These laws, however, proceed from the Highest Source and are not merely to be found in the work of Creation!

THE REGIONS OF DARKNESS AND DAMNATION

WHEN one looks at pictures supposed to represent life in the so-called hell, one shrugs one's shoulders and dismisses them with a half-ironical, half-contemptuous smile, thinking that only morbid imagination or fanatical blind faith can conjure up such scenes. Very rarely will anyone seek even for the slightest grain of truth in these pictures. And yet the most gruesome imagination can hardly contrive a picture that comes anywhere near depicting the torments of life in the dark regions!

Poor deluded fools who imagine they can carelessly dismiss it with a mocking shrug of the shoulders! In the moment when the appalling truth dawns upon them such carelessness will revenge itself bitterly! It will be of no avail to struggle or turn aside; they will be drawn into the whirlpool awaiting them, unless they can rid themselves in time of the deep-seated ignorance which always characterises the hollowness and narrow-mindedness of such people!

The ethereal body will hardly have detached itself from the physical body* before these souls receive their first great surprise by experiencing that this has not brought conscious being and life to an end. As a result they first of all become confused, and then follows an unexpected apprehension, which again often gives place to a state of dull resignation or dreadful despair. All resistance is vain; vain are their lamentations and even their pleading, for they must reap what they have sown during their life on earth!

If they ridiculed the Word brought down to them from God, which points towards life after physical death and the consequent responsibility for every serious thought and action, the least that is awaiting them will be what they themselves willed – *utter darkness!* Their ethereal eyes, ears and mouths are closed through their own volition. They are blind, deaf and dumb in their new surroundings!

* See Lecture: "Death".

That is the most favourable thing that can happen to them! A guide and helper from the beyond cannot make himself understood because they keep themselves closed to such a possibility. A sad condition indeed, which can only be gradually changed by the slow inner maturing of such a soul, which in turn can only come about through an increasing desperation! Thus with this ever-increasing longing for light, rising upwards like a perpetual cry for help from such an oppressed and tormented soul, lighter conditions will ultimately prevail around it, until in fact it may also learn to discern others in the same need of help!

If such a one then feels a desire to help those souls still languishing in greater darkness towards lighter conditions, the exertion required by the effort to help will bring it increased strength, so that others still further advanced may in turn approach and help this soul onwards to more luminous regions.

Thus these souls squat about dejectedly because their ethereal bodies have become too enfeebled to walk owing to their negative attitude. And if there is any movement at all, it is but a cumbersome and uncertain crawling along the ground!

Others again grope about in this darkness, and stumble and fall, but quickly get up again, only to bump themselves against this and that, inevitably suffering painful injuries. Depending entirely on the nature of its own darkness, and on its consequent density and weight, a human soul sinks into that region which exactly accords with its own ethereal gravity and which is thus of the same ethereal species. Its new environment will therefore be just as tangible, perceptible and impenetrable as is the gross material environment for a physical body. Every knock, every fall, or every injury will be just as painfully felt there as the physical body experienced during its life on the gross material earth.

Such is the case in every region regardless of its depth or height! Everything of like substance has a like tangibleness and a like mutual impenetrability. But every higher region or, in other words, every lighter species of substance can penetrate the lower, denser species of substance unhindered; as, for instance, all ethereal substance can penetrate the different texture of the gross material substance.

The case is different with those souls who, in addition, have to atone for some kind of injustice. This is a question which stands on its own, but it can be redeemed the moment the perpetrator can obtain full and genuine pardon from the person he has harmed.

But what binds a human soul *more firmly* is a *propensity* or *craving* which is the mainspring to one or more deeds! This propensity lives on in a human soul, even when the latter has passed into the beyond after severance from its physical body. As soon as the limitations of everything to do with gross matter fall away, the propensity will immediately become even more pronounced in the ethereal body, because then the intuitive perceptions work with much greater animation and less restraint.

And again it is such a propensity which will define the density and thus the weight of the ethereal body! The result is that, after its liberation from the physical body, the ethereal body will immediately sink to that region which exactly corresponds to its weight and density. And there it will also find all those which indulge the same propensity. Through their radiations its propensity will be further nourished and intensified, causing it to rage madly while indulging it! All the others there will naturally do likewise!

That such unrestrained raging must be a torment for the surroundings is not hard to understand. As in those regions this happens only on a mutual basis, however, every single soul will have to suffer bitterly from the others what in turn it is trying continuously to inflict upon them. Thus life there becomes hell, until such a human soul gradually tires of and intuitively feels disgusted by it! Then, after a long while, the desire will gradually awaken to get away from such an environment!

This desire and disgust are the beginning of improvement. They will grow into a cry for help and finally into a prayer. Only then can a hand be stretched forth to help the soul ascend, but decades, centuries or sometimes even longer may often pass before this happens. It is thus the propensity of a human soul which weighs upon and encumbers it most!

Hence it follows that an unpremeditated deed can be much more easily and quickly atoned for than a propensity clinging to a human being, no matter whether it is expressed in a deed or not!

A person with an unclean propensity which he has never expressed in a deed because his earthly circumstances have favoured him will therefore have to make greater amends than a person who has inadvertently erred through one or more deeds without evil intent. The latter can be immediately forgiven his unpremeditated actions without developing evil karma, but a propensity can only be forgiven when it has been completely eradicated from a human being. And there are many kinds of propensities! Be it greed and its cousin avarice, sordid sensuality, the urge to steal or murder, incendiarism, or merely fraud or careless negligence; no matter what it is, such a propensity will make the soul concerned sink or be dragged to the region where it will be among its own kind!

It serves no purpose to give pictures of life in those regions. They are often so terrible that a human spirit on earth can hardly believe in their reality without seeing them. Even then he would still think they must only be the visions of a feverish and highly fanciful imagination! Thus he should be content intuitively to feel a moral shyness in regard to all such evils! This will liberate him from the bonds of all that is base so that there will no longer be any obstacle barring his ascent towards the Light.

Such are the dark regions resulting from the principle Lucifer strives to introduce. The eternal cycle of Creation rotates and reaches the point where disintegration begins and all matter loses its form and reverts to primordial seed which, in rotating further, brings a new blending and new forms with fresh power and virgin soil. What until then could not detach itself from gross and ethereal matter to cross over the highest, finest and lightest boundary and enter the Sphere of Spiritual Substantiality, thereby leaving all matter behind, will inevitably be drawn into the disintegration, whereby its form and whatever else is personal about it will be destroyed! And that alone is eternal damnation, the extinction of all conscious personality!

THE REGIONS OF LIGHT AND PARADISE

RADIANT light! Dazzling purity! A blissful feeling of lightness!

All this speaks for itself so clearly that it is hardly necessary to go into details. The less the ethereal body, i. e., the cloak of the human spirit in the beyond, is burdened with some base propensity or with a desire for material things and pleasures, the less it will be attracted by them. In this case the ethereal body, which is formed according to its volition, will be less dense and consequently less heavy. Through its lightness it will all the more quickly be uplifted to the luminous regions which correspond to its lesser density.

The less dense, the freer and finer this ethereal body becomes when it is cleansed of base desires, the brighter and the more luminous it must appear; for then the core of spiritual substantiality within the human soul, which as such is radiant by nature, will more and more shine forth from within as the ethereal body grows ever more transparent; whereas in the lower regions this radiant core is hidden through the greater density and gravity of the ethereal body and thus remains darkened!

In the regions of Light every human soul will also meet other souls with ethereal bodies homogeneous to its own, those of a like nature. As only that which is truly noble and of genuine goodwill is able to strive upwards free from all base desires, such a human soul will only encounter other souls of equal nobility. It is also easy to understand that the dweller in such a region has no torments to suffer, but only delights in the blessing of the nobleness radiating there, sharing in the joy of others which it also arouses by its own deeds. It can truly say that it is wandering in the fields of the blessed, where all is bliss.

Thus encouraged, its joy for all that is pure and sublime grows ever stronger, lifting it higher and higher! Permeated by this intuitive feeling, its ethereal body will become ever finer and less dense, enabling the shining core of spiritual substance to break through ever more radiantly, and finally causing the last remnants of the ethereal body to fall away as if consumed by flames.

Then the human spirit, having attained a complete and conscious personality by reason of its perfect spiritual nature, can cross the border into the Realm of Spiritual Substantiality. *Only then does it enter the Eternal Kingdom of God the Father, the everlasting Paradise!*

Just as it is impossible for a painter to portray the torments of real life in the dark regions, so is it equally impossible for him to depict the rapture which life holds in the light regions, even if these regions still belong to the transient World of Ethereal Matter before the boundary to the Eternal Kingdom of God has been crossed!

Every painting and every attempt to portray this life in pictures would definitely mean belittling it, and therefore inevitably harm instead of benefit the soul of man!

THERE is no greater danger to a cause than to leave a gap in its presentation which needs filling up, as may often be intuitively sensed. It is of no avail to pass it over because such a gap hinders all progress. Any building erected over it will inevitably collapse sooner or later, even if the greatest skill and best materials have been used.

Such is the case with the various Christian religious communities of today. They persistently close their eyes and ears to certain points in their teaching which can be sensed as illogical. They try to dismiss them with empty phrases instead of taking thought in all seriousness.

They readily apprehend the danger that one day the temporary bridges they have built over such gaps through a teaching of blind faith will no longer suffice, and they dread the moment when enlightenment will show up the flimsy character of these structures. Moreover they know that they will then no longer be able to persuade anybody to follow such a deceitful course, with the natural result that all the rest of their teaching, however sound, will also be discarded. They also realise that a single flash of fresh truth must sweep away such artificial constructions.

Still, for want of something better, they seek to maintain their swaying plank in spite of every danger. Even worse, they are prepared to defend their position by every means in their power, and would destroy him who dared to provide a firmer crossing over the gap through the Truth Itself! Without any hesitation they would try to repeat what occurred here on earth nearly two thousand years ago, and which still casts its shadow right down to the present day. Yet they themselves, while using that event as the subject of a great accusation against the blindness and pernicious stubbornness of mankind, also make it the focal point of their own teaching and faith.

It was the *church dignitaries* and scholars of that time, with their narrow dogmatism and a conceit which betrayed their weakness, who were unable to recognise the Truth and the Son of God. They also closed themselves against it, hating and persecuting Him and His followers out of envy and fear, whereas other people more readily opened themselves to the recognition and were quicker to perceive the Truth of the Word.

Although the present heads of Christian religious communities lay special stress on the Son of God's path of suffering, they have learned and profited nothing from this fact. It is just the present leaders of communities based on Christ's teaching, as well as the leaders of newer movements, who would to-day try to eliminate any man who, by revealing the Truth Itself, could endanger the swaying bridges over the precarious gaps in their teachings and interpretations. They would persecute him with a hatred born of fear and even more of vanity, exactly as happened once before.

They would lack the greatness to endure the fact that their own knowledge was insufficient to enable them to recognise the Truth and fill the gaps, and thus help to smooth the path for mankind towards an easier understanding and complete grasping of It.

And yet it is only possible for mankind to ascend by fully grasping the Truth; but they can never do so by blind ignorant faith!

One such gap created by an erroneous transmission concerns the concept of the "Son of Man". People cling to it morbidly, like the Pharisees who did not want to open themselves to the Truth brought by the Son of God, which opposed their conventional and rigid teachings. Christ spoke of Himself *only* as the Son of God. It was far from His thoughts to be so illogical as to call Himself also the Son of Man. Even if, as a result of their own doubts, people have tried with the greatest artistry and skill in every direction to clarify this obvious contradiction between the Son of God and the Son of Man, which is intuitively sensed by every person who reflects quietly, it cannot be asserted in spite of all their efforts that they have managed to *unify* them. The most favourable of all the interpretations could but repeatedly show a dual personality *each standing beside the other,* but never appearing as *one!*

This is quite in the natural order of things. The Son of God cannot become the Son of Man just because He had to be born of a human body so as to enable Him to walk on earth.

Every Christian knows that the Son of God came only on a *spiritual* mission, and that all His words referred to the *Spiritual Kingdom* and were thus meant *spiritually*. Consequently His repeated references to the Son of Man may not from the very outset be interpreted in any other way! Why should an exception be made here? In the spiritual sense, however, Christ was and remained only the *Son of God!*

Therefore when He spoke of the Son of Man He could not possibly mean Himself! There is something far more stupendous in all this than is indicated in the present interpretations of the Christian religions. This obvious contradiction should long ago have induced men to more serious reflection, had it not been for the fetters of dogmatism darkening everything! Instead of making the serious investigations which are absolutely necessary to such incisive matters, they clung tenaciously to the transmitted words, thus putting on "blinkers" that hindered a free view.

The natural consequence is that these interpreters and teachers, although they stand in the Creation of their God, are not even able to understand this Creation aright. Yet this carries the only possible prospect of coming closer to the Creator Himself, the Origin of all that is created!

In the first place Christ taught absolute naturalness, which means adjusting oneself to the Laws of Nature, and thus of Creation. But only he who knows these laws can adapt himself to them. Again these Laws of Nature embody the Will of the Creator, and therefore provide the path to the recognition of the Creator Himself.

Whoever knows the Laws of Nature will also experience with what absolute precision they gear into each other. He therefore knows that their activity is unchangeable in the steady consistency with which it drives forward, as is also the Will of the Creator, God the Father.

Every divergence would mean a change of the Divine Will. A change, however, would indicate imperfection. But since the Primordial Source of All Being, God the Father, is unity and perfection, it follows that even the minutest deviation in the Laws of Nature, thus the laws of development, would be simply impossible and out of the question from the very start. This fact imposes the condition that the philosophy of religion and the philosophy of natural science must in every respect coincide in perfect clarity and consistency if they are to represent the *Truth!*

That natural science today still has a very limited range of knowledge compared with the whole of Creation is not denied, as it has merely kept to the World of Gross Matter, because the intellect of today can only tackle what is bound to time and space. The one absolutely unpardonable mistake made is that the disciples of this science try to ridicule and deny the existence of anything which goes beyond its range, except for a few scientists who have lifted themselves above the average and become more far-sighted, and who refused to cloak their ignorance with conceit.

Although the science of religion extends much further, it nevertheless remains dependent upon the Natural Laws which reach out beyond all that is bound to time and space and which, coming from the Primordial Source, extend down into what is physically visible without a break or change in their nature.

For this reason there may be neither gaps nor contradictions in religious teachings if they are really to accord with the Truth and thus with the Laws of Nature or the Divine Will, that is if they are to harbour the *Truth*. Leading and responsible teachings cannot permit themselves the liberty of a blind faith!

The erroneous conception concerning the Son of Man therefore weighs heavily upon the followers of the true Christian teachings, because they quietly accept and carry on wrong transmissions, in spite of the fact that from time to time a contrary intuition quietly warns many people.

It is the very immutability and perfection of the Divine Will which precludes any arbitrary interference of God in Creation. And it is this same perfection which is unable simply to eliminate Lucifer after he had fallen through his wrong actions!* It also has to allow men to misuse the Natural Laws, the Divine Will, because the human spirit, in virtue of its origin from the eternal Sphere of Spiritual Substantiality, has been granted the freedom of decision.**

It is just because of this immutable perfection of the Creator's Will that it must appear bound to a certain extent when it evidences itself in the happenings of ethereal and gross material Creation! But upon this being recognised, only inferior and small human spirits will regard it as a limitation of the Power and Magnitude. Such a view would merely be the result of their own narrow-mindedness!

It is the vastness of the whole problem that confuses them, because actually they can only envisage it within the narrower limits which correspond to their own understanding!

* See Lecture: "The mystery of Lucifer".
** See Lecture: "Responsibility".

He, however, who makes an honest effort to recognise his Creator in His Work will, when he follows the sure road of the Natural Laws, receive a convincing idea of the vastness and extent of the manifestations that have their beginning in the Primordial Source, i. e., the starting point of all happenings, whence they spread through Creation like irremovable railway lines, along which all further life unrolls itself according to the position of the points.

The turning of the points, however, is done *automatically** by the *human spirit* on its journey through the World of Matter. Unfortunately the majority allow themselves to be induced through Lucifer's principle to turn the points in the wrong direction, and so their lives, in accordance with the immutable laws of continuous development which pervade all material Creation like railway lines, roll more and more downward towards a very definite final goal, a goal conforming to their attitude!

The direction in which the free decision turns the points can be exactly observed or intuitively perceived from the Point of Origin On High, making it possible clearly to recognise what will be the further course, which can only run along those lines which the Laws anchored in Creation have laid down according to the decision taken.

This circumstance enables many events to be foreseen, because the Laws of Nature or Creation never deviate in their urge to develop. Here millennia make no difference. Out of these clearly foreseen and final irrevocable goals come forth the great revelations shown to the specially blessed in spiritual pictures which, when passed on, come to the knowledge of mankind.

One thing, however, *cannot* be accurately predicted – *the earthly time* at which these revelations and promises find their fulfilment!

This will come to pass at the hour when such a life, travelling along the line it has chosen, reaches a foreseen intermediate station or the terminus. The fate of man, of the nation, indeed of all humanity, may be compared to a train standing and waiting on a single track connected to lines leading in all directions. Man switches the points as it pleases him, jumps on to the engine and turns on the steam, which means he animates it.

As soon as he turns on to the line he has chosen one can mention each station and the terminus only, but never give the exact hour of arrival, for this

---

* See Lecture: "Man and his free will".

depends on the speed at which the train travels, and that may vary according to the nature of people. For it is *man who animates* the engine, and he will drive it forward in accordance with his own nature, either with quiet evenness or impetuous temperament, or with alternate variations. The nearer such a train – whether representing a single individual, a nation, or all mankind – gets to a station lying on the line of its fate, the more surely can its arrival be foreseen and foretold!

Connected to the network of lines are a few branch lines which, by turning the points occasionally *during the journey,* can be used to change its direction and so reach another terminus than the one first contemplated. It is obviously necessary in this case to slow down when reaching such points, and then to stop and turn them. The slowing down represents the act of reflection, and the stopping the decision taken by man, which he is always free to make until he reaches the last opportunity to choose. The turning of the points is the deed that follows his decision.

The Divine Will which, like railway lines, penetrates the World of Matter in the form of the firmly established Natural Laws, may also be called the nerves in the work of Creation, which detect every unevenness in the gigantic body of Creation and report it to the starting point, the Creative Primordial Source.

This precise survey which, through the immutable laws, the Creator possesses over everything to its final end, causes Him to supplement His revelations with *promises* proclaiming the advent of helpers to be sent by Him in time, when a train is seen to be approaching the most dangerous curves, intermediary stations and termini!

Properly equipped by Him, such helpers are intended to open the eyes of those human spirits who are travelling along the wrong track, by proclaiming the Truth shortly before inevitable catastrophes and dangerous changes take place! This serves to enable mankind to change the points in time, thus avoiding the increasingly dangerous places and also escaping the fatal terminus by taking a new direction!

As the Creator cannot alter the Perfection of His own Will, He will also, in connection with this help, keep exactly to the existing laws. In other words, His Will is perfect from the Primordial beginning. Every new expression of His Will must naturally also be perfect! This presupposes that every new Act of Will issuing from Him must also bear within itself the same laws as those that preceded it. Consequently it will fit itself precisely into the course of development prevailing in the Ethereal and Gross Material Worlds.

By virtue of the Perfection of God any other possibility is absolutely excluded! It was through this already explained foreseeing that the promise of the coming of the Son of God in the flesh was given. By proclaiming the Truth He was to induce mankind to turn their points!

According to the laws, however, the act of turning the points is reserved to the human spirits themselves. As a result it is not possible to foresee how they will decide. It is only those lines *already chosen* by the human spirits, in which they have already fixed the points according to their free decisions, which can be exactly surveyed with all the stations and curves right to the terminus.

This naturally excludes those turning-points which are still to be determined by a free decision of mankind, for this right is also just as immutable as everything else, due to the natural lawfulness of coming into existence and development through the Perfection of God. And as the Creator has granted this right to the human spirits because of their origin in the Sphere of Spiritual Substantiality, He does not demand to know beforehand what their decision will be!

It is only *the consequence* of such a decision which He can clearly recognise to its very end, because it will then have to work itself out within His Will which rests in the laws governing Ethereal and Gross Material Creation. If it were otherwise the reason could only be found in a lack of perfection, and this is absolutely out of the question!

Thus man should always be fully aware of this his immense responsibility, that he is really independent in his basic decisions! Unfortunately, however, he imagines himself either as a totally dependent slave or, over-rating himself, as a part of the Divine!

The probable reason for this is that in both cases he considers himself relieved of all responsibility; in the one case as being too low and dependent a creature, and in the other as standing far above it! Both of these views are wrong! He should look upon himself as an administrator who has the free right of decision in certain matters, but also full responsibility; who thus enjoys great confidence, but who must not abuse it by being a bad householder!

And it is just this perfection which makes it necessary that, when sending direct help to mankind travelling on a wrong course, the Creator must reckon with the possibility of their failing to come to a right decision! In His Wisdom and Love, which are the inherent, lawful and natural attributes of the Creator, He has still other means in reserve to afford help in such cases. These join up as a continuation with the former course, which had been cut off through the failure of mankind.

Thus before the Son of God was incarnated upon earth, another revelation of the Truth was being prepared in the Eternal Kingdom of the Father, in case humanity should fail in spite of the Father's great sacrifice of Love. If mankind did not heed the warning of the Son of God, with His Pure Divine attitude, to the extent that they turned the points in the direction He indicated, but blindly continued on their course leading to destruction, then another Messenger should be sent out Who could stand closer to the inmost nature of mankind than did the Son of God. He was once more to admonish and lead them in the last hour if ... they desired to listen to His call of Truth! *That is the Son of Man!*

Christ as the Son of God knew about this! On recognising during His Mission how choked and parched were the souls of men, it became clear to Him that His Ministration on earth would not bear the fruit which, given the good volition of mankind, should have ripened. He grieved deeply about this, for He knew so well the Laws of Creation that bear the Will of His Father, and He could clearly foresee the way things were bound to develop towards the inevitable end, which the nature and volition of man were certain to bring about!

It was then that he began to speak about the Son of Man, Whose advent would become necessary because of the course events had taken. His great Mission left two ways open for mankind to decide upon – either to follow His teaching and so ascend, avoiding all that brings destruction, or to fail and descend still further on the downward road leading to destruction. The further He came towards the fulfilment of His great Mission the more clearly He saw that the decision of the great majority of mankind was inclined towards failure and thus towards destruction!

Consequently His utterances about the Son of Man formed themselves into direct promises and proclamations, such as when He declared: "But when the Son of Man cometh ...", etc.!

Therewith He marked the time just prior to the danger of destruction, which was bound to be the ultimate end according to the Divine Laws operating in the World of Matter, because of the failure of mankind towards His Mission and their insistence on continuing their chosen course. This realisation caused Him intense suffering, for He was Love incarnate!

Every transmission affirming that Jesus, the Son of God, at the same time called Himself the Son of Man is wrong! The Divine Laws cannot hold anything so illogical, nor can it be ascribed to the Son of God Who Himself knew the Laws and carried them within Him!

The *disciples* could not grasp this, as was evident from their questions. They alone spread the error which has prevailed up to the present day. They thought that the Son of God meant Himself when He used the expression "the Son of Man" and, acting on this assumption, transmitted this error to posterity! Neither did succeeding generations trouble to concern themselves more seriously with the want of logic inherent in it than did the disciples themselves! They simply disregarded it, partly from diffidence and partly from indolence, although the all-embracing Love of the Creator would have evidenced itself all the more clearly and powerfully by a rectification of the error.

Following in the footsteps of the Son of God, that is, taking up and carrying on His Mission, the Son of Man will face mankind on earth as the Envoy of God the Father, so as to drag them back from their present course by proclaiming the Truth, and induce them voluntarily to decide to change their attitude. This will lead them away from the destruction that now awaits them!

Son of God and Son of Man! Surely it is not so hard to discover that there must be a difference between these Two? Each of these words has its own clearly defined, strictly marked meaning, and those who would mix and fuse them into one must forthwith be stamped as too indolent to think. Hearers and readers of my lectures will be aware of how the natural process of development, beginning with Primordial Light, which is God the Father, descends right down to the globes of the Gross Material World. The Son of God came from Divinity Unsubstantiate, quickly passing through all the spheres until He was incarnated in the World of Gross Matter. This is a process of radiation! Therefore it is absolutely right to call Him the Son of God Who became flesh. His rapid transit through the Sphere of Spiritual Substantiality (it is only there that the human spirit has its origin) permitted Him neither there, nor subsequently in the ethereal part of Creation, to gain a foothold strong enough so that His core of Divine Unsubstantiality could obtain the strong protecting covers of these different natures. Consequently these covers, which otherwise serve as a protective armour, remained thin!

This had the advantage that His innermost Divine nature burst through and shone forth more easily and strongly, but it also had the drawback that in the regions of the earth hostile to the Light it was all the more quickly opposed and furiously attacked because it stood out. The strong Divine part, which was only thinly veiled in the physical vessel, had to remain a stranger among men, something which stood too far apart.

Figuratively speaking, one might say that His Divine core was insufficiently armed and equipped for the lower Gross Material Sphere, through lack of absorption from the Sphere of Spiritual Substantiality and the Ethereal World. The gulf between the Divine and earthly parts was but slightly bridged.

As mankind neither heeded nor treasured this gift of Divine Love but, through the natural driving power of all Darkness, faced the luminous Son of God with animosity and hatred, a second Envoy, better equipped for the World of Gross Matter, had to come – the Son of Man!

The Son of Man is also an Envoy of God and has issued from Divinity Unsubstantiate, which was also a process of radiation! Before beginning His Mission in the World of Gross Matter, He was incarnated in the World of Primordial Spiritual Substantiality, and was thus closely connected with that spiritual species in which the seed-germ of the human spirit originates. Thus the Divine Unsubstantiate core of this second Envoy comes nearer to the origin of the human spirit; thereby gaining greater protection and direct power against it!

It was only after being in this sphere that He was sent down on His Mission to the World of Gross Matter at that time which enabled Him to arrive at the proper hour on the field of battle, there to show the right way into the Kingdom of the Father to all those seriously seeking God and asking for spiritual guidance and, at the same time, to protect them against the attacks of those who are hostile and striving downwards!

Therefore, be on your guard, so that you may recognise Him as soon as His time is come, for that will also be your time!

THE DIFFERENCE IN ORIGIN OF MAN AND ANIMAL

To MAKE clear the difference in origin of man and animal it is necessary to go more deeply into the various spheres of Creation than has been done hitherto.

Such conventional catch-words as the "group soul" of the animal as distinct from the personal "ego" of man no longer suffice for this purpose, although as such they are quite correct. For these give only a general outline and deal with what lies nearest the earth, but do not indicate the *essential* difference!

It is necessary to know about the development of Creation as explained in the lecture: "The development of Creation"!

For the sake of a more comprehensive view, the main spheres from above downwards are reproduced here: –

1. The Divine:	Divinity Unsubstantiate = God Divine Substantiality
2. *Spiritual* Substantiality:	Conscious Spiritual Substantiality Unconscious Spiritual Substantiality
3. Animistic Substantiality:	Conscious Animistic Substantiality Unconscious Animistic Substantiality
4. The Spheres of Matter:	Ethereal Substance Gross Matter

Man has his spiritual origin in Unconscious Spiritual Substantiality, whereas the animal has its animistic origin in Unconscious Animistic Substantiality. There is a huge difference between these two spheres. The animating core of man is *spirit*. The animating core of the animal, however, is *animistic substantiality*.

In this case a spirit stands above animistic substantiality; the origin of the inner man is consequently higher than that of the animal, while both have only the origin of their physical bodies in common. The spirit of man, however, has over the ages developed his original purely animal body to a higher state of perfection than was possible for the animistic substantiality of the animal.

The theory of the natural development of the physical body from the lowest form of animal body right up to the human body is therefore correct. It shows in every respect the continuous and uninterrupted working upwards of the Creative Will in Nature, a proof of its perfection.

But with this theory one very great mistake was made, that man did not take into account what lay beyond the World of Gross Matter!

If it is said that the human body, i. e. the gross material cloak of man, originates from the animal body which existed before the human body, this is correct. These bodies, however, comprise neither the human being as such nor the animal as such, but solely serve as something necessary in the World of Gross Matter. If one were to infer from this that the inner life of man also originated from that of the animal, this is an unpardonable and misleading error that must cause a conflict!

As a result of this conflict a sound intuitive feeling arises in many people *against* such a false assumption. On the one hand they are attracted by the correctness of the assumption as far as the body is concerned, but on the other hand they are repulsed by the gross negligence which without further argument wants to apply the same precept to the origin of the inner man!

It is true that up till now science could hardly do otherwise than assert that in his natural development man must finally have originated from the animal and, above all, from an ape-like animal which in its form most closely resembled the human body. This was because science was hitherto only able to concern itself with matter, and mainly with gross matter, which constitutes only a very minute part of Creation. And of this science knows only the coarsest manifestations, thus very little indeed!

Today at last science has become capable of making use of various things that are valuable without, however, knowing their essential nature, but it is forced to use certain alien terms to do duty for lack of knowledge! These terms merely denote the provisional classification of something existing which they can already use, but the essential nature of which they do not know, much less its origin!

Animistic substantiality and, to a far greater degree, spiritual substantiality stand *above* all matter. Regarded from the earth upwards, they are the continuation up to the origin of all that exists, or looking downwards from On High, which is the more natural way, they are what preceded the World of Matter in the process of development.

It must be remembered that all that belongs to spiritual substantiality as well as to animistic substantiality naturally, and in accordance with its development, needs the cloak of a physical body as soon as, in obedience to the laws of development, it penetrates into the World of Gross Matter as an entity with a living core able to shape matter! Every dissension will immediately be eliminated when at last all men's investigations either penetrate higher into the regions beyond the Sphere of Matter, or they become capable of following the natural process of development from On High downwards.

The time has come when the first move in this direction should be made. But the greatest care must be exercised lest the spiritual knowledge which bears the unmistakable stamp of logic is imperceptibly degraded to the level of ignorant phantasy! It should be noted that animistic substantiality and spiritual substantiality can only be approached with a *free, clear* spirit, and not, as is the case in the World of Matter, with scales, scalpels and test tubes!

Nor can it be done with a *constrained* spirit or one hampered by prejudice, as is so often attempted! The existing Laws of Creation make this automatically and irrevocably impossible. In this matter the small human creature, even when possessed of the greatest presumption, can alter nothing of the perfection of the adamant Will of its Creator!

The essential difference between man and animal lies solely within. An animal can only return to animistic substantiality after casting aside its physical body, whereas man returns to spiritual substantiality, which is far higher.

It is true that in a certain sense man can often descend to the level of the animal, but he must nevertheless always remain a human being, as he cannot shirk his responsibility, which is an inherent part of his spiritual origin! On the other hand an animal, originating as it does from animistic substantiality, can never swing itself upwards to the level of a human being. The difference between the bodies, however, lies only in the outer form, which has been more nobly developed in man by the *spirit* after it had entered the physical body.*

* See Lecture: "The creation of man".

THE SEPARATION BETWEEN MANKIND
AND SCIENCE

THIS separation need not exist, for all mankind is fully entitled to make use of science. For after all science merely tries to make the Divine gift that is Creation more understandable, and the real task of each of its branches is to attempt to probe more deeply into the Laws of the Creator, so that through a more exact knowledge of them they can be used with greater benefit to mankind!

All this is nothing more than a desire voluntarily to submit to the Divine Will!

Now as Creation and the Natural or Divine Laws on which it is based are in their perfection so absolutely clear and simple, it naturally follows that those who really recognise them should be able to give a plain and simple explanation!

Here, however, a noticeable difference sets in which, in its unhealthy tendency, is creating an ever-increasing gap between mankind and those who call themselves disciples of science, thus disciples of knowledge or truth!

They do not express themselves with such natural simplicity as would be consistent with the truth and thus with real knowledge, indeed, with what truth requires as a natural consequence.

There are two, indeed three, reasons for this. These disciples expect to take an exceptional position on account of what they consider to be their hard study. They will not see that with this study they are only taking over something which already existed in Creation. They are doing the same as a simple peasant does when necessity requires him quietly to observe the working of Nature, and also what others must do in their ordinary practical work!

Moreover, as long as a disciple of science does not really approach the truth with his knowledge, he will naturally have to express himself in obscure terms. Only when he has really grasped the truth will he also, out of necessity, have to become simple and natural in his dissertations!

It is no secret that just those people without any knowledge have a liking during their period of study to hold forth to a greater extent than those who actually possess knowledge. In so doing they will always be obliged to use obscure terms, because they cannot do otherwise as long as they have not attained to the truth and thus to real knowledge!

In the third place there is a real danger that most people would pay very little attention to science if it revealed itself in the natural cloak of truth. They would think it "too natural" to be of much importance!

They do not reflect that *this* is the only right thing, and that it also furnishes the standard by which to measure what is genuine and true. The guarantee of truth lies only in the simple naturalness of things!

But it is not so easy to convince men of this! They would not even recognise the Son of God in Jesus because He came to them in "too simple a manner"!

The disciples of science were very well aware of this danger from the earliest days. That is why, in their shrewdness, they closed themselves more and more to the simple naturalness of truth. In their cogitations as to how they could make themselves and their science appear of more importance, they created ever greater obstacles!

Finally, any scholar who had attained to some eminence disdained to express himself so simply that all could understand him. This often happened for a reason he himself was hardly conscious of, namely, that there would be little left to make him stand out unless he used a mode of expression which could only be learned by years of special study!

By not making himself generally understood, in due course he created for himself a position of artificial superiority which was upheld by his pupils and successors at all costs, as otherwise for many the long years of study and corresponding financial sacrifice would really have been in vain!

And today it has even gone so far that many scholars are no longer capable of expressing themselves clearly and comprehensively, thus simply, to ordinary people! To achieve *this* again would indeed require the *hardest study* and take more than a whole generation. But above all it would have the result (distasteful to many) of bringing into prominence only those who, by virtue of their *real abilities* have something to give mankind, and who are willing to serve them with it!

At present the practice of mystifying the public with incomprehensibilities is a particularly prominent characteristic of the scientific world; similar to what was customary in religious observances, where ministers ordained by men on earth as guides and leaders spoke to those who came to worship and to be uplifted in Latin, which they could not understand and therefore could not grasp and make their own, which alone would benefit them. These ministers might just as well have spoken in Siamese; the result would have been equally ineffective!

True knowledge need not be incomprehensible, for at the same time it holds the capacity, indeed the inherent desire, to express itself in simple terms!

The truth is intended for *all* men without exception, for they issue from it, as the truth is an integral part of the Sphere of Spiritual Substantiality, the point of origin of the human spirit. For this reason the truth in its natural simplicity can also be understood by all people. However, as soon as it is turned into something complicated and incomprehensible, it either remains no longer pure and true, or the descriptions are lost in paltry details which are of less importance than the fundament!

This fundament, the true knowledge, must be comprehensible to everyone! Artificial highbrow expressions are far remote from what is natural and contain as little wisdom! Every person who cannot transmit true knowledge simply and naturally has *not* grasped it himself. He is either trying subconsciously to cover up something or he is like a gaily attired doll without life!

He who still leaves gaps in the logical course and demands blind faith instead, makes his perfect God into an imperfect idol. He proves that he himself has not found the right way and cannot therefore be a trustworthy guide. May this be a warning to every serious seeker!

SPIRIT

THE WORD "spirit" is often used without the speaker being aware of what spirit really is. Some simply call spirit the inner life of man, while others regard soul and spirit as being the same. It is often used to describe a "spirited" person, but this goes no further than mere brain activity. There are also many other ways of using it, but no one tries to explain what spirit really means.

The most exalted meaning yet given to the word lies in the expression "God is spirit", from which all else is deduced. Through this expression one sought to understand God and thus to explain Him.

But just this was again bound to lead away from reality and disseminate errors, for it is *wrong* simply to say "God is spirit".

God is *Divine* and not spiritual! This in itself explains everything. One may never call Divinity spirit! Only spirituality is spirit. This hitherto erroneous view can be explained by the fact that man originates in the Spiritual Sphere, and is therefore unable to think beyond that sphere. Thus he regards all that is spiritual as being the highest.

So it is quite natural that he likes to regard what is most perfect and undimmed in this sphere as the origin of all Creation, thus as God. Hence one may assume that the reason for this wrong conception sprang not only from the desire to depict his God as being of his own nature, although perfect in every respect, so as to feel more closely united with Him, but lay mainly in his inability to grasp the real Sublimity of God.

God is Divine, His Will is spirit! Out of this, His Living Will, His immediate spiritual surrounding came into being – Paradise and its inhabitants. Out of this Paradise came man as a spirit-germ to begin his journey through the further Creation. Thus man is the bearer *of spirit* in the whole material Creation! For this reason he is bound to the pure Primordial Will of God in all his actions. He must bear full responsibility if he permits external influences from the material world to smother his spirit with impurity and, in certain circumstances, to allow it from time to time to be completely buried!

This is the treasure or the talent which at his hand was to bring compound interest. From the erroneous assumption that God Himself was spirit, thus of the same nature as the origin of man, it is evident that man could never form the right conception of the Godhead. He should not only picture Him as being the absolute perfection of his own species, but go far beyond this to a species that will forever remain incomprehensible to him, because his own spiritual nature would never be capable of grasping it!

Spirit, therefore, is the *Will of God,* the life-elixir of all Creation which, if it is to continue to exist, must be permeated by the Divine Will. Man being part-bearer of this spirit should, in becoming self-conscious, contribute towards the *upliftment* and further development of all Creation. To do this, however, it is necessary that he should learn to use the powers of Nature aright and make them collectively serve the furtherance of Creation!

What is said here is only meant as a preliminary explanation. It will be followed later by more detailed lectures, in which the various species of spirit will be depicted within their own well-defined spheres.

THE DEVELOPMENT OF CREATION

ONCE before I have pointed out that the written accounts of Creation should not be taken in an earthly sense. The Bible narrative also does not refer to this earth. The creation of the earth was simply the natural consequence of the further development of the *first* Creation.

It is almost incredible how scriptural scholars could have jumped to such an illogical and incomplete assumption as that God out of His own Perfection could, without any transition, have immediately created the gross material earth!

To get nearer to the truth of what actually happened, it is not necessary to change the "Word" of the Scriptures. On the contrary, the description of the history of Creation represents the truth much more clearly than do all the false and incomplete assumptions! It is only the erroneous interpretations which have caused a misunderstanding on the part of so many people!

These people quite rightly sense the mistake that is made by persistently placing the Paradise referred to in the Bible on this gross material earth, which is so far remote from the Divine. It surely cannot be so little known that the Bible is primarily a *spiritual* book! It gives clarification about *spiritual* events, man only being mentioned where he has an immediate relationship with these spiritual things in order to illustrate and make them clear.

Finally even the human intellect can understand – because it is so natural – that the Bible narrative of Creation does *not* refer to the earth, which is so far away from the Creator!

Hardly anybody will dare to dispute the fact that this immediate Creation of God, designated as the *first* Creation, can only be looked for in His immediate neighbourhood, because it was the *first* to emanate from Him, and is thus *bound to be* in closer connection with Him! No calm and clear thinker will expect that this first and *original* Creation was enacted just on this earth, which is furthest removed from the Divine Sphere, and which only came into being in the further course of development!

Thus there could be no question of a Paradise *on earth!* What God created, as expressly stated in the story of Creation, naturally remained *immediately* connected with Him and could only be situated in His near vicinity. It is likewise quite understandable and natural that consequently all that was created in or emanated from His immediate proximity must most nearly resemble the Creator's own Perfection.

However, to suppose this to be on the gross material earth must breed doubters! The thought of a "driving out" from the *earthly* Paradise, whereby those driven out would still have to remain on the same earth, is so unhealthy, is so evidently and grossly material in its concept, as to be almost grotesque! It is a lifeless picture, bearing the stamp of such a rigidly compiled dogma that no sensible human being knows what to do with it!

The less perfect a thing is the further removed it is from Perfection. Hence the spiritual beings who were created out of Perfection cannot be the human beings on earth, but must have their place closest to this Perfection, and therefore represent the most ideal examples for humanity! They are the eternal spiritual beings who never descend into the World of Matter and therefore never become human beings. They are radiant, ideal figures who attract like magnets and, at the same time, exercise a strengthening influence on all the abilities in the human spirit-germs, and later in the spirits which have attained to consciousness.

The Paradise mentioned in the Bible may therefore *not* be confused with the earth!

For a better understanding it is necessary once again to give a complete picture of all that exists in order to make it easier for the seeker to find his way to the Eternal Kingdom of God, the Paradise from which he originates in his very first spiritual beginning.

Let man imagine Divinity as absolutely the highest over all! God Himself, as the starting point of all that exists, as the Primordial Source of all Life, is in His absolute Perfection *unsubstantiate.* Next to God Himself in His very own Unsubstantiality follows the Sphere of Divine *Substantiality.* In this originate the first beings to take form and shape. To these belong in the first place the Primordial Queen and the Archangels, and finally a small number of Elders. The Elders are of great importance for the further development towards spiritual substantiality, much in the same way as, later on, the conscious beings of the Animistic Sphere are of great importance for the development of matter. Lucifer was sent from the Sphere of Divine Substantiality to be a direct support for Creation as it automatically developed further.

The Son of God, however, issued from Divine Unsubstantiality as a part of It, and after fulfilling His Mission of help had to return to Divine Unsubstantiality and again become One with the Father. The Son of Man also issues from Divine Unsubstantiality. Through the connection with conscious spiritual substantiality His Part, which was severed, remained of necessity separate from Divine Unsubstantiality, and yet also directly connected with It, so that He may stand as the Eternal Mediator between God and His Work.

As Lucifer, who proceeded from the Sphere of Divine *Substantiality*, failed in his mission, it became necessary to send in his place someone stronger who could bind him and bring help to Creation. For this reason the Son of Man, who was entrusted with this office, issued from Divine *Unsubstantiality*.

Adjoining the Sphere of Divine Substantiality is Primordial Creation, the Eternal Kingdom of God. Closest to Divine Substantiality there is first of all *conscious spiritual substantiality*, consisting of the created eternal spiritual beings who are also called spirits. These are the perfect, ideal forms of all that human spirits, in their most perfect development, can and should aspire to. Like magnets they draw up those who strive to ascend. Through this automatic connection those who are seeking and those who strive to ascend often feel an inexplicable longing, which gives rise to the urge to seek and strive upwards.

These spirits were never born into the World of Matter, and were created by God Himself, the Primordial Source of all Being and all Life, as the first Primordial Spirits, thus coming nearest to Him in perfection. *They* are the ones *made after His Own Image!*

It must not be overlooked that the story of Creation expressly states: "*After His Image!*" This statement is not without importance, for they can only be after His *Image*, not after *Himself*, i.e., only after that in which He *shows* Himself, because only pure Divinity Itself is *un*substantiate.

In order to show Himself God must first clothe Himself in Divine Substantiality, as has already been said above, but even then He cannot be seen by those who dwell in spiritual substantiality, but only by those dwelling in Divine Substantiality, and that only to a minor degree, because all that is purely Divine must in its perfect purity and radiance blind what is not so Divine. Even those of Divine Substantiality cannot look upon God's Countenance!

The difference between Divine Unsubstantiality and Divine Substantiality is still far too great!

This Paradise of conscious spiritual substantiality also contains *unconscious spiritual substantiality* which holds the same fundamental components as conscious spiritual substantiality, i.e., the germs. These germs have life, and all life in the whole Creation strives to develop in obedience to Divine Will, to develop towards consciousness. This is quite a natural and healthy process!

The unconscious, however, can only achieve this consciousness through experiencing, and this urge towards further development through experiencing finally causes such maturing or ambitious germs of unconscious spiritual substantiality to be automatically expelled or ejected, whichever you wish to call it, over the boundary of the Sphere of Spiritual Substantiality. Since this expulsion or ejection of a germ cannot take place in an upward direction, it must necessarily proceed in the only way open to it, and that is downwards.

And this is the natural expulsion from Paradise, from the Sphere of Spiritual Substantiality, necessary to every spirit-germ striving to become conscious!

When it is said: "In the sweat of thy brow thou shalt eat thy bread", this is metaphorically quite correct. In other words, the turmoil of experiencing makes it necessary for it to defend itself and struggle against the onrushing influences of the lower sphere into which it penetrates as a stranger!

This expulsion, ejection, or being driven out from Paradise is in no wise a punishment, but becomes an absolutely natural and automatic necessity when the spirit-germ is nearing a certain stage of maturity as a result of the urge to develop self-consciousness. It is the birth from the Sphere of Unconscious Spiritual Substantiality into the Sphere of Animistic Substantiality*, and later into the World of Matter for the purpose of developing. It is *progress*, not retrogression!

The Fall of Man, which occurred only later, and from which hereditary sin developed, was a happening all on its own, about which I shall still give a detailed explanation. It has nothing whatever to do with the continuously recurring process described here!

It is also quite a correct description when it is said in the story of Creation that man felt the desire to "cover his nakedness" after the conception of good

---

* See Appendix.

and evil awakened within him, which was the beginning of self-consciousness.

With the increasing urge to become conscious, ejection or expulsion from Paradise follows automatically, so as to journey through the Animistic Sphere and enter the World of Matter. Now as soon as the spirit-germ steps out of the Realm of Spiritual Substantiality it would stand "naked" as such in the lower, different and denser surrounding. One could also say "uncovered". It is then that the human spirit feels not only the urge but the absolute necessity to cover itself protectingly with the essence and nature of the substance surrounding it; to wrap itself in a sort of cloak and take on first the animistic covering, then the ethereal body and finally also the gross material body.

Not until it has clothed itself in a gross material cloak or body does sexual instinct fully awaken and with it physical shame!

The greater this feeling of shame is the nobler is this instinct and the higher the man also ranks spiritually! *The inner spiritual worth of a human being* on earth may be directly *measured* by the greater or lesser degree of his physical shame.

This is an infallible standard and easily recognised by any man! When this feeling of outward shame has been choked or eradicated, the soul's far finer and quite different feeling of shame will always be simultaneously choked and the inner man consequently debased.

It is an infallible sign of a deep fall and certain deterioration when humanity, under the guise of progress, begin to want to "lift" themselves above the feeling of shame, this precious jewel which could help them in every respect. No matter whether this is done under cover of sport, hygiene, fashion, children's education or many another welcome pretence! Decline and fall cannot then be stayed, and only the greatest of shocks can perhaps still bring to their senses a few of all those who so thoughtlessly allowed themselves to be drawn along this course!

Following its natural expulsion and during its journey through the animistic sphere and material parts of Creation, not only one but ever more urgent necessities arise for the existence of the spirit-germ in these lower regions of Creation so as further to develop and uplift them. This also works in return to strengthen and fortify the germ, not only contributing to its own development towards self-consciousness but actually making it possible.

It is a gigantic working and weaving, with the threads in the cosmic loom, as it were, intermingling in a thousand ways. Yet in spite of all the lively individual activity there is such an absolutely logical interlocking with the reciprocal actions that the path of a single spirit-germ, right to its very end, appears to be part of a beautiful many-coloured carpet, deliberately formed by the hand of an artist. It is a path either leading upwards towards self-consciousness or descending to eventual annihilation in order to protect the others.

There are so many laws working silently but surely in the wonderful work of Creation that one could write an essay upon each of the thousand different processes in the life of man, but they would always lead back to the one great basic truth – *the Perfection of the Creator as the Source of all that exists, Whose Will is the Living Creative Spirit. The Holy Spirit! All that is of spirit is Its Work!*

As man originates in this work of spiritual substantiality he bears within himself a particle of the volition of this spirit. This, it is true, brings with it the freedom of decision and the responsibility attaching to it, but it is in no way the same as Divinity Itself, as is so often erroneously assumed and asserted.

Those who can survey with understanding every manifestation of the Divine Will, which through the Laws of Nature works to help and further Creation, will join in a wonderful harmonious hymn of praise, in one united feeling of gratitude and joy rising through millions of channels towards the Source!

The eternally recurring process of development in Creation, which brings about the consequent expulsion of the spirit-germ from Paradise at a certain stage of maturity, can also be seen with the physical eyes in all earthly happenings, because everywhere the process is reflected in the same way.

One could also call this expulsion, which is quite a natural development, the process of automatic release. It is exactly the same as a ripe apple or any other ripe fruit falling from a tree, so as to release the seed in the process of decomposition according to the Creative Will. *Only then,* under the outside influences brought to bear directly upon it, can it *burst* the covering, germinate and become a tender plant! The plant again can only develop resistance through exposure to rain, storm and sunshine and thus grow into a strong tree.

Thus the expulsion of the mature spirit-germ from Paradise is an inevitable result of development, in much the same way as the Animistic and Material Spheres, and finally the Gross Material World, are basically only a consequential development from the Sphere of Spiritual Substantiality! In this the fundamental characteristics of Original Creation continually repeat themselves, but with the necessary distinction that the manifestations always correspond to the essence and nature of the particular substance.

The expulsion of the soul also occurs in the World of Gross Matter as soon as its time of maturity has arrived. This is called physical death, and it is the automatic expulsion or severance of the soul from physical matter and its birth into ethereal matter. Here also one can liken the process to fruit falling from a tree. In calm weather only the ripe fruit fall, but during storms the unripe fruit also fall. The ripe fruit are those who pass over into the ethereal beyond at the right time and with their seeds inwardly matured. They are spiritually "ready" for the beyond, and therefore will quickly take root and be able to grow up securely!

The unripe fruit, however, are those whose fall or death, with the accompanying decay of the protecting physical body, lays bare the *as yet unripe* ethereal seeds, thus exposing them prematurely to all the influences, whereby they either have to perish or will be forced to complete their process of ripening before they can take root (adjust themselves) in the ethereal soil (conditions) and thus grow up.

And so development continually proceeds step by step unless in the meantime decay sets in and destroys the seeds insufficiently ripened. Such a seed is then lost and naturally with it the inherent possibility to become an independent fruit-bearing tree which, in its turn, can help to continue the process of development.

He who looks around attentively can often clearly observe this fundamental picture of all the happenings in Creation in his immediate vicinity, for in the most minute there is always mirrored a reflection of the greatest.

Next in order downwards from this Paradise of Spiritual Substantiality comes the Sphere of all *Animistic Substantiality*. This sphere is again divided into two parts. There is first *conscious animistic substantiality,* consisting of the elementals and nature-beings to which, as the last of many, belong the elves, gnomes, nixies, etc. These elementals and nature-beings were the necessary preparation for the further development towards the eventual creation of matter, for matter could only come into existence in unison with animistic substantiality.

The elementals and nature-beings had to co-operate creatively in the developing World of Matter just as they still do today!

Secondly, in the Sphere of Animistic Substantiality there exists *unconscious animistic substantiality*. From this issues the life of the animal soul*. Here should be noted the difference between the Sphere of Spiritual Substantiality and the Sphere of Animistic Substantiality. Only that which is *spirit* bears within it from the very beginning onwards the power to make a free decision, and the resulting full responsibility. This is not the case with the beings of animistic substantiality!

A further result of the process of development was the creation of matter. This is divided into *ethereal substance,* in which there are many divisions, and *gross material substance* which, commencing with the finest nebulae, is visible to the physical eye. But there is no question of a Paradise on earth, as the earth is one of the furthest outposts of gross matter. The time will arrive when a *reflection* of the real Paradise *must* come on earth under the rule of the Son of Man at the beginning of the Millennium! Then at the same time there will be erected an earthly replica of the Grail Castle, the original of which stands on the highest heights of Creation as the hitherto only true Temple of God!

---

* Lecture: "The difference in origin of man and animal".

I AM THE LORD THY GOD!

WHERE are those who really obey this highest of all commandments? Where is the priest who teaches it purely and truly? "I am the Lord thy God; thou shalt have none other gods but Me!" These words are given so plainly, so *straightforwardly*, that any variation should be utterly impossible! Christ also repeatedly pointed this out quite clearly and emphatically.

It is all the more deplorable that millions heedlessly overlook it and devote themselves to cults which are directly opposed to this highest of all commandments! Worst of all is that they disregard this commandment of their God and their Lord with devout fervour, under the delusion that they are honouring and pleasing Him with what is an obvious transgression of His commandment!

This great error can only be kept alive through a *blind* faith which excludes all investigation. For blind faith is nothing but thoughtlessness and spiritual indolence on the part of those who, like the sluggard and lie-a-bed, try to put off as long as possible the moment of awakening and getting up because it involves duties they would much rather evade! They loathe all exertion, for it is much easier to let others work and think for them!

However, he who lets others think for him puts himself in their power! He reduces himself to slavery and thus surrenders his freedom! But God gave man the power to decide freely and the ability to think and perceive intuitively, in return for which man must naturally render account of everything brought about by this ability to make free decisions! Thus God wanted *free* men and not slaves!

It is indeed sad when out of laziness man makes himself a slave *in the earthly sense*, but the consequences are fearful when he debases himself *spiritually* so far as to become the dull-witted adherent of teachings which are in opposition to the explicit commandments of God! It avails mankind nothing to try and lull the misgivings which now and then assail them with the excuse that those who introduced the errors into the teachings must, after all, carry the greater responsibility. This is fundamentally true, but in addition each individual is specifically responsible for everything he thinks and does! In short nothing of this can be remitted to any man!

He who does not practise to its fullest extent the ability granted him to think and perceive intuitively makes himself guilty!

It is not a sin but a duty for every man who is approaching maturity, and thus becoming a fully responsible being, to begin to think about what he has been taught up till then. If he cannot bring his intuition to harmonise with some point in the teaching, he must not blindly accept it as being correct! He then harms himself as if he had made a bad bargain! That which he cannot retain out of conviction he should leave alone, otherwise his thoughts and actions will become hypocritical!

He who neglects something which is really good because he cannot understand it is not nearly as despicable as he who without conviction adheres to a cult he does not quite understand. All the thoughts and actions resulting from this want of right comprehension are empty and, because of this emptiness, there can naturally be no good reciprocal action. There is no *living* basis for anything good in emptiness. Thus it becomes hypocrisy, which amounts to blasphemy, because it is an attempt to deceive God with something which does not exist! That makes him who practises it despicable, an outcast, because the living intuition is lacking!

Although they may be devout and fervent, millions who thoughtlessly do homage to things that are directly opposed to the Divine Commandments are absolutely fettered and completely cut off from spiritual ascent!

Only a free conviction has real life and can therefore create living values! Such a conviction, however, can only arise from a rigorous testing and from intuitive perception! Where there is the slightest lack of understanding, not to mention any doubt, conviction can never be attained!

Only a complete understanding, free of any gaps, is synonymous with conviction, which alone has spiritual value!

It is truly painful to observe how thoughtlessly the masses make the sign of the Cross, bow down and kneel in church! Such automatons should not be numbered among thinking men. The sign of the Cross is the sign of Truth, and therefore a sign of God! He who uses this sign of Truth at a moment when his inmost being is not genuine in every respect, or when his entire intuition is not fully adjusted to absolute Truth, burdens himself with guilt. It would be a hundred times better for such a person to refrain from crossing himself until such time as his whole soul has become attuned to the Truth, thus also to God Himself and to His Holy Will. For God, his Lord, is the Truth!

It is idolatry and an open transgression against the holiest of all Divine Commandments when he renders to a *symbol* the homage which is due only to God!

"I am the Lord thy God; thou shalt have none other gods but Me!" This is stated so explicitly, in such brief, distinct and clear terms, as not to permit of the slightest deviation. Christ also specifically pointed to the necessity of keeping this commandment. Purposely and designedly He called it the *supreme* law when speaking to the Pharisees, i. e., the law that must not be broken or perverted in any circumstances. At the same time this implies that nothing else that is good nor any other faith can come to full value unless this *supreme* law is strictly obeyed! Indeed *everything* depends upon this!

Let us, for example, consider without prejudice the homage paid to the monstrance! Here we find many people conflicting with this clear, supreme commandment!

In order to provide an explanation as to why he accords it Divine honours, does man expect his God to descend into this consecrated wafer, which can be changed at will? Or that God is compelled to enter the host on account of its consecration? One is as unthinkable as the other! Neither can such a consecration bring about a direct connection with God, for the way to God is not so simple and so easy! Nor will man or the spirit of man ever be able to reach that goal!

When one man prostrates himself before a carven image, another before the sun, and a third before the monstrance, they are all trespassing against God's supreme law *if in doing so they see in it* the Living God Himself, and consequently expect from it immediate Divine Grace and Blessing! The *actual* trespass and open idolatry lie in such a false assumption, expectation and intuition!

This kind of idolatry is often practised with the greatest fervour, although in different forms, by the adherents of many religions.

Every man who thinks seriously, as his capacities oblige him to do, *must* come into a conflict which can only be forcibly silenced from time to time through wrong indulgence in blind faith, like the lazy sluggard who prefers to sleep the time away rather than attend to his daily duties!

Every earnest man, however, will definitely perceive that in the first place he must seek *clarity* in all that is to become holy to him.

How often did Christ explain that men should *live* His teaching in order to derive any profit from it, i.e., in order to commence spiritual ascent and attain everlasting life! The words "everlasting life" in themselves express spiritual *activity*, not spiritual indolence. When He spoke of *living* His teaching He expressly and clearly warned that a dull acceptance of it would be false and useless.

Genuine experiencing can naturally always only come through conviction, never otherwise! Conviction, however, can only arise through complete understanding, and understanding in turn presupposes deep reflection and personal examination. The teaching must be weighed with one's own intuition. It therefore obviously follows that blind faith is utterly wrong! All that is wrong, however, can easily lead downwards, towards perdition, but it can never lead upwards.

Ascent is synonymous with liberation from all pressure. As long as there is still pressure somewhere, there can be no question of liberation or redemption. That which is not understood, however, *comprises* a pressure, which is not released until the point of pressure or gap is eliminated through complete understanding.

Blind faith will always remain synonymous with lack of understanding, and therefore it can never equal conviction, nor can it bring liberation and redemption! People who have imprisoned themselves within a blind faith cannot be spiritually alive. They are as if dead and therefore worthless!

If a man begins to think aright, to consider all happenings calmly and attentively and to arrange them logically, he will of his own accord come to the conviction that God in His Perfect Purity *cannot,* on account of His Own Creative Will, *descend to this earth!*

The absolute Purity and Perfection of Divinity exclude the possibility of His descent into the World of Matter. The difference is too great for a direct union to be at all possible, unless the necessary transition stages comprising animistic and material substance are taken into account. Compliance with the transition stages can only be accomplished by an incarnation in the flesh, as happened in the case of the Son of God!

As the Son of God "has been re-united with the Father", has returned to the sphere of His origin, He is again part of Divinity and thus separated from what is terrestrial to a like degree.

Any exception to this would mean a perversion of the Divine Creative Will, and would once more show a lack of perfection.

But since perfection is inseparable from Divinity, there remains no other possibility than that His Creative Will is also perfect, which is the same as being unalterable. If all men were perfect, each one would naturally take the same road as the other.

It is only imperfection which allows of variations!

After the Son of God's "return to the Father", the operation of the perfect Divine Laws made it impossible for Him as for the Father to be personally in the sphere of matter or to descend to the earth, unless indeed He were incarnated in the flesh in accordance with the Creative Laws!

For these reasons the adoration of any object of physical substance as Divine represents a transgression against the supreme Law of God. Divine adoration should only be accorded to the Living God, and just on account of His Divinity He cannot be on earth!

In accordance with the Perfection of God as expressed in His Creative Will, the gross material body of the Son of God could likewise only be a *purely physical* body and must not be called or considered as Divine*.

It follows that everything which contradicts this will cast doubt on the absolute *Perfection of God* and must therefore be wrong! This is an unquestionable and infallible standard for an appraisal of the right faith in God!

It is different with pure symbolism. Every symbol serves a good and helpful purpose as long as it is seriously regarded as *such*. It will help very many people when they gaze upon it to a greater and deeper concentration. Many a man who looks upon the symbols of his religion will find it easier to direct his thoughts more clearly towards the Creator, no matter by what name he has learned to call Him. It would therefore be wrong to doubt the high value of religious ceremonies and symbolism, as long as they do not degenerate into direct adoration and worship of the material *object*.

As God Himself cannot descend to the earth in the Gross Material Sphere, it lies with the human spirit itself to make its way upward to the Sphere of Spiritual Substantiality from which it originates. And it was *to show this way*

---

* Lecture: "The resurrection of Christ's physical body".

that Divinity was incarnated in the flesh, for in Divinity alone lies that Primordial Power from which the Living Word can flow. But man must not imagine that Divinity remained on earth in order that every person wishing for it might at once be accorded grace in a very special manner! For the purpose of obtaining grace *the immutable Laws of God lie in Creation, and it is only through strict adherence to them that grace can be received!* He who wishes to ascend to the Luminous Heights must adjust himself accordingly!

Nobody shall compare God in His Perfection with an earthly king who can arbitrarily repeal sentence passed by his equally arbitrary judges. *The Perfection of the Creator and of His Will, which is One with Him, would never permit such a thing!*

The human spirit should at last get accustomed to the thought that it must bestir *itself* most energetically to obtain grace and forgiveness and thus fulfil the duty it has slothfully neglected! It must pull itself together and work on itself if it would not fall into the darkness of the damned!

When it is said that we are to trust in our Saviour, this means that we are to trust in His words, to let His words come to life in deeds! *Nothing else will help!* Mere empty faith is of no avail! To believe in Him means just to believe Him! And he who does not assiduously climb the rope tendered him through the Word of the Son of God is irretrievably lost!

If a man really longs for his Saviour he must ultimately bestir himself to spiritual mobility and exertion directed to more than mere earthly advantages and enjoyments! He must not in his presumption expect his Saviour to descend, but must strive to climb up to Him! The way upwards is shown in the Word!

God will not run begging after mankind when they build up a false picture of Him and thereby turn away and go on wrong paths. It is not as easy as that! Because such an absurd notion is deeply rooted in many people through a false understanding mankind must first learn to *fear* their God again! They must recognise through the inevitable reactions to their comfortable and dead faith that His Will is adamant in its Perfection and cannot be turned aside!

He who will not conform to the Divine Laws will be hurt or even crushed, as must also happen ultimately to those who practise idolatry by according Divine homage to something that is not Divine! Man must learn to recognise the fact that *the Saviour is waiting for him, but He will not come and fetch him!*

The faith, or rather the delusion, held by the greater part of mankind of the present day *was bound to fail them,* and even lead to misery and destruction, *because it is dead* and without real life!

As Christ once drove out the money-changers who were defiling the Temple, *so* must men first be lashed out of all indolence regarding their thoughts and intuitive perception about God! But let him who does not wish otherwise sleep on quietly, let him recline comfortably on the soft pillow of self-delusion that although he does not think about things very much, yet his faith is right, and that it is even sinful to investigate further! The awakening which is nearer to him than he expects will be terrible! It will be meted out to him according to his indolence!

How can a man who believes in God, who has reflected upon His Nature and His Greatness, and who, above all, knows how the perfect Divine Will rests in Creation as the active Laws of Nature – how can he expect that, contrary to the Divine Law of absolute Reciprocal Action, his sins can be forgiven him through some penance imposed upon him? This would be impossible even for the Creator; for the Laws of Creation and of Development, which have issued from His *Perfection,* are in their effects solely and completely responsible for the automatic dispensation of reward or punishment, which they carry out with immutable justice, in the ripening and harvesting of the good and evil seeds sown by the human spirit.

Every fresh manifestation of God's Will will always continue in perfection, and therefore cannot deviate in the slightest degree from previous manifestations, but must be in complete agreement with them. God's Perfection necessitates that everything, literally everything, must continually follow the same course! Any remission of sins and consequently any immediate atonement is utterly impossible unless there has been fulfilment of the Divine Laws resting in Creation, to which every human spirit is subject if he wishes to enter the Kingdom of Heaven.

How can a man who even thinks a little expect any deviation? This would be a complete belittlement of his Perfect God! When Christ during His life on earth said to this or that man: "Thy sins are forgiven thee", this was quite correct; for in his earnest prayer and firm faith lay the best guarantee that in future the man concerned would live according to Christ's teaching. Therefore in doing so he was *bound* to receive forgiveness of his sins, because he had adjusted himself aright to the Divine Laws of Creation and no longer opposed them.

If now a man of his own discretion dictates penance to another, after which he declares the other's sins to be remitted, he deceives himself and also the man who came to seek his help, whether he is conscious of the fact or not, and unscrupulously sets himself far above Divinity Itself!

If men would at last only think of their God in a more *natural* way, of their God Whose Volition created living nature! But in their blind and erroneous faith they build up a picture of Him which is a delusion, something which is much less than they imagine it to be. It is just in the Natural Perfection or Perfect Naturalness of God, the Primordial Source of all being and the Starting Point of all that lives, that His Magnitude is so overwhelming and beyond the grasp of the human spirit! Many of the teachings, however, contain so much wilful distortion and confusion as to make it unnecessarily difficult and sometimes quite impossible for man to preserve a pure belief because of the lack of all naturalness! And how many incredible contradictions are contained in some of them!

For instance, one frequently finds as a basic tenet the Omniscience and Perfection of the Will of God and the Word that issues from It! Quite naturally this must carry with it an *unchangeableness* that cannot be moved by a hair's breadth, because Perfection cannot be thought of in any other way!

The actions of many religious ministers, however, indicate *doubt* in their own teaching, because they stand in direct contradiction to it, and by their deeds they openly disavow its basic tenets. For example, the hearing of confession and the imposition of penance, the sale of indulgences whether for money or for prayer, which is supposed to be followed by the immediate forgiveness of sins, and other similar customs, are, if considered calmly, a denial of the Divine Will resting in the Laws of Creation. He who does no more than merely engage in a desultory consideration of these practices will see in them nothing else but an absolute belittlement of the Perfection of God!

It is quite natural that man's erroneous presumption in considering himself capable of forgiving sins, and similar transgressions against the Perfection of the Divine Will, were bound to lead to gross abuse! How much longer will man continue under the foolish delusion that he is able to drive such an unsavoury bargain with the Just God and His unalterable Will!

When Jesus the Son of God once said to His disciples: *"Whose soever sins ye remit, they are remitted unto them..."*, these words were not meant as a general licence to act arbitrarily.

That would have been equivalent to upsetting the Divine Will as embodied in the immutable power of reciprocal action, which in its active working carries reward and punishment with incorruptible and Divine (and therefore perfect) Justice. It would have meant a permitted interruption of this law!

This Jesus could never have done, neither did He do it, because He had come to "fulfil" the laws, not to overthrow them!

With these words He meant the lawful operations which rest in the Creative Will, whereby one human being can forgive *that injury* which he has suffered *at the hands of another* human being! Being the victim he has the right and also the power to forgive! His sincere forgiveness will turn aside and break the power of the karma which would otherwise surely develop for the other through reciprocal action, and in this actual happening lies at the same time real forgiveness!

This forgiveness of the culprit can *only* come from the person who suffered the offence, not otherwise! It is for this reason that there is so much blessing and deliverance in personal forgiveness when it is honestly meant and intuitively felt.

A person not immediately involved is quite naturally excluded from the threads of reciprocal action and therefore cannot actively and effectively intervene because of this fact. He can only *intercede by prayer* in such cases, the effect of which, however, depends on the condition of the souls of those immediately concerned. He himself must remain on the outside and therefore cannot bring about forgiveness! *This alone rests in God's Will,* which reveals Itself in the laws of just reciprocal actions, against which He Himself would never act, because they were perfect from the beginning according to His Will.

It lies in the Justice of God that whatever will happen or has happened *can only be forgiven by the injured person,* either here on earth or later in the Ethereal World. Otherwise the weight of reciprocal action must hit the offender to such effect that the debt would then be redeemed. Simultaneously this reaction would in some way bring about the forgiveness of the injured person, whose attitude is interwoven in the working of karma. There is no other possibility, as until this happens the connecting threads remain unbroken. This is not only an advantage for the offender, but also for the person offended, because the latter could not wholly enter into the Light without first having granted this forgiveness. His unrelenting attitude would inevitably retain him.

Thus no man can forgive another an offence unless he has personally been the sufferer! The Law of Reciprocal Action would remain uninfluenced by anything not interwoven in it with the living thread, and this can only come about through being directly involved. Reformation alone is the living road to forgiveness!*

"I am the Lord thy God; thou shalt have none other gods but Me", should remain burned into man's spirit in letters of fire as a natural protection against any idolatry!

He who truly acknowledges God in all His Magnitude must regard all other practices as sacrilege!

A man may and should go to a priest to receive *instruction*, providing the latter is really capable of giving it. If, however, a demand is made upon him to belittle God's Perfection through carrying out some action or adopting a false way of thinking, then he must turn away from the priest, for a *servant* of God is not at the same time an *Envoy* of God who could have the right to demand and to grant in His Name.

This matter also has quite a natural and simple explanation which shows what is the right way without any digression.

An Envoy of God can naturally never be a man, unless he comes directly from Divinity and thus bears the attributes of Divinity within himself! That alone makes him an Envoy!

But since man is not Divine, it is therefore impossible for him to be an Envoy of God. The Power of God cannot be conferred upon any man, *because Divine Power lies only in Divinity Itself!*

This logical fact in its very simplicity automatically and absolutely precludes all possibility of the *election by men* of a worldly substitute for God, or of the *proclamation of a Christ.* Every effort to do so must bear the stamp of impossibility!

It follows that in such matters neither an election nor a proclamation by man has any validity, but only a *Messenger direct* from God Himself!

---

* Lecture: "Fate".

Man's opinions in these matters are of no account; on the contrary, judging from *all* that has happened in the past, they have *always been far from realistic* and did not harmonise with the Will of God! Thinking people cannot comprehend the morbid exaggeration with which men try again and again to reach out beyond their actual value; men who, in their highest state of spiritual perfection, can only ascend to the *lowest* level in the conscious part of the eternal Sphere of Spiritual Substantiality; whereas, except for a greater intellect, a large number of men today differ very little in their intuition, their thinking and their striving from the most highly developed animals!

Like insects they hustle and bustle about as diligently as if it were a question of attaining to the highest goal with the utmost haste. When their aims are more closely and carefully scrutinised, however, the hollowness and insignificance of their feverish efforts, which are indeed unworthy of such diligence, will very soon become apparent. And out of this chaotic medley rises the insane audacity which presumes that it can choose, acknowledge or reject an Envoy of God. This would mean exercising judgment on something which they would never be able to comprehend, unless the Supreme Being graciously inclines to them and makes Himself understood. Today people are everywhere relying on science, intellect and logic, yet accepting the great inconsistencies inherent in so many current opinions!

In the case of thousands it would be a pity to waste any further words on this matter! They are so taken with their own knowledge that they have lost all ability to consider anything simply and unpretentiously! These words are only addressed to those who are still natural enough to develop their own sound power of judgment as soon as they are given a lead, and who do not blindly join first this and then that movement which happens to be popular, only to desert the new cause with equal speed when they hear the first doubt uttered by an ignorant critic!

A little quiet thought will surely enable a man to recognise that one species of being cannot evolve from another species which has nothing in common with the first. The simplest knowledge of the Natural Sciences will verify this! As the ramifications of the Natural Laws operating in the World of Gross Matter have their origin in the living Primordial Source of God, it is clear that these same laws must also be found in operation in the intervening spheres with the same immovable logic and consistency, becoming still purer and clearer the more nearly they approach their Starting Point.

It is just as impossible to transplant a human spirit into an animal here on earth, thus turning the living animal into a man, as it is to transplant the element of Divinity into a man! Nothing can ever develop except what was *originally* implanted. The original substance does permit of different kinds and forms of compositions being developed, as can be seen in the grafting of trees or in cross-breeding, but even the most astonishing results must remain within the range of the basic substance as determined by its origin!

It is impossible either to add something to or to take something away from that which stands *above* the point of origin, i. e., something that was not contained in the original substance, as is the case with the difference between the *spiritual* origin of man and Divinity!

Christ, as the Son of God, came from Divinity Unsubstantiate. He bore Divinity within Himself on account of His origin. But it would have been impossible for Him to transmit this Living Divinity to any other man, since such a man can only originate from the Sphere of Spiritual Substantiality! Therefore He could not *invest* anybody with the powers that belong to Divinity alone as, for example, the forgiving of sins. This forgiveness can *only* be obtained through the effects of the automatic Law of Reciprocal Action carrying out the fundamental *Divine* Purpose in Creation, and embodying the unalterable Justice of the Creator with a Perfection that is beyond the comprehension of the human spirit.

Therefore the authority with which the Son of God could invest man related merely to such human things as corresponded with the human spirit's origin, but never to anything Divine!

It is true, of course, that ultimately man's origin can be logically traced back to God, yet it does *not lie in God Himself,* but *outside* Divinity. Therefore man's descent from God is merely an *indirect* one, and *therein lies the greatest difference!*

The authority, for instance, that attaches to the office of a regent could *only be automatic* if it were acquired through the same *direct* descent. Everyone can readily understand this, because an envoy must possess all the qualifications of his superior in order to represent him in a mission or an office. Such an envoy would therefore have to come directly from Divinity Unsubstantiate, as did Christ.

If a man, in all good faith, undertakes this office in spite of everything, it naturally follows that his edicts could have no far reaching validity or life as they are *purely earthly*. Those, however, who see something greater in him are suffering from a delusion, which they will only recognise as such after they have passed over, and the time they have spent on earth towards spiritual ascent will be entirely lost! Lost sheep following a false shepherd!

What holds true for this supreme commandment: "I am the Lord thy God; thou shalt have none other gods but Me", also holds true for the other commandments, which are often disregarded and trespassed against because they are not understood!

And yet the commandments are in reality nothing but an explanation of the Divine Will which has been resting in Creation from the very beginning, and which cannot be circumvented by a hair's breadth!

Viewed in this light, how foolish becomes the principle of so many men that *"the end justifies the means"*, which contradicts every Divine Thought and all Perfection! What mad confusion would ensue in the Laws of the Divine Will if they could be shifted about in such a way!

Anyone having the slightest idea of what perfection means cannot but reject such impossibilities from the very beginning. As soon as a man tries to form a *true* picture of the *Perfection* of God he will find that this will not only serve him as a guide, but will lead to a quicker understanding of all things in Creation. To know full well the *Perfection* of God and always bear it in mind is the key to the understanding of God's *work*, of which man himself is a part!

Then he will recognise the compelling power, the serious warning of the Word: "God is not mocked!" In other words His laws are fulfilled or operate irrevocably! He just lets the wheels He set in motion during the Creation run on. Little man will alter nothing in this! Should he try to do so all he would accomplish would be that he and all who followed him would be torn to pieces! It will be of no avail to him if he *believes* otherwise!

Blessing can only descend upon him who fully and completely adjusts himself to the Will of God, which bears Creation in its Natural Laws! But only he can do this who understands them rightly!

The teachings which demand *blind* faith are to be discarded as dead and therefore pernicious! Only those teachings can bring liberation and redemption which, like Christ's, prompt man to *greater mobility,* that is, make him consider and examine and thus gain conviction through real understanding!

Only those exhibiting the most reprehensible thoughtlessness can imagine that the purpose of man's existence consists primarily of pursuing and gaining physical necessities and enjoyments, and that at the last moment, through a few beautiful words and some external ceremonies, he could be conveniently freed from all guilt and from the consequences of his own indolent careless-ness during his life on earth! The passage through life and the step into the beyond at physical death is not the same as an everyday journey for which one only needs to buy a ticket at the last moment!

With such a belief man *doubles* his guilt, for every doubt in the incorrupt-ible Justice of the Perfect God is *blasphemy!* To believe in an arbitrary, easy forgiveness of sins, however, is a manifest proof of *doubt* in the incorruptible Justice of God and His Laws and, what is more, such a person directly con-firms his belief that God acts arbitrarily, which amounts to the same thing as being deficient and imperfect.

Poor wretched believers!

It would be better for them if they were still unbelievers, for then they would be unhindered and could more easily find the way they imagine they have already found!

Their salvation does not lie in anxiously suppressing the thoughts that come and the doubts which these thoughts awaken in so many questions, for they are but the healthy urge for Truth!

To wrestle with doubt is a process of examining which must invariably be followed by the rejection of all dogmatic ballast! Only a spirit completely lib-erated from all misunderstanding can rise in joyful conviction to the Lumin-ous Heights, to Paradise!

THE IMMACULATE CONCEPTION AND
THE BIRTH OF THE SON OF GOD

THE IMMACULATE conception is not only meant in a physical sense, but is more especially meant in a purely spiritual sense, like so much else in the Bible. Only he who recognises and perceives that the spiritual world really exists and is in vital activity can find the key to an understanding of the Bible; this alone will make the Word come to life! To all others it will always remain a book with seven seals!

Every conception arising out of *pure* love and a heartfelt looking upwards to the Creator, in which the sensual instinct is only an adjunct and not the basis, is an immaculate conception in the physical sense.

In reality this occurs so seldom that there was every justification for laying special stress upon it. The relegation of sensual instincts into the background was assured by the fact of the Annunciation, which for this reason is especially mentioned, because otherwise a link in the chain of natural happenings and strict co-operation with the spiritual world would be missing.

The Virgin Mary, already provided with all the gifts needed to fulfil her high mission, was at the requisite time led through spiritual guidance into contact with persons who had deeply penetrated into the revelations and prophecies about the coming Messiah. This was the first preparation on earth which urged Mary on to the path leading to her real goal, and acquainted her with all the circumstances in which she herself was later destined to play such an important role, without being aware of it at that time.

The bandage which blindfolds the eye of the specially chosen ones is only carefully and gradually loosened so as not to disturb the necessary process of development, for every intermediary step must be seriously experienced in order finally to ensure the possibility of fulfilment. To be conscious of the actual task too early would leave gaps in their development which would render a later fulfilment more difficult.

To have the goal constantly in sight incurs the danger of pressing forward too rapidly, whereby much that must absolutely be experienced in all seriousness to qualify for the appointed task would be overlooked or learned too easily. However, a man can only experience seriously what at any particular time he regards as his real life's task. So it was with Mary!

Thus, during a moment of perfect rest and psychic tranquillity, after her preparation had been completed both inwardly and outwardly, she became clairvoyant and clairaudient, that is, her inmost being opened itself to the world of different substance and she experienced the Annunciation described in the Bible. The bandage fell from her eyes and she consciously entered into her mission!

The Annunciation became such a stupendous and shaking spiritual experience for Mary that from that hour it completely filled the life of her soul. From that time it was only concentrated in one direction, to be allowed to expect a high Divine Grace. Through the Annunciation the Light *wanted* to bring about this condition of her soul so as to drive back from the very outset all base instincts, and create the soil upon which a pure physical vessel (the child's body) could come into being for the immaculate spiritual conception. Through this exceptionally strong psychic adjustment Mary's physical conception, in accordance with the Laws of Nature, became an "immaculate one"!

For those who have some knowledge of the spiritual world and its tremendously widespread activities, which easily span thousands of years in preparing for all great events, it is not difficult to understand that Mary came already equipped with all the gifts needed for her mission, that is, she was pre-natally chosen to become the earthly mother of Jesus, the coming Bringer of Truth!

With the child's body developing in such circumstances as the purest vessel, the earthly conditions were provided for an "immaculate *spiritual* conception", the incarnation, which takes place in the middle of pregnancy.

In this case it was not a question of the incarnation of one of the many waiting souls or spirit-sparks who wish or are compelled for the sake of development to live a life on earth, and whose ethereal bodies or garments are more or less tarnished and soiled, so that their direct connection with the Light is dimmed and at times completely severed!

Here it was a process of radiation from God, given out of love to mankind erring in darkness, which was strong enough to prevent the direct connection with Primordial Light ever being broken!

This resulted in a close connection between the Godhead and mankind through this One, Who resembled a shining pillar of inexhaustible purity and power before which all baseness was forced to retreat. The possibility was thus created for the transmission of undimmed Truth direct from the Light, and also of the power for the actions which appeared to be miracles.

The account of the temptation in the wilderness shows how the attempts of dark influences to defile Him were repelled by the purity of His intuition without being able to do any harm.

After Mary's immaculate physical conception the incarnation which occurs in the middle of pregnancy could take place from the Light with a strength which excluded the possibility of any dimming on the intermediate steps between the Light and the mother's body, thus bringing about an "immaculate *spiritual* conception" as well.

Therefore it is quite right to speak of an immaculate conception, which occurred both physically and spiritually without the necessity of circumventing, altering or remodelling a Law of Creation for this particular case!

Now man must not think that because it had been promised that the Saviour should be born of a virgin that therein lies a contradiction!

The contradiction lies solely in the wrong interpretation of the word "virgin" mentioned in the prophecy. If this prophecy speaks of a virgin, it does not infer a limited conception of the word, much less the opinion of any State, but it can only be a question of a broad conception concerning all mankind!

Putting aside all thought of procreation, those who take a limited view of the word should note the fact that pregnancy and birth of themselves exclude virginity in its ordinary sense! The prophecy, however, does not mean such things! It meant that Christ would definitely be born as the *first* child of a virgin, that is, of a woman who had never been a mother. In such a case all the organs that have to do with the development of the human body *are* virginal, that is, they have never before come into activity in this way, meaning that no child has issued from this womb. The organs of the mother's body must be virginal in the case of *every* first-born child. Only in this sense could such a far-reaching prophecy be understood, because every prophecy can only be fulfilled within the strict logic of the active Laws of Creation and is so made on the basis of such reliable foresight.

Thus in this prophecy "the *first* child" is meant, and therefore a distinction has been made between *virgin* and *mother!* Any other distinction is out of the question because the conceptions of virgin and married woman have merely arisen out of the purely civil or social institution of marriage, which are in no case meant by such a prophecy!

The very perfection of Creation as the Work of God makes the act of procreation absolutely necessary, because the All-Wisdom of the Creator has ordered all things in Creation from the Primordial beginning so that there should be nothing too much or superfluous! He who thinks otherwise must also hold that the Work of the Creator is imperfect! It is the same with the person who affirms that the birth of Christ occurred *without* there first being a normal procreation, as is prescribed by the Creator for all mankind. A normal procreation through a human being of flesh and blood *must have* taken place! Even in this case!

Every man who truly understands this praises his Lord and Creator more than he who wants to permit other possibilities! The former shows such unshaken faith in the Perfection of his God as to be convinced that any exception or change in the Laws He has ordained is absolutely impossible. And *that* is the *greater* faith! Besides, all the other events entirely agree with this! Christ became a *human being on earth.* It having been thus resolved, as the Perfection of God ordained, He was obliged to submit to all the Laws God had decreed for physical procreation!

If it should be objected that "with God nothing is impossible", such a concealed explanation brings no satisfaction, for again another and quite different meaning lies in these words than that which so many people imagine in their indolence. In order to refute the *wording* of this sentence as commonly understood, it need only be said that imperfection, want of logic, injustice, arbitrariness and many other things are impossible with God!

It could further be argued that if in *this* sense nothing is impossible with God, He could just as easily with a single act of His Will have made every man on earth a believer! Then He need not have permitted His Son to become man and exposed Him to earthly hardships and death on the cross! He would have been spared that stupendous sacrifice!

That things happened *as they did* shows the inflexible nature of the Divine Laws which have been active in Creation from the very beginning, and the perfection of which makes a forced intervention for the purpose of changing them in one way or another quite impossible.

The blind and contentious opponent could now stubbornly assert that the way it happened was according to God's Will. That is quite right, but in no way a counter-proof! On the contrary it merely *confirms* the previous reasoning, provided one drops the more naive interpretation and follows the deeper explanation necessarily demanded by all utterances of a spiritual nature.

It was the Will of God! However, that has nothing in common with arbitrariness! On the contrary, it means nothing less than the confirmation of the laws God placed in Creation and which bear His Will; it means absolute obedience to them, allowing of no exception or circumvention whatever! *It is just in the necessity for compliance that the Will of God reveals and manifests itself!* Otherwise Jesus need not have been born of a woman on earth, but could quite simply have made a sudden appearance!

In order to fulfil His mission Christ had therefore inevitably to submit to all the Natural Laws, that is, to the Will of His Father. That Christ did so is proved by His whole life – His normal birth and growth, His feeling both of hunger and fatigue, His suffering and finally His death on the cross. He was subject to everything to which man's earthly body is subject. Why then should His procreation alone have been different, when there was absolutely no necessity for it? It is just because of the naturalness of everything that the Saviour's task appears even greater, by no means smaller! Likewise Mary was no less blessed in her high calling on that account!

THE CRUCIFIXION OF THE SON OF
GOD AND THE LORD'S SUPPER

AT THE death of Christ the veil which shut out the Holy of Holies from mankind was rent in twain. This happening is taken as a symbol that the separation between Divinity and mankind ceased at the moment of the Saviour's sacrifice on the cross, and that direct communication was established in its stead.

However, this interpretation is *wrong!* Through His crucifixion men rejected the Son of God as their expected Messiah, and this made the separation all the *greater!* The veil was rent because henceforth the Holy of Holies was no longer necessary! It was exposed to all eyes as well as to impure currents because, symbolically speaking, after this deed Divinity would no longer set foot on this earth, thus rendering the Holy of Holies superfluous!

This is the exact contrary of the existing interpretations, which express nothing but a great presumption on the part of the human spirit!

Neither was the death on the cross a *necessary* sacrifice, but a murder, a dastardly crime! Every other explanation is a misinterpretation which either has its origin in ignorance or is meant as an excuse. Christ certainly did not come to this earth with the intention of letting Himself be crucified; *neither does redemption lie in the crucifixion!* Christ was crucified because of His teaching, as a troublesome Bringer of Truth!

It was not His death on the cross that could and should bring redemption, but the *Truth* He gave to mankind *in His Word!*

The Truth, however, was irksome to the religious leaders and heads of the temples of that time. It was an annoyance because it severely undermined their influence. *It would be exactly the same today in many places!* Mankind has not changed in this respect. The teachers of that time took their standing, it is true, on the good old traditions as do those of today, but through those who practised and interpreted them these traditions had become nothing but rigid and empty forms, wholly wanting in life, the same as may often be observed today!

434

But He Who wanted to bring the necessary life into the existing Word naturally also *upset* their practices and explanations, but He did not upset the Word itself. He liberated and redeemed the people from the debasing rigidity and emptiness, and this was naturally a great vexation to those who soon recognised how effectively this would interfere with their false leadership!

For this reason the Bringer of Truth, the Liberator from the burden of erroneous interpretations, had to be rendered suspect and persecuted. As in spite of all their efforts they did not succeed in ridiculing Him, they sought to discredit Him. His "earthly upbringing" as the son of a carpenter served to brand Him as "unlearned and therefore incompetent to give explanations", as "a layman"! Just as it is today with everyone who exposes the rigid dogma that chokes every free and vital aspiration from the very start!

His opponents carefully avoided going into His explanations as such, because they quite rightly felt that they would lose in a purely *objective* discussion. They contented themselves with slandering Him maliciously through their bribed agents, and finally did not shrink from availing themselves of an opportune moment to accuse Him publicly and falsely and bring Him to the cross, in order to remove the danger He represented to their authority and power!

His violent death, in the form at the time used by the Romans to execute people, was not in itself the redemption, nor did it bring redemption. *It atoned for none of mankind's guilt,* liberated them from nothing, but *burdened them still more with a dastardly murder!*

If still here and there a cult has arisen which sees in this murder a necessary and principal part of the Son of God's Work of Redemption, this only distracts man's attention from the greater value which alone could bring this redemption. It diverts him from the *true* mission of the Saviour, from that which necessitated His coming from the Divine Sphere to the earth!

The purpose of His Mission, however, was not to suffer death on the cross, *but to bring the Truth into the maze of dogmatic rigidity and emptiness* which debase the human spirit, and to explain the relations between God, the Creation and mankind as they actually are!

Through this knowledge the illusions which the constricted spirit of man added, and which covered up the reality, had feebly to fall away of their own accord. Not till then could man see clearly before him the way leading upwards!

Redemption lies solely in the bringing of this Truth and the consequent liberation from errors!

It is redemption from obscured vision, from blind faith! The word "blind" most suitably depicts this false state!

The Last Supper before Christ's death was a farewell meal. When He said: "Take, eat, this is my body!" and: "Drink ye all of it, this is my blood of the New Testament, which is shed for many for the remission of sins", He declared thereby that he was willing even to embrace death on the cross if only as an opportunity of bringing the Truth to erring mankind through His teaching, which alone shows the way to the forgiveness of sins!

He says expressly: "Forgiveness for *many*", not "forgiveness for *all!*" Thus only for those who take His teachings to heart and make vital use of them!

The destruction of His body and the shedding of His blood through death on the cross are meant to help mankind recognise the necessity for and seriousness of the explanations He gave. The *repeated* celebration of Holy Communion and the taking of Holy Communion as such are merely intended to emphasise this urgency!

That the Son of God did not shrink even from such enmity on the part of mankind, the *probability* of which was already recognised before His coming,* should especially indicate the desperate plight of the human spirits who could only be dragged back from perdition if they grasped the rope of salvation, of undimmed Truth.

When during the Last Supper the Son of God referred to His death on the cross, it was only to lay special emphasis for the last time on the compelling necessity of the teaching He had come to bring!

In partaking of Holy Communion each person should always realise afresh that the Son of God did not even shun the probability of death on the cross through mankind, and actually sacrificed His body and His blood so that mankind might have the opportunity to receive an explanation of the actual happenings in the cosmos, which clearly show the operation of the inflexible Laws of Creation that bear the Divine Will!

With this realisation of the profound gravity of the situation, emphasising as it does the burning necessity of the Message of Salvation, ever new strength should arise in man, a new encouragement *truly to live* the clear teaching of

* Lecture: "World events".

Christ, not only to understand it aright, but also to act accordingly in every-thing. *Through this* he will also find redemption and forgiveness for his sins. Not otherwise! And also not immediately! But he will surely find them through following the way Christ pointed out in His Message!

For this reason Holy Communion is meant to vitalise this process ever again, so that the zeal to follow the teaching brought at the cost of so great a sacrifice, which could free him, does not weaken; for once indifference or mere outward ceremony develops people lose their hold on the rope of salva-tion and sink back into errors and perdition!

It is a great mistake for men to believe that through the death on the cross the forgiveness of their sins is guaranteed. This thought is followed by the ter-rible harm that all those who believe this are *held back* from the true road to redemption, which lies *only and solely* in *living the Word* of the Saviour, ac-cording to the explanations given by Him, Who knew and could overlook all. And these explanations give practical examples of the need to obey and ob-serve the Divine Will as expressed in the Laws of Creation, and also show what happens if It is obeyed and what follows on disobedience!

His Work of Redemption lay in bringing this enlightenment, which expos-ed the defects and abuses of religious practices because it carried the Truth within itself and thus brought Light into the ever-increasing darkness of the human spirit. His Work of Redemption did not lie in His death on the cross, neither can Holy Communion nor the Consecrated Host bring immediate forgiveness of sins! Such a thought is contrary to all Divine Law! And conse-quently the power of men to forgive sins falls away! A man only has the right and also the power to forgive what he has personally suffered at the hands of another, and then only when, quite freely, his heart bids him do it.

He who seriously reflects upon these things will recognise the Truth and thus the true path! Those, however, who are too indolent to think and who, like the foolish virgins in the parable, are too lazy to exercise the necessary care and attention to keep in constant order and readiness the little lamp left to them by the Creator, i. e., their ability to examine and illuminate, may eas-ily miss the hour when the "Word of Truth" comes to them! As they allowed themselves to be lulled into inert ease and blind faith they will consequently through their slothfulness be incapable of recognising the Bringer of Truth, the Bridegroom! They will then perforce stay behind when the wakeful enter into the Kingdom of Bliss!

COME DOWN FROM THE CROSS!

"IF THOU art the Son of God, come down from the cross and save Thyself and us!" These were the scornful words addressed to the Son of God as He hung in agony on the cross in the burning rays of the sun!

Those who shouted this considered themselves specially clever! They scoffed, they triumphed and they laughed hatefully without any real cause, for surely Christ's sufferings were no reason for mockery and ridicule, much less for laughter! If but for one moment they could have "seen" the simultaneous happenings in the Ethereal and Spiritual Realms, where their souls were being firmly bound for thousands of years, their laughter would have ceased! Even though their punishment could not become immediately visible in the material world, it did come in *all* the subsequent earth-lives which these wicked souls were forced to live on account of it!

The scoffers of that time thought themselves clever, but they could have given no better proof of their limitation than these words, for they reveal the most childish view one can think of. Those who speak thus are far from understanding Creation and the Will of God operating therein! How depressing and sad it therefore is to know that even today a great number of those who still believe in God and in the Mission of His Son at that time are quite convinced that Jesus of Nazareth could have come down from the cross if He had only so willed!

After two thousand years there is still the same sluggish obtuseness – no change or progress! According to the naive opinions of many believers Christ, having issued from God, must be unrestricted in His actions here on earth!

To expect this shows both poverty of intellect and inertia in thinking!

Through becoming flesh the Son of God was also "placed under the law", that is, He subjected Himself to the Laws of Creation, the unalterable Will of God in Creation. There could be no change in connection with the physical and earthbound body. In obedience to the Will of God Christ voluntarily

438

submitted to this Law. He did not come to overthrow it, but to fulfil it through becoming flesh on this earth.

He was therefore bound to everything in the same way as man on earth is bound! Even as the Son of God, with all His Divine Might and Power, He could not come down from the cross as long as He was in a physical body of flesh and blood! That would have been equivalent to upsetting the Divine Will in Creation!

This Divine Will, however, has been perfect from the very beginning; everywhere, not only in the World of Gross Matter here on earth, but also in the Ethereal World and in the Worlds of Animistic and Spiritual Substantiality, with all their sub-divisions and transitional stages! Just the same as in the Divine Sphere and also in God Himself!

Divine Activity, Divine Power and Might, never unduly obtrude themselves. The Divine only lives in the strict fulfilment of the Divine Will, and never wishes to do anything else. The same holds true for the human being who is highly developed spiritually. The more highly matured he is the more strictly will he submit to the Divine Laws in Creation, voluntarily and joyfully! But he will never expect arbitrary acts which lie outside the valid Laws of Creation, because he believes in the perfection of the Divine Will.

If a physical body is firmly nailed to a cross it cannot free itself without extraneous physical help. That is the Law according to the Divine Will in Creation, which permits of no exceptions. He who thinks differently and expects something else does not believe in the Perfection of God and in the immutability of His Will.

That men still have not changed despite their alleged progress in the sciences and in their abilities, that they still stand where they stood in those times, is demonstrated when today they again call out: "If He be the Son of Man He can bring about the catastrophes that have been prophesied as soon as He so wills!" To them this is a foregone conclusion! In other words, however, this means that "if He cannot do so He is not the Son of Man"!

Yet men are very well aware, as Christ the Son of God Himself already pointed out, that no one but God the Father knows the hour in which the Judgment begins. Therefore if men now utter the afore-mentioned words they express a double doubt! They doubt the Son of Man and doubt the Son of God's word! It is also a proof of their lack of understanding of the entire

Creation, and of their complete ignorance just in all those questions which it is so urgently necessary for every man to know!

If in becoming man the Son of God had to submit to the Will of God in Creation, it is evident that the Son of Man also cannot stand above these Laws. Indeed it is utterly impossible to stand above these Laws in Creation! He who enters Creation thereby also becomes subject to the Law of the Divine Will, which never changes! Thus also the Son of God and the Son of Man!

A great handicap to their ability to comprehend all these things is imposed upon men by the fact that they have never sought these Laws in Creation and thus, except for small fragments upon which they happened to stumble here and there, they have had no knowledge of them up to today.

When Christ performed miracles that are quite beyond man's ability this does not justify the thought that He did not need to observe the Laws of the Divine Will resting in Creation, that He reached out beyond them. That is impossible! Even with miracles He acted in complete accordance with the Laws of God, and not arbitrarily! He only proved thereby that He worked in *Divine* Power, not in spiritual power, and naturally the effects also far surpassed what is possible to men. Nevertheless these miracles were not performed independent of the Laws in Creation, but were completely in accordance with them!

Man is so far lagging behind in his spiritual development that he cannot even fully develop the spiritual powers at his command. Otherwise he, too, would achieve results that would appear miraculous in the present times!

Naturally, however, it is possible to create quite different works with Divine Power, which can never be attained with spiritual power, and which even differ in their nature from those done with the highest spiritual power. But despite this every happening remains within the bounds of Divine lawfulness, and nothing goes beyond it!

Men are the only beings guilty of arbitrary actions within the limits of the free will given to them, for where they do have a certain liberty to act in accordance with their own will, they have never really subjected themselves to the Will of God. They have always put their own will first. And in so doing they paralysed themselves and could never soar above what was permitted by their own earthbound intellectual will!

Thus men do not even know those laws in Creation which release and set free their spiritual power, those laws in which they can unfold their spiritual power!

And then they are all the more amazed at the display of Divine Power! For the same reason they are unable to recognise the Divine Power or expect it to accomplish things that lie outside the Divine Laws in Creation. This would include the descent of a physical body from a cross made of material substance.

The raising of the dead through Divine Power is *not* beyond Divine Laws as long as it happens within a certain time after death, the length of which differs for each human being. The more spiritually mature the soul is when severing itself from the physical body the quicker it will be released, and the shorter will be the time during which the lawful opportunity exists to recall it, because this can only happen while the soul is still connected with the body!

The soul, which is animated by the spirit, must obey the Divine Will, i. e., the Divine Power, and must upon Its call return along the ethereal bridge, as long as this bridge has not been pulled down, and re-enter the already forsaken physical body.

When we speak of Divine Power and spiritual power, this does not refute the fact that in reality there is but *one* Power which has issued from God and which permeates all Creation. Yet there is a difference between Divine Power and spiritual power! The spiritual power is dominated by the Divine Power from which it has issued. It is not really a weakened Divine Power but rather a *transformed* power which, through its transformation, has taken on a different nature, and the effectiveness of which has thereby been somewhat limited. Thus there are two species working differently, yet in reality only one power!

In addition to these we have animistic power. Hence there are three basic powers, of which the spiritual and the animistic powers are nourished and governed by the Divine Power! All three may be called one!

There are no other powers, only many sub-species which have arisen through the basic spiritual and basic animistic species, and each of which is also different in its effect. Each species in its own way again produces correspondingly changed laws which, however, are always a logical consequence of the fundamental species although, due to the change of power that has taken place, they may appear somewhat different outwardly.

All the species, however, including the fundamental species, are bound to the highest Divine Law of Power, and within their own changed laws can only be different in their outward forms. They appear different because, with the exception of the Divine Will Itself, every species and every sub-species form only part-species, thus piecework, which can naturally also only have part-laws. These strive to unite with the perfect whole, the Pure Divine Power from which they are derived, and which is identical with Divine Will and becomes manifest as immutable adamantine law.

Each power with all its sub-species works in the existing ethereal and gross material substances according to its nature, forming therein on account of its own particular variety *different* worlds or planes. Individually judged, each of these worlds or planes, if compared with the whole of Creation, is in each case no more than piecework, because the power that formed it is also only a correspondingly altered part of the perfect Power of God, containing not complete but only part-laws.

Only when all the laws of the various world planes *are combined* do they again result in the perfect laws which were established through the Divine Will in Primordial Creation, in the Primordial Spiritual Realm.

Therefore the seed-germ of the human spirit has to traverse all the world-planes in order personally to experience their individual laws and bring them to life within itself. When it has gathered all the good possible out of them, these laws will really have become a part of its inner consciousness. If it makes proper use of them according to the Will of God it may then enter Paradise; indeed these laws will bear it there in the course of their normal activity. From there it will consciously work, helping and furthering, in the part-planes below, this being the highest task of every mature human spirit.

There can never be overcrowding because, as they float in the Infinite, the world-planes now existing can be extended without limit.

Thus the Kingdom of God will become larger and larger, forever being developed and extended by the power of the pure human spirits, whose field of activity will be Subsequent Creation. This they will be able to direct from Paradise, having themselves already wandered through all its parts and thereby become thoroughly acquainted with them.

These explanations are only given here so that no misconceptions will arise through the reference to Divine Power and spiritual power, for in reality there exists but one Power which has issued from God and out of which the different species are formed.

442

He who knows of all these processes will never childishly expect things to happen which can never happen because they lie outside the various laws in question. Thus neither will the Son of Man stretch forth His hand to give rise to catastrophes which are supposed to come about *immediately!* That would be against the existing and immutable Laws of Nature!

The spiritual is more mobile and lighter, and therefore also faster, than the animistic. For this reason the animistic will require more time to manifest than does the spiritual. Consequently the animistic, i. e., the elemental, happening must naturally also take place after the spiritual happening. Likewise ethereal matter can be moved faster through these powers than gross matter. All these laws must be fulfilled; they can neither be circumvented nor over-ridden!

These laws are known to the Light, and the despatch of the executive messengers or of special orders are *so* arranged that the final effects converge as God willed it!

An apparatus of a magnitude far beyond man's power of comprehension has been necessary for the Judgment that is now at hand. But it works so exactly that in reality there are no delays – except in those points where human volition is required to co-operate! With foolish obstinacy men alone forever try to remain outside every fulfilment, or even malevolently interfere with its accomplishment ... in earth-binding vanity!

But fortunately this was taken into account after the great failure of mankind during the life on earth of the Son of God! Through their failure men can only make the earthly path of the Son of Man more difficult up to a certain point, causing Him to wander on by-ways and make detours. They cannot, however, prevent the happenings ordained by God, nor in any way postpone the predestined outcome, for the backing of the Darkness which gave them strength for their folly has already been taken away from them! And as for that bulwark of intellectual activity behind which they shelter while shooting off their poisoned arrows, it will soon collapse under the pressure of the advancing Light! Then all will tumble about their ears, and no mercy will be shown to them after all the evil they have constantly created in their thoughts! Thus the day so ardently longed for by those who strive for the Light will come not one hour later than was originally ordained!

THIS IS MY BODY! THIS IS MY BLOOD!

THE SON of God said to His disciples: "He who absorbs My Word absorbs Me. He really eats of My Body and drinks of My Blood!"

Such is the sense of the words the Son of God spoke when He instituted the Last Supper; words which, through the Last Supper, He symbolised as a remembrance of His Life on earth! How then could it happen that they were the cause of violent conflicts between the learned and the churches? Their sense is so simple and so clear when man bases them on the fact that the Son of God, Christ Jesus, was the Word of God which had *become flesh!*

How could He express Himself more clearly than by simply saying: "He who absorbs My Word eats of My Body and drinks of My Blood!" Also when He said: "The Word is truly My Body and My Blood." He had to speak in this way because He Himself was the Living Word in flesh and blood. But when such words were passed on the most important point was always omitted again and again – the reference to *the Word* which was *walking* on earth! Because they did not understand it they thought it of secondary importance. Through this the whole Mission of Christ was misunderstood, mutilated and distorted!

Despite their belief, even the disciples of the Son of God were not at that time capable of understanding the words of their Master aright, just as they had never fully grasped so much of what He had said! Indeed Christ Himself often enough expressed sorrow at this! They simply portrayed the meaning of the Last Supper according to *the* manner in which, in their childlike simplicity, they had understood it. It is therefore quite natural that they passed on words which were not quite clear to them merely as they comprehended them, and not as the Son of God had meant them!

Jesus was the Word of God become flesh! Thus he who absorbed His Word aright also received Jesus Himself!

And if a man lets this Word of God that is offered to him come to life within himself so that it becomes an integral part of himself, of his thoughts and his

444

actions, he thereby lets the spirit of Christ come to life within himself, for the Son of God was the incarnate living Word of God!

Man must at last make an effort really to fathom this train of thought *aright!* He should not merely read and talk about it, but he must also try to animate it by quietly experiencing its meaning in living pictures. Then he will also *truly* experience the Last Supper, providing he recognises that what he receives is the Living Word of God, and that he has already made himself thoroughly familiar with Its meaning and purpose.

It is not quite so easy as many believers think. To partake of Holy Communion apathetically will bring no profit! For what is living, as is the Word of God, must be *taken* in by a man who is fully alive! The Church cannot animate Holy Communion unless the communicant has prepared himself beforehand to receive it in the *right frame of mind!*

One also sees pictures intended to illustrate the beautiful words: "I am knocking!" Such pictures are quite right! The Son of God is standing at the door of the hut and knocking, desiring admittance. But here already man has again added some of his own thoughts, for through the partly-open door one can see a table laid in the hut. This gives rise to the idea that no one who begs for food and drink should be turned away. The thought is beautiful and also corresponds to Christ's Word, but it has been interpreted in too narrow a sense. "I am knocking" means much more! Charity forms but a small part of the contents of God's Word!

When Christ says: "I am knocking" He means that the Word of God embodied in Him is knocking at the door of the human soul, not *begging* to be admitted, but *demanding* admittance! The *Word* in its entirety, as it has been given to man, is to be received by him! His *soul* is to open its door to admit the Word and have the table within itself prepared for it! The word "table" is here identical with altar. If the soul complies with this demand, the physical actions of the earth-man will naturally accord with what the "Word" demands.

Man invariably tries to grasp a question with his intellect only, which means that he analyses and thus belittles it, compressing it into narrow limits, and thereby always running the risk of only recognising fragments of all that is great, just as happened in this case!

The Incarnation of the Living Word of God is always bound to remain a mystery to man on earth because the beginning of this happening lies in the Divine Sphere! The human spirit does not possess the perceptive capacity to penetrate into the Divine Sphere, and therefore the forging of the first link in the chain of events which led to the later Incarnation will always remain closed to human understanding.

It is therefore not surprising that just *this* symbolic action of the Son of God, as expressed in the distribution of the bread and wine, could not up till now be understood by mankind. However, if after this explanation, which enables him to construct a picture in his mind, man still persists in inveighing against it, he merely proves that the limit of his perception ceases in the Spiritual Sphere! In defending the absolutely unnatural explanation of the Words of Christ which has hitherto prevailed he would only indicate an unscrupulous obstinacy!

THE RESURRECTION OF CHRIST'S PHYSICAL BODY

PERFECT is God the Lord! Perfect is His Will, which is in Him and which issues from Him in order to produce and maintain the Work of Creation! Perfect, therefore, are also the laws that permeate Creation according to His Will!

Perfection, however, excludes any changes from the very beginning. This is the fundamental fact which absolutely *justifies* doubt in so many assertions! Some doctrines contradict themselves in that although they quite rightly teach the Perfection of God, yet at the same time they make assertions exactly to the contrary, demanding belief in things which exclude the Perfection of God and of His Will which rests in the Laws of Creation!

As a result there was implanted in many a doctrine the germ of disease which, boring like a worm from within, will one day cause the whole structure to collapse! This collapse is all the more inevitable wherever such contradictions are made the *pillars* of a doctrine, which not only drag into doubt the Perfection of God but directly deny it! This denial of the Perfection of God has even been made part of the qualified declaration of belief required for membership in some congregations!

Thus we have talk of the *resurrection of the flesh*, referring to the resurrection of the physical body of the Son of God! This is quite thoughtlessly accepted by most people without the faintest trace of an understanding being apparent in them. Others again accept this assertion although fully aware of their own ignorance, because they lacked a teacher who could give them the proper explanation for it.

What a sad picture this presents to the calm and serious observer! How pitiable such a group appears in his eyes! When they exhibit their zeal by unhesitatingly looking down in ignorant presumption upon those of different opinion, as they quite often do, they even go so far as proudly to consider themselves zealots of their faith, strict believers, not realising that in so doing they give an infallible sign of their helpless stupidity!

He who accepts important matters *without question* and professes them as his own conviction shows boundless indifference and no true belief!

And it is in *this* light that such a person stands before Him Whom he customarily calls the Highest and the Holiest, Who should represent the purpose and the support of his whole being!

As such he is not a live member of his religion who may expect ascent and redemption, rather he is but "sounding brass", only an empty "tinkling cymbal", one who neither understands the Laws of his Creator nor troubles to recognise them!

For all who act thus it means standstill and retrogression on the road meant to lead them in their development and advancement through the World of Matter towards the Light of Truth!

Like any other erroneous opinion, the wrong conception of the resurrection of the flesh is also an artificially constructed obstacle which they take over with them into the beyond, and before which they will then have to halt! They can make no further progress as they cannot get rid of it of their own accord, because a false belief tightly clings to and binds them in such a way that they are cut off from every independent view towards the Luminous Truth.

They do not dare to think otherwise, and thus cannot advance! Through this the danger arises that these souls, who keep themselves thus fettered, miss the last opportunity of becoming free and cannot ascend to the Light in time. As a consequence they will have to slide down into disintegration, with eternal damnation as their final goal!

Eternal damnation is exclusion in perpetuity from the Light! It is the self-determined *separation from* the opportunity of being able to return to the Light as a fully conscious and mature personality, which would be brought about in the natural and logical course of events. This condition becomes effective through being drawn into the disintegration which not only disperses and dissolves the ethereal body, but also all the personal consciousness acquired spiritually*. That, then, is the so-called "spiritual death", from which there can be no further ascent towards the Light for the conscious "ego" developed up to that point. On the other hand, where an ascent does take place, that particular ego not only remains intact but continues to mature till it reaches spiritual perfection!

* Lecture: "The World".

A man who has passed into the beyond with a wrongly or thoughtlessly accepted belief remains hampered until another conviction awakens him to life *inwardly* and sets him free, thus shattering the obstacle which through his own faith keeps him from striding forward along the right and true path!

It requires an enormous exertion to conquer oneself and to develop the strength necessary to become free from such a false belief. The mere step towards indulging in such a thought calls for an immense spiritual effort! Thus millions keep themselves imprisoned and therefore cannot gain sufficient strength even to move a step, under the fatal delusion that they would be doing wrong thereby! They are as if paralysed and would indeed be lost unless the Living Power of God Itself sought a way to them. But again this Power cannot intervene and help unless there rests in the human soul the spark of a volition which reaches out towards it!

The condition of paralysis arising through this simple and natural happening is such that nothing could be more terrible and fatal, for here the blessing of free decision entrusted to man becomes a curse by being wrongly used! Each individual is always free to adhere or to exclude himself. But it is just when a man blindly embraces a doctrine without careful and serious examination that a terrible punishment will be exacted! Indolence in this matter may cost him his entire being!

Man's worst enemy in purely earthly matters is indolence! Indolence in matters of faith, however, will result in his spiritual death!

Woe unto those who do not awaken soon, pull themselves together and submit all they call faith to the keenest scrutiny! Perdition indeed awaits those who cause such great misery, those false shepherds who lead their sheep into the desolate wilderness! Nothing can help them unless they lead their misguided sheep back onto the true path. The great question, however, is whether there will still be time enough left for them to do so. Hence everyone should carefully examine himself before he attempts to teach his neighbour!

To believe what is erroneous means delusion! This holds the human spirit closely and tightly bound here as well as in the beyond, and with such a strength that only the Living Power of the true Word of God can break it! Therefore when it hits home let all such men harken to its call! It is only meant for him who perceives it! Such a person should then examine, consider and free himself!

He should not forget that *only through his own resolution* can he burst the fetters with which he had previously bound himself through a false belief! Just as he once resolved, out of sloth or indolence, blindly to embrace some doctrine he had not seriously examined in *all its aspects,* or just as perhaps he tried to deny God because up till then he could not find a way to Him that satisfied his justifiable desire for logical completeness, so now it is again necessary that the *first volition* for an inflexible examination in all his seeking should issue *from himself! Only then* will he be able to raise the foot held so firmly down by his own will, and so take the first step that will lead him to the Truth and thereby to freedom in the Light!

It is always and only *man himself* who *can, shall* and *must* weigh these matters because he possesses the gift to do so. He himself must also shoulder all responsibility for everything he wills and does! Whatever it may be, it is all the same!

This knowledge alone should impel him to the keenest scrutiny!

It is just this responsibility which not only gives every man the unlimited right to carry out such an examination, but which even makes it an imperative necessity! May he regard it as a healthy instinct for self-preservation! This is not at all wrong! No doubt he would never sign any earthly contract burdening him with some responsibility without examining it carefully word by word, and considering whether he could comply with the conditions! Nor is it any different, but far more serious, in spiritual matters, such as the decision to devote himself to a particular belief! If men would only exercise a little more of the sound instinct for self-preservation in this respect it would not be a sin but a blessing!

Resurrection of the flesh! How can flesh of gross material substance ascend to the Primordial Spiritual Realm of God the Father, gross material substance that cannot even enter the ethereal substance of the beyond? All gross matter, and even all ethereal matter, is subject to disintegration in accordance with the eternal Laws of Nature. There are no exceptions or deviations in this because the laws are perfect. Hence gross matter cannot ascend into the Kingdom of the Father after death has set in, nor even into the ethereal beyond, which is also subject to disintegration. Due to the perfection of the Divine Laws of Nature such deviations are simply an impossibility!

All this can be quite distinctly observed in a small way in the laws of physics for these, too, demonstrate nothing but the immovable Laws of the Creator, which also penetrate this field as they do everything else in the entire existence.

All that exists is subject to the uniform Laws of Origin which clearly and distinctly carry within them the simple but inexorable Divine Will! Nothing can be exempted from them!

Thus it is all the more regrettable if some teachings refuse to acknowledge the great magnitude of God revealing itself in these matters, which brings Him so manifestly close to the understanding of mankind!

Quite correctly every doctrine points to the Perfection of God. If, however, the Origin or the Primordial Source as such is perfect it follows that all that issues from It cannot be otherwise than perfect. Consequently the Laws of Creation, resting as they do in the Acts of Will that have issued from the Primordial Source, must necessarily be perfect also! Quite naturally the one cannot be separated from the other. These perfect Laws of Creation, namely the Laws of Nature, penetrate and support all that has come into existence.

Perfection, however, means immutability! Hence it follows that a change in these fundamental or natural laws is completely impossible. In other words: In no circumstances can there occur exceptions which are contrary to the naturalness of all the other events!

Thus no resurrection of the flesh can take place because the flesh is gross material substance and remains absolutely bound to gross matter!

As all the primordial laws have proceeded from Divine Perfection, no new manifestation of God's Will can take a form different from that which was laid down at the primordial beginning of Creation.

If some teachings refuse to accept this self-evident fact, which is absolutely representative of God's Perfection, they prove thereby that their foundation is *faulty,* that they are based upon the human intellect which is bound to space and time. Therefore such teachings may not lay claim to be a Message of God, because such a Message would be without gaps; It can only come from Perfection, from the Truth Itself, which is without flaw and also understandable in Its simple magnitude! In the first place it is *natural,* because what man so often called Nature issued from the Perfection of the Divine Will, and still maintains its vitality unchanged and therefore cannot be subject to any exceptions!

Consequently when Christ came to this earth to proclaim God's Message of Truth He was obliged to make use of a physical body, i. e., a body of flesh.

Every thinking man should recognise in this the immutability of the Laws of Nature, as also in His physical death which occurred through crucifixion!

This gross material flesh could not, however, be the subject of any exception after death, but had to remain in the Gross Material World! It could *not* rise from the dead in order to enter another world! The immutable Divine or Natural Laws, through their Perfection which issued from the Divine Will, do not permit of such a thing. They cannot permit it, otherwise they would not be perfect, which in turn would also imply that the Will of God, His Power and He Himself are not perfect!

Since this remains forever impossible, however, as any science in Creation can observe for itself, it follows that it is wrong and a doubt in God's Perfection if it should be asserted that this gross material flesh was resurrected and ascended into another world after forty days.

If the flesh is really to come to life again, this can only be done if the soul, which for a time is still connected to the physical body by an ethereal cord, is called back into the body*. In accordance with the Natural Laws this is only possible as long as this cord still exists. Once this cord is severed a raising from the dead, i. e., a recalling of the soul into its physical body, would be impossible!

This also is strictly subject to the perfect Laws of Nature, and even God Himself could not do it because it would be against His Own Perfect Laws, against His Own Perfect Will which operates automatically in Nature! It is just on account of this very Perfection that there could never occur to Him such an imperfect thought, which would only be an arbitrary action!

Here again God appears to be bound within the work of Creation through His flawless Perfection, which must be fulfilled in every case and which permits of no change; nor indeed is such a change intended or necessary. But this restraint is not real at all, it only *appears so* in some things because man is unable to overlook the *entire* happening. And this inability to overlook the *whole* is the cause of his expecting – in all goodwill and respect – arbitrary acts from his God which, to the keen observer, must only belittle Divine Perfection!

What a man thinks in all humility is good does not in this case become a

* Lecture: "Death".

looking upward in veneration, but merely a dragging down into the quite natural limitation of the human spirit!

The strict observance of the Laws of the Divine Will or the Laws of Nature also became evident in the raising of Lazarus and of the youth of Nain. These could be raised because the cord connecting body and soul was still intact. At the Master's call the soul could re-unite with the body, which was then compelled to remain in the Gross Material World, according to the Laws of Nature, until a new separation between the gross material body and ethereal body took place, i. e., until a new physical death occurred, permitting the ethereal body to enter the ethereal beyond.

However, it is impossible for a gross material body to pass over into another world! If the Spirit of Christ had again returned into His gross material body, or had It perhaps not even left the body at all, He would have been forced to remain in gross matter till He died again, not otherwise!

The resurrection of the flesh into another world is completely out of the question for men, as it was then for Christ!

The physical body of the Redeemer followed the same course as every other physical body has to follow in accordance with the Natural Laws of the Creator.

Consequently Jesus of Nazareth, the Son of God, did not rise again in the flesh!

Yet in spite of all logic and the far greater reverence towards God expressed in this, there will still be many who, in the blindness and indolence of their erroneous faith, will not be willing to follow such simple paths of the Truth. There are also some who cannot do so because of their self-imposed limitations. Others again will purposely and furiously try to fight against it on account of their well-founded fear that their laboriously erected edifice of comfortable faith must collapse.

It is of no avail to them to base their assertions on nothing but literal transmissions, for the disciples were also human beings. It is only human if at that time the disciples, who were greatly agitated by all the dreadful happenings, also wove some of their own thoughts into the accounts they gave from memory; thoughts which, through having witnessed miracles they themselves could still not explain, caused them to report some things differently from what they had been in reality!

Their writings and stories were repeatedly based too strongly on their *own* human assumptions, which then later on became the basis for many an error, as for instance in the erroneous combining of the Son of God and the Son of Man into one person!

Even though they were helped by the strongest spiritual inspiration, their own preconceived ideas nevertheless interfered strongly with their transmission and often dimmed the clearest and best meant picture!

Jesus Himself, however, never wrote down anything, and thus nothing was left upon which one could absolutely and indisputably rely!

He never would have said or written anything that was not wholly and fully in accord with the Laws of His Father, the Divine Laws of Nature or the Creative Will. For He said expressly:

"I am come to fulfil the Laws of God!"

The Laws of God, however, are clearly evident in Nature which, indeed, extends further than the mere Gross Material Sphere, yet remaining also "natural" everywhere, in the Ethereal as well as in the Animistic and Spiritual Worlds! Any man who thinks can surely find something in these important words of the Redeemer which goes beyond the confusing religious dogmas and shows a way to all who are really serious in their seeking!

In addition, however, everybody can find important points about this in the Bible, for Jesus appeared to many – and what happened? Mary did not recognise Him at first, Mary Magdalene did not recognise Him immediately, the two disciples on their way to Emmaus did not recognise Him for hours, although He walked and spoke with them ... What must be inferred from this? *That it must have been another body* they saw, otherwise they would all have recognised Him *at once!*

However, let him who does not wish to hear remain deaf, and let him who is too lazy to open his eyes remain blind!

The general conception "resurrection of the flesh" finds its justification when applied to *earthly* births, which will never cease as long as there are men on earth! It is a great promise that repeated lives here on earth are possible, repeated incarnations for the purpose of a more rapid advance and a necessary redemption of the baser reciprocal actions, which is synonymous with the forgiveness of sins! A proof of the immeasurable Love of the Creator Who graciously permits that departed souls, which have wholly or partly frittered away their time on earth and who were therefore still immature when they entered the beyond in order to ascend, are given another opportunity to clothe themselves in a new gross material body or cloak, whereby the flesh they laid aside celebrates a resurrection in the new flesh! The soul that had already passed over thereby celebrates a new resurrection *in* the flesh.

The spirit of man, which cannot overlook all things, will only later on be able to grasp the blessing that rests in the constant recurrence of this high Grace!

HUMAN OPINIONS AND GOD'S WILL IN
THE LAW OF RECIPROCAL ACTION

WHEN human opinions are considered, including the subject of earthly justice, one must not expect the latter to be the same as Divine Justice, or even to come near to it. On the contrary it must unfortunately be said that in most cases they are as far apart as heaven and earth! The popular expression "as far apart as heaven and earth" is truly appropriate in this connection!

Often this difference could be explained as being due to the human intellect, which is limited to space and time, and which because of this limitation cannot recognise and distinguish *real* injustice from justice. This can seldom be perceived clearly by external means, for it really lies only deep within each human being, and cannot be sufficiently interpreted by rigid paragraphs of the law or by scholarly erudition. It is saddening that on account of this so many judgments of the earthly courts are bound to be in direct opposition to Divine Justice!

We need not talk about the time of the Middle Ages, of the sad times when there were agonising tortures, as well as so-called witch burnings and other juridical crimes! Nor need we touch upon the numerous burnings at the stake, the tortures and murders which have to be charged to the *religious* communities! The retribution for such crimes must be doubly terrible upon those who carried them out, because they abused the Name of the Perfect God in so doing, committing all these crimes in His Name as if they were supposed to be agreeable to Him, and thereby stamping Him in the eyes of men as answerable for it.

These abuses and cruelties should not be so quickly forgotten, but should always be recalled as a warning when passing judgments today, particularly since those practising such evils at the time did so enthusiastically, under the pretext of acting in all good faith and of having every right to do so!

Much has changed since then! But the time will also inevitably come when one will look with similar horror upon the existing administration of justice,

456

just as with our present enlightenment we look today upon the times mentioned above in which so much injustice was done. That is the way of the world, and gives evidence of a certain progress!

If we look deeper, however, we shall find that the apparently great progress made between then and now lies *merely in the outward forms.* The immense power held by some individuals, which cuts so deeply into the whole existence of many a man without the one wielding it being held responsible here on earth, is still the same in many respects. Nor have men and the motives which dictate their actions changed very much! And where the *inner* life is still the same the reciprocal actions carrying out *Divine* Justice will also be the same.

If mankind could suddenly become *seeing in these matters* there could only follow a long-drawn-out cry of despair, and horror would afflict all the peoples! No one would then raise his hand in reproach against his neighbour, for in one way or another *each individual* would be bound to feel the same burden of guilt oppressing him. Indeed no one has the right to rebuke his neighbour because up till now *every one* has wrongly judged from appearances only, *overlooking all real life!*

If the first ray of Light could penetrate them without their being prepared for it many would despair of themselves, while others who have hitherto never taken the time to reflect would be embittered beyond words at having been asleep for so long!

Therefore the time has come to urge man to serious thought and to develop *his own impartial power of judgment,* which will refuse to lean blindly on the opinions of others but only *accept, think, speak and act* according to its *own* intuitions!

Man must never forget that he *personally* must take full and complete responsibility for everything *he* perceives, thinks and does, even if he has accepted it from others without question!

Blessed is he who reaches this height and weighs every judgment he is confronted with, and then acts in accordance with his *own* intuitions! By so doing he will not become so deeply implicated as thousands of others who often burden themselves with heavy karma through mere thoughtlessness and love of sensation, or by showing prejudice and slandering, which will lead them into regions of suffering and torment they need never have experienced. Thus they often allow themselves to be deterred here on earth from a great deal that is really good, and thereby not only miss much for themselves but perhaps risk everything, even their whole existence!

Such was the case with the senseless and blazing hatred against Jesus of Nazareth! Only a few of the malevolent clamourers knew the actual reason for it while all the others, who had never come into personal contact with Him, merely worked themselves up into a completely blind and ignorant passion and joined in the general outcry. Just as lost are all those who turned their backs upon Him because of the false opinions of others, and who did not even listen to His words, much less gave themselves the trouble of examining them objectively, whereby they might have recognised their value after all!

Only thus could the insane tragedy develop in which, of all men, the *Son of God* was being charged with *blasphemy* and brought to the cross! He Who alone came directly from God and proclaimed to mankind the Truth about God and His Will!

This happening is so grotesque that it shows up with glaring clarity the whole narrow-mindedness of mankind!

And mankind have by no means progressed inwardly since then! Instead they have retrogressed even further in this respect, in spite of all their other discoveries and inventions!

On account of their outward successes mankind advanced in conceit only, and thereby became even more presumptuous! It is just conceit that is born of and cultivated by narrow-mindedness, indeed it is a definite sign of narrow-mindedness!

And it is from this soil, which has become more and more fertile in the last two thousand years, that the present opinions of mankind have developed! The effect is both decisive and *devastating*, the while men, without realising it, continue to entangle themselves more and more in their opinions, thus preparing their own terrible doom!

So far it has very rarely become clear to anyone how many have drawn upon themselves the evil effects of reciprocal currents, that is to say, how many, often well-meaningly, have transgressed against the Divine Laws through their false opinions! Their number is large, indeed many in their unsuspecting arrogance are even proud of the fact until the day when, to their agonising horror, they will have to face the Truth, which is entirely different from what their convictions had allowed them to depict!

Then, however, it is too late! The guilt with which they have burdened themselves must be expiated in a laborious struggle with themselves which often lasts decades!

As soon as a man has lost his opportunity while on earth, when either wilfully or through ignorance he even burdened himself with new guilt, the way to recognition is long and arduous.

Excuses never carry any weight in these matters! *Every one* can know it if he *wishes!*

He who feels the urge to distinguish between Divine Justice and earthly opinions in the course of the reciprocal actions should make an effort by taking any example in earth-life and examining it to find out which side is right and which side is wrong. He will find very many every day!

Soon his intuitive capacity will unfold more strongly and actively, until he finally casts off all the prejudices derived from faulty opinions. Thereby a conception of justice will arise which can depend upon itself because, in recognising all the reciprocal actions, it will absorb the Will of God, stand in It and work in It!

THE SON OF MAN

EVER since the crime committed against the Son of God, the Bringer of Truth, Jesus of Nazareth, the fact that men did not recognise this most important prophecy has lain like a curse upon mankind, and even today they stand before it unsuspectingly as if their eyes were closely blindfolded! The terrible consequence will be that a great part of mankind will stumble on towards destruction, past the only possibility of saving themselves from being cast out!

This is the prophecy of the Coming of the Son of Man, which the Son of God held forth as a star of hope and also as a serious warning in face of the constant attacks upon Him by the masses, who through their subservience to the Darkness naturally hated the Bringer of Truth.

The same deceptive feelings and thoughts which prevented the Son of God from being recognised as such also caused confusion in their minds regarding the importance of this prophecy at the time it was made. The human spirit was too dark and too conceited to be able to receive still undimmed such high Messages of God! Messages coming from a height above their own sphere of origin passed them by without leaving any impression!

For a real understanding of this Message a belief backed by conscious conviction would have been needed, and this even His followers were not capable of at the time. The soil upon which the words of the Redeemer fell was still much too overgrown with weeds. Furthermore, the momentous experiences and psychic shocks of a life in the Saviour's vicinity were crowded into only a few short years. Consequently everything was bound to be concentrated on the Person of Jesus, so much so that when He spoke of another Person in the distant future what He said was also again interwoven with Him personally!

Thus the error has lived on in the opinions of men until the present day! The unbelievers did not bother themselves about the Saviour's words, while the believers, just because of their belief, forcibly suppressed every serious criticism of the transmissions out of holy awe that they must not come too close to these words of the Saviour! But in doing so they overlooked the fact that it was not a question of His own real original words, but merely of transmissions written down long after His life on earth. Thus the words were naturally subject to unconscious modifications through the human intellect and personal opinions!

A certain greatness is indicated in this reverential upholding of purely human transmissions, and therefore no reproach shall be voiced about it!

All this, however, does not prevent the hampering consequences of erroneous opinions which have arisen through faulty transmissions, because the Laws of Reciprocal Action cannot be overthrown in this case either. Even if the only effect of such errors is to raise obstructions barring the human spirit in its further ascent, this still constitutes a disastrous standstill preventing all progress as long as the liberating Word of Enlightenment cannot come to life within them.

He who believes in the Son of God and in His words and has made them come to life within himself, thus carrying them within him in their *true* interpretation and acting accordingly, naturally need not wait for the promised Son of Man because the Son of Man has nothing else to bring than the Son of God has already brought! It is a condition, however, that such a person has *really understood* the words of the Son of God, and does not stubbornly cling to erroneous transmissions. If somewhere he has bound himself to errors he will not be able to complete his ascent until he has received enlightenment. It was reserved for the Son of Man to bring this because the limited human spirit is unable to free itself from the dense undergrowth which now obscures the Truth!

Jesus spoke of the Coming of the Son of Man as the last possibility of salvation, and also pointed out that with His Coming the Judgment would commence. Therefore those who are still not willing or, to express it differently, those who are too stiff-necked or too indolent to be prepared to accept enlightenment would be irretrievably cast out! From this the conclusion is to be drawn that there will be no further opportunity for consideration and decision. This undoubtedly contains the announcement of great tribulation which will bring to an end a period of patient forbearance! This in turn indicates the impending struggle of the Light against all darkness, which must end with the violent destruction of darkness!

It is not to be assumed that all these events will coincide with human expectations, wishes and conceptions, because *all* past happenings indicate to the contrary. Never as yet have human ideas agreed with the manifestations of the Divine Will! The reality was always different to what men had imagined, and it was only long, long afterwards that they sometimes slowly grasped the meaning of what had happened!

Neither is there any hope that it will be different this time, because human ideas and views have gained nothing in comparison with former times! On the contrary they have become much more "realistic"!

The Son of Man! A veil still lies over Him and His time! Even if here and there a vague presentiment arises in many a spirit, a longing for the Day of His Coming, many of those who feel this will probably pass Him by unsuspectingly and will not wish to know Him, because their expectations promised them a different kind of fulfilment! It is only with great difficulty that man can accustom himself to the idea that, in obedience to the Law of God, a Divine Being on earth cannot differ outwardly from human beings themselves. He insists on picturing the Divine in supernatural form only, and yet he has unfortunately so fettered himself that he would not be capable of recognising *aright* what is supernatural, much less would he be able to bear it! Nor is this in the least necessary!

The man who seeks the Will of his God in the Natural Laws of all Creation will soon recognise it therein, and finally realise that the Divine can come only on the paths of these adamantine laws, not otherwise. As a result such a person will become vigilant and carefully scrutinise everything he meets on these paths, but only in the light of the *Divine* Laws and not with regard to human opinions. Thus through his personal examination of what is brought, and not through the clamour of the masses, he will at the right hour recognise Him Who brings liberation in the Word!

It will have occurred already to every thinking person that the Son of God and the Son of Man cannot be one! The difference is quite clearly expressed in the words themselves.

Just on account of the very purity of His Divinity, during His emission and incarnation the Pure Divinity of the Son of God bore within itself the *condition of becoming One again* with Divinity as such. In the natural order of things there is simply no other possibility! This is also confirmed by the Son of God Himself when He hinted at His "becoming One with the Father" and His "being reunited with the Father".

462

For this reason the Son of God's Mission as Mediator between the God-head and Creation could only *last a limited time*. The Son of God, after having laid aside all that was not Divine, was inevitably drawn back by the power of the attraction of the stronger homogeneous species to the Divine Origin and forced to remain there. Therefore He could not remain the *eternal* Mediator between the Godhead and the Creation in which mankind lives. Thus through the reunion of the Son of God and the Father a new gulf would have arisen, and the Mediator between pure Divinity and Creation would again have been missing!

The Son of God personally proclaimed to mankind the Coming of the Son of Man, Who will then remain the *eternal* Mediator between the Divine and Creation! This expresses the sublime love of the Creator for His Creation!

The difference between the Son of Man and the Son of God is that, though born out of the purely Divine, the Son of Man was at the same time connected with the Sphere of Conscious Spiritual Substantiality, so that it is as if He stands simultaneously with one foot in the Divine and with the other in the highest part of Conscious Spiritual Substantiality. He is a part of *each*, and thus forms the eternal bridge between the Divine and the summit of Creation. This union, however, involves the obligation of remaining separated from the pure Divine, yet in spite of this permits and even conditions admittance to Divinity.

The addition of the spiritual to the Divine merely prevents a reunion which would otherwise be unavoidable. Mankind will hardly ever grasp that this is another sacrifice of love on the part of the Creator, and the fulfilment of a promise of such magnitude as only God Himself is capable of giving and ful-filling! *That* is the difference between the Son of God and the Son of Man!

The Mission of the Son of Man on earth is the continuation and completion of the Mission of the Son of God, as the Mission of the Son of God could only be a transient one. Hence this continuation and completion is at the same time a *consolidation* of Christ's Mission!

Whereas the Son of God was born directly into His earthly Mission, the Son of Man had to traverse a far wider sphere before He could enter upon the beginning of His actual Mission. As a condition for the fulfilment of His task, which in comparison to that of the Son of God was more terrestrial, the Son of Man, coming as He did from the highest Heights, also had to descend into the deepest depths; not only in the beyond but also here on earth, so that He might personally "experience" all the misery and suffering man is heir to. Only then will He be in the position, when His Hour comes, to intervene effectively in their shortcomings and help to bring about changes!

For this reason He could not merely stand *beside* the experiences of mankind, but had to stand in the midst of them through His own personal experiences. He even had to stand in and suffer under the bitter side of life. Again it was only for the sake of men that He had to serve His time of apprenticeship in this way! But it is just on account of this that people will try to reproach Him in order to make His task more difficult as they had done previously with Christ, because the human spirit with all its limitations can never understand such high guidance, being only able to judge by externals!

Just what He had to suffer for the sake of men in order to learn to recognise the worst points in their errors, that is, what He suffered or came to know through His own experiences in the interests of the future welfare of mankind, they will wish to use as stones to throw at Him when their rising hatred is inflamed by the Darkness as it trembles in fear of annihilation!

That something so incredible can happen again in spite of the events during the Son of God's wanderings on earth is not inexplicable, because in reality more than half of the present inhabitants of the earth do not belong here at all but should be maturing in much deeper and darker regions! The foundation for this was laid through constant psychic retrogression, which in turn was brought about by those who became slaves of their own tool, the limited intellect, and gained the upper hand!

When the limited intellect gains the sole direction it will, because it is purely earthly, always further everything that is material and therefore cultivate all the accompanying secondary effects. The resulting decline from a higher conception created a breach through which a hand was stretched downwards to assist those souls in climbing up for earthly incarnation which otherwise, owing to their spiritual heaviness and the denser darkness, could never have penetrated to the surface of the earth.

But, above all, there are the purely animal sensations accompanying procreation, as well as the general striving for earthly enjoyments which, during the demoralising times for centuries past, have enabled inferior souls to rise! These inferior souls then constantly circle round expectant mothers, and if an opportunity presents itself they incarnate, because up till now all that is light had voluntarily retired before what is dark in order to avoid becoming soiled.

So it has gradually come to pass that the ethereal surrounding of the earth has grown ever denser and darker and thus heavier, so heavy in fact that it even keeps the gross material earth from a course that would have made it more accessible to higher spiritual influences.

As the majority of all incarnated souls actually belong to regions that lie much deeper than the earth itself, it will therefore be but Divine Justice if such souls are swept away and sink back to where they properly belong; to the region where, due to their absolute homogeneity, they have no further opportunity to burden themselves with new guilt; and where consequently they are better able to mature and begin to ascend through the suffering inflicted upon them in their own sphere!

It does not lie with mankind to elect the Son of Man sent by God. But the Power of God will uplift Him at the hour when mankind in their helplessness are whining for deliverance! Then they will cease to revile, because horror will silence them, and they will willingly accept all the gifts the Creator offers His creatures through His Envoy! But he who will not accept them from Him shall be cast forth for all eternity!

THE SIGNIFICANCE OF MAN'S GENERATIVE
POWER FOR HIS SPIRITUAL ASCENT

I would again point out that all *life* in Creation is of two kinds – conscious and unconscious. Only in the process of becoming conscious does the likeness of the Creator, by which we mean the human form, evolve. This goes uniformly hand in hand with the development of consciousness.

In the *first* actual Creation, which stands closest to the Creative Spirit and which can therefore be only spiritual in nature, *unconscious* spiritual substantiality exists beside the first created conscious spirit beings. In this unconsciousness, which has the same qualities as consciousness, there naturally lies dormant the urge for further development, which can only take place when there is an increase in consciousness.

If now the urge to become conscious has increased to a certain degree in this spiritual unconsciousness, a process similar to an earthly birth takes place in the normal and natural order of things. We need only observe our own environment to see that the physical body automatically throws off every fruit that has ripened, both in man and beast. Every tree, too, casts off its fruit. This process is a repetition of development and follows the basic order established in the *first* Creation.

There likewise, at a certain stage of maturity, unconscious substance striving to become conscious is automatically cast off, a severance, or what is also called an expulsion, from the other unconscious substance in which the urge is not yet developed. *These spiritually unconscious particles which have thus been ejected now form the spirit-germs of developing human beings.*

This process *must* take place because unconsciousness is without *responsibility,* while a growing consciousness calls forth a corresponding sense of responsibility.

This severance of the maturing unconscious is therefore necessary for the spirit which wishes to follow its natural urge and develop towards consciousness. This is progress, not retrogression!

Since these living germs cannot be ejected upwards, i. e., towards perfection, they can only take the road leading downwards. Here, however, they enter the Realm of Animistic Substantiality*, which is heavier in weight and contains nothing spiritual.

In this sphere the spirit-germ striving towards consciousness suddenly finds itself in a *strange* surrounding of a different consistency from its own and, as it were, *uncovered*. Being spiritual it feels naked and bare in the denser animistic substantiality. If it is to stay there or advance it naturally needs to clothe itself in an animistic *cloak* of the same nature as its surroundings. Otherwise it can neither become active nor maintain itself there. Thus it not only has the desire to cover its nakedness in its pursuit of knowledge, as is depicted in the Bible, but this is also a necessary step in its evolution.

The germ of the developing human spirit is now guided along the natural paths into the World of Matter.

Here again it needs and is covered by a cloak of the same nature as its new material environment.

Now the spirit-germ stands at the outer boundary of the Ethereal World!

This earth, however, is *that* gross material point at which *all* that rests in Creation meets. From *all* sections, which are otherwise strictly separated owing to their different characteristics, the species come together here. All threads, all roads converge upon this earth as if to a common centre. There they combine and also create new effects, which flare up strongly and send forth currents of power into the Universe, such as come from no other part of the World of Matter.

As *all* kinds of species in Creation combine through the medium of the World of Matter, experiencing is most intense here. But it is only a combination of all species in *Creation,* nothing Divine or of the Holy Spirit, Which stands *above* and outside Creation.

The last vibrations of this experiencing on earth now stream towards the spirit-germ as soon as it enters the Ethereal World. It is surrounded by these effects, which attract it but also help to awaken it to consciousness and to develop it.

While it still stands unfettered, that is, without guilt, on the threshold of all matter, the spirit-germ perceives the last effects of the vibrations of strong experiences which take place in the birth and decay of all matter.

* See Appendix.

The wish then arises within it to have *closer* contact. As soon as it forms such a wish, however, the spirit-germ voluntarily adjusts itself to one of these vibrations, be it good or evil. Through the Law of Attraction of Homogeneous Species it is thereupon immediately drawn to a homogeneous species stronger than its own. It is then driven towards a point where greater homage is rendered to the wished-for species than was its own desire.

Such an inner craving immediately increases the density of its ethereal cloak, and the Law of Gravitation causes it to sink further downwards.

Only on the gross material earth, however, can it truly *experience* the craving that lies within it! Therefore, as it wishes to proceed from nipping to enjoying, the spirit-germ is further encouraged to incarnate on earth. The stronger the desire for *earthly* enjoyments becomes in the spirit-germ awakening through this nipping, the denser becomes the ethereal cloak it bears. As a result its weight also increases, and it sinks slowly downwards to the earth-plane where there is an opportunity to realise its wishes. Having arrived on this earth-plane, however, it is then ripe for an earthly birth.

The Law of the Power of Attraction of Homogeneous Species now manifests itself *more conspicuously*. Each of the undeveloped spirits, exactly according to the wish or propensity within it, is magnetically attracted to a spot where the main substance of its wish is realised by men on earth. If, for example, the spirit has the desire to rule, it is by no means born into circumstances where it can indulge its wish, but is attracted by a person who has a strong craving for power, that is, to one who thinks and perceives in the same way, and so on. In this manner it can in part already atone for wrong desires or can be made happy by having wished rightly, at least it is given the opportunity to do so!

From this process it is erroneously concluded that characteristics or spiritual abilities are inherited. *This is wrong!* Outwardly it may appear to be so, but in reality a human being can bequeath *nothing* of his living spirit to his children.

There is no such thing as spiritual heredity!

No man is in a position to give away even the least particle of his living spirit!

In this matter an error has been fostered that casts its hindering and confusing shadow over many things. No child need thank its parents for any spiritual abilities, any more than it may reproach them for its deficiencies! That would be wrong and unjust!

The wonderful work of Creation is so complete and perfect that it could never allow arbitrary acts or acts of chance such as would be involved in spiritual heredity!

This power of attraction of all that is of the same nature, which is so important in the birth of a child, can proceed from the father, from the mother, or from anyone in the vicinity of the expectant mother. *Therefore an expectant mother ought to be very careful whom she allows around her!* Consideration must be given to the fact that it is not in the outward character, but primarily in one's *weaknesses* that inner strength lies! Weaknesses bring important periods of inner experiencing which produce a strong power of attraction!

The coming of man to this earth is comprised of procreation, incarnation and birth. The incarnation, that is, the entrance of the soul, takes place about *the middle of pregnancy.* The growing state of maturity, both of the expectant mother and of the soul preparing to incarnate, also produces a special and *more earthly* tie. This comprises radiations created by their mutual state of maturity, which irresistibly strive towards one another in natural release. These radiations increase more and more and unite the soul and the expectant mother ever more closely in their longing for each other, until finally, when the developing body in the mother's womb has reached a certain maturity, the soul is literally absorbed by it.

The moment when the soul enters, or is being absorbed, naturally brings about the first shock to the little body, which shows itself in twitchings called the first movements of the child. When this occurs the expectant mother very often experiences a change in her inner feelings, either uplifting or oppressive according to the kind of soul that has entered.

On entering the little body the human soul which has developed thus far now takes on a cloak of gross matter, which is needed to enable it fully to experience, to hear, to see and to feel everything in the World of Gross Matter. This only becomes possible through a cloak of a *homogeneous* kind or a tool of the same substance. Only now can it proceed from nipping to actual tasting and thence *to discriminating!* It is understandable that the soul must first learn to make use of and control this new body as if it were a tool!

This in short is the process of man's development till his first birth on earth!

But already for a long time, in the natural course of events, it is impossible for any soul to embark upon its *first* incarnation on this earth. Instead souls were incarnated which have wandered through *at least* one life on earth before. Thus they come grievously burdened with much and diverse karma at birth. *The opportunity to free themselves from this karma is offered through the generative power.*

Through the protection afforded by the gross material body the soul of man is kept isolated during its childhood years from currents which try to reach it from *outside*. All that is dark and evil on this earth-plane finds its way to the soul barred by the gross material body, and thus it cannot influence or harm the child. But naturally the evil a reincarnated soul brings over from previous experiences also remains with it during childhood.

The body forms this protective wall as long as it is still undeveloped and immature. It is as if the soul had withdrawn into a castle with the drawbridge pulled up. During these years an impassable gulf yawns between the soul of the child and Ethereal Creation, in which latter the ethereal vibrations of guilt and atonement live.

Thus the soul lies sheltered in its earthly cloak, maturing towards responsibility and waiting for the moment when the lowering of the drawbridge will mark the real beginning of its life in the World of Matter.

Through the Natural Laws the Creator has endowed *every* creature with an *imitative instinct* to take the place of the free will before the latter has become active. It is generally spoken of as the "receptivity of youth". The imitative instinct is a preparatory step in development for life on earth until the time when, in the case of animals, it is enriched and supported by experiences, and in the case of human beings it is uplifted to self-conscious activity through the spirit and the free will.

The spirit incarnated in the child's body lacks a bridge of radiations, which can only be formed with the help of the generative power at the time of physical maturity. The spirit needs this bridge to become fully and truly active in Creation, which can only be accomplished through the uninterrupted exchange of radiations between all species in Creation. For there is life only in radiation, and only in and through radiation is movement generated.

During this time the child, which can only have a full effect on its environment through its *animistic* part and not through its spiritual core, has little more responsibility towards the Laws of Creation than the most highly developed animal.

Meanwhile the young body matures and gradually *generative power*, which is only to be found in *gross matter*, awakens within it. It is *the finest and noblest flower of all gross matter*, the highest that the Gross Material Creation has to offer! In its *finest nature* it forms *the summit of all that is gross material*, that is, of all that is earthly, and as the highest of the living ramifications of the World of Matter it comes closest to the Animistic Realm! Generative power is the pulsating life of the World of Matter, and it alone can form the *bridge* to the World of Animistic Substantiality, which in turn acts as intermediary to the World of Spiritual Substantiality.

It is for this reason that the awakening of generative power in the physical body may be likened to the lowering of the drawbridge in a castle that had hitherto proved inaccessible. This permits the inhabitant of the castle, the human soul, to step forth fully armed and ready for battle. At the same time, however, it allows friends or foes lying in wait outside to enter. These friends or foes are first of all ethereal currents of good or evil nature, but also include those in the beyond who only wait until a hand is stretched forth to them through some wish, as it were, which enables them to attach themselves firmly to the soul and exercise a like influence upon it.

However, in the natural course of development the laws of the Creator do not allow the influences from without to be stronger than the power of resistance within, so that an unequal struggle is completely out of the question, providing no sins are committed in the process. For every sexual instinct which is rendered unnatural through artificial stimulation opens this strong castle prematurely and causes the soul not yet equally strong to be exposed! It must then succumb to the onrushing evil ethereal currents which it could otherwise easily have coped with!

As the soul matures normally in the natural course of things there can only be equal strength on both sides. The decisive factor in this, however, is the will of the dweller in the castle, not that of the besieger. Thus if his volition is good he will always be victorious in the Ethereal World, that is, in the happenings of the beyond, which the average human being cannot see as long as he remains on earth, but which have a closer and more lively connection with him than the gross material surroundings visible to him.

But when the dweller in the castle *of his own free will*, that is, through his own wish or free decision, stretches forth his hand either to an ethereal friend or foe, or even to vibrations from outside, the case is naturally quite different. Since he thereby attunes himself to a certain type among the besiegers waiting outside, these can easily assail him with a power ten or a hundred times stronger than his own. If this power is good he will receive help and blessing! If it is evil he will reap destruction!

This free choice constitutes an action of his own free will. Having once made a decision, however, he is irrevocably subject to the consequences, for which his free will is then eliminated. By his own choice he has incurred good or bad karma, to which he is naturally subject until he changes inwardly.

Generative power has the task and also the ability to send an earthly *"glow"* through all the *spiritual* perceptions of the soul. Only when this happens can the spirit obtain real connection with the entire World of Matter and thereby become of full value on earth! Not until then can it embrace all that it needs to enable it to assert itself authoritatively in the World of Matter, to stand firmly in it, to influence it effectively, to be protected, and to be so armed as to defend itself victoriously.

There is something stupendous in this union. *That* is the *principal purpose* of this mysterious and immeasurable natural instinct! It is to help the spirit unfold its full power of action in the World of Matter! This would be impossible without generative power, because there would be no bridge or means for the animation and control of all matter. Otherwise the spirit would remain too estranged from matter to work really effectively in it!

Through generative power, however, the human spirit attains to its full power, its warmth and vitality. Only through this development does the spirit become ready for battle here on earth!

It is just at this stage that responsibility sets in! A serious turning-point in every man's existence!

At this important moment in a man's life the wise Justice of the Creator provides not only the opportunity but also the natural urge to shake off *easily and without effort* any karma with which he has so far burdened his free will.

If a man misses this time it is *his* fault! Consider a moment! As soon as generative power sets in there is first of all a mighty surge upwards towards all that is ideal, beautiful and pure. In unspoiled youth of both sexes this can be clearly observed, and produces the enthusiasms of the young so often smiled at by their elders, and also the inexplicable, somewhat melancholy intuitions which beset them in these years.

The moods in which it seems as if the youth or maid were burdened with the sorrows of the whole world, where premonitions of a deep seriousness assail them, are not altogether without cause!

Even their frequent feelings about not being understood contain in reality much that is true. These periodically arise through a recognition of the perverted conditions of their environment. Those around them neither wish nor are able to understand such sacred beginnings to a pure soaring upwards. They are not satisfied until these strong warning intuitions in the maturing soul are dragged down to a sober "reality" which they can understand better, which they consider more suitable for mankind and which, with their one-sided intellectual thinking, they regard as the only normal condition of life!

The inexplicable charm which radiates from an unspoilt maiden or youth is nothing but the *pure* soaring upwards of the awakening generative power towards what is high and noble in union with the spiritual power. This is also sensed by their surroundings.

The Creator has carefully provided that this should not occur until a human being is old enough to be fully conscious of his volition and actions. The time has then arrived when, in conjunction with the full power vested in him, he could and should easily shake off all that lies behind him. Indeed it would fall away of its own accord if only a man would keep his volition intent on what is good, which he is unceasingly urged to do during this time. Then he could, as his intuitions quite rightly indicate, ascend without any trouble to that eminence to which he as a human being belongs.

Observe the day-dreams of unspoilt youth! They are nothing but an inward yearning to tear themselves away from all that is base, an ardent longing for what is ideal! This restless urge, however, is a sign not to miss the opportunity, but energetically to shake off karma and *begin* with the ascent of the spirit!

It is a wonderful experience to stand in the fullness of this power, to work *in it* and *with it!* But this is only as long as the direction a man chooses is a good one! On the other hand there is nothing more deplorable than to squander these powers one-sidedly in blind sensual activity, and thus paralyse one's spirit!

But alas, in most cases man unfortunately does not avail himself of this precious time of transition, but allows himself to be guided by the "wiseacres" around him on to wrong paths, which not only keep him down but lead him still further downwards! Thereby not only is he *unable* to throw off the impure vibrations clinging to him, but these receive a reinforcement of power of the same kind. As a consequence his free will is entangled more and more until it becomes unrecognisable beneath these unnecessary growths. It is much like the creepers to which a sound tree first lends a helping hand, but which finally choke it to death through their luxuriant growth!

If a man would observe himself and the happenings in the whole of Creation more closely, no karma could prove stronger than his spirit as it comes to full strength when the generative power connects it firmly with the World of Matter to which such karma belongs.

Even if man misses this opportunity, if he entangles himself still more and perhaps even sinks deeply, despite all this a further opportunity to ascend is offered him ... through love!

Not the covetous love of the World of Gross Matter, but the sublime, pure love which has no other thought, no other desire, but the welfare of the beloved one! This love also belongs to the World of Matter and it requires no renunciation, no asceticism, but always and only wills the best for the other. And this volition, which *never thinks of self,* also offers the best protection against any interference!

The basis of love, even in people of the most advanced age, is always the idealistic yearnings which unspoiled youth feel when generative power begins to exert itself in them. But it shows itself differently! A mature person is spurred on to the height of his ability, even to deeds of heroism. In this no limit is set as to age! Generative power remains even when the baser sexual instinct is eliminated, for generative power and sexual instinct are not identical.

As soon as a man gives room to pure love, whether it be the love of a man for a woman or the reverse, love for a man or a woman friend, for parents or for children, it is all the same! So long as it is truly pure it will bring as a first gift the opportunity for casting off karma, which can be redeemed very quickly in a "symbolical" manner. It "dries up" because it no longer finds any affinity with him, receives no further nourishment within him. Thus he is set free and can begin his ascent through redemption from the unworthy fetters that hold him down!

The first intuition this love awakens is the feeling of being unworthy of the one beloved. One can call this the beginning of modesty and humility, thus the acquiring of two great virtues! This is followed by the urge to hold one's hands protectingly above the other so that no harm may befall him from any side. This desire to "wait hand and foot on the other" is no empty saying, but signifies the rising intuitions quite correctly. This, however, means renouncing one's personality and feeling a strong desire to serve, which alone would suffice to cast off all karma within a short time, provided this volition remains constant and does not give way to purely sensual instinct!

Finally pure love engenders the ardent wish to do something really great and noble for the loved one, never to hurt or offend him by thought or word, much less by an unfair action, thus always showing him the most delicate consideration!

The purity of this intuition must then be preserved at all costs, and placed above and before all else. No one will ever think or do any evil in such circumstances! He simply cannot do so! On the contrary, through these intuitions he has the best protection, the greatest strength and the most benevolent adviser and helper!

The Creator in His Wisdom has thereby thrown out a lifebelt to mankind, and offers *each* human being during his time on earth more than one opportunity to grasp and lift himself up by it.

This help is available to *all!* It makes no distinction as to age or sex, whether a person be rich or poor, of high or lowly birth! Hence love is the greatest of all God's gifts! He who grasps it is sure of salvation from *every* sorrow, *every* depth!

Like a whirlwind love can seize and uplift him to the Light, to God, Who is Love Himself!

As soon as love stirs in a man's heart, inspiring him to bring light and joy to another, rather than to drag him down through impure thoughts, but to protect and uplift him, he thus *serves* the other without being conscious of it, for he thereby becomes a selfless and joyful giver. And through such serving he frees himself!

To find the right way in these matters it is only necessary to observe one thing! All men have one great and strong desire in common – *really to be* in their own eyes what they are considered to be in the eyes of *those who love them!* Such a desire is along the right lines! It leads directly upwards!

Many opportunities are offered to men to pull themselves together and soar upwards, but they do not grasp them!

The man of today is just like a man to whom a kingdom is given, but who prefers to fritter away his time with a child's toy!

It is quite understandable, and hardly to be expected otherwise, that the mighty powers which are given to man must *smash* him if he does not know how to *master* them!

Thus also generative power must destroy individual human beings and entire nations wherever its *principal function* is misused! The purpose of procreation is only of *secondary* importance.

And what help the generative power gives to every man, so that he may recognise and *live* this principal function!

One need only think of the feeling of physical shame! It awakens along with generative power and is given as a *protection*.

Here, too, as everywhere in Creation, there is a triad, and in the process of descending one can observe that things become ever coarser. The feeling of shame which develops as the first consequence of generative power is intended to form an *impediment* to sexual instinct, so that man should not descend from his height and yield to sexual indulgence in an animal-like manner.

Woe to the people who disregard this!

A strong feeling of shame provides against the possibility of a man ever succumbing to sexual indulgence! It protects him from physical passion, for in the natural course of events it will never permit him an opportunity to forget himself even for a fraction of a second!

Only *forcibly* and wilfully can man push aside this precious gift in order to behave in a *bestial* manner! But such forcible interference in the Creator's cosmic order *must* bring a curse upon him, for the thus unleashed power of the physical sexual instinct in its uncontrolled state no longer accords with what is natural.

Wherever the feeling of shame is lacking man becomes the slave instead of being the master. He is hurled from man's estate to below the level of an animal!

Man should realise that a strong feeling of shame alone precludes all possibility of falling. It is thus his surest defence!

The more intense this feeling of shame the *nobler* is the instinct and therefore the higher man stands spiritually. Indeed this is *the best measure of his*

476

inner spiritual worth! This standard is infallible and can easily be recognised by everybody. In suppressing or pushing aside this outward feeling of shame the finer and most valuable psychic qualities are also simultaneously suppressed, as a result of which the inner man is rendered worthless.

It is an unmistakable sign of a deep fall and certain decay when, under the pretext of progress, mankind want to set themselves "above" the feeling of shame, this precious jewel that brings them nothing but benefit! Whether it is under the guise of sports, of hygiene, of fashion, of children's education, or many another welcome excuse, the decline and fall cannot then be prevented, and only horrors of the worst kind can still bring a few individuals back to their senses!

And yet it is made so easy for man on earth to follow the path leading upwards!

All he needs to do is to become more "natural"! To be natural, however, does not mean to go about half-naked or to disport himself barefoot in eccentric clothing! To be natural means to listen attentively to one's inner voice and not forcibly to disregard its warnings!

Unfortunately more than half of all the people today have fallen so far and become so dull that they can no longer understand these natural intuitions. Through their own actions they have become much too narrow-minded to do so! A great cry of horror and dismay will be the end!

Happy is he who can then re-awaken the feeling of shame! It will be his shield and support when all else crumbles!

I AM THE RESURRECTION AND THE LIFE, NO MAN
COMETH TO THE FATHER BUT BY ME!

As Jesus came from the Divine He was right in using these words because He was the only One who could overlook and really explain everything. His Message, which cannot be separated from Him personally, shows the *clear* path up to the Light amid the confusion arising from erroneous views. For all human spirits this means the possibility of rising or *resurrection from the World of Matter* into which they had been immersed for their further development. Such resurrection means *life* for everyone!

Now listen attentively! All that is base and all that is evil, i.e., all that is called Darkness, exists *only* in the World of Matter, both in gross matter and in ethereal matter. He who grasps *this* aright has already gained much!

As soon as a man thinks in an evil or base manner he does immense harm to *himself*. The main strength of his volition then flows forth like a magnetic ray towards all that is base where it attracts ethereal matter which, due to its weight, is denser and thus darker. As a result the human *spirit* from which this volition issues is enveloped in this dense kind of matter.

Even if a human mind is primarily bent on worldly things, i.e., if a man is under the spell of a passion for something which need not necessarily be immorality, gambling or drinking, but can also be a marked partiality for anything of an earthly nature, his spirit will be covered by a more or less dense ethereal cloak through the process I have already mentioned.

This dense and consequently dark covering prevents all possibility of the spirit rising upwards, and *remains* with it as long as it does not change the nature of its volition.

Only an earnest volition and an earnest striving for *sublime spirituality* can loosen and at last completely detach such a cloak, because it then no longer receives a supply of strength of a like nature and gradually loosens its grip. Finally it is dissolved and sinks away, thus freeing the spirit for its ascent.

Ethereal matter must not be regarded as refinement of visible gross matter, for it is a species quite *alien* to gross matter and of *different* consistency, which however can still be called matter. It forms a transition to animistic substantiality from which the animal soul originates.

If men remain in the World of Matter they must naturally be drawn at some time or other into the disintegration to which all matter is subject, because owing to their cloak they can no longer free themselves from matter in time.

Those who of their own desire have descended into the World of Matter for their development will remain bound in it *unless they continue on the right path!* They are unable to sever themselves from it, which if they did would be tantamount to a resurrection towards the Light!

It should be further explained that *every* development of a spirit-germ longing for personal consciousness *necessitates* a descent into the World of Matter. *Only through experiences in the World of Matter can it so develop.* No other way is open to it! The spirit-germ, however, is not forced to make this descent, it only happens when its *own desire* to do so awakens within it. Its own *wishes* then impel it towards the necessary course of development, out of the so-called Paradise of unconsciousness and thus out of its state of non-responsibility.

If through their wrong desires men lose the right path which leads upwards again, back to the Light, they remain wandering about in the World of Matter.

Now try and observe the happenings in the *World of Gross Matter,* the development and the decaying in your immediate and visible surroundings!

Observe in the germination, growing, ripening and decaying how the process of forming goes on, i. e., how the basic substances become merged, the development which takes place, followed again by deterioration into the same basic substances through disintegration, that is, through the falling apart in the process of decaying of what has been formed! You can distinctly see this with water, also with the so-called decomposition of stones, with plants and also with animal and human bodies. And in the same way that this happens with small things it also happens with great things, and ultimately with all world events! And not only in the Gross Material World which is *visible* to man on earth, but also in the Ethereal World, in the so-called beyond which, however, has nothing to do with Paradise!

As the lowest part of Creation the entire World of Matter hangs like a huge wreath, rotating in an immense circle which it takes millions of years to complete. Thus in the great cosmic happenings everything not only revolves around itself, but the whole of Creation also continually rotates in an immense circle. Just as this great cycle *resulted* from the first union and developed to its present perfection, so it *continues* unswervingly on its course *in the same manner* until disintegration sets in and returns the component parts to their primeval substance. The circle, however, calmly continues to rotate along with this primeval substance in order to form new worlds with new and virgin powers through newly-effected unions.

Such is the great process of evolution, eternally repeating itself on the smallest as well as on the greatest scale! And *above* this rotating circle there stands firmly anchored the first spiritually pure Creation, the so-called Paradise. In contrast to the formed World of Matter, Paradise is *not* subject to disintegration.

In this Eternal Spiritual Sphere, which stands luminously above the rotating circle, lies the origin of the unconscious spirit-germ of man. This spiritual sphere again becomes the *final goal* of the human spirit after it has become self-conscious and thus *personal* in the World of Matter.

It comes forth as an unconscious and non-responsible germ. It returns as a self-conscious and therefore responsible personality provided that ... it does not get lost on its necessary journey through the World of Matter (thereby becoming entangled in it), but celebrates its resurrection from it as a human spirit which has become fully conscious. A joyful emergence from the World of Matter towards this luminous and eternal part of Creation!

As long as the human spirit remains in the World of Matter it joins in part of this great and eternal rotating movement without, of course, realising it. Thus one day it will at last arrive at the boundary line where that part of Creation inhabited by the human spirits slowly drifts towards disintegration!

Then, however, it is high time for all human spirits which are still *within* the World of Matter to make haste and improve themselves to *such* an extent that they can ascend to the safe and luminous haven of the Eternal Kingdom, which means to find the right way and above all the *shortest* way of escape from the impending dangers in the World of Matter before being overtaken by them!

If they do not do so it will become more and more difficult, and finally too late for them!

With all the rest they will then be slowly drawn into disintegration, in which process the *personal* "ego" they have acquired will be torn to pieces.

Suffering a thousand torments they will again become unconscious spirit-germs, the most dreadful fate which can befall a spirit that has attained self-consciousness!

This concerns all those who have developed their personality in the wrong direction. As their personality is both useless and detrimental it must therefore again be forfeited. It should be noted that disintegration is not the same as destruction. Nothing can be destroyed! It only relapses into a primeval state. What will be destroyed in these lost ones is the personal "ego" they had acquired up to that time, and this will be accompanied by unspeakable torments!

Such lost or damned ones then cease to be complete human spirits, while the others are permitted to return home to the Eternal Kingdom of Joy and Light as self-conscious spirits, consciously enjoying all its splendour.

In the same way as a field after a number of years yields an ever-decreasing harvest of grain, and only receives new strength through planting different crops, so it is with the whole World of Matter. This, too, becomes exhausted after a time and must refresh its strength through disintegration and a new composition. Such events, however, cover millions of years, but even in happenings extending over many millions of years there comes *one definite year* which is absolutely decisive for the necessary separation of what is useful from what is useless.

And the earth has now reached this point of time in the great cycle! The human spirit still dwelling in the World of Matter *must* at last decide to make its ascent, or the World of Matter will clasp it firmly for the ensuing disintegration. This is the eternal damnation from which it will never be possible to rise as a conscious spiritual personality and ascend towards the luminous eternal part of Creation which stands above such disintegration!

In the natural development of the whole every possibility that spirit-germs striving to become conscious can incarnate upon this over-ripe earth-plane has long since been forfeited, because they would require too long a period to make a timely departure from the World of Matter as personal self-conscious spirits. In the natural course of events the spirit-germs can only flow to *such parts of the cosmos* as are of the same nature *in respect of the fact* that their necessary development requires just as much time as a spirit-germ also needs if it were to use all the time allotted to it to gain perfection. Only the fact that they are on the same stage of development opens the way for a spirit-germ, while if any part of the cosmos were of greater maturity it would create quite insurmountable barriers. Thus here too there can be absolutely no question of an injustice and a deficiency! *Every* human spirit can therefore stand equally matured with the greatest maturity of the material environment in which it has its being, and at the same point as that now reached by the particular part of the World of Matter we at present inhabit.

There is not one human being who could not be mature! The disparity among men is but the necessary consequence of their own free volition. Because it is over-ripe the World of Matter is now entering a period of disintegration and simultaneously drifting towards a new birth.

For the human spirits, however, the time of harvesting has arrived, and with it the separation! That which is mature will be uplifted towards the Light through the effects of the Natural Laws which permit the ethereal cloak gradually to be cast off, leaving the spirit thus freed from its burden consciously to swing upwards to the realm of its own nature, of all that is eternally spiritual. That which is useless, however, will be retained in the World of Matter by the self-imposed density of their ethereal bodies.

The fate of these latter is that their ethereal bodies will remain subject to the changes now beginning in the World of Matter, and they will have to suffer under the most painful disintegration covering thousands of years. The magnitude of their suffering will finally affect the human spirit in such a manner as to make it lose its self-consciousness. And with it the form of the image of God, the form of man, acquired in the course of becoming conscious, again disintegrates!

After the complete disintegration of matter back into primeval substance, that which has become *unconscious* spiritual substance is again set free and, in accordance with its nature, rises upwards. Then, however, it does not return as a conscious human spirit, but as an unconscious seed which at some time or other, through a newly-awakened desire, sets out from the very beginning on a new course of development in a new part of the world.

Looking down from His infinitely high standpoint, that is, from *On High,* Christ, *as always,* chose His words in such a way as to describe the quite natural process of the spirit rising out of the World of Matter into which it had descended as a spirit-germ.

Try to imagine yourself standing *above* the World of Matter!

Below you, spread out like a field, lies the World of Matter in its many varieties! The spirit-germs, coming from above, now descend into the World of Matter. After a long time and at many different intervals there gradually emerges a number of complete human spirits which have become self-conscious through their experiences in the World of Matter, and which through their urge to strive upwards have been able to cast off all that is material and leave it behind. These then celebrate their resurrection from the World of Matter!

But not all germs rise as matured spirits above the surface. A good many of them never emerge and must perish without being of any use!

It is exactly the same as with a field of grain!

Just as with the seed of wheat all the mysterious and *real* development takes place *in* the soil needed for the purpose, so the principal development of the spirit-germ takes place in the general World of Matter.

In *each one* of His sentences Christ invariably *illustrates* some natural happening in Creation!

Whether He said: "No man cometh to the Father but by My Message, or by My Word, or by Me", it is one and the same thing! It means: "No man can find the way except through what I say!" One expression means the same as the other! It is also the same whether He says: "Through My Message I bring you the possibility of resurrection from the World of Matter and with it life" or "I am, by My Word, resurrection and life for you!"

Men should grasp the *meaning* and not persist in confusing themselves by haggling over words!

The processes in the cycle of the World of Matter indicated here only in broad outline may also produce a few exceptions which, however, are not caused by any changes or distortions in the effective Laws of Creation, but which contain complete and inexorable fulfilment.

In order to avoid errors creeping in I now wish to give a few brief explanations in advance of later lectures where the subject is dealt with more fully.

The afore-mentioned periodic disintegration of all matter at a certain definite point in its cycle is a consequence of the fact that the human spirit-germs, which have the capacity to make a free decision, are permitted to develop in the Worlds of Matter.

Since with this ability to make a free descision the spirit-germs do not always choose the way upwards to the Light, a certain increase in the density of the World of Matter not willed by the Light takes place, causing it to become heavier and forcing it down onto a course that leads to over-ripeness and to the funnel which acts like a cleansing filter upon everything, and in which disintegration simultaneously occurs.

Any part of the Cosmos or any celestial body in the World of Matter in which the developing human spirits adjust all their desires and pure volitions only to the Light remains more luminous, and therefore lighter, on a plane where it can uninterruptedly absorb the living radiating powers out of the Light. It always remains fresh and healthy and swings in the Laws of Creation, thus avoiding a course which must otherwise lead to over-ripeness and disintegration.

Such parts quite naturally, i.e., by the Will of the Light, wing their way high above the boundary where disintegration sets in.

Unfortunately there are only very few of these! The guilt for this must lie at the door of the spirit of man which is allowed to develop but which chose wrong paths and, despite all admonitions, clung to them persistently!

Where, however, by an act of Grace the Creator wishes to offer help when distress is at its highest, that is, shortly before the particular part enters the sucking power of the vortex of disintegration, there the process is changed!

Without the participation of the human spirits the anchoring of the Light through the coming of an Envoy of God so strengthens the Power of the Light that a purification takes place which then, in the last moment, pulls up the thus blessed part of the World of Matter towards more luminous regions so that it passes above the funnel of disintegration and thereby remains in existence.

The purification naturally sweeps away all that is dark along with all its creatures, its servants and all their abominations, while the human spirits which still remain must gratefully strive upwards to the Light with all their strength!

Even this extraordinary event swings completely in the Laws of Creation and its effects do not deviate from them by a hair's breadth. The compulsory purification connected with the anchoring of the Light is the same as an absolutely new birth!

GROSS MATTER, ETHEREAL MATTER, RADIATIONS, SPACE AND TIME

THERE have been many enquiries about the meaning of my expressions "gross matter" and "ethereal matter". Gross matter comprises everything that man can see with his *physical* eyes, and what he can feel and hear *physically*. To this also belongs what he can see with the help of material aids, such as everything to be observed through the microscope, and what he will be able to see through further inventions. Gross matter is only a *certain* species in the World of Matter.

The great field of the *whole* World of Matter, however, comprises *several* species which are basically entirely different, and which therefore *never blend with each other*.

The different species of matter form the lowest strata or end of Creation. As with every sphere in Creation, it begins with the lightest species above and, in continuing downwards, ends with what is heaviest and densest. All these species of matter merely serve as a means for the development of everything that is spiritual which, as a germ, descends into it as if into a fertile field, in the same manner as a seed of grain needs the earth in which to germinate and grow.

The World of Matter with its various strata remains inactive and helpless of itself. Not until it is penetrated and bound together by the animistic substantiality above it does it receive warmth and vitality and serve as the coverings or bodies of a great variety of forms and species!

As I have already mentioned, the different species of matter *cannot be blended*, but they can be united through animistic substantiality, and also linked up in many ways. The resultant unions and alliances produce heat-emanations and radiations. Each individual species of matter thus produces its own definite radiation which blends with the radiations of the other species to which it is connected, and together these form a halo of radiations which is today already recognised and called "Od" or emanation.

485

Thus every stone, every plant and every animal has its own particular radiation which one can observe and which, according to the *condition* of the body, i. e., the cloak or form, is entirely different! It is also possible to observe disturbances in this halo of radiations and recognise points of disorder in the cloak.

This halo of radiations gives each form or body a special aura which constitutes a protection and defence, but at the same time also a bridge connecting it with its wider environment. It also affects the interior in order to take part in the development of the inner core in its *coarsest* sense. For in reality there are many things which contribute to the overall activity in Creation which I may only explain very gradually in order to make it easy for serious seekers to fathom the Laws of Creation.

The World of Matter is as nothing unless it is permeated by animistic substantiality. What we have now so far been considering, however, was only the uniting of animistic substantiality with the various species of matter. And it is this union alone which provides the fertile *soil* for the *spirit!* Animistic substantiality binds, unites and animates the World of Matter. The spirit, however, controls all matter and animistic substantiality. As soon as the spirit, i. e., all that is spiritual, descends for its development into this union, the latter quite naturally becomes subordinate to it, including animistic substantiality itself.

Spirituality is thus endowed with sovereignty in the most natural manner! It is sad if it misuses or abuses it! *The real equipment of the spirit* for its development in the World of Matter *consists of the radiations* just mentioned. The soil needed for its development has already been carefully prepared by the animistic substantiality before the spirit descends into it. The coverings automatically form around it as a protection, and it is the spirit's task to make proper use of this equipment, which is given to it for its well-being and ascent, not to be used in a harmful way and cause its downfall!

It is not difficult to understand that *that* species of matter which predominates in the covering of the spirit must also be decisive for the composition of its emanation. In this the radiation of the species of matter most strongly represented will naturally always predominate. And that which predominates will in turn exert the greatest influence upon the inside as well as upon the outside.

The composition of the radiation, however, is of much greater significance than mankind have been able to fathom up to now. Not the tenth part of its real purpose has been envisaged as yet!

The quality of the radiating halo decides the strength of the waves which have to absorb the vibrations from the radiating system of the entire Universe. The hearer and reader should not superficially pass over this thought, but penetrate deeply into it. Then he will suddenly see spread out before him all the nerve-strands of Creation, which he should learn to tap and to use.

He should picture to himself the Primordial Power poured radiatingly out upon the Work of Creation! It streams through Creation, through every part and every species. And every part and every species thereof will pass it on in modified form. Thus the varying consistencies of the different parts of Creation produce changes in the Primordial Radiation which also alter its colour!

Thus the whole of Creation presents a wonderful picture of the most glorious colour-radiations such as no painter could reproduce! And every part of Creation itself, every star, indeed every single object, be it ever so small or minute, resembles a finely-cut prism passing on every ray it receives in numberless different radiant hues!

These colours in turn give forth ringing sounds that blend into harmonious accords!

And confronting this magnificent realm of radiations stands the human spirit with its equipment of radiations derived from the various cloaks given to it! Until the generative power awakens the process is the same as with a babe. Through their radiations the material cloaks absorb only what they need in order to mature. When the generative power sets in, however, the spirit stands there fully equipped, the gates are then thrown open, and an immediate connection is established. It now comes into contact in many and varied ways with the powerful radiations of the great Universe.

As the human being, i. e., the spirit, develops and controls the colours of his own radiations so, as with a radio, he attunes his own vibrations to these same colours and absorbs those from the Universe. This receiving may also be called an attracting, or the Power of Attraction of Homogeneous Species. Regardless of what it is called the process as such remains the same! The colours merely indicate the species, and the species determine the colours.

This also contains the lost key to the *truly* royal art of astrology, the key to the knowledge of healing with herbs as well as to the much discussed art of magnetic healing, the key to the art of living and also to the step-ladder of spiritual ascent. For by this step-ladder, the so-called ladder leading to Heaven, is meant nothing but a simple *appliance* which one is to use. And the mesh of this network of radiations in Creation constitutes the rungs of this ladder. In it lies *everything,* all knowledge and the last secrets in Creation!

You who are seeking should grasp the mesh of this network of radiations! Consciously, but with a *good* volition, and humbly acknowledging your God Who gave this wonderful Creation which you may use to make you as happy as a child at play, providing you at last *honestly* wish to do so and throw off your presumptuous knowledge! The false burden must first be cast from your shoulders, from your spirit, before you can stand upright and free!

Absolute harmony must also prevail in the composition of the radiations of the human body in order to provide the spirit with the best means for its protection, development and advancement, such as are meant for it in the normal course of development in Creation. In particular it is through the choice of foods and manner of exercising the body, and in general through the whole conditions of living in many ways, that these radiations have become one-sidedly disordered, which calls for a readjustment if there is to be any possibility of ascent at all. *Today everything is diseased in this respect!* Nothing can be called healthy!

Man can now imagine what effect the choice of foods alone has upon this system of radiations! Through the choice of foods for his nourishment man may help his body to acquire the right balance by strengthening or perhaps weakening certain radiations or by displacing the predominant ones, whether favourable or hampering in their effect, so that *that* radiation takes the lead which is *favourable* to him and thereby also normal, for only what is favourable is the normal condition!

All this, however, cannot of itself bring about ascent. It only provides a healthy soil for the full activity of the spirit, *to the volition of which* it is reserved to determine whether the road is to lead upwards, to one side, or downwards.

However, the body as well as the spirit are bound to be strengthened as soon as one begins to pay attention to these things! At present almost everywhere grievous sins are committed in these matters through ignorance!

When I speak of gross matter and ethereal matter it should not be assumed that ethereal matter is a refinement of gross matter. Ethereal matter is a completely *different* species and of different consistency. It can never become gross matter, but it forms an intermediate step in the upward direction. Furthermore, both ethereal matter and gross matter represent *coverings* only, which must be united with animistic substantiality in order to be animated by it!

In dealing with this subject I must point out that those already mentioned by no means exhaust the number of divisions. Therefore I wish to state here and now that, besides conscious and unconscious spirituality and animistic substantiality, *currents of energy* of various kinds penetrate Creation, animating the different species of matter and contributing in different ways to their development and progress, each according to its nature.

These streams of energy again are only the next of the forces which adjoin the activity of spiritual and animistic substantiality or, more correctly, which precede the two latter and prepare the field of their activity. The further we analyse and go into the details the more will be revealed.

One follows the other in a continuous flow in order to create ever new gradations in unison with what already existed before. Everything, however, also has a logical explanation, because after the First Creation only what was consistent with logic could come into being. Nothing else exists! And this fact absolutely guarantees a complete solution and a clear survey. In my lectures I now offer the *key!* With it every hearer can then unravel the entire Creation for himself!

To give this all at once, however, would create a picture the vastness of which would only confuse mankind! But if I permit, as I have done hitherto, one thing to issue quietly from the other in the course of coming decades, it will be easy to follow and finally to survey everything calmly, consciously and quite clearly. It will be easy for him who wishes to follow me. In the beginning, before I touch all the finer points, I first want to explain the main pillars of Creation.

The hearer and reader will probably feel like a creature to whom a human skeleton is first shown, and then next to it a living man in the fullness of his vigour and activity. If it has no conception of man it would not recognise the skeleton in the living man. It might even aver that the two do not belong together or, indeed, that they are not the same.

And so it will be with those who do not calmly follow my explanations to the end! He who does not earnestly and persistently strive to understand from the beginning will not be able to grasp the entire Creation *when* I come to the last explanations. In these matters he *must* attempt to follow only step by step!

Since so far I have been obliged to speak in broad outline, I shall now *gradually* turn to the *new* things. Otherwise I would leave gaps! Moreover I have often been told that I offer only the gist of a subject, which is not so easily understandable to the majority. But I cannot act differently in order to say everything I wish to say. Otherwise I would only get one fourth of my task done, because a lifetime on earth would hardly suffice for more than that if one were to go into details. Others will come who will be able to write one or even several books about each one of my lectures. I cannot spend my time on it now!

Since, as I have mentioned before, ethereal matter is of a *different* nature from gross matter, this implies something I have not touched upon so far. In order not to cause confusion I have hitherto in many instances used popular terms, which I must now enlarge. This, for instance, includes the expression *"beyond time and space"*.

This always pointed to everything that is above the earthly. But in order to continue we must now say: Life in the World of Ethereal Matter "stands above the earthly conceptions of time and space", for in the World of Ethereal Matter there is also a conception of time and space, but of a *different nature* and adjusted to ethereal conditions. Indeed, the conception of time and space is to be found in the whole of Creation, but it is always bound up with the nature of the species concerned! Creation itself has its limits and that involves the idea of space even for Creation itself!

It is the same with all the basic laws which uniformly permeate the entire Creation – in their *effects* they are always influenced by the particular species in Creation and are subject to its peculiarities! Therefore the effects of a *certain law* must manifest themselves *differently* in the various sections of Creation! This has led to great misunderstandings, to contradictions and doubts in the uniformity of the Laws of Creation and of the Divine Will, and also to belief in arbitrary acts by the Creator. In reality, however, every such thing is caused through man's ignorance about Creation!

I shall postpone going into these subjects in detail until much later, as at present it would only divert the attention of the hearer and reader and confuse them. I will give this information as soon as it becomes necessary for a further understanding, so that no gaps will then remain!

THE ERROR ABOUT CLAIRVOYANCE

CLAIRVOYANCE! How much glory has been woven around it! What ridicule is heaped upon it by some, while others approach it with timid curiosity, and the rest in respectful silence! Those who have the gift strut about proudly like peacocks in a chicken yard! They imagine themselves to be endowed with Divine Grace, and in their conceited form of humility feel far superior to other people. They love to receive admiration for something which, in reality, is just as strange to them as to the many curious enquirers around them.

They hide their actual ignorance behind a meaningless smile, which is supposed to create the impression that they "know". However, it comes much nearer to an expression of helplessness, which has developed into a habit when they are confronted with questions which test their personal knowledge about this process.

In reality they know no more than the hammer and chisel which a sculptor uses to form some work of art! Here again it is only mankind themselves who wish to turn those endowed with the gift of clairvoyance into something different from that which they really are, thereby doing them great harm!

This is the unhealthy state of affairs that is to be found everywhere today! In most cases the "seeing" is *real* enough, but it is nothing special, nothing worthy of admiration let alone trepidation, because in reality it should be quite a natural thing. But it only remains natural as long as it comes about of its own accord, and is left quietly to develop without extraneous or personal aid. To give such *help* is just as damnable as to help forward physical death!

Seeing, however, only becomes of value when it is accompanied by real *knowledge*. Knowledge alone can provide a sound foundation for this natural ability, and thereby induce the *right* attitude and the right goal. That this is lacking in the majority of clairvoyant persons is readily evident by the manner in which they like to display an over-zealousness based on presumption and a barely-concealed sham knowledge!

It is just this imagined knowledge that not only prevents such people from advancing further, but which indeed becomes absolute perdition for them, because it directs their efforts on to wrong paths which lead *downwards* instead of upwards, without those persons who think they know more being aware of it! The best thing that can happen to some of these people is that their clairvoyant or clairaudient abilities should gradually diminish and disappear through some favourable circumstances, of which there are several kinds! That is salvation!

Let us now look more closely at these clairvoyant people and at the erroneous convictions they spread among men! They alone are responsible for this whole field being dragged into the mud and branded as false and unreliable up till now!

What these people see in the most favourable and advanced cases is the second step of the so-called beyond, if one wishes to divide the beyond into steps (and not to think in spheres), the plane of the Light being about the twentieth step, in order to obtain an approximate picture of the difference. Those, however, who are really able to see to the second step imagine they have achieved something stupendous, while those who can see only to the first step are in most cases even more conceited.

Now it should be realised that a person with the highest gifts can in reality see only as far as his own inner maturity will permit. *He is thereby bound by his own inner condition!* In the nature of things it is simply impossible for him to see, really to *see,* anything other than his own species, that is, within the region in which he could move about freely after his physical death. But no further, for in the moment when he would step over the boundary prescribed for him in the beyond by his own state of maturity he would immediately become unconscious of his environment! In any case he would not be able to cross this boundary of his own accord!

If after it had severed itself from its earthly body his soul were to be taken along by a dweller on the next higher step of the beyond, it would, on crossing the border to the next higher step, at once lose consciousness in his arms, that is, it would fall asleep. On being brought back he would only be able to remember as far as his own maturity permitted his soul to look about while it was still awake, despite its clairvoyant gifts. Thus no benefit would be derived, but his ethereal body would be harmed.

Whatever he imagines he sees in regions beyond, whether landscapes or persons, is never truly or actually experienced or personally seen by him! It is merely a question of *pictures* being shown to him and voices which he imagines he hears! They are never reality! These pictures appear so lifelike that he himself cannot distinguish between what is only shown to him and what he really experiences, because an act of will of a stronger spirit can create such lifelike pictures.

Thus it is that many clairvoyant and clairaudient people imagine they are on a much higher plane during their excursions into the beyond than is actually the case, and this leads to many errors!

Even if many think that they see or hear Christ this is a great delusion! Due to the great gulf caused by the lack of homogeneity, this would be utterly impossible because it would be contrary to the Creative Laws of the Divine Will! The Son of God cannot come to afternoon tea in a spiritist circle in order to confer some favour or distinction on the visitors, neither can great prophets nor higher spirits!

No human spirit still in the flesh is granted such a sure and firm intercourse with the beyond during his earth-life as to be able to see and hear everything there unveiled, and perhaps climb the steps as if there were nothing more to it! It is not quite so simple as all that despite its entire naturalness, for it remains subject to the immutable laws!

And if a clairvoyant or clairaudient person neglects his earthly task in his eagerness to penetrate into the beyond he loses more than he ever gains! As soon as the time arrives for him to continue his maturing in the beyond, he will take with him a gap in his experiencing which he can *only* fill *upon the earth!* Thus he cannot ascend any further and remains bound at a certain point! Before he can think about a further serious ascent he must go back to make up for what he missed. Everything about this is quite simple and natural, and always merely a necessary consequence of what lies behind, which can never, never be turned aside.

Every step in a man's existence requires to be really experienced in all seriousness, with all the receptive abilities trained upon what is happening at the time. To neglect to do this causes a disruption which makes itself felt with increasing acuteness the further he advances! Eventually it will lead him to a breakdown and finally to collapse, unless he returns in time and, through further experience, bridges the gap so that it is made firm and secure!

This applies to all happenings! Unfortunately, however, man has acquired the morbid habit of always reaching beyond himself, because he imagines himself to be more than he actually is!

VARIOUS ASPECTS OF CLAIRVOYANCE

FOR A LONG time I have hesitated to answer the various questions about clairvoyance, because any man who has read my Grail Message *aright* must be completely informed on the subject. Provided, of course, that he has not read the Message as he would a novel, merely to pass the time away, or from a prejudiced point of view, but has delved into it seriously and considered every sentence as important! Quite naturally he must *exert* himself to fathom every sentence, as well as its connection with the whole Message, because this is how it was intended from the very beginning!

The spirit must be awake in so doing! This is in order automatically to exclude superficial people!

I have repeatedly pointed out that a particular *species* can only be recognised by the *same species*. The species referred to here naturally mean species of Creation.

Considering them from below upwards there are the species of *gross matter*, of *ethereal matter*, of *animistic substantiality*, and of *spiritual substantiality*. Each of these species is again divided into many grades or steps, so that the danger easily arises of confusing the steps of fine gross matter with the steps of coarse ethereal matter. The transitions are quite imperceptible, and in their operation and effects are not really firmly connected but only interlinked with each other.

On each of these steps life manifests itself in a different manner. Man has a cloak of each species of Creation *below* the spiritual. The core itself is spiritual. Each cloak is equivalent to a body. Thus man is a spiritual core which, in developing self-consciousness, takes on human form! The more its development inclines towards the Light the more ideal it becomes, till it attains perfect beauty, but if development proceeds in a downward direction this has the opposite effect and produces grotesque deformities. In order to avoid any errors I wish especially to mention that the gross material covering or body is

494

not subject to this development. It must co-operate only for a short time, and on the gross material earth-plane can be subject only to very limited changes. Thus a human being on earth who is outwardly beautiful may be inwardly evil, and vice versa!

Man on earth, that is, man living in the World of Gross Matter, bears the cloaks of *all* the species in Creation *simultaneously*. Each cloak, each body of the different species, also has its own separate organs of sense. The gross material organs, for example, can function *only within the same species*, the gross material species. A more refined development under the most favourable conditions might perhaps provide the possibility to see finer gross matter to a certain degree.

This finer gross matter is called "astral" by the people who occupy themselves with it, a conception which is not even really understood by those who introduced the term, much less by those who repeat it!

I use this definition because it is already known. It should be realised that like other terms used by occult investigators, the word "astral" serves only as a sort of collective name for everything that is known and felt to exist, but which cannot rightly be understood, much less explained!

The mass of pseudo-knowledge that occultists have established up till now is nothing but a great, self-created labyrinth of ignorance, a rubbish heap of presumptions produced by intellectual thinking, which does not suffice for these things. Nevertheless I wish to retain this much-used term "astral"! That which men see and mean by "astral", however, does not even belong to the World of Ethereal Matter, but merely to fine gross matter!

The investigators, filled with human imaginings, have not yet stepped beyond the World of Gross Matter in these fields, but have remained in the *lowest species* of Subsequent Creation, and therefore make much ado with all kinds of "high-sounding" words! They do not even see with their ethereal eye, but merely with *a transitory perception* which functions between gross material and ethereal sight. This could be called transitory or intermediate sight!

When a human spirit lays aside its gross material body through physical death, naturally the gross material organs of sense are also laid aside, because these belong to the cloak concerned. Thus earthly death is nothing but the stripping off of the outermost cloak or shell which enabled man to see and work in the World of Gross Matter! Immediately after the human spirit has cast aside this cloak it stands in the so-called other world or, more precisely, in the planes of the World of Ethereal Matter. Here again it can only work with the same sense organs of the ethereal body, which has now become its outer shell or covering. Thus it sees with the eyes and hears with the ears, etc., of the ethereal body.

It is natural that on entering the Ethereal World the human spirit must first learn to make proper use of the sense organs of the ethereal cloak which has suddenly been forced into activity, as formerly it had to learn to use the organs of the physical body in the World of Gross Matter. As this different species of matter is not so ponderous as gross matter, this learning to use the organs in the proper way takes place more quickly and easily. And this applies to each of the other species also!

It is to help the spirit to become acclimatised to the various species that this transitory or intermediate sight has been given to it for use upon the intermediate planes. Thus through certain exertions and in special physical circumstances the gross material eye may be able to get a glimpse in advance of the intermediate plane between gross matter and ethereal matter, while the ethereal eye in the initial stages of its activity may also, upon looking back, reach in a half-seeing way this same plane where fine gross matter and coarse ethereal matter join hands.

This half-seeing affords a certain support to the human spirit on its transit so that it never need feel completely lost. This applies to *every* border between two different species. Waves of *animistic* power, the magnetic quality of which has a holding and binding effect, ensure that the two different species of matter cling to each other, and do not form a gulf because they cannot mix.

After the human spirit has passed through the different sections of the World of Ethereal Matter it also lays aside its ethereal body and then enters the *World of Animistic Substantiality*. Only the *animistic* body then remains with it as its outermost cloak, with the eyes and ears of which it must now see and hear, until the possibility also arises for it to lay aside this animistic cloak and enter the Spiritual Realm! It is only here that *it is really itself*, unveiled, and it must see, hear and speak, and so on, with its *spiritual* organs. Also its garments and everything round about it consist of *spiritual* substantiality!

These statements of mine must have the deep consideration of readers so that they can formulate a proper picture for themselves.

Materialisations of those who have left the earth are nothing more than the process by which those departed ones who are wearing the ethereal body can, with the help of a medium, envelop themselves with a cloak of fine gross matter. This is probably the only exception which allows earthly men of today *clearly* to see and grasp fine gross matter with their physical eyes and other physical senses respectively, because in this case a specially strong binding and densening of fine gross matter occurs through the unusual blood radiations of the medium. They can see it and feel it because, in spite of its fineness, the same kind of sense organs are still involved, that is, those of gross matter.

Man should therefore realise that gross matter can only be "perceived" by what is of gross matter, ethereal matter by what is of ethereal matter, animistic substantiality by what is of animistic substantiality, and spiritual substantiality by what is of spiritual substantiality. No intermingling is possible. By the above-mentioned "animistic substantiality" a very definite species of its own is meant. Divine substantiality and spiritual substantiality are again of entirely different species.

However, one thing is possible – a man on earth who is able to see with his physical or gross material eye may also, while still in the flesh, open his ethereal eye, at least from time to time; that is to say, not simultaneously, but each one after the other. When he sees with his ethereal eye his physical sight is wholly or in part inactive, and vice versa. He will never be able properly to see ethereal things with his physical eye, nor gross material things with his ethereal eye. That is impossible!

Statements to the contrary would only rest upon errors caused through ignorance about the Laws of Creation! They are delusions to which those people fall victim who assert that they can recognise ethereal matter with their physical eyes or spiritual substantiality with their ethereal eyes!

He who considers this truly and tries to picture the process clearly to himself will recognise what indescribable confusion must exist at present in judging clairvoyance, so that it is quite impossible to obtain reliable information on this subject as long as the laws governing it are not made known. This *cannot* be done through inspiration or through revelations in spiritist circles, because neither the "inspiring" souls nor the "revealing" spirits in the beyond can survey the whole question, for each one must always move within the limits set by his own state of maturity!

It is only possible to achieve an orderly explanation of the wonderful weaving of Subsequent Creation if there is an all-embracing *knowledge*. Otherwise it is impossible! In their well-known morbid faith in human "learnedness", however, men never recognise this, but take a hostile attitude to all such correction from the very beginning!

They prefer to go on strutting jauntily about in their pitiful seeking, with the result that they can never agree with others nor achieve any real success. If they would but *once* show enough greatness to conquer their conceit and *really* to apply themselves *in all seriousness* and without prejudice to the Grail Message as offering an explanation of the world, eliminating all faith in their own learnedness while studying it, then there would soon be revealed new aspects which, in logical sequence, would clarify every happening not understood, and in one broad sweep pave the way to what was hitherto unknown.

However, it is well known that obstinacy is *only one* of the unmistakable signs of real stupidity and narrow-mindedness. None of these people ever suspect that through such behaviour they brand themselves as utterly incapable, and that in the near future such a brand will burn them with shame and eliminate them because they can no longer hide or deny it!

In judging clairvoyance one should first of all know with which eye the clairvoyant sees in each particular case, to which plane his "seeing" belongs, and how far he is developed therein. Only then can further conclusions be drawn! The person who superintends such investigations would need to have an absolutely clear knowledge about the various steps within the different species, and also regarding the various effects and activities in them. The present time is suffering through this, because it is just those people who imagine that they know who do not understand anything at all about it!

It is deplorable to see the flood of publications in the form of magazines and books about all kinds of occult observations and experiments, and to read the more or less illogical and untenable efforts at explanation, which in most cases presumptuously receive the stamp of definite authority, while on the whole they not only remain divorced from the facts, but even give *the opposite*. And how infuriated and hostile the army of such wiseacres becomes when the structure of Subsequent Creation is put before them in simple sequence, which can indeed be easily examined, and yet without the exact knowledge of which they cannot understand anything at all! We must leave Primordial Creation out of the discussions altogether for the time being!

He who would judge or even condemn clairvoyants must know, really know, the entire Creation! As long as this is not the case he should keep silent about it! And similarly the zealous champions of the facts of clairvoyance should also never make assertions which cannot be substantiated without an exact knowledge of Creation!

So many calamitous errors are current about all the happenings outside the World of Gross Matter that it is now high time to bring some order and lawfulness into it!

Fortunately the time is not far off when a clean sweep will be made among the many and indeed ridiculous figures in the serious fields of occultism who, as everybody knows, vociferate the loudest and who are the most obtrusive with their theories! It is regrettable, however, that it is just these prattlers who have already led many seekers astray through their behaviour. They will be unable to avoid the responsibility for this; it will fall with dreadful force upon all those who have tried to deal with this most serious field in such a frivolous manner. But those who have gone astray and been seduced thereby will derive little benefit from it. Instead they must suffer for allowing themselves to be so easily influenced into adopting false opinions.

On the average it can be said that at the moment it is just in the occult fields that prattling has been given the beautiful name of "investigation", and that consequently most investigators are mere prattlers!

Thus among clairvoyants there are those who can see fine gross matter, those who can see ethereal matter, and those who can see animistic substantiality, each with the eyes belonging to the same species! A spiritual seeing, however, has been denied to men, unless it be to a specially "called one" who, for a certain purpose, is also endowed with the ability to open his spiritual eye while still here on earth!

But the countless present-day clairvoyants do *not* belong to these! Many of them can only recognise *one* of the various steps in the World of Ethereal Matter, and in time perhaps also several steps. Thus their ethereal eye is opened! It happens only rarely that the eye of the animistic body is also able to see!

If in connection with special earthly events, such as criminal or other cases, a clairvoyant human being is called in to solve the mystery, the interested person must know the following – that the clairvoyant sees with his ethereal eye, and is therefore *not* able to see the *gross material* happening as it actually took place. But every earthly happening has at the same time its ethereal counterpart, which is often the same as the earthly happening, or at least similar.

For instance, in the case of murder the clairvoyant will see the *ethereal* happening which occurs at the same time, not the actual earthly event which, in accordance with the existing mundane laws, is alone decisive for the exercise of jurisdiction. This ethereal happening, moreover, may vary in detail to a greater or lesser degree from the earthly event. Consequently it would be wrong hastily to condemn the clairvoyant for having failed or for a wrong seeing!

Let us consider a murder or a theft! The clairvoyant who has been asked to help solve the mystery will see partly on the astral plane and partly on the ethereal plane – astral, that is, in fine gross matter, showing the scene of the action; and ethereal, showing the action itself. To this must be added the fact that he can also see various thought-forms which came into being through the train of thought of the murderer as well as of the murdered person, or of the thief. How to distinguish between all these must be part of the knowledge of the person superintending the investigation. Only then will the result be correct! However, there is not yet a person proficient enough to conduct such an investigation!

Although it may sound grotesque, since it really has no relation to the matter, I would still like to give a secondary example by mentioning the work of a police dog, which is also used to help in the uncovering of crimes. Naturally the leader of a police dog must be thoroughly acquainted with the manner in which the dog works, and must closely and very actively collaborate with it, as is well known to those who are experts! We only need to think of this kind of work in a more noble form and we have the activity of the director of an investigation collaborating with a clairvoyant in the uncovering of a crime!

Here also the leader of the investigation is the one who actually does the work, observing and combining the various factors, and taking the greater part of the activity upon himself, whereas the clairvoyant merely remains the passive working assistant! Every judge must go through a protracted study of such activities before he should be allowed to deal with them! It is a far more difficult study than the study of the law!

IN ORDER to follow this explanation it is necessary to know that man on earth does not live in Primordial Creation but in a subsequent Creation. Primordial Creation consists solely of the *Spiritual Realm,* which exists quite independently and is known to men as Paradise. The Grail Castle stands at the summit of Paradise with the gate facing towards the Divine, which as such lies outside Creation.

Subsequent Creation, on the other hand, is the so-called "world", eternally rotating *below* Primordial Creation, the various solar systems of which are subject to evolution and dissolution, that is, they ripen, grow old and decay, because they were not created by Divinity directly like the Eternal Primordial Creation, Paradise.

Subsequent Creation came into existence through the volition of the Primordial Beings and is subject to the influence of the maturing human spirits, whose path of development leads through this Subsequent Creation. For this reason it also contains an imperfection not to be found in Primordial Creation, which is open to the direct influence of the Divine Holy Spirit.

To comfort the Primordial Beings, who were extremely perturbed about the ever-increasing and more noticeable imperfections in Subsequent Creation, a Voice from Divinity called: "Wait for Him Whom I have chosen ... to bring you help" – which to a certain extent is accurately transmitted from Primordial Creation in the legend of the Grail.

Now to the subject at hand! *Every* earthly action can only be considered as the outward expression of an inward process. By "inward process" is meant a spiritual intuitive volition. Each volition of the intuitive perception is a spiritual *action* which becomes decisive for every man's existence, because it brings about ascent or descent. In no case may it be put on the same level with thought volition!

Intuitive volition concerns the core of man proper, thought volition merely a weaker outer circle! It is not always necessary for either of these to become visible on earth, despite their unfailing effect. An earthly gross material action is not necessary for the creation of karma. But, on the other hand, there is no earthly gross material activity that does not have to be preceded by a thought volition or an intuitive volition. The earthly visible action, therefore, is dependent upon either a thought volition or an intuitive volition, but not vice versa.

However, what is really decisive for the existence of a human spirit, for his ascent or for his descent, is *most strongly* anchored in the *intuitive volition*, to which man pays the least attention, and yet from the absolute and never-failing effects of which there is no escape, also no mitigation or falsification! This alone contains the real "experiencing" of the human spirit, for *the intuitive volition is the sole lever for the release of the spiritual power waves* which rest in the work of the Creator, waiting only for an impulse from the intuitive volition of the human spirits, which they immediately put into effect with manifold strength! Up till now mankind have hardly paid any attention to this so important, even most important, process!

For this reason I shall again and again draw attention to an apparently simple but essential point which contains *everything:* The spiritual power permeating the work of Creation can make contact *only* with the *intuitive volition* of the human spirits, all else being excluded from making such contacts!

Even the thought volition can no longer make any such contact, much less any *products* of the thought volition. This fact excludes *every* hope that the *actual* principal power in Creation could ever be associated with some "invention"! This is irretrievably blocked! Man does not know this principal power nor its effects, although he stands in it!

What this or that thinker and inventor imagines as Primordial Power is not so! It is invariably a far inferior form of energy only, of which there can still be found many kinds with astonishing effects, but without mankind approaching even a step closer to the real power which the human spirit uses daily without being conscious of it. Unfortunately man trifles with it without being aware of the dreadful consequences of his boundless frivolity! And in his unbounded ignorance he always wantonly tries to cast the responsibility for the consequences upon God which, however, does not free him from the great guilt he has incurred by his refusal to gain knowledge!

I want to try and give a clear picture here! As an example, let us assume that a man *intuitively feels* envy! Usually it is said: "Envy arises within him!" At first this is a general intuitive feeling, of which quite often the human spirit is not even clearly conscious. This intuitive perception, however, which as yet is not clad in definite thoughts, that is, which as yet has not "risen" to the brain, carries within it *the key* which *alone* can establish contact with the *"Living Power"*, can build a bridge to it.

Immediately this is done, as much of the "Living Power" resting in Creation passes into this particular intuitive perception as it is capable of absorbing, this in each case depending on the strength of the perception. Only *through this* is the *human* or *"spiritualised"* intuitive perception called to life within itself, thus receiving an enormous capacity to generate (not to create) in the Ethereal World. This makes man lord among all creatures, the highest of all creatures in Creation! This process also permits him to exert an immense influence upon the entire *Subsequent Creation*, thereby ... investing him with personal responsibility which no other creature besides him can have in Subsequent Creation, because only man possesses the ability which is decisive in this matter and which rests in the very nature of the *spirit!*

And only *he* alone in the entire Subsequent Creation bears spirit in his innermost core, and *as such* he alone receives connection with the *Supreme Living Power* resting in Subsequent Creation! The Primordial Beings in Paradise are of a *different* species of spirit to the world wanderers, the so-called earth-men, and their capacity for connection is therefore directed towards another, a higher and far stronger wave of power. This they use consciously, being naturally able to create with it things quite different to those of the world wanderers to whom the earth-men belong. The highest wave of power of the earth-men is but a gradation of the power resting in Primordial Creation, just as they themselves are but a gradation of the Primordial Beings!

The main lack in human knowledge so far is the realisation of the many gradations which become ever weaker as they descend from Primordial Creation, and the recognition that men themselves belong to these *gradations* only. Once this understanding has really penetrated, their hitherto presumptuous attitude will fall away and clear the path for ascent!

The stupid vaingloriousness exhibited by men in claiming supremacy, even of carrying Divinity within themselves, will suffer an ignominious collapse, and finally there will only remain a liberating shame. The Primordial Beings, who stand so much higher and who are of much greater value, are not possess-

503

ed of such conceit. They only smile indulgently at the straying earthworms, just as many parents smile at the fantastic chatter of their children!

But let us return to the intuitive perception! A man's intuitive perception which has thus been strengthened now, in a further gradation, immediately and automatically produces a form which exactly embodies *the nature* of the intuition, in this case of envy. In the beginning the form stands within its creator and later beside him, connected to him by a cord through which it receives nourishment. At the same time, however, in obedience to the Law of the Attraction of Homogeneous Species, it immediately and automatically makes contact with the power-centre of the same species of forms and receives strong reinforcements therefrom. Together with the young form, these then fashion the ethereal environment of the person concerned.

Meanwhile this intuitive perception rises higher and finally reaches the brain, exciting *thoughts* of a like nature which set themselves a very definite aim. Thus the thoughts become channels or roads upon which these forms drift towards a very definite goal, there to do harm if they find the proper soil.

However, if the man who is to be the target of these forms is only pure within, that is, if he has a pure volition, he offers no point of attack for these forms, no anchorage! Still, this does not mean that they are rendered harmless again! Instead they continue to wander about singly, or unite themselves with their homogeneous species in places of assembly which one may well call "planes", because they are subject to the law of their spiritual gravity and therefore must form *definite* planes which can only admit and hold the same species.

Thus they remain an absolute danger to all those human spirits whose volition to do what is good is not of sufficient strength and purity! Finally they also bring destruction upon their authors, who constantly remain in touch with them, and who through the cord of nourishment continually permit new envy-energy to flow back to them, which the forms themselves receive from the power-centres.

This makes it difficult for such a creator to indulge again in purer intuitions, because he remains very badly handicapped by the return flow of envy-energies, which continually tear him away from it. He is forced to expend far greater efforts for his ascent than a human spirit not so hampered. And it is only through a constantly pure volition that such a nourishing-cord of evil gradually decays, until it finally shrivels up and falls feebly away.

This means the liberation of the author of such evil, provided that his form has meanwhile done no harm; but if it has done some harm *new* ties are *then* immediately formed which must also be redeemed!

To effect the redemption of such threads it is absolutely necessary that the author should again cross the path, either on this earth or in the beyond, of any person harmed by the evil, so that recognition and forgiveness can be obtained. Consequently the ascent of the author of such forms cannot take place before those persons who have suffered injury have made their ascent. The connecting thread or threads of fate hold him back until redemption has been effected through compensation and forgiveness.

But this is not all! This intuitive volition, under the strengthening influence of the "Living Power", has a far greater effect, for it not only populates the Ethereal World, but also influences the World of Gross Matter, either building up or destroying!

This should at last make man recognise the folly which he has already perpetrated, instead of fulfilling the duties ordained through the abilities of his spirit for the benefit of Subsequent Creation and of all creatures. Man often asks why there should be such a conflict in nature, and yet what is of animistic substantiality adjusts itself in Subsequent Creation ... to the nature of man! With the exception of the Primordial Elemental Beings!

But let us continue! The creations of the intuitive volition of the human spirit, the forms mentioned above, do not cease to exist when detached from their author, but continue to exist *independently* as long as they receive nourishment from human spirits who by nature are like-minded! It need not be the author himself. They seek an opportunity to attach themselves to this or that person who is open to their influence, or even to those whose power of resistance is weak. If evil they are *the demons* born of envy, hatred and all that is similar. If good they are benevolent beings which only lovingly make peace and further ascent!

With all these processes a visible earthly action by a human being is not in the least necessary; it only adds further chains or threads which must be redeemed on the gross material plane, and would require a reincarnation if redemption cannot take place in one life on earth.

These forms of the human intuitive volition have power *within themselves* because they come into being through *spiritual* volition in combination with the "neutral principal power" and, what is most important, because *thereby* during the process of their formation they also absorb *animistic substantiality**, that is, *that* species from which gnomes and their like develop.

The volition of an animal cannot achieve this because the animal soul is not of a spiritual nature, but only animistic. Thus this is a process which *only* takes place with the forms of the human intuitive volition and which must therefore bring great blessings if the volition is *good,* but incalculable mischief if the volition is evil, because the animistic core of such forms carries its *own motive power,* and is thus able to influence all that is gross material. And thereby the responsibility of the human spirit becomes enormous! According to its nature its intuitive volition creates *benevolent entities* as well as *demons!*

Both are merely the products of man's spiritual abilities in Subsequent Creation. Their cores, self-motivated and thus unpredictable in their influence, *do not* originate in *that part of Animistic Substantiality which has the capacity to will,* and from which the animal souls come, but issue from *a gradation therein which does not possess the personal ability to will.* In the World of Animistic Substantiality, as well as in the Spiritual Sphere above it, there are also many gradations and special species, about which I shall have to speak separately.

Let me add as a further explanation that animistic substantiality *also* has contact with a living power resting in Creation which, however, is not the same as the Living Power with which the volition of the human spirit is connected, but a gradation of it.

It is just these possibilities and impossibilities of combination which are the strictest maintainers of order in Subsequent Creation and bring about a firm, immutable system in all evolution and dissolution!

So far-reaching, then, is the activity of the human spirit! Now look closely at men of the present day, and you can imagine what mischief they have already done, especially when you consider the further consequences of the activity of these living forms which are let loose upon all creatures! These resemble a stone which, once it has left the hand, is no longer subject to the control and will of the thrower!

Besides these forms, the far-reaching activity and influence of which it would take a whole book to describe, there is another species which is next to and closely connected with these, but forming a *weaker* section. Yet it is still

* See Appendix.

dangerous enough to molest many people, to hinder them and even cause them to fall! These are the forms of thoughts, that is to say, the thought-forms or phantoms.

The volition of the thoughts, being the product of the earthly brain, in contrast to the volition of the intuitive perception, does not have the ability to make direct contact with the neutral principal power resting in Creation. Therefore these forms lack the self-acting core of the intuitive forms, which latter we might call "animistic *shadows* of the soul". Thought-forms remain absolutely dependent upon their creator, with whom they are connected in a similar way as the forms of the intuitive volition, that is, through a cord of nourishment which simultaneously constitutes the road for the returning reciprocal actions. I have already spoken about this species in the lecture on "Thought-forms", and therefore I need not repeat it here.

Thought-forms have the weakest effect according to the Law of Reciprocal Action. Despite this they still work dangerously enough, and can not only bring about the doom of individual human spirits, but even that of great masses! They can also contribute to the devastation of whole parts of the world as soon as they are over-nourished and over-cultivated by men, thus receiving undreamt of power, as has happened in the last few thousand years.

Thus the whole of this evil has been brought about by men *alone*, due to their uncontrolled and false intuitive volition and thought volition, as well as through their levity in these matters!

These two realms, the realm of the forms of the human intuitive volition and the realm of the forms of the human thought volition, in which naturally real human spirits are also forced to live, alone formed the field of action and the range of vision of the greatest "magicians" and "masters" of all time, who became entangled in them and who finally are retained there when they pass over. And what do we find today?

The "great masters of occultism", the "enlightened ones" of so many different sects and lodges ... are no better off! They are masters only in *these* realms! They live amid forms of their own devising, and only *there* can they be "masters", but not in *the real life of the beyond!* Their power and mastership never extend so far!

Pitiable people, regardless of whether they have followed the black or the white art, according to their evil or good volition ... they imagined and still believe themselves mighty in their spiritual power, whereas in reality they are less than a man *ignorant* in these matters! In his childlike simplicity such a man stands far *above* these actually low fields of activity of such "ignorant" spiritual princes, that is, he stands *higher* spiritually than they do!

All would be well if the retroactive effects of the work of such eminent ones could fall back upon themselves *only,* but such "masters" through their efforts and activities agitate these nether regions, which are of no particular importance in themselves, stirring them up unnecessarily and thereby increasing their strength, so that they become a danger to all whose resistance is weak! For others, happily, they hold no danger, because a harmless human spirit, one who enjoys his life like a child, rises without any difficulty *above* these nether regions, into which the pseudo-scientists burrow and probe, finally being retained there by the forms and images which they themselves have helped to strengthen!

Although this should all be taken seriously, yet seen from above it makes an unspeakably ridiculous and sad impression, entirely unworthy of the human spirit! Tricked out with ridiculous frippery and puffed up with false conceit, they creep and crawl about in this realm, busily endeavouring to animate it! A shadow-land in the truest sense, an entire world of *sham,* which becomes capable of deception with everything possible and impossible! And he who first conjured it into existence can in the end no longer cast it out, but must succumb to it!

Many eagerly dig and delve into these nether regions, priding themselves on the tremendous height they have reached thereby! A clear and simple human spirit, however, can pass through these nether regions without heed or further ado – there is no need to be detained there in any way!

What else shall I say about these "great ones"? Not one of them would listen to it, for in their sham world they can pretend for a time to be what, in the real existence of the *living spirit,* they could never hope to become, for there they must "serve", and their desire to be master would quickly cease. For this reason many fight against it, because much is taken from them through the Truth! And they lack the courage to bear this! Who likes to have all that his imagination and vanity have created pulled down? He would indeed have to be a *right* and really *great man!* Such a person would never have fallen into these snares laid by vanity!

But there is one distressing feature – how many or, better said, how few human beings are so clear and firm within themselves, how few still command such a childlike, gay simplicity that they could *safely* traverse these planes, which are so wantonly created and constantly reinforced by man's volition? For all others, however, a continually increasing danger is evoked!

If only men could at last become *really seeing* in these things, how much harm could be avoided! A purer intuitive perception and pure thinking on the part of every individual would soon so weaken the dark and dismal planes of the beyond that even the struggling human spirits retained there would be released the sooner, because they could more easily free themselves from their weakening surroundings!

What holds true for many great "masters" here on earth also holds true for the human spirits in the beyond. They experience everything as being quite *genuine* in the various environments, in the forms and images, regardless of whether it be in the lower or gloomier regions or in the already higher ethereal and more friendly regions ... fear as well as joy, despair and also liberating release ... and yet they are not in the realm of real life at all, but *only they themselves are really alive!* All else, their quite diversified and changing surroundings, can only exist through them and through those on earth who think as they do!

Even hell itself is but a product of the human spirits! Hell exists, it is true, and it also holds serious dangers and causes terrible suffering, but it is completely dependent on the volition of all those human beings whose intuitive perceptions supply hell with strength to exist from the neutral Divine Power which rests in Creation for the use of human spirits. Thus hell is not a Divine institution, but the work of man!

He who recognises *this* aright, and then consciously makes use of this knowledge, will help many, and he himself will also ascend more easily towards the Light, *in which alone lies all real Life!*

If men would only just open themselves once *so far* as to be able to perceive what a treasure rests in Creation for them! A treasure which should be discovered and unearthed by every human spirit, which means that *it should be used consciously* – the neutral principal power that I have so often mentioned! It makes no distinction between good or evil, but stands outside these conceptions. It simply is *"Living Power"*!

Every intuitive volition of a human being is *the equivalent of a key* to this treasure chamber and makes contact with this sublime power, the good volitions as well as the evil volitions. Both are reinforced and animated by this "power" because it immediately reacts upon the intuitive volition of the human spirit, but *only* upon this, and upon nothing else. Man determines the *nature* of the volition, this being in his hand alone. The power as such brings neither good nor evil, but is simply "power", and it vitalises what man has willed.

It is important, however, to know that man does not bear this life-giving power within himself, *but only possesses the key to it in the ability of his intuitive perception.* Thus he is the steward of this creative forming power which works in accordance with his volition! For this reason he has to render account of his stewardship which he exercises every hour. But he unconsciously plays with fire in these matters like an ignorant child, and therefore causes great damage, as a child is apt to do! Yet he need not be so ignorant! That is *his* fault alone! All the prophets and finally the Son of God Himself tried in their parables and teachings to enlighten men on this point, to show the way they should take, and *how* they should intuitively perceive, think and act in order to tread the *right path!*

But it was in vain! Men continued to play with this tremendous power entrusted to them only in accordance with *their* opinions, without listening to the warnings and advice from the Light! Ultimately, therefore, they will bring about the collapse, the destruction of their works and also of themselves! For this power works in a completely neutral manner, strengthening the good as well as the evil volitions of the human spirit, and thus will not hesitate coldly to wreck the car and its driver, just as happens with any motor vehicle that is badly driven!

Surely the picture has now been made clear enough! Through their volition and thoughts men direct the destiny of the entire Subsequent Creation as well as their own, without knowing anything about it! They further either progress or decadence, they can achieve either development in the fullest harmony or *that* wild confusion which *now* reigns! Instead of building up in a reasonable manner they waste their time and energy unnecessarily in a great deal of petty trifling!

Intelligent people now call this punishment and judgment, which is correct in a certain sense. Yet it is men *themselves* who have forcibly brought about everything that must now happen!

Often there have been thinkers and observers who already surmised all 'this, but they erred when they falsely assumed that in its manifestation this power of the human spirit is a sign of personal divinity. This is an error which only originates through a one-sided judging by appearances. The human spirit is neither God nor Divine! Such wiseacres see only the external shell and not the core of the happening! They confuse the effect with the cause!

Unfortunately many false doctrines and much presumption originated from this inadequacy. Therefore let me stress once more: The Divine Power which continually permeates and rests in Creation is *only lent* to all human spirits. As they *use* it they can *guide* it, but they do not have it within themselves, *nor is it their own!* Divinity alone possesses this power, but uses it only for the good, because Divinity does not know Darkness at all. The human spirits to whom it is lent, however, only dig their own grave with it!

Therefore I once more adjure all men: Keep the hearth of your volition and your thoughts pure, and you will become peacemakers and be happy! Then at last Subsequent Creation will begin to resemble Primordial Creation, where all is Light and Joy! All this lies in the hands of man, in the capacity of every self-conscious human spirit, who will no longer remain a stranger in this Subsequent Creation.

Many of my readers and hearers will quietly wish that I should give some suitable picture of such a happening in addition to my explanations, a living illustration that would help them to understand better. Others again might think this disturbing. There may also be some who think that I would thereby weaken the seriousness of what has been said, because the reproduction of a living happening in these planes might easily be construed as a flight of fancy or clairvoyance. I already heard similar remarks when I published my lectures "The Holy Grail" and "Lucifer". Those who investigate deeply, however, and whose spiritual ears are not closed, will understand the reason which prompts me. And the picture I wish to give about it is for these persons alone, for they will know that it is neither fantasy nor clairvoyance, but more!

Therefore let us take an example! A mother has taken her life by drowning herself, and in so doing has carried her two-year-old child to its earthly death along with her! Upon awakening in the beyond she finds herself sinking in a dismal, muddy expanse of water, for the last terrible moment of the soul has come to life in the Ethereal World. This is the place where all those who belong to the same species suffer continual torment with her in a similar way. She has the child in her arms, and it clings to its mother in deadly terror, even though she had flung it into the water *before* throwing herself in!

511

Depending on her psychic condition, she has to live through these agonising moments for a shorter or longer period, that is, she must always be on the verge of drowning but never accomplishing it, never losing consciousness! It may take decades and even longer before a genuine cry for help, uttered in pure humility, awakens in her soul! This is not so easily done, for round about her there is only what is of the same species, but no light. She hears only ghastly cursing, maledictions and coarse language, and sees nothing but the most callous brutality!

First of all there may gradually awaken within her the urge at least to protect her child from this, or to remove it from such dreadful surroundings, with their perpetual danger and torment! Trembling with fear, while still on the verge of drowning, she therefore holds her child above the stinking, slimy surface, while many another being in the vicinity clings to her and tries to drag her down into the depths!

This heavy, leaden-coloured water is composed of the thoughts of those who have committed suicide by drowning, thoughts which have not yet taken precise shape but which have come to life ethereally, as well as of the thoughts of those still on earth who harbour similar ideas. These thoughts have contact with one another and, in the process of mutual attraction, constantly reinforce each other, whereby the torment is endlessly renewed. But these waters would have to dry up if, instead of receiving reinforcements of the same nature, waves of fresh, happy and joyful thoughts would stream forth from the earth!

Grief over the child, which the maternal instinct might gradually fan into apprehensive and fearful love, receives enough strength to form the first step of salvation towards the stairway leading the mother out of the torments, which she herself created through bringing her life on earth to a premature end! In trying to save the child from the horror into which she herself has plunged it, she nourishes within herself more noble qualities which can ultimately lift her into the next and less dismal environment!

The child in her arms, however, is not in reality the living soul of the child she murdered when she dragged it into the water with herself. No such injustice would be possible! In most cases the *living* soul of the child is merrily gambolling about in sunny meadows, whereas the child in the arms of the struggling mother is only ... a phantom, a living form of the intuitive perception of the murderess and also ... of the intuitive perception of the child! This may be a guilt-form, arising perhaps from the pressure of a guilty conscience, or it may be a desperation-form, a hatred-form, a love-form, but whichever it is the mother imagines it to be the living child itself, because the form exactly resembles the child, also moves like it, cries like it, etc! I do not wish to go into such details nor into their many variations!

It would be possible to describe numberless happenings, the nature of which is always bound precisely to the deeds which preceded them.

But I wish to mention one more example as to how this world is interlocked with the beyond!

Take the case of a woman or girl who, contrary to her wishes, has become pregnant and who has, as unfortunately very often happens, done something against it. Even if in specially favourable cases all went well without any *bodily* harm ensuing, it is not thereby simultaneously redeemed! The Ethereal World, as the environment in which the soul lives after physical death, records everything exactly and impartially.

From the moment it happened an ethereal body of the growing child has fastened itself to the ethereal neck of the unnatural mother, where it remains clinging until the deed is atoned for. Naturally the woman or girl in question does not notice this as long as she lives in her physical body here on earth. She may perhaps have an uneasy feeling now and then as a reaction, for the small ethereal body is as light as a feather in comparison with the physical body, and today most girls are much too obtuse to be able to feel this little burden! This dullness, however, is not in the least a sign of progress, nor of robust health, but indicates retrogression; it is a sign of being psychically buried!

But at the moment of physical death the weight and density of the clinging child's body become the *same in nature* as that of the ethereal body of the mother (which has now left its earthly vessel), and it is thus a distinct burden! It will immediately cause as much discomfort to the ethereal body of the mother as would a child's physical body when clinging round her neck here on earth. Depending on the nature of the happening which preceded this, it may well increase to a breath-taking agony! The mother must drag the child's body around with her in the beyond, and she does not become free of it until mother love awakens within her and, setting aside her own comfort, she faithfully tries to labour and provide for the relief and care of the little body. Very often a long and thorny path has to be traversed to reach that point!

These happenings are naturally not without a certain tragicomic aspect! One need only imagine a man from whom the partition between this world and the beyond has been removed, entering a family gathering or a party! Perhaps there is a group of ladies sitting there in lively conversation. One of the women or "virgins", in a tone of moral indignation, voices a disdainful opinion of her fellow-men, and all the while the visitor sees one or even several little children's bodies hanging from the neck of this proud and zealous disclaimer! Not only that, but *every* other person also has the works of his real volition hanging on to him, distinctly visible, and often in the most grotesque contrast to his words, to how he wishes to appear and maintain himself before the world!

Many a judge sitting before the person on whom he passes sentence has a much greater burden of sin on his shoulders than the delinquent! How quickly his few years on earth will be over! Then he will stand before *his* Judge where other laws are valid! What then?

Unhappily in most cases man is easily able to deceive the Gross Material World! In the Ethereal World, however, this is impossible! Fortunately there a man *must* really reap what he has sown! Therefore no one need despair if here on earth injustice temporarily has the upper hand! Not one single evil thought will remain unexpiated, even when it has not developed into a physical deed!

THE EFFORTS of the occult schools as well as of those aiming to reform our way of living have set a high goal for themselves, the attainment of which will mean a further epoch in the development of humanity. The time when these valuable *aims* will be fulfilled will surely come, but the present rapidly growing efforts in this direction are only part of the process of fermentation of this new period.

While with the best of intentions the leaders of occult schools have taken an entirely wrong road in this field which is unknown to them, thereby accomplishing nothing but clearing the road to darkness and exposing mankind to increased dangers from the beyond, the so-called health reformers in their efforts to reach their valuable goal far exceed what is possible in the *present time!*

The activities of both parties must be directed differently! Fundamentally the psychic exercises must be carried out on a *higher* level than has been the practice so far. In these matters an entirely different road must be taken in order to reach the summit. The present road only leads into the undergrowth of the beyond, in which the majority of the followers are totally enveloped in darkness and dragged down!

The *right* way must *lead upwards from the very start,* and must not first lose itself in a lower environment and perhaps in an environment on the same level. These two roads are not in any way similar, but entirely different basically. The right way immediately uplifts the inner man, and thus goes upward from the very beginning, without first making contact with the ethereal environment on its own level, much less with one that is lower; for this is not necessary, as normally there should only be a striving upwards from the earth. Therefore let me again warn you seriously against all spiritual acrobatics!

During its life on earth the spirit positively needs a strong and healthy body in a normal physical condition, in order *completely* to fulfil the purpose of its existence. If the condition of the body is disturbed, this derangement upsets the absolutely necessary harmony between body and spirit. Only *such complete harmony* brings about a healthy and strong development of the spirit, preventing the possibility of any morbid eccentricity!

Due to its normal condition a healthy and unrestrained body will always quite naturally harmonise with the spirit, thereby providing it with a firm foundation in the World of Matter. The spirit does not stand in the World of Matter without a purpose, and therefore a healthy body will give it the best help wholly to fulfil the purpose of developing itself and simultaneously furthering Creation.

Each body creates certain definite radiations which are absolutely essential to the spirit for its work in the World of Matter. Foremost of these is the so mysterious generative power, which is quite independent of sexual instinct. If the harmony between body and spirit is disturbed, the power of this penetrating radiation and emanation is drawn off in another direction, and thus weakened for its real purpose.

This hinders or paralyses the fulfilment of the purpose of the spirit during its existence in the World of Matter, and consequently it cannot achieve normal development either. At some later point in its efforts to ascend it must therefore irrevocably sink back exhausted, and in the natural course of events will have to repeat a great part of its development. For what it misses in the World of Gross Matter it cannot make up in the Ethereal World, because there it does not have the radiations of its physical body at its disposal. It must go back in order to fill this gap!

Such a clear objectivity is to be found in these events, such naturalness and simplicity, that it just cannot be any different! Every child will understand this and take it for granted once it has grasped the basic laws aright! It will require a whole series of lectures to bring the vast Creation so close to mankind that they can survey all the great web of events and trace all the accompanying threads and influences in this incomparably glorious lawfulness.

There are many ways in which this generative power so necessary for the spirit in the World of Matter can be diverted; through over-indulgence in sexual intercourse, or even merely by stimulating the desire for it; also through occult training or wrong psychic exercises in which the spirit forcibly appropriates this power of the mature body, only to dissipate it in this false and unnecessary activity. In both cases it is a wrong application, which will also gradually bring in its train a weakening of the physical body!

In turn the weakened body can then no longer send forth such strong radiations as are really needed by the spirit, and thus each becomes more and more ill through the other. This produces a one-sidedness which is *always* detrimental to the right goal and therefore harmful. Here I do not wish to deal with other by-paths on which the spirit also absorbs too much of the generative power for wrong purposes, such as through the reading of books which conjure up a false world in the imagination, and so on, as a result of which there is not enough power left for the main purpose.

In all these cases the spirit arrives in the Ethereal World still *immature* and also takes a *weak* ethereal body along with it. The consequences of such earthly sins are so decisive for his entire existence that every man must atone for them heavily in manifold ways! Such a delay and such false actions during his time on earth cling to a man, hinder him and become ever heavier until, as already mentioned, at one point in his ascent he can continue no further and sinks back to the place where he began his wrongdoing! This is the border-line up to which he still possessed his harmony.

The strength a spirit has cultivated through occult training at the cost of the body is also only *apparent*. The spirit then is actually *not strong,* but like a hot-house plant which can hardly withstand a wind, much less a storm! Such a spirit is *sick,* and not advanced. Its condition resembles that of artificially produced fever. Periodically the fever patient may have considerable strength at his command, only to relapse into even greater weakness. What lasts only seconds or minutes in the case of a fever patient, lasts decades or centuries in the case of the spirit. The moment arrives when all this comes home to it bitterly!

Harmony is the only right thing in every case! And harmony is only to be found in the *middle way!* When the beauty and power of harmony are so much extolled, why is it not approved in these matters and why is everything done to destroy it?

The way all occult training has been carried out so far is wrong, even though the goal is a high and necessary one!

The case is quite different with the leaders and adherents of the movements aimed at reforming our way of living. Although they are on the right road, they wish to accomplish already *today what* will *only* be proper for *future* generations, and for this reason they are at present no less dangerous in their ultimate influence on most human beings. *The necessary transition is lacking!* The time to begin is now at hand, but one must not jump into it with both feet without further ado! Man must be *gradually* led to accept it! Decades do not suffice for this! As practised today, the rapidity of the transition actually causes a weakening of the body, even if it appears to be in good health. And a body weakened in this way will never be able to regain its vigour!

Vegetarianism! It is quite true that it brings about a refinement of the human body, ennobling it and also strengthening it and helping it towards a good recovery! The spirit is also still further uplifted thereby. *But all this is not meant to be adopted immediately by mankind of the present day!* In all these efforts and struggles circumspect leadership is lacking!

The human body of today should on no account be suddenly subjected to a vegetarian diet, as is so often tried! It is quite good when used temporarily, and perhaps even for years at a time in the case of sick people; indeed, it may even be necessary in order to cure some ailment, or to assist in one-sidedly strengthening some physical organ, but it must not be lasting. If his body is to maintain its full vigour the patient must gradually return to the diet to which he is so much accustomed today. The appearance of well-being is deceptive!

Certainly it is very beneficial if healthy people also adopt a strict vegetarian diet for a time. Without doubt they will feel well and will also feel a free soaring upward of the spirit. This, however, is the result of the *change,* just as every change is refreshing, spiritually as well!

If, however, they suddenly start this one-sided diet on a permanent basis, they will not notice that they are actually becoming weaker and much more sensitive over many things. In most cases the attributes of composure and equanimity do not indicate strength, but a definite kind of weakness. This shows itself in an agreeable manner and has nothing depressing about it, because it does not originate from any disease!

This equanimity resembles the equanimity of healthy *old age* where only the body is becoming weaker. At least it resembles this sort of weakness much more than the weakness resulting from illness! Suddenly deprived of what it has been accustomed to for thousands of years, the body cannot produce the generative power the spirit needs for the full accomplishment of its purpose in the World of Matter.

Many confirmed vegetarians notice this in a slight abatement of their sexual

518

instinct, which they joyfully acclaim as progress. But this is by no means a sign that their spirit has been ennobled through vegetarian diet, only that their generative power has been *lowered*, which must subsequently lessen their spiritual capacity to soar upwards in the World of Matter.

The errors about this continue to grow, because man almost invariably sees only what is closest to him. Certainly it is to be welcomed, and may be regarded as a measure of progress, if by ennobling the spirit the baser sexual instinct is greatly moderated compared with what it is today! It is also true that eating meat aggravates sexual desire, but in these matters we must not judge by mankind of today, for in their case the sexual instinct has been *cultivated one-sidedly and abnormally!* It is altogether unnatural today. However, this cannot be attributed to the enjoyment of meat alone!

The moderation of the sexual instinct is by no means dependent on the lessening of the generative power. On the contrary, the latter is able to help the human spirit *advance,* and *liberate* it from its dependence upon the coarse instinct, which is so marked today. In fact, the generative power is the *best means* to accomplish this!

The first step in the transition is to restrict oneself only to *white meat* such as poultry, veal, lamb, and so on, together with an increased amount of vegetable food.

"Do not neglect your body!" I would call out as a warning to the one party! And "Think of your spirit!" I would say to the other party! The right way will then grow out of the present-day confusion!

HEALING BY MAGNETISM

HEALING by magnetism is taking a leading role in the further development of the human race.

When I speak of magnetopaths I only mean serious practitioners who are prepared to help mankind with an honest volition. Not the group of those who, with a low average radiation, make many words and mysterious gestures, and imagine that they are accomplishing great things!

There is a nervous disquiet in the ranks of those courageous pioneers who for many years and in numerous cases have brought to their fellow-men the best earthly gift they could bring – recovery from many an illness through the so-called magnetism of their bodies, or through the transmission of similar currents from the Ethereal World, the beyond!

Unfortunately there are continued and repeated attempts to represent the whole class of magnetopaths as inferior, if not even worse, to hinder them and to suppress them! With much clamour their opponents magnify out of all proportion the individual exceptions where a low desire for money-making created dishonest characters, or where fraudulent intentions were the basis from the beginning, but in those cases this beautiful gift did not even exist with those who "practised" it!

Just look around you! Where do you *not* find impostors and swindlers? You will find them everywhere – even more so in other vocations! For this reason the *deliberate* injustice characterising such enmity immediately makes itself clear to everyone!

But envy, and still more fear, causes the number of opponents and enemies to increase. Naturally *this* art of healing *cannot* be acquired at beer and wine orgies!

It demands serious and, above all, abstemious and healthy human beings!

This perhaps is the deepest root of all the envy, of which the great animosity is a consequence, for today such conditions are not so easily fulfilled. And what has once been neglected in this respect cannot be retrieved!

Besides, the *genuine*, strong healing power cannot be acquired by learning. It is a gift, which ordained the one thus gifted as a "called one"!

He who wishes to suppress such people proves that he is *not* interested in the welfare of humanity, much less has it in his heart. He thereby burdens himself with a guilt which must become fatal to him!

The little group of courageous pioneers need have no fear, for the obstacles are only temporary! In truth they are a sure sign of an early, joyful and proud ascent!

LIVE IN THE PRESENT!

IF YOU study mankind you will find that they fall into different groups. There is one group which lives exclusively in the past. That is to say, they begin to understand an event only when it is past! As a result they can neither truly rejoice about something that is happening, nor intuitively perceive its full gravity. Only afterwards do they begin to talk about it, to enthuse about it, or to feel regret. And while constantly speaking of the past, either feeling happy about it or lamenting it, they continually overlook present events. Such must first become old and past before they begin to value them!

Again, there is another group which lives in the future! They set all their wishes and hopes on the future, and thereby forget that the present has so much to offer them. They also forget to bestir themselves sufficiently to enable many of their dreams about the future to become reality!

Both groups, to which the majority of men belong, have not, so to speak, really lived on earth at all; they just fritter away their time!

Then there will be men who, on hearing the call to "live in the present", will imagine something entirely wrong, thinking perhaps that I would encourage them to relish and enjoy every moment, and incite them to live in a somewhat frivolous way! There are more than enough of these sauntering through life, senselessly indulging the moment in this fashion!

With this call I do indeed encourage the full enjoyment of every minute, but *inwardly,* not only outwardly! Every single hour of the present must become a real experience for a human being, sorrow as well as joy! In all his reflection, his thinking and his intuition he must be open to the present moment, and thus *awake!* Only *in this way* can he profit from his life on earth as it is meant that he should! Neither in his thoughts about the past, nor in his dreams of the future, can he find real experiences so strong as to impress his spirit with a stamp which he can take over with him into the beyond as something gained!

If he does not *live* in the present he cannot *mature,* for maturing depends on experiencing only!

If during his life on earth he has not always experienced the *present* within himself, then he will return empty-handed. He must therefore once more wander through the time he lost, because he was not awake and did not gain anything for himself through experiencing!

Life on earth is like one step in the entire existence of a man, but so great that he cannot omit it. Unless he sets his foot firmly and securely on this step, it will be quite impossible for him to ascend to the next one, for he needs the first as a foundation!

If a man will envisage his whole existence as it rises upwards in steps, beginning from this earth and returning to the Light, it must then become clear that he cannot reach the next step unless he has stood firmly upon the previous one and fulfilled what awaited him there properly! It should even be expressed more strongly: Only through the complete and absolute fulfilment of each step to be experienced can the next higher one develop itself. Experiencing alone serves to give a man maturity, and if he does not fully experience on the step on which he happens to be, then the new step will not become visible to him, because for this to happen he needs the experiencing of the previous step. Only when he is equipped with these experiences does he receive the power to recognise and ascend to the next higher step!

And so it goes on from one step to another! If he keeps his eyes fixed *only* on the high goal, without paying careful attention to the individual steps leading him there, he will never reach it. The steps which he must build for his own ascent would then be far too unsubstantial and flimsy and would collapse when he tried to climb them.

But there is always a safeguard against this danger in the natural course of events, inasmuch as the next step can only develop after the complete fulfilment of the present step. Thus he who does not wish to spend half his existence standing upon one and the same step, nor constantly to return there, should force himself always to belong completely to the present, to grasp it aright deep within himself, and to experience it so that he gains spiritually from it!

Neither will he lose from a worldly point of view, for the first advantage he gains is not to expect either from the people or from the time more than they can *really* give him! Thus he will never be disappointed, and also remain in harmony with his environment!

If, on the other hand, he lives only in the past or dreams only of the future, his expectations will easily reach beyond the compass of the present, which must bring him into disharmony with his time, not *only* making *him* suffer but also *his nearer surroundings!*

It is right to think of the past in order to learn the lessons it teaches, and also to dream of the future to receive encouragement therefrom, but in the present one must do nothing but *live* fully and consciously!

WHAT MUST A MAN DO TO ENTER
THE KINGDOM OF HEAVEN?

ONE IS often approached with this question, but it would be wrong to reply with a definite rule and to say "Do this" and "Do that"! *That is not showing the way!* It would be completely devoid of life, and for this reason nothing living, such as is absolutely necessary for soaring upwards, can arise from it, for *life* alone contains the key necessary for ascent!

If now I say "Do this and that, and don't do the other," I am only giving weak, external crutches on which no one can walk properly and independently, for these crutches do not at the same time help him to "see"! And yet he must *see* the "*way*" clearly before him, otherwise the crutches are of no use to him! Such a person would only hobble about aimlessly, like a blind man on a road he does not know. No, that is not the right thing, and would once more only lead to another dogma, which would hinder and delay every ascent!

Let man consider: If he wishes to enter the Realm of the Spirit he must naturally journey there! *He* must walk there – it does not come to him! The Spiritual Realm lies at the summit of Creation, indeed it *is* the highest point itself!

The human spirit, however, is still in the nether regions of the World of Gross Matter. Therefore it will probably be clear to everyone that he must first wander from these nether regions to the longed-for height in order to reach the goal!

In order not to lose his way it is imperative that he should have a *thorough knowledge* of the whole distance he has to traverse! Not only the way itself, but also everything he may meet en route, the dangers which threaten him, and the help he can count upon! Since the road lies entirely *within Creation*, in fact *is* Creation, the wanderer who journeys towards the Spiritual Realm must become absolutely *familiar* beforehand with the Creation which leads him there. For he needs must pass through it, otherwise he will not reach his goal!

Up till now there has been no man able to give *such* a description of Creation as it is necessary to absorb in order to ascend. In other words, there was no one who could make *the way to the Grail Castle,* the summit of Creation, visible and distinct. It is the way to the Castle which stands as the Temple of the Almighty in the Spiritual Realm, where alone *pure* worship takes place. This is not only meant allegorically, but it exists in all reality!

The Message of the Son of God pointed out the way once before. But in his eagerness to show how clever he was, man *interpreted it wrongly* in many respects and consequently *misplaced* the *signposts,* thereby misleading the human spirit and preventing it from rising!

Now, however, the hour has arrived in which *every* human spirit *must* decide for itself, whether it is to be *"yes"* or *"no",* day or night, ascent to the Luminous Heights or descent, finally and irrevocably, without any further possibility for it to reconsider! For this reason another Message from the Luminous Castle has now been given. This Message puts the misplaced signposts back into their *proper* places, so that the right road may be recognised by all *serious* seekers!

Happy are all those who adjust themselves to this Message with an open mind and a free heart! They will find in it *all* they must know of Creation, and see *all* the rungs which their spirit must use on its ladder of ascent in order to enter into the Spiritual Realm, Paradise!

Each individual will find in it what *he* needs for his climb towards the Light with the abilities *he* possesses!

That alone brings *life,* freedom for ascent, and development of the abilities necessary for each individual, as against the uniform yoke of a fixed dogma which makes him a slave without a will of his own, suppresses all independent development, and thereby not only hinders but completely destroys the possibility of ascent for many!

The man who knows Creation in all its lawful activity will soon comprehend the sublime Will of God in it. If he adjusts himself to it in the right manner Creation, and also the way itself, will serve him *only* for a joyful ascent, because then he also stands correctly in the Will of God. His way and his life must therewith be right!

It is not the attitude of a canting devotee, writhing on his knees with eyes upturned in contrite prayer, but prayer made a *living reality* in fresh, pure-minded and joyful activity! It is not begging and whining to have the way pointed out, but *recognising* it with a thankful upward glance to the Creator and *travelling* upon it cheerfully!

Thus a life which can be described as devoted to God is quite different from what has been presumed hitherto! It will be much more free and beautiful! It means *standing aright in Creation* as is willed by your Creator through His Creation, in which (metaphorically speaking) one grasps the hand of God which He thereby stretches out to mankind!

Therefore I call out once more: Take all these things as *factual,* as *real,* and no longer regard them as figurative! Then you yourselves will become *living* realities instead of the lifeless shadows you now are! Learn to understand Creation aright *in its laws!*

Therein lies the way upward to the Light!

THOU BEHOLDEST THE MOTE THAT IS IN THY BROTHER'S EYE AND CONSIDEREST NOT THE BEAM THAT IS IN THINE OWN EYE!

EVERYONE believes that he has fully understood these simple words, and yet there will be but few who have grasped their actual meaning! It is one-sided and wrong to interpret this saying as if it was only meant to teach man to be lenient with his neighbour. If a man really experiences these words, leniency towards his neighbour will come entirely and quite naturally of its own accord, but only in the second place!

He who searches in the words of Christ in this fashion does not search deeply enough, and thus shows either that he is far from being able to call the words of the Son of God to life, or that he under-estimates the wisdom of His utterances from the very beginning. And in the interpretation of many preachers, as with all else, these words are associated with the weakness and feebleness of *that* love which the church likes to try and hold forth as Christian love!

However, man can *and shall* use these words of the Son of God only as a measure for his own faults! If he looks around with open eyes, and also studies himself at the same time, he will soon recognise that the faults which most disturb him in others are very strongly marked in himself and a cause of annoyance to his neighbours!

In order to learn to observe properly it is perhaps best if you first closely observe your fellow-men only. It is doubtful if there will be even one among them who does not have to criticise this or that in others, and who does not also talk about it openly or covertly! As soon as this happens, you should take this particular person who is so critical or even indignant about the faults of others under close scrutiny! It will not be long before you discover with surprise that it is just those faults which he so sharply censures in others that are present in him to a far greater degree!

This fact will amaze you at first, but it is *always* so without exception!

When judging people in the future you may be quite certain of this without fear of making a mistake! The fact remains that a man who gets excited about this or that fault in another person is sure to have these same faults to a far greater extent within himself!

Just set about such tests quietly one day! You will find you can do so and you will recognise the truth at once, because you yourself are not directly concerned and therefore do not attempt to screen either party!

Take the case of a person who is habitually morose and discourteous, who seldom shows a friendly face and whom one would gladly avoid for this reason! These are the very people who expect and require to be treated with special kindness, and who become enraged, even to the point of tears with girls and women, if they meet with but a single reproachful glance, however justified it may be! This strikes a serious observer as so unspeakably ridiculous, yet sad, that he forgets to be indignant about it!

And so it is in a thousand and more different ways! It will be easy for you to learn and recognise that this is so! And when you have advanced to that stage, you must also have the courage to assume that you yourself are no exception to this rule which you proved never to fail with others! Then at last your eyes will be opened to your true self! This means a great step forward, perhaps even the greatest one, towards your development! You thereby cut a knot that today holds down all mankind! Free yourself, and also joyfully help others to do likewise!

This is what the Son of God meant to say with His simple words! Such was the value of the enlightenment He offered with His plain statements! But man did not honestly *seek* their real meaning. As always he wanted to set himself above them and merely learn to look down forbearingly upon others! This flattered his disgusting arrogance!

The whole wretchedness of his false thinking, the unconcealed hypocritical pharisaism, becomes clearly evident in all his past interpretations! It has transplanted itself in identical manner into Christendom! For even those who call themselves seekers have taken, and still take, everything much too superficially under their usual and customary illusion that by reading the words they must also have grasped their real meaning! They make themselves believe this, just in accordance with *their* prevalent opinions!

That is not honest seeking, and therefore they cannot find the real treasure, nor could there be any progress! The Word remained dead for those who were supposed to have called it to *life* within themselves in order to derive values from it which would uplift them!

And every sentence the Son of God gave to mankind contains such values, only they have not been found because no one has ever sought for them diligently!

WARFARE IN NATURE

How FOOLISH are you who always ask whether the struggle in Creation is right, who only perceive it as cruel! Do you not know that you thereby appear as weaklings who endanger every *present-day* possibility of ascent?

Rouse yourselves at last out of this shocking weakness, which only allows both body and spirit gradually to *sink,* but never to rise!

Look about you, seeing and recognising, and you must *bless* the great impulse which induces the need to struggle and consequently to defend, to act cautiously, to be *alert* and really to *live!* It protects the creature from the deadly embrace of sloth!

Can an artist ever reach the peak of his skill and maintain himself there unless he continually practises and fights for it, no matter what his profession and how great the abilities he possesses? The voice of a singer would soon lose in power and dependability, if he did not force himself constantly to practise and learn afresh!

An arm can only grow strong if it is constantly exercised! If there is any relaxation in this respect it must weaken. And so it is with every body and every spirit! However, no man can be brought to do this voluntarily! There must be some compulsion!

If you wish to be healthy you must *care* for your body and your spirit, that is to say, keep them in strict activity!

But what man today understands and what he has always understood by "caring" is not the right thing! Either he means indulging in sweet idleness, which as such already implies a weakening and paralysis, or he practises this "caring" only one-sidedly, as with every sport, thus making the caring a "sport", a *one-sided exaggeration,* and thereby a frivolous and ambitious abuse that is utterly unworthy of serious humanity!

True humanity must indeed have in view the *highest goal,* which cannot be reached by high jumping, swimming, running, riding or furious driving! Mankind and the entire Creation derive no benefit from such individual accomplishments, for which many a man often sacrifices the greater part of his thoughts, his time and his life on earth!

That such extravagant activities could develop at all shows how false is the road on which mankind travel, and also how they divert this great motive power in Creation into nothing but wrong channels, thereby frittering it away in useless toying, if not even causing injury by hindering healthy progress, all the possibilities for which have been provided in Creation!

In their human conceit men so distort the course of the strong currents of the spirit, which are meant to further ascent, that instead of the intended progress stoppages occur which act as a hindrance! In their reaction these stoppages increase the struggling instinct until finally, bursting all bounds, they carry everything along with themselves into the depths!

It is with *such* hollow pseudo-scientific toying and ambitions that man of today primarily occupies himself! A *mischief-maker*, destructive of all harmony in Creation!

He would have long since fallen into the lazy sleep of idleness which must lead to decay had it not fortunately been for the fighting instinct resting in Creation which *forces* him to bestir himself *in spite of* everything! Otherwise he would long ago have arrogantly assumed that God must care for him through His Creation, just as in the dream of a fool's paradise! And if he offers his thanks for it in a spiritless prayer, then that is more than enough reward for his God! Indeed there are many who never thank Him for it at all!

Such is man, and in truth not otherwise!

He talks of cruelty in Nature, but it never occurs to him to examine himself first of all! He only wants to criticise!

Even in the fighting among animals there lies only blessing, and not cruelty!

One only needs to observe some animal closely! As an example let us take a dog! The more considerately a dog is treated the lazier and more slothful it will become. If a dog is in the study of its master and the latter always carefully refrains from stepping upon or pushing the animal, even if it lies down in those places where it is in constant danger of being hurt unintentionally, as for instance near a door, this is to the *detriment* of the animal!

In a very short time the dog will lose its alertness. "Kind-hearted" people will say in "loving" extenuation, perhaps even moved by the wonderful "trust" the dog shows in this, that it knows nobody will hurt it! In reality, however, this is nothing but a gross diminution in its capacity to "be alert", a marked falling-off in psychic activity!

If, on the other hand, an animal has constantly to be on the alert and ready to defend itself, it will not only become and remain psychically awake, but its intelligence will steadily grow keener and it will *gain* in every way. It remains alive in all respects, and that means progress! It is the same with *every* creature! Otherwise it will perish, because its body gradually weakens and, having no longer any power of resistance, it becomes more liable to disease!

The fact that man takes an absolutely wrong attitude towards the animal in various ways will not surprise a keen observer, for man does the same towards *everything*, towards himself and towards the entire Creation, doing harm spiritually everywhere instead of bringing benefit!

If today there was no longer in Creation the fighting instinct which so many indolent people call cruel, the World of Matter would already long ago have been in a state of rottenness and disintegration. This instinct has a *preserving* effect on the body and soul. It is certainly not destructive, although it may appear so on the surface! Otherwise there would no longer be anything left to keep this sluggish World of Gross Matter in motion, and consequently in good health and vigour, since man, through his errors, has so wantonly diverted the quickening effects of the all-pervading *spiritual power* actually destined for this purpose, so that it cannot act in the way it really should!

If man had not failed so miserably to carry out the task for which he was destined, then much, *everything*, would look different today! Neither would the so-called "fight" have taken on *the* form in which it shows itself *at present!*

The fighting instinct would have been ennobled, spiritualised by the upward surging will of man. Its original uncouth effect, instead of increasing as it does now, would gradually have changed under the *right* spiritual influence and become a united, cheerful incentive to help one another forward, which would require the same energy as the most violent struggle. But with this difference, that a struggle is followed by exhaustion, while in mutually helping one another a great increase in energy would be the consequence!

Also in the reproduction of Creation, in which the *spiritual* will of man is the strongest influence, there would finally have set in for *all* creatures the Paradise-like state, just as it is in the real Creation, where there is no struggle and no apparent cruelty required any longer! This Paradise-like condition, however, does not consist of idleness, but is equivalent to being most energetically *astir,* to real personal fully-conscious life!

That this could not happen is the guilt of the human spirit! I must again and again revert to the decisive fall of man, which I describe in detail in the lecture "Once upon a time".

Only the complete failure of the human spirit in Creation through the *misuse* of the spiritual power entrusted to it, the effects of which were diverted *downwards* instead of upwards to Luminous Heights, has brought about the present unsound aberrations!

Man has already trifled or gambled away even the ability to see his mistake! Thus if I wanted to say more about it I would only be *preaching to deaf ears!* He who really *wishes* to "listen" and *is able* to seek earnestly will find *all* he needs in my Message. And he will also find everywhere explanations about the great failure which has brought on such unspeakably serious disasters in so many varied forms!

He, however, who is *spiritually deaf,* as so many are, has only the inane laugh of those who are devoid of understanding, a laugh that is meant to *simulate knowledge,* but which in reality merely indicates a careless superficiality, and is the same as gross narrow-mindedness! And those on whom the idiotic laughing of such spiritually limited human beings makes any impression today are themselves worthless. To *such* Christ's words are applicable: "Let the dead bury their dead", for he who is *spiritually* deaf and blind is spiritually dead!

With his ability the human spirit could make the earth, this replica of Creation, a paradise! He has not done so, and therefore he now sees the world before him as he has distorted it through his false actions. *Everything lies therein!* Therefore do not out of false sentimentality disdain such an important matter as the warfare in Nature, for it restores the necessary balance to something which man neglected to carry out! Nor be so bold as to call your sweet and sultry sentimentality "love", with which man likes so much to cover his weaknesses! Such falsehood and hypocrisy must avenge themselves bitterly!

Therefore, woe unto you, man, you degenerate product of your imagination! You caricature of what you *should be!*

Try to observe calmly what you usually call Nature – the mountains, the lakes, the woods, and the meadows, at all seasons! Man is enraptured by the beauty that meets his gaze! And now reflect: That which gives you so much happiness and refreshment is the fruit of the activity of all that comprises *animistic substantiality** which, in Creation, ranks *below* the spiritual, with the power of which you have been endowed!

Then seek out the fruits of *your* work, you who are spiritual and who should accomplish higher things than animistic substantiality, which is actually ahead of you!

And what do you find? Only feeble imitations of what animistic substantiality has already achieved, but no progress towards ideal heights in all that is living and thus in Creation! With nothing but degenerated creative instincts mankind only try lifelessly to imitate existing forms, whereas with a free and conscious spirit, and their eyes uplifted to the Divine, they would be capable of producing very different and much more sublime things!

Men have wantonly cut themselves off from the greatness which is born only of a *free spirit,* and besides childish imitations they can therefore produce nothing but machines, constructions, and technical achievements in general. All earth-bound, on a lowly plane, hollow and lifeless, just like themselves!

These are the fruits which man, as a spiritual being, can now compare with the activity of the elemental beings! *This* is how he has fulfilled the spiritual task in the Subsequent Creation given to him for that purpose!

How do they expect to pass when the reckoning comes? Is it any wonder if the sublime Paradise *must* remain closed to people with such base propensities? And can one be surprised if now in the end the elementals, in reaction, will completely destroy the work so wrongly led by the human spirit?

And when now, owing to the lack of ability you showed, everything will collapse upon you, then cover your face and acknowledge with shame the terrible guilt with which *you* have burdened yourselves! Do not again try to accuse your Creator of it, or to call Him cruel and unjust!

You who are seeking, however, examine yourselves seriously and unsparingly, and then try to *readjust* your whole thinking and intuitive perception, indeed your whole being, upon a *spiritual* foundation, which will no longer rock like the intellectual and thus very limited foundation of the past!

* See Appendix.

THE OUTPOURING OF THE HOLY SPIRIT

THE EVENT described in the Bible of the outpouring of the Holy Spirit upon the disciples of the Son of God is still an inexplicable happening to many people, and is mostly regarded as extraordinary, as having occurred only on this one occasion, and therefore as an arbitrary act!

It is just in this erroneous view that there lies the cause for what is apparently "inexplicable"!

The happening was not an isolated one, not one specially brought about for the disciples, but one that has *recurred regularly* ever since Creation existed. With *this* recognition it will immediately lose its inexplicability, and it will become understandable to the seriously seeking readers of the Grail Message without forfeiting any of its greatness, but on the contrary making it even more stupendous!

He who has attentively studied my Grail Message will already have found the solution for this event in it, for he must also have read the explanation given in the lecture "The Holy Grail". There I mentioned the *regularly recurring* yearly renewal of power for the entire Creation. It is the moment in which new Divine Power streams into the Holy Grail for the maintenance of Creation!

For some moments the "Holy Dove" appears above the Grail. This is the spiritually visible form of the presence of the Holy Spirit, which directly belongs to the "form" of the Holy Spirit, and is therefore a part of this "form".

Just as the Cross is the spiritually visible form of Divine Truth, so is the "Dove" the visible form of the Holy Spirit. This actually *is* the form, not merely an imaginary conception!

This renewal of power by the Holy Spirit, the Living Will of God which is this Power, recurs every year at a certain definite time in the Holy of Holies of the highest castle or temple harbouring the Holy Grail. This temple is the only point of connection of Creation with the Creator, and is therefore called *the Grail Castle*.

This renewal may also be called the outpouring of power, thus the Outpouring of the Holy Spirit or, still more explicitly, the outpouring of power *by* the Holy Spirit, for it is not the Holy Spirit that is poured out, but the Holy Spirit pours out the power!

Now the disciples were assembled on this day in commemoration of their ascended Lord Who had promised to send the Spirit, that is, the Living Power. The fact of their commemorating provided an anchorage *for this,* an anchorage for the event which took place at this time in the Primordial Sphere, enabling the Living Power to descend to a certain and corresponding degree directly upon the disciples on earth, who had assembled in devotion and accordingly adjusted themselves to it. All the more so as the way to these disciples had been opened up and smoothed by the life of the Son of God on earth!

And for *this* reason the miraculous happened, which could not otherwise have been possible on earth, and the experiencing of which is related in the Bible. The evangelists were able to describe their own *experiences* but not the actual happening, which they themselves did not understand.

The festival of Whitsuntide has been instituted by Christians in memory of this occurrence, without their ever suspecting that at this approximate time each year the Day of the Holy Dove occurs in the Grail Castle, that is, the day of the renewal of power for Creation by the Holy Spirit. Naturally this does not always correspond exactly with the Whitsuntide holiday as figured out on earth, but at its approximate time!

At that time the meeting of the disciples coincided *exactly* with the actual happening! Later on it will also be celebrated here on earth regularly and at the *right* time as the most supreme and holy festival of mankind, the day on which the Creator always renews His gift of sustaining power to Creation, as the "Day of the Holy Dove", or the Day of the Holy Spirit, a great prayer of thanksgiving to God the Father!

It will be celebrated by *those* human beings who at last stand *consciously* in this Creation, and who have finally learned to understand it aright in all its manifestations. Their devout attitude at the exact time will also make it possible that, through opening themselves, the living blessing can again flow down to this earth in return, and pour itself into the thirsting souls as it did long ago with the disciples!

This period, which is not too far distant, will bring peace and happiness if men do not fail and do not want to be lost for all eternity!

SEX

MANY people on earth are sorely troubled by the question of intercourse between the two sexes, male and female! The only exceptions are those frivolous persons who do not allow themselves to be disturbed by anything at all. The rest, however, much as they may otherwise differ, do seek for a solution either openly or pondering quietly within themselves!

Fortunately there are many people who are really longing for a guide in this matter! Whether they would then adjust themselves accordingly remains to be seen! But it is a fact that they are very preoccupied with this problem, and that the majority are oppressed by the realisation of their ignorance about it!

Efforts were made to solve or anchor this in marriage problems, but no satisfactory basic thought has yet been arrived at, because here as elsewhere the main thing is that man should know what he is dealing with. Otherwise he can never cope with it, and will still continue to worry!

As a result, from the very start many people are frequently confused about the meaning of this word "sex". It is taken in a general sense, whereas it has actually a far deeper meaning!

If we wish to obtain a correct picture, we must not be so one-sided as to compress it into definitions which merely serve a purely mundane social order, and which are in many ways absolutely contrary to the Laws of Creation. In such grave matters it is necessary to meditate deeply upon Creation in order to grasp the *fundamental thought!*

We call the conceptions male and female simply the different sexes! But because in their thoughts they automatically connect the word sex with procreation, the majority are decisively led astray from the very beginning. And this is wrong! The separation of female and male in *this* sense has, in the great conception of Creation, only some significance for the outermost and deepest gross material portion, and none for the *principal happenings!*

What is sex? When the spirit-germ issues from the Spiritual Sphere it is then sexless, nor does any bisection occur, as is often assumed!

538

Fundamentally the spirit-germ always remains an independent entity. In becoming conscious during its wanderings through Subsequent Creation, i. e., through the automatic replica of actual Creation, the spirit-germ, as I have mentioned several times already, takes on according to its degree of consciousness the human forms known to us, which are an imitation of the Primordial Beings, who are themselves in the image of God.

Here it is the *nature* of the spirit-germ's *activity* which is decisive, that is, in which direction such a spirit-germ, in becoming conscious, strives mainly to develop the abilities resting within it, whether in a positive, compelling and energetic manner, or in a negative, quietly preserving way, wherever its principal desires urge it.

And in this activity of the spirit-germ, even if it consists at the start of no more than strong desires which increase to an urge, *the form shapes itself!*

That which is positive shapes the male form, and that which is negative the female form. Here male and female are already outwardly recognisable through their forms. Each in its forms is the expression of the *nature* of the activity which it chooses or desires. In the beginning these desires are really only the expression of the actual nature of the spirit-germ in question, either negative or positive.

Female and male therefore have nothing to do with the usual conception of sex, but merely indicate *the nature of their activity in Creation.* It is only in the World of Gross Matter, so familiar to man, that these forms evolve the procreative organs which we designate as male and female. Only the physical body, i. e., the earthly body, needs these organs for its procreation!

Thus *the nature of the activity in Creation* shapes the form of the actual body, male or female, of which the gross material earthly body is again but a coarsely constructed copy!

Hence sexual intercourse is placed on the step where it belongs, that is, on the lowest step in Creation, the gross material step which lies far removed from the Spiritual Sphere!

It is all the more deplorable, therefore, if a human spirit indulges to such an extent in this activity, which is a function of his outermost covering, that he becomes a slave to it! And unfortunately this has become so general today that it illustrates how the priceless and high-ranking spirituality, when clothed in a covering of the coarsest matter, will voluntarily allow itself to be downtrodden and suppressed!

It is understandable that such unnatural proceedings must bring about an evil end. They are unnatural because in the natural order of things that which is spiritual is the highest in the entire Creation, and harmony can only exist in Creation as long as spirituality, as the highest, holds the dominating position with all else remaining *subordinate* to it, even in a union with gross matter here on earth.

I do not especially need to point out what a sad role a man takes in placing his spirit under the control of the coarsest material covering; a covering which only gains its sensitiveness through the spirit and which must lose it again on being cast aside; a tool in the hand of the spirit which must be cared for to keep it proficient, but which must always remain under control!

The spiritual, animistic and ethereal form of the body changes as soon as the spirit-germ changes its activity. If it changes from a negative to a predominantly positive activity, then the female form must change into a male one, and vice versa, for the *predominant* nature of the activity shapes the form!

The transformation of the gross material physical shell, however, cannot follow so quickly; it is not so easily changeable, as it is only intended to last for a very short time. Here the change manifests itself in *reincarnations*, of which in most cases there are many!

Hence it happens that a human spirit sometimes wanders through its lives on earth *alternately* in male and female bodies, depending on its changing inner attitude. But this is an unnatural condition, brought about by a stubborn and violent distortion!

The opinion that men hold that there is a complementing soul for each person is correct as such, but not in the sense of a bisection having preceded it. The dual soul is merely *the harmonious complement* to another soul, that is, a soul which has developed just *those* abilities which the other soul left slumbering within itself. This then comes to a full completion, to a united working together of all the abilities of the spirit, both positive and negative. There is not merely one such complementing soul in existence, but many, so that a person seeking a complement is not limited merely to one other particular human being. He may meet with many during his life on earth, if he only keeps his capacity to perceive intuitively pure and alert!

Thus the conditions for a life of happiness are not nearly so difficult to fulfil as it appears at first glance to those who have only part-knowledge! Happiness is much easier to achieve than many think! But it is first necessary for mankind to know the laws which rest in Creation. If they live accordingly then they *must* become happy! At the present time, however, this is far from being the case, and for this reason those who come closer to the Truth in Creation will at first have mostly to feel lonely which, however, does not make them at all unhappy, but brings great peace!

IS OLD AGE AN OBSTACLE TO SPIRITUAL ASCENT?

OLD AGE forms no obstacle, but is a *spur!* For in old age the hour of passing over comes visibly closer! Those who still hesitate only burden themselves through indolence and love of ease (which I have already frequently described as the greatest enemies of mankind), and will thus perish!

The time of spiritual vagabondage has ceased, as also the time when men took their ease and comfortably awaited what the future would bring them. Within a short period the sleepers and sluggards will be smitten in all directions with such terrible force and harshness that even the deafest will then awaken!

From the very beginning the study of my lectures stipulates the need for self-exertion, for a forceful concentration of all the senses, and thus for spiritual vitality and *full* alertness! Only *then* does it become possible to penetrate deeply into my words and truly grasp them!

And that is so willed! I reject all spiritual sluggards!

Even if men have buried *all but one* of the grains of Truth they brought with them from their home in the Spiritual Sphere, the Word *must* hit them just like a call, provided they take the trouble to read it impartially and in all earnestness! If they *then* perceive nothing that re-echoes in their hearts, it will also hardly be possible any longer to awaken them in the beyond, because there also they will not be able to receive *anything else!* Such people remain standing where they place themselves through their own will! No one will compel them to move away, but neither will they be able to leave this World of Matter in time to escape from the disintegration which is everlasting damnation!

They will naturally take their "refusal to listen" over with them from this earth into the Ethereal World, but they will not cut any better figure there than they did here!

How can old age form an obstacle? It is a call from Eternity which hits them out of the Word, but which they do not wish to hear, because it is more comfortable for them otherwise! In the end, however, their slothfulness will destroy them, unless they wish to rouse themselves in time! The question put above points very clearly to this love of ease! It is the same with so many people who constantly wish to deceive themselves with any more or less acceptable pretext! They belong to the chaff which, far from being fortified by the coming storms of purification, will be blown away as useless for the seriousness of real life!

They would always demand more time for consideration from their Creator, without ever beginning an ascent, for that would involve exerting themselves spiritually! For this reason it would serve no purpose to expend much time on this. They are eternally intending to do something, but never fulfil their intentions as regards themselves! Thus they are also lost!

FATHER, FORGIVE THEM, FOR THEY
KNOW NOT WHAT THEY DO!

WHO DOES not know these momentous words which Jesus of Nazareth uttered when He hung on the cross? They are one of the greatest prayers of intercession ever spoken. Clear and explicit! And yet, despite this, for two thousand years these words have never been understood! They were interpreted *one-sidedly*, and only in *that* way which appeared to be agreeable to men. There was not one person to raise his voice and call out their proper meaning in all clearness to mankind, and especially to Christians!

But not only that! *Every* soul-stirring event in the earth-life of the Son of God was put into a false light by the one-sidedness of the transmission. But these faults are not only exhibited in Christianity, they are to be found in *every* religion!

It is understandable if disciples place first and foremost all that is personal about their teacher and master, especially when this master was so abruptly and brutally torn from their midst and, although utterly innocent, exposed to the most terrible suffering and coarsest mockery, and finally put to the most agonising death!

Such events would be deeply engraved on the souls of those who had come to know their teacher in the most ideal way while they lived together, and would quite naturally cause them to place the personal element foremost in everything they remembered. But the sacred *Mission* of the Son of God lay in His *Word*, in bringing the Truth from Luminous Heights, in order to show mankind their way to the Light! This had been closed to them up till then, because their spiritual development had previously made it impossible for them to *walk* on that road!

The suffering thereby wrought upon this great Bringer of Truth by mankind stands entirely on its own!

However, what was quite understandable and natural with the disciples resulted in many great errors in the later religion! The *essence* of the Divine

Message receded far into the background before the personal cult of the Bringer of Truth, which Christ never intended!

For this reason mistakes are now evident in the Christian religion which will lead to the danger of a breakdown unless the errors are recognised in time and, through open confession, are courageously set right.

It cannot be expected otherwise than that the smallest amount of serious progress must make all these gaps visible! But then it is decidedly better not to avoid them, but to tackle them boldly. Why should not this purification be instituted by the leadership itself, freshly and cheerfully, with a free upward gaze towards the Supreme Godhead? Great numbers of men would feel as if freed from a pressure, which they had indeed perceived but never really recognised as such, and would gratefully follow a call leading them into the light of joyful conviction!

In following the habit of *those* who blindly subject themselves to an unlimited control of their intellect, and who thereby severely diminish their ability to comprehend, they placed the same value on Christ's earth life as on His Mission. His family relationships and all the earthly events received even greater attention than the main purpose of His Coming, which consisted of bringing enlightenment to the matured human spirits about all the *real* happenings in Creation, wherein alone they would find the Will of God, which is woven into it and thus made available to them!

It was the bringing of this Truth, up till then still unknown, which *quite by itself* necessitated Christ's coming upon the earth. Nothing else! For without truly recognising the Will of God in Creation no man can find the road of ascent to the Luminous Realm, much less walk upon it!

Instead of simply accepting these facts as such, becoming absorbed in the *Message* and *living* accordingly, as the Bringer of Truth repeatedly and emphatically demanded, the founders of the Christian religions and churches created a *personal* cult as the principal foundation, which forced them to make the suffering of Christ mean something entirely different from what it really was!

They needed it for this cult! Finally, in the course of further development, this quite naturally produced one great error after another, which became obstacles for a great number of people, preventing them as yet from properly recognising the *right way*.

This wrong structure, based on *lack of objectivity*, alone brought about the distortion of all the happenings, it being inevitable that factual impartiality was bound to cease from the moment when the principal cult became purely personal! Thus the urge developed to anchor the Mission of the Son of God mainly in His *life on earth*. Indeed this became a necessity!

That this is a *wrong* step to take Christ Himself proved by His whole attitude. More than once He clearly and sharply rejected the personal attitude taken towards Him! In every word and every action he continually pointed to God the Father, Whose Will He fulfilled and in Whose Power He stood and acted. He explained how mankind should henceforth learn to look up to *God the Father,* but He never spoke of Himself in this connection.

Since His words dealing with this point were not heeded, it became inevitable in the end that Christ's *suffering on earth* was supposed to be regarded as *necessary* and as ordained by God, and it was even declared to be part of His main task in *coming* to earth. According to this view He came from the Luminous Heights only in order to suffer here on earth!

As He had not burdened Himself with *any* guilt, there remained only one explanation: He must have taken the sins of others upon Himself in order to redeem them from those sins!

What else was there left but to continue to build *in that manner* on the foundation thus established?

And the exaggerated self-esteem which is not altogether unknown, and from which all mankind suffer, provided the nourishing power and fruitful soil for this. It is the result of the great Fall of Man, which was directed against the spirit, and which I have often explained in detail. In evaluating his intellect too highly man only comes to know himself and not his God, all the bridges to Whom he has thus destroyed. Only a few here and there have a very weak connection with the Spiritual Sphere which, however, allows them to perceive very little, and *never* really to *know*.

Thus the right and natural thought completely *to separate the earthly sufferings of Christ, as a special happening, from the Divine Message* occurred to no one! Nor did anyone recognise all the enmity, persecution and torment as the serious and grievous crimes they really were! It is a new and great wrong to gloss over them as a necessity!

Indeed His sufferings and agonising death on the cross deserve the radiant light of highest glory, because the Son of God did not shrink from an evil reception among the tyrannical and revengeful people! This was anticipated after the Fall of Man, but in spite of this He brought His so urgently needed Message of Truth to earth for the sake of the few who were good!

This deed is to be appraised all the higher, because it is actually a question of only a small proportion of mankind who thereby wish to save themselves!

But it is a new sacrilege against God when the crimes mankind committed at that time are supposed to be so mitigated through false assumptions as to make it appear that men had only been the tools of a necessary fulfilment!

These *errors* give rise to a feeling of uncertainty among many *thinking* men about the consequences of Judas Iscariot's deed. With full justification! For if the death on the cross was necessary for mankind, then Judas and his betrayal provided the necessary means towards it, and in the spiritual sense he was not really punishable for what he did! The truth about the actual happening, however, abolishes all these disagreements, the justified appearance of which only confirms the fact that the assumptions accepted in the past must really be false! Where the *right* view prevails there is no room for such unexplained questions, and the quite natural happening can be considered from *every* point of view without meeting with any hindrance.

Man should at last have the courage to recognise the cowardice in this glossing over, which is only kept concealed by the sagacity of his earthbound intellect, the greatest enemy of everything that is able to rise *above* it, a fact that is always clearly visible with every base companion! Or let him consider it a veiled self-aggrandisement which springs from the same source! It is wonderful to have such an imagination as to consider oneself so precious that a Divine Being would fight for one and take upon Himself every kind of suffering only in order to be allowed to offer poor wretched man a place of honour in the Divine Realm of Bliss!

Such, plainly and bluntly expressed, is *really* man's basic view, which looks no different if one removes with a firm hand all the frippery from its outer forms!

I need hardly point out that such a view can only arise through a most seriously restricted capacity to perceive all non-earthly happenings. This again is one of the grave consequences of the glorification of the earthly intellect which intercepts every free, broad outlook. The worship of this idol "intellect" has naturally grown steadily since the Fall of Man, until it has now developed into the powerful earthly Antichrist or, more explicitly, into all that is *anti-spiritual*. This is clearly evident today wherever one looks, and does not require a keen eye to observe it.

And since the spiritual *alone* can provide the bridge by which to approach and to understand all that is Divine, the granting of supreme power to the earthly intellect, to which all the sciences proudly confess today, is nothing but *an open declaration of warfare against God!*

Not only the sciences, but *all mankind* today move under this sign! Even everybody who calls himself a serious seeker carries this poison about with him!

Thus it is not unnatural that the Church must also have much of this within it. In the rendering and interpreting of all the words of the Saviour, therefore, much has crept in which has its origin only in the earthly cleverness of the intellect!

This also is the serpent of which the Bible story warns and which entices man ever again – the serpent of intellectual sagacity which alone is always confronting man with the subtle question: *"Yea, hath God said, ye shall not eat of every tree of the garden?"*

As soon as every decision is left to the serpent, i. e., to the intellect alone, it will always, as has been rightly indicated in the Bible, choose what is *hostile to or what leads away from* God, that which is purely earthly and much lower, to which the intellect belongs as its highest manifestation. Thus it cannot grasp what is higher!

Man has been endowed with the intellect so that in every life on earth he has *a counterpoise pulling downwards* to balance the upward-striving *spirituality.* It was given to him for the purpose of preventing him from floating in spiritual heights only, and thereby forgetting his task on earth. The intellect is also meant to facilitate his whole life on earth. But, above all, it is intended to transmit the strong upward urge for what is sublime, pure and perfect, which is *an absolutely inherent quality of the spirit,* to the small earthly, so that it has a visible effect in the material world! It should act as the handyman of the living spirit, as its servant, not as the one to make decisions and take the lead. It is to help create the earthly or material opportunities for the carrying out of spiritual urges. The intellect is to be the tool and the servant of the spirit.

If, however, all decisions are left to the intellect *alone,* as is done now, then it ceases to be a counterbalance and helper, but throws *only its own weight* into the scale of every decision. This can quite naturally *only* be followed by a *sinking downward,* because the intellect draws down. No other course is possible because the intellect belongs to the World of Matter and is firmly bound to it, whereas that which is spiritual comes from above. Instead of extending a helping hand to the spiritual, and becoming strong and great in so doing, the intellect, as soon as everything is left to it, rejects and repudiates the stronger hand proffered by the spiritual. It cannot do otherwise and acts in these matters only in accordance with the laws of its own nature!

It should be noted that the earthly intellect becomes an enemy of the spirit *only* when it is elevated *above* the latter, not before! For if it stands *under* the dominion of the spirit, as it naturally should in accordance with the Creative Will, it remains a faithful servant which can be *appreciated* as such. But if, contrary to the Laws of Nature, the intellect is given a position of authority, where it does not belong, the consequence is that it will suppress everything that could disturb it in order to maintain itself on the usurped throne. It automatically closes the doors which, if kept open, would throw light upon its deficiencies and narrow limitations!

This is a counterpart of the actions of *those* people who feel their abilities developing in well-ordered circumstances and under good leadership, and who then over-estimate them and, in throwing over the old order, through their inability to achieve what is higher plunge a nation into want and misery! Just as these can never realise their error and, both to themselves and before others, always try to blame past circumstances alone for their own incapacity, so will it be equally hard for the human intellect to recognise that it can never undertake the work of the higher-ranking spirit without causing grievous harm and finally bringing about destruction. It is always the same picture everywhere, an eternal repetition of the same happening!

Man himself should meditate deeply and calmly upon this process! Everything would then soon become clearly understandable, and must also appear very natural!

It was the same with the founders of churches and religions; this condition drew a veil over the great simplicity of Divine Truth and prevented every possibility of a right understanding.

Mankind could not burden themselves with anything more terrible than this voluntary limitation, this incapacity to perceive all that lies beyond earthly matters, i. e., by far the greater part of all happenings. However, as a consequence, this literally lies *above* their so narrow horizon!

Now let a man try to fight against the impenetrability of this wall! He would be very soon obliged to acknowledge the truth of the poet's words: "The gods themselves fight *in vain* against stupidity!"

This stout wall can only be penetrated by each individual personally from within, for it was built up from within! *But they do not wish to do so!*

Therefore there is failure everywhere today! A picture of desolate confusion and much distress wherever one looks!

And on top of this pile of ruins there stands, hollow and puffed up with pride, the author of all this wild confusion ... "modern man" as he most of all likes to describe himself! The "progressive" who in reality has constantly retrogressed! The man who also calls himself a "sober materialist", expecting to be admired for it!

To this must now be added the many schisms and the ever-increasing hatred for one another, despite the uniformity of their voluntary enslavement! The cause lies neither with employer nor employee, neither with capital nor lack of it, nor is it due to the church or the state, or to the different nations, but it is only the wrong attitude of each individual which has brought about the present state of affairs.

Even the so-called seekers for the Truth are now seldom on the right road! Nine-tenths of them turn into nothing but Pharisees who look arrogantly down upon their fellow-men and criticise them, while at the same time quarrelling among themselves! Everything is wrong! First of all there must come the inevitable fulfilment of a dreadful end before some few can awaken out of their sleep!

As yet it is still possible for everyone to turn back! But soon and at last there will come a "too late" for all time, contrary to the hopes of so many believers who favour the erroneous view that it probably needs a longer or shorter period for the necessary purification, depending on the individual himself, but that in the end his path must again lead to the Light, to eternal joy and to happiness in God's proximity!

This thought is an agreeable consolation, but it is not correct, and it does not correspond to the Truth!

Let us once again calmly and clearly, but in broad outline, survey the great evolution of Creation and of man who belongs to it! In so doing observe closely the operation of the *Primordial Law of Homogeneous Species,* and all it embraces in the way of immutable and necessary consequences in every happening, as I have so often explained!

The World of Matter is like a huge cultivated field which, being the heaviest section, moves in a gigantic circular course at the *lowest* part of the entire Creation. There, beginning with the primordial seed, all is in constant motion, perpetually developing, increasingly uniting and forming, right up to the visible globes, of which the earth is one. In the process of maturing they reach the greatest perfection and bear fruit, a condition which corresponds with our present time, only automatically to decay again in the approaching state of over-ripeness according to the Laws of Creation, and to dissolve back into primordial seed, which in turn will continually receive opportunities of entering into fresh combinations and of evolving anew.

Such is the overall picture presenting itself when quietly viewed from On High!

Matter as such is nothing but the substance used to *create forms* or coverings. It only comes to life when it is penetrated by the non-material animistic substantiality in the sphere *above* it. Through this union it is set aglow!

This amalgamation of matter with the non-material animistic substantiality provides the basis for further development. All the souls of animals are formed out of animistic substantiality.

Above the two basic divisions of matter and animistic substantiality lies as the highest division of Creation the *spiritual.* As my readers already know, this has its own special nature. From this spiritual substantiality issue the seed-germs which are intent on developing into self-conscious human spirits.

It is *only* in the field of matter that such a seed-germ of spiritual substantiality can develop into a self-conscious human spirit, much the same as a wheat seed will grow in the soil of a field into a ripe ear of corn.

Its entry into the field of material substance, however, is not possible until the latter has reached a certain stage of development, when its nature is suited to absorb the spirit, which ranks highest in the entire Creation.

That is the time in which Creation produces the most highly developed animal body, after which it is no longer possible for any further development to take place through an animal soul issuing from animistic substantiality!

A small counterpart, a repetition of this great cosmic event, is for example continually provided later on by the earthly birth of the human soul. Indeed, with man who is the crown of Creation, and thus the highest created being, the whole course of cosmic events is reflected. The human soul, too, can enter the child's body developing in its mother's womb only when this body has reached a certain stage of maturity, not before! In fact it is only the requisite stage of development as such which opens the way for the soul to enter. This moment lies *in the middle* of pregnancy.

Thus in the great cycle of cosmic events the time of the highest development of the animal body also falls in the middle, i.e., midway in the cycle of all matter! Let the reader mark this closely!

When the *animistic substantiality* of the animal soul had at this particular point achieved *the highest it could achieve* in the development of the body from the World of Matter, this automatically opened the way for the entrance of the *spiritual* standing *above it*.

The spirit-germ, on the other hand, being the lowest of its spiritual species, could only enter into the highest masterpiece that animistic substantiality below it had produced, i.e., into the most highly developed animal body.

Due to its higher quality the spirit naturally takes over all direction immediately upon entering, and can henceforth lead the body it inhabits, as well as its entire earthly environment, further along the road of development, something which animistic *substantiality* would have been unable to accomplish! In this process the spirit itself naturally develops simultaneously.

This is a cursory sketch of the activity *within* Creation, the exact details of which I shall give in later lectures right down to the most minute parts.

But let us return to the first entry of the human spirit-germs into this World of Matter, i.e., let us return to the point midway in the cycle of the World of Matter! The most highly developed animals of that time, which are today erroneously described as Primeval Men, became extinct. Only *those* bodies among them were developed towards ennoblement into which *spirit-germs* had entered instead of animistic animal souls. The spirit-germs in them matured through varied experiences, raised the animal body to the human body known to us now, and separated themselves into races and nations.

The great Fall of Man lay behind them. It was the first act involving a voluntary decision after the spirit-germs had become self-conscious, and was caused by their placing the intellect *above* the spirit. This in turn permitted the portentous hereditary sin to grow, which very soon made the hollow fruits of the governing intellect become clearly and easily recognisable. The hereditary sin is the one-sided development of the brain through the exaggerated activity of the intellect, which as such is then perpetually inherited. I have often mentioned this fact and shall in due course speak about it in much greater detail. There will probably also be men who, when they grasp the way pointed out to them, will be able to help joyfully with the great work of enlightenment!

Without ceasing the great cosmic cycle continued on its course. But erring mankind brought standstill and confusion into the progress which was necessary. In the midst of this turmoil the Jewish people came under the well-known and oppressive scourge of the Egyptians. Their tribulation and great longing for liberation hastened the maturity of their souls. Thus they outstripped all others spiritually, because this strong emotional upheaval enabled them above all to see themselves as they really were, and also to look into the souls of their oppressors!

After they had clearly perceived that neither anything earthly nor the keenest cleverness of the intellect could help any longer, whereby they also recognised the emptiness of their own souls, their spiritual eye learned to see more keenly, and gradually there arose at last a conception of the actual Godhead truer and higher than any they had had before! And stricken with grief, their prayers rose once again with much greater fervour.

Through this the Jewish people were able to become "the chosen people", who for a period preceded all other people spiritually, because for their time they possessed the purest conception of Divinity, a conception as high as possible considering the existing maturity of the human soul.

Maturity of the spirit, however, must not be confused with knowledge acquired by learning, but you must always bear in mind that being *spiritual* is the same as having *deep inner feeling (gemütvoll)*.

The advanced spiritual maturity of the Jews at that time enabled them to receive through Moses the Will of God clearly expressed in the form of laws, which constituted the greatest treasure and the best and most powerful support for the further development.

Just as world happenings will quite naturally always concentrate only where the maturity is greatest, so it gradually came to focus at that time upon the human race of the Jews, who were increasing in spiritual maturity.

But here again world events must not be confused with earthly world history, which is far removed from actual world events, and which mostly only portrays the effects of the often wrongly applied *free will* of the human spirit, which in turn always casts many stones into the actual happening, thereby often producing temporary distortions and earthly confusion!

The Jewish people of that time were ahead of the others in their religious cult and therefore stood closest to Truth in their views.

The natural consequence of this was that in accordance with the Law of Reciprocal Action the annunciation of an incarnation out of the Light was also bound to come upon this road which, being the most correct, led closest to the proximity of Truth! Through their greater distance from the Truth all the other roads were closed to such a possibility, because they were lost in errors!

Again, in conformity with the Law of Attraction of Homogeneous Species, so absolutely necessary for any activity, it was not possible for a Bringer of Truth from the Light to come to an incarnation by any other road than *that* which lies closest to the Truth, and which therefore resembles His homogeneity most nearly. Only this provides the necessary hold and attracts, whereas erroneous views repel and directly close the road upon which the Light might come and enter!

The Law of Reciprocal Action and the Law of Attraction of Homogeneous Species must also operate in this case without fail! The Primordial Laws either open or close a road in their uniform and unswerving effects.

When in the course of time the Jews again allowed the intellect to dominate in their religion, breeding sordid place-hunting, the heavy hand of the Roman helped to keep a small group in the right recognition, so that the Word could be fulfilled!

Just as a spirit-germ in its still unfinished but yet higher spiritual nature can only enter that part of the world which is in a corresponding state of development, but never one which is unripe, nor one which is too ripe (as is the case today with our part of the world where only souls can live which have already been incarnated several times), so the process is no different with the incarnation of a Bringer of Truth from the Light. His Coming can only take place in that section of humanity which is most matured for this purpose. In the case of a *Divine* Messenger the conditions of all the laws had to be observed *most exactly!* He could only be born among *those* whose conceptions came closest to the Truth.

Just as a spirit-germ can enter the World of Matter *only* after the animistic has achieved the highest peak in its working, when standstill and thereby retrogression must occur unless the spirit-germ enters, so just before Christ's Coming a point was reached in the World of Matter where the spiritual, through the *confusion* caused by hereditary sin, *could not continue to develop.* The free will resting in the spirit, instead of furthering all that existed, had *cut off* the upward development towards the Heights which is willed in Creation and, through the elevation of the intellect, had *one-sidedly* directed all its abilities to what is material only.

The animistic, which *does not* possess free will, had carried out the development of Creation exactly in conformity with Nature, that is, *completely* in accordance with the Divine Will of the Creator. The spiritual, however, *with* its gift of free will, had through the Fall of Man rendered itself incapable of playing its part, and brought only confusion and standstill into the further development of matter. The false application of the ability given to it to direct the Divine Creative Power, as a necessary step forward in the development of matter, was even bound to lead to *descent* instead of to the highest development! Through the Fall of Man the human spirit forcibly retarded all *real* further development, for mundane technical achievements are not actual progress in the sense of cosmic events willed by God. *Therefore the quickest aid, intervention by the Creator Himself, was necessary!*

With every further century evil would have so increased that the possibility of a way to Divine Help would gradually have become entirely out of the question, because the dominion of the intellect would in the course of time have completely cut off any understanding of all that is truly spiritual, and even more so of what is Divine! Thus there would have been no anchorage available for an incarnation from the Light!

It was out of this distress that there arose the great Divine Mystery that God in His Love made the sacrifice for Creation of sending down to earth a portion of Divinity in order to bring Light to those who had gone astray.

The *animistic* in the World of Matter had *fulfilled* its task in the development of Creation. The *spiritual,* however, had completely *failed* through mankind. But, even worse, the spiritual had used the power of decision, which was granted to it for the furthering of Creation, to achieve exactly the contrary! Thus it became *hostile* to Divine Volition, using for this purpose Divinity's own power supplied to it to do God's Will! Man may well ponder how great is his guilt in this!

The birth of Christ was a *Divine Act of Love* for the entire Creation, which was in danger of being undermined by the erring human spirit!

This also necessitated that the Divine part then incarnated in Jesus of Nazareth must reunite completely with the Father, as Christ Himself had repeatedly emphasised! He must again become One with Him!

It was only through Christ's Message that the gates to Paradise were unlocked for *mature* human spirits. The ability to understand the way there aright did not exist until then. This Message was meant for earth-men as well as for those already departed, as is *every* Divine Message and every Word of Luminous Truth!

After learning about the severity of the Laws, men also heard in the Message of a Love which up till then they would not have been able to comprehend, but which they were now meant to engender within themselves. Yet this Message of Love did not overthrow the laws, but only developed them! They were meant to remain as the firm foundation which, in their effects, would produce such love!

Later on attempts were made to build upon this Word of the Son of God, but I have already pointed out in the beginning of my lecture the errors that crept into these attempts through many wrong assumptions.

Let us cast a glance at the history of Christianity! It will teach us the best lesson and at the same time throw a ray of light upon *all* religions. We find the same faults everywhere!

Without exception every Bringer of Truth, whether great or small, has had to suffer mockery and scorn, persecution and attack by his dear fellow-men, who in just the same way today always like to consider themselves too clever and too wise to accept the explanations of the Will of their Creator from His Messengers, especially since these Messengers never in fact issued from any of mankind's great institutions of learning!

An explanation of the Divine Will is fundamentally nothing but the interpretation of the course of His Creation, in which men live and of which they are also a part. To know Creation, then, means everything! If a man has this knowledge it is very easy for him to make use of all it contains and offers. This ability to make use of it in turn brings him *every* advantage. Thus he will soon recognise and fulfil the real purpose of his existence and, furthering everything, he will rise towards the Light, a joy to himself and nothing but a blessing to his surroundings!

But men scoffed at every Messenger and thus also at the Message itself. Not once did it happen that such a Messenger was made welcome, no matter how much good He did! He always remained an annoyance, as can of course be easily explained if one considers the enmity of the intellect towards God, which in itself proves that this enmity towards God is a definite fact. Christ clearly sums up all these happenings when He speaks of the master who sent out his servants to collect what was due to him from his tenants. But instead of receiving the rent the servants were scoffed at and beaten before they were scornfully sent back empty-handed!

Once again this is glossed over by calling it a *parable!* In snug comfort one always seats oneself *beside* these facts, without ever applying them to oneself! Or one has the desire to explain that it is a *distinction* conferred by God upon His Messengers if they have to suffer in this manner, instead of regarding it as a crime on the part of mankind which is not willed by God!

Because the intellect needs tinsel and sham to cover its limitations, which would otherwise become plainly visible, it makes almost desperate efforts to look down with absolute contempt upon the simplicity of Truth, *which* it fears will become a danger! It needs jingling bells for the cap it is wearing, and many great words to keep attention centred upon itself! But its contempt for the unvarnished simplicity of Truth has long since turned to uneasiness! More and more bells are added to this gaudy fool's cap which, through convulsive contortions and antics, are made to jingle louder and ever louder in order to maintain itself for as long as possible on the usurped throne!

But of late these antics have become a dance of despair, which will soon become the last dance of death! The exertions are increasing, they *must* increase, because ever more distinctly the hollowness is forced to reveal itself in spite of all this jingling! And in the greatest and most furious antic which is being prepared the gaudy cap will at last fall from the head!

Then the crown of unvarnished Truth will lift itself, radiant and steadying, up to that place which alone is its due!

And those serious seekers who have become quite confused by these grotesque and incomprehensible distortions will at last receive a firm foothold and support for their view! Without any exertion they will be able fully to comprehend the *whole* Truth, whereas up till now it was certain to cost great trouble to unearth even a minute particle!

Let us return to simplicity in thinking! Otherwise no one can *fully* grasp that which is great and can thus never attain to it! Think as simply as children! That is the true meaning of the great words: "If ye do not become as little children, ye shall in no wise enter into the Kingdom of Heaven!"

The way there can never be found with the complicated present-day thinking! Even in the churches and religions it is no different as yet! If these maintain that *sufferings* help one to *ascend* and that therefore they come under the mercy of God, this contains a small grain of Truth, but badly distorted in a glossing over sort of way! *For God does not will that His people should suffer!* He wills only joy, love and happiness! The way *within* the Light cannot be otherwise! The way *towards* the Light has stones only if man first places them there!

The grain of Truth in the doctrine of suffering is that with this suffering a certain guilt may be redeemed. This can only happen, however, when a man consciously *recognises* that he deserves this suffering, as did the penitent thief on the cross.

The way all the world goes on living today is just senseless! Even those who talk about the redemption of karma in such a clever way! They err, because it is still much more difficult than these would-be sages imagine. For karma *reactions* do not always bring *atonements*. Let every man mark this well! On the contrary, they may *drag him still further down!*

Notwithstanding the reaction due to guilt, the ascent of every man solely depends on his inner attitude. How he sets his course inwardly, whether upwards, straight on, or downwards, *thus* and not otherwise will he proceed in spite of all he experiences!

Here it becomes clear that he is not, nor ever can be, the plaything of fortune, but *must direct* his actual course alone through the power of his *free* will! *In this respect a man's will always remains free up to the last moment.* In this every man is truly his own free master, only he must never forget that according to his attitude the consequences lead him upwards or downwards!

If, however, he sets his course in an *upwards* direction with insight and a firm will, evil reactions will hit him less and less, and will finally have only a symbolical effect, because through his ascent he has already been removed from the nether regions of evil reactions, even though he may still be on this earth. It is not at all necessary that a man must *suffer* if he strives towards the Light!

Away, therefore, with the bandage which many placed before their eyes so that they would not tremble at the sight of the abyss that has yawned before them for a long time! Temporary relief from anxiety afforded by such a bandage is not strength-giving help, but only a loss of time through negligence which can never be retrieved!

There has never yet been a right explanation and justification for the suffering on earth. Therefore narcotics were offered in the form of palliatives, which over and over again are thoughtlessly handed out to the sufferers in more or less clever language. The great fault of one-sidedness in all religions!

And if a desperate seeker for once requires *too* precise an answer, then that which is not understood is simply pushed into the realm of Divine mystery. All unsolved questions have finally to end up there, as in a harbour of refuge, clearly showing thereby that they are on the *wrong* course!

For the end of every *right* course is clearly visible and does not terminate in something that is impenetrable! Wherever the "inscrutable ways of God" have to serve as an explanation, there ignorance is unmistakably in evidence!

There need not and must not be *any* mystery *within* Creation for man! For God wills that His Laws working in Creation should be quite *familiar* to man, so that he can adjust himself accordingly, and with their help can complete and fulfil his course through the world more easily and without ignorantly going astray!

Thus it remains one of the most fatal conceptions to consider the brutal murder of the Son of God as *a necessary propitiatory sacrifice* for mankind!

To think that this brutal murder of His Son would reconcile God!

Because no logical explanation can be advanced for this peculiar conception, in the ensuing confusion one again slips behind the frequently used protective screen of Divine mystery, making it something which can never become understandable to man.

Yet God is so clear in everything He does! He is lucidity itself! He created Nature out of His Will, and therefore what is natural must also be right, since the Will of God is absolutely perfect!

But the propitiatory sacrifice on the cross must be *unnatural* to every sane mind, because being against the innocent Son of God it is also unjust! All twisting and turning is useless! Rather should a man frankly confess that such a thing is truly beyond all comprehension! However much he likes to exercise his mind he will never come to any conclusion. The fact is that in this case he can no longer understand his God. *But it is God's Will that He should be understood!* And He can be understood, since the expression of His Will clearly rests in Creation and never contradicts itself. Only men take the trouble to introduce what is incomprehensible when making religious investigations!

The structure men so laboriously erected with the fundamentally false idea of a *necessary* vicarious sacrifice in the death on the cross is already destroyed by the words of the Saviour Himself at the time He was nailed to the cross!

"Father, forgive them, for they know not what they do!"

Would this intercession have been necessary if the death on the cross was meant to be a necessary propitiatory sacrifice? "For they know not what they do!" This is an accusation of the gravest kind! A clear indication that what they were doing was *wrong,* that this deed was nothing but an ordinary crime!

Would Christ have prayed in Gethsemane that this cup of suffering might pass from Him if His death on the cross was necessary as a vicarious sacrifice? Never! Christ would not have done so! It was because He knew that the tortures awaiting Him were *nothing but the consequence of the free will of man* that He prayed *thus!*

For two thousand years men have blindly passed this by, accepting with their empty minds what is absolutely impossible instead!

It is indeed distressing frequently to hear it seriously affirmed that the more favoured ones among today's disciples of Jesus, male as well as female, are endowed with physical suffering, such as stigmata!

Such a view, of course, only originates in the false interpretation of Christ's suffering on earth! Indeed it could not be otherwise! I still have to mention how personally serious these consequences can become!

How much thoughtlessness and what rigid servility are required so to depict the Almighty Creator that He could be thought to act in such a way! It is without doubt the most sinful debasement of the Sublime Godhead, for the conception of Whose Essential Nature the most beautiful cannot be beautiful enough and the best is still not good enough, in order to come only a little closer to reality! And to think that this great God should be capable of demanding that man whom He has created is to writhe in pain before Him when He accords him grace!

How can anyone holding such views ascend?

Men shape their God as *they* wish to have Him; *they* dictate the direction of

His Volition! And woe to Him if He is not what they think He ought to be! Then He is rejected forthwith, just as they condemn and fight against all *those* who dare to see God as much greater and more sublime! But no greatness is to be found in the past conceptions of man! On the contrary they merely bear witness to man's unshakable belief in his *own* worth. God has to beg for the favour of mankind! He Who was allowed to receive back from their blood-stained hands His Son Whom He had once sent to help them with the saving Message – scorned, mocked, scourged and tortured!

Does one still wish even today to affirm that all this was a necessary propitiatory sacrifice for God? When Christ Himself in His agony and absolute despair at their blindness cried out: "They know not *what* they do"?

Is there any possibility at all to lead mankind on to the right road? The most drastic happening is still too weak to accomplish this! When will man at last recognise to what depths he has actually sunk! How empty and hollow are the conceptions he has conjured up for himself!

As soon, however, as one digs a trifle deeper one comes upon selfishness in its most undisguised form neatly hidden away. Even if now people on all sides speak of seeking God in high-sounding words, this *again* is great hypocrisy and the usual self-complacency entirely devoid of any really serious longing for pure Truth! They only seek for self-worship – for nothing else! No man seriously strives to *understand God!*

With a benign smile they disregard and quickly push aside the simplicity of Truth, for they imagine themselves to be much too knowledgeable, much too high and much too important as that *their* God could still deal with simplicity. To uphold their honour He must be much more complicated! Otherwise it would not be worth believing in Him! In their view how can they possibly be expected to recognise something that is easily understandable to every unlearned person! Anything like that cannot be considered *great!* Today they dare not occupy themselves with such things, otherwise they would be liable to make great fools of themselves! Let this be for children, old women and the unlettered! Anyhow it is not for men with such well-trained intellects, with such intelligence, as are so much in evidence among the "cultured" of today! Let the *ordinary man* concern himself with that! Education and learnedness apply their standard of greatness only to what holds *the possibility of being the most difficult to comprehend!*

Ignorant indeed are those who think thus! They are not worthy to receive one further drop of water from the Hand of the Creator in the weaving of Creation!

They have so limited themselves as to preclude the possibility of recognising the radiant sublimity which lies in the simplicity of the Divine Laws. They are literally incapable of doing so or, to put it more bluntly, too stupid owing to their one-sidedly stunted brain, which from the hour of their birth right up till now they carry around with them like a trophy of the highest achievement!

It is indeed an act of mercy if the Creator will leave them to perish in the structure they have erected! For wherever one looks all is hostile towards God, distorted by the morbid ambition of every man of intellect, whose incapacity is evident everywhere!

And this has been going on with increasing intensity for thousands of years! It has inevitably carried the poison into the churches and religions, a corrosive evil which was the inevitable consequence of the Fall of Man, wherein man decided in favour of the absolute dominion of the intellect!

This wrongfully usurped authority has at all times deceived those it has enslaved in everything that concerns the Divine, even in all that is spiritual!

He who does not cast down this throne within himself and thereby become free must perish with it!

One can no longer speak of *poor* mankind, for they are *consciously* guilty, as guilty as ever a creature could be! The words: "Forgive them, for they know not what they do" are *no longer* appropriate for mankind of today. They had more than one opportunity to open their eyes and their ears. They act in full consciousness, and all reactions must therefore hit them with full force, unabated!

If now the ring of all the past happenings closes, then the reaping, the harvest, and the separation for this part of Creation will take place. Since the creation of the entire World of Matter this has never occurred before!

THE GODS, OLYMPUS AND VALHALLA

FOR A LONG time now attempts have been made to find the right interpretation about the gods known in past ages and their connection with the present time. Called ones and scholars alike are seeking for a solution which will bring complete clarification!

However this will only be possible if the solution provides a comprehensive and unbroken survey over *all* the ages, from the beginning of the human race to the present day. Otherwise it will again remain incomplete. It is of no value just to pick out the period in which the well-known cults of the Greeks, Romans and Teutons regarding gods were at their height. So long as the explanations do not also freely and quite naturally embrace all evolution and disintegration they are wrong! In spite of much cleverness the attempts so far begun have always finally resulted in failure. They could never stand their ground before the deeper intuitive perception, and without a connection with the previous and succeeding periods could only hang in the air!

Nothing else can be expected when one closely scrutinises the development of man!

The hearers and readers of my Grail Message should be able to discover for themselves how these matters actually stand! They have even been partly relegated to the realm of sagas and legends, or efforts were made to accept them only as phantasies conjured up by religious beliefs, formed and thought out through observation of Nature and in context with everyday life.

Yet it should not be hard for the thinker and investigator to find *more* in the old lore than mere *myths!* He must even clearly see the *actual happening!* Those who wish to do so should follow my explanation!

Here I would refer back to my lecture: "Father, forgive them, for they know not what they do!" In that lecture I briefly described the history of mankind on earth from the very beginning until now. I also gave a glimpse into the future. In so doing I showed how midway in the cycle of Creation the animistic, which stands lower than the spiritual, had achieved fulfilment to the highest of its abilities in the World of Matter below it, and in the course of this fulfilment had opened the way for the entrance into matter of the higher spiritual – a process which repeats itself continually in Creation. I also explained how in the highest animal body developed by the animistic, and called Primeval Man, there was created the opportunity which *only then,* that is, during the climax of its development, permitted a spirit-germ to enter, which promptly took place. It is an opportunity which will always be provided anew at this point of development in Creation. Thus into the most highly developed animal of that time there entered something new, the spiritual, which had never been in it before!

It should not be hastily concluded from the foregoing that this process continuously repeats itself in the *same* part of the Universe as that part develops further, for this is not the case! It happens *only once in each part!*

In the further development the Law of the Attraction of Homogeneous Species also here effectively blocks a repetition in the same part of the Universe. In this case the attraction of the homogeneous species is equivalent to the *admission* of spirit-germs to the World of Matter during a certain definite period in its development. When it has reached a certain state of half-ripeness and receptivity, the spirit-germs whirling about on its border are able to rush like meteoric showers into the World of Matter. There they are absorbed and enveloped, i. e., neatly protected and retained by the elements which have become receptive for this purpose, which in this case were the most highly developed animal bodies.

It is just the same on a small scale with the chemical process of amalgamation, in which a foreign substance can only amalgamate with the absorbing substance when the latter has reached a very definite temperature, this degree of heat having in turn produced a very special and outstanding state of the absorbing substance which can only be attained at this particular temperature. The slightest divergence from this exact condition again prevents an amalgamation, the substances repelling and remaining unapproachable to each other!

In this case the homogeneity of the two species lies in a certain condition of mutual maturity, which *appears* to indicate a great contradiction, but the balance is maintained through the difference in elevation of the two parts to be amalgamated. The maturity of the lowest point of the spiritual is similar to the maturity of the highest point of the animistic lying below it. Only at this *exact* point of meeting is amalgamation possible. And since in its development the World of Matter unceasingly moves in a gigantic cycle – budding, blossoming, ripening, and decaying through over-ripeness, while the spiritual reposes above it – this process can only be sparked at a very definite point during the time the World of Matter passes by. It is a spiritual fructification of the World of Matter, which has been developed for this purpose by the working of the animistic, and longingly awaits consummation!

If a certain part of the world in its cycle passes this point, the possibility of spiritual fructification *by spirit-germs* ceases for this part, and the part following it moves into position. For the first part, however, a new stage commences in which maturing spirits can later find access to it, and so on. In this lecture I have no room to unfold the whole world picture, but a serious investigator may well conjecture the further development.

Due to its higher nature the spiritual, even in its then *unconscious* state, exercised its vital influence in a noticeable manner upon everything as soon as it entered the World of Matter – it began to dominate on its arrival in the World of Matter! How the spiritual then gradually raised the animal body to the level of the present human body my readers already comprehend!

The animal bodies of the most highly developed race of that time, into which no spirit-germs incarnated, came to a standstill in their development, however, because the animistic element within them had already attained to the highest it could attain to, and they lacked the power of the spirit to advance further. And with the standstill over-ripeness quickly set in, to be followed by retrogression and disintegration! For these races there were only two possibilities, either development into a human body through the power of the spirit, or decay and extinction. And as a result these matured animal species became completely extinct!

Let us now follow up the slow *development* of the at first unconscious spirit-germ to a state of *consciousness* as a human spirit, and *let us accompany it spiritually as step by step it penetrates the coverings enveloping it and the surroundings in which it lives!*

This is not so difficult because the process of development is quite plainly visible externally. One need only observe the human races *still* in existence on earth *today!*

The spirit of the most primitive people, for instance, which include the so-called savage tribes, and also the Bushmen, Hottentots, and so on, has perhaps been in the World of Matter just as long as that of other peoples, but has not kept pace in development, *or after already ascending in this world or in the beyond has again retrogressed so far* that it could be incarnated *only* in such *lowly* surroundings. Through their *own guilt* and in the natural course of events they either *remain* or are *again* on a very low step, as a result of which their outlook upon the *non-gross material* environment is far from being of an uplifting nature!

The spiritual urge of desiring to see more than that which is on its own step has always resided within the spirit-germ as a part of its essential nature, and therefore has a strong effect even in the lowest stages of development! This is the living motive power *within the spirit,* the special element which is lacking in other kinds or species in Creation. The possibility of thus wishing to see or perceive is always provided, but for *one* step only *above* the one it stands upon at the time, and no further. It is for this reason that the human souls standing on such a low step, who have so sinfully neglected their development, can similarly see or perceive only *base* entities through clairvoyance!

There are mediums and clairvoyant people among *all* races, regardless of what step they belong to.

Here I must once more mention especially that when I speak of "seeing" or "perceiving" I really only mean that which is *"personally* seen" by the clairvoyant, according to my explanation! But that which the "seeing ones" of all times can actually "see" is only the fourth part *at the most* of what they see. And this again can be but one step above their own inner maturity, and no more! There is no other possibility! But this circumstance constitutes at the same time a great natural protection for every clairvoyant, as I have repeatedly stated before.

It must not be assumed that mediums and clairvoyants are necessarily so matured and inwardly advanced as are the things which they describe as having "seen", for the purer and more luminous heights, the happenings and the spirits are *shown* to them only in *living pictures* by spirit guides and higher entities! The clairvoyants, however, erroneously imagine that they have actually experienced all this, thus deceiving themselves about it. Great surprise is often occasioned by the baseness of the characters of so many mediums, who describe things as though they had experienced and seen them, things which do not at all seem to fit their own characters, or very little!

Therefore I speak *here* only of the narrow field of *actual personal seeing* by mediums and clairvoyants! The rest is not considered!

The mediums and clairvoyants of *all* times should actually only serve the purpose of helping mankind more and more upwards through their gifts, not as leaders but as instruments! Mediums could never be leaders because they are much too dependent upon vibrations and other influences. They are meant to be doors which open from time to time for the purpose of furthering development, rungs in the ladder of ascent!

If you now realise that races standing on a low level of spiritual development can only see into the same base environment, with but little scope in an upward direction, it is not hard to understand that among the *lower* human races we find primarily the fear and worship of demons! That is what they are able to see and perceive!

So much for a superficial consideration, but I shall go deeper with my explanation, although in so doing we branch off from the clear survey!

The spirit of the lower human races which has either never been developed or has again degenerated is naturally still *spiritually blind* and *deaf,* or has again become so. Such a person cannot see with his spiritual eye, *nor unfortunately has this become possible to any man even to this day!*

The man still on the lower stage, however, cannot even see with his animistic eye, and just as little with his ethereal eye – he can only see with his gross material eye, which becomes ever sharper in the wilderness through the necessary personal struggle with his fellow-men, the animals and the elements, whereby he gradually learns to distinguish *finer* and *finest* gross matter!

Thus in the beginning they notice the *phantoms,* entities which have only been *formed* through men's fear and anxiety, and which are also sustained by these emotions!

These phantoms, *which have no life of their own,* are completely dependent upon the intuitions of man. They are attracted or repulsed by them. Here the Law of the Power of Attraction of all Homogeneous Species takes effect. Fear always attracts these forms produced by fear and anxiety, so that it appears as if they were absolutely rushing at the frightened human beings!

Since these phantoms are connected with their authors – themselves very frightened human beings – through flexible nourishing-strands, every fearful man is therefore always indirectly connected with the mass of anxious and fearful people, thus receiving additional nourishment which increases his own fear and anxiety all the more, and which may finally even drive him to despair and insanity!

Fearlessness or courage, on the other hand, absolutely repels such phantoms in a natural manner! Therefore, as is well known, the fearless man always has the advantage!

Is it then surprising if among the lower races the so-called medicine-men and sorcerers came into being, whose caste was founded by *clairvoyant persons,* because the latter were able to observe how such forms, erroneously considered entities with a life of their own, are "repelled" through a little inner composure, by warding off fear through leaps and contortions, or through concentration or courage-instilling exorcisms!

If in our opinion they consequently think up ideas which appear impossible and ridiculous to us, that does not alter the fact that they are doing something *which is quite right within the limits of their horizon* and their power of comprehension, and that *we* alone are the ignorant ones who lack understanding for such things!

It happens that among the successors of these sorcerers and medicine-men there are naturally many men who have neither mediumistic nor clairvoyant abilities in any way, especially since this position brings them influence and income, at which men on the most inferior steps grab just as unscrupulously as those of the high white race. These non-clairvoyant successors then simply imitated all the actions of their predecessors without understanding what they were doing. They even added a few more follies in order to make a greater impression, because they only valued the respect of their fellow-men! Thus they became the crafty impostors who seek only their own advantage, and have not the slightest idea about the real meaning! And today the whole caste is judged and condemned on their account!

This is the real reason why we first of all find only the fear and worship of demons among the lower human races! It is what they are able to see and what they fear on account of its different nature!

Let us now proceed to somewhat higher stages of development! Here the ability to see reaches further, be it through clairvoyance or only unconsciously through perception, which is also a part of inner seeing. Through these higher developments, further enveloping layers are pushed through from the inside upwards by the encased spirits, which are awakening more and more.

These spirits already see more friendly entities or know about them by perception, and thus they will gradually lose their demon-worship. And so it goes on higher and higher, becoming more and more luminous! With normal development the spirit pushes ahead further and further!

The Greeks, the Romans and the Teutons, for instance, could see still further! Their inner seeing reached beyond the World of Matter into the Animistic Sphere lying above it. In their more advanced development they could finally even see *the Lords of the Elementals and of the Elements.* A few mediumistic individuals among them, by virtue of their ability, could even enjoy a closer relationship with them, because these created beings of the Conscious Animistic Sphere have a certain affinity to *that* animistic substantiality of which man also carries a part within himself in addition to the spiritual!

To see, to feel and to hear the elementals was the highest the peoples could achieve in their stage of development *at that time.* It is only natural that these peoples should then look upon the mighty Lords of the Elements, whose activity and nature were so different from their own, as the highest possible, calling them gods, and their high impregnable fastnesses, which really exist, Olympus and Valhalla!

Any outward expression of the inner seeing and hearing of men is always dependent upon their *personal* ability to comprehend and to express at the time. Thus it is that the Greeks, the Romans and the Teutons depicted the *same* Lords of the Elements and of all that is animistic in form and conception, but always in accordance with the views prevailing in their surroundings! Despite some differences in their descriptions they were the same, however!

If today, for example, five or more really good clairaudients are assembled, and all of them simultaneously hear a very definite sentence *spoken in the beyond,* then only *the sense* of what they heard will be rendered uniformly, but not the actual words. Each will report the words differently, even hear them differently, because even in the reception much that is *personal* makes itself felt! It is the same as with music, which is perceived quite differently by the various listeners, yet recognised as being fundamentally the same! I must only gradually reveal the details regarding the far-reaching secondary phenomena in the relation between earth-man and the Universe, as today it would divert us too far from the subject under discussion!

When in later times *called* peoples, that is, those who were most highly developed inwardly (intellectual development does *not* count in these matters), were able to burst through this boundary of the Animistic Sphere as they matured through their experiences, their seeing or perception penetrated *to the threshold of the Spiritual Realm!*

The natural consequence was that they had to dethrone the past gods as such and replace them with what was higher. Despite this, however, they unfortunately *did not advance* so far as to become able *to see what is spiritual!*

Thus the Spiritual Realm remained *closed* to them, because the normal course of development was halted at this point, restrained by the ever-increasing growth of intellectual conceit!

Only a few exceptions saved themselves from this standstill, such as Buddha and a few others who, by renouncing the world, succeeded in continuing their development in a normal manner, and in seeing spiritually to a certain degree!

This renunciation of the world, or turning away from mankind for the purpose of further spiritual development, became necessary only through the one-sided training of the intellect, which generally increased its domination more and more and is antagonistic to all that is spiritual. It was a natural form of self-protection against the increasing spiritual decline, which would not be necessary at all if the *general* development is normal! On the contrary, for when a man reaches a certain height in his spiritual development he must continue to strengthen himself through further activity, otherwise he will become lax, which would quickly put a stop to further advance! Standstill would then ensue, speedily followed by retrogression!

Although the further spiritual development of Buddha and others succeeded only to a certain degree, i. e., it was incomplete, still this greatly increased their remoteness from their fellow-men, so that such normally developed human beings came to be regarded as Divine Envoys, whereas what in fact happened was that only a new conception arose quite naturally through their further spiritual progress!

Those human beings who had risen above the masses (which had halted and partly retrogressed spiritually) stood only at the open door to the Spiritual World, where they could perceive certain things vaguely, *but could never see clearly*. Yet they distinctly sensed and intuitively perceived a powerful conscious *uniform* guidance coming from above, from a world into which they were never able to see!

Yielding to this intuition they now formed the idea of the *one invisible God,* without knowing anything further about Him!

It is therefore understandable that they regarded this God, Whom they had merely sensed, as the highest *spiritual* being, because the spiritual region was new to them and they were still standing only on its *threshold*.

Thus it was that their new idea of an invisible God was only correct as to the fact, *but not as to the conception,* for their conception of Him was wrong! The human spirit has *never* envisaged *the* God *as He really is!* Man thought of Him merely as the *Highest Spiritual Being!* And this gap in the further development even shows itself today in that many human beings persistently cling to the idea that they have something of the *same nature* as they perceive to be their God's!

The fault lies in the *standstill* that occurred in *spiritual development.*

Had this development *continued* then maturing mankind, during the transition from the old gods of the Animistic Sphere, would not have thought next of this One God as an Invisible God, but would first of all have been able to perceive, standing above the Lords of the Elements called gods, the *Spiritual Primordial Beings who have their seat in the Grail Castle,* the highest fastness of the *Spiritual World.* And in the beginning they would have again considered these Primordial Beings as gods, until they had *developed themselves inwardly to such an extent* that they would not merely have been able to perceive the Primordial Beings, who are the true *images* of God, but also to *hear* them spiritually through mediators. From these they would have received information of the existence outside of Creation of the *"One Supreme God"!*

Had their intuitive perception been directed in this manner they would, through further spiritual maturing and development, have finally become capable of joyfully receiving *Divine Messages* out of the actual Divine Sphere from a Messenger of God, i.e., from outside of Creation, and therefore beyond their capacity to see!

That would have been the normal way!

As it was, however, their development came to a halt on the threshold of the Spiritual Sphere, and even declined quickly through the fault of man!

Thus the time came when, as *an act of emergency,* a strong Envoy from God had to be incarnated in Jesus of Nazareth, in order to bring to a humanity still too immature *for it* a Message from the Divine Sphere to help and enlighten them, so that seekers lacking the necessary maturity *could for the time being at least pin their faith in it!*

For this reason the Son of God, who had been sent to the aid of erring mankind, could do nothing more than demand *faith and trust* in His Word!

A desperate task! *Christ could not even say everything He wished to say!* Therefore He did *not* speak of many things, such as reincarnation, and so on! In these matters He was confronted with too great a spiritual immaturity. And He Himself sorrowfully said to His disciples: *"I would say many things unto you, but you would not understand!"*

Thus even His disciples misunderstood Him in many things! And if Christ Himself already knew while He was on earth that He was not understood *by His disciples*, it is obvious that later on there arose during the transmission of His Word many errors to which, unfortunately, even today man tries to cling tenaciously! Although Christ demanded only *faith* in His Word on account of the immaturity of that time, yet He requested from those who were of serious volition that their initial faith should also become "alive" within them!

That means that they would thereby become convinced! For he who confidently followed His Word would again progress in his spiritual development, and would thus be bound gradually to advance from faith to conviction as to the truth of what Christ had said!

Therefore the Son of Man will now demand *conviction* instead of faith! Also from all those who profess to carry Christ's Message within themselves and pretend to follow it! For he who has not been able to replace his faith with the *conviction* of the truth of Christ's Divine Message, which is *one* with and inseparable from the Grail Message, has not attained the maturity of spirit necessary to enter Paradise. Such a person will be cast out!

Even the greatest intellectual knowledge will not permit him to slip through! He must naturally remain behind and be lost for evermore!

That in their stage of development mankind in this part of the Universe still stand on the *threshold* of the Spiritual Realm, the greater part even far *below* it, is merely caused by their personal lack of volition, their intellectual conceit and their belief that they know everything better than others! As a result it is absolutely impossible for them to develop in the normal way, as has probably become clear to many persons in the meantime!

The various religious cults of mankind do not originate from phantasy, but indicate sections of *life* in the so-called beyond. Even the existence of the medicine-man of a Negro or Red Indian tribe is justified in view of the *low stage of development* of his people! That there are rogues and impostors among them does not discredit this fact as such!

Demons, wood-nymphs and sylphs, as also the so-called old gods, are to-day still in the same place and carry on the same activity as before! Even the high fastnesses of the great Lords of the Elements, Olympus or Valhalla, were never fairy tales, but were really seen! However, what mankind *has never been able to* see, having come to a standstill in their development, are the prime-spiritual Primordial images of God, who also have a lofty fastness which they call the Grail Castle, the highest castle in the Primordial Sphere, and thus in all Creation!

Standing as he did on the threshold of the Spiritual Sphere man could only receive knowledge of the existence of this Castle through inspiration, because he was not spiritually mature enough *intuitively* to "perceive" it!

All is life! Only men, who consider themselves advanced, have turned aside and back again towards the depths, instead of progressing!

Now it must not be thought that in a further development the conception of God as taught by Christ and in my Grail Message would change again! This will remain forever as it is, because there is nothing further!

When entering the Spiritual Realm, which mankind still fails to accomplish today, and achieving perfection therein, every human spirit can ascend to that point where in the end he gains absolute conviction of this fact in his inward experiences. Then, standing consciously in the Power of God, he could bring about those great things for which he already had been ordained from the beginning! He would then never again imagine he possessed Divinity within himself! This delusion is nothing but the stamp and the seal of his present immaturity!

Having achieved a *right* consciousness he would then feel true humility and a liberating desire to serve, which had always been *demanded* by the pure teachings of Christ!

Only when missionaries, preachers and teachers begin their activities by using as their foundation the knowledge of the natural development of all Creation, and thus the exact knowledge about the Laws of the Divine Will, without being desultory or leaving any gaps, will they really be able to achieve successes that are *spiritually alive!*

Unfortunately every religion is now nothing but a rigid form, only holding together its dull doctrine with a great deal of trouble! After the necessary change, however, the hitherto dull doctrine will become invigorated, burst asunder the cold, dead and rigid forms, and jubilantly and tumultuously flow forth over the entire world and among all peoples!

THE CREATURE THAT IS MAN

MY ASSERTION that mankind do not bear within themselves anything that is Divine continually evokes new waves of indignation which flood over the borders of one country after another. This shows how deeply conceit has taken root in the souls of men, and how much they dislike separating themselves from it, even though their intuitive perception calls out warningly now and then, giving them the opportunity to recognise that this must be true after all!

But struggling against it does not alter the fact! As soon as the human spirits have come to the conviction that they are void of anything Divine, they will recognise that they are *still* smaller, indeed much less, than they imagine they are!

Therefore I wish to go further than I have done as yet, and explain Creation in a little more detail in order to show on which step man belongs. Indeed it is hardly possible for him to begin his ascent without knowing exactly beforehand what he *is* and what he *can do!* Once this becomes clear to him he will also finally realise what he *must do!*

That, however, is greatly at variance with everything he *wills* today! Indeed, what a difference there is!

This no longer awakens compassion in the person who is privileged to see clearly! By "seeing" I do not mean the seeing of a clairvoyant, but that of a man who possesses true knowledge! Instead of compassion and pity today only *anger* is engendered, anger and contempt at the stupendous presumption shown towards God, of which hundreds of thousands of conceited ones are guilty daily and hourly! Their conceit contains no grain of knowledge to justify it! It is not worth wasting a single word upon it!

What I have to say from now onwards is meant for the few who, in pure humility, can still attain to a certain degree of recognition without first having to be so crushed as will soon happen in accordance with the Divine Laws, in order finally to force an entrance and prepare a fertile soil for His *true* Word!

Then all the empty and wordy effusions of earthly wiseacres will crumble away, together with the absolutely unfruitful soil of the present day!

It is indeed high time that this empty profusion of words, which acts like a poison upon all that strives upwards, should collapse in all its hollowness!

Hardly had I made my assertion that the Son of God and the Son of Man are two separate Personalities than there appeared treatises intended to *clarify* in confused theological-philosophical jargon that this is not so! Without going into my arguments impartially, attempts are made to maintain the old error *at all costs,* even at the cost of all logical objectiveness, citing for this purpose the obscure terms of the existing dogma! They stubbornly rely upon single sentences out of ancient manuscripts to the exclusion of all independent thought; thus making it a condition (which is never expressed in words) that hearers and readers must not think, much less sense intuitively! For otherwise it would be quickly recognised that nothing is explained by this multitude of words, because whichever way they are examined it remains impossible to draw the right inference! But it is still more obvious that this verbosity lacks all connection with actual events!

He who finally succeeds in opening his eyes and ears in these matters must without difficulty recognise the emptiness of such "apologia"! It is but a last convulsive clinging (one can no longer call it real adherence) to what has hitherto been their support, which will soon prove to be *useless!*

The only foundation for their arguments is composed of sentences, the correct transmission of which cannot be proved. On the contrary, it is impossible logically to fit them into the course of world events, thereby clearly showing that their sense has been distorted by the human brain in the course of transmission. Not one of these sentences can be assimilated with the chain of events and man's intuitive perception without leaving a gap. Yet only where everything comes to a conclusion through *the completion of its cycle,* without any phantasy or expressions of blind faith, only *there* is every happening explained *in the right manner!*

But why exert oneself if man *does not wish* to be freed from such obstinate fatuity? Therefore let that calmly come to pass which in the circumstances *must* come to pass!

It is with a shudder that I turn away from all the believers and from all those who in their false humility think they know better, who do not recognise a simple truth but even smile indulgently at it and want to correct it! How quickly will just these persons become little, so very little, and lose every support, although in fact neither in their faith nor in their knowledge do they have such! They will be *permitted* to walk upon the road which they so persistently desire, but upon which they can no longer return to life! The right to choose has never been denied them!

Those who have followed me so far know that man originates in the highest sphere of Creation, in the Spiritual Sphere. But there are still many differences to be noted in the Realm of the Spiritual. Man on earth, who audaciously considers himself great, who often does not shrink from dragging his God down by regarding Him merely as the highest on *that* step to which *he himself* belongs, who sometimes even ventures to deny or revile Him, man in reality is not even that which many a humble soul imagines himself to be in all good faith! Man on earth is *not a created being,* but merely a *developed being!* That is a difference which man is unable to perceive, and which he will never be able to survey freely!

Beautiful and agreeable to many are the words which numerous teachers utter in their efforts to increase the number of their adherents! Yet these ignorant teachers are themselves convinced that all the errors they spread abroad are the truth, and do not realise what great harm they thereby do to mankind!

Only certainty about the answer to that great question *"What am I?"* can lead to *ascent!* If the significance of this question has not been completely recognised and the solution found beforehand ascent will become bitterly difficult! For men do not *voluntarily* submit themselves to that humbleness which will help them on to the right path on which they can really progress! That has been clearly proved by all the past events right up to the present time!

Even in their efforts to be humble these men either turned themselves into slaves, which is just as wrong as being presumptuous, or reached far beyond their actual goal, placing themselves upon a road the end of which they can never reach, because the nature of their spirits does not suffice for this! As they aspired to what is too exalted for them they will now fall headlong into the depths, which will destroy them!

Only the *Created Ones* are images of God! These are the Primordial Beings, the Prime-Spiritual Beings, in that Original Creation out of which all else developed. In their hands lies the main guidance of all that is spiritual.

They are the ideals, the eternal prototypes for all humanity. Earthman, on the other hand, has only been able to develop himself as a copy out of this complete Creation, starting as a small unconscious spirit-germ and evolving into a self-conscious personality.

Only when he has reached perfection by keeping to the right path in Creation will he take on the likeness of the images of God! He himself is never an actual image of God! There is a great gulf all the way down to him from the Divine!

But even from the actual images of God the next step is far from being to God! Therefore man on earth should at last recognise all that lies between him and the Sublimity of the Godhead, which he tries so hard to usurp! Man on earth imagines that he will become Divine once he has reached perfection, or at least be a part of Divinity, while actually at his greatest height he will only be the *likeness* of an *image* of God. He is permitted to enter the forecourt in the entrance hall of a Grail Castle as the highest distinction which can be bestowed upon a human spirit!

Cast aside this presumption at last! It can only hinder you and make you miss the luminous path! Dwellers in the beyond who wish to give well-meaning advice in spiritist circles do *not* know about it, for they themselves lack the necessary recognition. They would rejoice if they were permitted to hear about it! Among these also the great lamentation will not fail to come, once they recognise how much time they have wasted in fruitless toying and obstinacy!

What applies to the Spiritual World also holds true for the Animistic Sphere. Here the Lords of all the Elements are the *Prime-Elemental Beings.* All those elementals which gain consciousness, such as the nixies, elves, gnomes, salamanders, and so on, are *not* Created Ones, but merely beings which have been developed out of Creation. They have developed out of the Realm of Animistic Substantiality, starting as unconscious *elemental* seed-germs and evolving into conscious elementals, in the course of which, as they gain consciousness, they also assume human forms. This latter always occurs simultaneously with becoming conscious. There is the same gradation here in the Animistic Sphere as exists in the Spiritual Sphere.

According to the nature of their activity the Prime-Elemental Beings in the Animistic Sphere are clothed in male and female forms, just the same as the Primordial Beings in the Spiritual Sphere. Hence the conception of *gods* and *goddesses* in the olden times, which I have already dealt with in my lecture: "The Gods, Olympus and Valhalla"!

There is one great uniform feature permeating all Creation and the World!

The reader and hearer of my lectures should always work within himself, keenly scrutinising my lectures and constructing bridges from one to the other, as well as outside to the great and small happenings in the world! *Not until he does so* will he be able to understand the Grail Message! He will find that it will gradually shape itself into one complete whole, leaving no gaps. Again and again in all the happenings the reader will come back to the basic features. He can explain everything and deduce everything without having to change one single sentence. He who detects gaps lacks full understanding! He who does not realise its great depth and all-embracing character is superficial, and has never tried to penetrate with real animation into the spirit of the Truth brought here!

He may join those masses who, full of self-complacency and believing they already possess the highest knowledge, follow the broad road! The belief that they possess this knowledge prevents such mistaken persons from recognising in other statements the vitality lacking in their own pseudo-knowledge. Wherever they look, whatever they hear, everywhere their self-satisfaction with what they imagine they hold firmly in their hands blocks them!

Not until they reach the boundary line, where all untruth and sham are inevitably rejected, will they recognise on revealing their hands that these contain *nothing* which makes it at all possible for them to continue on their present road and ultimately enter the Kingdom of the Spirit. Then, however, it will prove too late to retrace their steps and receive what they previously rejected and disregarded! There is no longer sufficient time for that! The gate to the entrance is locked! The last opportunity is missed!

Only when man *actually* becomes what he *should* be and ceases to cling to what he wishes to be can he speak of a true humanity! He must always remember that he only issued out of *Creation,* not directly from the Hand of the Creator!

"That is quibbling with words, for basically it is just the same, only expressed differently!" So say the boastful and lazy ones, barren products of this humanity because they will forever remain incapable of perceiving the great gulf indicated by these words. Once more they let themselves be deceived by the simplicity of the words!

He who is inwardly alert will not carelessly pass this by! He will try to perceive the immeasurable distances and sharp lines of demarcation involved!

Were I now to indicate *all* the divisions of Creation, many a man who today considers he is great would prostrate himself in despair on recognising that such words contain the Truth, crushed by the realisation of his own emptiness and insignificance! The frequently used expression "earth-worm" is justified when applied to those who today still boast of their cleverness and "spiritual superiority", but who soon, very soon, will be made the lowest in all Creation if, indeed, they are not numbered among those who are rejected!

The time has now come to comprehend the world aright! It is not wrong to separate that which is temporal from that which is spiritual, also in earthly life. These terms have probably arisen through the ability of many human beings to sense correctly, for they reflect the difference existing right through the entire Creation. We can also divide Creation into Paradise and the World, i. e., into the spiritual and the temporal. Here also the spiritual is not excluded from the temporal, but the temporal is excluded from the spiritual!

We must call the World the World of Matter, which is also penetrated by the spirit! The spiritual is the Spiritual Realm of Creation, Paradise, from which everything that is material is excluded. Thus we have Paradise and the World, the spiritual and the material, Original Creation and the development therefrom, which may also be called an automatic copy!

Creation proper merely consists of Paradise, the Spiritual Kingdom of today. Everything else is only *developed*, i. e., no longer really created! And what has been *developed* must be designated as the *World!* The World is transient. It develops from the emanations of Creation, imitating the latter in reflections, being driven and sustained by spiritual emanations. It comes to maturity and then disintegrates again through over-ripeness. The spiritual, however, does not age, but remains forever young or, in other words, eternally the same!

Guilt and atonement are only possible in the *World!* This is due to the faultiness of the subsequent development. Guilt of any kind is utterly impossible in the Realm of the Spirit!

He who has seriously read my lectures will be absolutely clear about this. He knows that any spirit which penetrates the world can never return to its source of origin as long as but a *minute speck* of a different species still clings to it from its wanderings! The smallest particle makes it impossible to step over the border into the Spiritual Realm! The spirit would be retained, even if it had advanced to the very threshold! Owing to its different and baser consistency this last particle does not permit the spirit to enter as long as it remains clinging thereto!

Not until the moment when this minute speck severs itself and sinks back does the spirit become completely free, thus attaining the same consistency as prevails in the *lowest* plane of the Spiritual Sphere, which consistency exists as the law for this lowest spiritual plane! Then the spirit not only *can* but *must* enter by crossing the threshold at which it was previously held back by the last particle!

This process can be considered and described from many angles, but it remains exactly the same, regardless of the words used to illustrate it. I can embellish it with the most fantastic stories, can use many parables to make it understood, but the fact in itself is quite plain and simple, and is produced by the effect of the three laws I have so often mentioned.

It may also rightfully be said that no sin can occur in Paradise, that it is not touched by any guilt. Consequently only that which has been created is of full value. But in that which has subsequently evolved out of it as a copy of Creation, and which has been set aside as a training ground for the development and strengthening of the human spirit, guilt can be incurred through the false volition of indolent human spirits, which must be balanced through atonement before they are able to return!

If in following a self-engendered urge spirit-germs issue from Creation, i. e., from Paradise, in order to wander through the aforementioned world, one can naturally say by way of illustration that they are like children who leave home in order to learn and finally return fully matured. This mode of expression is justified if it is regarded merely as a *picture*. However, everything must always remain a picture, and must not be taken personally, as is attempted everywhere!

Since the human spirit only burdens itself with guilt in the world, such a thing not being possible in the Spiritual Sphere, it is also natural that it cannot return to the Spiritual Realm until it frees itself from this burden of guilt! I could give a thousand different illustrations of this, but they would *all* have the same fundamental meaning, which I have so often depicted in the working of the three simple basic laws.

It sounds strange to many people when I describe the process *objectively*, because illustrations flatter man's conceit and self-love! He much prefers to live in a dreamland, because everything sounds much nicer there, and he imagines himself to be much more important than he really is! In so doing he makes the mistake of refusing to examine what is objective, but instead indulges increasingly in imaginative phantasy, thus losing his way and his support! He is then horrified, perhaps even indignant, if I show him soberly and in all simplicity *how* Creation is and what part he actually plays in it!

For him the transition is somewhat like that of a small child which, in the loving hands of mother or grandmother, listens happily to fairy stories with sparkling eyes and cheeks flushed with enthusiasm, and then, out in the world, sees men as they really are! So altogether different from the beautiful tales, and yet, when you look more keenly and retrospectively at these fairy tales, it is basically the same! This moment is bitter but necessary, otherwise the child would be unable to make any progress and, as "a stranger in the world", would perish under much suffering!

It is no different here! He who wishes to ascend further must at last come to understand Creation as it *really* is! He must stride firmly on his feet, and no longer lose himself in emotional impressions, which may be all very well for an irresponsible child, but not for a mature man whose power of volition penetrates Creation, either furthering or retarding it, and uplifting or destroying him in the process!

Young girls who read novels which misrepresent the truth and only veil the reality of life will, through the fanciful illusions thus awakened, quickly experience bitter disappointments, and even very often become broken for their entire time on earth, falling an easy prey to this unscrupulous deception which they so trustingly approached. It is no different with the development of a human spirit in Creation!

Therefore away with all illustrations! Man never learned to understand them, because he was much too lazy to apply himself seriously to the discovery of the right interpretation. It is time for the veils to fall so that man can see clearly whence he came, what duties his task bestows upon him, and also what is his destination! *He needs to be shown the right path!* And he will find this path clearly marked in my Grail Message, providing he *wishes* to see it.

The Word of the Grail Message lives! It only permits those people to find abundantly in it who really carry the honest desire in their souls! All others are automatically rejected! To those who are conceited and who only seek superficially the Message will remain a book with seven seals!

Only he who willingly opens himself will receive! If from the beginning he starts to read with a sincere and honest mind, then everything he seeks will be revealed in one glorious fulfilment! But those whose hearts are not completely pure will be repelled by this Word; it will remain closed to those of deceitful eye! They will find nothing therein!

AND A THOUSAND YEARS ARE AS ONE DAY!

WHO AMONG all mankind has already grasped the meaning of these words? In what church are they truly interpreted? In many cases they are taken as a conception of life without time. But there is nothing in Creation which is not limited in time and space. The very meaning of the word "Creation" must contradict such a conception, for what is created is a work, and every work has a limit! And whatever is limited must have boundaries! And what has boundaries can also not be timeless!

There are a number of spheres where human spirits dwell according to their spiritual maturity. These spheres vary in density as they are near to or more remote from Paradise. The further they are from Paradise the denser and thus heavier they will be.

The conception of time and space becomes narrower as density increases, as substance becomes more solid in the World of Matter, and as the distance from the Spiritual Realm increases.

The different conceptions of time and space arise from the more or less elastic ability of man's brain to absorb experiences which, in turn, is adapted to the density of his environment, that is, to the nature of the sphere in the Cosmos in which his body happens to be at the time. Thus it is that we have to speak of different conceptions of time and space in the different spheres of the Cosmos!

There are spheres in the Cosmos situated much nearer to Paradise than the sphere to which the earth belongs. Those spheres lying nearer to it are of a different material consistency, which is lighter and less solid. Consequently they offer more extensive opportunities to experience in full consciousness. Here on earth we call it experiencing which registers in our day-consciousness.

The worlds of matter which are of a different nature belong to fine gross matter, as well as to coarse ethereal matter, and also to pure ethereal matter, while we at present live in the World of absolute Gross Matter. The more rarified matter is, the more pervious it also is. The more pervious a species of matter is, however, the more extensive become the possibilities for conscious experiencing or, let us call it, the possibilities for receiving impressions, on the part of a human spirit living in the body.

In a coarser and denser body, with its correspondingly denser brain as a transit point for external happenings, the human spirit living therein is naturally more firmly segregated or walled in than in a more pervious and less dense species of matter. Therefore in the denser medium it can only inwardly perceive or let itself be impressed by happenings on a more limited scale.

The less dense a species of matter, however, the lighter it naturally is, and the higher it must also be. It will likewise be more translucent and thus also brighter! The nearer it is situated to Paradise due to its lightness, the more luminous and sunny it will be, because it permits the radiations issuing from Paradise to pass through it.

The further a human spirit shining forth from out of its body receives the possibility of sensing real life through a lighter, less dense environment, the more it will be able to experience inwardly, so that in the time of one earth-day it can absorb far more experiences in its particular environment than can an earthman with his denser brain in his heavier and more solid surroundings. According to the nature of the perviousness, i. e., according to the less dense and more luminous nature of its environment, a human spirit is able, through easier receptivity, to experience in the time of one earth-day as much as in the time of one earth-*year*, until in the Spiritual Realm itself it can experience in the time of one earth-day as much as in a thousand earth-years!

That is why it is said: "There a thousand years are as one *day!" Thus it rests on the wealth of experiences,* the increase of which depends on the growing maturity of the human spirit!

Man can best picture this if he thinks of his *dreams!* In a dream lasting a single minute of earth-time he is often able to perceive, really experience in his spirit, an entire lifetime! He lives through the happiest as well as the most painful things, he laughs and weeps and experiences his ageing, and yet he has used the time of only a single minute! In his earth-life the same experiencing would consume many decades, because the time and space of earthly experiencing have too narrow a limit, as a result of which each single stage advances more slowly.

69. AND A THOUSAND YEARS ARE AS ONE DAY!

Just as man on earth can experience as rapidly as that in his dreams only because during sleep the fettering influence of the brain has been partially removed by the spirit, so in the more luminous spheres of the Cosmos, when he is no longer so strongly fettered and later becomes a completely free spirit, he *always* stands in this vivid and rapid experiencing! For the actual experiencing of a thousand earth-years he needs no more time than one day!

INTUITIVE PERCEPTION

EVERY intuitive perception that a person has immediately forms a picture. In the formation of this picture the small brain or cerebellum participates as the bridge across which the soul should control the body. It is *that* part of the brain through which you receive your dreams. It is in turn connected with the frontal brain or cerebrum, through the activity of which thoughts are generated that are more closely tied to space and time and which eventually constitute the intellect.

Now pay close attention to the process! You will then be able clearly to distinguish when the intuition speaks to you through the spirit, or when feeling addresses you through the intellect!

The activity of the human spirit awakens intuitive perception within the solar plexus, thereby simultaneously making an impression upon the cerebellum. It is the *effect* of the spirit, that is, a wave of power *issuing* from the spirit. Man naturally perceives this wave in that spot where the spirit within the soul is connected with the body – in the centre of the so-called solar plexus, which passes on the wave to the cerebellum where it creates an impression.

In accordance with the specific nature of the various impressions received the cerebellum, like a photographic plate, forms a picture of the process as willed by the spirit or as created with the strong power of the spirit through its volition. *A picture without words!* The frontal brain takes over this picture and seeks to describe it in words, thereby generating thoughts which then find expression in language.

In truth the whole process is very simple! I will repeat it once more: With the help of the solar plexus the spirit makes an impression on the bridge provided for it, thus impressing a definite volition in power waves upon the small brain, the instrument given to it for this purpose, which immediately passes on what it received to the frontal brain. In the process of transmission a slight change through consolidation has already occurred, because the small brain adds something of its own nature to it.

The instruments within the human body which are at the disposal of the spirit work like the connecting links of a chain. But they all serve in a *forming* capacity *only*, because they cannot do otherwise. Everything transmitted to them they form in accordance with their own special nature. Thus the frontal brain takes up the pictures transmitted to it by the cerebellum and, in accordance with its somewhat coarser nature, first of all compresses them into narrower conceptions of space and time, thereby condensing them and bringing them into the ethereal world of thought-forms, which is of a more tangible substance.

Next the frontal brain forms words and sentences which, through the organs of speech, penetrate as formed sound-waves into the World of Fine Gross Matter, there again producing a new effect brought about by the movement of these waves.

Thus the spoken word is the resultant effect of the pictures transmitted through the frontal brain! The latter can also direct the course of the effect towards the organs of locomotion instead of to the organs of speech, whereby words are replaced by writing or action.

That is the normal course of the activity of the human spirit in the World of Gross Matter as willed by the Creator!

It is the *right* way, which would have brought about a healthy subsequent development in Creation, making it utterly impossible for mankind to go astray.

Man, however, voluntarily abandoned the course prescribed for him through the constitution of his body. He stubbornly interfered in the normal working of "the chain" of his instruments by making the intellect his idol. Thus he concentrated his whole energy upon the training of the intellect in an entirely one-sided manner! As a result the frontal brain, having now become the producer, was forced to exert itself out of all proportion to what was required of the other co-operating instruments.

This naturally incurred a heavy penalty! The uniform and harmonious co-operation of all the individual links was upset and hindered, and with it every right development. The excessive strain to which the frontal brain *alone* was subjected for thousands of years forced its development far beyond everything else.

This consequently curtailed the activity of all the neglected parts which, because of their lack of use, were bound to remain weak. Foremost among these is the cerebellum, which is the instrument of the spirit. Thus it follows that the activity of the human spirit proper was not only severely obstructed, but it is often completely cut off and remains excluded! The possibility of proper intercourse with the frontal brain over the bridge of the small brain is buried, while a direct connection between the human spirit and the frontal brain is utterly impossible owing to the latter's nature. The frontal brain is absolutely dependent on the full activity of the cerebellum, to which it stands *next in succession* according to God's Will, in order properly to fulfil the task assigned to it.

The specific quality of the cerebellum is needed in order to receive the vibrations of the spirit. It is impossible to bypass it, for the work of the frontal brain is to prepare their transition to the World of Fine Gross Matter, and therefore it is of a quite different and much coarser nature.

In the one-sided cultivation of the frontal brain lies the hereditary sin of earth-man against his God or, more precisely, against the Divine Laws, which manifest through the right apportionment of the bodily instruments, as in the entire Creation!

The observance of the correct apportionment would have automatically indicated the straight and right road of ascent to the human spirit. As it was, however, man in his ambitious conceit interfered with this machinery of healthy activity, singled out one part and cultivated it specially while disregarding all the others! This was *bound* to bring disproportion and stagnation in its train. If the course of natural events is hampered in such a way disease and failure must ensue, ending finally in wild confusion and collapse.

Here it is not only a question of the body but in the first place of the spirit! Through this interference – the unequal cultivation of the two brains – the cerebellum was suppressed through neglect in the course of thousands of years, and thereby the spirit was hampered in its activity. This became the *hereditary sin*, because the one-sided over-cultivation of the frontal brain is in the course of time passed on to each child through physical inheritance. Thus from the outset it becomes immensely difficult for the child's spirit to awaken and grow more powerful, because the bridge necessary for this purpose, the cerebellum, is no longer so easy to cross and is even very often completely cut off!

Man has not the faintest idea what irony and strong censure lie in the expressions "large brain" and "small brain" which he created! No indictment regarding his transgression against Divine ordinance could be set forth in a more devastating manner! This precisely indicates the gravest of his earthly sins, for in his wanton obstinacy he so mutilated this fine instrument of his physical body, which is meant to help him on earth, that not only is it unable to serve him any longer *in the way* the Creator ordained, but it *must* even lead him to the depths of destruction! In this man has failed to a far greater extent than the drunkards or those who destroy their bodies by becoming slaves to their passions!

In addition they now have the presumption to expect that God should make Himself manifest to them *in a manner they can understand* in their wantonly distorted physical bodies! After committing such a sin they would also make *this demand!*

How easily and joyfully man could have ascended the steps to Luminous Heights in the natural course of development if he had not so wantonly interfered with the Work of God!

The man of the future will have *normal* brains which will work uniformly and thus support each other harmoniously. The cerebellum, called the small brain because it is stunted in its growth, will now grow in strength as it attains to its proper field of activity until it is in the right proportion to the frontal brain. Then there will be harmony again, and all that is petrified and unhealthy must disappear!

But let us now turn to the *further* consequences of the false mode of living in the past! The cerebellum, which is relatively much too small, makes it difficult for the truly serious seekers of today to distinguish between what is genuine intuitive perception within them and what is merely feeling. I have already said that feeling is produced by the frontal brain; the thoughts it sends out influence the bodily nerves in such a way that, in reaction, they forcibly incite the frontal brain to indulge in so-called imagination!

Imagination consists of pictures generated by the frontal brain, but they are not to be compared with the pictures the cerebellum forms under the pressure of the spirit! Here we have the difference between the mode of expression of the intuitive perception as the consequence of an activity of the spirit, and the results of feeling issuing from the bodily nerves. Both produce pictures between which the ignorant person finds it almost or entirely impossible to distinguish, although they differ tremendously! The pictures of the intuitive perception are genuine and full of living power, while the pictures of the feeling, i. e., the imagination, are deceptions produced with borrowed power!

But the difference is easily detected by anyone who knows the process of development in Creation as a whole and then studies himself attentively!

In the case of intuitive pictures, which arise through the cerebellum acting as a bridge for the spirit, the picture immediately appears *first,* and only thereafter is it transmuted into thoughts which then influence the feeling of the body!

In the case of pictures produced by the frontal brain the process is reversed. Here the thoughts must *precede* in order to form the basis for the pictures. All this occurs so rapidly that it almost seems to be one and the same thing. With a little practice in observation, however, man can very soon learn to distinguish the nature of the process exactly!

A further consequence of this hereditary sin is presented by the confusion in dreams. For this reason man can today no longer give *that* value to his dreams which is really their due. The normal cerebellum, influenced by the spirit, would render dreams clear and unconfused. That is to say, they would not be *dreams* at all, but *experiences* of the spirit, received and reproduced by the cerebellum while the frontal brain rests in sleep. The radiation of the now overwhelmingly strong frontal or day-brain, however, makes its influence felt upon the sensitive cerebellum even during the night. In its present weakened condition the latter absorbs the strong radiations of the frontal brain simultaneously with the experiences of the spirit, creating a mixture like a double exposure on a photographic plate. The result is the confused dreams of today!

The best proof of this double influence is the frequent appearance in dreams of words and sentences which *only* originate in the activity of the *frontal* brain. Only the frontal brain forms words and sentences, because it is more closely bound to space and time.

For this reason man is no longer, or at least very inadequately, susceptible to spiritual warnings and instructions through the cerebellum, and is consequently far more exposed to dangers which he could otherwise escape through spiritual warnings.

Thus, besides the evil consequences already mentioned, there are many others brought about by man's interference with Divine Ordinance, for in reality *all* evil proceeded only from this failure, so clearly visible to everybody today! It was a fruit of vanity, which developed through the appearance of woman in Creation!

If man does not wish to be lost he should at last tear himself away from the results of this hereditary sin!

Naturally, since he has to take trouble over everything, this is no exception! Man *must* awaken from his comfortable indolence to become at last what he should have been from the beginning – one who is bent on furthering Creation and a mediator of Light to all creatures!

MAN'S conception of life has so far been erroneous! All that he has called life is nothing but impelled motion, which may only be considered as the natural effect of life proper.

Therefore in the whole of Creation there are only the after-effects of this more or less strong motion, which form, mature, maintain and disintegrate everything. The human intellect has investigated this motion as being the highest force conceivable, and thus found therein the limit of its capacity to comprehend! Man cannot proceed further in his investigation because he himself is a product of this motion. As it was the highest he could comprehend he simply called it "power" or "living power" or even "life".

It is neither power nor life, however, but only a natural and inevitable effect of these, for power only exists in life itself, is one with it and inseparable from it. Since power and life are inseparable, and since Creation is formed, maintained and again disintegrated by movement alone, it is impossible to speak either of power or of life within Creation.

Thus he who desires to speak of the discovery of Primordial Power, or even of the exploitation of Primordial Power by machinery, is greatly in error, because Primordial Power is not to be found within Creation at all! He mistakes something else for it and erroneously expresses his opinion that it is "power". Such a man thereby proves that he has no idea of the processes in Creation, nor of Creation itself! However, he cannot be reproached about this, for he shares his ignorance with *all* his fellow-men, whether they are learned or otherwise!

For this reason I have spoken from the very beginning in my Message of one "power" streaming through all Creation, as it was only thus that I could explain many things for men's understanding.

Otherwise they would not have grasped my explanations at all! Now, however, I can go further in these matters and furnish a picture which soberly reflects the processes in all that happens. This description is novel, but it changes *nothing* of my previous descriptions. Everything remains exactly as I have stated, and *it is real!* What I am now saying only appears new because this time I put it in a new light!

In so doing I provide a solid foundation – a large bowl, so to speak, into which man can place everything already mentioned in the Message as the constantly moving, effervescent contents, combined into one whole, something which unquestionably belongs together and intermixes. Thereby man can obtain a comprehensive survey of all the great happenings hitherto unknown to him, including his own existence and inner development, which survey is quite inexhaustible to him and harmonises in every way!

The hearer and reader should now try to picture in his mind what I am about to unfold!

Life, real Life, is something completely autonomous, something completely independent. Otherwise it could not be designated as "Life". Such Life is in *God* alone! And since besides God nothing is truly "living" it follows that He alone holds the power which lies in Life. Thus He and He alone is the Primordial Power, or simply the "Power", so often referred to! And again, in this Power there is Light! Here again the expression "Primordial Light" is just as false as the expression "Primordial Power", for there is but One Light and One Power – *God!*

The existence of God, of Power, of Light, i. e., of Life, alone inevitably brings into being the Creations, for the Living Light, the Living Power, cannot but *radiate! And these radiations contain all that is necessary for Creation!*

The radiations, however, are not the Light Itself!

Hence all that exists outside of God has its origin only in the radiation of God. This radiation is a natural effect of the Light, however, an effect that has *always* existed from all eternity.

The strength of the radiation is naturally greatest in the proximity of the Light, so much so that there can be no other movement in it than the *"perfectly straight line"* movement, which is an intrinsic quality of the radiation. Thus it issues from God and proceeds for fabulous distances, the extent of which a human spirit is unable to imagine!

When, however, this inflexible forward propulsion, which is equivalent to an immense and constant pressure, comes to the point where it at last eases off a little, the nature of the movement changes from the hitherto straight line *to a circular movement.* This circular movement is produced by the attraction of the Living Power simultaneously pulling back all that has been flung beyond the border of the full radiation to that point where only the straight line movement predominates. In this process the rotating movements take on an *elliptical* form, because they are *not independent* movements, but only produced by this flinging-out-of-the-mainstream and the subsequent pulling back through the attraction which rests in the Power, that is, in God Himself!

Moreover the process of dividing the radiation into positive and negative species, which takes place after the radiation leaves the Sphere of Divine White-Heat, also plays a part here!

In these rotating movements, in which the immense pressure of the original radiation has diminished, a slight cooling off also takes place in the course of nature. This in turn causes a certain deposit to be precipitated.

This deposit sinks deeper or recedes further away from the original strongest radiation, but is still held by the all-pervading attraction of the Power. Yet it simultaneously retains enough of the straight line impetus of the radiation to again produce new rotating movements, which always remain within very definite but quite different limits. Thus one deposit after another is precipitated and corresponding elliptically rotating planes of motion form, which bring accumulations of substance and finally ever more solid forms, receding further and further away from the Original Radiation and its enormous forward pressure!

The gradations thus produced form planes in which definite species link together and settle, conforming to the degree their temperature has cooled off. I have already described these planes or species in my Message as being the great fundamental planes of Spiritual Substantiality in the uppermost region of Creation, under which successively range the Spheres of Animistic Substantiality, of Ethereal Substance, and finally of Gross Matter, with their many sub-divisions. It is quite natural that the more perfect species should remain higher, thus closest to the Point of Origin, because they most nearly resemble It and are most strongly affected by the attraction of the Living Power!

As I have already said this radiation of the Light working in such an incomprehensible way has always existed from all eternity!

But God did not allow this radiation to penetrate further and act beyond the limits at which the forward drive of the stream still forms an absolutely straight line, so that the pure Divine Radiation still remained luminous and clear without any cooling off and consequent precipitations. This formed the Divine Sphere which, as with God Himself, is eternal! In this clear transparency there could never be any dimming, nor can there be any swerving aside or change. Only perfect harmony with the Source, with the Light Itself, was possible. And this Sphere is inseparably connected with God, because *this* radiation of the Living Power, being its natural effect, can never be avoided!

To this Divine Sphere, which because of its close proximity to the Living Power is subjected to a pressure incomprehensible to the human spirit, belongs the actual Castle of the Grail as the most extreme outpost and anchorage, as a terminating counter-pole, so to speak! This still stands within the Circle of Divinity and has therefore existed from all eternity and will remain unchanged for all eternity, even if in times to come Creation would have to fall to ruin!

Thus it was from all eternity! It is something the human spirit is unable to comprehend!

It was not till God, in His Volition, sent forth the great words: "Let there be Light!" that the rays shot out over the limit hitherto set them into the Universe, then in utter darkness, carrying movement and warmth! This was the beginning of Creation, which gave birth to the human spirit and could become his home!

God, Who is Light, does not need this Creation! Should He again limit His Radiation to its unavoidable minimum, so that only a Sphere of Divine Purity would remain into which no dimness can ever enter, as it was in the beginning, then the end of all that has been subsequently created would be at hand! Man would then also cease to exist, as he can be conscious only *within* Creation!

The immediate radiation of the Light can produce *only* what is perfect. In the changes from this first pressure, caused by the ever-increasing distances, however, this original perfection diminishes because, in the progressive cooling off, individual particles constantly separate themselves and remain behind. Purity in perfection necessitates *the pressure of Divine Radiation at its greatest intensity*, which is possible only in the proximity of God. The pressure creates motion which in turn produces warmth, heat and white heat.

Pressure, however, is but the resultant effect of the power, and not the power itself, just as the radiations come into existence only under the pressure of the power, but they are not the power itself! Therefore the radiations within

Creation are but the consequence of a corresponding motion, which in turn must adjust itself to the particular pressure at the time! Thus where there are no radiations in Creation there is also no motion or, as man erroneously calls it, no "life"! For all motion radiates, while stagnation is nothingness, an absence of motion which men call death!

Thus the Great Judgment comes about only through the increased pressure of a Divine Ray, passed on through an Envoy from God incarnated in the World of Gross Matter, to Whom God has given a spark of *His Living Power!* Only that which swings *aright* in the Laws manifesting the Power of God can withstand the pressure of this Living Power-*Spark,* which naturally cannot be as strong as the enormous pressure of the Living Power in God the Father Himself. That which swings aright will be strengthened by this pressure, but not brought to white heat, for which the radiation of the power-spark is insufficient.

The radiation of the power-spark, however, is amply sufficient to unhinge all disturbing elements, thrust them out of their false movements, and crush and disintegrate them. Thus the Great Judgment of God follows quite automatically and in no wise depends on an arbitrary act of the Divine Envoy! It is simply the result of the Law of Radiation, which was bound to come into being in consequence of the radiation of God's Power. For all that moves *aright* in thought and deed radiates a violet colour in the World of Gross Matter.

That which is of the Darkness, either evil or striving towards it, albeit in thought or desire, emits a dull *yellow* colour. These two colours are fundamental for the Judgment! According to the strength of a volition or deed the radiations are either weak or strong. With the coming of God's Envoy an absolutely unmodified Ray of *Divine* Light enters Creation and thereby also this earth. Divine Light strengthens and uplifts all that is good, i. e., all that is of a violet colour on earth, while all that is of a dull earthly yellow will be disintegrated and destroyed by It!

The radiation is stronger or weaker according to the nature and strength of a volition or deed. And this again influences the nature and strength of the judging effect of the Divine Light-Ray with unswerving justice!

It may quite well be said that Creation is encompassed and penetrated by a gigantic network of many-coloured radiations. These radiations are nothing but the expression of the diversified movements having their origin in the pressure of the Living Power in God. In other words: God holds Creation in

His Living Power! All this is right, no matter in what form it is expressed! But if one wishes to put it to good account the real origin and process of further development must be known accurately.

Just as the highest degree of heat throws out a *white* glow, so is it the same in the Divine Sphere! With a decrease in temperature other colours gradually appear, and in the cooling off process everything becomes more and more dense!

To continue my explanations with the aid of these earthly conceptions, I wish to say that the human spirit can never come to white-heat, because it came into being in a sphere where the pressure was already becoming weaker and where it was consequently no longer able to produce this highest degree of heat. Thus in its origin the human spirit is of a species which cannot consciously withstand this highest degree of power! Or one can also say: "That which is spirit cannot evolve and become conscious until the temperature has fallen to a certain level!" Furthermore, the species in which the "spirit" originates is nothing more than a *deposit* precipitated from the Divine Sphere, which was bound to form itself owing to the slight decrease in temperature, and so on!

But there are still further graduated extensions! The first precipitation from the Divine Sphere forms the Primordial Spiritual Sphere in which the Primordial Beings originate. It is only the deposit the Primordial Beings precipitate which produces the species from which the human spirits can evolve. The deposit precipitated from the latter species in turn produces the Sphere of Animistic Substantiality, out of which the World of Ethereal Substance emerges, which again is finally followed by the World of Gross Matter. But each of the fundamental species named here, including the Divine, contains many intermediate spheres, which are bridges that have to act as connecting links from one sphere to another!

The *first* deposit from the Divine Sphere, as is easily understandable, holds the greatest values and could therefore produce self-consciousness immediately. It produced the so-called Primordial Beings, whereas the deposit precipitated after this first deposit is not quite so strong and must gradually develop towards consciousness. From this second deposit the human spirits originate.

Due to the greater value and significance of their species, and because they constitute the *first* deposit from the Divine Sphere, the Primordial Beings therefore stand at the highest heights in Creation, while the human spirits emerged only from a still further deposit. Naturally even at their full maturity the human spirits cannot reach the height of the much more valuable and significant Primordial Beings, but must remain on the level of their own species!

In order to rise higher they lack something which it is impossible to supplement, unless this something was given to them directly by the Living Power of God which, however, cannot take place in the natural course of events. Instead it would have to issue from a Living Part of God placed in Creation because, being the personal and truly *Living Power* Himself, the radiation has not cooled, which ordinarily it is bound to do in transition. He alone, therefore, is in a position to add to a human spirit through His own immediate radiation something which makes it possible for the spirit to cross the border to the region in which the Primordial Beings live!

When the radiation first shot over the boundary-line of the Divine Sphere, i.e., at the beginning of Creation, a new section was added to the eternal Castle of the Grail situated at the most remote border of the Divine Sphere. This section protruded towards the further side, towards the most spiritual part of Creation, so that the Primordial Beings on their side can also visit this new section of the Castle in the Spiritual World, at least as far as the limit set by their species permits!

One step beyond this border, i. e., into the Divine Sphere, would mean immediate unconsciousness, for they would be consumed in white-heat, if ... they were able to take such a step! But this is impossible, because the much greater pressure of the Divine Sphere, to which they are not accustomed, would simply fling them back or, in other words, would prevent them from entering. In an absolutely natural manner it bars their entrance without the necessity of any further action!

The position is similar as between the developed human spirits and the Primordial Beings in the plane in which they live!

Thus the Castle of the Grail with its spiritual extension today constitutes the intermediary point between the Divine and Creation! Through the Castle all the radiation necessary for Creation must flow, and the Son of Man as King of the Grail and as the only Mediator is, owing to the nature of His Origin (which combines Divinity with Spirituality), able to cross the border into the Divine Sphere from Creation! For this reason the mystery of this union *had to be* brought about!

It is only far below this Castle of the Grail and the Sphere of the Primordial Beings that Paradise lies! It is the highest and most beautiful sphere for those human spirits who have fully matured in the Divine Will through obeying the Laws of His Radiations!

To avoid enlarging the picture of these happenings too far I will not enter into details here. I shall be publishing books on these matters so that earthly scientists can study the individual processes, such as the development within the various spheres, their relationship to one another, etc. Nothing must be passed over lest there be a gap, which would immediately call a halt to human knowledge!

Thus when the spirit of an earthman in all its maturity returns from its long wandering and arrives at the boundary ordained for its species, i. e., to the point where it encounters stronger pressure, it cannot increase its own luminosity beyond what its own full maturity has already brought about! The higher pressure of a much greater power would disintegrate and consume its particular species. In the greater degree of heat to which it was exposed its ego would be lost. It could then no longer exist as a human spirit, for in merging with the White Light it would be dissolved, while in the region of the Primordial Beings it would become unconscious through the higher pressure prevailing there!

The White-Light, i. e., the Radiation of God, in which only what is Divine can exist consciously, *thus carries within itself all the fundamental components of Creation* which, in the gradual process of cooling off, deposit themselves in a downward direction, manifesting in forms through motion, and as such uniting themselves with each other. But they no longer merge with each other, because the pressure needed for this is lacking. With every degree that the temperature decreases a definite precipitation forms and remains behind. First the Divine, later the Spiritual and then the Animistic, until finally only Ethereal Substance and Gross Matter sink still further!

Thus Creation is actually the deposit formed through the increasing cooling off of the White Light, of the Radiation of the Living Light! The spiritual, as also the animistic, can only form and become conscious at a very definite degree in the process of cooling off, which is equivalent to the decrease in pressure of God's Radiation.

If I here speak of the melting or dissolution of the human spirit when the pressure of the Light Radiation becomes too great, this does not refer to the

Nirvana of the Buddhists as these would perhaps like to interpret my explanation. My present explanation merely concerns the happenings as they occur from the Light downwards, whereas Nirvana is meant to be the climax on the way upwards!

Here the way would be blocked, for in order to ascend from the earth into the Spiritual Kingdom, into Paradise (at the highest boundary of which this point of dissolution is to be found), every human spirit as "a conscious ego" must have already attained to the highest maturity, a maturity according to the Divine Will and not perhaps as man thinks it should be. Otherwise it cannot enter this Kingdom. But if as a self-conscious spirit it has matured so far, it will be strictly held back and repulsed at the boundary by the increased pressure of the Divine Sphere. It *cannot* proceed any further! Nor does it want to do so! It would never be able to enjoy bliss in the Divine Sphere because it cannot live there as a human spirit but would have dissolved, while in the Spiritual Kingdom, in Paradise, it finds eternal bliss, and in its gratitude thinks no more of wanting to be completely dissolved!

Besides, in the fullness of its maturity, the human spirit is *needed* for the uplifting and perfecting of the spheres lying below it. These spheres being still further deposits can withstand even less pressure than the human spirit. There *it,* the human spirit, is the greatest, because it can endure and even has need of a stronger pressure!

It is the task of the human spirit in these lower regions, through the power inherent in it, to open everything that stands below it as much as possible to the influence of the pure Radiations of the Light; and thereby, as a mediator through which the stronger pressure can operate, to dispense blessing to all else, because it can receive this higher pressure and distribute it as a purifying element that destroys all uncleanness!

Unfortunately man has made sad havoc of this! It is true that everything in Creation that was meant to develop did develop up to the present time following the pressure or urge. However, it developed in the wrong way, because here man not only failed, but even misdirected this development downwards instead of upwards! For this reason only hideous caricatures of everything came into being instead of natural beauty!

To be natural, however, means to ascend, to strive upwards, following the attraction of the Living Power! For where there is naturalness everything strives upwards only, just like every blade of grass, every flower and every tree. Thus what man's volition brought about unfortunately bears only an external *resemblance* to that which he was supposed to accomplish!

A rich inner life, for instance, may to the superficial observer outwardly resemble the emptiness which comes of a blasé attitude to knowledge. Reverential love of all that is beautiful, at starting, bears some resemblance to lustful desire, for both exhibit a certain enthusiasm, except that the one is genuine, and the other false and only a means to an end. Vanity becomes a substitute for real charm, and place hunting for honest service. And so it is with everything that man brings forth! Only rarely do his ways lead towards the Light! Almost everything is inclined towards darkness!

All this must be eliminated so that in place of this Sodom and Gomorrah the Kingdom of God may now come upon the earth! Everything must finally turn towards the Light, and for this man is the mediator!

Of the Light Itself, of God, I will not speak here! The subject is too sacred! Besides which man would never be able to grasp it! He must be eternally content to know *that God is!*

EXPAND YOUR KNOWLEDGE!

THE WISDOM

OF GOD RULES THE WORLD!

STRIVE THROUGH YOUR RECOGNITION, MEN,

TO PERCEIVE HIS MAGNITUDE!

VOLUME 3

IN THE LAND OF TWILIGHT

LET ME take you a step into the Ethereal Realm, soul of man! We will hurry through the Land of Shadows without stopping, for I have already spoken about this. It is *that* plane where *those* must linger who are still too stupid to use their ethereal bodies properly, particularly those who while on earth considered themselves especially clever. In the Ethereal Realm they are dumb, blind and deaf because the earthly intellect, as a product of their gross material body, could not accompany them into the beyond. Being earthbound it remained in the narrow confines of the World of Matter, which it can never overstep.

The first consequence of this great error becomes immediately clear to a human soul after earthly death, for it stands useless in the Ethereal Realm, helpless and weak, much worse than a newly-born child on the gross material earth. Therefore they are called *shadows*, souls which still sense their existence but which cannot be conscious of it.

Let us leave these foolish ones behind us – those who, in their conceited belief that they know everything better, prattled enough trivial nonsense on this earth, and who must now be silent. *We are now entering the plane of twilight!* A whispering reaches our ears, in complete accord with the dim twilight around us, in which we can vaguely recognise the outlines of hills, meadows and bushes. Thus *everything* here corresponds to the state of *twilight,* which *may* be followed by an awakening. This only *may* be so, not necessarily must be so!

No happy cheerful sound, no clear vision is possible here! Only twilight or a restriction which conforms to the condition of the souls sojourning here! These drag themselves sluggishly about, tired and indifferent, except for an indefinable urge driving them in one direction, towards a faint roseate glow which seems to rise in the distance and which, like a harbinger of light, affects these seemingly tired souls like sweet enchantment. They only *appear* to be tired. Actually they are *indolent* in spirit, and *therefore* their ethereal bodies are *weak!*

The roseate glow in the far distance beckons them onward, full of promise. Hope awakens within them and they are stirred to quickened movement. Their desire to reach this glow gives fresh strength to their ethereal bodies; their eyes reflect a keener consciousness, and they step out towards it with ever greater assurance.

We accompany them! The number of souls around us increases; everything grows more active and distinct; the speaking becomes somewhat louder, swelling to a strong murmuring. Soon we discern words, words that evolve into prayers uttered by those jostling forward, uttered unceasingly, hastily, feverishly! The crowds now grow ever more dense. The forward movement becomes spasmodic, and whole groups in front of us come to a halt. They are being thrust back by those ahead of them, only to push forward again. Thus the jammed masses surge to and fro! Cries of despair, frightened entreaties, timid demands, and here and there a suppressed whimpering of utter helplessness arise from the prayers!

Quickly we swing ourselves above this struggle of millions of souls! We see that before them, inflexible and cold, an obstacle checks their advance; an obstacle against which they hurl themselves, and which they wet with their tears in vain!

A series of high, strong and closely-set bars relentlessly halts their forward movement!

More brightly gleams the roseate glow in the distance, and still stronger grows the longing for it within those who have made it their goal. Beseechingly they stretch out their hands, still convulsively clasping their rosaries and letting one bead after another slip through their fingers as they continue to stammer their prayers. The barrier, however, stands rigid and immovable, separating them from their beautiful goal!

We walk past the dense crowds, which seem to be endless. Not hundreds of thousands, but millions! All faithful "believers", at least so they thought while on earth! How different they had imagined everything to be! They thought they would be joyfully awaited and welcomed with respect!

Call out to them: "Of what use are your prayers, you believers, if you did not allow the Word of the Lord to become active *within yourselves,* a natural conviction?

"The roseate glow you see in the distance is the longing for the Kingdom of God burning within you! You carry this longing within yourselves, but you blocked the road leading there with the rigid forms of your false opinions, which are represented in the bars of the fence you now see obstructing you. Discard all the false views you accepted, and those you yourselves built up in addition during your time on earth! Throw them aside and boldly step out for the Truth *as it is* in its great and simple naturalness! Then you are free to attain the goal you long for!

"But see, you dare not! You are in constant fear that it might perhaps be wrong, because you have thought differently up to now! But you only hinder yourselves through this and must remain where you are until it becomes too late to stride onward, and you are bound to be drawn along into perdition! Nobody can help you with this unless *you* yourselves begin to leave behind all that is wrong!"

Call out to them! Point out the way of salvation to these souls! You will see it is utterly in vain! The noise of their endless prayers only grows louder and *prevents* them *from hearing* a single word that might help them to stride forward towards the roseate glow and the Light! In spite of many a good volition they must now perish as victims of their indolence, which prevented them from recognising and absorbing anything *more* than the *externals* connected with their churches, temples and mosques!

Sad at heart, we want to move on! But there before us we notice the soul of a woman, whose face suddenly takes on an expression of peace and calm; her eyes lose their troubled, anxious look and shine more brightly. As she attains to greater consciousness her body becomes more erect and more transparent... a strong volition of purest hope helps her to raise her foot... and then, uttering a sigh of relief, she stands *on the other side* of the barrier! To the soul of this woman the bars no longer formed any obstacle, for through deep meditation and delicate intuition she became convinced that all she had hitherto thought must have been wrong, and with a joyous belief in the love of God she fearlessly cast aside all her mistaken ideas!

Now she is astonished when she realises how easy it was! Gratefully she raises her arms, her supreme happiness makes her want to sing with joy! But the magnitude of the experience overwhelms her and her lips remain mute! She trembles slightly, her head sinks down upon her breast, and she closes her eyes as big tears course slowly down her cheeks. She clasps her hands in prayer, but this time she prays in a *different* way. A prayer of thanks, and a heartfelt intercession on behalf of all those who are still behind these hard bars because of the false opinions they refuse to surrender!

A sigh of profound sympathy swells her breast, and it is as if the last of her fetters falls away. Now she is free, free to tread the path to the goal she inwardly longs for!

Lifting her eyes she sees a guide standing before her, and joyfully she follows him into the new, unknown land, towards the roseate glow which becomes ever brighter.

Thus many a soul still detaches itself from these masses which must wait behind the bars erected by their erroneous opinions for their own decision; for their own resolution which may lead them onward or which retains them till the hour strikes when everything that cannot brace itself to cast off that which was formerly wrong will be destroyed. Few only will still be able to free themselves from the clutches of their false views, in which they are too deeply entangled. The bars that prevent their progress toward ascent are as rigid as their own stubbornness in clinging to these erroneous views. It is impossible to lend them a helping hand to overcome this obstacle, because it is absolutely necessary that the initiative should come from the souls *themselves!* It is their inner *personal* experiencing which activates their limbs!

Thus an ominous curse falls upon all those who teach mankind wrong conceptions about the Will of God in Creation, which was at that time to be found in the Word of the Saviour. But it was not purely preserved in the Word of the Bible, still less in earthly explanations!

Let them in their rigidity continue to prattle their prayers under the delusion that the number thereof can and must help them because the church has taught them so – as if some bargain could be driven with the Will of God!

Let us continue our journey in the Land of Twilight! The stronghold of bars seems to stretch endlessly into the distance, and the multitude it imprisons reaches far beyond our gaze!

But here we see other groups holding Bibles in their hands instead of rosaries, and desperately searching through the pages. They gather round a few souls who try to give instruction and information by continually reading passages from the Bible. Here and there various souls lift their Bibles in a demanding manner. Others kneel and raise them as if in prayer...however, the bars remain immovable, preventing all possibility of advance!

Many souls point to their Biblical knowledge; others demand their right to walk into the Kingdom of Heaven. But the bars do not budge!

Then we observe the soul of a man smilingly forcing his way through the multitude. Triumphantly he waves his hand!

"You fools," he cries, "why did you not want to listen? I spent half my time on earth studying the other world, which for us is now this life. The bars in front of you will quickly disappear through one act of your will – they are the product of your imagination! Just follow me, I will lead you! I am already familiar with all this!"

The souls around him give way! He strides towards the bars as if they do not exist, but instantly staggers back with a cry of pain. The impact was too hard and very soon convinced him that the bars were real enough. He puts both hands to his forehead. The bars before him stand immovable. In a fit of rage he seizes them and shakes them violently!

Angrily he cries out: "Then the medium has deceived me! And year after year I devoted to studying this!"

He does not realise that it was *he* who originated and spread these errors both verbally and through his writings, after interpreting the pictures transmitted to him by the medium according to *his* ideas, and without first studying the Laws of God in Creation!

Do not try to help this man or others! They are all so wrapped up in themselves that they have no wish whatever to listen to any but their own perceiving. They must first become weary of their plight, must recognise or comprehend its futility, for this alone holds the possibility of escape from the entanglement of wrong convictions after long wanderings in the Land of Twilight!

These are not bad persons, but those who in their seeking have merely clung tenaciously to false conceptions, or who were too lazy to ponder over everything thoroughly, when they should have examined what they accepted with the most careful intuition to see whether it could be considered correct, or whether it contained flaws which their own healthy intuition must reject as unnatural. Therefore drop all empty superficiality!

The human spirit should reject all mysticism, because it can never be of any value to him. Only that which he himself enters into with his intuitive perception, thereby bringing it to personal experience within himself, will be useful to him in the maturing of his spirit.

The word *"Awake"* which Christ used so frequently means *"Experience"*. Do not go through life on earth sleeping or dreaming! "Pray and work" means: "Make your *work* a prayer", spiritualise the work of your hands! In its performance every task should become a reverential worship of God, in gratitude that God has given you the chance to accomplish something extraordinary among all the creatures of this Subsequent Creation, *if only you so wish!*

Begin timely with this awakening, with this personal experiencing of everything, including what you read and hear, which is the same as consciously perceiving it, so that you do not have to remain in the Land of Twilight, of which I have explained only a very small part today!

610

PONDERERS

THE MAN who spends his days on earth in pondering about himself can never ascend, but remains hampered.

So many people live in the belief, however, that just such pondering and self-observation is something specially great which helps them to ascend. They have many words for it that veil its true nature. One person ponders in repentance, another in humility; still others ponder assiduously in order to discover their faults and the way to avoid them, and so on. But it all remains a continuous pondering which seldom or never permits them to experience true joy!

That is not what is willed! It is a false road and never leads upwards to luminous and free realms. For through this pondering man *binds* himself! He directs his gaze forcibly upon himself only, instead of upon a high, pure luminous goal!

Cheerful, hearty laughter is the strongest antidote to darkness. Only it must not be a laugh of malicious pleasure!

On the other hand pondering weighs a person down, and this alone is enough to explain that it keeps *down* and also pulls down!

Nor is the real basis of continual pondering a good volition, but only vanity, ambition and conceit! It is not the pure longing for the Light that gives cause to this pondering, but a craving for self-esteem that kindles it ever anew and perpetually nourishes it!

The continued concentration of his thoughts upon himself is a form of self-torment. He zealously observes the alternate pros and cons working within his soul, feeling vexed at times and then finding solace again, so that finally he can personally note with a deep breath of quiet self-satisfaction that once more he has "overcome" something and gone a step forward. I purposely say *"personally note"*, for it is really he alone who does most of the observing, and such personal observations are invariably nothing but self-delusions. In reality he has not advanced a *single* step, but goes on

611

making the same mistakes over and over again, although he imagines they are *no longer* the same. But they *are* the same, always the old mistakes, only their form changes!

Such a man never advances in this way, although his personal observations give him cause to imagine that he is overcoming one fault after another. But he always revolves in a circle around himself, while the basic evil hidden within him does nothing but continuously create new forms.

A man who is always observing and pondering over himself is the personification of the fighter against the nine-headed snake! No sooner is each head cut off than it grows afresh, making the struggle endless, with nothing to mark in the way of progress on the fighter's side!

As a matter of fact this is also the ethereal process resulting from the activity of a ponderer. In the olden days, when men considered everything not gross material to be gods, demigods or other kinds of entities, they were still able to see this.

Only a man of cheerful volition who keeps his gaze freely concentrated *upon a sublime goal,* instead of continually focussing all his attention upon himself, only *he* will advance and ascend towards the Luminous Heights. No child learns to walk without frequently tumbling, but it almost invariably gets up with a smile until it is able to walk in safety. *That* is what man must do on his path through the world! Do not despair, lament or complain when you sometimes fall! Get up briskly and try again! You must learn the lesson from each fall through your *intuitive perception,* however, and not through mental observation! Then there will quite suddenly come a time when you need no longer fear another fall, because you have inwardly absorbed everything the previous ones have taught you!

Thus man can only absorb through actual *experiencing,* and not through observation. A ponderer never comes to the point of experiencing! Through his observing he always places himself *outside* every experience; looking at himself with his dissecting and analytic mind as if at a stranger, instead of exercising his intuitive perception to the full on his own behalf! If he *looks* at himself he *must* stand *beside* the intuitive perception. The very words "to look at" oneself, to observe oneself, imply this!

This also explains that he is but serving *the intellect,* which not only hinders every genuine experience *with the intuitive perception,* but utterly eliminates it. He prevents the effect of every outward happening in the material world from penetrating further than the frontal brain where it is first received. There it is arrested, presumptuously dissected and analysed, so that it does not reach the intuitional brain, through which alone the spirit could accept it for experiencing.

For mark my words: Just as the human spirit must direct its activity from within outwards, i. e., in proper sequence over the intuitional brain to the intellectual brain, so the effects of outward happenings can only take the reverse course if they are to be absorbed by the human spirit as experiences.

Thus the impression of outward happenings in the material world must, in coming from the outside, always go through the intellectual frontal brain and thence via the intuitional back brain to the spirit, not otherwise! And the activity of the spirit must take exactly the reverse direction towards the outside, because the intuitional brain alone has the ability to absorb *spiritual* impressions.

The ponderer, however, clings convulsively to the impression of an outward happening in his intellectual frontal brain. There he dissects and analyses it, and does not pass it on to the intuitional brain in its full value, but only partly (in addition these parts are distorted through excessive intellectual activity), and thus it is no longer as real as it was.

For this reason there can be no progress for him, no spiritual maturing, which can only come about through the real experiencing of outward happenings.

Be like children in this! Absorb everything fully and experience it immediately within yourselves! Then it will again stream back through the intuitional brain to the intellectual brain. From there it can either serve for a strong and successful defence or increase the receptive capacity, depending on the nature of the outward happenings, the radiations of which are called influences or impressions from without.

Man will receive his training for this during the Millennium, which shall become the Kingdom of Peace and Happiness, the Kingdom of God on earth. Owing to his *exacting desires* man again misunderstands what this means, because in his conceit he can no longer form anything in the right and healthy way. The expression "the Kingdom of God on earth" calls forth a tremulous joy in the ranks of all those hoping for it. They really think of it as a gift of joy and happiness which will fully correspond to their longing for tranquil enjoyment. Actually however, it will be a time of the strictest obedience for all mankind!

Today nobody is willing to accept the fact that therein lies a demand that man's volition and desires *must* at last completely subordinate themselves to the Will of God!

Peace and happiness will then ensue because all disturbing elements will be *forcibly* removed from the earth, and will be kept away from it in the future. To these in the first place belongs the man of today, for he alone caused the disturbances in Creation and here on earth. But after a certain hour has struck no disturbing one will be able to live on this earth any longer.

This will come about through the transforming of the radiations, which takes place through the Star of the Son of Man. Peace will be *enforced,* not come as a gift, and to keep the peace will then be demanded, firmly and relentlessly!

Such will be the Kingdom of Peace and Happiness, the Kingdom of God on earth, in which man must be *deprived* of ruling by *his* volition, which he was permitted to keep hitherto; for being spiritual among the developed ones upon this earth he must, as the highest creature, therefore rule in strict accordance with the Primordial Laws of Creation.

In future there will be only able to exist *that* man and all those creatures which voluntarily adjust themselves to the Will of God! Those which live and think and work accordingly! *This* alone offers the possibility to live in the coming Millennium!

VOLUNTARY MARTYRS, RELIGIOUS FANATICS

MEN WHO voluntarily inflict pain and privation upon themselves in order to become pleasing to God are repulsive! None of them will ever attain to the Kingdom of Heaven!

Instead of showing gratitude for their existence by enjoying the beautiful Creation, they torment and torture their bodies, which before were often quite healthy, in the most wanton manner, or harm them by various self-imposed privations and renunciations only ... in order to be considered great *in the eyes of men,* or to achieve personal satisfaction and exaltation under the delusion that they have accomplished quite an exceptional feat!

All this is nothing but an evil and obnoxious outgrowth of the most gross and base conceit – the desire by every means and at all costs to pass for something before others! Generally such persons fully realise that they can never command attention in any other way, thereby clearly perceiving their inability to distinguish themselves by achieving something great. They have become convinced of their insignificance!

In their self-delusion they consider this conviction as to their insignificance to be humility. But it is not humility, and they immediately prove it by their desire to attract attention! Only self-complacency and vanity drive them to such repugnant acts. These are not pious ones or humble servants of God, nor should they be considered saints, but only wilful *sinners* – sinners who even expect to be admired for their sins and to be rewarded for their indolent attitude towards work!

If it never dawns upon many of them that this is a great sin, because in striving for "self-exaltation" they themselves do not wish to recognise it as such, this does not alter the fact that ultimately every action remains always and only what it *really* is, and not what man wishes to make himself and others believe it is!

Such men are nothing but *sinners* before God, because by their wilful or stubborn behaviour they oppose His Primordial Laws of Creation. They do not give the bodies entrusted to them the necessary nourishment and care in order to develop that strength which will enable them to provide a strong soil for the spirit on earth, and to make healthy and vigorous tools for defence and reception, serving the spirit powerfully both as shield and as sword at the same time.

Wilfully to oppose the Laws of Nature in order to stand out and attract attention is nothing but the result of a diseased brain. For a healthy man will never imagine that he can change or improve the Will of God expressed in the Primordial Laws of Creation, even by as much as a hair's breadth, without harming himself!

How foolish, how childishly wayward or ridiculous does it appear when a man spends a lifetime in a hollow tree, when he allows a limb of his body to become completely paralysed, or when he lacerates or defiles himself!

Let man exert himself as he will to find a reason which would justify such behaviour, or which would even offer some sense for it, it is and remains a crime against the body entrusted to him, and therefore a crime against the Will of God!

To these also belong the innumerable martyrs to vanity and fashion!

Pay no further attention to such people! You will see how quickly they change, how shallow are their convictions!

A fanatic ruins himself by his stubbornness! He is not worth grieving over, for such a human spirit never has any *values* to show!

And just as thousands of people severely maltreat their physical bodies in this manner, therewith maliciously turning against the Will of God, so is it also done in a thousand ways against the soul!

Great is the number of those, for instance, who continually live under the self-imposed delusion that they are outcasts in the world, bereft of happiness, neglected by their fellow-men, and so on! Yet they themselves make demands upon their fellow-men which are far from justified; their envy has a disintegrating effect upon their surroundings, whereby they heap an ever-growing and heavy burden of guilt upon their shoulders. These comprise the vermin which must be crushed under foot in the Judgment, so that undimmed peace, .joy and happiness may at last reign among men!

However, not only do they torment their neighbours with their moods, but they also injure *their own* soul bodies in much the same way as religious fanatics harm their physical bodies. In so doing they *especially* transgress against the Divine Laws, for they recklessly injure all those necessary cloaks which are entrusted to their spirit, so that they cannot be used by the spirit in their fresh health and full vigour!

Far-reaching indeed are the consequences of such deeds on the part of those who thus abuse their physical or soul bodies! Their spirits are hampered and harmed in their urgent and necessary development, and may even be led into eternal disintegration, into perdition! But even as they fall they will still suffer from the delusion that they are the victims of injustice!

Basically, however, they are only contemptible creatures, unworthy to enjoy any happiness!

Disregard and avoid them, therefore, for they do not merit even one good word!

WITHOUT any reason to justify it many people have hitherto assumed that servants of churches, temples and religious movements in general must also be regarded as the equivalent of servants of God.

This idea was disseminated at the time of the founding and development of all sorts of cults by the servants of these cults, who thereby sought to gain respect for themselves, which they would hardly have been able to achieve personally. And it has been retained ever since without anybody attempting to realise the fact that this is harmful instead of beneficial to mankind and, most important of all, that it leads to a wrong conception of God.

A man standing in Creation with an alert spirit, one who does not remain closed to the delicate intuitive vibrations of his soul, will never be able to accept as true that the Great and Living God can really be served through the practices of cults, through the begging that men call "praying", or through mortification of the flesh! With these practices you do not *give* anything to your God! You do not offer Him anything! What then is your real aim? You yourselves do not know how to answer this question when you stand before the Judgment Seat of God! You will have to remain silent, for you have done all this only *for yourselves,* for *your* inner composure and exaltation, or in despair and affliction!

But I say unto you: Only *that* man who stands aright in the Creation of his God, who recognises himself as a part of Creation and *lives accordingly,* only he is the true servant of God, no matter in what way he earns his necessary living on earth. As a part of Creation he will always strive to adjust himself to *those* laws that have a *furthering* effect therein. Thus he himself furthers Creation, and serves his God in the only right way. For through the right adjustment *only* happiness, joy and further progress can arise!

For this reason he must naturally become familiar with Creation!

And this is something you badly need – to *recognise* the Will of God resting in Creation and its constant self-acting effects therein! But so far you have never troubled yourselves to do just this in the correct manner. And yet it is the same for all of you, namely, that you stand and must move in the midst of a mighty mechanism, so to speak, without ever being able to alter or improve upon it.

Unless you stand and move in it *aright,* however, danger threatens you from all sides! You are sure to hit yourselves, and may fall and be torn to pieces! Exactly as in a gigantic machine-shop, with numerous driving belts constantly moving in all directions, confusing the eye and seriously threatening at every step all those not acquainted with it, but only of real service and use to the expert! It is no different for man in Creation!

At last learn to understand its mechanism aright, then you may and shall use it for your own happiness. But to do this you must first become an apprentice, as in everything! The greatest of all works, this Creation, is no exception; the same applies here as with all men's productions. Even an automobile gives pleasure only to the *expert!* It brings death, however, to him who does not know how to control it!

There are thousands of such minor examples available to you! Why have you never learned anything from them as yet?

All this may be recognised in such a simple and natural way. But just in this matter you stand as if before a wall – apathetic, indifferent and with an inexplicable stubbornness! After all it is your life, your entire existence, which is at stake here!

Only the constructor himself can explain the working of a machine to you, or a man whom *he* has trained for the task. It is the same in Creation as here on earth! But it is just in regard to Creation that men, who are themselves only a part of it, imagine that they of themselves know everything better than their Master, and refuse to be trained in the use of the mechanism! They themselves want to teach the basic laws, which they try to establish through superficial observation of the very faint, last ramifications of what is great and true, to the *perception* of which they always kept themselves closed. Thus there can never be any question of knowledge!

And yet the possibility of recognition was already lovingly offered to you by the Son of God, Who tried to teach you through parables and pictures!

However, their meaning was not grasped, but instead by insisting that they knew better men badly distorted, darkened and perverted it!

Now again you are granted the opportunity clearly to see the Laws of God in Creation, so that men may become true servants of God, fully conscious and in joyous and cheerful activity, as the true worship of God requires!

Joy and happiness can exist in all Creation! You men alone bring about distress and sorrow, disease and crime, for right up to the present day you did not *want* to recognise the source of the vast power which was given to you for your journey through all the worlds, in which by your own desire you must all wander for your development!

If only you adjust yourselves aright this power will forcibly bring sunshine and happiness into your lives. Unless you do this you stand small and helpless in the all-embracing mechanism, yet still boasting with big words of yourselves and your knowledge, until finally you must fall through these faults, which arose only out of your ignorance and unwillingness to learn anything!

Wake up at last! First start *learning* in order to acquire the *knowledge,* otherwise you will never make any progress!

In the eyes of the Creator you are now far less than an insect! An insect faithfully fulfils its allotted task, while you as human spirits fail! You fail through your vain pseudo-knowledge that is no knowledge! Your schools founded on this sham knowledge are fetters that hold you firmly bound, even choking every attempt at spiritual ascent, because the teachers in these schools cannot set about this spiritual ascent themselves.

Thank the Lord that the possibility of continuing to live on such an empty and thoroughly detrimental basis will now be forcibly taken from you! Otherwise you would never recognise the contemptibleness surrounding you everywhere today, which must bring ridicule upon you throughout Creation for being empty, grotesquely dressed-up dolls, whose spirits are asleep within them!

THE INSTINCT OF ANIMALS

MEN ARE often struck with admiration when they observe the instinctive actions of animals. They ascribe a special sense to animals which mankind either lack completely or which they have allowed to degenerate.

They are perplexed, for example, when they see a horse, a dog or some other animal suddenly refusing to pass a certain place on a road it is accustomed to and which it has perhaps taken daily, and when they subsequently learn that an accident occurred on that very spot shortly afterwards.

Quite often the lives of one or more persons have been saved through such incidents. So many of these cases have been published that there is no need to go into the matter more deeply here.

Instinct or unconscious presentiment are the terms man has used to describe this characteristic of the animal! Having found a name for a thing men are usually well satisfied! They envisage something in their imagination and accept it as fact, irrespective of whether they are right or wrong. It is the same with this!

The reason for such actions on the part of an animal, however, is quite a different one. It possesses neither the quality nor the ability of instinct as man understands the word. In such incidents it merely heeds a warning that is given to it. These warnings can be *seen* quite well by the animal, whereas only a few people are able to observe them.

As I have already explained in one of my earlier lectures, the soul of an animal does not originate in the Spiritual Sphere from which man comes, but from the Animistic Sphere. The elemental beings also originate there, such as the gnomes, elves, nixies, and so on, whose field of activity lies in what men usually call Nature, i. e., water, air, earth and fire. The same applies to other beings which occupy themselves with the development and growth of stones, plants and the like. All these elemental beings originate in another section of the Animistic Sphere to that of the animal souls. However, the mutual homogeneity of their origin provides a greater possibility for them to recognise each other. Thus an animal is far better equipped to recognise these elemental beings than is man, whose origin lies in the Spiritual Sphere.

The elemental beings know exactly when and where sudden changes in Nature are about to take place, such as landslides, rocks being dislodged from mountains, trees falling, the caving-in of land undermined by water, the bursting of a dam, sudden water eruptions, volcanic and fire eruptions, tidal waves and floods, earthquakes, and everything else coming within the same category, because they themselves are occupied with the preparation and bringing about of such changes, which men call disasters and catastrophes.

If such a happening is imminent it may well be that an animal or a person approaching the spot is warned by these elementals. They block the way and try, through vehement motions, shouting or sudden impressions upon their feelings, to induce them to return. The animal is startled, its hair "bristles", and it energetically refuses to continue, quite contrary to its usual behaviour, so that often as an exception even the best-trained animal disobeys its master. *This* is the reason for the striking behaviour of the animal in such cases. Man, however, does not see these elemental beings and very often runs into the danger, thereby perishing or suffering great harm.

For this reason man should pay more attention to animals so that he learns to understand them. Then animals will truly become man's friends, able to fill gaps and thus be much more useful to him than they have been in the past.

THE KISS OF FRIENDSHIP

THERE has been much discussion on this subject all over the world. Both in poetry and prose the kiss of friendship has been beautified and exalted to a high position in the world of thoughts. However, all this is only a phantasy far removed from what is natural!

It is a pretty little cloak which, as with so many things, earthman has manufactured in order to admire himself or others in it. Yet admiration is absolutely out of place, for in reality it is nothing but hypocrisy, a shameful attempt to disarrange and distort the Laws of Creation, and thus divest them of their glorious and simple naturalness!

It is true that the intention behind a kiss often varies, but this does not alter the fact that each kiss as such remains a kiss, i.e., a physical contact which, according to the Natural Laws, causes a feeling that can never be other than merely physical. He who knows my Message is aware of this already. Man must not always behave in such a cowardly manner in his efforts to deny the *true nature* of his deeds! On the contrary he must remain clearly conscious of them at all times. A hypocrite is even worse than an evil-doer!

The term "kiss of friendship" definitely presupposes the age of maturity.

The kiss between a man and a woman who have reached a mature age, however, is subject to the vibrations of the Primordial Laws in Creation, no matter how pure their intentions. It is ridiculous to make excuses. Man knows very well that the Laws of Nature do not ask for his opinion. The kiss given by a friend, a brother, or a father to a mature girl or woman always remains a kiss between the different sexes, despite the strongest self-delusion. It is no different with the kiss given by a mother to her son as soon as he has reached a mature age. The Laws of Nature neither know of nor grant any distinction in these matters. Every person must therefore practise much greater self-restraint!

Only man's mania for wishing to adapt the Natural Laws to his own desires creates ideas so *opposed* to those laws, such as kisses of friendship, embracing among relatives, and the many other trespasses existing in these matters. Under the most hypocritical cloaks man often tries to sin, even *deliberately!*

Because many people believe they are acting quite harmlessly with such transgressions, and imagine their intentions to be absolutely pure, this does not alter the fact that such behaviour is contrary to the Laws of Nature. It is and remains a distortion of the purest Laws of Nature when they are robbed of their beautiful simplicity by false interpretation. Only what is unhealthy arises from this, because every abuse and distortion only devalues, defiles and debases the original soundness of the law.

Therefore away with such hypocrisy! At last honour the Laws of Nature as they really are in their simple and thus sublime greatness! Adjust *yourselves* to them and live accordingly! Also adjust all your thinking, your actions and your habits to them, both within your families and outside! Therefore become natural in the purest sense and you will then also be happy! Every unhealthy aspect of life will then fall away from you. Honesty will be the rule among you, and you will be spared many unnecessary inner conflicts, which only result from such foolish illusions, and often molest and torment you all through your earthly lives.

The unhealthiness of this injurious toying, this wrongful caressing, which invariably indicates a purely physical basis, can be most clearly observed in immature and guileless children of a *tender* age. Children who are continually showered with or, to put it quite frankly, "molested" by these family caresses always have an unhealthy appearance. Besides nearly every child shows an intuitive repulsion against such obtrusive fondling and never any desire for it, because in reality a child is "naturally innocent". To start with it must first always be trained to tolerate and return caresses.

Such training, however, is only desired by the grown-ups, who through the maturity of their physical bodies instinctively feel the need for it, but it is not the wish of the child! All this shows clearly enough the dangerous coercion which is being insidiously brought to bear upon the child. Gradually, however, it gets accustomed to this fondling and finally comes to desire it out of sheer habit, until the maturing body itself awakens in the instinct.

Shame on a mankind who continually try to hide their base desires and personal weaknesses under a cloak of hypocrisy, or who act thoughtlessly in such matters!

Man must *know* that genuine love is of the soul only! Everything else is merely instinct! Psychic love, however, has nothing to do with the physical body, nor has it any physical desires, for the separation between all the species in Creation always remains complete. Spiritual is spiritual, psychic is psychic, and physical is and always remains only physical!

When the physical body dies not a single particle of the soul dies with it. This proves in all simplicity that everything stands on its own, that no intermingling occurs.

A soulful kiss, for example, exists only in the imagination, because every kiss is and always remains merely a gross material act. What a man experiences in his soul thereby is an entirely separate matter. Psychic love goes *beside* the physical instinct, not with it or even in it.

Any other conception is a gross self-deception because it does not correspond with the Laws of Nature. It was only the intellect which invented differences therein to serve as an excuse, and in order to create a new caricature with which to mutilate the Truth. In its pure form the Truth should bring mankind to awakening and recognition, thus to purity and truthfulness of character, and finally to ascent towards the Light.

Now at last, man, have the courage to be *true* in all you do! Also in regard to the kiss! Break through the deceptive images your vanity and sensual lust have created! Wake up!

THE DISTORTED TOOL

THE GREATEST burden with which the human soul has encumbered itself, and which will hinder every possibility of ascent, is vanity! It has spread ruin throughout the entire Creation. Vanity has become the most powerful poison for the soul, because man has cherished it as a shield and mask for all his shortcomings.

Like a narcotic it always helps to overcome psychic shocks easily. It is of no consideration to earthmen that this is merely an illusion, so long as it affords them satisfaction and therewith the possibility to attain some earthly goal, if only a few minutes of ridiculous self-complacency. It does not need to be genuine, a mere semblance will suffice!

People speak of this vanity, of conceit, spiritual arrogance, malicious joy and so many characteristics of all earthmen in a benevolent and glossing-over way as being snares of the Lucifer principle. All this, however, is nothing but feeble self-excuse! Lucifer had no need whatever to exert himself so very much. It sufficed for him to tempt man to enjoy the fruit of the "tree of knowledge", and thus to indulge in the knowledge, thereby inducing him to over-develop his intellect. All that followed was brought about by man himself.

As the worst outgrowth of the intellect (which is earthbound and gaining the upper hand), vanity must be disposed of – vanity which is the root of so many evils, such as envy, hatred, slander, and the craving for all kinds of earthly pleasures and possessions. Everything that is ugly in this world is really anchored in vanity, which expresses itself in a great variety of ways.

It was the urge towards outward sham which produced the "caricature of man" so predominant today! The sham being who does not deserve to be called "man", because in his vanity he undermined the possibility of the necessary spiritual ascent for the sake of sham, stubbornly blocking all the natural connecting lines given to him for his activity and spiritual maturing, and wantonly burying them entirely against the Creator's Will!

The effect of raising the earthbound intellect to the position of an idol was in itself sufficient to change the entire course which the Creator had designed for man in His Creation.

Lucifer claimed it as a triumph for himself that the human soul had ventured to interfere with its physical body in such a manner as to make it utterly impossible for the soul to fulfil its willed activity in Creation. In order to sharpen the intellect man feverishly promoted the one-sided cultivation of *that* part of the brain which is exclusively devoted to working in the World of Gross Matter, namely the frontal brain. This resulted in the automatic repression and curtailment of the activity of the spiritually *receiving* part of the human brain. Consequently the ability to comprehend spiritual things was rendered more difficult, and in the course of thousands of years earthman even entirely lost *spiritual* understanding.

Thus he now stands forsaken and *useless* in Creation! Cut off from the possibility of spiritual recognition and ascent, and consequently also cut off from God!

That is the work of Lucifer! He had no need to do anything more! He could then leave earthman to himself, watching him sink from one step to another and thus remove himself further and further from God, all as a consequence of this single act!

For those men who make the genuine effort to *think* objectively just for once it is not at all difficult to observe this. It is easily understandable that intellectual activity also bears within itself the conceit which comes of an insistence on knowing better, the obstinate perseverance in everything which such activity considers right, for man has "thought" as far as he was able to think in these matters. He has reached *his* highest limit in thinking!

Man cannot know that this limit is a *low* one because of the earthbound condition of his frontal brain, and that therefore he *cannot* penetrate any further with his intellect. For *this reason* he will always believe and aver that with *his* limit he has also achieved what is *right*. If he hears something different he will always give greater credence to and consider right what *he* has thought out. This remains the peculiarity of every intellect, and thus of all intellectuals!

As I have already pointed out once it is the task of one portion of the brain substance *to receive what is spiritual like an antenna,* while the other portion, which produces the intellect, transforms what has been received for use in the Gross Material World. Conversely the frontal brain which produces the intellect is likewise supposed to take in all the impressions from the World of Matter, and so transform them that the back brain can receive them and use them for the further development and maturing of the spirit. Both parts, however, are intended to work *together*, for it has been so decreed by the Creator!

Due to the intervention caused by the one-sided cultivation of the frontal brain, the latter became over-dominating in its activity, thus disturbing the necessary harmonious co-operation between the two brains, and consequently all healthy activity in Creation. The development of the portion meant to receive spiritual impressions lagged behind, while the frontal brain, which became more and more active through training, had long since ceased to receive through the back brain the pure vibrations from Luminous Heights necessary for its work, and for transmission into the World of Gross Matter. Instead it absorbs its working substance for the most part from its material environment and from thought-forms only, which it sends out again remodelled as its own production.

There are only a few people today whose *receptive* portion of the brain co-operates harmoniously at least *to some extent* with the frontal brain. These people rise above the ordinary level and distinguish themselves through great inventions or through an amazing reliability in their capacity to perceive intuitively, which enables them quickly to grasp many things that can only be attained by others through laborious study.

These are the people of whom it is enviously said that they "receive it in their sleep!" They confirm the saying: "The Lord gives it to His own in their sleep!"

By "His own" are meant those who still use their implements in accordance with the Creator's decree, i. e., those who are what He wills them to be and who, like the wise virgins, continually replenished the oil in their lamps; for these alone can "recognise" the Bridegroom when He comes. Only they are really "awake"! All the others are "asleep" in their self-imposed limitations! They rendered themselves incapable of "recognising" because they did not keep the requisite "tools" in proper order. Without the *harmonious* co-operation of that portion of the brain meant to receive spiritual impressions, the frontal brain is like a lamp without oil!

Persons of mediumistic ability *cannot* so easily be included in the above category. While it is true that the receptive part of their brain necessarily functions more or less well, during this receptive activity the frontal brain of such mediums, which is meant for the earthly transmission of what is received, becomes fatigued. Due to the determined volition of some dweller in the beyond, the proceedings bring exceptional pressure to bear upon the receptive portion of the medium's brain, and this consequently calls for a more powerful counter-pressure, which in turn automatically draws blood from the frontal brain, i.e., the warmth which is engendered by movement, with the result that the frontal brain comes to a partial or complete standstill. It co-operates only sluggishly or not at all. This withdrawal of blood would not be necessary if the receptive brain had not been seriously weakened by the suppression.

This gives the cause why the transmission of a medium, either verbally or in writing, does not appear to be *so well* remodelled for earthly comprehension as it must necessarily be if it is to be *correctly* understood by earthly conceptions, such as computation of space and time.

This also gives the cause why mediums who often foresee earthly events, catastrophes or the like, can rarely in their utterances or writings forecast the earthly time accurately.

A medium receives the *ethereal* impression and passes it on verbally or in writing with little or no alteration at all for the Gross Material World. This naturally results in misunderstanding on the part of those who view things from a purely gross material standpoint. The ethereal impression differs from the gross material effect which manifests later on. For in the World of Ethereal Matter the contrasts are sharper and richer, with corresponding effects. Now it frequently happens that mediums depict nothing but ethereal things without alteration, because the frontal brain cannot follow up with its work of remodelling and is quiescent. Then the *picture* of an event and the *times* given differ, for ethereal conceptions of time also differ from earthly conceptions.

Consequently predictions and descriptions of the same happening will sound different from almost every mediumistic person, depending on the degree of co-operation possible by their frontal brain, which can only in very rare cases achieve the complete transformation necessary for earthly conceptions.

If those dwelling in the beyond, however, are striving to re-establish connection between the World of Ethereal Matter and the World of Gross Matter, which had been severed by earthmen, then no exactions or ridiculously presumptuous judgments on the part of ignoramuses and intellectuals shall be further tolerated, for such efforts must be taken with absolute seriousness, so that what has been spoiled by conceited vanity can again be restored.

All fantastics, zealots and mystics must also be excluded from participating, for in reality they are even more detrimental than the intellectuals!

If both parts of the brain of earthmen could co-operate harmoniously, as the Creator ordained they should, then the transmissions of the mediums would be given in conceptions of time suitable to the World of Gross Matter. As it is, however, the more or less extensive withdrawal of blood from the frontal brain causes derangements and distortions. To correct them requires diligent study through observation. But it deserves neither the ridicule nor the aspersion of fraudulent intentions, such as the spiritually indolent love to suggest.

As in all fields so also in this there will naturally always be people with a pretence to knowledge who bask in their "proficiency" in these things, and who make themselves completely ridiculous, not to mention others with sordid aims! But such can be found everywhere, and it affords no justification for besmirching the work itself or those seriously engaged upon it in such a flagrant manner!

This kind of conduct which disparages everything that cannot yet be understood is again nothing but an expression of ridiculous vanity, a sign of irresponsible stupidity which has become habitual among these people. But there is nothing that is great or sublime which has *not* in the beginning incurred the enmity of mankind. Not excluding the utterances of Christ Jesus, Who fared no differently Himself!

Such scoffers show only too clearly that they go through life blindfolded, or at least with obvious narrow-mindedness!

Let us take a glance around us! He who goes on his way scoffing at the previsions and forecasts of terrible happenings which accumulate from all sides, and who refuses to see that many of them are already being fulfilled, that natural catastrophes are increasing from one week to the next, *is* either narrow-minded or does not yet want to recognise anything because of a certain fear!

These are the narrow-minded or cowardly who dare not face the facts! In any case they are harmful creatures!

He who does not yet wish to recognise the great economic distress which steadily increases in every country on earth, nor see in the consequent confusion and helplessness a disastrous setback, just because he himself still happens to have enough to eat and drink – such a person no longer deserves to be called man, for he must be inwardly corrupt and blunted to the suffering of others.

"All this has already happened before!" That is what they thoughtlessly reply! It is true that such events have taken place before, *but singly,* and not in the same conditions as today, not with all this knowledge men boast of and with all the precautionary measures which can now be taken. That is as different as day is from night!

Above all there was never such an *accumulation* of events! In past times a gap of years occurred between natural catastrophes. Such happenings excited all civilised nations and were talked and written about for months, while today they are dismissed from the mind within a few hours at a dance or in everyday conversation. This is a difference which people do not want to see on account of a fear which manifests itself in frivolity, in a wanton refusal to understand!

"The people must not be disturbed!" That is the order which has gone forth! Not out of love for humanity, however, but only for fear that mankind might make demands with which no one could cope any longer!

The attempts made to calm the public are often so crude that none but the *indifferent* humanity, with that obtuseness that prevails today, can listen to them in silence! Nobody bothers to recognise and remonstrate against these efforts as being antagonistic to the Sublime Will of God!

God *wills* that men should recognise these warnings which speak so plainly to them in the march of events! They *are meant* to awaken out of their irresponsible spiritual lethargy in order to reflect and retrace their steps in time, before it becomes necessary that they themselves must experience all the afflictions they can still see their fellow-men suffering. It is rebellion against God on the part of those who try to prevent this with comforting words!

Unfortunately, however, mankind are only too susceptible to every word which tends to absolve them from personal spiritual activity, hence they like to listen to the most peculiar utterances, accept them faithfully, and in fact *desire* to have them; even spread and advocate them rather than be disturbed from their peace and comfort!

And beloved vanity beats time to this, proving the best support of all those weeds which, like vanity itself, grow as the fruit of the intellectual domination which is hostile to God!

Vanity will never permit the recognition of the Truth, no matter where it is to be found. What it achieves in this respect is proved by the attitude of this mankind to the life on earth of the Son of God which, in its true and great simplicity, does not satisfy the vain minds of men. The believer wants "his" Saviour only in accordance with *his own* ideas. Therefore he embellishes the earthly mission of the Son of God, Christ Jesus, with events of his own fabrication!

According to man's opinion and solely because of his "humility" towards all that is Divine, this Saviour, being the Son of God, must also be absolutely "supernatural"! But in so thinking they do not realise that God Himself is *the Perfection of all that is natural,* and that Creation developed out of this His perfect Naturalness through His Will. Perfection, however, also bears the unchangeable within itself. If there could possibly be an exception in the Laws of Creation, which correspond with the Will of God, they would be bound to contain a gap and thus lack perfection.

Man's humility, however, sets itself above all this! For as regards the life of the Son of God on earth it expects, indeed *demands,* an alteration in the existing Laws in Creation, thus a trespass against them. And just from Him Who had come to fulfil all the Laws of His Father, as He Himself said! They expect from Him things which must simply be impossible according to the laws of natural development. And just *by that* is His Divinity to manifest Itself, the Divine Which carries the Living Source of the Natural Laws within Itself!

Yes, man's humility can achieve a great deal! But its true face bears the stamp of *exaction,* and not of genuine humility! The greatest presumption and the worst form of spiritual arrogance! Sweet vanity just covers this with a thin cloak which bears a semblance of humility!

It is indeed sad that so often even those who have a really good volition allow themselves, in their initial and quite genuine humility, unwittingly to be carried away by their enthusiasm to commit the most incredible things!

They gave play to their imagination, and the subsequent transmissions did great harm!

Thus the child Jesus was already supposed to have performed the greatest miracles, even during the childhood games played by every child who is healthy and spiritually alert. The small birds which he modelled from ordinary clay *came to life* and flew into the air singing merrily, and many other such things! Such happenings are *simply impossible, because they are contrary to all the Divine Laws in Creation!*

Otherwise God the Father might just as well have placed His Son upon the earth as *a fully mature man!* What was the need of a human mother? Why the inconvenience of a birth? Are men unable to think in *simple* terms for once? It is their personal vanity which deters them! In their opinion the life of the Son of God on earth *must* be different. *They* want it this way so that "their" Saviour and "their" Redeemer should not be subject to the Laws of God in Creation. Actually in their view this would not have been too small for *Him,* the Son of God, but it surely would have been for all those who wish to recognise their Redeemer in Him! Human vanity, and nothing else!

They fail to realise how even greater it was for Jesus voluntarily to subject Himself to these Laws by becoming flesh in order to bring the Truth in the Word to those who, through the distortion of their earthly tool, had wantonly rendered themselves incapable of receiving and recognising the Truth of their own accord. They were much too conceited to see Christ's Mission fulfilled in the Word Itself. For them, vain men that they are, *greater* things had to come to pass!

And when the Son of God suffered physical death upon the cross, dying just as any man must die when crucified because it corresponds with the Divine Laws in Creation, when His human body could not simply descend unharmed from the cross, then vanity had no other choice but to assert that the Son of God had to die in this way, that in order to bear the sins of the poor little men *He did not wish to step down from the cross,* so that they can now be joyfully received into the Kingdom of Heaven!

And thus the foundation was laid for the later belief in the *necessity* of the death on the cross, that great and tragic error prevalent among Christians today, which is entirely due to the vanity of men!

If there is no longer any man who wishes to recognise that such thinking can only arise out of shameless conceit – to the joy of Lucifer who presented man with vanity in order to ruin him – then there is no longer any help for humanity and all is in vain! Even the greatest and strongest warnings in Nature cannot arouse them from their spiritual sleep! Why does not man think any further?

If it would have been possible for Christ to have risen from the dead in the flesh, then it follows that one could just as logically expect it to be possible for Him to descend to the earth already matured in the flesh, from that sphere to which He was supposed to have ascended physically at His resurrection! That this did not happen, however, that on the contrary from the very beginning He had to live through the phases that every human body is subject to from birth onwards, with all their great and minor troubles, and also face the many other needs of His earthly life, clearly enough speaks against this conception. Quite apart from the fact that it could not be otherwise because the Son of God also had to submit Himself to the Perfect Laws of His Father in Creation!

He who wishes to enter Creation and live upon the earth is subject to the Immutable Laws of Creation!

All assertions to the contrary are inventions, created in their enthusiasm by men themselves, and then bequeathed as the truth! The same happened with all traditions, regardless of whether they were passed on verbally or in writing. Human vanity plays a great role in this! Very seldom indeed do they issue from the human hand, voice or even brain without something being added! Second-hand records never constitute a proof on which posterity should rely. Man only needs to observe current events closely! Let us take just one example which received world-wide publicity!

Newspapers in all countries *published reports* of the mysterious "castle" on Vomperberg, of which I was supposed to be the owner! I was described as "the Messiah of the Tyrol" or "the Prophet of Vomperberg" with great and prominent headlines, even in the leading newspapers which wish to be taken seriously! There were weird and mysterious accounts of numerous underground tunnels, of temples, of knights both in black and silver armour, of an unheard-of cult, also of great parks, automobiles, stables, and whatever else could be invented by the diseased brains that can report such things. Details were quoted, some based on beautiful phantasy and others so disgustingly filthy that anyone giving a little thought to the matter could not fail immediately to recognise the lies and malevolence behind it!

And there was *not one word of truth* in any of these reports!

If, however, after centuries or, better still, in thousands of years to come, some person reads one of these evil and scurrilous articles... who can blame him for wanting to believe it and saying: "Here it is, reported and published, and the same in nearly every newspaper and language!"

And all this was nothing but a reflection of the decadent brains of this time! With their own works they stamped themselves with the proof of their depravity, ready for the coming Judgment!

This happened even *today* in spite of every facility for speedily obtaining accurate information *before* publication. What must it have been like in former times, in the days of Jesus, when everything could only be passed on by word of mouth? How greatly subject to alteration are such verbal transmissions! This applies equally to written records and letters. It takes on the characteristics of an avalanche! Already partially misunderstood at the start, in this way there always arises something different to the original facts. How much of what has been heard has been written down at second, third or even tenth hand only, but which has now come to be regarded as the original basis! Surely men should know their fellow-men!

As soon as they can no longer make use of the scaffolding of their intellect – which is the case with all truth *on account of its great simplicity* – they are not satisfied. They either reject or change it in a manner that suits their beloved vanity!

For this reason "mysticism" is preferred to the simple truth! The great craving for "mysticism", for everything mysterious, which is engrained within every person is vanity, and not the urge for truth as is so often depicted! *Self-complacency* constructed the unhealthy way upon which hosts of idle enthusiasts can sun themselves, and upon which many who are spiritually indolent allow themselves leisurely to drift!

In all these matters the vanity of man plays a devastating and dismal role, dragging him tenaciously and irretrievably down to destruction, because he has come to love it!

He would be seized with consternation if he could but once master himself sufficiently to reflect about it objectively and without self-complacency! But again that is just the difficulty! He cannot do anything without being self-complacent! Thus many will probably have to remain in this state until they perish from it!

This fact in all its tragedy is the result which, consequent upon the Fall of Man, was forcibly brought about by the prevention of the harmonious development of the brain in the earthly body entrusted to him. The distortion of the tool indispensable to man in this Gross Material World through its one-sided development has thereby exacted its revenge. Now man stands *un-harmoniously* in Creation with his gross material tool, his physical body, incapable of performing the task he has to fulfil therein, rendered useless by himself!

To eradicate the root of all this evil the intervention of God is necessary! Every other power and authority, however great, is inadequate to achieve this! It constitutes the greatest and most devastating contamination in man's false volition that ever found its way into Creation. *Everything* on this earth will have to collapse before any improvement can come about, because there is nothing in existence which is not already irretrievably pervaded by it!

THE CHILD

WHEN people ask themselves what is *the right way* to bring up their children they must first of all consider and adjust themselves *to the particular child*. The personal wishes of the educator in this matter must be put completely aside. The child must go *its own* way on earth, but not that of its educator.

It is well meant if an educator sincerely wishes to put at the disposal and use of his child *those* experiences which he himself had to undergo in his life on earth, with a view to sparing the child much in the way of disappointment, loss and pain. But in most cases he achieves very little!

In the end he has to recognise that all his efforts and good intentions in this matter have been utterly in vain, for at a certain time the maturing child quite suddenly and unexpectedly goes its own way, and in decisions of importance to itself has forgotten or disregarded all admonitions.

The educator is not justified in bewailing this, for with all his good volition he entirely failed to realise that the child he wished to educate has by no means to follow in his footsteps, in order *properly* to fulfil the purpose of its existence here on earth.

All the experiences which the educator could or was obliged to undergo in the past were intended and necessary *for him*. They were therefore only of use *to him,* provided he was capable of absorbing them in the right manner.

The experiences of the educator, however, cannot bring the same benefit *to the child* because, for the purpose of its own development, the child's spirit must pass through entirely different experiences that accord with the threads of fate connected with *it*.

Not two of the many men on earth follow the *same* path for the purpose of furthering their spiritual maturing!

The experiences of one man are therefore *spiritually* valueless for any other man. And if one person exactly follows and *imitates* the footsteps of another he has just frittered away his own time on earth!

Until the child reaches maturity you shall only prepare the *tool* which it needs for its life on earth, and nothing else, namely, the physical body with all its gross material functions.

Exercise the greatest care to see that you do not distort or even completely disable it through excesses or one-sidedness! Next to the necessary physical training, schooling in the right activity of its brains plays an important part. The first period of this training ends with the beginning of maturity, and not until then must the second period begin, which is to teach the spirit to control the entire body *correctly*.

Until the spirit breaks through in the years of their maturity the children of earthmen have *only a predominantly animistic* intuitive perception. Naturally they are already set aglow inwardly by the spirit, i. e., they are not merely like noble animals in the highest state of development, but already very much more. Nevertheless the *animistic* prevails and is therefore decisive. It is absolutely imperative that this be borne in mind by every educator, and the basis of an education strictly adjusted *in accordance with it,* if the result is to become complete and without harmful effects on the child. The child must first receive full understanding in the great activity of all that is animistic, to which at this time it is still more open than to that which is spiritual. In this way its eyes will open in joy and purity to the beauties of Nature which it sees around it!

The streams, the mountains, the forests, the meadows and the flowers, as well as the animals, will then become familiar to every child, who will be securely anchored in this realm, which is to provide the field of activity during its sojourn on earth. It will then stand quite firmly and fully conscious in Nature, in the whole world of animistic activity, full of understanding and thus well equipped and quite ready to work with its spirit also, uplifting and furthering to an even greater extent all that surrounds it like a huge garden! Only *thus* can it become a true gardener in Creation!

On this basis and not otherwise must each maturing child stand when the spirit breaks through, healthy in body and soul, joyfully developed and prepared on *that* soil to which every child belongs. The brain must not be one-sidedly over-burdened with things that will never be needed during its life on earth, things which do cost great pains to acquire, consequently wasting its strength and weakening body and soul!

If, however, a preliminary education already takes all his strength, then man has nothing left for his real task!

With the *right* training and preparation for real life, however, work becomes only a joy, a pleasure, for then everything in Creation is also able to vibrate in full harmony, thus supporting the maturing of youth by furthering and strengthening it.

But how senselessly men act towards their children! What crimes are they guilty of against posterity!

Just when the spirit within the young girl's body breaks forth so that it can make use of the gross material and ethereal tools entrusted and given to it, in order that she may become a real human being, this young representative of womanhood is dragged off to earthly pleasures ... with the idea of getting her quickly linked up with a man!

The spirit, the true human being, which has yet to face earthly activity, thus never gets a start. Becoming paralysed, it must watch how the earthly intellect, which was exclusively and wrongly trained, expends itself in nothing but glittering nonsense in order to *appear* clever and witty and thus cover the lack of true spirit. It must observe how the intellect becomes implicated in all sorts of impossible things, thereby requiring and squandering the entire strength the tool is able to give. Finally the woman becomes a mother without ever having been a real human being!

Thus there is no field left for the spirit, no possibility for it to become active!

And things are not much better for the young man! He is weary and fatigued from over-burdening study in schools, his nerves overwrought! He provides only a diseased soil for the spirit breaking through, a brain distorted by and satiated with useless things. Thus the spirit cannot work as it should, and in turn cannot develop itself properly, but is stunted and completely smothered by the weight of the dross! There only remains an unquenchable yearning to give some inkling as to the presence of the immured and suppressed human spirit. Finally even this longing is lost in the mad whirl of earthly haste and greed which is first meant to act as a bridge over this spiritual vacuum, and which later on becomes a habit and a need!

This is the manner in which man *now* goes through his earthly life! And for the most part the faulty upbringing is to blame for it!

If man wishes to stand aright here on earth the first part of his training, i.e., of his education, must absolutely be changed. Let children really be children in these matters! Never allow them to enjoy equal privileges with grown-ups, nor indeed expect that grown-ups should adjust themselves to children! You are giving them a strong poison by doing so! For the spirit of the children has not yet broken through from within, they are still largely dominated by their animistic nature, and therefore they are not on a level with grown-ups.

Children feel this very distinctly! Therefore do not allow them to play a role which deprives them of this consciousness! You only make them unhappy! They become unsteady upon the firm soil of the childhood which is their rightful due, and which is ordained for them in Creation. But they can never feel at home on an equal footing with grown-ups, because they lack the principal quality which entitles them and makes them able to exist on that level – the complete connection of their spirits with the outer world through their bodies!

You rob them of the genuine childhood to which they are fully entitled according to the Laws of Creation, and which they even need urgently, because the experiences of childhood are absolutely necessary for the later development of the spirit. Instead you often allow them to mingle with grown-ups in whose company they cannot move freely since they lack every quality to do so. Such children become unsteady and precocious, which naturally only appears repulsive to grown-ups, giving an unhealthy impression, and disturbing pure intuition and all harmony. For a precocious child is like a fruit the kernel of which is still unripe, whereas the shell is already about to grow old!

Beware of this, parents and educators, for it is a crime against the Laws of God! Let children remain as children! Children that know they are *in need* of the protection of all grown-ups!

The task of the grown-up is only to furnish the *protection* which he is able and also in duty bound to give where the child *deserves* it.

Unless you yourselves destroy this Law of Nature the child, in its animistic state, quite distinctly senses the need of the grown-up's protection and consequently looks up to him, by way of balance voluntarily showing him the respect which implies the desire for support.

But in most cases you do destroy this Law! You tear every child out of its quite natural intuitive perceiving through the false methods you apply to them, very often just to satisfy your own desires, since for the most part the child is a lovable plaything to you which *you* wish to enjoy, and which you try to make prematurely intelligent so that you may be proud of it!

All this is of no benefit *to the child*, but only harmful! In the days of its youth, which must be considered as the first stage of its development, already starting with the earliest years, you have to fulfil *more serious* duties towards the child. Not your wishes, but the Laws of Creation must be the decisive factor in this matter! And the decree that every child must *be* a child in all things!

A human being who has really been a child will grow up to give full value as an adult. *But only then!* And a normal child can be solely recognised *by the fact* that it has a genuine respect for grown-ups in *its personal intuitive perception,* which *thus* precisely corresponds to the Law of Nature.

All this every child already bears within itself as a gift of God. It will develop this if you do not bury it! Therefore keep children away when grown-ups converse together, for they do not belong there. In this also they must always know that they are children, and as such not yet of full value, not yet matured for their work on earth. Much more is contained in these apparent trifles than you think today. They fulfil a basic law in Creation which you often disregard. Children, *all* of whom still stand predominantly in the animistic, *are in need* of this as an outward support, in accordance with the Law of the Animistic!

Grown-ups must give protection to children! Therein lies more than the words alone indicate! But they must grant protection only where the child deserves it! Children must return something to balance this protection, so that they may already learn *through experiencing* that *there must be equilibrium everywhere,* and that *therein* lie harmony and peace. This also *is demanded* by the nature of the animistic.

It is just *this,* however, which many parents and educators have often neglected, although it is the fundamental condition for a proper upbringing, if such is to be carried out in accordance with the Primordial Laws of Creation. Everyone lacking the conception of unconditional equilibrium is bound to waver and fall, no matter whether sooner or later. And the consciousness of the unavoidable necessity of this conception must be hammered into the minds of children from their very first days so that it becomes *as much* their own, as much a part of their flesh and blood, and *as natural* as the feeling for physical balance which they develop, and which is based on the same fundamental law.

If this principle is carefully applied in all education, there will at last be free men who are pleasing to God!

But just this most indispensable and main fundamental Law in this Creation was disregarded by men everywhere. Except for the sense of physical balance this law is not observed and practised in the field of education. This necessarily brings about one-sidedness of an unhealthy kind, causing every man to flounder about psychically on his course through Creation and continually to stumble and fall!

It is sad that this intuitive sense of equilibrium is only accepted as necessary for all movements of the physical body, but does not receive the proper care and is often altogether neglected, in things psychical and spiritual. The child must be carefully guided in these matters by imposing external restrictions upon him from the first weeks. To neglect this brings about dreadful consequences for the entire existence of every human being through the Law of Reciprocal Action!

Just look around you! In the life of the individual, as well as in the family, in state activities and in the attitude of the churches, indeed everywhere, there is a serious lack of consideration in this and *only* in this! And yet you find this law manifesting clearly everywhere, if only you wish to observe it! Even the physical body indicates it; you can find it in regard to food-intake and waste-elimination, also, indeed, in the various kinds of food you eat if the body is to keep well, in the balance between work and rest in all its details, quite apart from the afore-mentioned Law of Equilibrium which enables every individual body to move, and only thus to become fit for its task on earth. This law also holds and sustains *the entire world,* for only through the balance of equilibrium can stars and globes pursue their respective courses and maintain themselves.

And you, you little men in Creation, no more than a speck of dust before the Sublime Creator, you overthrow this law by refusing to heed and obey it fully!

For a time it was possible for you to distort it, but now it jerks back into its original form, and in doing so it must hit you painfully!

Out of this one fault has grown all the affliction which hits Creation today! It is also the cause of dissatisfaction and rebellion within nations where a proper balance is lacking on the one side. However, this is nothing but a continuation and development of *those* mistakes which the educators make in regard to youth!

The new kingdom, the Kingdom of God on earth, will create equilibrium and with it a new generation. But before it can be understood force will have to be used to bring about the right conception of equilibrium. It will bring it about forcibly by remodelling all that is distorted, a process which is already taking place, because all that is false and unhealthy must run itself to death, urged on by the invincible power and force of the Light. Then will follow the gift of the true conception of all the Primordial Laws of Creation. Strive to recognise them correctly already, and you will stand aright in this Creation. This in turn will result in bringing you nothing but happiness and peace!

WOMAN AND HER VOCATION

A HEAVY burden presses upon all earthly womanhood since the delusion was spread abroad that woman's main vocation is motherhood. Some people look upon girls who do not marry, and also upon women whose marriages are childless, with false pity and frequently even with hidden malicious joy. The expression "old maid" or "elderly spinster", which is really an *honourable name,* is frequently used with an undertone of mockery and a pitying shrug of the shoulders, as if marriage were the highest goal for woman on earth, indeed her absolute vocation!

That this false opinion has gained a foothold and spread so devastatingly over thousands of years is one of the supreme achievements of Lucifer, who in aiming at the debasement of womanhood delivered the most crushing blow at true humanity. For look around you! The evil outgrowths of this false opinion have from the very start trained the thoughts of parents and girls to concentrate upon earthly security through marriage. Everything is directed towards this – even a girl's education, all her thinking, all her speaking and all her activities from the days of her childhood until she has attained maturity. Then the opportunity is sought or offered, or if this fails is even brought about by force, to make acquaintances with the final aim of marriage!

It is thoroughly hammered into the girl that her life will be joyless unless she can go through it at the side of a husband, and that otherwise she will never be taken seriously. Wherever a member of the female sex turns she sees the glorification of *earthly* love, with maternal bliss as its highest aim! Thus, due to artificial pressure, the idea is formed that every girl who cannot achieve this is to be pitied and has partly wasted her time on earth. From the moment of her birth all thoughts, all desires and all plans are aimed at this, which is so deeply engrained as to become a part of her very flesh and blood. But all this is a very clever move by Lucifer with the purpose of debasing human womanhood!

This constraint must now be removed from womanhood on earth if they are to ascend. Only from the ruins of the present delusion can greatness and purity arise! The God-Willed *noble* womanhood could not unfold through this most cunning of Lucifer's plots against the human spirits, *all* of whom could originally have done nothing but strive towards the Light had they unerringly followed and submitted to the guidance of the Primordial Laws of Creation.

Become *spiritual* at last, you men, for you are of the spirit! Recognise and also have the courage to accept the fact that maternal bliss, which was considered the highest goal and most sacred destiny of earthly womanhood, is rooted only *in the animistic!* Woman's most sacred vocation, however, lies much higher, lies *in the spiritual!*

Not *once* did the thought occur to you that everything you have praised so far was merely meant for the earth, for life on earth, with all its restrictions! For marriage and procreation exist *only* in the gross material part of this Subsequent Creation, whereas womanhood exists in all Creation. This fact should give you cause to consider! But no, this was expecting too much of you!

Just as in the case of wild animals which you try gradually to drive into a carefully-built and well-concealed path which they cannot distinguish from the free and beautiful forest, but which leads them into captivity, so have you always driven your daughters only towards the one goal...towards the man! As if that was their main destiny!

The delusion created by this false view was akin to placing barriers to right and left, which ultimately also prevented the poor children from thinking in any but this one direction. And many a girl "escaped" by suddenly embarking upon a marriage which she contracted with great reluctance, only because she refused to fall a miserable prey in her old age to the consequences of this wrong opinion, which hang like threatening swords over every girl's head!

When in the first upheavals of a new epoch youth wished to flee from this unhealthy situation which, however, they had not recognised for what it really was, this merely indicated an inner contradiction developing quite subconsciously, a rebellion of the spirit which had been hitherto so suppressed. Unfortunately they slipped into something much worse, into the idea of free companionship and thus also of companionate marriage. Although in a different form, yet it is basically still the same excrescence of

Lucifer's idea aiming at the *debasement* of womanhood. No purity could arise therefrom because the Darkness lays a sinister spell upon everyone, holding them firmly in its grip and oppressing them continually!

That which was false *was bound* to remain, even when it appeared in a different form. The stroke that will liberate true womanhood can now only come from on High. Mankind themselves are unable to achieve it because they entangled and enslaved themselves too much!

Neither laws nor new forms can help here any longer! Salvation lies only in an understanding of all the Primordial Laws of Creation. At last you must accept *the truth* as it really *is*, and not as you imagined it to be because you were so susceptible to Lucifer's promptings!

Human womanhood was debased and dishonoured by the thought that every woman is supposed to consider motherhood as the principal purpose of her existence. For she was thereby degraded and bound to the *animistic*. Lucifer had no need to do more than disseminate this idea, which was thus absorbed and gradually developed into the definite belief still dominating the human mind today, forcing it into the *very* direction that prevents the spirit from soaring upwards towards Pure and Luminous Heights!

Thus the dirty fists of the Luciferian henchmen oppress the whole of earthly womanhood. Away with them! Free yourselves now from the clutches that hold you down! For this belief alone has brought in its train everything which must dishonour woman. The beautiful little cloak of sacred motherhood, the high praise bestowed upon mother-love, can never alleviate this pressure of the dark fists, nor make these black fists luminous!

Listen to my words! Through this belief earthwoman was made into a mother-animal! Wake up, you girls, you women and you men, so that you may at last recognise the absolute horror of this idea! One of your Sacred Rights is at stake!

Lucifer could well be proud of this achievement!

I have already stated once before that through womanhood Lucifer sought to deliver the most crushing blow against real humanity and, alas, he *succeeded* only too well!

Follow for yourselves the thought he has sown among you with great cunning and malice! He deceitfully flattered you with the thought that motherhood was woman's highest task. But to attain to motherhood the *earthly instinct* is needed, and it is *this latter* which he wanted to place on a higher pedestal through the thought of motherhood, so that it would become the dominant factor and force the thinking of mankind on earth into *one* direction. A plan which was conceived with admirable cunning! He played upon your feelings as carefully as a first class artiste plays upon his instrument, dangling motherhood and mother-love alluringly before your eyes as a shield for his intentions, so that you were unable to recognise what was lurking in the background! And he succeeded *completely!*

You heard the alluring tune vibrating *purely* within you, but you overlooked the dirty, greedily clutching hands that brought forth the melody! The highest goal and most sacred calling! That was before your eyes, you saw it bright and luminous! But in spite of all its brightness it is merely the purest radiation of the *animistic*, not of the spiritual! The *animal* is set aglow and attains its greatest height in motherhood, becoming merged in it and yielding itself *completely* to it, because the animal itself originates in the Animistic Sphere. It attains greatness therein and becomes bright and luminous. Man, however, possesses something still stronger which should and must stand *above* the animistic if he wishes to be a complete human being ... the spirit!

Being of the spirit he cannot and must not remain in the animistic. He must refrain from making the highest of *his* goals something which belongs unconditionally to the Animistic Realm, and which must forever remain there in accordance with the Primordial Laws of Creation. With exceptional cleverness Lucifer thus laid his snare, forcing the human spirit into the animistic and holding it captive there. This was achieved all the more easily because man saw all the beauty and luminosity which emanates from everything that is pure, and which is therefore also a part of the highest animistic radiation.

Yes, motherhood is certainly sacred, and its crown mother-love, but nevertheless this is not the highest goal of *human* womanhood, not their mission in Creation! Motherhood is rooted in the animistic and is only set aglow by a pure volition. Even if this is not always so with human beings, it is definitely always the case with animals.

In spite of this, however, motherhood remains within the highest radiation of the animistic, which alone can directly coalesce with gross matter. But only he who has thoroughly studied and absorbed the Grail Message will understand me *fully* here!

What Lucifer intended with his scheming came to pass, for he knew precisely what would be the consequences of distorting the Divinely-instituted Primordial Laws, which he thereby achieved through men themselves! He only gave men a false goal which was nicely suited to their spiritual indolence and weaknesses, and all their thinking and perceiving were adjusted accordingly, causing them inevitably to take wrong paths!

Thus Lucifer only *shifted the points,* and the catastrophe of derailment was bound to follow! Lucifer had merely flattered the physical instinct in a deceitful manner, thereby elevating it to an immense force and power.

Furthermore, he knew very well that the intellectual development of man was bound to strengthen this powerful instinct through the corresponding effect of thoughts which may increase the pernicious desires to fever heat. Thus man finally became completely enslaved within, something which can never happen to an animal!

The beautiful word "motherhood" remained nothing but the deceptive shield which Lucifer deceitfully conjured up in your imagination. However, the strengthening of the physical instinct, which was the inevitable consequence, was his goal. As he had plainly foreseen, it finally developed into morbidity, enslaved the minds of all people of both sexes, and turned for many into the baffling sphinx – the form in which the unhealthy instinct shows itself today, and against which man so often fights a losing battle!

The root of the problem, as also its solution, lie solely in this Luciferian thought, which was thrown out to you in defiance of the Laws which the Will of God instituted in Creation for your benefit and for the general development. And you, you reached out for it and were caught on it like a hungry fish on the angler's hook, just because you found pleasure in it! As for the male sex, its effect was like a serious and incurable plague!

In all truth grasp and hold within yourselves the idea of pure, sublime womanhood, and then you will be free from these heavy chains that caused you such unspeakable suffering and such anguish to your souls! Through this Luciferian thought all earthly womanhood was robbed of what is noblest, woman became the puppet and the prey of degraded male beings and, what is more, a lovable mother-animal even to the serious-minded man! The air then became charged with this false belief, as the popular saying goes; in reality it came to life and took form in the Ethereal World, hovering around you constantly and influencing you continually until you could not help but absorb it!

I sever this evil connection, for it is false!

Only when she has become truly conscious of her womanhood does woman stand at the *highest* place *spiritually!* And her task is not primarily dedicated to motherhood! As I have already stated motherhood exists for your earthly body only, that is all! Yet womanhood is to be found in all spheres, even in the *Primordial Realm* among the Primordial Beings, at the *highest* point! But it is *true* womanhood in all its sublime, unapproachable dignity!

It may seem as if I am taking much away from you when I now say that motherhood belongs only to the *Animistic* Realm. It is a keen cut that I am now forced to make if I am to help you! Motherhood *remains* within the realm of the animistic, and manifests on that plane. If this were her highest goal, woman would be in a very sad plight!

Just observe the animal! In truth it is very often much stronger in its instinctive mother-love than a human being can ever be. For it gives itself *wholly* in everything it does, because it acts only on impulse and without any pondering. Thus it readily faces death for its young and fears no enemy. The self-same basis is also stipulated for human mother-love by the Laws of Nature, unless it is suppressed through intellectual thinking. But it remains bound up with the body, and the body with all its radiations is animistic and not otherwise!

It is true that some human beings have already felt what is right in these matters. Not without reason is it said even today that only *that* woman is a true mother who is also able to become a friend to her children at the proper time!

What wisdom lies in this! When a mother can become a friend to her maturing daughter! This means that as soon as the girl outgrows her childhood the mother must also change or lay aside her motherly ways altogether, if she wishes to stride onward with her child, whose spirit is breaking through in the process of maturing, as I have already clearly explained in my lecture on generative power.

Up to that moment the child is exclusively dominated by the animistic, and the original mother-love fully satisfied it. When the spirit breaks through, however, it demands *more* than merely the motherhood which has so far prevailed. The spirit has little connection with such motherhood, because spiritual heredity can never take place; instead the spirit in each child's body is a stranger even to the mother, and it can only feel any link through homogeneity.

The "more" that the spirit then demands can only be given to the girl by *that* mother who at this time becomes her friend, who thus connects herself *spiritually* with her daughter. That is a process which it was not possible to set in motion either at birth or during childhood, but which only develops with the break-through of the spirit at the time of the girl's maturing, with which motherhood *and* mother-love have nothing to do. *Not until then* is there established in such cases a spiritual relationship standing higher than the mother-love, which is rooted only in the Animistic Sphere.

Where such a spiritual relationship proves impossible there is bound to be a separation after maturity, just as is the case with animals. Among human beings, however, this remains an *inward* separation; it seldom becomes visible, because *externally* conditions and education maintain a sham bridge which does not exist among animals.

The highest task in the life of woman on earth is the same as it has always been in the higher regions – to ennoble her surroundings and ensure a continuous flow of radiation from the Light, which only woman through the delicacy of her intuitive perception can mediate. Ennoblement, however, is bound to bring about ascent towards the Luminous Heights. That is spiritual law! For this reason the existence of *genuine* womanhood is alone enough irrevocably to ensure the ascent, ennoblement and continuous purity of the entire Creation.

Lucifer knew this, because it is contained in the Laws of Creation, and he tried to cut off the development of this natural process with the harmful and false basic idea which, in an enticing manner, portrayed the instinct of the physical body and its effects as of the highest value. He thereby poured poison into all *true* humanity, which thereupon unsuspectingly – and to its own detriment – distorted the purely upward movement of the straight paths of these Primordial Laws of Creation, so that they were compelled to bring about a standstill and thereafter lead downwards, thus bringing harm instead of blessing to all human spirits.

He knew what he was doing thereby! By submerging and losing themselves in the animistic, women on earth could not develop properly; they were bound to become confused about themselves and their main vocation, and thus even brought confusion into the Animistic World because they do not belong there.

Thus woman's principal task also here on earth, in the World of Matter, is to ennoble her environment. Coming as she does from above, holding herself above with her delicate intuitive perception, and thus leading upwards in turn, she forms *the anchorage of man with the Light,* the support which he needs for his work in Creation. No marriage is required to accomplish this, not even an acquaintanceship or personal meeting! The mere *existence* of woman on earth already brings about fulfilment!

Man stands in Creation facing outward ready for battle while woman, in shielding his back, maintains the connection with the Light, thus constituting the core, the supply of power and the strengthening. Wherever decay is permitted to creep into this core, however, the "front" is also lost. Bear this in mind at all times! Nor is it then of any avail for woman to try and place herself at the front beside the man, where she does not belong. Her delicate intuitive perception only hardens through such a struggle, and thus the highest ability and power once bestowed upon her as her own becomes exhausted, and everything *must* fall into ruin!

It is known to everybody, however, that even in the most remote regions of the earth men immediately pull themselves together and try to behave in a more respectful manner as soon as even one woman comes near them, with whom they need not necessarily exchange a single word!

Such is the effect of the mere presence and appearance of a woman! Even in its curtailed expression this quite clearly reveals the mystery of woman, the power and the sustaining force that emanate from her in accordance with the Laws in Creation, which are not directly related to procreation on earth. Procreation is for the most part animistic in character!

You girls and you women, *you* must first of all remember that you are the bearers in this Creation of the highest tasks, with which God has endowed *you!* Neither marriage nor motherhood are your *highest* goal, sacred as they are! You stand alone and firmly for yourselves as soon as you stand *aright!*

How ridiculous and disgusting will the present fashion craze appear, to which you have always readily and even unconditionally submitted! Every nonsensical creation thrown on to the market for the sake of money-making by the fashion designers you seized like an animal to which titbits are thrown!

You will live to recognise the disgrace contained in this, even in the reception you gave to the sometimes quite questionable aberrations from the concepts of true beauty, not to mention purity at all! Purity has always been soiled in these matters with an impudence that could not be further increased.

Years afterwards you will still blush with shame at the recognition of how deep you really sank in this respect!

What is still worse is the conscious and deliberate exposure of the body (which should be sacred to everyone), as fashion so often demands. Only the basest form of vanity could cause woman to sink to such a depth. And this vanity, which has long since been proverbially associated with woman, is but the abominable caricature of the effect womanhood should *really* have in accordance with the Divine Laws!

Man, however, is just as guilty as woman! It is only necessary for him to show contempt for such things, and woman would soon stand aside, solitary and ashamed, even if her first reaction was unjust anger! But instead man welcomed the fall of woman because she therewith corresponded more nearly to the weaknesses and desires which he already carried within himself, increased to a state of morbidity by the Luciferian idea!

Woman can never fulfil her vocation on earth while she has any vanity, which always involves shamelessness, *but only through that grace* with which *she alone* is endowed as the most beautiful spiritual gift. *Every look, every movement, every word of a woman must bear the stamp of her nobility of soul.* Therein lie her task, as well as her power and her greatness!

Develop yourselves and take advice *in these matters,* so as to let that become *genuine* which you now seek to substitute with base vanity! It is *grace* which holds your earthly power, it is grace which you must cultivate and use. Grace, however, cannot be contemplated without purity! The very word, in its conception, directs thought and mind towards purity and the heights; it has a commanding, inviolable and sublime effect! *Grace* makes the woman! Grace alone holds true beauty for *every* age and every physical form, for it *makes* everything beautiful, because it is the expression of a pure *spirit,* from which it issues. Grace, however, must not be confused with the physical litheness which originates in the animistic.

It is *thus* that you shall and *must* stand in Creation! Therefore become spiritually free within yourselves, you women and girls! The woman who is content to live *merely* as a mother in her life on earth has missed her real purpose and vocation!

OMNIPRESENCE

GOD IS omnipresent! Children are taught this even at school! To those who still believe in God at all this is so familiar and so self-evident that they do not consider it necessary to ponder seriously as to whether they really know what they are saying with these words.

But if an explanation is demanded as to how they picture this, then their wisdom immediately fails them and they themselves recognise that, after all, the word "omnipresent" as such does not hold the knowledge as to its real significance.

Men indeed have the word, but not the understanding of it! And that, after all, is the main point in everything. Even knowledge is of no avail where understanding is lacking. Man knows the meaning of the term "omnipresent", but to know the meaning is not the same as understanding or grasping its sense.

I must therefore refer you to my lecture "Life". God is Life! He alone! All else is but a consequence of the motion which as such only comes into being through the pressure of the radiation of Life!

The man who in a really fervent prayer seeks help for something, obtains connection through his attitude with that sphere from which help can be proffered. This I have mentioned once before in my explanations about the effect of prayer. Do not think of prayer as pleading, but as worship – worship and veneration! Every plunge into such deep meditation by the human spirit, however, is nothing but an effort to establish a connection, a seeking for connection with the Light, with Purity and with Life! The desire and *longing* of the human spirit expand in such cases. In its spiritual seeking it reaches out to Luminous Heights. And if it thereby seeks in true *earnestness* it will then find, as Christ has already promised. It finds the *connection* with Life. But only the connection, not Life Itself!

Thus through prayer or earnest seeking you find a *path connecting* you with God, and it is on account of this that He appears *as* omnipresent as you have imagined in the past. But God can *never* be seen by any creature!

Omnipresence has been misunderstood. Omnipresence might perhaps be even better interpreted with the words "always present", always to be found if one seeks!

It is only the outward manifestation of the happening that has misled mankind. They have approached the subject from the false assumption that God personally looks after them, pleads with them, and also surrounds them with His protection. It never occurred to them that *they themselves must do everything* in order to strive for the necessary connection, which they have always unconsciously fulfilled in accordance with the Laws of Creation in their genuine prayers. They did not like to believe that it is only the Laws of God resting in Creation that encompass them, and that these act automatically to mete out every reward and every punishment.

To be omnipresent really means nothing else than to be accessible from every part of Creation!

But even this must again only be taken in a restricted sense, for when it is said: *"Before God everything dissolves!"* this is literally true. There is a tremendous gulf! Not a single creature can step directly before God and thus come into His Presence, unless it is One who issued directly from God. This is possible for two only – the Son of God and the Son of Man! All else would and must be dissolved in His Presence, i.e., could never stand consciously before Him.

It is only possible for the human spirit to find the connecting path to God!

CHRIST SAID...!

You can hear these words repeated unctuously in a thousand ways today! *Christ said!* With this introduction every contrary opinion is supposed to be quashed from the very beginning. Every person using these words, however, also desires to absolve himself of all personal liability, but instead of this he burdens himself with an enormous responsibility ... before God!

But this does not occur to him until it descends upon him with such a force that he will be compelled to remain silent for ever after! The hour is approaching, already the first stones of retribution are rolling. But the biggest stone of retribution for many human spirits was formed through using the introductory words: *Christ said ...!*

These words are then followed by some quotation from the "Holy Scriptures" which is meant to soothe and comfort, to encourage, also to warn and even to threaten, or in defence and argument. They are used both as a balm and as a sword, as a shield and also as a soft cushion.

All this would be beautiful and great, and would even be the *right thing,* if the words quoted still existed in the *same sense* as Christ *actually* spoke them.

But this *is* not so! Many of these words were fashioned out of themselves by *men* who had a very deficient memory. Consequently they could not reproduce the same sense as was intended by the words of Christ.

You only need to observe how it is today! Anyone wishing to explain in his *own* words or to write down from memory alone a passage from the Grail Message, which is available in printed form and written by myself, even *today* does not reproduce it according to the original sense. A second mouth, a second pen always introduces alterations. New words change the original meaning, sometimes even distort it, although the writer may be absolutely willing to answer for it. It is never *that* word which *I* have spoken!

And how much worse it was at the time of the Son of God when He Himself had not written down any of His words, and when everything could *only* be transmitted to posterity at second or third hand! Indeed, not until a long time after Christ had left the World of Gross Matter! Everything – the writings and narratives, and all the words which today are customarily prefaced with a definite: *Christ said!* – evolved only out of the imperfect human memory!

Even at that time Lucifer's efforts to elevate the human intellect to the status of an idol had progressed so ominously as to prevent Christ's words from finding *that* soil which provides the possibility of a right understanding. This was an exceptionally clever move out of the Darkness. For the ability to grasp aright all those words which tell of other things than the gross material can only arise through the *unimpaired* co-operation of the intuitive brain. Even during the time of Christ on earth, however, this was already sadly neglected by all men, and had consequently become degenerate and incapable of playing its full part.

Thus Lucifer also had mankind on earth in his power! And that was his weapon against the Light! –

It is the human intuitive brain only, i. e., the back brain, which possesses the capacity of keeping memories *undistorted,* which is impossible for the intellect of the frontal brain.

Thus their hereditary sin was sharply and decisively brought home to mankind, who lightheartedly allowed their back brain to become so terribly degenerate, the back brain which alone is capable of retaining in pictures and intuitive impressions all happenings and experiences *as such,* and *in such a manner* that they can be *exactly* reproduced at any time as they really were, unchanged and even *undimmed.*

The frontal brain cannot do this because it is more closely bound to the gross material conceptions of time and space. It was not created for *reception,* but for *transmission into the earthly world.*

Thus it was that the descriptions of what was experienced and heard during Christ's days on earth were transmitted from memory, intermingled with earthly human opinions and quite unconsciously formed in an earthly way, but not with that purity with which a powerful intuitive brain would have seen and recorded them. The claws of Lucifer's minions had already embedded themselves too deeply, preventing their slaves of the intellect from escape, so that they could no longer grasp aright or hold fast to the greatest treasure, the Message of God, which was their only possibility of salvation, but had to let it pass by unused.

656

Just try to realise this situation! It does not require much trouble to under-stand it! Many people approached Christ with questions, asking His advice about this or that. Gladly He advised them out of His great love, which never failed, because He was and also today *still is* Living Love!

Thus He gave to the person who asked and begged for it as *he* needed it! Let us take an example: –

That rich young man who was eager to know the way which could lead him to the Kingdom of Heaven! The Son of God advised him to distribute all that he possessed among the poor and then to follow Him!

To follow Christ means nothing else than to live strictly in accordance with His words!

The bystanders quickly seized upon this happening as they had seized upon so many others, passing it on in that manner in which each as an indivi-dual had humanly perceived it. And that very seldom or never coincided with the actual meaning of Christ's original words, for a few words arranged in a different form can change the entire sense.

The first persons to pass it on, however, contented themselves with *relating,* giving a simple account of the happening. But later on such pieces of individual advice were turned into basic laws for the whole of mankind. It was *mankind* who did this, however, and not Christ Himself, the Son of God.

And this same mankind also have the effrontery simply to assert: *Christ said!* They attribute to *Him* what men themselves out of their memory and a wrong interpretation alone had clothed in forms and words which, as *the Word of God,* are today supposed to remain authoritative and irrefutable for Christians!

Therein lies a *thousandfold murder* of the *true* Word of the Son of God!

Everybody knows quite well that after weeks or months have elapsed he is unable to describe *without error* what he once experienced and heard, that he can *never* repeat it literally word for word. And if there are two, three, four or even ten persons who simultaneously heard or saw the same thing, they will give just as many different versions of it. Nobody today still doubts this fact!

On recognising this it is therefore natural that you should come to some conclusions as to what happened in the past, conclusions that are convincing and irrefutable!

For it was also no different when the Son of God was on earth. You can observe it clearly enough with the evangelists. Their reports plainly bear the stamp of it in many instances, as for example when Peter, the first among the disciples to declare his recognition, said to the Son of God: "Thou art the Christ, the Son of the Living God!"

The evangelists recorded these portentous words and also Christ's answer, but not at all uniformly. Matthew reports that the Son of God thereupon figuratively endowed Peter with a key to the Kingdom of Heaven and made him the rock upon which a future community was to be built, while the other evangelists give Christ's answer in a more general form, which is more correct.

Peter spoke only as *the first* to put this conviction into words. And such happenings remain not only as words, but immediately become a deed in Creation, quickly *taking form* in the Ethereal World, directly! The honest conviction which Peter thus anchored in the World of Matter through his words, his profession of belief, became at the same moment a rock in the Ethereal Sphere which represented the foundation stone for the building of a later community for all those who can become able to believe in the Son of God with the *same* simple and honest conviction.

And *with this* Peter also held the key to Paradise in his hand! For the conviction that Jesus is the Son of God quite naturally brings in its train the urge *to live* in accordance with His Word. *That,* however, is at the same time the *key* to the Kingdom of Heaven for *every* man. This confession *is* the key, provided such a believer absorbs the Word of God in *undistorted* form, understands It aright and lives accordingly. Christ knew about this happening which, when Peter uttered his words of conviction, took place ethereally according to the Laws of Creation, and He spoke about it in order to explain it to the disciples. The lawfulness of ethereal happenings is also known to every reader of my Grail Message.

Thus merely through being the first to confess in words what he intuitively perceived, Peter consequently became the first to receive the key to Paradise. And to whomsoever on earth he could later on mediate this same conviction he would also open the Kingdom of Heaven! For those, however, who did not wish to share his conviction it was bound to remain shut. All this is a quite natural and automatic happening, clear and simple, and it is neither bound up with Peter nor dependent upon him!

Christ wished to and *could* only lay the foundations for a community upon *such a conviction,* but not upon any person! Peter merely happened to be the first who really expressed this conviction in words. The *conviction* developed, formed and *became* the rock, but not Peter as a person!

But Matthew, in accordance with his own interpretation, gives to Christ's answer a meaning which is purely personal, concerning Peter only, and this he passes on.

Matthew in particular shows that he misunderstood many things which he then thoughtlessly passes on after interpreting them in his own way. Just as he has already done at the beginning of his writings with the announcement of the angel to Joseph in Matthew 1.v.21: "And she shall bring forth a son, and thou shalt call his name Jesus; for he shall save his people from their sins"!

And then Matthew follows in verses 22 and 23 with: "Now all this was done that it might be fulfilled which was spoken of the Lord by the prophet, saying, Behold a virgin shall be with child, and shall bring forth a son, and they shall call his name Imanuel, which being interpreted is, God with us."

In explaining this Matthew wants to form a close link between the prophecy of Isaiah and the birth of the Son of God, but the way in which he does it shows only too plainly that in his writings he expresses only his personal interpretations and does not remain objective.

This should have served *as a warning* to everybody that these writings must not be considered as the Word of God, but only as the personal opinion of their author.

Matthew, for example, does not even see the difference between the announcement made by Isaiah, which he himself quotes, and that of the Angel, but mixes them together with a childlike innocence because *he* "imagines" it to be so, and is quite unconcerned as to whether it is also correct! He does not even notice that the *names* mentioned in them are different!

But it was not without purpose that they were so precisely named!

Isaiah prophesied *"Imanuel",* but the Angel *"Jesus".* Therefore it was not Imanuel to whom Mary gave birth, nor was her child the one of whom Isaiah prophesied!

Isaiah announced "Imanuel", the Son of Man; the Angel, however, "Jesus", the Son of God! It is clear that these are two different announcements requiring two different fulfilments which, again, must be carried out by two different Persons. A mixing of these two happenings is impossible and can only be maintained by a human volition which *deliberately* ignores all basic facts.

Matthew had no evil intentions in this, he merely wrote down his own simple opinion in a most thoughtless manner. It could easily happen that he linked up these two events because at that time, more so than today, people were waiting and longing for the fulfilment of the promises of the old prophets. He did not foresee the evil of still greater misunderstanding that would grow out of it!

I do not need to speak further here about the fulfilment of the prophecy of "Imanuel", as I have already dealt with this in detail several times in the Grail Message. –

Thus the misunderstanding was as great at Jesus' time on earth as it is today. Indeed He Himself often lamented that His disciples did not understand Him, could not understand Him! Do you think it was any different when He was no longer with them?

"Later on the spirit came upon them," many will say here, those who give little or no thought to the matter at all! The spirit, however, did not at the same time correct the deficiencies of the brain. Weaklings consider it sinful to think in such a way, but this is really nothing but an excuse for their spiritual indolence, which they imagine they can gloss over thereby.

You will soon be awakened from the half-heartedness of such thoughts however! "But when the Son of Man will come..." declared Christ, as a warning and a threat! Think of it when now the hour of announcement comes in which the Lord Himself reveals that He *sent* the Son of Man to this earth! Remember that with those words Christ threatened all the spiritually indolent among mankind! – –

When at that time He told the rich young man to give away all his earthly possessions, this was necessary only for *him,* since he had asked: "What shall *I* do...?" And Christ gave *him* the answer, which in this sense was not meant to apply to all mankind!

Only the rich youth could profit *quite personally* from this advice. Amid all the comforts provided by his wealth he was too weak to exert himself to rise inwardly. Therefore his riches formed a hindrance to his spiritual ascent. The best advice which Christ could therefore give him was naturally to remove every obstacle, which in his case was the wealth inducing him to live a life of comfort!

But only for that reason! Not because a man should never possess wealth!

A man who does not pile up riches needlessly just for self-gratification, but who uses them *aright* by *revaluing* them and applying them for the benefit of many, is much greater and worthier than one who gives all his wealth away. He stands much higher in Creation because he furthers it.

Through his wealth such a man is able to provide employment for thousands during the whole earth-life, thereby giving them the satisfaction of having earned their own living, which strengthens and supports them both spiritually and physically. It is quite natural, of course, that a correct attitude must be preserved as regards work and rest, as also in giving the right remuneration for all work done, so that a strict and just equilibrium is upheld.

That assures *movement* in Creation, which is indispensable to healthy development and harmony. A one-sided giving away without asking for an equivalent value, however, is contrary to the Laws of Creation, and only brings stagnation and disorders as can be seen in *everything,* including our physical bodies, where lack of movement causes a thickening and stagnation of the blood, because only *movement* permits the blood to flow more freely and purely through the veins.

Man finds this law of essential movement *everywhere,* in a thousand different forms, but always the same in basic principle. It arises with every individual happening, and yet in its reciprocal action it works harmoniously throughout Creation, through all the spheres. Even the spirit needs uninterruptedly to obey this law if it wishes to continue in existence, remain strong and soar upwards!

There is nothing without this law! Movement everywhere in an absolute balance of give and take!

It was not a universal precept which the Son of God proclaimed in the advice He gave to the rich young man, but it was meant exclusively and entirely for the young man himself, or perhaps for those who are *like* him, those who are also too weak to control their riches. He who allows himself to be dominated by his wealth shall not have it either, for it does not serve him, but serves only that person who controls it, for in the latter's hand it will also bring benefits! He *shall* possess it, because he knows how to help himself and many others with it, thereby maintaining and furthering movement in Creation.

This is never or very seldom the case when things are given away. Many people are only brought to an awakening and to activity through suffering. If others help them too soon they slacken, depend upon this help and succumb spiritually, because without some stimulus they cannot remain active. Then they live on aimlessly, often spending their time *only* in observing *what* is to be criticised in others instead of looking within themselves, and yet wishing to possess what others possess. A corrupt generation is created by such one-sided giving, worthless for a robust and cheerful life, and therefore harmful to the entire Creation!

That was not the meaning of the advice given to the rich young man!

Nor did the Son of God ever speak against wealth as such, but always and only against those rich men who through their riches allowed all feelings of compassion at the suffering of others to dry up, who thereby sacrificed their spirit to their wealth, who had no interest beside their earthly possessions, in short who let themselves be entirely dominated by their riches.

That Christ Himself neither despised nor disapproved of wealth was proved by his frequent visits to the houses of the rich, where He was a welcome guest.

Neither was He Himself poor, as is strangely enough often assumed! There is no foundation for the assumption, now almost proverbial, that Christ was poverty stricken!

Christ never knew of worries caused by the struggle of life. He was born into circumstances similar to those now designated as the good middle class, because it was just this soil alone which had remained the most healthy. It was neither affected by the over-cultivation of all the rich and aristocratic circles, nor by the bitterness of the working classes. It was carefully selected. Joseph, the carpenter, could be described as well-to-do, but by no means poor.

That Christ was born in a stable at Bethlehem was merely a consequence of the overcrowding of Bethlehem due to the taking of the census, to which Joseph had also come. Joseph could simply find no lodging anywhere, something which can easily happen here and there to many a person attending some special gathering today. All this had nothing to do with poverty! In Joseph's house there would have been bedrooms such as are customary among well-to-do citizens.

Nor did Christ have to live in poverty! This idea only arose because any earthly possessions which exceeded the necessities of earthly life had no meaning for the One coming out of God. The task He had come to fulfil was not an earthly one, but purely *spiritual.*

Christ's allusion to people as being "brothers and sisters" is also being used in the wrong way today. How earthly unhealthy, akin to communistic ideas, how sickly sweet and repugnant in regard to religion! It plays directly into the hands of Darkness, for in its present interpretation it absolutely suppresses the free upward striving of the individual human spirit as willed by God. No ennoblement can ever develop out of this. Once more all these things are nothing but the unhealthy caricatures of what Christ intended!

When He spoke of all men being brothers and sisters He was far from thinking of the manifold eccentricities such as are in vogue today. He was giving enlightenment for *that* time, when the wicked custom of keeping slaves flourished greatly, when men were given away and sold, and thus considered as having no will of their own!

People, however, are brothers and sisters *from out of the spirit, from out of their origin.* They are *human spirits* which may not be considered as chattels without a will of their own, since every human spirit carries within itself the ability consciously to exercise its own will.

It was meant only *in that way,* and never intended to signify *that* equality of rights for which one looks in the words today! In fact no human spirit may enter Paradise just because it can call itself a human spirit. No such equality of rights exists in the general sense there. The conditions of *maturity* play a decisive role. The human spirit must first of all fulfil everything and do everything which it is able to do with its volition set on what is good. Only in this way will it so mature that it can gain access to Paradise!

Inflexible laws permeate Creation which can never be overthrown or deflected by the designation little brother and little sister because of our common origin. Nor here on earth either! How sharply the Son of God demanded the separation of the mundane from the spiritual, yet fulfilment towards both, lies clearly and distinctly in His statement: "Render unto the Emperor that which is due to the Emperor, and unto God that which is due to God!" –

And so it is with many sentences and reports in the Bible that men have based on their *own* views when transmitting them.

Yet all these writers did not intend at the time to make any law out of them for the whole of mankind, they only wanted to report!

It is also to be forgiven that the contemporary earthmen, and also Christ's disciples, did not understand much of what the Son of God told them, which often made Him very sad; and that later on they transmitted everything in terms of their own lack of understanding, which they did with the best of intentions, just as it was retained in their memories, but which for the reasons already stated must not be considered as wholly authoritative.

But it is unpardonable that *later on* men simply and boldly assert as if it were a fact: *Christ said*...! And thus without further ado attribute these erroneous human views, these products of a faulty human capacity to remember, categorically and finally to the Son of God! But only in order to establish and maintain by their selfish endeavours a system of teaching, the gaps in which from the very outset were bound to reveal to every powerful intuition that the entire structure was rotten and unsafe! Only the demand for blind faith offered the possibility to prevent these numerous shortcomings in the structure from being discovered immediately!

Such systems have been upheld, and are still today being upheld, *only* through the strict demand for blind faith and the decisive words: *"Christ said..."!*

And this word, this scheming assertion, shall become a dreadful Judgment for them! For it is just as wrong as the presumptuous assertion that the Crucifixion of Christ was willed by God in order to wash away all the sins of humanity through this sacrifice. What lies within all this, how much impudent wantonness and unbelievable human conceit were necessary to distort the murder of the Son of God in this fashion, that the future will reveal and mankind will experience in themselves!

Woe unto those men who once murdered the Son of God upon the cross! A hundredfold woe unto you, however, who since then have nailed Him to the cross a thousandfold in His Word, and who still murder Him daily and hourly over and over again! A heavy Judgment will fall upon you!

Look about you, men, and you will see how you have to live here on earth! It is not difficult to recognise the Primordial Laws in Creation if you only strive to *observe* everything around you in the right way.

Motion is a basic law in the entire Creation, thus also on earth. Motion of the *right* kind! But it is just *this* law which has been disregarded and also applied in the wrong way.

It was only through motion that everything could come into being. Upon motion, incessant motion, therefore depends the *preservation and restoration* of all that Creation embraces. Man cannot be considered an exception. He cannot be the only one among the creatures to remain stationary in the midst of this animating movement, or go his own way without harm to himself.

The intellectual goal of many people on earth today is rest and a comfortable life. To spend the last years of their life on earth in comfort is for many human beings the crowning of all their activity. But what they are longing for is poison, and they bring about the beginning of their end therewith!

Surely you have often heard it sympathetically expressed in cases of death: "He has not been able to enjoy his rest very long; it was only a year ago that he retired to private life!"

Such remarks are very often made. No matter whether it is a business man, an official or a soldier, as soon as a person "retires", as it is popularly called, he quickly begins to decline and death is not far off.

He who observes his surroundings with a keen eye will notice much in this respect. He will see that he experiences such things *surprisingly* often, and he will finally search for a very definite reason for this and recognise a law governing it.

The man who really retires here on earth, who wishes to rest from his activities until the end of his life, such a man will be cast aside by the law of rhythmic movements of this Creation as being an over-ripe fruit, because all the swinging, the movement around him, is much stronger than the move-

665

ment *within himself,* which must keep in step. Such a man *is bound to* grow weak and fall ill. Only when his individual swinging and alertness keep pace with the prevailing movement in Creation, only then can he remain healthy, hearty and happy.

The saying: "Stagnation is retrogression" gives an idea of this great law. Movement alone assures progress and preservation for everything that is to be found in Creation. I have already firmly established this in my lecture: "Life".

He who literally wishes to retire completely here on earth has no longer any goal before him, and thus no right to continue living in this Creation, because he has set an "end" to himself through his volition. The swinging of Creation, however, does not *show* any end, it *has* no end. Continuous development through movement is a law in the Will of God and can therefore never be circumvented without ill effect.

You will surely have noticed that those people who have continually to exert themselves in order to earn their living are often much healthier and live longer than those who have been very well off since their youth, who have been watched over and looked after in the most careful manner. You will also have observed that people who have grown up in wealthy circumstances and who use all the remedies for their bodies they can get, and who live comfortably and without excitement; that such people show the outward signs of approaching old age much earlier than those not endowed with earthly possessions, who always have to spend their days in working.

As an example I am pointing to *those* cases of a life filled with work where there is no unnecessary exaggeration, where there is no mad craving to accumulate earthly riches or to attain to some earthly prominence, which prevents the worker from ever really resting. He who becomes a slave to such a mania is always under high tension, and *also* brings disharmony into the rhythm of Creation. The consequences for him are the same as for those who swing too slowly. Thus the happy medium is also necessary here for everyone who wishes to stand *aright* in Creation and on earth.

Whatever you do, man, do it with *your whole heart!* Work during your working hours, and rest during the necessary time of rest. Do not mix the two!

The greatest poison threatening the harmonious fulfilment of your humanity is one-sidedness!

666

A life full of work but without any spiritual aim, for instance, is of no avail. The physical body would swing in the rhythm of Creation but the spirit would stand still. And if the spirit does not simultaneously swing in the God-willed rhythm of Creation, then the body that does swing in with it will not be maintained and strengthened through its work, but become worn out and exhausted, because it does not receive the spiritual strength which it needs through the mediation of the animistic. The stagnation of the spirit hampers the full development of the body. Consequently the body in its swinging must consume itself, causing it to wither and decay. It can no longer be regenerated because the source for this, the spiritual swinging, is lacking.

It is therefore of no use for a man who has retired from his earthly work to take regular walks in order to exercise his body, or to undertake all sorts of other earthly things to keep his body fit. He will quickly grow old and decay unless his spirit maintains the same swinging. And nothing but some definite goal which moves *the spirit* can bring about this spiritual swinging.

A spiritual goal, however, is not to be sought upon earth, but will only be found towards the Spiritual Realm, in the homogeneous plane of this wonderful Creation! It must therefore be a goal which stands above what is earthly, a goal which towers high above this life on earth!

The goal must *live,* must be alive! Otherwise it has nothing to do with the spirit!

The man of today, however, no longer knows what is spiritual. He has substituted the working of the intellect for it, and considers intellectual activity to be spiritual activity. This now gives him the final blow which brings about his downfall, for he is clinging to something that remains on this earth together with his body when he himself must enter the beyond!

A spiritual goal is *always* something which contains *furthering values.* You will always recognise it by this! Eternal values, nothing that is transitory! Therefore whatever you wish to accomplish, whatever you now endeavour to strive for, always ask yourself first of all for the values you will consequently bring about and find. It is not too difficult if you really wish to do so!

Nine-tenths of today's sciences must be accounted as false activity and useless striving in Creation. The sciences as they are *now* practised hinder the ascent of those who are concerned with them; they bring about stagnation and retrogression, but never that progress which leads to ascent. Man cannot unfold his wings in the so-called sciences of today; he can never achieve what he could achieve, for his wings have been pitifully clipped and destroyed. Only in simplicity of thought and action does greatness lie and power develop, for simplicity alone strives towards the Primordial Laws of Creation and harmonises with them.

Man, however, has bound and blocked himself up with his earthly sciences!

Of what use is it when a man attempts to spend his life on earth in finding out when the creature fly came into existence and how long it is likely to remain on this earth, and many other similar questions that seem to be important for human knowledge. Just ask yourselves whom he really benefits with such knowledge! Only his vanity! Nobody else in the world! For this knowledge has nothing to do with ascent in any way whatever. Man derives no advantage from it, nor does it uplift him! Nobody gains anything from it!

Thus you must seriously scrutinise one thing after another for the actual value each proffers you. You will find that all that happens in this respect today reveals itself like a useless house of cards. Indeed the time allotted to you for your development on earth is too precious to allow you to sacrifice even one hour for such things with impunity. You become the slaves of vanity and toying thereby, for there is nothing in it which could really uplift you. It is nothing but hollow inside and dead!

Do not think that during the Judgment you can step before God's Throne and repeat some such brief scientific formula! Deeds are demanded of you in Creation. With your false knowledge, however, you are nothing but sounding brass, whereas your task in this Creation is to live vitally and build up. The man who enjoys each flower of the field, and who lifts his eyes to Heaven in gratitude for it, stands much higher before God than he who can scientifically analyse each flower without recognising the greatness of his Creator therein.

Man does not gain anything by being the fastest runner, a skilful boxer, a bold driver, or if he knows whether the horse appeared on earth before or after the fly! Such a volition only strives for something ridiculous, i. e., for vanity. It brings no blessing to humanity, no progress, and no gain for their existence in this Creation, but only encourages them to fritter away their time upon earth.

Look about you, men! Examine everything in *this light!* What does your own occupation and that of your fellow-men really mean, what value does it have? You will find little that is worthy of true humanity. So far your endeavours have proved you to be useless servants in the vineyard of the Lord. For you fritter away your time in utterly useless toying, and burden the great talent lying within you as a gift from God with the unnecessary trifles of the vain earthly intellectual volition, all of which you must leave behind when you depart this life.

Awake, so that you can create for yourselves a dignified garment of the *spirit* here upon earth, and will not have to enter the beyond like paupers as you have done hitherto, in spite of the fact that you were given such great treasures for your sojourn on earth. You are like a king who childishly plays with the sceptre, and who imagines that this sceptre and the wearing of the crown alone suffice to make him a king!

What man needs to investigate in the first place is only that which helps in his ascent and thus also serves to further Creation. In all his activities he should ask himself what advantage they will bring both to himself and to mankind. *One* goal must henceforth dominate every man – to recognise and also to fulfil the place he, as a human being, must occupy in Creation!

I will tell you how it is done in other parts of Creation, and how it must now be done also here on earth in accordance with the Will of God.

If here on earth a man accomplishes something great he is honoured, unless his deed arouses nothing but envy. The fame remains his until he dies, very often even beyond that time, for decades and centuries, for thousands of years.

However, this is *only on earth,* as a result of false human opinions! It became the custom in this heavy gross material mass, but not in the higher and more luminous worlds. There the rotating movement is not as sluggish as it is on earth. There the reciprocal action takes effect more speedily, depending on the increasing lightness. There deeds are measured from quite different and natural points of view, whereas human opinions make many a deed appear great that is not great at all, and place no value upon some things of true worth.

The higher, more luminous and lighter the environment, the clearer and quicker will be the reward and the consequences. A human spirit which has a good volition thus always ascends faster under these conditions, a really great action often pulling him upwards at the very same moment. But he cannot then rest upon his laurels as is the case here on earth, for he must continually regain this height ever anew if he wishes to remain there, and exert himself to rise ever higher. If he relaxes his efforts but once he will very quickly become over-ripe in his present environment and will decay, to use a gross material picture!

Man is nothing else fundamentally than a fruit of Creation! He is never Creation itself, much less the Creator! Within every apple slumbers the capacity to enrich this Creation with new apple trees, with flowers and fruit, but that does not make the apple the Creator: It is the automatic course of the Primordial Laws of Creation which endowed the apple with that capacity, and which forces it to act as it does in order to fulfil its task in Creation. It always and inevitably fulfils *one* task!

Men or animals may do with this apple as they wish. It either serves to preserve the species or acts as food to maintain other bodies. There is nothing in this Creation without a task. Also in all decay there is movement, value and gain.

Therefore as soon as a human being has risen to a certain height he must *maintain* himself there. He cannot and must not rest and think that he has done enough for a while, but must continually bestir himself like a bird in the air that is forced to use its wings if it wishes to remain aloft. The same simple law applies to everything, to the finest spiritual as well as to the most coarse and earthly, without change and without distortion. It operates everywhere and must be observed. It works more quickly in what is luminous and light, and correspondingly slower in the more sluggish and gross material world, but in all cases it works with *absolute certainty*.

Such is the simplicity that lies in the working of the Laws of Creation, as well as in the laws themselves, that no college education is required to recognise them properly! Every man has the ability to understand them if only he so wills. It is extremely easy to observe them. It is only made difficult by the conceited learnedness of men who love to coin big words for the most simple things, and who thus clumsily splash about in Creation, as if in clear water, assuming an air of importance and consequently dimming the original healthy clearness.

With all his false learning man is the only one among the creatures who neglects to fill his place in Creation by swinging in its rhythm and acting correctly.

But it is the Will of God that man *must* at last come to his senses and completely fulfil his task in this Creation. If he neglects to do so he will now become over-ripe and decay as a rotten fruit of Creation. The Divine Light which God is now sending into Creation affects it in the same way as the plants in a greenhouse are affected by the increased warmth, which forces them to produce flowers and fruit more quickly.

What is moving aright in the Laws of Creation is thereby revealed, also what has acted falsely. The fruits will correspond with this. The man who has toiled over things which can offer no basis for his necessary ascent has wasted his time and his strength. He has deviated from the swinging of Creation and can no longer adjust himself to it, can no longer recover in the necessary harmony, because he himself disturbs it.

Therefore learn through observation to value and use for yourself the simplicity of the Divine Laws in all their greatness, otherwise they must now crush you, because you stand as an obstacle in the way of their working. They will brush you aside as a dangerous obstruction!

Motion is the main commandment for everything that lies in this Creation, for Creation developed out of motion, and is maintained and renewed by motion.

As it is in the beyond, especially in the more luminous spheres, so must it now become here on earth also, brought about by the Power of the Light. That man who swings in with the Primordial Laws of Creation will be preserved, but he who wastes his time in morbid intellectual pondering will now be destroyed by the buoyant power of movement, which has been strengthened by the Light.

Therefore you must at last become acquainted with all the Laws and adjust yourself accordingly!

He who does not embrace a high and luminous goal in his earthly activities cannot exist in the future. He must disintegrate in accordance with the Divine Laws which permeate Creation strengthened by the Light. Also spiritually he will be reduced to dust as a useless fruit that does not fulfil its purpose in this Creation.

This happening is quite simple and real, but its effects upon mankind as they still show themselves today will be formidable in the extreme! You will be spared nothing! You will still be able to exercise your will in making decisions, because this is inherent in the nature of all that is spiritual, but you will now immediately receive the retroactive effects up to the final point, with *such* speed as you do not deem possible here on earth in the sluggishness of this World of Matter.

On earth mankind will also be forced from now onwards to adjust themselves completely to all the Primordial Laws of Creation.

It will not suffice in the future if a person has been able to attain to a certain height here. But he will be obliged to maintain himself on that level by constant effort, for otherwise he will quickly go downwards again. Every man must again leave the position where he cannot maintain himself, for it can only be taken into account as to *how* he really *is,* not how he *was!* The "was" passes away with every change and *is* no more. The "*is*" alone is of value and valid in the Millennium.

Therefore, man, always in future remain through your real being that which you want to be taken for! You fall or rise with every new change!

Without constant movement you can no longer maintain yourself in Creation. You cannot bask in the splendour of your ancestors, the son in the glory of his father! The wife has no share in the deeds of her husband. Each individual stands entirely alone, by himself, in this matter. Only the present is what counts for you, for it is the present which really "*is*" for a human spirit. This is how it is in the entire Creation, and this is how it shall also be in the future among the hitherto sluggish human beings on earth!

THE PHYSICAL BODY

MAN WEARS the physical garment which he needs for the maturing of his spirit in the World of Gross Matter with an irresponsible indifference and lack of understanding. As long as he has no pains he neglects the gift he has received and does not even dream of giving to the body what it needs, above all what would benefit it. He never attends to his body until he has damaged it and consequently feels pain, or until it somehow hampers him in carrying on his daily work, or in following some trifling pursuit or hobby.

It is true that he eats and drinks, but without due consideration and often excessively, just as it appears pleasant to him, quite indifferent to the fact that he injures his body in so doing. Nobody thinks of tending his body carefully as long as it causes him no pain. However, it is just the care of the *healthy* body which is an urgent necessity.

Man shall give to the *healthy* body what it needs. He shall observe it with all the care requisite for the proper activity of this most necessary implement in the World of Gross Matter. For indeed it is *the most precious possession* which every human being has received for his time here on earth.

But look at adolescent youth, how frivolously and carelessly they neglect their bodies, and how they abuse them with all kinds of over-exertions.

Observe students who predominantly cultivate their intellects in a *one-sided* manner through their studies! How proudly have they sung, and still sing today, the songs glorifying their college days!

But if, for once, you ask yourselves honestly what it is they are so proud of, you must examine the contents of their songs in order to find the reason. All sound-thinking people will then feel greatly ashamed, for these songs contain nothing but a glorification of drinking and flirtation, of idleness and frittering away the best time of development in man's existence on earth. The very time when man must begin to soar upwards in order to become a full-fledged human being in this Creation, in order to attain the spiritual maturity needed to enable him to fill the position which man as such must fill and fulfil in Creation in accordance with the Laws of his Creator, his Lord!

These songs show only too clearly what is considered to be most beautiful and ideal at a time when man, filled with gratitude and joy, should perceive in purity how, through his physical body, his spirit makes contact with his entire surroundings in order to work fully conscious therein, and thus with full responsibility to his Creator! At a time when every spirit, through the radiations of the generative power, begins to send its volition formingly far out into the World of Gross Matter with its many gradations!

These songs, however, are a cry of mockery against the Primordial Laws of Creation, which they oppose to the last word!

As against this there are those youths who do not go through the higher educational institutions! Here you find all the foundations to be more suitable, healthy and natural for the proper treatment of their physical bodies, provided that these young people do not indulge in some sport, for in so doing everything that is reasonable and healthy also ceases even here!

Wherever you turn to investigate you must recognise that man has no knowledge as yet of the Laws of Creation!

He has no idea of the responsibility he must unfailingly bear for the physical body entrusted to him! Nor does he realise the value of the physical body for his position in Creation, but keeps his eyes fixed only upon this earth. However, the physical body has only the least significance in its connection with the earth as such.

And this complete ignorance about the Laws of Creation has permitted errors to creep in which continue to cause harm to many people. They permeate and infect everything!

This is the only reason why it was possible even among all the present-day churches for the nonsensical opinion to develop that sacrificial suffering and sacrificial death are pleasing to God in certain circumstances! This erroneous view has also become deeply anchored in the arts, for there the thought is frequently glorified that one person through his voluntary sacrificial or love-death can bring "redemption" to another!

This only confused mankind still further!

The Law of God, however, in its inflexible justice, does not permit one person to intervene for the guilt of another. Such a deed brings nothing but guilt upon the person who sacrifices himself, and who thereby forcibly shortens his life on earth. In addition the soul suffers from the delusion that it is doing something great and pleasing to God. The one who sacrifices himself becomes *doubly* guilty through his presumption that he is able to release *another person* from his sins. He would supposedly have done better to implore forgiveness for himself alone as a great sinner before the Lord, for by his action he calls his God an unjust judge, capable of such an arbitrary act and one who can be bargained with!

In addition this is also really a blasphemy! Thus bringing a third guilt upon him through such a deed, which stands absolutely and diametrically opposed to any intuitive perception of justice!

It is personal conceit, not pure love, which brings forth such deeds. In the beyond, when they must suffer the consequences of their deeds, these souls are soon set right, while the other person is not helped in any way by such an action and, if he knew about it and hoped for it, must become burdened still further.

It is therefore deplorable that even great artists indulged in this accursed delusion about redemption in their works. A sensitive artist should take objection to it, because it is unnatural, contrary to all lawfulness and completely unfounded.

The true Magnitude of God is diminished thereby!

Again, nothing but human conceit dares to expect from Divine Justice, which cannot be influenced, that it would be capable of accepting such a sacrifice. In this man has a higher regard for his earthly judiciary, for such a thought never occurs to him in legal practice.

By such actions man shows disregard for his physical body, not gratitude for the gross material implement lent to him for his development. He cannot do too much in caring for it, in keeping it clean and pure, because it is indispensable for this particular life on earth.

Therefore, man, learn to understand your physical body properly so that you can treat it accordingly. Only then will you become able to use it aright, to master it so that it becomes what it is meant to be for you here on earth. The first consequence of real control over your physical body shows itself in the grace and beauty of your movements, which enables the power of the spirit in the harmony with its implement to become visible.

In order that you may learn to distinguish properly in these matters, observe the people who indulge in some kind of sport! You will quickly recognise that the steeling of the body of itself does not necessarily bring about beauty of movement because it produces too much one-sidedness unless the spirit also swings in the necessary harmony. The walk of the athlete is very often anything but beautiful, his carriage seldom graceful. The sportsman is very far from really controlling his body.

For power is derived from the spirit only, strength from the body!

Thus a *heavy* step is evidence of ponderousness, not of power. A body which is maintained and permeated by spiritual power has *elastic* movements and strides along with a light, springy step, regardless of whether its weight is heavy or light.

A man with a heavy step always gives proof of nothing but a lack of the proper mastery of his body through his spirit. It is spiritual control which distinguishes man from the animal. In this respect the animal is subject to different laws, because its soul comes from the Animistic Realm. However, the animal fulfils these laws, its body and soul harmonise, and in its movements it always shows a very definite kind of beauty adapted to its body. In contrast to man it has a light step despite its physical weight, which is often enormous!

Go into the zoological gardens! Look at the animals there and also at the human beings! Observe them very closely just for once! You will very soon be struck by the consequences of the lack of harmony between soul and body in all *human beings,* while the animals are absolutely "natural" unless handicapped by some ailment. You will observe for yourself that man's mode of living is wrong, that he does not control his body, does not live properly in it, and that he is not at all in harmony with it!

The same also applies to the nourishment and maintenance of the body. The animal will never overfeed its body as so many men do. It is satisfied when it no longer feels hungry, whereas in many cases man is not satisfied until he can eat no more! That is a great difference, again only called forth through the over-cultivated intellect by its endeavour to suppress all natural sense in these matters.

The animal also drinks only to quench its thirst. Man, however, cultivates within himself illusions about enjoyment which, if carried to excess, are bound to harm his body greatly. Here again I only refer to the custom among students' associations as regards drinking, and also deprivation of sleep which this false mode of living always entails.

It is not necessary to give further explanations on this subject, for these actions are probably well enough known for their gross foolishness. Neither the person who is most benevolent nor the person who is most narrow-minded in this matter can assert that such practices could be useful or would do no harm!

Those people who "walk" (wandeln)* through the zoological gardens to see the animals show plainly that they should take a lesson from the animals how to stand aright in Creation with their physical bodies. "Walking" is hardly the correct word, for only a few of the visitors "walk". The expression contains a conception of gracefulness and natural control, but many people hobble or stump along, either thoughtlessly or deep in thought, or they hasten along nervously, distraught and absent-minded. There is absolutely no beauty in it! You can see quite clearly that they pay no attention to the movement of their bodies, but hamper the naturalness of their movements through their false and one-sided thinking. There has been neglect ever since their youth. Many an omission therein shows itself only later, but then without fail! The consequences are inevitable!

What beauty alone lies in the words: to stride (schreiten)**, to walk! You can hardly perceive the high value inherent in them. Through all this neglect of his earthly body man shows the immaturity of his spirit! A mature spirit will *always respect* his body as the necessary implement for the achievement of his earthly maturity, and he will not abuse it senselessly. He will care for it in *such a manner* as is *wholesome* for it, not as is occasionally required by its nerves, which are often whipped up through a perversion of natural conceptions.

Wherever pure spiritual power completely permeates and controls the physical body, there its movements are also *bound to* show beauty, because in such circumstances it cannot be otherwise. There the gross material senses also become completely permeated with beauty, so that they will ennoble everything they do, regardless of what it is.

Beauty and grace are the expression of a pure human spirit in all its *activity*, which also includes the movements of the physical body.

Look about you, everything is being shown to you! You *are bound to* recognise it quickly if you stand alive in this Creation!

---

* This applies to the German language.
** This refers to the German language only.

You will then discover how impossible man's actions have been up till now, how little he has recognised the Creation which forever remains his home. He is born into it, yet he always wishes to tear himself away, to place himself above it. This odd volition never allows him to become secure in it, because he does not thereby learn to know his home.

The earthly body of each human being is in every respect closely linked with *that* soil upon which he was born. This is in accordance with the Law of Creation governing all matter. He has to take this into account at all times. Yet he has but seldom observed it in the past. He thinks himself free in this matter, but he is not. He is just as closely connected with it as is the body of an animal. *Both* physical species are formed by the animistic. In the case of the animal, man has closely observed everything and knows about it, too. But he does not wish to place *his own* body under the homogeneous laws! That is wrong!

The earthly body is connected with *that part* of the earth where it was born. It is also closely connected with all the stars of this particular region and with all the radiations that belong thereto. Quite extensively, far more than you can imagine! Only *that* part of this earth gives the body exactly what it needs to blossom forth properly and remain vigorous. The earth also provides this in its different zones always at the proper time, and in the manner in which the gross material bodies that have been *born* into each particular zone need it. Herbs and fruit, therefore, are advantageous and upbuilding for the human body at *that* time when the earth *produces* them.

At those times the body *needs* just such nourishment as is provided by *that* zone in which it came into existence, and with which it remains continuously connected.

Strawberries at the time of the strawberry harvest, apples at the time of the apple harvest, and so on! The same applies to all fruits and herbs. Herbal treatments are therefore beneficial at the time when the herbs are in their full vigour, also for healthy bodies!

The animistic itself offers the physical body a continuous change of foods just as it really needs them, even as the sun, rain and wind remain *best* for a healthy activity of the skin. Creation gives man everything he needs for his earthly body, and also gives it in the proper sequence and at the right time.

With all his special arts man can never achieve *that* which Creation grants him of its own accord!

Just observe this! On this earth the earthly *body* is closely connected *with that zone* in which the place of birth is located. If it is also to remain healthy in a foreign zone, if it is to retain its *full vigour* for its activity on earth, then it is necessary that the basis for the feeding of the body must be that provided by the zone where it was born. With care he will then be able to create a bridge which for a time makes it possible to unfold his full powers, but never permanently. Now and then he must return in order to obtain new vitality. But in spite of everything he will also *shorten* his life on earth.

It is not arbitrary or accidental that earthmen are of different form and colour.

The Primordial Laws of Creation place them in the exact region which alone serves for their maturing on earth, and also equip them accordingly.

The animistic fashions your earthly bodies, and at the same time the nourishment for their maintenance. But the effects are only uniform in a particular zone in a particular part of the earth. You men are no different in these matters from the plants and the animals, for you, too, are a fruit of Creation; nothing but creatures who are and remain closely connected with the zone and the radiations of that part of the earth where you came into being.

Therefore observe and learn from every activity in Creation! It is your duty to obey the Primordial Laws of Creation if you wish to achieve that which will benefit you and help in your ascent!

THE MYSTERY OF THE BLOOD

THE BLOOD! How much swings forth from this word, how rich and strong are all the impressions it is able to produce, and what a never-ending source of conjecture is contained in this one significant word!

And much knowledge, which has proved to be full of blessing for the bodies of earth-men, has evolved from these suppositions. Through troublesome investigation and devoted work gifted ones, with their keen observation and pure volition to render unselfish help to mankind, found many a *path* leading to the *real* purpose of the blood, none of which, however, is this purpose itself.

Here are further hints on the matter, with which those who carry within them the calling will be able to build up through their knowledge of the swinging Laws of God. They will then become *helpers* of mankind here on earth in the truest sense, and as a most precious reward their ways will be brightened by the grateful prayers of all those to whom their knowledge of the secrets of the blood could bring help of a nature not believed possible, and such as there has never been before.

I will immediately name the main purpose of all human blood! *It is meant to form the bridge for the activity of the spirit on earth,* i. e., in the World of Gross Matter!

This sounds so simple, and yet it holds the key to *all* knowledge about the human blood.

Hence the blood is meant to act as a bridge for the activity of the spirit, or let us say "soul" in this case so that readers will understand me better, for they are more familiar with the expression "soul".

The spirit forms the human blood so that the activity of the spirit from out of man may proceed in the proper manner.

The connection between the blood and the spirit can easily be substantiated. It need only be realised that until the spirit has entered the developing body of a child at incarnation, which takes place at a very definite stage of development in the middle of pregnancy, causing the child's first movements; that until this stage has been reached its *own* blood does not begin to circulate; while at physical death, when the spirit has left the body, the blood ceases to pulsate and to exist altogether.

Therefore the blood itself is only present during the time between the entrance and departure of the spirit, when the spirit dwells in the body. Indeed it can be noted through the lack of blood that the spirit has finally severed its connection with the earthly body, i.e., that death has occurred.

In reality it is as follows: The human blood can form itself only when the spirit enters the body, and when the spirit leaves the body the blood can no longer exist in its actual nature.

However, we will not rest content with this knowledge, but I will go further! The spirit or the "soul" contributes to the formation of the blood, but it cannot come into outward earthly activity directly through the blood. The difference between the two species is too great to permit this. The soul, of which the spirit is the core, is still far too fine in its coarsest layer to be able to accomplish this, and can become outwardly active only through the *radiation of the blood.*

The radiation of the blood is therefore in reality the actual bridge for the activity of the soul, and then only if this blood is of a very particular *composition suitable for the soul concerned.*

In future every conscientious doctor can consciously help and intervene in these matters, as soon as he has absorbed and grasped this knowledge aright. It is just this which will become one of the greatest and most decisive aids doctors can offer to the whole of humanity, for the effects in this respect are so manifold that, with the right application, the peoples are bound to blossom forth most splendidly in their volitions and in their capacities, because they will be able to unfold all their power, which will not urge them on to destruction, but towards peace and a grateful striving for the Light.

I have often pointed to the significance of the composition of the blood. When the composition changes this naturally also alters the radiation, producing therewith correspondingly alternating effects upon the person concerned as well as upon his earthly environment.

In my lecture about the significance of the generative power I stated that the latter does not set in until the body has attained a very definite maturity.

Then a drawbridge is lowered to enable the soul to sally forth into the outer world, from which it has been protected and separated up to that time. Naturally this bridge not only permits the soul to exercise an influence on the outside, but it also permits influences from outside to obtain access to the soul by the same route.

It is not until then that the individual person becomes fully responsible before the Divine Laws of Creation, a point which has also been given similar consideration in the earthly laws.

The lowering of the drawbridge, however, takes place automatically, through nothing other than a transformation in the composition of the blood, which in turn is produced by the maturing of the physical body and the urging of the soul, and which then, through the change in radiation, affords the spirit the possibility to become active upon earth.

Here I naturally do not refer to the mechanical actions and work of the physical body, but to that which actually "leads" in these things, to that which is willed, and which the brain and the body as implements then turn into earthly deeds.

In my lecture on the temperaments I likewise referred to the blood which, through its various radiations, forms the basis for the temperaments, because up to a certain point the activity of the soul is bound up with the various kinds of blood radiations.

Since, however, the maturity, state of health and age of a body contribute to the changing of the blood composition, such a constraint might prove unjust. This is balanced by the fact that the *spirit* can change this composition, which at the same time explains the secret of the saying that "the spirit forms the body".

But wherever a spirit is too weak to accomplish this, or wherever it is hindered in its efforts by some outside influence, such as an accident or a physical ailment, there the doctor can soon help by intervening through his knowledge!

And he will be amazed at the recognition of how much depends in each case upon the right composition of the blood for earthman. No hard and fast rule must be made in these matters, for the procedure is entirely different with every person. So far only the coarsest differences have been found. There are still innumerable refinements which have not yet been recognised, and which are of far-reaching importance and influence.

The establishment of the various blood groups which have now already been discovered, and which can only confirm my statements, does not yet suffice.

It is true that these discoveries are in the right direction and have already proved very beneficial in their application. However, they remain only *one* of many ways and are not *the goal itself,* which is not merely restricted to physical recovery and invigoration, but which is able to uplift man in every respect.

In my lecture "Possessed" I point out that only the blood composition of some particular person offers the possibility for the occurrence of spookish manifestations such as knocking, making noises, throwing of objects, etc. During such incidents this person must always be in close proximity, as it is from his radiations that the power to manifest is drawn.

Even these things could be quickly remedied by the skilful intervention of a doctor who understands, and who helps by changing the composition of the blood, which also alters the radiation and thereby prevents such disagreeable possibilities.

It is the same with the so-called possessed ones, of whom there are many in spite of all doubts. The process in itself is quite simple, even if dreadfully decisive for the person concerned and for his environment, and painful to the relatives.

The composition of the blood of these persons has formed in such a manner that it offers the soul inhabiting the body only a feeble possibility, or none whatever, to manifest in full vigour towards the outer world. However, the radiation of the blood provides the opportunity to another soul, with less good or even malicious qualities, and which is perhaps already free from its body, to interfere from outside and, what is more, to control brain and body either periodically or perpetually.

Here, too, a doctor can give effective relief by changing the composition of the blood, which in turn alters the radiation, thereby cutting off alien influences and granting the opportunity for the indwelling volition to unfold its own personal powers.

As I have already mentioned, the investigators are doing very good and beneficial work in establishing the blood groups, and it is just in the application of this knowledge that their observations are bound to confirm my statements.

If a different blood group was used in the case of a blood transfusion, then the soul living in such a body would find itself prevented from fully developing its volition, would perhaps be entirely cut off from it, because with the blood of different composition the radiation also changes and is then no longer adapted to the soul. It cannot make full use of the different type of radiation or even none whatever!

To the outside world such a person would then appear handicapped in his thinking and acting, because his soul cannot work properly. It can even go so far that the soul, hindered in its capacity to work, slowly severs itself from the body and leaves it altogether, which is equivalent to physical death.

Doctors will recognise with amazement how far-reaching and comprehensive is the influence of the proper blood composition in each human body in relation to the effectiveness of the soul on earth. They will recognise which diseases and other ailments can be abolished by the right knowledge, and how the hitherto existing "secret of the blood" is solved and thus becomes the key to joyous activity in God's wonderful Creation.

It is not through injections that *lasting* changes can be brought about, but in the natural way, through appropriate food and drink, which over a short period will vary with every individual person, yet always without one-sided limitations.

From these considerations it also follows that a great number of so-called "mentally backward" children can be fundamentally helped. Give their souls the right bridge for the development of their powers, and you will see how they begin to blossom forth and work with joy upon this earth; for in reality there are no sick souls.

Unless that which hinders the soul, or better said the spirit, is forcibly brought about by a disease of the brain, it will always and only be due to the insufficient or false radiation of the blood.

Indeed, all is so wonderfully arranged in the weaving of Creation that probably none of my readers will be surprised when I further explain that even the type of blood radiation of an expectant mother can become an additional decisive factor as to the kind of spirit to be incarnated, which must follow the Law of Attraction of Homogeneous Species; for each of the different kinds of blood radiations will prepare only for the approach and entry of a type of soul which completely corresponds with it. It is likewise understandable that the same species of soul must try and bring about similar blood compositions, because they can only become truly effective by a very definite kind of radiation, which again changes during the different periods of life.

He who wishes to grasp this hint with regard to birth correctly should at the same time become acquainted with my explanations in the lecture "The mystery of birth", because in tracing the automatic working of the Laws of Creation I must elucidate one point at one time and another point at another time, although everything forms an inseparable whole and no part of it can be described as something which exists independently, but only as a part which is closely linked with the whole; which part in its co-operation becomes ever again visible at various places as a coloured thread woven through the entire fabric in accordance with the laws.

Later on I shall elaborate more fully on all the details necessary completely to fill in the picture, which I have today given only in broad outline.

I hope that in times to come it may prove a great blessing for mankind.

A further hint is perhaps in order: It can easily be recognised that the blood cannot be solely dependent upon the body because of the difference between human blood and animal blood, which can be discerned immediately.

The basic composition of these two types of blood is so different that it must be obvious. If the body alone would form the blood then there would need to be a far greater similarity. It therefore depends on something else – in the case of the human blood it is the *spirit*. On the other hand the soul of the animal, which becomes active through the body, consists of a different species, and is not of the spiritual species which makes man a human being. Therefore the blood is also *bound* to be quite different!

THERE are people who excuse many of their faults, even to themselves, as being due to their temperament!

That is wrong! He who acts in this manner shows that he has become nothing but a slave to himself. Man is of the *spirit,* which remains as the highest form of all that is self-conscious in this Subsequent Creation, thereby influencing, forming and leading all else, no matter whether he acts in full awareness of it or whether he knows nothing at all about it.

This ruling or influencing in Subsequent Creation is anchored in the *nature of the spirit* in accordance with the Laws of Creation. Through its very existence, therefore, the human spirit works in Subsequent Creation in this manner, because it issues from the Spiritual Realm. The temperament, however, cannot be attributed to the spirit, for it is only produced by the radiations of a certain species of matter when the latter is animated and completely permeated by the animistic, which moves, warms and forms all that is of matter. This radiation emanates from the blood.

Thus it is not wrong to use the popular expression concerning certain qualities which people possess: "It runs in the blood!" In most cases they mean that it has been "inherited". And often this is the case because *gross material* heredity does occur, while spiritual heredity is impossible. With that which is spiritual it is the Law of Attraction of Homogeneous Species which counts, the effects of which do *outwardly* resemble heredity in our life on earth, and can therefore easily be confused with it.

Temperament, however, comes from the World of Matter and may therefore be partly inherited, and it also remains closely connected with all that is matter. Its cause lies in *animistic* activity. Here again some idea of this is contained in another popular saying. The wisdom of such expressions has always originated in the natural intuitive perception of those people of sound mind whose manner of living in Creation has remained simple and undistorted. This popular saying speaks of light blood, hot blood, heavy blood, and blood which can be easily excited. All these terms are applied to the temperament with the correct perception that the blood plays the major role in these matters. In reality it is a definite radiation which develops through the type of blood composition in each case. It first of all produces an equivalent effect in the brain, which subsequently becomes strongly perceptible in the feeling of the entire body.

In accordance with the blood composition there will therefore always be a type of temperament predominating in different people which is decisive for them.

In the *healthy* blood of a human being are anchored *all* the radiations which the blood is capable of producing and consequently *all* the temperaments. I am always and only referring to the healthy physical body, for sickness brings confusion into the radiations.

As the physical body ages the blood composition also changes. Thus when healthy blood changes through increasing age a corresponding change of temperament occurs at the same time.

Besides advancing age in the body, however, there are still other things which have an influence on the change in blood composition, such as the characteristics of the different regions and everything pertaining to them, i.e., the climate, the radiations of the stars, different kinds of nourishment, and many other things as well. They all affect the temperaments directly because they are part of the World of Matter and therefore linked very closely with it.

In general one can distinguish between four basic temperaments in mankind – the sanguine, the melancholic, the choleric and the phlegmatic – and men themselves are described accordingly. In reality, however, there are seven temperaments and, with all the gradations, even twelve. But the principal temperaments are four in number.

In a person with an absolutely healthy blood condition they can be classified into four age periods, in each of which the composition of the blood changes. First of all there is the period of childhood, resembling the sanguine temperament, the carefree life of the moment. Then comes early manhood or womanhood, which is like the melancholic temperament of dreaming and longing. Thereafter follow the years of man's and woman's full estate which is the choleric temperament urging them to action. And finally comes old age, or the phlegmatic temperament of quiet reflection.

This is the normal and healthy condition in the temperate zone as distinct from the *abnormal* zone.

How closely all this is connected with and works in a similar way in the World of Matter you can even witness on the gross material earth in the seasons of spring, summer, autumn and winter. In spring an impetuous awakening, in summer a dreamy development with an urge towards ripening, in autumn the full activity of the fruits, and in winter a quiet transition with all the gathered experiences to a new awakening!

Even nations and races bear very definite characteristics of common temperaments. This may be traced back to the part of the earth where they came into existence and where they live, to the consequent form of nutrition there, to their exposure to similar gross material radiations by the stars, and last but not least to the spiritual maturity of the entire nation. A people of sanguine temperament are still, figuratively speaking, in their childhood, or have through some circumstances retrogressed to this stage. The latter category not only comprises the sunny South Sea islanders but to a greater extent the Latin peoples. People of melancholic temperament stand before their actual deeds. The Germans and all Germanic people belong to this group. They stand at their awakening, prepared for action!

That is why the period of early manhood and womanhood is also the age of the melancholic temperament, because only as the spirit breaks through in the generative power does it find a direct connection with the species of Creation. Thus man becomes responsible for his deeds in Creation, fully responsible for every individual thought, for every word, and for every one of his actions, because all the vibrations thereof are pressing in full power, thereby penetrating the spheres of animistic species and producing forms. Thus forms arise in Subsequent Creation in accordance with the vibrations sent forth by man.

Consequently if a person is unrestrained in his temperament he thereby creates new and unhealthy forms in Creation which can never produce harmony, but which are bound to have a disturbing influence upon all that exists.

Since by virtue of his origin the human spirit stands at the highest point in Subsequent Creation, he has not only the power but also the duty to control every species different to him in Creation. In fact he cannot do otherwise, he *must* dominate owing to his nature!

He must now think of this every moment! With each individual thought, with each stirring of his soul, he creates ever new forms in this Subsequent Creation! Try to grasp this clearly, as you are indeed responsible for it, and everything you form in the course of your existence clings to you. What is good uplifts you, what is low must pull you down in accordance with the Law of Gravity, which takes effect irrevocably, regardless of whether you yourselves are aware of it or completely indifferent to it. It operates and works around you in a constant weaving. It is true that you are the starting point of all that must be formed or produced in this loom, yet you are unable to stop it even for one moment!

Just try to envisage *this one picture* clearly! It must suffice to rouse you from the trifling things for which you are often willing to sacrifice so much time and strength. You must be horrified at the frivolous manner in which you have hitherto spent your life, and stand ashamed before your Creator, Who thereby bestowed such a great gift upon you. But you have paid no attention to it, you only dabbled with this enormous power to the detriment of the Subsequent Creation entrusted to you, which you can transform into a Paradise for yourselves if at last you wish to do so.

Consider! The entire disorder which you have brought about through your ignorance of the Divine Laws is now bound to confuse and overwhelm you! It is *your* fault that you do not yet know these laws. Since you stand in Creation it is your most sacred duty personally to concern yourselves with them.

But instead men have mocked and sneered at the messengers who were able to indicate the way which is bound to bring recognition. Without effort, however, no prize can be won, for that is against the Law of unceasing Movement in Creation, which is a necessary factor for the maintenance and further development of everything. Movement in the spirit *and* of the body! Everything which does not move, or which does not move in the right way, will be ejected, because it does nothing but disturb the swinging harmony of Creation. It is ejected as being a diseased part which does not want to move along in rhythm.

I have already spoken to you about the necessity of continual movement as a law.

The spirit *must* dominate, no matter whether it wants to or not. It cannot do otherwise! And thus it must now also exert itself at last to dominate spiritually in *full consciousness*, unless it wishes to bring nothing but harm. However, it can only dominate consciously if it is familiar with and adjusts itself to all the laws resting in Creation. There is no alternative! Only then does it fill the post to which it has been appointed, and which it can never alter or rearrange.

Thus the human spirit must also stand above the temperaments, it must restrain and rule them, so that harmony will be achieved first of all in its own body and then extend beneficially to the immediate surroundings; they will radiate and manifest in forms in the entire Subsequent Creation.

Only that man who makes good use of all the four temperaments in proper sequence and at the appropriate times stands truly firm in this Creation. For he needs these temperaments so as to climb the steps of his earth-life with security and certainty and to neglect nothing which is necessary for his spiritual maturing.

Temperaments which are well controlled and properly employed are like wearing good boots on the road through material substance on earth! Pay greater attention to them than you have done so far! You cannot do without them, but neither must you yield to them, as then they become tyrants which torment you and your surroundings also, instead of serving you.

But *make use* of them, for they are your best companions during your life on earth! They are your friends if you control them. The child develops best when it is sanguine, therefore the composition of its blood is such as to produce the sanguine temperament. The blood composition changes at the time of increasing physical maturity and then brings with it the melancholic temperament.

This in turn is the best aid for the time of maturing! It can direct the spirit towards the Light, towards purity and loyalty, during the years when the spirit's connection with Creation is being completed, at which time it takes the active lead and gears into the entire weaving and working which is in constant movements therein. In this way it may become the greatest helper to the human spirit in its essential being, more decisive than he is now able to imagine.

Therefore the child must be allowed the undimmed joy of the moment which is derived from the sanguine temperament and, on the other hand, the youth and maiden must be left to the healthy daydreams in which they so often indulge. He who destroys such reveries in order to make these young people conform to the sobriety of their surroundings becomes a brigand of the spirit on its way to the Light! Beware of this, for all the consequences will also fall upon you!

The choleric temperament in a clarified form is needed by every man of action! I purposely say in a clarified form, for the spirit *must* dominate in the years of manhood and womanhood, it must ennoble and transfigure everything, it must send forth and spread light radiations throughout the entire Creation!

In old age, however, the phlegmatic temperament gradually helps to loosen the spirit more and more from its body, to re-examine past experiences of earth-life in order to retain the lessons learned as something personal, and to prepare itself little by little in this way for the necessary step into the Ethereal World of Creation. It is thereby made easy for such a person, becoming quite a natural event which means nothing but progress, and involves no suffering in obeying the Law of this Creation.

Pay attention to the temperaments, therefore, and further them whenever you can, but always and only at their proper time and so long as they do not become tyrants through lack of restraint! He who wishes to change or suppress them destroys the best help there is for the development of earthman as willed by God. In so doing he also disturbs all healthiness, causing confusion as well as undreamt-of eccentricities, which will bring discord, envy, hatred and anger, not to mention robbery and murder. All this because the temperaments were disregarded at the essential time by the coldly-calculating intellect, and broken when they should have been developed and observed!

The temperaments are given to you by the Will of God in the Laws of Nature, which are always tended and kept fresh for you by the elemental beings in order to facilitate the course of your life on earth if you live as God wills that you should. Thank the Lord for this and joyously take up the gifts which lie ready for you everywhere in Creation! Exert yourselves in order to recognise them aright at last!

BEHOLD, MAN, HOW YOU SHOULD WANDER THROUGH THIS CREATION SO THAT THREADS OF FATE WILL NOT HINDER BUT FURTHER YOUR ASCENT!

ALTHOUGH the Message contains everything that is needed to show the way which men must take through Creation if they wish to ascend to the Luminous Heights, yet for each individual there is a repeated anxious questioning: What shall I do really to proceed aright?

Very many persons are troubled by this intuitive perception, because man likes to make everything more complicated than it really is. He *needs* this curious method of making everything more difficult for himself, because he does not possess the inner strength to pursue with earnestness and zeal *that which is simple*. He has no longer sufficient ability to do so!

If he sees no difficulties confronting him he never succeeds in putting forth powers in order to use them, for a lack of difficulties soon makes him slothful and finally paralyses his entire activity. Therefore he pays no attention to what is simple but, as soon as he can, he even distorts everything that is simple into something which is incomprehensible, purely for the purpose of giving himself a hard time to recognise yet again in this distortion just what is right, which remains anchored only in simplicity. Thus man constantly wastes time and energy!

Man needs *obstacles* in order to attain to the goal; only in this way does he still gather all his strength, which he is no longer able to do when he is confronted with it in a *simple* way!

This at first sounds as if it were something great, yet it is only the sign of deepest weakness! Just as a weakened body needs stimulants to enable it to carry on its activity, so the human spirit, in order to attain any goal, first needs the incentive of knowing that it must overcome something and thereby exert its strength to do so! Out of this there once came into existence the so-called science, which disdains all that is simple, reaching out to the ridiculous for the sole purpose of excelling others and "shining"!

But it is not only science which has been acting in this manner over a long period, erecting with much trouble a false structure which is supposed to lend

692

an air of greatness to something that in Creation is actually inferior, artificial, cramped and distorted, indeed often hindering!

Even from the very beginning each individual has allowed his earth-life to be built up on a wrong basis. It is much too complicated to be healthy, and only incites the indolent spirit in its conceit to distinguish itself before others. For it is *this* aspiration alone which is the true reason for the mutilation and confusion of all naturalness and simplicity by these human spirits. The ambition to excel, the conceit to investigate and lay down laws from a knowledge that can never really become knowledge as long as man struggles against *receiving* humbly and simply in devotion to God's Magnitude – all this holds him down!

There is not a single thing that man could really create without taking it from that which has already come into existence through the Will of God! He would be unable to create anew a single grain of sand without finding all the material for it already to hand in Creation!

As yet he cannot recognise how ridiculous he appears, but the day will come when he will be unspeakably ashamed of himself and only too glad to efface the time when he imagined himself as being so great and knowing!

With tolerant indulgence, sometimes even with a sarcastic smile, man now passes by every great simplicity of the Divine Laws. He does not realise that in so doing he exposes the greatest weakness of which a human being is capable and puts himself in the lowest place among all creatures, because *he alone* forgot how *to receive* and use the gifts from Creation rightly. Man considers himself too great and too exalted to accept gratefully from his Creator all that he needs, and therefore he is no longer worthy to enjoy such mercies further!

And yet the Laws in Creation should be quite natural, simple and without confusion to every creature, because each creature came into existence through them!

But what has man made of them in his vain imaginings!

What he can produce in the way of unintelligible and unwieldy institutions you can observe for yourselves in all the human laws governing the social order! A lifetime hardly suffices to study all of them thoroughly for *one* country alone. Specially trained scholars are needed to interpret them aright. And these often dispute among themselves as to how and where they can be applied. This proves that even among these lawyers there is no clarity about the actual meaning.

But wherever there is room for dispute there *is* also no clarity. Where there is no clarity, accuracy and thus also justification are lacking!

At present every individual person would have to become a learned scholar of these laws established by men in order to go through life unscathed! What folly lies in this fact! And yet it is so! Often enough experts have been heard to observe that according to mundane law *every* person living on earth could be indicted and in some way found guilty, wherever this was tried! Unfortunately this is true! And yet every individual is made subject to these laws without being able to be properly informed about them!

This will also have to fall into ruin of its own accord, because it is an impossible outgrowth of a most unhealthy confusion.

The human spirit has now thoroughly proved its incompetence in these matters. An unworthy enslavement resulted from its failure to link up the earthly laws with the Primordial Laws of Creation, which it never endeavoured to study. Only if it is built upon *their* soil can any benefit arise, no matter what! It is the same with *justice!* And this again, like all basic laws, lies only in clear and great *simplicity*.

That which is not inherently simple will never last! The simplicity of the Divine Laws does not permit otherwise! Will man never learn to understand?

He can quite clearly recognise in the events of every era that great success could only come about *where* all the power was focussed upon *one* point! This indicates clearly enough the necessity of simplification! You should at last discover something in this! Everybody knows the danger which *always* threatens through a splitting up.

Observe therein the Law of the Power of every *Simplification;* the victorious greatness which only becomes effective in *simplicity!*

But you can no longer perceive the value of all that is simple! It is only in simplicity that true strength, genuine nobility, knowledge, and grace become manifest. Also in simplicity of expression and movement!

You all know about this quite well! And yet you do not learn to appreciate the actual value, and therefore you cannot grasp it, cannot transfer it to your *thinking* so that it can find expression in your words and in your deeds!

Man is unable to be as simple as he should learn to be in Creation. It not only comes hard to man to attain to the greatness of simplicity in his thinking and activity, but he is utterly unable to achieve it! It has already passed beyond his reach!

He therefore no longer understands the simplicity of the language and the explanations resting in the Message. In the perversity of his thinking he assumes that this only right and great way is too childlike *for him,* and therefore cannot contain anything of value. Thus its actual values remain closed to him because *he* is incapable of absorbing them. He neither sees nor recognises what is great and powerful as soon as it is clothed in simple words!

This is due to *his* incapacity! For simplicity and clearness the spirit must develop strength *within itself,* while in the case of obstacles due to confusion the impulse for the development of strength approaches man from *without.* Unfortunately, however, the human spirit of today *needs* this impetus *from outside* in order to enable it to be at least a little astir. Therefore man cannot stand simplicity and clearness. Simplicity lulls him to sleep, it paralyses him because he is too indolent to develop of his own accord that inner strength which alone can bring him real benefit and help him to ascend.

He is unable to keep himself active with simplicity and clearness around him. His strength is no longer sufficient for this because he never developed it. It is natural that owing to this indolence he creates for himself continual obstacles. Today these obstacles serve a few people as incentives or stimulants in the sense already explained. But in order to overcome these self-created obstacles the strength arising at the sight of them, which is lamentably small, is used up and nothing remains for real progress and ascent, which could only begin after overcoming the obstacles.

When the path before them again becomes simple and clear they weary on account of this simplicity. It is not "interesting" enough, because they can no longer conceive of their personal greatness, and once more they bring about further confusion, so that what they do will "appear" or "sound" like something important!

All this happens over and over again because the human spirits of today lack real greatness of their own.

You can observe the same physically with gymnasts. During the presentation of their gymnastic exercises they develop strength and suppleness with a grace of movement which shows the control over their bodies. But only a few of all the gymnasts upon earth show continual bodily control, i.e., also in every-day life.

Their posture when sitting, speaking, standing, and also when walking is often deplorable! This proves that they develop strength only when they practise or appear in public, i.e., when they want to exhibit something. However, to control the body energetically all day long, which requires *real* strength and from which the body derives ten times more benefit than from a few hours of gymnastics, this strength they are *unable* to bring up without some impetus from outside, for this requires more, much more!

All gymnastics and special exercises could safely be abolished if man *really* controlled himself and his body; for then every muscle must remain in constant movement, which demands strength and will. All special exercises offer nothing but a pitiful substitute for the conscious strength of that great simplicity which lies in the naturalness of perpetual self-control.

As it is with gymnastics so it is with *all* things! Man does not need to perform anything extraordinary if he wanders through Creation *in the right way*. Everything is given to him in simplicity and everything is within him, without his having to resort to artificial assistance. In the same way as men add all kinds of possible and impossible stimulants to their nourishment in order to energise their bodies, as they use such things as smoking and intoxicating narcotics in order to whip up the nerves of their body and the brain, deluding themselves into the belief that it will enhance their thought processes, so they use confusion for their spirit in order to indulge their conceit.

That is why I am compelled again and again to formulate many words about things just to make them to some extent comprehensible to you, when in reality they should be grasped immediately in one very simple conception. I continually struggle to find new interpretations for everything that has already been said because you are incapable of accepting that which is simple and plain, both in regard to truth and to life as well as to Creation, in which your path and your entire existence also lie anchored.

You should not at all need to ask what you must or must not do! Just demolish the maze *within you*, which you so carefully nurse and foster, thereby creating ever new entanglements by your thoughts! You think *too much*, and for this reason you can think *nothing real*, nothing which is of benefit to you.

The Law of Almighty God for you is:

You are permitted to wander through Creation! Go in such a manner as to cause no harm to others in pursuit of your personal desires! Otherwise threads will be woven into the carpet of your paths which will hold you down and prevent you from ascending to the Luminous Heights of conscious and joyful activity in the gardens of all the Realms of your God!

That is the basic law containing everything you need to know! If you follow this nothing can happen to you. You will only be led *upwards* by all the threads created by your thinking, volition and actions.

That is why the Son of God once said in all simplicity: "Love thy neighbour as thyself"! Fundamentally this has exactly the same meaning!

You are allowed to wander through the Creations! This holds the command to constant *movement!* You must not stand still! You could not in fact do so, because the self-created threads which form your paths *always* drive you forward according to their nature – either upwards or straight ahead for a time or also downwards. You can never stop, even if you yourselves should wish to do so!

And during this wandering you shall not harm any others, who like you are also journeying through Creation, just to satisfy some personal desire!

It is not difficult to grasp this aright, for when your perception is calm you are quite well aware of when, where and how you harm others. All that remains for you to do in this matter is to become clear as to everything which falls into the category of *desiring!* However, you have already been told this clearly in the Commandments! It is not necessary for me to repeat it again!

You may enjoy *everything* here in Creation, you may taste of everything, but it must not bring harm to your fellow-man! Again, this only occurs if you become a slave to your desires!

But you must not get too one-sided an idea of what this desiring implies! Not only earthly property and the physical body are included, but also the desire to undermine the reputation of your fellow-man, giving way to your own weaknesses, and many other things!

Today in particular far too little attention is paid to this giving way to one's own weaknesses, and yet it falls into the category of fulfilling one's own desires to the detriment or suffering of your neighbour! The threads which become knotted thereby are dense and thus hold down every soul which has acted in this fashion.

Such weaknesses comprise distrust and envy, irritability, coarseness and rudeness, in a word the lack of self-control and refinement, the latter signifying nothing less than the necessary consideration for your fellow-men, which *must* be present if harmony is to prevail. For harmony alone furthers Creation and yourselves!

It is a close weaving which comes about through such weaknesses, forcing many to fall just because so little attention is paid to it, although it inflicts disquietude, pressure, annoyance and often even severe suffering upon your fellow-men. But in each case harm!

If men let themselves go to such an extent there immediately arises through the radiation of the slightly or greatly excited blood a strongly dimmed layer which places itself *separatingly* between man's spirit and his luminous guidance! He thus immediately stands alone and also completely unprotected, which may cause such damage as proves to be irreparable.

Everyone wishing to ascend should engrave this upon his mind!

This advice is a lifebelt which may save him from drowning, from destruction. It is of the *utmost importance* for everybody in their earthly existence.

You may journey through Creation consciously! However, you must not harm others in order to satisfy your personal desires. Live accordingly, and you will then be happy and wander upwards into the Luminous Gardens of your God, there to help in joyful activity with the further and eternal development of this Creation!

A NEW LAW

I HAVE told you: "At your desire you are allowed to wander through the Creations, thereby becoming self-conscious, but in so doing you must not harm others in order to satisfy your *personal* desires!"

There is nothing in Creation you would not be allowed to enjoy in the sense in which Creation gives it to you, i.e., for the same purpose as that for which it is developed. However, you do not know the real purpose of so many things, and erroneously commit many excesses which are bound to bring harm instead of benefit. Thus the desire to taste, to get to know and to enjoy often increases until it becomes a *propensity,* which finally keeps you enchained and quickly enslaves your free volition, so that through your own selves you become *servants* instead of masters.

Never let yourselves be subjugated through enjoying, but take only what is necessary in life on earth for the maintenance and development of the good things entrusted to you. You hinder all development by excess, no matter whether the body or the soul is involved. Just as you hold things up through excess, so also through negligence or imperfection! You disturb the great God-willed development! Everything which you now wish to do with the best volition to adjust and compensate for such mistakes remains nothing but patchwork, leaving traces of repair which do not look nice and which can never be the same as one uniform and unpatched work.

The fulfilment of the promise that "everything must become new" does not contain the sense of remodelling, but of forming *anew* everything that has been distorted and poisoned by the human spirit after it has collapsed. And as there is nothing which has not yet been touched and poisoned by man in his conceit, *everything* must collapse in order *afterwards* to become new again; not, however, in accordance with men's volition as hitherto, but according to the Will of God, which has never yet been understood by the human soul that has begun to decay through its obstinacy.

Mankind has *touched* everything created by the Will of God, but has *not recognised* it, as it should have been the task of every human spirit to do. In his presumptuous imagining that he was master man *touched* everything, but thereby only devalued and soiled all purity.

What does man really know of the conception of purity! What has he already made of the boundless sublimity of true purity in his atrocious pettiness! He has dimmed and debased this conception, dragging it down to his own low and dirty cravings, wherein he no longer knows the intuitive perception of his spirit but only follows the narrow limitations of his feeling, which is produced by his intellect through the retrospective effect of its thinking. But in the future the feeling shall again become pure!

Feeling in relation to the intuitive perception is what the intellect should become in relation to the spirit – a *tool* for activity in gross material life! Today, however, the feeling is debased and dragged down to be the implement of the intellect, and has thus become dishonoured. In the same manner as the spirit bearing the intuitive perception with which to express its working has already been forced down and fettered by the hereditary sin of intellectual domination, so also the coarser feeling produced by the intellect was simultaneously and automatically bound to triumph over the purity of the spiritual intuitive perception, suppressing the latter and cutting it off from the possibility of a wholesome working in Creation.

In the natural course of things one fault consequently brought the other in its train. Thus it is that today men also in this matter only hold lead in their hands instead of gold without realising it, and they consider this lead to be gold, although they no longer have any knowledge whatever of pure intuitive perception.

However, as the spirit must be rightly balanced and connected with the intellect, i. e., the spirit dominating and leading, and the intellect as an implement serving, preparing the way and bringing about possibilities for carrying the spiritual volition into effect in the World of Matter, so also must the intuitive perception at the same time have a leading and animating influence, while the feeling in following this lead transforms the activity into the gross material. Then at last will the feeling also very soon and speedily take on nobler forms, quickly effacing by its upward soaring the wretched moral breakdown in conceptions, which could only arise out of the domination of the present-day feeling!

If the activity of the feeling is guided by the intuitive perception, all thinking and doing is filled only with beauty, balance, and ennoblement. There is never any desiring, only the sacred wish to give! This must be taken to heart in everything, including love and marriage!

With your short-sighted and narrow-minded attitude you often consider certain persons to be pure when in reality, according to the Laws in Creation, they belong to the most depraved class of men. There are many actions which without further ado you think in your narrow-mindedness are impure, yet which radiate with purity, while many things considered pure by you are impure.

The purity of the intuitive perception uplifts many an action to heights undreamt-of by you, yet which here you still wish to soil with your scorn and mockery. For this reason first of all liberate your *intuitive perception* so that you may judge aright and weigh good and evil, otherwise you are bound to go astray!

Also do not think that you have "overcome" this or that within you so long as you have not *been endangered,* and faced the possibility of yielding to your weaknesses in the certainty that nobody will hear about it! Neither does an escape into solitude bring real benefit to anyone! This merely proves that such a person feels himself too weak or is too tired for the struggle, is perhaps even afraid of himself that he will fall at a given opportunity.

Being strong is different, it *manifests* in a different way! The strong one pursues his path unswervingly and unerringly amid all dangers. He cannot be upset, nor does he deviate of his own accord, but he knows and sees his high goal, the personal attainment of which is more valuable than anything else that may present itself before him.

Man must now become *new* in everything, new and strong *within himself!*

I give you some advice regarding this new activity: "No longer cause any harm to your fellow men in order to fulfil your personal desires thereby!"

You have not yet grasped all that this contains. It is the best staff for a man's journey through the various parts of Creation to Paradise.

In addition I give you a second piece of advice: "Take care of the good things entrusted to you upon earth, which also include your physical body, *in the right manner.* Never let pleasure become a propensity, and you will then remain free from the chains holding you down!"

It should be a condition for everyone striving seriously upon earth that the addressing of a person as "Thou" ("Du" in German) must be kept strictly sacred among each other.* Only in exceptional cases may it be used or offered. This is different in the Ethereal World, the so-called "beyond". There the barriers of spiritual maturity are *strictly established* and cannot just be transgressed. *There* the real homogeneous species live together in accordance with the Law of Creation, *and it is solely the homogeneous species which justifies the address of "Du"!*

In the Gross Material World, however, these barriers must first be established. Here the gross material earth body makes it possible for spirits of *all* degrees of maturity to live closely together in a way which occurs nowhere on other planes again.

Therefore establish a barrier for the future, the necessity and great value of which you probably cannot quite understand.

Already once in my Message I have pointed this out in the lecture: "The Kiss of Friendship". Part of this is the *poison-spreading* habit of calling each other "Du", and thus bursting through and transgressing one of the most necessary barriers in the World of Gross Matter. A barrier offering you support, the value of which you are not capable of measuring!

Thus it must become a *command* for everyone striving for the Light that he follows the habit of offering the familiar "Du" to his fellow-men sparingly. Best of all he should avoid it entirely!

If it should be offered to you reject it, except in those cases where a serious union for earth-life is intended, i. e., in marriage! *Years later* you will recognise the value resting in this command. A shudder always comes over me when I hear of it, for I know the corruption contained in this habit. But no man has any idea of it!

With this German "Du", which embodies a very special conception, every soul enters into a bond capable of reaching beyond the earthly grave!

Special threads which are by no means harmless immediately link one to the other with the use of this "Du" – threads which may hold the spirits down, even those capable of ascent! For very seldom will it happen that two spirits of the same maturity in all things are thereby linked together, two which actually stand on the same step spiritually.

And wherever two link up who are unequal, the law ordains that the higher one is *pulled down*, but the lower one never ascends! For in Creation the

* This refers to the German language only.

higher one alone can descend to lower planes, but no spirit can ever succeed in raising itself even one step above the place where it stands!

Thus in the case of a voluntary and close union between two spirits who are unequal in their maturity the higher one *must* either descend or be retarded by the other, who remained backward in his maturity and hangs upon him like a weight through this tie. Not everyone possesses the strength to lead the less mature one in such a way that he comes upward to him. These are exceptions which one may not take into account. And a complete severance from a voluntary union is not easy!

This contains a fact the dreadfulness of which earthman has never yet taken into account. He frivolously passes over this unfathomable deep in earthly existence, and is hampered in *every case* without exception as soon as he trespasses against the law. Like a swimmer who dives into the water at places he does not know he is often hampered by invisible creepers!

The time will come when you will one day be free from this danger, to which many fall victim every day and every hour upon earth. You will become free through the knowledge! But then marriages will also be different, as well as friendships and other unions, all of which quite distinctly bear the name "binding". Then all quarrels between friends will be ended, all spitefulness and misunderstandings will disappear. In observing this law, which until today has not been understood, everything will turn into the fullest harmony.

Until then, however, you can only be helped by the advice to be careful with the familiar "Du"! If you observe this you will be protected from great suffering! You can shorten your spiritual ascent by thousands of years! Do not forget this, even when you do not understand it today. I thereby give you the best weapon with which to avoid creepers of an ethereal nature!

You need more commandments in the World of Gross Matter than is necessary in the Ethereal Worlds, where all human spirits cannot but associate with their homogeneous species, even if this species carries many gradations and therefore also shows very many and varied forms.

In following this advice you will now become free from the heavy and unnecessary load with which mankind burden themselves ever anew.

Do not look for an example to the beyond, which is subject to simpler laws. Those in the beyond must also first learn for themselves in the new time, in the promised Millennium. They are no wiser than you yourselves and only know what is necessary for their plane. Therefore the bond will still have to be torn asunder for spiritists, where it brings nothing but harm due to misunderstandings and stupid conceit; the conceit which has already brought so many wrong interpretations of much that is valuable, thus leading the masses astray or preventing them from recognising the Truth *now*.

Do not let yourselves be misled, but *heed* my advice! It is for *your* help, and you could easily recognise its value even now if you looked around you more attentively! You must not perhaps break off without cause what exists. That would bring no solution! It would be an attempt at false and unhealthy transformation! But now you must act *differently* in these matters, no longer in a thoughtless and frivolous manner! You must build up entirely anew. What is old will fall away of itself.

And when I now also say to you: "Man shall never live together with another whom he cannot respect!" then you have for your earth-life *that* which will enable you to stay free from karma. Take these principles along with you on your path!

So that you may ascend there must in addition to all this be the inner yearning for the pure and luminous Realm of God! The *yearning* for it carries the spirit upwards! Therefore *think* upon God and His Will at all times! But do not make a picture of it for yourselves! It would certainly prove wrong because the human spirit cannot grasp the conception of God. Therefore it is given to him to grasp the *Will* of God, for which he must seek honestly and in humility. *If he has found the Will he will then recognise God therein!* That is the only way to Him!

So far, however, man has not yet exerted himself in the right way to grasp the Will of God, to find It, but he has always given precedence to the *human volition* which originated within himself, embodying the human wishes and the instinct for self-preservation. This is not in harmony with the automatic upward swinging of all the Primordial Laws of Creation.

Therefore find the way to the true Will of God in Creation, and then you will recognise God therein!

DUTY AND LOYALTY

THE FULFILMENT of duty has always been considered man's greatest virtue. Among all peoples it ranked higher than everything else, higher even than life itself. It was held in such esteem that it retained first place even among the intellectuals who ultimately regarded nothing as sacred any more but their own intellect, to which they submitted like slaves.

The consciousness of the need to fulfil one's duty remained; not even the domination of the intellect was able to upset this! However, the Darkness found a point of attack after all, and gnawed at its *root*. As everywhere so also here it distorted the *conception*. The idea of the fulfilment of duty remained, but the *duties themselves* were set up by the intellect and thus became earthbound, piecework and imperfect.

It is therefore only natural that a person of intuitive perception is often unable to acknowledge that the duties assigned to him are right. He comes into conflict with himself. He, too, considers the fulfilment of duty to be one of the supreme laws which a person must observe, and yet at the same time he is bound to admit to himself that in fulfilling the duties laid upon him he sometimes acts against his own convictions.

As a result of this condition forms arise not only in the inner man, who thus torments himself, but also in the Ethereal World, forms which also cause discontent and discord in others. Thus a craving for fault-finding and grumbling spreads over the widest circles without anybody being able to discover the actual cause, which cannot be recognised because the effect comes from the Ethereal World through the living forms created by a person of intuitive perception, arising out of the conflict between his urge to fulfil his duty and his intuitive perception which wills otherwise.

There must now be a change in this matter in order to redress the evil. Duty and inner conviction must always *harmonise* with each other. It is wrong for a person to risk his life in the fulfilment of a duty which he cannot acknowledge within himself as being right.

Each sacrifice becomes of genuine value only when conviction harmonises with duty. But if a man only risks his life in the fulfilment of duty *without* conviction he thereby degrades himself to the position of a mercenary who, in the service of another, fights for the sake of money, similar to the lansquenets. Fighting of that kind thus becomes murder!

If, however, someone risks his life out of conviction, he also bears within himself love for the cause for which he voluntarily resolved to fight.

And this alone has high value for him! He must do it for the sake of love, out of love for the *cause!* Thereby the duty he thus fulfils comes to *life* and is so uplifted that he places its fulfilment before everything else.

Thus the dead, rigid performance of duty automatically separates itself from the living. And only the living has spiritual value and effect! Everything else can only serve and advantage earthly and intellectual purposes. Not for any length of time either, but only temporarily, because only what is living becomes of lasting duration!

Thus the fulfilment of duty arising out of conviction becomes genuine, self-willed loyalty, and natural to the one carrying it out. He is neither desirous nor capable of acting otherwise. He cannot stumble and fall because with him loyalty is genuine, is closely connected with him, indeed it is a part of him which he is unable to lay aside.

Blind obedience and blind fulfilment of duty are therefore of as little worth as is blind belief! Both are lacking life because they lack love!

From this alone man immediately recognises the difference between a genuine sense of duty and a feeling of duty which has only been imparted to him. The one bursts forth from out of the intuitive perception, and the other is grasped by the intellect only. Therefore love and duty can never oppose each other but are *one* where the perception is *genuine,* and from this blossoms forth loyalty.

Where love is missing there is also no life, there all is dead! Christ has often pointed this out. It is inherent in the Primordial Laws of Creation, and is therefore universal without exception.

The performance of duty which voluntarily breaks forth radiantly from a human soul can never be confused with a duty carried out for the sake of earthly reward, but each can quite easily be recognised. Therefore let genuine loyalty arise within you, or hold aloof where you cannot be loyal!

Loyalty! So often praised, yet never understood! As with everything else, earthman has also deeply debased the conception of loyalty, narrowing and compressing it into rigid forms. Its greatness, freedom and beauty became cold and devoid of all expression. Its naturalness became *forced!*

According to present conceptions loyalty ceased to be part of the soul's nobility and was made a quality of the character. A difference like day and night! Thus loyalty became soulless. Where it is required it has devolved into a duty. Man has thus declared it to be independent, it stands upon its own feet, all by itself, and therefore ... wrong! Loyalty, too, was twisted and distorted by the human mind!

Loyalty is *not* something which is independent, but only a quality of love! Of the *right* love, which embraces everything! To embrace everything, however, does not hold the meaning of embracing everything at once in accordance with human understanding, which is expressed in the well-known words "embracing the whole world"! To embrace everything means: *To have the capacity of being directed upon everything,* upon personal as well as upon impersonal matters. It is not merely bound to something specific, nor is it meant to be one-sided.

Right love does not exclude anything that is pure or kept pure, no matter whether this concerns persons or one's native land, also such things as work or Nature. That is what is meant by embracing. And *the quality of this right love* is loyalty, which must no more be considered of small, earthly narrowness than is the conception of chastity.

There is no real loyalty without love, just as there is no true love without loyalty either. But the earthman of today regards fulfilment of duty as loyalty, a *rigid* form with which the soul does not need to vibrate. This is wrong! Loyalty is *nothing but* a quality of true love, which is merged with justice, but has nothing to do with being "in love".

Loyalty rests in the vibrations of the intuitive perception of the spirit, and thus becomes a quality of the soul.

In performing his duty today a person often gives reliable service to someone whom he must inwardly despise. This, of course, cannot be described as loyalty, but remains merely the fulfilment of earthly duties which he has undertaken. It is purely an *external* affair, which in the reciprocal action can *also bring nothing but outward benefit* to the person concerned, be it improvement in his earthly means or earthly reputation.

In such cases true loyalty cannot manifest because it wants to be offered *freely* with love, from which it cannot be separated. Therefore loyalty cannot exert an influence of itself either!

However, if men would live on a basis of true love, as is willed by God, this condition alone would provide the impetus to alter many things among them, in fact everything! No man who is inwardly base would then be able to exist any longer, much less gain any success here upon earth. A great purification would set in immediately!

Men who are inwardly base would not enjoy earthly honours, nor would they hold office, for intellectual knowledge of itself shall not suffice to place them in authoritative positions.

Thus the fulfilment of duty would then always become an absolute pleasure and all work would become enjoyment, because all thinking and all working would be completely penetrated by true, God-willed love, and bring in its train not only an unshakable intuitive perception of justice but also loyalty, that loyalty which as a matter of course remains unchangeable in its essence, and does not consider this as a merit that must be rewarded.

THE BEAUTY OF THE PEOPLES

THE EARTH is now being encompassed by the Light. A strong cloak firmly envelops the globe so that the Darkness cannot escape. Ever stronger becomes the pressure, sharply forcing together all that is evil, so that one cycle after another of all that has happened must come to a close, and the end be connected with the beginning. Spears and arrows of Light dart here and there, swords of Light flash forth, and Lucifer's minions are being sorely afflicted to their destruction.

Holy victory for the Light here upon earth! That is God's Almighty Will! Light shall be everywhere, also among all the errors of mankind so that they may now recognise truthfulness!

The great new time shall be ushered in as a blessing for all the peoples, so that they may feel happy upon the soil to which they belong, and thus come to full blossom in exact accordance with their race, bearing rich fruit and working only towards the harmonious development of the whole of mankind upon earth.

Thus beauty will arise afresh! The entire earth will become a picture of beauty as though it had issued from the Hand of the Sublime Creator Himself, for all human spirits will then swing in the same sense, their joyful activity ascending in jubilant prayers of thanks to the Luminous Heights, there to mirror all the harmony of happiness manifesting on earth!

But this God-willed beauty cannot come about as long as the leaders try to force upon their people and upon their country foreign habits and customs, foreign clothing, and foreign architectural styles in the illusion that this makes for the progress of their people. Imitation is not uplifting, there is no personal achievement in it! Uniformity through copying is wrong!

The best measure of this is the sense of beauty which is given to you so that you may recognise what is right and what is wrong in these matters. Devote yourselves to the original, *true sense of beauty,* and then you can never err! For this is linked with the Primordial Laws of Creation, and is the expression of a knowledge of perfection which still remains hidden. It is an infallible signpost for every *spirit*, because only that which is *spiritual* in this Subsequent Creation possesses the ability, at a very definite stage of maturity and in full consciousness, to recognise real beauty.

But here also you have unfortunately long since extinguished the unbiassed intuitive perception through the fall of man (which you now know about), with its disastrous consequences arising from the domination of the intellect, which created caricatures of everything. The form which the intellect substituted for the conception of true beauty is the folly of fashion, to which your vanity only too gladly submitted. This slavery to fashion has completely buried your sense of beauty for-noble, graceful forms, which is given to your *spirit* as a guide and a staff in this coarse existence upon earth, thus causing you to lose a strong support through your own guilt.

Otherwise, in *every* circumstance of life and in *all* places, you would always and at once intuitively perceive and *know* if something is not in order because wherever your sense of beauty is unable to vibrate joyfully the harmony which is a strict condition for Creation does not exist *as it should*. And where there is no harmony there is no beauty either!

Look at a Chinaman when he wears a top-hat, or a Japanese or Turk for that matter! Caricatures of European culture! Look at the Japanese woman who nowadays dresses herself in European clothes, and then see her when she wears the costume of her own country! What a difference! How much she loses when wearing clothes alien to her country! It is indeed a great loss for her!

In the advancement of its own culture alone lies true progress for each of the peoples! There must naturally be *ascent* in everything, and no standstill. But this upward progress must always take place upon and out of its *own* soil, not through adopting foreign things, otherwise it is never progress. The word itself in its true sense rejects any imitation. A people can only *progress* through the upward development of what it already possesses, and not by the adoption of something it has borrowed. Taking something over is not progress, for progress shows itself in the improvement of what already exists. This alone should cause some reflection! Nor is that which is borrowed or taken over really one's property, even if one wishes to make it so! It is not something personally achieved, not a result of the people's own spirit, of which alone it could and must be proud!

A great task rests therein for everyone overseas: To let each people there become great *within itself*, entirely out of itself, through its own abilities, which vary so greatly among the many peoples of this earth. *All* must come to full blossom *according to the nature of the soil upon which they have developed*. They must remain adapted to this soil in order to unfold *that* beauty which swings harmoniously upon earth with the others. It is just through the *difference in kind* that right harmony comes into existence, and not through uniformity among all the peoples. If this had been willed then there would have been only *one* country and one people. This, however, would soon bring about a standstill and ultimately decay and death, because the refreshing influence of the complementary would be missing.

Here again just look at the flowers in the meadows, which stimulate and refresh and indeed spread happiness around on account of their variety!

But failure to observe such laws of development will come home severely to the peoples, for this, too, will finally lead to retrogression and collapse; there can be no upward soaring because all healthiness is lacking. Man cannot strive against those things to which he like every other creature is subject, in as much as he will never achieve anything unless he takes into account the Living Laws which are woven into this Creation. Wherever he acts against and disregards them he *is bound to* suffer shipwreck sooner or later. The later it happens the more violently it will occur! Thus every leader must also bear the main responsibility for that which he mismanages due to *his* wrong attitude. He must then suffer for his entire people, who in their distress cling firmly to him spiritually!

I repeat once more: True progress for each people lies solely in the development of its own culture adapted to the soil, the climate and the race. Man must become *indigenous* in the purest sense, if he wishes to develop and expect help from the Light. He should beware of adopting the habits and customs of peoples alien to his nature, not to mention foreign opinions. To be rooted in one's native soil is a basic condition and alone guarantees health, strength and maturity!

Has man not yet learned enough from the bitter experiences he often called forth through the gift of his own culture to foreign peoples, the decline of which he then had to experience? Only a very few have been induced to reflect upon this! But even this reflection has so far seeped away in the sand, unable to find any ground which could hold an anchor!

To sweep away the evil and inaugurate a new, happy and rich life in the countries overseas is an incisive task. It is of revolutionary character, because its results will affect *all* peoples upon earth, bringing them support and recovery, indeed happiness!

IT IS FINISHED!

"It is finished!" These momentous words of the Son of God were taken and interpreted by mankind as the end of the work of redemption, as the crowning act of a propitiatory sacrifice which God offered to earthmen for all their guilt.

Trembling with gratitude, faithful Christians are therefore stirred by the sound of these words and, with a deep sigh of relief, feel themselves comfortably protected through them.

However, this *feeling* has no genuine foundation, but only originates from an empty imagination. In every human soul there always lies more or less hidden this anxious question: How was such a great sacrifice on the part of God possible? Is humanity so precious to Him?

And this anxious question is justified, for it comes from the intuitive perception and is intended as a warning!

The spirit rebels and wishes to speak through the intuitive perception. Therefore this warning can never be silenced with empty words which hint that God Himself is *Love* and that Divine Love remains incomprehensible to mankind!

One seeks to use such words to fill the gaps that arise wherever true knowledge is lacking.

But the time is now past for empty phrases! The spirit must now awaken! It *must,* for it has no other choice!

He who is satisfied with shallow excuses in matters concerning men's salvation proves himself spiritually indolent in the most important questions of this Creation, and thus indifferent and lazy about the Laws of God which rest in this Creation.

"It is finished!" That was the last sigh of Jesus as He ended His earth-life and thereby His sufferings through mankind!

Not *for* mankind, as they in their irresponsible conceit try to deceive themselves, but *through* mankind! It was the cry of relief that now the suffering was coming to an end, and thus the special confirmation of the hardships He had already suffered.

In uttering it He did not wish to make an accusation for, being the personification of Love, He would never do so. Yet in spite of this the Laws of God work on everywhere, and thus also here, unswervingly and inevitably! And just here with double severity, for this great *suffering without hatred* falls back tenfold upon the originators of the suffering in accordance with the law!

Man must not forget that God is also *Justice* Himself in Inviolable Perfection! He who doubts this commits an outrage against God, and mocks at Perfection!

God is the Living and Inflexible Law from Eternity to Eternity! How then can any person dare to doubt this by supposing that God is able to accept an atonement through someone who did not himself also place the guilt in Creation, who is not himself the author of it?

Such a thing is not even possible *on earth,* and how much less then in the Divine Realm? Who among you, you men, would believe it likely that an earthly judge would be capable quite deliberately of allowing a person utterly innocent of the crime to be executed in place of a murderer, and that instead he would then allow the actual murderer to go free without punishment? Not one of you would consider such an absurdity to be right! However, you allow men to tell you such things about God without even inwardly resisting it!

You even accept it thankfully and always endeavour to suppress as wrong the voice stirring within you which tries to induce you to reflect upon it!

I say unto you: The effect of the Living Law of God pays no heed to the wrong opinions which you seek to cultivate in these matters against your personal conviction, but it now falls upon you severely, simultaneously bringing about the reactions to the culpable neglect of such wrong thinking! Wake up, so that it is not too late for you! Tear yourselves loose from opinions which lull you to sleep, and which can never be brought into harmony with Divine Justice! Otherwise it may well happen that such indolent drowsiness turns into a death-like sleep for you, with spiritual death as the inevitable consequence!

Hitherto you believed that the Divine should allow Itself to be scorned and persecuted without exacting punishment, while you earthmen wish to claim true justice for yourselves! To your mind the Greatness of God shall consist in His being allowed to suffer for you, and in offering you good for the evil which you do unto Him! That is what you call Divine, because only a god in accordance with your conceptions can accomplish this!

In so doing you are declaring that man is much more just than God! You only wish to recognise in God all that is improbable, but even then only when it serves you for the best! Never otherwise! For when it threatens to turn against you, you immediately cry out for the just God!

You must yourselves recognise the childishness of such one-sided opinions! You would surely blush if just for once you attempted to think about it in the right way!

According to your way of thinking God in His indulgence would cultivate and strengthen that which is mean and ignoble! You fools, accept the truth:

God manifests towards all creatures in this Creation, thus also towards you, only through His adamantine Laws, which are firmly anchored therein from the beginning. They are inflexible and inviolable, and their activity takes effect at all times with infallible certainty. This activity proceeds irresistibly, crushing all that tries to stand in its way instead of *adapting* itself *in full knowledge* to their swinging.

Knowledge, however, is humbleness! For he who has true knowledge can never be other than humble! They are as if inseparable! True knowledge simultaneously brings humility into being as a matter of course! Where there is no humility there is also never true knowledge! *Humility, however, is freedom!* Genuine freedom for each human spirit lies solely in humility!

Take this also for your guidance! And never again forget that the *Love* of God is inseparable from the *Justice!*

As God is Love, so also is He Living Justice! Indeed He *is* the Law! Absorb this fact at last and use it as a basis for your thinking for all time! You will then never miss the right path to the conviction of the Greatness of God, and you will *recognise* it in your surroundings as well as through the observation of every-day life. Therefore be spiritually alert!

AT THE BOUNDARY OF GROSS MATTER

MILLIONS of earthmen call themselves seekers, but they are not so! There is a great difference between humble seeking and self-complacent and vainglorious investigating!

But in spite of this they call themselves seekers after the truth, and even imagine that they have already become "knowing" as a result of their investigations.

Such conceit could easily be classed as ridiculously grotesque but for the fact that it so often contains dangers, was indeed always dangerous! For investigating and prospecting is the work of the intellect *only!* But what can this intellect, which comes from the gross material brains and which is therefore also subject to the gross material Primordial Laws of Creation, investigate of the *spiritual,* to the nature of which it is in no wise related? *Everything immediately collapses on account of this one quite natural fact!*

In his desire to investigate man is unable to continue even beyond the furthest point of fine gross matter!

For the human intellect ethereal matter is and will remain an alien species with which it can make no connection. But without such connection there can never be any understanding, not even seeing or hearing, much less any investigating, scrutinising or classifying into gross material conceptions, which the intellect cannot do without, proving that it is subject to gross material laws to which it remains firmly linked.

Thus every "seeker" or *"spiritual investigator"* has hitherto always remained closely tied to the World of Gross Matter, and he could never get beyond its finest boundaries, not even through really high accomplishments. The Primordial Law of Creation holds him adamantly back. There is no possibility whatever for him to go any further!

That is why many so-called boards of examiners who condescended or felt themselves called to "investigate" the authenticity of mediumistic qualities and their results, in order to pronounce an opinion with which mankind is supposed to conform, were often bound to fail miserably.

The miserable failure was always on the side of these *examiners,* even if they wish to make it appear the other way round, and probably also believe in their judgment. The inference to be drawn from the immutable Laws of Creation, however, proves it to be otherwise and speaks *against* them. And every other form of argument opposes the irrevocable nature of the Divine Laws, and is thus the wrong and erroneous work of men, the motive of which is base vanity and self-complacency of the narrowest kind.

For the same reason the earthly law courts are also hostile towards all ethereal happenings, because they are simply incapable of delving into things which are so utterly remote from their understanding.

That, however, is their own fault, a consequence of the limited conditions which they created for themselves through the indolence of their spirit, which they permit to sleep on quietly, while they mistake the earthly *intellect* originating in the World of Gross Matter for the *spirit* and value it accordingly. It is by no means always the fault of those who are summonsed to appear before them. But despite this the courts have never shrunk from judging about things which they do not understand in a manner contrary to the Laws of God. What is more, on account of their lack of understanding they very often tried to impute the intention of wilful deception and even of fraud to these actual ethereal happenings and to the spiritual ones as well!

It is the same procedure as was once applied by the churches and worldly judges in the trials for witchcraft, nothing less! It is just as repugnant and narrow, and as much a violation now as it was then of all the Primordial Laws of Creation.

Such exceptions as where actual impostors wish to benefit personally from something are to be found in *all* fields of activity of these earthmen, but that provides no justification for always treating the entire field with distrust from the very outset! Such things occur in every trade, in every kind of scientific pursuit, and in every branch of the various professions! But ultimately these deceivers can always be recognised without any difficulty, for an evil volition cannot be permanently hidden.

Therefore this singular enmity on the part of the earthly courts, as well as by all intellectuals, must appear all the more striking to the calm observer!

On closer consideration it can easily be found that the motive behind this complete antagonism and the desire to suppress originates in nothing but the pressure of utter helplessness in these matters.

Today, indeed, no man has any idea of the greatness, the purity, and yet the overwhelming simplicity and really quite easily understandable nature of the basic Laws in Creation, to which churches and mundane laws *must* adapt themselves if they wish to be right and just, and consequently pleasing to God. They can and may not do otherwise without causing harm both to themselves and to their fellow-men.

There is in fact for all creatures nothing other than these irrevocable Laws of God in Creation, from which they issued and to which they must also adapt themselves if they do not wish to be detrimental to Creation. Being a creature, man must also at last condescend to adjust himself accordingly, if he does not wish to perish through his carelessness, his presumption and, closely connected with these, his intellectual sophistry. For the intellect plays but a small part in the greatness of Creation and serves purely to make movement possible in the coarsest material. What is beyond its boundaries the intellect can never grasp, and it is thus unable to work therein, much less pass judgment upon it!

The entire knowledge which mankind on earth possess today, the knowledge of which they are so proud, moves *only* within the Realm of the Gross Material and goes no further! This proves how narrow and limited such knowledge is, for gross matter is the *lowest* of all the rings in Creation, the densest and the heaviest, and consequently also the most narrow and limited in its conceptions in this Subsequent Creation.

Your thoughts, too, are only of gross material nature, being the products of your brain. They belong to fine gross matter, which consequently also embraces all the thought-forms that can so often be seen by mediums. They imagine, however, that these lie in the Ethereal Realm or even in the Spiritual Realm. In one of my earlier lectures I have already mentioned thought-forms, and I also spoke about the centres formed by these, but not about the regions or the kinds to which they belong. Thoughts as well as thought-forms are still of a *gross material nature* even though they are part of *fine* gross matter. They are not *ethereal.* That which is ethereal has nothing to do with fine gross matter.

It is of an entirely different species, and the two cannot blend but must always stand side by side, because a different species is also subject to different law *forms.* It is true that the Laws of God are uniform in each species of Creation; they penetrate the entire Creation; but despite their individual uniformity the laws manifest in each species of Creation in a different form corresponding to that particular species. Therefore a person will never be able to examine or judge things of ethereal substance by means of his gross material implements, to which the brain with its intellect belongs; and just as little can he do so with things taking place in the Spiritual Realm as long as he lacks the connection thereto, which can only be attained through radiations.

The path of radiation out of gross material substance, however, is still closed to all those who have unconditionally submitted to the domination of the intellect, which is firmly bound to the World of Gross Matter and its conceptions. It is utterly impossible for these downright slaves of the intellect to send out radiations to other regions, because they themselves closed the borders and allowed everything that is necessary for sending out to perish within themselves.

Men are now only creeping along the ground, for their power to swing upward to the Heights fell away from them long ago, when they ceased to apply it or make use of it after giving their intellect the highest place, which bound them to the earth.

You thus had to become subject to the Law of Adaptation, which works automatically in the World of Matter. It is the same with you as with the animals whose wings, when never used, first gradually deteriorate and then cease to develop altogether; or with fish which, in the course of time, lose the air-bladder they use to raise and support them in the water, if they continually stay only at the bottom because of currents which are too strong for them.

Naturally this does not take effect quickly from one day to another, but only in the course of centuries and even thousands of years. But it does come about! And it *has* already taken effect with the human spirit!

Everything you do not use zealously in the right way must gradually become stunted and lost to you! Automatic adjustment is nothing but the consequence of the Law of *Movement* in Creation. This is only *one* of its many-sided effects. That which does not move in the right manner, and naturally also that which is not always *kept* in the necessary movement, *must* degenerate and be finally discarded altogether, also from every gross material form; for each form is shaped only in accordance with the kind of movement.

Do not protest that this is contradicted by knowledge of the sentence that the *spirit* forms the body! That only confirms it, and shows the immutability of this law, for every spiritual volition *is* movement, which in its continuing activity produces further movements.

Go out and seek in Nature! Observe Creation itself! You will find fish which cannot swim, because they had difficulty in holding themselves in turbulent waters and thus preferred to remain on the bottom. Their air-bladder degenerated and in the course of time they lost it entirely. There are also birds which cannot fly. Think of the penguins and ostriches and many others! Only *that* part and *that* ability is developed and maintained which is *used*, thus participating in the Law of necessary Movement.

You, however, have spent thousands of years for the purpose of clinging almost convulsively to the lowest and most narrowly limited Realm of Gross Matter, because it meant everything to you; you dug yourselves into it and now you are *no longer able* to look upwards! You have lost the ability to do so, you yourselves have broken the habit through the indolence of your spirit, which no longer wishes to move upwards and which with many today is no longer *able* to move!

Therefore it now becomes hard for you to grasp the *Word* from the Highest Heights, and it will be utterly impossible for many! He who wants to measure it with his *intellect* alone will never recognise its true value; for he will then have to drag the Word of God down to the low gross material comprehension. He who can do nothing but think within narrow limits will also belittle the Word in his own understanding, and thus not recognise it and will lightly put it aside, because he does not see *what* it really contains!

However, in his smallness he will be glad to talk about it and criticise it, perhaps even wish to bring it into contempt; for such people do precisely *that* which *proves* the narrow limitations of their pseudo-knowledge, which clearly points to their inability to dig deeper. You can daily experience the same everywhere, that it is just the really stupid persons who consider themselves especially clever and try to discuss everything, when the intelligent man keeps silent. Stupidity is always obtrusive!

Just observe all those who like to make themselves conspicuous with their talk about ethereal or even spiritual happenings! You will soon recognise that they really know nothing at all about it! Particularly those who often speak about karma! Just let such people give you an explanation of karma! You will shudder as you listen to their confused and muddled words!

And as for the person who does not talk, but modestly asks about it, you should first observe him more closely before you answer. Most of the inquirers only wish to find in karma an excuse for themselves and their weaknesses! *It is this* which they long for so eagerly – that through their belief in karma they may quietly continue with their weaknesses, sometimes even ill-breeding or impudence, with the self-excuse when they consequently meet with unpleasantness that it is their karma. With hypocritical mien they love to sigh: "It is my karma which I have to redeem!" They leave it at this sighing and become tyrants in their environment, destroying all harmony even if they could change and avoid many a thing by a little self-education and by showing a little consideration for their fellow-men!

They do not think of this and do not *want* to think of it – that they only burden themselves thereby with a karma which throws them back for centuries!

Prattle, nothing but empty prattle, is all such, emanating from vanity and the lack of genuine fresh volition! It is a pity for every single minute that a person sacrifices for such spiritually indolent ones. Let them carry on and take this to heart: A person with real knowledge will never indulge in idle talk!

He does *not* take his knowledge to be the *subject for conversation,* nor does he offer it for that purpose! He will answer a serious question only, and even then will hesitate until he knows the inquirer is driven by a really honest volition.

Men's talk in these matters is for the greater part but empty sound! For the comprehension of all earthmen has been unable to step beyond the boundary of gross material substance, due to the mistakes they made in Creation, which hold them down through the indolence of their spirit. They confuse the spirit with their earthly intellect, and thus create for themselves this low boundary.

In future, you earthmen of the present time, refrain from forming opinions about things which you cannot understand! *Too* heavy is the guilt with which you burden yourselves thereby! It is no less heavy than that which people in their stupid delusion once imposed upon themselves by plunging countless thousands into suffering and misery, even taking the earth-life of many through death by fire after days of torture. By the Law of the Lord it is the same whether you today accuse such persons of fraud or of practising gross deception only!

Exert yourselves at last to fulfil *your* duties towards your God and to *recognise the Laws of God* before wishing to judge! You have no right to expect forgiveness! You yourselves have forfeited the claim to that through your own law – that ignorance can protect no one from punishment! An eye for an eye and a tooth for a tooth, *that* is how it will now happen to *those* who do not wish it otherwise, and who do not obey the Law of the Lord!

THE RECOGNITION OF GOD

ALTHOUGH I have already explained that a human being can never really *see* God, because his nature is in no way endowed with the capacity to do so, yet he does carry within himself the gift to *recognise* God in His works.

This, however, does not come to him overnight, nor does it fall to him in his sleep, but it requires earnest efforts, a great and strong volition, which must not lack in purity.

You human beings have had the unquenched longing for the recognition of God bestowed upon you. It is so implanted within you that you cannot find any peace during your wanderings through Subsequent Creation, which you are permitted to undertake for the purpose of your development, so that in becoming self-conscious you learn gratefully to enjoy the blessings which the worlds hold for you and offer to you.

If during these wanderings you were to find rest within yourselves, then this rest would ultimately bring about stagnation, which holds exhaustion and decay for your spirit, and finally inevitable disintegration, because it does not thereby obey the Primordial Law of necessary Movement. The working of the self-acting laws in Creation, however, is like a conveyor belt which pulls the human spirit along without interruption. But all those who do not know how to keep their balance, however, will slip and thus stumble and fall.

Keeping the balance in this case is equivalent to keeping the harmony in Creation undisturbed by observing the Primordial Laws of Creation. He who wavers and falls, he who cannot keep himself upright therein, will be *dragged* along, because the machinery does not halt for his sake even for a single second. This being dragged along, however, causes injury. And to be able to stand upright again demands increased exertion, and still more effort is needed to find the necessary balance again. It is not so easy in an environment where there is continual movement. If he does not succeed in doing so man will be flung completely out of his course right into the middle of the machinery and be crushed.

Therefore be grateful, you men, that the longing for the recognition of God does not leave you in peace during your wanderings. In this way without realising it you escape all sorts of dangers in the machinery of the world. But you have not understood the longing which lies within you; this you have also distorted, making only a low kind of restlessness out of it.

This restlessness you again strive to calm or satisfy in the wrong way by some means or other. As you only use your intellect to do this you naturally reach out for earthly desires, hoping to satisfy this urge by accumulating earthly treasures, through the rush of work, by pleasurable diversions, in weakening comfort or, at its best, perhaps through a pure kind of earthly love for a woman.

All this, however, brings you no benefit, nor does it help you onwards. It may perhaps for a short period deaden the longing which you have perverted into disquietude, yet this distorted longing cannot be obliterated for ever, only repressed here and there. This unrecognised longing spurs on the human soul ever again, and unless earthman finally tries to grasp its meaning, it drives him through many earth-lives without achieving that maturity which will enable him to ascend, as is willed, to the lighter, more luminous and more beautiful fields of this Subsequent Creation.

The fault lies with man himself! He pays far too little attention, or even none whatever, to all the help given to him, suffering under the delusion of his desire to be sufficient unto himself. This arose through the snares of the intellect, with which he bound the wings of his spirit.

Now at last he has come to the *end* of his strength! He is exhausted through being driven by powers he has not yet recognised, the help of which he has stubbornly opposed in his obstinate attitude of childishly thinking he knew and could do everything better himself, which manifests itself as a result of the enforced and self-inflicted crippling of his brain.

And yet it would have been so easy for every man, had he but simply and modestly permitted all those gifts to mature within himself, which the Creator bestowed upon him for his wandering through all the planes of Subsequent Creation, gifts which are absolutely necessary for the development of the human spirit. He would have become great thereby, much greater and much wiser than he ever dreamed of being. But without humbleness and modesty these gifts can never blossom into abilities!

It is a childish plaything, this knowledge of which you are so inordinately proud! A speck of dust compared with what you could know, and above all with what you could *achieve* and what already today you *should* achieve! What do you earthmen know of this wonderful Creation, which manifests inviolably everywhere in its respective species and beauty, but above all in its laws? It is with dull indifference that you stand before all this greatness! Now at last, men, seek *the recognition of your God* in Creation, of which you are the smallest part of that species which is allowed to develop to self-consciousness through the Grace of the Creator, in fulfilment of the longing that lies within it!

Do not merely seek to satisfy your vanity in this matter, as you have hitherto done through being the slave of your intellect! You have come to an end of this! You and your imagined abilities are about to collapse! And you are very far from real ability!

The results of your actions will now prove what little bunglers you have been! In obedience to the Divine Laws in Creation these results will now return like heavy waves to their originators, either greatly uplifting them or burying them beneath with all their works. It will then become quite definitely evident as to what was right and what was wrong. That which in recent times you could have already seen clearly enough if you had only *wished* to do so – the failure everywhere of all efforts to avert the decline which has already set in – should have been a warning to you to turn back while there was yet time! And at last to think about examining *yourselves!*

But men neither hear nor see; despair drives them ever more frantically to the belief that help can come through their own abilities!

But I say unto you: He who does not stand and work in the Laws of God will no longer receive help from the Light. The condition is the knowledge of God's Laws in Creation! And without help from the Light the *real* upbuilding is utterly impossible *today!*

The belief of a man in his own mission and the belief of those who follow him are of no avail to any human being. Everything will break down with him at that point where the effect of the Divine Laws in Creation touches him.

And *every* person is now confronted with these effects in accordance with the Holy Law of God. Therein lies the Judgment which all the believers dread!

The believers! All you who count yourselves among the believers in God, just examine yourselves to ascertain whether the belief you carry within yourselves is really the *right one!* By that I do not mean *the form* your belief takes, whether Catholic or Protestant, Buddhist or Mohammedan, or any other form, but *I mean the nature* of your belief, to what extent it is *living!*

For God is God! And *how* you approach Him *in your inmost self, that* alone is decisive for the strength and genuineness of your belief!

Examine yourselves carefully *as to that* for once! I will show you how you can find the way in order to obtain support for this.

Just go with me in spirit to Africa to any negro tribe! Think of such people's power of comprehension! Make an effort clearly to envisage their inner life and way of thinking!

These people believed in demons and all sorts of things! They possessed idols of roughly carved wood, and then Christian missionaries visited them. They told and taught them about that great invisible God of their religion.

Picture this to yourselves, and then ask what, after being baptised, the intuitive perceptions of these natural men will be like when they pray to the Christian God Who is so new to them. Not much different to when they formerly prayed to their idols of carved wood! Most of them simply replace their former idols with the new God. That is the only difference! In doing so they have not changed their intuitive perceptions, but in the most favourable instances they adhere solely to the *doctrine*. Real *experiencing,* however, is lacking. With these ignorant men it cannot possibly be otherwise!

Accepting the doctrine itself does not make them *knowing,* for their acceptance of the belief rests solely upon a pretended knowledge of what others passed on to them. The profitable inner experiencing, and thus the true support, are lacking! It is always and everywhere the same! The missionaries and converters throw themselves upon the people and want to convert them to Christianity *without* any further transition!

The same thing takes place today with the instruction of children, and yet children are no different inwardly to the heathens, for baptism has not made them any more knowing.

But if man does not follow in sequence the steps which are designed in Creation, and which Creation offers him in the automatic Primordial Laws, since it is composed of those steps, he can never attain to the true recognition of God. Even *good* teachings will be of no avail to him, but only entangle his paths.

All missionary work has so far suffered from this. It simply *cannot* achieve a result which is really living because it does not proceed in accordance with the Laws of Creation. The Law of Development in this Creation does not tolerate any jumps when genuine maturity is to be attained. And man will never be able to lift himself out of and above this Creation to which he belongs, with which he is closely connected by innumerable threads, and of which he shall now form the most precious of fruits.

But if he really desires to become the fruit which this Creation is capable of producing in the pure power of the Lord, then there must not be any interruption in the process of his maturing. It is the same as with animistic activity in regard to the fruit of the tree. Wherever there is an interruption or some other interference in the development towards ripeness, be it through an early frost, too violent a storm, or the harmful arbitrary action of man, the fruit can never grow to full ripeness and thus cannot attain real perfection.

It is no different with earthman, who is a fruit of *spiritual* activity!

Nothing must be missing in the course of his development, not a single step, because a gap or gulf would then remain which does not permit of a continuous live upbuilding, and thus of a further ascent towards the Heights; it makes it utterly impossible. Where *but one* step is missing or faulty a collapse *is bound* to come, and a headlong fall. He can twist or turn as he likes, but man *must* submit to this! Least of all could the cunning and subtle sham wisdom of his intellect erect a substitute bridge to help him onwards!

And man himself has undertaken a harmful interference by the *one-sided* cultivation of his earthly intellect, which now fetters him with a firm grip, as if with steel clamps, to the World of Gross Matter only, from which the intellect originates.

Through this the gap arose which an acquired faith in what is highly spiritual and Divine cannot bridge.

Thus the human fruit of Subsequent Creation must wither on its way to maturity through its own guilt!

That is why even today many a man, after he leaves school to enter upon life, experiences how he entirely loses the faith acquired in his childhood, although struggling bravely to retain it. Sooner or later, if he is an earnest seeker for the Truth, he has to build up entirely anew from the very beginning.

Being rushed along with the enthusiasm of the masses is of no use whatever to the individual. It never offers him that firm ground which he needs for his ascent, nor is he able thereby to find the necessary hold *within himself* – *that* support which alone permits him always to stand firm!

Thus at present all the instruction for growing children in matters of faith is not yet right. *Therefore* everywhere *that* faith which leads to the *true recognition* of God, and which alone grants real happiness and also peace, is missing!

The instruction given today is wrong and without life. The support the individual believes he possesses is imaginary. It is only a formal faith to which everybody clings. The peace and security with which they try to lull themselves are a pretence, often adopted only to prevent giving outward offence, sometimes in order to enjoy earthly advantage, or anyhow to be held in esteem. It is never genuine, and it *cannot* be so, because the foundations in accordance with the Laws of Creation are still lacking. And without these it is simply impossible!

Let us go back into the past, and consider the former conversions in the German lands! The thinking person who does not allow himself to be carried along with the average indolent masses must also recognise here how empty – and for the inner being *useless* – were the forms created at that time, which could not bring about any recognition of God!

Within every nation, indeed within every individual, as also within the people of the present time, there must *first of all* exist the *foundation for the acceptance* of the high recognitions of God which is contained in the teachings of Christ. Only out of such a mature foundation may and must the human spirit then be led into all the possibilities of a recognition of God through the teachings of Christ.

So it is and so it will remain for all eternity!

Could it be otherwise, then God would have permitted an *earlier* revelation of Himself among the peoples on earth. He did not do so!

Not until a nation had advanced so far in its development that it knew about the activity of all that is animistic could it learn about the spiritual, the Primordial Spiritual, the Divine, and finally also about God.

But always and only in such a manner that it was led intelligently upwards into a *higher* understanding by prophets called for the purpose, who never overthrew the old in doing so. *They built up!* Just as Jesus Christ Himself did, and often emphasised in His Word, which is something you hitherto *did not wish to understand!*

With their conversions, however, the Christian churches want to destroy much that is old and declare it to be wrong, or at least to get rid of it by disregarding it, instead of carefully continuing to build up on the old, and in so doing to pay due regard to the necessary bridging over. They expect and demand that the human spirit should jump immediately into this most exalted Christian teaching!

Thus the Laws of God are not observed in these matters, although the intention is often good!

The Germanic peoples were also closely connected with the elemental (animistic) beings at that time. Many of them were able to see and experience them, so that no doubts could remain with them about their actual existence, and just as little about their activity. They *saw* this and therefore *knew* about it!

It was the purest conviction for them and therefore sacred!

And with brutal fist Boniface attacked their existing shrine! He wanted to deny the Teutons the truth of such knowledge and declare it to be false. In its place he wanted to force upon them the forms of his Christian teaching. From the very beginning such an ignorant way must have made the Teutons doubt the truth of what *he* proclaimed to them, must have robbed them of all trust!

He should have confirmed the truth of their knowledge and then led them onwards with explanations to higher recognitions. But he himself lacked the knowledge of Creation. He revealed his ignorance about the weaving in Creation only too clearly by calling Wotan (Odin) and the other elemental (animistic) beings, whom the Teutons considered as active gods, an erroneous faith and non-existent. Although they are not gods yet they do exist through the power of God and work in Creation.

Without the working of the elemental beings the spiritual could not possibly become anchored in the World of Matter and thus could not accomplish anything therein. The spiritual, from which the human spirit originates, thus needs the co-operation of that which is animistic in the World of Matter to further its own development.

Religious zeal can never replace knowledge in these matters!

However, the mistake made by Boniface and all those who wished to convert is still kept alive today.

The Greek *myths* are spoken about and taught. They were no myths, however, but real *knowledge,* which the men of today lack. Unfortunately the churches also do not know the working of the Holy Will of God in Creation, which still remains the home of all human spirits. They blindly overlook past happenings and are therefore unable to lead anyone to the *true* and living recognition of God. With the best volition they cannot achieve it!

It is only through the Laws of Creation themselves, which God has given, that the human spirit can come to the recognition of God. And this recognition is absolutely necessary for its ascent. Only through this does it receive *that* support which permits it to journey steadfastly along the path prescribed and useful for it towards perfection! Not otherwise!

He who wants to jump over the activity of the elemental beings, about which the peoples of olden times had an exact knowledge, can never come to the true recognition of God. This exact knowledge is an unavoidable step towards recognition, because the human spirit has to struggle from below upwards. Unless it first possesses as a foundation an exact knowledge of the lower steps in Creation to which it belongs, the human spirit can never learn to obtain a faint conception of the Primordial Spiritual and the Divine Spheres, which are above his ability to comprehend. This is an unavoidable necessity as a preparation for the possibility of higher recognition.

As I have already stated the knowledge of God was always first given to those peoples who stood in the knowledge of the activity of the elemental beings, and never otherwise! For the possibility to comprehend is never provided before this is achieved. In these matters the entire human race was carefully led by the Light.

A man who in purity stands and lives only in the knowledge of the Animistic Realm is to be valued more highly in Creation than one who merely stands in an acquired Christian faith and smiles about that which is animistic, considering it as fairy tales or myths; the latter is thus ignorant about it and thereby never obtains a true support, while the former still possesses the full possibilities for ascent in a strong, undimmed longing for it, which has not been undermined.

With a good volition he can animatedly grow within a few days into the spiritual recognitions and the spiritual experiencing, because he did not lose the firm ground beneath him.

In all missionary work and school teaching in future, therefore, the knowledge of God should be brought by way of the knowledge of the animistic forces that have taken on form and their activities, for only out of this can there develop the higher recognition of the spiritual and of the Primordial Spiritual, and finally also of the Divine and of God. The *entire* knowledge of the Creation is necessary in order finally to arrive at a faint idea of the greatness of God and thus in the end also at the true recognition of God. There cannot be anything vital in the Christian faith of *today* because it lacks all this! What is necessary for it is always left out, and the gulf can only be bridged by that which was given by God for the purpose in this Subsequent Creation, not by anything else!

Nobody, however, has learned from a calm observation of the past entire development of mankind here on earth what is *most important:* That all the stages through which men had to live *were necessary* and therefore may not be avoided or jumped over today either! The entire Creation gives you the clear picture and all the basic requirements to carry this out.

Therefore listen to what I say to you: Until it has achieved maturity the child of today is directly and closely connected only with the Animistic World. During this time it must become thoroughly acquainted with the animistic through experiencing. Only when maturity sets in does it proceed to the point of spiritual connection, building up and ascending as it develops. In so doing, however, it must firmly and consciously set its foot upon the animistic as the foundation, and must not sever the connection as mankind does today by never calling it to life within the children, but on the contrary suppressing it forcibly in their irresponsible conceit. For ascent, however, both want to and need to be connected knowingly.

The man of today shall be so far ripened as a fruit of Creation that he bears within himself the *accumulated* and *complete* result of the past development of mankind.

Therefore what *childhood* alone represents to each individual today was formerly (being a total development) a great epoch of mankind within the entire development of Creation.

Pay close attention to what I am saying therewith!

The first development covering *millions of years is now,* for men at *today's* stage of development in Creation, compressed into the *years of childhood.*

He who is incapable of keeping pace with this must put it down to his own guilt; he remains behind and must finally perish. The development of Creation cannot be retarded by the indolence of men, but strides forward unceasingly in accordance with the laws inherent therein, which bear the Will of God.

Formerly Creation was at such a stage of development that for many earth-lives men had to remain inwardly as children are today. They were directly connected with animistic activity only, slowly developing through experiencing, which alone grows into knowledge and recognition.

For a long time already, however, Creation has through continual advancing arrived at that point where the first stages of development of the human fruit here on earth, which covered millions of years, are now crowded into the period of their childhood. The former epoch of mankind must and can now be hastened through inwardly during these few earth years, because the experiences of former lives now slumber in readily available form within the spirit.

However, they must be awakened and thereby come to consciousness; for they must not remain slumbering or even be pushed away, as happens today. Everything *must* come to life and be kept alive through the work of "knowing" educators and teachers, so that the child receives the firm foundation and support in the animistic world which it needs for the recognition of God in the spiritual world. One step only grows out of the other when the latter is completed, and not before. Nor must the previous one be taken away if the stairway is to remain intact and not to collapse.

Only as the child matures physically does the break-through occur which establishes connection with the spiritual. But this impulse can *only* have vital consequences when it is based on a knowledge of the animistic. Neither fairy tales nor legends are of any avail here, but solely the experiencing which must be achieved and completed by the beginning of maturity. It must also *remain* entirely alive in order to permit the spiritual to come consciously to life. That is an irrevocable stipulation of Creation, which you should all have learned by observation of the past!

You need it now or you cannot proceed. Without the clear knowledge of the animistic activity there is never a spiritual recognition. Without the clear knowledge of the spiritual and its activity the recognition of God cannot arise! Everything which stands outside this lawfulness is presumptuous conceit and imagination, also very often quite a deliberate lie!

Question your fellow-man about the irrevocable Laws of God in Creation!

If he cannot give you the right answer he is nothing but a hypocrite, who deceives himself when he talks of the recognition of God and of the *right* faith in God!

For in accordance with the unswerving Laws of God he *cannot* possess it, because in no other way can he ever attain it.

Everything in Creation strides forward uniformly without interruption in accordance with an immovable law! It is only you human beings who still do not go along owing to your delusion, your ridiculous conceited knowledge, which is lacking in humble observation!

The children and grown-ups of the present time walk as if on stilts in the re-cognition of God! Truly they struggle for it, but they float in the air with it, having no living connection with the ground as is absolutely necessary for their support. Between their volition and the foundation which is needed for the upbuilding there is dead wood, without any ability for intuitive percep-tion, just as with the stilts.

The dead wood of the stilts is the *taught* faith, which is entirely devoid of mobility and vitality. Man certainly has the volition but no firm basis and no proper support, both of which lie only in the knowledge of the past develop-ment of Creation, to which the human spirit always belongs inseparably. Therefore it is and always remains closely connected with this Creation, and can never go beyond it.

Men, awake! Retrieve what you have been neglecting! Once more I will show you your way! At last bring life and movement into your rigid volition, and then you will find the great recognition of God which you should already have possessed a long time ago, if you had not remained behind in the pro-gressive development of the great Creations!

Remember that you must not eliminate anything of that which the entire humanity was already compelled to experience here upon earth; for it always experienced what was necessary for it. And when mankind went wrong through its own volition destruction ensued. Creation hurries onward un-swervingly and casts off all rotten fruit!

THE NAME

It is a pity that men pass by even serious matters with indifference, and that owing to their spiritual indolence they only recognise everything when they *must* recognise it. The root cause of this fateful indolence is to be found in the effects of mankind's hitherto wanton misuse of their *free volition*.

All men stand in the Law as does every creature; they are enveloped and penetrated by the Law, and in the Law and through the Law they have also come into existence. They live in it, and with their free volition they themselves weave their own fate, choose their own ways.

When incarnated here upon earth these self-chosen paths also lead them unfailingly to those parents whom they absolutely need for their childhood. Thus they also enter into *those* circumstances which are useful to them, because they receive just *that* which has ripened for them as the fruit of the threads of their own volition.

In the resulting experiences they also continue to mature, for if their previous volition was evil then the fruits they will have to taste will be exactly in accordance therewith. This happening with its inescapable final consequences is at the same time the continuous fulfilment of wishes once cherished, which always lie hidden in every volition, and which indeed form the central motive of every volition. Except that such fruits often do not appear till the next earth-life, yet they never fail to appear!

In addition these consequences simultaneously hold the *redemption* for everything which man has formed up till then, be it good or evil. As soon as he learns the lessons from these experiences and thereby comes to recognise how he is, then it is also definitely possible for him to ascend at any moment, as well as out of *any* set of circumstances; for no burden is *so* weighty that it could not be changed by an earnest volition for what is good.

Thus it operates in constant and uninterrupted movement throughout the entire Creation, and the human being also, along with every other creature, keeps on weaving his fate, his particular kind of path in the threads of the

Law. Every stirring of his spirit, every wavering of his soul, every action of his body, and every word he utters automatically and unconsciously ties ever new threads to the existing ones, *attaching* them, *connecting* one with the other, and *interweaving* them. The human being forms and forms, and *even thereby forms in advance the earth-name which he must bear in his next life on earth*, and which he *will* inevitably bear because the threads of his own weaving surely and unswervingly lead him to it.

Thus every earth-name also stands in the Law. It is never accidental and never without the bearer himself having provided the basis for it beforehand, because in the process of incarnating every soul runs irresistibly along the threads of its *own* weaving, as if on rails, to the place where it exactly belongs in accordance with the Primordial Law of Creation.

As this happens the threads finally become ever more taut in the increasing material condensation at those points where the radiations of coarse ethereal matter are in close contact with the radiations of fine gross matter, and join hands for a firm *union, as if magnetised,* for the period of a new life on earth.

The particular earth-life then lasts until the original strength of these radiations of the soul changes on account of various redeeming experiences during life on earth. Therewith this magnetic power of attraction is also directed more upwards than downwards to the gross material; whereby in turn the separation of the ethereal matter of the soul from the gross material body finally takes effect in accordance with the Law, because a real fusion has never taken place, but merely a *union,* which was held together magnetically through a very definite strength arising from the degree of heat of their mutual radiation.

Thus it also happens that the soul must separate from a body which has been forcibly destroyed, ruined by disease, or weakened by old age at the very moment when *this body,* owing to its changed condition, can no longer produce *that* strength of radiation which brings about such a magnetic power of attraction as is necessary to play its part in the firm union between soul and body.

This results in earthly death, or the falling back or falling off of the gross material body from the ethereal cloak of the spirit, thus separation. This is a process in accordance with firmly established laws and takes place between two species, which only unite at a precisely corresponding degree of heat through the radiation thus produced. But they can never merge into each other, and they fall apart again when one of the two different species can no longer fulfil the condition ordained.

Even when the gross material body is asleep its firm union with the soul is loosened, because during sleep the body produces a different radiation which does not bind as solidly as the one required for the firm union. However, since the union still exists only a *loosening* takes place, but no separation. This loosening is immediately eliminated at each awakening.

But if a person inclines only towards gross material things, for example, as with those who so proudly call themselves realists or materialists, then hand in hand with this goes the fact that through this desire their soul produces a specially strong radiation directed towards the World of Gross Matter. This process involves a very hard physical death because the soul tries to cling one-sidedly to the gross material body, and thus a condition arises which is called a heavy death-struggle. The kind of radiation is therefore decisive for much, indeed for everything in Creation. It provides an explanation for every process!

How a soul comes just to the gross material body ordained for it I have already explained in my lecture about the mystery of birth. The threads linking it with the prospective parents have been knotted through their mutual homogeneity, which at first had an attracting influence that increased more and more, until at a certain maturity of the growing body the threads joined and knotted themselves to this body, thus forcing a soul to incarnate.

And the parents also bear *that* name which they acquired through the way in which they wove the threads for themselves. For this reason the same name must be suitable for the approaching homogeneous soul which has to incarnate. In spite of the apparent reflection given to the matter even the first names of the new earthman are always and only given in such a way as will correspond to *the homogeneous species,* because the thinking and reflecting always and only conform to that particular species. The *species* can always be accurately recognised in the thinking, and therefore in spite of their thousandfold variations *those* species to which particular thought-forms belong can be clearly and sharply distinguished. I have already spoken about this in my explanations about thought-forms.

The *species* is fundamental for everything. Consequently even with the greatest pondering about the names to be given to an infant at its christening they will always be so chosen as to correspond with the Law to which the spe-

736

cies is subject or which it merits, for man cannot act any differently because he stands in the Laws, which affect him according to his species.

Notwithstanding all this the free will is never excluded, since each *species* of man is in reality only a fruit of the personal and actual volition which he carries within himself.

It is nothing but an utterly detestable excuse if he seeks to deceive himself that under the compulsion of the Laws of Creation he has no freedom of his will. Whatever he is forced to experience for himself under the compulsion of these Laws are fruits of his *personal* volition, which has preceded these fruits and woven the threads leading to them, allowing them to ripen correspondingly.

Thus every person on earth bears precisely *that* name which he earned for himself. Therefore his name is not only what it is, he is not only called by this name, but he *is* this name. Man *is* what his name says!

There is no chance about the matter! In some way the prescribed combination is *achieved;* for man cannot tear apart these threads until they are *lived* off by the human spirits concerned with them and to which they cling.

That is a knowledge which mankind of today does not yet possess, and which they will therefore very probably smile about as they do with everything they cannot comprehend. But neither does this mankind know the Divine Laws which have been hewn firmly into Creation from its primordial beginning, the Laws to which Creation owes its very existence, which also affect man every single second, which are likewise his helpers and judges in everything he does and thinks, and without which he would be absolutely unable to draw a single breath! And all this he does not know!

Neither is it astonishing, therefore, that he does not want to recognise many things as the immutable consequences of these Laws, but tries to mock and laugh at them. However, just in those things which man *should* and *must* definitely know he is utterly inexperienced or, to put it bluntly, he is more stupid than any other creature in this Creation whose whole life simply swings therein! And just through this *stupidity* he laughs about everything he cannot understand! His mockery and ridicule are the direct proof and admission of his ignorance, of which he will soon be ashamed when it causes him to be overcome with despair.

Only despair can still achieve the destruction of the hard casing which now envelops men and keeps them so much imprisoned!

SUBSTANTIALITY

In my Message I have often spoken of Animistic Substantiality in Creation. I spoke of its nature and its working, also of its significance for the human spirit, whose paths in Creation it smoothes as he develops towards perfection.

All this you already know!

In spite of this I now consider it necessary to speak once more in greater detail of all Substantiality, so that man is given the opportunity to absorb within himself the entire picture of this activity. –

"Substantiality" is an expression which I myself gave to you, because it best expresses *that* which can provide you with a definite form for your conceptions about the working and also the nature of this component part of Creation, which is so important for every activity that is brought into existence.

"Substantiality"! Let us also call it for once that which is "essential" for *Creation* or, better still, that which "visibly manifests" in Creation; then perhaps what I actually want to say by the expression "Substantiality" will become even more comprehensible to you.

We can also use other conceptions from the vocabulary of your language (German) in order to fashion it even better. The expression appertaining here is "that which unites and combines" or, in short, "that which binds" and is thereby itself "bound".

After all these transitory expressions I can now also safely say "that which shapes forms", without you thereby thinking that Substantiality would create forms out of its *own* volition; for this would be wrong, because Substantiality is only able to create forms when behind it stands the Will of God, the living Primordial Law of Creation, setting it in motion.

We may just as well call Substantiality the executive and preservative motivating power in the creating of forms! Perhaps this is the easiest way to provide your mental capacity with the approximately *correct* conception.

That which is substantiate, i. e., that which manifests visibly in a form and which can therefore also be reproduced in a picture, comprises *everything* but God. God alone is Unsubstantiate, so called in order to differentiate from the conception of substantiate.

Therefore everything existing outside the Unsubstantiality of God is substantiate and formed!

Take this as a basic conception for your understanding!

Thus everything is substantiate but God. And since nothing but the radiation of God exists outside God it follows that Substantiality is the natural and inevitable radiation of God.

Thus Substantiality is much more comprehensive and higher than you thought it to be. It comprises *everything* outside of God, but it is divided into many gradations depending on the degree of cooling off and the consequent distance from God.

If you understand the Message *aright* you will know that I have already spoken of Divine Substantiality, which exists in the Divine Sphere, also of Spiritual Substantiality, which in turn is divided into Primordial Spiritual Substantiality and Spiritual Substantiality. Thereafter I mentioned the gradation of that Substantiality which is only Animistic, which is followed further downwards by the World of Ethereal Matter and finally by the World of Gross Matter, with all their various transitional planes.

Since *everything* is substantiate, however, outside of God Himself, I simply called the various species Divine, Primordial Spiritual, Spiritual and Animistic, as well as Ethereal Matter and Gross Matter, these being the various gradations downwards.

In the great basic structure, however, there are only two – that which is Unsubstantiate and that which is substantiate. God is Unsubstantiate, while His Radiation must be called substantiate. There is nothing else; for everything which is outside of God issues and develops solely from the Radiation of God.

Although if you study it *aright* this follows quite clearly from the Message already, yet many hearers and readers at present still think of the substantiate as being only the sphere of Creation between the Spiritual Sphere and the Ethereal World, the region from which the elementals originate, such as the elves, nixies, gnomes and salamanders; and also the soul of animals, which do not bear anything spiritual within them.*

* We have hitherto described this sphere as "The Realm of Animistic Substantiality", "the Animistic Sphere", or "the World of Animism".

Actually the thought was not wrong up till now, because this region between the Spiritual Sphere and the Ethereal World is the simple Substantiality which is only Animistic, from which the Divine, the Primordial Spiritual and the Spiritual have already separated. It is the heaviest of the layers still mobile within itself, from which in the process of further cooling off the World of Matter detaches itself and sinks. In the first stage of this cooling off process there remains the ponderous World of Ethereal Matter, from which in addition the mass of the Gross Material World severs itself, which is without inherent mobility.

But even within these two planes of matter, the species of which are alien to each other, there are still many special gradations. Thus the earth, for instance, is not the most ponderous of them. There are within the World of Gross Matter further gradations which are far heavier and denser, and where consequently the conceptions of space and time become much narrower still, quite different from what they are here on earth; and where the resultant mobility is even slower and the possibility of development consequently also more cumbersome.

The conceptions of space and time in each gradation are formed according to the capacity for movement, for not only do the stars journey more slowly in the greater density and heaviness, but the bodies of flesh are also plumper and firmer, and the brains therefore less mobile too. In short, everything is different due to the resulting entirely different character and effect of the mutual radiations, which are the impulse towards movement and also at the same time, after having been transformed, the consequences of this movement.

It is just because everything is subject to *one* Law in Creation that the forms and conceptions must always manifest differently in the various gradations, depending on the nature of the mobility. This in turn is related to the particular cooling off and the resultant density.

But I am again straying too far from the subject with this, for today I want first of all to enlarge the conception about Substantiality a little more.

In doing so I refer to an illustration which I gave once before, and say briefly:

That which is Unsubstantiate is God. That which is substantiate is the mantle of God. There is nothing else whatever! And this mantle of God must be kept pure by those who weave it or who may shelter in its folds, which also include the human spirits.

Since everything outside of God is substantiate, Substantiality therefore extends right into the Divine Sphere; indeed this Sphere itself must be called substantiate.

In order to prevent any errors from creeping in we must now make a finer distinction. It is best if we separate the conception *"the substantiate"* and the conception *"the animistic (elemental) beings"*.*

"The substantiate" comprises everything outside of God because it is the opposite of the Unsubstantiate. But the substantiate also bears within itself the Divine, the Primordial Spiritual, and the Spiritual with all its special gradations, which I have not yet explained because at present this would be beyond your capacity to understand. It is necessary that the exact *foundations* should first be unshakably established in the consciousness of the human spirit, from which we can always and only gradually undertake the extensions by small steps, until the comprehension possible to the human spirit has become sufficiently embracing.

Thus in future when we speak of Substantiality *as such* this means the Substantiality which comprises everything but God. Only in the course of further lectures will you recognise how great this is; for there are not only the already known gradations leading downwards but also various important related species *side by side,* through the activity of which Creation develops.

If, however, we speak (in German) of *the* elemental beings in the plural, then this refers to *those* elementals which you have hitherto thought about as comprising the Substantiality which is only Animistic.

This includes all those beings which deal with *that* which men in a very superficial way call *Nature,* which include the seas, the mountains, the rivers, the forests, the meadows and the countryside, as well as the soil, the rocks and the plants, while the soul of the animal is again something different, although it also comes from this Sphere of Substantiality which is only Animistic.

All this is quite correctly designated by the expression: "Beings". Elves, nixies, gnomes and salamanders are thus beings, whose activities lie *solely in the World of Matter.* It is *therein* that we now find the real possibility to classify them.

---

* The author called these terms in the German language "Das Wesenhafte" and "Die Wesenhaften", hence his emphasis on the need to distinguish carefully between these closely similar expressions.

But there are also beings active in the Spiritual Sphere, others working in the Primordial Spiritual Sphere, and still others busy even in the Divine Sphere.

This recognition must completely undermine the conception you have hitherto held, based on your assumption that the spiritual stands above the elemental beings. But this is true only for a very definite species of elementals, for those which are active solely in the World of Matter, such as the already-mentioned elves, nixies, gnomes and salamanders, and also for the souls of animals. But not for others!

You surely cannot imagine that a being active in the Primordial Spiritual Sphere and even in the Divine Sphere should stand *under* you human spirits!

To further an understanding of this matter I must first give a more precise explanation as to the difference between spirit and being; for only thus can I give you a key to the right conception.

In Creation there is actually no difference in *value* between the creature "spirit" and the creature "being". The only difference lies in the difference of species and the consequent necessity for a difference in their activities. The spirit, which also belongs to the great Substantiality, is permitted to follow roads of its own choosing and work correspondingly in Creation. The being, however, stands directly in the pressure of the Will of God, and therefore it has no possibility to make personal decisions or, as man expresses it, it does not possess its own free will.

The elemental beings are the builders and administrators of the House of God, i.e., of Creation. The spirits are the guests therein.

At present, however, all the beings stand *higher* in Subsequent Creation than the human spirits, because the human spirits did not place themselves voluntarily under the Will of God, which the *normal* course of development would have automatically assured. Instead they turned their will in a different direction, pushing it in between and thus disturbing all harmony and upbuilding, and going other ways than those willed by God.

Thus the only standard of value for a creature in Creation is *the quality of the activity* in which it is engaged.

The smaller beings working in the World of Matter, however, suffered greatly through this disturbing work of the human spirits with their wrong volition. But now they eagerly draw from the Living Source of Power which came to earth with the Will of God, and all the harm caused by the human spirits now rolls back upon its originators.

But more of this later! Today it is a question of forming the conception as a basis for a further understanding.

The Archangels in the Divine Sphere are beings, because under the immeasurably great pressure of the proximity of God no other volition but that which swings pure and undistorted in the Will of God would be at all possible.

Only at a distance so vast that it is beyond your power to grasp, at the extreme boundary of the Divine Sphere, there where the Grail Castle is anchored in the Divine as a counter-pole, only there for the first time can an ego-consciousness manifest itself in the Eternal Ones or, as they are also sometimes called, the Elders, who at the same time are the Divine Guardians of the Holy Grail. It is only their remoteness from the proximity of God which made this possible.

And only further downwards therefrom, at an ever greater distance from the proximity of God, could there also develop the smaller ego-conscious ones. Unfortunately, however, they also lost their real support thereby and finally strayed away from the swinging of the pure Will of God.

Likewise it was only due to the ever-increasing distance that Lucifer was able long ago to change, and through his wilfulness to cut himself off from the connection, thereby automatically opening up chasms which in time became unbridgeable, so that he himself became darker and heavier and sank ever deeper. Thus in the process of densification and cooling off he became a spirit possessing free volition, and with the great capacities bestowed upon him by his origin he finally stood under the World of Matter as the *strongest spirit*.

His wrong volition then brought the evil upon everything spiritual in the World of Matter, which at first felt attracted by him and then *voluntarily* succumbed to his enticements. Of their own free will because, in accordance with the Law in Creation, the human spirits *themselves* had to make the decision leading to their fall! Without their own decision to do so it would have become impossible for them to sink and now consequently to fall.

However, this also is but the logical fulfilment of the Perfect Law! –

Thus spirits with a volition of their own cannot possibly exist in the immediate proximity of God. This is a lawful condition of the Almighty Power of the Living Light! –

Where there are archangels there must also be other angels, as the word implies. There are very many of them in the Divine Sphere, also in the Primordial Spiritual and Spiritual Spheres, but they are all *beings*.

The beings which are called angels *swing* in the Will of God and are His messengers. They carry out the Will of God and spread it abroad.

Besides the angels, however, there are also innumerable beings, all linked together like small wheels in a great machine, and yet apparently working independently and faithfully in the building up and maintenance of the entire Creation, because they are firmly anchored in the Law. And above all these stand individual leaders equipped with a power incomprehensible to man; and again above these there are still higher and more powerful leaders, always of a species alien to the one below.

And so it goes on and on right up into the Divine Sphere. It is like a great chain, the links of which penetrate the whole of Creation without a break, their joyful activity like the verses of a hymn of praise resounding to the honour and glory of their Lord.

Remember that what you see around you here is but a coarse image of everything which lies higher, which takes on ever more glorious, more noble and lighter forms the nearer it is permitted to be to the Circle of the Divine. In all these circles, however, the *beings* always work exactly in accordance with the Will of God that rests in the Laws!

All beings stand in the service of God, which spirits themselves must first acknowledge voluntarily if they wish to work beneficially in Creation. If spirits follow the path which is exactly designed for them, and which they can easily recognise if they only wish to do so, then a way of happiness and joy is assured for them; for they will then swing together *with* the beings which help to smooth their paths.

But the spirits must compel themselves to take any wrong path by a very special decision. They only bring about failure, however, and create suffering for themselves therewith, and ultimately their fall and the necessity to expel them from Creation into the funnel of disintegration, as being useless for the God-willed and lawfully conditioned development of everything that has so far come into existence.

The developed spiritual alone has evolved in the wrong direction and to the disturbance of harmony. After the Judgment it is now once more granted a period in which to change through the God-willed Millennium. If it does not by then become absolutely firm in its striving for the good, the developed human-spiritual must again be drawn back to that border where it *cannot* develop itself to become self-conscious, so that at last peace and joy will prevail for all creatures in the Realms of God.

Thus you, man, are the only one who has a *disturbing* effect in the desired beauty of this Creation when it is now to be uplifted for its necessary change to the state of a gross material Paradise. Make haste! For only in the *knowledge* can you still swing yourselves up, you men! You will receive the strength to do so as soon as you open your souls for it!

THE LITTLE ELEMENTAL BEINGS

I CONTINUE with my explanations about Substantiality and its function in Creation. To do so it is necessary that I first give you a small glimpse into the *nearer* surroundings of earthman, which is easier for the earthly understanding, before I bring to life before your gaze the vast picture of all the happenings, beginning from above and continuing downwards.

Let us therefore first consider *those* elemental beings which are concerned with the Gross Material World. These consist of many special groups formed through the nature of their activities. There are, for example, groups which work entirely independent of the human spirits and which, being led only from above, busy themselves with the continuous development of new celestial bodies. They further their maintenance as well as their course, and likewise their disintegration wherever this becomes necessary due to their over-ripeness, in order that they may come into existence again in a new form in accordance with the Primordial Laws of Creation, and so on. But those are not the *particular* groups with which we want to deal today!

Rather it is the *little beings* we want to consider! You have often heard of the elves, the nixies, the gnomes and the salamanders, which are occupied with the gross matter of the earth here which is visible to you, also similarly on all the other gross material globes. They are the densest of all and can therefore also be most easily seen by you.

You *know* about them, but you are not yet acquainted with their actual work. At least you imagine you already know *what* they occupy themselves with; but you are absolutely ignorant as to the manner in which they perform their task, and how their activity is always carried out strictly in accordance with the Laws of Creation.

Generally speaking, everything that you already call knowledge is not yet real and authoritative recognition, but merely an uncertain groping: indeed a great shout goes up when here and there something is found through this groping, i. e., when these desultory and, in comparison with Creation, trifling attempts to clutch at something happen to reveal a little speck of dust, the existence of which is often a surprise.

However, today I still do not want to unveil this for you either, but I first want to tell you of *that* which is closely connected *with you personally*, which is linked up with your thoughts and actions, so that you will gradually achieve the capacity of careful observation at least in *such* matters.

These groups about which I speak to you today also belong to the *little* elementals. But you must not forget that every tiniest one of them is immensely *important* and more reliable in its activity than a human spirit.

They carry out the work assigned to them with an accuracy so great that you cannot even imagine it, because even the apparently most insignificant of the elementals is *one* with the whole and therefore through it also works the power of the whole, behind which stands the *one* Will furthering, strengthening, protecting and leading: the Will of God!

It is like this throughout the whole of the realms where "beings" are active, and it could and *should* also have been the same long ago with you, the spirits of Subsequent Creation which have developed to ego-consciousness.

This firmly-established connection automatically ensures that, should any one of these elementals fail in some way or other, it is immediately expelled by the pressure of the whole and thus remains cut off. It would then wither away because the power no longer flows to it.

All that is weak is quickly shaken off in this way and does not even have a chance to become harmful.

I now want to talk about these elemental beings which, though seemingly small, are yet so great in their activity; these you still have no knowledge about whatever, of the existence of which you have hitherto not known anything.

But you have already heard about their *activity* in my Message. However, you will not have associated it with Substantiality, since I myself did not link them with this because it would have been premature at that time.

What I then revealed in short sentences *objectively* I am now giving to you in its real working.

I have already once observed that the little elemental beings around you are influenced by the human spirit and can accordingly produce either good or even evil.

However, this influence does not take effect in *that* sense as you imagine it.

It is not that you could be *masters* over these beings, that you could direct them!

In a sense, of course, it could be described like that without saying anything wrong. It is actually expressed in the right way as far as *your* conceptions and your language are concerned, because you look at everything *from your point of view* and also judge accordingly. Therefore I very often had to speak to you in my Message in the same manner to make myself understood. I could also do it *here* because in this case it makes no difference as regards your acting in the right way.

Because it more closely corresponded with the attitude of your intellect it was much easier for you to understand at that time when I told you that with your volition you always strongly influence everything of the animistic around you, and that it adjusts itself to your thoughts and actions because you are spiritual.

That in itself remains literally true, but the reason for it is different; for the actual guidance of all creatures standing in the Law of this Creation, which thus live in the Will of God, is exercised solely *from above!* This includes *all* the elemental beings!

They are never subject to an alien volition, not even temporarily, nor in cases where it seems to you as if they were.

The little elementals which I mentioned do indeed adjust their activity to your *volition* and your *actions*, you human spirits, but nevertheless their work stands entirely in the Will of God!

This appears to be a riddle, but its solution is not so difficult; for now I only need to show you the other side as against that from which *you* consider everything!

Looked at from your angle you do influence the little elementals! Looked at from the Light, however, these only fulfil the Will of God, the Law! And since any power to act can only come exclusively from the Light, therefore this side which is *different* to you is the *right one!*

But nevertheless, for the sake of a better understanding, let us first consider their activity as seen *from your side*. In accordance with the Law that with every volition the spirit exerts a pressure here in the Material World, also upon the small Substantiality that is only Animistic, so you leave an imprint upon the little elemental beings with your thoughts and deeds. These little elementals then form in *fine gross matter* everything which is transferred to them by this pressure. Let us therefore say, from your point of view, that they carry out all your volitions!

In the *first* place your *spiritual* volition! *Spiritual* volition, however, is *intuitive perception!* The little elementals form it in fine gross matter exactly according to the volition that has issued from the spirit. They immediately take up the thread which springs forth from your volition and from your deed, and fashion at the end of the thread *that* form which corresponds exactly with this thread of will.

Such is the nature of the activity of the little elementals, which you do not yet know in their actual working.

In this way they create or, better said, they *form* the plane of Fine Gross Matter, which awaits you when you have to pass over into the Ethereal World! It is *the threshold* thereto for your soul where, to use your expression, it must first "purify" itself after earthly death, before it is able to enter the Ethereal World.

The stay of the soul on this plane is of longer or shorter duration depending upon its inner quality and upon whether, through its various propensities and weaknesses, it strove with greater or lesser strength after the gross material.

This plane of finer gross matter has already been seen by many people. It still belongs to the World of Gross Matter and is formed by the elemental beings which prepare the path of the human spirit everywhere.

This is very important for you to know: The elemental beings prepare for the human spirit, and thus also for the human soul as well as for earthman, that path which he *must* follow whether he wants to or not!

These elemental beings are influenced by man and also apparently directed by him. But only apparently, for the *actual* direction in this matter does not come from man but from *the Will of God,* the adamantine Law of Creation, which stationed this group of elementals at this place and directs their activity in the swinging of the Law.

All the thought-forms also come about through a similar activity of the elementals. However, this work is again carried out by a different group and a different species of the elementals, which also develop a special plane in fine gross matter alongside the first.

In this way landscapes, villages and towns also arise. That which is beautiful and that which is ugly! However, the different kinds are always precisely linked together, i. e., the ugly with the ugly, the beautiful with the beautiful, corresponding to the homogeneous species.

These are the places, the planes, in which you must still move about after your earthly death, *before* you can enter the Ethereal World. The coarsest which still clings to your soul in the earthly sense is cast off and left behind here. Not one little speck of this dust can you take along with you into the Ethereal World. It would hold you back until it has fallen off, i. e., until you have lived it off through recognition.

Thus the soul must journey slowly onwards after earthly death; it must climb step by step, i. e., plane by plane, through constant recognition by personal experience of that which it acquired.

Wearisome is the path if the elementals had to build dark or gloomy places for you, depending on your volition here upon earth. It is always you who give the cause for it! –

Now you know what the little elementals do and how they work for you under your influence: It is in the Law of Reciprocal Action! The little elementals thereby weave your fate! They are the little master weavers which work for you, because they always and only weave *in such a manner* as *you* wish it through your inner intuitive perception, likewise through your thinking and also your actions!

Yet in spite of this they are not in your service! –

There are three species of such elemental beings alone which are busy with this. The one species weaves all the threads of your intuitive perception, the second one the threads of your thinking, and the third the threads of your actions.

It is not to be assumed that this is *one* weaving only, but there are three; however, they are linked with each other and also again linked with many other weavings besides. A whole army is busy at this work. And these threads are coloured according to their nature. But I must not carry my explanations so far yet, or we shall get into depths which are still incomprehensible to you and would never find an end. You could not get a clear picture thereby!

Therefore let us concern ourselves with the individual person for the time being. Apart from other things there issue *three* weavings from him, each of a different nature, because his intuitive perception is not always identical with his thinking, nor is his thinking always in strict accord with his actions! In addition, the threads of the intuitive perception are of an altogether different nature, for they reach into the Ethereal and Spiritual Spheres and are anchored *there,* while the threads of his thinking remain in *fine* gross matter *only,* and must be lived off *there.*

The threads issuing from the actions, however, are *still* more dense and heavy, and they are therefore anchored closest to life on earth, and must *first* be journeyed through and lived off after departure from the earth before it is at all possible for a soul to continue.

You have no idea how far many a soul must travel just to be able to enter the Ethereal World, not to speak of the Spiritual Sphere!

In his superficial way man simply calls all this "the beyond" and is satisfied with that. In his indolence he pours everything into one pot!

Many souls are earthbound over a long period because they are suspended on threads which are firmly anchored close to this heavy gross matter. The soul cannot release itself from them until it has lived itself free of them, i. e., when in the course of its compulsory journey through them it came to the re-cognition that all these things possess neither the value nor the importance which the soul had attached to them, and that it was futile and wrong to waste so much time on them while on earth. This often takes a very long time and it is sometimes very bitter!

Meanwhile many souls are again attracted from out of heavy gross matter, and they are incarnated again and ever again on earth without ever having been in the Ethereal World during that time. They had to remain in fine gross matter because they were unable to free themselves quickly enough. The threads held them too tightly therein. And in this it is impossible to slip through by cunning!

So much is possible for man here upon earth which he is unable to do after his departure. He then hangs more firmly in the Law of this Creation, exper-iencing everything instantly without the interference of a ponderous gross material cloak to delay matters. The earthly cloak is able to *delay* through its dense heaviness and impermeability, but it can never actually prevent. There-fore many things awaiting redemption are only postponed, but nothing is ever cancelled.

Everything that man here upon earth has perceived and thought is awaiting him, as well as the strict and just consequences of his actions!

When a man perceives intuitively then the threads thereby produced, which seem like small seeds sprouting forth from the soil, are taken up and cared for by the little elementals. And just as it is in heavy gross matter, the weeds receive exactly the same careful attention as the best plants. As the threads develop they are anchored for the first time at the border of fine gross matter, where they pass into the hands of a different species of the elementals, which lead them onward through the Ethereal World. They are again anchored at the border of the Ethereal World, and passed on into the Animistic Sphere. From the Animistic Sphere they then reach the Spiritual Sphere, where they are finally anchored again by a different species of the elementals.

Such is the path of a *good* volition which leads *upwards*. The path of an evil volition is guided *downwards* in the same way.

With each anchorage at a border these threads lose a certain species of their substance, which they leave behind in order to be able to proceed into the next sphere. This, too, takes place in a lawful manner, exactly corresponding to the particular species of the spheres. And all these developments are subject to the activity of the elementals.

As the intuitive perception of a good volition originates in the mobility of the *spirit,* these threads are consequently carried into the Spiritual Sphere. From there they pull at the soul or at least *hold* it fast when it still has to live through or redeem many a thing in fine gross matter. Thus, if there are many such threads anchored in the Spiritual Sphere, the soul cannot sink and fall so quickly as can a soul which carries with itself threads only for fine gross matter, because the latter was spiritually indolent while on earth and only bound itself to the World of Gross Matter, considering its pleasures alone worth striving for.

The soul that is being pulled by the threads of its volition no more sees these threads than does man here on earth, because they are always of a somewhat finer substance than the outermost cloak in which the soul still moves about. At the very moment, however, when the process of living off these threads through recognition enables the cloak to attain the same consistency as the densest among the still existing threads, whereby the soul through the homogeneous nature of its outer cloak could see them, these threads have already fallen off as being redeemed. Consequently it never happens that the soul connected with such threads actually sees them. –

Thus from the *earthly* point of view these little elementals are in the service of the human spirit because they adjust their activities to the nature of the conscious or unconscious volitions of men. And yet in reality they only act in accordance with the Will of God, Whose Law they thereby fulfil.

Thus their activity is only *apparently* influenced by the human spirit. For the difference to become evident it depends entirely from which side you look at the matter.

When in the lectures about reciprocal action I spoke of threads which, as they issue from you, are thrust out and attracted, you perhaps until now saw only a conglomeration of threads before your mind's eye. However, it was not to be supposed that these threads would continue by themselves like worms, but they must pass through hands, must be guided. And these hands belong to the little elementals working therein, of which you could have no knowledge up till now.

But now the picture has come to life and stands before you! Imagine that you are constantly surrounded by these elementals, which observe you and at once take up every thread and guide it to where it belongs. Not only that, but they anchor it and care for it until the seed springs up, indeed until the blossoms and fruit appear! Just as it is here in the World of heavy Gross Matter with the seeds of plants, which are tended by the elemental beings until you can eventually have the fruits thereof!

It is the same basic Law, the same activity, but carried out by other species of the elemental beings which, as we would express it in an earthly way, are specialists in this field. And thus the same weaving, the same activity – the producing of seed, the germination, the growth, the blossoming and the fruit-bearing – under the supervision and care of the elementals, penetrates the entire Creation for *everything*, no matter what it is and to which species it belongs. The activities of the elemental beings cover every single species, and without their activity there would in turn be no species.

Thus through the activity of the elemental beings, under the impulse of the base volition of men, and through the anchoring of the threads springing forth from this volition, there also came into existence the so-called hell. The threads of the evil volition were anchored there, grew, blossomed and finally bore the corresponding fruit, which *those* human beings who produced the seed had to accept.

Therefore a consuming lustfulness has dominion in these nether regions, the lust for murder, for quarrelling and for all the aberrations of human passions, each with its corresponding place. However, everything springs forth from the same Law, in the fulfilment of which the little elemental beings also fashion the fairy-like *beauty* of the more Luminous Realms! –

Thus I shall let one picture after another arise from Creation until you receive a great and uniform survey, which will never allow you to waver upon your ways nor let you go astray, because you are then "knowing". Whoever even *then* would still *not* wish to direct his path towards the Luminous Heights would fundamentally prove himself as absolutely depraved and only worthy to be cast out!

IN THE GROSS MATERIAL WORKSHOP
OF THE ELEMENTAL BEINGS

SO FAR we have been considering the activity of the little elemental beings in regard to that which *issues* from earthmen, such as their intuitive perception, their thinking and their actions.

Now, however, we want to remain just as close to earthmen as before, but observe therewith the activities of *those* elemental beings which develop their sphere of work in a direction *leading towards* earthmen. Thus they are not the beings which build the paths of the soul leading out of the heavy gross material substance of the earth, but those which strive in the opposite direction towards the gross material substance of this earth.

Everything shows movement, nothing is without form. Thus it appears as if man is surrounded by a huge workshop, the activities of which partly stream towards him and partly diverge from him, thereby intertwining, knotting and loosening, building up and pulling down, in constant change, continually growing, blossoming, ripening and decaying in order to offer new seed the opportunity to develop in fulfilment of the cycle which is in accordance with the Laws of Creation, the cycle of the necessary development and decay of all forms in the World of Matter. This is ordained by the Law of continuous Movement under the pressure of the radiation of God, the Only Living One!

It effervesces and surges, melts and cools off, hammers and pounds without ceasing. Vigorous fists push and pull, loving hands guide and protect, unite and separate the wandering spirits in all this tumult.

But the man of this earth is dull, blind and deaf to all this as he staggers about in his gross material attire. Greedy in his pleasures and knowledge, his intellect shows only this as its goal: Earthly joys and earthly power as the reward for his work and the crown of his existence! For the sluggish and indolent, the intellect tries to conjure up pictures of quiet comfort which, like a narcotic – hostile to the spirit, paralyse the will for activity in Creation.

He does not want to submit, the man of this earth, because the choice was left to his volition. And therefore he chains his living spirit to the dying form, the origin of which he does not even know.

He remains a stranger to this Creation, instead of using its gifts to build up for himself. Only the right knowledge offers the possibility of a conscious adaptation. Therefore man *must* step out of his ignorance now! In future he can only work *knowingly* under the rays of the new star, which will separate the useful from the useless in the whole of Creation.

That which is useful – not judged according to human thinking, but only according to *God's* Holy Law! Thus all that is useless in the first place includes every person who is incapable of receiving the blessings and mercies of God in humility, something which he can only achieve through the knowledge of all the activities in Creation.

Only out of the *Word* can he receive all the knowledge which he needs for this. He will *find* it therein if he seeks earnestly. He finds exactly what *he needs for himself!* But Christ's words are now more than ever a law: "*Seek, and ye shall find!*"

Whoever does not seek with true eagerness of his spirit shall not and will not receive anything either. And therefore he who sleeps or is spiritually indolent will also find nothing in the Word which is living. It does not give him anything!

Every soul must first open itself for this of its own accord and strike the Source which lies in the Word. Therein rests an adamantine and sifting law, which now fulfils in all severity.

You must become *knowing*, otherwise you will lose every hold and will stumble and fall when now, during the course of the onrolling world events, you are forcibly compelled to take *that* course which you must take in accordance with the Holy Will of your God, in Whose Works of Grace you have so far trampled about like ignorant animals in the most beautiful flower garden – destroying instead of furthering the upbuilding and helping, indulging in conceited audacity without exerting yourselves to obtain the understanding as to *why* you are allowed consciously to stay and enjoy everything in the beautiful Creation.

You never thought of giving the necessary service in return, you did not observe that great Law of God which ordains that the right to take lies in *giving* alone! But you have taken thoughtlessly; with or without petitions you have made boundless *demands* without even once thinking of your *duty* towards Creation, in which you guests wanted to make yourselves unscrupulous masters!

The Creator was expected to give, always to give! You did not even once in serious reflection ask how you really came to deserve this, but you only complained when you had to undergo suffering which you yourselves brought about, and you grumbled when something you had hoped for was not fulfilled for once. And your hoping, your wishes, were directed always and only towards *earthly happiness!* You have never as yet properly concerned yourselves with genuine longing for all else, for that which is more real! Where you *did* so it was the urge for earthly knowledge, nothing else!

You wanted to find in order to make yourselves prominent thereby! And when it happened that because of some distress you tried to investigate, then it was only done in order to escape from this trouble, no matter whether it was earthly distress or distress of the *soul. But it was never done for the purpose of honouring God!*

Now, however, learn at last to know the structure of this Creation in which you dwell and through part of which you also have to wander, so that you will no longer remain as foreign substance therein. With the recognition which will then become ever stronger you will also receive *that* humbleness which you need in order to absorb the last and great gift: that of being allowed to exist eternally!

With the cognition, which must lead to recognition, you also shorten the period of your wanderings through Creation by thousands of years, and arrive much more quickly and surely at those Luminous Heights which must remain the longing and the goal of *that* human spirit which does not wish to become lost through being useless.

Thus follow me today further along the paths through the nearer surroundings of your existence upon earth!

Imagine that you are striving towards this earth as it is with every incarnation, no matter whether it be the first or already the fiftieth!

Thereby it is not possible for the soul which is waiting for incarnation to slip into a physical body without further ado. The soul itself, which on account of its nature never unites with the physical body, but which is capable of *joining* a physical body only when the conditions required for this are fulfilled, could never move or set aglow the physical body without a special bridge. The threads which are tied through the attraction of homogeneous species are not sufficient for such a purpose.

In order to give an absolutely clear picture I will go back once more and in brief outline touch upon a few requirements for an incarnation which are already known.

The effects of the Law of Attraction of Homogeneous Species are not decisive in *all* cases for incarnations, but there are also other possibilities and compelling reasons.

The Law of Reciprocal Action also intervenes in this matter and sometimes with a strength which eclipses all else. A soul outside of the physical bodies, which through threads of reciprocal action is strongly linked with another soul dwelling upon earth within a female physical body, will absolutely be led to this woman upon earth by way of these threads as soon as there is an opportunity for an incarnation with her.

In addition to such conditions, which cannot be avoided, there is then also the Law of Attraction of Homogeneous Species. But there are also besides these two happenings other kinds and possibilities about which we shall talk in the course of time only, because today any superfluous deviation would only dim the clearness of the necessary picture.

So for the present let us only say that all the threads, no matter what their nature, cannot suffice to enable the soul to move the gross material body and to set it aglow.

Even when the condition is fulfilled that, due to some threads, the soul remains in the neighbourhood of the growing body, and that the body in its radiation also reaches that degree which is able to *hold* the soul (as I have already mentioned in an earlier lecture), then although it is true that the soul would thereby be bound to the body, yet it would still not on that account be in a position to move or set aglow the physical body connected with it.

A bridge for this is still lacking. Instead of saying bridge we can also call it an implement, which is especially needed by the soul in addition. And this bridge must again be built by the little elemental beings!

Like everything else this also takes place within the laws of the exact *meeting together* of very specific radiations, which in this case concern earthly manhood and womanhood, as well as various active threads of fate concerning these two human beings and also the soul. This process, too, needs a special explanation later on. Today it should be sufficient to hint that all of this

forms the decisive starting-point for the activities of *those* little elemental beings which build the bridges for the incarnation of souls.

And these bridges are what many today already call the "astral body".

The astral body consists of medium gross matter. It must be formed by the
little elementals directly *preceding* the heavy gross material earth body, so
that it almost appears as if it were being fashioned simultaneously. But this is
not so, for the astral body – I still want to retain this known designation for
the sake of simplicity – must precede *everything* which is to be formed in the
heavy gross material substance.

There are many people who have arrived at the knowledge of the *existence*
of so-called astral things. But they neither know their actual purpose nor the
real process of their coming into existence!

Those who have hitherto known about astral things again looked at everything only from their angle, and therefore thought of them as having originated from the heavy gross material substance. In most cases they consider
them to be *images* of heavy gross matter, because every plant, every stone,
and in fact *everything* of heavy gross matter seems to be reflected in the astral
world.

These, however, are not *images* but *prototypes* of things in heavy gross
matter. Without them nothing whatever would or could form in the World of
heavy Gross Matter. That is the difference!

According to earthly conceptions this field of medium gross matter could
best be called the workshop for models. Just as an artist first fashions a model, so the so-called astral body comes into existence *before* the heavy physical
body. Except that there is nothing in Creation which would serve one such
purpose *only* and then just be put aside, as it is with earthman! Instead everything, even that which appears the smallest, necessarily has a many-sided
value in Creation.

In the working of the elemental beings every single thing belongs as a necessary part to the whole. Each part is also flooded through and pulsated
through *uniformly* by the whole and with the whole.

So every piece upon the earth, even the earth itself, has a co-operating
model. Some of those who are allowed to see call it the "shadow", while
others, as already mentioned, call it the "astral body". There are other
lesser known designations for this, but they all mean the same thing. None of
them, however, hits upon that which is right, because it was again consider-

ed from the wrong side, whereas there is no knowledge whatever about the origin.

There is nothing on earth which has not already been fashioned beforehand in an even more beautiful and more perfect way by the little elemental beings in medium gross matter.

Everything taking place in the World of heavy Gross Matter, even the skill of the craftsmen, the creations of the artists, etc., is only *drawn from* the preceding activities of the little elemental beings. They have already completed this and much more besides in medium and finer gross matter. There all this is even more perfect in its forms, because the elementals work directly in the laws of the Will of God which is perfect, and which can therefore only give expression to what is perfect in form.

Every invention, even the most surprising one, is only *borrowed* from things already achieved by the beings on other planes. There are very many such things yet, ready for men to draw upon in order to transfer them here upon earth into the World of heavy Gross Matter.

And yet, although the models are so easily attainable for those who are not only serious but also humble seekers, much has again been distorted here upon earth through the intellect, because in most cases those endowed with the ability lacked the requisite humility to draw in purity, and furthermore because the inhabitants of the earth, through their conceit which hampers everything, have so far paid no attention to the Laws of God in Creation. Not until they obtain exact knowledge of these Laws will the inventing or, more correctly expressed, the discovering on other planes, and consequently also the *correct* transfer into the heavy gross material substance of this earth, become much easier and more accurate than it has been so far. It will also become much more extensive.

The astral plane is therefore *not* a reflection of the World of Gross Matter! In the first place this plane in itself still consists of gross matter, only of a somewhat finer species than the earth, and secondly the *reverse* obtains – the heavy earthly gross matter is a reproduction of medium gross matter, of the so-called astral plane.

However, the astral plane contains two ways and thereby also two great basic divisions, one leading towards the heavy gross matter and another leading away from it again! The part striving towards heavy gross matter is the bridge which is necessary for the upbuilding in the earthly; the part striving away from it, however, is the formed expression of the thoughts and actions of the human spirits which are upon earth in earthly garments.

Men's knowledge of this has so far been isolated piecework only, whereby owing to their ignorance these few pieces are in a confused medley without any real connection. Thus nothing but a fantastically composed picture floating in the air was devised, which seems like a mirage, and therefore probably exerts a special fascination upon many people who are inwardly unstable. Man can then revel so beautifully in irresponsible things! He can allow himself to establish daring suppositions in these matters, which he naturally likes others to consider as knowledge and certainty, knowing that nobody can hold him responsible thereby if he errs. In his opinion he has been given the opportunity to be held in esteem for once without having any responsibility!

Yes, before men! But not before the Laws of God! Towards these everybody is *fully* responsible for everything he says! For every word! And all those who follow his wrong opinions, even those whom he merely incites with his erroneous teachings to new and fantastic ideas of their own, all are firmly chained to him, and he must help to free them again individually before he can think of himself and his ascent.

After having again taken a brief glimpse at these matters, we must now return to details. Thus the little elemental beings fashion the astral body beforehand as the necessary bridge for the soul, so that it is able to control, direct and move the growing body.

The soul is connected with *the astral body* and works *through this* upon the heavy physical body. Likewise the physical body with the radiation necessary for this can really bind the soul to itself only through the astral body acting as a mediator. The radiations issuing from heavy gross matter, through which the animistic pulsates, must first penetrate the medium gross matter of the astral body, for otherwise they cannot connect with the radiations of the soul, the outermost cloak of which is by then already of finest gross matter.

Let us at present distinguish only between three basic species of gross matter, although there are still various intermediate and side species in addition. For the time being we will only consider the fine, the medium heavy and the heaviest gross material substance. In this sense the physical body also belongs to the heaviest earthly species, and the astral body to the transitional species of medium heavy gross matter, i.e., to that species which *lies next* to the heaviest.

When an incarnation is to take place this astral body is *first* fashioned by the elemental beings, and immediately afterwards the physical body is formed so that it appears as if both occur simultaneously. In reality, however, the fashioning of the astral body precedes the process in heavy gross matter; it *must* precede it, otherwise the physical body could not be completed and the soul would be unable to do anything with it.

I am only giving you the *picture* of the process here, so that the conception can arise therefrom. Later on we shall perhaps follow *step by step* the growing, the maturing and the decaying, with all the logical order and with all the threads which are part of it, as soon as *the whole* stands before you *like a picture*.

The astral body is connected *with* the physical body, but is not dependent upon it, as has been assumed in the past. The lack of knowledge of the actual process of development in Creation brought in its train the many errors, especially since man always basically presented the little knowledge he acquired by considering it from his point of view.

As long as *he* imagines *himself* as the *most important* point in Creation, where in reality he does not at all play a special main role, but where he is nothing but a creature like innumerable others, he will always go wrong, also in his investigations.

It is true that after the soul has severed itself from the physical body the astral body decays along with the physical body. But this must not be taken as a proof that it is therefore dependent upon it. This does not even give a justifiable foundation for such an assumption!

In reality the process is different: When it severs itself the soul, being the mobile part, draws the astral body away from the physical body. Figuratively speaking: The soul upon stepping out of and leaving the physical body pulls the astral body out with it. That is how it appears! In reality the soul only pulls it *off* the physical body, because a fusion has never taken place but only a telescoping, as it is with field glasses which go in and out.

In so doing the soul does not draw this astral body along very far, because the latter is not only anchored with the soul but also with the physical body; and, moreover, the soul from which the essential movement issues also wants to sever itself from the astral body and consequently strives away from it too.

Thus after the earthly departure of the soul the astral body always remains near the physical body. The further the soul then moves away the weaker the astral body also becomes; and the ever-increasing severance of the soul finally brings about the decay and decomposition of the astral body, which in turn immediately brings in its train the decay of the physical body, in the same way as it also influenced its formation. This is the normal process in accordance with the Laws of Creation. Naturally special acts of intervention also bring about special conditions and disarrangements, but without being able to eliminate the lawfulness.

The astral body, which is first and foremost dependent *upon the soul,* is the mediator to the physical body. Whatever happens to the astral body is also definitely suffered by the physical body. The sufferings of the physical body, however, touch the astral body much less, although they are closely connected with each other.

If, for example, some part of the physical body is taken away (let us suppose it is a finger), then the finger of the astral body is not also taken away simultaneously, but it still *remains* as before. That is why a person on earth can actually still feel pain or a pressure periodically at that spot where he no longer possesses a member of his physical body.

Cases of this kind are well enough known, but man never found the proper explanation of it because he lacked the survey.

Thus the elemental beings knot and connect all the souls to their astral bodies, which we shall call the bodies of medium gross matter, while the heavy earth bodies, even when coming into existence, are directly connected with the body of medium gross matter and form and develop accordingly.

It must be reserved until possible later lectures to show the way in which the soul works through this cloak upon the heavy physical body, for to reach such a point much has still to be clarified beforehand in order to presuppose the right understanding.

All this, however, is also pervaded by one *single* law, which is zealously and faithfully fulfilled by the little elemental beings without any deviation. In this they are models for the human spirits, which can and also *shall* learn therefrom, until at last they work hand in hand and without presumption with the little master-builders in this Creation, so that through deeds which lead to complete harmony they will jubilantly and gratefully praise the Wisdom and Love of their Creator!

A SOUL WANDERS

In the last two lectures I explained the happenings in the planes of medium gross matter (formerly called the astral plane by those who knew about it), which are *directly* connected with men's existence upon earth.

There are many other happenings besides those mentioned therein which also belong to the fields of activity of the elemental beings. But since these types of work only touch men's souls *indirectly,* we do not yet want to speak about them but first to consider what lies nearest at hand: *the human soul itself* in connection with what has already been explained.

Therefore follow me for a short distance along the path upon which a soul must wander after departure from its physical body. Let us, then, observe its first steps!

We are standing in medium gross matter. Before us we see threads of fate of various colours and strengths, of which we talked in the last lectures when considering the activities of the little elemental beings. Let us eliminate everything else this time; for in reality there exists in this region much more, flowing closely together and through each other, than just these threads. Everything swings in the strictest order in accordance with the Laws in Creation. We look neither right nor left, but stay only by these threads.

These threads appear to trail along with only slight movement, showing no particular activity; for they are such as were already spun a long time ago. Suddenly one of them begins to quiver. It vibrates and increases its movement more and more, swells out, deepens its colour, and starts to become more active in every respect... A soul which is connected with this thread has released itself from a physical body. It approaches the place where we are waiting.

This bears a resemblance to a fire hose into which water is suddenly driven. One can accurately observe the path of the oncoming water as it forces its way forward in the hose. It is the *same* process with the threads of fate, which become released when the soul is forced to wander along the path thus marked out for it. The radiation of the spirit within the soul streams ahead of it and animates the thread of its path, even if this thread was only in weak activity up till then. Through this stimulation the tension becomes stronger and pulls the soul more vigorously to the nearest anchorage of this thread.

This place of anchorage abounds with homogeneous species of such threads, which in turn are connected with souls still dwelling upon earth in gross material earth bodies. Yet other souls which have previously left the earth are already at the anchorage, and must now at this place partake of the fruit which ripened through the activity and care of the little elemental beings according to the species of the threads, which work like seed stalks.

The forms of the fruit are of a very definite and uniform nature at this particular place. Let us assume it is a place of envy, which is very widespread upon earth and finds excellent soil among earthmen!

That is why the anchorage for these threads is such an immensely large and many-sided place. Landscape upon landscape, towns and villages, with corresponding activities of every kind!

But envy lies in wait everywhere, arousing repugnance. Everything is permeated by it. Envy has taken on grotesque forms which move about and work in these regions. They work on all the souls drawn to this place in the most decisive and increased way, so that these souls may themselves experience with greater intensity that which they so obtrusively favoured their fellow-men with here on earth.

Let us not occupy ourselves with individual descriptions of this place; for it is of such a thousandfold variety that no firmly given picture would suffice to provide even the shadow of a conception. But the expression "nauseating" is a mild and exceedingly glossed-over description of it!

It is to this place that the thread which we observed leads; the thread which we suddenly saw becoming more active, richer in colour, and fresher through the approach of the soul which had left the earth.

As the soul now moves towards the place itself, there also at a very definite spot where the thread is firmly anchored everything gradually becomes more mobile and colourful – let us call it more animated. Everything flares up!

This revival, however, issues quite unconsciously from the *spirit of the soul;* it comes about through the radiation of the spirit, even though this soul, as occurs in most cases, journeys along the path with eyes still closed. It then awakens at its destination, *at this very place,* where everything had just become more lively at its approach through the radiation. For here are the fruits of *that* thread, or perhaps also of various threads connected with *this* very soul, because they were produced by it.

Through this coming to life under the personal radiation of the soul concerned, the spirit living in this soul impresses a certain *personal* note *of its own* upon its new environment, which was already awaiting it – a note which always differs from that of the other souls. This always makes it, so to speak, a quite distinctive world in itself for each soul, despite the fact that everything is closely interwoven, that the souls molest each other to excess, and that the whole place can be considered as one single, great, uniform plane.

Thus it happens that in spite of the experience which so many souls simultaneously share in this place, and also basically in the same form, each individual soul always experiences and lives through it only according to its very own nature, i. e., each soul receives an entirely different impression of it from the other souls which have to live through the same with it. What is more, this soul will also see things differently from a second or third soul which has the same picture before it.

Picture this to yourself! A soul awakens at such a place. This place or plane possesses a very definite picture as regards its formation and everything that moves therein. Even the happenings there may be called uniform, because they also remain subject to one single great law through which they take effect.

This soul which we are considering now sees the other souls already there or those arriving later experience *the same* which this soul is also forced to experience. However, the soul sees this of itself and of the others in a very definite way which is entirely *its own,* and it also lives through these things correspondingly.

One must not come to the conclusion from this that the other souls too see and experience everything in exactly the same way as does this one soul which we named; for this is *not* the case, but each of these souls sees and experiences things in accordance with its *own personal* nature and quite differently from the others! They see the *happenings* differently, likewise the *colours* and the *landscapes!*

This is because the radiation of the inherent spirit also lends to the environment there the personal expression which belongs only to this particular spirit, and the expression is animated according to *its* nature. In the first moment this may seem very strange to you!

But perhaps I can furnish you with a few similar although much more clumsy illustrations from the heavy terrestrial World of Matter, which will give you an idea towards a better understanding.

Let us take two persons who are visiting a beautiful park! Without a special understanding between them it is seldom that both will designate the same point as being the most beautiful therein, even if they walk through the park side by side. Each will find something different as beautiful for himself. One of them perhaps nothing whatever, but he only says otherwise out of politeness, though he prefers the wild forest to the cultivated park!

This is then simply done away with by saying that the one has no "sense" for what the other declares to be beautiful. This, however, does contain a certain truth. The "sensing" of the one simply goes in another direction! Therefore the scene looks different to him from that viewed by his companion!

In the recognition of a picture, in the way as to how one sees it, it is the purely *personal sensing* or the direction of the sensing of him who looks at it which is decisive, not the picture or the landscape which is being observed. One person experiences it differently from another.

That which becomes evident here in such a clumsy way is more lively and impressive in the more easily mobile layers of matter. This is why it happens that the same place with the same events calls forth different experiences in the individual souls, depending on *their* own particular natures.

We can delve more deeply into this matter, however!

Let us again take two persons to serve as an example! While they are young a colour is shown to them and they are told it is blue. Thereafter each of them always considers this particular colour he saw as being blue. But this does not prove that both of them also *see* this particular colour *in the same way*. The opposite is the case. In reality each one sees the colour which he calls blue differently from the other. Even here already in the physical body!

Even if you closely examine the physical eyes and find them of an exactly similar quality, this condition is not decisive to define how the colours are seen. The brain also has a say in this, and in addition, as *the main thing,* the *personal nature* of the human *spirit* itself!

Let me try to take the explanation further! Let us stick to blue! You yourselves have thereby quite a definite colour before you which, with all its shades, was once pointed out to you as being blue. And if your fellow-man who was taught likewise will also pick out from all the colours when questioned the same colour which you yourself call blue, it does not prove that he sees the colour which he also calls blue in the same way as you do!

As for him, it is just *this* very particular kind which is blue. You do not know *how* it looks to him in reality. Naturally he will and is bound to regard everything of this colour which he sees, and which is thus designated, as being blue, just as he would also call the white colour black if he had been told it was so from the very beginning. He will always say blue to this one definite colour which you also call blue. *In spite of this, however, he does not see it in the same way as you do!*

It is the same with the tone. A certain tone you hear *is*, for example, an "E" to you. To every person! Because he learned to hear and call it as such. He will also form it in this way with his mouth, but always in accordance with his *own* sensing, which will naturally always bring forth the same tone for what is also considered "E" by you. However, this does not at all mean that he actually *hears* it *in the same way* as *you* hear it. But in reality he always hears it only in accordance with the nature of *his* spirit, *differently* from his fellow-man.

Now I come to what I wish to explain with this. In Creation the colour *in itself* is *constant* and each one for itself remains unchanged. The same applies to the tone. But the *experiencing* of this colour and of the tone *differs with every person* in accordance with his personal nature. That is *not* uniform!

Part of the experiencing is also the seeing, no matter whether gross material with its different species, or ethereal, animistic or spiritual. As it is with the *colour* and the *tone,* so is it also with the *form.*

Each one of you experiences his surroundings in a different way, sees and hears it differently from his neighbour. *You have merely become accustomed to finding uniform designations for things,* but these lack vitality. Thus you have pressed that which is mobile into fixed forms, and you think that with these fixed forms of your language all movement in Creation must also become rigid for you!

This is not so! Each person lives and experiences absolutely according to *his own nature!* Therefore he will some day also see and recognise Paradise in a different way from his fellow-man!

And yet if one of them would design a picture of it as *he* sees it, the others would also immediately recognise and see as being right in the picture *that* which they themselves experienced by Paradise; for they again see the *picture* according to their own nature, and not as the one who reproduced Paradise in the picture sees it.

The thing in itself is always the same, it is only the way in which the human spirits see it which varies. Colour is colour, but it is absorbed in different ways by the human spirits. Tone is tone, and form is form, of a very definite kind in the entire Creation. The various human spirits, however, experience them differently, always according to *their* maturity and *their* nature.

That is how a person can suddenly experience Spring and all the awakening in Nature in an entirely different way to that in which he experienced it in past decades, just as if he had never really observed or "enjoyed" it. This occurs in particular when a man has had to pass through some critical period in his life which enabled him to *mature* inwardly.

Nature and Spring have always been like this; but it is *he* who has changed, and according to *his* maturity he experiences them *differently!*

Everything depends on *him alone*. And thus it is with the entire Creation. *You human beings* change and not Creation! Therefore you could already have Paradise here on earth if *you* were mature for it. Creation can remain the same but you, you and always again only you, must change in order to *see* it differently and therewith to *experience* it differently. For seeing, hearing and feeling belong to experiencing, are part of it.

That is why the *World* is seen and experienced in millions of different ways by human spirits. These differences, however, are put into it by men alone; for Creation itself actually has quite simple basic forms, which always repeat themselves. They are formed, ripen and decay in accordance with *one* uniform law in order to arise anew in these same forms. Everything which is real is simple, but this simplicity is *experienced* by men in a thousandfold ways.

With this knowledge you now already come nearer to the process of what happens to the soul once it is released from heavy matter on earth. It experiences the so-called beyond *in accordance with* its *inner nature; for it animates the forms* which had to be connected with it *through its personal radiation,* it vitalises them in accordance with its own character, which must spend itself out therein.

The fact that the soul may thereby come to the recognition of whether that which it created for itself was right or wrong, i. e., to the recognition of which paths it took, remains a special act of grace in itself. *One* of those which the Creator wove into *everything,* so that the struggling soul will *always* have lifebelts in every place and at all times in order to rise above the entanglements, and so that with a really good volition and recognition at the right time it need not become lost!

The many-sided indispensable value of everything that exists in Creation always proffers the possibility of ascent again in *some* way or other, even amid the greatest confusion caused by men. Whether or not the soul recognises and uses these possibilities is *its* affair alone. The lifebelts are there! The soul only needs to reach out for them with a good volition in order to swing itself up on them. –

Having changed inwardly man also sees everything differently, as the popular saying goes! However, this is not a mere saying, but in reality man does then see everything differently. With his inner change his seeing and his hearing change to a certain degree; for it is the *spirit* which sees, hears and feels through the corresponding tools in the various different planes, and not the physical or ethereal eye itself. If the spirit changes then the way of seeing changes with it, and consequently also the way of experiencing. The tools play no part in this whatever; they are merely mediators.

The *radiation of the spirit* absorbs the resistances which it meets and leads them back to the spirit in a sort of reciprocal action. In this World of heavy Gross Matter the leading back goes through the gross material organs provided for the purpose, such as the eyes, ears and brain. Thereby the brain is the meeting place for the mediations of all the lower organs.

Only later shall we speak about this in more detail!

Today I am only trying in this way to make it clear to you that the nature of the impression of the outer world, i.e., of the surroundings, is dependent upon the particular spirit *itself!* For this reason one and the same form always affects the various spectators differently, even when they have become equally clear as to its beauty. And if one person sees a certain form differently from his fellow-man, then a sketch of the form seen by the one must yield for the other a picture identical with the form itself.

At this point everything must indeed come together again in one; for only the seeing is different, and not the actual form.

Men have created a common name for every form. *Only* the *name* for it is *common*, but not the way in which it is recognised or seen.

In this you have also so far gone wrong in your opinions. But if you now seek to approach the experiencing in the so-called beyond more closely from the viewpoints newly shown to you, much will become clearer to you. You will be able to understand many things more easily when I now continue with my explanations, and so much that is puzzling will become clear.

What has been shown to you also explains why two or more persons with mediumistic abilities see, hear and interpret one and the same thing quite differently, without there being any justification for reproaching them; for they see it according to *their* nature, and therefore always in a different way from the other. The subject being dealt with, however, is only of a very definite type. And only he who has learned to reckon with these happenings through the knowledge of the Laws of the Divine Will in Creation also knows exactly how to find the connection in the various reports and thus to recognise what is right therein, how it *really* is!

But you have sought to press Creation and yourselves into rigid and stationary forms by means of *the language* with which you make yourselves understood. You will never succeed in this; for Creation is *mobile,* as is your inner life also. When you seek to reflect about this, however, you think in the firmly-moulded words of your language!

Just think how foolish this is! The firmly-moulded language never suffices to reproduce correctly anything that is mobile!

Here again the impediment is your intellect, which can *only* work with very definite words, and which is also capable of absorbing only very *definite* words. You can realise from this how you have firmly chained and enslaved yourselves by considering the intellect to be the *highest* for man, whereas it is only useful for and applicable to the heavy gross matter of this earth. And even then only to a limited extent and not for everything! Little by little you recognise how really paltry the intellectuals are!

For this reason I have already called out to you often that you must try to absorb my Word *in such a manner* that as you read it you see *pictures* of it before you! For you can understand it only in pictures, not with the paltry words of these earthmen which I am compelled to use in order to tell you about it.

You will *never* learn to understand Creation in words, nor that which is *within* you, because all of that is and must remain *mobile,* whereas *words* press everything into firm and rigid forms only. And that is impossible, an entirely vain effort with and for everything that is mobile! Understanding will not come to you with words!

771

However, as soon as the soul lays aside the terrestrial heaviness of the physical body it enters the mobility of Creation. It is drawn into the constant surging and seething, and will then experience its surroundings in a much more mobile way. The surroundings often change in the redemptions awaiting every soul, to which the soul is drawn by the animating of all the threads clinging to it.

And all this is again reciprocal in its effects. When the soul withdraws from the physical body, when it strives away from it and lets it fall back, i. e., when it no longer radiates through it, then its radiations, which manifest even more strongly through becoming freer, go in one direction *only* with their full strength – towards medium gross matter, the nearest anchorage of the threads of fate.

The threads receive a much greater animation thereby, called forth by the soul's radiation, which is now guided in this one direction. Through this animation their capacity to attract is also intensified, which retroactively strikes the connected soul and attracts it more keenly. All these are automatic, absolutely lawful and thus completely natural happenings, which you can also easily understand if you try to go deeply into it.

Thus the soul is drawn along on its path by threads which it animates through its radiations, which it cannot hold back or avoid. And in this way it goes either towards its purification or towards its destruction. All this happens ever again through the soul itself. The elemental beings only *form* and build in accordance with the Law. The *animation* of the forms and the releasing are brought about by the souls themselves through their radiations. And according to the *nature* of the radiations, the forms which are animated in such a variety of ways then exercise a more or less strong retroactive effect on the soul.

Here, too, the saying becomes valid: As you call it into the wood so it echoes! In this case it *means:* As it radiates into the forms so are they animated and *work* accordingly. A great lawful simplicity and unswerving justice is inherent in all this! –

What I have described to you herein *solely* concerns the *human spirits alone,* for it is also inherent in the activity of the free will. With the elemental beings it is again different! –

Let these happenings come to life before your eyes for once! Exert yourselves to achieve it, for the effort is worthwhile and the reciprocal action will bring you rich reward. You will thereby again become *knowing* as regards a part of this Creation. –

I have described to you how it has been so far. But now it comes like a lightning flash out of the Light! Divine Power suddenly strikes unexpectedly into the threads of fate of all earthmen, as well as of all the souls which dwell on the planes of Subsequent Creation.

Thus everything now comes to its final release, immediately and unexpectedly! The elemental beings are newly strengthened to unprecedented power. In their activity they turn against all those human beings who through their doings and dealings have compelled them in the past to create ugly forms in obedience to the Law of Creation. Now, however, the Power of God is *above* all human volition in the entire Creation; the Will of God which permits only the pure, the good and the beautiful to be formed, and destroys all else!

The Power of God has already penetrated into Subsequent Creation also in order to work here Itself, and all the elemental beings, supported by this Highest Power, quickly, joyfully and proudly seize the countless meshes of the weaving of all the threads of fate for men in order to guide them jubilantly to their end.

In obedience to the Command of the Light they tear the threads which are only weakly anchored in the spiritual, so that the souls will remain completely severed from the Light when the dark cords, with everything clinging to them, rebound sharply upon their originators.

But the tearing of these threads also proceeds in an absolutely lawful manner, whereby the *nature* of men themselves is decisive; for the elemental beings do nothing arbitrarily.

The Divine Power of the Light now strikes like lightning into all threads! Those threads which bear corresponding similarities to the species striving for the Light, and which through the really strong volition of those attached to them also became strong enough to bear the sudden penetration of this unaccustomed Light-Power, will gain firmness and freshness thereby, so that the human souls attached to them will by the strong attraction be wrenched upwards from out of the dangers of Darkness, and thus from out of the danger of being dragged along into disintegration also.

However, the weak threads of light produced only by a weak volition cannot stand the sudden and tremendous pressure of Divine Power, but they become singed and are *thereby* severed by the elemental helpers; thus those who were tied to these threads remain a prey to Darkness. The cause of this natural happening is their own lukewarmness, which was incapable of producing threads of sufficient strength and firmness.

Thus you find nothing but justice in every happening! Therefore it is promised that the lukewarm will be spewed out, as it literally happens therewith from the Light.

All the elemental helpers, great and small, now become *free* from having to form what is dark under the compulsion of the evil or false volition of men and in fulfilment of the Law. And simultaneously everything that is animistic (all the elemental beings) is drawn back from this severed Darkness by the Power of the Light, to which they closely attach themselves in jubilant joy so that they may now form and maintain what is willed by the Light. Thereby they become strengthened in new power in order to swing in exultant accord with the entire Creation amid the surging Light of God!

Honour be to God Who sows but Love! Love also in the Law of the annihilation of the Darkness!

WOMAN AND MAN

WITH my lectures on "Substantiality", "The little elemental beings", "In the gross material workshop of the elemental beings", and "A soul wanders" I gave a piece of knowledge about the constant activity in Creation. I explained a small part of your nearer surroundings, and only about that which is very closely connected with you personally. However, I did not just give it so that you might become aware of it, but for the *very* purpose of enabling you to draw benefit from it for your life upon earth, *now,* in the physical body. At the same time also as a blessing for those who are with you and around you!

The *knowledge* of it brings you no advantage; for it is the sacred duty of every human spirit to apply any knowledge for the development in Creation, for the progress and happiness of all those who are connected with him or who just come in contact with him. *Then* his spirit profits greatly from it, but never otherwise!

The spirit will become free of all repressions, and in the Law of Reciprocal Action it will be uplifted unfailingly to a height upon which it can perpetually draw powers, powers which are penetrated by the Light, and which must bring blessing where they strike the right soil here upon earth. Thus the knowing one becomes a strong mediator of high Divine Power.

Therefore I want to show you what you could draw from the last lectures for your path on earth, and what you must also draw from them; for the Word must not remain without practical application.

In broad outlines I called your attention to a small part of the weaving and working of very definite species of the elemental beings in Creation, and I also showed you that the human spirit has so far walked about in Creation in a completely ignorant manner.

The beings of Substantiality supervise and weave in loyalty in the household of the great Creation, while that which is spiritual is to be considered as a guest journeying therein, a guest who has the duty to adapt himself harmoniously to the order of the great household and to use his best abilities to further and support the ministration of these beings. Thus he should lend a hand in the maintenance of the great work which offers him a dwelling, the possibility to subsist and a home.

To view it aright you must put it *thus: The high Substantiality has released the spirit from out of itself or given birth to it, and offers it the possibility of a joyful existence in its great household of Creation!*

Provided, of course, that this spirit does not disturb the harmony of the household; for then it is a disagreeable guest and will be treated accordingly. Then it will never be able to receive and enjoy a really happy existence!

The guest is also naturally obliged not to hamper the household, but to adapt itself to the existing order, and even *to support and to protect* it in return for the hospitality.

Finally, for a better understanding one can also express it differently without altering the actual sense: The great all-embracing Divine Substantiality has divided itself into two parts, into an active part and a passive part, or into a positive part and a negative part.

The passive or negative part is the *finer* part, the more sensitive, gentler part; the active or positive part is the *coarser* and not so sensitive part!

The more sensitive part, i. e., the passive part, is, however, the *stronger* and predominant part, which in reality has a *leading* effect. Through its delicate sensitiveness it is more capable of absorbing and is more responsive to pressure, and consequently qualified to stand and act more securely in the power of the Holy Will of God, this being the highest pressure. Pressure here means the lawful *impressing of the higher species* upon the lower species, but not perhaps some arbitrary act of force, no pressure of a violent and unstable craving for power!

Therewith you see the great picture before you, coming from above, and it is no longer difficult to comprehend that the after-effects in Creation are always and quite naturally repeated *in the same way*, and are ultimately also to be transmitted to the split-off parts, the human spirits of *Subsequent Creation*, being the effect of one uniform Law which penetrates the entire Creation. Only it is named differently on the various planes and cooling-off stages.

Thus in the grading the human *woman* of Subsequent Creation embodies the more sensitive element of Substantiality as being the negative, passive part, and the man embodies the coarser spiritual as the positive, active part;

for the splitting that has once set in is also further repeated in the parts which already split off ever again and continuously, so that one can say that *the entire Creation actually consists only of splittings!* That part which is really stronger, which actually dominates, is at the same time always the more sensitive part; thus among human beings it is *womanhood!* According to her nature it is much easier for her intuitively to perceive the pressure of the Will of God and to obey it. Thereby womanhood has and provides the best connection with the only real Living Power!

This Law of Creation should also be observed by investigators and taken into account by inventors. The part which is really the stronger and more powerful is always the more sensitive, i. e., the negative or passive part. The more sensitive part is really the *deciding* one, while the active part is only the *executing* one.

Therefore in every normal development all that is womanly exercises a strong and solely *uplifting* influence (which in its unconscious beginnings always swings purely) upon the male as soon as the latter attains physical maturity. With physical maturity there simultaneously awakens the great generative sensing, which forms the connection or the bridge for the activity of the *spiritual core* of earthman in the plane of coarse matter, i. e., here on earth.

You already know this from my Message. All this takes place *simultaneously.* One immediately necessitates the other. In this you recognise the enormous help which a human spirit on earth receives through the Laws of Creation! You see the almost indescribable protection and the merciful, scarcely-to-be-overlooked supports provided for ascent. Also the secure *paths* precisely given therein, from which no one can go astray unintentionally. A very evil will indeed is needed, even opposing efforts, when a person tries wantonly to push all these things aside and leave them unheeded. In fact man must even forcibly resist all these automatic aids in order *not* to use them!

In spite of this, however, he does it! I therefore purposely said that in the "unconscious" beginnings of maturity the womanly influence will *always* result in a pure upward swinging to the heights on the part of the male, because it then operates uninfluenced by the decadent intellect and only according to the Laws of God in Creation! Not until the intellect with all its cunning is also awakened in this, and sets to work, does this purity and all the aids with it become dragged into the dirt and debased through evil thinking!

The evil thinking is brought about through the impurity of womanhood, moral corruption, persuasions by false friends, bad examples, and last but not least also through the false trend in art and literature.

However, when once the many bridges to Luminous and Pure Heights are burst and broken down then it is very difficult to find a way back! And yet also in this matter the All-Wise Creator in His Grace gives through the Laws of Creation a thousand possibilities and also further automatic aids, if only a human spirit which has gone astray tries to bring up within itself the really earnest volition towards purity.

The Message already throws sufficient light on all these things, so that it is no longer necessary to give you any further references to it.

Men, you do not at all know what mercies you tread underfoot ever anew and almost daily, and therefore you likewise do not know how great and ever greater your burden of guilt becomes with every hour, which you must *pay* for in *any case*, for all the Laws of God which rest in Creation and help you also turn against you when you refuse to observe them.

You cannot get around the *necessity* of recognising them. Not one among all the creatures! And the Laws are the *Love* of God, which remained incomprehensible to you because you tried to make something entirely different of it from what it really is.

Learn and recognise! Woman, if you do not awaken to your *real* value in Creation and then act accordingly, the reaction of the great guilt will shatter you before you divine it! And you, man, at last recognise in woman that great help which you need and can never dispense with if you want to swing in the Laws of God. And honour in woman that for which God destined her! The way in which you intuitively feel towards the woman will become the Gate to the Light for you. Never forget this!

Besides, really strong and genuine manhood never manifests otherwise than in gentle consideration towards genuine womanhood; with increasing spiritual values this becomes ever more clearly expressed.

Just as with the body real strength never becomes evident in weighty, heavy steps, but through the control of all movements results in an elastic and light step clearly indicating security and firmness, so genuine manliness shows itself in respectful gentleness towards all womanhood which swings in purity.

This is the absolutely natural process in the swinging of the undimmed radiations in accordance with the Laws in Creation. All else is distorted!

Just meditate deeply upon all these descriptions for once! You will find them confirmed everywhere by your experiences. Always let these words form a basis for your observations. Thereby you will *see* much quite differently, and you will also recognise it more readily than you did in the past. Even in the smallest things the effects are quite evident, not only on earth but in all Creation!

You will now perhaps ask yourselves *why* the human woman is the *more sensitive* part! Therefore I also want to answer this right away:

In the separations or splittings-off the woman forms *the bridge* between Substantiality and Spirituality! Therefore the Primordial Mother also had to come into existence *first*, before further splittings could follow or take place.

And always the woman of the particular separated plane is the bridge between the next higher form of Substantiality and the Spirituality which has emanated from the latter. For this reason woman has still kept within herself a special part of the higher Substantiality which is closest to her own plane, and man lacks this part.

The popular saying is also again quite right when it noted that woman is *more closely connected with Nature* than is man! Woman, indeed, is actually nearer to Nature in *every* respect. You students of the Message, however, know that the expression "connected with Nature" means nothing else than being more closely connected with Substantiality.

This is how it is in the great household of Creation! From this you must draw lessons for yourselves and wisely apply them to life upon earth. I will tell you today *how* you can do this. When you neglect to do so, you do *not* submit to the swinging harmony of the household in which you are guests. And if you wish to act differently and go on other paths than those Creation clearly points out to you, then you will never be successful, nor will you receive genuine joy and the peace for which you long so much!

Everything which does not swing in the sense and the Laws of this Creation is bound to fail and collapse; for then it not only loses all support, but it creates for itself opposing currents which are stronger than any human spirit and which in the end will always overpower him and his work.

Therefore adjust yourselves now and at last to the perfection of the harmony of Creation, then you will find peace and success!

In this the woman has failed first and foremost; but the man is also mainly guilty of this. Of course, not by a hair's breadth less the woman on that account, for she had no need at all to adjust herself to him. Each is responsible in this for himself or herself alone. The greatest evil of all herein was again the voluntary subordination to the intellect.

The woman of Subsequent Creation should have formed the bridge from Substantiality to the Spiritual; the bridge from *that* Substantiality from which the spiritual element of Subsequent Creation originally severed itself! Not from that animistic substantiality which, after the separation of the last remnants of what was spiritual, sank down still further in order to form the bridge to the World of Matter, and to provide the origin for all the animal souls!

In the values of Creation, grading downwards, there thus comes first of all the woman and *then* the man. But the woman of Subsequent Creation has utterly failed therein. She does not stand in *that* place which Creation assigned to and ordained for her.

Woman kept the great part of Substantiality (not of the lower animistic kind but of the higher kind) as a bridge within herself and thus could and *should* remain accessible to the Will of God as is Substantiality itself, which always swings only in the Will of God. Naturally it was a condition that she kept this part of Substantiality *pure,* pure for perceiving the Divine Will, the Laws in Creation!

Instead she opened this intuitive perception only too quickly and too easily to all the seductive arts of Lucifer. And since through her speciality, which lies in the connection to Substantiality in Creation, woman is stronger than the coarser spiritual species of man, and consequently the *decisive* factor, or let us say in the most literal sense, she "sets the standard", she very easily dragged man down with her into the depths.

For this reason I have already called out to all womanhood in my Message that she must *take the lead* over man in ascent; for this is her duty, because it is inherent in her capacity! Not just because she thereby redeems the guilt with which she has burdened herself from the very beginning! That in itself is an act of Grace, the retroactive effect of which sets in automatically through the volition for ascent!

The woman of Subsequent Creation *could* fall so deeply despite her attribute of substantiality because, being the *last of her species,* she is *furthest away* from the proximity of God. As a compensation for this, however, she had through that part of the higher Substantiality a strong anchor within herself to which she could cling, and she would indeed have clung to it if it had only been the woman's earnest will to do so. However, the coarser spiritual element within her wanted it otherwise. And the distance from the proximity of God allowed it to triumph!

Woman *could* fall but she did not *have* to do so! For she had help enough at her side. But by not making use of it she never accepted the help!

In the Millennium, however, she must be *different*. Woman will now change and live only according to the Will of God! She will be purified or perish in the Judgment, for she is now receiving the Power of God on earth direct! Therewith *every* excuse for all womanhood has already fallen away! And every woman who has not yet *entirely* buried the element of substantiality within herself through frivolity and sinfulness *must* intuitively perceive the Power of God, and therein gather strength for higher power. In accordance with the living Laws in Creation! But only those who are still capable of gratefully recognising the pressure of the pure Power of God as such will have this automatic help.

Whoever is *unable* intuitively to perceive this Power any longer, nor wants to do so, will wither away, and will not much longer have the possibility to call herself woman!

You will now, of course, ask yourselves how it can then happen that many a human soul can be incarnated on earth alternately, at one time as a woman and at another as a man. The solution to this is not as difficult as you think; for a woman who is genuine in *every respect* will *never* get into the position of having to be incarnated in the gross material as a man.

Such a happening is again merely one of the evil consequences of the domination of the intellect, strange as this might sound!

The earthwoman who subjugates herself to the intellect, just by doing so represses her *genuine womanliness*. This becomes suppressed because the *delicacy of perception* which it represents is walled in by the cold intellect. The threads of fate are thereby so knotted that such a woman *must* be incarnated as a man the next time, because after this repression and walling in only the coarser spiritual element prevails, and in accordance with the Laws in Creation the threads simply cannot be knotted otherwise.

Such changes in incarnation are then necessary because *everything* that is touched in the spiritual core of man *must* develop. In particular the present unnatural imitation of men by women, which is contrary to the Laws of Creation, as well as the pronounced intellectual work, are bound to have serious consequences for womanhood because they disturb the harmony in Creation.

All such women suppress their genuine womanliness and *must* thereupon be incarnated in male bodies the next time. This in itself would not be so bad, but although the circumstance is such that the soul of the woman through this distortion of her task may well work *cleverly* in the male body, nevertheless this is only physical, and she will never be a truly genuine man in spirit and soul! It is and remains an aberration!

In the distortion of Creation these things have happened *hitherto*, but it will no longer be possible in the Millennium; for then all such souls of women who have walled in their womanliness will be absolutely unable to incarnate on earth but, being useless, they will fall into the category of those masses which are drawn into disintegration during the Judgment. They are all lost unless they remember their task as women in time and work accordingly.

But the reverse is also true! The soul of a man which through weakening has inclined itself too much towards the female species in thought and action, has thereby forced itself through the threads which have thus come into existence to enter a female body at a later incarnation. But here, too, it was just as little possible for such souls to become *genuine* women, because they lack that part of the higher Substantiality which belongs to womanhood.

For this reason we often find on earth men with predominant feminine characteristics and women with predominant masculine qualities! In neither case, however, is the respective *species* of soul genuine, but it is distorted. In Creation itself they are useless except for the possibility of physical procreation.

In this also the *first resolution* of the spirit-germ is decisive and fundamental for its whole existence; this resolution, however, is not made consciously but lies only in an inner, awakening urge! If this urge leads to a more delicate activity, then the existence of the spirit-germ is determined to be of a female kind; for thereby it keeps or holds a part of the higher Substantiality from which it severs or splits itself off. If it is inclined towards the coarser, active or positive working, then gradually the delicate and finer part of the higher Substantiality entirely severs itself and stays behind; in fact it is automatically cast off, so that for such a spirit-germ the masculine nature has therewith been determined as fundamental.

Thus right at the beginning the guarantee of the one-time free resolution, which is called the free volition, is fulfilled for the spiritual also here.

Woman! How much does this word alone express as a collective or radiating conception in the way of purity, grace and longing for the Luminous Heights!

What was meant to become of you, you earthwoman – something so great, so high, so noble – and *what* have you made of yourself!

You can no longer even perceive that your wish to enjoy admiration and appear desirable in the social trifling you so much favour, and every *word*, even every *glance* therein from the male side, are really insults to your womanly dignity...a besmirching of your God-willed purity!

If there were not still a *few* among you on earth in whose souls the Will of God could yet be anchored, verily it would be better if a movement of the Hand of God would sweep away these caricatures of womanhood from the smooth soil of this glorious Creation!

But for the sake of those few faithful ones the earthwoman, through the nearness of God, shall be permitted to rise to that height which was already ordained for her from the very beginning!

The *purity* of earthly woman lies in her *faithfulness!* For *faithfulness is* purity! A woman without faithfulness is unworthy to be called woman. And unfaithful is every woman who playfully trifles with men, either in words or in thoughts! Unfaithful to herself and to her high task in this Creation, therefore also on earth!

Faithfulness alone calls forth *all* the virtues in woman. Not one of them will be lacking!

Just as mankind had formed for themselves a one-sided, rigid, thus utterly wrong and narrow conception of chastity, so through their base thinking they have whittled down the high conception of purity to become something clumsy and ridiculous! They made a caricature, an unnatural fetter of it, which is contrary to the Laws in Creation, is utterly wrong, and merely shows the narrow limits of their paltry intellectual thinking!

The purity of the human woman rests solely in her *faithfulness!* Indeed, purity for mankind *is* faithfulness!

In absolutely plain words: Purity among men is *personified* in faithfulness!

He who grasps this *aright* will always be able to find and to walk upon the right path therein, and not push aside the Law of Creation through psychic distortions. Therefore you must try and learn to understand it aright!

Purity as such is *Divine!* Therefore *man* himself cannot possess purity in its original form at all; for he is but a small part in Creation and as such is subject to very definite laws. *Purity, however, can lie only in Divine Perfection; it is a part of this Perfection!*

Man cannot therefore just possess purity in the true sense, but he can only *personify* it figuratively in accordance with his nature, by expressing it in a changed form in faithfulness! Faithfulness is thus the gradation of purity for mankind. Man puts faithfulness in the place of Divine Purity. And above all and in the most noble sense woman does so! Whatever she does is *pure* when it is done in faithfulness. Nor is it otherwise with man. Faithfulness *is* purity for every human being!

Naturally faithfulness must be *genuine;* it must not merely spring from the imagination. Genuine faithfulness can only live in true love, never in passion or phantasy. This again contains a protection and also a standard which serves for self-examination!

Man cannot be divine and must adjust himself to the laws of *his own species.* All else becomes distorted, unnatural and unhealthy, merely the consequence of false opinions, of a conceited craving which strives to draw attention to himself at all costs, or to stand apart from his fellow-men, to be admired or also perhaps to do something special before God. Never does it hold anything genuine and natural, but it is a nonsensical, forceful crippling of the soul which also brings physical detriment. It by no means contains anything great or sublime, but merely shows a grotesque distortion which has a ludicrous effect in Creation.

Man can only come to useful value in Creation when he remains what he is meant to be, and when he tries to bring *his species* to perfection through ennoblement. However, he can only achieve this through swinging in the laws, not when he places himself outside them.

Therefore faithfulness is the *highest virtue* of every woman; it also enables her fully to accomplish her high task in this Creation!

Heed *this* well, ye men:

The high, fine Substantiality, that which is most perceptive and more gentle, *leads the household* in the great Creation! Therewith woman is also appointed to her office, which she is completely capable of fulfilling: To lead the *household* in the earthly existence, to offer a home in the right sense! It is the task of the woman to make this earth homelike and harmonious, and she can develop this task to artistic heights. Therein lies everything, and upon this everything must be founded if it is to thrive and blossom forth!

The *home* must become a *sanctuary* through the woman! It must become a Temple for the Will of God! *This* contains worship of God when you listen in to His Holy Volition in Creation and when you adjust your life and your activity on earth accordingly.

And also man, whose profession in the past has proved to be based exclusively on slavish subjection to the intellect, will change through the nature of woman when he is forced to recognise in her the hint to what is more noble.

Always look into the household of this Creation and you will know how you have to arrange your life *on earth!*

However, man must not disregard the order of a household in an inconsiderate way, no matter whether through neglectful non-observance or a craving for power; for the activity of the woman in the household is just as important as is that of the man in his profession. It is merely of a different nature, but it cannot be dispensed with. Woman's task in the home swings in the Law of God of which you are urgently reminded by the physical body, in that the latter seeks recreation, rest and nourishment, and last but not least... *harmony among the souls* therein, which refreshes and provides a new incentive and new strength for *all* man's activities.

The balance in this, however, must be absolutely harmonious. For this reason the woman, too, must respect the work of the man, and not think that *her* activity may alone be decisive. The activity of both parts shall be joined *to* each other in an even swinging. The one may not disturb the other!

Thus man must not wilfully upset or confuse the orders in the household, but through being punctual and showing a growing understanding he must even help so that everything can keep its harmonious course.

This is what you can and *must* learn from Creation. In the Millennium you will yet be compelled to do so, otherwise you could never exist therein!

All those who now do not wish to obey the Laws of this Creation are rebels against their home, against their Creator, their God! They will be cast out and destroyed by the Laws themselves, which through the increased Power of

God now quickly and invincibly turn against everything that destroys the God-Willed harmony.

Therefore pay heed to your home, men, and learn to understand this Subsequent Creation! You *must* become familiar with it and now at last adjust yourselves to the order also here on earth!

MAN ASKS question upon question! As soon as I offer him a new knowledge he immediately comes with new questions, even before he has understood and absorbed everything which I proffered to him.

This is his great mistake! He wants to *hasten* forward! If I were to adjust myself to *him* in this matter he could never accomplish anything; for with his questioning he always remains stationary only at his spot, like a lazy wanderer who seats himself comfortably in the shade of the woods and lets others tell him of his goal, instead of pulling himself together and striding towards the goal.

On his way he himself would then *notice* and *experience* everything he would like to know in answer to the questions which he always allows to arise within himself. He must *move,* otherwise he will not get to the goal!

In my lecture "Woman and man", I said that each person should draw from my words practical applications for his present life on earth. If he wishes to follow this advice then there is nothing else for him to do but to *make* my Word *come to life* within him just as I give it to him; for I know exactly what man needs for this, and I always arrange my lectures accordingly. He must follow the discourse word for word, for they contain a step-ladder which carefully leads his soul upwards. A path which the soul *is able to* follow if it only will!

His quick questioning, however, shows that he wants to *learn* in his hitherto accustomed intellectual way, and again brushes aside the necessary experiencing. *Learning* is of no avail to the *soul,* for that which has been learned stays behind with the body as soon as the first step is taken away from this earth. The soul takes along only that which has been *experienced.* I have said this often before, and yet despite this earthman always approaches the Holy Word in the wrong way again! He wants to know better, or he does not like to relinquish his long-accustomed manner of doing things.

There is a guidance in the structure of my lectures which he does not understand. Nor is it even necessary for him to recognise it therein as long as he only follows it and does not seek to hurry on ahead in his desire to know, like the superficial readers of a book who read for the sake of the *suspense,* just to fill in free hours with it, and to divert themselves from one-sided thinking about their everyday activity.

While reading they do not see the characters in the book coming to life before them, they pay no attention to the various developments which the persons acting therein have to live through inwardly, they do not perceive the precise consequences arising therefrom, which are continually capable of changing the circumstances and the surroundings. All this they disregard, but they advance by leaps and bounds just to learn quickly about this or that in the action. They derive no profit from the *best* books describing a part of life on earth, from which the reader could draw much for himself if he *experienced* everything within himself aright!

Just as those readers who absolutely seek to devour all books in their zeal without ever recognising their true purpose and sense, but knowing how to differentiate between only two kinds – the fascinating and the non-fascinating books, *so* are men who immediately allow questions to arise within themselves again as soon as they read a lecture concerning the knowledge of Creation!

First of all with the greatest effort and expenditure of energy they should seek to *draw* from each lecture what it offers!

If then something does not immediately appear quite clear to them they must not look *ahead* in their seeking, but they *must look back in the Message* in order to delve *therein and* find enlightenment *there.*

And man will *find* it if in his spirit he lets the Message arise in pictures before him! He finds *everything* when he really seeks. Through this necessary seeking, however, the Message becomes continually clearer, stronger and more secure within him. Thus he learns to know it ever better and...to *experience* it! Just *in this way* I force him to do something that he would never do voluntarily owing to his spiritual indolence, which in part still hangs over all men.

Therein lies a guidance which he did not recognise, but which is an invaluable help to him in bringing my Message to life. He thus learns to recognise all that is expressed in the Message, all that it contains, about which he had so far no idea in spite of reading it. He sees *how* he can delve into this Message and makes what appears to him the ever new discovery that indeed he does find *everything* therein; that it was only due to himself, to his weak manner of seeking, when so much escaped his attention previously.

Not *one* passage can be avoided thereby! And this is not asking too much for a knowledge of Creation! Whoever finds this too much will never be able to make an end of it!

I am trying to guide you along the path which is best for you. However, you must go along *with me* with firm steps, and you must not always desire to try and hurry ahead as do the readers whose superficiality I quoted to you as an example.

It is the same, too, with my last lecture about "Woman and man". From what I know of people they will again have questions arising in their brains before they take the trouble to find an answer from the Message or in the lecture itself, and by no means last *through observation of their fellow-men in the present life on earth*. It is just *in this* that you will discover the most, because in observing it through my Message it offers you abundant confirmation of everything I explained to you! But mark well, only when you regard it from the contents of my Message!

This stipulates that you must stand in the Message aright. If you are able to do so then you can immediately and exactly recognise everything, absolutely everything in your surroundings, and thus you become knowing, you become wise! You will then read in the life on earth just as one reads in a book. It is opened up to you for this purpose through the Message!

Just try it! Your eyes will then be quickly opened, and you will therewith have awakened. Do not shun any trouble to achieve what is so necessary!

It is not that you should only see the faults of your fellow-men in this way! That is not how it is meant, but you shall recognise *life itself* therein with all its consequences and changes, to which my Message is your guide and always will remain as guide in unchangeable faithfulness! Only *in* life or *through* life itself will you recognise all the values of my Message, and not with your pretended knowledge. And through the Message you can in turn view life aright, in such a way as is beneficial for you. Here, too, everything works in a reciprocal way, and true knowledge only comes through experiencing!

In this way you will soon become *one* with the Message; it becomes life for you, because only from out of this life are you able to recognise it; for it speaks to you of life.

Therefore you must not seek to recognise the value of the Message in the book itself, but through the observation of life! With eager and most careful observation of all that happens around and within yourselves you must contribute to the possibility of *finding* the Message *again* in life, out of which it speaks to you.

That is your path to the true recognition of my Words, which must bring you benefit and in the end victory over Darkness! Therewith quite automatically you will receive the Crown of Eternal Life, which is being permitted to exist eternally as a self-conscious being in this Creation. Thereby you can then co-operate in its further development by spreading blessings for the joy and peace of all creatures.

And after my last lecture there indeed *arose* questions within you again! Questions which are bound to bring a certain oppression even, though an answer is easily to be found in the Message; for there it states consolingly that each consequence of a wrong action also contains the possibility of release and thus of redemption, as soon as the human spirit learns from it and recognises the wrong.

And yet a certain anxiety exists when a person with advanced knowledge says to himself that he is a distorted human soul, if once he was a woman on earth and the next time a man, or vice-versa. His soul becomes oppressed.

That, of course, is wrong and once again throwing the child out with the bath! For what lies nearest to this is the recognition that such a person *had* distorted his soul! The distortion does *not* necessarily *still exist*. In reality he has only changed his garment, the body! But in spite of all the changes the *spirit* itself always remained that which it had originally resolved upon at the start of its wanderings through Creation; for in this respect there is also for him, as with everything in Creation, only *one single* and decisive free resolve to which the spirit then remains bound.

Thus the oppression arises only from a too superficial absorption of the Message; for everyone should know from the Message that just such a change could be of benefit for the one concerned. It does give him the possibility of putting things straight again; it induces him, indeed it helps him in the strongest way to make everything good again. The soul can even *grow strong* through compulsory experiences of this nature.

Now it must not be imagined again that those whose path remained straight have missed something! This is not so! But where a distortion occurred through one's own wrong volition, only *there* can the change mercifully become beneficial in order to strengthen this distorted soul which showed such a weakness, to strengthen it to such an extent that it will not repeat the mistake. With this, of course, the fault has also fallen away from it!

Now look around you for once and observe your fellow-men! You will soon find among them women who bear *masculine* characteristics in their nature. Just today there are more of them than ever. One can say that much that is womanly appears to be absolutely *infected* with this; for it is not difficult to understand that a woman or a girl of this kind has and *must* have something in her nature which is *distorted*, because a woman naturally neither can nor should be a man.

With that, of course, I never mean the body; for this is almost always markedly female with the exception of the hips, which in most such cases are reminiscent of the male through their narrowness, which is therefore actually *not womanly*.

I mention this purposely because I immediately name therewith a distinctive *outward* mark. In most cases the female body harbouring a distorted male soul will have this distinctive mark of the narrow hips inclining towards the male structure, in contradistinction to those whose soul is just beginning to strive towards the masculine in some way, be it in their opinions or in their activities, causing a propensity through which the threads develop for the next incarnation into a male body. It is the same with the male bodies which receive broader hips inclining towards the female structure, as soon as they harbour a distorted female soul.

Of course there are also exceptions through the degeneration of the physical structure of women, which are due to over-breeding, also to one-sided sports or wrong physical activity indulged in by mothers, the consequences of which are transferred to the children.

We have therewith also designated two principal groups which we must keep separate from each other.

The one group of women and girls on earth who already bear a distorted male soul within themselves, and the other group who still harbour female souls but who are striving towards the masculine due to distorted conceptions, which they have either adopted voluntarily or received through a wrong upbringing!

I probably need not specially mention that in the last-named cases not only the female souls themselves have to bear the consequences, but those who gave cause for this will also be woven into the threads of guilt.

However, we do not want to digress too much with this, but remain with the two groups we have found for the present. Let us eliminate those still developing, for they are female souls in the process of distortion whose physical bodies, due to the density and heaviness connected therewith, naturally cannot change any more in this present life on earth. This is reserved for them in their next incarnation.

But they are offered deliverance even from this! When in *this* present life they still pull themselves together and energetically shake off all that is unwomanly! Through this new threads must immediately form which will incline and pull towards *female* incarnation, while the other threads no longer receive any supply of power.

What is finally decisive, however, is the *exact condition* of the soul *at its departure*, the side towards which it is personally inclined most strongly. If up till then the female volition, thinking and activity has regained the upper hand within the soul, its radiation at its departure from earth will mainly strive towards *those* threads, and thereby revive *such* as lead towards the womanly; while the others after only a short and light experience in the beyond can then quickly dry up and fall off, providing they were not knotted *too strongly* beforehand.

It is also possible that these wrong threads are already redeemed during the time on earth through a strong womanly volition, and that the soul becomes free from them before it has to pass over. All this depends on the nature and strength of each particular volition, and on whether the soul incarnated on earth has still sufficient time left before its necessary departure to do this; for the Law must be fulfilled in any case, either here on earth or after passing over.

However, for our consideration today let us take *only* those distorted souls which are already incarnated in corresponding physical bodies as a result of this distortion.

First among them the earthly womanhood in which weak masculine souls were incarnated, because in their former lives they deviated too much from the purely male thinking and activity! This already explains that in the case of such earthwomen only *weak* male souls can be concerned. Thus it is not at all praiseworthy when a woman, contrary to the feminine nature, seeks to push male characteristics into the foreground or even to show them.

A woman of this kind is not really strong in any direction as regards her thoughts and actions, neither towards the male nor towards the female direction. She would also gain more for herself *in the earthly sense* if she tries to suppress the distortion.

Her experience, however, helps her to change; for she must soon notice that a genuine man never feels happy in her proximity. He finds within himself no understanding for her. Much less can any harmony arise, because genuine manhood is repulsed by everything false, thus also by the masculine striving of a woman! A marriage between a genuine man and a woman who carries within herself a distorted male soul can only take place on a purely intellectual basis. Genuine harmony will never arise therewith.

Such a woman will in any case be automatically drawn to *those* men who carry within themselves a distorted female soul!

Also the latter are subconsciously not taken seriously by men with undistorted souls. This unconscious intuitive perception and action, however, contains the force of truth, of reality.

However, all the consequences of such instinctive and intuitive actions, which we can describe as *natural,* produce an educational effect on the distorted souls who, through the painful experiences arising from their disappointments, are again bent towards the right direction, at least in many cases. But this does not preclude that later on they may ever again relapse into such or similar faults. Unless they become stronger through these experiences they will remain like reeds swaying in the wind. Much, much, however, can men *now* spare themselves in the future by becoming knowing in these matters. Much suffering and much time! For not until now could a soul become conscious of being distorted.

Just as it is with male souls in women's bodies so it also is with female souls in men's bodies. The same consequences arise for both parts out of one uniform, immutable law.

One thing which I have already mentioned will strike you when observing your surroundings: that strangely enough female souls in men's bodies feel drawn to male souls in women's bodies, and vice versa. Thus here the woman with a stronger intellectual volition and with predominant male characteristics feels in most cases unconsciously drawn to a man with more delicate characteristics.

Therein lies not only an unconscious seeking for balance, but also the great Law of the Attraction of Homogeneous Species is at work here.

The homogeneous species lies *in the distortion of the souls!* The souls of both are distorted, and through this there exists a real homogeneity, the species of which attract each other in accordance with the Law.

The attraction of the man towards the woman (sexual instinct being excluded from this) is the consequence or the effect of *another* law, and not that of the attraction of homogeneous species. For the sake of a better understanding it is appropriate if at this point I say something about the homogeneous species and explain what is to be understood by that term; for therein lies that which is decisive here.

The attraction of the homogeneous species is not the only kind which seems to have an *attracting* effect. There is a great difference in the process of the apparent attraction. The attraction of homogeneous species, this great Law of Creation, however, is *fundamental* for *everything striving for union* in Creation, no matter how this happens. This great Law as such is the *cause* of all these happenings, brings them about and also regulates them. It floats above everything and works like a motive force in them and through them in the entire weaving of Creation.

Therefore I first want to *separate* the species of attraction according to the character of their actual working, i. e., according to their manifestation, into the genuine *attraction* and into the *desire for a union* of split parts of a definite species, such desire being forcibly brought about by this great Law which overtops and conditions everything.

Consequently there is an *attracting* and a *desiring for union* in the working of Creation. The effects of both processes appear to be the same outwardly. The inner motivating power for this, however, is entirely different.

The *attraction* results from similar species which are complete within themselves, and the *desire for union* arises in the *split* species which continue to strive for the formation of a species again!

The assertion made by people that opposites attract each other but like poles repel each other is therefore only an *apparent* contradiction of the Law of the Attraction of Homogeneous Species.

In reality, however, this holds no contradiction; for this man-made assertion is valid and correct for the process in which there is the desire by the various split species for union into a definite species of full value. *But only in this!* Only among the complete species themselves does there come into force the actual Law of the Attraction of Homogeneous Species, which in addition calls forth the motivating effect of seeking union to establish a definite species of full value. It swings above and in it!

What man has hitherto recognised through his science are but the small happenings among the *split* species. He has not at all so far discovered the effect and manifestation of the real species, because on earth and in its nearer circle there exist only *split* species, i. e., *small parts* the activities and effects of which he was able to observe.

Thus the female spirit and the male spirit are also nothing but a *split* species each, which in accordance with the Laws of Creation strive towards each other seeking a union, i. e., they are only small parts which by their union in turn furnish but a part to the real *spiritual species*.

What is here stated, however, concerns only the *fundamental feature* between the female and the spiritual; whereas the soul-cloaks and finally the gross material cloaks are much smaller parts of consequent splittings from other species which, according to their particular basic species, produce a desire for union and therein show definite results.

The human being himself, for example, is no definite species, but only a splitting which carries within itself the desire for union.

But his evil thoughts or evil deeds are a definite species which attracts the homogeneous species and is attracted by it! From this you see that from a split species there can issue not only split parts but a complete species.

Let me give another hint here: There lies a very definite and immutable limitation in the attraction of homogeneous species. This also holds a greater power which is anchored in the basic law. The desire for union on the part of the split species, however, contains a greater freedom of movement granted through weakened power. For this reason *split* species can unite in *various* ways, and thus result in changing effects and forms.

Today I can only give a brief illustration of this because all these points vary a thousandfold and we should find no end. Unless *I* open up for you a *very definite* path in this, which is adapted to your human capacity, you would never be able to receive a really well-rounded picture of the happenings in Creation.

Therefore you must also follow me slowly! You must not try to go one step further before you have inwardly absorbed everything I explained to you correctly and ineffaceably; for otherwise you could and would become helpless on your way despite my guidance. You will derive no benefit from an *unconscious* following.

Reflect that you are following me along a path on which I do not return with you! We climb up a ladder together on which there must be no single rung missing, and thus we go up rung by rung!

If you do not experience each rung in the right way so that they become really familiar to you, it may easily happen that you suddenly lose your support on your way and must fall. If the rungs have not become familiar to you, have not become your own, then some day perhaps you may already stand at a considerable height, but confused; you can no longer continue upwards because you lack the secure support for this beneath your feet. But neither can you go back any more, because the rungs have not become sufficiently familiar for you to do so, and thus you must crash headlong down in a sudden fall!

Do not take such a warning and admonition too lightly, for your entire existence is at stake!

AFTER having considered the nearest surroundings of man upon earth, the basis is now provided to cast a glance also at the guidance standing by his side and helping him.

It is indeed necessary that something should be mentioned about it, for much nonsense is spoken just in and about this matter by those who on the whole believe in a guidance or know something of it, so that sometimes one would like to smile if it were not so sad.

It is sad because through his odd efforts to regard himself at any cost as extremely valuable, the condition of the human spirit is once again clearly demonstrated. I do not think it is still necessary to quote examples in this matter, for each of my listeners has probably at one time or another become acquainted with such persons who talk about their "high" guidance or about the guide himself, whom they declare they clearly perceive and ... still they do not act according to his gentle urging!

They do not add the latter, it is true; but just those who talk so much about their guidance, who imagine they are on intimate and companionable terms with it, seldom or only in part act as their guidance would like them to. Mostly they do not act like it at all! This can be rather safely assumed with such people! It is merely a pleasant entertainment for them and nothing else. To some extent they behave like rather spoilt children, giving themselves airs about it, and mainly and above all wanting to indicate how much effort is expended upon them "from above"!

Naturally their guide is always a "very high one", wherever they do not prefer to divine in him a beloved and affectionate relative who is very concerned about them. In more than a thousand cases, however, it is supposed to be Jesus Himself Who comes from the Light in order to warn them or to strengthen them with praise and, what is more, Who if asked about people well known to them sometimes commends such persons or criticises them adversely!

They love to speak of this with respectful awe, but one can easily recognise that this veneration is not meant for the Son of God but for the fact that they are personally deemed worthy of such solicitude! In plain words: It is veneration for themselves!

Anybody who is taken into the confidence of such persons – and they are eager to tell as many people as possible about it – can quickly experience the truth of what I have stated in this matter by meeting such information with scepticism. Then such communicative ones show a displeasure which can only issue from an injured vanity!

They are finished with you or "through" with you, as the popular saying so aptly describes the frame of mind of those who have been hurt thereby. They look down upon you only with contempt!

It is also certain that they will then consult their guidance about you as soon as an opportunity arises, and receive the answer (which already they did not expect to be otherwise) with great content; for this guide is at the same time their friend, and if in their opinion he is not the Son of God Himself they look upon him more like an obliging valet in whom they confide everything, because anyway he knows it already, and only awaits opportunities to confirm what they say or give necessary advice.

Go out and investigate, and observe in the right way! You will very soon find all this confirmed ad nauseam! If just once you are so bold as to call much of it stupid, then you must promptly seek shelter for yourselves unless you want to be stoned. Even if this cannot happen today in the physical sense yet it is certain to be done morally, you can be sure of that!

In a hypocritical pitying manner it then passes from mouth to mouth and from one letter to another, in complete confidence and with deep earnestness! In an underhand way a grave is dug for you, but with great zeal and such assurance as indicates practice, in order to put a well-deserved end to your depravity and also to your dangerousness!

These people smell the danger in the wind which threatens their credibility! Above all, however, they do not wish to be deprived of opportunities so well adapted to enhance the value of their personality in such a wonderful way. Their "high" guidance proves it, even if their poor fellow-men cannot yet perceive anything of it! And *therefore* they fight for it!

Such, and not otherwise, is the conceit of these people, which becomes clearly evident in the nature of the gossip about their guidance. They want to be *esteemed* for this and not perchance to help their fellow-men in all kindness. They love to be envied and admired!

I would like to lead you to the recognition of the laws *governing* the guidances so that you may also now become knowing in this matter; for the guidances are also not subject to arbitrariness, but are interwoven with you into the threads of your fate!

Everything is subject to reciprocal activity in Creation, and this Law of Reciprocal Action also lies behind the secret of the appointment of your guidances. You find no gap, nowhere a loophole in which it would be possible to insert something that does not unconditionally belong there according to the Law.

After the last lectures you will readily be able to conceive how many threads are coursing around you, which are interwoven with you and you with them. But this is only a small part of it. And there is no gap in the great weaving which envelops you. Nothing can be slipped in or inserted arbitrarily, there is no squeezing in between, neither is it possible to cast anything off or to become free unless it has been worn off, lived to its dead end by you according to the Law.

Nor is it otherwise therefore with your guidance! The guidance you have is firmly linked with you in some way or other, in many cases through the attraction of homogeneous species!

Many a guide can and must through the act of guiding redeem happenings *for himself,* happenings which bind him to the World of heavy Gross Matter. This is new to you, but easy to understand. In as much as a guiding one seeks by his guidance to prevent some earthman from making the same mistakes on earth as he himself committed, although the dweller on earth may be predisposed to do so, the guide *therewith* also redeems his guilt in the World of heavy Matter without having to be specially incarnated on that account. For the effect of his guidance becomes manifest *on earth* (where at one time he had failed) through the protégé he is allowed to guide. In this way the cycle of many a happening also closes for those in the beyond precisely where it must close, without the one in the beyond attached to the threads having to be incarnated on earth once more for this purpose.

It is a simple happening corresponding to the Law, and yet it offers relief to him who guides a man on earth, and benefits are at the same time given to the earthmen.

It is just the Law of Attraction of Homogeneous Species which easily brings very many of those who want to guide into the proximity of *such* earthmen as carry within themselves some similar quality, and who threaten to fall into the same mistakes as the one desirous of guiding them committed himself at one time. And the Law then creates the threads which connect the guide with his protégé.

Consider in all strictness the blessing which lies retroactively in this process for *both* parties, for the guide and for the one he is automatically compelled or, let us say, mercifully granted to guide through the reciprocal action in the Law of the Attraction of Homogeneous Species!

And there are in addition many other mercies which arise from this *one* process alone, for thereby new threads go out in all directions, which again carry within themselves reciprocal action, and which in some places connected with these two main parties strengthen, uplift, further and redeem. For mercy and love alone are contained in the final effects of *all* the laws in Creation, which in the end rise upwards and meet in the one great basic Law: The Law of Love!

Indeed love is *everything!* Love is justice and likewise purity! There is no separation between these three. These three are one, and therein again perfection rests. Heed these my words, take them as a key for all happenings in Creation!

It will be absolutely natural for you who know my Message that only that can always find connection with you which lies closest to you, because very definite requirements which permit of no gap must be fulfilled for this purpose.

Thus it is contained in the Law of Creation that a guide wishing to be connected with you can only be so connected *when* he himself is still enveloped by a cloak, i. e., by a body which in its species comes nearest to your own, so that the thread which is to connect you with him can adhere.

From this you must conclude that he can by no means be a "specially high spirit" who guides you; for only he who is still sufficiently close to this earth can guide an earthman; otherwise he would already be too much of a stranger to everything; neither would there be any sense in it nor could it bring you great benefit if there was a gap in this. Both would then fail to understand each other; the guide his protégé, and the latter his guide!

A *single* gap would be bound to render successful guidance impossible.

However, there is no gap in the lawfulness of the happenings in Creation! Thus not in this either; for a single gap would cause the great work of Creation itself to collapse completely.

Thus between the guide and the one guided there exists a close reciprocal activity which is conditioned by the Law of Attraction of Homogeneous Species.

If you now wish to ask how it can become possible that at times something comes to the guided one on earth from a higher spiritual place, then these exceptions do not overthrow the Law. You need only remember that the same Law providing you with your direct guide also gives *the latter* a guide, and provides the latter with one again, and so on. There is only *one* Law forming an *entire chain* which must swing in this Law!

Thus it may happen that a guide from a higher place mediates something to you through this chain, or better, through the threads of this chain. This, however, happens only when very special matters are in question. But the development always takes place within the immovable laws because there are no other ways for it whatever.

It is a ladder which must be taken rung by rung, both upwards and downwards, and there is no other possibility at all. I shall give special explanations about the happenings in connection with mediumistic abilities, but these do not belong here.

For a person on earth the blessing of the Law lies in the fact that he always has a guide, who is precisely acquainted with the faults from which the guided one suffers, because these faults were also the guide's, who has already lived through all the *consequences* thereof.

Therefore the guide is able to advise and help in all cases from his own experience. In this way he can also protect the one he guides from many things, provided that the latter pays close attention to his hidden urging or admonition; for he must not coerce him. He may likewise only help *where* the guided person carries within himself the desire, the yearning or the demand for it, and not otherwise. He must leave the decision of the free will to the earthman, this again being according to the Law, to which the guide himself remains bound; bound by a reciprocal action which can generally let him intuitively perceive something only *when through your volition you urge him to it.*

The threads connecting you with your guidances become taut through the radiation of this your volition. Only through these threads does your guide then intuitively perceive *with* you, and only in *this way* can he also support you! He cannot perhaps turn you, but merely strengthen and support you! It is also a condition thereby that you must *first* and *seriously* occupy yourselves with it! Do not think it is so easy!

Apart from this great mercy through the possibility of redemption, such processes sometimes hold a punishment as well for the guide, when in such wise *he is also bound to perceive* that in spite of his warning you act differently, just as he himself acted at one time. He thereby experiences within you a repetition which causes him to become sad, but which also strengthens and matures him in his intention never to fail again in such a manner!

However, all the greater is also his joy when he perceives the *success* of his guidance *with* you. Therewith he is also redeemed from his guilt!

After such a redemption a change takes place in your guidance; for many in the beyond are waiting to be allowed to guide an earthman in order thereby to redeem their own guilt through giving such help. Yet the desire for redemption must naturally *not* be *the motive* for the longing to guide! If it is to redeem him from a guilt then it is necessary that he actually wishes to do it *out of love for his fellow-men* in order to save them from the consequences of erroneous ways on earth! *Only* when one in the beyond has reached *this point* is he allowed to guide earthmen, and the redemption comes to him as a mercy for his good volition! And this compulsion as well as the later granting of redemption are contained in the final effects of his threads of fate, which adjust themselves to the nature of his radiating volition in the most perfect justice.

You must not forget that beyond the ponderousness of the earth everything is always *experiencing!* The pseudo-cleverness of the intellectual thinking has ceased there. Thus everything is genuine. It does not happen that a human spirit wants to act *in a scheming manner* there, nor can he do so, but he really lives himself to the end in everything! *Without forethought,* exactly as the human spirit is in his particular condition!

The afore-mentioned circumstances pertain to *one* kind of guide. Then there are other kinds which are connected with you especially strongly, and whom you have perhaps already known on earth. Relationship does not count in this matter. But the earthly *conception* about physical kinship ties many firm threads which then keep you connected for a time.

It is only the *conception* which you yourselves created that links you up and not the relationship, as you have imagined in the past. Your conception of it creates the threads or your love, your hate, and thus it is that departed relatives can also still guide you.

However, they must be capable of guiding; they must be able to have something *to give* you through their own experiencing, for otherwise they cannot guide you. It is not sufficient just to cling to you!

But here again there is much that has a say in it. Thus it is possible that someone on earth has somehow or other brought you up in a wrong way. He thereby remains connected with you. If after his departure he has by some means come to a personal recognition of his faults in this matter then these threads draw him to you. Let us call them threads of *repentance* in this case! Only when he has succeeded in changing you will he too be freed from this, not before!

If, however, you do not lay aside the wrong you learned from him, but transfer it again to your children, then he is thereby bound with you also to these children, and so on, until he at last succeeds in making good his error with one child.

Thus there are many kinds which provide you with guides, all of whom can only serve you for the best as soon as you pay attention to their quiet influence. However, they can *never force* you, but in their activity they mould the "*conscience*" which admonishes and warns you!

Pay heed to this! The activity of the guides forms a part of your conscience, the origin and nature of which you were never able to unravel properly! Now I give you a clue to this today!

As everywhere in this Creation it is always the *specific condition* of the guided human spirit *himself* which alone is decisive for the nature of the guide. The more the spirit of earthman matures inwardly the higher he himself can rise, even if he is *unconscious* of this on earth, as is nearly always the case.

The plane of the particular guide, who changes with the maturing of the guided human spirit, is at the *limit* of the latter's personal and safe ascent. Through his own experiences the guide will always stand half a step higher than the one whom he is allowed or also compelled to guide. Yet all these cases are *so* different in nature that it would be wrong for me to name and explain very definite ones. You might become confused through this, because with very definite pictures you only bind yourselves to *fixed* ideas.

For this reason I only make known to you the final effects without describing special species thereof. In this way you remain absolutely free and unbound in your knowledge about it, for later all this will become manifest in so many forms through your own experiences. –

As soon as a guide can be detached from you a new one immediately approaches you. In many cases they are guides who have suffered from another of your faults, different to that which the previous guide was able to redeem for himself. Thus when one guide is relieved it does not necessarily follow that his successor must be standing on a higher plane.

A higher guide can only approach you when in the meantime *you too* have attained a higher step spiritually; for the guide can never stand below you but often *by your side*. It is only that through his personal experiences he has *come to know more* than *you* have, but by no means is he always an entire step higher. For he must still be able to *understand* you, he must be able intuitively to perceive with you or, better still, be able to *enter* into your intuitive perception. This stipulates that he cannot be far away from you.

And any person possessing a little knowledge about the unswerving lawfulness in Creation will scarcely imagine that he is directly connected with the Son of God Jesus, which is *utterly impossible* for a human spirit!

But just numerous minor mediums lay claim to this privilege without realising that they could not even bear the power of an *approach!* And thousands of self-complacent people allow themselves to be duped and enticed through these errors, because they are agreeable to them and they like to indulge in such self-delusions; for they are flattered by them!

My explanations have nothing to do with the numerous confused gabblings of the minor mediumistic persons. I speak of serious guidances only and not of prattlers, who are also to be found among *those* departed ones *strongly* populating the *nearer surroundings* of this gross material earth. That is another chapter which we shall deal with more closely when the opportunity presents itself.

I am only giving you all that which can be really beneficial and which consequently leads you upwards. The sections which you do not need to become acquainted with more closely we only touch in passing. For the present they do not merit any attention at all.

It is a sad feature of the present low spiritual state that men just love to busy themselves with and hear about this most of all. Let such enthusiasts go their own way; they only want to entertain themselves or wrap themselves in self-complacent comfort, which can never hold ascent nor the possibility of it.

Prattlers from the beyond merely keep you from serious activity and earnest thinking; for it is their peculiarity, since they also dawdle and fritter away their time instead of using it full of gratitude.

It will be a great horror for them when they must suddenly recognise this and slide downwards as useless for the new time!

To sum it up let me tell you once more:

First of all there are only *helpers,* who through the same kind of *faults* as *yours* were able to become connected with you. Only later, when you no longer have faults to carry about with you, and when you only bear within yourselves the longing for the Luminous Heights, are real *guides then* taken into consideration for you, who are connected to you through the same kind of *qualities* and *virtues* as *yours.*

These in truth only lead you upwards by strengthening your virtues, and by affecting you through their great strength like a powerful magnet.

Only *these* are the *guides* whom you can really call guides. It is true that even now they already hold you firmly in a mysterious way, quite unknown to you, because their power penetrates the Universe. But naturally they hold only those who still have *virtues* active within them, virtues which are not buried too deeply.

But you cannot yet speak of these guides here on earth because first of all the *helpers* must develop their activity for you in order to support you, so that you can purify your garments from all the dirt you have drawn upon yourselves. But all the helpers still have to atone *themselves,* which they achieve by helping you.

The true guides, however, are already standing above all these, waiting for you and meanwhile holding you, so that you do not fall – and perish – during your great purification.

Here, too, everything takes effect through the Law of Attraction of Homogeneous Species. They are the *Primordial Beings,* who work powerfully in this way.

That Primordial Being, for instance, who embodies heroism correspondingly affects *all* those subsequently created ones who carry heroism as a virtue within themselves, and so also the other Primordial Beings, each according to his distinctive kind.

The Primordial Being in the Primordial Spiritual Realm always manifests by himself alone for each kind. Through his radiation he then influences *groups* of the same nature which are still in the Primordial Spiritual Sphere but further below. And *groups* of each kind exist even further downwards in Paradise, among the perfected ones of the subsequently created, developed human spirits; and from there the radiations extend ever further downwards into the entire Subsequent Creation, to those with whom they can still find connection.

Thus at the highest place of the Primordial Spiritual Sphere there is for *each* of the virtues only *one* embodiment who is the *guide* therein for *all* the human spirits of the same nature! And only these few are the *actual* guides, but solely in the most pure and comprehensive objectivity through their radiation, *never personally!*

All this is already clearly stated in the Message!

Man is consequently not even able to designate a Primordial Being as his *personal* guide. It would be wrong! And how much less Jesus, the Son of God!

Become familiar with the fact, you men, that only the really awakened ones can notice something of this great fundamental guidance through their true knowledge, which brings *conviction.* And not everybody who boasts of it is really awakened in his spirit, and thus newly born!

It is much better if you first speak about *helpers,* for they are much closer to you than the guides and bring you great benefit through the immense trouble they take on your behalf! Give them your hand in joy and gratitude and listen to their admonishing, which is part of your conscience!

THREADS OF LIGHT ABOVE YOU!

You SHOULD now put together the lectures I gave about Substantiality and the closest surroundings of earthman, in which I spoke of the undulating and weaving constantly going on around you, and try to regard them as being assembled into *one* picture.

It is really not so difficult. You will be able to recognise their connection with each other and also with yourselves very quickly and easily. In your imagination set everything in motion just as you do with a jigsaw puzzle, first of all as regards the individual effects working in the various directions, *taking them one after another,* and finally in *their combined effects upon each other as a whole.* You will see how clearly in the course of time the picture unfolds and comes alive before you.

In doing so try to see how each evil thought or volition runs through the weaving like a shadow, more or less dimming what is clear and destroying the beauty here and there, whereas clear, good thinking or volition penetrates the threads luminously, spreading beauty and lustre on the paths it follows.

The mechanism will soon become so familiar to you that it will form a support for you which will only permit you to think or desire, and also finally to carry out, that which is good.

Spare no pains in this matter, for you will obtain such rich reward as nobody can reduce. And when you then have the activated picture before you absorb something else in addition, which will give a termination and a frame worthy of the picture.

Instead of a ceiling imagine many luminous, delicate threads hanging above the "weaving around you" like the thinnest and daintiest of gossamer veils, which sends forth a delightful fragrance that can animate and strengthen in a singular way as soon as one is able to become aware and take notice of it.

Innumerable are these threads, possessing manifold possibilities of application, and ready at any time to lower themselves to *those* places where a longing for them is revealed.

If somewhere in the depths of the mechanism a small spark glows from which a longing, a prayer or a strong desire arises, then the threads of the same species immediately reach out towards this little spark, connect themselves with it magnetically and strengthen it, so that it can become brighter and more luminous and thus quickly push aside all that is more dark and gloomy around it. And when it blazes up brightly it scorches all the spots which still connect *that* strand with darkness or evil on which this spark sought to develop itself. Thus this strand is very quickly freed from all that is holding it down.

But only light, pure wishes or prayers can achieve the connections with the luminous threads continually hanging above the mechanism which always surrounds a human soul or an earthman. Dark wishes never find any support therefrom because they are unable to bring about a connection.

For every earthman the connection with these threads coming from Substantiality takes place through the cloak or body of medium gross matter, which is usually called the astral body. The soul radiates through the astral body according to the nature of each of its emotions. If the emotions of the soul are of a dark nature then the luminous threads hanging in readiness do not find a channel for the help. Only when the emotions are luminous can the astral body radiate *in such a way* that it quite automatically opens itself for *those* threads coming from on high which are of the same nature as the particular emotions of the soul.

Therefore this astral body of medium gross matter is the true entrance and exit gate of the soul. In reality the threads mentioned are consequently active on the plane of medium gross matter, which is called the astral plane, and work through the latter's mediation according to the nature of its glowing.

Picture all this to yourselves! It is so simple, and yet so dependable and just, that it is never possible for any thought or volition towards what is good to remain without help. It is always made so easy for the human spirit. *Too easy* that with his strange ways he would still respect it according to the value belonging to and inherent in these processes!

In order to avoid a gap in your ability to depict it I will also show you the origin of these threads, otherwise they will remain hanging in the air for you, which is really impossible because everything has – indeed *must* have – a very definite starting point in this Creation, nor could it exist without such!

The threads are the radiations of many substantiate mediators, the activities of which have not yet become very familiar to you, but which mediators were already well known to the ancient peoples.

In the same way as you human spirits on earth should have become the collectors and then the mediators for passing on all the radiations of such human spirits as are more matured than you are and who stand on higher planes in Creation; and just as these in turn carry this out in regard to even higher and more luminous matured human spirits, until ultimately this results in the connection with Paradise, where the completed and perfected ones of the human spirits of this Subsequent Creation dwell in joyous activity, who are likewise in touch through a chain of mediators reaching up to the most perfect ones of the Primordial Beings in the Primordial Spiritual; so is it also in like manner and like sequence with all the substantiate beings helping and working with you in the entire Creation, but in each case they are always half a step higher than you are.

Whatever of this unfolds its activity beside you and below you is also partly connected with you, but not in this manner. Let us first keep to *those* threads which I have mentioned.

The threads are so many-sided that there is nothing in which the earthman, and also the soul already distant from the earth, could not find and receive help, invigoration, comfort and support at the actual moment when his longing or prayer for it has a very definite intensity of genuine volition. Not before, because formed words alone never suffice to bring about the connection, neither does a casual thought!

It must be ardent, genuine and true yearning or desiring without any intellectual scheming, without expecting a reward, without something memorised, which can never really come from the heart or the soul! For the formed *earthly word* binds too strongly for that! The earthly word can only give the direction for the volition of a soul, it can construct a street for the way which the intuitive perception wants to take, yet it must never be meant to represent *everything!*

If man cannot combine both, i. e., the word and his volition, if he must *think* too much about the right forming of his words, then it is better only to pray and to thank, or to petition intuitively *without* words! Then it will surely be undimmed. The firmly formed word blurs much too easily and cramps every intuitive perception.

Much more beautiful is it, and also stronger, if you can drop your words and replace them *only* with *one picture* arising spiritually before you, into which you can pour intuitive sensing, great and pure! You must try which is easier for you and which does not restrict you!

As soon as you can dispense with earthly words then it is your *soul* which speaks – the soul as it will speak when it has departed from this earth and also from all the planes of gross matter, for then the formed word remains *behind*.

Probably you will again already question within yourselves how it is that souls from the Ethereal World are still able to speak through people with mediumistic abilities, or that mediums *hear* such souls speak, taking this in and passing it on in writing or verbally. I know that many such questions immediately arise within you!

If, however, you search thoroughly in my Message you will already find the answer to all such questions, which are nothing but intellectual doubts. Just absorb *aright* what I tell you, and then you will be able to build up everything for yourselves in *such* a logical way that doubts will no longer arise.

Already long ago I explained to you the activity of the earthly brain, which we divided into the back brain and the frontal brain. The back brain is *impressed* by *intuitive perceptions.* It only absorbs pictures of the volition of the intuitive perception, and after preparing them accordingly it passes them on to the frontal brain. The frontal brain then takes this up and makes it *more earthly* by remodelling everything again, condensing it according to the frontal brain's respective radiating capacity and transforming it into coarser earthly substance. In this way it is compressed into a still narrower form, more firmly put together, and coined anew for the expression of the earthly word.

Such is the activity of the brains of this earthly cloak of every earthman! The brains form a widely ramified workshop, and are a marvellous mechanism full of the most stirring activity. And since the frontal brain performs the so-called hard labour, i. e., it transforms all the impressions conveyed to it by the back brain into heavier, denser forms, which due to their increased density have much narrower limits in order to become intelligible to earthly understanding; therefore the frontal brain grows weary and needs sleep, whereas the back brain does not need to share this sleep and continues to work on calmly. Even the body itself would not require this sleep, but merely *rest,* repose!

Sleep is solely a necessity of the frontal brain!

However, this too you can easily grasp and understand!

You need only reflect calmly and logically upon everything! Therefore realise that while the body rests you can be awake and do not need to sleep. You have frequently experienced this with yourselves already. But when a rest is taken by the frontal brain which provides you with the *thinking,* i. e., which brings about the remodelling of the impressions of the intuitive perception into coarser and narrower forms and heavier density; once this brain must rest then of course the thinking also ceases. Naturally you are unable to think anything while the frontal brain is resting!

And here on earth you only designate the ability to think as being awake, and the inability to think as sleep or unconsciousness! Here it is a matter only of the so-called *day*-consciousness, which is exclusively the activity of the frontal brain. The back brain is always awake.

After this digression let us return again to the language of the souls; with the latter the limited word-forms fall away and only pictures exist which have to form the conception. When the departed souls communicate something to an earthman these pictures of their volition or experiences are impressed upon his back brain, in the same way as his own volition; and according to its nature the back brain absorbs these pictures, properly prepares them and immediately transmits them to the frontal brain which in turn, following its own nature, condenses the pictures received and expresses them in thoughts, words or writing.

For many a mediumistic person this is, of course, as if he actually *heard* these words, this again being due to the activity of the frontal brain, which is also connected with the *hearing* and takes up *its* impressions in order to work them over accordingly.

In *these* cases mentioned here, however, if it concerns the so-called "clairaudience" from the Ethereal World, the frontal brain, during the transformation into greater density, radiates the pictures of the intuitive perception which it received from the back brain also to the hearing in the *reverse* way. The hearing is then induced to vibrate in the word forms while they are being fashioned, because the connection is provided and is likewise always ready to receive.

Due to this *reversed* order of transmission to the gross material ear, it then naturally sounds somewhat different to the mediumistic person, because the nature of the vibrations is different from those producing the gross material sound-waves and striking the ear of the heavy physical body which passes them on to the frontal brain.

For this process of clairaudience, however, the heaviest outer gross material substance of the ear is not taken into consideration, but the finer gross material substance. This you can imagine, because the outer and heaviest material substance is much too coarse and rigid to respond to the more delicate vibrations coming from the brain. Only the finer gross material substance vibrates with it, being of the same nature as the vibrations of the frontal brain.

The admission or reception points of the *outer* ear are effectively hit and moved only by the coarser sound-waves *coming from outside.*

As I think you could easily follow me in these observations I have gone into greater detail in order to make everything fully understandable to you. Such is therefore the process of the mediations through pictures rather than through words as used by the souls in the Ethereal World, in order to form the conception of their volition within earthmen.

Likewise the "hearing" of the souls which have become more luminous and lighter takes place there *from within outwards!* The process is in the *reverse* order to that in the World of Gross Matter, where owing to its density the cloak has a protecting but also hindering effect, which protection is no longer necessary in theEthereal World.

Thus you can more easily account for the circumstance that souls which do not open themselves *inwardly* are *deaf* there as well as *blind,* for I have already explained in an earlier lecture that the actual seeing is a seeing *of the spirit.*

Many a subtle, specially clever intellectualist (but who may better be described as being bound only to his earthly brain) will perhaps come across *the fact* that the manner of expression of various departed souls through one and the same medium is *also* very often entirely different, although the same brain is being used as the tool.

This circumstance should really point more *to the fact* that they are still *nevertheless* using a language with word expression in order to make themselves understood, especially since such manifestations also sometimes come in languages of which the medium is totally ignorant, like English or French, Latin, as well as Japanese, Turkish, and many another.

However, this does not stand the test because such manifestations come only from planes that *still belong to the World of Gross Matter,* which indeed comprises many planes. There the process is still similar to that of heavy gross matter on earth. Furthermore, those in the beyond periodically take complete possession of the brains of some mediums as tools for direct expression.

Only in the *World of Ethereal Matter,* which is of an entirely different nature from that of gross material substance, does the form of expression of the same Laws of Creation change with this species, as I have already pointed out in the Message several times.

You must not make the mistake of wanting to press my Message – which comprises the entire Work of Creation and even goes far beyond this – just as it *is* into your small world of thoughts! You would not get far with it; for I have often crowded immense spaces into one single small sentence in order to make at least a well-rounded basic picture available to your comprehension, a picture which you can use as a support so that you no longer need go astray in aimless confusion in a field which does not even form the smallest part of your closer surroundings. To understand my Message aright you must *assimilate it!*

First of all I want to give you the *connections* only, and not the details! Not until you have firmly grasped the great connection can you also deliberately go into the details without needing to lose the connection.

The higher you come the less it can be framed in words. Finally everything is solely *radiation* for you, and all else ceases!

I especially emphasise *for you,* i.e., for the spirit of earthman, the spirit of Subsequent Creation which has become form! All else, that which is not beneath or beside you, you can never grasp anyway!

That which becomes radiation for you is still visible, prehensible and formed to that which is higher than you are. Thus it goes on ever higher, until ultimately only the Divine in the Divine Realm can recognise everything as having form, with the exception of God Himself, Who in His Unsubstantiality cannot be recognised by the Divine Ones either.

Make this ever again clear to yourselves, and use what I give you *by always assimilating it yourselves, having regard to the present time and to your immediate surroundings!* With your desire for knowledge do not in fantasy climb to *those* heights where after all you could neither work nor recognise anything. However, it is necessary for you to know the *connections* therewith if you want to go *aright* wherever, according to the Law, you have to abide. And it is for this purpose that I want to mediate the *connections* to you!

But now let us return to our threads hanging above the weaving which is in perpetual movement around you! These are the radiations of the substantiate mediators which stand in the great chain coming down from above. Running down from *above,* that you must not forget, for otherwise you lose the connection! I only explained it previously by going upwards because I was then near the *ends* of the threads hanging down, and in order to complete the picture which we allowed to arise before us.

Thus there are different kinds of such threads. They originate in the radiation of the beings concerned, which have absorbed the power passed on by the particular mediator higher than themselves, and pass it on again, whereby a change takes place in this streaming through, and in this way the radiation is adjusted to *that* species which it then next contacts in its leading downwards.

From these threads earthmen can receive increased strength for *every* virtue and for *every* good volition! At any time! For these threads are *always* suspended above you, ready and waiting for you to express a desire for them!

Just for once I will tell you about *one* kind so that you know how these happenings take place in exact obedience to the Primordial Laws of Creation through the operation of the Laws themselves.

Elizabeth, the Primordial Queen of Womanhood, embraces in Her perfection *all* the virtues and all the qualities.

The radiations corresponding with Her nature proceed from Her further downwards within the Region of the Divine, and also emerge into the Primordial Spiritual Realm, where there are the many gradations of all the Primordial Beings.

At each stage downwards the radiations are split into various individual species, which are forthwith embodied in the substantiate as reproductions of their origin, i.e., as reproductions of Elizabeth, the point of origin of these radiations. This takes place in the Substantial *and* in the Spiritual, because *both* kinds of radiation emanate from the Primordial Queen and are united in her.

Their forms mould themselves exactly according to the very definite and individual kind of the radiations which they embody and *are* themselves. Therewith naturally various deviations occur in the appearance or in the manifestation of the reproductions, which always clearly and distinctly express *that* which the nature of the particular radiation contains and produces.

Thus finally ever more individual species come into existence, which are visibly personified. The older races called them goddesses and gods because at that time they could see no further, and already imagined the female mediators of these radiations to be the actual points of origin, consequently regarding them as the highest in existence.

Proceeding from the human spirits upwards, which is for once in the reverse direction, we therefore find many such female intermediaries in the Realms of Substantiality, as well as male ones. Each earthman can receive *everything* through them if he only longs for something of it in purity. For instance chastity (which, however, is entirely different from man's conception of it), loyalty, productivity, truthfulness, grace, modesty, diligence (swinging in the Law of Movement), and much else. A female mediator for all that is womanly embodies each single womanly virtue, in the same way as there are also mediators for all that is masculine, such as strength, courage, daring, adroitness, genuine and pure gentlemanliness, and all else which need not be mentioned here, since I merely want to develop a rough picture of it to enable you to understand better what I am giving you today.

From each of these mediators, which became necessary due to the splittings of the single parts, come these threads which I am describing to you. And in turn each of these mediators has very many helpers, which surround him and are active in the radiations. It is a happy surging which is contained in all this activity!

But if you look at the threads *today*, in the *present* time, then a picture of despair opens up before your eyes; for many of these threads, indeed the greater part of them, hang down without finding any connection with earthmen. They flutter about loose, entirely unused, not taken up by the places for which they were intended through the helping love.

Hanging in this way the threads point out *your guilt*, you earthmen, just as so much else already cries out your guilt into Creation and up to the Creator Who has hitherto so showered you with His Love, and Who made it so easy for you in His Holy Laws exactly to recognise the paths which you were meant to take!

How great must be your shame when recognition comes at last! You human beings are just those and the only ones who do not pass on what they receive in the right way, and who in this case also failed completely as mediators, because already for a long time you have been unable to receive as such.

There is not much more to be said about this! All the mediators which are in connection with you, you men, stand sadly in the Realms of Substantiality. Accusingly they hold up the threads which through being used by earthmen were also meant to bring them retroactive currents. These would animate the one-sidedness of the purely outgoing radiations, making them more brilliantly colourful, and thus inducing them to become even more powerful and strongly beneficial and to begin to glow. They are dried up at the ends and withered!

Only those mediators connected with the animals, plants and stones still stand firm and joyful; for their threads of radiation are taut through the alternating rotation of giving and taking (which must also lie therein) in cheerful obedience to the Law of Creation, and in gratitude that the possibility was given for this through the Infinite Love of God manifesting in it.

Thus due to the wrong thinking you fostered you made a harmful, ugly-looking crack in the picture showing that part of the weaving in Creation which is very closely connected with you. Wherever you go and stand, you men, you spread around you that which is ugly. Wherever your thoughts could reach there you destroyed the harmony and thus the beauty, as well as the lawful possibility to mature. You have much to account for and also to redeem!

THERE has always been vibrating within men a knowledge about the Primordial Queen, Who is also called by some the Primordial Mother or the Queen of Heaven. There are still many other designations for this and, as always, through such a designation men envisage something very definite which approximately corresponds with the particular *designation,* and which in fact exists for the sole purpose of awakening a picture thereof in the spirit.

This picture then naturally always conforms with the particular kind of designation, and not least also strongly with the nature of the character and education of the person who, after hearing the designation, lets the picture arise within himself. However, each *different* designation will also always call forth a different picture. It cannot possibly be otherwise with the human spirit. Through the word of the designation a picture is created, and this picture then successively forms the *conception.* This sequence contains the circle of movement of earthman or, better said, of the human spirit incarnated on earth.

When he has departed from the earth the designation formed by the word, such as is conditional and customary during the stay on earth, also falls away for him, and only the picture remains with him which has then to form the conception.

Thus the earthly word and the picture arising in the spirit are the aids the human spirit uses to form the conception. In the end colour and tone also join these aids in order to complete the conception aright. The higher the human spirit rises in Creation the stronger colour and tone stand forth in their effects; in reality they are not two separate things but only *one.* They only *appear* to man as two, because in his earthly way he is unable to grasp the two of them as one!

Here on earth in this World of Gross Matter we already find the co-operation of colour and tone in the forming of a conception, although it is only relatively faintly indicated; for often, when forming a conception of a person, the latter's selection of colours for his surroundings and his clothing plays a part which is not to be under-estimated, even if in most cases it is unconscious.

And in conversation the use of a change in tone really underlines something or other that is said; either intentionally or unintentionally it is stressed, and as one quite rightly says: It is "emphasised" in order to evoke a very *special* "impression" through what is spoken. This means nothing else than the intention to foster the right conception within the listener.

In most cases this is also attained, because it is in fact easier for the listener to get a more correct "idea" of what was said through the use of the particular intonation.

Naturally it is no different with the consequences of the various designations about the Primordial Queen. With the designation Primordial Queen an entirely different picture arises than with the designation Primordial Mother. Furthermore, Primordial Queen immediately implies a certain and justified distance, whereas Primordial Mother suggests a more intimate connection.

Moreover, everything about this in particular is always bound to remain only a *shadow-like* conception for man, because with every attempt to arrive at an understanding he can only bring about a tremendous limitation and belittlement of the reality; it does not give him *that* which it really *is!*

In spite of this I will say something about it because otherwise the unhealthy fantasy of men, stimulated and also directed along this course by their conceit, creates ideas of it which again as always seek to push conspicuously into the foreground some kind of importance and value for the spirit of earthman.

In order to render this impossible and to avoid misdirections I will speak about it for once, especially since the ideas already existing about it also contain much that is wrong.

Too much of men's personal thinking and wishing interferes therewith. And this always produces confusion when it concerns matters which man is utterly unable to think out, but which he can simply receive as a gift from above, provided he has prepared the soil within himself for reception; part of this being *humbleness,* which man of the present day does not possess!

To add still more to the confusion many people also call *the earthly mother of Jesus* the Queen of Heaven, which with some understanding of the strict Primordial Laws of Creation could not have become possible at all, because a human spirit such as was Mary of Nazareth is never able to become the Queen of Heaven!

Nor was Mary of Nazareth ever meant with the inspirations and visions some artists and other men had of the Queen of Heaven with the Crown, if in this matter it really was a question of pictures given from above! In many cases they were but fanciful images of their own!

Genuine visions, however, always showed pictures of Elizabeth with the infant Parsifal or also without the latter. These were only live pictures shown by guides, but never Elizabeth Herself, Who cannot be seen by men.

But these pictures were never understood by men. It is true that they were right – it was the Queen of Heaven, for they mostly directed their longing and their prayers towards Her, but She was not identical with Mary of Nazareth. Here again men have devised something without finding the real and true connection. Unfortunately they always and only make it *as they* themselves think it is, and they imagine it must then also be correct, whereas they are not at all capable of thinking right into the Divine!

In this also earthmen have done much harm through their presumptuous pseudo-knowledge, thereby making the path of Mary of Nazareth unspeakably difficult. It was a torment for her to be linked so forcibly by earthmen with these wrong paths they have taken.

Such errors again have their quite understandable origin in the greatest plague of the human spirits, in their *spiritual indolence* which is hostile to the Light, and which under the domination of the intellect either makes them conceited earthbound creatures or, if their volition turns to religion, allows them to go to the other extreme, adopting childish ideas which consider anything possible! I explicitly call it *"childish"* because it is not childlike; for that which is childlike manifests in much healthier forms, whereas that which is conceited and earthbound, as also the childish type of imagination, results only in unhealthy and disjointed piecework.

Therefore today I again call out: *Learn to receive*, men, for not until then can you become really great in this Creation!

Everything is contained in this if you want to become happy, "knowing"! But you *must* comply with it, otherwise you cannot receive anything. And therefore you have so far been denied the enjoyment of the real *treasures* of this Creation!

Today I can explain many things to you who wish to receive if you have absorbed the lecture about "Substantiality" aright, for this enables you to understand me. It had to precede the explanations which will now follow little by little.

I already spoke in the Message of the Primordial Queen of Womanhood, Who bears the name "Elizabeth". The designation Primordial Mother is also quite rightly applied to Her, but man must envisage the right thing if he wishes to come closer to truth in the conception.

The "envisaging" is the picture I spoke about which fashions the aid for forming the conception through the activity of the human spirit.

First of all let my lectures about Substantiality arise before you, in which I said that the feminine, thus also woman, always forms the transition, the bridge, from one step of Creation to the next, both downwards and upwards!

This is a law which begins to operate at *that* step where the ego-consciousness of the individual species of beings becomes capable of manifesting. And this step is *first of all in the Divine,* in the Divine Region!

As you already know, God alone is Unsubstantiate!

All else is substantiate. This includes in the first place the Archangels as the pillars of the Throne. These still swing completely and solely in the Will of God, without desiring anything else from within themselves. And as according to the Law of God there is nothing which would not automatically turn into a form in Creation, these angels, which do not activate a will from within themselves but which only swing in the Will of God, wear pinions, thus *wings!*

The wings are the expression of their nature, which has taken on form, and a proof that they swing purely in the Will of God and do not desire anything else. If they were to change in this, which would only be possible at cosmic distances from God, as once happened with Lucifer, their wings would automatically become stunted and paralysed and finally fall off altogether, as soon as a swinging in the Will of God no longer exists.

And the more purely they swing in the Will of God the more luminous and pure are also their wings!

Wherever ego-consciousness can arise these wings fall away. From the very outset they are not at all developed with the spirits, because the spiritual must develop *personal* volition and does not swing unconditionally in the Will of God.

Here you need only accustom yourselves to the thought that everything in

Creation exists immediately in *actual fact;* and this is all the more pronounced in Substantiality, where personal volition is absolutely out of the question; instead everything therein submits unconditionally to the Will of God.

But a strength which you cannot at all realise lies just in *this* fact. In this giving up or devoting of oneself there is rooted the power to transform also that which you call Nature.

But I want to speak to you about the *Primordial Queen!*

A transformation embracing complete worlds is necessary in the Divine Realm *between* the Archangels and the Eternal Ones who have become conscious of themselves; these latter are called the Elders in the Divine Realm, and have their existence before the steps of the Throne of God, where the Grail Castle is to be found in the Divine Sphere.

You must not envisage this picture too narrowly. Distances of worlds lie between the Archangels and the starting-out point from the Divine Sphere, where the Grail Castle in the Divine is anchored from eternity, thus at the boundary of the *direct* effect of the Radiations of God.

This has nothing to do with the part of the Grail Castle which was revealed to you in pictures as being the highest *in Creation!* For this part known to you through the descriptions is only in the Primordial Spiritual, beyond the direct Radiations of God.

The *steps* of the Throne of God *to that point* only, however, already comprise world distances, and in reality also comprise worlds.

With a little reflection you can already gather from the lecture "Woman and Man" that it is necessary that the womanly must definitely be present to act as a bridge at each transformation in Creation. Neither is this law circumvented in the Divine Sphere!

The eternal Elders in the Divine, who were able to become self-conscious at the boundary of the Divine Sphere because the great distance from the immediate proximity of God then permitted it, could not have come into existence, and just as little could the Archangels have been formed, unless the Primordial Queen representing Primordial Womanhood had stood *in advance* of them as the mediator, as the necessary bridge for this change and forming.

Naturally this has nothing at all to do with the earthly gross material species and thinking. There is nothing personal whatever in it, but it contains much greater happenings than you will probably ever be able to imagine. You must try to follow in this matter as best you can!

Elizabeth is the very foremost *Divine-Substantiate* embodiment of radiation, which as the only one therein took on the most ideal womanly conformation. Thus She is the Primordial conformation of the *radiation* of the Love of God which, as the first, is embodied in Her.

Jesus is the conformation of the living Unsubstantiate Love of God Itself, being a Part out of God.

I only speak of these things in order to prevent any false picture from arising within you, and so that you can at least divine the further connection from that place where, as you go upwards in your comprehension, you must stay behind, if you take as a basis that also further above the laws remain *uniform*, because they do come from there. There they are even much more simplified, because only later on in descending must they also split owing to the many divisions, and therefore appear much more extensive than they really are.

When I say to you that every intuitive perception, every movement up there becomes an event which radiates its effect into all the worlds and sinks down upon milliards of smaller personalities, not to mention upon all that is objective, then the words I am able to give you about this are insufficient; they are only words of your own language, from which you must try to obtain a conception!

It is utterly impossible to express the real greatness of the matter itself in words; it is hardly possible to indicate it!

And there the Primordial Queen has Her being!

She has Her origin in the Divine, possesses the great Divine-Substantiality of the Archangels, and in spite of this carries personal ego-consciousness within Herself in a transfigured way. Beside Her are the Archangels, and further downwards lie the Eternal Gardens of all the Virtues, in each of which one main conformation is active; the uppermost thereof being the Garden of Purity, of the "Pure Lily", at the feet of the Primordial Queen, from Whose radiations it issued.

At the lowest end of this Divine Sphere there are then the Elders, who are only called the Old Ones or Elders because they are eternal, and who have therefore always existed from eternity; in the same way as the Grail Castle in the Divine exists as an anchorage of the Radiation of God, which like Him was and is eternal, as also is Elizabeth, the Primordial Queen of Womanhood.

However, She is *virgin!* Although She is called Primordial Mother and Parsifal calls Her Mother! A Divine Mystery which the human spirit will never understand, it is too far removed from them, and must always remain so! She is in the Divine the Primordial Prototype of all Womanhood, after which the womanhood of the Primordial Beings formed themselves into likenesses!

THE CYCLE OF RADIATIONS

THERE is much I have yet to explain about the greater and great substantiate beings, not to mention at present the small helpers of these great ones; for there are so many of the smaller and very small ones as you can hardly imagine.

I could often despair when trying to ponder *how* I shall still explain all this to you in the available words of the language without you thereby losing the comprehensive survey, and above all in such a manner that you nevertheless fully grasp the connections.

The difficulty arises just from the great simplicity which lies in what is to you a boundless diversity; it is difficult because earthman is only capable of clearly overlooking a very definite number of things, and consequently he can never come into a position simultaneously to grasp *everything* as *one whole,* from which simplicity alone results.

Each separation into different parts must render the necessary comprehensive view more difficult for you, since each part is again so great in itself and so closely connected with the others through reciprocal effects, that it is utterly impossible to give a really *self-contained* part, because in this Creation, which in itself is a whole, there is no self-contained part!

And man *cannot* overlook the whole! He will never be able to do so, because he lacks the ability, for he himself is only a part of Creation, and a very small one, who cannot go beyond his own boundaries and naturally not in his understanding either.

I am thus compelled to remain within your boundaries, and in addition I can only give you glimpses into or upon everything which will and must remain inaccessible to you. No amount of effort will be of use here!

However, when at last through the knowledge you resign yourselves to *the fact* that you are not capable of *everything* in Creation, then you will also call *humbleness* your own, and you will be happy about the enlargement to your existing knowledge given to you through my Message.

You will then occupy yourselves with the present and with your immediate surroundings much more thoroughly even than now, because you will learn to know and to use it all much more accurately through all the glimpses which I could give into what is inaccessible to you, but which permit you exactly to recognise the close link with yourselves and with everything existing around you.

And *that* is what you needed in order to understand and make profitable use of the present, profitable for your ascent!

These glimpses can bring you *upwards* to the highest border which you will ever be able to reach. It is just because I allow you to glimpse into what is inaccessible to you that you are able to make use of all *that* which is given to you *here,* much of which was still unknown to you.

Valuable is this knowledge concerning the *links* between your existence and everything still lying *beyond* that boundary which, owing to the origin of your spirit, will always remain strictly drawn in regard to your ability to understand!

That is also what I want to give you with the Message: The knowledge of the connections! The serious seeker and the person with a really honest volition will gain much thereby. You will yet learn to recognise the value of everything; for what men have so far called knowledge is hardly the hundredth part of what they really *could* know. It is true that the limit of the knowledge of mankind in relation to the entire Creation is small, yet in comparison to the existing knowledge it is of a greatness which you can hardly conceive and which verges on the wonderful!

And the glimpses alone into that which is always inaccessible to you will aid you in reaching these highest borders, when I give you a description of your connections therewith, as well as of the connections of your surroundings. This knowledge will in time give you the possibility to know with *absolute accuracy* the laws within the part formed by your boundaries, which would remain impossible without the help given in describing the connections with what is inaccessible to you.

Try now to understand me in this, and recognise *what* I want to give you! Do not seek to reach beyond the reality in this; for I only want to give you *that* which can *further* and benefit *you within your boundaries,* nothing more! More would be of no avail to mankind!

Therefore do not torment yourselves *therewith,* wishing to make your *knowledge* all *that* which lies in what is inaccessible for you! You will never be able to do this, and I do not speak of it so that you should now turn your knowledge in that direction or worry yourselves with vain attempts really and fully to *grasp* everything! You cannot possibly do so, nor do I give it to you for that reason, but you receive it from me for the very purpose of becoming acquainted with all the *connections* leading to you therefrom.

If later on you will always unswervingly base your future investigations and your desires to find upon this knowledge of the connections as giving you the direction, you will rise higher in all your capacities and achieve results in *every* field which must put all that has been obtained so far into the shade!

Thus, men, your *masterpieces are yet to come*, the achievements which you can actually bring about within the boundaries which are set up firmly for you and which you can never cross! In reality, however, these boundaries are set so wide for you that you may rejoice about this, and should only thank God for all the grace He bestows upon you.

Thus you must remain on the basis and soil of all humanity in your thoughts and actions, and in all your duties towards your Creator. Nothing more is demanded of you; for therein lies the highest which you can offer to Him as gratitude, and everything *you* do in this way is also done in *His* honour!

Indeed, it is in the performance of the greatest achievements, of which you as men can and must become masters, that you offer and present your gratitude for the fact that the Creator has *granted you* to achieve such *great things* through His Will in Creation, which holds His Laws.

And with these splendid achievements *you* also simultaneously *honour Him* because the *greatness of your works* at the same time manifests the greatness of *His Grace!* The more you can achieve in Creation from out of Creation the more clearly do you prove how great are the Laws of God therein, and what wealth and blessing they hold for you!

You honour God in the *truest* and *purest* sense *when* in *joyful activity* you *make use of* everything Creation offers you; for this you can only do when you know and also understand its Laws and, above all, when you really *act* accordingly! Only *then* does this Creation offer you everything of beauty that it contains! Gladly does it give, and give to help you!

And when you act in this way according to the Laws in Creation you are already changed and entirely different from what you were before. You are then men who are pleasing to God, you are men as they always should have been, you are men according to the Will of God because you *live* His Laws!

No fault can then be found with you any longer. Wherever you may be you stand in Creation radiatingly and jubilantly, everywhere, whether on earth or in some other plane, and you would no longer do anything other than praise God through the *deed;* for such works resemble a hymn of praise which is living and swings in all the Laws of this Creation!

This is a goal so beautiful, so glorious and yet so easily attainable for you that I exert myself *for that reason* to pave a way there for you through my Message!

You will be *human beings!* Creative human beings to whom everything in Creation flows because you swing with it in the joyfulness of the greatest happiness!

That then is human existence to the honour of God! To be happy in the *truest* sense is indeed the greatest thanks which you can give to God. This, however, does not mean the sham happiness of the lazy ease which lies in slothful rest. That is an intoxicating drug for the spirit, much worse in its effect than opium for your body!

You will attain to this true happiness, however, if you carry the strong volition for it within yourselves! And you shall be the rock for all those who want to save themselves from the tidal wave of base passions and desires which now flow over mankind on earth as the fruit of their past wrong volition when, it is true, they very often had the name of God in their mouths, but they never seriously thought of obeying His Will unless at the same time it coincided with their own.

Try to absorb my volition aright in *that sense* in which I give it to you, and use it for yourselves accordingly; *then* you will have grasped the core which lies at the very root of the purpose of my Message. And only *then* can you derive true benefit from it!

Now let us try to go a step further in the knowledge of the weaving in Creation!

You are now perhaps faced with a new riddle; for it is unlikely that there is one among you who considers some error or contradiction possible in my explanations. Nevertheless you still consider many a thing as unsettled which you could not clearly arrange with a logical structure of thinking, which latter you need to be able to understand.

I spoke of the great Primordial Spiritual guides as embodying the virtues, but I also spoke of the many substantiate intermediaries embodying the same virtues. I characterised both species as having an effect upon men according to their particular types.

In this matter you still lack the right connection which can complete a clear picture for you, without disarranging what you have heard up till now.

Actually all this can be described in a few words, but it is better when I try to demonstrate it pictorially as it really is in its *forms*.

You know that radiations divide and separate into very definite sub-species. On each further plane going downwards a new sub-species is ever again severed, i. e., detached in the cooling off. This sub-species could not sever itself under the still existing stronger pressure reaching to this particular boundary, and only through this further cooling off and subsequently reduced pressure or degree of heat was it able to loosen itself and make itself independent.

Every such severance or detachment simultaneously results in a new formation of the severed species into a corresponding substantiate form. This process takes place automatically according to the Law of Creation. Thus there arises a whole chain, with its various additional links of helping and building substantiate beings, of which I have already spoken to you.

And all of them are connected with each other so that one can say that they extend their hands to each other.

This whole chain of the *substantiate beings* stands solely in the Will of God. They are embodiments, transitory points of the radiations *themselves*, which pass on; in their very definite species they are always the *dispensers* in Creation, which by working in this way and *radiating downwards* penetrate the entire Creation.

Thus mark well that the substantiate beings are the *dispensers* of the radiating powers of the Divine Radiation, which in obeying the pressure or in standing *from above downwards* in the pressure *always radiate downwards*.

The counter-current is provided by the embodied spiritual ones, who receive of these radiations and who, in *making use* of them, *radiate* them *upwards!*

Therein lies the cycle of the radiations throughout Creation! At first you are somewhat confused and imagine this contains a contradiction, because we also talked about the fact that the Primordial Beings in the Primordial Spiritual Sphere radiate downwards onto all the human spirits, and now you think that two kinds of radiations flow downwards side by side in Creation, the substantiate one and the spiritual one!

This is not in itself wrong, for these two kinds of radiations do stand next to each other, but there is a difference in their activity which brings about the cycle.

You know I spoke about the radiations of the primordially created Primordial Spiritual Beings. However, the effect of *these* radiations is different from those of the primordially created substantiate beings. The radiation of the substantiate beings is *dispensing, passing on, mediating,* as I have emphasised. However, already from the very beginning in my Message I have pointed to the fact that the Primordial Beings in the Primordial Spiritual Sphere, i. e., the Primordial Spiritual Beings in their various kinds, affect mankind *like gigantic magnets,* thus *attracting* or *sucking.*

Only today can I supplement the picture for you because the other lectures had to precede and prepare the soil for this by way of explanation. In reality we are today merely extending what has been said up till now, of which you probably did not have an absolutely clear idea when the radiations were discussed, in that you imagined them as *always working only in a downwards direction.*

However, of these there are two kinds differing in their effects. It is true that the radiations quite naturally also go downwards with the primordially created Primordial Spiritual Beings, but their *effect is of an upward striving* nature through the power of attraction, which the substantiate beings do not possess; the latter are always and only *dispensing,* i. e., *giving out!*

The spiritual is *demanding* through the capacity of *attracting.* And the so-called free will to decide actually lies anchored solely in this activity of attracting, if you think it over properly for once. What is even more, it also contains the absolutely just distribution of reward or punishment for the one concerned consequent upon his decision!

Think about this quietly for once and picture these happenings to yourselves in all the details. You will suddenly see before you the astounding *simplicity* of the lawfulness in Creation, the absolute clearness in it, and although the volition of free decision is granted to the spiritual, you also see the latter's subjection to the consequences, which is linked up with it and takes effect in *the same* law.

One *single* ability of the spiritual thus produces something many-sided, in *such* a just and logical way that you must stand amazed before it as soon as you recognise it aright.

It is indeed quite comprehensible that this magnetic ability of the spiritual to attract through the Law of Attraction of Homogeneous Species always attracts only *that* which is *willed* through the ability to decide, and nothing else. And this is done with absolute accuracy, with all the finest shades and tones of good as well as of evil. Just go deeply into this! It is not difficult! *Every* person must be able to develop that much imaginative power!

In order to counterbalance this ability to attract, the ability to decide is given to the spiritual, but the substantiate does not need this because it always and only dispenses according to its particular inherent species. Naturally the spiritual always attracts only that which corresponds with its particular volition, because each volition immediately seizes the entire spirit, illuminates it or glows through it, only thereby releasing the ability to attract, which develops accordingly.

The spirit is unable to shake off the ability to attract because it possesses this ability or, to express it more clearly, this ability is the property or a part of the spirit's nature. The spirit cannot free itself from this. And as another part belonging to the spiritual nature, the ability to decide is also bestowed upon it as a decisive factor – the desiring or the volition, which cannot be shaken off either, because it is meant to *help;* for otherwise the spiritual would simply attract *everything* that exists in a wild confusion and could thus become heavily burdened.

However, such mistakes are impossible in Creation through the just Law of the Attraction of Homogeneous Species, which in its effect is like a great incorruptible guardian of order. Now combine all this, let it come to life in pictures before your eyes, and you will thereby have gained much in your knowledge! You must take pains, however, and if necessary go deeply into it for hours and days, for such a length of time as enables you to grasp it aright. Therewith you are again handed a key which will open many, almost all, gates in Creation for your understanding!

Therefore do not neglect to do so! It is important to do it, for *your* inmost core and *your* real being, as well as your *origin*, are also *spiritual*, and you are thus subject to these abilities of your spirit. Until now we have characterised this process as a law.

830

In reality, however, this is a simple ability, a component part of the spirit, which works automatically and therefore appears to be a law!

On the whole and strictly speaking there are no real laws in Creation but solely abilities which, corresponding to each particular species, operate automatically and thereby, but only thereby, appear to be immutable laws!

Therefore learn to know your *own* abilities, as well as those of the other parts of Creation, and thus you will know the laws which in reality unite in one *single* law that is many-sided only in its effects. As soon as you have advanced deeply enough with your recognitions it will suddenly fall from your eyes like scales and you will stand shaken before the simplicity of it all.

Through this, as soon as the true knowledge has set in, there finally no longer remain any laws for you at all, for with this knowledge everything becomes only *a wise use of all the abilities,* and therewith you become free; for it is just as though all the laws are fulfilled.

Thus you should now think deeply about it once more and seek to grasp the great pulsating in Creation. Therefore I will repeat:

The substantiate radiates and *dispenses* in a downwards direction; the Primordial Spiritual also radiates downwards, but it operates with a magnetic attraction as well.

And since according to their nature the primordially created Primordial Spiritual Beings are to be found at the uppermost border of Creation, and since they also possess the strongest power of attraction in the Spiritual, they operate like enormous magnets upon everything of a spiritual nature, they *hold* it, and allow to stream *upwards* that which corresponds with their nature, i. e., in this and in all cases *always and only the good* fashioned from all the planes; while everything which in turn is fashioned by them is absorbed or drawn off by the Divine, the power of attraction of which is naturally even stronger.

And mark well, always and only the good which is *fashioned* is attracted upwards, i. e., only the *radiations* themselves, which may also be called the result of spiritual activity.

Now you lack the conception of the necessary *fashioning!* This takes place *solely in the volition* of the spiritual, which is inherent in it, and which therefore cannot help always and absolutely willing something, even if it is only through some inner urge.

And in becoming aglow this process or activity, which we can also call *movement* of the volition, attracts from the radiations dispensed by the substantiate that which is homogeneous to the particular kind of volition.

Through the *union* of the radiation of the spiritual volition with the dispensing homogeneous to this volition from the substantiate, each in turn becomes more intensely aglow, and the still closer connection formed through this glowing results in a new radiation of a different and also stronger content.

Therein lies the so-called *fashioning*. And the *radiations thus transformed through the new connection* are attracted from the next *higher* plane and thus uplifted, thereby ascending.

This process is continually repeated from one plane to the next going upwards, unless...the upward striving is held back and cut off through evil volition or spiritual lukewarmness, because only the good volition leads upward.

Lukewarmness is a hindrance because it does not sustain the necessary movement. Stagnation will then occur throughout the entire Creation. And it is in *this* that mankind on earth have so badly sinned, sinned against the entire Creation, and therewith against the Will of God, against the Holy Ghost!

It caused a standstill in the cycle, which only now is again being brought into the correct and even more intensified movement, thus tearing down everything which has opposed and hampered it in the past.

You must first try to become clear in your minds that it is not the radiations of the spiritual alone which lead upwards of their own accord. These simple personal radiations are already *adapted* to the particular plane in which the spiritual in its human embodiments is to be found in each case; and they are therefore also cooled off correspondingly, and would have to remain constantly on the same plane were it not that the urging volition of the spiritual attracts the dispensing or radiations of the substantiate and then simultaneously transforms them.

This likewise all takes place automatically. A corresponding union of the radiations sets in, which through the spiritual movement of the volition receives a greater degree of heat, thereby offering the possibility to link up with the attraction from the higher plane, which takes effect immediately.

You can imagine the rotary movement of the radiations as somewhat *like* the blood circulation in the human body, which does give an approximate copy of the process in Creation.

The movement of the radiations in Creation is therefore quite simple and yet strictly conditioned: That which is substantiate radiates downwards only and is always and only *dispensing,* giving out. That which is spiritual also radiates downwards of its own accord, but nevertheless has an upward striving effect according to the description which I just gave you.

Of course this again concerns only the *radiations* themselves and not perhaps the spirits which have become *personal,* the human spirits. These find their way upwards or downwards through or in the Law of Gravitation, which in reality is closely linked with the Law of Attraction of Homogeneous Species; these two laws having the same effect as if they were one.

If the striving, thus the volition and desiring of a human spirit, goes upwards then the radiations fashioned by him, which are always attracted from above, form *the way,* the road upward for him personally, on which he strides upward in an absolutely lawful manner. He thereby also attracts the radiations from the substantiate, situated higher and ever higher, which help him to ascend like ropes or threads; for in fashioning these his spiritual form itself receives ever more heat which permits him to ascend, to become constantly lighter and more luminous, more glowed through.

Despite the close connection of all these processes there are always numerous special secondary happenings in addition which, however, remain conditioned by and interwoven with each other, in that one results from the other.

If I do not want to make it more difficult for you to comprehend this, however, I must not touch upon the secondary happenings yet. But what I have said today is already sufficient to offer you a firm support to advance further and for later personal investigation.

That which is substantiate stands always and only in the Will of God *dispensing,* whereas everything that is spiritual, by its ability to attract through the volition, always remained actually demanding and taking only.

As I have already said, being spiritual man always and only takes as a guest what has already been laid upon the table of this Creation by the substantiate beings. Unfortunately he takes it in a wilful and demanding manner, instead of showing joyful gratitude and looking reverently up to Him Who proffers all this. And *in this* he must now change!

Here I want to touch upon one more point from the lecture "Woman and Man", which could probably bring thoughts to many among you which are not correct. In the stories of Creation in various nations mention is frequently made that man and woman came into existence *at the same time;* in some, however, that man came into existence *first.*

The representations of this, given in simple pictures, cannot at all be taken into consideration here, because they were given according to the stages of development of the various nations and of the times, whereas we *here* are dealing with the *strictly lawful and real knowledge of Creation;* yet despite this you do not find any contradiction therein because through the lawful happenings described to you so far you know that naturally the coarser, purely masculine, the positive part, had to be ejected or had to sever itself first from that which is substantiate before the purely feminine part was able to remain!

From this it would be possible to describe man as having come into existence first, while it can be stated with equal justification that both came into existence *at the same time. Both* of these former pictorial descriptions may be considered as correctly described in the actual, great and *objective* happening; for the finer spiritual-feminine or the spiritual woman can in turn come into existence only when the coarse spiritual-masculine has severed itself from that which is substantiate, not otherwise.

Therefore considered from *all* sides it is *correctly* expressed in the representations of those times, despite the various ways of illustrating it; for the descriptions about Creation are not concerned with the development in coarsest matter, *but with the beginning of Creation in general.* This started in the Realm of the Primordial Spiritual, at the uppermost point of Creation, from which in sinking downwards it continually developed further.

It is the same with these descriptions as with everything earthmen do, nor was it any different with the description of the happening about Parsifal and the Grail Castle: People who become deeply absorbed spiritually are presented with inspirations which they are unable to recognise clearly. In view of this the transmission is already distorted, and they then simply force these inspirations into their particular surroundings, as well as into the happenings, habits and customs known to them on earth. In this process the intellect in particular does not neglect to contribute its part, which is not so small either! I probably do not need especially to emphasise the fact that this is not particularly helpful, nor can it have an enlightening effect, but is bound to cause distortion in matters which the earthly intellect is absolutely unable to grasp.

And thus all such descriptions always and only came into existence in slightly or seriously distorted renderings, to which you as now-knowing ones must never cling too firmly, however!

Nor do the ancient descriptions, which are now already in great need of a more exact delineation for the new time, offer any contradiction to the fact that the womanly always forms and remains the bridge to the next higher step in Creation, and being the passive part is the dispensing and stronger one; this is conditioned and brought about through its special nature, which still retains and carries within itself part of the next higher step of substantiality.

But since that which is substantiate is always and only dispensing and not attracting, it could not prevent the downfall of the earthly woman's will in spite of its higher nature. Indeed it is only prepared to give where the demand for it arises!

Now strive to grasp my Message aright and to act accordingly!

I do not intend to place everything before you in a comfortable way after I have severed it into tiny pieces; for you, too, must bestir yourselves and add *whatever* lies in your strength.

I know precisely the limits of everything which the human spirits on earth are able to think, to perceive intuitively and to do, better even than you yourselves, and from the readers and listeners of my Message and of my explanations I expect *the highest* which the man of Subsequent Creation is able to achieve if they really want to follow me; for this is the right way which will benefit you according to the Will of God, Who demands movement and swinging along in the cycle of all the radiations penetrating Creation.

Therefore swing yourselves upward for this! What is possible to receive within the limits of *your* understanding that *you* must do! I leave it entirely to you and only give you the direction for it, laying foundations upon which you can and must now continue to build.

If you indolently want to refrain from *personal* work in these matters, and if you are only satisfied with absorbing within yourselves the sense of the Message without also *applying* it aright for further building, then you will derive no benefit from the Word; for its *real* value must thereby remain closed to you like a book with seven seals.

Only through your *own* movement will the Message open itself up for you, and pour rich blessings upon you! Therefore become *active* in spirit! With my Word I give you the *impulse* to do so!

SHUN THE PHARISEES!

THE DESIGNATION "Pharisee" has become a conception containing nothing good, but signifying a combination of spiritual arrogance, hypocrisy, cunning and occasionally also malice.

Persons deserving this designation can be found everywhere today, in all countries and in every walk of life. This has nothing whatever to do with race or nation, and there are many more of them now than there ever were before. Every profession has its Pharisees, but they can still mostly be found where they could formerly be encountered at any time in great numbers – among the servants and representatives of the temples and churches!

And, strangely enough, wherever some messenger of the Light had to proclaim the Truth according to the Will of God, he was attacked, defiled, slandered and persecuted. This was done first and foremost by the representatives and servants of the prevailing religious dogmas who pretended to serve God, and by those who even had the effrontery to profess themselves as representatives of the Divine Will.

This has always been the case from the most primitive medicine man and sorcerer up to the highest priests. Without exception they always felt themselves menaced by the Truth, and thus either carried on a veiled agitation or quite openly made mischief against every person who was ordained, mercifully granted or sent by God to bring Light to these earthmen.

No denial of this irrefutable fact is of any avail, nor any perversion or glossing over, for *world history gives proof of it!* Clearly and distinctly it testifies to the ineffaceable fact that it has never been otherwise; among the many instances that have occurred there has not been a single exception. Always and ever again it was just the priests who were the most definite adversaries of the Light and thus enemies of God, Whose Will they did not want to observe. Instead they fought against the Will of God, and opposed it with their own volition.

Of what use was it when recognition sometimes came *afterwards*, but often not until it had become too late for many things!

On the contrary, this only proves that it was just the priests who were never in the position to recognise the Truth and the Light in time!

Recognition lay always and only with a few among the people, but not with the priests or those who made a pretence of recognising God purely on account of their profession.

And these few among the people clung to it firmly until later on the priests also considered it wiser to go along in *their* way so as not to lose the upper hand. The servants and representatives of a religion have never voluntarily and joyfully harboured a messenger from God. It is characteristic that neither such messengers nor the Son of God could issue from their ranks. And, strange to say, no person thinks about the fact that God Himself always declared His *judgment* in these matters and therewith *clearly* manifested His Will.

Experiences over many thousands of years confirm ever and always again that the priests were never capable of recognising Divine Truth, but in their conceit they always closed themselves to It, sometimes also because of fear or lazy comfort. This they also proved ever anew, because they *constantly* fought against *every* messenger from God with the vilest methods a man can use. There can be no dispute about it whatever; for past times themselves offer the most irrefutable evidence!

In every way, even with the Son of God! Nor was it love of humanity which drove the priests to this, but professional envy and nothing else! It was the Truth which *disturbed* them, because they have never yet faithfully taught the Truth – they themselves did not know It!

And, humanlike, they were much too weak to admit that there were many things they did not yet know, and that therefore they spread wrong opinions in some matters; nor were they capable of admitting this, for fear their authority might begin to wane!

Just delve into the history of the world and investigate it seriously, and you will find that it was never otherwise! But nobody has so far wanted to learn a lesson from it! Nobody takes it as a warning, because although it always remains basically the same this is continually appearing in a new form. Therefore, due once more to indolence, man imagines that just in *his* time it is different after all. But it is still the same today as it used to be. There is *no difference* now to what it was in the past. Nothing has changed therein, but if anything it has become worse!

837

Go and ask earnest people who serve the church, but who are nevertheless still courageous enough openly to confess their inner stirrings, people who do not shrink from being honest with themselves... they will all have to admit to you that even today the church would still want to make every person impossible, and carry on an agitation against him, if he is able to endanger the rigid dogmas supporting the churches! Even if Christ Jesus would now suddenly walk among them as a human being in the same way as before! If He did not agree that their conceptions were the only right way they would immediately treat Him *as an enemy,* and without any hesitation would again accuse Him of blasphemy! They would pelt Him with dirt, and be unsparing with their ugly slanders in the process!

That is how it is, and not otherwise! The reason for all this wrong-doing, however, is not the urge to honour Almighty God, but the struggle to influence men and acquire earthly power and wealth! –

But you men draw no beneficial consequences whatever for yourselves and for your seeking from these many facts, which are indeed so easily discernible in the disputes among all the churches. You thoughtlessly overlook it!

But do not imagine that God in His Holy Laws will thereby leave it at that for you! You will be roused suddenly and severely from this irresponsible indolence!

The second group of persons hostile to the Truth are the spiritually arrogant among those who do not belong to the clergy.

For one reason or another they are self-complacent. Perhaps one such person has gone through an inner experience in accordance with his nature, no matter what caused it. It need not always have been suffering. Sometimes it is also joy, some vision, or a celebration, in brief there are many incitements for it!

He then clings to this one-time experience which proved capable of moving him so much, not thinking that it very likely arose out of himself, and that it was therefore not a real experience at all. However, he quickly seeks to raise himself above his fellow-men with the self-comforting assertion: "I had my experience and so I know I am standing in the true recognition of God!"

The wretched man! A human spirit must have a thousandfold experiences if he really wishes to mature to a higher recognition! And such a spiritually indolent human spirit on earth, who holds himself in high esteem, clings fast as if in a shrine to one *single* experience within himself and does not strive to proceed further, because he believes that with this *everything* has already happened and that he has achieved enough for his life! The fools who act in such a manner will now come to the awakening; for they must realise that they were asleep!

It is all right when a person has once had an inner experience, but not enough is achieved with that alone. He must not stagnate there but unswervingly stride onwards – he must keep alert in spirit! On this path he would very soon realise that his experience was only a transition serving to awaken him to real recognition.

However, his spiritual arrogance only comes more than ever to the fore, and he fancies he is of greater worth than those who go another way and follow a different creed.

Onward, ever *onward,* must man proceed on his way through Creation, ever onward also in the recognition of everything he finds in Creation! He must never feel safe and bask in a *single* experience which came to him once. Onward, only onward, proceeding with all his strength! To remain stationary means to stay behind. And danger threatens those who stay behind. With ascent, however, the dangers always lie *behind* every human spirit and never *in front of* him – he should be aware of this!

Therefore calmly leave *those* people alone who seek so proudly to *talk* about themselves. Look at their *actions,* their manner, and you will quickly recognise what they are worth! There are very many who belong to this group. They are hollow fruit which have to be cast out; they no longer absorb anything, for in their conceit they imagine they already have everything. –

The third big group of useless ones comprises the visionaries and enthusiasts who, easily stirred over anything that is new, harm everything which is really good. They always want to conquer the world immediately, but quickly collapse inwardly when it comes to proving their strength through *perseverance,* in working *upon themselves* unceasingly!

They would sometimes be useful as stormers provided the resistance does not last long, and when it is a question of assailing their fellow-men – wishing to teach them without already possessing a firm basis for themselves! Fireworks which quickly begin to glow and soon fade away! They belong to the superficial ones who have no great value!

Next to this group comes still another comprising *those* persons who cannot abstain from adding their own thoughts to something they are given, so that through the opportunity to absorb one particle of truth they *themselves* can also achieve some distinction or other by spreading it! They cannot refrain from weaving their own opinions into what they have read or heard, and continuing to follow up everything just as it arises in their imagination.

Fortunately they are not very numerous, but they are all the more dangerous because they create and spread false doctrines out of one little grain of truth. Thus they are not only very harmful to themselves, but also to many of their fellow-men by the ever-changing form of their activities. Let us take a minor example which everybody knows about – the fanciful novels and stories. What is so wantonly achieved therein on the basis of seemingly small grains of truth or, to express it better, what do some people burdened with fantasy achieve therewith!

It cannot always be assumed that the reason is that the writer merely wants to make money by stimulating the diseased fantasies of his fellow-men, and offering them the most incredible stories in which they can revel with a shudder. In most cases the reason lies deeper. Such people principally wish to shine with their work and revelations. They wish to let their spirit flare up before others, thinking to provide further realms for investigation and to incite others to important work in this connection.

But what nonsense is often brought forth by this! Let us only consider a few of the fantastic accounts written and printed about the inhabitants of Mars! Every line shows the lack of comprehension regarding the Divine Laws in Creation! And in the end we are bound to include Mars in *Creation* as well as everything else!

Creatures are described which really spring forth from a *diseased* imagination, based on the belief that men there must be of quite a different shape to those here on earth because Mars is a *different* planet!

Enlightenment on such matters will come through learning to know the Laws of Creation. A knowledge of the Laws then opens up entirely different prospects, with exact foundations, to the scholars and technicians, and thus also brings about an entirely different kind of progress and success in every realm.

I have already said quite often that there is no reason whatever to think that something is different in Creation because it happens to be further from the earth or because it cannot be seen with the physical eyes. Creation has come into existence through *uniform* laws; it is equally uniform in its development, and is also maintained with the same uniformity. It is wrong to let a sickly imagination have a free run in these matters or even to heed it!

Every *man* of Subsequent Creation is in the likeness of the primordial images of God. Therefore throughout the entire Creation men bear only the one form, more or less ennobled and ordained for them as human beings. The form itself, however, can always be recognised, and cannot, for instance, have three legs or in general only one eye in the middle of the head, unless there is an occasional deformity, which only occurs in isolated cases. However, this does not contain anything fundamental!

That which does *not* bear the fundamental human form cannot be called "human" either! In its individual stages of development a spirit germ, for example, is not yet a human being, yet it would still not have such divergent forms as are described by the harmful fantasts!

In the realms of medium and fine gross matter of the darker and dark planes there can be found fantastic forms with human faces, forms which resemble animals and which always correspond with the manner in which a human spirit has thought and acted upon earth, but these forms are mostly produced only by the *thinking* of men. Periodically they bear the face of *that* person who produced them, because being the children of his thoughts they issue from him.

And when a person has become *such* that he continually indulges in hatred, envy and other evil passions, then it happens that outside the materiality of the earth a body of this kind forms around his spirit. With this occurrence, however, he has lost every claim to be human, and consequently he is no longer permitted to, nor can he bear any resemblance to the form of the likenesses of the images of God. In reality he is then no longer a human being, but has sunk down to something as yet unknown to earthmen, and for which they therefore still have no name. –

However, soon the false chimeras of the fantasts will no longer be spread, because the time is drawing near when the knowledge of the Laws of God in Creation will have advanced so far that such untrue things will disappear of their own accord. Men will laugh when they look back at the present time, which gives plain evidence of their ignorance in so many ways. –

POSSESSED

PEOPLE are only too ready to express an opinion about things they do not understand. In itself this would not be so bad if such utterances were not spread abroad so often, and then suddenly stand as a firm judgment, which is accepted in many spiritually indolent circles as definite knowledge.

It then simply exists, maintaining itself with a remarkable tenacity, although nobody is able to state *how* this has come about!

And how often do these frivolous remarks cause great harm! But this does not worry men – they continue to prattle because they like it that way! They prattle unceasingly, either out of stubbornness, spitefulness, frivolity, thoughtlessness, as a pastime, not infrequently also from a craving to be heard, or with deliberately malicious intent. An evil motive can always be found for it. One meets only a few people who actually indulge in this devastating custom just for the pleasure of talking.

This talking epidemic has also only arisen as a consequence of the disintegrating rule of the intellect. Much talking, however, suppresses the purer capacity to perceive intuitively, which requires a greater *"personal" deepening!*

It is not without reason that a prattler, even when harmless, does not enjoy any confidence, but only he *who can be silent.* So much lies in the instinctive reserve towards prattlers that everybody should become aware of it, in order to learn lessons therefrom for his personal relations with his fellow-men.

However, in the truest sense prattlers are, above all, those persons who are so quick and ready with words where it concerns things which they do not understand.

In their superficiality they are destructive persons who cause a great deal of harm and untold suffering.

Let us just take one case! Newspapers very often report so-called ghostly apparitions, which suddenly appear in houses where nothing like it has occurred before. Objects are disarranged or lifted, pots are flung about and similar incidents!

This kind of news comes from various regions and countries. In every case the happening always takes place around some very definite person.

Wherever *this person* is these happenings take place!

Immediately the opinion is bandied about that such a person must be *"possessed"!* No other possibility is even thought about, but thoughtlessly and unscrupulously they simply talk of being possessed!

Officials and churches in the various countries were often induced to take an interest in it, and if there was no evidence of fraud on anybody's part the church would occasionally attempt to exorcise the demons. Such efforts, however, are not of much use, because they are ignorant of the facts!

Formerly such a person – it mostly concerns children or young girls – would simply have been submitted to a regular witch's trial of a penal character, until the tormented person explained everything *in the way* the judges and servants of the churches wanted it. Then, as a final disgusting spectacle, came the death of the tortured one by fire in order to free devout humanity from such a person!

In reality, however, all this only happened in order to indulge the wanton craving for earthly power, and to obtain a strong influence over the people who were at that time such childish believers – an influence which thus became ever greater. The reason for this did not lie with the pure conviction to serve God thereby! This sacrilegious conduct aroused nothing but fear of men, suppressing all trust in God and giving full vent to the infamy of the most base slander.

In each case the sad end could always be reliably foreseen already at the beginning, and all those so frivolously accused could just as well have been murdered immediately without further ceremony. In that case the guilt of the murderers would have been even less than the guilt of the then fiends who were attired as God's servants and in judges' robes!

I do not want to draw any comparisons between the olden times and the present, nor do I want to build bridges by giving special explanations, but through thoughtless talk the process is still exactly the same *spiritually!* In the *earthly gross material sense* it is now only modified through newer laws. Nevertheless ignorant mankind think wrongly as ever in this matter, and they would act accordingly if the laws did not prevent them from doing so.

Among low negro tribes such persons are still persecuted out of superstition, killed or also...venerated! These two extremes in human behaviour have always been found very close to one another!

Among the low and ignorant tribes their sorcerers come in order to expel such evil spirits from the hut, by torturing the "possessed one" in their own special way.

Similar happenings can be found all over the world and among all peoples. I only quote these facts for a better understanding.

In all these cases, however, people who are considered as being "possessed" in this way are completely innocent. There is no trace of possession, even less of the demons which one seeks to exorcise! All this is but childish prattle and medieval superstition – a remnant from the time of the witches! In reality only those burden themselves with guilt who in their ignorance due to erroneous conceptions and superficial opinions want to help.

It is in *lunatic asylums* that the possessed can be found, and more than people imagine! And these *can* be cured!

Today, however, these pitiable persons are still simply regarded as insane, and no difference whatever is made between the really sick and those who are possessed, because as yet nothing is understood about it.

The lack of understanding in these matters is due solely to the ignorance about Creation. What is lacking is the *knowledge of Creation*, which can provide the foundation for the recognition of *all* happenings and of the changes within and around man, i.e., the foundation which leads to true knowledge, to that future science which has no need to grope about with pitiful efforts in order *therewith* only to arrive at a *theory*, which in many cases and after decades proves ever again to be wrong.

Learn to know *Creation* and the Laws operating therein, you men, and you will no longer need to grope and to seek; for you will then possess everything you need in order to help yourselves in the events occurring during your earthly life, and also even far beyond this – throughout your *entire existence!*

Then there will no longer be any pseudo-scientists, for they will have become *knowing ones*, who cannot be confronted with anything in the existence of men which holds something unknown to them.

A surprisingly great part of those today called incurably insane, who are forced to spend their lives confined in lunatic asylums, are not insane but possessed. It is the same here as with so many things. One does not *seek* for it therein, and consequently one cannot find anything either in the effect of Christ's Word, which clearly stipulates and undoubtedly demands: *Seek* and ye shall find!

This Word of Truth can be applied to *everything* in life! In any form! Therefore I, too, have already pointed out several times that only *that* person will find values in my Message who in all earnestness *seeks values therein.*

Nobody else! For the Living Word only gives when earnest seeking from within the soul touches it! Only then does it open up in rich abundance! –

Indeed today the word "possessed" is still heard and found always and only where there is no question of it!

And wherever it is appropriate nobody thinks of using it!

However, here also the expression coined in the human word has already *unintentionally* and at the *right* place hit upon the right thing; for you will find many in the lunatic asylums of whom it is said, with a shrug of the shoulders: "He is only possessed of a fixed idea, but otherwise seems normal!"

Here again men *unintentionally* hit upon what is right, but without themselves giving it any *further* thought.

However, not only this type should be called possessed – those who have a fixed idea and so-called lucid hours or moments, but also those who talk irrationally all the time may be possessed. In reality they are not always sick! –

As an example let us now consider one of the many cases where a young girl is regarded by her surroundings as possessed, or where at least she is suspected of it, because *in her presence* some such peculiar things suddenly occur, the origin of which is not known.

There are many different and possible explanations which correspond with reality, but not a single one is consistent with being possessed.

In the house concerned a *human spirit* may be *earthbound* through some cause or other; for *in all cases* it can only be a question of *human spirits* which have departed from the earth. Demons or the like are utterly out of the question in this matter.

Through some deed such a human spirit is perhaps bound to the house or only to the place, the spot. Thus it need not necessarily have done something during *the period* when the house existed, but it may have already been *before* then, at or near the spot where the house now stands.

Sometimes this spirit is tied to the place for decades or centuries, either through a murder or through some grave act of negligence, through harming some other person as well as through other happenings, many of which can bind a person.

Therefore it is not absolutely necessary for it to be connected with the people inhabiting the house *now*. Despite its perpetual presence in the house it has at all events never before had an opportunity enabling it to manifest itself in the gross material on earth, which *now only* takes place through the girl on account of her special, *but also only present,* peculiarity.

This peculiarity of the girl is a matter all by itself, which merely gives the spirit the opportunity of expressing its volition in the gross material world in a certain way. It has otherwise nothing to do with the spirit.

The cause of the peculiarity lies in the radiation of her blood at that time, the instant it has *a very definite composition.* It is *from this* that the human spirit without a gross material earth cloak derives strength for carrying out its desires to make itself conspicuous, which often develop into irksome bad behaviour.

As I have once already pointed out every person has different blood radiations, and this blood composition is changed several times during life on earth, whereby the type of radiation of the blood also changes at the same time. Thus in most cases the singular effect some persons exercise in being able to set free the unusual happenings occurs over a very definite period only, i. e., *temporarily.* There is hardly a single case where it lasts during the whole earth life. Sometimes it continues only for weeks or months, but seldom for years.

Therefore when such a happening suddenly ceases this does not prove that the spirit concerned no longer exists or is released, but in most cases it has suddenly no further possibility of making itself conspicuous in such a crude way.

Consequently it is by no means "exorcised" nor has it vanished, just in the same way as it may have already been confined to the place for a long period without people ever noticing it. Moreover it remains just as imperceptible to people as their permanent spiritual environment. People are never alone in reality!

With this example I have given only *one* possibility for consideration, in which the spirit is bound to a *particular place.*

However, it can also be a human spirit chained to a *person* living in the house, chained through any of the happenings which have so often been mentioned in my Message. It need not involve the particular child which through its blood composition offers the temporary possibility for earthly visible activity. The real cause may also be the father, the mother, the brother, the sister, or some other person living in the same house or merely frequenting it.

And there is still another difference, for the guilt of this happening can lie either with the departed human spirit or with one of the occupants of the house, and may date from the present life on earth or from a previous one.

So many and varied are the possibilities that no definite outline whatever should be prescribed in this matter without running the risk of arousing and supporting wrong thinking in people, and an over-hasty, thoughtless judgment in individual cases.

I only mention all these possible causes in order to show the comprehensiveness of these matters, and thus warn people not to be so quick with some superficial expression; for a suspicion is often thereby voiced which is unjustified.

Therefore be careful with your conversation about things you do not understand! You bear the full responsibility for it, and you may also perhaps bind yourselves with as little as one word for years and decades!

The spirit concerned in such a happening may have been evil and detained through some guilt. It does not change so easily in this, and it will, according to its nature, show its hatred towards people provided it receives the strength from somewhere to carry this into effect on the earthly gross material plane. Or the spirit itself was the one harmed and attaches itself spiritually to the person who at one time harmed it and who now lives in the house. However, in every case the spirit binds itself ever anew by such spiteful and disturbing activities and entangles itself still more, whereas with a *good* volition it could sever itself and would be able to ascend. Such a blustering spirit always harms itself most of all by this!

But the person who through his blood radiation temporarily offers the opportunity for this manifestation need not be connected at all with such an affair. It is, of course, possible that he is linked with it through some former guilt or, alternatively, that the spirit is bound to him. All this is not excluded. But on no account is it a question of *being possessed!*

Were a person possessed by another spirit, i.e., should an alien spirit periodically or continually make use of a body not belonging to it for the purpose of manifesting on the earthly gross material plane, then the physical body concerned would *itself* have to carry out everything that happens, such as throwing, hitting, scratching, and destroying, or in whatever way it is expressed.

As soon as someone is possessed the alien spirit concerned will *always* work *directly through that* physical body with which it has been able to connect itself, of which it has partly taken possession and which it uses for its purposes. It was only through this that the expression "possessed" arose, because an alien spirit takes possession of an earthman's body, appropriating it in order to work with it in an earthly gross material way. The spirit also lays claim to the possession of the physical body alien to it. And this body is then "possessed" by the spirit, or we may also say it is "occupied". The spirit places itself within the physical body, possesses it or has periodically possessed it.

It is quite natural that the process of taking possession occurs first of all *in the brains*. Those earthmen to whom this happens are then described as being insane or not normal mentally, because there are often two different human spirits quarrelling and fighting to use the brains.

Thus thoughts and words and deeds are expressed which contradict each other, often in confused succession and in incomprehensible chaos, because two different spirits are trying to impress their volition – the rightful owner and the intruder! Naturally this also causes an over-straining of the nerves of the brain, which are literally shaken up and thrown into confusion; and man, observing this from outside, can only conclude there is cerebral confusion, although the brain itself may be quite healthy otherwise. It is only the fight and conflict between the two different spirits which causes the confusion.

Occasionally it also happens that the alien human spirit which forcibly takes possession of a physical body not only makes complete use of the brain, but even carries the encroachment further by subjugating still other parts of the body for itself and its purposes, even pushing out the soul which is the rightful owner of the body, crowding it out with the exception of a small part which it cannot steal without endangering the life of this body itself.

In such serious cases there occurs the "double life" of a person, already often mentioned in reports which have caused learned scholars quite some brain-racking; a double life which could even drive those afflicted with it to commit suicide because they became desperate over the way they acted.

But these happenings can also be explained in accordance with the Laws of Creation. They are always strictly linked with very definite conditions which must first be fulfilled by *both* parties. Man is not just simply at the mercy of an alien spirit's desire to intrude upon him!

For instance, the *spirit* of such a person whose body offers the possibility for an alien spirit to take advantage of it in this way, and who also more or less surrenders his body to the spirit for this purpose, will always be lazy or weak; for otherwise his own natural defence should remain strong enough to prevent this happening.

Indolence or weakness of the spirit is always due to one's own guilt, though mankind is unable to recognise it. This condition is again a consequence of the domination of the intellect, which oppresses and confines the spirit, stifling it. Thus it is the result of the hereditary sin, which I accurately described in my Message together with all its evil outworkings, one of which is also the possibility of becoming possessed.

A person with a weary spirit, however, may be exceptionally lively in his thinking, also in his learning, because spiritual indolence has nothing whatever to do with intellectual keenness, as readers of my Message know.

Indeed it is just the spirit of distinguished scholars which is often very strongly earthbound and confined. As a fitting expression for this one could use the term "a spirit with drooping wings", because this gives the best conception. In reality the spirit of some great intellectual scholars is already slumbering towards spiritual death, although among men on earth the person concerned is particularly honoured as a shining light!

Therefore a person so afflicted may be exceptionally fresh intellectually and clever, and yet have a weary spirit which allows his physical body to become in part the subject of dispute by another bodiless human spirit.

Therefore, you men, gain *greater knowledge* of God's Primordial Laws of Creation, and you will be able to prevent much evil from assailing you! Tear yourselves away from your hollow knowledge-*conceit*, which brings forth only piecework, hardly of any use in the smallest need!

Science today lacks the *knowledge* which will enable it to recognise *these* things, for what science still teaches to date and what it pretends to know only proves clearly and distinctly that it really does not yet know anything about Creation at all. It lacks all the great connections and thus at the same time the actual picture of the real happening. It is only shortsighted and cramped, and

849

has passed by all the great truths. However, this is the beginning of a new era, which will also in this matter let *everything arise anew!*

Thus a child or a grown-up is not always to be suspected if he sets free such things as knocking or the throwing of physical objects. The basis for such causes is so manifold that a statement can only be made in each individual case and on the very spot by those who really know.

What has been said here does not nearly exhaust all the possibilities, but one thing is certain: *There is no question here of being possessed!*

People who through the temporary state of their blood radiation offer the possibility for such actions on the part of an alien and earthbound spirit, may during such happenings naturally be subject to bodily convulsions, fever symptoms, and also indeed to unconsciousness.

This all comes about, however, because the alien human spirit seizes the helping radiations concerned and literally draws them forcibly from the physical body, thus causing disturbances in the harmony of the normal bodily radiation, which naturally becomes immediately noticeable in the body itself.

All these are very simple happenings which through careful observation can easily and conclusively be substantiated as soon as the proper connections are known.

Useless prattling and suppositions about it serve no purpose; they can only harm other people who have absolutely nothing to do with the whole matter.

Therefore, guard your words, you men! For they, too, are bound to drag you down, because all that is *unnecessary* is disturbing in Creation, and all that is disturbing sinks downwards according to the Law of Gravity.

But if your speech is true and good you will have a furthering effect, and you yourselves will become lighter and be uplifted in the light of your words, because they also hold threads which run and knot in the same way as the threads of your thoughts and actions. And then, when you no longer wish to speak needlessly, you will become more silent and reserved, and in this way powers will be stored up within you which I already described as the power of silence!

As soon as you desire to say only what is *useful,* as man should always have done from the outset, it will become natural to you. Then man will hardly take up a third of *that* time with his talking which he still spends upon it to-day.

Unfortunately, however, he prefers superficial chatter to a noble silence, thus allowing himself to be drawn ever further downwards in accordance with the Law of Gravitation, which presses downwards all that is unnecessary in Creation, allowing it to sink away as being useless!

Therefore heed your words, you men, and do not regard the evil of thoughtless prattling too lightly!

MAN IS still in doubt about how to form his prayers. He desires to do what is right and not to omit anything. Although he gives the matter the most sincere and willing thought, he is still not really sure that he is not doing something wrong.

But such pondering is utterly useless; it only proves that man is ever again trying to approach God with his *intellect*, and this he will never achieve, for he *always* remains far away from the Almighty with such efforts!

Whoever has absorbed my Message *aright* is clear about the fact that words are much too limited in their nature to be able to ascend to the Luminous Heights. It is only the *intuitive perceptions* embraced by the words which, depending upon their strength and their purity, ascend above the boundaries of formed words.

Words are meant in part only as signposts to indicate the direction which the rays of the intuitive perception should take. In part they also release *the nature* of the rays within man himself, who uses the formed word as a support and as a cloak. The *word* which is thought during prayer reverberates within man, if he experiences it within himself or if he exerts himself to call it to life within himself.

With this explanation you already see two kinds of prayer arising before you. The one arises within you out of your intuitive perception, without reflection, through the experiencing itself, which is therefore the strong intuitive perception of some moment, and which while springing forth yet veils itself in words; and then the other kind, which in the process of reflection forms words *beforehand*, and in working backwards through the words it only seeks to set free the corresponding intuitive perception, i. e., it wishes to fill the already formed words with intuitive perception.

There is no need to state which of these kinds of prayer counts as the more powerful one, for you yourselves know that that which is *more natural* is always *more correct*. Thus in these cases it is *that* prayer which arises through the bursting forth of a sudden intuitive perception, and which only afterwards seeks to compress itself into words.

Just assume that you are unexpectedly hit by a very heavy blow of fate, which shakes you to the depths. Fear for someone or something you love grips your heart! In your need a cry for help arises within you with a strength which shakes your body!

It is in this that you see the strength of the intuitive perception which is capable of ascending to Luminous Heights, if ... this intuitive perception bears within itself *humble purity;* for without this every ascent is already halted on its way at a very definite point, no matter how strong and powerful the intuitive perception is. It is utterly impossible without humility; it could never advance to that purity which in an immense circle surrounds all that is Divine.

Such a strong intuitive perception will also bring in its train only a *stammering* of words because its strength does not permit it to be squeezed into narrow words. The power streams far beyond the confines of all words, foaming over and tearing down the boundaries which words want to erect through the narrow limits of the earthly brain's activity.

Every one of you will already have had such an experience in his life. Therefore you can grasp what I am trying to convey to you. *That* is the intuitive perception which you should have if you expect your prayer to be able to ascend to the Heights of Pure Light, from which all granting comes to you.

However, not only on account of fear shall you turn to the Heights, but also pure joy as well as happiness and gratitude can well up within you with the same strength! And this *joyful* kind swings upwards even faster, because it remains more undimmed. Fear very easily dims your purity of intuitive perception and forms a wrong kind. Too often it is connected with a silent reproach or even grudge that whatever hit your soul so severely just had to happen *to you,* and naturally this is not right. It must then hold back your cries!

It is not necessary to form words in order to pray. The words are *for you,* in order to grant *you* the support of your intuitive perception, so that it remains more concentrated and does not become dissipated in many varieties.

You are not accustomed to think clearly without words and to become absorbed without losing the straight direction, because through too much talk you actually became far too superficial and distracted. *You* still *need* the words as signposts and also as cloaks to keep certain types of your intuitive perceptions together, and to envisage more clearly through words whatever you wish to express in prayer.

Such is the way to pray if the urge to do so arises from the intuitive perception, i. e., if it is a volition of your *spirit!* But this rarely happens with the mankind of today – only when they are hit in some way or other by a very strong impulse, through suffering, joy or also through some physical pain! Nobody takes the trouble any more to think now and then about God the Dispenser of all mercies, voluntarily and without some impulse!

Now let us turn to the second kind of prayer! It comprises those which are intended to be said at very definite times and without the kind of cause we have just discussed. Man takes it upon himself to pray. It is a deliberate, especially *willed* prayer.

This brings about a change in the process. Man thinks or speaks certain words of the prayer, which he himself has composed or which he has learned. Usually these prayers have little of intuitive perception. Man thinks far too much *about* getting the words right, and *this alone* already diverts him from really perceiving intuitively that which he speaks or merely thinks.

Without any difficulty you will recognise that this explanation is right, if only you think back and examine yourselves carefully in this respect. It is not easy to fill such prayers with the capacity of pure intuitive perception. Even the slightest constraint weakens it, claiming part of the concentration for itself.

Here the formed words must first be called to life within yourselves, i. e., *the words* must arouse *that kind of intuitive perception* within you which in their form they express. The procedure does not then follow the course of bursting forth from within, and passing through the back brain into your frontal brain, which quickly forms words according to the impressions received; but the frontal brain begins by *first* forming words which only thereafter must be absorbed retroactively and assimilated by the back brain, in order to exercise from there a corresponding pressure on the nerve system of the solar plexus, which only after further proceedings can arouse an *intuitive perception* in accordance with the word.

It is true that everything in the sequence takes place at such an enormous speed that it appears to the observer as if it happens *simultaneously*, but nevertheless such forms are not so powerful or so original as those arising in the reverse manner. Therefore they cannot attain the effect, and in most cases remain devoid of intuitive perception. Even with a repetition of the *same* words *ever again* daily, they lose their power for you, they become habitual and thus meaningless.

Therefore become *natural* in your praying, men, become free and unaffected! What you have learned by heart so easily becomes a recitation. You only make it difficult for yourselves by this!

If you begin your day with truly heartfelt gratitude to God, and if you also finish it with equally heartfelt gratitude, be it only gratitude for the lesson you have learned on this day through experiencing, you live well! Through diligence and care let everything you *do* arise as a prayer of gratitude! Let each word you speak reflect the love which God grants you! Then life on this earth will soon become a joy for everyone who is allowed to live upon it!

It is not nearly so difficult, nor does it take up any of your time. A short moment of honest heartfelt gratitude is much better than praying for hours what you have learned by heart, and which you could not in any case follow with your intuitive perception. Moreover, such outward praying only takes up the time you should use for genuine thanksgiving through joyous activity.

A child which really loves its parents will demonstrate this love by *its ways,* by its actions, and not with flattering words, which in many cases remain nothing but an expression of nestling self-complacency, unless it is even a selfish desire. The so-called wheedlers are seldom of any value and only think of themselves, and of satisfying their own wishes!

You stand no differently before your God! Prove through the deed what you wish to say to Him!

You now know *how* you have to pray and already again you are anxiously facing the question as to *what* you shall pray!

If you wish to recognise the right way for this you must first *separate* your prayer from your petitions. Differentiate between prayer and petition! Do not always try to stamp your petitioning as prayer!

Prayer and petition must signify *two different things* to you; for prayer belongs to worship, whereas a petition cannot count as worship if you really want to adjust yourselves to the conception.

And it is necessary that henceforth you should adjust yourselves to it, and not intermingle everything!

When you pray *give* yourselves! This only I wish to call out to you, and in the word itself you have the explanation. *Give* yourselves to the Lord in your prayer, give yourselves entirely to Him and without reserve! Prayer must be the unfolding of your spirit at the feet of God in veneration, praise and gratitude for everything He grants you out of His great Love!

It is so inexhaustibly much! Up till now you just have not understood it; you have lost the way which would enable you to enjoy it in the full consciousness of all the capacities of your spirit!

Once you have found *this* way through recognising all the treasures of my Message *you will no longer have any petition left.* You will have nothing but praise and thanksgiving as soon as you turn your hands and eyes upward to the Highest, Who reveals Himself to you in His Love. Then you will stand in a *perpetual* state of prayer, such as the Lord cannot expect otherwise from you; for in Creation you may indeed take for yourselves whatever you need. The table is prepared therein at all times!

And you may choose from it through the abilities of your spirit. The table always offers you *everything* you need, and petitions are unnecessary if you only make the *right* kind of effort to move within the Laws of God.

All this has already been said in words well known to you: "Seek, and ye shall find! Ask, and it shall be given unto you! Knock, and it shall be opened unto you!"

These words teach you the *necessary* activity of the human spirit in Creation, and above all the *right* application of his abilities. They point out exactly the way *in which* he must comprehend Creation, and also the path which will help him *onwards*.

The words must not be regarded merely in a commonplace sense, for their meaning goes deeper, encompassing the existence of the human spirit in Creation in accordance with the Law of necessary Movement.

The words "Ask, and it shall be given unto you!" point very clearly to the ability of the spirit (which I mentioned in the lecture: "The cycle of radiations"), causing it through a certain urge which cannot be shaken off always to will or to wish something; through its radiation this immediately attracts the *homogeneous species*, as a result of which it is automatically *given* what it desired.

The urge impelling the desire, however, must always remain *a petition* and must not become a one-sided demand, as unfortunately every human being of the present time has accustomed himself to making. For if it remains a petition it also holds *humbleness*, and consequently it will always contain what is good and will also bring in its train what is good.

With His words Jesus clearly showed *how* man has to adjust himself in order to direct all the self-acting abilities of his spirit onto the *right* course!

It is the same with all His words. Unfortunately, however, they were pressed into the narrow mould of the human earthly intellect, and thus became badly distorted, with the result that they were never understood any more, nor interpreted in the right way.

For it will probably be easily understandable to everybody that this does not refer to the ordinary relations between men, because men's attitude was neither then, nor is it today, of *such* a nature that one could expect from *them* the fulfilment of such hints.

Go among men and ask, and you will be given *nothing!* Knock, and the door will *not* be opened unto you! Seek among men and their works, and you will *not* find what you are seeking!

Nor did Jesus refer to the attitude of man towards God personally, omitting all the huge worlds lying in between, which cannot be pushed aside as if non-existent. Neither did He mean the Living Word alone therewith, but Jesus always spoke out of the primordial wisdom, and this He never compressed into small earthly thinking or conditions. When He spoke He depicted man *standing in Creation*, and He chose His words in an *all-embracing* manner!

All reproductions, translations and interpretations, however, suffer from the neglect to think *of this!* They were always intermingled with and carried out by earthly, petty human thinking and thus distorted and misrepresented. And where understanding was lacking their own ideas were added, which could never answer the purpose, however good the intention!

That which is human always remained petty human; the Divine, however, is always all-embracing! In this way wine was badly mixed with water, and finally there emerged something different from the original. This you must never forget!

Similarly with "The Lord's Prayer", through the petitions stated therein Jesus merely sought to direct the human spirit's volition in the most simple form, towards *that* which would permit the human spirit to desire only what is useful for its ascent, so that it could receive such from Creation.

This does not hold a contradiction, but it was the best signpost, the infallible staff for every human spirit of *that* time.

The man of today, however, needs the entire stock of words he has meantime created for himself, and the application of every conception arising therefrom, if he is to find a path out of the confusion of his intellectual sham wisdom.

Therefore, men of the *present* time, I must now grant you more extensive explanations, which in reality convey exactly the same again, only in *your* way!

It is *now your* duty to learn this, for your knowledge of Creation has become greater! So long as with this knowledge you do not now fulfil the duties laid upon you by your spirit's abilities, which have to be developed, so long have you no right to ask either!

With the faithful fulfilment of your duty in Creation, however, you receive *everything* through the reciprocal effect, and there is no longer a reason for any petition; from within your soul there then streams forth only *gratitude* to Him Who in His Omniscience and Love ever again loads you with gifts every day!

You men, could you but *pray* aright at last! *Really pray!* How rich would your existence then be! For in prayer lies the greatest happiness you can receive. It uplifts you to immeasurable heights so that supreme happiness streams through you blissfully. Could you but *pray*, men! That shall now be my wish for you!

In your small thinking you will then no longer ask to *Whom* you shall and may pray. There is but *One* to Whom you are allowed to dedicate your prayers, only One: GOD!

Approach Him in solemn moments with a sacred intuitive perception, and pour out before Him what your spirit can bring up in the way of gratitude! Turn *only to Him* when you pray; for it is to Him alone that gratitude is due and to Him alone you yourself belong, Oh Man, because only through His great Love were you able to come into existence!

THANKS

"THANKS! A thousand thanks!" Everybody has probably heard these words quite often. They are uttered with such a variety of expression that they cannot so easily be classified into *one* single and definite kind, as is actually required by the *sense* of the words.

In fact the meaning *of the words* is here only of secondary or even third consideration! It is more the *inflection*, the *tone of voice* used, which gives value to the words or indicates their worthlessness.

In many cases, probably in the majority, it is merely a superficial habit expressing the customary form of social politeness. In such instances the words might just as well have never been uttered at all, for they remain a hollow phrase which is more of an insult than an acknowledgement to all those for whom it is intended. Only occasionally, indeed very seldom, can there be sensed a vibration indicating an intuitive stirring of the soul.

One's hearing does not need to be so keen in order to recognise just *what* the person uttering these words means. They do not always contain something good, for the vibrations of the souls vary greatly with the same words.

They may reflect discontent or disappointment, yes, even envy and hatred, deceit and many an evil volition. These beautiful words of genuine gratitude are often misused in all sorts of ways so as carefully to gloss over something else, unless they are completely empty and only spoken in order to conform to manner and custom, or to habit!

These words are generally expressed by those who are accustomed to receiving, who use them constantly and who always keep them ready for every occasion without giving any thought to it. This is similar to the frequently encountered babbling of endless chains of all kinds of formulated prayers, but which through being rattled off without any inner intuitive response are nothing but an offence against the Holiness and Greatness of God!

But where the words are really used in accordance with *that* sense which they seek to express, i. e., where the soul vibrates in the wording, where the words formed remain indeed the expression of the pure vibrations of the soul, as it always should be when man forms words – then *such* cases shine forth brilliantly in Creation like beautiful blossoms springing forth from stony ground!

If you consider it aright, in fact, everything uttered without intuitive prompting is bound to remain nothing but empty prattle, wherewith man fritters away the time which he should value differently; or it can only contain a false volition, with the words representing something to his fellow-men not in accord with the speaker's intuition. Nothing healthy and constructive can ever come from it – the Laws of Creation prevent it!

Thus it is, and not otherwise, although it remains very sad, clearly showing all the mire men are piling up through their varied prattling in the field of fine gross matter, which has a retroactive effect upon life on earth, and through which every human soul must first journey before it can enter the lighter spheres.

Never forget that each of your words allows a form to arise which clearly shows the contradiction between your intuitive perception and the words, no matter whether you wish it or not. You cannot alter this fact! Consider this with everything you say! Although fortunately they are but lighter forms which quickly vanish again, yet there is always the danger for you that such products may suddenly obtain reinforcement from a completely strange source, strengthening and condensing them in the same species and thus permitting them to extend their activity, which is bound to become a curse to you!

For this reason try to reach the point where you only utter *that* in which your soul vibrates.

You imagine this would be quite impossible on earth, because otherwise, in comparison to your present custom, you could say so little to each other that life would thereby threaten to become monotonous and boring, especially at social gatherings. There must be many who think in this way and who are afraid of it!

However, if man only advances to this point in his thinking, he will also see how much of his time on earth so far was bound to remain utterly empty, without value and thus without a purpose. Then he will no longer be sorry at the loss of so many empty hours, but quite on the contrary he will be afraid *to indulge in them* in the future.

The person who must seek to fill his time with empty words, just for the purpose of keeping on social terms with his fellow-men, is empty himself, as are his surroundings. However, he will not admit this to himself. He will console himself by saying that he cannot always talk about serious matters, that he will become boring to the others, in short that it is only the fault of the *others* if he does not speak of that which perhaps still stirs him personally.

With this, however, he deludes himself. For if his fellow-men are really as he supposes them to be, then this proves that he himself has nothing else to offer either, because it is only through the attraction of homogeneous species that the surroundings with which he associates come into existence. Or his surroundings have attracted him because of the homogeneity! It is the same in both cases! The popular saying about this is quite right when it asserts: "You can judge a man by the company he keeps!"

Empty people who do not strive to fill their life with genuine contents will flee from such people bearing spiritual values within them!

Nobody can conceal spiritual values; for as soon as it is not buried within man but still really alive, the spirit has quite a natural urge towards activity through Creation's Law of Movement. It irresistibly presses towards the outside, and such a person will again find men to whom he can give something as recompense through his spiritual activity, so that he in turn may receive from them, if only through new stimulation or through questions of serious purport.

It is absolutely impossible for boredom to find any room in such cases! On the contrary, the days are then far too short, time passes by ever faster, and there is not enough of it to hold everything a spirit can give when it is really astir!

Go among your fellow-men and listen to how much of the many things they talk about contains anything worth mentioning. Speedily and without any trouble you will recognise how spiritually dead humanity is at present – the humanity who should *work* spiritually, which means that every word they utter should be of great and upbuilding value, because they are of the spirit! You yourselves have deprived your words of all the high power which they should contain in the Law of Creation due to your wrong application of the ultimate expression of your thoughts. The language is intended to serve man with power and as a sword in order to promote and protect harmony, not to spread suffering and conflict.

He who speaks out of his spirit *cannot* make many words. But with him every word becomes a deed, because he swings in his word and this swinging brings fulfilment in the Law of Reciprocal Action, which itself is fulfilled in the Law of Attraction of Homogeneous Species.

For this reason man shall never utter words of *gratitude* in a superficial way; for they do not offer gratitude unless penetrated by the soul!

Does it not sound like a jubilant song as soon as human lips form these plain words with a blissful heartfelt emotion: "Thanks! A thousand thanks!"

And it is more, in reality much more, for such gratitude from a soul which is stirred is at the same time a prayer – gratitude to God!

In all such cases the intuitive perceptions contained in the words rise unconditionally towards the heights, and the blessing descends reciprocally upon that person or those persons who called forth these intuitive perceptions, i. e., upon that place which the words of genuine thanks are meant for, the place to which they were directed.

Therein lies the just equilibrium which is fulfilled with the blessing, which also takes on form and is bound to become visible on earth.

But ... the blessing cannot flourish visibly everywhere, for the process requires this one condition: No matter what has been done by the one for whom the words of such genuine gratitude are meant, *he must have done it with love and with the intention of giving joy to the other!* Whether it has been a gift or some action, or only some really well-meant and good word of advice!

If this requirement is not met by the giver, then the blessing sinking down in reciprocal action for the gratitude which ascended does not find the soil in which it could become anchored, and thus in all these cases the just blessing *must* nevertheless fail to materialise, because the one who should have received it is incapable of accepting or receiving it.

Therein lies a justice which man on earth does not know, and which is only contained in the Laws of Creation working so vitally and automatically, the Laws of Creation which can neither be distorted nor influenced in this matter.

For example, a person who does something in a calculating way, either to attain fame or some other pleasant reputation, will never be able to receive the true blessing arising out of his kind actions, because he does not carry within himself the soil which is *required* according to the Law to receive this blessing. At the most he can receive transitory, dead and thus nothing but temporary *earthly* advantage, but never a true reward of God, which can only be received by a person who himself stands and lives in the sense of the Divine Will in Creation.

Even if a person would give away millions for the poor or, as so often happens, sacrifices them for the sciences, if his impulse is not genuine love, if his urge to help does not come from his soul, then he will not get any reward of God either, because it *cannot possibly* come about, since such a person is incapable of absorbing, of receiving it!

As a consequence of many a genuine expression of thanks from those who received from him, the blessing in accordance with the Law already hovers above him, it has descended upon him, but such a person cannot partake of it due to his own fault, because he does not offer the soil within himself for its reception.

When genuine gratitude is uttered the reaction will come in any case. However, the extent of the effect depends in turn – and according to the Law – upon the attitude adopted by the soul of him for whom the blessing came through the reciprocal action.

The one who should receive is therefore himself at fault when such a blessing cannot take shape for him, because he does not possess the inner capacity to receive it in accordance with the requirements of the Primordial Law of Creation, since he lacks the right warmth of soul.

The misuse of beautiful words of thanks, however, is not only carried on by the one party, not only by the receiving ones, but also by the giving ones, who entirely displace and distort the conception of gratitude.

There are more than a few among mankind who to all appearances do a lot of good, and yet extend their help just to reap gratitude for themselves.

In their giving they are coldly calculating! Only the cleverness of their intellect is at work. Among these there are also a few whose momentary feeling prompts them to offer help, but who later on constantly try to throw this at the one-time recipient, expecting gratitude from him for the rest of their life!

Persons of this kind are even worse than the most evil usurers. They do not shrink from expecting *life enslavement* from those who at one time or other received help from them.

With this they not only destroy their self-respect and the value they should receive for the help once given, but they fetter and burden themselves with tremendous guilt. They are despicable creatures, not worthy to breathe another hour in Creation or to enjoy its blessings, which the Creator grants them ever anew with each moment. They are the most unfaithful of servants who, due to themselves, must be cast out.

But just these insist upon morals on earth and are also supported by earthly moralists, who always seek with high-sounding words to further the same wrong opinions about obligatory thankfulness, thereby cultivating something which, according to the Primordial Laws of Creation, is akin to the grossest immorality.

Many now praise gratefulness as a virtue, others as a duty of honour! Through one-sidedness and lack of understanding opinions are uttered and frivolously spread, which have already caused severe suffering to many a person.

Therefore man must now become clear as to *what* gratitude really is, what it calls forth and how it works!

Then much will become different, and all the chains binding slaves, which were forged through wrong opinions about gratitude, will fall away. Mankind will at last be freed from them. You have no idea what travail has spread over mankind on earth like a shroud draping all human dignity and the noble, joyful desire to help, due to this mutilation and the false conceptions of pure gratitude forced upon men. Countless families in particular are infected with this, and have been producing accusing victims for thousands of years.

Away with this false delusion, which seeks with deliberate intent to drag every noble action which is natural to human dignity deep into the mud!

Gratitude is *not a virtue!* It must not, nor does it want to be counted among the virtues! For each virtue emanates from God and is therefore unlimited!

Nor may genuine gratitude be stamped as a duty! For then it would be unable inwardly to unfold *that* life and warmth which it needs in order to receive the blessing of God from Creation through the reciprocal action.

Gratitude is closely linked with joy! Gratitude itself is an expression of purest joy. Thus wherever there is no joy included, where no joyful elation is the cause for gratitude, there the expression gratitude is used *wrongly*, there it is misused!

In such cases it will never be able to set free *those* forces which are automatically released by true gratitude in accordance with the Laws of this Creation. The blessing is then lacking. Confusion must come in its place.

Such misuse, however, is found almost everywhere when men speak of gratitude, of thanks *today!*

The gratitude really felt intuitively is a *compensatory value* willed by God, which mediates the counter-value to whomsoever gratitude is due. This is contained in the Law of necessary Equilibrium in this Creation, which can only be upheld and furthered by harmony, which lies in the fulfilment of all the Primordial Laws of Creation.

You men, however, bring entanglement into all the running threads of the Laws through your false practices, your erroneous conceptions! Therefore you make it difficult for yourselves to attain to true happiness, to peace! In most cases you are hypocrites with your words! How then can you expect that truth and happiness can blossom forth for you? You must indeed always reap what you sow!

Thus you must also reap everything you sow with your words, and through the manner in which you utter your words! Your own attitude towards these words!

Nothing other can develop out of this for you – this you must always remember in regard to *everything* you say!

Just think over everything once again each evening, and seek to recognise the worth of the words you have exchanged with your fellow-men in the course of the day; you will be horrified at their emptiness! Even at the emptiness of many hours of but a single day! Attempt this without any extenuation of yourselves! With a shudder you will realise what must also arise out of this for you in the workshop of Creation, well known to you through my Message, in which everything automatically manifests which issues from you through your intuitive perception, your thinking, your speaking and your actions!

Examine yourselves seriously and with an honest confession! From that hour onwards you will change yourselves in many things!

You must not on that account become sparing with words in your life on earth in order to proceed on the right path. But in talking you must avoid superficiality as well as lack of sincerity, which lie behind the major part of all the speaking of these earthmen.

For you act with all your talking in the same way that you deal with expres-

865

sions of gratitude, and yet inwardly you highly praise such moments as earnest, solemn and significant when with your words you simultaneously express your intuitive perception!

This happens only seldom, however, but it should *always* be thus! So many men consider themselves very clever and wise, even highly developed spiritually, when they know how to conceal their intuitive perceptions and their actual volition behind their words, never permitting their fellow-men to see their true face in spite of lively conversation.

This method is called diplomatic, as a soothing expression for the strange mixture of crafty cheating, of hypocrisy and falsehood, and of the greed which is always lying in wait triumphantly to create advantages for oneself at the expense of weaknesses discovered in others.

In the Law of Creation, however, it makes no difference whatever whether all this is done by someone acting for himself personally or only for the benefit of a state. In this matter acting is acting, and is bound to release all the effects of these Laws.

He who knows the Laws and their effects need not first be a prophet in order to recognise quite clearly the end of all that is bound up in the fate of individual nations and of mankind on earth; for the whole of mankind is incapable of displacing or distorting anything in this matter!

Only through recognition and genuine observance of the Laws, and thus acting differently *in time,* could mankind have sought to diminish a great deal in order to ease many afflictions for themselves. However, it is now too late for this! For all the effects of their past actions are already rolling!

But all that is burdensome therein truly serves only as a blessing! It is a mercy! It brings about purification where there is something wrong which now causes the collapse as the final consequence, no matter whether in the state or in the family, in the people themselves, or in association with others generally. We stand in the great final reckoning, which rules over the force of the human means of power. Nothing can shut itself out or hide from this!

Only the Laws of God still speak, which with superhuman accuracy and in an unswerving manner take automatic effect in everything that has happened so far; for new energy has penetrated them from the Will of God, which energy now permits them to enclose men as with immovable walls, protecting them or also destroying them, depending upon the nature of men's attitude towards them.

For a long time in the future they will also remain like walls, surrounding everything with the same power, in order to prevent such confusion as has occurred in the past from coming about once more. Soon men will be thereby compelled to move only in the forms willed by God, for their own salvation and for their deliverance, so far as this is still possible, until they themselves go consciously forward again on the right paths in accordance with the Will of God.

Therefore look around you, men, and learn to swing in your words, so that you will not neglect anything!

LET THERE BE LIGHT!

LET THERE be Light! How far man still is from grasping this great Word of Creating! Far even from the right desire to learn to understand this happening! And yet he has never ceased to occupy himself with it for thousands of years. In *his* way, however! Not in humility does he wish to take a spark of recognition from the Truth, to receive in purity, but only to puzzle out everything himself intellectually!

In the course of doing so he stubbornly tries to substantiate every proposition he sets up in accordance with the nature and need of his earthly brain. This is quite right for *the things of the earth* and for everything gross material, which includes the brain from which the intellect issues; for the intellect is nothing but gross material comprehension. Thus all those who merely submit to the intellect, wanting only those things to be considered justified and correct which can be absolutely substantiated through the intellect, are very *narrow-minded* and inseparably bound to the World of Gross Matter.

With this, however, they are also furthest away from true knowledge and from knowledge in general, although just they in particular imagine themselves to be knowing!

Rightly considered, it is in this pitiable role that the whole of science presents itself to us today. Narrowing itself, convulsively suppressing and fearfully rejecting everything which it cannot also press into the limited confines of its so earthbound understanding! They really reject it with fear, because in spite of their rigidity these learned men cannot indeed deny that there exists *more* than merely that which they can classify in the gross material register of the brain, which thus still belongs unconditionally to the gross material plane, to the outermost ramifications at the lowest end of this great Creation!

In their anxiety some of them become malicious and even dangerous towards all those who refuse to be embraced by this rigidity, but who expect *more* from the human spirit. For this reason they not only investigate with their earthbound intellect, but reach out beyond gross material happenings with their *spirit,* just as is worthy of a still healthy human spirit and as remains its duty in this Creation.

The intellectuals want to suppress *alert* spirits *at all costs.* This has been so for thousands of years. And the darkness, spreading ever more rapidly mainly through the intellectuals – as a consequence of such gross material narrowness, gradually formed the soil which made it possible for the intellect to expand its power on earth.

Whatever could not be substantiated by the intellect was persecuted, if at all possible was ridiculed, to prevent it from getting a foothold and disquieting the intellectuals.

As a precautionary measure they tried to disseminate as wisdom, that everything which cannot be fathomed and proved by the intellect belongs only to an untenable theory.

For thousands of years this established principle of the intellectuals has been their pride, also their weapon and their shield. It has even been their throne, which is now bound to collapse as soon as the *spiritual* awakening commences! The spiritual awakening shows that this principle has been absolutely wrong, and that with boundless effrontery it was so twisted as just to protect the earthbound narrow-mindedness and to keep the human spirit in idle sleep!

Nobody realised that just this reasoning proved at the same time how far removed intellectual work lies from true knowledge.

Break the narrow bounds drawn around you in such a clever way as to render you incapable of developing beyond the pompous earthly erudition of the human intellect! You will quickly learn to perceive intuitively that it is precisely those things which the intellect can substantiate that belong to *theory;* for only earth-built theory can be substantiated as a structure, *never true knowledge!*

Thus in this matter, too, it is just the contrary of what has been asserted hitherto. Here also everything must now become new, as mankind was promised by the Lord! –

Everything that can be *proved* by the intellect is earthly theory, nothing else! And the scholarship of today is based on this, and presents itself to us *in this way!* But that has nothing to do with intelligence, i. e., with true knowledge! There are scholars who, according to the Primordial Laws of Creation,

i. e., according to reality, count among *the most narrow-minded* of human spirits, even though they possess a great reputation on earth and are highly esteemed by men. In Creation itself they only play a ridiculous role!

Some of them, however, can become really dangerous to the human spirits of this earth, because they lead them along false and narrow ways on which the spirit is never able to unfold itself. They suppress them, seeking to impose upon them their own scholarship, which is fundamentally nothing but narrow-minded earthly intellectualism veiled with tinsel.

Awake and expand, you human spirits, make room for upward flight. You are not made for the purpose of remaining only in the gross material sphere; you are to *make use* of it, but not to consider it your home.

In these perverted days many a farm labourer is more *spiritually* awake and thus more *valuable* in Creation than a scholar who has entirely lost his pure intuitive perception. It has really a deep meaning when people talk of *dry* intellectual work or of dry scholarship. How often does the most simple person hit unswervingly on the right thing with an expression of the intuitive perception! The expression "dry" here means "without life", thus dead! There is no life in it! And the saying carries truth within it!

For this reason man will never be capable of grasping with his intellect the high conception of the Holy Words: "Let there be Light!" Nevertheless, or perhaps just because of this, the words "Let there be" leave him no peace of mind! He tries time and again to picture this to himself in order to arrive at the *how*. Once he knows about the how he is soon confronted with the question of *"why?"*

Finally he also wants to know *why* God let Creation come into existence at all! Such is man's nature! However, he desires to *fathom* everything himself, but he will *never* succeed in *fathoming* it! For to do so he would have to work with his spirit. In view of the present decisively dominating activity of the intellect, however, the spirit would be quite unable to set to work, because it is too badly confined and tied to what is *gross material only,* whereas the beginning of Creation, as part of an utterly different species, lies so infinitely far above the gross material.

For this reason man in his present state would never have any prospect of divining this, even if he had the inner capacity to do so. But he *has not* the capacity to do so either! The human spirit simply cannot fathom happenings in such heights, because they are far *above* that point where the human spirit can "know" something, i. e., above where it is capable of absorbing anything consciously!

Wanting to fathom these matters can thus never enter into it! Therefore it is of no avail for man to attempt to concern himself with it! He can merely receive it in pictures as soon as he is willing to absorb a knowing of it in true humility. This "knowing of it" is naturally not the knowledge itself, which latter he can never receive.

Thus if he desires seriously but humbly to know something about it, he may picture it to himself. I will describe the process in such a way that he is able to absorb it. To unfold it in its entire greatness before the human spirit, even if only in picture form, is impossible, because *those* modes of expression given to the human spirit to understand things do not suffice. –

In my lecture "Life" I have already explained how, upon the Act of the Will of God expressed in the words "Let there be Light!", the rays shot beyond the border of the Divine Sphere, and how then, as they proceeded downwards, they cooled off more and more and were bound to manifest. Through the ever diminishing elasticity or pressure caused by the cooling off, various entities could gradually come to personal consciousness, first in the intuitive perception and then also by strengthening themselves little by little in outward activity. However, it is better for me to say that the pressure does not diminish through the cooling off, but that the cooling off takes place through and within the slackening pressure.

I do not need to emphasise that each individual happening, each minute change in the cooling off process, spans immense spaces and distances, which again the human spirit can never understand and conceive.

In that lecture I contented myself with simply saying that the radiations were impelled beyond the boundary of the Divine Sphere through the Act of Will. I did not speak further about the Act of Will itself.

Today I want to go further and explain why the radiations *were* then *bound* to shoot across the boundary of the Divine Sphere; for everything in the development of Creation happens only because it cannot be otherwise, thus strictly according to the Law. –

From all eternity the Holy Grail was the extreme pole of the direct Radiation of God; a vessel in which the radiation was collected at the last and furthest point in order, by flowing back, to become renewed ever again. *Around* it stood the Divine Castle of the Grail, with its gates shut fast towards the out-

871

side so that nothing could penetrate it any more and there was no possibility of any further cooling off. Everything was guarded and watched over by the "Elders", i.e., the Eternal Unchangeable Ones who, at the outermost boundary in the Divine Sphere of Radiation, are able to live conscious of their existence. –

Now if man wishes to follow my description aright he must first realise that Will and Deed are always one in the *Divine Sphere.* Each word is directly followed by the deed or, more precisely, each word as such *is* already the deed itself, because the Divine Word possesses creative power, and thus immediately forms itself into the deed. So it also was with the great Word: "Let there be Light!"

Only God Himself is Light! And His Natural Radiation forms what to the human mind is the immeasurable circle of the Divine Sphere, the outermost anchorage of which is and was the Grail Castle from eternity. When God wished that there should also be Light beyond the boundary of the immediate Divine Radiation, there could be no question of a simple arbitrary *extension* of radiation, *but Light had to be placed at the outermost point of the immediate boundary of the Radiation of Divine Perfection,* in order to radiate forth from there through that which had not hitherto been illumined.

Thus God not only uttered the Words: "Let there be Light!" according to human conceptions, but it was simultaneously a deed! This was the great happening when a Part of Imanuel was sent out or born out from the Divine Sphere! The placing out of a Light-Part from the Primordial Light in order that this Part might radiate and illuminate independently beyond the direct Radiation of God! The beginning of the great development of Creation was the simultaneous consequence of the sending out of a Part of Imanuel.

Thus Imanuel is the cause and the starting point of Creation through the sending out of a Part of Him. He is the Will of God, Who carries the Word: "Let there be Light!" living within Himself, Who is this Word Himself! The Will of God, the Living Cross of Creation, around Which Creation could and had to form! Therefore He also is the Truth as well as the Law of Creation, which was allowed to form through Him, from out of Him!

He is the bridge from the Divine outward, the way to the Truth and to Life, the Creative Source and the Power which issues from God!

It is a new picture which unfolds before mankind, and yet a picture which does not distort anything, but which only sets right what has been distorted in human opinions.

Now you still have the question as to "why"! Why did God send out Imanuel! Although this is a rather strange, indeed presumptuous, question asked by the human spirit, I will nevertheless explain it to you, because so many men on earth feel themselves to be victims of this Creation through imagining that if they can make mistakes God has created them faulty!

Their presumption even goes so far as to make a *reproach* of this, with the personal excuse that God only needed to create man in such a manner that he could never think and act wrongly, and therewith the Fall of Man would not have occurred either!

But it is only the human spirit's capacity for free decision which brought about his decline and fall! Had he always heeded and followed the Laws in Creation there could have been *nothing but* ascent, happiness and peace for him; for that is how these Laws wish it to be. When he disregards them he naturally bumps against them, stumbles and falls. –

In the Circle of Divine Perfection the *Divine* alone can partake of the joys of *conscious* existence which the Radiation of God bestows. It is the purest of the pure in the radiation which can take on form, such as Archangels, for example; still further away at the outermost limit of the sphere of radiation also the Elders, who at the same time are the Guardians of the Grail in the Grail Castle within the Divine Sphere.

When this is accomplished that which is most powerful and strong is drawn out of the radiation. From what is left animal forms, landscapes and buildings then arise in the Divine. Therewith the nature of the last remnants changes ever more, but it is subject to the highest tension in the tremendous pressure brought about by the nearness of God, although even here His distance away must still remain vast and incomprehensible to the human spirit.

These last remnants, which as the ramifications and exhausted residues of the radiations can no longer take on form *in the Divine Sphere,* and which float along and surge about at the outermost boundaries of the Divine like little luminous clouds, also contain the spiritual. Under the high pressure the latter cannot unfold and become conscious. *The strong urge to do so,* however, is inherent in all that is spiritual, and *it is this urge* which like one great petition ascends out of the perpetual surging, which surging cannot at the boundary come to the point of weaving and forming.

And again it was this petition within the unconscious urge to which God yielded in His great Love, which He allowed to be fulfilled; for only *outside* the boundaries of all that is Divine was it possible for the spiritual, in following its urge, to unfold; so as in part consciously to enjoy the blessings of the Divine radiations, to live in them joyfully, and to build up and create a realm for itself which, flourishing and abounding in harmony, may become a monument raised to the honour of God, in gratitude for His Goodness in granting all that is spiritual the opportunity for the freest development and thus for the forming of all their wishes!

In accordance with the nature and laws of the Radiations of God, *nothing but happiness and joy was bound to ensue* for all those becoming conscious therefrom. It simply could not be otherwise, because any darkness is altogether foreign and incomprehensible to the Light itself.

Thus the great deed was a sacrifice of love on the part of God, Who severed and sent out a small Part of Imanuel just in order to grant a conscious enjoyment of existence in response to the perpetual petitioning urge of the spiritual.

To attain this the spiritual had to cross the boundaries of the Divine Sphere towards the outside. However, only a part of the Living Light could pave the way for such a happening, because the attraction of the Primordial Light is so strong that all else was held back at the boundary of its own immediate radiation and was unable to proceed further.

Thus there was but *one* possibility to grant the fulfilment of the urge of all that is spiritual: To send forth a Part from out of the Light Itself! Only in Its Power, by using the way of the radiation of this Part of the Light as a bridge, could the spiritual cross the boundary toward becoming self-conscious.

But even this did not suffice, because according to the Law this small Part of the Light would Itself also be drawn back by the Primordial Light. Therefore the Part of the Light had to be *anchored* outside the boundaries of the Divine Sphere, otherwise the spiritual there would have been as good as lost.

Once having crossed the boundary of the immediate Radiation of God, which could only occur with the help of a Part of the Light, the spiritual was no longer subjected to this original power of attraction, because the ever-increasing distance permitted a cooling off and a subsequent partial becoming conscious. Thus it no longer had this firm support, because in the cooling off another species came into existence, creating a separating gulf. Only the

Part of the Light, being homogeneous with the Primordial Light, always remained connected with the Primordial Light and also directly subject to Its Law of Attraction.

Thus the inevitable consequence would have been the drawing back of this emitted Part of the Light to the Primordial Light, which would have necessitated a constant repetition of the emission, and thus continual interruption of the Act of Grace. This had to be prevented because, with a return of the Part of the Light across the border into the Divine Region to the Primordial Light, the spiritual outside the border would have immediately been left to itself and thus without any support, and without the supply of power it would have become unable to live. This would have meant the destruction of everything in existence outside.

Now for this reason the Primordial Light, God, connected the Part He sent out from Imanuel with a part of the purest extraction from all that is spiritual as a cloak, which acted as an anchorage of the Part of the Light with everything outside the border. This was a sacrifice of love on the part of God for the sake of the spiritual, which was therewith able to become conscious and *to remain so.*

The spiritual and everything issuing from it had thus found a support outside the border of the Divine and an eternal Source of Life, from which it could perpetually develop further. Simultaneously the bridge (in character similar to a lowered drawbridge) was built therewith from out of the Divine, so that the spiritual could perpetually renew and expand itself.

Thus a Part of Imanuel manifesting as "Let there be Light" became the starting-point and perpetual Stream of Life for Creation, the core around which all Creation could form.

First of all of the Primordial Spiritual Region as the Basic Creation, to which Imanuel formed the bridge. This made Him the *Outborn* Son of God in the Radiation of Whom the Primordial Spiritual World could come to self-consciousness, the Son in Whose Radiation mankind developed, from which happening the surname "the Son of Man" originated; *that* Son Who directly stands above the human spirits because they could only develop to consciousness through Him.

In the mystery of the separation and sending forth of a Part of Imanuel this Part remained in the Grail Castle of the *Divine* Region by the Law, corresponding with His origin as King of the Holy Grail. He opened the gate towards the outside and therewith formed the bridge over which the spiritual could pass. He did *not* also *cross the threshold* in person; only His Radiations issued from this border into the space which up till then had been void of Light.

Thus Parsifal came into existence in the Primordial Spiritual as coming from Imanuel, always being connected with Imanuel by a tie or, still more accurately, by an unbreakable radiation. *This* is the *way* in which man can imagine this connection. They are Two, and yet They are but One in Their working – the Part of Imanuel in the Divine Part of the Grail Castle at the outermost border of the Divine Region, still standing within it and only forming the bridge, which remains kept open towards the Primordial Spiritual Sphere through Him, indeed within Him; and Parsifal in the Primordial Spiritual Part of the Grail Castle, which came into existence with the spiritual becoming conscious and with the forming of all the landscapes and buildings connected with this process, both Persons being inseparably linked and working as *one* Person, thus also being One!

Parsifal is linked with Imanuel by a tie of radiation, at the same time also by a tie of radiation with Elizabeth, the Queen of Womanhood in the Divine, as His Mother, and thus He forms the permanent anchorage through the radiation connection. From the radiations of Her mantle Elizabeth gave the first form-giving cloak for the Unsubstantiate radiating core of Parsifal.

Subsequent Creation could come into existence *through the activity of the Prime-Spiritual* Primordial Beings. In descending the process is always a constant but weaker repetition of the Primordial Creation, which proceeds according to the respective laws. As a matter of course the nature of the happening changes according to the respective transformation of the Laws.

There was no longer any direct link from Imanuel for Subsequent Creation, because this only developed as a consequence of Primordial Creation from the volition of the Primordial Spiritual Beings. This process, however, was likewise based only on the Love towards the spiritual which, remaining unconscious in the Primordial Spiritual Realm, developed the same urge to become conscious as was the case previously with the Primordial Spiritual in the Divine Region. But the power of the spiritual did not suffice to form itself immediately and at once to the state of consciousness in Subsequent Creation, as was possible for the stronger Primordial Spiritual to do.

The last precipitation of the spiritual, not being as strong as the Primordial

Spiritual, had first slowly to develop in Subsequent Creation under the influence of the Prime-Spiritual Primordial Beings.

Since Subsequent Creation grew dark through the slowly developing human spirits and their fall, which was due to the one-sided cultivation of the intellect, it was necessary to intervene. In order helpfully to put right again everything in which mankind had failed, Parsifal was linked with the World of Gross Matter in Abd-ru-shin. Therefore Abd-ru-shin was Parsifal through the continued direct connection of the radiations, which cost great preparation and trouble to bring about. Through His Life on earth Subsequent Creation could again be given corresponding Light-Power to clarify, strengthen and help all that is spiritual, and passing through this the entire Subsequent Creation.

However, mankind of Subsequent Creation stubbornly opposed it and in their conceit refused to accept it, because they did not trouble themselves about the Laws in Creation and clung instead to their man-made theories! Nor did they heed the mission of the Son of God, which was to bring them help *before* the World Judgment.

The World Judgment itself is a natural happening, and the consequence of establishing a straight line to the Light, which was accomplished by Parsifal's wandering through the parts of the world.

In this wandering the earth was the turning-point, being the outermost boundary in the World of Gross Matter, for due to the spiritual nature of a few men it still offered an anchorage for this. Thus the earth is the last planet that can be saved, although it already belongs to the Realm of Darkness. Whatever lies *even* lower in this respect than the earth, i. e., whatever is encompassed even more by the Darkness, is left to disintegration, to which all darkness is bound to fall a prey with everything it holds fast.

The earth has thus become the *last* stronghold of the Light on soil which is hostile to the Light. Therefore the terminal point of the Light is now anchored *here*. The tighter the direct line of the Triune of the Light Activity, Imanuel – Parsifal – Abd-ru-shin, stretches from one day to the other, the more tangible and visible becomes the outworking of the power in the Divine Will, which creates order and forcefully straightens everything which mankind has distorted, that is, in so far as it can still be put right. That which *cannot* be made straight will have to break. The Power of the Light never permits of anything intermediate!

Only when this line of the Light is stretched taut and *straight* does the world tremble from the Divine Power, does mankind then recognise Imanuel in Abd-ru-shin!

Such is the process of development in all simplicity! Out of love, the innate desire of all creatures consciously to experience was fulfilled! However, out of love for all those who wish to have happiness and peace by obeying the Natural Laws of this Creation, everything that disturbs the peace therein will now also be destroyed, because it proved unworthy of the permission to be self-conscious. This is the World Judgment, rightfully dreaded! The great Cosmic Turning Point!

The human spirit has no right whatever to ask about the "why" of Creation, for this is a demand upon God which he must not make, because through the voluntary fall of man he *closed himself* to all wisdom and the possibility of higher recognition!

But I gave an explanation in order to counteract the senseless illusions of the intellectuals, so that such human spirits as strive seriously for the Truth, and who are ready to receive it in humility, shall not allow themselves to be led astray by such wanton, blasphemous presumption in the moment of final decision – to be or not to be – for every creature! –

The true seeker will now gain much from knowing about this, for you all cannot live otherwise but in the Law! The *Living* Law!

Whether you are capable of absorbing it is your affair! For I cannot help you with this either! Mankind asked, begged, and I have answered in matters far above the human spirit's ability to comprehend, which are fulfilled vast distances away from him, following the adamantine course of Divine Justice and Divine Perfection. Man should bow down in humility!

UNSUBSTANTIATE

THE WORD "substantiate" is an expression of Creation. It is so comprehensive that the human spirit as a particle of Creation will never be able to get a right conception of it.

As the counterpart of substantiate the expression "Unsubstantiate" is named. Less than ever can man imagine what is the meaning of Unsubstantiate. He will always have a confused idea of it, because it is something which must perpetually remain an enigma to him. He cannot even form a conception of it, because there exists no form for Unsubstantiate that comes within the understanding of the human spirit.

However, in order to bring you at least a little closer to an understanding I will for once substitute earthly expressions for the expressions of Creation, although these can only be considered the vaguest shadow in comparison to the reality.

For substantiate imagine *dependent*, and for Unsubstantiate that which alone is *independent*.

According to human thought this gives you the best possibility to approach the matter *objectively*, although it can neither render nor designate *that* which it really is, or how it is; for you would always be unable to comprehend the *"what"*, whereas in this way you can at least approximately envisage the *"how"* to yourselves.

The Unsubstantiate is therefore that which alone is independent, while all else is dependent upon it *in every respect* and is thus called substantiate, of which latter everything that is spiritual is also a part and likewise everything that is Divine, whereas the Unsubstantiate is only God.

From this you can realise that there is still a great difference between the Divine and God. The Divine is not yet God; for the Divine is substantiate, but God is Unsubstantiate. The Divine and all else that exists is dependent upon God, it cannot exist without God. God, however, is absolutely independent, if we are to use the earthly conceptions which, however, can naturally not convey what it really is, because earthly or human conceptions cannot span such greatness.

Thus heed this well, God is not Divine, but God is *God*, because He is Unsubstantiate, and the Unsubstantiate is not Divine, but God!

HOLY Night! Exultant singing in jubilant gratitude once streamed through all the spheres of Creation when the Son of God Jesus was born in the stable in Bethlehem! And shepherds in the fields, from whose spiritual eyes the bandage was removed during this joyous upheaval of the Universe, so that they could bear witness to this immense happening and thus call people's attention to it, fell upon their knees *apprehensively* because they were overwhelmed by what was so new and incomprehensible to them.

It was *fear* on the part of the shepherds, who for this purpose were temporarily made clairvoyant and also clairaudient. Fear of the greatness of the happening, of the Omnipotence of God thus made manifest! For this reason the herald from the Luminous Heights first spoke to them reassuringly: *"Be not afraid!"*

Whenever a herald from the Luminous Heights speaks to human beings you will ever again find these words, for it is fear that earthmen always perceive first when seeing and hearing heralds from on high. This is called forth by the pressure of the power, to which they are also opened a little in such moments. But only to the smallest part, for anything more would surely smother and burn them.

And yet it should be joy, not fear, as soon as the spirit of man strives for the Luminous Heights!

This did not become manifest to all mankind during the Holy Night! The Star became physically visible, but nobody on earth saw this luminous herald and the luminous hosts surrounding him. None saw and heard this but the few shepherds chosen for the purpose, who through their simplicity and close connection with Nature could be most easily opened to receive it.

And such great revelations on earth can never take place other than through a few chosen for the purpose! Remember this always! For the lawfulness in Creation cannot be annulled on your account! Therefore do not build up any fanciful pictures about various happenings, which can never be *as you* imagine them to be! These are unspoken demands, which never emanate from genuine conviction, but they are a sign of hidden unbelief and spiritual indolence, which has not absorbed my Word of the Message *in such a manner* as it demands to enable it to come to life in the human spirit.

In those days people *believed* the shepherds, at least for a short period! Today such people are only derided, considered eccentric, or even as impostors wishing to obtain earthly benefits thereby! For mankind has sunk far too deeply to be still able to accept calls from the Luminous Heights as genuine, especially when they themselves cannot hear or see anything.

Do you really believe, men, that on account of your great downfall God will now set aside the perfect Laws in Creation just to serve you, to bridge over your faults Himself, and to balance your spiritual indolence? The Perfection of His Laws in Creation is and will always remain inviolable, immutable; for they bear the Holy Will of God!

Thus the great revelations which you expect cannot possibly take place on earth except in that form which you have already known for a long time, and which you also *acknowledge* as long as they lie in the distant past.

Without any hesitation a so-called good Christian would designate as a blasphemer and see as a great sinner *that* person who would dare to assert that the announcement to the shepherds of the birth of the Son of God Jesus is a fairy tale.

Yet the same good Christian rejects with zealous indignation the announcements of the present time, although these are given *in the same way* through persons mercifully blessed to do so; and without further ado he calls the bearers blasphemers *too*, or in the most favourable cases perhaps he calls them simply fantasts or sickly persons, often misguided ones!

But reflect for yourselves – where is any healthy thinking to be found, where exact deduction, and where justice? These opinions of the strict believers – as they like to call themselves – are one-sided and abnormally limited. In most cases, however, it is indolence of their spirit and the human conceit always resulting from such indolence on the part of the spiritually weak, who find it difficult to remain clinging convulsively – at least for the sake of appearances – to what they once learned about some former happening, but never really *experienced inwardly*. But they are quite incapable of making spiritual progress, and *therefore* reject all the new revelations.

Who of all the believers has yet obtained any idea of the Sublimity of God contained in the happening which took place quietly during that Holy Night through the birth of the Son of God! Who can begin to conceive the Grace which was thus granted as a gift to the earth!

There was jubilation in the spheres at that time, today sorrow! Only on earth many a person seeks to give pleasure to *himself* or to others! But all this is not done as it ought to be done if the recognition or, for that matter, the true conception of God were astir within the human spirit.

Could they but vaguely sense the reality all men would experience the same as did the shepherds! Indeed the very Greatness of the happening would not possibly permit it to be otherwise – they would immediately fall upon their knees ... *out of fear!* For in beginning to perceive this, fear would first of all be bound to arise powerfully and force man down, because with this sensing of God the great guilt with which man has burdened himself on earth also becomes evident, merely through the indifferent manner in which he accepts God's blessings without really doing anything in return in the service of God!

How strange it is that every man who once in a while really and truly wishes to experience the Christmas Festival tries to recall his childhood!

This clearly enough indicates *the fact* that he is absolutely incapable of experiencing the Christmas Festival as *a grown-up* with his *intuitive perception!* It proves that he has *lost* something he *possessed* as a child! Why does this not make men think?

Again it is spiritual indolence which prevents them from earnestly considering these matters. "That is for children" they think, and grown-ups have no time for it whatever! They have *more serious matters* to think about!

More serious matters! By this they only mean the pursuit of earthly things, which is the work of the intellect! The intellect quickly subdues memories in order not to lose pre-eminence when the intuitive perception is given the chance to express itself for once!

In all these apparently small facts the *greatest* things could be recognised if the intellect would only allow time for it. But it has the upper hand and fights to retain it with every form of cunning and malice. Actually it is not the intellect which fights but that which uses it as a tool and hides behind it – the Darkness!

Darkness does not want the Light to be found through memories. And *how* the spirit longs to find the Light, to draw new strength from it, can be recognised from the fact that with memories of the Holy Nights of their childhood an undefined, almost painful longing also awakens, which is able to move many persons to pathos for a brief while.

If such a tender mood is used at once and with all one's powers it could become the best soil for an *awakening*. But unfortunately this only sends adults into reveries whereby the rising power is wasted and lost. And through such reveries the opportunity passes by without being able to bring any benefit or having been used.

Even if many a person sheds a few tears thereby he feels ashamed and tries to hide them, pulling himself together with a physical jerk which often betrays unconscious defiance.

How much could people learn from all this! It is not coincidence that a feeling of tender sadness weaves itself into the memories of childhood days. It is a subconscious sensing that they have lost something, leaving an emptiness, the inability still to perceive intuitively like a child!

Surely you have often noticed how wonderful and refreshing is the mere quiet presence of every person from whose eyes there emanates now and then a *childlike* glow!

The adult must not forget that childlike is not the same as childish. But you do not know why to be childlike has such an effect, what it really is, and why Jesus said: "Become as little children!"

In order to fathom what it is you must first realise that to be childlike is by no means confined to the child itself. No doubt you know children who lack the trait of beautiful childlikeness. Thus there are children who are not childlike. A malicious child can never have a childlike effect, and just as little one who is ill-mannered, who is really not brought up properly.

This clearly proves that childlikeness and the child are two things independent of each other.

That which is called childlike on earth is part of the manifestation of *purity!* Purity in its higher sense, not merely in its earthly human sense! The human being who lives in the ray of Divine Purity, who makes room for the ray of purity within himself, has thereby also become childlike, be it while still a child or later as an adult.

Childlikeness is the result of inner purity, or the sign that such a human being has submitted to purity and serves it. All these are merely different ways of expressing it, but in reality they always amount to the same thing.

Thus only a child which is pure within itself, and an adult who cultivates purity within himself, can be childlike. That is why he has such a *refreshing* and vitalising effect, and also inspires confidence!

And wherever there is true purity, genuine love can also enter, because Divine Love works in the Ray of Purity. The Ray of Purity is the path It treads. It could not possibly walk upon any other!

The Ray of Divine Love can never find Its way to him who has not absorbed the Ray of Purity.

Always remember this, and as a Christmas gift for *yourselves* make the firm resolution to open yourselves to Purity, so that at the Festival of the Radiant Star, which is the Festival of the Rose in the Divine Love, the Ray of Love can penetrate to you on the Path of Purity!

Then you will *really* have celebrated this Festival of Christmas as it should be celebrated according to the Will of God! Therewith you bring up true gratitude for God's incomprehensible Grace, which He gives ever again to the earth with the Holy Night!

Many Divine Services are held today to commemorate the birth of the Son of God. Hurry through the churches of all kinds in spirit or also in memory! Let your intuitive perceptions speak when doing so, and you will turn away resolutely from the gatherings called Divine Services!

In the first moment man is astonished that I talk in this way, for he does not know what I wish to indicate thereby. But this is only because in the past he has never exerted himself to think about the expression "Divine service", and then compared it with the proceedings called Divine Service. You simply accepted it like so many things which have existed for centuries as customary.

And yet the expression "Divine service" has only one meaning and simply *cannot* be applied in the wrong sense, unless man ever again *indifferently* and unhesitatingly accepts and perpetuates the custom of centuries. What is *at present* called Divine Service is at best a prayer connected with human attempts at interpretation of those words which, taken as having been uttered by the Son of God, were only written down by human hands later.

This fact cannot be altered, and no man can contradict such remarks if he wishes to remain honest with himself and honest about the actual happening! Above all, if he does not stay too indolent to ponder this thoroughly, and does not use empty catchwords obtained from others to excuse himself!

And yet it is just the expression "Divine service" which in its essence is so vital, and which through itself speaks *so* clearly to men, that with only a little intuitive perception it could hardly be used for the purpose for which it is still used today, although man on earth deems himself far advanced.

Divine service must now become *living* if the Word is to rise to reality, with all that it contains! It must manifest itself in *life*. When I ask what you men understand by service, thus what it means *to serve*, not a single person will answer otherwise than with the words: *"To work!"* This is already clearly implied in the word "service", and one cannot think of it as meaning anything else.

Divine *service* on earth is also naturally nothing other than to *work* in the sense of the Laws of God here on earth, to swing actively in them terrestrially! To transform the Will of God into deeds on earth!

And this is lacking everywhere!

Who seeks to serve God in his earthly activity? Everyone only thinks of himself, and partly of those who are near to him on earth. But he believes he is *serving* God when he prays to Him!

Just think it over yourselves – where is there any real service to God in this? It is indeed anything but *serving!* Such is the one part of today's so-called Divine Service, which comprises the *prayer*. The other part, the interpretation of the Word written by human hands, can again only be looked upon as learning on the part of those who really exert themselves to obtain an understanding of it. The indifferent and superficial ones are of no importance anyway!

It is quite justified when people speak of *"going to"* or "attending" a Divine Service. These are the *proper* expressions, which speak for themselves!

However, man shall *perform* Divine *service himself* and not stand apart from it! "Petitioning" is not serving, for when he petitions man usually wants something from God, that God shall do something for him, which after all is far removed from the conception of "serving"! Thus petitioning and prayer have nothing to do with Divine *service!*

This will probably be easily understood by *every* person! Everything a person does on earth must have some meaning; he cannot misuse the language given to him as he pleases without causing himself harm. That he acquired no knowledge about the power also inherent in the human word will not protect him from it.

It is *his* fault if he neglects this! He is then subject to the effects of a wrong application of words, which becomes a hindrance rather than a help to him.

The independent weaving of all the Primordial Laws of Creation neither halts nor hesitates on account of men's neglect, but everything which has been established in Creation proceeds on its course with the most unswerving precision.

This is what men never think about and therefore, to their detriment, never observe. Even in the smallest and most insignificant things it always has a corresponding effect.

The inherently wrong designation of the gatherings under the name of "Divine Service" has also contributed a great deal to the fact that genuine Divine service was not accomplished by men, because everyone believed that he had already done enough by attending such a Divine Service, which has never been the genuine Divine *service*.

Call these meetings an hour of *joint worship* of God, which would at least come closer to its meaning, and to a certain degree also justify the institution of special hours for this purpose, although worship of God can also be expressed in every look, in all thinking and acting.

Many a person will now probably think that this is not at all possible without appearing too artificial and too obvious. But this is not so! The more the true worship of God breaks through the more natural will man become in all he does, even in his most simple movements. He then swings in honest gratitude to his Creator and enjoys the blessings in the *purest* form.

Today, for the Festival of Holy Night, go back to any one of the earthly Divine Services!

Jubilant thanks, supreme bliss, should vibrate in every word for the Grace which God once bestowed upon mankind. In so far as this Grace can at all be valued among men; for the human spirit is incapable of grasping the real greatness of it in its *entirety!*

But for *that* you seek in vain everywhere. The joyful swinging upward to the Luminous Heights is lacking! There is no trace of jubilant gratitude! Even some pressure is frequently perceptible, originating in disappointment for which man has no explanation.

Only one thing can be found everywhere, something which renders or characterises the nature of Divine Services in all confessions as if engraved with the sharpest chisel, or something which forces the nature of the Divine Services audibly to embody everything swinging therein – a woeful sound vibrating monotonously through all the voices of the preachers, which in its constant repetition produces a wearying effect and rests like a grey veil over souls falling asleep.

Yet it sometimes also sounds like a hidden lamenting over something which is lost! Or over something which has never been found! Go there yourselves and listen! You will find this peculiar and striking characteristic everywhere!

Men are not conscious of it but, to use the customary phrase, it just happens to be so!

And herein lies truth! It happens without any intention on the part of the speaker, and plainly shows the nature in which the whole vibrates. There can be no question of a joyful upward swinging, nor of blazing fires bursting forth, but it is like a dull, subdued smouldering which cannot bring up the strength to penetrate freely upwards.

Wherever the speaker does not allow himself to be "upheld" by the dull, weak vibration of these Divine Services, when he remains untouched by it (which would be equivalent to a certain lukewarmness or to deliberately standing aloof), there all words will seem *unctuous* and can be regarded in the same way as sounding brass – cold, without warmth, without conviction!

In both cases the ardour of conviction is lacking, as well as the power of victorious knowledge, which wants to preach about it to all his fellow-men in jubilant exultation!

When, as with the expression "Divine Service", a misleading designation is employed for something the contents of which are different from what the expression indicates, then this mistake takes effect. The power it could have is broken from the very outset by the employment of a false designation and no real and uniform swinging can arise, because through this designation another conception arose which is consequently not fulfilled. The holding of the Divine Service stands in contrast to that which arises as a picture in the inmost intuitive perception of every human spirit with the word "Divine Service".

Go out and learn and you will soon recognise where you are offered the true bread of life! Above all make use of the joint gatherings as *hours for the solemn worship of God*. But do express Divine *service* in the entire activity of your being, in life itself; for it is *with this* that you shall *serve* your Creator, thankful and jubilant for the grace of being allowed to *exist!*

Make everything you think and do into a *service* to God! Then it will bring you *that* peace which you long for. And even if people harass you severely, be it through envy, malice or base habits, you bear peace *within* yourselves forever, and this will finally help you to overcome all difficulties!

WATCH and pray that you do not *fall* in temptation! Up till now men have regarded this warning from the Light as nothing but kindly advice given by the Son of God Jesus, in view of the weak nature falsely imputed to the Son of God as a consequence of mankind's pronounced conceit.

Today I must repeat this warning!

But it is more than advice alone; for it is God's *demand* to you, men, if you want to save yourselves from the poisonous fruits of your wrong opinions and conceptions.

Do not imagine that God will now simply lift you out of the loathsome swamp which keeps clinging to you with great tenacity, with the same tenacity as you applied in forming such a swamp through your rigid stubbornness against the Will of God!

God does not lift you out of it through gratitude that you at last show some signs of being willing! Oh no, *you* must work *yourselves* out of it, just as you allowed yourselves to sink into it!

You must exert yourselves, exert yourselves honestly and with great diligence, so as to be able to come up again on to healthy ground! *Only* when you *do* this will you be given the strength you need, but always and only in the same measure as your volition. This is inexorably demanded by the Justice which lies in God.

And *therein* lies the help which is promised you, the help you will receive in the very moment when your inner volition has at last become deed, not before!

To help you achieve this, however, the Word has been brought to you as a *gift* from God, the Word which shows in all clearness the path you must follow if you wish to save yourselves! In the *Word* lies the Grace which God gives in His incomprehensible Love, as has already happened once through Jesus.

The *Word* is the *gift!* The great *sacrifice* of God, however, is the *deed* – to send the Word as far as to the Gross Material Worlds, to you men here, a mission always connected with great suffering because of man's attitude, which through his stubborn conceit is one of hostility towards the Light! And nobody else can give the true Word to mankind but a Part of the Word Itself. The Bringer of the Living Word must therefore also *be* from the Word *Itself!*

If, however, the Word had *not* been given to them after the darkening had taken place among men on earth, they would have had to sink into disintegration together with the Darkness which closely surrounds them.

And for the sake of the small number nevertheless still carrying within themselves the yearning for the Light in spite of the Darkness which men had formed for themselves, God in His Justice and Love once again sent the Living Word into this Darkness, so that for the sake of Justice the few should not be lost with the others, but may still save themselves by following the path shown to them in the Word.

However, so that the Word could indicate the path leading out of the Darkness, It first had to learn to know and experience the effects of the Darkness upon Itself; It had to sink Itself into this Darkness in order to tread the path out of it first, and thus open up the way for those men who want to follow It.

It was only because the Word trod the path out of this Darkness that It could also explain and thus bring the path closer to mankind!

Men would never have been able to do this of their own accord without this help. Understand then, you men, that such a decision, which became necessary only for the sake of a small number of men, was indeed a great sacrifice of love, such as only *God* alone can consummate through His unswerving Justice!

That was the *sacrifice* which *had to be* fulfilled in complete accord with the Laws for the sake of Justice and Love in the inviolable and adamantine Perfection of the Will of God.

But this is no excuse whatever for men, since the need for this sacrifice only arose out of the failure of mankind through turning away from the Light.

Although the sacrifice came about through the lawfulness of the Holy Will of God Himself, the guilt of mankind does not become less but even heavier still, because through the distortion and confusion of all that God entrusted to them they wantonly made everything more difficult.

Therefore the great sacrifice stands for itself alone as a consequence of the God-Perfection of the All-Holy Will.

Whether you really still wish to save yourselves is solely *your concern;* for this God-Perfection, which made the great sacrifice of God a necessary consequence, now also demands the destruction of everything in the entire Creation that cannot voluntarily adjust itself according to the Laws of His Will.

There is neither mercy nor escape in this matter, no exception or deviation, but solely the outworking according to the Laws in Creation through the closing of the cycle of all past actions.

Hence the demand: Watch and pray so that you do not *fall* in temptation!

First comprehend these words aright, then you will indeed learn to recognise the strict demand they contain! *"Watch"* calls upon the alertness of your *intuitive perception* and thus demands mobility of your spirit! This alone harbours true vigilance. And it is *here*, too, that *womanhood* must again take the lead, because she is given a more extended and more delicate ability of intuitive perception.

Womanhood must be vigilant in the strength of her purity, which she must serve if she faithfully wishes to fulfil the task of womanhood in this Creation. But this she can only do as a priestess of purity!

Watch and *pray* are the words which you are once more given on your path! The *watching* concerns your life on earth, during which you must at any moment be ready of your own accord clearly to perceive the impressions assailing you, and also to weigh and scrutinise them, as well as carefully to examine beforehand everything emanating from you.

Praying, however, ensures the maintenance of the connection with the Luminous Heights, and the opening of oneself to holy streams of power for earthly application.

That is the purpose of prayer, which compels your mind to turn away from this earth upwards! *Hence* this demand, the fulfilment of which will bring you nothing but inestimable gain through strong help, to the supply of which you otherwise close yourselves by not observing the Laws in Creation!

If you fulfil *both* you can never *fall* in temptation. Interpret this hint aright also, for when it is said to you "that you do not fall in temptation" this does not perhaps mean that you will no longer be afflicted by temptation, that such keeps aloof from you if you watch and pray, i.e., that you do not come into temptation, but it signifies that if you always remain alert and pray, you can never fall when temptation approaches you – you are able to face all dangers victoriously!

Just emphasise this sentence aright, in the sense in which it is meant! Therefore do not put the stress on the word "temptation", but on the word "fall"! Then you have immediately grasped the right meaning! It says: "Watch and pray so that you do not *fall* in temptation." Thus watching and praying is a protection against *falling*, but here amid the Darkness do not rule out the approach of temptation. Indeed, temptation can only strengthen you if your attitude is right; under the compulsion of the necessary resistance it will kindle your spirit to become more glowing and burst into flames, and thus is bound to bring you great benefit.

All this, however, will no longer endanger mankind but become a joy to them, an agreeable spiritual activity which only furthers rather than hinders, *as soon as womanhood faithfully fulfils the task* granted to her by the Creator, for which she was very specially equipped.

If only her volition is at last honest, then it will not be difficult for her really to fulfil. Her task lies in the priesthood of purity!

This she can apply *everywhere*, at any time! She does not need special responsibilities for this, but she can exercise it without further ado in *every look* and *every word* that comes from her lips, even in every movement – it must become quite natural to her! To swing in the Light of Purity is her real element, the element to which she has kept herself closed till now through frivolity and ridiculous vanity!

Wake up, you women and girls! In fulfilment of your human womanhood proceed along the path which the Creator has precisely marked out for you, and on account of which you are really allowed to stand in this Creation!

Then very soon miracle after miracle will be revealed before you; for wherever you look everything will begin to bloom, because God's blessing streams through you abundantly as soon as the purity of your volition smoothes the path to it and opens the gates within you!

Happiness, peace and joy such as never existed before will cover this earth radiantly when womanhood forms the bridge to the more luminous spheres, as is intended in Creation, and when through her exemplary existence she keeps awake the longing for the Light in every spirit, and becomes the guardian of the Holy Flame!

Oh woman, how much was given unto you, and how have you wantonly abused all the treasures of God's High Grace!

Ponder this and become a priestess of purity in the deepest intuitive sensing, so that filled with bliss you may stride through a flourishing land in which human beings with radiant eyes give jubilant thanks to their Creator for the mercy of their existence on earth, which they use as a step to the gate of the Eternal Gardens!

See your task before you, you women and girls, as the future priestesses of Divine Purity here on earth, and do not rest until you have acquired what you are lacking towards it!

THE FAMILY BOND

The intimate home! These words vibrate in a way which clearly indicates *what* a home that man establishes for himself here on earth must be *like*.

The *expression* is quite right, as is everything given to men by the word, but here also man has distorted the clear meaning and dragged it down with him through his decline.

Thus man deprived himself of one foothold after another which could offer him support during his life on earth. And due to men's wrong way of thinking all that was originally pure was badly obscured, and frequently it was even wantonly changed into a slough which developed into a mass grave for souls.

This also includes the family bond in its *past* form, the family bond so often praised and emphasised as something noble and rich in character with a specially high value, as something proffering man great support, strengthening and furthering him and making him an estimable citizen on earth, who becomes capable of stepping out secure and protected in his struggle for existence, as men today like to call every life on earth.

But how foolish you are, you men, how narrowly you have constricted your outlook on everything, particularly on that which concerns *you* and your wanderings through the Creations.

It is just the family bond you value so highly which is one of those pits that with absolute certainty demands innumerable victims – and gets them too! For through the unwritten laws of human customs many people are flung into it without consideration and held fast by a thousand arms until, with their souls languishing piteously, they adapt themselves defencelessly to the indolent mass, which drags them along into the depths of feeble impersonality!

And strangely enough it is particularly all those people tenaciously trying to cling to such wrong forms who imagine they can thereby stand successfully before God as being especially valuable. But I say to you that they, too, must be counted among those who are dangerous, who *impede* instead of furthering the development and strengthening of many human spirits!

Tear open the gates of your intuitive perception at last, so that you may now recognise for yourselves the wrong that has settled itself into *all* matters and habits which man made for himself, for he formed them under the domination of the distorted intellect, which was led by Lucifer!

I will try to give you a picture which can bring you nearer to an understanding. It is closely connected with the great and lawful rotation in Creation which, stimulated by the Law of Movement, is meant to keep everything healthy, because vigour and strength can only be maintained through right movement.

Let us assume what it *is intended* to be like on earth, not what it is like now! Then all that is spiritual on earth would resemble a clear liquid, which is and remains in a perpetual rotating movement, so that it does not thicken or perhaps even congeal.

Also imagine a lively, babbling brook! How delicious is its water, how refreshing and invigorating, offering a restorative to all who are thirsty, and thereby bringing joy and dispensing blessing along the course it pursues.

But if here and there a small portion separates from this water, leaping to the side independently, then in most cases the part which has severed itself soon becomes stagnant as a small pool. Through its isolation it quickly loses its freshness and clearness and gives off a stale smell, because without movement it gradually becomes putrid, it is bound to become bad and foul!

It is exactly the same with the spiritual swinging of men on earth. As long as it rotates harmoniously according to the Law of Movement, without any retardation or haste, it will also develop beneficially to unsuspected strength, thereby bringing continuous ascent in its train, because it is simultaneously furthered by every species of vibration in the entire Creation. Nothing obstructs it, but everything unites with it joyously, helping and strengthening its working.

Such was once the swinging a long, long time ago, and with a healthy unconstraint and naturalness every human spirit developed joyfully and rose ever higher in his recognising. He gratefully absorbed all the rays that could be sent from the Light to help him. And thus a fresh stream of spiritual power of the Living Water flooded as far down as to the earth, and from there peacefully back again to the Source of Preservation, in the form of grateful worship and as the outflow of continual experiencing.

Everywhere the consequence was a glorious thriving, and spontaneous chords of undimmed purity resounded throughout the entire Creation like a jubilant song of praise in the happy, unhindered rotation of harmonious movement.

This is how it was until the distortion of the recognitions through forming wrong basic conceptions began in man's vanity. This brought about disturbances in the wonderful co-operation of all the rays in Creation which, through their continually increasing power, must finally enforce the collapse of everything that closely united with them.

In addition to many other things these disturbances also include the present-day rigid family bond in its wrong form and its almost unbelievable extension.

You need only picture it to yourselves! In the harmonious swinging and rotating of the upward striving spirit, which radiated around the earth invigoratingly and which, together with the Animistic, dispensed blessings, penetrated it brightly and pulled it upwards with itself through the strong longing for the Light, obstructions suddenly appeared in the form of small solidifications which went along only sluggishly with the rotation.

It is like a soup which is cooling off, where the fat congeals and separates. You can perhaps understand it even better when I compare the process with unhealthy blood which thickens here and there, and which can only flow sluggishly through the body, thus hampering the necessary and preserving movement of pulsation.

This picture will enable you better to recognise the fundamental, serious significance of the *spiritual* pulsation in Creation, which – as a minor reflection – finds its coarsest expression in the blood of the physical body. You can understand this more clearly than you can the illustrations of the soup and the gurgling brook.

Another comparison which may also help is when disturbing grains of sand are thrown into a well-oiled machine!

As soon as the family bond, which in itself is quite natural, develops along unhealthy and wrong lines, it is bound to have a hampering and debasing effect in the necessary swinging of the Law of Movement of joyful upward striving; for the present idea about the family sticking closely together is only based on the upbringing, and on the preservation of *gross material* advantages and comforts as well, nothing else!

Thus there gradually came into being the family "lumps", which due to their peculiar characteristics simply cannot be called anything different, and which burden and paralyse all spiritual swinging. For those who belong to them *bind* each other, hang upon each other, and thereby form a heaviness which holds and drags them down ever further.

They make themselves dependent upon each other, and gradually lose the pronounced *individual personality* which as characteristic of a spiritual being thus also obliges them to be so.

With this they heedlessly push aside the command contained for them in the Will of God, and turn themselves into a kind of group souls, which due to their nature they can never really become.

Each member interferes with the path taken by the other, often even wanting to prevail over the other, thus knotting untearable binding threads which chain them all together and press them down.

They make it difficult for the individual to sever himself from it when his spirit awakens, and to stride by himself along the path on which he can develop and which fate also prescribes for him. Thus it becomes impossible to rid himself of his karma for the God-willed ascent of his spirit.

As soon as he wishes to undertake only the first step along the path to freedom of *his* spirit, which will be the right one only *for him* and *his* particular nature (but not at the same time for all those who call themselves members of the family), then a great shout is immediately set up, together with admonitions, petitions, reproaches or even threats from all those who seek to pull this "ungrateful one" back into the constraint of their family love or views!

What all is achieved with this, what is quoted about it, especially when it concerns the most precious things a man possesses, such as the power of decision of his free volition in *spiritual* matters, the power of decision which is given him by God and which is also necessary, for which *solely he alone* and nobody else in his place is held responsible by the Law of Reciprocal Action!

It is the Will of God that man should absolutely develop an individuality of *his own*, with the most pronounced awareness of his responsibility for his thoughts, volition and actions! However, the possibilities for developing one's own personality for the strengthening of an independent capacity of decision, and above all the necessary fortification of the spirit and the preservation of its mobility for constant wakefulness – all of which can arise only as a result of being dependent upon oneself – *all this becomes utterly submerged in the fettered family bond!* It dulls and suffocates the budding and joyful blossoming of what is most precious in man, of that which marks him before other gross material creatures as a human being, that which is the *individual personality*, for which his spiritual origin qualifies and destines him.

It cannot come to the point of unfolding; for if the family bond is of an *unfair* kind, if it lays claim to rights which do not really exist at all, then it often becomes a shocking torment, ruptures the peace and destroys all happiness. The consequence is that finally any buoyancy is blown away.

Just for once call upon *those* people who already had to suffer under this and whose souls thereby languished – they will comprise numbers almost beyond counting!

And when the love of earthmen, or at least the feeling which earthmen call love, penetrates the family bond in a benevolent way, this is not much better either; for then each one constantly tries to make everything as comfortable as possible for the other, to spare him just that which would force his spiritual powers to develop ... out of love, solicitude, or family duty!

And persons whose every path is smoothed are often envied, and perhaps even hated on account of it! In reality, however, they are only to be pitied! For the love so wrongly directed, or the customs of a family bond applied in the wrong way, should never be considered as a good action; instead they have the effect of a slow poison which with infallible certainty prevents the powers of those concerned from developing, thereby only weakening their spirits.

The periodic compulsion which is provided for in the natural course of things is taken away from men, the compulsion which challenges all their spiritual powers to unfold, and which especially in this way offers the best and surest aid for their spiritual development, as a Grace of the Omnipotent Creator in which great blessings for the preservation and furthering of everything are contained.

Today's notorious and valued family bond in its wider meaning is like a dangerous sleeping draught for every human spirit, tiring and paralysing him. It obstructs and hinders the necessary spiritual ascent, because the individual members of the family are spared the very things that can help to strengthen them. Spiritually weary hothouse plants are raised and cultivated, but not strong spirits!

A thousandfold are the kinds of harmful, hampering customs which the wrongly-applied family bond brings in its wake as evil consequences. You shall yet learn to recognise them very quickly and easily if you only become capable of considering everything from the right point of view, which must bring life and movement into this hitherto sluggish mass of easy-going family "lumps". These family lumps wallow about, dam and block the God-willed circulation of healthy spiritual movement, which accords with the Laws of Creation, paralysing and poisoning all joyous vitality, while at the same time they embrace as if with a thousand clasps the upward striving human spirits, so that they will not escape or bring disquietude into the long-accustomed run of things, which would disturb the self-complacent attitude of these family lumps.

You will realise with horror how you yourselves are still stuck in many such threads, similar to a fly caught in the web of a death-dealing spider!

Once you only make a move, once you try to struggle free from this in order to attain to your God-willed spiritual independence (because you alone have to bear the responsibility), then you will realise with a shudder how far-reaching the effect of your mere attempt to move suddenly becomes; and only through this can you recognise how manifold are these threads into which wrong customs have relentlessly woven you!

You will be seized with alarm at this recognition, which you can only find through *experiencing*. However, you will get the experience quickly, it will flare up around you as soon as your surroundings see that you are *in earnest* about changing your way of thinking and intuitive perception, that your spirit wants to awaken and wander along its *own* paths, the paths which are ordained for its development, and also at the same time for its liberation and redemption as the reciprocal action arising out of former decisions.

You will be surprised, indeed dismayed, to see that they are perfectly willing to forgive you every gross error, everything, even the very worst, except the effort to become *spiritually* free and to have *personal* convictions about it! Even if you do not want to say anything at all about it, if you leave others in peace over it, you will see that all this can change nothing, because they do not leave *you* in peace!

If you calmly observe and investigate, however, it must only strengthen you in recognising all the wrong that people carry within themselves. For they *show* it very plainly by the *way in which* they present themselves in their sudden and newly-awakened zeal to hold you back! A zeal which only arises on account of the disquietude brought about by the unaccustomed, and which comes from the urge to remain in the usual lukewarmness and not to be disturbed therefrom!

It is fear of being suddenly confronted with a *truth*, which is utterly different from that with which they have so far lulled themselves in indolent self-complacency!

A THOUSANDFOLD are the entanglements in which men squirm with apparent ease. Only those who feel God's law of spiritual movement within themselves, and who long for the awakening, experience these fetters in an extremely painful manner, because they only hurt when the one caught in the web tries to free himself from it.

And yet this struggle to free himself is the only thing that can save man from sinking into a spiritual death-sleep!

Today you will hardly grasp aright the full incisive truth of these my words, because mankind laced themselves in too tightly in these matters, leaving themselves hardly any possibility for a free outlook from this state, or a full understanding of it.

For this reason the bonds are now *cut* by the Justice of God, smashed to pieces, although this is bound to be very painful for men, excruciatingly so when there is no alternative. Only *after* the bonds and lacings have been cut and fallen away will you then be able to grasp my words aright, looking back horrified at your past wrong thinking!

Nevertheless, from among the many examples I want to pick out a few small ones which may perhaps after all give you some idea!

Let us cast a glance into human life as it is today!

It is right to see children through their childhood faithfully, guarding and watching them, and to give adolescent youth the tools for their path through life on earth by means of adequate education!

But then each individual must be left with the possibility – indeed, it must be *given* to him – to work *his own* way up from the smallest beginning. Not everything must be made easy for him from the very outset.

To make it comfortable or easy for the other person harbours the greatest danger – that of fostering spiritual indolence! And this has always been the case in the past by the well-meant family bond!

It is already poison for a human spirit when as a child he is brought up in the belief that he has a legal right to the earthly possessions acquired by his parents.

I am now talking of the harm in a purely spiritual aspect, which is the *essential thing* in all a man's activities. He must also remain aware of this in the future if he and his surrounding circumstances are really to become healthy.

However, a change in these matters would immediately transform much in an *earthly* respect as well, and do away with many an evil! For example, supposing a child was also legally entitled only to enjoy the protection and care of its parents, together with a corresponding education, up to a certain age, after which it remains purely the free will of the parents how they wish to dispose of their personal property!

How different would so many children become by this mere fact alone! How much more *personal* effort would then have to arise, how much more seriousness towards life on earth, how much increased diligence! And not as the last thing also more love towards the parents, which would remain far from so one-sided as is often exhibited today!

Sacrifices on the part of loving parents would even be given much greater value, because they would then really issue only from a freely bestowed love, whereas nowadays such sacrifices are often not at all valued by children, but only expected and demanded as a matter of course, without giving rise to any real joy.

A change in these matters would contribute right away to the bringing up of human beings of greater worth and greater self-consciousness, having a stronger spirit and increased energy.

Crimes would often be avoided, too, if property *rights* in the personal possessions of others did not exist!

Children will be more concerned with acquiring their parents' love instead of standing on their childhood status and its rights, which in any case has an entirely different meaning from what is assumed today. For children must be thankful to their parents for having given them the opportunity to incarnate on earth, even if the redemption and advancement thereby is mutual, as is the case with everything connected with the working out of the Laws of God.

In reality these children are all alien spirits to their parents, *each with its own individual personality*, which could only be attracted for incarnation through being of homogeneous species or through some former connection.

The parents on earth offer protection and help for the time which the spirit needs in order to direct its new physical body in a worthy and fully responsible manner. Thereafter, however, man on earth must remain completely free and dependent on himself, otherwise he can never become as strong as is useful for him in the great swinging of the Laws of God. He *must* do battle and have opposition so that in gaining the victory he can ascend spiritually and come towards the Heights.

A change in the idea held up till now about children being entitled to their parents' possessions, however, would have far greater effects than those already mentioned, provided that the government ministers concerned with the development would adjust themselves accordingly in their efforts for the people, and pioneer the way to help parents and children alike.

Thus the acquisitive sense of each individual must develop on a different basis. Today many people seek to increase their property more and more, merely to make life easy for their children later on, i.e., in order to bequeath it to their children. Their every thought and every wish is exclusively directed to this aim, which becomes the basis for an egoistic accumulation of earthly possessions.

Although this will not cease entirely because one or other person will still base his whole life's activity on this idea, yet numerous people would prescribe a higher and more general goal to their earthly activity for the benefit of many!

Thus the immoral "calculated" marriages would cease to exist, along with the fraudulent and deplorable practice of dowry hunting! Much evil would therewith be automatically eliminated, giving way to healthier conditions in which honesty of the intuitive perception could prevail and marriages become *genuine*. From the very beginning there would be a much more serious approach to any marriage.

Opportunities should be offered to adolescent youth which would *compel* them to unfold their spiritual powers in order to acquire the necessities of life, not only to make them able to do it! This alone would be the right thing, for then, and only then, will they *advance* spiritually, because they *will have to bestir* themselves spiritually.

But instead of this parents or other members of the family make just this path, which is necessary for the children's spiritual health, too easy for so many of them – it is made *as* completely *comfortable as* possible for those concerned. That is then called the family bond and love, or also family duty!

I do not wish to outline the harm arising from this, even through the best volition. For every good person needs an impetus here and there, and a force from outside, in order to be strengthened. Only seldom would he place himself *voluntarily* in a position where he is forced to exert himself, to employ all his spiritual powers, in order to master the situation and to solve it well. In most cases, provided he can choose, he would select the *most comfortable* way in order to take it easy, but this does not bring him any spiritual benefit!

However, his self-respect and self-confidence is increased when with exertion and diligence he struggles upwards himself on earth and when all this is a result of *his* work.

He then values his possessions much more in the right sense, he values the work and even every small joy; he also values each kindness done to him by others correspondingly, and he can enjoy everything with much greater vitality than a person to whom luck comes overnight without trouble, and who only needs to fill in his time by amusing himself.

One must seek to assist a person to attain to the *possibility of striving aright*, if one really wishes to help. *Those* fruits which someone has acquired through his own efforts must never be thrown into anybody's lap without that person having to fulfil certain duties.

Of course parents can still give everything to their children if they wish to do so, or out of false love they may sacrifice the meaning and time of their entire life on earth to them – they can make themselves slaves of their children, for they retain free will in these matters! But since no earthly law will force them to do anything in this, in the reciprocal effect of the Will of God they bear the full responsibility *entirely alone* for their own neglect in Creation, and in part also for the spiritual harm that consequently befalls their children.

Men are not here on earth for their children in the *first* place, but for *themselves*, so that *they* can become spiritually mature and strong. But due to a false idea of love this was no longer observed. Only animals still live in the law in this matter!

Just take a close look at family customs!

Two persons want to contract a marriage, they want to set up a household of their own in order to journey through life on earth together, and for this purpose they become engaged.

The engagement is therefore the first step towards marriage. It is the mutual promise and obligation, so that on the strength of the promise the serious preparation for setting up the household can begin.

An engagement is nothing more than the earthly basis for the establishment of the new home, and the first step towards procuring everything necessary for this on earth.

With this, however, wrong customs immediately set in again!

In reality this engagement concerns *those* two persons alone who wish to set up a household together. The fact that the families or the parents take part in procuring all that is necessary for this on earth is a matter entirely for itself, which should remain a purely external affair in order to be correct. If they wish they may give something or help in some other way. All this remains an *outward* matter, and it does not connect them, does not tie any threads of fate.

But the engagement should also be absolutely the last and *outermost boundary* for any family ties. Just as a ripe fruit falls from the tree, if tree and fruit wish to fulfil the purpose of their existence without harming one another, so after his maturity must a person separate from his family, from his parents, for like himself they also still have tasks *of their own!*

However, families look at it in a different light, even at the *last* time limit for it, which comes when two persons find each other and become engaged. In these matters they very often arrogate to themselves rights which they do not at all possess.

Only through the Power of God is each child they wished for given to them, otherwise they would have been unable to receive it. It is purely the fulfilling of a desire which shows itself through the intimate relationship between two persons!

They have no right to the child, which is only lent to them but which never belongs to them! It is also indeed taken away without their being able to retain it, or without their being first asked about it! From this they can quite clearly see that they are not given any rights over it from the Light, from the Origin of all Life!

The fact that they also take over duties up to the time of maturity is only natural and a balance for the fulfilment of their wish, for they would not have received a child if they had not brought about the opportunity for this, which in the Primordial Laws of this Creation is equivalent to a petition. And as compensation for the duties they have joys, provided they fulfil these duties *aright!*

On reaching the period of maturity, however, they must leave each person to journey along *his* paths, which are not theirs!

In any case through engagement and marriage the two persons step *out* of their families in order to form a union together for their own household. Instead of this, however, the two families imagine they were likewise connected through this engagement and marriage and belong to it, although when considered objectively this is not at all the case, and the mere thought of it seems very strange!

An engagement of two people does not extend the family circles by bringing a daughter to one and a son to the other, but the two individual human beings unite together *entirely alone*, having no intention whatever of dragging their former families along!

If men had but a faint idea of the harm these peculiar opinions and customs *are bound to do*, they would perhaps leave it alone of their own accord, but they do not realise how much damage is caused thereby.

The wrong customs do not occur without creating ties in the World of Fine Gross Matter. Threads thereby wind themselves around the couple preparing to set up a home of their own, and these threads gradually impede, entangle and become ever more knotted, often leading to unpleasant things, the origin of which men cannot explain, although they themselves laid the foundation for this with their ludicrous and annoying customs, in which real deep earnestness is *always* lacking.

It may be said without exaggeration that it is *always* lacking, for he who really grasps the seriousness of the union between two people, the seriousness that is attached to engagement and marriage, will greatly reject the customary family habits and prefer to hold quiet hours of self-communion which will lead with far greater confidence to a happy life together than all outward bad customs – for they cannot be called good customs! –

After the engagement of the couple, if circumstances permit a home is set up in the best way possible, but from the very start it leaves little to be desired. This is therefore bound to *eliminate* a joyful ascent from the very outset, or at least over a long period, because everything was thought of and nothing more is lacking.

All possibility is taken from the couple to participate in adorning their home through *personal* acquisition by diligence and industry, to take pleasure *in the fact* that they *jointly* strive towards the gradual completion of their own home as an earthly goal, so that with pride and love they can then value each individual, self-earned piece, connected as it is with memories of many a dear word, of many a necessary struggle which they have fought through joyfully and courageously side by side, and also of many a peaceful happiness!

This joy is already taken from many right in the beginning, and it is seen to that things are made as *comfortable* as possible. However, the two persons will always be strangers therein as long as among the other things they do not have objects which they were able to acquire for themselves.

I do not need to say much more to you about this, for you yourselves will gradually recognise what is false in these matters and, above all, what is spiritually as well as terrestrially harmful, no matter whether you wish to do so or not. For here, too, everything must at last become new and right, just as lies clearly enough in the Laws of God.

Give people and young couples the possibility for *personal* upward striving; only *that* will give them lasting pleasure because it increases their self-respect and also their self-confidence, thus awakening the intuitive perception of personal responsibility; and with this you will do the *right* thing! You will give more in this way than if you want to take all the cares of life from them or at least if you seek to relieve them as much as possible, whereby you can only weaken them, and you retard them from the necessary strengthening.

This makes you their enemies and not the true friends that you want to be. By spoiling them and making things easy for them you deprive them of more than you perhaps think after my words today.

Many a person will also be painfully hit thereby, but I am pulling him back from a mass grave by freeing him from the wrong and corrupting family bond, which paralyses the spirit and which was gradually formed on entirely wrong assumptions.

In this also everything must finally become *new,* for after the purification that kind of disturbance-centre will no longer be possible in this Creation.

PEOPLE will have noticed how often I mention the unlimited domination of the intellect and the great spiritual indolence as fatal, but it is necessary to do so; for both processes are inseparably linked together and can be designated as starting points of many evils, indeed as the *real* hostile-to-the-Light cause of the decline and fall of the developed beings.

Hostile to the Light, because it prevents recognition of all that happens through the Light and all the help available from the Light; for when it attains a dominating position the earthbound intellect, as a reaction, first of all severs the connection which makes it possible for the spirit to recognise the Light, and thus *binds* it to the physical cloak in which it is awaiting its development, to the cloak which should be its servant.

The process, which takes effect as a matter of course and in complete accord with the Laws of Creation, is of such a horrible nature as man can hardly picture to himself aright, for otherwise he would surely break down inwardly out of fear.

It is especially dreadful *because* on that account everything *is bound* to develop towards destruction. It simply cannot do otherwise, since the human spirit on earth, through its malicious, stubborn opposition against the All-Holy Will of God, *gave the wrong direction to its own development* – something which forms all the evil under the pressure of the automatic Laws of this Creation, the activity of which man cannot recognise because he deprived himself of the possibility to do so.

In the perfectly running mechanism of the wonderful Work of God man frivolously and forcibly altered a switch so that now, as *his* train of fate continues to roll on, derailment must follow as an inevitable happening.

And in turn this happening, which first of all strikes mankind on earth, also at the same time very severely endangers their environment, which has no part in this failure, but which always had to suffer under it and was thereby retarded in its development.

Just contemplate quietly what it must mean when that implement the intellect (with which the Creator graciously endowed each human spirit on earth as an aid for his necessary *development* in the World of Gross Matter), contrary to its task even *chokes off* the spirit from any possibility of connection with the uplifting streams of power from the Light – and this *as a consequence of your deed;* instead of submitting to the spirit and serving it, and spreading the volition of the Light in the material environment, thus ever more ennobling and forming it into the Paradise on earth which should have come about!

This failure, forcibly brought about in the free volition by greed and conceit, is *so* unprecedented that such guilt on the part of the indolent human spirit on earth now appears far too great to enable those who are awakening to obtain forgiveness once again in the Love of the Almighty!

Only damnation by withdrawal of all the blessings from the Light, and disintegration, should be the well-deserved lot of the human spirits on earth, who with their conceited stubbornness have steadily driven an entire part of Creation towards inevitable destruction, were it not that this Love of the Almighty is also simultaneously connected with Perfect Justice – because it is *God's Love* which will forever remain incomprehensible to the human spirits!

And the Justice of God cannot *entirely* abandon something to destruction as long as tiny sparks are glowing therein which do not deserve this!

For the sake of this minute number of little spirit sparks longing for the Light, *the Word of the Lord* was once more brought to this so-near-to-disintegrating part of Creation, that all those who carry the right inner volition for it, and who really *bestir* themselves with all the strength still left to them, may save themselves.

However, this volition must be *differently* constituted from how so many of the numerous believers in God on earth imagine it!

The domination of the intellect entirely shuts off the spirit from every possibility for its necessary development. This actually is not malevolent on the part of the intellect, but only a quite natural effect.

In this the intellect merely acts according to *its nature,* because it cannot do otherwise than only develop *its nature* to blossom and to full strength when it is cultivated one-sidedly and put in the wrong place by unreservedly subjecting the whole of life on earth to it!

And this its nature is *earthbound* and will never be otherwise, because as the product of the physical body it must also remain within the latter's boundaries, i. e., within the purely earthly gross material; for gross matter cannot produce what is spiritual.

The fault lies solely with man himself and with the fact that he surrendered the mastery to the intellect, thus also gradually enslaving himself to it, i. e., binding himself to the earth. In doing so he completely lost the real purport of his life on earth – the possibility of spiritual recognition and spiritual maturing.

He simply cannot grasp it any more because the channels for this are choked up. The spirit lies in the physical body as if in a sack which is tied at the top by the intellect. Thus the spirit can no longer see and hear anything, and any path leading to the spirit is cut off in the same manner as is the spirit's path towards the outside!

That it could be so tightly blocked by the earthly intellect is due to the fact that the binding up already takes place *before* physical maturity, i. e., before the period of adolescence, during which the spirit is meant effectively to work its way through the body towards the outside in order to take up a leading connection with its surrounding World of Matter for the tempering of its volition.

At this time, however, the intellect has already been one-sidedly and much too strongly developed through the wrong schooling, and it already keeps the physical cloak around the spirit closely locked, so that the latter simply *cannot* come to development or gain authority.

Pernicious, one-sided education which was lacking in spiritual balance! Nothing but a rigid dogma that cannot give it anything was forced upon the *spirit;* it does not warm up the spirit towards its own free conviction about all that is connected with God, since what is taught itself lacks vitality and has *no* connection with the Light, because in the teachings everywhere the intellect and conceit of earthman has caused much devastation.

The past schooling about the knowledge of the Creator stood on feet much too weak or, better expressed, on feet already too weakened by men, for it to remain capable of keeping pace with the intellect, which quickly grew stronger through its one-sided cultivation.

The instruction intended for the *spirit,* i. e., for the mind of strong activity on the part of the intuitive perception, always remained rigid and therewith lifeless, so that it could consequently never really be *received* spiritually.

Thus everything was directed only towards *learning*, which could never become experiencing. Consequently whatever was meant predominantly for the *spirit* had to be absorbed, like everything else, by the *intellect*, and was held fast by it without being able to penetrate to the spirit! In this way the drops of the Living Water, in so far as here and there a few did exist, were also lost in the sand!

The *inevitable* result was that the spirit received *nothing* and the intellect everything! Thus *that* condition was finally reached when the spirit was no longer capable of absorbing anything at all. This brought standstill to the spirit germ, which without an impulse from outside was in any case always inclined towards inactivity, and also its inevitable retrogression.

In this state of inactivity and lack of friction the spirit germ languished more and more until today a pitiful picture presents itself on earth: Human beings saturated with earthbound intellectual cleverness and with completely languid spirits which for the greater part are also really asleep!

With many of them the sleep has already turned into the sleep of death! *These* are the *dead* who must now awaken for the Judgment! *These* are the ones meant when it was proclaimed: He shall come to judge both the quick and the dead! This implies those *spiritually* alive and those *spiritually* dead; for there are no others, since the physical body cannot be considered as either alive or dead. It has never been alive of itself, but *has* only *been animated* for a time.

You men indeed do not realise the danger in which you stand, and it will already be too late for many when you now *have* to recognise it; for they no longer have strength to shake off this lethargy which has caused such frightful harm.

In connection with all the evils of mankind I must for this reason ever again revert to their actual cause – the domination of the intellect, and connected therewith the spiritual indolence which has come about as the immediate consequence.

Also the majority of today's believers in God count in *the first place* among the spiritually indolent, who are like the lukewarm that must be cast out in the Judgment!

If with a little volition you would for once examine the situation *aright,* and would then wish to draw the corresponding conclusions, you should see clearly and be able without any doubt to form the correct opinion. You need only think logically about it, nothing else!

Look around you and see how people today accept the *extension of the knowledge of Creation* which is necessary for them! From this alone you can already draw sufficient conclusions about their true condition!

When today statements are made about the necessity for the advance of *spiritual* knowledge, because for human beings the time has now arrived for this, you hear all kinds of reasons for the rejection of the new revelation from the Light!

I do not want to name all of them, for there are too many widely ramified varieties; and there would be no end. However, *in their actual sense* they are *all alike* because they have but *one* origin – spiritual indolence!

Let us take just one of them; for many an apparently quite good-willing church believer among the Christians says: "The Word of the Message is actually correct in many things, but it does not tell me anything new!"

Whoever speaks in this way has *not* grasped nor does he know the *past* which he believes he has already learned in his school or church, despite imagining to the contrary; for otherwise he should know that there is very much which is *utterly new* in the Message, but which is naturally not *opposed* to *that* Message which Jesus brought, because both issue from *the same* source, from the Living *Truth!*

What is new is *not* always equivalent to a *negation* of what is past, but it can also swing in the old and *lead onwards* in the *upbuilding,* in such a manner as it unites the actual Message of Jesus with mine.

However, just because my Message is *completely* in accord with the *true* words of *Jesus,* so many people when reading it intuitively perceive that there is nothing new in it! But only for the reason that the Message of Jesus and my Message are in reality *one!*

Therefore everything does swing *uniformly,* with the exception of what people in their sham wisdom have added to the words brought by Jesus, which is mostly wrong! Naturally my words cannot conform with what has been added or rendered *differently.* But with the words of Jesus Himself they agree absolutely!

And this intuitive perception about a similar swinging from the same origin, which the *spirit* recognises without the intellect being conscious of it, permits men to think, without giving it any reflection, that nothing new was given therein.

Such is one part of men! But others accept the new as a matter of course and as something already given once before, because they do not really know the old they thought they possessed, and therefore they have no idea what the new is that is contained in my Message for them.

Yet there is no lecture in my Message which would not indeed bring something that is perfectly new to the human spirits, something they have *not yet* known *up till now!*

Many people therefore neither know what they imagine they possess nor what I bring them! They are also much too indolent *really* to absorb anything at all from it within themselves!

For all *those,* however, whose spirit is at least capable of perceiving the *uniform* vibration of both Messages, this very fact should be proof that both Messages issue from *one* Source.

But those who are indolent do not become conscious of this. They simply prattle away about it, thereby laying themselves open so that everybody must clearly and immediately recognise them as being spiritually indolent.

Other believers again struggle against extending their knowledge, assuming or fearing that they could thereby do something wrong! However, this is fear in only a few cases, rather is it merely *conceit* rooted in stupidity, and only able to flourish on such soil; for conceit in itself is already stupidity – the two cannot be separated!

However, the stupidity is meant here in a *spiritual* and not an earthly respect, because just those persons who are considered particularly strong and clever in the earthly intellectual sense are in most cases spiritually languid, and as human beings in Creation possess no value before God; for they have failed as regards their actual existence, and are in no position with their intellectual knowledge to create any values for eternity, or to use their intellect for that purpose.

But let us leave everything else aside, let us take only the believers among *Christians,* of whom there are not in any case many who can be considered truly believing; for the greater number are nominal Christians only, inwardly empty and nothing else!

In a certain sense these people speak just as do the first ones mentioned, or they explain with a certain theatrical expression that is supposed to be reverential awe (at least as they try to delude themselves): "We have our Jesus, our Saviour, we shall not renounce Him, nor do we need anything more!"

This is just about the sense of all their words, although the words themselves sound different according to the person speaking.

These genuine reproductions of the Pharisees, whom Jesus so often sharply censured, are in reality nothing but spiritually indolent, and in this case also very *self-complacent.* Their occasional repugnant way of talking alone characterises them all too plainly!

If you ever try to enter deeply into the thoughts of this type of person, you will recognise that they do not really hold a true conviction inwardly, but just a simple, empty *habit* since their youth! They no longer wish to be disturbed in their indolence, for if they occupied themselves with it thoroughly it could cause them spiritual unrest.

They seek carefully to avoid this without realising that they thereby sin against the important Law of God, the Law of Spiritual Movement, which offers them the preservation of their soul as well as of their body, and in the activity of which, when obeyed, the ascent and the possibility to mature towards perfection alone rest!

Just the very thing they consider great and proudly seek to display in order to continue feigning support for themselves, which they do not at all carry inwardly, will become their doom and destruction!

If in obedience to the Law they would for once only bestir themselves a little *spiritually,* they would very quickly have to recognise that their past belief was no belief at all, but something they had *learned* which became a welcome habit, because apart from a few formalities it required nothing from them and they *thereby* considered it pleasant and *right!*

However, they should not avoid this restlessness but should be *grateful* for it; for it is the best sign that their spirit is awakening, which must naturally be first preceded by restlessness before the security of a real, free conviction can arise, the conviction which only unfolds its power through serious and zealous examination, and in the actual *experiencing* in the spirit that is closely linked with the examining.

Wherever restlessness arises, there the irrefutable proof is thus given that the spirit has been *asleep* and wants to awaken. But wherever rejection takes place with the proud reference to a personal, possessive claim to Jesus, there it merely shows that this human spirit has already lapsed into the agony that leads to the sleep of death!

It furthermore proves that just *these* spirits would also have sternly rejected Jesus and His Word during His life on earth. They would have done so with the same empty, overweening pride by clinging to what they had already learned, had it been offered to them for their choice and personal decision as the new revelation at the necessary turning point of that time!

For the same merely convenient reason they would have held fast to the old, which must furnish the soil for *advancement* if no standstill is to ensue.

They are rejectors of *all* that is new because they do not feel capable or strong enough to examine that which is incisive earnestly and without prejudice, or because they are already too indolent and prefer to try and cling to past habits!

It can be assumed with certainty that they would definitely have rejected Jesus had they not been *compulsorily* taught about this already from childhood!

Nor is it any different with those who try to reject everything that is new by referring to the prophecy about the appearance of false prophets! This likewise contains nothing but *spiritual indolence* again; for in this prophecy on which they insist it is simultaneously and also clearly enough stated that the *Right One*, the *Promised One, will come* just *at this time* when the false prophets appear!

How then do they think they can recognise Him if for their convenience they simply dispose of everything lightheartedly with such a reference! No person has as yet propounded this fundamental question to himself!

But *they themselves* have to find the proof of identity *in the Word,* which with a very few exceptions people did not want to heed during the time of Jesus either, but still expected other proofs.

His Word of Truth, which was the real proof of identity, did not have any value for them at that time. Personal spiritual indolence in everyone wherever you look, and as it was then so it is again today, only much worse even; for now every spirit-spark is buried almost completely!

The believers of today have accepted everything merely as a *doctrine* without digesting any of it or making it their own! They are too spiritually sluggish to perceive intuitively that their belief is nothing but *habit from child-*

hood on, which in complete ignorance about themselves they now call their conviction.

Often their behaviour towards their fellow-men very clearly indicates that they are no *real* Christians, but only empty, spiritually indolent pseudo-Christians!

With my words I lead to God and also to Jesus! However, in a *more vital* way than has been known in the past, and not as people have trimmed it through their propensity for spiritual comfort!

I point to the fact that God wishes to have spirits in Creation who are alive and conscious of their *personal* responsibility, *such* as lies in the Primordial Laws of Creation! That everyone must personally and fully account for everything he thinks, speaks and does, and that this could not be effaced for mankind by the murder of the Son of God at that time!

Jesus was murdered because with His demands of a like nature He *too* was felt to be irksome; he appeared dangerous to *those priests* who taught differently, who taught much more leniently so as to attract ever larger congregations in an *earthly* way only, which at the same time was meant to bring about and preserve an increase of their mundane power through mounting earthly *influence.*

This they did not wish to give up! Men did not want to surrender their comfort, nor the priests their influence, their power! The priests did not want to be *teachers* and *helpers* at all, but only rulers!

As true *helpers* they would have had to educate people to become *inwardly independent,* dignified and great spiritually, so that these people would adjust themselves to the Will of God and act joyfully in accordance with it out of free conviction.

The priests did the opposite and *bound* the spirit, so that it would remain tractable for their earthly purposes.

In His Laws of Creation, however, God demands striving towards spiritual perfection from mankind! Constant progress in extending their knowledge of Creation, so that they stand and work in it aright and do not become a hindrance in the swinging, rotating movement!

But whoever does not wish to go *further* now, and tries to insist on *what* he already believes he knows, consequently rejecting or in hostility opposing new revelations from God, will remain behind and be flung out in the World Judgment, because this tears down any obstacle in order at last to let clarity arise again in Creation, the clarity which in future will *further* the progressive development which rests in the Will of God for His Creation.

Jesus was a new revelation and brought further revelations in His Word. *All this* was new for that time, and as necessary a progress then as it is today; at which point, however, there should not be a final halt!

Jesus shall not be given up as the Son of God through my Message! He must now be recognised *as such* all the more, but not as the servant and slave of a decayed humanity in order to carry their burden of guilt, or to redeem it so that they may have it easier!

And just those who have *really* accepted Jesus as the Son of God *can* do no other than welcome my Message with *joyful gratitude,* and the new revelations from the Grace of God connected with it! Nor will it come hard to them to grasp everything I say aright and make it their own!

Whoever does not or cannot do this has not recognised the Message nor the true Being of the Son of God Jesus, but has built up for himself something only alien and wrong out of *his own* judgment and conceit and ... not as the least ... out of the laziness of his easy-going spirit, which shuns the movement demanded by God.

The meaning and purpose of the Message from the Light through me in the fulfilment of God's All-Holy Will is the necessary extension of the knowledge for mankind.

Neither the excuses of the spiritually indolent nor vain pharasaical phrases are of any value then; and also the malicious slanders and attacks will have to give way before the Justice of the Triune God and vanish like chaff; for there is nothing which is greater and mightier than God the Lord and what issues from His Will!

The spirit of earthman must now become *alive* and strong in the Will of God, to serve which he is allowed to dwell in this Creation. The time has come! No longer are any enslaved spirits tolerated by God! And man's self-will shall be broken unless he is prepared to adjust himself to the Primordial Laws of God which He placed into Creation!

To these also belongs the Law of constant Movement, which demands unhampered progress in development. The extension of knowledge remains connected with this! The knowledge of Creation, spiritual knowledge, is the real purport of all life!

For this reason you were given new revelations. If you reject them through the indolence of your spirit, if you want to let your spirit sleep on quietly as in the past, then it will awaken in the Judgment in order to deteriorate in the disintegration!

And woe unto all those who still wish to keep the human spirit bound! They will suffer tenfold harm and in the last moment, full of horror, will *have* to recognise too late what they burdened themselves with, in order then to collapse under their burden and sink into the horrible abyss.

The day has come! The Darkness must perish! The glorious Light of God now breaks in two all that is wrong and burns what is indolent in this Creation, so that it can pursue its course only in light and joy for the blessing of all creatures, as a jubilant prayer of thanks for every Grace of their Creator, to the Honour of God, the Only One, the Almighty!

919

CONSIDER WHAT IS OF BENEFIT TO YOU!

WHY, YOU men, do you always wish for something *different* spiritually from that which you really *need* and which will really benefit you? This peculiar characteristic is spreading abroad among all seekers with the devastating effect of a serious plague.

It would be of little avail for me to ask you about it; for you cannot account for it yourselves, even if you would exert yourselves to think about it day and night.

Just observe yourselves in all calmness for once, consider the questions that come to life within you, follow where your train of thought leads to, and you will soon recognise that for the greater part it always concerns such spheres as you will never reach because they lie above your origin, which you will therefore never be able to grasp.

However, it is a basic condition that you must be capable of grasping everything intended to *benefit* you!

Make this clear to yourselves in all your thoughts and deeds and adjust yourselves accordingly. Then everything will also become easier for you! So only deal with that which you can really grasp, i.e., with that which is anchored within the compass of your human existence.

Towards the Luminous Heights there is a sharp limitation to the sphere in which you have the capacity to be conscious as a human spirit, but it is not small on that account. It offers you room for all eternity and therewith fields of activity that are correspondingly great.

The possibility of your *development* alone is *without* limits, manifesting itself in the ever greater perfecting of your work within these spheres of activity. Therefore observe very closely what I am revealing to you herewith!

There is absolutely no limit to the greater perfecting of your spiritual *activity* – there is no end to it! You can become ever stronger in it, and with this becoming stronger the sphere of activity will always automatically expand, as a result of which you will find peace, joy, happiness and bliss.

In the past everyone has also formed a false idea about bliss. This lies solely in the radiant joy of an activity which is full of blessing, and not in lazy idleness and indulgence or, as the false is cleverly concealed by the expression, in *"sweet* idleness!"

For this reason I often call the human Paradise the "Luminous Realm of Joyful Activity"!

The human spirit cannot obtain bliss *in any other way* but through joyful activity for the Light! Through this alone will the crown of eternal life be finally bestowed upon it, granting the guarantee to the human spirit to be *eternally* permitted to co-operate in the cycle of Creation without the danger of falling into disintegration as a useless building stone.

In spite of the possibility graciously bestowed upon them continually to perfect their spirit, human beings will never be able to overstep the bounds of their sphere of existence in Creation, nor to tear down the strictly established boundaries of the human consciousness granted to them. In the simple *not being able to do so* there lies for them the very natural *not being allowed to do so,* which always manifests itself automatically, but just because of this has an invincible effect.

Increased perfection lies in the radiations of the spirit becoming ever more luminous, which is manifested correspondingly through increased strength of activity.

The increasing luminosity of the spirit arises in turn from the purification and cleansing of the soul, if in the volition for the good it strives upwards. One always develops out of the other in this matter in strict consistency.

If you deal *exclusively* and earnestly with what is good all else follows of its own accord. Thus it is not at all so difficult! But in your volition you constantly reach far beyond this, thus from the outset making the most simple things not only very hard for yourselves but quite often even impossible.

Consider that in the growth of the perfecting process even the strongest radiation of your spirit can never change its *species* but only its *condition!*

Therefore it is never possible to overstep the bounds of the limits of human consciousness, because the limits are defined through the *species* and not just through the condition. Within this great framework of the species, however, the condition builds very special small part-boundaries for itself, which can also be crossed through the change in condition.

Within this compass lie enormous expanses, worlds that are also spiritually immeasurable for you, in which you can sojourn and work without end for all eternity.

If you thoroughly and also deeply occupy yourselves *with this, then* you will be happy! In my Message I gave you the exact knowledge of what you are connected with and what is connected with you, how through your thoughts and actions you work in it, and what you *must* therewith achieve.

But instead of now devoting yourselves in the right sense and with all seriousness to what is offered to you, and therewith at last filling the post which each individual must occupy in this Creation, all your thoughts, your questions and also your wishes go ever again far above this into regions which the human spirit can never consciously reach.

Thus it is impossible for man really to grasp anything of this. All the weaving, radiating, striving, in brief the entire life in these regions, will forever remain incomprehensible to man, far remote from him. Therefore it can be of no benefit to him when he ponders over it. He only wastes the time and strength proffered to him for his own necessary development and must finally perish as useless.

Bestir yourselves at last with all your strength in *that* sphere which the Creator has given *you,* so that you will lead it to purest beauty, making it into a Garden of God similar to Paradise; a garden resembling a prayer of gratitude that has taken on form, in which everything arises jubilantly to the steps of God's Throne, in order through the deed humbly to praise the Creator of all things for His bountiful mercies.

Men, how small you are and yet how immeasurably exacting and conceited! If only you would bestir yourselves a little in the *right* manner, in such a way that you will swing undimmed and harmoniously *with* the Primordial Laws of Creation (and not always as in the past have only a hampering effect due to your ignorance), then richest blessings would spring forth over everything, wherever you lend a helping hand, no matter what you exert yourselves to undertake.

It simply could not be otherwise; and with the same unswerving certainty with which over a long period already you have been gliding towards destruction, you would see yourselves uplifted by the same power, leading to spiritual wealth and trouble-free earthly life.

But first you must *know* your home in Creation, and also everything in it that helps and furthers you! You must know how you yourselves have to wander and work in it before the blossoming can begin!

Try first of all to adjust yourselves aright *in the earthly sense* to the vibrations of the Divine Laws, which you can never circumvent without bringing great harm upon yourselves and upon your surroundings; and also make *your* laws accordingly, let them arise from this, then you will quickly have that peace and happiness which furthers the upbuilding for which you long so much; for without this all effort is utterly in vain, and even the greatest ability of the most skilled intellect is useless and brings ill success.

It lies with *you*, with you alone, with each individual, and not as you so much like to delude yourselves – always with the others! Try it with yourselves first of all – but this you do not wish to do! For you imagine yourselves too superior for this, or it appears too small and incidental to begin with!

In reality, however, it is but the indolence of your spirit which is capable of keeping you back from this, and to which you have all enslaved yourselves for thousands of years. Your intellect which bound the faculties of your spirit can now no longer help you when it is a matter henceforth of either humbling yourselves before the Pure Power of God or of perishing.

You must rouse your spirit, awaken it within you in order to recognise the Will of God and hear what it demands of you; for since the very beginning man is subject only to this Will and to none other, and he must now render account to this Will for everything he did in the part of Creation that was lent to him for a home.

And your accursed propensity for always reaching out only towards something higher, of longing for what is alien to you instead of enjoying your surroundings will, as proving one of your worst evils, direct itself against you. The evil has issued from the indolence of your spirit, which must not be confused with the intellect – for intellect is not spirit!

Indeed you have always done the same in the earthly sense. Instead of forming your environment more beautifully with all your strength and joy, making it more perfect and bringing it to full blossom, you often want *to get out* of it, because that seems easier for you and promises a quicker success. You wish to separate yourselves from it in order to find the desired improvement, because in all that is alien you also at the same time expect betterment and embellishment!

First of all try to *evaluate* aright that which is *given* to you! Then you will discover one marvel after another!

However, in order to make use of something in the right way you must first thoroughly *know* it beforehand. And this you are completely lacking! You were always too indolent to recognise the Will of your God, which becomes clearly and distinctly visible to you from out of Creation.

Ever again I must touch the old wound that you men bear, from which I have already often torn off all the coverings, but which you ever again seek to apply to it carefully. The wound that forms the origin of all evil, under which you must now suffer until you either free yourselves from it or completely collapse, is and remains the voluntary indolence of your spirit!

Many among these earthmen will no longer be capable of freeing themselves from the deadening clutches of this evil, for they have hesitated too long to recover from it.

It is natural that the sagacity of the intellect tries to cover up all spiritual slumber, because with the awakening of your spirit the domination of the intellect is also quickly ended.

It is only through indolence that the spirit pays too little attention to what is given to it! It does not take the trouble to discover its beauty and to make it ever more perfect, but imagines it can only find improvement in *change* and seeks happiness in everything that seems *alien* to it.

Man does not consider that a change first necessitates an uprooting, and then places the uprooted one on *alien* soil with which he does not yet know what to do. For this reason he very easily makes big mistakes which bring unsuspected harmful consequences. He who places his hope in *changes,* who does not know what properly to do with what is *given* to him, lacks the serious volition as well as the ability. From the very outset he stands on the precarious ground of an adventurer!

First recognise yourselves aright and avail yourselves of that which God offers for your use, employing it in such a way that it *can* also blossom forth; then the earth and the entire sphere of Creation left to the human spirit for his activity *must* and *will* become a *Paradise* where only joy and peace dwell; for the Law of Creation will then work *for* you with the same certainty as it must *now* work against your activities, and it is immovable, stronger than the will of men; for it rests in the Ray of the Primordial Light!

The hour is not far off when men *must* already recognise that it will not be at all difficult to live differently than hitherto, to get along with their fel-low-men in *peace!* Man will become seeing, because all possibility for his hitherto prevailing *wrong* doing and thinking will now be taken away from him by God.

He must then acknowledge with shame how ridiculously he has behaved in the haste of his bustle that is so unimportant for *real* life, and how *dangerous* he was to the whole of that part of Creation with which he was graciously en-trusted for his use and enjoyment.

In the future he will live only to the *joy* of his fellow-men, just as they will to his joy, and he will not always carry about envious desires for what he does not yet possess. The ability will awaken to develop the beauty of his personal environment to the most glorious blossom, to fashion it in complete accord-ance with his nature as soon as he brings it into the great blissful swinging of the simple Primordial Laws of Creation; such as I could teach him with the Message through the Love of God, which this time helps by punishing in or-der to save those who still possess good volition and humility of spirit!

If you wish to build up *clarify your spirit* first and make it strong and pure. *Clarify* it, which means let it come to maturity! Creation is already standing in the time of *harvest,* and man as a creature with it!

However, he remained behind in this through his stubbornly wrong voli-tion; he placed himself apart from all the swinging willed by the Light, and must be flung out of the already *intensified* and more joyful rotation of Crea-tion, because in his immaturity he cannot maintain himself therein.

The popular saying about the *clarified* spirit is quite right! A mature or clarified person can very easily be recognised, for he stands in the Light and avoids all that is dark! He will also radiate peace around him through his nature!

There will be no more hissing up, but calm objectivity in the great swinging of joyous activity, or cool severity which in all friendliness will clear up and throw light upon the frailties of those who have not yet been able to become strong in spirit, but who are still subject to fermentation, which must bring about purification and clarification or … destruction!

Only the Darkness can hiss up, never the Light! The Light always exhibits cool purity and peaceful circumspection in the conscious power of the high knowledge!

Wherever anger can still *hiss up* in a person there weaknesses must still be burned out; such a spirit can also still succumb to attacks of the Darkness or serve it as a tool. He is not "clarified", not yet purified enough!

It is the same with *all* the weaknesses you carry within you, which you seem utterly unable to dispose of, or at least only with great difficulty.

In reality it would not be difficult as soon as you are finally able to agree to deal sensibly with *that* which God has given you, to apply *in the right way what* you already hold in your hands, and to adapt yourselves to the swinging of the Laws, the knowledge of which you could already gain through my Message. Then in the truest sense it is as easy as child's play!

Refrain from occupying yourselves predominantly with questions which go beyond the sphere assigned to you, and learn first of all to recognise thoroughly all of *that* which is *within* and *around* you! Then ascent will come of its own accord; for you will be automatically uplifted by the consequences of your activities.

Be *simple* in your thoughts and deeds; for greatness and also strength lie in simplicity! You do not retrogress thereby, but advance and erect a *firm* structure for a new life in which every person finds his way about because it is no longer confused and entangled, but in full view in every respect, bright and clear, in a word healthy, natural!

Develop yourselves as inwardly upright, genuine *human beings,* and you will thereby immediately have the intimate connection with the entire Creation, which will further you in everything that you need for yourselves and for your ascent! You cannot achieve this in any other way!

Then everything you have need of, everything that brings you joy and peace, will stream towards you in rich abundance! In no case will it happen before you do this, no matter how hard you would exert yourselves for it; for the time has now arrived when man on earth *must* open himself to the Word of God, which is the same as adjusting himself to the existing Laws of God's Holy Will, which sustain and further Creation!

OMNISCIENCE

With my Word I lead you back to God, from Whom you gradually allowed yourselves to become estranged through all those who placed their human pseudo-knowledge above the Wisdom of God.

And those who are still profoundly convinced of the Omniscience of God, who wish humbly to bow before the great, loving guidance contained therein through the effects of the irrevocable Laws of this Creation, they think of this Omniscience of God as different from what it is!

They picture the Wisdom of God as much too *human* and consequently much too small, compressed into much too narrow boundaries! With the best of volition they make nothing but an earthly *should-know-everything* out of Omniscience.

However, all their good thinking in this matter is too human, for ever and again they commit the one big mistake of seeking to picture God and the Divine as the *crowning point* of what is *human!*

They simply do not get away from the human basis, but contemplate everything only from their own particular status; proceeding upwards from the *human* level they come to conclusions which are perfected to the highest and most ideal point of the same species. In spite of everything they do not leave their own level in their conception of God!

Even when they seek to raise their expectation to something which is utterly incomprehensible to them, everything still remains in one mental groove, and thus although the volition is there to perceive it faintly, they will never find even a shadow of the conception of the true greatness of God!

It is no different with the conception of Divine Omniscience! With your most venturesome thinking you make nothing of it but a petty and earthly *all-knowing!*

You imagine that Divine Omniscience should *"know"* your *human* thinking and perceiving. This conception therefore demands or expects from Divine Wisdom an unlimited entrance into and adjustment to the most personal and smallest thinking of every individual here on earth and in all the worlds! A taking care and understanding of each little human spirit, and what is more – a troubling itself over each one!

Such "should-knowing" is not wisdom! Wisdom is much greater, standing far above this!

Providence lies in wisdom!

Providence, however, is not identical in meaning with foreseeing by the guidance, as people so often understand the expression "wise providence", i. e., as they imagine it. In this matter they also err, because in their human way of thinking they again *start from below,* and for every kind of greatness picture an *enhancement* of everything they bear within themselves *as human beings!*

Even with the best attitude they do not deviate from this habit, never thinking of the fact that God and the Divine are utterly *alien to their species,* and that all thinking about this must result in nothing but errors, if they use the human species as a basis for it!

Herein lies all that has been wrong in the past, all the errors as regards concepts. It can be said quite calmly that not a single one of the past concepts resulting from thinking, pondering and investigating about this has really been *right;* in their human narrow-mindedness they have never been able to come near to the actual truth!

Providence is *Divine* activity; it lies anchored in the Divine Wisdom, in Omniscience. And this Omniscience has become deed in the Divine Laws of this Creation! It rests in them, as also does Providence, which latter takes effect upon the human beings.

Therefore do not think that God's Omniscience should know your thoughts and how you are faring on earth. The working of God is entirely different, greater and more comprehensive. With His Will God spans everything, maintains everything, and furthers everything from out of the Living Law which brings to each individual *that* which he deserves, i. e., that which he wove for himself!

Not one can thereby escape the consequences of his deeds, be they evil or good! *It is in this* that God's Omniscience, which is united with Justice and Love, manifests itself! In the working of this Creation *everything* for man has been wisely provided! Also that he *must* judge himself!

That which comes in the Judgment of God is the *release* of the sentences which men had to pass upon themselves in wise Providence according to the Law of God!

For years now, strangely enough, mankind have been talking about the *Cosmic Turning-Point* which is supposed to come, and in this they are as an exception right for once. But the Turning-Point has already come! Mankind stand amid the world-embracing happening which they are still awaiting, and they do not notice it because they do *not want to!*

As always they think about it *differently* and do not wish to acknowledge how it *really* is. Through this, however, they miss for themselves the right time for the possibility of individual maturing, and they fall short. As always they fall short, for never as yet have mankind *fulfilled what* God can and must expect of them if He is to permit them to stay any longer in this Creation.

In men's actions there is such a stubborn limitation, which is repeated in the same way at *every* Light Happening! There is such childish wilfulness and ridiculous conceit that not much hope remains for any possibilities of salvation!

For this reason Creation is now being purified from all such evil. The All-Holy Will brings the purification in the closing of the cycle of all happenings, all actions!

The closing of the cycle is brought about through the Power of the Light, in which everything must judge itself, must purify itself, or must perish and sink into terrible disintegration!

It is natural, conditioned by the Laws of Creation, that now towards the end all the evil characteristics must bring forth their strongest blossoms and most repulsive fruit in order to live themselves to extinction thereby, through each other and in each other!

Everything must come to the boiling point in the Power of the Light! However, this time only a *matured* mankind can emerge from the effervescing, those who are able and also willing to accept the new revelations from God gratefully and jubilantly, and to live accordingly so that they wander through Creation by working in the right way. –

At each Turning-Point the Creator offered the maturing human spirits new revelations unknown to them until then, which were meant to serve as an extension of their knowledge so that through further recognition their spirits would become capable of swinging themselves upwards to the Luminous Heights, which once they left as unconscious spirit germs.

However, there have always been just a few who proved themselves willing gratefully to accept descriptions descending from the Divine Sphere, and who could thereby gain as much in value and spiritual power as it was necessary for human beings to have. The majority of all mankind rejected these high gifts from God due to their constantly increasing limitation in spiritual comprehension.

The periods for such Cosmic Turning-Points were always connected with the condition of Creation's state of maturity at the time. In its development according to the Holy Law of God the maturity of Creation was always exactly fulfilled, but due to their spiritual indolence the *human beings* in Creation often placed themselves *hinderingly* in the way of these developments.

During the dissemination among human beings of the increasing recognition of all God's Activity in Creation – which was arranged in world epochs – they closed themselves to it almost every time.

Since human beings elevated themselves to be the starting-point of all existence, they did not wish to believe that something existed which they could not grasp with their earthly senses. They limited their knowledge to this alone, and did not therefore want to approve of anything else – they, the smallest ramifications of Creation, most remote from genuine existence and real life, who wantonly fritter away the time of grace allowed them in order to mature through advancing recognition!

Now comes a new, great Turning-Point which also brings new knowledge! They already speak about this Turning-Point themselves, but again they only envisage it as the fulfilment of conceited human wishes of a kind they thought up themselves. Not that *they* would have duties thereby, no, again they only await an improvement in earthly comforts which the Light throws into their laps! *That* is how the Turning-Point shall be, for their thinking does not reach any further!

The new compulsion to knowledge closely connected with this Turning-Point, which enables man to ascend spiritually and thus at last to transform the surroundings in the material realms as well, does not interest them! What did not exist before they simply reject out of spiritual indolence!

But now the human beings are *forced* by God to accept it, for otherwise they can no longer ascend spiritually; for they *must* know about it! –

It lies within the working of Omniscience that at very definite periods of maturing in Creation ever new revelations are given to the human spirits about the working of God. –

For this reason *Created Ones* were already sent down to this earth primeval ages ago after the spirit-germs in their slow development had already trained the animal bodies chosen for this purpose to become human body forms, something which went hand in hand with the development of spiritual self-consciousness in the physical body. This was unutterably long times *before* the known glacial age of this earth!

Since I have already given the knowledge about *Primordial* Created Beings there must also exist Subsequent Created Beings or Created Ones, because I have also talked of Developed Beings, only to whom the human beings on earth belong.

These Created Ones, of whom I have not so far spoken, inhabit spheres in Creation which lie between those of the Primordial Beings of Primordial Creation and those of the Developed Beings of Subsequent Creation.

In the times of the beginning a Created Being was also incarnated here and there among the maturing tribes of the ones developing from the spirit-germs. His task was to lead and to proffer the connection to the particular next step in the necessary upward striving of all that is spiritual. These were the great Turning-Points *there* in the times of the beginning.

Later on came the Prophets as blessed ones! *In this way* the Infinite Love from the Light worked to help and assist the human spirits with ever new revelations whenever Creation was mature for it, until finally there came also the Sacred Tidings about the Divine and Its Working.

Thus at the great Cosmic Turning-Point now operating there also comes the absolute necessity for an extension of knowledge.

Either the human spirit must swing itself upwards to knowledge or remain stationary, which latter is equivalent to the setting in of decay, due to uselessness consequent upon a stationary human spirit becoming over-ripe through inactivity; a human spirit which no longer knows how to apply the Power of the Light accumulating within it in the right way. Thus that which can and would *help* it becomes its ruin, as is the case with all energy that is wrongly applied!

God is the Lord, *He absolutely alone,* and whoever does not want to acknowledge Him humbly just as He really *is,* and not as *you imagine Him* to be, cannot rise up to the new life.

I was allowed to unfold before you the picture of the weaving in Creation to which you belong, so that you will become seeing and may consciously enjoy and use for your benefit the blessings contained in Creation for you; so that in future they may only *help* you to advance upwards, and not have to punish you painfully or even be compelled to reject you! Thank the Lord that He thinks of you with such Love as to allow me to tell you with my Message what will help you, and also what is dangerous for you!

I showed you *those* paths which lead to the Luminous Heights! Now *follow* them!

THE WEAK SEX

IF YOU want to recognise how much wrong there is in the hitherto prevailing ideas, habits and customs of these earthmen, the search for it will not cause you much trouble; for you do not need to do anything else than to take some expression and reflect upon it *deeply*. It will be wrong, because even the foundation of all the thinking done by these earthmen is already utterly distorted. On a false basis, however, the *right* way of thinking can never develop, but in view of such a foundation it is also bound to be wrong.

Today let us take the designation which is generally disseminated about womanhood on earth as being the "weak sex". There will hardly be anyone among my hearers who has not already heard this expression. It is used in an affectionate way as well as sneeringly, kind-heartedly and also ironically, but it is always taken up without reflection as something that is established, and adhered to thoughtlessly, or at least without being examined.

In reality, however, womanhood is just as strong as manhood on earth, only in a different way.

In my lectures I have already often explained that the *actual concept* of womanhood and manhood issues from the *nature of their activity* in Creation, i. e., that the nature of their activity is fundamental for this and determines the form which allows human beings on earth to be recognised as female or male.

The difference immediately shows itself as soon as the human spirit-germs leave their sphere of origin. Those inclined towards the active, i. e., the coarser working, take on male forms, whereas female forms shape themselves around those who wish to work passively, i. e., in a more delicate way. These are two different kinds of activity, but of equal strength; there can be no question whatever of a weaker species.

These two species also give the meaning of the Living Cross, which in itself is perfect! The vertical beam of the Cross represents the positive, i. e., the active life, and the horizontal beam of equal length and strength represents the negative or passive life. The Living Cross bears both within Itself!

The Cross of Creation from out of which and around which the whole of Creation develops itself says and indicates the same. The vertical beam is the positive, active working, and the horizontal beam the negative, passive working.

The Elders in the Divine Sphere, who at the same time are the Guardians of the Holy Grail in the Divine part of the Grail Castle, likewise show the cross with beams of equal length in their radiation. In their case, however, it is not the Living Cross which Itself forms their radiation, but it enables one to recognise that these Elders are perfected spirits of their species, and that they carry *both* the active and the passive within themselves, uncurtailed and working in harmony.

In Creation, however, the active is *separated* from the passive as regards their working. Every spirit carries within itself either the active *only* or the passive *only,* which is later also repeated with the spirit seed-germs.

These work either passively or actively *side by side,* and yet they constantly strive towards one another, since the two species can only achieve something which is perfect through their *joint* activity. However, it only becomes perfect when the two work with *equal strength* and strive for *one* goal – towards the Light!

They do not need to live together in earthly marriage in order to achieve this, nor to be at all close together gross-materially – they need not even be personally acquainted! Only the *goal* must be the same – towards the Light!

I mention this particularly so that no wrong conclusions may be drawn from my lecture; for marriages and physical gross-material approaches in general are things entirely for themselves, which are not a requirement connected with striving for the Light, though if they are pure they do not hinder it either!

But this lecture is primarily concerned with the erroneous expression "the weaker sex"! I must not digress too much, for I want to show how the expression once originated and how it could be continuously maintained.

This is not so difficult fundamentally! You can also recognise it easily if you are willing to take the trouble closely to examine everything your fellow-men utter!

You know that all womanhood on earth must keep awake the longing for the Light as the guardian of the flame of the preserving-and-upward-leading-longing for the Light.

For this purpose a more delicate capacity to perceive intuitively develops within woman for, in her urge towards a more delicate activity, less of the spiritual substantiality detaches itself from her than from the man, who inclines towards coarser activity.

Through this every woman is the receiver and mediator of radiations which men can no longer receive. Womanhood stands therein half a step higher, turned more towards the Light than any man. Provided, of course, that she stands *aright* and does not fritter away her abilities or obstruct them herself!

Man subconsciously senses that woman thereby possesses refinements which he no longer bears within himself, nor can he bear them within him in view of the nature of his activity, since they would restrain him from many a coarse matter which has still to be dealt with. It is true that he does not become quite clear about this, or at least very rarely, but he perceives a treasure therein which needs to be *preserved*. He feels urged to *protect* this invisible treasure in the World of Gross Matter, because he feels himself the *stronger one* in the earthly, i. e., in the gross material sense.

There are only a few men who do not intuitively perceive this. But these have in any case become brutalised and can no longer be counted as men in the true sense.

The desire to protect which remains unuttered because only subconsciously felt, has now brought man gradually and erroneously to view womanhood as the *weaker* sex, the sex which needs his protection. Thus this designation does not perhaps originate from an evil volition or a depreciatory judgment, but only from ignorance of the true reason for his own intuitive perceptions.

Along with the beginning and advancing dullness due to earthmen's false ways of thinking, and along with the ever-increasing limitation of their ability to understand things lying outside the coarsest World of Matter, there also naturally arose an interpretation of the expression that became ever more base.

In reality man is not the *stronger* sex but only the *coarser* sex, i. e., the more gross material one, and therefore the denser one; womanhood, however, is not the weaker sex, but merely the *more delicate,* the more "loosened" one, which has nothing to do with weaknesses.

Due to his greater activity man is gross materially more strongly *solidified*, but this is no fault since he needs it in order to work effectively in Creation, to stand more firmly on earthly soil, and to have a more direct effect in and upon the dense gross material substance. Thus he is more firmly connected with the earth and more inclined towards it.

Woman, however, tends to be drawn more in an upward direction, to what is finer, more delicate and less dense. In this she supplements human spirituality, holding it and uplifting it ... naturally only if she stands at *the* post to which the Creator appointed her!

Through retaining a very definite species of the higher substantiality in her body the latter is not so strongly solidified, because this substantiality penetrates her physical body and keeps it loose.

This again is neither a deficiency nor a weakness, but a *necessity* for the reception and mediation of radiations, the help of which man in his working cannot do without, although through his coarser nature he does not have the ability to take up these radiations directly.

All this naturally also includes gross material things in the most simple way. Let us take a birth, for example! *For this reason* alone a man would simply be unable to offer the possibility for a soul to approach him for the purpose of incarnating on earth, even if the organs for this were present in his body.

He lacks *the bridge* for the soul that is contained in the delicate substantiality which womanhood still carries within, and which was bound to sever itself automatically from manhood owing to their active volition.

Therefore even if the organs for this were present, only the *beginning* of a physical body could develop, nothing more, because then the co-operation of the new soul is missing, the soul which cannot approach unless the more delicate bridge of the substantiate is at hand. With some women, too, a soul can sometimes approach, but it is unable to maintain itself if this bridge has become damaged, because the woman has acquired male characteristics which pushed aside the delicate substantiate addition to womanhood. The souls then release themselves again before an earthly birth can take place!

All this reaches much further than you can imagine. Even the earthly health of your children is conditioned, retarded or furthered through the flawlessness and purity of this higher substantiate bridge which the mother offers.

It is not only the organs alone which are the cause of childlessness or of the fact that many births do not occur *as* they normally should do. The main cause for the difficulties, illnesses or weaknesses very often lies only in the defectiveness of the bridges, which the souls need for striding along their earthly path securely and vigorously.

How often has a woman either through stupid trifling or condemnable vanity accepted male characteristics which were bound to weaken or push aside completely the higher substantiate part that was given to her as a privilege. The results of this are so varied as to the nature and form of their conditions that men often rack their brains how many a thing is possible.

But worse even than the injuries arising out of these happenings, which still become physically visible immediately, are the injuries on the planes of fine gross matter, brought about through such a failure on the part of womanhood and which then also manifest on earth, although only a long time afterwards.

You will hear even more about this when later on I deal with these subjects, and you will be struck with horror at the frivolous guilt of womanhood, which was even furthered by men and strengthened through wanton conduct, because such guilt was very welcome to them!

For decades you will still blush about this, because this period of degradation will oppress you through your memories like a loathsome burden for a long time.

At present these happenings are still a mystery to mankind, which I shall yet unveil when they have matured to the point where they can grasp it; for I also work absolutely according to the Laws in these matters. Mankind can come to know *everything* from me; however I only open my mouth for it when they have become capable of absorbing it through their inner maturity. This process acts in the same way as an opening or ignition connection is established, quite automatic! For this reason mankind will get to know only as much from me as they are capable of digesting, not more!

However, they need not always be conscious of this; for I perceive the *inner* awakening and stirring of the spirit, which is very different from the day-consciousness of the intellect. And *that* to me gives the release for my Word!

For this reason it seems as if today I already give much more than you are able to absorb really consciously. But your spirit to which I speak does take it up without your knowing about this in the earthly sense. Thus it looks as if

937

I am now giving much that is meant for later times, whereas your *spirit* has already taken it up.

The "day-conscious" understanding only comes to you later, perhaps not for decades, so that only *then* will you become capable of knowing how to apply it also *in the earthly sense* with perfect understanding.

As soon as you vigorously stride along with me spiritually I can reveal the entire Creation to you. It always lies only with you, you men! Therefore remain awake and alert in spirit, so that I need not withhold anything from you!

I like to give and give joyously, but I am bound to the Law because I myself have no choice! I am allowed to give to you according to your ability to receive and no more! Bear this in mind! Therefore make use of the time as long as I am with you so that you will not miss anything!

Guard my Word and use It; It can give you *everything!*

THE DESTROYED BRIDGE

IT IS pitiable to see how diligently man on earth works at his retrogression and thus at his destruction under the delusion that he is thereby striding upwards!

Earthman! A bitter taste is attached to the name of this creature for everything in Creation weaving in the Will of God, and it would seem better for man if this name were no longer uttered, because whenever it is mentioned vexation and uneasiness penetrate the entire Creation at the same time, something that lays a burden upon mankind on earth; for this vexation, this uneasiness, are a living accusation which forms itself automatically and must confront all mankind on earth adversely.

Due to his wrong activity, which made itself conspicuous in this Creation by hindering, disturbing, and continually doing harm, man on earth has at last become an outlaw through himself, through his ridiculous pretence of knowing everything better! He has stubbornly and forcibly brought on his expulsion, because he made himself incapable of simply *receiving* God's blessings in humility.

He wanted to make himself the creator, the achiever, he wanted to force the activity of the Almighty into complete submission to his earthly will!

There is no word which could properly describe such conceited arrogance in its boundless stupidity! Just delve into this hardly credible behaviour yourselves! Imagine man on earth, and how by assuming an air of importance he wishes to place himself above the mechanism of this marvellous work of a Divine Creation (which has up till now remained unknown to him) in order to direct it, rather than willingly fitting himself into it as a small part thereof... you will not then know whether to laugh or to weep!

A toad standing before a high rock and wanting to order it to move out of its way does not produce quite so ludicrous an effect as does present-day man in his mad ambition towards his Creator!

To envisage this must also arouse disgust within every human spirit who now comes to awakening in the Judgment. He will be seized with dismay, shuddering and horror when, through recognising the Luminous Truth, he suddenly sees everything before him just *as* it has *really* been for a long time, although he was unable in the past to notice it in this way. Filled with shame, he then wants to flee to the end of all the worlds!

And the covering veil will now be torn to pieces, ground to powder as the grey remnants flutter here and there, until the Ray of Light can stream freely into the souls which are deeply tormented with remorse, those who in newly awakened humbleness want to bow before their Lord and God, Whom they were no longer able to recognise through the chaos which the earthbound intellect brought about at all times when it was allowed unlimited domination.

But you must thoroughly experience disgust at the deeds and thoughts of the earthmen *upon* yourselves, and also *within* yourselves first, before you can be redeemed from it. You must taste disgust *as* thoroughly as every Envoy from the Light always had to experience it through the villainous depravity of mankind on earth, which is hostile to the Light! In no other way can you obtain redemption!

It is the sole redeeming reciprocal action of your guilt, which you are now *compelled* to live through yourselves, because it cannot be forgiven you in any other way!

You will already enter upon this experience very soon – the sooner it touches you the easier it will become for you! May it at the same time open up the way for you to the Luminous Heights!

And again womanhood will have to feel the ignominy *first,* because her downfall now compels her to expose herself to these things. Frivolously she has put herself into a position where she will now be forced down at the feet of brutalised manhood. It is with anger and contempt that manhood on earth will now flare up and look down upon all women who are no longer capable of giving *that* for which the Creator had designated them, that which man so urgently needs for his activity.

This is *self-respect,* which first makes every true man a man! Self-respect, not self-conceit! However, man can only have self-respect through looking up to *womanly dignity,* to protect which gives him respect for himself – and upholds it!

That is the great secret between woman and man, the secret which has never been uttered before, which is able to spur him on to great and pure deeds here on earth, which glows purifyingly through all thinking, thus spreading a holy shimmer of high longing for the Light over the whole of life on earth.

But all this has been taken away from man through woman, who quickly succumbed to Lucifer's enticements through the ludicrous vanities of the earthly intellect. With the awakening of the recognition of this great guilt, man will now regard womanhood as only *that* which she was really bound to become on account of her wilfulness.

But although this disgrace brings pain it is nothing but a strong help for *those* female souls who awaken under the just blows of the Judgment, and who through their recognition see the enormity of the theft which they perpetrated on man with their false vanity; for they will have to muster all their strength to regain the dignity they lost, the dignity which they threw from themselves like some worthless property which hindered them on their chosen path downwards.

You have not yet become quite clear about the burden of the harmful consequences, the burden which was bound to fall upon the whole of earth's humanity when earthly womanhood, through wrong actions, zealously sought for the greater part to destroy the bridges that connected her with the streams of Light.

The harmful consequences are a *hundredfold* and multiform, working in all directions. You need only try and place yourselves in the course of the inevitable outworkings that accord with the Laws of Creation! The recognition is then not at all difficult!

Once again think of the simple process which takes place in strict lawfulness:

As soon as woman tries to become masculine in her thoughts and actions this volition already takes corresponding effect – first of all upon everything of her which is closely connected with (higher) substantiality, then also with ethereal substance, as well as after a very definite period with fine gross matter!

The consequence is that with her attempts at positive activity, which is contrary to the task of woman on earth, all the more refined elements of her womanly nature are repressed because they are passive, and they finally release themselves from her, since through lack of use they gradually lose strength and are drawn off the woman by the same basic species.

The bridge is then broken down which enables earthwoman through her passive nature to absorb higher radiations and to mediate them to the coarser World of Matter, in which she is anchored with a very definite strength by her body.

But this is also the *very* bridge a soul needs for earthly incarnation into the physical body! If this bridge is missing it is made impossible for any soul to enter the growing body; for the soul of itself cannot step across the gulf that was bound to arise in this way.

If this bridge is only partly broken down, however, which depends on the nature and strength of woman's desire to become masculine through her activities, it is nevertheless possible for souls to incarnate which are in the same way neither completely masculine nor completely feminine, and which therefore form ugly, unharmonious mixtures; later on these hold all sorts of unquenchable longings, they never feel understood during their life on earth, and are thus a constant source of unrest and discontent to themselves and to their surroundings.

It would be better for such souls, as well as for their later earthly surroundings, if they had never found an opportunity to incarnate; for they only burden themselves with guilt and will never redeem anything, because in reality they do not belong on this earth.

The opportunity and possibility for such incarnations which are not willed by Creation, thus by the Will of God, is proffered only by *those* women who through their capricious ways and ridiculous vanity, as well as through the degrading craving for a sham importance, are inclined to become to some extent masculine, no matter how it is expressed!

Delicate, *genuinely female* souls are never incarnated through such unwomanly women, and thus the female sex on earth is gradually completely poisoned, because this eccentricity has become ever more widespread, attracting more and more new souls of this kind, souls which can neither be wholly female nor wholly male, thus spreading what is neither genuine nor harmonious on earth.

Fortunately the wise Laws of Creation have also drawn a sharp line even in such matters; for through a distortion of this nature, violently brought about by a wrong volition, there first of all occur difficult or premature births, then children who are liable to illness, who are nervous and have torn intuitive perceptions, and finally after a very definite period sterility sets in, so that a nation which allows its womanhood to strive towards the unsuitable state of manliness is sentenced to slow extinction.

Naturally this does not happen from one day to the next, so that it would become glaringly conspicuous to the people living at the time, but a happening of this kind must also proceed along the path of development. Even if slowly, it will yet be surely! And a few generations need to vanish first before the consequences of such an evil on the part of womanhood can be halted or made good in order to restore a people from a decline to a state of health and save it from total extinction.

It is an adamantine Law that wherever the size and strength of the two beams of the Cross of Creation are unable to swing in perfect harmony and purity, i.e., where the positive masculine as well as the negative feminine do not remain equally strong and undistorted (whereby the equal-armed Cross would also become distorted), decline and finally also destruction are bound to follow so that Creation will again become free of such absurdities.

Therefore no people can ascend or be happy unless they possess genuine, unadulterated womanhood, in whose wake alone genuine manhood can and must develop itself.

A thousand things spoil genuine womanhood in this way. Therefore all the consequences show themselves in quite different ways, more or less severe in their harmful effects! But they will always appear without fail!

I do not yet wish to speak here of the frivolous imitation of men's evil habits by women, of which smoking probably counts as the first; for this is a plague entirely by itself, forming a crime against humanity such as man of the present time hardly dares to imagine.

With a closer recognition of the Laws in Creation, the unjustified and thoughtless presumption of the smoker even to indulge in his vice out of doors, thereby poisoning God's gift of fresh, upbuilding air, which is meant to be available to every creature, will very soon vanish, especially when he must experience that this bad habit is the seat of many a disease under the scourge of which today's humanity groans.

Quite apart from the smokers themselves, having to breathe in such tobacco smoke hampers the normal development of many an organ in infants and children, especially the necessary firmness and strengthening of the liver, which is particularly important for every person, because when functioning in the *right* and healthy manner it can prevent the establishment of a cancerous centre as the surest and best means of resistance to this plague.

In most cases the woman of today has chosen a wrong path for herself. She strives to *rid* herself of womanliness, be it in sports, in excesses or diversions, but mostly through participating in *positive spheres of activity* which fall to and must also remain with manhood if there is to be genuine ascent and peace.

Through this everything on earth has already become fundamentally disarranged, has lost its equilibrium. Even the ever-increasing and more violent disputations, as well as the failures, can only be traced to the wilful *mixing* of the positive and negative activities among all human beings on earth, which activities Creation stipulated should *remain pure* only. The confusion forcibly brought about in this way can have no other consequence but decline and destruction.

How foolish are you human beings that you do not wish to learn to recognise the simplicity of God's Laws, which in their absolute consistency are so easy to observe!

It is true that you possess wise sayings which you like to quote! Even this one sentence tells you much: Small causes, great effects! But you do not follow them! It never occurs to you to look for the small cause first of all in the things happening around you which threaten, afflict and oppress you, so that by avoiding *this* the great effects cannot even arise!

This is much too simple for you! Therefore you prefer first to tackle the severe effects only, if at all possible with a lot of noise, so that the action will also be fully valued and bring you earthly fame!

But you will *never* attain victory in this way, no matter how well you believe yourselves to be equipped for it, unless you condescend in all simplicity to look for *the causes*, so that by avoiding all of them you can for ever banish the severe consequences.

And again you cannot find the causes unless you learn to recognise in humility the mercies of God, Who gave you everything in Creation that can protect you from every misfortune!

As long as you lack the humility to receive God's mercies gratefully you will remain entangled in your wrong actions and thoughts until the final fall which must inevitably lead you to eternal damnation! And this last moment lies before you! You are already standing with one foot in the gate! The next step will let you fall into bottomless depths!

Consider this well! Pull yourselves back and leave behind the flat earthly life, without form and warmth, which you preferred to lead hitherto! At last become *such* human beings as the Will of God wishes further to tolerate in Creation in the future! In doing so you fight *for yourselves*, since your God, by Whose Grace you were granted to fulfil your urge for a conscious existence in this Creation, does not need you! Remember this at all times, and thank Him with every breath which you are allowed to take through His boundless Love!

UNGRATEFUL and devoid of understanding, even reproachful – that is how men often face the greatest help from the Light!

It is distressing to observe how even those of good volition behave lamentably in these things, or turn away doubtingly from the Light because of unfulfilled hopes regarding wrong earthly wishes. And yet, through non-fulfilment, the Light very often grants salvation and gain.

But, sulking like the most stubborn children, men close themselves to the recognition of the All-Wise Love, thereby harming themselves to *such* an extent that frequently they can never again ascend, and become lost like a useless grain of seed in this Creation.

The smallest of all the evils which they thereby inflict upon themselves during their wanderings are multifarious incarnations on earth that result from the reciprocal action. These incarnations take up centuries, perhaps thousands of years, ever again delaying the possibility of the spirit's ascent, permitting new suffering to arise, and resulting in continual new chains of unnecessary entanglements, which must all be redeemed without fail down to the last and finest speck of dust, before the spirit can rise from the confusion brought about through stubbornness.

Were the Light as *human nature* is, then It would drop Creation out of weariness, for truly an unbelievable patience is needed to allow such disgusting, stupid stubbornness to live itself out so that those of good volition still emerging from such a state will not lose their possibilities of salvation, and need not perish in the whirlpool of destruction created by those who no longer wish to change themselves.

But even among those of good volition only a small part will attain to real salvation, for many weaken too soon and lose heart, and also sometimes think they have taken wrong courses, because so much opposes them and causes vexation, worry and suffering from the moment the good volition sets in; whereas formerly they did not notice it so much.

Along with the resolution for ascent contained in the firm volition for what is good, there first comes a time of refining for many persons which lets them experience their past wrong ways of thinking or acting, and transforms them for what is right! The more conspicuous this becomes the more such a person is endowed with grace, and the stronger the help already extended from the Light.

It is already the beginning of salvation, the severance from Darkness, which in the process seems to keep him clasped even more *firmly*. But this firmer and harder embrace only seems to be such because the spirit which is already awakening and growing strong *is striving away* from the Darkness that holds it.

It is only the *upward striving of the spirit* which makes the grip of the Darkness appear more painful, because until then the grip could not become as noticeable so long as the spirit voluntarily adapted itself to or nestled itself in this embrace. Previously the spirit offered no counter-pressure, but always yielded without struggling against it.

Only when it wishes to uplift itself is the hindrance through the Darkness bound to become perceptible and incisive to the upward striving spirit, until finally it *tears* itself forcibly *away* in order to become free of the ties retaining it. The very word already indicates that this tearing away cannot always take place without pains; for a *tearing* away cannot be accomplished with gentleness. But no time is left for a quiet *severance*. For this earth has already sunk far too deeply and the World Judgment is in full swing in its final fulfilment.

Man does not reflect about all this! Many a person thinks his resolution cannot be right because he never perceived such hindrances before, and could perhaps even feel quite comfortable. Thus through such false thinking he again lets himself sink into the hands of Darkness.

He then no longer resists it, and consequently fails to perceive its embrace as hostile. He is pulled down without sensing any pain until aroused by the call of Judgment, to which he cannot close himself, but then ... it will be too late for him!

He is only stirred up so as to come to the dreadful recognition of his fall into the bottomless pit of final disintegration, of being cast out! And with this begin the torments which will never ease off, but which are bound to increase until the horrible end comes to his being permitted to be self-conscious, i.e., of being allowed to be a human being, something that could have brought him bliss for all eternity!

Consider, you men, that you are deeply embedded in Darkness, that you have embedded yourselves therein! If you wish to be saved you must wrench yourselves free from it, and my Word shows you the way to do so, giving you the possibility through the knowledge and the strength to carry out your liberation and redemption!

As soon as you have resolved to escape from the collapsing Darkness which embraces you firmly and pulls you down into the depths, there already comes like a flash with this resolution a ray of light and of strength to help you!

You have tied innumerable knots into the threads of your fate through your past wrong thinking, and through the actions that so pulled you down. But, held in the fist of Darkness, you no longer thought of them at all, neither could you see or perceive them because they still lie *above* you, blocking your path and your connection with the Luminous Heights.

With your upward striving, however, you will naturally find them all again upon your path, and you must untie the knots one after the other so that your path will become free for ascent.

When it concerns the knots of your vanities and so much else, this then seems to you like misfortune and sorrow, anguish of the soul. In reality, however, it is the only possible way to liberation and salvation and simply cannot be otherwise, because you yourselves had prepared your path beforehand in this manner, and must now return along it if you wish to attain the height again.

Such is the way towards your liberation and redemption, *such* the path towards ascent into the Luminous Heights! It simply cannot be otherwise! And since you now find yourselves in Darkness it is natural that everything hampers and opposes you in the *very* moment when through your resolution you want to proceed upwards into the Light!

You need only reflect a little in order to understand the correctness of the process and also to hit upon it yourselves!

But very many think that at the moment of their volition to ascend everything must reveal itself to them in sunshine and joy, that they must succeed in everything without a struggle, that their path is immediately smoothed for them, and that without effort sweet fruits will even drop into their laps as a reward from the very beginning.

And if it turns out quite differently they will quickly tire in their volition, give up and sink lazily back into their old course, if they do not even show enmity towards the person who pointed out to them the path leading to freedom, and who in their opinion caused them nothing but disquiet thereby.

Such are the majority of these earthmen! Stupid and lazy, presumptuous, demanding, and even requiring reward and gratitude when they *permit* the way to be *offered* to them that leads them out of the swamp in which they indolently wallow, finally to become engulfed therein.

But you who wish to fight for yourselves honestly, never forget that you are actually in the *Darkness*, where a good volition is immediately attacked. Your surroundings will also quickly seek to make their claims felt if you dare to sever yourselves from them. Although previously nobody ever bothered about what your soul desired, no one paid any attention as to whether it was already near to starvation and dying of thirst, nobody proved willing to refresh you...yet at the very moment you dare to place your foot on the only true path towards your redemption, *then* they suddenly and quickly make themselves heard so that you will not leave them.

They are then apparently worried about the welfare of your soul, although on more than one occasion they already proved that your soul *and* your life on earth were really of utter indifference to them!

It is so conspicuous that it even appears ridiculous, as can be frequently observed; and it clearly shows that all these dear earthly relatives or other acquaintances are nothing but blind tools of the Darkness, whose urge they obey without being conscious of it. If you do not then listen to them they will show through their actions that it was *not* really worry about you which caused them to do such things, for real concern would embrace love for one's neighbour. But love is not shown when they annoy you with malicious remarks or spiteful talking about you, when they even seek to harm you in some way or other!

Plainly and quickly hatred also flares up, which all that is dark harbours against anything striving for the Light! Observe this and now learn to recognise the Darkness *thereby!* Just *through this* you can also see that you have chosen the *right* path; for the Darkness *must reveal* itself in the way that is *solely* its own!

You will easily learn to differentiate! And finally, the real hatred of the

Darkness and also of its slaves is directed beyond you, towards Him Who offers the Word to human beings for their redemption!

Heed this! For in this way you will now immediately recognise all the henchmen of Lucifer who are already cast out in the Judgment!

Turn away from them, and no longer try to help them with the Word, for it shall no longer be offered to them! Henceforth you must *eliminate* them from it unless you yourselves want to suffer harm through ill-considered friendly advances!

Your love must be directed to the *Light* and to all those striving towards the Light through their pure and humble volition, but not to those who must be cast out of this Creation because they are harmful.

Above all the call is directed to *womanhood* once more! Through their more delicate intuitive perception womanhood has the ability to distinguish with infallible certainty what belongs to the Light and where there is still hope for it, and what irretrievably remains a prey to the Darkness and must perish with it.

For this, however, womanhood must first be purified itself and rise from the swamp into which it has frivolously led the whole of mankind! And only when vanity has fallen away from her will woman again be able to perceive intuitively in the *right* way!

Of all the developed ones womanhood has allowed itself to be seduced *too* willingly, to descend from that step which the Creator graciously assigned to woman, to spread ruination instead of God's blessing, and to distort all that is noble, when she was meant to *keep* it upright and also undimmed.

She tore womanly dignity down into the dust! Her every thought, her every wish was subjugated to the most base calculation, and all the innate charm bestowed upon her as a gift by the Creator, in order thereby to keep awake the longing for the beauty of the Luminous Heights in human souls, and to set ablaze the urge to protect all that is pure – this charm, so sublime in itself, was scornfully dragged down into the deep mire by womanhood on earth in order sinfully to exploit it for *earthly aims* only!

Never before has any creature of Creation sunk as deeply as has woman on earth!

The reciprocal action in the power of the Light now strikes with unfettered force every woman who does not wish to awaken for pure and high deeds, which through His Grace the Creator once placed in her hands and also endowed her accordingly!

It is womanhood, the woman, whom the Creator once chose to be the Guardian of the Flame of Holy Longing for the Light in all His Creations, bestowing the most delicate intuitive ability upon her for this purpose! She came into existence in order to absorb the radiations of the Light without hindrance, and to pass them on in the purest way to the man as well as to her particular surroundings.

For this reason she exercises an influence no matter where she may be! Through her nature she has been blessed for this! And she has used this Gift of Grace for the opposite!

The influence given to her by God she exercises to attain egoistic and often condemnable ends, instead of uplifting her surroundings, keeping the longing for the Light alive within the souls during their wanderings through the dense planes that have to serve for their development and maturing towards the Spiritual Height!

Thus they were meant to be a steadying and supporting influence to the wanderers, to offer upliftment and strength through their being, and to keep open the connection to the Light, the Prime Source of all Life!

They could have already turned this earth into a Paradise in the World of Gross Matter, swinging joyously in the purest Will of the Almighty!

The Guardian of the Flame of Holy Longing for the Light, however, has failed as no creature has ever failed before, because she was equipped with gifts the possession of which should never have allowed her to fall! And she has dragged down an entire section of the World with her into the swamp of Darkness!

The way is far and great the exertion which still confronts *that* woman who longs to co-operate in the future. But again only if she really wishes to do so, will the Grace of the increased strength fall to her share! But she must not think it so easy! The high distinction of now again being permitted to become the Guardian of the Longing for the Light, to keep it alive in the material world through the purity of her womanly dignity, *must be won by severe exertion* through perpetual alertness and unswerving faith.

Wake up, woman of this earth! Become pure again and faithful in your thinking and your actions, and keep your entire volition firmly anchored in the Holiness of the Will of God!

MANY readers have not yet clearly pictured to themselves the gradations between the Primordial Beings, the Created Beings and the Developed Beings. In many conceptions thereof everything still appears to be markedly confused. And yet it is all quite simple!

This disorder only arises because man confuses the expressions somewhat, and pays insufficient attention to the strict boundaries existing in this matter.

For this reason it is best if he simply envisages Creation as explained to him *so far* with the gradations as follows: –

1. The Primordial Spiritual Part.
2. The Spiritual Part.
3. The Material Part.

It can also be described as: –

1. Primordial Creation.
2. Creation.
3. Subsequent Creation.

In doing this the thought quite naturally occurs that the Primordial Beings are in Primordial Creation, the Created Beings in Creation, and the Developed Beings in Subsequent Creation.

These are not actually wrong designations if one wishes to describe the whole of Creation in big outlines only. When dealing with the matter more closely, however, the division must be more precise and extended even further, although this changes nothing in the basic expressions.

In more accurate explanations there also occur many intermediate steps, which cannot be avoided when a picture without gaps is to be given.

Today I will refrain from mentioning the substantiate part, because what is substantiate is present in all parts anyway; except to say that between the spiritual part and the material part there exists a big *layer* of a *special* kind of Substantiality (the World of Animism, the Animistic Sphere) which, however, need not be regarded as a part of Creation in itself; for in its activity this layer serves primarily to promote movement, thus to generate heat and form the material worlds; and therefore does not in itself form a distinct part of Creation.

This animistic layer does not need to be mentioned as a *part* of Creation, but as a *species* of Creation which, through setting into motion and forming, belongs to the material part of Creation.

I purposely speak of the foundations of Creation as it has been *so far* explained; for I have not yet finished with it by a long chalk, and gradually I must stretch everything so far described much further even, as I have always done bit by bit already. This necessitates inserting new sections in that which has been explained in the past, thus extending your view. To have stated everything at once would have been too much for the human spirit!

Even with this method as prepared by myself, he will still have to summon all his strength in order to be able to make a knowledge of it to some extent his own!

Let us not speak today about Primordial Creation, Creation and Subsequent Creation, but basically simply about the Primordial Spiritual Part, the Spiritual Part, and the Material Part. Then man can no longer confuse everything so easily!

I myself, however, *had* to mention *all* the designations possible for this, so that they may be used for stricter divisions of the gradations.

Gradually they shall penetrate to human knowledge ever more clearly and definitely, and in spite of their comprehensiveness they must no longer cause any confusion!

As foremost and strongest in Creation there is the *Primordial Spiritual* Part of Creation. This consists of *two* basic sections. The uppermost, highest section of the Primordial Spiritual Realm carries the actual *Primordial* Beings, who immediately came into existence as *fully matured* from the radiations of Parsifal, and did not need any development. This section reaches as far as Vasitha, whose activities lie at the boundary downwards.*

The second section holds developed ones in the Primordial Spiritual Realm. Therefore children are to be found there for the first time, which do not appear in the uppermost section; for children can only exist where development takes place.

Both sections, however, have the *Primordial Spiritual* in common. But

* Lecture: "The Primordial Spiritual Spheres V."

only the *uppermost* section can be called *Primordial Creation* in the right sense, and only the Primordial Spiritual Beings dwelling therein can be considered the real Primordial Beings.

With this I stretch out Creation a little for the better understanding of the human spirit in Subsequent Creation!

We cannot therefore actually talk of a Primordial Creation reaching down as far as Patmos, as we have done in the past for the sake of greater simplicity. But to be more strict we must already here speak of a *Primordial Creation* which is uppermost and which came into existence in full maturity, and of a developed Primordial Spiritual Creation following the first, while both sections together form the *Primordial Spiritual Realm* or the Primordial Spiritual Part of Creation.

Primordial Spiritual or *the Primordial Spiritual Realm* is therefore the great collective designation for the uppermost part of Creation, considered as a *species* of Creation, whereas the designation Primordial Creation in the stricter sense applies only to the highest part of it.

If now we wish to penetrate further into the knowledge of Creation, then we must no longer take the Primordial Spiritual and Primordial Creation as *one* conception, as was done up till now.

It is true, Primordial Creation is Primordial Spiritual, but there is also a world of development in the Primordial Spiritual which is below Primordial Creation proper and, connected with the latter, they both form the Primordial Spiritual Realm, where there are consequently Primordial Spiritual Primordial Beings who were immediately able to be fully matured without any transition as being the strongest and most powerful ones; and then following, Primordial Spiritual Developed Beings, who must begin their life as children.

The first section, Primordial Creation, comprises three principal steps or planes; the second section of the Primordial Spiritual Realm contains four. Consequently there are *seven* basic steps, which are again divided into many sub-divisions.

This Primordial Spiritual Realm comprising so many sections is followed by the great *Spiritual* Realm.

The Spiritual is not perchance a weaker species issuing from the Primordial Spiritual, but a species *alien* to the Primordial Spiritual which, however, is really weaker, and therefore needs a greater distance from the Primordial Light in order to be able to form and in part to become conscious.

Therefore it sinks down further in order to be able to form a realm at a greater distance from the Light; however, it has no share in the Primordial Spiritual but exists by itself.

It is all so easy and natural, and yet difficult to explain in a way that will initiate the human spirits into a knowledge which lies above their origin.

However, you must now grasp the connection between all the happenings so that you do not dangle about as an ignorant appendage in the rotation of this Creation with the same discordant buzz as a humming top, because you do not manage to obey it like faithful children.

You do not wish to fulfil the word "Become like children!", and thus there remains as the last of all help for your salvation this one way only – the *knowledge* of Creation!

You must at least know so much about it that you are able to adjust yourselves to the lawful swinging, which will uplift you and lead you along, or which in destroying you flings you as chaff far out into disintegration.

The swinging is intensified at present for the purpose of the great purification, and is carried by the Omnipotence of God. It therefore irresistibly forces each creature to swing along harmoniously or to perish in the wild pain of the most boundless despair, which as a consequence of wayward stubbornness arises out of the hopelessness brought about by a final recognition that it is on the wrong path, and has no prospect of turning back. For this reason seek to assimilate the knowledge of the Truth, which grants you support and leads straight to the goal.

If you look around you in an alert manner you can immediately recognise the fact that you really have the Word of Truth in my Message; for your entire life on earth in the past, as well as the new experience of every moment outwardly and inwardly, will become absolutely clear to you as soon as you illuminate and regard it from what my Message contains.

Not a single question remains unsolved for you; a great understanding arises within you for the working of that which has so far been a mystery to you, of the adamantine Laws in Creation, the Laws which guide you with the results of your volition; and as a crown for all your trouble there comes the wonderful divining of a Wisdom, of an Omnipotence, of a Love and of a Justice that can only issue from *God*, Whose Being you therewith discover!

But let us return to Creation!

The Primordial Spiritual Realm is then joined by the *Spiritual* Realm, the Spiritual to be considered as a *different* species and not as a weaker residue of the Primordial Spiritual.

After crossing the boundary at a certain distance from the Light, the boundary necessary for the possibility to form the Spiritual, there also come into immediate existence in the Spiritual, without any transition for development, fully matured spirits which must be called *Created Beings,* in contradistinction to the Primordial Beings in the Primordial Spiritual.

Thus the Created Beings are the strongest and most powerful in the Spiritual, similar to the Primordial Beings in the Primordial Spiritual, which was already able to form earlier.

And just as previously in the Primordial Spiritual, there is also a second section in the Spiritual in need of development, and where there are consequently children in addition to those who have matured through development. These two sections together form the Spiritual Part of Creation.

This Spiritual Part is then again joined by a large ring of very special animistic species enclosing the Material Part, affecting it, penetrating it, moving it, and thereby bringing heat and forming.

The Material Part of Creation in turn also has two sections. The first part, Ethereal Matter, forms immediately through the influence of the animistic, because it can easily be penetrated. The second part, Gross Matter, must first owing to its greater density go through a process of development with the help of the elementals. Naturally these two basic sections also fall into many sub-divisions.

Each section of the species of Creation splits into many planes, of which each individual plane is again so multiform that it appears like a huge world in itself.

However, I shall only accurately explain to you *what* comes within the boundaries of your human spirit! This is already so vast that your spirit must bestir itself specially, indeed perpetually without interruption, in order to grasp aright here on earth one *part* only. But this part brings you so far that you cannot easily get lost!

You can work yourselves laboriously out of the swamp of your intellectual conceit with the true *knowledge* only, for you can now no longer become *children* in spirit. Today you lack every capacity to devote yourselves to high guidance without contradiction, in a childlike and confident way, without worrying; for the misguided and too highly-strung activity of your earthly intellect no longer permits this!

Thus there is only *one* way left to you for your salvation – *the path of true knowledge* which leads from faith to conviction!

With the Message I have given I wish to help you to proceed along this path! But do exert yourselves to absorb this knowledge inwardly, and to keep it alive so that you will never again lose it but take it along with you on all your paths!

The word will then come true which has already remained alive in people's sayings since olden times: "The more man becomes capable of advancing in true knowledge, the more clearly he recognises the fact that in reality...he knows nothing!"

Expressed in other words: "One who is really knowing becomes small within himself before that greatness, the traces of which he finds in the process of becoming knowing! This means that he becomes humble and loses the conceit that keeps the human spirit imprisoned, he becomes free and rises up!"

Try to engrave upon your mind today what I have already said in my lectures, but of which you do not appear to have formed the right picture for yourselves after all, at least not all of you, namely that in the gradation the Created Beings do not immediately follow the Primordial Beings of the Primordial Spiritual Realm, but first the developed Primordial Beings in the lower part of the Primordial Spiritual Realm form a big intermediate step.

Only thereafter follow as the uppermost in the Spiritual Realm the Created Beings, which are not Primordial Spiritual but Spiritual, as an entirely different species, which are then again followed by Developed Spiritual Beings.

But from there we are still far, very far away from the Worlds of Matter, before which there swings the ring of the special kind of animistic powers, which I want to discuss more closely only later, because they work with you very closely and you could not remain in the World of Matter at all without their help.

Without this help your development would also be impossible. You would have to remain spirit-germs with the burning desire to be able to become conscious through the Grace of God, of the Only One, of the Almighty!

However, with the abnormal contention that they must come within the realm of saga and legend, because you blocked the ability to see and hear them, you disdain to give thanks for the necessary activity of those always ready to help from the animistic ring around the Worlds of Matter.

So often have you smiled scornfully whenever this was discussed, and you have no idea how ridiculous *you* made *yourselves* in doing so, and what a repulsive effect you were bound to have upon the helpers so urgently necessary for you!

There is much you have to make good and retrieve in order to mend the rungs in the ladder for the upward climb of the spirit, the rungs which you have so frivolously and presumptuously broken. But you cannot stride upwards without them. The foot of the spirit *needs* this support and cannot miss one of these rungs.

In these brief explanations I have not mentioned that Sphere which surpasses by far the magnitude of all the combined rings of Creation, the Sphere which is in the immediate radiation of God and which we called the Divine Sphere. I shall probably never again revert to this subject, because man is and always will remain too far away from it. The descriptions I gave about it so far he only needed in order to be able at least once to form a coherent picture from the Origin of all Life downwards.

Learn, you men, for it is high time!

SOUL

MANY people who have absorbed my Message very well are nevertheless not yet quite clear about the expression "soul"! But it is necessary to be clear about this too!

It is just about the soul that mankind have always talked much too much, thus forming an everyday picture which in its superficiality has become a common conception containing nothing whatever!

Whenever the word "soul" is mentioned it rises before man like a discoloured and well-thumbed painting. Faded and devoid of meaning, it passes quietly by them. It can tell the individual nothing because it has been used too much!

But just because it can no longer say anything it was gladly appropriated by *those* people who, with meaningless eloquence, wish to let their false light shine on fields that could not be opened to human knowledge because the human being of today keeps himself closed to them.

Those very people also fall into this category who pretend to deal seriously with the subject. They keep themselves closed to it on account of their wrong way of seeking that is no seeking, because they approach such work with preconceived and much too narrowly limited opinions, which work they want to press into the interpretation of the earthbound intellect, whereas the intellect can never attain to the possibility of absorbing anything thereof of its own accord.

Give a magnifying glass which has been ground for short-sightedness to a far-sighted eye ... you will see that the eye cannot recognise anything with it!

It is the same with the activity of these seeking ones whose work is based on erroneous principles from the start. If they can find anything at all it will only appear blurred and distorted, and in no case will it correspond with the facts!

And the expression "soul" was also pushed into this seemingly obscure pool of conceptions, which appeared always distorted for lack of sufficient support, but it was rendered in such a way as if based on firm knowledge.

This was dared because each one said to himself that in any case there was nobody who could refute this assertion!

However, all this has become so deep-rooted that nobody now wants to relinquish it, because an unstable and unlimited picture presents itself ever again at mention of the word "soul".

Man probably imagines that he cannot so easily go astray if he leaves as extensive a picture as possible instead of drawing a strict boundary.

But that which is extensive does not at the same time convey anything definite; it is difficult to survey, if not vague and indistinct, as in this case. It does not give you anything, because it is not right.

For this reason I once again wish to explain in clear words what *soul* actually *is,* so that you will at last see it absolutely clearly and no longer vaguely make use of expressions, the true meaning of which you really do not know.

The fact that people talked so much about the soul was also due to the *spirit* of man not bestirring itself sufficiently to show that it *also* exists.

That people always spoke of their soul only, and preferred to imagine the spirit as a product of the earthbound intellect, was really the best and most striking evidence of the true and sad condition of all mankind of the present time!

The soul was considered the innermost and that was all, because the spirit indeed is asleep, or at least much too weak and indolent in order to make itself noticeable as such. For this reason, with apparent justification, it played a subordinate role. It, the spirit which is really *everything,* and also the only thing that really *lives* within man or, better said, that *should* live but which alas sleeps!

From many well-known designations the fact can be quite clearly seen that the spirit had to content itself with a subordinate role. For example, man thinks about spirits in the first place as ghosts, and says they "haunt" this or that.

Wherever the expression "spirit" (ghost) is used in ordinary conversation there is always something associated with it which is either unwelcome and which one would rather avoid, or which is a little doubtful, not quite clean or even malicious; in short, something that manifests and takes effect in an inferior manner, except when the term "spirit" is meant to relate to the intellect.

In such cases where the expression is used in connection with the intellect it even assumes a kind of respect. *So* badly distorted is the pseudo-knowledge in these fields! You only need to consider these two expressions by interpreting them according to present conceptions:

Spiritualised (intellectualised) and *soulful!*

According to the old habit you will also here instinctively place the expression "spiritualised" (intellectualised) closer to earthly, colder activity, i. e., to masculine activity, especially to intellectual knowledge, and you will intuitively sense the expression "soulful" as being more womanly, warmer, more exalted, but at the same time also more vague, not to be bound in words, and as being less earthly. In other words: Of greater intensity, but indefinite, and therefore without strict boundaries, being more unearthly.

Just try it, you are sure to find the confirmation within yourselves!

These are the fruits of men's opinions, which were so wrong and bound to bring wrong conceptions, because the *spirit's* connection with its spiritual home had been cut off, and consequently it was also cut off from the supplies of power from the Light.

It was bound to become stunted and also forgotten, because here on earth it remained immured in the physical bodies, and thus as a matter of course all the opinions were also bound to change correspondingly.

A person who disappears in lifelong imprisonment is soon forgotten by the public, while all those who did not at one time live in his immediate vicinity know nothing about him whatever.

It is the same with the spirit during its captivity on earth!

However, you already know through the Message that it is this spirit which *alone* turns man into a human being – that man can only become a human being through the spirit!

This again proves that all those creatures on earth today who keep their spirit imprisoned cannot be regarded by the Light as human beings either!

The animal has nothing of the spirit, therefore it can never become a human being. And that man who buries his spirit and does not let it work, which is just what makes him a human being, is in reality no human being!

At this point we arrive at a fact which has so far been observed too little: I say that it is the spirit which stamps a man as a human being, which makes him one. The expression "to *make* a human being" contains the hint that *only* through its *activity* does the spirit form the creature into a human being!

Therefore to carry the spirit within does not suffice to be a human being, for a creature does not become a human being unless it allows the spirit *as such* to *work* within!

Take this as a basis for your life on earth! Take this as a basic conception for your future life here on earth! It will then become evident of its own accord outside the coarse World of Matter as soon as you no longer wear your physical body.

But whoever allows his spirit to *work* within himself as such will never again be able to let the Darkness arise anew, nor would he let himself be caught by the Darkness.

You were allowed to recognise, and you must now also see the end to which everything leads when the spirit within men cannot come to activity, because it is gagged and kept away from any supply of power from the All-Holy Light of God!

Just as only *he* who allows the spirit to work within himself is considered a human being by the Light, so shall it also become on this earth! *That is the foundation for ascent and for peace!*

For whoever allows the spirit to come to activity within himself can *only* walk on the path to the Light. This will ennoble and uplift him ever more, so that finally wherever he goes he will spread blessing around him!

Now I wish to repeat what the soul is, so that you will drop all the old opinions and henceforward have a firm support in this matter!

It is best if you first of all tell yourselves that before all the gross material creatures on earth it is the *spirit* that makes man a *human being*.

But we may equally well and justifiably declare that the *spirit is* the real *human being*, which must develop in various cloaks from the germ to completion, because it always carries the urge to do so within itself.

The outermost point of its development (which as being farthest away from the Light is also *that* point where the spirit under the pressure of the heaviest, densest cloak must develop its own volition to the greatest strength, whereby it can and also must become aglow to enable it to ascend closer to the Light again) in Ephesus is the gross material substance of this earth.

Therewith the sojourn on earth becomes the *turning-point* of all the wanderings! Thus it is especially important!

But it was just here on earth that the spirit was fettered and walled-in by men themselves through the wrong volition under the influence of the creeping Darkness. Thus at the very place where it was meant to achieve the most resplendent radiance through the most intense and strong activity, the spirit was compelled to inactivity from the very outset, which brought in its train the failure of mankind.

Therefore the activity of the Darkness is most intense at this turning-point which is so important for the human spirit, and consequently the battle is fought out *here*. The end of the struggle must bring the complete defeat and destruction of Darkness if humanity on earth is ever again to be helped so that they will not become utterly lost. –

Thus the Darkness has always been most actively astir here on earth, because it is here that the turning-point of the wanderings of the human spirit is formed; and secondly, because it was easiest for the Darkness to interfere just here, as here man is furthest away from the starting-point of the helping power of the Light, and can therefore become more easily susceptible to other influences.

Nevertheless this is no excuse for the falling human spirit; for he only needed to *will* through honest prayer in order to receive a pure connection with the Power of the Light immediately. Besides, on account of its density, his physical body in particular gives him a special protection against influences of another nature than those which he himself seeks to bring along through his wishes.

However, you already know all this through the Message, if you *wish* to find it therein!

Therefore think of the *spirit* as being the real essence of man, as the core wearing many cloaks for the purpose of development and unfolding its inherent strength, which core must rise to the most severe test through the physical body in order to attain to victorious perfection.

These ever-increasing loading tests, however, are through their simultaneous reciprocal effect also the furthering stages of development, the earth thereby being the outermost plane for the turning.

Thus let us confidently assert that *the spirit is the actual human being,* all else being only the cloaks. By wearing them the spirit becomes strong, and the consequent compulsion to bestir itself ever more increases its glowing.

The glow into which the spirit is thus transposed does not die down when the cloaks are laid aside, but raises the spirit and leads it upwards into the Spiritual Realm.

Just through being forced to bestir itself under the weight of its cloaks the spirit finally grows so strong that it can bear the stronger pressure in the Spiritual Realm and remain conscious, something it was unable to do as a spirit-germ.

Such is the course of its development which took place for the sake of the spirit. The cloaks themselves are to be considered nothing but the means towards the end.

Therefore nothing changes when man on earth lays aside his physical body. He is still the same human being, only without the physical cloak, with which there also remains the so-called astral covering necessary for forming the gross material earthly body, and which originates from medium gross matter.

As soon as the heavy earthly body together with the astral body has fallen away the spirit remains clad in the more delicate cloaks only. In *this condition* the spirit is called *"the soul"* in contradistinction to the earthman of flesh and blood!

In his further ascent the human being also gradually lays aside all the other cloaks, until finally he only keeps the spirit body with a spiritual cloak, and in this way enters the Spiritual Realm as a spirit without any cloaks of other species.

This is a natural happening because then no alien cloak can keep him back any longer, and consequently he *must* in the natural course of things be uplifted through the species of his own nature.

Therefore *this* is the difference which very often causes you difficulty in your desire to understand, because you had no clarity and thus the conception of it remained vague.

In reality only *the spirit* comes into question with a human being. All the other designations depend purely on the cloaks he wears.

The spirit is everything, it is the *essence,* thus the human being. If together with the other cloaks he also wears the earthly cloak he is called earthman; when he lays aside his earthly cloak he is considered by earthman as soul; when he also lays aside these delicate cloaks he remains spirit alone, which he always has been in his species.

Thus the various designations are merely adjusted to the species of the cloaks, which could themselves be nothing without the spirit, which glows through them.

It is something other with animals; for they have within themselves something animistic *as soul,* the nature of which men do *not* possess!

Perhaps so many errors arose through men thinking that animals *also* have a soul which permits them to act. For this reason they think that, since man has spirit in addition, spirit and soul should be something separate and perhaps even able to work separately.

But this is *wrong,* for man has nothing of the species of the animal soul within himself. With man it is the spirit alone which glows through all the cloaks, even when it is walled-in and bound. When the spirit is fettered through the intellect the animating warmth of the spirit is directed into wrong channels, which the unperverted spirit would never itself choose if left a free hand.

However, the *Message* gives clear information about all the distortions and faults of men, especially about *how* man has to think and to act if he wishes to reach the Luminous Heights.

Today it is only a matter of clarifying once more the expression "soul", so that false thinking about it may come to an end.

The best for human beings would be if I would now proceed one step further in this, and tell you that *only the animal* has a *soul* that guides it. Man, however, has spirit!

Therewith the difference is *precisely* designated and in the right manner.

If up till now I have still used the expression "soul" it was only because it is so deeply rooted within you that you cannot so quickly give it up!

Now, however, I can see that it will leave nothing but errors unless I make a sharp cut of separation in this matter. Therefore as a foundation impress firmly upon your minds:

The *animal* has *soul,* but man has *spirit!*

In this way it is correct, although it now appears strange to you because you have often praised the soul. But, believe me, it is only being tied to the known expression which gives an uplifting feeling when you hear the word soul, as a consequence of the songs which you always sought to weave around the term "soul".

Now praise the *spirit* instead, and soon this expression will rise brilliantly before you, much clearer still and purer than the expression "soul" could ever give it to you!

Accustom yourselves to it, and then you will also have advanced one step further in the knowledge leading to the Truth!

However, it is solely as *the foundation of your thinking* that you shall now carry this difference knowingly within you. Besides this you may continue to retain the expression "soul" also for man, because otherwise it would be very difficult for you to keep the necessary steps of development properly separated.

The soul is the spirit which has already been severed from the World of Gross Matter and which *retains* both ethereal and animistic cloaks.

For your conception the spirit must remain soul until it lays aside the last cloak when, being nothing but spiritual, it is able to enter the Spiritual Realm.

If you carry the knowledge within you *in this way*, then the expression soul may also be appropriated and retained for men.

It is best if you form the development of the spirit-germ into these three sections:

Earthman – human soul – human spirit!

As long as you have the right conception thereof let it go at that, but otherwise it would not be advisable, because really the animal alone possesses a "soul" in *the truest sense.* A soul which is something for itself alone! Besides his spirit, however, man has no soul which is independent as such.

However, in connection with the human being you cannot very well state in place of soul: The spirit with cloaks, and just as little the veiled spirit, or later on the spirit without cloaks, the unveiled spirit.

This would actually be right, but it is too involved for the purpose of forming a conception!

Therefore we want to retain the former expression, as Jesus also did when He spoke of the soul. You will now understand even better His reference to the necessity for the soul to sever itself; for to sever the soul means nothing else than to lay aside the still existing cloaks holding back the spirit, thereby severing the latter from their heaviness and freeing it for further ascent.

But Jesus could not speak to the earthmen of that time in such an intellectually adapted manner. He had to express Himself more simply and thus retain the customary way.

It may remain in this way even today as long as you only know the precise facts!

Engrave it upon your minds:

The animal has a soul, but man has spirit!

NATURE

IN THE same way as the expression "soul" became a vague general conception among men, so is it also with the expression "nature"! This word has also been used far too often as a great collective conception for everything they liked to dispose of easily, without having to rack their brains over it. It was especially used for those things where man knew in advance that he would be unable to come to a clear solution.

How often is the word "natural" used without the user having anything definite in mind? Man speaks of being "close to nature", of beautiful nature, of boisterous nature, of natural instincts, and so on in numberless terms, by which they seek to define something in big outlines that can be more or less related to nature.

But what *is* nature? It is just this basic expression which must *first of all* be quite clearly understood before it is applied to every conceivable thing!

However, when you raise this question you will no doubt receive many explanations, presented with a greater or lesser degree of conviction as to the details; but you can clearly recognise from all this that men's conceptions in this matter are very varied, and lack a uniform knowledge.

For this reason let us open up a way in this matter so as to obtain a definite picture in our conception of this word "nature"!

The best thing to do is to divide the conception about this into *sections* in our imaginative faculty in order to arrive more easily at an understanding of the whole.

Let us first take the *coarse form* of "nature", thus the outward appearance! For the sake of simplicity I will make an exception and begin with the thinking of earthman, and only at the end shall I reverse everything so that the correct course, i.e., from above downwards, is again placed before your gaze.

When nature is considered in its coarsest sense, thus viewed with your physical eyes on earth, it comprises material substance which has been "set aglow" and consequently animated and formed. By material substance you must imagine the various layers of the World of Matter.

This includes in the first place all the pictures which you can perceive with your physical eyes, such as landscapes and all the stationary and mobile forms of plants and animals; expressed more comprehensively – everything you are able to perceive through your physical body with your gross material senses!

Excluded from this, however, is everything *men have formed artificially* whereby they introduce changes into what exists, as with houses and any other products. This has then ceased to count as nature.

Here we already come closer to a fundamental distinction: That which man *changes,* i.e., that which be does not leave in its original state, no longer belongs to nature in its *real* sense!

However, since I also say that nature in its outermost manifestation is the World of Gross Matter, which has been set aglow and thus animated and formed, and since you already know from my Message that *animistic* forces permeate and set the Worlds of Matter aglow, you can directly conclude from this that *nature* can only be *that* which is most closely associated with the *animistic forces.*

Here I am referring to *those* animistic (substantiate) forces which form a ring round the Worlds of Matter.

This is a very special species of which we must now soon speak. As a special species of Creation it must be separated from the great general conception of that which is Substantiate, which exists as a foundation in *all* spheres, reaching right up to the boundary where the Unsubstantiality of God begins.

The present conceptions of the Substantiate which I could already give you I shall have gradually to draw still further apart, if I wish to complete the picture which, with the increasing maturity of your spirit, you will be able to absorb.

Therefore nature is everything in the World of Matter which, being permeated and set aglow by the animistic forces (these I must yet describe more fully to you), was able to form and to unite, and which in its basic species was not changed by the human spirit.

Not to change the *basic species* given by the animistic – that is the prerequisite for the *correct* expression: "Nature"!

Thus the term "nature" is quite inseparably linked with the *animistic* which permeates the World of Matter. From this you can also rightly conclude that nature is not necessarily bound to matter but only to the *animistic,* and that to be natural, and nature in general, are the undistorted effects of animistic activity.

Thus step by step we come ever nearer to the Truth; for in going further we can now also conclude that nature and spirit can only be comprehended separately! Nature is based upon the activity of a very definite animistic species, while spirit, as you know, is something entirely different.

It is true that spirit is often placed right into the middle of nature through incarnations, but it *is* not nature nor a part of it, in the same way as nature is not a part of the human spirit either!

I know it is not easy for you to recognise clearly from these brief words what the question is, but if you delve into it properly you *will be able to* grasp it; and in the end it is your spirit above all which *must* become *mobile* through exerting itself to penetrate the Word which I can give you.

It is just the *exertion* required to achieve this which brings you the mobility that protects your spirit, keeping it from slumber and death, and pulling it up from the claws of the creeping Darkness.

Although people very often try with intellectual subtlety and malice to reproach me that it is just to gain influence that I oppress, scare and threaten men through my Word with hints as to the ever-lurking danger of spiritual slumber and death, I shall never cease to illustrate the dangers threatening your spirit, so that you will know them and no longer fall blindly into snares and temptations. For *I serve God* and not men! With this I give what *benefits* men, and not merely what pleases them in the earthly sense but kills them spiritually.

It is just that with which people seek to attack my Word maliciously in service to the Darkness (which is already defending itself desperately), it is *just that which gives evidence of nothing but the fact* that I serve God in truth and do not also try to please men with the Word in order to catch them for my Word!

Men *must* indeed be torn out of their self-chosen spiritual comfort, which can only put them to sleep instead of strengthening them and animating them. Just as Jesus once said admonishingly that only he who is born anew inwardly can enter the Kingdom of God, together with His often repeated reference to the fact that *everything* must become *new* in order to pass before God!

And ever again men themselves speak about these weighty words with a ringing sincerity of conviction as to the truth contained in them. But if they are confronted with the demand that they must *first* let themselves become new in spirit, then they cry out one lament after another, for they never thought about themselves in this respect!

Now they feel harassed in their comfort, and yet they were hoping to be admitted to Heaven with jubilant songs without themselves doing anything about it except to enjoy all the pleasures!

Now they try to drown the inconvenient Caller with their clamour in the conviction that they will once more accomplish the same as was done with Jesus, Whom they first morally branded and murdered as a criminal, rebel and blasphemer before all men, so that thereafter He could even be sentenced and killed with the apparent justification of the human laws!

Even if it is different in many things today there is no lack on earth of a cunning cleverness of the intellect which serves the Darkness for the purpose of skilfully distorting what is most simple and clear, and thus influencing the inoffensive and disinterested; in the same way as there have been at all times willing false witnesses, who can achieve much through envy and hatred or through the prospect of gain!

But the Holy Will of God is mightier than the actions of such people! It does not err in its adamantine Justice, as is possible among men!

Thus *in the end* all Darkness with its evil volition must serve only the Light, hence bear witness for the Light.

But those men who exert themselves seriously to grasp the Truth of God will learn from this, will recognise the Sublimity of God, His Wisdom and His Love, and serve Him joyfully!

Beware of the indolence of your spirit, of comfort and superficiality, you men, and remember the parable of the wise and the foolish virgins! It is plain enough in its great simplicity, so that *everybody* can easily grasp the sense. Act upon it inwardly, then all else will come of itself. Nothing can confuse you, for you go quietly and with firm strides along your path!

But now let us return to the expression "nature", the conception of which I wish to mediate to you as a necessity!

I have already explained the first and most dense section thereof in broad outline. As soon as man in his activities will, as a basis, allow nature really to remain nature, and will not seek to interfere with its species and change them, but simply achieve the upbuilding by fostering a healthy, i.e., an undistorted development, *then* he will also find and receive a crowning of his works in everything; which he could never previously hope for, because everything that has been forcibly perverted from its natural state can in its growth only bring forth what is distorted, which possesses neither firm support nor continual existence.

This, being fundamental, will also some time hence be of great value to the sciences. Only in the way in which nature, with its animistic working in accordance with the Laws of Creation, brings about unions of material substances, only *therein* lies an upbuilding power and radiation; whereas in the case of other unions devised by men, which do not precisely accord with these Laws, radiations form which harm one another, perhaps even destroy and disintegrate one another, of the actual final results of which men have no idea.

Nature in its perfection according to the Laws of Creation is the most beautiful gift that God presented to His creatures! It can bring *only* benefit as long as it is not distorted by change, and guided into wrong channels by the stubborn pseudo-knowledge of these earthmen!

Now let us pass over to a second section of "nature" which is not immediately visible to the physical eye!

This section consists mainly of *medium* gross matter, i.e., not the most dense and heavy kind which must be immediately perceptible to the earthly eye on account of its heaviness.

As regards medium gross matter the physical eye can only *observe* its *effects* in heavy gross matter. To these, for example, belong the strengthening of everything that was formed through being "set aglow", and its unfolding as it grows and ripens.

A third section of "nature" is the propagation, which occurs automatically at a very definite stage in the process of being set aglow and of development. The propagation in the "glowed-through" gross material substance has therefore nothing to do with the spirit, but belongs to *"nature"*!

Therefore the urge for propagation is *correctly* designated as a *natural instinct*. A very definite ripeness of the material substance, permeated and set aglow by the animistic, results in radiations which, when positive and negative kinds meet, unite and react upon the gross material, pressing upon it and causing it to become active.

The spirit has nothing to do with this, rather this activity is a *tribute to nature!* It stands quite apart from the spiritual, as I have already hinted once before.

If we therefore call this exchange of radiations and uniting a *tribute to nature* this is right; for this is the way of the entire World of Matter that has been permeated and set aglow by the animistic up to a certain definite degree. With it the World of Matter always seeks to bring about a renewal that accords with the Laws of Creation, which renewal on the one hand acts as a *preserving* agency and on the other hand requires *propagation*.

This Law of Nature as it manifests itself is the result of definite radiations. It brings about preservation through the accompanying stimulation and renewal of the cells.

This is the *primary* and main purpose of this tribute which nature demands from the mobile creatures. Nature knows no distinction therein and all the effects are useful and good.

But here again man has aggravated everything in his own case to the point of abnormality, and thus distorted and twisted it, although it is just he who could find a normal balance through special kinds of earthly activity.

But he pays no attention to what nature demands of him through its quiet reminder or warning. By exaggerating everything abnormally he wants to direct or master nature with his ignorant stubborn volition; he often wants to force nature in a manner that must harm and weaken gross matter or even destroy it; and thus in this, too, he has brought about devastation, just as he has done in the entire Creation.

The human being who was at first only a disturbing agent has now become a *destroying* one with everything he thinks and does, wherever he may be!

He has therewith placed himself *beneath* all creatures!

First learn thoroughly to know the *nature* from which you long ago turned aside, then it will be possible for you to become *human beings* again, human beings who live in the Creative Will of God, and who will thus reap health through nature for a joyful upbuilding activity on earth, which alone can help and further the spirit towards its necessary maturity.

SPIRIT-GERMS

SPIRIT-GERMS! I have often spoken about them already, explaining their development and course. I have also said that earthmen are developed from spirit-germs. Therefore it is *your* development, you human beings, that I am going to describe here!

Today I want to bring still closer to you the starting point of your development towards consciousness.

I have already spoken about a second and lower section in the Spiritual Part of Creation, in which the spiritual beings could not come into existence fully matured immediately, but must develop from children.

The developed ones of Subsequent Creation, to which you human beings also belong, still do *not* originate from this part. They only come from a precipitation thereof, which does not possess the strength to develop itself without outside influence.

This precipitation consists of the spirit seed-grains, of the spirit-germs, from which the developed human spirits of the Material Worlds evolve.

The precipitation sinks down from the Spiritual Part of Creation and thus enters into an animistic ring surrounding the Worlds of Matter.

I shall not yet speak about the process of attraction, of being set aglow, and the consequent changes in radiation, the process that takes place according to the Laws of Creation. Instead I only wish to talk about the *helpers* active therein, and of the individual happenings that can give a *picture* which will become understandable to you.

For as soon as I show you tangible *forms* in my descriptions you will then be able to envisage something very definite, something that nearly corresponds with the facts and helps your earthly understanding.

Thus I do not wish to explain *how* everything is fulfilled as it swings in the Law of Creation, but how it *manifests* in the process of forming itself.

In this animistic ring into which the spirit-germ sinks there exist entities of very different species, not intermingled with each other but again standing below one another on individual planes, according to the nature of the activity in which they swing.

Coming from the Spiritual, we find at the uppermost point of the ring wonderfully delicate female beings swinging in the rays of Love and Purity. These receive the spirit-germs and cover them with an animistic cloak with motherly solicitude. They then forward the thus-veiled spirit-germs, which still slumber in complete unconsciousness, into the hands of other female beings which stand nearer to the World of Ethereal Matter.

These in turn veil the germ with a second cloak, again of a different nature and corresponding with the *particular* surrounding in which these entities dwell. They then accompany the germs, which have through this process again become a little heavier, downwards to the topmost layer of the Ethereal World.

All these delicate female beings *support* with their help the lawful, automatic happenings. They are of perfect beauty and were in former times already known to many men, to whom they could occasionally show themselves here and there. They were called kind fairies, concerned with furthering the developing souls of men.

At the border of the Ethereal World other female beings once more await the descending spirit-germs in order to *tend* them lovingly. For *protection* there are also beings of a male nature at hand here, which do not work in this tending way but act more positively.

Thus the spirit-germ is guarded and cared for by animistic helpers while still unconsciously following its urge towards the possibility of becoming self-conscious, moving ever further onwards until it strikes a density in the Ethereal World which no longer permits it to travel further with the unconscious urge. Thus its gliding down comes to a halt, and it must tarry awhile to awaken for development before it can continue its journey.

This is again quite a natural process, conditioned by the nature of the surroundings, but a great turning-point for the spirit-germs. They are now in a plane of the Ethereal World, the density of which retains them, and as a result their unconscious wandering is brought to an end.

Thus they suddenly lie softly embedded in a layer which halts their progress. Only an awakening volition, even if but weak yet nevertheless already *conscious*, can bring up the strength which will enable them to wander through and recognise their surroundings and travel further.

Just at this point I must proceed slowly and especially carefully with my explanations, so that men can form the right picture thereof and nothing is displaced.

For here, where the spirit-germs in their initial unconscious wandering are literally bound to become stuck, due to a very definite density of the ethereal substance that is permeated with animistic streams, much happens affecting the path of the human spirit as it descends into the Worlds of Matter for the purpose of development, and also concerning the path upwards again after maturity has set in through development.

Just *this* layer is an important boundary plane in the existence of the human spirit. Therefore I want to dwell upon the subject a little, and speak more of it.

To the human spirit as it ascends this plane already appears immensely high and wondrous in its beauty. It stretches before the eyes bathed in a mild light; in a light which appears mild and yet which is much brighter than our sunshine here on earth. The rays have an awakening, furthering and strengthening effect.

This plane appears like a single endless series of gardens. One flower garden follows another over vast distances, each filled with beautiful flowers of all sizes and many colours; flowers which are tended by delicate beings and preserved and guarded by earnest, manly figures, who stride through the rows keeping order, watching and sorting.

Floral arbours stand all around, an invitation to rest and recuperate and ... for quiet and grateful self-communion!

The denser mass forming the ground is the ethereal substance which has held fast the spirit-germs, the mass in which they became stuck on their march.

And then the miraculous happens: While anchored in the ethereal ground and tended by the female animistic gardeners, the animistic cloak (in which the delicate female beings had veiled each of the spirit-germs after it had left the Spiritual Realm) develops under the radiation of this ethereal plane into a glorious flower in the cup of which the spirit-germ sleeps quietly and becomes ever stronger.

Due to the fact that it is roused through the effects which, in spite of the delicacy of this plane, are of a coarser nature than in the Spiritual Realm, and through the stronger sound of the activity, the spirit-germ can at a definite stage of ripeness, simultaneously with the bursting open of the bud, awaken to become gradually conscious. This coming to consciousness, however, is not yet self-consciousness.

There is still a big step from the *consciousness* of the awakening spirit to the *self-consciousness* of the matured spirit. The animal is also conscious, but it is never self-conscious! But let us not dwell upon this subject now!

Thus the bursting open of each bud is caused by the ripeness of the spirit-germ and is a natural, automatic effect, and the crack of this bursting open simultaneously awakens the spirit-germ to consciousness of its existence.

These processes can be explained accurately later on in all their details in order to find the lawfulness also inherent therein, through which everything becomes simple and natural, as can be recognised ever again in the whole of Creation.

The flower in whose cup the spirit-germ ripened needed only part of the spirit-germ's animistic cloak, whereas the other part remained round the spirit-germ and, during the awakening to consciousness, took on the human form of a child. Thus when the bud bursts open a child in human form lies in the cup of the flower.

Here, too, I must insert a few explanations before I can proceed further:

The spirit-germ had already passed through the care of *two* different female entities before it came into the hands of the female gardeners. We may call the two species "fairies". The first one, which received the spirit-germ as it left the Spiritual Realm, veiled it with a delicate cloak of the finest substance of this plane or ring, the second adding a cloak of a different kind.

Therefore when the spirit-germ came to a halt in fine matter it had already received two different cloaks through the fairies, thus two gifts from the fairies!

These happenings gave rise later on to the stories of the fairies giving presents at the children's cradle!

Now in the denser Ethereal World the outer cloak developed under the awakening radiations as the protecting flower-bud, and as it awakened the most delicate inner cloak immediately developed as a small body in human form. I also wish to explain why the finer cloak was bound to form into a *human body*.

In my Message I have already stated that when the *spirit* becomes conscious the human form also comes into existence, because the special nature of the spirit stipulates the human form.

This statement is made in broad outline. Now I must also enlarge upon this explanation and point out the fact that during this awakening to first consciousness the spirit-germ as such does *not* yet fashion itself into a human form, but only the delicate, animistic cloak which the spirit-germ received through the first fairy does so.

This cloak takes on human form because, in awakening, the spirit-germ already unconsciously sets this cloak aglow. Therefore, since it is "glowed through" *spiritually* even if unconsciously, the cloak, also adapting itself to the nature of being glowed through, consequently takes on human form as a matter of course.

As it becomes *self*-conscious on its wanderings through the Worlds of Matter, however, the spirit itself only gradually receives a more or less beautiful human form, depending on the nature and goal of its development. In this process the spirit's outer animistic and ethereal cloaks also change correspondingly.

As long as the spirit-germ remains in its merely conscious state, the animistic and ethereal cloaks are *always beautiful,* because only when the spirit becomes conscious of *itself*, thereby also receiving its free will, can the cloak be *mal*formed!

Just think carefully over this one sentence! You will find the solution to very many things contained therein!

You will also find the explanation as to why the beings consciously swinging in service to the Will of God are, without exception, of the most delicate beauty and perfect shape; for they all carry what is spiritual within themselves, but they cannot malform their figures through a self-consciousness that goes astray.

With this explanation you will also find a difference in that which in the past we have described under the great collective term "substantiate (animistic) beings". For the first time I bring you today a very definite gradation in this matter which, however, can for the moment only be explained in very broad outlines so that we do not widen the subject too much.

There are substantiate (animistic) beings carrying within themselves what is spiritual, and swinging and serving consciously in the Will of God; and also substantiate (animistic) beings which have nothing within themselves but that which is animistic, which lack what is spiritual. The animals, for instance, are part of the latter!

In order to prevent unnecessary questions in regard to this I want to mention at the same time that many divisions have yet to be made among the substantiate (animistic) helpers in Creation in order to give men a proper understanding. However, I shall always and only deal with each case individually as soon as an opportunity presents itself. In this way it will be easier to grasp. Men can themselves make classifications in regard to this from the Message later on.

Now I only wish to say that various classifications can also be made among the substantiate (animistic) beings carrying what is spiritual within themselves. That part which is by far the greater swings and serves *only in the Will of God,* and is completely independent of everything else.

A small part, however, which exists far from the Luminous Heights and works in close connection with the coarsest World of Matter, such as gnomes, etc., could like much else be temporarily influenced by the developed human spirits living in the World of Gross Matter.

But this possibility of the human spirit to influence has already been *annulled,* and even these little animistic (elemental) helpers stand at present only serving in the Will of God, during the Judgment and the time of the Millennium.

However, I must not yet go into these details; for I should divert you too much from the basic features, whereas now I wish above all to form a *basic knowledge* for you, which will give you the support you need for ascent and for perfecting your spirit, to mature it for the Luminous Heights.

All else must still be left aside until the great purification is over. Until then, however, you have no more time for details leading you into distances that will make your head swim!

You must first be able to *save* yourselves from the maze of pseudo-knowledge. That is now the most necessary thing for you to do, as you will recognise for yourselves later on!

But you must not take all this in too earthly a way when forming a picture of these happenings for yourselves, for ponderous earthliness does not come into the matter. And yet you will find similar happenings even in this *coarse* material world on earth.

Just take the butterfly developing under the protection of the cloak of the cocoon, which it bursts as soon as it has come to the necessary state of ripeness!

In the case of the spirit-germ the protective cloak receives the form of a flower, which through connection with the qualities of the soil in the Ethereal World must develop. The why and the how can also be precisely explained according to law, so that you will recognise that it can only occur in such a manner and form, and *not* by any means *otherwise*!

But years of explaining are still necessary to get to the point when you human beings will recognise with amazement the great simplicity penetrating Creation with a thousand different effects, and yet it is ever again precisely the same in all things, developing according to *one* basic Law.

You will be dumbfounded to realise that the difficulties of recognition have only arisen through you. You prepared them and made everything difficult for yourselves, you followed diversions and wrong courses which were bound to tire you, and which prevented you altogether from reaching the goal without help from the Light.

But if your intellectual conceit had not beguiled you so nastily, even if well-deservedly, and tricked you into so much artificial confusion, you would, with childlike confidence faithfully guided by the Light, have attained to full maturity easily and quickly on a path that held nothing but joy for you.

Now, however, it is very hard for you, for all the stones with which you blocked the path you must first remove again. Nor can you get with one leap into the right road, but you must retrace your steps over all diversions and wrong courses to that place where you turned aside, so that you can then set out once more at the beginning of the right road.

For this reason I first had to follow you on all your diversions and wrong courses so as to catch up with and call out to you, and carefully lead back those who would follow my call, because you are unable of your own accord to find a way out of the maze.

Not from the Light directly, but *on your own paths* I had to come to you when I wanted to bring you help!

Soon you will understand all this through recognition – it will not be very long till then! Then many things will become easier for you! –

Although *everything* in this Creation is of importance and has purpose, yet there is one straight line which offers you support as you become knowing, a support by means of which you can stride securely upwards.

And this support alone I want to give you *first of all*, because it is urgently necessary!

Today I offered you an entirely new picture of that plane which remains the actual starting-point for you earthmen, and which therefore plays a great part. You now know *how* you awaken and *where* this awakening takes place.

And this plane which mediates and renders possible your coming into the world, thus granting you a foundation stone for your personal existence as a human being, this plane is also important for the mature spirit which has developed aright in the sense of the Will of God and becomes capable of ascent.

Just as here the first cloak blossoms forth in human form, so the mature spirit again lays aside the same cloak on this plane. In ascending this first cloak becomes the last to be laid aside!

It remains behind on this plane in order to sever itself again, to disintegrate, to become submerged in the same species from which it first arose through the gift of the fairy.

However the cloak of a mature spirit brings along new powers refreshing and strengthening the same species, because it has been strongly penetrated by the glowing of the self-conscious spirit, which ascended in the right sense carrying this glowing within it.

As a result this species of cloak becomes all the more powerful in the animistic ring round the Worlds of Matter, and it can help even more strongly with the new development and awakening of many human spirit-germs.

After the last cloak of delicate animistic substance has been laid aside, the spirit as such, being conscious of itself, leaves this plane of gardens again for the Spiritual Realm which it once left as an unconscious spirit-germ, merely yielding to its undefined urge for development produced by the longing to become conscious.

Strive for the ability to enter the Spiritual Realm as fully matured spirits, you earthmen! You will then be united with *those* who could develop in the Spiritual without having to plunge into the World of Matter first.

You will then be no less strong than these, for you have overcome many obstacles, and through the requisite exertion you became a flame! There will then be joy over you, as is already indicated in the parable about the prodigal son!

I HAVE spoken of the awakening of the spirit-germs to consciousness of existence.

Just as there are spirit-germs as the last precipitation in the Spiritual Sphere, so there is finally also a precipitation of unconscious animistic-germs in the Animistic Sphere; and just as the spirit-germs sink into the most delicate layer of ethereal matter, so the animistic-germs sink into the most delicate layer of gross matter, where later on they work as developed animistic helpers.

These animistic-germs are also veiled with cloaks and, having thus become heavier, they sink into a somewhat denser layer of gross matter, where they likewise remain literally stuck.

Before proceeding with explanations, however, I must mention something of which I have already briefly spoken, but about which I so far intentionally avoided giving closer descriptions, because if I say too much prematurely it might easily lead to confusing entanglements for the human spirit.

I once pointed out the fact that, in addition to those things which have taken on form, there are also *currents* which flow through and penetrate Creation.

But with the expression "currents" we already have the form itself again; for it is actually so – they are streams flowing through Creation just as rivers flow upon the earth, and also like the currents of air!

And just as these two differing gross material species of currents exist on earth, so we also have two species that stream through Creation – animistic currents and spiritual currents!

There is nothing in Creation which is not formed. We have individual forms and collective forms. To the collective forms belong the currents of the species which work beside or, better said, *with* the special forms or individual forms. Each of these currents has very definite tasks which precisely correspond with their species; we may also say, which issue from the species.

Thus it is a spiritual current which among other things also guides the spirit-germs as long as they are unconscious along the path which brings them to where development may begin.

On this path the spirit-germs' inner urge to become conscious has a *pushing* and *pressing* effect upon them, while the effect of the stream of the spiritual current is to *carry* them along.

At the time when the first spirit-germs approached *that* part of the world which includes the earth, the World of Matter was not yet as dense as it is today; for it was only later on through men's volition developing in the wrong way that greater density and heaviness came about, resulting in a greater distancing from the Light and more sluggish and hampering movement.

In view of the lightness of the World of Matter at that time, the spirit-germ's inherent urge, together with being carried along by the stream, were sufficient for it to reach the first goal for development. Further development was also easier, since even the *faint* beginnings of consciousness provided a sufficient impulse to proceed along another stretch of the path.

All this has become considerably more difficult today!

Here I must again insert something! The sinking down of spirit-germs is a process which proceeds *without interruption* for Creation. When I formerly stated that a very definite stage of maturity must be present in the World of Matter for the reception of spirit-germs, and that this can no longer be repeated as the maturity increases, this did not concern the whole of Creation, but only *individual* celestial bodies such as *the earth*, for example!

Finally, only such human souls as were older, and which had already been previously incarnated, could come to the earth; those which have to complete their course in the closing of the cycles, but not spirit-germs, i. e., souls which have never before been in the dense World of Gross Matter.

But there are always parts in Creation prepared to receive spirit-germs which have already attained to consciousness of their existence, but which must first develop towards self-consciousness through experiencing.

As long as the human spirit leads nothing but a life of being conscious of its existence it must retain the name "spirit-germ", although its cloak may already bear the human form. Only with its further development towards self-consciousness does it cease to be a human spirit-*germ* and become a *human spirit!*

It is necessary to say this here in order to avoid misinterpretations or erroneous conceptions. That is why I have already mentioned in my last lecture that it is a big step from consciousness of existence to human self-consciousness, which latter alone brings in its train the *free* and conscious will to decide, but also the full responsibility for it.

As I proceed with my explanations I must make ever keener divisions in the conceptions, whereas in the past I could still leave many things under collective conceptions. This is not perhaps a sort of play upon words, which many clever intellectuals in their spiritual indolence held in readiness as a designation for certain passages in my Message; with which, however, they plainly enough showed nothing but their utter ignorance and lack of comprehension for the seriousness and greatness of the matter! Instead, it is an urgent and unavoidable necessity if man wants to fathom the movement of Creation at all!

Then he cannot get along for ever with a few earthly expressions, but he must in fact accommodate himself to the necessity of gradually learning ever more exact limits and of clearly weighing the real meaning of each individual word.

We must also do the same if we want to advance, and not come to a halt or leave unclarified areas behind us!

There must be movement in this, too, instead of rigid and stubborn adherence! When first I explain something in broad outlines I can name it differently than when I go into details and have to separate things more and more, all of which I could at first take as a collective conception.

And I must *always* give collective conceptions first in order to go into details *later on,* once your apprehending faculty has gained to some degree a clear picture of the collective conception; otherwise you would never be able to come to an understanding in view of the vast magnitude of Creation. You would quickly lose the firm soil of real knowledge, and fall into the desultory obscurities which are customary among men, and which characterise the adherents of the numerous sects and of the churches as well.

For this reason let such persons continue to talk! They only give evidence of their superficiality and of their dread of taking the trouble to go into things more closely. Follow me joyfully *in the way* in which I give it to you! Then you will gain nothing but benefit therefrom, for not only do I make it easier for the human spirit, but I first make it possible for him to grasp the magnitude at least in *those* parts with which he is connected and upon which his activity remains dependent.

Just as the spiritual currents carry the *spirit*-germs, so the animistic currents carry the *animistic*-germs along their courses. Only later on can one talk specifically about the starting-point, the species and activities of all these currents. As a beginning today let us simply accept the conception that all these currents, like the air and waters of the earth, are fructifying, preserving and purifying – in short furthering in every respect!

Moreover these currents were also in part already known to former earthmen!

But let us now return to the purpose of today's lecture after these digressions!

The animistic-germs are carried by currents of an animistic nature. Despite the animistic *basic species* of the currents there are, however, quite different, even many-sided individual species; and for this reason ever more side-currents seeking their own path gradually separate from the original main current as it follows its course through the various planes. For as the distance from the Light increases the various individual species separate as side-currents, which ultimately contain the whole of only *one* very definite species of being; and in obedience to the Law these side-currents only lead along with them the corresponding homogeneous species of animistic-germs.

In this way such animistic-germs proceed towards their destined places, fulfilling the Law of Creation. They are divided into such germs as are closely connected with flowers, with other plants, likewise with water, air, with the earth and rocks, with fire, and with many other individual things in the Worlds of Matter as well.

As the currents stream through the planes, the corresponding beings are always deposited in each individual plane, indeed in each intermediate plane as well – those beings that are of the same homogeneity as the plane where they are deposited! They stay behind in the plane where they have to work, because they become conscious there. All this takes place through the natural and most simple operation of the laws, in such a way that it could not possibly be different!

In each intermediate plane specific kinds of beings awaken to consciousness in a manner that in each case corresponds with their strength, and begin to work there in a forming, protecting and tending way.

Finally there remain in these currents merely those beings which can only come to consciousness on the celestial bodies of the *coarsest Worlds of Mat-*

ter. And as the last deposit thereof there are also animistic-germs, which cannot immediately awaken in the coarse World of Matter, but which need a special development.

However, this again is only a large picture I am giving you for the time being, which you can best take in at first as if you were looking at a *flat* map, observing the courses of the streams, rivers and brooks with their many branches and apparently self-chosen paths!

Only *then* can you *round off* the picture and envisage that water arteries also stream through the interior of the earth and not merely flow on the surface, and the same with air currents. In this way you will have finally gained in picture form a part of *this* kind of happening in Creation.

If men of the earth would swing and serve *aright* in the Will of God, the earth would actually be a harmonious although coarse reproduction of Creation. It is only due to the perversity of mankind that this has not yet happened.

Now let us at last talk of animistic-*germs*, which we had taken as our subject. Those that are most closely related to the spirit-germs of earthmen as regards their development are the small flower-elves of the earth.

As you regard it, these awaken in the cups of earthly flowers, but not in the way you imagine it! It is true that they are in the flower-buds which form their coarsest protective cloak until they awaken, but there is something else in addition.

In reality they lie softly embedded in a layer of fine, delicate gross matter, not visible to you in the earthly sense. But at the same time they also lie in a flower-bud of the earth. The delicate layer of gross matter not only penetrates the bud but also the entire earth and its surroundings, something which is invisible to you.

It is in this layer that the actual development to consciousness of the flower-elves takes place, while the earthly flower-bud remains but the coarsest *outer* protection, of which the flower-elves are pretty well *independent* despite a certain connection.

Nor do they die as the flowers wither, but their development continues through their helpful tending of new earthly flowers, and partly also of new elf-children. Their strength grows with their ability.

So it goes on and ever onwards to the point where they can lift themselves in full maturity to another and new field of activity; for as with the spirit-germ so with the animistic-germ...both are subject to *one Divine Law* of development which is uniform in its effect!

Nor are the small elves left unprotected from danger as they develop, so that their habitation, even while a flower-bud, could be eaten by animals or destroyed by an inconsiderate human hand, as it would seem in the gross material sense.

The flowers are, of course, *tended* by developed elves, but an elf-child does not live in every flower, only in those that are specially protected and inaccessible to danger, as far as one can speak of inaccessibility. Also in cases where danger approaches they are immediately carried away as long as they have not yet become conscious.

I first mention the flower-elves because they have always been and still are standing in the swinging of the Will of God. They *cannot* be influenced by the will of men, but they always weave and breathe in the vibrations of the Light!

In this fact lies the secret as to why *every* flower, even the most simple, is radiant with beauty; for the flower-elves stand in the Light! Owing to their delicacy they have female forms and, because they are attuned to the Light, they are of the most exquisite beauty!

On the basis of the Message you will now already be able to follow that there are also elves which have male forms according to their activity!

They are denser and more positive, because they occupy themselves with a harder material. The tree elf, for instance, has a male form.

The form and density always correspond with the activity!

Thus, because they are working with earth and rocks, the gnomes also have male forms. They are denser, while the nixies or water sprites of the liquid element, again bear female forms.

You yourselves can draw further conclusions and will always hit upon what is right, if you use the Message in which you find the Laws of Creation as a basis!

What is said here concerns the developed animistic beings of your surroundings on earth! Everything which is closely connected with the *coarsest* World of Matter can really only count on a result which is quickly visible through positive activity and in greater density. Therefore that which is male is always the part inclined towards what is denser and thus lower, the part which acts positively; on the other hand, that which is female is the part inclined towards the more delicate and thus higher, the part which receives negatively.

Such is the arrangement of Creation according to the Will of God, and only when man also adjusts himself accordingly and swings therein will real ascent come to him, which he cannot achieve in any other way. For then all his activity swings in the Cross of Creation, in which positive with negative, working actively and receiving passively, hold the balance!

And ever again it is still the *woman* of humanity who does *not* fill her post in Creation!

If you reflect upon all this quietly you can come to undreamed-of conclusions, and to clarifications that have so far seemed almost insoluble to you. But your intellect will not acquiesce so readily and quietly, but will ever again want to sow doubt in order to confuse you and thus hold you fast in the spell which it was able to inflict upon you almost unopposed during the past centuries.

There are probably many people in whom the questioning thought arises: And the furies? Do they not also have female forms although their activity is of a very positive nature?

Therefore I already want to deal with this subject now and explain to you: The furies exist in both male and female form, yet both have *one* aim alone in spite of their diverse effects ... destruction!

The furies, however, are *not animistic beings.* Such a thing does not originate from the Will of the Light! Furies are nothing but productions of men's volition. They belong to the demons that must immediately perish when men's volition improves and turns to the Light!

True, they are very dangerous, and in the Judgment they are set free so that they can rush upon all mankind! But they can only do harm where they can attach themselves, i. e., where they find homogeneous evil or fear in a person.

Through this the furies must also serve the Light, for they do away with the evil men on earth and thus further the great purification! As soon as this is completed the furies also obtain no further nourishment, and must automatically perish!

But whoever has fear in the Judgment lacks conviction about the Word of Truth, and thus also confidence in the Omnipotence of God and in His Justice, which so often manifest in the helping Love!

Such a person will then *rightly* fall a victim to his lukewarmness or indolence. He is *meant* to be seized and destroyed by the furies during the Judgment!

Therefore in the end *that* also is a simple happening which in its dreadfulness must proceed along the paths of the Holy Law of God!

The furies unleashed! This means they are not restrained, but for a time will be allowed to have a completely free run!

Men will not be protected therefrom, but abandoned to the raging!

However, it is quite natural that *those* people who have the right inner conviction and who are connected with the Light cannot be attacked, for no response can be found within them to which the furies can cling in order to confuse them.

During this raging those connected with the Light stand as if in a cloak which cannot be penetrated, and upon which every attacking evil volition injures itself. This cloak has automatically grown during the hours of danger through the firm trust in God.

But men who in their conceit or presumption think they are faithful, and yet have faith only in their church but not in *God,* and who are thus not inwardly alive, will be tossed hither and thither like a withered leaf in a storm. They must also perish in this turmoil unless they recognise in time through this happening that they have been hollow in their rigid belief, and ardently exert themselves to absorb life from the Light of Truth which shines above all the storms.

Remain wakeful and strong so that the furies cannot find support within you! Become in your deeds like the many small animistic helpers which in their faithful service are an example for men!

I HAVE already spoken several times about Creation's Ring of Animistic Substantiality, which embraces the Worlds of Matter as the transition from the spiritual to the material.

This substantiality is a very special species by itself and really forms the final ring for the entire Creation, and simultaneously also the bridge for Subsequent Creation.

Once again let us envisage everything outside the Divine Sphere, thus below the Grail Castle, in three big divisions!

Let us enumerate Primordial Creation as uppermost and first, Creation as second, and Subsequent Creation as third.

The Grail Castle itself is not strictly speaking part of Primordial Creation, but is something entirely by itself that is *above* Primordial Creation. The Grail Castle *stands!* I deliberately choose this expression, for the Grail Castle does not float, but is firmly anchored.

Also that part of it which is outside the Divine Sphere, from which Primordial Creation issues, is firmly connected with the Grail Castle in the Divine Sphere like an annexe, and is therewith anchored immovably in the Divine.

Down to that point the only activity is a streaming *down*wards and *up*wards of Divine Waves of Light. Only in the Grail Castle does a change in this activity take place, and outside the Castle, streaming downwards, the *rotational movement* sets in, bringing all the Creations into existence and keeping them in motion. Here, too, they are *held* by waves that are descending and rising!

Such is the large picture of the form in which all the movements take place!

I have already spoken in greater detail about the Primordial Creation and named the two basic divisions. They are Primordial Spiritual. The one part immediately took on form and came to consciousness, while the other could only develop to it. It is the same in Creation, which in the conception as being Spiritual we separated from the Primordial Spiritual.

Creation is also separated into two divisions. The first could again immediately take on form, and the second had to develop to this point.

After this comes as a termination the afore-mentioned ring of *that* substantiality of which you do not yet have a clear picture, because I have only made a slight reference to it in my past explanations.

Today let us name it as a division of Creation by itself – *the Ring of Animistic Substantiality!*

From now on we must understand by this *ring* something quite different from that which we simply called *the elemental* (animistic, substantiate) beings. Those which I have so far designated in this way are the Light-waves that have taken on form through their activity, which stream *downwards* and again *upwards,* thus being connected with the Grail Castle in a straight line or chain. They are not the *rotational* forces!

There lies the difference! The rotational forces are also formed in their working, but they are of a different nature and could only come into existence through the *intersection* of radiations. You do not yet know anything about this, though you already know many of them!

This rotational movement originates or begins with the separation of the positive from the negative, thus of the active from the passive, which occurs in the Grail Castle and which, at the beginning of today's explanations, I called the *change* in the currents – the rotational movement that results through the separation in the Castle.

As the radiations of the Light begin to cool off, the positive separates from the negative and through this *two* kinds of radiations form, whereas down to the Grail Castle there is only *one uniform* ray in activity fashioning the Divine Sphere, where all that has become form bears within itself both positive and negative in a harmonious union!

Picture all this to yourselves just as I sketch it with very simple strokes, then you will grasp it in the quickest and surest manner. Only then can you try to penetrate ever deeper through your desire to understand!

If you act in this way then the whole will gradually become alive before you, and as "knowing" onlookers you can let the floating and weaving of Creation pass before you in spirit.

However, if you should wish to try it the other way round and already at the first hearing seek to follow me with the power of your intellect, you will become stuck at my very first sentences and will never be able to attain to any goal.

You must absorb it *simply* and only *then,* by gradually following the individual strokes, can you let everything come to life within you! In this way you will succeed!

Therefore today we want to talk of the ring of animistic substantiality which forms the termination of all that is *mobile.*

Just as the precipitation of the spiritual is known to you as spirit-germs, so the ring of animistic substantiality can also be called a precipitation, though in quite a different way; which precipitation trickles and drops down from out of the *rotation* of the self-moving Creations, from out of the substantiate waves, in order to assemble at the termination of the Creations and to maintain itself through the attraction of the same basic species.

Therewith we again hit upon an extension of the conceptions of Creation!

Consequently we have *self-moving* parts, which include Primordial Creation and Creation, and then follows Subsequent Creation, unable to move of its own accord and needing to be driven.

The self-moving parts are activated by their own warmth, whereas Subsequent Creation, which must be set in motion, is activated by the effect of alien warmth. Thus individual parts thereof can also become cold when that which supplies warmth is withdrawn, something which is quite impossible in Primordial Creation and in Creation, because they possess their own warmth.

Pay strict attention to all the details I am telling you herewith, for they lay the foundation in advance for many further explanations, which will be of great use for every aspect of man's earthly life.

This ring of the animistic substantiate precipitation is *below* the spirit-germs, therefore below the ring of the spiritual precipitation, and forms the termination of all that is mobile; for also the ring of the spiritual precipitation as the last of the spiritual, and the ring of the animistic substantiate precipitation as the last of the substantiate, have their own movement and thus warmth within, although still unconscious in the beginning. *This is important to know!*

Then follow the various Worlds of Matter. They are called like this because they can only serve as cloaks and possess neither their own warmth nor movement. They must first be permeated with warmth before they pass on warmth, and they are again cold and immobile when the dispenser of warmth is withdrawn. *That* is the peculiarity shown *only* by the Worlds of Matter.

Now the expressions material and the World of Matter have not perhaps been named according to the material with which man on earth covers himself, but the reverse is the case. Earthman has caught up these designations and then transferred them according to the proper meaning also to his earthly products, with which he covers himself.

The ring of animistic substantiality, however, not only forms the *termination* of that which is mobile and has inherent warmth but, since this ring also contains warmth and movement in itself, it presses even further into the World of Matter, thus warming it up and driving it from static inactivity into rotational movement, which in turn warms it increasingly and causes it to glow through friction, as is conditioned by the density of its nature.

In the movement thus forcibly brought about the material substance *takes on form,* and permits the radiations to penetrate it very easily through this activity of the even greater warming of the driving animistic, in order to spread ever new warmth and thus movement for the forming.

After this comprehensive picture let us go into details! Thus we return to the ring of animistic substantiality, which serves as the bridge for the unwarmed and consequently immobile stratifications of all the Material Worlds.

In this ring of animistic substantiality the corresponding special types of all the animistic-germs draw closely together in accordance with the Law. Groups then form which may also be called centres or accumulations.

Thus, for example, there is a separation between the groups of *those* germs which, as they penetrate the Worlds of Matter, co-operate through their development and awakening in the forming and preservation of fire, water, air and earth, of rocks, plants, and also animals.

I have already spoken of the process of the *penetration* of the animistic-germs, and I only want to point especially *to the fact* that all this happening is carefully directed by animistic helpers, which *serve* like a chain in the straight streaming downward of the Light-waves from the Castle, and also help to guide them upwards again.

All this you already know, and you can easily put together the basic knowledge for this out of my Message, but you must proceed in this matter like children, who make the effort to put the parts of a Chinese puzzle together *correctly* until a very definite picture arises therefrom.

It is *in this way* that you must make use of the knowledge from the Message, for it contains the foundation stones for *all* knowledge, and gives explanations for *every* happening in the whole of Creation!

If you want to achieve clarity about some matter in Creation or in your own life, about how this experience in the effect of the Primordial Laws must absolutely take place, you only need to lift any one of the many little individual stones containing something of the question which moves you, from among all the precious stones that can be found in the Message as a treasure that wants to be unearthed for you.

Just as with the game of putting Chinese puzzles or toy constructions together, you then seek *to join from the Message* that which fits this first little individual part. Finally you will obtain in this way a large picture standing completely by itself and compact in itself, which gives you a precise answer in pictorial form of that weaving of Creation which you desire to know.

If you follow my advice you will always succeed in obtaining a solution to everything in a form which will *in any case* become intelligible to you, and which will never let you go astray.

Just place the individual stones *in such a way* that they will fit in *precisely with the first stone* which you take from the treasure for your question. It is all the same whether this stone indicates the centre or should lie only to one side. The others belonging to it can always and only be *so* dovetailed or added that the final result is the very picture you need for an answer and the clarification of your question!

The stones never let themselves be placed in any other way, and you immediately realise when you have put just one part wrongly. This part simply does not fit in with the whole, and thus compels you to put it where it belongs, or to leave it out altogether if it does not belong there.

When you do this just think of a Chinese puzzle, which results in complete pictures or constructions when the individual parts given in a definite form for this purpose are put together logically.

This is the way I have given you my Message, which contains *everything*, but which forces you *to co-operate in this yourselves!* It does not allow itself to be taken up lazily as something standing there complete, but upon each of your questions you must exert yourselves to extract from it and put together that which will form the perfect picture.

That is the peculiarity *of the Living Word,* which forms and educates you and forces you to movement of your spirit!

Should you put a picture together wrongly, through error or superficiality, you will quickly come to a stop and realise that it brings no harmony, perhaps because you put just one little stone in the wrong place or, according to its form, put it in such a way that it cannot fit *that* picture or construction you are striving for. Thus you cannot complete it, and must try ever again until it stands firmly and correctly put together before you!

Each stone can be used for *many* pictures, not only for one, but through its peculiarity you are forced to place it differently for each picture, always so that it will fit in exactly with the other stones.

If, however, the individual picture results in a complete whole, then you may be sure that your work in seeking was right!

You will never lack a stone in this, not the smallest part, for the Message contains *everything* you need! Just try it until this work becomes easy to you, then you will yourselves stand firmly in the entire Creation!

In my Word of the Message I give you the perfect "box of bricks" consisting of the best-cut precious stones, so that you can build with it yourselves! From the very beginning they are precisely arranged to meet all your needs. But you alone must construct the building, for this is how it is willed!

Now you know how you have to act, and I can proceed with my explanations about the animistic ring and its effect upon the Material Worlds, to which it simultaneously forms a bridge through its working, the ring which is really the termination of all that is mobile.

Among other species there has gathered in this ring an accumulation of a species of *that* animistic substantiate precipitation from which the animal soul with its many ramifications is formed.

It is just this part, however, which needs a very special course of instruction, which must be connected with *observation,* in order to arouse complete clearness in earthman, but at least I will give a few hints about this.

The soul of every animal *forms* itself, it puts itself together first, something which is indicated in the expression "to form".

To show the difference and make it easier to understand I point once again to the human spirit. The spirit of earthman already carries everything within itself in the spirit-germ and only needs to develop to become conscious.

The soul of the gross material animal, however, puts itself together first, it *forms* itself, so as gradually to become strong through development. As it becomes strong it is able to form ever more firmly and durably.

The soul of the animal that belongs to the World of Gross Matter can only gradually receive a permanent form. In most cases, following severance from the physical body, after a shorter or sometimes longer period the animal soul again loses its form and is absorbed by the accumulation of homogeneous species, absorbed as a homogeneous species which indeed brings *increased* warmth, but which does not yet remain in a stable form. Hence the expression "group soul"!

Only one thing can maintain the form of the animal soul, the strongest thing there is – *the love!*

If an animal has taken to loving a person it is thereby uplifted, and through the voluntary connection with the spirit it receives a supply of power which also keeps its soul together more firmly. But more about this later! There are not only animals from the terminating ring of the animistic but also in higher, even up to the highest planes.

In the very highest planes there are thus *knowing* animals which are perfectly pure in their serving.

It can also occur that animals from the higher planes are incarnated on earth for very special purposes. We will not deal with this now but remain with the animals that are known on earth, the souls of which form out of the animistic ring round the Worlds of Matter.

I only want to give *one* other hint about this concerning your nearest visible earthly environment, thus your gross material surroundings.

All forms that are *bound to a definite spot* on earth have *no soul of their own,* for it would indeed become too dependent upon that which approaches it and would thus be at the mercy of every arbitrary action in the World of Gross Matter.

But such a lack of balance is utterly impossible in the wise arrangement of the Creator in His Work!

That is why such forms have no souls of their own, but serve solely as habitations for beings which are quite independent of the forms, which forms they merely protect and tend.

Plants and rocks belong to these forms! Thus you will gain further enlightenment which can benefit you, through which you can clearly recognise wrong opinions.

Only those creatures which are *independent of a place,* such as animals which can move freely from their spot, have within themselves *a mobile core of their own* that guides them.

With animals this core is the animistic soul, with men it is the spirit! Plants and rocks, however, merely serve as habitations for alien entities that are independent, and which therefore cannot be called the soul of the forms concerned.

THE PRIMORDIAL SPIRITUAL PLANES I

For all those who have already absorbed my Message aright, for those *alone* will I again extend the picture of Creation a little further in order to increase their knowledge of it.

In this way you will be initiated into higher recognitions, which have not been given to mankind in the past because they would not have understood it, because they would have been far too immature spiritually to absorb it. And no man *himself, of his own accord,* could ever attain to these recognitions.

It is given as a grace from the Light! Often in the past I have spoken of the Primordial Beings who are active in Primordial Creation, the Primordial Spiritual Realm.

Instead of saying primordial spiritual I could with equal justification also use the expressions "highly spiritual" and "completely spiritual". I could likewise designate it as the *highest* spiritual. All would be correct!

But I preferred the term "primordial spiritual". It is the *strongest* out of the spiritual capable of becoming fully conscious of itself, and in remaining conscious also to be active, under the highest pressure of the Light which the spiritual as being spiritual can bear at all.

In becoming conscious of itself the form also simultaneously came into existence without having first to undergo a slow process of development, as becomes necessary in those spheres of movement of this Creation which lie deeper, which have cooled off even further, and which are consequently denser and also slower.

After the strongest out of the spiritual was immediately able to sever itself and take on form, remaining in the closest proximity to the Divine Sphere and held fast by the latter's strong attraction through the Light-Pressure, the remainder was pushed further away by this pressure because it was unable to resist and had to give way to the too strong pressure, after the strongest thereof had become form.

The spiritual species which had been pushed still further away and remain-

997

ed unformed was able to cool off even more in the greater distance from the Light, and with this a new world again came into existence; for in the cooling off that which was *this time* considered the strongest in the remainder of the spiritual could now again simultaneously release itself and take on form in order to be active in conscious state in this plane which had cooled off more.

However, the second as well as the first, the uppermost, plane contain many gradations within themselves, forming themselves with these gradations, which latter formed according to the *speed* of their ability to be conscious.

The differences therein were again conditioned by the varieties that even occur within the *homogeneous species,* in so far as they have a *greater* or *lesser* capacity to bear the nearness of the Light-Pressure.

Thus here, too, there are still fine distinctions. Therefore each plane of a definite homogeneous species has nevertheless within its boundaries numerous planes which can be active either nearer to the highest point of this corresponding plane or only further away.

This often results in barely noticeable transitions which are drawn in this way through the whole of Creation without interruption, resulting in glorious, absolutely gapless connections for the flowing through of the Light-Power – we may also call them steps which, despite their delicate nature, can never be surmounted upwards unless the corresponding degree of consistency in the homogeneous species has been attained for this purpose.

But the developed human spirits, to which earthmen belong, originate neither in the afore-mentioned first nor in the second collective spiritual plane, but they issue from the *last precipitation* of spiritual substance, which does not hold enough strength to enable it to form itself by becoming conscious in the second plane of the spirit.

Neither could this precipitation stay there because it was no longer able to withstand the pressure of the Light even at this more remote place, after *that* part had severed and formed itself which was able to do so on this second plane. Thus the part left over, being the last precipitation, had to recede still further into yet deeper cooling-off possibilities.

But here also, being the weakest part and last precipitation of the spiritual, it was not possible for this precipitation to come to consciousness *of its own accord* without receiving an impulse from outside. That is why they remained only human spirit-*germs*, capable of development it is true, and filled with the urge towards it by their spiritual nature. But they were not strong enough to awaken of *themselves*, and thus to take on form in the process of becoming conscious.

That alone is the place where the spirit of earthman as such *originates* in the great Creation; *there* arose and also is the Paradise of the human spirits that develop to completion, thus the plane from which they actually set out and likewise to which they return in the completion!

Looking downwards from above it lies at an immense depth, yet looking upwards from the earth it lies nevertheless at an indescribable height; for the planes of the Worlds of Matter, which are the spheres of development and fields of activity for the human spirits, are far flung!

Their inability to awaken of themselves, even at this outermost place which is furthest away from the Light and the last point of support of the spiritual, forces these spirit-germs as they follow the inner urge for development to move even further in order gradually to develop to spiritual consciousness by wandering through the more and more distant fine and coarse Worlds of Matter, because the friction and colliding therein due to the density and heaviness contribute to and compel them to awaken and grow strong.

That is the approximate picture of the growth of your human spirit!

Only to those who are to be taken seriously and to those who plead for it do I give the extended view into the wonderful Creation, which surrounds you as the Work of God in clear greatness, with the activity of the most perfect and thereby irrevocable self-acting laws.

To this there must later be added special descriptions about the origin and coming into existence of everything which, corresponding to its species, can be found in *every* Realm of Creation, such as plants, animals, soil, rocks, seas, air and fire, etc., which here on earth we can only consider as the coarsest reproductions, as are earthmen themselves!

It is a vast field, and yet no gaps shall be left, but everything only at its time! Now I am first giving only that with which earthman is connected in an absolutely straight line.

It remains unpleasant enough to know in what an unworthy manner earthly mankind have been exerting themselves for thousands of years to narrow and oppress in a destructive way their most valuable possession, indeed that which really makes them human beings – their *spirit!* So that now man on earth is even ashamed to speak of something *spiritual*, to admit to a spiritual experience! But it becomes agonising to experience ever again that men, with a stupidity which has an incredibly ridiculous effect, take this voluntarily enforced narrow-mindedness even for *cleverness*, regard it indeed as learnedness!

There is only *one* consolation in this matter – the knowledge of the *turning-point* in these things which is already so near at hand as nobody would divine or believe; and the knowledge of the fact that a part of these same men will then ashamedly look back to the time of their disgraceful aberration which separates them widely from their real humanity and human dignity, while the other part will no longer be a matter of concern, for it will have ceased to exist!

Only *with this* in view do I continue my explanations! –

However, I wish to lift the veil even more for the human spirit after having already given a very compact picture of the path of the Light down to him, along which path with its various anchorages the Light had to proceed each time help was extended from above, only in the end to be rewarded with outrageous conceit on the part of these small earthmen, as has always happened in the past!

It is true that revelations from these planes have often descended to you, but you only absorbed miserable fragments and formed them according to your human nature, so that the renditions can be found only as badly distorted fragments in legends and poetic writings. Confused and impossible according to the Laws of Creation in their presentation, interwoven with various happenings of a purely earthly nature...the result is a mixture which seems sublime to you, but which appears ridiculous when compared to the Truth, and only to be excused by your complete lack of knowledge!

Already before my Message people here and there heard of the existence of such planes, but they were unable to keep them apart and so, due to the usual conceit of human trying-to-be-clever, the most impossible productions arose!

It can readily be understood that serious people shook their heads and kept at a proper distance therefrom, while among enthusiasts and visionaries the most devastating aberrations arose, quite apart from the fact that especially the many small "would-be-greats" sought to use such opportunities to swing themselves upwards without effort, so as to be able at least *once* to satisfy their morbid craving for easily achieved respect, which propensity always clings to them.

All that resulted from this was a disgusting ethereal swamp which became a great danger to the human spirits, because it hindered them from taking up the Truth uninfluenced and thus recognising the *right* path to ascent!

Despite everything, however, it is *none the less* the *personal* and *free* will, and the result of a self-created indolence of the spirit of each individual, which hold him back from recognition.

Whoever exerts himself only *a little must* very soon clearly recognise the truth in these writings through his intuitive perception!

Let us take the legend about Parsifal! Starting in his thinking *from this small earth* man seeks to fathom and to find something about Parsifal in order to discover how this legend originated, came into existence.

No doubt these earthly writers had in mind earthly persons who gave an outward impulse to the *form* of the poetic production, but in their spiritual absorption as they worked they unconsciously drew some things from sources which they themselves did not know.

Since in the end, however, they again polished it up with their intellect, thus seeking to make it beautiful in the *earthly sense* and more easily intelligible, even the little which could flow to them from unknown planes was compressed into the World of Gross Matter, diminished and distorted!

It is not worth while to go especially into this with further explanations! I am giving what is *founded on fact,* and every person can take out of it for himself whatever his spirit is able to.

However, it is necessary at the outset to point to certain things which must clarify for many people much that is erroneous, and which will make many things easier for those who can be initiated into higher recognitions, because through this they will be able right from the beginning to swing themselves above all the wrong that has settled down on the earth.

There actually *is* a Castle where an Amfortas dwelt, who for a time was considered the first guardian there. In this Castle there is a vessel called the "Grail", which is faithfully guarded by the knights. It was indeed there that Amfortas actually met his downfall, and where a great helper was promised.

But this happened neither on earth nor in the high Light Castle of Primordial Creation!

The Castle which is revealed *there* (where Amfortas was) is even today still to be found as the highest point on a plane in which the *Created Beings* have their field of activity towards the developed ones. In their purest volition and worship of God they possess only an *imitation* of the Light Castle. This Light Castle radiates down from the highest place in Primordial Creation and, as the actual Castle of the Holy Grail, also forms the exit gate from the Divine Sphere of Radiation.

In this lower lying *imitation* Amfortas was once active, and he fell when he succumbed to the evil influence of Lucifer. His mistake was that by following this influence he once, for a short time, sought to devote himself comfortably to the enjoyment of a proud knightly life!

Therewith he stepped out of the harmony of the necessary movement of his plane, which movement the Primordial Law of Creation automatically compels him who wishes to stay on the same height to maintain. For a short time Amfortas came to a standstill, thereby hindering and creating a gap for the streaming through of the Power of the Light.

Thus his fall was unavoidable and it tore him down. The gap was the wound he carried. Upon the supplication of the faithful knighthood the coming of the helping Pure One who could arrest the destruction was proclaimed.

And Parsifal fulfilled the promise as He journeyed through all the parts of Creation, just as He fulfils all the promises that were ever given to the creatures of the entire Creation. But the fulfilment was entirely different to what is described in the poetic writings.

The description of Creation also brings full enlightenment about this, and eliminates all that has been wrong in the past.

Thus only parts of a revelation from the lowest *imitation of the Light Castle* could penetrate to the opened spirits of these earthly poets, who absorbed them during their work. They did not come from the luminous Grail Castle itself, for there it was impossible to proclaim Parsifal's coming, because Parsifal was and is the *First* in the whole of Creation, only with Him could the entire Creation come into existence. He is part of the God-Spirit Imanuel, anchored into the Primordial Spiritual in order to create the Primordial Spiritual.

It was out of His Light-Radiation that the Primordial Beings came into existence, and with them the Castle and everything that took on form. Thus He could not be proclaimed to anyone, because He Himself was the First and all else could only come into existence *after* Him. No one but He has ever been King of the Holy Grail!

For this reason it was only natural that the Castle of which the poets speak had to be *further down* than the actual Grail Castle, because later on Parsifal hastened through the world in order to redeem it from the evil influence of Lucifer, and to shackle him for the Kingdom of God lasting a thousand years in the World of Matter.

Thus during His wandering through all the parts of Creation He also came to that Castle which is wrongly described in the poetic writings. He made His entry there *as King of the Holy Grail,* Who He is from the beginning and will remain so eternally, because He Himself originates from the Light. Nor did He remain there, but in place of Amfortas appointed a new highest guardian for the vessel, which they honour as the *image* of the Holy Grail.

In the Holy Light Castle which surrounds the actual Grail it is absolutely impossible for any of Its guardians to be found wanting, because Parsifal remains present therein; in Whom an Unsubstantiate part of the Light Itself is anchored, which was guided down from out of Imanuel through the Primordial Queen Elizabeth at the Word of God: Let there be Light!

PARSIFAL! How well known is this word as such among earthmen, of whom none, however, has any idea as to the real significance!

A poetic work, a legend! This hits upon the right thing if they mean *that* which is known about the word today; for in reality it is nothing else but a legend that has become a poetic work, which as a fragment of a former knowledge has been preserved as such!

As I have already pointed out, it was always small fragments only which came down from spiritual planes into the gross matter of this earth long, long ago.

The authors of the Grail legends known *today* are by no means the first who concerned themselves with this and who, as they became absorbed in their work, were once again able to divine a few gleams of light.

Far, far back lies the time when the *first* hints as to the Light Castle and its inhabitants descended to the earth from the spiritual planes, together with the tidings of the Holy Grail.

At that time it was received with reverential awe and childlike confidence by the inhabitants of the earth, who were still working undisturbed in co-operation with the elemental beings, whose advice they liked to heed. Without knowing it the human beings in turn helped the elementals with the radiations of their spirit-sparks. Thus Creation increasingly unfolded itself in the World of Gross Matter with the spirit sparks, which gave promise of a wonderful blossoming.

At that time, long before the revolutionary changes which we know about today took place on earth, even before men made an idol of their intellect, thus bringing about their defection from the Light and their downfall, a connection with the Luminous Castle was created; for the rays could flow unhindered all the way down to the earth, and in these rays men on earth could already divine Parsifal.

But then, proceeding from the human beings, the reign of intellectual idolatry set in, causing the connection with the Light Castle to be cut off, which was automatically followed by ignorance about it, the impossibility of a spiritual divining through the intuitive perception.

Finally the ability to absorb anything of the *animistic* also dried up, and all the natural experiencing in the knowledge about the animistic helpers sank into the realm of fables, so that the development which up till then had been striving upwards in a straight line was quite unexpectedly torn apart.

If men had remained *as* they were at the time I have mentioned, when the first tidings of the Luminous Castle and of Parsifal came down to the earth, then through their steady ascent they would indeed be lords of all the World of Gross Matter today in the best upbuilding sense. Nor would any person have been destroyed during the revolutionary changes, which were bound to occur from time to time in the maturing development.

The great *catastrophes* were always a necessity of the development, but not the destruction of so many nations, something which has up till now always invariably remained connected with this.

If men had not frivolously and wantonly given up the connection with the animistic helpers and the Luminous Heights, they would always have been warned in time of any emergency and led away from the endangered regions in order to escape destruction! For that is how it also happened at the time when men allowed themselves willingly to be guided by the helpers, which the Creator assigned to them from the animistic and spiritual worlds, and with which they sought to maintain the connection with joy and gratitude.

But later on they always robbed themselves of these invaluable aids due to the conceited wanting-to-be-clever of their intellect, and thus several times they enforced their own painful destruction in the same way as they are now bringing it about again, because they no longer want to listen to the last calls from the Light and even think they know everything better, as was so often their attitude in the past!

Tribulation, despair and destruction are always and only the lawful reciprocal effects of wrong actions. Surely this is not difficult to grasp if one only *wills* it so! This contains such a simple and clear naturalness that you will later on hardly understand how it could happen that such a thing could be overlooked and not strictly heeded, in order not only to spare all personal suffering but even to change it into joy.

Today you yourselves see clearly enough that no person can really defend himself against this! No nation, nor a joint volition of the whole of mankind, would manage to achieve it; for every being in Creation remains nothing but a creature dependent upon the Will of God! It will *never* be otherwise!

Thus it was always and only the wrong action of submitting to the bound and binding intellect, to the natural consequences of which many individuals and whole nations were certain to fall a prey, because they kept themselves outside every possibility of salvation through higher guidance!

You can easily recognise the great simplicity of the effect of the Divine Laws therein, and also see what men missed for themselves.

With this I have given you a brief glimpse today into that great activity of Creation which caused men many a headache already, so that by way of the Message you can see that all the distress, all the fear and suffering can only be ascribed by man to himself; and he could have avoided a great deal had he not stubbornly entered upon wrong courses!

Through the Message you can clearly recognise and *substantiate every* happening that takes place in Creation. You know about the unalterable effects of the Laws of Creation, which I have explained to you, you know of their simplicity and greatness which can be easily surveyed.

You will experience ever more that, with the Message, I have given you the key to the right explanation of *every* happening, and therewith of the entire Creation!

Let your fervour and untiring watchfulness gradually fathom it, then you will have the path to eternal life, which you only need to tread in order to reach it. –

Thus primeval ages ago men had already received the first and right tidings about Parsifal. This knowledge was passed on by word of mouth from parents to children.

But through the retrogression in the purity of the connection with the activity of Creation, the transmission of the original knowledge also gradually became clouded. It was imperceptibly distorted and finally curtailed by the growing intellect, remaining only as a legend which no longer bore any resemblance to the former knowledge.

Those human beings who were striving for noble-mindedness continued to interest themselves in these fragmentary legends and tried to make something of them here on earth *gross materially*, because they imagined that the origin of these transmissions must once have existed in an *earthly* prototype ages ago.

They wanted to renew this, and they often tried to do so over great intervals of time. Thus it is that even today many an investigator imagines he has found an *origin* in one of the earthly attempts of past centuries, but without hitting on what is right therewith.

Man does *not* emerge from the confusion however hard he tries to exert himself, for he lacks connection with the reality, which I want to restore to him in order to eradicate all that is wrong!

Parsifal! He cannot be separated from Imanuel; for Imanuel is in Him and He works out of Parsifal. It may also be said that Parsifal is a cloak of Imanuel formed by the Primordial Queen Elizabeth, through which Imanuel, standing at the head of Creation, works; which Creation could only come into existence out of Him – it would not and simply could not exist otherwise; for Imanuel in Parsifal is in fact the origin and starting point of Creation.

He is the Creative Will of God and God is with Him, in Him. That something like this could be dragged down to become *that* figure which people imagine Parsifal to be today is only possible for this mankind on earth, who press everything into the dust through their intellect, which itself is born of the dust!

Whatever this mankind try to absorb with their intellect they consequently also press into the dust in the natural course of events, thus dragging it down into the range of the *earthly* ability to understand. With this everything is confined within the narrow limits of coarse matter, that which is highest being wrapped in the density and ponderousness of a slow movement in the zone of the most extreme cooling-off. And thus quite naturally it cannot even bear any resemblance to the reality of that which was so dragged down, which reality is found in altogether different conditions and in *such heights* as the human *spirit* is unable to grasp, much less the earthbound intellect!

The expression "to drag into the dust" does not here mean to press into the dirt, but merely to *make it earthly!*

The expressions "dust" and "born of the dust" are inserted in the place of the conception "gross matter", something which will perhaps be more easily understood by some men, because it is a popular saying.

Thus *that* is Parsifal! The *First* in Creation! He bears within Himself an *Unsubstantiate* core out of God, is connected with Imanuel and remains so connected in all eternity, because Imanuel works out of Him and thus rules the Creations. With this He is the King of all kings, the Son of the Light, also called the Prince of the Light!

Now compare this with the figure contained in the poetic writings! What an impossible caricature you see before you! But when one can overlook the whole and separate it into *three great sections,* it can readily be understood how all this happened.

But let each of these three sections, one by one, come to life in picture form in front of your spirit! Only in this way can you survey the *whole* and understand what I am trying to make clear to you!

The *first* thing which is *fundamental* for an understanding is:

To think of Parsifal as the Son of the Light, Who descends into Creation *from above,* Who is not perchance lifted up from below; to think of Him as the beginning and the end in Creation, the A and the O for all the weaving outside of the Divine, and therewith King of the Holy Grail, King of Creation!

The *second:*

Parsifal's great work of purification which leads Him personally through the worlds, with the unreserved condition that He must through His own experiencing learn to know all the evil, which work was bound to end with the fettering of Lucifer for the protection of the Creations and of all the creatures that remain after the purification.

The *third:*

The fall and great failure of the developed ones, i. e., of the human spirits in the World of Matter, which necessitates the breaking of their wrong self-will; the immediate institution of God's Will in the establishment of the Millennium, until the voluntary submission of mankind's entire volition to the Will of God comes about, thus completely ensuring the undisturbed further development of the Creations in the swinging of the Light-pervaded spheres of movement. –

He who grasps these three sections well, *one by one,* and who is at least able to envisage them clearly as a picture, can quite easily understand how the wrong poetic writings of today gradually came into existence. Part tidings of the three happenings penetrated to the earth here and there, announcing much of it beforehand.

Through the lack of understanding men pressed everything into the coarse conceptions of the densest World of Matter, transferring it onto the earth and thus mixing a concoction from which the last writings emerged.

You must follow my words precisely, you must also *obey* them and picture to yourselves living illustrations of the three sections as tremendous individual happenings, of which only a part-knowledge could reach the earth through channels open for this purpose, channels which are badly clogged up and which in any case only let through that which has been dimmed, that which has already been mixed with what men themselves thought, which was deposited as mud in these channels!

For thousands of years it has been unable to penetrate to the earth clearly and purely!

With all this I am referring only to *happenings in Creation* which forcibly arose out of the development through the wrong volition of failing creatures, and for the time being I am following this *one* path in my explanations! I am still leaving everything else aside! Therefore this does not include the attempted redemption of earthmen by the Son of God Jesus either, for this was a Work of Love standing all by itself.

You must follow me precisely, otherwise you will be unable to understand! Perhaps it is quite good when I therefore also explain to you what the happening is like when I speak to you.

I see before me the *entire* happening, for I overlook it in its complete activity down to the most delicate ramifications. I see everything *at the same time in the knowledge!*

Now through what I want to explain I am trying to prepare a straight road on which you can *so* grasp the main points that you receive a basic picture for *that* particular point which you are meant to take in through the lecture. But all this I must first press into *such* a narrow form as is adapted to the perceptive faculty of the developed human spirit. When I have achieved that then I must still seek suitable words and forms of expression to let *the very* picture arise before you which I want to give.

All this, however, does not happen *successively* but *simultaneously* within myself, and then I give in a form which is accessible to you the happening which you can neither overlook nor grasp, in which past and future are consummated in the present, a process the nature of which human spirits are absolutely unable to imagine!

You receive it drop by drop from out of that which is incomprehensible to you, and yet in such a way that the drops together yield an enjoyable and powerful draught which strengthens you in your knowledge and helps you upwards, if only you wish to accept this restorative as nourishment on your way!

There is very often a great deal which I must first leave out in order to bring it in other places much later, but then always in such a way that it completes the picture to which it actually belongs; for all the weaving of Creation *above* him is far too intricately patterned, much too alive and mobile to enable the earthly human spirit to grasp anything thereof, even pictorially, unless he receives it in a form made accessible to him through special descriptions.

Just take one tenth of *that* trouble which *I* must take merely in order to make it accessible to you, and you will have attained to *everything* for yourselves!

Later on I shall perhaps also describe how it *is* in the Light Castle, and then illuminate those planes which could develop at a greater distance, until we finally come down to that place where the human spirit-germs remain as the last precipitation of the spiritual in order to find development in wandering through all the Worlds of Matter, the urge and longing towards the fulfilment of which they all bear within themselves.

First I shall give pictures of *how it is,* and perhaps later on about how at one time it came into existence; for the happening is too great. First you must know how it *is,* for *this* is what you need, because for yourselves you must always count with the present and with the future that opens up from the present. If you stand firmly *in this* then we can stride onwards in the knowledge.

Learn to recognise the three basic sections for today that are connected with the name *Parsifal.*

PRIMORDIAL Beings! These words are familar to you but you cannot imagine anything by them, or what you imagine can never correspond with the real facts.

Therefore I want to lead you towards a better understanding of them, so that you may become knowing in this matter, as far as this is possible for a human being!

In telling you about the Realm of the Primordial Beings I must once again begin with Parsifal, *out of Whom Primordial Creation came into existence.*

You already know the main facts about Parsifal. You know where He came from and what He is!

Adjoining the Unsubstantiate Light-Core of the Triune Godhead is the plane of the direct radiation of God's Power, something which is incomprehensible to everything that has been created. It is the sphere embracing the surroundings that live from eternity to eternity in the radiation of God's Power, which radiation cannot be restrained. So was it ever!

And when *Creation* was meant to arise out of the Will of God the Father, everything could only develop in the course of the action or happening necessary for this purpose, which course you are today able to envisage logically through the Message.

Creation had to come into existence through the *Creative Will* of God the Father! As such the Creative Will of God the Father is Imanuel, Who is personal in His Creating and yet stands or remains completely in the Father, and the Father is within Him as He creates.

I believe that *in this way* many things will become increasingly comprehensible to you!

Just as the Creative *Will* Imanuel is *personal* so also the *Love* became *personal* in the activity in Jesus.

Both being Parts of the Father are one with Him, and the Father is within Them. From eternity unto all eternity!

1011

Jesus is the Love of God, Imanuel the Will of God! Creation therefore swings in His Name. Everything that occurs, that is fulfilled therein, is inscribed in the Name which carries Creation, from the smallest to the greatest happening! There is nothing that does not come out of this Name and that would not have to be fulfilled therein!

You men have no idea of the greatness that rests in this; for this Name is the Living Law in its origin and in the fulfilment – it carries the Universe with all that it contains!

The fate of each individual rests in this Name, because you must pass judgment upon yourselves through it, since you are all firmly anchored in it.

And the Name *is!* It is *living* and *personal,* for the Name and its Bearer are inseparably one!

The work of creating had to devolve upon the *Creative Will,* i. e., upon Imanuel, Who *is* the Creative Will in God!

And since the creating could only take place *outside* the *immediate* radiation of the Primordial Light, which radiation has existed from eternity and cannot be held back, the necessity arose to *place* a small Part of the Creative Will of God Himself *outside* of, *beyond the boundary* of the direct radiation. A Part Who remains eternally united with the Creative Will in the Unsubstantiate, and yet Who remains standing and working by Himself outside the Divine Sphere, so that through His radiation Creation can form itself and be maintained.

And this small Part Who out of the Creative Will of God was placed outside, so that Creation can form from His radiation and also remain preserved, is *Parsifal!*

His Unsubstantiate Core out of Imanuel received form through the Primordial Queen Elizabeth, i. e., a cloak which became His anchor, so that He can remain standing *outside* the Divine Sphere! And this cloak, this form, is the Holy Vessel in which Imanuel is anchored and out of which He works.

At that time it was *Parsifal* Who was on earth in Abd-ru-shin, whereas in the hour of fulfilment Imanuel as such will take possession of the physical cloak of Parsifal after troublesome purification of this cloak.

Only then can the full power gradually sink down into this cloak in order, through merciful dispensation, to fulfil the Divine Promises for humanity!

In this way I once again unfold immeasurable happenings before your spirit as a foundation for the understanding about Parsifal!

It is exceedingly troublesome to give a clear picture for earthly comprehension, and I must not fight shy of the number of lectures if I want to attain it!

Thus I already clearly stated in advance in the first lecture that the explanations can *only* be for *those* people who were already able to bring the Message to *complete* experience within themselves. Only *those* will be able to follow me if they exert themselves with all their strength again and again until they can grasp it; for I narrow it down in such a way that it becomes possible for their spirit to do so.

Above all, you must *not* think of the term *"Son" in the human way,* not like a son in a human family!

For the Divine "Son" means a "Part", a Part of the Father that works specially by Itself. Son and Father are completely *one* and can never be separated!

Therefore never in any case think about it according to the human way, for that *would be certain* to give an absolutely *false* picture. It would lead you to errors in conception that would completely eliminate the actual facts, and would consequently never let you come nearer to the Truth!

Perhaps one should rather say: It is all *only* God the Father, He works threefold as One!

It probably comes closer to your understanding as you picture it! And considered from the Origin it is also described *more correctly,* for there is but *One* God! Whatever God the Son works that He works out of the Father, in the Father, for the Father! He would be nothing without the Father; for He is Part of the Father and the Father Himself is within Him and works in Him.

Here we can perhaps again come a little closer to earthly comprehension if you imagine: The Father does not perchance work *out of* the Son, thus not *through* Him, but *in* Him! Herein lies the mystery for the human conception, which despite my efforts will probably always remain a mystery too; for it cannot be described in earthly words. Words are in the end only words, strictly limited; they cannot render that which is mobile, that which in truth is living, such being inherent in everything concerning God and the Divine.

That which is with God can never be with men. In the human family the son is by himself and the father is by himself, they are and remain *two.* At the utmost they can become *united in their working,* but never one! It is different with the expression God the Son! Just the opposite! God the Father and God

1013

the Son *are one* and can only be considered as two in *Their working,* as also the two Sons of God Imanuel and Jesus are one in the Father and only in Their working two, in *the nature* of Their working!

With this I have once more tried to explain to you the *origin* of Parsifal, Who through Imanuel is in God and therewith God in Him.

Now I will also try to show Him to you as a picture, as a person, how He *is!* And *then* in His working!

It will be hard for you to imagine that the Light Castle was also bound to issue from His radiation, the Castle that surrounds Him protectingly in the Primordial Spiritual Sphere, in Primordial Creation. The Castle that must be considered like an annexe to *that* Castle which is situated since Prime Eternity at the boundary of the Divine Sphere, in which Castle the Elders, the Eternal Ones, have their home and activity in the Divine Sphere! In the *Divine,* that is in the immediate radiation of God, not perchance in God Himself!

I do *not* include the Castle in the Divine Sphere in the range of my explanations because mankind has nothing to do with it, but I always and only speak of the Castle *in the Primordial Spiritual Sphere,* which is the summit and starting-point of the entire Creation.

The Castle in the Primordial Spiritual, in Primordial Creation, may be looked upon as an annexe of the Castle in the Divine Sphere. At its uppermost end is the golden screen and the curtain through which the Primordial Beings cannot pass and which forms the boundary.

Imagine Parsifal at this boundary as the First and Uppermost in the whole of Creation, from Whom Creation issued! In a hall of pillars that has closed around Him in the most faithful and pure volition of all the Primordial Beings and their Love for the Light!

The first Primordial Beings, the uppermost of Primordial Creation, could only become conscious as they severed themselves within and out of the creative radiation of Parsifal, outside the boundary of the Divine Sphere, i.e., beyond the immediate radiation of God!

I am repeating the expressions and designations so often that they may become hammered into you as unshakable conceptions!

Thus Parsifal stands there as the First One! He has stepped out of the Divine Sphere. From out of His radiation there first severed themselves the uppermost Primordial Beings as they became conscious, and their love

1014

and loyalty to the Light, towards Parsifal, formed itself in the volition to the glorious Hall, to the Temple, to the Castle!

However, I want to mention this living forming and weaving only fleetingly today. Perhaps I shall give more detailed enlightenment about it later on. It has only to be mentioned now for the sake of the whole picture I want to give.

For you Parsifal Himself is only undulating Light, His Unsubstantiate Core out of Imanuel puts all else deep into the shadow, if shadow can be spoken of at all in the Luminous Castle. Therefore this is only stated *pictorially,* for actually there is no trace of shadow whatever.

However, to the eye of the Primordial Spiritual Beings, of the Primordial Beings, the form takes shape, the Primordial Spiritual Form of the Son of the Light, brilliantly penetrated with radiation by His Unsubstantiate Core!

What shall I now tell you about that which simply cannot be limited by earthly words?

A luminous head in the most perfect form, cloaked in the eternal movement of the Living Light, which causes every Created One who looks at it to lose consciousness and throws him down. The body enveloped in a radiant cloak which gives the impression of a flexible scaly mail, above the head the wings of the Dove spread protectingly... thus can you envisage Him, powerful, imperious, invincible, unapproachable, the Power of God embodied, the Radiance of God that has taken on form: Parsifal, the Son of Light, in the Primordial Spiritual, standing at the summit of Creation! *The Pure Gate* that has opened from the Divine to Creation, that leads from God to man!

According to its meaning the name Parsifal signifies among other things: *From God to man!* He is therefore the gate or the bridge from God to man. He is not the pure simpleton (in German *"der* reine Tor"), but the Pure Gate (in German *"das* reine Tor") of Life to Creation!

For His work of purifying Creation which was granted by God the Father, and which became necessary through the fall of the human spirits in the World of Matter, Parsifal's *volition* as a Part of Him took on form for His wandering through all the parts of the world, so that through gathering experiences therein He would recognise all the weaknesses and wounds of the human spirits.

Parsifal always remained in the Castle while His living volition, as a part out of Him become form, wandered through the parts of the world learning.

Being of an alien nature, particularly towards everything that is wrong, the *form* of His volition for this task was naturally bound to be like that of a child first, then like that of a youth who had to learn and so mature to become a man, which in the swinging of the Laws of Creation naturally also manifested in the outward form, corresponding to the nature of the particular plane.

As in wandering downwards Parsifal arrived at the boundary where the World of Matter began, i. e., the area of the human spirits developing from spirit-germs, he reached that plane in which the effects of the dark currents that had also already touched Amfortas first became manifest.

At this boundary there is the Castle in which Amfortas was priest-king. It is the lowest image of the actual Grail Castle, furthest away from it and most different from it in nature. Also therefore the nearest one to the earth, although in terms of human thinking at such a great distance as can hardly be grasped! In this Castle there are indeed the purest of the developed human spirits as guardians of the vessel and as knights.

Upon entering this plane it was necessary for Parsifal to become veiled with a cloak of the same kind, even though of the very fine material substance such as existed there, which was like a bandage that temporarily blots out all memories of higher regions.

Coming from the Light He now in pure innocence faced the evil that was completely unknown to Him, and He could only take notice of it through suffering under it. He thereby had to learn laboriously what human spirits are capable of in this respect.

Thus He did indeed obtain a thorough knowledge of it, but since it was completely alien to His nature He could never understand such things.

Thus it was here that the currents from the Darkness, which had naturally taken on form, rushed for the first time upon the wandering stranger, who in the struggles connected therewith gained strength and awoke to the recognition of Himself.

It is of this path, difficult and full of suffering, that mankind on earth received knowledge, because it took place in the World of Matter, although only at its highest boundary. That is why the errors could arise, because the human spirit on earth can never picture to itself such happenings as lie far above its species.

However, I shall give closer explanations about all this some time later, explanations that will bring light and therewith clarity!

MAN HAS burdened himself with much that acts as a hindrance and prevents an unfolding of his spirit, which strives of its own accord to tread the path *upwards* as soon as it is not fettered or earthbound by anything.

The main evil, however, remains the one-sided and too greatly cultivated intellect which, puffed up, lolls about on a ruler's throne that it is not entitled to.

It resembles an animal that renders very good service only when controlled, but which in any event has a *harmful* effect *as soon as* it is allowed to be independent.

It is like a beast of prey which at first remains friendly and gives pleasure to him who cares for and feeds it, but which once it has reached a certain size becomes dangerous also to him who has first reared it.

It then becomes the tyrant of the caretaker, who must fear it and who completely loses his hitherto accustomed freedom of movement in the cage, the habitation of this animal. All of a sudden the animal controls him within the bounds of its ability to move about.

It is the same with every person and his intellect. And since the intellect not only remained dependent upon the habitation assigned to it, i. e., upon the particular human body, but enforced *complete freedom of movement* for itself, which is without limit on earth, *the whole of mankind* had to accommodate themselves to its volition.

Nowhere are they safe from it, it lurks dangerously everywhere, ready to apply its sharp claws or destructive teeth wherever a person appears who is *not* willing to submit to it!

This is how it looks on earth *today!* The animal at first so tenderly cared for has grown to an immense strength, it cannot again be compelled by any man to give *useful* service! And so it now creates sad havoc, in which you are already partly involved, and which will become even worse because you are incapable of commanding the beast to stop!

Many persons will become a prey to it in spite of the fact that they could easily have controlled the animal if they had only trained it *aright* at the proper time.

The strength which the beast now consumes in its ravages was meant to be used in a beneficial way under the judicious guidance of your spirit, to beautify and uplift yourselves and your surroundings for the peace and joy of all.

Instead of devastation, flowering gardens would lie before you, inviting you to blissful activity in the grateful productivity of peace-loving earthly citizens!

Without exception you would have to come to grief over this monstrous beast you have reared if God Himself does not now set a limit to it, divesting it of its power and leading it again on paths where it can only work *beneficially!*

But before that you must experience what harm you have therewith committed, you must see and undergo the serious consequences which it brings and draws in its train, so that you will be completely cured of such wrong deeds and striving, and no desire for such can again arise within you in the future!

This is how God punishes you, by giving you the fulfilment of everything which you tried to enforce through your stubborn volition against His command, after you not only disregarded all those sent to warn you out of love from the Light, but persecuted them with your hatred and finally murdered them in blind rage because they were inconvenient to your plans, although *only they* could really have helped you.

And through this mistake you also make it impossible for the *spirit* to loosen itself within you in order gradually to unfold and receive connection with *its own* kind, with the Spiritual Plane in the Ray of Light of the Divine Grace.

The domination of the intellect never permitted this; for its artificially enforced false glory would very quickly have melted away like a snowman in the rays of the sun. It would have inevitably sunk down from the throne and would *have had to serve* again instead of playing the master.

This accounts for the strenuous resistance, which did not even shy at murder where its prestige could in any way be endangered.

That is why even today you simply cannot think differently, and press everything you hear, that is revealed to you, into forms that are well known to you in the *earthly* sense, thus permitting ideas to arise within you that do not nearly correspond with reality; for the animal that you have nursed and cultivated without making it subject to you is *above* you and holds you down! It has placed itself separatingly between you and all that is spiritual, and does not let anything pass to that which is higher than is this ambitious beast, your intellect, which remains earthly, which is the alluringly iridescent but most dangerous and certain implement for your destruction in Lucifer's hand.

Now *free* yourselves from it and lift yourselves *above* it! Otherwise you will never be able to grasp the values that are offered to you from the Light or make use of them for yourselves!

Become again *like* the earthmen used to be before intellectual conceit enveloped them and pressed them down onto *that* ground which was suitable for them in their narrowness.

At that time the people were swinging *with* and *in* their surroundings, and they could therefore be spiritually uplifted in the swinging without having to fear they would lose earthly ground and earthly thinking!

How small you have become in comparison with those whom you characterise today as standing in the beginning of development and not yet of full value in the human sense!

They were of greater worth in Creation than you are today, and therefore more valuable and useful in the eyes of the Creator than you are with your accursed perversity, which can only leave devastation instead of improving what already exists.

You must again return to this point, must again unfold the wings within you that have become completely stunted, if you do not wish to fall; for your spirit is now forcibly *freed* by the Power of the Light from all obstruction! The obstruction is shattered! Then woe to the spirit that cannot *maintain* itself in *harmonious swinging,* it must fall because it has no longer any strength for the flight due to lack of any practice and activity, of which you maliciously deprived it!

Man on earth must heed one thing in particular in which he has sinned severely: The connection with the animistic helpers must *never* be *eliminated!* Otherwise you tear a great gap therewith which harms *you!*

You must not look upon the *great* strong animistic beings as gods; for they are not gods but faithful servants *of the Almighty,* and they are *great* in their serving! But they are never subject to *you!*

However, you must not look in arrogance at the *small* animistic beings as if from above; for they are not *your* servants, but like the great ones they serve only *God,* the Creator. Only in their working do they approach you, but you should approach them!

You can learn very much from them, especially from their faithful serving, which they gratefully dedicate to their Creator! You men absolutely *need* the great and small helpers, for only through completely harmonious *co-operation* with them can your souls mature aright and attain to ascent.

Therefore learn to *esteem all* the animistic helpers, for they can be your best and most loyal friends!

Then you will swing more lightly again, but first you must be *free* of *any constriction* caused by your earthly intellect! Especially when you want to grasp *that* which I am revealing to you of the Luminous Realms, which can never become intelligible to you if you want to think only in the *earthly* way; for they are of a nature that can only be absorbed by *your spirit!*

Only when you have *opened* yourselves for it will you know what I have given you with my explanations. I am speaking about these things already to-day, but it is given for a *later* grasping; for I *fulfil,* as with everything I say to you! I fulfil, because it was once promised that I should reveal Creation to the Developed Ones as well as to the Created Ones, that I should give you the key to the understanding of every happening in Creation!

Just administer all the knowledge *faithfully!* As I reveal all this to you, you become *the guardians of all the keys!* If you allow blemishes to come upon them or twist only a small part, they will no longer open these secrets of Creation, and the gates will again remain locked.

You therewith became capable of *knowingly* enjoying all the Grace in Creation, in eternity, if only you proceed aright and become a useful link in this Creation, and provided you do not envy others over anything; for there is room and the possibility of existence for *all* who in following the Law of Movement swing harmoniously with the others!

You small group are now the *leaven* which I have prepared for mankind, which must now penetrate and further everything, bringing spiritual movement into the ponderous masses so that they need not uselessly collapse and perish.

Faithfully guard the keys that I give you with my words, and always transmit them in the right manner to those who come *after* you!

As soon as you have become free from the pressure of intellectual compulsion, *then* all my words that I have already spoken to you and that I shall yet speak are clear to you. *Then* you will also absorb what you have heard about Primordial Creation and about the Primordial Beings, who stand at the highest place of all the Creations, in the Temple of the Holy Grail.

The *first* ring around Parsifal, facing towards Creation, consists of *four* Primordial Beings, who could immediately become conscious from the radiations of Parsifal and take on form as the first ones. Working joyfully, they swing steadfastly in absorbing and transmitting, and again in receiving and radiating back.

There are *several* rings of Primordial Beings around Parsifal. But all of them, even the first ring, are a great distance from Parsifal and His Throne, which on account of the pressure they cannot traverse.

The four of the first ring are the strongest of all the Primordial Beings. They are able to bear a greater Light Pressure than the others without having to lose consciousness.

They are:

Od-shi-mat-no-ke, the Server and Light-Protection of the Perfect Triune. He is the most ideal embodiment of a kingly ruler.

Leilak, the embodiment of manly courage and manly strength.

These two in their nature are understandable to men. But it is different with the two whom I am going to name now, for these species are beyond human conception.

The Lion. It comes closer to the human conception when I say that the Lion as a Grail Knight is the embodiment of the most noble *heroism*, whose radiation supports and furthers heroic loyalty in Creation.

Mercury, the Primordial Leader of the forces of all the elements. They are anchored within him!

Man will think he has understood without difficulty what I have stated here, but that is not so! He cannot understand it unless I give him an extended explanation about the special nature of the Lion.

In order to do this I must ascend still further into the Divine Sphere. Men know allegorically that Animals keep watch at the Steps of God's Throne – winged, powerful Animals, among which there is also a Lion!

These Animals are not a legend, but they actually exist there! I have never as yet mentioned them because it would have become too much in the beginning. Therefore we shall only talk about them when the human spirits are more matured than today.

What I say about it today is only for those who have already absorbed my Message within themselves, and really seek to make it alive within themselves. Thus it is only for the *more mature* earthmen!

Man will now ask himself how it is that *Animals* come into the Divine Sphere, and what is more even up to the Steps of God's Throne, indeed *onto* those Steps, which a human spirit can never reach, no matter how much grace he might be endowed with.

However, this is very simple to explain! Man has formed a false conception of the *animal,* for he only sees the animals of the earth which can develop themselves in the World of Gross Matter!

And that is wrong! Whether man or animal, both are *creatures* in Creation, one as necessary as the other, or one can be just as well dispensed with as the other!

The Animals at the Steps of God's Throne are of an entirely different species from that which human beings think of as animals. They are *knowing* Animals! Of this alone you are unable to form any idea, nor will you ever be able to do so in the right way, for all this is too far removed for the human spirit of the developed beings.

Knowing Animals, whose loyalty and devotion are absolutely incorruptible! There is no wavering or hesitation about them, but only an enthusiastic unchangeable serving! Serving in immediate action, without deliberating, without first needing a volition to do so! A living swinging in the Law as a matter of course and as a need for existence!

They also stand much higher than the developed human spirit, by the mere fact alone that in their inviolable purity of activity and strength they are in the *Divine* Sphere.

Thus it is not a question of animal in the human *sense,* but of a special species of radiation which has taken on form and is called Animal, just as another but lower species of radiation is called *man!* Very special explanations are yet needed about this that can only follow much later!

Just as the Lion at the Steps of the Throne of the Unsubstantiate God-Trinity issues from the latter's radiation, lives and works in it, so the Lion in Primordial Creation has issued from the radiation of the likewise Unsubstantiate Core in Parsifal and its "glowed-through" cloak, and has taken on form in the Primordial Spiritual Plane of the first Primordial Creation as Knight of the Holy Grail!

It is a similarity of species in a different form; for the Lion of Primordial Creation bears other things within himself besides, something of the spiritual-human nature about which I shall speak later in greater detail. He is already a combination within himself, whereas the knowing Lion at the Steps of God's Throne does not carry another combination within himself.

The Lion of the Primordial Creation is already prepared for the radiation *in the Creation* as a necessary kind of transition. His radiating activity is many-sided and nevertheless more limited than that of the Lion in the Divine Sphere.

All the heroic virtues which manifest here and there in Creation issue from him!

I must not go into details about it today, for this branches out too much from what I want to say in this lecture. I only want to remark in passing that from the radiations of this heroic spirit a share was also given to the spirit of those *earth* men who were active as real *heroes*.

This was well known to the ancient Germanic people and to the Greeks, as well as to many other former human races who still kept up conscious connection with the Animistic.

At the earthly death of such a hero the animistic beings guided the animistic radiation-part of the heroism to Valhalla, the uppermost Castle in the Animistic Ring of Creation, whereas the spirit had to go to the plane destined for it. Despite this, if the spirit had been active in the *good* sense, both parts remained connected with each other by means of threads.

These two parts were only separated when the spirit stepped downwards, so that the animistic part could not be dragged along. Otherwise the two parts flowed together again at earthly incarnations.

This attribute of heroism is a special gift for earthman, the reception of which is prepared through a definite maturity of the spirit concerned, as well as through a definite *path* thereof.

For certain tasks on earth a part of these animistic rays of the Lion is needed, because an aggressiveness (which swings *in purity*, however) is anchored therein, and is connected with an absolute devoting of oneself, which the spiritual as such does not carry within because its highest goal is upbuilding and peaceful activity.

All the real heroism in Creation is anchored in the Lion, who as Knight of the Holy Grail stands in the first ring of the Primordial Beings.

Now I have also simultaneously lifted the edge of a veil a little from the Animals on the Steps of God's Throne. They are four winged knowing Animals who guard the Throne: an Eagle, a Lion, a Bull and a Ram. The Ram, however, bears a human countenance, for the Ram carries the *human-spiritual* within itself!

The four knowing Animals on the Steps of God's Throne have issued from the *immediate* radiations of God and can live therein knowingly. They bear within themselves *the basic species for the Creations,* whereas the Archangels swing in a different kind of radiation. It is not without significance that the birth of the Son of Man on earth falls within the sign of Aries (the Ram) according to Law!

But to solve these mysteries is not the task of today's lecture. Accept with gratitude to God what I am allowed to offer you, try to understand everything, and do not perhaps toy fitfully with it! You cannot afford to do so in these things, for they are much too powerful and too high for the trifling thoughts customary to mankind!

However, the *more keenly* and *earnestly* you exert yourselves really to *grasp* the Truth of my Word, the more I am able to reveal to you. For you the key to the gate of my knowledge lies in your effort! Therefore strive in such a way that I can give to you with full hands!

I HAVE explained the first ring of the Primordial Beings around Parsifal, i. e., not yet explained, but only spoken of them!

Before continuing I must yet explain many things in greater detail, otherwise you lack something for the ring of the great swinging, and cannot let it come to life within yourselves. Everything must be without a gap, although it can only be given to you in *pictures*. For this reason we can only advance very slowly.

Therefore we must once again dwell upon the first Primordial Beings whom I named in the last lecture. They are the strongest pillars *for* and *in* the Creations.

And again I must in doing this ascend to the nearest proximity of God, in so far as one can at all speak about proximity; for there is nothing of which one could say it is in the proximity of God, if the proximity is measured according to earthly conceptions.

Even the greatest distance which exists in human conception is not yet sufficient to give an approximate picture of *that* distance which one wants to designate as the nearest proximity to God. It is still infinitely greater; for that which one can call the actual proximity to God is a surging ocean of flames, still without the possibility to acquire form.

For this reason I merely make use of the *expression* for the designation "proximity" in this matter, not of the *conception*. In this proximity, upon the Steps of the Throne, which are entire planes, the four Animals in their very special species of swinging are to be found.

The Primordial Queen Elizabeth cannot be placed upon any gradations for She is *entirely by Herself,* through Her the Pure Lily.

The Archangels are again of a different species of the direct Radiations of God than are the four Animals. The species separate themselves in the process of their forming. One can also say: The forming *is* the separation, for it is an *automatic,* living occurrence!

Today, however, let us only talk about the four Animals! These Animals carry within themselves the suppositions for *Creation!* This means that all the radiations which the *Creations* need in order to take on form, in order to fashion themselves, are *accumulated* within these Animals.

For this reason the foundation of Creation already rests in these Animals. Four Animals which form a Square on the Steps of the Throne of God and drink in, absorb within themselves, all the Creative Radiations of God! This means that they not only form a Square, but they *are* the Square of Creation, or the Square of the later Circle of Creation.

I do not want to dwell upon this too long, but merely touch quickly upon that which is essential for us today in order to explain the relation of the Square of the Animals with Creation.

Thus the Square of the Animals, or better said *"Beings",* contains everything the *Creations* need, and *for this* purpose it is the first central gathering point out of the Radiations of the Divine Trinity above it.

Entirely different radiations go through the Primordial Queen, as again different ones through all the Archangels!

Therefore it is *only* this Square of the four Beings that deals directly from above with the later Circle of Creation; it is connected with it. All else having its home in the Divine Plane of Radiation, and which was and is thereby eternal, inclines towards all that is created *only* in a *helping,* uplifting and furthering way in the swinging of the Divine Love, which is quite natural to them. However, they are *not* firmly *connected* with Creation. Only the Square of the Four Animals is connected with it!

Very much lies in this fine distinction! Therefore impress it upon your mind very specially! Many a thing, much that has so far remained incomprehensible to you, will thus become clearer to you.

Of the four winged, knowing Beings by the Throne of God – the Ram, the Bull, the Lion and the Eagle – the Ram is *that* Being which bears a *human countenance;* for the Ram holds within itself *that Spirituality* of Creation out of which *the human beings* in Creation form themselves and develop!

This is *also* related to the expression: The Lamb of God and the wound it bears; for in conformity with nature it shows upon itself the wound of the failure and decline of the human spirits in Creation, since they issued from it, if not directly, then *indirectly.* The outstreaming human-spiritual does not pulsate harmoniously back from out of Creation, but is held fast in the Worlds of Matter because too much guilt clings to it.

With this I again extend the field of knowledge for you for another span. But it does not displace anything of what you have been able to learn in the past, all of which continues to exist nevertheless, swinging in full harmony with the new, although some things may not appear to do so in the first moment.

Now I want to pass on to the details. Parsifal stepped across the boundary of the direct radiation of the Divine Trinity, i. e., across the boundary of the Divine Plane.

With this He carried the radiation of His Unsubstantiate God-Core out, and now radiated outside the Divine Sphere as a small Part out of Imanuel into the Light-Void and, being the Source of Life, illuminating, warming, bringing everything into motion, and keeping it in motion.

Immediately and at an adequate distance there formed in a kind of combination the first four Pillars of the Creations, which contain everything necessary for Creation. They are not formed like the Beings by the Throne of God, but are human form, although to human conception absolutely unbelievable in size and beauty.

Standing before Parsifal as Knights of the Grail, i. e., as powerful protectors and faithful Guardians of the property and the Holy Vessel of His Unsubstantiate Part entrusted by God in Parsifal, they simultaneously comply with the effects of the four Beings on the Steps of the Throne. As the Quadrature of the Circling of Creation!

In their effect for the Creations they are of the following kinds:

1. *Od-shi-mat-no-ke:* The ideal figure of the human-spiritual which cannot be attained by others because it is perfect! Therefore appearing as a kingly ruler! He bears *only* the species of the Ram within, thus he is *its* mode of operation in Primordial Creation; one could say that the Ram is anchored within him.

2. *Leilak:* The ideal figure of man's courage, of man's strength. Within himself he bears a combination of the species of the Ram – therefore the spiritual-human form – and of the *Bull.*

3. *The Lion:* The ideal figure of heroism. He bears within himself the combination out of the Ram with the *Lion.*

4. *Mercury:* The ruler of all the forces of the elements. He bears within himself the connection out of the Ram with the *Eagle.*

All four of the Primordial Beings, apart from the other species that are expressed, must also be fundamentally connected with the *Ram,* because they are *spiritual* and *conscious,* something which is anchored in the Ram.

Just as the four Beings on the Steps of the Throne are the pillars and powerful Guardians in the Divine, naturally outside of the Unsubstantiate Godhead Himself, so the four Primordial Beings of the first ring around Parsifal in the Primordial Spiritual Sphere, in Primordial Creation, are the pillars and powerful Guardians whose co-operation brings about a perfect combination and radiates all the requirements of Creation.

The animation of these rays comes from the Light-Core of Parsifal, from Whose Radiation they were able to form as the first necessary basic pillars, which at the same time are the most powerful Guardians of the Sanctum.

It is not easy to explain to you something which is so great and mobile, to form it into stationary pictures for you, whereas the reality is *not* stationary, but remains in a continual flowing movement, in a movement of receiving, of radiating further, of withdrawing and again leading back to Parsifal. All this *simultaneously* without interruption! This alone you will never be able to picture to yourselves!

Therefore within these four first Primordial Beings all the powers of creating streaming out of Parsifal are gathered, connected and strengthened through the same species of radiation as those of the four Animals, are maintained in a pushing or pressing away movement by the Living Light within Parsifal, and guided by the volition of the Primordial Beings which arises out of their species.

Perhaps you are able *in this way* to imagine a happening which comes closest to the Truth expressed in earthly words!

Keep this thoroughly in mind first of all and hammer it into yourselves, in the same way as I formed it into earthly words!

Do not perchance jump about again in your thoughts and do not ask yourselves where is then the feminine, which according to my earlier lectures is always supposed to stand half a step higher! Also do not ponder as to where Maria is and Irmingard, Who certainly cannot stand deeper than the Primordial Beings! Here, too, there is no gap, but it all accords precisely!

To begin with the four named Primordial Beings are the *main pillars* of the structure of Creation, and *from these* it then goes downwards or into greater distances according to the explanations of Creation which I have already given; for these four bear all the powers of creating combined within themselves, whereas all the others are *helpers!*

Here, too, I first indicate again only the *straight* line downwards which leads to the developed human spirits and I leave all the branch lines untouched and unnamed, as for example Loherangrin, because he is not the *starting-point* of a radiation which has an incisive effect for the forming in Creation. I shall come to it later on. First of all I give the points of support in the structure of Creation!

Maria does not enter into all this at all, nor does Irmingard. Coming from above, They are, it is true, *anchored* into the Creations, but *not* firmly *connected* with them. Therein lies a great difference again.

Despite the anchorages They are not tied to them, but completely free from them and their currents. The currents of Creation can *approach* Them through these anchorages, so that they become clearly recognisable, but they can never penetrate *into* Them, because the necessary *connection* for this is lacking.

Maria and Irmingard are active, but without the possibility of anything reacting upon Them! They work in a helping and uplifting way, strengthening, purifying, healing or also repelling, but in Their Radiations They do not *connect* Themselves with the Creation. Heed this well!

Maria did come into holy union as a Part of the Love of God, which is Jesus, and as a Part of Imanuel. She has nothing to do with womanhood *as such*, but as the Love of God She faces the *whole of mankind!*

The womanhood of Creation as such has *only* to do with Irmingard. And She *descended* to the Grail Castle into Primordial Creation, out of the Divine Plane, and there merely stepped into a Primordial Spiritual vessel which had already been prepared for Her.

Quite aside from the fact that through an Act of God's Will a spark of Unsubstantiality was sunk into Her, so that Imanuel can now work in the whole of Creation as a *Triad!* The Triad of Imanuel in Creation is: Parsifal – Maria – Irmingard, thus Justice, Love and Purity!

Therefore in the last, most sacred fulfilment Imanuel now works in Creation simultaneously *in* Parsifal, Maria and Irmingard.

This is a fresh Act of Love which God fulfilled for the aid and stronger protection of *that* humanity which will surmount the Judgment, so that Creation then cannot again suffer harm through the weakness of the human spirits.

Therefore do not confuse yourselves with unnecessary thinking! I am at present speaking *only* of the Primordial Creation out of Parsifal. Neither Maria nor Irmingard are part of this, but They *work* there in Their species.

After the four Primordial Pillars there is a second ring, which is somewhat further distant, let us say half a step further away in earthly thinking. This second arc or plane is filled with the activity of the three female Primordial Beings: *Johanna, Cella, Josepha.*

Now you must not picture this to yourselves as if these Primordial Beings simply stand there in an arc, but according to their special species they work in big gardens or planes which arise around them and from out of them, with many helping entities and inhabitants of Primordial Creation, who swing and work around each of these leading female and male Primordial Beings in their like species.

Thus in the retinue of each of the four first Primordial Beings there is a great number of knights, while a great number of female beings co-operate with the female Primordial Beings.

But we must not dwell on this for the moment, otherwise the picture I want to give you will dissolve into distances which you can no longer grasp or survey.

Today I merely wish briefly to indicate the manner in which the activity through the radiation of the three female Primordial Beings swings as it penetrates the whole of Creation.

Each one has a special activity, and yet the entire activity of these three *so* gears into the activity of each other that it can appear almost as one. One can hardly recognise any boundary in this. Their activity is purely *womanly,* of which they are the ideal embodiments.

First *Johanna:* Her activity cannot be put into definite *words,* because the conception would then be immediately diminished. For this reason I only want to state briefly that it concerns the *home.* To fashion it as "homely", attractive, harmonious! However, the home considered in the *broad* sense, not perchance merely as a small residence of earthmen!

True, men's earthly home is also included, for this activity takes effect in great things as well as in small, indeed down to the most minute! But here it is a question of *the matter itself,* not merely of a small form thereof!

For instance, it also embraces the intuitive sensing of a joyful connection with one's native soil, which can set whole nations ablaze with the most genuine enthusiasm if an enemy seeks to damage it in a covetous way.

I could quote a thousand different things, but despite this you would never recognise therein the true greatness which lies in the activity of Johanna, who also tries to impress it upon each human spirit as a holy legacy which can uplift it to great heights and give it firm support. And this legacy is given above all to *womanhood,* and for this reason the fate of an entire nation often rests within them.

Cella's activity is of no less a delicate nature! With care she plants into the spiritual the serene respect for developing motherhood! With all the inviolability and sublimity inherent therein! In the noblest way and with the respectful reserve which comes to the fore in such proximity with all who are still pure in spirit!

Josepha lays the foundation for *that purpose,* to care for the *cloaks,* i. e., the bodies, as property entrusted by the Grace of God, and to treat them accordingly. Naturally not only the earthly bodies, but *all* the cloaks in Creation, which in the first place are always and only given as a support for the development of the spiritual or animistic core, and which as such must always be considered in purity!

Diseased cloaks also contribute to the development of *that* core which would perhaps not come so quickly to awakening if the cloak was healthy.

Josepha's activity is of the same value as that of the others, and also of the same *importance* on the paths of all the wanderings through Creation. These are fundamental conditions for a normal, God-Willed maturing of all the creatures in the Creations. They penetrate everything as if with the finest threads and manifest in their effects in quite different forms, because they remain mobile, reposing unuttered and unformed in the spirit. All this urges and drives, but only in the intuitive perception can it be understood *aright* and brought to beneficial realisation.

When the capacity to perceive intuitively is buried through the domination of the intellect, then a gulf is torn between all the Weaving Ones serving the Will of God in Primordial Creation, and with this the disturbance in the necessary swinging of Creation is also forcibly brought about.

The radiating activities of the three Primordial Beings Johanna, Cella and Josepha comprise one great, *combined,* fundamental working, gearing into each other and yet remaining separate.

Now let us once again proceed half a step further which, of course, really signifies distances that appear hardly conceivable to you. There again we find a female Primordial Being: Vasitha.

She is the protecting gatekeeper at the exit of the uppermost and purest part in Primordial Creation, on the summit of which there radiantly arises the glorious Castle of the Holy Grail in sublimity and peace!

With Vasitha and her surroundings the uppermost part of the Primordial Creation comes to a close. She stands at the gate and directs all that is spiritual (which must move onwards as a necessity for their own development) towards the way out to the bridge which, like an immense rainbow, spans deep chasms to those regions which needed a further cooling-off and greater distance from the Light of God to enable them to become conscious for their own existence, to form themselves and unfold to full blossom therein.

High stands Vasitha there, pointing with her spear, while her keen gaze scrutinises and penetrates everything which is unable to remain in the first part of Primordial Creation and which must then pass before her! Her words of direction give strength to all and a faithful accompaniment!

So they move out, those who are able to form themselves as Created Ones, together with those who still remain lying in the last precipitation, and who must first wander along the path of slow development in order to become conscious of their existence. They move out into great remote distances with the longing for the Light of God. –

In conclusion, make a short survey for yourselves again of what has been said:

The path of the Radiations of God for Creation, and thus naturally also for all mankind, goes through the Square of the four Animals on the Steps of the Throne, hitherto only known to you by name. The four first Primordial Beings of Creation carry within themselves these radiations of the Animals, thus they form the Square in the Primordial Spiritual for the circling of Creation. The circle of Creation is then driven and kept in constant movement by the Power of the Light, which works in a living manner out of the Unsubstantiate Core of Parsifal.

Let this basic picture be firmly anchored within you, so that I can now broaden out, adding one picture after another in order to extend your knowledge without your gaze becoming confused! You will succeed if you wish to!

TODAY I once again call up before the eye of your spirit the picture of Primordial Creation as I have given it to you so far. After Parsifal you see the first four of the Primordial Beings who occupy the uppermost of the seven steps in the Primordial Spiritual: Od-shi-mat-no-ke, Leilak, the Lion and Mercury.

On the next step I named three female Primordial Beings: Johanna, Cella, Josepha, and again a little further distant, upon the third step or plane, Vasitha as the protecting gatekeeper.

With this I revealed in their basic species three steps or planes of the highest Primordial Creation. But before I further extend the picture and go into details I want as a fundamental to name the four other steps; for there are *seven* steps or main sections in the Primordial Spiritual, which I designate as Primordial Creation, just as later on there are also seven steps or parts of the world in the Material Spheres.

Everywhere as a matter of course you will find the *seven*-division where the *Will* of God is working, Who also carries the seven in His name: Imanuel.

Let us now enter the fourth step in the Primordial Spiritual Realms!

Wondrous, infinitely beneficent light streams through this glorious plane, which like an immense crystal-clear sea extends into shimmering distances.

Out of this flowing weaving there arises like an island a luminous place abounding in the most exquisite roses. Grateful jubilation pervades the terraces which, as they rise up to the radiant hill in ineffable beauty, offer a perfect wealth of colour, compelling the most fastidious gaze to admiring worship. The colours swing in the most glorious splendour, radiating blessing and forming the delightful gardens into the source of all hope and all life. Here and there innumerable rosy children play happily, and much-blest matured women move about joyfully!

But these are not perchance the spirits which later incarnate in the Creations. Rather are they starting-points of radiations which, in the special nature of the Isle of Roses, affect the human womanhood of Creation as a help for their development on all their wanderings through the Material Worlds. The children affect children, according to size and nature, even according to colour, and grown-ups affect *those* grown-ups whose *forms* resemble them as regards the state of the maturing spirit.

The sizes of the bodies on the Isle of Roses are therefore a counterpart of each particular and differing state of maturity also of those human *spirits* who, during their wanderings through the Material Worlds, are gradually able to develop from germs to being allowed complete consciousness.

Thus everything also exists in the Primordial Spiritual on the Isle of Roses which is later repeated in the Spiritual and Material Worlds like an image or like imitations.

In reality this *is* the lawful repetition in all parts of the world of everything that has already occurred in the Primordial Spiritual, because it can never be otherwise with the simplicity and clarity of the Divine Laws, both of which are incomprehensible to human beings. Thus everything which has already taken place in the Primordial Spiritual is then precisely repeated in the Spiritual.

Also in the Primordial Spiritual everything which could neither form itself immediately to ego-consciousness, nor maintain itself under the enormous pressure of, and in such nearness to, the Unsubstantiate Core, moved out of the uppermost part of Primordial Creation, passing by Vasitha into a greater distance, into a next plane in order to maintain itself in the greater cooling-off and thereby achieve self-consciousness. This also includes germs of the *Primordial Spiritual,* which already develop to consciousness in the fourth step of cooling-off, as here on the Isle of Roses.

When I speak about steps of Creation or planes these are steps of *cooling-off,* for nothing else lets steps come into existence; they may also be called steps of distance instead of cooling-off steps, thus in reality they are also steps or gradations according to *earthly* conceptions.

Therefore as we descend from above we find *children* and *development* on the Isle of Roses *for the first time* in the Primordial Spiritual. This is important for you to know as it signifies a great division of Creation.

Thus in the upper steps of the Primordial Spiritual there are first of all those who are able immediately to be conscious of themselves, i. e., the strongest and therefore the most powerful ones, the pillars. Then on more distant steps follow those who are still able to *develop* in the Primordial Spiritual. Therefore for the first time we find *Primordial Spiritual children* there!

In the next great division of Creation, the *Spiritual,* which is somewhat weaker than the Primordial Spiritual, because it can only become self-conscious at an even greater distance from the Unsubstantiate Core of Parsifal, the process is repeated in exactly the same manner as it was in Primordial Creation.

First the strongest parts of the Spiritual become self-conscious immediately, while the others must still be pushed a further distance away in order to mature there to self-consciousness in a slow development.

There also, beginning only with the step of the spirit-germs concerned with this, spirit *children* exist who may develop to a greater spiritual maturity or who remain children; for spirit-germs which do not grow to full maturity, i. e., to a spiritual adulthood, are *not destroyed,* not cast out, as long as they remain *pure!*

This is a point which I have not so far mentioned. *Spiritually* they remain children and as such radiate to children, until finally they gradually mature after all and become grown-ups. What is *pure* can *never* fall into disintegration.

There is still another point I want to mention here. The Primordial Spiritual in this Creation is not perhaps the stronger part and the Spiritual the weaker part of *exactly the same species,* but the Spiritual is a *completely different* species from the Primordial Spiritual.

Both species in themselves have a stronger and a weaker part. True, the Spiritual is a *precipitation* from the Primordial Spiritual, but only because it is of a *different* nature, which can therefore sever itself and only in fact form at a greater distance from the Unsubstantiate Light-Core of Parsifal.

If it were of the same species, then the Primordial Spiritual would not have passed this same species further on, but on the contrary would have *held* it *fast* through the Law of Attraction of Homogeneous Species, although as a result it would not have been able to become conscious and form.

The further I go with my explanations the more I must draw apart the structure of Creation. Thereby many a picture which you have formed in the past changes for you, but it is merely divided into ever more pictures without the actual basic picture needing to be somehow disarranged.

It is the same as if describing a long journey. If only the main experiences are first of all strung together and described, it appears quite different than the picture where all the intermediate experiences, each standing on its own, are gradually added, although the journey as such remains unchanged. –

But now let us return once more to the Isle of Roses!

On the summit of the Isle a glorious Temple radiates in roseate hue. Peace descends into the heart of whoever beholds it, his breast will almost burst with happiness!

And with this peace, with the melodious sounding of the colours, there blends the jubilant singing of friendly birds, which scintillate brilliantly with every movement as if studded with diamonds, thus enhancing the splendour around them.

The human expression of blissfulness is much too weak to press the Light-rapture prevailing here even approximately into a form that can become understandable to the spirit of earthman. And over all this lies a sacred sublimity!

Red roses like chalices of ruby are in full bloom around the Temple!

Isle of Roses! The anchorage of the Love of God for Creation! On this Isle there works and weaves the fundamental upbuilding of the healing, uniting, reconciling Love, which radiates from here out into the Universe! The Isle stands under the protection of the Primordial Queen Elizabeth, as does everything that is womanly in the whole of Creation.

Under the protection of the Primordial Queen Elizabeth, Maria often inclines to this Isle, visiting the Temple in order to give ever-new and direct strength to all those serving on the Isle, who then transform and mediate this strength into their kind and send it out as a help for all creatures.

At times the gaze of those serving on the Isle of Roses opens even further and they behold Parsifal in the Holy Castle, receiving directly of His Power as a sacred fulfilment of blessed promises.

At the same height in this plane a second island strives upwards out of the weaving of the Light! *The Isle of Lilies!*

As with the roses in their glowing splendour on the Isle of Roses, so here only lilies predominate, radiating in unutterable purity over vast distances. Here, too, terraces rise to the summit, on which stands a Temple.

In this Temple there is a wonderful radiance resembling the delicate lustre of pearls, but gleaming at the same time with a rosy hue and settling upon this Isle with a keen severity like the soothing coolness of the sea.

Whoever is allowed to behold this Temple will always be forced to devout humbleness by the sight of it, for it shines down with a sharp and demanding severity; with the coolness of Light, the proud calm of Purity sinks down and penetrates the spirits, refreshing and strengthening them and pulling them up to the liberating worship of Divine Sublimity.

Here, too, everything came into existence with a beauty that is beyond human conception; here, too, wondrous melodies swing, ascending to the Creator as a living prayer of gratitude which sounds eternally in His Honour!

Here, too, the Primordial Queen Elizabeth reigns supreme, and under Her protection Irmingard, the Pure Lily, inclines at very definite times to this Isle in order to renew the power of Purity for those who serve upon it, which they transform and send out to refresh and uplift all creatures.

The inhabitants of the Isle of Lilies, like those of the Isle of Roses, belong exclusively to womanhood. Among them all statures are represented!

Here, too, only that which is *upbuilding* in the Will of God dominates, just as on the Isle of Roses, but the upbuilding is of a different kind on the Isle of Lilies – in purity and justice it is *demanding, strictly exacting,* unrelenting!

It is the same on the Isle of Lilies as it is on the Isle of Roses, where the serving ones see Parsifal at times and receive of His Power.

And there is a third island which rises out of the Plane of Light of the fourth step in the Primordial Spiritual! It is the *Isle of Swans!* It stands a little further downwards between the two islands first mentioned!

This bears delicious fruit which is enjoyed by the Swan Maidens living there. Here the radiations from the Isle of Roses and the Isle of Lilies concentrate and, in exemplary serving, are passed on unchanged for the Creations.

Therefore the Isle of Swans could also be called the island or main junction of *exemplary serving,* of *selfless* serving. Here the serving in purest love is spread and uplifted. The inhabitants of the Isle of Swans are not spirits but executive *beings,* which have a *uniting* effect between the radiations of the Isle of Roses and those of the Isle of Lilies.

In accordance with their graceful nature these entities swing blissfully in the direct radiations of the Isle of Roses and the Isle of Lilies, and with their inherent characteristic of exemplary serving in purest love they closely unite the radiations of Love and Purity, passing them on linked together, it is true, but unchanged.

Swanhild is the responsible Guardian of the Isle of Swans! Swanhild is responsible to the Primordial Queen Elizabeth, Who is the Protector and Ruler of the Isle of Swans as well. This responsibility gives increased strength to Swanhild and an enhanced existence!

Like the Swan Maidens she wears a flowing gown which, similar to the plumage of swans, clings brightly to the body that in its harmony surpasses the divining of all earthly artists.

A peculiarity of the Swan Maidens is that they have only *blue* eyes, and also as a head ornament they wear a star of lustrous blue. They distinguish themselves especially by their wonderful, moving singing, and they swing in the harmony of the tones, which from here streams downwards to all parts of Creation.

The worship of the Swan Maidens is manifested in the Temple of the Swans through their enchanting singing, which is softly penetrated by the magnificent sounds of the harp. On this account the harmony of the tones forms a part of the elixir of life for each Maiden on the Isle of Swans. She revives therein, swings joyously in the waves of pure tones and absorbs them inwardly like an elixir of life that gives her joyful activity.

Tidings of this especially moving singing of the Swan Maidens has already reached the Material Spheres. For this reason they still speak here and there of a swan's song, which in its special nature is supposed to have a shaking effect. As always, only a *part* of the old revelations has been preserved also in this, and through the intellect it has been distorted and made earthly.

Now many of you will probably understand why, at the time of the most sacred fulfilments on earth, when the Rose and the Lily work on earth, there is also a Swan Maiden from the Isle of Swans needed as a connection, in a physical body prepared for this purpose, in order not to leave a gap in the swinging.

God's Mercy is *so* great that He allows wonder upon wonder to arise, so that the help for mankind in the Millennium may be absolutely complete!

Bow down in humility before His great Goodness!

LAST time I spoke about the Isle of Roses, the Isle of Lilies, and the Isle of Swans.

These points of support are like three radiating jewels in a gold ring, if we compare the entire plane of the fourth step with a gold ring, with a golden band in which the three jewels are wonderfully mounted.

Naturally there is also other life on this step as well as on all the other planes, but now I am first mentioning the points of support that *shine forth*, which have an incisive, indeed a *decisive,* effect upon the human spirits.

It is the same on the next, the fifth step of Primordial Creation. If the previous steps were the *basic planes* for the *issuing forth* of all the powers of radiation for everything further, then the fifth step is the land or the plane for the *preparation,* the *training,* of the helps for everything that is *below* Primordial Creation. Working on this fifth step are the leading, strong preparers of all the supports for the *human race.*

You will understand me best if I give you *one* name therefrom: *Is-ma-el!*

Here he lives, from here his activity goes forth! Is-ma-el, who once brought up Abd-ru-shin on this earth, who was incarnated on earth for His sake, who then as John the Baptist also proclaimed Jesus, and who had to prepare all the seven parts of the World for the coming of Parsifal!

He is the *uppermost* on this step, numerous helpers surround him, and it was *he* who received the tidings from the Light for his great, comprehensive working, which he always faithfully fulfilled. It was also *he* who gave men the great revelation of the present-day happenings, which have become generally known as the Revelation of John.

With this great work of preparing all the incisive Light-happenings for the Creations, this fifth step is filled and full of flaming life! –

The next step, the sixth one, again shows also for human beings a point which stands out strongly and luminously: *The White Castle!*

The White Castle is not to be thought of according to earthly conceptions.

It has this designation as the *shelter of the two pure vessels!* Faithfully guarded therein are the two Primordial Spiritual female vessels of the most holy Light-Fulfilments on earth.

They are the two Primordial Spiritual vessels for the earthly mothers of Jesus and Abd-ru-shin!

However, the two Primordial Spiritual Vessels were also in need of a *spiritual* cloak, without which they would have been unable to fulfil their task *on earth.* This *spiritual* part was the earth mother at the particular time.

Thereby each spiritual cloak was a human being of herself, thus a self-conscious earthwoman, with whom the chosen *Primordial Spiritual* woman must first be connected for an earthly birth of the Light of God in each case.

Such an earthly Light-birth needs the greatest and most comprehensive preparations from above, and after centuries of trouble such a small earthly human spirit, due to its weaknesses, may necessitate further changes even at the last moment.

When I speak of a Primordial Spiritual and of a Spiritual vessel or cloak, then in each case this is a *woman* of herself. The two Primordial Spiritual vessels are two women *in the Primordial Creation* chosen for this purpose who, under a definite high guidance for this from the Primordial Spiritual, were able to develop conscious of their aim, and who always remained under the most faithful guardianship in the White Castle.

The *spiritual* vessels or cloaks are those earthly women who could be chosen and also prepared to unite themselves closely with these cloaks or women out of Primordial Creation for the purpose of the most sacred fulfilment.

Once again I briefly want to summarise this, which is difficult for you, so that it will stand before you absolutely clear!

In the White Castle of the sixth step of the Primordial Spiritual, there are two chosen women who carry down all Those born of the Light (Who sink Themselves into the Worlds of Matter for the fulfilment of Divine promises) in order to connect themselves with a woman on earth; because this transition must occur when incarnations of Those born of the Light take place on earth, since a gap in the operation of the Divine Primordial Laws of Creation is impossible.

The two women bear names that stand in the Law: *Maria,* swinging in the *Love,* and *Therese,* swinging in the *Will!* Thus Maria is chosen for the *Love* of

God according to the law of the number and her nature, and Therese for the *Will* of God!

For earthly birth they were in each case closely united with a human woman on earth, with her *spirit*.

This human earthwoman had naturally to have a similar vibration. For the birth of the Love an earthly human spirit was needed who vibrated in the *Love*, for the birth of the Will an earthly human spirit who vibrated in the *Will!*

The earthly women who were to give Those born of the Light into the World of Matter are connected by threads with the Primordial Spiritual vessels *only*, but not with the Envoys of the Light Themselves.

You must pay close attention to this in order to understand the entire happening aright!

Therefore the spirit of the mothers on earth is only indirectly linked with the Envoys of the Light through the Primordial Spiritual vessels, with which latter they are directly linked for a time by carefully woven threads. The Primordial Spiritual vessels carry the Envoys of the Light down to the earthly mothers, with whom they connect themselves only at the time of incarnation, remaining connected until forty days after the earthly birth.

During *this* period, through the Primordial Spiritual vessel, a Light-connection also exists for the spirit of the earthly mothers, but this connection is again dissolved in that the Primordial Spiritual vessel again severs itself and returns.

Through this the female human spirit on earth is again left to herself, because a *direct* connection with the Core of Light of her child does *not* exist.

It is all so simple and natural, and yet nevertheless so hard to narrow down into earthly words in order to make it understandable in the coarse World of Matter! –

The last step of Primordial Creation, the seventh, carries the Isle of the Chosen Ones!

I have not much to say about it in this lecture, for the name is already enough for you: *Patmos!*

A great deal has already been said about this Isle of the Blessed Ones, and much more will be spoken about it yet, for at the same time it is the Isle of Promises or the Mountain of Holy Proclamations!

Like the Grail Castle which arises at the outermost boundary in the Divine Sphere, and which at the same time has a replica as the summit in Primordial Creation, so Patmos is also situated at the last boundary of the Primordial Spiritual and has a replica on the highest height of the adjoining Spiritual; and whatever happens on Patmos in the Primordial Spiritual can be seen in the Spiritual like a reflection.

In this way, despite the separation, there is always a common experiencing in the two realms, and thus a connection is established.

Thus on Patmos, the summit of the human spiritual, there is also a Created One who bears the name Is-ma-el, and who swings and works in the rays of Is-ma-el in the Primordial Spiritual.

Later on we can perhaps return to this in greater detail, for today it would far exceed the purpose of this lecture! Therefore I only want to bring the conclusion for the great Realm of the Primordial Creation in the straight line downwards.

After the last step in the Primordial Creation, the seventh, there follows a protective cloak, which has the effect of a separating layer between the Primordial Spiritual and the adjoining Spiritual part of Creation, the latter being in its extent no less vast to the minds of earthmen than is the Primordial Spiritual.

This protective cloak is also a plane of great extent by itself. It is not uninhabited, but animated by many beings, though not a permanent stopping place of self-conscious spirits.

It forms the unsurmountable border of the Primordial Spiritual, of Primordial Creation, which border cannot be broken through, and yet again acts as a transition stage.

But in order to cross over it is necessary to have an escort of the entities populating this plane, which in their working again resemble a protective cloak towards the one crossing over, just as their plane is towards the whole of Primordial Creation.

And such an escort through this protective plane can only be granted by these entities under very definite conditions which swing adamantly in the Laws of Creation.

Therefore it is only possible to cross this plane of protection by fulfilling very special stipulations. The fulfilment of the conditions, which lies partly in the *species* and partly also in the *nature* of this species, i. e., in the particular state of maturity, results in the passage through, bringing it about automatically as a necessary and natural consequence.

Thus everywhere there is an exact interlocking movement, just as with a most delicately manufactured gearing put together skilfully, which is kept in motion by vitally working Laws.

Whatever keeps to its path *in the right way* therein is polished and purified, pushed along and lifted up, but always towards the height of a pure ability; but that which strays from the right path and which carelessly or even wantonly steps aside in this machinery is struck and damaged, until it again stands on its right path and can then swing along smoothly, or until it is ground and crushed between the wheels that never stop.

Therefore, you human beings, adjust yourselves to the adamantine machinery of this masterpiece that is Creation, which is far greater than anything you can comprehend, and in the uniform swinging you will be happy for all eternity!

Epilogue

HOW THE MESSAGE SHOULD BE ABSORBED

MAN ON earth makes *one* great mistake when seeking for spiritual knowledge! He wants to strive forward with leaps and bounds instead of proceeding step by step in calmness and sure certainty. No sooner is he aware of some impulse that wants to direct him to seek for spiritual values than he already asks about the highest things, things far beyond the capacity of a human spirit to comprehend!

He thereby renders himself incapable from the very outset of absorbing anything! Perplexed and discouraged, he soon gives up the search. Quite often even resentment arises in his soul and he derides, mocks and scorns other seekers, facing them with enmity. But such hostility is actually based on the feeling of a depressing recognition that he was himself incapable of finding values in the spiritual. The *knowledge of his impotence* lets him who is joined by envy and jealousy become an enemy!

A person who scoffs is not superior but merely embittered. Scorn and ridicule hold an open confession of personal inadequacy, personal weakness, of inability to grasp a matter which a scoffer lacks the capacity to understand. Or it is envy that speaks from him – envy because another person can comprehend something which remains incomprehensible to himself!

It is also characteristic of the human spirit that when he fancies he possesses a greater knowledge he does not indulge in mockery and scorn. If he is really convinced of his knowledge he has no incentive to malice and enmity. –

But fear can also cause a human spirit to be filled with hatred. Especially fear of being treated with disdain in public opinion, fear of it becoming known that the personal knowledge he so proudly displayed in the past will receive a jolt through some matter which *he* himself is incapable of following, or which he cannot follow without designating his hitherto imagined knowledge as deficient, if not wrong!

For a human spirit on earth *this* is then the *most potent* incentive for attacking, for scorn and mockery, indeed for the most repulsive kinds of hostility that do not shrink from lying and slandering, and which finally even degenerate into acts of violence if there is no other way of achieving success!

It is the same in the smallest things as in the greatest! The more influence a person exerted with his supposed knowledge upon his fellow-men, the more they are informed as to his pseudo-knowledge, the more energetically will he always close himself to new recognitions when they come from an alien source, the more desperately will he also work against them!

Many a person on earth would gladly open himself to new knowledge, even if it is opposed to his hitherto imagined and false pseudo-knowledge, so long as nobody knows of his old views!

But when his fellow-men know about it then his vanity does not permit him to throw in his lot with a new knowledge which changes his own, for in doing so he would show that he has so far been wrong. He then rejects it, sometimes even against his innermost conviction, which often gives him anxious hours!

Out of cowardice he then seeks for high-sounding words to cover up his vanity, and the subtle intellect helps him to do so. It then allows him to declare in a dignified manner that he considers himself responsible for those who have so far followed him along his path. Out of "love" for the others he rejects the new knowledge so that no disquiet will arise in that peace which the souls of his believers found in their past thinking.

Damnable hypocrites who speak thus! For their much-praised peace is nothing but *slumber,* which holds the human spirit fettered and prevents it from bestirring itself according to God's Law of Movement, from unfolding the spirit so that its wings will grow for the flight to the Luminous Heights, from which those slumbering peacefully must remain far removed!

But many people gladly run after such mischievous detractors of God's Laws, because the comfort they teach is so alluring to the indolent human spirits! It is the broad and all-too-comfortable road to damnation, to the regions of disintegration! Not without purpose did the Son of God Jesus point so often to the hard, stony and narrow path to the Height and warn against the broad road of comfort! He knew the slothful indolence of these human spirits only too well, and the temptations by Lucifer's henchmen who make use of this weakness!

Man must bestir himself if he wishes to reach the Luminous Heights! Paradise awaits him, but it does not come down of itself unless he strives for it. To strive does not mean just to think, to plead and to beg as you are doing today! To strive means to *act,* to *exert oneself* to get there!

But men only beg and then imagine that they will even be carried aloft by the very hands through which, in their hatred, they once thrust nails! Only *the path* is shown and will be shown to all of you, you indolent ones, but you yourselves must walk upon it! You must exert yourselves to do so!

How often did Christ say this, and yet you believe that you can be forgiven your sins without difficulty, immediately, if only you pray for it! You live according to *your* wishes and desires, and even beg for Divine Help to do so! And again you expect this help to be only in *that* form which *you* wish for, thus even making conditions about it!

Indolence and presumption wherever you look! Nothing else! *This* also is spiritual laziness, when in the very beginning of your spiritual awakening you already ask, leaping forward, for the highest things. In doing so you only want to see at the outset whether it will pay to walk along the path which will cost so much toil! Indeed you have no idea how ludicrous a person appears when putting such questions to Him Who can give you the answer. For such questions can only be explained by One Who comes consciously from Above, One Who was among the Highest Things!

And He Who comes from Above also knows that not a single one of the human spirits can even divine these things, much less absorb them *knowingly!*

I brought you the Message which earthmen need if they want to ascend spiritually! Just examine it aright! At best, however, you find it beautiful... and immediately ask about things which in any case you will never be able to understand! And which are therefore of no use to you either!

But when once you have inwardly absorbed the entire Message aright, and have experienced every word of it within yourselves, once you have lived it through in order to transform it into deeds as a matter of course in your existence on earth, then it will become your own like the flesh and blood you need for the fulfilment of your wandering on earth.

If you act *in this way* it follows that you will no longer ask these questions; for then you will have become *knowing,* as knowing as a human spirit is capable of becoming! And with this the nonsensical wishing also simultaneously ceases; for through the knowledge you have become truly humble, have cast off the weaknesses of your human vanity, of haughtiness, of the conceit of your own pseudo-knowledge, and all the many faults which a human spirit has acquired.

Thus whoever asks these and similar questions still sleeps on in the indolence of his spirit, only imagining he is thereby emphasising alertness of spirit and the strong urge to seek. He is no different from a child who wants to run a race before it has even learned to walk!

Neither can you pick out individual passages from the Message just as they suit you or interest you; for interest is not sufficient for spiritual learning, it extends only to the intellect, not to the spirit, which requires more!

You must take all or nothing!

It is true that genuine seeking can arise out of interest, but not easily, only very seldom! Zeal is also harmful, for it induces one to make jumps that paralyse the powers. Stride forward calmly, word by word and sentence by sentence, not reading and not learning, but trying to absorb everything I gave you in pictures just as in life. Dig yourselves into my words, and then, indeed only then, will you be able to get a faint idea that you hold the Word of Life in your hands, the Word which lives Itself, which was not composed of anything that was learned or thought out!

Only when you thus force yourselves to life in God's Law of harmonious Movement can the Word come to life within you, enabling you to ascend into the Luminous Heights which are your real home. But before that can happen you must shatter all the walls around you which, during thousands of years, your spiritual indolence permitted to become so very rigid, which constrict the wings of your spirit and keep them down in such a manner that the rigid dead dogma satisfies you, indeed even seems great to you; with which dogma you today seek to serve *that* God Who Himself is the *Life* with an empty form *only!* –

Nevertheless I have also finally explained to you in descriptions that which you call the last things, but which in reality are the *first,* so that in the whole existence there no longer remains any question for you to ask. I gave it to you as a *reward;* for in order to recognise the descriptions you must have taken the *trouble beforehand* to absorb the entire Message word by word, making it live within you! Whoever neglects to do this work will never be able to understand me, even if he thinks he does!

Therefore avoid anything desultory, but fathom each of my words from the beginning, and sentence by sentence. No person is able to exhaust the value of the Message here on earth, for it is intended for all parts of the World. Do not pick out certain passages of the Message at random! It is *one whole,* indivisible, like God's Laws of this Creation. No human spirit can alter or distort anything without being harmed in the process. Nor can you introduce anything into it from outside either; you cannot insert anything alien which is more pleasant to you into individual passages, no matter whether it originates from a known teaching or comes from yourselves!

You must leave my Message unchanged from the first to the last word if it is to benefit you! You must first experience it *within yourselves* so as to form your outward life in accordance with it!

If you do this you will proceed in the right way, and Luminous Heights will open themselves before your spirit in order to permit you to pass through to the highest realm of joyful activity of the blessed human spirits, which you call Paradise! There you will obtain a faint idea of the Primordial Spiritual, and will perceive the Power of the Divine which I have described to you. But then you will no longer desire to ask any questions, for in your happiness you are without a wish! Then the intellect will no longer torment you, because you experience everything!

Abd-ru-shin

APPENDIX

READERS will observe from certain footnotes in this Volume that their attention is called to the terms "the Realm of Animistic Substantiality", "the Animistic Sphere", "the World of Animism", etc. The translators feel that the words "animism" and "animistic" best describe the nature of this particular Sphere, which the Author reveals for the first time. It must therefore be borne in mind that these words have to be interpreted as embracing much wider and, in part, very different conceptions from those given in any dictionary. However, as the reader makes genuine efforts to follow the Author's guidance and explanations step by step through the Grail Message, he will be able to grasp, intuitively absorb and picture to himself the actual meaning and significance of these words.

CHRONOLOGICAL INDEX

VOLUME I

VOLUME II

VOLUME III

ALPHABETICAL INDEX

If you have questions about this Work,
please contact Reader Services at:

Grail Foundation Press
P. O. Box 45
Gambier, Ohio 43022
Telephone: 614-427-9410
Fax: 614-427-4954